ECONOMICS

Visit the *Economics, sixth edition* Companion Website at **www.pearsoned.co.uk/sloman** to find valuable **student** learning material including:

- Learning objectives and chapter overview for each chapter
- Multiple choice questions to test your learning
- Extra case studies with questions per chapter
- Maths cases with exercises, related to the Looking at the Maths boxes in the book
- Answers to all in-chapter questions
- Topical Economic Issues, with analysis and links to key concepts, updated regularly
- Economics News Articles with questions, updated monthly
- Extensive annotated Hotlinks to relevant sites on the Internet, regularly updated
- An online glossary to explain key terms

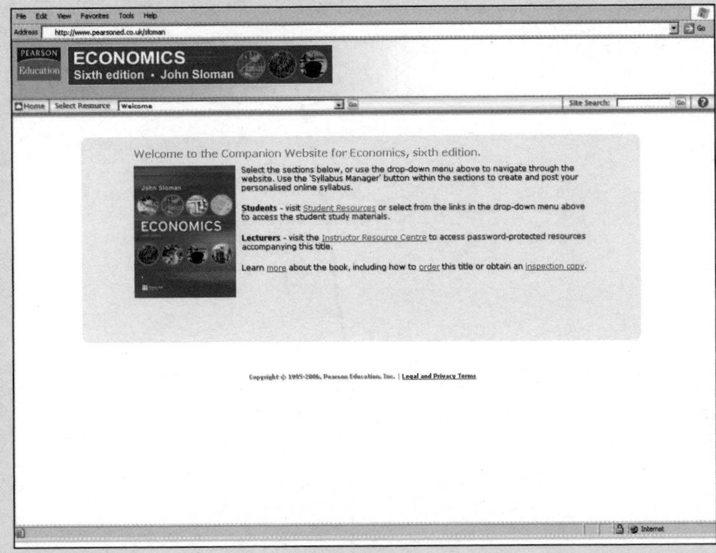

We work with leading authors to develop the strongest educational materials in economics, bringing cutting-edge thinking and best learning practice to a global market.

Under a range of well-known imprints, including Financial Times Prentice Hall, we craft high quality print and electronic publications which help readers to understand and apply their content, whether studying or at work.

To find out more about the complete range of our publishing, please visit us on the World Wide Web at: www.pearsoned.co.uk

John Sloman
University of the West of England and
the Economics Network

ECONOMICS

Sixth edition

An imprint of Pearson Education
Harlow, England • London • New York • Boston • San Francisco • Toronto • Sydney • Singapore • Hong Kong
Tokyo • Seoul • Taipei • New Delhi • Cape Town • Madrid • Mexico City • Amsterdam • Munich • Paris • Milan

Pearson Education Limited
Edinburgh Gate
Harlow
Essex CM20 2JE
England

and Associated Companies throughout the world

Visit us on the World Wide Web at:
www.pearsoned.co.uk

First edition published 1991
Second edition published 1994
Updated second edition published 1995
Third edition published 1997
Updated third edition published 1998
Fourth edition published 2000
Fifth edition published 2003
Sixth edition published 2006

ISBN-13: 978-0-273-70512-3
ISBN-10: 0-273-70512-1

British Library Cataloguing-in-Publication Data
A catalogue record for this book is available from the British Library

Library of Congress Cataloging-in-Publication Data
A catalog record for this book is available from the Library of Congress

10 9 8 7 6 5 4 3 2
10 09 08 07 06

Typeset in 8/12 pt Stone Serif by 35
Printed and bound by Graficas Estella, Bilboa, Spain

Brief Contents

Contents

* Denotes more advanced sections of the text.

Supporting resources

Visit **www.pearsoned.co.uk/sloman** to find valuable online resources

Companion Website for students

- Learning objectives and chapter overview for each chapter
- Multiple choice questions to test your learning
- Extra case studies with questions per chapter
- Maths cases with exercises, related to the Looking at the Maths boxes in the book
- Answers to all in-chapter questions
- Topical Economic Issues, with analysis and links to key concepts, updated regularly
- Economics News Articles with questions, updated monthly
- Extensive annotated Hotlinks to relevant sites on the Internet, regularly updated
- An online glossary to explain key terms

For lecturers

- Tutor guide to using chapters and discussion of learning/teaching issues
- Testbank of question material
- Customisable lecture plans in PowerPoint
- Key models animated as full-colour PowerPoint slide shows
- Downloadable PowerPoint slides of all figures and tables from the book
- A range of teaching and learning case studies
- Workshops with answers
- Answers to End of Chapter Questions
- Answers to the case studies found on the student Companion Website

These lecturer resources are also available on CD-ROM from your Pearson Education sales representative.

Also: The regularly maintained Companion Website provides the following features:

- Search tool to help locate specific items of content
- E-mail results and profile tools to send results of quizzes to lecturers
- Online help and support to assist with website usage and troubleshooting

For more information please contact your local Pearson Education sales representative or visit **www.pearsoned.co.uk/sloman**

MyEconLab: *Get Ahead of the Curve*

MyEconLab offers extensive online resources delivered inside CourseCompass.

MyEconLab is a one-stop online location for a variety of tools that will help students increase their understanding of economics and raise test scores.

MyEconLab for *Economics, sixth edition* enables students to assess their own learning, and provides a personalised Study Plan which identifies areas they need to concentrate on to improve grades. Specific tools are provided to direct their study in the most efficient way. Access to MyEconLab is provided with every new purchase of the main text.

For more information about the MyEconLab product please contact your local Pearson Education sales representative or visit **www.pearsoned.co.uk/sloman**

Preface

TO THE STUDENT

Economics affects all our lives. As consumers we try to make the best of our limited incomes. As workers – or future workers! – we take our place in the job market. As citizens of a country our lives are affected by the decisions of our government: decisions over taxes, decisions over spending on health and education, decisions on interest rates, decisions that affect unemployment, inflation and growth. As dwellers on the planet Earth we are affected by the economic decisions of each other: the air we breathe, the water we drink and the environment we leave to our children are all affected by the economic decisions taken by the human race.

Economics thus deals with some of the most challenging issues we face. It is this that still excites me about economics after many years of teaching the subject. I hope that some of this excitement rubs off on you.

The first five editions of *Economics* have been widely used in Britain and throughout the world. Like them, this new edition is suitable for all students of economics at first-year degree level, A level or on various professional courses where a broad grounding in both principles and applications is required. It is structured to be easily understood by those of you who are new to the subject, with various sections and boxes that can be left out on first reading or on shorter courses; yet it also has sufficient depth to challenge those of you who have studied the subject before, with starred sections (*) and case studies that will provide much that is new. There are also optional short mathematical sections for those of you studying a more rigorous course.

The book gives a self-contained introduction to the world of economics and is thus ideal for those who will not study the subject beyond introductory level. But by carefully laying a comprehensive foundation and by the inclusion of certain materials in starred sections that bridge the gap between introductory and second-level economics, it provides the necessary coverage for those of you going on to specialise in economics.

The book is designed with one overriding aim: to make this exciting and highly relevant subject as clear to understand as possible. To this end the book has a number of important features (see also the Guided Tour):

- Full and consistent use of colour to guide you through the text and make the structure easy to follow.
- A direct and straightforward written style; short paragraphs to aid rapid comprehension.
- Key ideas highlighted and explained where they first appear. These ideas are key elements in the economist's 'toolkit' and whenever they recur later in the book, an icon appears in the margin and you are referred back to the page where they are defined and explained.
- Fifteen 'threshold concepts' (a new feature for this edition). Each one is explained in a separate panel. Grasping these fundamental concepts that recur throughout the subject will help you to 'think like an economist'. Like the key ideas, an icon is used to refer to them whenever they occur.
- Full-page chapter introductions that raise the key issues of the chapter and also give a map to help you 'navigate' through the contents of the various sections.
- Numerous examples given from around the world: some serious, some lighthearted.
- Summaries at the end of each section (rather than each chapter).
- Definitions of all key terms at the bottom of the page.
- A comprehensive index, including reference to all defined terms.
- Questions throughout the text (typically one or two per page) to test comprehension and stimulate thought while you are learning. Answers to all these questions are given on the book's website at www.pearsoned.co.uk/sloman.
- Questions at the end of each chapter for either individual or class use.
- Many boxes (around seven per chapter) providing case studies, institutional material, news items, contemporary and historical debates and issues, anecdotes and advanced topics.
- Advanced material in starred sections/boxes, which can be omitted without affecting the flow of argument.
- Many additional case studies, which are listed at the end of each chapter, can be accessed on the book's website.
- Many issues are examined in their historical as well as contemporary context.
- 'Looking at the maths' sections. These optional sections are designed for students on more rigorous courses that make use of mathematics. These sections express things

mathematically that have just been covered in words and/or graphically. Most of them link to Maths Cases on the book's website. These cases give worked mathematical examples and also include one or more numerical questions for you to work through, either at home or in class.

- Website references. Extensive web references are given at the end of each chapter. These refer you to the websites listed at the end of the book in Appendix 2. These can all be accessed directly from the 'hotlinks' section of the book's website at www.pearsoned.co.uk/sloman.

All these features are designed to make your studies more interesting and to help you learn in a deeper and more active way.

The book looks at the world of the early 21st century. Despite huge advances in technology and despite the comfortable lives led by many people in the industrialised world, we still suffer from unemployment, poverty and inequality, and in many countries (the UK included) the gap between rich and poor has grown much wider; our environment is polluted; our economy still goes through periodic recessions; conflict and disagreement often dominate over peace and harmony.

What is more, the world order has been changing. With repeated bouts of turmoil on international financial markets; with a growing interdependence of the economies of the world; with an inexorable process of 'globalisation', which links us all through a web of telecommunications and international trade into a world of Coca-Cola, Nike trainers, Microsoft, football and American chat shows; with Japan, once seen as the most dynamic of all industrialised countries, struggling to emerge from a paralysing recession; with Chinese economic growth increasingly becoming the powerhouse of the global economy; with fears that economic problems in one country will spread like a contagion, not only to its direct neighbours, but possibly around the world; with the move away from the ideological simplicity of a 'free-market' solution to all economic problems; with a powerful but economically sluggish 'eurozone' and a rapidly evolving European Union with ten new members and soon three more; with an uncertain future for the USA with its ever-growing level of debt; and with an ever deepening crisis for many developing countries; so there are many new economic challenges that face us. Economists are called on to offer solutions.

But despite our changing environment, there are certain economic fundamentals that do not change. Despite disagreements among economists – and there are plenty – there is a wide measure of agreement on how to analyse these fundamentals.

I hope that this book will give you an enjoyable introduction to the economist's world and that it will equip you with the tools to understand and criticise the economic policies that others pursue.

Good luck and have fun.

TO TUTORS

This new edition retains many of the popular features of the previous edition (see also the Guided Tour):

- A style that is direct and to the point, with the aim all the time to provide maximum clarity. There are numerous examples to aid comprehension.
- All key terms highlighted in the text where they first appear and defined at the foot of that page. Each term is also highlighted in the index, so that the student can simply look up a given definition as required. By defining them on the page where they appear, the student can also see the terms used in context in the text.
- Key ideas highlighted and explained when they first appear. There are 36 of these ideas, which are fundamental to the study of economics. Students can see them recurring throughout the book, and an icon appears in the margin to refer back to the page where the idea first appears.
- (New to this edition) Fifteen 'threshold concepts'. Understanding and being able to relate and apply these core economic concepts helps students to 'think like an economist' and to relate the different parts of the subject to each other.
- A wealth of applied material in boxes (167 in all), making learning more interesting for students and, by relating economics to the real world, bringing the subject alive. The boxes allow the book to be comprehensive without the text becoming daunting. Many of the boxes can be used as class exercises and virtually all have questions at the end.
- Full-page chapter introductions. These set the scene for the chapter by introducing the students to the topics covered and relating them to the everyday world. The introductions also include a 'chapter map'. This provides a detailed contents listing, helping students to see how the chapter is structured and how the various topics relate to each other.
- A consistent use of colour in graphs and diagrams that makes them easier to comprehend and more appealing.
- Starred sections and boxes for more advanced material. These can be omitted without interrupting the flow of the argument. This allows the book to be used by students with different abilities and experience, and on courses of different levels of difficulty.
- (New to this edition) 'Looking at the maths' sections. These short sections express a topic mathematically.

Some use calculus; some do not. They are designed to be used on more rigorous courses and go further than other textbooks at introductory level in meeting the needs of students on such courses. Most refer students to worked examples in Maths Cases on the book's website. Some of these use simultaneous equations; some use simple unconstrained optimisation techniques; others use constrained optimisation, using both substitution and Lagrange multipliers. The 'Looking at the maths' sections are short and can be omitted by students on non-mathematical courses without any loss of continuity.

- An open learning approach, with questions incorporated into the text so as to test and reinforce students' understanding as they progress. This makes learning a much more active process.
- End-of-chapter questions. These can be set as work for students to do in class or at home. Alternatively, students can simply use them to check their comprehension at the end of a topic.
- Summaries given at the end of each section, thus providing a point for reflection and checking on comprehension at reasonably frequent intervals.
- An even micro/macro split.
- The book is divided into six parts. This makes the structure more transparent and makes it easier for the student to navigate.

Despite retaining these popular features, there have been many changes to this sixth edition.

Extensive revision

Economics (sixth edition) uses a lot of applied material, both to illustrate theory and policy, and to bring the subject alive for students by relating it to contemporary issues. This has meant that, as with the previous edition, much of the book has had to be rewritten to reflect contemporary issues. Specifically this means that:

- Many of the boxes are new or extensively revised.
- There are many new examples given in the text.
- All policy sections reflect the changes that have taken place in the last three years. For example, changes in competition policy, monetary policy and environmental policy are fully discussed.
- There is extended coverage of various aspects of globalisation, including strategic alliances in business, the growth in the US trade deficit, the rapid economic growth in China, attempts to reduce developing-country debt, the ratification of the Kyoto Treaty, the advent of emissions trading and the volatility of world financial markets.
- All tables and charts have been updated, as have factual references in the text.
- Theoretical coverage has been strengthened at various points of the books. For example, there is an expanded section on oligopoly and game theory, which now includes discussion of the Cournot and Bertrand models. The sections on monetary and fiscal policies, in both the closed and open economy contexts, have been tightened. The sections on the Romer/Taylor model have been sharpened and extended (in Box 20.2) to distinguish different types of inflation. Also the sections on inflation targeting have been expanded.

Most importantly, every single section and every single sentence of the book has been carefully considered, and if necessary redrafted, to ensure both maximum clarity and contemporary relevance. The result, I hope, is a text that your students will find exciting and relevant to today's world.

SUGGESTIONS FOR SHORTER OR LESS ADVANCED COURSES

The book is designed to be used on a number of different types of course. Because of its comprehensive nature, the inclusion of a lot of optional material and the self-contained nature of many of the chapters and sections, it can be used very flexibly.

It is suitable for one-year principles courses at first-year degree level, two-year economics courses on non-economics degrees, A level, HND and professional courses. It is also highly suitable for single-semester courses, either with a micro or a macro focus, or giving a broad outline of the subject.

The following shows which chapters are appropriate to which types of course.

Alternative 1: Less advanced but comprehensive courses

Omit all starred sections, starred sub-sections and starred boxes.

Alternative 2: Business studies courses

Chapters 1–3, 5–9, 12–14, 17, 19, 22–5.

Alternative 3: Introduction to microeconomics

Chapters 1–12, 23. The level of difficulty can be varied by including or omitting starred sections and boxes from these chapters.

Alternative 4: Introduction to macroeconomics

Chapters 1, 2, 13–25. The level of difficulty can be varied by including or omitting starred sections and boxes from these chapters.

Alternative 5: Outline courses

Chapters 1, 2, 5, 6, 13, 14, 16, 17, 23, 24 (section 24.1). Omit boxes at will.

Alternative 6: Courses with a theory bias

Chapters 1, 2, 4–9, 11, 13–18, 20, 21, 23, 24. The level of difficulty can be varied by including or omitting starred sections and boxes from these chapters.

Alternative 7: Courses with a policy bias (and only basic theory)

Chapters 1–3, 5, 6, 10–14, (16), 19, 22–5.

COMPANION BOOKS AND MATERIALS

Student Workbook, 6th Edition (by John Sloman and Peter Smith)

A new edition of the Student Workbook has been designed to accompany this text. Each chapter of the workbook matches a chapter of *Economics* and consists of four sections.

A. Review questions. This section is a mixture of narrative and questions and goes through all the key material in the textbook chapter. Questions are a mixture of multiple choice, true/false, either/or, filling in blank words or phrases, matching a series of answers to a series of questions, short written answers and brief calculations. Each type of question is clearly marked with an appropriate symbol.

B. Problems, exercises and projects. This section includes multiple-part calculations and exercises, and student projects (including data search exercises, games, role playing and questionnaires).

C. Discussion topics and essays. This includes various thought-provoking questions that can be used for class discussion and more traditional essay questions.

D. Answers and comments. This includes answers to *and* comments on all questions in section A of each chapter (answers to section B questions are given on the CD and in the Tutor's section of the website).

MyEconLab

MyEconLab is a new set of online resources developed for the sixth edition of *Economics*. Access is provided with every new purchase of this text. MyEconLab provides a variety of tools to enable students to assess their own learning. A personalised Study Plan identifies areas to concentrate on to improve grades, and specific tools are provided to each student to direct their studies in the most efficient way. See Guided Tour (pages xx–xxvi) for more details.

Website

Visit the *Economics* companion website at

www.pearsoned.co.uk/sloman

to find an extensive range of valuable teaching and learning material including:

For students:

- Study material designed to help you improve your results.
- Learning Objectives for each chapter written in 'student-friendly' language.
- Topical Economic Issues, with analysis and links to key concepts.
- Over 170 case studies with questions for self study. These are ordered chapter by chapter and are referred to in the text.
- Maths cases with exercises, related to the 'Looking at the Maths' sections in the book.
- 20 self-test questions per chapter.
- Updated list of 200 hotlinks to sites of use for economics.
- Answers to all in-chapter questions.
- Economics news articles. These are updated monthly. As well as hyperlinks to some 20 articles per month, there is an introduction to each article and questions at the end.

For lecturers:

- A secure, password-protected site with material designed to help you teach.
- Customisable lecture plans in PowerPoint®, including diagrams.
- Key models animated as full-colour PowerPoint® slide shows.
- Downloadable PowerPoint® slides of all figures and most tables from the book.
- A range of teaching and learning case studies, with the focus on improving student learning outcomes.

- Tutor guide to using chapters and discussion of teaching/learning issues.
- Answers to end-of-chapter questions (password protected).
- Testbank with over 2000 questions to help you prepare tests and exams (password protected).
- Workshops, with answers (password protected).
- Answers to the Case Studies and Maths Cases found on the Student Companion Website (password protected).

This site is regularly updated.

CD-ROM (new edition)

The CD produced for tutors using the 5th edition of *Economics* has proved very popular. The CD has been updated, revised and extended for the 6th edition. It is available free of charge from Pearson Education to tutors using the book as a course text. The CD contains the following:

- PowerPoint® slide shows in full colour for use with a data projector in lectures and classes. These can also be made available to students by loading them on to a local network. All PowerPoint® files are available in light on dark background, and dark on light background versions. The CD contains several types of these slide shows:
  - All figures from the book and most of the tables. Each figure is built up in a logical sequence, thereby allowing tutors to show them in lectures in an animated form.
  - A range of models. There are 39 files, each containing one of the key models from the book, developed in an animated sequence of between 20 and 80 screens.
  - Lecture plans. These are a series of bullet-point lecture plans. There is one for each chapter of the book. Each one can be easily edited, with points added, deleted or moved, so as to suit particular lectures. A consistent use of colour is made to show how the points tie together.
  - Lecture plans with integrated diagrams. These lecture plans include animated diagrams and charts at the appropriate points.
- PowerPoint® slides for printing on to acetate for use with a conventional OHP. These are reverse image slides (i.e. dark lines on a clear background) designed to minimise printer ink. They can be printed in colour, or in black and white (and grey). These slides contain the figures, tables and lecture plans referred to above.
- Tutor's Guide in Word®. This contains the following features:
  - Answers to all questions in *Economics* (6th edition): i.e. questions embedded in the text, box questions and end-of-chapter questions. These can be edited as desired and distributed to students.
  - Suggestions on how to use the text.
  - Learning objectives that can be used for syllabus design and course planning.
- Multiple-choice questions. This test bank is completely redesigned and contains many new questions. It is more flexible and easier to use.
- Case studies. These, also available on the book's website, can be reproduced and used for classroom exercises or for student assignments. Answers are also provided.
- Workshops. There are 18 of these (9 micro and 9 macro/international). They are in Word® and can be reproduced for use with large groups of students (up to 200). Suggestions for use are given on the CD. Answers to all workshop questions are given in separate Word® files.

WinEcon (Sloman version)

The widely acclaimed *WinEcon* software, produced and authored by the Economics Consortium of the Teaching and Learning Technology Programme (TLTP) and designed to support courses in introductory economics, is now available on CD in a version specially designed for *Economics* (6th edition). There is a separate chapter in the Sloman version of *WinEcon* to correspond with the relevant chapter in the book. The software is highly interactive and is attractive to use.

ACKNOWLEDGEMENTS

As with previous editions, I owe a debt to various people. The whole team from Pearson has, as always, been very helpful and supportive. Thanks in particular to Justinia Seaman, Linda Dhondy and Peter Hooper who have been of great help at editorial level and to Karen Mclaren and Sarah Wild who have steered the book smoothly through production. Thanks also to Chris Bessant, who has once again copy-edited the manuscript. He's done this since the first edition and has helped to ensure that it remains error free!

Thanks too to colleagues and students from many universities who have been helpful and encouraging and, as in previous editions, have made useful suggestions for improvement. As before, I have attempted to incorporate their ideas wherever possible. Please do write or email if you have any suggestions. Especially I should like to thank the following reviewers of the 5th edition. Their analysis and comments have helped to shape this new edition.

Lars Bach, The International Business Academy, Kolding, Denmark
Roy Bailey, University of Essex, UK
Professor Sue Bowden, University of York, UK
Leslie Christensen, CBS, Copenhagen Business School, Denmark

Dr Christopher J. Gerry, University College London, SSESS, UK
Professor Mark J. Holmes, Waikato University, New Zealand
Ian Jackson, Staffordshire University, UK
Tony McGough, Course Director, Cass Business School, City University, London, UK
Wilfried Pauwels, University of Antwerp, Belgium
Stuart Sayer, University of Edinburgh, UK
Walter Vanthielen, Hasselt University, Belgium

A special thanks to Peter Smith from the University of Southampton who has revised the Workbook to accompany this edition of the book and has contributed to the Tutor Guide and the MyEconLab online course. It's great to have his input and ideas for improvements to the books and supplements.

My biggest thanks go to my family, and especially to Alison, my wife and soulmate. As always she remains patient and supportive, despite my long hours at the computer.

Credits

We are grateful to the following for permission to reproduce copyright material:

Box 5.8 table (b) from *Economies of Scale, The Single Market Review* Subseries V Vol. 4, Office for Official Publications of the European Communities (European Commission/Economists Advisory Group Ltd. 1997); Box 7.3 figure from chart showing crude oil prices, 1970–2004 in *Annual Statistical Bulletin 2004*, (Organization of the Petroleum Exporting Countries 2004); Box 8.5 figure (b) from *Mergers & Acquisitions Note*, graph 2, DG ECFIN (European Commission/Economists Advisory Group Ltd., October 2004); Box 9.7 tables from *Annual Survey of Hours and Earnings*, Figure 10.1 from *The Effect of Taxes and Benefits on Household Income, 2003–4*, Figures 10.5, 10.7, 10.8, 12.4 and Table 10.1 from *Family Spending*, Figure 10.6 from *Annual Survey of Hours and Earnings*, Figure 10.9 and Table 10.2 from *Inland Revenue Statistics*, Box 10.6 table from the Inland Revenue, Table 12.3 from *Transport Statistics of Great Britain* (Department for Transport), Figures A13.1 and A13.2 and Tables A13.1 and A13.2 from *UK National Income and Expenditure*, Tables 14.2 and 14.3 from *Labour Market Trends*, Table 14.6 from *UK Economic Accounts*, Box 16.2 figure from *Financial Statistics*, Box 19.4 figure (b) from *Financial Statement and Budget Report* (HM Treasury 2005), Table 19.6 from www.statistics.gov.uk, Figure 21.1 from National Statistics time series data, Box 21.1 figure (b) from *Advancing Long-term Prosperity: Economic Reform in an Enlarged Europe*, p. 20 (HM Treasury 2004), Table 22.2 from National Statistics, Table 22.3 from *The Communities Plan* (Office of the Deputy Prime Minister), Box 24.1 figure from *Financial Statement and Budget Report* (HM Treasury 2005), Table A1:3 from *Social Trends*, Table A1:5 from *Economic Trends*, Crown copyright material is reproduced with the permission of the Controller of Her Majesty's Stationery Office and the Queen's Printer for Scotland; Box 12.7 figure from Electricity supply: reorganization and privatization in *Economic Review* Vol. 7 No. 4, March, Philip Allan Updates (Green, R. 1991); Box 14.2 table from *German Macroeconomic History 1880–1979: A Study of the Effects of Economic Policy on Inflation, Currency Depreciation and Growth*, Palgrave Macmillan (Sommariva, A. and Tullio, G. 1987); Box 19.11 figure from *Inflation Report*, Charts 1 and 2 (Bank of England 2005); Table 23.5 from The competition effects of the single market in Europe in *Economic Policy* Vol. 27, 441–486, Blackwell Publishing (Allen, C., Gasiorek M. and Smith A. 1998); Box 23.10 figure from *Internal Market Scoreboard*, Figure 1, Office for Official Publications of the European Communities (European Commission/Economists Advisory Group Ltd. 2005); Box 24.3 table from *The Economist*, 9 June (The Economist 2005); Box 26.1 table in *Human Development Report 2004 – Human Development Index* (Human Development Report Office and Oxford University Press 2004).

We are also grateful to the following for permission to reproduce textual material; PFD for permission to reproduce the poem 'The Castaways or Vote for Caliban' by Adrian Mitchell © Adrian Mitchell 1997 published in *Heart on the Left*. Educational Health Warning! Adrian Mitchell asks that none of his poems be used in connection with any examinations whatsoever!; and The Economist for an extract from 'Fast Food and Strong Currencies' published in *The Economist* 9th June 2005.

In some instances we have been unable to trace the owners of copyright material, and we would appreciate any information that would enable us to do so.

Guided Tour

NAVIGATION AND SETTING THE SCENE

The book is divided into six **parts**, each with a full page introduction and part map to help you navigate around the book.

Full page **chapter openers** provide an overview of the topics to be covered in each chapter, and a map of all chapter sections and sub-sections. These overviews, as well as full learning objectives per chapter, can be found in MyEconLab or at www.pearsoned.co.uk/sloman.

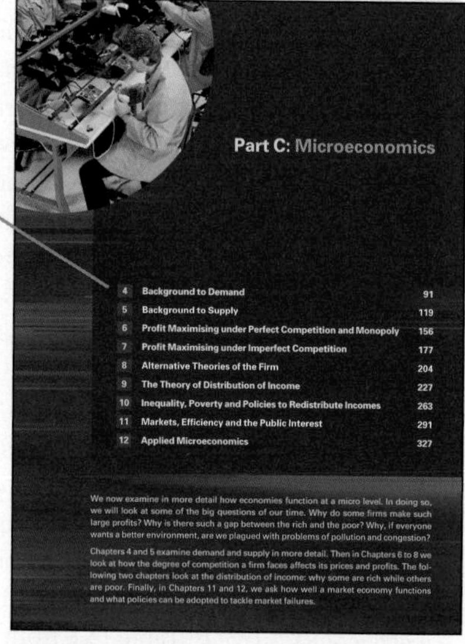

Part C: Microeconomics

We now examine in more detail how economies function at a micro level. In doing so, we will look at some of the big questions of our time. Why do some firms make such large profits? Why is there such a gap between the rich and the poor? Why, if everyone wants a better environment, are we plagued with problems of pollution and congestion?

Chapters 4 and 5 examine demand and supply in more detail. Then in Chapters 6 to 8 we look at how the degree of competition a firm faces affects its prices and profits. The following two chapters look at the distribution of income: why some are rich while others are poor. Finally, in Chapters 11 and 12, we ask how well a market economy functions and what policies can be adopted to tackle market failures.

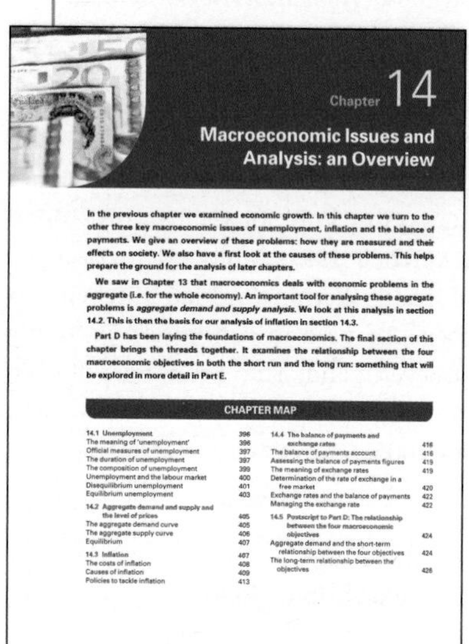

Chapter 14

Macroeconomic Issues and Analysis: an Overview

In the previous chapter we examined economic growth. In this chapter we turn to the other three key macroeconomic issues of unemployment, inflation and the balance of payments. We give an overview of these problems: how they are measured and their effects on society. We also have a first look at the causes of these problems. This helps prepare the ground for the analysis of later chapters.

We saw in Chapter 13 that macroeconomics deals with economic problems in the aggregate (i.e. for the whole economy). An important tool for analysing these aggregate problems is *aggregate demand and supply analysis*. We look at this analysis in section 14.2. This is then the basis for our analysis of inflation in section 14.3.

Part D has been laying the foundations of macroeconomics. The final section of this chapter brings the threads together. It examines the relationship between the four macroeconomic objectives in both the short run and the long run: something that will be explored in more detail in Part E.

CHAPTER MAP

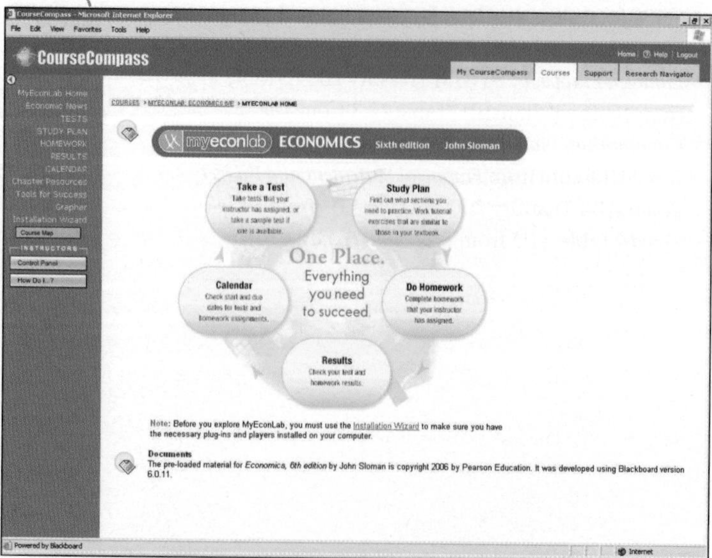

PRACTISING AND TESTING YOUR LEARNING

Questions throughout the text enable you to test your understanding of what you have just read. Answers appear in MyEconLab.

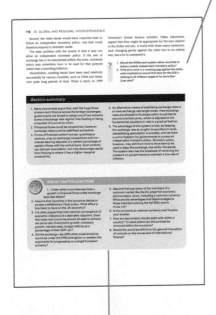

718 25 GLOBAL AND REGIONAL INTERDEPENDENCE

Second, the wider bands would leave countries freer to follow an independent monetary policy: one that could therefore respond to domestic needs.

The main problem with the system is that it may not allow an independent monetary policy. If the rate of exchange has to be maintained within the zone, monetary policy may sometimes have to be used for that purpose rather than controlling inflation.

Nevertheless, crawling bands have been used relatively successfully by various countries, such as Chile and Israel, over quite long periods of time. What is more, in 1999 Germany's former finance minister, Oskar Lafontaine, argued that they might be appropriate for the euro relative to the dollar and yen. A world with three major currencies, each changing gently against the other two in an orderly way, has a lot to commend it.

?
1. *Would the Williamson system allow countries to follow a totally independent monetary policy?*
2. *If the euro were in a crawling peg against the dollar, what implications would this have for the ECB in sticking to its inflation target of no more than 2 per cent?*

Section summary

1. Many economists argue that, with the huge flows of short-term finance across the foreign exchanges, governments are forced to adopt one of two extreme forms of exchange rate regime: free floating or being a member of a currency union.
2. If financial flows could be constrained, however, exchange rates could be stabilised somewhat.
3. Forms of financial control include: quantitative controls, a tax on exchange transactions and non-interest-bearing deposits of a certain percentage of capital inflows with the central bank. Such controls can dampen speculation, but may discourage capital from flowing to where it has a higher marginal productivity.
4. An alternative means of stabilising exchange rates is to have exchange rate target zones. Here exchange rates are allowed to fluctuate within broad bands around a central parity, which is adjusted to the fundamental equilibrium rate in a gradual fashion.
5. The advantage of this system is that, by keeping the exchange rate at roughly its equilibrium level, destabilising speculation is avoided, and yet there is some freedom for governments to pursue an independent monetary policy. Monetary policy, however, may still from time to time have to be used to keep the exchange rate within the bands. The system also has the drawback of removing the pressure on governments to maintain a low rate of inflation.

END OF CHAPTER QUESTIONS

1. Under what circumstances does a growth in financial flows make exchange rates less stable?
2. Assume that countries in the eurozone decide to pursue a deflationary fiscal policy. What effect is this likely to have on the UK economy?
3. It is often argued that international convergence of economic indicators is a desirable objective. Does this mean that countries should all seek to achieve the same rate of economic growth, monetary growth, interest rates, budget deficits as a percentage of their GDP, etc?
4. Did the exchange rate difficulties experienced by countries under the ERM strengthen or weaken the arguments for progressing to a single European currency?
5. Assume that just some of the members of a common market like the EU adopt full economic and monetary union, including a common currency. What are the advantages and disadvantages to those members joining the full EMU and to those not?
6. Is the eurozone an optimal currency area? Explain your answer.
7. How are asymmetric shocks dealt with within a country? To what extent can this process be mirrored within the eurozone?
8. Would the world benefit from the general imposition of controls on the movement of international finance?

Answers to in-text Questions in *Economics* (6th edition)

Chapter 2

Page 35 ➢ *Assume that there are 200 consumers in the market. Of these, 100 have schedules like Tracey's and 100 have schedules like Darren's. What would be the total market demand schedule for potatoes now?*

Price (pence per kg)	Total market demand (kg)
20	4400
40	2600
60	1400
80	800
100	600

➢ *1. How much would be demanded at a price of 6p per kilogram?*

Reading off from the graph: at a price of 6p per kg, total market demand is 600 000 tonnes per month (or a little under).

➢ *2. Assuming that demand does not change from month to month, plot the annual market demand for potatoes.*

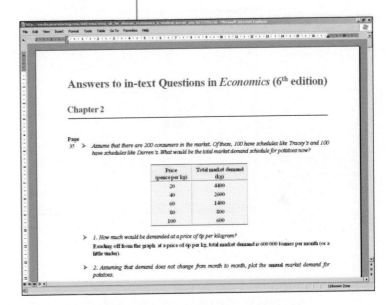

End of chapter questions can be used for self-testing or in class.

Take the **Chapter Tests in MyEconLab** to generate a personalised Study Plan. You will then be directed to specific resources in MyEconLab to help you focus your studies and improve your grades. For details on how to access MyEconLab, see the access card that is packaged with every new copy of this book.

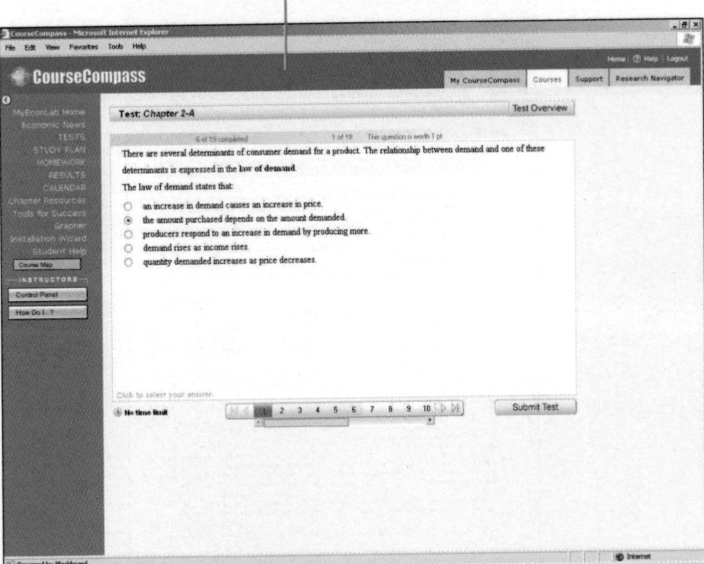

Graphical problems help you explore economic concepts visually.

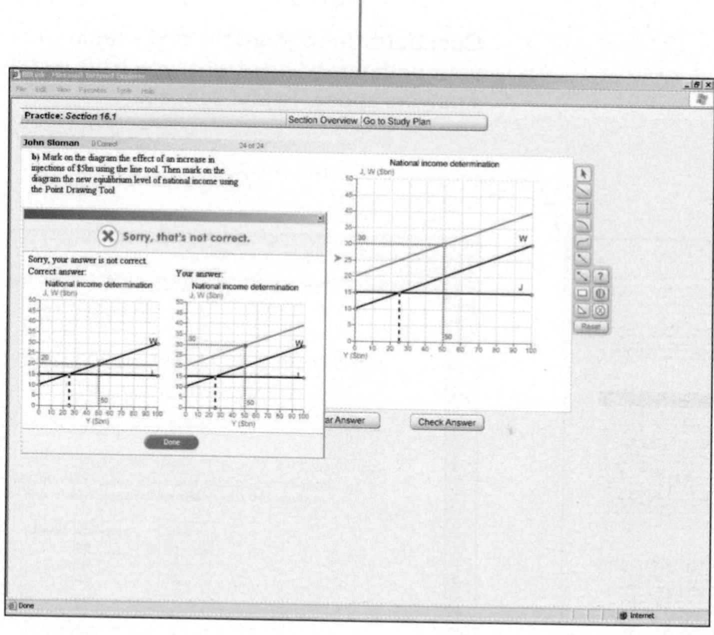

A printed **Workbook** is available for purchase (from www.pearson-books.com, ISBN 0 273 70517 2), which contains over 1500 questions of various types, carefully matched to the content of the main text.

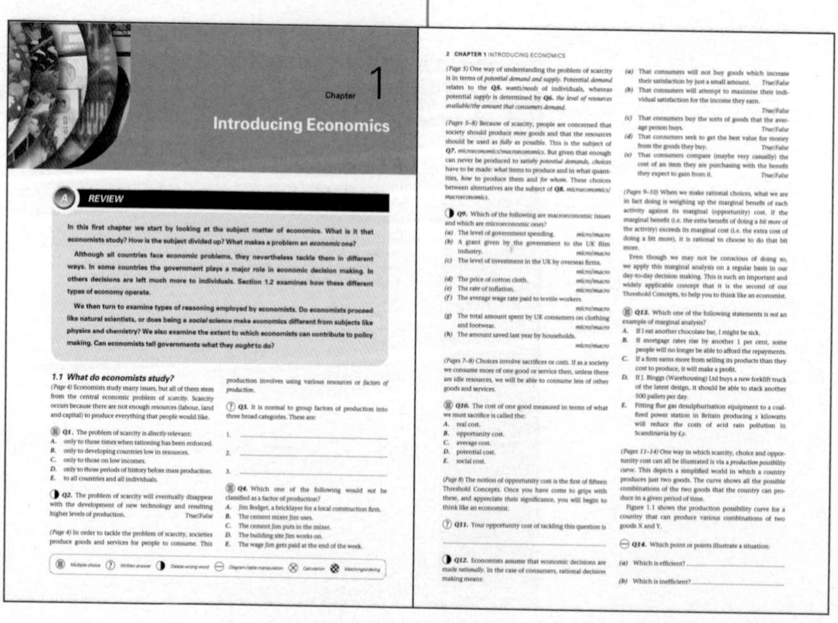

AIDING YOUR UNDERSTANDING

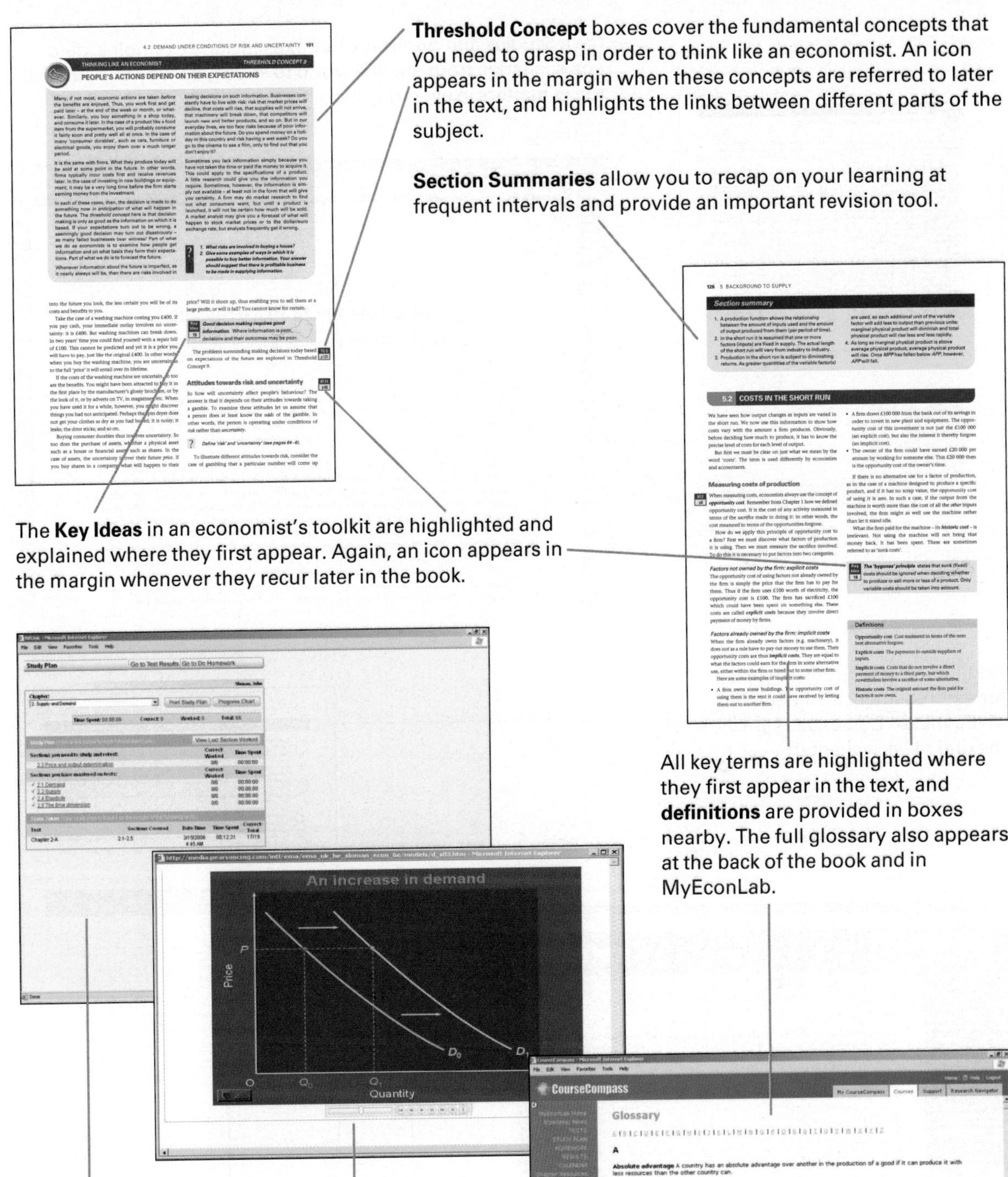

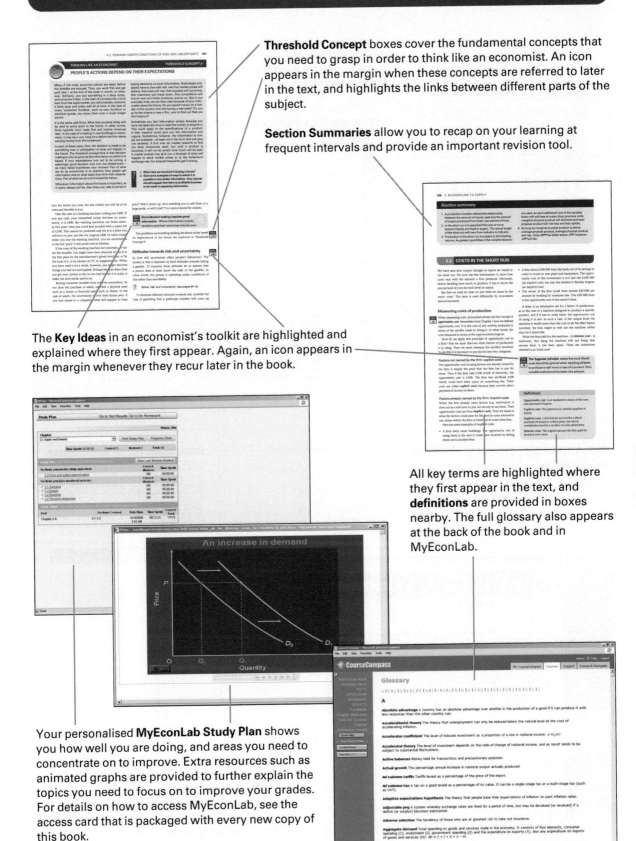

Threshold Concept boxes cover the fundamental concepts that you need to grasp in order to think like an economist. An icon appears in the margin when these concepts are referred to later in the text, and highlights the links between different parts of the subject.

Section Summaries allow you to recap on your learning at frequent intervals and provide an important revision tool.

The **Key Ideas** in an economist's toolkit are highlighted and explained where they first appear. Again, an icon appears in the margin whenever they recur later in the book.

All key terms are highlighted where they first appear in the text, and **definitions** are provided in boxes nearby. The full glossary also appears at the back of the book and in MyEconLab.

Your personalised **MyEconLab Study Plan** shows you how well you are doing, and areas you need to concentrate on to improve. Extra resources such as animated graphs are provided to further explain the topics you need to focus on to improve your grades. For details on how to access MyEconLab, see the access card that is packaged with every new copy of this book.

APPLYING ECONOMICS TO THE REAL WORLD

Case Studies and Applications boxes include examples, data and scenarios from the real world to show you why this subject really matters in everyday life.

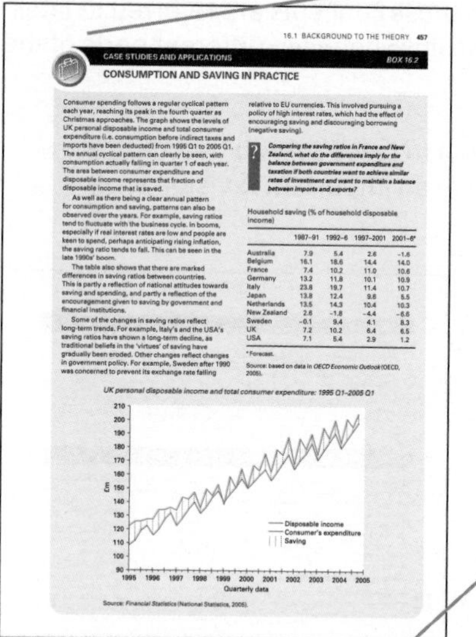

16.1 BACKGROUND TO THE THEORY 457

CASE STUDIES AND APPLICATIONS — BOX 16.2

CONSUMPTION AND SAVING IN PRACTICE

Consumer spending follows a regular cyclical pattern each year, reaching its peak in the fourth quarter as Christmas approaches. The graph shows the levels of UK personal disposable income and total consumer expenditure (i.e. consumption before indirect taxes and imports have been deducted) from 1995 Q1 to 2005 Q1. The annual cyclical pattern can clearly be seen, with consumption actually falling in quarter 1 of each year. The area between consumer expenditure and disposable income represents that fraction of disposable income that is saved.

As well as there being a clear annual pattern for consumption and saving, patterns can also be observed over the years. For example, saving ratios tend to fluctuate with the business cycle. In booms, especially if real interest rates are low and people are keen to spend, perhaps anticipating rising inflation, the saving ratio tends to fall. This can be seen in the late 1990s' boom.

The table also shows that there are marked differences in saving ratios between countries. This is partly a reflection of national attitudes towards saving and spending, and partly a reflection of the encouragement given to saving by government and financial institutions.

Some of the changes in saving ratios reflect long-term trends. For example, Italy's and the USA's saving ratios have shown a long-term decline, as traditional beliefs in the 'virtues' of saving have gradually been eroded. Other changes reflect changes in government policy. For example, Sweden after 1990 was concerned to prevent its exchange rate falling relative to EU currencies. This involved pursuing a policy of high interest rates, which had the effect of encouraging saving and discouraging borrowing (negative saving).

Comparing the saving ratios in France and New Zealand, what do the differences imply for the balance between government expenditure and taxation if both countries want to achieve similar rates of investment and want to maintain a balance between imports and exports?

Household saving (% of household disposable income)

	1987–91	1992–6	1997–2001	2001–6*
Australia	7.9	5.4	2.6	−1.6
Belgium	16.1	18.6	14.4	14.0
France	7.4	10.2	11.0	10.6
Germany	13.2	11.8	10.1	10.9
Italy	23.8	19.7	11.4	10.7
Japan	13.8	12.4	9.6	5.5
Netherlands	13.5	14.3	10.4	10.3
New Zealand	2.6	−1.8	−4.4	−6.6
Sweden	−0.1	9.4	4.1	8.3
UK	7.2	10.2	6.4	6.5
USA	7.1	5.4	2.9	1.2

* Forecast.

Source: based on data in *OECD Economic Outlook* (OECD, 2006).

UK personal disposable income and total consumer expenditure: 1995 Q1–2005 Q1

Source: *Financial Statistics* (National Statistics, 2005).

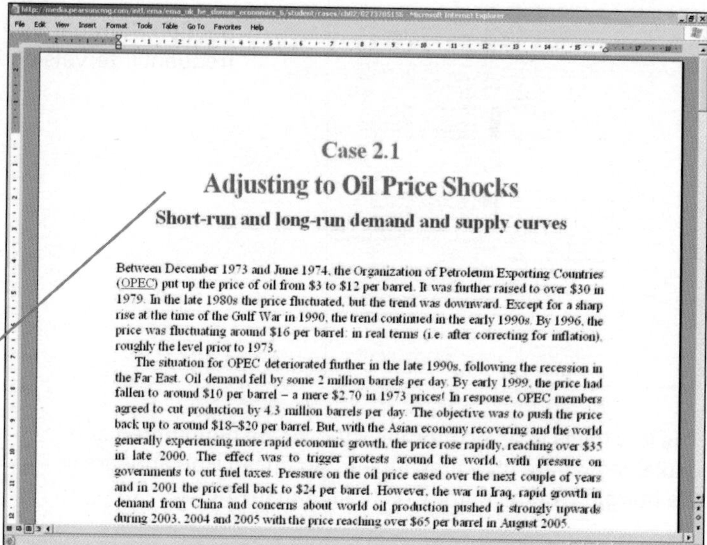

Case 2.1

Adjusting to Oil Price Shocks

Short-run and long-run demand and supply curves

Between December 1973 and June 1974, the Organization of Petroleum Exporting Countries (OPEC) put up the price of oil from $3 to $12 per barrel. It was further raised to over $30 in 1979. In the late 1980s the price fluctuated, but the trend was downward. Except for a sharp rise at the time of the Gulf War in 1990, the trend continued in the early 1990s. By 1996, the price was fluctuating around $16 per barrel: in real terms (i.e. after correcting for inflation), roughly the level prior to 1973.

The situation for OPEC deteriorated further in the late 1990s, following the recession in the Far East. Oil demand fell by some 2 million barrels per day. By early 1999, the price had fallen to around $10 per barrel – a mere $2.70 in 1973 prices! In response, OPEC members agreed to cut production by 4.3 million barrels per day. The objective was to push the price back up to around $18–$20 per barrel. But, with the Asian economy recovering and the world generally experiencing more rapid economic growth, the price rose rapidly, reaching over $35 in late 2000. The effect was to trigger protests around the world, with pressure on governments to cut fuel taxes. Pressure on the oil price eased over the next couple of years and in 2001 the price fell back to $24 per barrel. However, the war in Iraq, rapid growth in demand from China and concerns about world oil production pushed it strongly upwards during 2003, 2004 and 2005 with the price reaching over $65 per barrel in August 2005.

Additional **Case Studies** relevant for each chapter can be found in MyEconLab. These cases are listed at the end of each chapter.

364 12 APPLIED MICROECONOMICS

Additional case studies on the book's website (www.pearsoned.co.uk/sloman)

12.1 **Perverse subsidies.** An examination of the use of subsidies around the world that are harmful to the environment.

12.2 **Selling the environment.** This looks at the proposals made at international climate conferences to use market-based solutions to global warming.

12.3 **Environmental auditing.** Are businesses becoming greener? A growing number of firms are subjecting themselves to an 'environmental audit' to judge just how 'green' they are.

12.4 **Evaluating new road schemes.** The system used in the UK of assessing the costs and benefits of proposed new roads.

12.5 **Cartels set in concrete, steel and cardboard.** This examines some of the best-known Europe-wide cartels of recent years.

12.6 **Price-cap regulation in the UK.** How *RPI* – *X* regulation has been applied to the various privatised industries.

12.7 **Regulation US-style.** This examines rate-of-return regulation: an alternative to price-cap regulation.

12.8 **The right track to reform?** How successful has rail privatisation been in the UK?

12.9 **Privatisation in transition economies.** This extended case study examines state ownership under former communist countries of the USSR and how the transition of these countries to market economies involved a process of privatisation.

12.10 **Forms of privatisation in transition countries.** This focuses on how different types of privatisation are likely to affect the way industries are run.

WEBSITES RELEVANT TO CHAPTERS 11 AND 12

Numbers and sections refer to websites listed in the Web Appendix and hotlinked from this book's website at www.pearsoned.co.uk/sloman.

- For news articles relevant to this and the previous chapter, see the *Economics News Articles* link from the book's website.
- For general news on market failures and government intervention, see websites in section A, and particularly A1–5, 18, 19, 24, 31. See also links to newspapers in A38, 39, 43 and 44; and see A41 and 42 for links to economics news articles from newspapers worldwide.
- Sites I7 and 11 contain links to *Competition and monopoly*, *Policy and regulation* and *Transport* in the *Microeconomics* section; they also have an *Industry and commerce* section. Site I4 has links to *Environmental* and *Environmental Economics* in the *EconDirectory* section. Site I17 has several sections of links in the *Issues in Society* section.
- UK and EU departments relevant to competition policy can be found at sites E10; G7, 8.
- UK regulatory bodies can be found at sites E4, 11, 15, 16, 18, 19, 22, 25, 29.
- For information on taxes and subsidies, see E30, 36; G13. For use of green taxes (Box 12.1), see H5; G11; E2, 14, 30.
- For information on health and the economics of health care (Box 11.2), see E8; H9. See also links in I8 and 17.
- For sites favouring the free market, see C17; D34. See also C18 for the development of ideas on the market and government intervention.
- For the economics of the environment, see links in I4, 7, 11, 17. For policy on the environment and transport, see E2, 7, 11, 14, 21, 29; G10, 11. See also H11.
- For student resources relevant to these two chapters, see sites C1–7, 9, 10, 19.
- For a simulation on tackling traffic congestion, see site D3.

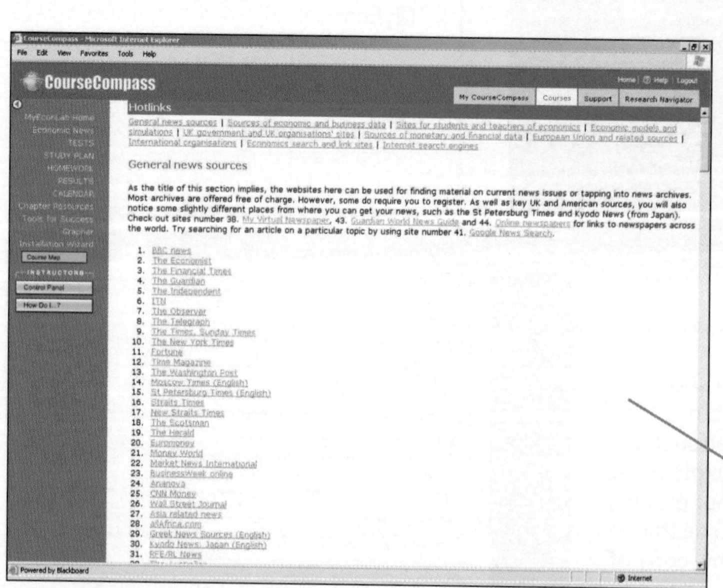

Websites relevant to each chapter are listed at the end of the chapter, and are linked to from the chapter resources area of MyEconLab.

Topical Economic Issues in the Economics News area of MyEconLab provide discussion of some of the key economic issues over the past six months related to passages in the book, with links to relevant websites.

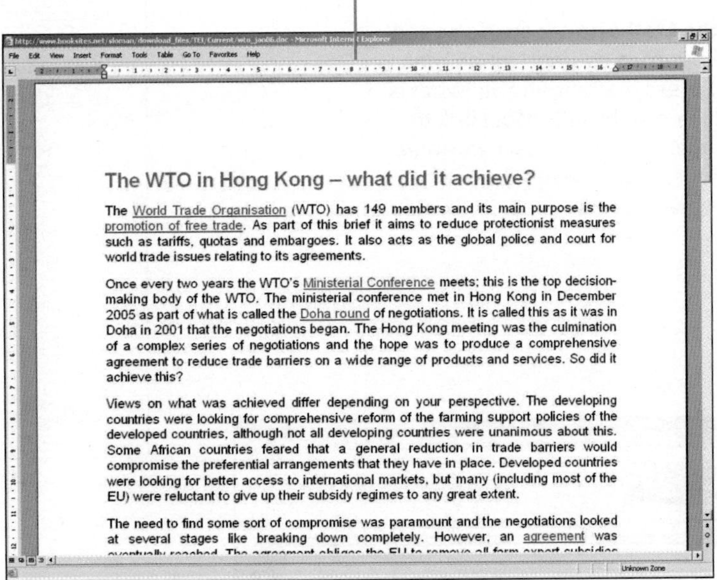

The WTO in Hong Kong – what did it achieve?

The World Trade Organisation (WTO) has 149 members and its main purpose is the promotion of free trade. As part of this brief it aims to reduce protectionist measures such as tariffs, quotas and embargoes. It also acts as the global police and court for world trade issues relating to its agreements.

Once every two years the WTO's Ministerial Conference meets; this is the top decision-making body of the WTO. The ministerial conference met in Hong Kong in December 2005 as part of what is called the Doha round of negotiations. It is called this as it was in Doha in 2001 that the negotiations began. The Hong Kong meeting was the culmination of a complex series of negotiations and the hope was to produce a comprehensive agreement to reduce trade barriers on a wide range of products and services. So did it achieve this?

Views on what was achieved differ depending on your perspective. The developing countries were looking for comprehensive reform of the farming support policies of the developed countries, although not all developing countries were unanimous about this. Some African countries feared that a general reduction in trade barriers would compromise the preferential arrangements that they have in place. Developed countries were looking for better access to international markets, but many (including most of the EU) were reluctant to give up their subsidy regimes to any great extent.

The need to find some sort of compromise was paramount and the negotiations looked at several stages like breaking down completely. However, an agreement was

Economics News Articles in MyEconLab are updated monthly, and provide hotlinks to recent economics articles from newspapers and magazines related to passages in the book.

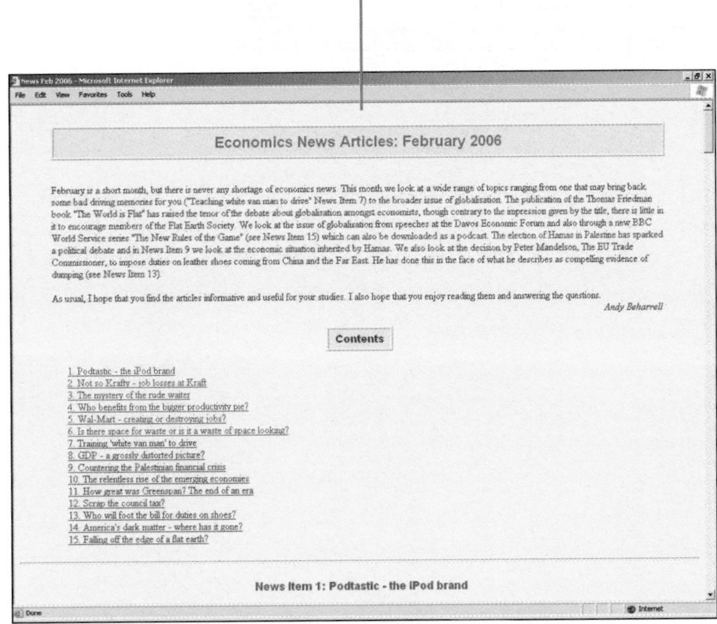

Economics News Articles: February 2006

February is a short month, but there is never any shortage of economics news. This month we look at a wide range of topics ranging from one that may bring back some bad driving memories for you ("Teaching white van man to drive" News Item 7) to the broader issue of globalisation. The publication of the Thomas Friedman book "The World is Flat" has raised the tenor of the debate about globalisation amongst economists, though contrary to the impression given by the title, there is little in it to encourage members of the Flat Earth Society. We look at the issue of globalisation from speeches at the Davos Economic Forum and also through a new BBC World Service series "The New Rules of the Game" (see News Item 15) which can also be downloaded as a podcast. The election of Hamas in Palestine has sparked a political debate and in News Item 9 we look at the economic situation inherited by Hamas. We also look at the decision by Peter Mandelson, The EU Trade Commissioner, to impose duties on leather shoes coming from China and the Far East. He has done this in the face of what he describes as compelling evidence of dumping (see News Item 13).

As usual, I hope that you find the articles informative and useful for your studies. I also hope that you enjoy reading them and answering the questions.

Andy Beharrell

Contents

News Item 1: Podtastic - the iPod brand

FLEXIBLE LEARNING

Starred sections contain optional, more advanced material. These can be omitted without interrupting the flow of the argument.

Optional **Looking at the Maths** boxes are designed for students on more rigorous courses which make use of maths. They express mathematically what is also covered in words or graphically. Most link to **Maths Cases** with worked mathematical examples and numerical questions, found on the Student Companion Website at www.pearsoned.co.uk/sloman or in MyEconLab.

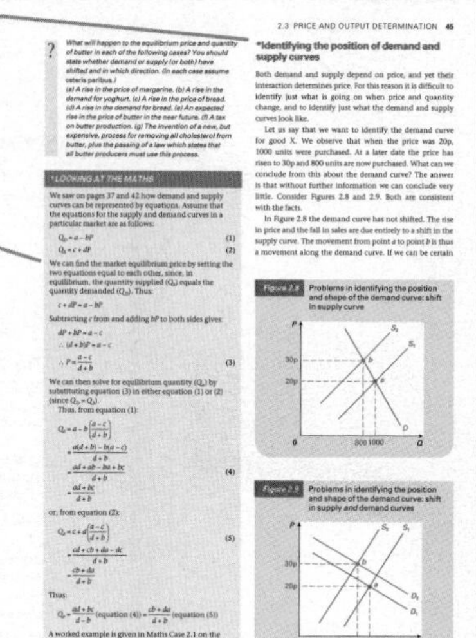

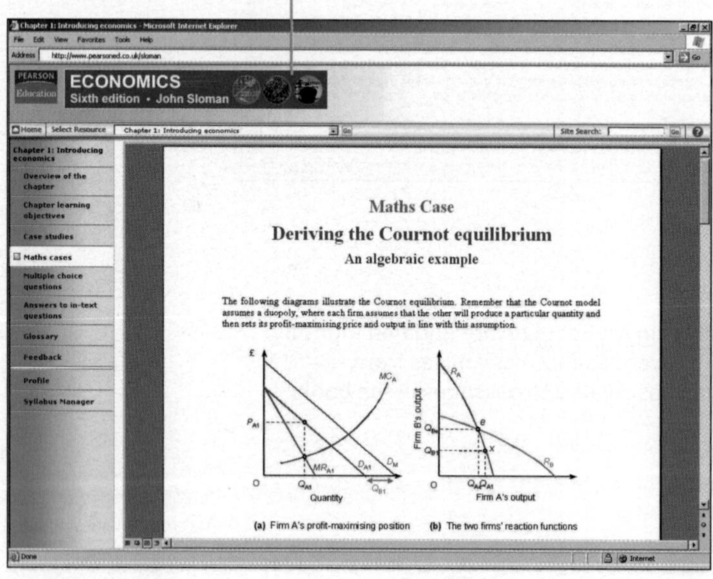

Part A: Introduction

In this opening part of the book you will get a glimpse of what the subject of economics is all about. One thing to be stressed right from the outset: economics is not just a set of facts or theories to be memorised. Studying economics gives you a way of thinking about the world. It helps you to make sense of the decisions people are making all the time: decisions we make about what to buy or what job to do; decisions our government makes about how much to tax us or what to spend those taxes on.

Economics contains some core ideas. These ideas are simple, but can be applied to a wide range of economic problems. We start examining these ideas in Chapter 1.

Chapter 1

Introducing Economics

You may never have studied economics before, and yet when you open a newspaper what do you read? – a report from 'our economics correspondent'. Turn on the television news and what do you see? – an item on the state of the economy. Talk to friends and often the topic will turn to the price of this or that product, or whether you have got enough money to afford to do this or that.

The fact is that economics affects our daily lives. Continually we are being made aware of local, national and international economic issues: whether it be price increases, interest rate changes, fluctuations in exchange rates, unemployment, economic recessions or the effects of globalisation.

We are also continually faced with economic problems and decisions of our own. What should I buy in the supermarket? Should I save up for a summer holiday, or spend more on day-to-day living? Should I go to university, or should I try to find a job now?

So just what is economics about? In this chapter we will attempt to answer this question and give you some insights into the subject that you will be studying by using this book. We will see how the subject is divided up, and in particular we will distinguish between the two major branches of economics: microeconomics and macroeconomics.

We will also look at the ways in which different types of economy operate: from the centrally planned economies of the former communist countries, to the free-market economies of most of the world today. We will ask just how do 'markets' work?

CHAPTER MAP

1.1 WHAT DO ECONOMISTS STUDY?

Many people think that economics is about *money*. Well, to some extent this is true. Economics has a lot to do with money: with how much money people are paid; how much they spend; what it costs to buy various items; how much money firms earn; how much money there is in total in the economy. But despite the large number of areas in which our lives are concerned with money, economics is more than just the study of money.

It is concerned with the following:

- The ***production*** of goods and services: how much the economy produces, both in total and of individual items; how much each firm or person produces; what techniques of production are used; how many people are employed.
- The ***consumption*** of goods and services: how much the population as a whole spends (and how much it saves); what the pattern of consumption is in the economy; how much people buy of particular items; what particular individuals choose to buy; how people's consumption is affected by prices, advertising, fashion and other factors.

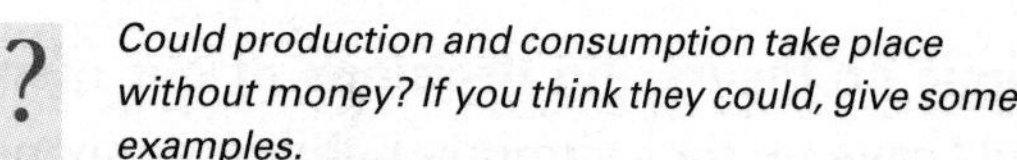

? *Could production and consumption take place without money? If you think they could, give some examples.*

But we still have not quite got to the bottom of what economics is about. What is the crucial ingredient that makes a problem an *economic* one? The answer is that there is one central problem faced by all individuals and all societies. From this one problem stem all the other economic problems we shall be looking at throughout this book.

This central economic problem is the problem of *scarcity*. This applies not only in countries like Ethiopia and the Sudan, but also in the UK, the USA, Japan, France and all other countries of the world. For an economist, scarcity has a very specific definition . . .

? *Before reading on, how would you define 'scarcity'? Must goods be at least temporarily unattainable to be scarce?*

The problem of scarcity

Ask people if they would like more money, and the vast majority would answer 'Yes'. They want more money so that they can buy more goods and services; and this applies not only to poor people but also to most wealthy people too. The point is that human wants are virtually unlimited.

Yet the means of fulfilling human wants are limited. At any one time the world can only produce a limited amount of goods and services. This is because the world only has a limited amount of resources. These resources, or ***factors of production*** as they are often called, are of three broad types:

- Human resources: ***labour***. The labour force is limited both in number and in skills.
- Natural resources: ***land and raw materials***. The world's land area is limited, as are its raw materials.
- Manufactured resources: ***capital***. Capital consists of all those inputs that have each had to be produced in the first place. The world has a limited stock of capital: a limited supply of factories, machines, transportation and other equipment. The productivity of capital is limited by the state of technology.

So here is the reason for scarcity: human wants are virtually unlimited, whereas the resources available to satisfy these wants *are* limited. We can thus define ***scarcity*** as follows:

Key Idea 1

Scarcity is the excess of human wants over what can actually be produced. Because of scarcity, various choices have to be made between alternatives.

? *If we would all like more money, why does the government not print a lot more? Could it not thereby solve the problem of scarcity 'at a stroke'?*

Of course, we do not all face the problem of scarcity to the same degree. A poor person unable to afford enough to eat or a decent place to live will hardly see it as a 'problem' that a rich person cannot afford a second BMW. But

Definitions

Production The transformation of inputs into outputs by firms in order to earn profit (or meet some other objective).

Consumption The act of using goods and services to satisfy wants. This will normally involve purchasing the goods and services.

Factors of production (or resources) The inputs into the production of goods and services: labour, land and raw materials, and capital.

Labour All forms of human input, both physical and mental, into current production.

Land and raw materials Inputs into production that are provided by nature: e.g. unimproved land and mineral deposits in the ground.

Capital All inputs into production that have themselves been produced: e.g. factories, machines and tools.

Scarcity The excess of human wants over what can actually be produced to fulfil these wants.

CASE STUDIES AND APPLICATIONS 

BOX 1.1

WHAT'S THE LATEST ECONOMICS NEWS?

- Budget news: Chancellor cuts 2p off the basic rate of income tax; government hopes that this will provide an incentive for people to work harder.
- Mortgage interest rates reduced: resulting boost to the housing market expected to lead to higher house prices.
- Recent survey reveals that business confidence is low: fall in investment predicted.
- The country continues to bask in a heatwave: record ice-cream sales reported.
- Floods hit Bangladesh: two-thirds of the country's crops ruined; massive food price rises expected.
- Consumer spending growing too fast: forecasters predict that inflation will soon begin to rise.
- Increased expenditure on education announced: government claims that this will help the economy to become more competitive and unemployment to fall. Opposition claims that it will lead to rising prices and to higher unemployment.
- Record balance of trade deficit announced today: further rises in interest rates seem inevitable.
- Rumours of a takeover bid for ABC plc: ABC shares close 25p up on the day.
- Tuition fees increased: Student Union president says that this will create real hardship for many students.

What is it that makes each one of the above news items an* economics *item?

economists do not claim that we all face an *equal* problem of scarcity. In fact this is one of the major issues economists study: how resources are *distributed*, whether between different individuals, different regions of a country or different countries of the world.

But given that people, both rich and poor, want more than they can have, this makes them behave in certain ways. Economics studies that behaviour. It studies people at work, producing the goods that people want. It studies people as consumers, buying the goods that they themselves want. It studies governments influencing the level and pattern of production and consumption. In short, it studies anything to do with the process of satisfying human wants.

Demand and supply

We said that economics is concerned with consumption and production. Another way of looking at this is in terms of *demand* and *supply*. In fact, demand and supply and the relationship between them lie at the very centre of economics. But what do we mean by the terms, and what is their relationship with the problem of scarcity?

Demand is related to wants. If goods and services were free, people would simply demand whatever they wanted. Such wants are virtually boundless: perhaps only limited by people's imagination. *Supply*, on the other hand, is limited. It is related to resources. The amount that firms can supply depends on the resources and technology available.

KI 1 p4

Given the problem of scarcity, given that human wants exceed what can actually be produced, *potential* demands will exceed *potential* supplies. Society therefore has to find some way of dealing with this problem. Somehow it has got to try to match demand with supply. This applies at the level of the economy overall: *aggregate* demand will need to be balanced against *aggregate* supply. In other words, total spending in the economy should balance total production. It also applies at the level of individual goods and services. The demand and supply of cabbages should balance, and so should the demand and supply of DVD recorders, cars, houses and package holidays.

But if potential demand exceeds potential supply, how are *actual* demand and supply to be made equal? Either demand has to be curtailed, or supply has to be increased, or a combination of the two. Economics studies this process. It studies how demand adjusts to available supplies, and how supply adjusts to consumer demands.

Dividing up the subject

Economics is traditionally divided into two main branches – *macroeconomics* and *microeconomics,* where 'macro' means big, and 'micro' means small.

Macroeconomics is concerned with the economy as a whole. It is thus concerned with ***aggregate demand*** and ***aggregate supply***. By 'aggregate demand' we mean the total amount of spending in the economy, whether by consumers, by customers outside the country for our exports, by the government, or by firms when they buy capital equipment or stock up on raw materials. By 'aggregate supply' we mean the total national output of goods and services.

Definitions

Macroeconomics The branch of economics that studies economic aggregates (grand totals): e.g. the overall level of prices, output and employment in the economy.

Aggregate demand The total level of spending in the economy.

Aggregate supply The total amount of output in the economy.

Microeconomics is concerned with the individual parts of the economy. It is concerned with the demand and supply of *particular* goods and services and resources: cars, butter, clothes and haircuts; electricians, secretaries, blast furnaces, computers and oil.

?

Which of the following are macroeconomic issues, which are microeconomic ones and which could be either depending on the context?

(a) Inflation.
(b) Low wages in certain service industries.
(c) The rate of exchange between the pound and the euro.
(d) Why the price of cabbages fluctuates more than that of cars.
(e) The rate of economic growth this year compared with last year.
(f) The decline of traditional manufacturing industries.

Macroeconomics

Because things are scarce, societies are concerned that their resources should be used *as fully as possible*, and that over time their national output should *grow*.

The achievement of growth and the full use of resources is not easy, however, as demonstrated by the periods of high unemployment and stagnation that have occurred from time to time throughout the world (for example, in the 1930s, the early 1980s, the early 1990s and the early 2000s). Furthermore, attempts by government to stimulate growth and employment have often resulted in inflation and a large rise in imports. Even when societies do achieve growth, it can be short lived. Economies have often experienced cycles, where periods of growth alternate with periods of stagnation, such periods varying from a few months to a few years.

Macroeconomic problems are closely related to the balance between aggregate demand and aggregate supply.

If aggregate demand is *too high* relative to aggregate supply, inflation and trade deficits are likely to result.

- ***Inflation*** refers to a general rise in the level of prices throughout the economy. If aggregate demand rises substantially, firms are likely to respond by raising their prices. After all, if demand is high, they can probably still sell as much as before (if not more) even at the higher prices, and thus make more profits. If firms in general put up their prices, inflation results.
- ***Balance of trade*** deficits are the excess of imports over exports. If aggregate demand rises, people are likely to buy more imports. In other words, part of the extra expenditure will go on Japanese LCD TVs, German cars, French wine, etc. Also if inflation is high, home-produced goods will become uncompetitive with foreign goods. We are likely, therefore, to buy more foreign imports and people abroad are likely to buy fewer of our exports.

If aggregate demand is *too low* relative to aggregate supply, unemployment and recession may well result.

- ***Recession*** is where output in the economy declines: in other words, growth becomes negative. A recession is associated with a low level of consumer spending. If people spend less, shops are likely to find themselves with unsold stock. As a result they will buy less from the manufacturers, which in turn will cut down on production.
- ***Unemployment*** is likely to result from cutbacks in production. If firms are producing less, they will need to employ fewer people.

Macroeconomic *policy*, therefore, tends to focus on the balance of aggregate demand and aggregate supply. It can be ***demand-side policy***, which seeks to influence the level of spending in the economy. This in turn will affect the level of production, prices and employment. Or it can be ***supply-side policy***. This is designed to influence the level of production directly: for example, by trying to create more incentives for firms to innovate.

Microeconomics

Microeconomics and choice

Because resources are scarce, choices have to be made. There are three main categories of choice that must be made in any society.

KI 1 p4

Definitions

Microeconomics The branch of economics that studies individual units: e.g. households, firms and industries. It studies the interrelationships between these units in determining the pattern of production and distribution of goods and services.

Rate of inflation The percentage increase in the level of prices over a 12-month period.

Balance of trade Exports of goods and services minus imports of goods and services. If exports exceed imports, there is a 'balance of trade surplus' (a positive figure). If imports exceed exports, there is a 'balance of trade deficit' (a negative figure).

Recession A period where national output falls for six months or more.

Unemployment The number of people who are actively looking for work but are currently without a job. (Note that there is much debate as to who should officially be counted as unemployed.)

Demand-side policy Government policy designed to alter the level of aggregate demand, and thereby the level of output, employment and prices.

Supply-side policy Government policy that attempts to alter the level of aggregate supply directly.

CASE STUDIES AND APPLICATIONS **BOX 1.2**

LOOKING AT MACROECONOMIC DATA

Assessing different countries' macroeconomic performance

Rapid economic growth, low unemployment, low inflation and the avoidance of current account deficits[1] are major macroeconomic policy objectives of most governments round the world. To help them achieve these objectives they employ economic advisers. But when we look at the performance of various economies, the success of government macroeconomic policies seems decidedly 'mixed'.

The table shows data for the USA, Japan, Germany[2] and the UK from 1961–2005.

Macroeconomic performance of four industrialised economies (average annual figures)

	Unemployment (% of workforce)				Inflation (%)				Economic growth (%)				Balance on current account (% of national income)			
	USA	Japan	Germany	UK	USA	Japan	Germany	UK	USA	Japan	Germany	UK	USA	Japan	Germany	UK
1961–70	4.8	1.3	0.6	1.7	2.4	5.6	2.7	3.9	4.2	10.1	4.4	3.0	0.5	0.6	0.7	0.2
1971–80	6.4	1.8	2.2	3.8	7.0	8.8	5.1	13.2	3.2	4.4	2.8	2.0	0.9	0.5	1.1	−0.7
1981–90	2.5	2.5	6.0	9.6	4.5	2.2	2.5	6.2	3.2	3.9	2.3	2.6	−1.7	2.3	2.6	−1.4
1990–2000	3.3	3.3	7.9	7.9	2.2	0.4	2.3	3.3	3.3	1.5	1.9	2.4	−1.6	2.5	−0.7	−1.5
2000–05	5.0	5.0	9.2	5.0	2.1	−1.3	1.3	1.9	2.6	1.7	0.8	2.5	−4.8	2.9	2.8	−1.9

Source: European Economy Statistical Annex, various tables (European Commission).

?

1. ***Has the UK generally fared better or worse than the other three countries?***
2. ***Was there a common pattern in the macroeconomic performance of each of the four countries over these 45 years?***

If the government does not have much success in managing the economy, it could be for the following reasons:

- Economists have incorrectly analysed the problems and hence have given the wrong advice.
- Economists disagree and hence have given conflicting advice.
- Economists have based their advice on inaccurate forecasts.
- Governments have not heeded the advice of economists.
- There is little else that governments could have done: the problems were insoluble.

[1] The current account balance is the trade balance plus any incomes earned from abroad minus any incomes paid abroad. These incomes could be wages, investment incomes or government revenues (see section 14.4 for details).

[2] West Germany from 1961 to 1991.

- *What* goods and services are going to be produced and in what quantities, since there are not enough resources to produce all the things people desire? How many cars, how much wheat, how much insurance, how many rock concerts, how many coats, etc. will be produced?
- *How* are things going to be produced, given that there is normally more than one way of producing things? What resources are going to be used and in what quantities? What techniques of production are going to be adopted? Will cars be produced by robots or by assembly line workers? Will electricity be produced from coal, oil, gas, nuclear fission, renewable resources or a mixture of these?
- *For whom* are things going to be produced? In other words, how will the nation's income be distributed? After all, the higher your income, the more you can consume of the nation's output. What will be the wages of farm workers, printers, cleaners and accountants? How much will pensioners receive? How much of the nation's income will go to shareholders or landowners?

All societies have to make these choices, whether they be made by individuals, groups or the government. These choices can be seen as *micro*economic choices, since they are concerned not with the *total* amount of national output, but with the *individual* goods and services that make it up: what they are, how they are made, and who gets the incomes to buy them.

Choice and opportunity cost

Choice involves sacrifice. The more food you choose to buy, the less money you will have to spend on other goods. The more food a nation produces, the fewer resources will there be for producing other goods. In other words, the production or consumption of one thing involves the sacrifice of alternatives. This sacrifice of alternatives in

THINKING LIKE AN ECONOMIST

THRESHOLD CONCEPT 1

CHOICE AND OPPORTUNITY COST

Scarcity, as we have seen, is at the heart of economics.

We face scarcity as individuals. Each of us has a limited income and hence we cannot buy everything we want. And it's not just a question of what we can afford. Even the richest person has limited time. There are only 24 hours in a day and we will all die. So even if we had the money, we would not be able to enjoy every possible good we would like to consume or take part in every possible activity.

The same applies to nations. A nation has limited resources and hence cannot produce everything people would like. So too with the world. Our planet has finite resources, and the technology and human abilities to exploit these resources are also limited.

We thus have to make choices. In fact, virtually every time we do something, we are making a choice between alternatives. If you choose to spend your time staying in and watching television, you are choosing *not* to go out. It's the same when you spend money. If you buy a CD for £10, you are choosing *not* to spend that £10 on something else. Likewise, if a nation devotes more of its resources to producing manufactured goods, there will be less to devote to the production of services or agricultural goods. If we devote more resources to producing a cleaner environment, we may have to produce less of the material goods that people want to consume.

What we give up in order to do something is known as its *opportunity cost*. Opportunity cost is the cost of doing something measured in terms of the best alternative forgone. It's what you *would* have chosen to do with your time or money, if you had not made the choice you did. This is one of the most fundamental concepts in economics. It is a *threshold concept*: once you have seen its importance, it affects the way you look at economic problems. When you use the concept of opportunity cost, you are *thinking like an economist*. And this may be different from thinking like an accountant or from the way you thought before. We will come across this concept many times throughout this book.

By looking at opportunity cost we are recognising that we face *trade-offs*. To do more of one thing involves doing less of something else. For example, we trade off work and leisure. The more we work, the less leisure time we will have. In other words, the opportunity cost of working is the leisure we have sacrificed. Nations trade off producing one good against others. The more a country spends on defence, whether on weapons or employing military personnel, the less it will have to spend on consumer goods and services. This has become known as the 'guns versus butter' trade-off. In other words, if a country decides to use more of its resources for defence, the opportunity cost is the consumer goods sacrificed. We examine such trade-offs at a national level on pages 12–14, when we look at the 'production possibility curve'.

We thus have to make decisions between alternatives. To make sensible decisions we must *weigh up* the benefits of doing something against its opportunity cost. Understanding this involves Threshold Concept 2 (see page 10).

1. ***Think of three things you did yesterday. What was the opportunity cost of each one?***
2. ***Assume that a supermarket has some fish that has reached its sell-by date. It was originally priced at £10, but yesterday was marked down to £5 'for quick sale'. It is now the end of the day and it still has not been sold. The supermarket is about to close and there is no one in the store who wants fish. What is the opportunity cost for the store of throwing the fish away?***

the production (or consumption) of a good is known as its ***opportunity cost***.

The ***opportunity cost*** of any activity is the sacrifice made to do it. It is the best thing that could have been done as an alternative.

If the workers on a farm can produce either 1000 tonnes of wheat or 2000 tonnes of barley, then the opportunity cost of producing 1 tonne of wheat is the 2 tonnes of barley forgone. The opportunity cost of buying a textbook is the new pair of jeans you also wanted that you have had to go without. The opportunity cost of working overtime is the leisure you have sacrificed.

Opportunity cost as the basis for choice is the first of our 'Threshold Concepts' (see panel below). There are 15 of these threshold concepts, which we shall be exploring throughout the book. Once you have grasped these concepts and seen their significance, they will affect the way that you understand and analyse economic problems. They will help you to 'think like an economist'.

Rational choices

Economists often refer to ***rational choices***. This simply means the weighing-up of the *costs* and *benefits* of any activity, whether it be firms choosing what and how much to

Definitions

Opportunity cost The cost of any activity measured in terms of the best alternative forgone.

Rational choices Choices that involve weighing up the benefit of any activity against its opportunity cost.

produce, workers choosing whether to take a particular job or to work extra hours, or consumers choosing what to buy.

Imagine you are doing your shopping in a supermarket and you want to buy a bottle of wine. Do you spend a lot of money and buy a top-quality French wine, or do you buy a cheap eastern European one instead? To make a rational (i.e. sensible) decision, you will need to weigh up the costs and benefits of each alternative. The top-quality wine may give you a lot of enjoyment, but it has a high opportunity cost: because it is expensive, you will need to sacrifice quite a lot of consumption of other goods if you decide to buy it. If you buy the cheap bottle, however, although you will not enjoy it so much, you will have more money left over to buy other things: it has a lower opportunity cost.

Thus rational decision making, as far as consumers are concerned, involves choosing those items that give you the best value for money – i.e. the *greatest benefit relative to cost*.

The same principles apply to firms when deciding what to produce. For example, should a car firm open up another production line? A rational decision will again involve weighing up the benefits and costs. The benefits are the revenues the firm will earn from selling the extra cars. The costs will include the extra labour costs, raw material costs, costs of component parts, etc. It will be profitable to open up the new production line only if the revenues earned exceed the costs entailed: in other words, if it adds to profit.

In the more complex situation of deciding which model of car to produce, or how many of each model, the firm must weigh up the relative benefits and costs of each – i.e. it will want to produce the most profitable product mix.

? *Assume that you are looking for a job and are offered two. One is more pleasant to do, but pays less. How would you make a rational choice between the two jobs?*

Marginal costs and benefits

In economics we argue that rational choices involve weighing up ***marginal costs*** and ***marginal benefits***. These are the costs and benefits of doing a little bit more or a little bit less of a specific activity. They can be contrasted with the *total* costs and benefits of the activity.

Take a familiar example. What time will you set the alarm clock to go off tomorrow morning? Let us say that you have to leave home at 8.30. Perhaps you will set the alarm for 7.00. That will give you plenty of time to get up and get ready, but it will mean a relatively short night's sleep. Perhaps you will decide to set it for 7.30 or even 8.00. That will give you a longer night's sleep, but much more of a rush in the morning to get ready.

So how do you make a rational decision about when the alarm should go off? What you have to do is to weigh up the costs and benefits of *additional* sleep. Each extra minute in bed gives you more sleep (the marginal benefit), but gives you more of a rush when you get up (the marginal cost). The decision is therefore based on the costs and benefits of *extra* sleep, not on the *total* costs and benefits of a whole night's sleep.

This same principle applies to rational decisions made by consumers, workers and firms. For example, the car firm we were considering just now will weigh up the marginal costs and benefits of producing cars: in other words, it will compare the costs and revenue of producing *additional* cars. If additional cars add more to the firm's revenue than to its costs, it will be profitable to produce them.

Rational decision making, then, involves weighing up the marginal benefit and marginal cost of any activity. If the marginal benefit exceeds the marginal cost, it is rational to do the activity (or to do more of it). If the marginal cost exceeds the marginal benefit, it is rational not to do it (or to do less of it).

Rational decision making is Threshold Concept 2.

? *How would the principle of weighing up marginal costs and benefits apply to a worker deciding how much overtime to work in a given week?*

Microeconomic objectives

Microeconomics is concerned with the allocation of scarce resources: with the answering of the *what*, *how* and *for whom* questions. But how satisfactorily will these questions be answered? Clearly this depends on society's objectives. There are two major objectives that we can identify: *efficiency* and *equity*.

Efficiency. If, by altering what was produced or how it was produced, we could all be made better off (or at least some of us could without anyone losing), then it would be efficient to do so. For a society to achieve full ***economic efficiency***, three conditions must be met:

Definitions

Marginal costs The additional cost of doing a little bit more (or 1 unit more if a unit can be measured) of an activity.

Marginal benefits The additional benefits of doing a little bit more (or 1 unit more if a unit can be measured) of an activity.

Rational decision making Doing more of an activity if its marginal benefit exceeds its marginal cost and doing less if its marginal cost exceeds its marginal benefit.

Economic efficiency A situation where each good is produced at the minimum cost and where individual people and firms get the maximum benefit from their resources.

THINKING LIKE AN ECONOMIST — THRESHOLD CONCEPT 2

RATIONAL DECISION MAKING INVOLVES CHOICES AT THE MARGIN

Rational decision making involves weighing up the marginal benefit and marginal cost of any activity. If the marginal benefit exceeds the marginal cost, it is rational to do the activity (or to do more of it). If the marginal cost exceeds the marginal benefit, it is rational not to do it (or to do less of it).

Let's take the case of when you go to the supermarket to do shopping for the week. Assume that you have £30 to spend. Clearly, you will want to spend it wisely. With each item you consider buying, you should ask yourself what its marginal benefit is to you: in other words, how much you would be prepared to spend on it. This will depend on the prices and benefits of alternatives. Thus if you were considering spending £2 from the £30 on wholemeal bread, you should ask yourself whether the £2 would be better spent on some alternative, such as white bread, rolls or crackers. The *best* alternative (which might be a combination of products) is the marginal opportunity cost. If the answer is that you feel you are getting better value for money by spending it on the wholemeal bread, then you are saying that the marginal benefit exceeds the marginal opportunity cost. It is an efficient use of your money to buy the wholemeal bread and forgo the alternatives.

Most decisions are more complex than this, as they involve buying a whole range of products. In fact, that is what you are doing in the supermarket. But the principle is still the same. In each case, a rational decision involves weighing up marginal benefits and marginal costs. Is buying an extra jar of this, or packet of that, worth the sacrifice of the alternative you could have purchased with the money?

This is another example of a *threshold concept* because it is a way of thinking about economic problems. It is a general principle that can be applied in a whole host of contexts: whether it is individuals deciding what to buy, how much to work, what job to apply for, or whether to study for a degree or take a job; or firms deciding how much to produce, whether to invest in new capacity or new products, or what type of people to employ and how many; or governments deciding how much to spend on various projects, such as roads, hospitals and schools, or what rates of tax to impose on companies that pollute the environment.

In each case, better decisions will be made by weighing up marginal costs and marginal benefits.

?

1. ***Assume that a firm is selling 1000 units of a product at £20 each and that each unit on average costs £15 to produce. Assume also that to produce additional units will cost the firm £19 each and that the price will remain at £20. To produce additional products will therefore reduce the average profit per unit. Should the firm expand production? Explain.***
2. ***Assume that a ferry has capacity for 500 passengers. Its operator predicts that it will typically have only 200 passengers on each of its midweek sailings over the winter. Assume also that each sailing costs the company £10,000. This means that midweek winter sailings cost the company an average of £10,000/200 = £50 per passenger. Currently tickets cost £60. Should the company consider selling stand-by tickets during the winter for (a) less than £60; (b) less than £50? (Clue: think about the marginal cost of taking additional passengers.)***

- Efficiency in production (***productive efficiency***). This is where production of each item is at minimum costs. Producing any other way would cost more.
- Efficiency in consumption. This is where consumers allocate their expenditures so as to get maximum satisfaction from their income. Any other pattern of consumption would make people feel worse off.
- Efficiency in specialisation and exchange. This is where firms specialise in producing goods for sale to consumers, and where individuals specialise in doing jobs in order to buy goods, so that everyone maximises the benefits they achieve relative to the costs of achieving them.

These last two are collectively known as ***allocative efficiency***. In any economic activity, allocative efficiency will be increased as long as doing more of that activity (and hence less of an alternative) involves a greater marginal benefit than marginal cost. Full efficiency will be achieved when all such improvements have been made.

Key Idea 3

Economic efficiency is thus achieved when each good is produced at the minimum cost and where individual people and firms get the maximum benefit from their resources.

Definitions

Productive efficiency A situation where firms are producing the maximum output for a given amount of inputs, or producing a given output at the least cost.

Allocative efficiency A situation where the current combination of goods produced and sold gives the maximum satisfaction for each consumer at their current levels of income. Note that a redistribution of income would lead to a different combination of goods that was allocatively efficient.

CASE STUDIES AND APPLICATIONS **BOX 1.3**

THE OPPORTUNITY COSTS OF STUDYING ECONOMICS

What are you sacrificing?

KI 2 p8

You may not have realised it, but you probably consider opportunity costs many times a day. The reason is that we are constantly making choices: what to buy, what to eat, what to wear, whether to go out, how much to study, and so on. Each time we make a choice to do something, we are in effect rejecting doing some alternative. This alternative forgone is the opportunity cost of the action we choose.

Sometimes the opportunity costs of our actions are the direct monetary costs we incur. Sometimes it is more complicated.

Take the opportunity costs of your choices as a student of economics.

Buying a textbook costing £42.99

This does involve a direct money payment. What you have to consider is the alternatives you could have bought with the £42.99. You then have to weigh up the benefit from the best alternative against the benefit of the textbook.

What might prevent you from making the best decision?

Coming to classes

You may or may not be paying your own course fees. Even if you are, there is no extra (marginal) monetary cost in coming to classes once the fees have been paid. You will not get a refund by skipping classes!

So are the opportunity costs zero? No: by coming to classes you are *not* working in the library; you are *not* having an extra hour in bed; you are *not* sitting drinking coffee with friends, and so on. If you are making a rational decision to come to classes, then you will consider such possible alternatives.

Choosing to study at university or college

What are the opportunity costs of being a student in higher education?

1. ***If there are several other things you could have done, is the opportunity cost the sum of all of them?***
2. ***What is the opportunity cost of spending an evening revising for an economics exam? What would you need to know in order to make a sensible decision about what to do that evening?***

At first it might seem that the costs would include the following:

- Tuition fees.
- Books, stationery, etc.
- Accommodation expenses.
- Transport.
- Food, entertainment and other living expenses.

But adding these up does *not* give the *opportunity* cost. The opportunity cost is the *sacrifice* entailed by going to university or college *rather* than doing something else. Let us assume that the alternative is to take a job that has been offered. The correct list of opportunity costs of higher education would include:

- Books, stationery, etc.
- *Additional* accommodation and transport expenses over what would have been incurred by taking the job.
- Wages that would have been earned in the job *less* any income received as a student.
- The proportion of tuition fees paid by the student.

1. ***Why is the cost of food not included?***
2. ***Make a list of the benefits of higher education.***
3. ***Is the opportunity cost to the individual of attending higher education different from the opportunity costs to society as a whole?***

Equity. Even though the current levels of production and consumption might be efficient, they might be regarded as unfair, if some people are rich while others are poor. Another microeconomic goal, therefore, is that of ***equity***. Income distribution is regarded as equitable if it is considered to be fair or just. The problem with this objective, however, is that people have different notions of fairness. A rich person will probably favour a much higher degree of inequality than will a poor person! Likewise socialist governments will generally be in favour of a larger redistribution of income from the rich to the poor than will conservative governments.

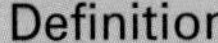

Definition

Equity A distribution of income that is considered to be fair or just. Note that an equitable distribution is not the same as an equal distribution and that different people have different views on what is equitable.

Key Idea 4

Equity is where income is distributed in a way that is considered to be fair or just. Note that an equitable distribution is not the same as an equal distribution and that different people have different views on what is equitable.

? *Would it ever be desirable to have total equality in an economy?*

Figure 1.1 A production possibility curve

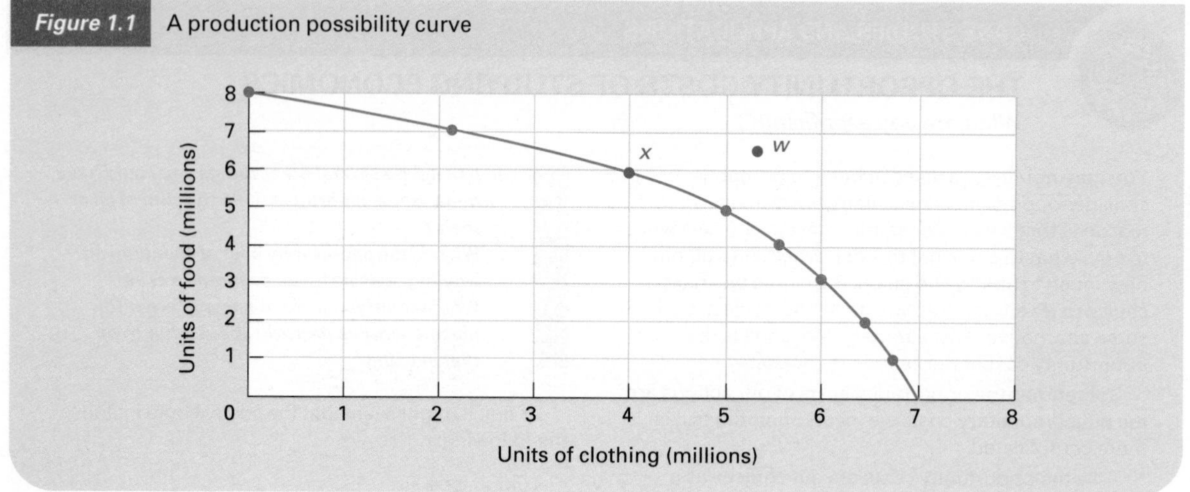

The social implications of choice

In practice, the consequences of the choices that people make may be neither efficient nor equitable. Firms may use inefficient techniques or be poorly managed; people often make wrong decisions about what to buy or what job to take; governments may be wasteful or inefficient in their use of tax revenues; there may be considerable inequality and injustice.

What is more, the effects of people's choices often spill over to other people. Take the case of pollution. It might be profitable for a firm to tip toxic waste into a river. But what is profitable for the firm will not necessarily be 'profitable' for society. Such an action may have serious environmental consequences.

Throughout the book we will be considering how well the economy meets various economic and social objectives: whether micro or macro. We will examine why problems occur and what can be done about them.

Illustrating economic issues: the production possibility curve

Economics books and articles frequently contain diagrams. The reason is that diagrams are very useful for illustrating economic relationships. Ideas and arguments that might take a long time to explain in words can often be expressed clearly and simply in a diagram.

Two of the most common types of diagram used in economics are graphs and flow diagrams. In this and the next section we will look at one example of each. These examples are chosen to illustrate the distinction between microeconomic and macroeconomic issues.

We start by having a look at a ***production possibility curve***. This diagram is a graph. Like many diagrams in economics it shows a simplified picture of reality – a picture stripped of all details that are unnecessary to illustrate the points being made. Of course, there are dangers in this. In the attempt to make a diagram simple enough to understand, we run the risk of oversimplifying. If this is the case, the diagram may be misleading.

Table 1.1 Maximum possible combinations of food and clothing that can be produced in a given time period

Units of food (millions)	Units of clothing (millions)
8.0	0.0
7.0	2.2
6.0	4.0
5.0	5.0
4.0	5.6
3.0	6.0
2.0	6.4
1.0	6.7
0.0	7.0

A production possibility curve is shown in Figure 1.1. The graph is based on the data shown in Table 1.1.

Assume that some imaginary nation devotes all its resources – land, labour and capital – to producing just two goods, food and clothing. Various possible combinations that could be produced over a given period of time (e.g. a year) are shown in the table. Thus the country, by devoting all its resources to producing food, could produce 8 million units of food but no clothing. Alternatively by producing, say, 7 million units of food it could release enough resources – land, labour and capital – to produce 2.2 million units of clothing. At the other extreme, it could

Definition

Production possibility curve A curve showing all the possible combinations of two goods that a country can produce within a specified time period with all its resources fully and efficiently employed.

CASE STUDIES AND APPLICATIONS — BOX 1.4

SCARCITY AND ABUNDANCE

Is lunch ever free?

The central economic problem is scarcity. But are *all* goods and services scarce? Is anything we desire truly abundant?

First, what do we mean by *abundance*? In the economic sense we mean something where supply exceeds demand at a *zero* price. In other words, even if it is free, there is no shortage. What is more, there must be no opportunity cost in supplying it. For example, if the government supplies health care free to the sick, it is still scarce in the economic sense because there is a cost to the government (and hence the taxpayer).

Two things that might seem to be abundant are air and water.

Air

In one sense air *is* abundant. There is no shortage of air to breathe for most people for most of the time.

But if we define air as clean, unpolluted air, then in some parts of the world it is scarce. In these cases, resources have to be used to make clean air available. If there is pollution in cities or near industrial plants, it will cost money to clean it up. The citizen may not pay directly – the cleaned-up air may be free to the 'consumer' – but the taxpayer or industry (and hence its customers) will have to pay.

Another example is when extractor fans have to be installed to freshen up air in buildings.

Even if you live in a non-polluted part of the country, you may well have spent money moving there to escape the pollution. Again there is an opportunity cost to obtain the clean air.

Water

Whether water is abundant depends again on where you live. It also depends on what the water is used for.

Water for growing crops in a country with plentiful rain *is* abundant. In drier countries, resources have to be spent on irrigation.

Water for drinking is not abundant. Reservoirs have to be built. The water has to be piped, purified and pumped.

1. ***There is a saying in economics, 'There is no such thing as a free lunch' (hence the sub-title for this box). What does this mean?***
2. ***Are any other (desirable) goods or services truly abundant?***

produce 7 million units of clothing with no resources at all being used to produce food.

The information in the table can be transferred to a graph (Figure 1.1). We measure units of food on one axis (in this case the vertical axis) and units of clothing on the other. The curve shows all the combinations of the two goods that can be produced with all the nation's resources fully and efficiently employed. For example, production could take place at point *x*, with 6 million units of food and 4 million units of clothing being produced. Production cannot take place beyond the curve. For example, production is not possible at point *w*: the nation does not have enough resources to do this.

Note that there are two simplifying assumptions in this diagram. First, it is assumed that there are just two types of good that can be produced. We have to assume this because we only have two axes on our graph. The other assumption is that there is only one type of food and one type of clothing. This is implied by measuring their output in particular units (e.g. tonnes). If food differed in type, it would be possible to produce a greater tonnage of food for a given amount of clothing simply by switching production from one foodstuff to another.

These two assumptions are obviously enormous simplifications when we consider the modern complex economies of the real world. But despite this, the diagram still allows important principles to be illustrated simply.

Microeconomics and the production possibility curve

A production possibility curve illustrates the microeconomic issues of *choice* and *opportunity cost*.

If the country chose to produce more clothing, it would have to sacrifice the production of some food. This sacrifice of food is the opportunity cost of the extra clothing.

KI 2 p8

The fact that to produce more of one good involves producing less of the other is illustrated by the downward-sloping nature of the curve. For example, the country could move from point *x* to point *y* in Figure 1.2. In doing so it would be producing an extra 1 million units of clothing, but 1 million units less of food. Thus the opportunity cost of the 1 million extra units of clothing would be the 1 million units of food forgone.

It also illustrates the phenomenon of ***increasing opportunity costs***. By this we mean that as a country produces more of one good it has to sacrifice ever *increasing* amounts of the other. The reason for this is that different factors of production have different properties. People have different skills; land differs in different parts of the country; raw

Definition

Increasing opportunity costs of production When additional production of one good involves ever increasing sacrifices of another.

Figure 1.2 Increasing opportunity costs

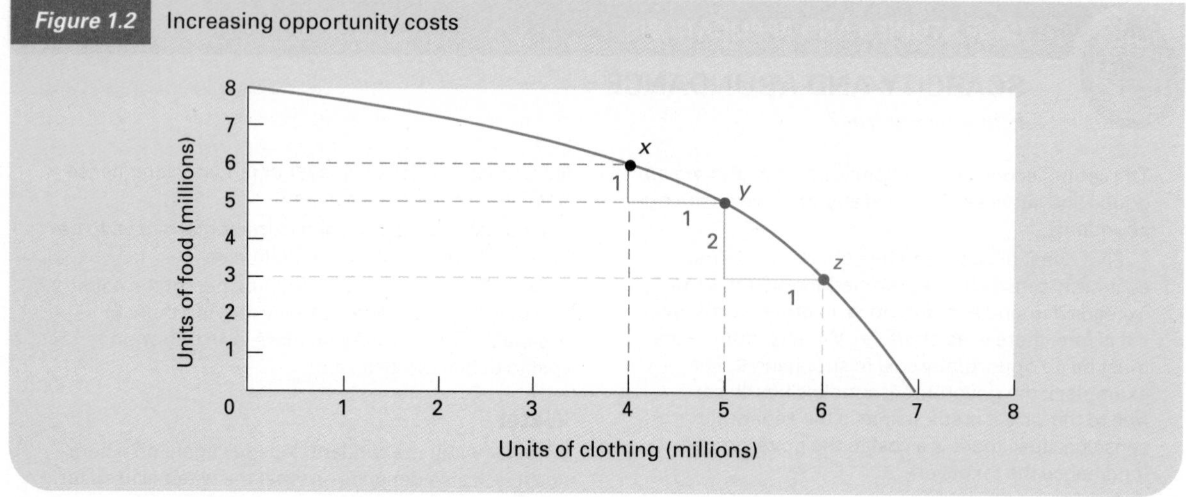

materials differ one from another; and so on. Thus as the nation concentrates more and more on the production of one good, it has to start using resources that are less and less suitable – resources that would have been better suited to producing other goods. In our example, then, the production of more and more clothing will involve a growing *marginal cost*: ever increasing amounts of food have to be sacrificed for each additional unit of clothing produced.

It is because opportunity costs increase that the production possibility curve is bowed outward rather than being a straight line. Thus in Figure 1.2 as production moves from point *x* to *y* to *z*, so the amount of food sacrificed rises for each additional unit of clothing produced. The opportunity cost of the fifth million units of clothing is 1 million units of food. The opportunity cost of the sixth million units of clothing is 2 million units of food.

1. *What is the opportunity cost of the seventh million units of clothing?*
2. *If the country moves upward along the curve and produces more food, does this also involve increasing opportunity costs?*
3. *Under what circumstances would the production possibility curve be (a) a straight line; (b) bowed in towards the origin? Are these circumstances ever likely?*

Macroeconomics and the production possibility curve

There is no guarantee that resources will be fully employed, or that they will be used in the most efficient way possible. The nation may thus be producing at a point inside the curve: for example, point *v* in Figure 1.3.

What we are saying here is that the economy is producing less of both goods than it could possibly produce, either because some resources are not being used (for example, workers may be unemployed), or because it is not using the most efficient methods of production possible, or a combination of the two. By using its resources to the full, however, the nation could move out on to the curve: to point *x* or *y*, for example. It could thus produce more clothing *and* more food.

Figure 1.3 Making a fuller use of resources

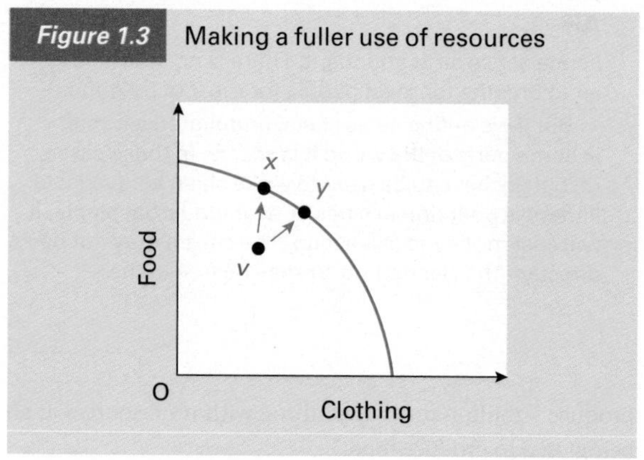

Here we are concerned not with the combination of goods produced (a microeconomic issue), but with whether the total amount produced is as much as it could be (a macroeconomic issue).

Over time, the production possibilities of a nation are likely to increase. ***Investment*** in new plant and machinery will increase the stock of capital; new raw materials may be discovered; technological advances are likely to take place; through education and training, labour is likely to become more productive. This growth in potential output is illustrated by an outward shift in the production possibility curve. This will then allow actual output to increase: for example, from point *x* to point *x′* in Figure 1.4.

Will economic growth necessarily involve a parallel outward shift of the production possibility curve?

Definition

Investment The production of items that are not for immediate consumption.

Figure 1.4 Growth in potential output

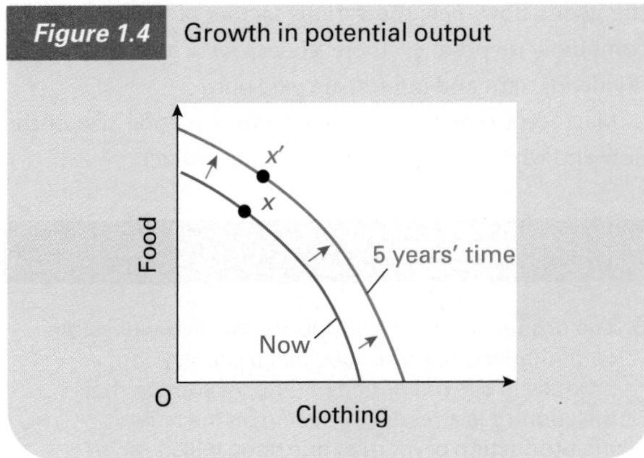

Illustrating economic issues: the circular flow of goods and incomes

The process of satisfying human wants involves producers and consumers. The relationship between them is two-sided and can be represented in a flow diagram (see Figure 1.5).

The consumers of goods and services are labelled 'households'. Some members of households, of course, are also workers, and in some cases are the owners of other factors of production too, such as land. The producers of goods and services are labelled 'firms'.[3]

Firms and households are in a twin 'demand and supply' relationship with each other.

First, in the top part of the diagram, households demand goods and services, and firms supply goods and services. In the process, exchange takes place. In a money economy (as opposed to a ***barter economy***), firms exchange goods and services for money. In other words, money flows from households to firms in the form of consumer expenditure, while goods and services flow the other way – from firms to households.

This coming together of buyers and sellers is known as a ***market*** – a street market, a shop, an auction, a mail-order system or whatever. Thus we talk about the market for apples, for oil, for cars, for houses, for televisions, and so on.

Second, firms and households come together in the market for factors of production. This is illustrated in the bottom half of Figure 1.5. This time the demand and supply roles are reversed. Firms demand the use of factors of production owned by households – labour, land and capital. Households supply them. Thus the services of labour and other factors flow from households to firms, and in exchange firms pay households money – namely, wages, rent, dividends and interest. Just as we referred to particular goods markets, so we can also refer to particular factor markets – the market for bricklayers, for secretaries, for hairdressers, for land, and so on.

There is thus a circular flow of incomes. Households earn incomes from firms and firms earn incomes from households. The money circulates. There is also a circular flow of goods and services, but in the opposite direction. Households supply factor services to firms who then use them to supply goods and services to households.

Definitions

Barter economy An economy where people exchange goods and services directly with one another without any payment of money. Workers would be paid with bundles of goods.

Market The interaction between buyers and sellers.

[3] In practice, much of society's production takes place *within* the household for its members' own consumption. Examples include cooking, washing, cleaning, growing vegetables, do-it-yourself activities and child care. Also, firms buy from and sell to each other – whether it be raw materials, capital goods or semi-finished goods. Nevertheless, it is still useful to depict the flows of goods and services and money *between* households and firms when explaining the operation of markets.

Figure 1.5 Circular flow of goods and incomes

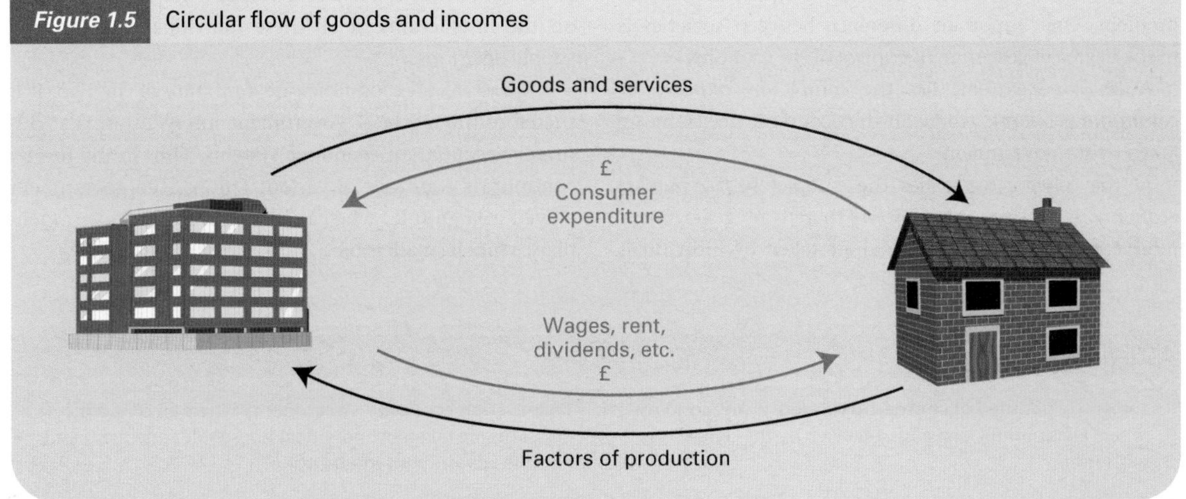

This flow diagram, like the production possibility curve, can help us to distinguish between microeconomics and macroeconomics.

Microeconomics is concerned with the composition of the circular flow: *what* combinations of goods make up the goods flow; *how* the various factors of production are combined to produce these goods; *for whom* the wages, dividends, rent and interest are paid out.

Macroeconomics is concerned with the total size of the flow and what causes it to expand and contract.

Section summary

1. The central economic problem is that of scarcity. Given that there is a limited supply of factors of production (labour, land and capital), it is impossible to provide everybody with everything they want. Potential demands exceed potential supplies.
2. The subject of economics is usually divided into two main branches, macroeconomics and microeconomics.
3. Macroeconomics deals with aggregates such as the overall levels of unemployment, output, growth and prices in the economy.
4. Microeconomics deals with the activities of individual units within the economy: firms, industries, consumers, workers, etc. Because resources are scarce, people have to make choices. Society has to choose by some means or other *what* goods and services to produce, *how* to produce them and *for whom* to produce them. Microeconomics studies these choices.
5. Rational choices involve weighing up the marginal benefits of each activity against its marginal opportunity costs. If the marginal benefits exceed the marginal costs, it is rational to choose to do more of that activity.
6. The production possibility curve shows the possible combinations of two goods that a country can produce in a given period of time. Assuming that the country is already producing on the curve, the production of more of one good will involve producing less of the other. This opportunity cost is illustrated by the slope of the curve. If the economy is producing within the curve as a result of idle resources or inefficiency, it can produce more of both goods by taking up this slack. In the longer term it can only produce more of both by shifting the curve outwards through investment, technological progress, etc.
7. The circular flow of goods and incomes shows the interrelationships between firms and households in a money economy. Firms and households come together in markets. In goods markets, firms supply goods and households demand goods. In the process, money flows from households to firms in return for the goods and services that the firms supply. In factor markets, firms demand factors of production and households supply them. In the process, money flows from firms to households in return for the services of the factors that households supply.

1.2 DIFFERENT ECONOMIC SYSTEMS

KI 1 p4

The classification of economic systems

All societies are faced with the problem of scarcity. They differ considerably, however, in the way they tackle the problem. One important difference between societies is in the degree of government control of the economy.

At the one extreme lies the completely ***planned or command economy***, where all the economic decisions are taken by the government.

At the other extreme lies the completely ***free-market economy***. In this type of economy there is no government intervention at all. All decisions are taken by individuals and firms. Households decide how much labour and other factors to supply, and what goods to consume. Firms decide what goods to produce and what factors to employ. The pattern of production and consumption that results depends on the interactions of all these individual demand and supply decisions.

In practice, all economies are a mixture of the two. It is therefore the *degree* of government intervention that distinguishes different economic systems. Thus in the former communist countries of eastern Europe, the government played a large role, whereas in the USA, the government plays a much smaller role.

Definitions

Centrally planned or command economy An economy where all economic decisions are taken by the central authorities.

Free-market economy An economy where all economic decisions are taken by individual households and firms and with no government intervention.

Figure 1.6 Classifying economic systems

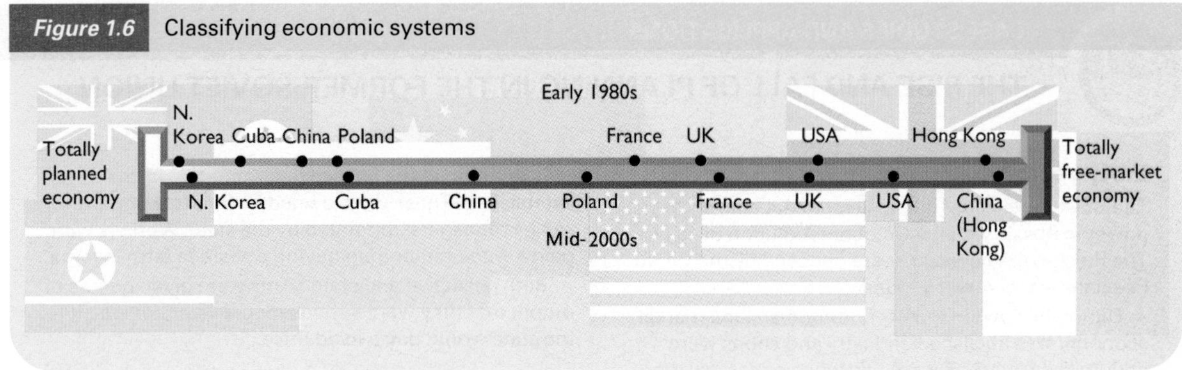

It is nevertheless useful to analyse the extremes, in order to put the different ***mixed economies*** of the real world into perspective. The mixture of government and the market can be shown by the use of a *spectrum diagram* such as Figure 1.6. It shows where particular economies of the real world lie along the spectrum between the two extremes.

The diagram is useful in that it provides a simple picture of the mixture of government and the market that exists in various economies. It can also be used to show changes in the mixture over time.

The problem with this type of classification is that it is 'unidimensional', and thus rather simplistic. Countries also differ in the *type* of government intervention as well as the level. For example, governments intervene through planning, public ownership, regulation, taxes and subsidies, partnership schemes with private industry, and so on. Thus two countries could be in a similar position along the spectrum but have quite different types of government intervention.

Notice that there has been a general movement to the right along the spectrum since the early 1980s. In former communist countries this has been a result of the abandonment of central planning and the adoption of a large measure of private enterprise, especially since the late 1980s. In western economies it has been a result of deregulation of private industry and privatisation (the selling of nationalised industries to the private sector).

Do you agree with the positions that the eight countries have been given in the spectrum diagram? Explain why or why not.

The informal sector: a third dimension

In all societies, many economic decisions are made, whether individually or in groups, which involve neither the government nor the market. For example, many of the activities taking place in the home, such as cooking, cleaning, decorating, clothes making, gardening and care for children or the elderly, can be seen as 'economic' activities. There is an output (such as a meal or a service provided) and there is an opportunity cost to the provider (in terms of alternative activities forgone). And yet no money changes hands. Similarly, many of the activities done in groups, such as clubs, societies and charities, involve the provision of goods and/or services, but again, no money changes hands.

These activities are taking place in the ***informal sector***. The relative size of the informal sector varies from one country to another and over time. In rich countries, as more and more mothers go out to work and as working hours have increased, many people employ others to do the jobs, such as cleaning and child care, that they once did themselves. What was once part of the informal sector is now part of the market sector.

In many developing countries, much of the economic activity in poorer areas involves ***subsistence production***. This is where people grow their own food, build their own shelter, make their own clothes, etc. While some of the inputs (e.g. yarn) may have to be purchased through the market, much of this production is in the informal sector and involves no exchange of money.

The command economy

The command economy is usually associated with a socialist or communist economic system, where land and capital are collectively owned. The state plans the allocation of resources at three important levels:

- It plans the allocation of resources between current consumption and investment for the future. By sacrificing some present consumption and diverting resources into investment, it could increase the economy's growth rate.

Definitions

Mixed economy An economy where economic decisions are made partly by the government and partly through the market.

Informal sector The parts of the economy that involve production and/or exchange, but where there are no money payments.

Subsistence production Where people produce things for their own consumption.

CASE STUDIES AND APPLICATIONS

THE RISE AND FALL OF PLANNING IN THE FORMER SOVIET UNION

Early years

The Bolsheviks under the leadership of Lenin came to power in Russia with the October revolution of 1917. The Bolsheviks, however, were opposed by the White Russians and civil war ensued.

During this period of *War Communism*, the market economy was abolished. Industry and shops were nationalised; workers were told what jobs to do; there were forced requisitions of food from peasants to feed the towns; the money economy collapsed as rampant inflation made money worthless; workers were allocated goods from distribution depots.

With the ending of the civil war in 1921, the economy was in bad shape. Lenin embarked on a *New Economic Policy*. This involved a return to the use of markets. Smaller businesses were returned to private hands, and peasants were able to sell their food rather than having it requisitioned. The economy began to recover.

Lenin died in 1924 and Stalin came to power.

The Stalinist system

The Soviet economy underwent a radical transformation from 1928 onwards. The key features of the Stalinist approach were collectivisation, industrialisation and central planning.

Collectivisation of agriculture

Peasant farms were abolished and replaced by large-scale collective farms where land was collectively owned and worked. Collectivisation initially caused massive disruption and famine, with peasants slaughtering their animals rather than giving them up to the collective. People died in their thousands. Despite an initial fall in output, more food was provided for the towns, and many workers left the land to work in the new industries.

In addition to the collective farms, state farms were established. These were owned by the state and were run by managers appointed by the state. Workers were paid a wage rather than having a share in farm income.

Both collective and state farms were given quotas of output that they were supposed to deliver, for which the state would pay a fixed price.

Industry and central planning

A massive drive to industrialisation took place. To achieve this a vast planning apparatus was developed. At the top was *Gosplan*, the central planning agency. This prepared five-year plans and annual plans.

The five-year plans specified the general direction in which the economy was to move. The annual plans gave the details of just what was to be produced and with what resources for some 200 or so key products. Other products were planned at a lower level – by various industrial ministries or regional authorities.

The effect was that all factories were given targets that had to be achieved. It was the task of the planning authorities to ensure that the targets were realistic: that there were sufficient resources to meet the targets. The system operated without the aid of the price mechanism and the profit motive. The main incentive was the *bonus*: bonuses were paid to managers and workers if targets were achieved.

Stalin died in 1953. The planning system, however, remained largely unchanged until the late 1980s. In the early years, very high growth rates were achieved; but this was at a cost of low efficiency. The poor flow of information from firms to the planners led to many inconsistencies in the plans. The targets were often totally unrealistic, and as a result there were frequent shortages and sometimes surpluses. With incentives

The amount of resources it chooses to devote to investment will depend on its broad macroeconomic strategy: the importance it attaches to growth as opposed to current consumption.

- At a microeconomic level, it plans the output of each industry and firm, the techniques that will be used, and the labour and other resources required by each industry and firm.

In order to ensure that the required inputs are available, the state would probably conduct some form of ***input–output analysis***. All industries are seen as users of *inputs* from other industries and as producers of *output* for consumers or other industries. For example, the steel industry uses inputs from the coal and iron-ore industries and produces output for the vehicle and construction industries. Input–output analysis shows, for each industry, the sources of all its inputs and the destination of all its output. By using such analysis the state attempts to match up the inputs and outputs of each industry so that the planned demand for each industry's product is equal to its planned supply.

- It plans the distribution of output between consumers. This will depend on the government's aims. It may distribute goods according to its judgement of people's *needs*; or it may give more to those who produce more, thereby providing an *incentive* for people to work harder.

Definition

Input–output analysis This involves dividing the economy into sectors where each sector is a user of inputs from and a supplier of outputs to other sectors. The technique examines how these inputs and outputs can be matched to the total resources available in the economy.

BOX 1.5

purely geared to meeting targets, there was little product innovation and goods were frequently of poor quality and finish.

The limits of planning

Although most resources were allocated through planning, there were nevertheless some goods that were sold in markets. Any surpluses above their quota that were produced by collective farms could be sold in collective farm markets (street markets) in the towns. In addition, the workers on collective farms were allowed to own their own small private plots of land, and they too could sell their produce in the collective farm markets.

A large 'underground economy' flourished in which goods were sold on the black market and in which people did second 'unofficial' jobs (e.g. as plumbers, electricians or garment makers).

Gorbachev's reforms

During the 1970s growth had slowed down and by the time Gorbachev came to power in 1985 many people were pressing for fundamental economic reforms. Gorbachev responded with his policy of *perestroika* (economic reconstruction), which among other things included the following:

- Making managers more involved in preparing their own plans rather than merely being given instructions.
- Insisting that firms cover their costs of production. If they could not, the state might refuse to bale them out and they could be declared bankrupt. The aim of this was to encourage firms to be more efficient.
- Improving the incentive system by making bonuses more related to genuine productivity. Workers had come to expect bonuses no matter how much or how little was produced.
- Organising workers into small teams or 'brigades' (typically of around 10–15 workers). Bonuses were then awarded to the whole brigade according to its productivity. The idea was to encourage people to work more effectively together.
- Stringent checks on quality by state officials and the rejection of substandard goods.
- Allowing one-person businesses and co-operatives (owned by the workers) to be set up.
- A greater willingness by the state to raise prices if there were substantial shortages.

These reforms, however, did not halt the economic decline. What is more, there was now an unhappy mix of planning and the market, with people unclear as to what to expect from the state. Many managers resented the extra responsibilities they were now expected to shoulder and many officials saw their jobs threatened. Queues lengthened in the shops and people increasingly became disillusioned with *perestroika*.

Following the failed coup of 1991, in which hard-line communists had attempted to reimpose greater state control, and with the consequent strengthening of the position of Boris Yeltsin, the Russian president and the main advocate of more radical reforms, both the Soviet Union and the system of central planning came to an end.

Russia embarked upon a radical programme of market reforms in which competition and enterprise were intended to replace state central planning (see Web Cases 12.9 and 12.10). The Stalinist system now appears to be but a fading memory. (See also Web Case 1.5, *Free-market medicine in Russia*.)

It may distribute goods and services directly (for example, by a system of rationing); or it may decide the distribution of money incomes and allow individuals to decide how to spend them. If it does the latter, it may still seek to influence the pattern of expenditure by setting appropriate prices: low prices to encourage consumption, and high prices to discourage consumption.

Assessment of the command economy

With central planning, the government could take an overall view of the economy. It could direct the nation's resources in accordance with specific national goals.

High growth rates could be achieved if the government directed large amounts of resources into investment. Unemployment could be largely avoided if the government carefully planned the allocation of labour in accordance with production requirements and labour skills. National income could be distributed more equally or in accordance with needs. The social repercussions of production and consumption (e.g. the effects on the environment) could be taken into account, provided the government was able to predict these effects and chose to take them into account. KI 4 p11

In practice, a command economy could achieve these goals only at considerable social and economic cost. The reasons are as follows:

- The larger and more complex the economy, the greater the task of collecting and analysing the information essential to planning, and the more complex the plan. Complicated plans are likely to be costly to administer and involve cumbersome bureaucracy.

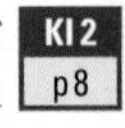

- If there is no system of prices, or if prices are set arbitrarily by the state, planning is likely to involve the inefficient use of resources. It is difficult to assess the

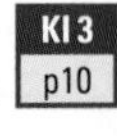

relative efficiency of two alternative techniques that use different inputs, if there is no way in which the value of those inputs can be ascertained. For example, how can a rational decision be made between an oil-fired and a coal-fired furnace if the prices of oil and coal do not reflect their relative scarcity?

- It is difficult to devise appropriate incentives to encourage workers and managers to be more productive without a reduction in quality. For example, if bonuses are given according to the quantity of output produced, a factory might produce shoddy goods, since it can probably produce a larger quantity of goods by cutting quality. To avoid this problem, a large number of officials may have to be employed to check quality.
- Complete state control over resource allocation would involve a considerable loss of individual liberty. Workers would have no choice where to work; consumers would have no choice what to buy.
- The government might enforce its plans even if they were unpopular.
- If production is planned, but consumers are free to spend money incomes as they wish, there will be a problem if the wishes of consumers change. Shortages will occur if consumers decide to buy more; surpluses will occur if they decide to buy less.

Most of these problems were experienced in the former Soviet Union and the other Eastern bloc countries, and were part of the reason for the overthrow of their communist regimes (see Box 1.5).

The free-market economy

Free decision making by individuals

In a free market, individuals are free to make their own economic decisions. Consumers are free to decide what to buy with their incomes: free to make demand decisions. Firms are free to choose what to sell and what production methods to use: free to make supply decisions. The demand and supply decisions of consumers and firms are transmitted to each other through their effect on *prices*: through the ***price mechanism***. The prices that result are the prices that firms and consumers have to accept.

The price mechanism

The price mechanism works as follows. Prices respond to *shortages* and *surpluses*. Shortages result in prices rising. Surpluses result in prices falling. Let us take each in turn.

If consumers decide they want more of a good (or if producers decide to cut back supply), demand will exceed supply. The resulting shortage will cause the price of the good to *rise*. This will act as an incentive to producers to supply more, since production will now be more profitable. At the same time it will discourage consumers from buying so much. *Price will continue rising until the shortage has thereby been eliminated.*

If, on the other hand, consumers decide they want less of a good (or if producers decide to produce more), supply will exceed demand. The resulting surplus will cause the price of the good to *fall*. This will act as a disincentive to producers, who will supply less, since production will now be less profitable. It will encourage consumers to buy more. *Price will continue falling until the surplus has thereby been eliminated.*

This price, where demand equals supply, is called the ***equilibrium price***. By ***equilibrium*** we mean a point of balance or a point of rest: in other words, a point towards which there is a tendency to move.

The same analysis can be applied to labour (and other factor) markets, except that here the demand and supply roles are reversed. Firms are the demanders of labour. Individuals are the suppliers. If the demand for a particular type of labour exceeded its supply, the resulting shortage would drive up the wage rate (i.e. the price of labour), thus reducing firms' demand for that type of labour and encouraging more workers to take up that type of job. Wages would continue rising until demand equalled supply: until the shortage was eliminated.

Likewise if there were a surplus of a particular type of labour, the wage would fall until demand equalled supply. As with price, the wage rate where the demand for labour equals the supply is known as the *equilibrium* wage rate.

? *Can you think of any examples where prices and wages do not adjust very rapidly to a shortage or surplus? For what reasons might they not do so?*

The response of demand and supply to changes in price illustrates a very important feature of how economies work: *People respond to incentives*. It is important, therefore, that incentives are appropriate and have the desired effect. This is the third of our fifteen threshold concepts (see panel).

The effect of changes in demand and supply

How will the price mechanism respond to changes in consumer demand or producer supply? After all, the pattern of consumer demand changes. For example, people may decide they want more mountain bikes and fewer racers.

Definitions

The price mechanism The system in a market economy whereby changes in price in response to changes in demand and supply have the effect of making demand equal to supply.

Equilibrium price The price where the quantity demanded equals the quantity supplied: the price where there is no shortage or surplus.

Equilibrium A position of balance. A position from which there is no inherent tendency to move away.

THINKING LIKE AN ECONOMIST — THRESHOLD CONCEPT 3

PEOPLE RESPOND TO INCENTIVES. IT IS IMPORTANT, THEREFORE, THAT THESE HAVE THE DESIRED EFFECT.

When there is a shortage of a good, its market price will rise. There will thus be an incentive for us to consume less. After all, the opportunity cost has risen. It might be better to switch to a cheaper alternative or simply to consume less and use the money saved to buy something entirely different.

Similarly, when the price of a good rises, there is an incentive for firms to produce more. After all, the good is now more profitable to produce and thus firms might consider producing more of this and cutting down the production of less profitable products.

These two incentives of a rise in price could be seen as desirable, as they result in the shortage being eliminated and consumers being able to buy more of a good where demand initially exceeds supply.

Incentives, however, could be 'perverse'. In other words, they could have undesirable effects. For example, if a particular course or module on your degree is assessed by two pieces of coursework, this may act as an incentive for you to concentrate solely on these two pieces and do little work on the remainder of the course!

There are plenty of other examples where incentives can be perverse. For example, making insurance compulsory may encourage people to take risks. Making cars safer may encourage people to drive faster. Increasing top rates of income tax may encourage high earners to work less or to evade paying taxes by not declaring income – tax revenues may end up falling.

If an economic system is to work well, it is important, therefore, that the incentives are appropriate and do not bring about undesirable side-effects. This is a *threshold concept* because virtually every action taken by households or firms is influenced by incentives. We need to understand just what the incentives are; what their effects are likely to be; and how the incentives could be improved.

This was something increasingly recognised in the former Soviet Union in the days of central planning: but too late! The targets given to factory managers (see Box 1.5) were often inappropriate. For example, if targets were specified in tonnes, the incentive was to produce heavy products. Soviet furniture and cooking utensils tended to be very heavy! If targets were set in area (e.g. sheet glass), then the incentive was to produce thin products. If targets were set simply in terms of number of units, then the incentive was to produce shoddy products.

The lessons of Soviet planning, however, have been lost on many in the West. Today across the public sector, and large parts of the private sector too, people are set targets. Thus if hospitals are given the target to reduce waiting lists, the incentive is to cut down on the quality of treatment so that as many patients as possible can be seen. If the target for universities is to reduce failure rates, then the incentive is to make it easier for students to pass.

One crucial incentive we shall be examining is that of profit. In a competitive environment, firms striving for increased profit may result in better products and a lower price for consumers as firms seek to undercut each other. In other cases, however, firms may be able to make bigger profits by controlling the market and keeping competitors out or by colluding with them. Here the profit incentive has a perverse effect: it leads to higher prices for consumers and less choice.

1. ***Give two other examples of perverse incentives. How could the incentives be improved?***
2. ***Find out just what the learning objectives are of the economics course or module that you are studying. What positive incentives are there for you to meet these learning objectives? Identify any perverse incentives and how you would change them.***

Likewise the pattern of supply changes. For example, changes in technology may allow the mass production of microchips at lower cost, while the production of hand-built furniture becomes relatively expensive.

In all cases of changes in demand and supply, the resulting changes in *price* act as both *signals* and *incentives*.

A change in demand. A rise in demand is signalled by a rise in price. This then acts as an incentive for supply to rise. What in effect is happening is that the high price of these goods relative to their costs of production is signalling that consumers are willing to see resources diverted from other uses. This is just what firms do. They divert resources from goods with lower prices relative to costs (and hence lower profits) to those goods that are more profitable.

A fall in demand is signalled by a fall in price. This then acts as an incentive for supply to fall. The goods are now less profitable to produce.

A change in supply. A rise in supply is signalled by a fall in price. This then acts as an incentive for demand to rise. A fall in supply is signalled by a rise in price. This then acts as an incentive for demand to fall.

Key Idea 5

Changes in demand or supply cause markets to adjust. Whenever such changes occur, the resulting 'disequilibrium' will bring an automatic change in prices, thereby restoring equilibrium (i.e. a balance of demand and supply).

THINKING LIKE AN ECONOMIST — *THRESHOLD CONCEPT 4*

MARKETS EQUATE DEMAND AND SUPPLY

Leave things up to the market. The market will sort it out. It's what the market wants. You can't buck the market.

These are typical sayings about the market and emphasise the power of market forces. The point is that our lives are affected massively by markets. Market forces affect the prices of the things we buy and the incomes we earn. Even governments find it difficult to control many key markets. Governments might not like it when stock market prices plummet or when oil prices soar, but there is precious little they can do about it.

In many ways a market is like a democracy. People, by choosing to buy goods, are voting for them to be produced. Firms finding 'a market' for their products are happy to oblige and produce them. The way it works is simple. If people want more of a product, they buy more and thereby 'cast their votes' (i.e. their money) in favour of more being produced. The resulting shortage drives up the price, which gives firms the incentive to produce more of the product. In other words, firms are doing what consumers want – not because of any 'love' for consumers, or because they are being told to produce more by the government – but because it is in their own self-interest. They supply more because the higher price has made it profitable to do so.

This is a *threshold concept* because to understand market forces – the forces of demand and supply – is to go straight to the heart of a market economy and understand what makes it tick. And in this process, prices are the key. It is changes in price that balance demand and supply. If demand exceeds supply, price will rise. This will choke off some of the demand and encourage more supply until demand equals supply – until an equilibrium has been reached. If supply exceeds demand, price will fall. This will discourage firms from supplying so much and encourage consumers to buy more, until, once more, an equilibrium has been reached.

In this process, markets act like an 'invisible hand' – a term coined by the famous economist Adam Smith (see Box 1.6). Market prices guide both producers to respond to consumer demand and consumers to respond to changes in producer supply.

In many circumstances, markets bring outcomes that people want. As we have seen, if consumers want more, then market forces will lead to more being produced. Sometimes, however, market forces can bring adverse effects. We explore these at various parts of the book. It is important, at this stage, however, to recognise that markets are rarely perfect. Market failures, from pollution to the domination of our lives by big business, are very real. Understanding this brings us to Threshold Concept 6 (see page 26).

Partial equilibrium

The type of equilibrium we will be examining for the next few chapters is known as 'partial equilibrium'. It is partial because what we are doing is examining just one tiny bit of the economy at a time: just one market (e.g. that for eggs). It is even partial within the market for eggs because we are assuming that price is the *only* thing that changes to balance demand and supply: that nothing else changes. In other words, when we refer to equilibrium price and quantity, we are assuming that all the other determinants of both demand and supply are held constant.

If another determinant of demand or supply *does* change, there would then be a new partial equilibrium as price adjusts and both demanders and suppliers respond. For example, if a health scare connected with egg consumption causes the demand for eggs to fall, the resulting surplus will lead to a fall in the equilibrium price and quantity.

1. ***If there is a shortage of certain skilled workers in the economy, how will market forces lead to an elimination of the skills shortage?***
2. ***If consumers want more of a product, is it always desirable that market forces result in more being produced?***

The fact that markets adjust so as to equate demand and supply is our fourth 'Threshold Concept' (see panel).

?

1. *Why do the prices of fresh vegetables fall when they are in season? Could an individual farmer prevent the price falling?*
2. *If you were the owner of a clothes shop, how would you set about deciding what prices to charge for each garment at the end-of-season sale?*

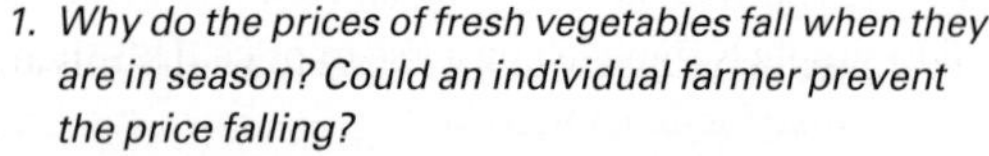

3. *The number of owners of compact disc players has grown rapidly and hence the demand for compact discs has also grown rapidly. Yet the prices of discs have fallen. Why?*

The interdependence of markets

The interdependence of goods and factor markets. A rise in demand for a good will raise its price and profitability. Firms will respond by supplying more. But to do this they will need more inputs. Thus the demand for the inputs will rise, which in turn will raise the price of the inputs. The suppliers of inputs will respond to this incentive by supplying more. This can be summarised as follows:

TC 3 p21

1. Goods market
   - Demand for the good rises.
   - This creates a shortage.

Figure 1.7 The price mechanism: the effect of a rise in demand

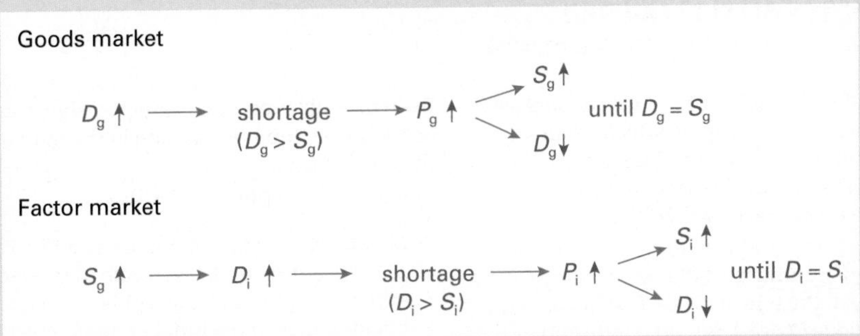

Goods market

$D_g \uparrow \longrightarrow$ shortage $(D_g > S_g) \longrightarrow P_g \uparrow$ $\nearrow S_g \uparrow$ / $\searrow D_g \downarrow$ until $D_g = S_g$

Factor market

$S_g \uparrow \longrightarrow D_i \uparrow \longrightarrow$ shortage $(D_i > S_i) \longrightarrow P_i \uparrow$ $\nearrow S_i \uparrow$ / $\searrow D_i \downarrow$ until $D_i = S_i$

(where D = demand, S = supply, P = price, g = the good, i = inputs, $\longrightarrow$ means 'leads to')

- This causes the price of the good to rise.
- This eliminates the shortage by choking off some of the demand and encouraging firms to produce more.

2. Factor market
   - The increased supply of the good causes an increase in the demand for factors of production (i.e. inputs) used in making it.
   - This causes a shortage of those inputs.
   - This causes their prices to rise.
   - This eliminates their shortage by choking off some of the demand and encouraging the suppliers of inputs to supply more.

It can thus be seen that changes in goods markets will cause changes in factor markets. Figure 1.7 summarises this sequence of events. (It is common in economics to summarise an argument like this by using symbols.)

Interdependence exists in the other direction too: factor markets affect goods markets. For example, the discovery of raw materials will lower their price. This will lower the costs of production of firms using these raw materials and will increase the supply of the finished goods. The resulting surplus will lower the price of the good, which will encourage consumers to buy more.

? *Summarise this last paragraph using symbols like those in Figure 1.7.*

The interdependence of different goods markets. A rise in the price of one good will encourage consumers to buy alternatives. This will drive up the price of alternatives. This in turn will encourage producers to supply more of the alternatives.

? *Are different factor markets similarly interdependent? Give examples.*

Conclusion

Even though all individuals are merely looking to their own self-interest in the free-market economy, they are in fact being encouraged to respond to the wishes of others through the incentive of the price mechanism. (See Web Case 1.4 *The interdependence of markets* on the book's website and Box 1.6.)

Assessment of the free-market economy

The fact that a free-market economy functions automatically is one of its major advantages. There is no need for costly and complex bureaucracies to co-ordinate economic decisions. The economy can respond quickly to changing demand and supply conditions.

When markets are highly competitive, no one has great power. Competition between firms keeps prices down and acts as an incentive to firms to become more efficient. The more firms there are competing, the more responsive they will be to consumer wishes.

The more efficiently firms can combine their factors of production, the more profit they will make. The more efficiently workers work, the more secure will be their jobs and the higher their wages. The more carefully consumers decide what to buy, the greater the value for money they will receive. KI 1 p4

Thus people pursuing their own self-interest through buying and selling in competitive markets helps to minimise the central economic problem of scarcity, by encouraging the efficient use of the nation's resources in line with consumer wishes. From this type of argument, the following conclusion is often drawn by defenders of the free market: 'The pursuit of private gain results in the social good.' This is obviously a highly significant claim and has profound moral implications (see Threshold Concept 5).

In practice, however, markets do not achieve maximum efficiency in the allocation of scarce resources, and governments feel it necessary to intervene to rectify this and other problems of the free market. The problems of a free market are as follows:

- Competition between firms is often limited. A few giant firms may dominate an industry. In these cases they may charge high prices and make large profits. Rather than merely responding to consumer wishes, they may attempt to persuade consumers by advertising. Consumers are

EXPLORING ECONOMICS

ADAM SMITH (1723–90)

and the 'invisible hand' of the market

Many economists would argue that modern economics dates from 1776. That was the year in which Adam Smith's *An Inquiry into the Nature and Causes of the Wealth of Nations* was published – one of the most important books on economics ever written.

Adam Smith was born in 1723 in Kirkcaldy, a small coastal town north of Edinburgh. After graduating from Glasgow University at the age of 17, he first became a fellow of Balliol College Oxford, but then returned to Scotland and at the age of 29 became professor of moral philosophy at the University of Glasgow. At the age of 40 he resigned and spent three years touring the continent where he met many influential economists and philosophers. He then returned to Scotland, to his home town of Kirkcaldy, and set to work on *The Wealth of Nations*.

KI 5 p21

The work, in five books, is very wide ranging, but the central argument is that market economies generally serve the public interest well. Markets guide production and consumption like an *invisible hand*. Even though everyone is looking after their own private self-interest, their interaction in the market will lead to the social good.

In book I, chapter 2, he writes:

> Man has almost constant occasion for the help of his brethren and it is in vain for him to expect it from their benevolence only. . . . It is not from the benevolence of the butcher, the brewer, or the baker that we expect our dinner, but from their regard to their own interest. We address ourselves, not to their humanity but to their self-love, and never talk to them of our own necessities, but of their advantages.

Later, in book IV, chapter 2, he continues:

> Every individual is continually exerting himself to find out the most advantageous employment of whatever capital he can command. It is his own advantage, indeed, and not that of the society, which he has in view. But the study of his own advantage

THINKING LIKE AN ECONOMIST — *THRESHOLD CONCEPT 5*

PEOPLE GAIN FROM VOLUNTARY ECONOMIC INTERACTION

Economic interaction between people can take a number of different forms. Sometimes it takes place in markets. For example, when goods are exchanged, there is interaction between the consumer and the shop. When someone is employed, there is interaction between the employer and the employee. When a firm buys raw materials, there is interaction between the purchasing firm and the selling firm.

In each case there is a mutual gain. If there wasn't, the interaction would not take place. If you choose to go on a package holiday costing £400, then assuming the holiday turns out as you expected, you will have gained. You would rather have the holiday than spend the £400 on something else. The marginal benefit to you exceeds the marginal cost. The travel agent and tour operator also gain. They make a profit on selling you the holiday. It is a 'win–win situation'. This is sometimes called a *positive sum game*: an interaction where there is a positive net gain.

Another example is international trade (the subject of Chapter 23). If two countries trade with each other, there will be a net gain to both of them. If there wasn't, they would not trade. Both countries will end up consuming a greater value of products than they could without trade. The reason is that each country can specialise in the products it is relatively good at producing (compared to the other country) and export them, and import from the other country the goods it is relatively poor at producing.

And it's not just in markets that human interaction results in a net gain. If you go out with friends, normally you will all benefit – unless you end up falling out or something else goes wrong! If you are a member of a football team, a political party or choir, you hope that it's not just you that gains, but the other members too.

That there is a net gain from voluntary interaction is a *threshold concept* because realising this tends to change the way we look at economic activity. Often it is important to identify what these overall gains are so that we can compare them with alternative forms of interaction. For example, even though both workers and their employer respectively gain from the wages currently paid and the output currently produced, it might still be possible to reorganise the workforce in a way that increases production. This could allow the employer to pay higher wages and still gain an increase in profits. Both sides could thus gain from constructive negotiation about wages and new work practices.

Sometimes it may appear that voluntary interaction results in one side gaining and the other losing. For example, a firm may raise its price. It gains and the consumer loses. But is this strictly true? Consumers are certainly worse off than *before*, but as long as they are still prepared to buy the product, they must consider that they are still gaining more by buying it than by not. There is still a gain to both sides: it's just that the firm is gaining more and the consumer is gaining less.

?

1. ***Would you ever swap things with friends if both of you did not gain? Explain your answer.***
2. ***Give one or two examples of* involuntary *(i.e. compulsory) economic interaction, where one side gains but the other loses.***

BOX 1.6

> naturally, or rather necessarily, leads him to prefer that employment which is most advantageous to the society . . . he intends only his own gain, and he is in this, as in many other cases, led by an invisible hand to promote an end which was no part of his intention. Nor is it always the worse for the society that it was no part of it. By pursuing his own interest he frequently promotes that of society more effectually than when he really intends to promote it.

He argued, therefore, with one or two exceptions, that the state should not interfere with the functioning of the economy. It should adopt a *laissez-faire* or 'hands-off' policy. It should allow free enterprise for firms and free trade between countries.

This praise of the free market has led many on the political right to regard him as the father of the 'libertarian movement' – the movement that advocates the absolute minimum amount of state intervention in the economy (see Box 11.6 on pages 324–5). In fact one of the most famous of the libertarian societies is called 'The Adam Smith Institute'.

But Smith was not blind to the drawbacks of unregulated markets. In book I, chapter 7, he looks at the problem of monopoly:

> A monopoly granted either to an individual or to a trading company has the same effect as a secret in trade or manufactures. The monopolists, by keeping the market constantly under-stocked, by never fully supplying the effectual demand, sell their commodities much above the natural price, and raise their emoluments, whether they consist in wages or profit, greatly above their natural rate.

Later on he looks at the dangers of firms getting together to pursue their mutual interest:

> People of the same trade seldom meet together, even for merriment or diversion, but the conversation ends in a conspiracy against the public or in some contrivance to raise prices.

particularly susceptible to advertisements for products that are unfamiliar to them.

- Lack of competition and high profits may remove the incentive for firms to be efficient.

- Power and property may be unequally distributed. Those who have power and/or property (e.g. big business, unions, landlords) will gain at the expense of those without power and property.
- The practices of some firms may be socially undesirable. For example, a chemical works may pollute the environment.
- Some socially desirable goods would simply not be produced by private enterprise. What firm would build and operate a lighthouse, unless it were paid for by the government?
- A free-market economy may lead to macroeconomic instability. There may be periods of recession with high unemployment and falling output, and other periods of rising prices.
- Finally, there is the ethical objection, that a free-market economy, by rewarding self-interested behaviour, may encourage selfishness, greed, materialism and the acquisition of power.

The fact that free markets may fail to meet various social objectives is Threshold Concept 6.

The mixed economy

Because of the problems of both free-market and command economies, all real-world economies are a mixture of the two systems.

In ***mixed market economies***, the government may control the following:

- ***Relative prices*** of goods and inputs, by taxing or subsidising them or by direct price controls.
- Relative incomes, by the use of income taxes, welfare payments or direct controls over wages, profits, rents, etc.
- The pattern of production and consumption, by the use of legislation (e.g. making it illegal to produce unsafe goods), by direct provision of goods and services (e.g. education and defence), by taxes and subsidies or by nationalisation.
- The macroeconomic problems of unemployment, inflation, lack of growth, balance of trade deficits and exchange-rate fluctuations, by the use of taxes and government expenditure, the control of bank lending and interest rates, the direct control of prices and the control of the foreign exchange rate.

The fact that government intervention can be used to rectify various failings of the market is Threshold Concept 7. Note, however, that governments are not perfect and their actions may bring adverse as well as beneficial consequences.

Just how the government intervenes, and what the effects of the various forms of intervention are, will be examined in detail in later chapters.

Definitions

Mixed market economy A market economy where there is some government intervention.

Relative price The price of one good compared with another (e.g. good x is twice the price of good y).

THINKING LIKE AN ECONOMIST — *THRESHOLD CONCEPT 6*

MARKETS MAY FAIL TO MEET SOCIAL OBJECTIVES

Although market forces can automatically equate demand and supply, and although the outcomes of the process may often be desirable, they are by no means always so. Unbridled market forces can result in severe problems for individuals, society and the environment.

Markets tend to reflect the collective actions of individual consumers and firms. But when consumers and firms make their decisions, they may fail to take account of the broader effects of their actions. They may act selfishly. If people want to buy guns and knives, market forces will make it profitable for firms to supply them. If people want to drive fuel-hungry cars and fit bull-bars to them, then this will create the market for firms to supply them. Market forces are not kind and caring. They mechanically reflect human behaviour.

And it's not just selfish behaviour that markets reflect; it's ignorance too. You may be blissfully unaware that a toy that you buy for a child is dangerous, but by doing so, you are encouraging unscrupulous firms to supply them. A firm may be unaware that a piece of machinery it uses is dangerous until an accident happens. In the meantime, it continues using it because it is profitable to do so.

If wages are determined purely by demand and supply, then some people, such as pop stars, footballers and accountants, may be very well paid. Others, such as cleaners, bar staff and security guards, may be very poorly paid. If the resulting inequality is seen as unfair, then market forces alone will not be enough to achieve a fair society.

Recognising the limitations and failings of markets is a *threshold concept*. It helps us to understand how laws or taxes or subsidies could be framed to counteract such failings. It helps us to relate the mechanical operation of demand and supply to a whole range of social objectives and ask whether the market system is the best way of meeting such objectives.

But to recognise market failures is only part of the way to finding a solution. Can the government and various public agencies, such as the police and health service, put things right, and if so, how? Or do the limitations of government mean that the solution is sometimes worse than the problem? We examine these issues in many parts of the book. We set the scene in Threshold Concept 7 below.

1. ***If global warming affects all of us adversely, why in a purely market economy would individuals and firms continue with activities that contribute towards global warming?***
2. ***In what ways do your own consumption patterns adversely affect other people?***

THINKING LIKE AN ECONOMIST — *THRESHOLD CONCEPT 7*

GOVERNMENTS CAN SOMETIMES IMPROVE MARKET OUTCOMES

Threshold Concept 6 was that markets may fail to meet social objectives. This is where government economic policy comes in. Governments have a number of policy instruments that they can use, either to influence markets or to replace them altogether. These policy instruments include taxation, benefits and subsidies, laws and regulations, licences and permits, and direct provision by government departments or agencies (such as the ministry of defence or the national health service).

The threshold concept here is not merely that governments intervene, but that they can correct, or at least lessen, market failures. Once we have understood the nature of a market failure, we can then set about designing a policy to correct it. For example, if we could identify that the cost to society of producing a product in a way which created pollution was £20 per unit more than the benefit that society gained from the product, then the government could tax the producer £20 per unit. This could be an argument for imposing taxes on airline tickets to reflect the adverse effects of air travel on the atmosphere.

In Chapters 10, 11 and 12 we consider a number of these policy instruments and seek to identify the *optimum* level of government intervention to meet social objectives.

Governments themselves, however, are not perfect – as opposition parties frequently remind us! For an economic adviser to recommend a particular policy as the best means of correcting a market failure does not mean that the government will carry it out efficiently or, indeed, carry it out at all.

1. ***How may welfare benefits be seen as a means of correcting market failures? Does the payment of such benefits create any problems for society?***
2. ***Assume that the government sees litter as a market failure that requires government action. Give some examples of policies it could adopt to reduce litter.***

Section summary

1. The economic systems of different countries vary according to the extent to which they rely on the market or the government to allocate resources.
2. At the one extreme, in a command economy, the state makes all the economic decisions. It plans how many resources to allocate for present consumption and how many for investment for future output. It plans the output of each industry, the methods of production it will use and the amount of resources it will be allocated. It plans the distribution of output between consumers.
3. A command economy has the advantage of being able to address directly various national economic goals, such as rapid growth and the avoidance of unemployment and inequality. A command economy, however, is likely to be inefficient: a large bureaucracy will be needed to collect and process information; prices and the choice of production methods are likely to be arbitrary; incentives may be inappropriate; shortages and surpluses may result.
4. At the other extreme is the free-market economy. In this economy, decisions are made by the interaction of demand and supply. Price changes act as the mechanism whereby demand and supply are balanced. If there is a shortage, price will rise until the shortage is eliminated. If there is a surplus, price will fall until that is eliminated.
5. A free-market economy functions automatically and if there is plenty of competition between producers this can help to protect consumers' interests. In practice, however, competition may be limited; there may be great inequality; there may be adverse social and environmental consequences; there may be macroeconomic instability.
6. In practice, all economies are some mixture of the market and government intervention. It is the degree and form of government intervention that distinguishes one type of economy from another.

1.3 THE NATURE OF ECONOMIC REASONING

Economics is one of the social sciences. So in what sense is it a *science*? Is it like the natural sciences such as physics and astronomy? What is the significance of the word 'social' in social science? What can economists do, and what is their role in helping governments devise economic policy?

Economics as a science

The methodology employed by economists has a lot in common with that employed by natural scientists. Both attempt to construct theories or ***models*** which are then used to *explain* and *predict*. An astronomer, for example, constructs models of planetary movements to *explain* why planets are in the position they are and to *predict* their position in the future.

Models in economics

In order to explain and predict, the economist constructs models of the economy or parts of the economy. These models show simplified relationships between various economic phenomena. For example, a model of a market shows the relationships between demand, supply and price. Although most models can be described verbally, they can normally be represented more precisely in graphical or mathematical form.

Building models

Models are constructed by making general hypotheses about the causes of economic phenomena: for example, that consumer demand will rise when consumer incomes rise. These hypotheses will often be based on observations. This process of making general statements from particular observations is known as ***induction***.

Using models

Explanation. Models explain by showing how things are caused: what are the causes of inflation, why do workers in some industries earn more than others, and so on.

Prediction. Models are sometimes used to make simple forecasts: for example, inflation will be below 5 per cent next year. Usually, however, predictions are of the 'If . . . then . . .' variety: for example, if demand for good x rises, its price will rise. This process of drawing conclusions from models is known as ***deduction***.

When making such deductions it has to be assumed that nothing else that can influence the outcome has changed in the meantime. For example, if demand for good x rises, its price will rise *assuming* the cost of producing good x has not fallen. This is known as the ***ceteris paribus*** assumption. *Ceteris paribus* is Latin for 'other things being equal'.

Assessing models

Models can be judged according to how *successful* they are in explaining and predicting.

Definitions

Economic model A formal presentation of an economic theory.

Induction Constructing general theories on the basis of specific observations.

Deduction Using a theory to draw conclusions about specific circumstances.

Ceteris paribus Latin for 'other things being equal'. This assumption has to be made when making deductions from theories.

CASE STUDIES AND APPLICATIONS BOX 1.7

CETERIS PARIBUS

Because of the complexities of the real world, economic models have to make various simplifying assumptions. Sometimes, however, economists are criticised for making unrealistic assumptions, assumptions that make their models irrelevant. The following joke illustrates the point . . .

There were three people cast away on a desert island: a chemist, an engineer and an economist. There was no food on the island and their plight seemed desperate.

Then they discovered a crate of canned food that had been washed up on the island. When they realised that they had no means of opening the cans, they decided that each of them should use their expertise to find a solution.

The chemist searched around for various minerals that could be heated up to produce a compound that would burn through the lids of the cans.

The engineer hunted around for rocks and then worked out what height of tree they would have to be dropped from in order to smash open the cans.

Meanwhile the economist sat down and thought, 'Assuming we had a can opener . . .'

If the predictions are wrong, the first thing to do is to check whether the deductions were correctly made. If they were, the model must be either adapted or abandoned in favour of an alternative model with better predictive ability.

Sometimes an economist will want to retain a model with poor predictive powers if it nevertheless helps to give some insight into the workings of the economy. For example, a model of some ideal world in which the goals of efficiency, growth and equality were all met might be extremely useful as a yardstick against which to compare the real world and to understand its shortcomings.

Economics as a social science

Economics concerns human behaviour. One problem here is that individuals often behave in very different ways. People have different tastes and different attitudes. This problem, however, is not as serious as it may seem at first sight. The reason is that people *on average* are likely to behave more predictably. For example, if the price of a product goes up by 5 per cent, we might be able to predict, *ceteris paribus*, that the quantity demanded will fall by approximately 10 per cent. This does not mean that every single individual's demand will fall by 10 per cent, only that *total* demand will. Some people may demand a lot less; others may demand the same as before.

Even so, there are still things about human behaviour that are very difficult to predict, even when we are talking about whole groups of people. How, for example, will firms react to a rise in interest rates when making their investment decisions? This will depend on things such as the state of business confidence: something that is notoriously difficult to predict.

For these reasons there is plenty of scope for competing models in economics, each making different assumptions and leading to different policy conclusions. As a result, economics can often be highly controversial. As we shall see later on in the book, different political parties may adhere to different schools of economic thought. Thus the political left may adhere to a model which implies that governments must intervene if unemployment is to be cured; whereas the political right may adhere to a model which implies that unemployment will be reduced if the government intervenes less and relies more on the free market.

This is not to say that economists always disagree. Despite the popular belief that 'if you laid all the economists of the world end to end they would still not reach a conclusion', there is in fact a large measure of agreement between economists about how to analyse the world and what conclusions to draw.

Economics and policy

Economists play a major role in helping governments to devise economic policy. In order to understand this role, it is necessary to distinguish between *positive* and *normative* statements.

A ***positive statement*** is a statement of fact. It may be right or wrong, but its accuracy can be tested by appealing to the facts. 'Unemployment is rising.' 'Inflation will be over 6 per cent by next year.' 'If the government cuts taxes, imports will rise.' These are all examples of positive statements.

A ***normative statement*** is a statement of value: a statement about what ought or ought not to be, about whether something is good or bad, desirable or undesirable. 'It is right to tax the rich more than the poor.' 'The government *ought* to reduce inflation.' 'Old-age pensions *ought* to be increased in line with inflation.' These are all examples of normative statements. They cannot be proved or disproved by a simple appeal to the facts.

Economists can only contribute to questions of policy in a positive way. That is, they can analyse the consequences of following certain policies. They can say which of two policies is more likely to achieve a given aim, but they cannot, as economists, say whether the aims of the policy

Definitions

Positive statement A value-free statement which can be tested by an appeal to the facts.

Normative statement A value judgement.

are desirable. For example, economists may argue that a policy of increasing government expenditure will reduce unemployment and raise inflation, but they cannot decide whether such a policy is desirable.

Key Idea 6 ***The importance of the positive/normative distinction.*** Economics can only contribute to policy issues in a positive way. Economists, as scientists, cannot make normative judgements. They can make them only as individual people, with no more moral right than any other individual.

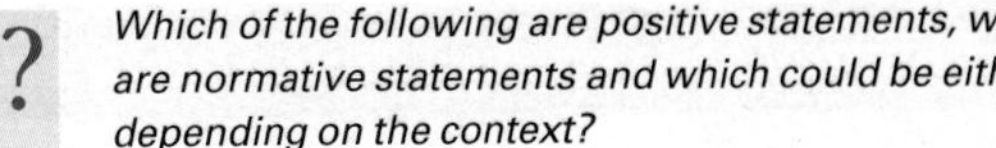

? *Which of the following are positive statements, which are normative statements and which could be either depending on the context?*

(a) Cutting the higher rates of income tax will redistribute incomes from the poor to the rich.
(b) It is wrong that inflation should be reduced if this means that there will be higher unemployment.
(c) It is wrong to state that putting up interest rates will reduce inflation.
(d) The government should raise interest rates to prevent the exchange rate falling.
(e) Current government policies should reduce unemployment.

Section summary

1. The methodology used by economists is similar to that used by natural scientists. Economists construct models which they use to explain and predict economic phenomena. These models can be tested by appealing to facts and seeing how successfully they have been predicted or explained by the model. Unsuccessful models can be either abandoned or amended.
2. Being a social science, economics is concerned with human actions. Making accurate predictions in economics is very difficult given that economics has to deal with a constantly changing environment.
3. Economists can help governments to devise policy by examining the consequences of alternative courses of action. In doing this, it is important to separate positive questions about what the effects of the policies are, from normative ones as to what the goals of policy should be. Economists in their role as economists have no superior right to make normative judgements. They do, however, play a major role in assessing whether a policy meets the political objectives of government (or opposition).

END OF CHAPTER QUESTIONS

1. Imagine that a country can produce just two things: goods and services. Assume that over a given period it could produce any of the following combinations:

Units of goods										
0	10	20	30	40	50	60	70	80	90	100
Units of services										
80	79	77	74	70	65	58	48	35	19	0

   (a) Draw the country's production possibility curve.
   (b) Assuming that the country is currently producing 40 units of goods and 70 units of services, what is the opportunity cost of producing another 10 units of goods?
   (c) Explain how the figures illustrate the principle of increasing opportunity cost.
   (d) Now assume that technical progress leads to a 10 per cent increase in the output of goods for any given amount of resources. Draw the new production possibility curve. How has the opportunity cost of producing extra units of services altered?

2. Imagine that you won millions of pounds on the National Lottery. Would your 'economic problem' be solved?
3. Assume that in a household one parent currently works full time and the other stays at home to look after the family. How would you set about identifying and calculating the opportunity costs of the second parent now taking a full-time job? How would such calculations be relevant in deciding whether it is worth taking that job?
4. When you made the decision to study economics, was it a 'rational' decision (albeit based on the limited information you had available at the time)? What additional information would you like to have had in order to ensure that your decision was the right one?
5. In what way does specialisation reduce the problem of scarcity?
6. Would redistributing incomes from the rich to the poor reduce the overall problem of scarcity?
7. Assume that oil begins to run out and that extraction becomes more expensive. Trace through the effects of this on the market for oil and the market for other fuels.
8. Give two examples of positive statements about the economy, and two examples of normative ones. Now give two examples that are seemingly positive, but which have normative implications or undertones.

Additional case studies on the book's website (www.pearsoned.co.uk/sloman)

1.1 Buddhist economics. A different perspective on economic problems and economic activity.

1.2 Green economics. This examines some of the environmental costs that society faces today. It also looks at the role of economics in analysing these costs and how the problems can be tackled.

1.3 Global economics. This examines how macroeconomics and microeconomics apply at the global level and identifies some key issues.

1.4 The interdependence of markets. A case study in the operation of markets, examining the effects on a local economy of the discovery of a large coal deposit.

1.5 Free-market medicine in Russia. This examines the operating of the fledgling market economy in Russia and the successes and difficulties in moving from a planned to a market economy.

WEBSITES RELEVANT TO THIS CHAPTER

Numbers and sections refer to websites listed in the Web Appendix and hotlinked from this book's website at www.pearsoned.co.uk/sloman.

- For news articles relevant to this chapter, see the *Economics News Articles* link from the book's website.
- For a tutorial on finding the best economics websites, see site C8 (*The Internet Economist*).
- For general economics news sources, see websites in section A of the Web Appendix at the end of the book, and particularly A1–9, 24, 38, 39. See also A38, 39, 43 and 44 for links to newspapers worldwide; and A41 and 42 for links to economics news articles from newspapers worldwide.
- For sources of economic data, see sites in section B and particularly B1–4, 33, 34.
- For general sites for students of economics, see sites in section C and particularly C1–7.
- For sites giving links to relevant economics websites, organised by topic, see sites I4, 7, 8, 11, 12, 17, 18.
- For news on the Russian economy (Box 1.5 and Web Case 1.5), see sites A14, 15. See also the *Economic Systems and Theories* > *Transition Economies* section of sites I7 and 11.
- For an excellent site giving details of the lives, works and theories of famous economists from the history of economic thought (including Adam Smith from Box 1.6), see C18.

Part B: Foundations of Microeconomics

In the first half of the book, we focus on microeconomics. Despite being 'small economics' – in other words, the economics of the individual parts of the economy, rather than the economy as a whole – it is still concerned with many of the big issues of today. To understand how the economy works at this micro level, we must understand how markets work. This involves an understanding of demand and supply.

In Chapter 2, we look at how demand and supply interact to determine prices in a free-market economy. Markets, however, are not always free: governments frequently intervene in markets. In Chapter 3, we examine government intervention in markets.

Chapter 2

Supply and Demand

As we saw in Chapter 1, in a free-market economy prices play a key role in transmitting information from buyers to sellers and from sellers to buyers. This chapter examines this 'price mechanism' in more detail.

We examine what determines demand; what determines supply; what the relationship is between demand, supply and price; how the price mechanism transmits information both from consumers to producers, and from producers to consumers; and how prices act as incentives – for example, if consumers want more mobile phones, how this increased demand leads to an increase in their price and hence to an incentive for firms to increase their production.

Changes in price affect the quantity demanded and supplied. But how much? How much will the demand for DVDs go up if the price of DVDs comes down? How much will the supply of new houses go up if the price of houses rises? We develop the concept of *elasticity* of demand and supply to examine this responsiveness.

Finally, we look at how quickly markets adjust and also examine how people's expectations of price changes affect what actually happens to prices. In particular, we look at speculation – people attempting to gain from anticipated price changes.

CHAPTER MAP

The markets we will be examining are highly competitive ones, with many firms competing against each other. In economics we call this ***perfect competition***. This is where consumers and producers are too numerous to have any control over prices: they are ***price takers***.

In the case of consumers, this means that they have to accept the prices as given for the things that they buy. On most occasions this is true. For example, when you get to the supermarket checkout you cannot start haggling with the checkout operator over the price of a can of beans or a tub of margarine.

In the case of firms, perfect competition means that producers are too small and face too much competition from other firms to be able to raise prices. Take the case of farmers selling wheat. They have to sell it at the current market price. If individually they try to sell at a higher price, no one will buy, since purchasers of wheat (e.g. flour millers) can get all the wheat they want at the market price.

Of course, many firms *do* have the power to choose their prices. This does not mean that they can simply charge whatever they like. They will still have to take account of overall consumer demand and their competitors' prices. Ford, when setting the price of its Focus cars, will have to ensure that they remain competitive with Astras, Golfs, Civics, etc. Nevertheless, most firms have some flexibility in setting their prices: they have a degree of 'market power'.

If this is the case, then why do we study *perfect* markets, where firms are price takers? One reason is that they provide a useful approximation to the real world and give us many insights into how a market economy works. Many markets do function very similarly to the markets we shall be describing.

Another is that perfect markets provide an ideal against which to compare the real world. It is often argued that perfect markets benefit the consumer, whereas markets dominated by big business may operate against the consumer's interests. Although these are normative issues, the economist can nevertheless compare the behaviour of prices, output, profit, etc. in different types of market. For example, will the consumer end up paying higher prices in a market dominated by just a few firms than in one operating under perfect competition? Will British Telecom respond to an increase in demand for telephone services in the same way as farmer Giles does to an increase in the demand for cauliflowers?

Markets with powerful firms are examined in Chapters 6 and 7. For now we concentrate on price takers.

2.1 DEMAND

The relationship between demand and price

The headlines announce, 'Major crop failures in Brazil and East Africa: coffee prices soar.' Shortly afterwards you find that coffee prices have doubled in the shops. What do you do? Presumably you will cut back on the amount of coffee you drink. Perhaps you will reduce it from, say, six cups per day to two. Perhaps you will give up drinking coffee altogether.

This is simply an illustration of the general relationship between price and consumption: *when the price of a good rises, the quantity demanded will fall*. This relationship is known as the ***law of demand***. There are two reasons for this law:

- People will feel poorer. They will not be able to afford to buy so much of the good with their money. The purchasing power of their income (their *real income*) has fallen. This is called the ***income effect*** of a price rise.
- The good will now cost more than alternative or 'substitute' goods, and people will switch to these. This is called the ***substitution effect*** of a price rise.

Similarly, when the price of a good falls, the quantity demanded will rise. People can afford to buy more (the income effect), and they will switch away from consuming alternative goods (the substitution effect).

Therefore, returning to our example of the increase in the price of coffee, we will not be able to afford to buy as

Definitions

Perfect competition (preliminary definition) A situation where the consumers and producers of a product are price takers. (There are other features of a perfectly competitive market; these are examined in Chapter 6.)

Price taker A person or firm with no power to be able to influence the market price.

Law of demand The quantity of a good demanded per period of time will fall as price rises and will rise as price falls, other things being equal (*ceteris paribus*).

Income effect The effect of a change in price on quantity demanded arising from the consumer becoming better or worse off as a result of the price change.

Substitution effect The effect of a change in price on quantity demanded arising from the consumer switching to or from alternative (substitute) products.

much as before, and we will probably drink more tea, cocoa, fruit juices or even water instead.

Key Idea 7 ***The income and substitution effects*** are useful concepts as they help to explain why people react to a price rise by buying less. The size of these effects depends on a range of factors. These factors determine the shape of the demand curve.

A word of warning: be careful about the meaning of the words ***quantity demanded***. They refer to the amount that consumers are willing and able to purchase at a given price over a given period (e.g. a week, or a month, or a year). They do not refer to what people would simply *like* to consume. You might like to own a luxury yacht, but your demand for luxury yachts will almost certainly be zero at the current price.

The demand curve

Consider the hypothetical data in Table 2.1, which shows how many kilograms of potatoes per month would be purchased at various prices.

Columns (2) and (3) show the ***demand schedules*** for two individuals, Tracey and Darren. Column (4) by contrast, shows the total ***market demand schedule***. This is the total demand by all consumers. To obtain the market demand schedule for potatoes, we simply add up the quantities demanded at each price by *all* consumers: i.e. Tracey, Darren and everyone else who demands potatoes. Notice that we are talking about demand *over a period of time* (not at *a point* in time). Thus we would talk about daily demand or weekly demand or annual demand or whatever.

?

Assume that there are 200 consumers in the market. Of these, 100 have schedules like Tracey's and 100 have schedules like Darren's. What would be the total market demand schedule for potatoes now?

The demand schedule can be represented graphically as a ***demand curve***. Figure 2.1 shows the market demand curve for potatoes corresponding to the schedule in Table 2.1. This price of potatoes is plotted on the vertical axis. The quantity demanded is plotted on the horizontal axis.

Point *E* shows that at a price of 100p per kilo, 100 000 tonnes of potatoes are demanded each month. When the price falls to 80p we move down the curve to point *D*. This shows that the quantity demanded has now risen to 200 000 tonnes per month. Similarly, if the price falls to 60p we move down the curve again to point *C*: 350 000 tonnes are now demanded. The five points on the graph (*A–E*) correspond to the figures in columns (1) and (4) of Table 2.1. The graph also enables us to read off the likely quantities demanded at prices other than those in the table.

1. *How much would be demanded at a price of 30p per kilogram?*
2. *Assuming that demand does not change from month to month, plot the annual market demand for potatoes.*

A demand curve could also be drawn for an individual consumer. Like market demand curves, individuals' demand curves generally slope downwards from left to right: they have negative slope. The lower the price of the product, the more is a person likely to buy.

Table 2.1 The demand for potatoes (monthly)

	Price (pence per kg) (1)	Tracey's demand (kg) (2)	Darren's demand (kg) (3)	Total market demand (tonnes: 000s) (4)
A	20	28	16	700
B	40	15	11	500
C	60	5	9	350
D	80	1	7	200
E	100	0	6	100

Definitions

Quantity demanded The amount of a good that a consumer is willing and able to buy at a given price over a given period of time.

Demand schedule for an individual A table showing the different quantities of a good that a person is willing and able to buy at various prices over a given period of time.

Market demand schedule A table showing the different total quantities of a good that consumers are willing and able to buy at various prices over a given period of time.

Demand curve A graph showing the relationship between the price of a good and the quantity of the good demanded over a given time period. Price is measured on the vertical axis; quantity demanded is measured on the horizontal axis. A demand curve can be for an individual consumer or group of consumers, or more usually for the whole market.

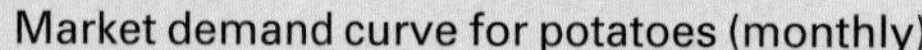

Figure 2.1 Market demand curve for potatoes (monthly)

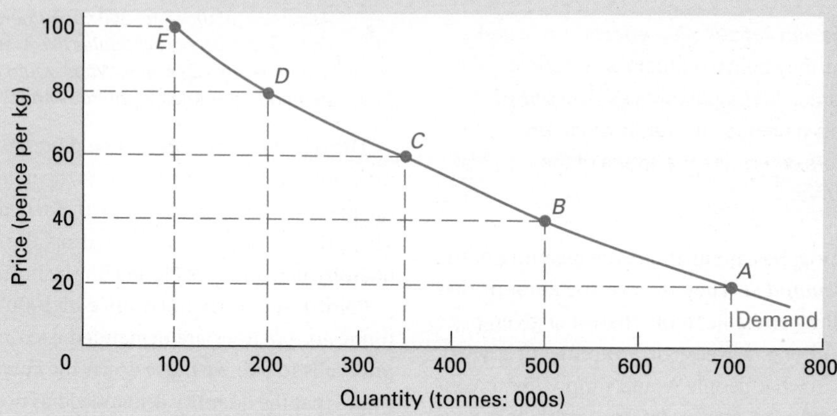

?

1. *Draw Tracey's and Darren's demand curves for potatoes on one diagram. Note that you will use the same vertical scale as in Figure 2.1, but you will need a quite different horizontal scale.*
2. *At what price is their demand the same?*
3. *What explanations could there be for the quite different shapes of their two demand curves? (This question is explored in section 2.4 below.)*

Two points should be noted at this stage:

- In textbooks, demand curves (and other curves too) are only occasionally used to plot specific data. More frequently they are used to illustrate general theoretical arguments. In such cases the axes will simply be price and quantity, with the units unspecified.
- The term 'curve' is used even when the graph is a straight line! In fact when using demand curves to illustrate arguments we frequently draw them as straight lines – it's easier.

Other determinants of demand

Price is not the only factor that determines how much of a good people will buy. Demand is also affected by the following.

Tastes. The more desirable people find the good, the more they will demand. Tastes are affected by advertising, by fashion, by observing other consumers, by considerations of health and by the experiences from consuming the good on previous occasions.

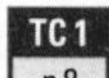
TC 1 p8

The number and price of substitute goods (i.e. competitive goods). The higher the price of ***substitute goods***, the higher will be the demand for this good as people switch from the substitutes. For example, the demand for coffee will depend on the price of tea. If tea goes up in price, the demand for coffee will rise.

The number and price of complementary goods. ***Complementary goods*** are those that are consumed together: cars and petrol, shoes and polish, fish and chips. The higher the price of complementary goods, the fewer of them will be bought and hence the less will be the demand for this good. For example, the demand for batteries will depend on the price of personal stereos. If the price of personal stereos goes up, so that fewer are bought, the demand for batteries will fall.

Income. As people's incomes rise, their demand for most goods will rise. Such goods are called ***normal goods***. There are exceptions to this general rule, however. As people get richer, they spend less on ***inferior goods***, such as cheap margarine, and switch to better quality goods.

Distribution of income. If national income were redistributed from the poor to the rich, the demand for luxury goods would rise. At the same time, as the poor got poorer they might have to turn to buying inferior goods, whose demand would thus rise too.

Expectations of future price changes. If people think that prices are going to rise in the future, they are likely to buy more now before the price does go up.

Definitions

Substitute goods A pair of goods which are considered by consumers to be alternatives to each other. As the price of one goes up, the demand for the other rises.

Complementary goods A pair of goods consumed together. As the price of one goes up, the demand for both goods will fall.

Normal good A good whose demand rises as people's incomes rise.

Inferior good A good whose demand falls as people's incomes rise.

CASE STUDIES AND APPLICATIONS *BOX 2.1

THE DEMAND FOR LAMB

A real-world demand function[1]

The following is an estimate of the UK's market demand curve for lamb. It has been estimated (using a computer regression package) from actual monthly data for the years 1966–99.

$$Q_d = 217.1 - 0.112P_L + 0.125P_B - 0.0198Y$$

where: Q_d is the quantity of lamb sold in grams per person per week.

P_L is the price of lamb (in pence per kg, at 1985 prices).

P_B is the price of beef (in pence per kg, at 1985 prices).

Y is annual personal disposable income per head (£, at 1995 prices).

From this, economists could forecast what would happen to the demand for lamb if any of three variables – the price of lamb, the price of beef or income – changed.

From this equation, calculate what would happen to the demand for lamb if:

(a) the price of lamb went up by 10p per kg (at 1985 prices).

(b) the price of beef went up by 10p per kg (at 1985 prices).

(c) personal disposable income per head went up by £100 per annum (at 1995 prices).

There is a serious problem with estimated demand functions like these: they assume that *other* determinants of demand have not changed. In the case of this demand-for-lamb function, one of the other determinants *did* change. This was tastes – during the 1980s and 1990s there was a shift in demand away from lamb and other meats, partly for health reasons, and partly because of an expansion in the availability of and demand for vegetarian and low-meat alternatives.

Assuming that this shift in taste took place steadily over time, a new demand equation was estimated for the same years:

$$Q_d = 192.3 - 0.530P_L + 0.0738P_B + 0.0261Y - 7.352TIME$$

where the *TIME* term is as follows: 1966 = 1, 1967 = 2, 1968 = 3 . . . 1999 = 34.

1. ***How does the introduction of the*** **TIME** ***term affect the relationship between the demand for butter and (a) the price of beef; (b) personal disposable income per head?***
2. ***Is lamb a normal good or an inferior good?***

Then in the mid-1990s, there was the BSE scare and a temporary shift in demand to lamb from beef. The following table shows this shift.

	Actual consumption of lamb	Actual consumption of beef	P_L	P_B	Y
1994	54	131	301.6	343.0	8266
1996	66	101	296.2	325.6	8607
2000	55	124	310.7	320.1	9604

Source: *http://www.defra.gov.uk/esg/Excel/allfood.xls*

Because of these large changes in demand, over just a few years, it is not possible to include their determinants in an equation in any meaningful way. But clearly, BSE did have a major effect and hence made the estimated equations less reliable for forecasting the demand for lamb.

Use the second equation to estimate the demand for lamb in 1994, 1996 and 2000. In which of these three years was the estimation closest to the actual figure? Explain the divergences in the actual figures from the figures derived from the equation.

[1] Thanks to Tony Flegg, my 'office mate' at UWE, for these calculations.

1. *Do all these six determinants of demand affect both an individual's demand and the market demand for a product?*
2. *Relate each of these six determinants to the demand for butter.*

Movements along and shifts in the demand curve

A demand curve is constructed on the assumption that 'other things remain equal' (*ceteris paribus*). In other words, it is assumed that none of the determinants of demand, other than price, changes. The effect of a change in price is then simply illustrated by a movement along the demand curve: for example, from point *B* to point *D* in Figure 2.1 when the price of potatoes rises from 40p to 80p per kilo.

What happens, then, when one of these other determinants does change? The answer is that we have to construct a whole new demand curve: the curve shifts. If a change in one of the other determinants causes demand to rise – say, income rises – the whole curve will shift to the right. This shows that at each price more will be demanded than before. Thus in Figure 2.2 at a price of P, a quantity of Q_0 was originally demanded. But now, after the increase in demand, Q_1 is demanded. (Note that D_1 is not necessarily parallel to D_0.)

If a change in a determinant other than price causes demand to fall, the whole curve will shift to the left.

Figure 2.2 An increase in demand

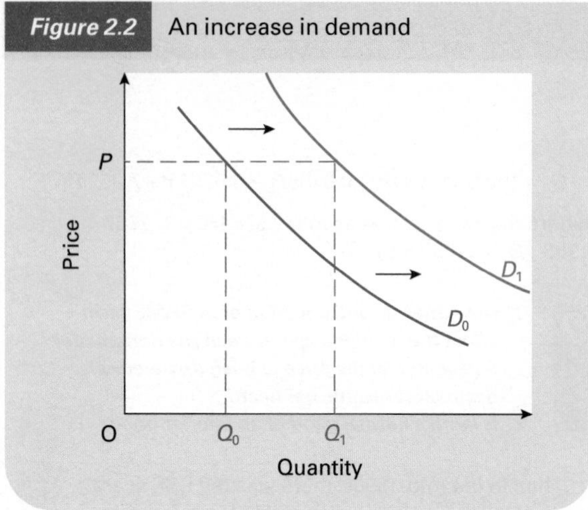

To distinguish between shifts in and movements along demand curves, it is usual to distinguish between a change in *demand* and a change in the *quantity demanded*. A shift in the demand curve is referred to as a ***change in demand***, whereas a movement along the demand curve as a result of a change in price is referred to as a ***change in the quantity demanded***.

1. *Assume that in Table 2.1 the total market demand for potatoes increases by 20 per cent at each price – due, say, to substantial increases in the prices of bread and rice. Plot the old and the new demand curves for potatoes. Is the new curve parallel to the old one?*
2. *The price of cashew nuts rises and yet it is observed that the sales of cashew nuts increase. Does this mean that the demand curve for cashew nuts is upward sloping? Explain.*

*LOOKING AT THE MATHS

We can represent the relationship between the market demand for a good and the determinants of demand in the form of an equation. This is called a ***demand function***. It can be expressed either in general terms or with specific values attached to the determinants.

Simple demand functions. Demand equations are often used to relate quantity demanded to just one determinant. Thus an equation relating quantity demanded to price could be in the form:

$$Q_d = a - bP \qquad (1)$$

For example, the actual equation might be:

$$Q_d = 10\,000 - 200P \qquad (2)$$

From this can be calculated a complete demand schedule or demand curve, as shown in the table and diagram. As price (P) changes, the equation tells us how much the quantity demanded (Q_d) changes.

Demand schedule for equation (2)

P	Q_d
5	9000
10	8000
15	7000
20	6000
25	5000

Demand curve for equation (2)

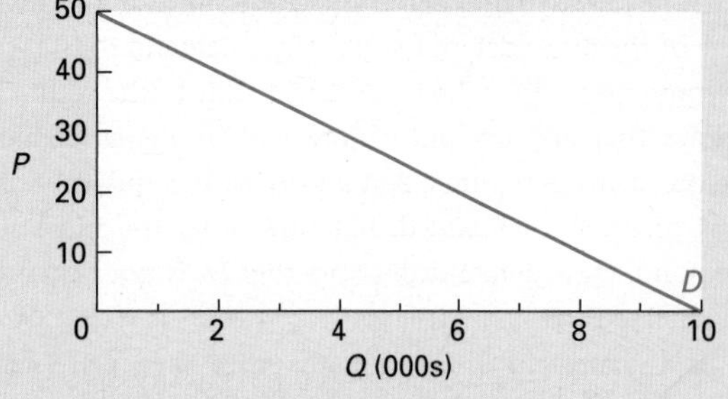

1. ***Complete the demand schedule in the table up to a price of 50.***
2. ***What is it about equation (2) that makes the demand curve (a) downward sloping; (b) a straight line?***

This equation is based on a *ceteris paribus* assumption: it is assumed that all the other determinants of demand remain constant. If one of these other determinants changed, the equation itself would change. There would be a shift in the curve: a change in demand. If the a term alone changed, there would be a parallel shift in the curve. If the b term changed, the slope of the curve would change.

Simple equations can be used to relate demand to other determinants too. For example, an equation relating quantity demanded to income would be in the form:

$$Q_d = a + bY \qquad (3)$$

1. ***Referring to equation (3), if the term 'a' has a value of –50 000 and the term 'b' a value of 0.001, construct a demand schedule with respect to total income (Y). Do this for incomes between £100 million and £300 million at £50 million intervals.***
2. ***Now use this schedule to plot a demand curve with respect to income. Comment on its shape.***

More complex demand functions. In a similar way, we can relate the quantity demanded to two or more determinants. For example, a demand function could be of the form:

$$Q_d = a - bP + cY + dP_s - eP_c \qquad (4)$$

This equation says that the quantity demanded (Q_d) will fall as the price of the good (P) rises, will rise as the level of consumer incomes (Y) rises, will rise as the price of a particular substitute (P_s) rises and will fall as the price of a particular complement (P_c) rises, by amounts b, c, d and e respectively.

Estimated demand equations. Surveys can be conducted to show how demand depends on each one of a number of determinants, while the rest are held constant. Using statistical techniques called ***regression analysis***, a demand equation can be estimated.

For example, assume that it was observed that the demand for butter (measured in 250g units) depended on its price (P_b), the price of margarine (P_m) and total annual consumer incomes (Y). The estimated weekly demand equation may then be something like:

$$Q_d = 2\,000\,000 - 50\,000P_b + 20\,000P_m + 0.01Y \quad (5)$$

Thus if the price of butter were 50p, the price of margarine were 35p and consumer incomes were £200 million, and if P_b and P_m were measured in pence and Y was measured in pounds, then the demand for butter would be 2 200 000 units. This is calculated as follows:

$$\begin{aligned} Q_d &= 2\,000\,000 - (50\,000 \times 50) + (20\,000 \times 35) \\ &\quad + (0.01 \times 200\,000\,000) \\ &= 2\,000\,000 - 2\,500\,000 + 700\,000 + 2\,000\,000 \\ &= 2\,200\,000 \end{aligned}$$

The branch of economics that applies statistical techniques to economic data is known as ***econometrics***. Econometrics is beyond the scope of this book. It is worth noting, however, that econometrics, like other branches of statistics, cannot produce equations and graphs that allow totally reliable predictions to be made. The data on which the equations are based are often incomplete or unreliable, and the underlying relationships on which they are based (often ones of human behaviour) may well change over time.

Section summary

1. When the price of a good rises, the quantity demanded per period of time will fall. This is known as the 'law of demand'. It applies both to individuals' demand and to the whole market demand.
2. The law of demand is explained by the income and substitution effects of a price change.
3. The relationship between price and quantity demanded per period of time can be shown in a table (or 'schedule') or as a graph. On the graph, price is plotted on the vertical axis and quantity demanded per period of time on the horizontal axis. The resulting demand curve is downward sloping (negatively sloped).
4. Other determinants of demand include tastes, the number and price of substitute goods, the number and price of complementary goods, income, the distribution of income and expectations of future price changes.
5. If price changes, the effect is shown by a movement along the demand curve. We call this effect 'a change in the quantity demanded'.
6. If any other determinant of demand changes, the whole curve will shift. We call this effect 'a change in demand'. A rightward shift represents an increase in demand; a leftward shift represents a decrease in demand.

*7. The relationship between the quantity demanded and the various determinants of demand (including price) can be expressed as an equation.

2.2 SUPPLY

Supply and price

Imagine you are a farmer deciding what to do with your land. Part of your land is in a fertile valley. Part is on a hillside where the soil is poor. Perhaps, then, you will consider growing vegetables in the valley and keeping sheep on the hillside.

Your decision will depend to a large extent on the price that various vegetables will fetch in the market and likewise the price you can expect to get from sheep and wool. As far as the valley is concerned, you will plant the vegetables that give the best return. If, for example, the price of potatoes is high, you will probably use a lot of the valley for growing potatoes. If the price gets higher, you may well use the whole of the valley, being prepared maybe to run the risk of potato disease. If the price is very high indeed, you may even consider growing potatoes on the hillside, even though the yield per acre is much lower there.

In other words, the higher the price of a particular farm output, the more land will be devoted to it. This illustrates the general relationship between supply and price: *when the price of a good rises, the quantity supplied will also rise.* There are three reasons for this:

Definitions

Change in demand The term used for a shift in the demand curve. It occurs when a determinant of demand other than price changes.

Change in the quantity demanded The term used for a movement along the demand curve to a new point. It occurs when there is a change in price.

Demand function An equation which shows the mathematical relationship between the quantity demanded of a good and the values of the various determinants of demand.

Regression analysis A statistical technique which allows a functional relationship between two or more variables to be estimated.

Econometrics The science of applying statistical techniques to economic data in order to identify and test economic relationships.

Table 2.2 The supply of potatoes (monthly)

	Price of potatoes (pence per kg)	Farmer X's supply (tonnes)	Total market supply (tonnes: 000s)
a	20	50	100
b	40	70	200
c	60	100	350
d	80	120	530
e	100	130	700

Figure 2.3 Market supply curve of potatoes (monthly)

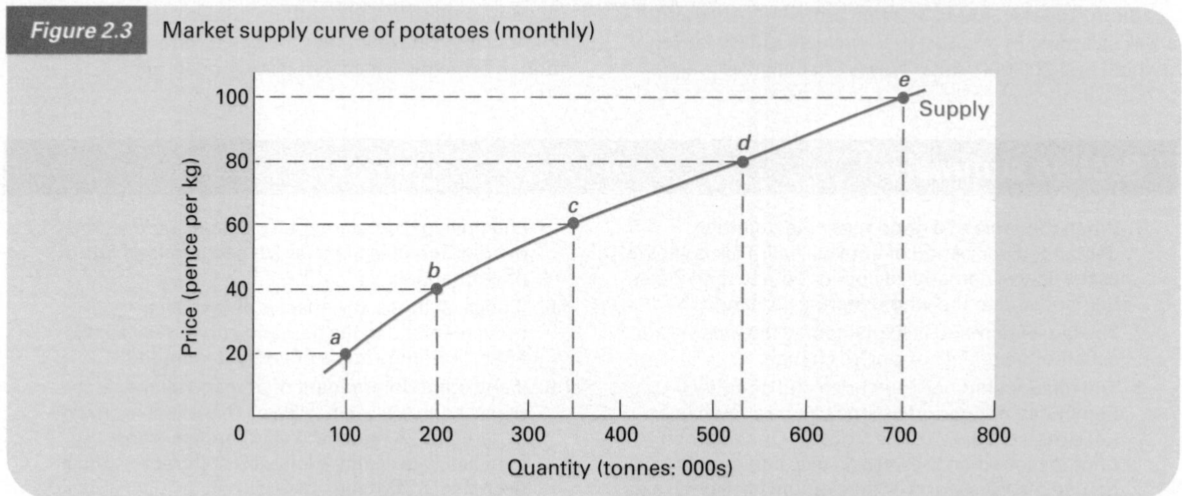

- As firms supply more, they are likely to find that beyond a certain level of output, costs rise more and more rapidly. In the case of the farm just considered, if more and more potatoes are grown, then land progressively less suitable to potato cultivation has to be used. This raises the cost of producing extra potatoes. It is the same for manufacturers. Beyond a certain level of output, costs are likely to rise rapidly as workers have to be paid overtime and as machines approach capacity working. If higher output involves higher costs of producing each unit, producers will need to get a higher price if they are to be persuaded to produce extra output.
- The higher the price of the good, the more profitable it becomes to produce. Firms will thus be encouraged to produce more of it by switching from producing less profitable goods.
- Given time, if the price of a good remains high, new producers will be encouraged to set up in production. Total market supply thus rises.

The first two determinants affect supply in the short run. The third affects supply in the long run. We distinguish between short-run and long-run supply later in the chapter on page 57.

The supply curve

The amount that producers would like to supply at various prices can be shown in a ***supply schedule***. Table 2.2 shows a monthly supply schedule for potatoes, both for an individual farmer (farmer X) and for all farmers together (the whole market).

The supply schedule can be represented graphically as a ***supply curve***. A supply curve may be an individual firm's supply curve or a market curve (i.e. that of the whole industry).

Figure 2.3 shows the *market* supply curve of potatoes. As with demand curves, price is plotted on the vertical axis and quantity on the horizontal axis. Each of the points *a*–*e* corresponds to a figure in Table 2.2. Thus, for example, a price rise from 60p per kilogram to 80p per kilogram will cause a movement along the supply curve from point *c* to point *d*: total market supply will rise from 350 000 tonnes per month to 530 000 tonnes per month.

1. *How much would be supplied at a price of 70p per kilo?*
2. *Draw a supply curve for farmer X. Are the axes drawn to the same scale as in Figure 2.3?*

Definitions

Supply schedule A table showing the different quantities of a good that producers are willing and able to supply at various prices over a given time period. A supply schedule can be for an individual producer or group of producers, or for all producers (the market supply schedule).

Supply curve A graph showing the relationship between the price of a good and the quantity of the good supplied over a given period of time.

Not all supply curves will be upward sloping (positively sloped). Sometimes they will be vertical, or horizontal or even downward sloping. This will depend largely on the time period over which firms' response to price changes is considered. This question is examined in the section on the elasticity of supply (see section 2.4 below) and in more detail in Chapters 5 and 6.

Other determinants of supply

Like demand, supply is not simply determined by price. The other determinants of supply are as follows.

The costs of production. The higher the costs of production, the less profit will be made at any price. As costs rise, firms will cut back on production, probably switching to alternative products whose costs have not risen so much.

The main reasons for a change in costs are as follows:

- Change in input prices: costs of production will rise if wages, raw material prices, rents, interest rates or any other input prices rise.
- Change in technology: technological advances can fundamentally alter the costs of production. Consider, for example, how the microchip revolution has changed production methods and information handling in virtually every industry in the world.
- Organisational changes: various cost savings can be made in many firms by reorganising production.
- Government policy: costs will be lowered by government subsidies and raised by various taxes.

The profitability of alternative products (substitutes in supply). If a product which is a ***substitute in supply*** becomes more profitable to supply than before, producers are likely to switch from the first good to this alternative. Supply of the first good falls. Other goods are likely to become more profitable if:

- their prices rise;
- their costs of production fall.

For example, if the price of carrots goes up, or the cost of producing carrots comes down, farmers may decide to cut down potato production in order to produce more carrots.

The profitability of goods in joint supply. Sometimes when one good is produced, another good is also produced at the same time. These are said to be ***goods in joint supply***. An example is the refining of crude oil to produce petrol. Other grade fuels will be produced as well, such as diesel and paraffin. If more petrol is produced, due to a rise in demand and hence its price, then the supply of these other fuels will rise too.

Nature, 'random shocks' and other unpredictable events. In this category we would include the weather and diseases affecting farm output, wars affecting the supply of imported raw materials, the breakdown of machinery, industrial disputes, earthquakes, floods and fire, etc.

The aims of producers. A profit-maximising firm will supply a different quantity from a firm that has a different aim, such as maximising sales. For most of the time we shall assume that firms are profit maximisers. In Chapter 8, however, we consider alternative aims.

Expectations of future price changes. If price is expected to rise, producers may temporarily reduce the amount they sell. Instead they are likely to build up their stocks and only release them on to the market when the price does rise. At the same time they may install new machines or take on more labour, so that they can be ready to supply more when the price has risen.

The number of suppliers. If new firms enter the market, supply is likely to increase.

By referring to each of the above determinants of supply, identify what would cause (a) the supply of potatoes to fall and (b) the supply of leather to rise.

Movements along and shifts in the supply curve

The principle here is the same as with demand curves. The effect of a change in price is illustrated by a movement along the supply curve: for example, from point *d* to point *e* in Figure 2.3 when price rises from 80p to 100p. Quantity supplied rises from 530 000 to 700 000 tonnes per month.

If any other determinant of supply changes, the whole supply curve will shift. A rightward shift illustrates an increase in supply. A leftward shift illustrates a decrease in supply. Thus in Figure 2.4, if the original curve is S_0, the curve S_1 represents an increase in supply (more is supplied at each price), whereas the curve S_2 represents a decrease in supply (less is supplied at each price).

A movement along a supply curve is often referred to as a ***change in the quantity supplied***, whereas a shift in the supply curve is simply referred to as a ***change in supply***.

Definitions

Substitutes in supply These are two goods where an increased production of one means diverting resources away from producing the other.

Goods in joint supply These are two goods where the production of more of one leads to the production of more of the other.

Change in the quantity supplied The term used for a movement along the supply curve to a new point. It occurs when there is a change in price.

Change in supply The term used for a shift in the supply curve. It occurs when a determinant other than price changes.

Figure 2.4 Shifts in the supply curve

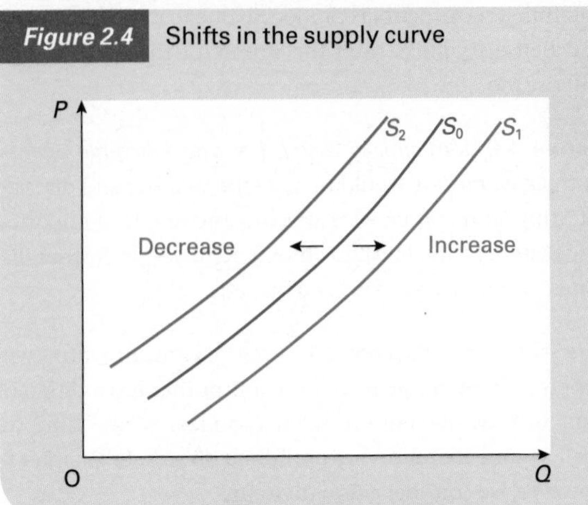

?

This question is concerned with the supply of oil for central heating. In each case consider whether there is a movement along the supply curve (and in which direction) or a shift in it (and whether left or right). (a) New oil fields start up in production. (b) The demand for central heating rises. (c) The price of gas falls. (d) Oil companies anticipate an upsurge in demand for central-heating oil. (e) The demand for petrol rises. (f) New technology decreases the costs of oil refining. (g) All oil products become more expensive.

*LOOKING AT THE MATHS

Using survey data and regression analysis, equations can be estimated relating supply to some of its determinants. Note that not all determinants can be easily quantified (e.g. nature and the aims of firms), and thus may be left out of the equation.

The simplest form of supply equation relates supply to just one determinant. Thus a function relating supply to price would be of the form:

$$Q_s = c + dP \tag{1}$$

Using regression analysis, values can be estimated for c and d. Thus an actual supply equation might be something like:

$$Q_s = 500 + 1000P \tag{2}$$

?

1. ***If P was originally measured in £s, what would happen to the value of the d term in equation (2) if P were now measured in pence?***
2. ***Draw the schedule (table) and graph for equation (2) for prices from £1 to £10. What is it in the equation that determines the slope of the supply 'curve'?***

If any determinant other than price changed, a new equation would result. For example, if costs of production fall, the equation may now be:

$$Q_s = 1000 + 1500P \tag{3}$$

More complex supply equations would relate supply to more than one determinant. For example:

$$Q_s = 200 + 80P - 20a_1 - 15a_2 + 30j \tag{4}$$

where P is the price of the good, a_1 and a_2 are the profitabilities of two alternative goods that could be supplied instead, and j is the profitability of a good in joint supply.

?

Explain why the P and j terms have a positive sign, whereas the a_1 and a_2 terms have a negative sign.

Section summary

1. When the price of a good rises, the quantity supplied per period of time will usually also rise. This applies both to individual producers' supply and to the whole market supply.
2. There are two reasons in the short run why a higher price encourages producers to supply more: (a) they are now willing to incur the higher costs per unit associated with producing more; (b) they will switch to producing this product and away from now less profitable ones. In the long run, there is a third reason: new producers will be attracted into the market.
3. The relationship between price and quantity supplied per period of time can be shown in a table (or schedule) or as a graph. As with a demand curve, price is plotted on the vertical axis and quantity per period of time on the horizontal axis. The resulting supply curve is upward sloping (positively sloped).
4. Other determinants of supply include the costs of production, the profitability of alternative products, the profitability of goods in joint supply, random shocks and expectations of future price changes.
5. If price changes, the effect is shown by a movement along the supply curve. We call this effect 'a change in the quantity supplied'.
6. If any determinant *other* than price changes, the effect is shown by a shift in the whole supply curve. We call this effect 'a change in supply'. A rightward shift represents an increase in supply; a leftward shift represents a decrease in supply.

*7. The relationship between the quantity supplied and the various determinants of supply can be expressed in the form of an equation.

2.3 PRICE AND OUTPUT DETERMINATION

Equilibrium price and output

We can now combine our analysis of demand and supply. This will show how the actual price of a product and the actual quantity bought and sold are determined in a free and competitive market.

Let us return to the example of the market demand and market supply of potatoes, and use the data from Tables 2.1 and 2.2. These figures are given again in Table 2.3.

What will be the price and output that actually prevail? If the price started at 20p per kilogram, demand would exceed supply by 600 000 tonnes (*A* – *a*). Consumers would be unable to obtain all they wanted and would thus be willing to pay a higher price. Producers, unable or unwilling to supply enough to meet the demand, will be only too happy to accept a higher price. The effect of the shortage, then, will be to drive up the price. The same would happen at a price of 40p per kilogram. There would still be a shortage; price would still rise. But as the price rises, the quantity demanded falls and the quantity supplied rises. The shortage is progressively eliminated.

? *Explain the process by which the price of houses would rise if there were a shortage.*

What would happen if the price started at a much higher level: say, at 100p per kilogram? In this case supply would exceed demand by 600 000 tonnes (*e* – *E*). The effect of this surplus would be to drive the price down as farmers competed against each other to sell their excess supplies. The same would happen at a price of 80p per kilogram. There would still be a surplus; price would still fall.

In fact, only one price is sustainable – the price where demand equals supply: namely, 60p per kilogram, where both demand and supply are 350 000 tonnes. When supply matches demand the market is said to ***clear***. There is no shortage and no surplus.

As we have already seen in section 1.2, the price where demand equals supply is called the *equilibrium price* (see Threshold Concept 4 on page 22). In Table 2.3, if the price starts at other than 60p per kilogram, it will tend to move towards 60p. The equilibrium price is the only price at which producers' and consumers' wishes are mutually reconciled: where the producers' plans to supply exactly match the consumers' plans to buy.

Equilibrium is the point where conflicting interests are balanced. Only at this point is the amount that demanders are willing to purchase the same as the amount that suppliers are willing to supply. It is a point that will be automatically reached in a free market through the operation of the price mechanism.

Demand and supply curves

The determination of equilibrium price and output can be shown using demand and supply curves. Equilibrium is where the two curves intersect.

Figure 2.5 shows the demand and supply curves of potatoes corresponding to the data in Table 2.3. Equilibrium price is P_e (60p) and equilibrium quantity is Q_e (350 000 tonnes).

At any price above 60p, there would be a surplus. Thus at 80p there is a surplus of 330 000 tonnes (*d* – *D*). More is supplied than consumers are willing and able to purchase at that price. Thus a price of 80p fails to clear the market. Price will fall to the equilibrium price of 60p. As it does so, there will be a movement along the demand curve from point *D* to point *C*, and a movement along the supply curve from point *d* to point *c*.

At any price below 60p, there would be a shortage. Thus at 40p there is a shortage of 300 000 tonnes (*B* – *b*). Price will rise to 60p. This will cause a movement along the supply curve from point *b* to point *c* and along the demand curve from point *B* to point *C*.

Point *Cc* is the equilibrium: where demand equals supply.

Movement to a new equilibrium

The equilibrium price will remain unchanged only so long as the demand and supply curves remain unchanged. If either of the curves shifts, a new equilibrium will be formed. KI 5 p21

Definition

Market clearing A market clears when supply matches demand, leaving no shortage or surplus.

Table 2.3 The market demand and supply of potatoes (monthly)

Price of potatoes (pence per kg)	Total market demand (tonnes: 000s)	Total market supply (tonnes: 000s)
20	700 (*A*)	100 (*a*)
40	500 (*B*)	200 (*b*)
60	350 (*C*)	350 (*c*)
80	200 (*D*)	530 (*d*)
100	100 (*E*)	700 (*e*)

Figure 2.5 The determination of market equilibrium (potatoes: monthly)

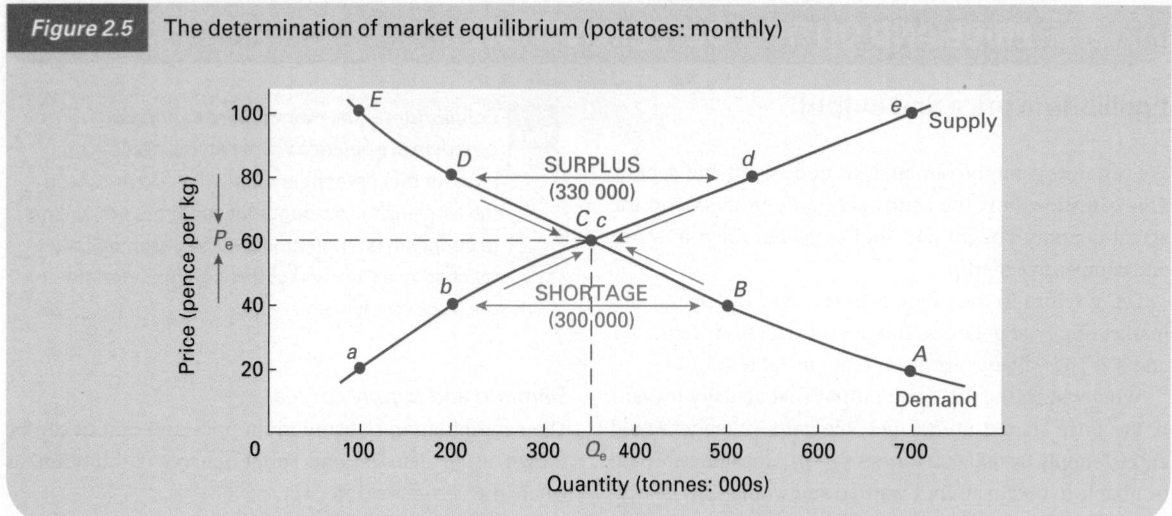

A change in demand

If one of the determinants of demand changes (other than price), the whole demand curve will shift. This will lead to a movement *along* the *supply* curve to the new intersection point.

For example, in Figure 2.6, if a rise in consumer incomes led to the demand curve shifting to D_2, there would be a shortage of $h - g$ at the original price P_{e_1}. This would cause price to rise to the new equilibrium P_{e_2}. As it did so, there would be a movement along the supply curve from point g to point i, and along the new demand curve (D_2) from point h to point i. Equilibrium quantity would rise from Q_{e_1} to Q_{e_2}.

The effect of the shift in demand, therefore, has been a movement *along* the supply curve from the old equilibrium to the new: from point g to point i.

? *What would happen to price and quantity if the demand curve shifted to the left? Draw a diagram to illustrate your answer.*

A change in supply

Likewise, if one of the determinants of supply changes (other than price), the whole supply curve will shift. This will lead to a movement *along* the *demand* curve to the new intersection point.

For example, in Figure 2.7, if costs of production rose, the supply curve would shift to the left: to S_2. There would be a shortage of $g - j$ at the old price of P_{e_1}. Price would rise from P_{e_1} to P_{e_3}. Quantity would fall from Q_{e_1} to Q_{e_3}. In other words, there would be a movement along the demand curve from point g to point k, and along the new supply curve (S_2) from point j to point k.

To summarise: a shift in one curve leads to a movement along the other curve to the new intersection point.

Sometimes a number of determinants might change. This might lead to a shift in *both* curves. When this happens, equilibrium simply moves from the point where the old curves intersected to the point where the new ones intersect.

Figure 2.6 Effect of a shift in the demand curve

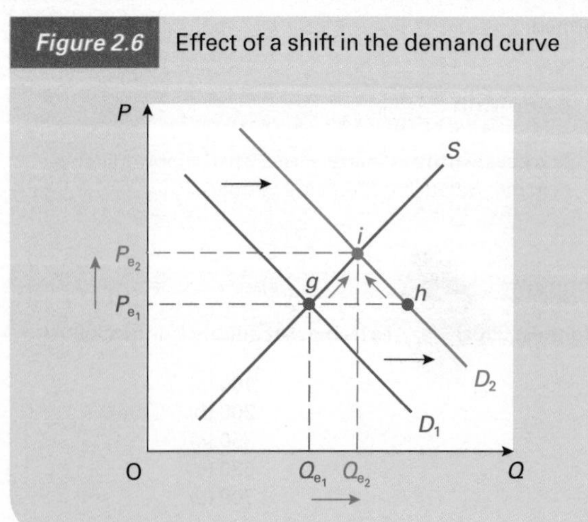

Figure 2.7 Effect of a shift in the supply curve

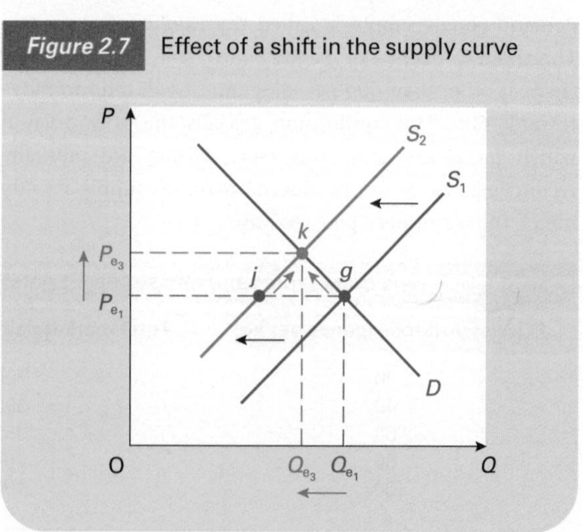

?

What will happen to the equilibrium price and quantity of butter in each of the following cases? You should state whether demand or supply (or both) have shifted and in which direction. (In each case assume ceteris paribus.*)*
(a) A rise in the price of margarine. (b) A rise in the demand for yoghurt. (c) A rise in the price of bread. (d) A rise in the demand for bread. (e) An expected rise in the price of butter in the near future. (f) A tax on butter production. (g) The invention of a new, but expensive, process for removing all cholesterol from butter, plus the passing of a law which states that all butter producers must use this process.

*LOOKING AT THE MATHS

We saw on pages 38–9 and 42 how demand and supply curves can be represented by equations. Assume that the equations for the supply and demand curves in a particular market are as follows:

$$Q_D = a - bP \quad (1)$$

$$Q_S = c + dP \quad (2)$$

We can find the market equilibrium price by setting the two equations equal to each other, since, in equilibrium, the quantity supplied (Q_S) equals the quantity demanded (Q_D). Thus:

$$c + dP = a - bP$$

Subtracting *c* from and adding *bP* to both sides gives:

$$dP + bP = a - c$$

$$\therefore (d + b)P = a - c$$

$$\therefore P = \frac{a - c}{d + b} \quad (3)$$

We can then solve for equilibrium quantity (Q_e) by substituting equation (3) in either equation (1) or (2) (since $Q_D = Q_S$).

Thus, from equation (1):

$$Q_e = a - b\left(\frac{a - c}{d + b}\right) = \frac{a(d + b) - b(a - c)}{d + b} = \frac{ad + ab - ba + bc}{d + b} = \frac{ad + bc}{d + b} \quad (4)$$

or, from equation (2):

$$Q_e = c + d\left(\frac{a - c}{d + b}\right) = \frac{cd + cb + da - dc}{d + b} = \frac{cb + da}{d + b} \quad (5)$$

Thus:

$$Q_e = \frac{ad + bc}{d + b} \text{ (equation (4))} = \frac{cb + da}{d + b} \text{ (equation (5))}$$

A worked example is given in Maths Case 2.1 on the book's website.

*Identifying the position of demand and supply curves

Both demand and supply depend on price, and yet their interaction determines price. For this reason it is difficult to identify just what is going on when price and quantity change, and to identify just what the demand and supply curves look like.

Let us say that we want to identify the demand curve for good X. We observe that when the price was 20p, 1000 units were purchased. At a later date the price has risen to 30p and 800 units are now purchased. What can we conclude from this about the demand curve? The answer is that without further information we can conclude very little. Consider Figures 2.8 and 2.9. Both are consistent with the facts.

In Figure 2.8 the demand curve has not shifted. The rise in price and the fall in sales are due entirely to a shift in the supply curve. The movement from point *a* to point *b* is thus a movement along the demand curve. If we can be certain

Figure 2.8 Problems in identifying the position and shape of the demand curve: shift in supply curve

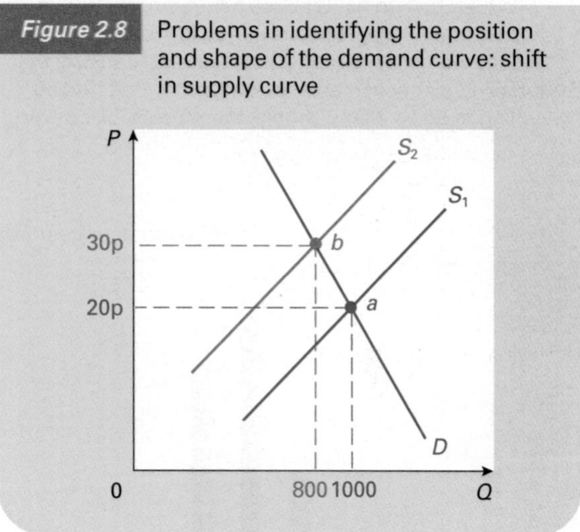

Figure 2.9 Problems in identifying the position and shape of the demand curve: shift in supply *and* demand curves

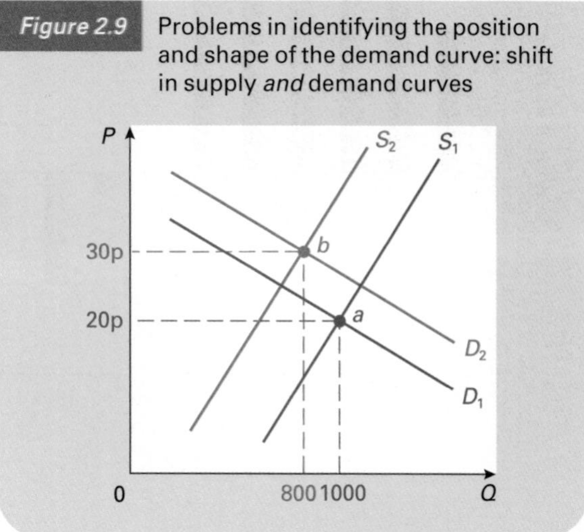

CASE STUDIES AND APPLICATIONS

UK HOUSE PRICES

The ups and downs of the housing market

If you are thinking of buying a house sometime in the future, then you may well follow the fortunes of the housing market with some trepidation. In the late 1980s there was a housing price explosion in the UK: in fact, between 1984 and 1989 house prices *doubled*. After several years of falling or gently rising house prices in the early and mid-1990s, there was another boom from 1996 to 2004, with house prices rising by 26 per cent per year at the peak (in the 12 months to January 2003). For many, owning a home of their own was becoming a mere dream.

House prices since the early 1980s

The diagram shows what happened to house prices in the period 1983 to 2005. The vertical axis measures the percentage by which average house prices rose in that particular year. You can see that house price inflation was very high in the late 1980s, reaching a peak of 23.3 per cent in 1988.

In their rush to buy a house before prices rose any further, many people in this period borrowed as much as they were able. Building societies and banks at that time had plenty of money to lend and were only too willing to do so. Many people, therefore, took out very large mortgages. In 1983 the average new mortgage was 2.08 times average annual earnings. By 1989 this figure had risen to 3.44.

After 1989 there followed a period of *falling* prices. From 1990 to 1995, house prices fell by 12.2 per cent. Many people now found themselves in a position of *negative equity*. This is the situation where the size of their mortgage is greater than the value of their house. In other words, if they sold their house, they would end up still owing money! For this reason many people found that they could not move house.

Then in 1996, house prices began to recover and for the next three years they rose moderately – by around 5 per cent per annum. But then they started rising rapidly again, and by 2002 house price inflation had returned to rates similar to those in the 1980s. Was this good news or bad news? For those who had been trapped in negative equity, it was good news. It was also good news for old people who wished to move into a retirement home and who had a house to sell. It was bad news for the first-time buyer, however! As we shall see in many parts of this book, what is good news for one person is often bad news for another.

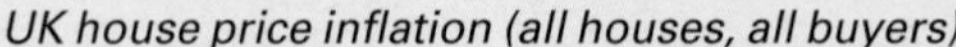

UK house price inflation (all houses, all buyers)

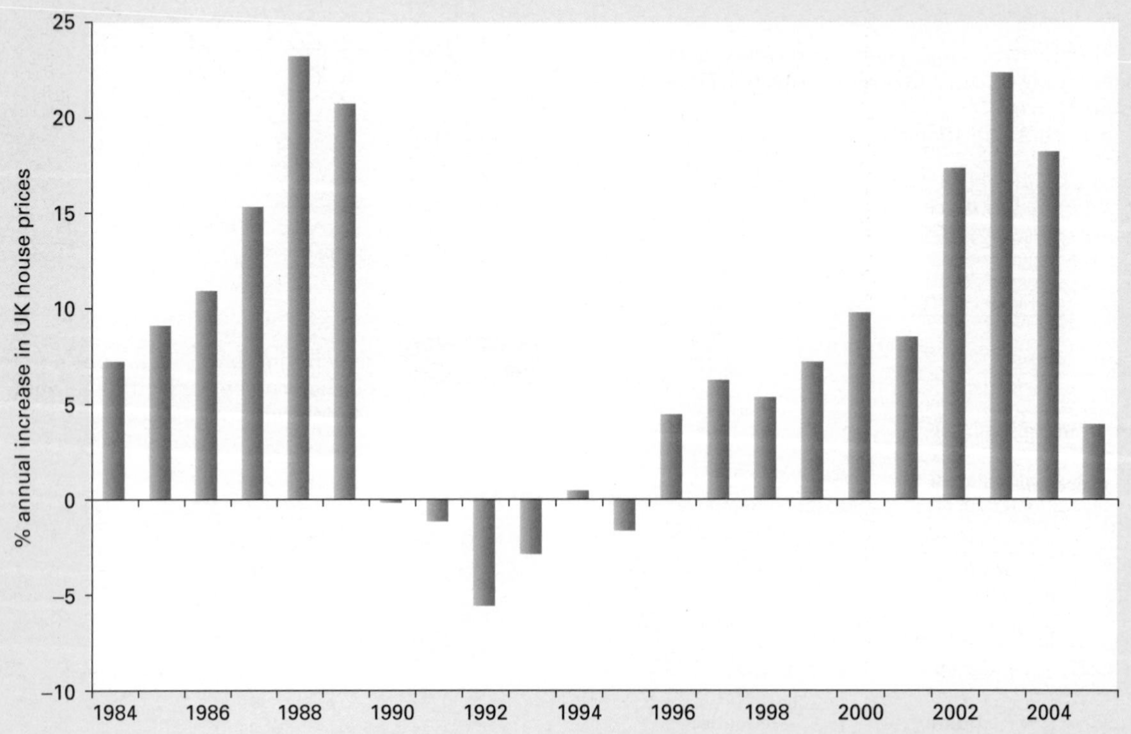

BOX 2.2

The determinants of house prices

House prices are determined by demand and supply. If demand rises (i.e. shifts to the right) or if supply falls (i.e. shifts to the left), the equilibrium price of houses will rise. Similarly, if demand falls or supply rises, the equilibrium price will fall.

So why did house prices rise so rapidly in the 1980s, only to fall in the early 1990s and then rise rapidly again in the late 1990s and early 2000s? The answer lies primarily in changes in the *demand* for housing. Let us examine the various factors that affected the demand for houses.

Incomes (actual and anticipated). The second half of the 1980s was a period of rapidly rising incomes. The economy was experiencing an economic 'boom'. Many people wanted to spend their extra incomes on housing: either buying a house for the first time, or moving to a better one. What is more, many people thought that their incomes would continue to grow, and were thus prepared to stretch themselves financially in the short term by buying an expensive house, confident that their mortgage payments would become more and more affordable over time.

The early 1990s, by contrast, was a period of recession, with rising unemployment and much more slowly growing incomes. People had much less confidence about their ability to afford large mortgages. The mid-1990s onwards saw incomes rising again.

The desire for home ownership. Mrs Thatcher (prime minister from 1979 to 1991) put great emphasis on the virtues of home ownership: a home-owning democracy. Certainly, the mood of the age was that it was very desirable to own one's own home. This fuelled the growth in demand in the 1980s.

The cost of mortgages. During the second half of the 1980s, mortgage interest rates were generally falling. This meant that people could afford larger mortgages, and thus afford to buy more expensive houses. In 1989, however, this trend was reversed. Mortgage interest rates were now rising. Many people found it difficult to maintain existing payments, let alone to take on a larger mortgage. From 1996 to 2003 mortgage rates were generally reduced again, once more fuelling the demand for houses.

The availability of mortgages. In the late 1980s, mortgages were readily available. Banks and building societies were prepared to accept smaller deposits on houses, and to grant mortgages of $3^1/_2$ times a person's annual income, compared with $2^1/_2$ times in the early 1980s. In the early 1990s, however, banks and building societies were more cautious about granting mortgages. They were aware that, with falling house prices, rising unemployment and the growing problem of negative equity, there was an increased danger that borrowers would default on payments. With the recovery of the economy in the mid-1990s, however, and with a growing number of mortgage lenders, mortgages became more readily available and for greater amounts relative to people's income.

Speculation. In the 1980s, people generally believed that house prices would continue rising. This encouraged people to buy as soon as possible, and to take out the biggest mortgage possible, before prices went up any further. There was also an effect on supply. Those with houses to sell held back until the last possible moment in the hope of getting a higher price. The net effect was a rightward shift in the demand curve for houses and a leftward shift in the supply curve. The effect of this speculation, therefore, was to help bring about the very effect that people were predicting (see section 2.5).

In the early 1990s, the opposite occurred. People thinking of buying houses held back, hoping to buy at a lower price. People with houses to sell tried to sell as quickly as possible before prices fell any further. Again the effect of this speculation was to aggravate the change in prices – this time a fall in prices.

Then, in the late 1990s, the return of rapidly rising prices encouraged people to buy more rapidly again, once more adding fuel to house price inflation. The speculation was compounded by worries about falling stock market prices. Many investors turned to buying property instead of shares.

What of the future?

By mid-2004, the boom in house prices seemed to be coming to an end. With interest rates rising, people were becoming increasingly worried about taking on large mortgage debt. And with house price inflation slowing down, speculation could go into reverse. It seemed unlikely that there would be a house price crash, however, with interest rates edging lower.

1. ***Draw supply and demand diagrams to illustrate what was happening to house prices (a) in the second half of the 1980s and the late 1990s and early 2000s; (b) in the early 1990s.***
2. ***Are there any factors on the* supply *side that influence house prices?***
3. ***Find out what has happened to house prices over the past three years. Attempt an explanation of what has happened.***

that the demand curve has not shifted, then the evidence allows us to identify its position (or, at least, two points on it).

In Figure 2.9, however, not only has the supply curve shifted, but so also has the demand curve. Let us assume that people's tastes for the product have increased. In this case a movement from *a* to *b* does *not* trace out the demand curve. We cannot derive the demand curve(s) from the evidence of price and quantity alone.

The problem is that when the supply curve shifts, we often cannot know whether or not the demand curve has shifted, and if so by how much. How would we know, for example, just how much people's tastes have changed?

The problem works the other way round too. It is difficult to identify a supply curve when the demand curve shifts. Is the change in price and quantity entirely due to the shift in the demand curve, or has the supply curve shifted too?

The problem is known as the ***identification problem***. It is difficult to identify just what is causing the change in price and quantity.

Section summary

1. If the demand for a good exceeds the supply, there will be a shortage. This will lead to a rise in the price of the good.
2. If the supply of a good exceeds the demand, there will be a surplus. This will lead to a fall in the price.
3. Price will settle at the equilibrium. The equilibrium price is the one that clears the market: the price where demand equals supply.
4. If the demand or supply curve shifts, this will lead either to a shortage or to a surplus. Price will therefore either rise or fall until a new equilibrium is reached at the position where the supply and demand curves *now* intersect.

*5. It is difficult to identify the position of a real-world supply (or demand) curve simply by looking at the relationship between price and quantity at different points in time. The problem is that the other curve may have shifted (by an unknown amount).

2.4 ELASTICITY

Price elasticity of demand

When the price of a good rises, the quantity demanded will fall. That much is fairly obvious. But in most cases we will want to know more than this. We will want to know by just *how much* the quantity demanded will fall. In other words, we will want to know how *responsive* demand is to a rise in price.

Take the case of two products: oil and cauliflowers. In the case of oil, a rise in price is likely to result in only a slight fall in the quantity demanded. If people want to continue driving, they have to pay the higher prices for fuel. A few may turn to riding bicycles, and some people may try to make fewer journeys, but for most people, a rise in the price of petrol and diesel will make little difference to how much they use their cars.

In the case of cauliflowers, however, a rise in price may lead to a substantial fall in the quantity demanded. The reason is that there are alternative vegetables that people can buy. Many people, when buying vegetables, are very conscious of their prices and will buy whatever is reasonably priced.

We call the responsiveness of demand to a change in price the ***price elasticity of demand***, and as we shall see on many occasions throughout this book, it is one of the most important concepts in economics. For example, if we know the price elasticity of demand for a product, we can predict the effect on price and quantity of a shift in the *supply* curve for that product.

Figure 2.10 shows the effect of a shift in supply with two quite different demand curves (*D* and *D'*). Curve *D'* is more elastic than curve *D* over any given price range. In other words, for any given change in price, there will be a larger change in quantity demanded along curve *D'* than along curve *D*.

Definitions

Identification problem The problem of identifying the relationship between two variables (e.g. price and quantity demanded) from the evidence when it is not known whether or how the variables have been affected by other determinants. For example, it is difficult to identify the shape of a demand curve simply by observing price and quantity when it is not known whether changes in other determinants have shifted the demand curve.

Price elasticity of demand The responsiveness of quantity demanded to a change in price.

Figure 2.10 Market supply and demand

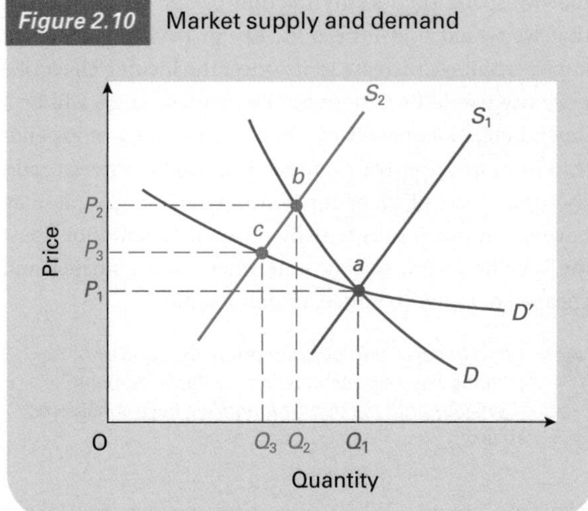

Assume that initially the supply curve is S_1, and that it intersects with both demand curves at point *a*, at a price of P_1 and a quantity of Q_1. Now supply shifts to S_2. What will happen to price and quantity? In the case of the less elastic demand curve *D*, there is a relatively large rise in price (to P_2) and a relatively small fall in quantity (to Q_2): equilibrium is at point *b*. In the case of the more elastic demand curve *D′*, however, there is only a relatively small rise in price (to P_3), but a relatively large fall in quantity (to Q_3): equilibrium is at point *c*.

Measuring the price elasticity of demand

What we want to compare is the size of the change in quantity demanded with the size of the change in price. But since price and quantity are measured in different units, the only sensible way we can do this is to use percentage or proportionate changes. This gives us the following ***formula for the price elasticity of demand ($P\epsilon_D$)*** for a product: percentage (or proportionate) change in quantity demanded divided by the percentage (or proportionate) change in price. Putting this in symbols gives:

$$P\epsilon_D = \frac{\%\Delta Q_D}{\%\Delta P}$$

where ϵ (the Greek epsilon) is the symbol we use for elasticity, and Δ (the capital Greek delta) is the symbol we use for a 'change in'.

Thus if a 40 per cent rise in the price of oil caused the quantity demanded to fall by a mere 10 per cent, the price elasticity of oil over this range will be:

$$-10\%/40\% = -0.25$$

Whereas, if a 5 per cent fall in the price of cauliflowers caused a 15 per cent rise in the quantity demanded, the price elasticity of demand for cauliflowers over this range would be:

$$15\%/-5\% = -3$$

Cauliflowers have a more elastic demand than oil, and this is shown by the figures. But just what do these two figures show? What is the significance of minus 0.25 and minus 3?

Interpreting the figure for elasticity

The use of proportionate or percentage measures

Elasticity is measured in proportionate or percentage terms for the following reasons:

- It allows comparison of changes in two qualitatively different things, which are thus measured in two different types of unit: i.e. it allows comparison of *quantity* changes with *monetary* changes.
- It is the only sensible way of deciding *how big* a change in price or quantity is. Take a simple example. An item goes up in price by £1. Is this a big increase or a small increase? We can answer this only if we know what the original price was. If a can of beans goes up in price by £1, that is a huge price increase. If, however, the price of a house goes up by £1, that is a tiny price increase. In other words, it is the percentage or proportionate increase in price that determines how big a price rise it is.

The sign (positive or negative)

Demand curves are generally downward sloping. This means that price and quantity change in opposite directions. A *rise* in price (a positive figure) will cause a *fall* in the quantity demanded (a negative figure). Similarly a *fall* in price will cause a *rise* in the quantity demanded. Thus when working out price elasticity of demand, we either divide a negative figure by a positive figure, or a positive figure by a negative. Either way, we end up with a negative figure.

The value (greater or less than 1)

If we now ignore the negative sign and just concentrate on the value of the figure, this tells us whether demand is ***elastic*** or ***inelastic***.

Definitions

Formula for price elasticity of demand ($P\epsilon_D$) The percentage (or proportionate) change in quantity demanded divided by the percentage (or proportionate) change in price: $\%\Delta Q_D \div \%\Delta P$.

Elastic demand Where quantity demanded changes by a larger percentage than price. Ignoring the negative sign, it will have a value greater than 1.

Elastic ($\epsilon > 1$). This is where a change in price causes a proportionately larger change in the quantity demanded. In this case the value of elasticity will be greater than 1, since we are dividing a larger figure by a smaller figure.

Inelastic ($\epsilon < 1$). This is where a change in a price causes a proportionately smaller change in the quantity demanded. In this case elasticity will be less than 1, since we are dividing a smaller figure by a larger figure.

Unit elastic ($\epsilon = 1$). ***Unit elasticity of demand*** occurs where price and quantity demanded change by the same proportion. This will give an elasticity equal to 1, since we are dividing a figure by itself.

Determinants of price elasticity of demand

The price elasticity of demand varies enormously from one product to another. For example, the demand for a holiday in any given resort typically has a price elasticity greater than 5, whereas the demand for electricity has a price elasticity less than 0.5 (ignoring the negative signs). But why do some products have a highly elastic demand, whereas others have a highly *in*elastic demand? What determines price elasticity of demand?

The number and closeness of substitute goods. This is the most important determinant. The more substitutes there are for a good, and the closer they are, the more will people switch to these alternatives when the price of the good rises: the greater, therefore, will be the price elasticity of demand.

Returning to our examples of oil and cauliflowers, there is no close substitute for oil and thus demand is relatively inelastic. There are plenty of alternatives to cauliflowers, however, and thus demand is relatively elastic.

Why will the price elasticity of demand for a particular brand of a product (e.g. Texaco) be greater than that for the product in general (e.g. petrol)? Is this difference the result of a difference in the size of the income effect or the substitution effect?

The proportion of income spent on the good. The higher the proportion of our income we spend on a good, the more we will be forced to cut consumption when its price rises: the bigger will be the income effect and the more elastic will be the demand.

Thus salt has a very low price elasticity of demand. Part of the reason is that there is no close substitute. But part is that we spend such a tiny fraction of our income on salt that we would find little difficulty in paying a relatively large percentage increase in its price: the income effect of a price rise would be very small. By contrast, there will be a much bigger income effect when a major item of expenditure rises in price. For example, if mortgage interest rates rise (the 'price' of loans for house purchase), people may have to cut down substantially on their demand for housing – being forced to buy somewhere much smaller and cheaper, or to live in rented accommodation.

Will a general item of expenditure like food or clothing have a price-elastic or inelastic demand? (Consider both the determinants we have considered so far.)

The time period. When price rises, people may take a time to adjust their consumption patterns and find alternatives. The longer the time period after a price change, then, the more elastic is the demand likely to be.

To illustrate this, let us return to our example of oil. Between December 1973 and June 1974 the price of crude oil quadrupled, which led to similar increases in the prices of petrol and central-heating oil. Over the next few months, there was only a very small reduction in the consumption of oil products. Demand was highly inelastic. The reason was that people still wanted to drive their cars and heat their houses.

Over time, however, as the higher oil prices persisted, new fuel-efficient cars were developed and many people switched to smaller cars or moved closer to their work. Similarly, people switched to gas or solid fuel central heating, and spent more money insulating their houses to save on fuel bills. Demand was thus much more elastic in the long run.

Demand for oil might be relatively elastic over the longer term, and yet it could still be observed that over time people consume more oil (or only very slightly less) despite rising oil prices. How can this apparent contradiction be explained?

Price elasticity of demand and consumer expenditure

One of the most important applications of price elasticity of demand concerns its relationship with the total amount of money consumers spend on a product. ***Total consumer expenditure (TE)*** is simply price times quantity purchased.

$$TE = P \times Q$$

Definitions

Inelastic demand Where quantity demanded changes by a smaller percentage than price. Ignoring the negative sign, it will have a value less than 1.

Unit elasticity of demand Where quantity demanded changes by the same percentage as price. Ignoring the negative sign, it will have a value equal to 1.

Figure 2.11 Elastic demand between two points

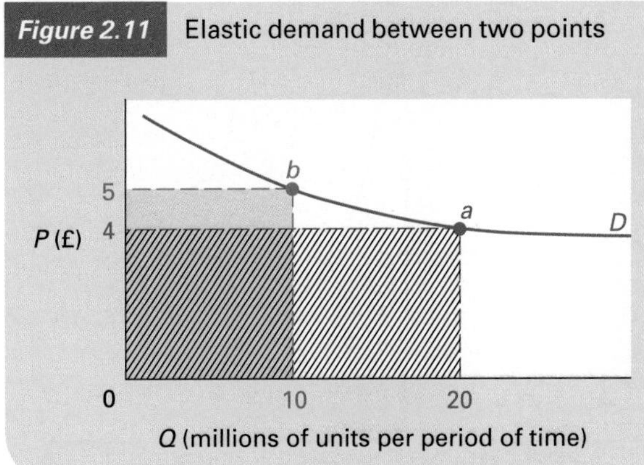

Figure 2.12 Inelastic demand between two points

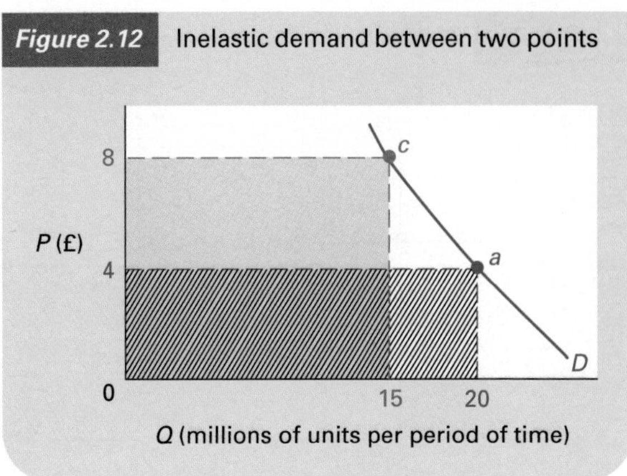

For example, if consumers buy 3 million units (Q) at a price of £2 per unit (P), they will spend a total of £6 million (TE).

Total consumer expenditure will be the same as the ***total revenue (TR)*** received by firms from the sale of the product (before any taxes or other deductions).

What will happen to consumer expenditure (and hence firms' revenue) if there is a change in price? The answer depends on the price elasticity of demand.

Elastic demand

As price rises so quantity demanded falls, and vice versa. When demand is elastic, quantity demanded changes proportionately more than price. Thus the change in quantity has a bigger effect on total consumer expenditure than does the change in price. For example, when the price rises, there will be such a large fall in consumer demand that *less* will be spent than before. This can be summarised as follows:

- *P* rises; *Q* falls proportionately more; thus *TE* falls.
- *P* falls; *Q* rises proportionately more; thus *TE* rises.

In other words, total expenditure changes in the same direction as *quantity*.

This is illustrated in Figure 2.11. The areas of the rectangles in the diagram represent total expenditure. Why? The area of a rectangle is its height multiplied by its length. In this case, this is price multiplied by quantity bought, which is total expenditure. Demand is elastic between points *a* and *b*. A rise in price from £4 to £5 causes a proportionately larger fall in quantity demanded: from 20 million to 10 million. Total expenditure *falls* from £80 million (the striped area) to £50 million (the pink area).

When demand is elastic, then, a rise in price will cause a fall in total consumer expenditure and thus a fall in the total revenue that firms selling the product receive. A reduction in price, however, will result in consumers spending more, and hence firms earning more.

Inelastic demand

When demand is inelastic, it is the other way around. Price changes proportionately more than quantity. Thus the change in price has a bigger effect on total consumer expenditure than does the change in quantity. To summarise the effects:

- *P* rises; *Q* falls proportionately less; *TE* rises.
- *P* falls; *Q* rises proportionately less; *TE* falls.

In other words, total consumer expenditure changes in the same direction as *price*.

This is illustrated in Figure 2.12. Demand is inelastic between points *a* and *c*. A rise in price from £4 to £8 causes a proportionately smaller fall in quantity demanded: from 20 million to 15 million. Total expenditure *rises* from £80 million (the striped area) to £120 million (the pink area).

In this case, firms' revenue will increase if there is a rise in price and fall if there is a fall in price.

Assume that demand for a product is inelastic. Will consumer expenditure go on increasing as price rises? Would there be any limit?

Special cases

Figure 2.13 shows three special cases: (a) a totally inelastic demand ($P\epsilon_D = 0$), (b) an infinitely elastic demand ($P\epsilon_D = \infty$) and (c) a unit elastic demand ($P\epsilon_D = -1$).

Totally inelastic demand. This is shown by a vertical straight line. No matter what happens to price, quantity demanded remains the same. It is obvious that the more

Definitions

Total consumer expenditure on a product (TE) (per period of time) The price of the product multiplied by the quantity purchased: $TE = P \times Q$.

Total revenue (TR) (per period of time) The total amount received by firms from the sale of a product, before the deduction of taxes or any other costs. The price multiplied by the quantity sold. $TR = P \times Q$.

Figure 2.13 Demand curves: three special cases

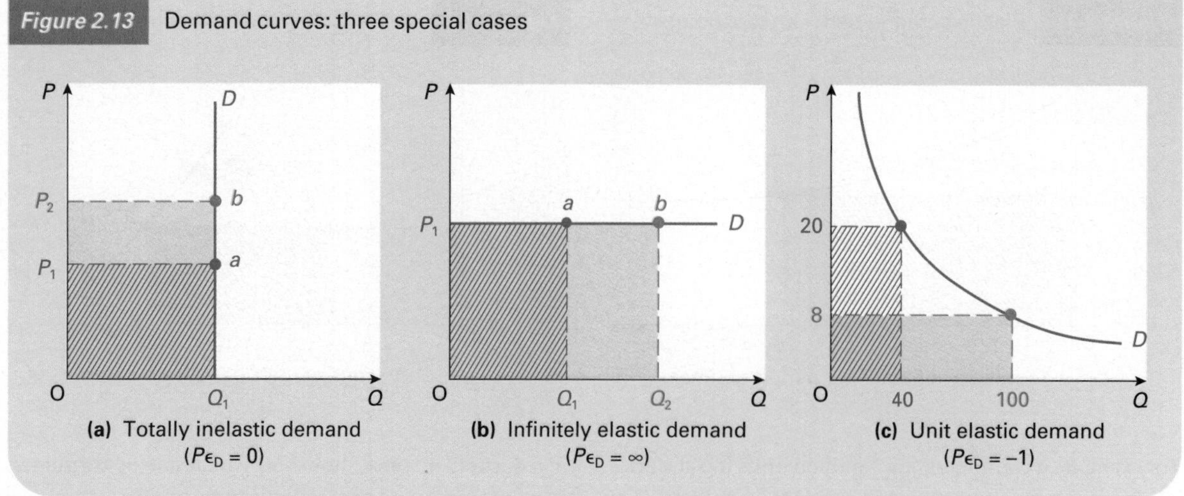

the price rises, the bigger will be the level of consumer expenditure. Thus in Figure 2.13(a), consumer expenditure will be higher at P_2 than at P_1.

? *Can you think of any examples of goods which have a totally inelastic demand (a) at* all *prices; (b) over a particular price range?*

Infinitely elastic demand. This is shown by a horizontal straight line. At any price above P_1 in Figure 2.13(b), demand is zero. But at P_1 (or any price below) demand is 'infinitely' large.

This seemingly unlikely demand curve is in fact relatively common for an *individual producer*. In a perfect market, as we have seen, firms are small relative to the whole market (like the small-scale grain farmer). They have to accept the price as given by supply and demand in the *whole market*, but at that price they can sell as much as they produce. (Demand is not *literally* infinite, but as far as the firm is concerned it is.) In this case, the more the individual firm produces, the more revenue will be earned. In Figure 2.13(b), more revenue is earned at Q_2 than at Q_1.

Unit elastic demand. This is where price and quantity change in exactly the same proportion. Any rise in price will be exactly offset by a fall in quantity, leaving total consumer expenditure unchanged. In Figure 2.13(c), the striped area is exactly equal to the pink area: in both cases, total expenditure is £800.

You might have thought that a demand curve with unit elasticity would be a straight line at 45° to the axes. Instead it is a curve called a *rectangular hyperbola*. The reason for its shape is that the proportionate *rise* in quantity must equal the proportionate *fall* in price (and vice versa). As we move down the demand curve, in order for the *proportionate* change in both price and quantity to remain constant there must be a bigger and bigger *absolute* rise in quantity and a smaller and smaller absolute fall in price. For example, a rise in quantity from 200 to 400 is the same proportionate change as a rise from 100 to 200, but its absolute size is double. A fall in price from £5 to £2.50 is the same percentage as a fall from £10 to £5, but its absolute size is only half.

? *To illustrate these figures, draw the demand curve corresponding to the following table.*

P	*Q*	*TE*
£2.50	*400*	*£1000*
£5	*200*	*£1000*
£10	*100*	*£1000*
£20	*50*	*£1000*
£40	*25*	*£1000*

If the curve had an elasticity of −1 throughout *its length, what would be the quantity demanded (a) at a price of £1; (b) at a price of 10p; (c) if the good were free?*

The measurement of elasticity: arc elasticity

We have defined price elasticity as the percentage or proportionate change in quantity demanded divided by the percentage or proportionate change in price. But how, in practice, do we measure these changes for a specific demand curve? We shall examine two methods. The first is called the *arc method*. The second (in an optional section) is called the *point method*.

A common mistake that students make is to think that you can talk about the elasticity of a *whole curve*. The mistake here is that in most cases the elasticity will vary along the length of the curve.

Take the case of the demand curve illustrated in Figure 2.14. Between points *a* and *b*, total expenditure rises ($P_2Q_2 > P_1Q_1$): demand is thus elastic between these two points. Between points *b* and *c*, however, total expenditure falls ($P_3Q_3 < P_2Q_2$). Demand here is inelastic.

Normally, then, we can only refer to the elasticity of a *portion* of the demand curve, not of the *whole* curve. There are, however, two exceptions to this rule.

CASE STUDIES AND APPLICATIONS **BOX 2.3**

ADVERTISING AND ITS EFFECT ON DEMAND CURVES

How to increase sales and price

When we are told that brand X will make us more beautiful, enrich our lives, wash our clothes whiter, give us get-up-and-go, give us a new taste sensation or make us the envy of our friends, just what are the advertisers up to? 'Trying to sell the product', you may reply.

In fact there is a bit more to it than this. Advertisers are trying to do two things:

- Shift the product's demand curve to the right.
- Make it less price elastic.

This is illustrated in the diagram.

Effect of advertising on the demand curve

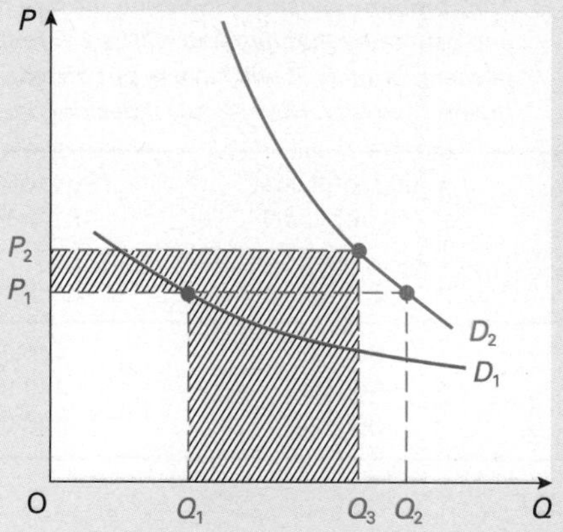

D_1 shows the original demand curve with price at P_1 and sales at Q_1. D_2 shows the curve after an advertising campaign. The rightward shift allows an increased quantity (Q_2) to be sold at the original price. If the demand is also made highly inelastic, the firm can also raise its price and still have a substantial increase in sales. Thus in the diagram, price can be raised to P_2 and sales will be Q_3 – still substantially above Q_1. The total gain in revenue is shown by the shaded area.

How can advertising bring about this new demand curve?

Shifting the demand curve to the right

This will occur if the advertising brings the product to more people's attention and if it increases people's desire for the product.

Making the demand curve less elastic

This will occur if the advertising creates greater brand loyalty. People must be led to believe (rightly or wrongly) that competitors' brands are inferior. This will allow the firm to raise its price above that of its rivals with no significant fall in sales. There will only be a small substitution effect because consumers have been led to believe that there are no close substitutes.

?

1. ***Think of some advertisements which deliberately seek to make demand less elastic.***
2. ***Imagine that 'Sunshine' sunflower margarine, a well-known brand, is advertised with the slogan, 'It helps you live longer'. What do you think would happen to the demand curve for a supermarket's own brand of sunflower margarine? Consider both the direction of shift and the effect on elasticity. Will the elasticity differ markedly at different prices? How will this affect the pricing policy and sales of the supermarket's own brand?***

Figure 2.14 Different elasticities along different portions of a demand curve

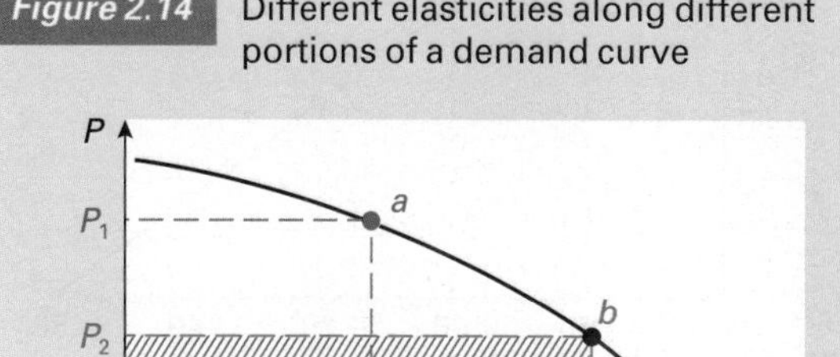

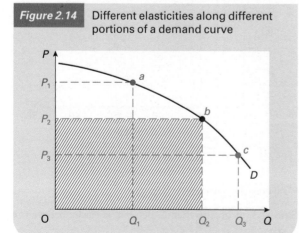

The first is when the elasticity just so happens to be the same all the way along a curve, as in the three special cases illustrated in Figure 2.13. The second is where two curves are drawn on the same diagram, as in Figure 2.10. Here we can say that demand curve D is less elastic than demand curve D' at any given price. Note, however, that each of these two curves will still have different elasticities along its length.

Although we cannot normally talk about the elasticity of a whole curve, we can nevertheless talk about the elasticity between any two points on it. This is known as ***arc elasticity***. In fact the formula for price elasticity of demand that we have used so far is the formula for arc elasticity. Let us examine it more closely. Remember the formula we used was:

$$\frac{\text{Proportionate } \Delta Q}{\text{Proportionate } \Delta P} \quad \text{(where } \Delta \text{ means 'change in')}$$

Definition

Arc elasticity The measurement of elasticity between two points on a curve.

CASE STUDIES AND APPLICATIONS

BOX 2.4

ANY MORE FARES?

Pricing on the buses

Imagine that a local bus company is faced with increased costs and fears that it will make a loss. What should it do?

The most likely response of the company will be to raise its fares. But this may be the wrong policy, especially if existing services are underutilised. To help it decide what to do, it commissions a survey to estimate passenger demand at three different fares: the current fare of 10p per mile, a higher fare of 12p and a lower fare of 8p. The results of the survey are shown in the first two columns of the table.

Demand turns out to be elastic. This is because of the existence of alternative means of transport. As a result of the elastic demand, total revenue can be increased by reducing the fare from the current 10p to 8p. Revenue rises from £400 000 to £480 000 per annum.

But what will happen to the company's profits? Its profit is the difference between the total revenue from passengers and its total costs of operating the service. If buses are currently underutilised, it is likely that the extra passengers can be carried without the need for extra buses, and hence at no extra cost.

At a fare of 10p, the old profit was £40 000 (£400 000 – £360 000). After the increase in costs, a 10p fare now gives a loss of £40 000 (£400 000 – £440 000).

By raising the fare to 12p, the loss is increased to £80 000. But by lowering the fare to 8p, a profit of £40 000 can again be made.

1. ***Estimate the price elasticity of demand between 8p and 10p and between 10p and 12p.***
2. ***Was the 10p fare the best fare originally?***
3. ***The company considers lowering the fare to 6p, and estimates that demand will be $8\frac{1}{2}$ million passenger miles. It will have to put on extra buses, however. How should it decide?***

Fare (pence per mile) (1)	Estimated demand (passenger miles per year: millions) (2)	Total revenue (£ per year) (3)	Old total cost (£ per year) (4)	New total cost (£ per year) (5)
8	6	480 000	360 000	440 000
10	4	400 000	360 000	440 000
12	3	360 000	360 000	440 000

The way we measure a proportionate change in quantity is to divide that change by the level of Q: i.e. $\Delta Q/Q$. Similarly, we measure a proportionate change in price by dividing that change by the level of P: i.e. $\Delta P/P$. Price elasticity of demand can thus now be rewritten as:

$$\frac{\Delta Q}{Q} \div \frac{\Delta P}{P}$$

But just what value do we give to P and Q? Consider the demand curve in Figure 2.15. What is the elasticity of demand between points m and n? Price has fallen by £2 (from £8 to £6), but what is the proportionate change? Is it $-^2/_8$ or $-^2/_6$? The convention is to express the change as a proportion of the average of the two prices, £8 and £6: in other words, to take the midpoint price, £7. Thus the proportionate change is $-^2/_7$.

Similarly, the proportionate change in quantity between points m and n is $^{10}/_{15}$, since 15 is midway between 10 and 20.

Thus using the ***average (or 'midpoint') formula***, elasticity between m and n is given by:

Figure 2.15 Measuring elasticity using the arc method

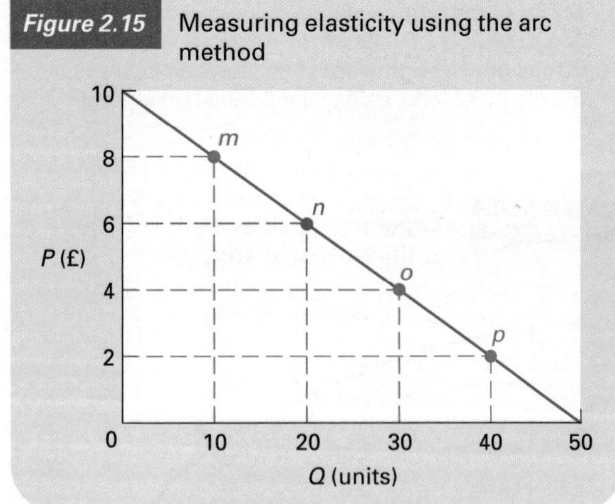

$$\frac{\Delta Q}{\text{average } Q} \div \frac{\Delta P}{\text{average } P} = \frac{10}{15} \div \frac{-2}{7} = -2.33$$

Since 2.33 is greater than 1, demand is elastic between m and n.

Definition

Average (or 'midpoint') formula for price elasticity of demand ΔQ_D/average $Q_D \div \Delta P$/average P.

?

Referring to Figure 2.15, use the midpoint formula to calculate the price elasticity of demand between (a) P = 6 and P = 4; (b) P = 4 and P = 2. What do you conclude about the elasticity of a straight-line demand curve as you move down it?

*The measurement of elasticity: point elasticity

Rather than measuring elasticity between two points on a demand curve, we may want to measure it at a single point: for example, point r in Figure 2.16. In order to measure ***point elasticity*** we must first rearrange the terms in the formula $\Delta Q/Q \div \Delta P/P$. By doing so we can rewrite the formula for price elasticity of demand as:

$$\frac{\Delta Q}{\Delta P} \times \frac{P}{Q}$$

Since we want to measure price elasticity at a *point* on the demand curve, rather than between two points, it is necessary to know how quantity demanded would react to an *infinitesimally small* change in price. In the case of point r in Figure 2.16, we want to know how the quantity demanded would react to an infinitesimally small change from a price of 30.

An infinitesimally small change is signified by the letter d. The formula for price elasticity of demand thus becomes:

$$\frac{dQ}{dP} \times \frac{P}{Q}$$

dQ/dP is the differential calculus term for the rate of change of quantity with respect to a change in price (see Appendix 1). And conversely, dP/dQ is the rate of change of price with respect to a change in quantity demanded. At any given point on the demand curve, dP/dQ is given by the *slope* of the curve (its rate of change). The slope is found by drawing a tangent to the curve at that point and finding the slope of the tangent.

The tangent to the demand curve at point r is shown in Figure 2.16. Its slope is $-50/100$. dP/dQ is thus $-50/100$ and dQ/dP is the inverse of this, $-100/50 = -2$.

Returning to the formula $dQ/dP \times P/Q$, elasticity at point r equals:

$$-2 \times 30/40 = -1.5$$

Rather than having to draw the graph and measure the slope of the tangent, the technique of differentiation can be used to work out point elasticity as long as the equation for the demand curve is known. An example of the use of this technique is given in Box 2.5 (on page 56).

Figure 2.16 Measuring elasticity at a point

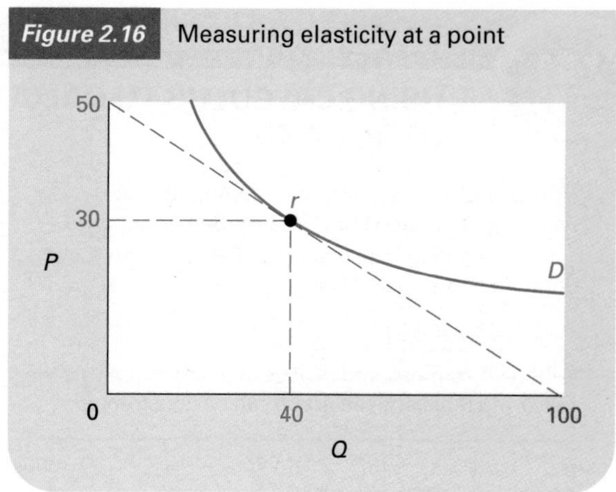

Definition

Point elasticity The measurement of elasticity at a point on a curve. The formula for price elasticity of demand using the point elasticity method is $dQ/dP \times P/Q$, where dQ/dP is the inverse of the slope of the tangent to the demand curve at the point in question.

*LOOKING AT THE MATHS

Elasticity of a straight-line demand curve. A straight-line demand curve has a different elasticity at each point on it. The only exceptions are a vertical demand curve ($P\epsilon_D = 0$) and a horizontal demand curve ($P\epsilon_D = \infty$). The reason for this differing elasticity can be demonstrated using the equation for a straight-line demand curve:

$$Q = a - bP$$

The term '$-b$' would give the slope of the demand curve if we were to plot Q on the vertical axis and P on the horizontal. Since we plot them the other way around,[2] the term '$-b$' gives the inverse of the slope as plotted. The slope of the curve as plotted is given by dP/dQ; the inverse of the slope is given by $dQ/dP = -b$).

The formula for price elasticity of demand (using the point elasticity method) is:

$$P\epsilon_D = \frac{dQ}{dP} \cdot \frac{P}{Q}$$

This can thus be rewritten as:

$$P\epsilon_D = -b\frac{P}{Q}$$

This is illustrated in the diagram, which plots the following demand curve:

$$Q = 50 - 5P$$

The slope of the demand curve (dP/dQ) is constant (i.e. $-10/50$ or -0.2). The inverse of the slope (dQ/dP) is thus -5, where 5 is the 'b' term in the equation. In this example, therefore, price elasticity of demand is given by:

$$P\epsilon_D = -5\frac{P}{Q}$$

The value of P/Q, however, differs along the length of the demand curve. At point n, $P/Q = 8/10$. Thus:

$$P\epsilon_D = -5(8/10) = -4$$

At point m, however, $P/Q = 6/20$. Thus:

$$P\epsilon_D = -5(6/20) = -1.5$$

EXPLORING ECONOMICS *BOX 2.5

USING CALCULUS TO CALCULATE THE PRICE ELASTICITY OF DEMAND

(A knowledge of the rules of differentiation is necessary to understand this box. See Appendix 1.)

The following is an example of an equation for a demand curve:

$$Q_d = 60 - 15P + P^2$$

(where Q_d is measured in 000s of units). From this the following table and the graph can be constructed.

P	60	$-15P$	$+P^2$	=	Q_d (000s)
0	60	−0	+0	=	60
1	60	−15	+1	=	46
2	60	−30	+4	=	34
3	60	−45	+9	=	24
4	60	−60	+16	=	16
5	60	−75	+25	=	10
6	60	−90	+36	=	6

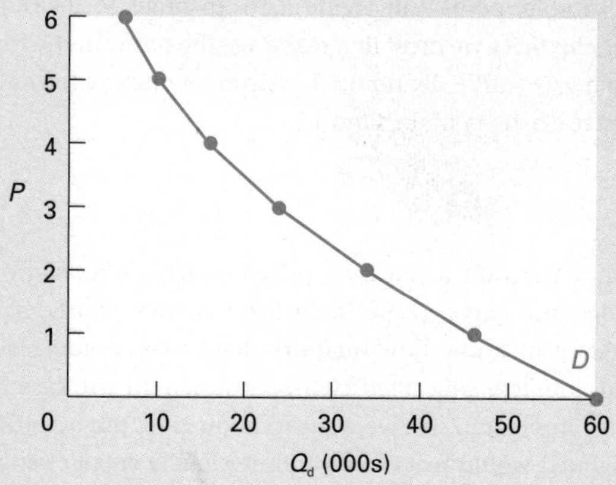

Point elasticity can be easily calculated from such a demand equation using calculus. To do this you will need to know the rules of differentiation (see pages A:9–12). Remember the formula for point elasticity:

$$P\epsilon_D = dQ/dP \times P/Q$$

The term dQ/dP can be calculated by differentiating the demand equation:

Given $Q_d = 60 - 15P + P^2$

then $dQ/dP = -15 + 2P$

Thus at a price of 3, for example,

$$dQ/dP = -15 + (2 \times 3)$$
$$= -9$$

Thus price elasticity of demand at a price of 3

$$= -9 \times P/Q$$
$$= -9 \times 3/24$$
$$= -9/8 \text{ (which is elastic)}$$

Calculate the price elasticity of demand on this demand curve at a price of (a) 5; (b) 2; (c) 0.

*LOOKING AT THE MATHS (continued)

Different elasticities along a straight-line demand curve

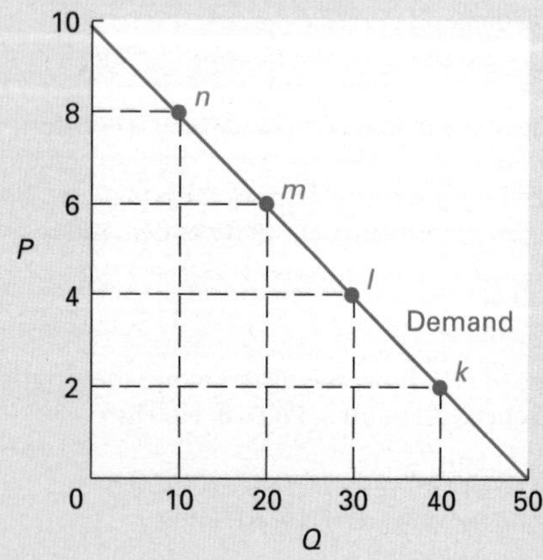

?

These questions still refer to the diagram.

1. ***What is the price elasticity of demand at points l and k?***
2. ***What is the price elasticity of demand at the point (a) where the demand curve crosses the vertical axis; (b) where it crosses the horizontal axis?***
3. ***As you move down a straight-line demand curve, what happens to elasticity? Why?***
4. ***Calculate price elasticity of demand between points n and l using the arc method. Does this give the same answer as the point method? Would it if the demand curve were actually curved?***

[2] It is contrary to normal convention to plot the independent variable (P) on the vertical axis and the dependent variable (Q) on the horizontal axis. The reason why we do this is because there are many other diagrams in economics where Q is the *independent* variable. Such diagrams include cost curves and revenue curves, which we will consider in Chapter 5. As you will see, it is much easier if we *always* plot Q on the horizontal axis even when, as in the case of demand curves, Q is the dependent variable.

Price elasticity of supply ($P\epsilon_S$)

When price changes, there will be not only a change in the quantity demanded, but also a change in the quantity supplied. Frequently we will want to know just how responsive quantity supplied is to a change in price. The measure we use is the ***price elasticity of supply***.

Figure 2.17 shows two supply curves. Curve S_2 is more elastic between any two prices than curve S_1. Thus, when price rises from P_1 to P_2 there is a larger increase in quantity supplied with S_2 (namely, Q_1 to Q_3) than there is with S_1 (namely, Q_1 to Q_2). For any shift in the demand curve there will be a larger change in quantity supplied and a smaller change in price with curve S_2 than with curve S_1. Thus the effect on price and quantity of a shift in the demand curve will depend on the price elasticity of supply.

The ***formula for the price elasticity of supply*** (***$P\epsilon_S$***) is: the percentage (or proportionate) change in quantity supplied divided by the percentage (or proportionate) change in price. Putting this in symbols gives:

$$P\epsilon_S = \frac{\%\Delta Q_S}{\%\Delta P}$$

In other words, the formula is identical to that for the price elasticity of demand, except that quantity in this case is quantity *supplied*. Thus if a 10 per cent rise in price caused a 25 per cent rise in the quantity supplied, the price elasticity of supply would be:

$$25\%/10\% = 2.5$$

and if a 10 per cent rise in price caused only a 5 per cent rise in the quantity, the price elasticity of supply would be:

$$5\%/10\% = 0.5$$

In the first case, supply is elastic ($P\epsilon_S > 1$); in the second it is inelastic ($P\epsilon_S < 1$). Notice that, unlike the price elasticity of demand, the figure is positive. This is because price and quantity supplied change in the *same* direction.

Figure 2.17 Two supply curves with different price elasticities of supply

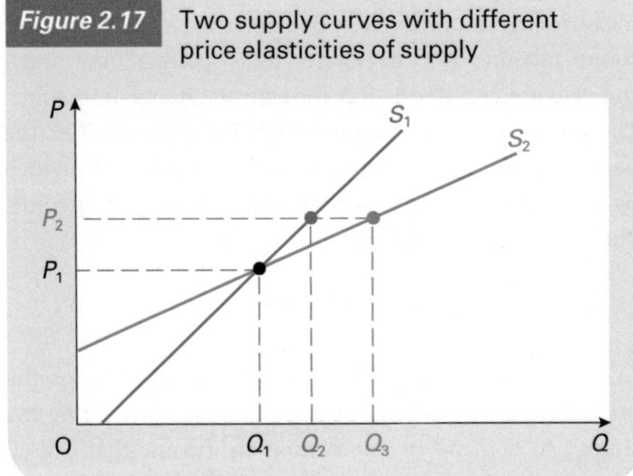

Definitions

Price elasticity of supply The responsiveness of quantity supplied to a change in price.

Formula for price elasticity of supply ($P\epsilon_S$) The percentage (or proportionate) change in quantity supplied divided by the percentage (or proportionate) change in price: $\%\Delta Q_S \div \%\Delta P$.

Determinants of price elasticity of supply

The amount that costs rise as output rises. The less the additional costs of producing additional output, the more firms will be encouraged to produce for a given price rise: the more elastic will supply be.

Supply is thus likely to be elastic if firms have plenty of spare capacity, if they can readily get extra supplies of raw materials, if they can easily switch away from producing alternative products and if they can avoid having to introduce overtime working (at higher rates of pay). The less these conditions apply, the less elastic will supply be.

Time period

- Immediate time period. Firms are unlikely to be able to increase supply by much immediately. Supply is virtually fixed, or can only vary according to available stocks. Supply is highly inelastic.
- Short run. If a slightly longer period of time is allowed to elapse, some inputs can be increased (e.g. raw materials) while others will remain fixed (e.g. heavy machinery). Supply can increase somewhat.
- Long run. In the long run, there will be sufficient time for all inputs to be increased and for new firms to enter the industry. Supply, therefore, is likely to be highly elastic. In some circumstances the long-run supply curve may even slope downwards. (See the section on economies of scale in Chapter 5, pages 131–3)

The measurement of price elasticity of supply

A vertical supply has zero elasticity. It is totally unresponsive to a change in price. A horizontal supply curve has infinite elasticity. There is no limit to the amount supplied at the price where the curve crosses the vertical axis.

When two supply curves cross, the steeper one will have the lower price elasticity of supply (e.g. curve S_1 in Figure 2.17). Any straight-line supply curve starting at the origin, however, will have an elasticity equal to 1 throughout its length, *irrespective of its slope*. This perhaps rather surprising result is illustrated in Figure 2.18 (on page 58). This shows three supply curves, each with a different slope, but each starting from the origin. On each curve two points are marked. In each case there is the *same* proportionate rise in Q as in P. For example, with curve S_1 a doubling in price from £3 to £6 leads to a doubling of output from 1 unit to 2 units.

This demonstrates nicely that it is not the *slope* of a curve that determines its elasticity, but its proportionate change.

Figure 2.18 Unit elastic supply curves

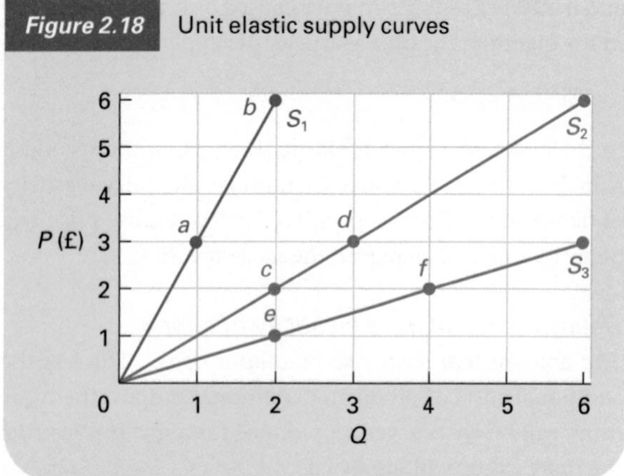

Other supply curves' elasticities will vary along their length. In such cases we have to refer to the elasticity either between two points on the curve, or at a specific point. Calculating elasticity between two points will involve the ***arc method***. Calculating elasticity at a point will involve the point method. These two methods are just the same for supply curves as for demand curves: the formulae are the same, only the term Q now refers to quantity supplied rather than quantity demanded.

*LOOKING AT THE MATHS

We can use a supply equation to demonstrate why a straight-line supply curve through the origin has an elasticity equal to 1. Assume that the supply equation is:

$$Q_S = a + bP \quad (1)$$

If the supply curve passes through the origin, the value of $a = 0$. Thus:

$$Q_S = bP \quad (2)$$

The point elasticity formula for price elasticity of supply is similar to that for price elasticity of demand (see page 55) and is given by:

$$P\epsilon_S = \frac{dQ_S}{dP} \cdot \frac{P}{Q_S} \quad (3)$$

But:

$$b = \frac{dQ_S}{dP} \quad (4)$$

since this is the slope of the equation (the inverse of the slope of the curve). Substituting equation (4) in equation (3) gives:

$$P\epsilon_S = b \cdot \frac{P}{Q_S} \quad (5)$$

Substituting equation (2) in equation (5) gives:

$$P\epsilon_S = b \cdot \frac{P}{bP}$$

$$= \frac{bp}{bP}$$

$$= 1$$

?

Given the following supply schedule:

P:	*2*	*4*	*6*	*8*	*10*
Q:	*0*	*10*	*20*	*30*	*40*

(a) Draw the supply curve.

(b) Using the arc method, calculate price elasticity of supply (i) between P = 2 and P = 4; (ii) between P = 8 and P = 10.

**(c) Using the point method, calculate price elasticity of supply at P = 6.*

(d) Does the elasticity of the supply curve increase or decrease as P and Q increase? Why?

(e) What would be the answer to (d) if the supply curve were a straight line but intersecting the horizontal axis to the right of the origin?

Income elasticity of demand ($Y\epsilon_D$)

So far we have looked at the responsiveness of demand and supply to a change in price. But price is just one of the determinants of demand and supply. In theory, we could look at the responsiveness of demand or supply to a change in *any* one of their determinants. We could have a whole range of different types of elasticity of demand and supply.

Key Idea 9

Elasticity. The responsiveness of one variable (e.g. demand) to a change in another (e.g. price). This concept is fundamental to understanding how markets work. The more elastic variables are, the more responsive is the market to changing circumstances.

In practice there are just two other elasticities that are particularly useful to us, and both are demand elasticities.

The first is the ***income elasticity of demand ($Y\epsilon_D$)***. This measures the responsiveness of demand to a change in consumer incomes (Y). It enables us to predict how much the demand curve will shift for a given change in income. The ***formula for the income elasticity of demand*** is: the percentage (or proportionate) change in demand divided by the percentage (or proportionate) change in income. Putting this in symbols gives:

$$Y\epsilon_D = \frac{\%\Delta Q_D}{\%\Delta Y}$$

In other words, the formula is identical to that for the price elasticity of demand, except that we are dividing the change in demand by the change in income that caused

Definitions

Formula for price elasticity of supply (arc method) ΔQ_S/average $Q_S \div \Delta P$/average P.

Income elasticity of demand The responsiveness of demand to a change in consumer incomes.

Formula for income elasticity of demand ($Y\epsilon_D$) The percentage (or proportionate) change in demand divided by the percentage (or proportionate) change in income: $\%\Delta Q_D \div \%\Delta Y$.

THINKING LIKE AN ECONOMIST — THRESHOLD CONCEPT 8

ELASTICITY: OF A VARIABLE TO A CHANGE IN A DETERMINANT

As we have seen in the case of price elasticity of demand, elasticity measures the responsiveness of one variable (e.g. quantity demanded) to change in another (e.g. price). This concept is fundamental to understanding how markets work. The more elastic variables are, the more responsive is the market to changing circumstances.

Elasticity is more than just a technical term. It's not difficult to learn the formula:

$$P\epsilon_D = \frac{\%\Delta Q_D}{\%\Delta P}$$

in the case of price elasticity of demand, and then to interpret this as

$$P\epsilon_D = \frac{\Delta Q_D}{\text{average } Q_D} \div \frac{\Delta P}{\text{average } P}$$

using the arc elasticity method, or as

$$P\epsilon_D = \frac{dQ_D}{dP} \times \frac{P}{Q}$$

using the point elasticity method.

We can also very simply state the general formula for any elasticity as

$$\epsilon_{XY} = \frac{\%\Delta X}{\%\Delta Y}$$

where the formula refers to the responsiveness of variable X to a change in variable Y (where X could be quantity supplied or demanded, and Y could be price, income, the price of substitutes, or any other determinant of demand or supply). Again, we could use the arc or point elasticity methods. Although students often find it hard at first to use the formulae, it's largely a question of practice in mastering them. No doubt, if you are attending classes, you will be given practice in working out elasticities!

What makes elasticity a *threshold concept* is that it lies at the heart of how economic systems operate. In a market economy, prices act as signals that demand or supply has changed. They also act as an incentive for people to respond to the new circumstances. The greater the elasticity of demand, the bigger will be the response to a change in supply; the greater the elasticity of supply, the bigger will be the response to a change in demand.

Understanding elasticity and what determines its magnitude helps us understand how an economy is likely to respond to the ever changing circumstances of the real world.

In a perfect market economy, firms face an infinitely elastic (horizontal) demand curve: they are price takers (see page 34 and Figure 2.13(b)). What this means is that they have no power to affect prices: they are highly dependent on market forces.

By contrast, big businesses (and some small ones too) are in a very different position. If there are only one or two firms in a market, each is likely to face a relatively inelastic demand. This gives them the power to raise prices and make more profit. As we have seen, if demand is price inelastic, then raising price will increase the firm's revenue (see Figure 2.13(b)). Even if demand is elastic (but still downward sloping) the firm could still increase profit by raising prices, provided that the fall in revenue was less than the reduction in costs from producing less. The general point here, is that the less elastic is the firm's demand curve, the greater will be its power to raise prices and make a bigger profit.

And it's not just price elasticity of demand that helps us understand how market economies operate. In a perfect market, market supply is likely to be highly elastic, especially in the long run after firms have had time to enter the industry. Thus if a new lower-cost technique is discovered, which increases profits in an industry, new firms will enter the market, attracted by the higher profits. This increased supply will then have the effect of driving prices down and hence profit rates will fall back. What this means is that in highly competitive industries firms are very responsive to changing economic circumstances. If they are not, they are likely to be forced out of business. It's a question of survival of the fittest. We explore this process in more detail in section 6.2.

If there is less competition, firms are likely to have a much cosier life. But what is good for them may be bad for us as consumers. We may end up paying higher prices and having poorer quality goods – but not necessarily. We explore this in sections 6.3 and 6.4 and in Chapter 7.

So, getting to grips with elasticity is not just about doing calculations. It's about understanding the very essence of how economies operate.

1. ***What would you understand by the 'wage elasticity of demand for labour'? How would the magnitude of this elasticity affect the working of the market for plumbers?***
2. ***How is the concept of income elasticity of demand relevant in understanding how the structure of economies changes over the years?***

it rather than by a change in price. Thus if a 2 per cent rise in income caused an 8 per cent rise in a product's demand, then its income elasticity of demand would be:

$$8\%/2\% = 4$$

The major determinant of income elasticity of demand is the degree of 'necessity' of the good. In a developed country, the demand for luxury goods expands rapidly as people's incomes rise, whereas the demand for basic goods rises only a little. Thus items such as cars and foreign holidays have a high income elasticity of demand, whereas items such as vegetables and bus journeys have a low income elasticity of demand.

The demand for some goods actually *decreases* as people's incomes rise beyond a certain level. These are inferior goods such as cheap margarine. As people earn more, so they switch to butter or better quality margarine. Unlike ***normal goods***, which have a positive income elasticity of demand, ***inferior goods*** have a negative income elasticity of demand.

? *Look ahead to Box 3.4 (page 79). It shows the income elasticity of demand for various foodstuffs. Explain the difference in the figures for milk, bread and fresh fish.*

Income elasticity of demand is an important concept to firms considering the future size of the market for their product. If the product has a high income elasticity of demand, sales are likely to expand rapidly as national income rises, but may also fall significantly if the economy moves into recession. (See Web Case 2.3, *Income elasticity of demand and the balance of payments*, on the book's website. This shows how the concept of income elasticity of demand can help us understand why so many developing countries have chronic balance of payments problems.)

Cross-price elasticity of demand ($C\epsilon_{D_{AB}}$)

This is often known by its less cumbersome title of ***cross elasticity of demand***. It is a measure of the responsiveness of demand for one product to a change in the price of another (either a substitute or a complement). It enables us to predict how much the demand curve for the first product will shift when the price of the second product changes.

The ***formula for the cross-price elasticity of demand*** ($C\epsilon_{D_{AB}}$) is: the percentage (or proportionate) change in demand for good A divided by the percentage (or proportionate) change in price of good B. Putting this in symbols gives:

$$C\epsilon_{D_{AB}} = \frac{\%\Delta Q_{D_A}}{\%\Delta P_B}$$

If good B is a *substitute* for good A, A's demand will *rise* as B's price rises. In this case, cross elasticity will be a positive figure. For example, if the demand for butter rose by 2 per cent when the price of margarine (a substitute) rose by 8 per cent, then the cross elasticity of demand for butter with respect to margarine would be:

$$2\%/8\% = 0.25$$

If good B is *complementary* to good A, however, A's demand will *fall* as B's price rises and thus as the quantity of B demanded falls. In this case, cross elasticity of demand will be a negative figure. For example, if a 4 per cent rise in the price of bread led to a 3 per cent fall in demand for butter, the cross elasticity of demand for butter with respect to bread would be:

$$-3\%/4\% = -0.75$$

The major determinant of cross elasticity of demand is the closeness of the substitute or complement. The closer it is, the bigger will be the effect on the first good of a change in the price of the substitute or complement, and hence the greater the cross elasticity – either positive or negative.

Firms need to know the cross elasticity of demand for their product when considering the effect on the demand for their product of a change in the price of a rival's product or of a complementary product. These are vital pieces of information for firms when making their production plans.

Another application of the concept of cross elasticity of demand is in the field of international trade and the balance of payments. How does a change in the price of domestic goods affect the demand for imports? If there is a high cross elasticity of demand for imports (because they are close substitutes for home-produced goods), and if prices at home rise due to inflation, the demand for imports will rise substantially, thus worsening the balance of trade.

? *Which are likely to have the highest cross elasticity of demand: two brands of coffee, or coffee and tea?*

Definitions

Normal goods Goods whose demand increases as consumer incomes increase. They have a positive income elasticity of demand. Luxury goods will have a higher income elasticity of demand than more basic goods.

Inferior goods Goods whose demand decreases as consumer incomes increase. Such goods have a negative income elasticity of demand.

Cross-price elasticity of demand The responsiveness of demand for one good to a change in the price of another.

Formula for cross-price elasticity of demand ($C\epsilon_{D_{AB}}$) The percentage (or proportionate) change in demand for good a divided by the percentage (or proportionate) change in price of good b: $\%\Delta Q_{D_A} \div \%\Delta P_B$.

*LOOKING AT THE MATHS

Calculating income and cross-price elasticities from a demand equation. The following demand equation relates quantity demanded (Q_A) for good A to its own price (P_A), consumer income (Y) and the price of a substitute good B (P_B).

$$Q_A = a - bP_A + cY + eP_B$$

Note that this is a 'linear' equation because[3] it has no power terms, such as P^2 or Y^2. The formula for income elasticity of demand for good A will be:

$$Y\epsilon_D = \frac{\partial Q_A}{\partial Y} \cdot \frac{Y}{Q_A}$$

But since the term $\partial Q_A/\partial Y$[3] represents the amount that Q_A will change for a given change in Y (i.e. the value of c), then:

$$Y\epsilon_D = c\frac{Y}{Q_A}$$

Similarly, the formula for cross-price elasticity of demand for good A with respect to good B will be:

$$C\epsilon_{DAB} = \frac{\partial Q_A}{\partial P_B} \cdot \frac{P_B}{Q_A} = e\frac{P_B}{Q_A}$$

A worked example of these two formulae is given in Maths Case 2.2 on the book's website. We can also use calculus to work out the two elasticities for both linear and non-linear demand equations. A worked example of this is given in Maths Case 2.3.

[3] Note that in this case we use the symbol '∂' rather than 'd' to represent an infinitely small change. This is the convention when the equation contains more than one independent variable (in this case P_A, Y and P_B). The term $\partial Q_A/\partial Y$ is the 'partial derivative' (see page A:12) and refers to the rate of change of Q_A to just *one* of the three variables (in this case Y).

Section summary

1. Elasticity is a measure of the responsiveness of demand (or supply) to a change in one of the determinants.
2. It is defined as the proportionate change in quantity demanded (or supplied) divided by the proportionate change in the determinant.
3. If quantity changes proportionately more than the determinant, the figure for elasticity will be greater than 1 (ignoring the sign): it is elastic. If the quantity changes proportionately less than the determinant, the figure for elasticity will be less than 1: it is inelastic. If they change by the same proportion, the elasticity has a value of 1: it is unit elastic.
4. Price elasticity of demand measures the responsiveness of demand to a change in price. Given that demand curves are downward sloping, price elasticity of demand will have a negative value. Demand will be more elastic the greater the number and closeness of substitute goods, the higher the proportion of income spent on the good and the longer the time period that elapses after the change in price.
5. When demand is price elastic, a rise in price will lead to a reduction in total expenditure on the good and hence a reduction in the total revenue of producers.
6. Demand curves normally have different elasticities along their length. We can thus normally refer only to the specific value for elasticity between two points on the curve or at a single point.
7. Elasticity measured between two points is known as *arc elasticity*. When applied to price elasticity of demand the formula is:

$$\frac{\Delta Q_d}{\text{average } Q_d} \div \frac{\Delta P}{\text{average } P}$$

*8. Elasticity measured at a point is known as *point elasticity*. When applied to price elasticity of demand the formula is:

$$\frac{dQ}{dP} \times \frac{P}{Q}$$

where dQ/dP is the inverse of the slope of the tangent to the demand curve at the point in question.

9. Price elasticity of supply measures the responsiveness of supply to a change in price. It has a positive value. Supply will be more elastic the less costs per unit rise as output rises and the longer the time period.
10. Income elasticity of demand measures the responsiveness of demand to a change in income. For normal goods it has a positive value. Demand will be more income elastic the more luxurious the good and the less rapidly demand is satisfied as consumption increases.
11. Cross-price elasticity of demand measures the responsiveness of demand for one good to a change in the price of another. For substitute goods the value will be positive; for complements it will be negative. The cross-price elasticity will be higher the closer the two goods are as substitutes or complements.

2.5 THE TIME DIMENSION

KI 5 p21

The full adjustment of price, demand and supply to a situation of disequilibrium will not be instantaneous. It is necessary, therefore, to analyse the time path which supply takes in responding to changes in demand, and which demand takes in responding to changes in supply.

Short-run and long-run adjustment

TC 8 p59

As we saw in the previous section, elasticity varies with the time period under consideration. The reason is that producers and consumers take time to respond to a change in price. The longer the time period, the bigger the response, and thus the greater the elasticity of supply and demand.

This is illustrated in Figures 2.19 and 2.20. In both cases, as equilibrium moves from points *a* to *b* to *c*, there is a large short-run price change (P_1 to P_2) and a small short-run quantity change (Q_1 to Q_2), but a small long-run price change (P_1 to P_3) and a large long-run quantity change (Q_1 to Q_3).

Price expectations and speculation

TC 9 p101

In a world of shifting demand and supply curves, prices do not stay the same. Sometimes they go up; sometimes they come down.

If prices are likely to change in the foreseeable future, this will affect the behaviour of buyers and sellers *now*. If, for example, it is now December and you are thinking of buying a new winter coat, you might decide to wait until the January sales, and in the meantime make do with your old coat. If, on the other hand, when January comes you see a new summer dress in the sales, you might well buy it now and not wait until the summer for fear that the price will have gone up by then. Thus a belief that prices will go up will cause people to buy now; a belief that prices will come down will cause them to wait.

The reverse applies to sellers. If you are thinking of selling your house and prices are falling, you will want to sell it as quickly as possible. If, on the other hand, prices are

Figure 2.19 Response of supply to an increase in demand

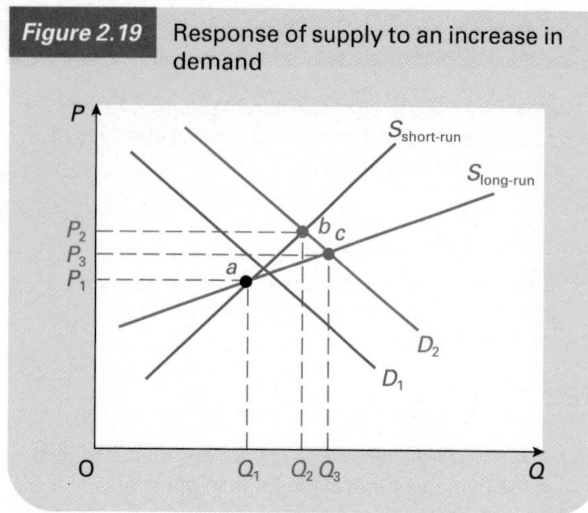

Figure 2.20 Response of demand to an increase in supply

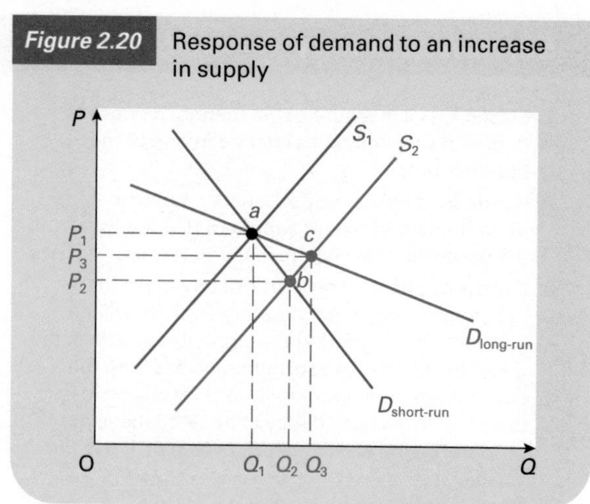

rising sharply, you will wait as long as possible so as to get the highest price. Thus a belief that prices will come down will cause people to sell now; a belief that prices will go up will cause them to wait.

> **Key Idea 10** ***People's actions are influenced by their expectations.*** People respond not just to what is happening now (such as a change in price), but to what they anticipate will happen in the future.

This behaviour of looking into the future and making buying and selling decisions based on your predictions is called ***speculation***. Speculation is often based on current trends in price behaviour. If prices are currently rising, people may then try to decide whether they are about to peak and go back down again, or whether they are likely to go on rising. Having made their prediction, they will then act on it. Their actions will then affect demand and supply, which in turn will affect price. Speculation is commonplace in many markets: the stock exchange, the foreign exchange market and the housing market are three examples.

Sometimes people will take advantage of expected price rises purely to make money and have no intention of keeping the item they have bought. For example, if shares in a particular company are expected to rise in price, people may buy them now while they are cheap and sell them later when the price has risen, thereby making a profit from the difference in price.

Similarly, people will sometimes take advantage of expected price reductions by selling something now only to buy it back later. For example, if you own shares and expect their price to fall, you may sell them now and buy them back later when their price has fallen. Again, you make a profit from the difference in price.

Sometimes the term *speculation* is used in this narrower sense of buying (or selling) commodities or financial assets simply to make money from later selling them (or buying them back) again at a higher (or lower) price. The term ***speculators*** usually refers to people engaged in such activities.

In the extreme case, speculators need not part with any money. If they buy an item and sell it back fairly soon at a higher price, they may be able to use the money from the sale to pay the original seller: the speculator merely pockets the difference! Alternatively, speculators may sell an item they do not even possess, as long as they can buy it back in time (at a lower price) to hand it over to the original purchaser. Again, they simply pocket the difference in price.

It may sound like speculators are on to a good thing, and often they are, but speculation does carry risks: the predictions of individual speculators may turn out to be wrong, and then they could make a loss.

Nevertheless, speculators on average tend to gain rather than lose. The reason is that speculation tends to be ***self-fulfilling***. In other words, the actions of speculators tend to bring about the very effect on prices that they had anticipated. For example, if speculators believe that the price of British Airways shares is about to rise, they will buy BA shares. But by doing this they will ensure that the price *will* rise. The prophecy has become self-fulfilling.

Definitions

Speculation Where people make buying or selling decisions based on their anticipations of future prices.

Speculators People who buy (or sell) commodities or financial assets with the intention of profiting by selling them (or buying them back) at a later date at a higher (lower) price.

Self-fulfilling speculation The actions of speculators tend to cause the very effect that they had anticipated.

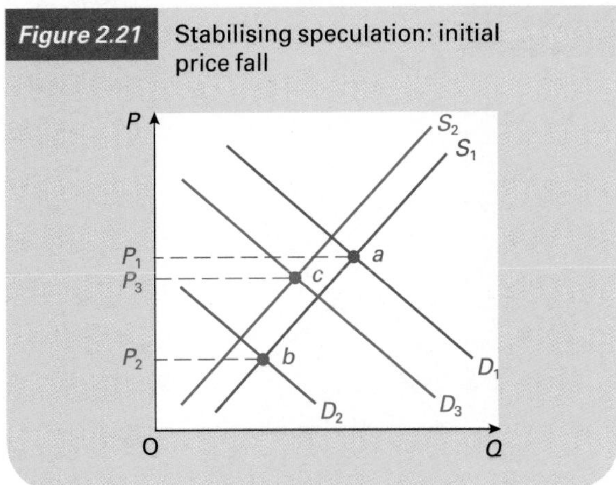

Figure 2.21 Stabilising speculation: initial price fall

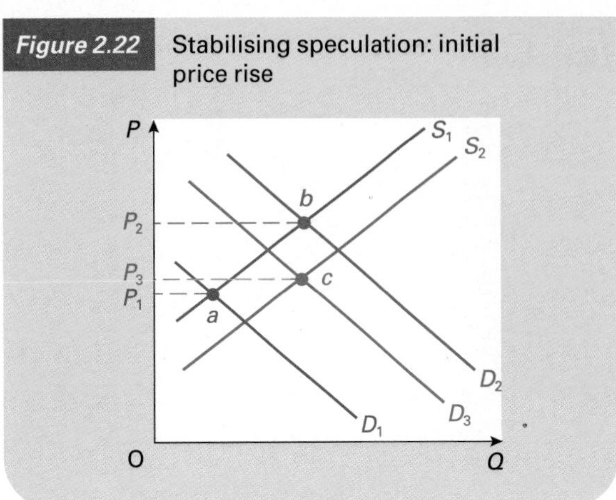

Figure 2.22 Stabilising speculation: initial price rise

Speculation can either help to reduce price fluctuations or aggravate them: it can be stabilising or destabilising.

Stabilising speculation

Speculation will tend to have a ***stabilising*** effect on price fluctuations when suppliers and/or demanders believe that a change in price is only *temporary*.

An initial fall in price. In Figure 2.21 demand has shifted from D_1 to D_2; equilibrium has moved from point *a* to point *b*, and price has fallen to P_2. How do people react to this fall in price?

Given that they believe this fall in price to be only temporary, suppliers *hold back*, expecting prices to rise again: supply shifts from S_1 to S_2. After all, why supply now when, by waiting, they could get a higher price?

Buyers *increase* their purchases, to take advantage of the temporary fall in price. Demand shifts from D_2 to D_3.

The equilibrium moves to point *c*, with price rising back towards P_1.

An initial rise in price. In Figure 2.22 demand has shifted from D_1 to D_2. Price has risen from P_1 to P_2.

Suppliers bring their goods to market now, before price falls again. Supply shifts from S_1 to S_2. Demanders, however, hold back until price falls. Demand shifts from D_2 to D_3. The equilibrium moves to point *c*, with price falling back towards P_1.

A good example of stabilising speculation is that which occurs in agricultural commodity markets. Take the case of wheat. When it is harvested in the autumn, there will be a plentiful supply. If all this wheat were to be put on the market, the price would fall to a very low level. Later in the year, when most of the wheat would have been sold, the price would then rise to a very high level. This is all easily predictable.

So what do farmers do? The answer is that they speculate. When the wheat is harvested, they know price will tend to fall, and so instead of bringing it all to market they put a lot of it into store. The more price falls, the more they will put into store *anticipating that the price will later rise*. But this holding back of supplies prevents prices from falling. In other words, it stabilises prices.

Later in the year, when the price begins to rise, they will gradually release grain on to the market from the stores. The more the price rises, the more they will release on to the market *anticipating that the price will fall again by the time of the next harvest*. But this releasing of supplies will again stabilise prices by preventing them from rising so much.

Rather than the farmers doing the speculation, it could be done by grain merchants. When there is a glut of wheat in the autumn, and prices are relatively low, they buy wheat on the grain market and put it into store. When there is a shortage in the spring and summer they sell wheat from their stores. In this way they stabilise prices just as the farmers did when they were the ones who operated the stores.

In Figures 2.21 and 2.22, the initial change in price was caused by a shift in the demand curve. Redraw these two diagrams to illustrate the situation where the initial change in price was caused by a shift in the supply *curve (as would be the case in the wheat market that we have just considered).*

Definitions

Stabilising speculation Where the actions of speculators tend to reduce price fluctuations.

Destabilising speculation Where the actions of speculators tend to make price movements larger.

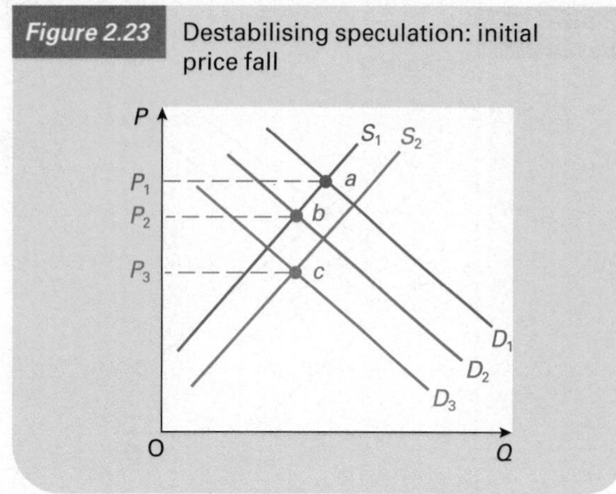

Figure 2.23 Destabilising speculation: initial price fall

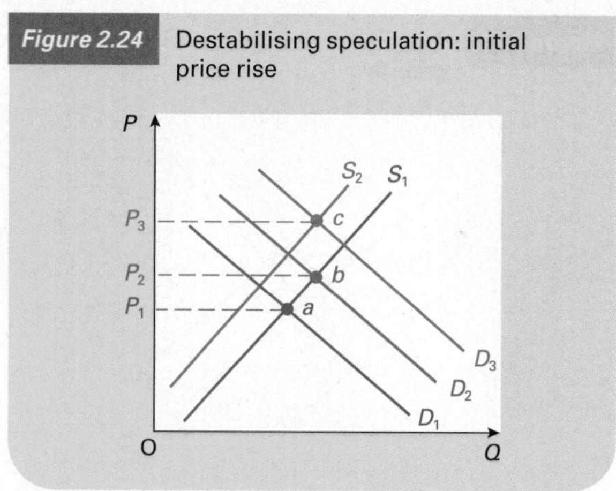

Figure 2.24 Destabilising speculation: initial price rise

Destabilising speculation

Speculation will tend to have a ***destabilising*** effect on price fluctuations when suppliers and/or buyers believe that a change in price heralds similar changes to come.

An initial fall in price. In Figure 2.23 demand has shifted from D_1 to D_2 and price has fallen from P_1 to P_2. This time, believing that the fall in price heralds further falls in price to come, suppliers sell now before the price does fall. Supply shifts from S_1 to S_2. And demanders wait: they wait until price does fall further. Demand shifts from D_2 to D_3.

Their actions ensure that price does fall further: to P_3.

An initial rise in price. In Figure 2.24 a price rise from P_1 to P_2 is caused by a rise in demand from D_1 to D_2. Suppliers wait until price rises further. Supply shifts from S_1 to S_2. Demanders buy now before any further rise in price. Demand shifts from D_2 to D_3. As a result, price continues to rise: to P_3.

Box 2.2 examined the housing market. In this market, speculation is frequently destabilising. Assume that people see house prices beginning to move upwards. This might be the result of increased demand brought about by a cut in mortgage interest rates or by growth in the economy. People may well believe that the rise in house prices signals a boom in the housing market: that prices will go on rising. Potential buyers will thus try to buy as soon as possible before prices rise any further. This increased demand (as in Figure 2.24) will thus lead to even bigger price rises. This is precisely what happened in the UK housing market in 1999–2004.

Conclusion

In some circumstances, then, the action of speculators can help to keep price fluctuations to a minimum (stabilising speculation). This is most likely when markets are relatively stable in the first place, with only moderate underlying shifts in demand and supply.

In other circumstances, however, speculation can make price fluctuations much worse. This is most likely in times of uncertainty, when there are significant changes in the determinants of demand and supply. Given this uncertainty, people may see price changes as signifying some trend. They then 'jump on the bandwagon' and do what the rest are doing, further fuelling the rise or fall in price.

? *Redraw Figures 2.23 and 2.24 assuming, as in the previous question, that the initial change in price was caused by a shift in the supply curve.*

Dealing with uncertainty and risk

When price changes are likely to occur, buyers and sellers will try to anticipate them. Unfortunately, on many occasions no one can be certain just what these price changes will be. Take the case of stocks and shares. If you anticipate that the price of, say, Toyota shares is likely to go up substantially in the near future, you may well decide to buy some now and then sell them later after the price has risen. But you cannot be certain that they will go up in price: they may fall instead. If you buy the shares, therefore, you will be taking a gamble.

Now gambles can be of two types. The first is where you know the odds. Let us take the simplest case of a gamble on the toss of a coin. Heads you win; tails you lose. You know that the odds of winning are precisely 50 per cent. If you bet on the toss of a coin, you are said to be operating under conditions of ***risk***. *Risk is when the probability of an outcome is known.* Risk itself is a measure of the *variability* of an

Definition

Risk When an outcome may or may not occur, but its probability of occurring is known.

EXPLORING ECONOMICS BOX 2.6

DEALING IN FUTURES MARKETS

A way of reducing uncertainty

One way of reducing or even eliminating uncertainty is by dealing in ***futures*** or ***forward markets***. Let us examine first the activities of sellers and then of buyers.

Sellers

Suppose you are a farmer and want to store grain to sell at some time in the future, expecting to get a better price then than now. The trouble is that there is a chance that the price will go down. Given this uncertainty, you may be unwilling to take a gamble.

An answer to your problem is provided by the *commodity futures market*. This is a market where prices are agreed between sellers and buyers *today* for delivery at some specified date in the *future*.

For example, if it is 20 October today, you could be quoted a price *today* for delivery in six months' time (i.e. on 20 April). This is known as the six-month ***future price***. Assume that the six-month future price is £60 per tonne. If you agree to this price and make a six-month forward contract, you are agreeing to sell a specified amount of wheat at £60 on 20 April. No matter what happens to the ***spot price*** (i.e. the current market price) in the meantime, your selling price has been agreed. The spot price could have fallen to £30 (or risen to £100) by April, but your selling price when 20 April arrives is fixed at £60. There is thus *no risk to you whatsoever of the price going down*. You will, of course, lose out if the spot price is *more* than £60 in April.

Buyers

Now suppose that you are a flour miller. In order to plan your expenditures, you would like to know the price you will have to pay for wheat, not just today, but also at various future dates. In other words, if you want to take delivery of wheat at some time in the future, you would like a price quoted *now*. You would like the risks removed of prices going *up*.

Let us assume that today (20 October) you want to *buy* the same amount of wheat on 20 April that a farmer wishes to sell on that same date. If you agree to the £60 future price, a future contract can be made with the farmer. You are then guaranteed that purchase price, no matter what happens to the spot price in the meantime. There is thus *no risk to you whatsoever of the price going up*. You will, of course, lose out if the spot price is *less* than £60 in April.

The determination of the future price

Prices in the futures market are determined in the same way as in other markets: by demand and supply. For example, the six-month wheat price or the three-month coffee price will be that which equates the demand for those futures with the supply. If the five-month sugar price is currently £200 per tonne and people expect by then, because of an anticipated good beet harvest, that the spot price for sugar will be £150 per tonne, there will be few who want to buy the futures at £200 (and many who want to sell). This excess of supply of futures over demand will push the price down.

Speculators

Many people operate in the futures market who never actually handle the commodities themselves. They are neither producers nor users of the commodities. They merely speculate. Such speculators may be individuals, but they are more likely to be financial institutions.

Let us take a simple example. Suppose that the six-month (April) coffee price is £1000 per tonne and that you, as a speculator, believe that the spot price of coffee is likely to rise above that level between now (October) and six months' time. You thus decide to buy 20 tonnes of April coffee futures now.

But you have no intention of taking delivery. After four months, let us say, true to your prediction, the spot price (February) has risen and as a result the April price (and other future prices) have risen too. You thus decide to *sell* 20 tonnes of April (two-month) coffee futures, whose price, let us say, is £1200. You are now 'covered'.

When April comes, what happens? You have agreed to buy 20 tonnes of coffee at £1000 per tonne and to sell 20 tonnes of coffee at £1200 per tonne. All you do is to hand the futures contract to buy to the person to whom you agreed to sell. They sort out delivery between them and you make £200 per tonne profit.

If, however, your prediction had been wrong and the price had *fallen*, you would have made a loss. You would have been forced to sell coffee contracts at a lower price than you bought them.

Speculators in the futures market thus incur risks, unlike the sellers and buyers of the commodities, for whom the futures market eliminates risk. Financial institutions offering futures contracts will charge for the service: for taking on the risks.

If speculators believed that the price of cocoa in six months was going to be **below** ***the six-month future price quoted today, how would they act?***

Definitions

Futures or forward market A market in which contracts are made to buy or sell at some future date at a price agreed today.

Future price A price agreed today at which an item (e.g. commodities) will be exchanged at some set date in the future.

Spot price The current market price.

outcome. For example, if you bet £1 on the toss of a coin, such that heads you win £1 and tails you lose £1, then the variability is –£1 to +£1.

The second form of gamble is the more usual. This is where the odds are not known or are known only roughly. Gambling on the stock exchange is like this. You may have a good idea that a share will go up in price, but is it a 90 per cent chance, an 80 per cent chance or what? You are not certain. Gambling under this sort of condition is known as operating under ***uncertainty***. *This is when the probability of an outcome is not known.*

You may well disapprove of gambling and want to dismiss people who engage in it as foolish or morally wrong. But 'gambling' is not just confined to horses, cards, roulette and the like. Risk and uncertainty pervade the whole of economic life, and decisions are constantly having to be made whose outcome cannot be known for certain. Even the most morally upright person will still have to decide which career to go into, whether and when to buy a house, or even something as trivial as whether or not to take an umbrella when going out. Each of these decisions and thousands of others are made under conditions of uncertainty (or occasionally risk).

People's actions are influenced by their attitudes towards risk. Many decisions are taken under conditions of risk or uncertainty. Generally, the lower the probability of (or the more uncertain) the desired outcome of an action, the less likely people will be to undertake the action.

?

Give some examples of decisions you have taken recently that were made under conditions of uncertainty. With hindsight do you think you made the right decisions?

We shall be examining how risk and uncertainty affect economic decisions on several occasions throughout the book. For example, in Chapter 4 we will see how it affects people's attitudes and actions as consumers and how taking out insurance can help to reduce their uncertainty. At this point, however, let us focus on firms' attitudes when supplying goods.

Stock holding as a way of reducing the problem of uncertanty

A simple way that suppliers can reduce the problem of uncertainty is by holding stocks. Take the case of the wheat farmers we saw in the previous section. At the time when they are planting the wheat in the spring, they are uncertain as to what the price of wheat will be when they bring it to market. If they keep no stores of wheat, they will just have to accept whatever the market price happens to be at harvest time. If, however, they have storage facilities, they can put the wheat into store if the price is low and then wait until it goes up. Alternatively, if the price of wheat is high at harvest time, they can sell it straight away. In other words, they can choose the time to sell.

Definition

Uncertainty When an outcome may or may not occur and its probability of occurring is not known.

Section summary

1. A complete understanding of markets must take into account the time dimension.
2. Given that producers and consumers take a time to respond fully to price changes, we can identify different equilibria after the lapse of different lengths of time. Generally, short-run supply and demand tend to be less price elastic than long-run supply and demand. As a result, any shifts in *D* or *S* curves tend to have a relatively bigger effect on price in the short run and a relatively bigger effect on quantity in the long run.
3. People often anticipate price changes and this will affect the amount they demand or supply. This speculation will tend to stabilise price fluctuations if people believe that the price changes are only temporary. However, speculation will tend to destabilise these fluctuations (i.e. make them more severe) if people believe that prices are likely to continue to move in the same direction as at present (at least for some time).
4. Many economic decisions are taken under conditions of risk or uncertainty. Uncertainty over future prices can be tackled by holding stocks. When prices are low, the stocks can be built up. When they are high, stocks can be sold.

END OF CHAPTER QUESTIONS

1. The weekly demand and supply schedules for T-shirts (in millions) in a free market are as follows:

Price (£)	8	7	6	5	4	3	2	1
Quantity demanded	6	8	10	12	14	16	18	20
Quantity supplied	18	16	14	12	10	8	6	4

(a) What is the equilibrium price and quantity?

(b) Assume that changes in fashion cause the demand for T-shirts to rise by 4 million at each price. What will be the new equilibrium price and quantity? Has equilibrium quantity risen as much as the rise in demand? Explain why or why not.

(c) Now plot the data in the table and mark the equilibrium. Also plot the new data corresponding to (b).

(d) Referring to the original data, what is the price elasticity of demand between a price of £7 and £5? Is it elastic or inelastic?

(e) Again referring to the original data and by reference simply to total expenditure, is demand elastic or inelastic with respect to price, between prices of (i) £8 and £7; (ii) £4 and £3? Again with reference simply to total expenditure, what is the price elasticity of demand at a price of £5.50?

2. On separate demand and supply diagrams for bread, sketch the effects of the following: (a) a rise in the price of wheat; (b) a rise in the price of butter and margarine; (c) a rise in the price of rice, pasta and potatoes. In each case, state your assumptions.

3. For what reasons might the price of foreign holidays rise? In each case, identify whether these are reasons affecting demand, or supply (or both).

4. If both demand and supply change, and if we know which direction they have shifted but not how much, why is it that we will be able to predict the direction in which *either* price *or* quantity will change, but not both? (Clue: consider the four possible combinations and sketch them if necessary: (a) *D* left, *S* left; (b) *D* right, *S* right; (c) *D* left, *S* right; (d) *D* right, *S* left.)

5. Which of the following will have positive signs and which will have negative ones: (a) price elasticity of demand; (b) income elasticity of demand (normal good); (c) income elasticity of demand (inferior good); (d) cross elasticity of demand (with respect to changes in price of a substitute good); (e) cross elasticity of demand (with respect to changes in price of a complementary good); (f) price elasticity of supply?

6. Two customers go to the fish counter at a supermarket to buy some cod. Neither looks at the price. Customer A orders 1 kilo. Customer B orders £3 worth. What is the price elasticity of demand for cod of each of the two customers?

7. Is there any truth in the saying that the price of a good is a reflection of its quality?

8. Why are both the price elasticity of demand and the price elasticity of supply likely to be greater in the long run?

9. What are the advantages and disadvantages of speculation from the point of view of (a) the consumer; (b) firms?

Additional case studies on the book's website (www.pearsoned.co.uk/sloman)

2.1 Adjusting to oil price shocks. A case study showing how demand and supply analysis can be used to examine the price changes in the oil market since 1973.

2.2 Shall we put up our price? This uses the concept of price elasticity of demand to explain why prices are higher where firms face little or no competition.

2.3 Income elasticity of demand and the balance of payments. This examines how a low income elasticity of demand for the exports of many developing countries can help to explain their chronic balance of payments problems.

2.4 The role of the speculator. This assesses whether the activities of speculators are beneficial or harmful to the rest of society.

2.5 The cobweb model. Illustrating the effect of time lags in production.

WEBSITES RELEVANT TO THIS CHAPTER

Numbers and sections refer to websites listed in the Web Appendix and hotlinked from this book's website at www.pearsoned.co.uk/sloman.

- For news articles relevant to this chapter, see the *Economics News Articles* link from the book's website.
- For general news on markets, see websites in section A, and particularly A2, 3, 4, 5, 8, 9, 18, 24, 25, 26, 36. See also links to newspapers worldwide in A38, 39, 43 and 44, and the news search feature in Google at A41.
- For links to sites on markets, see the relevant sections of I4, 7, 11, 17.
- For data on the housing market (Box 2.2), see sites B7, 8, 11.
- For sites favouring the free market, see C17 and E34.
- For student resources relevant to this chapter, see sites C1–7, 9, 10, 19.
- For a range of classroom games and simulations of markets, see sites C24 (computer based) and C20 (non-computer based).
- Site D3 contains simulations on elasticity, house prices and the relationships between markets.

Chapter 3

Government Intervention in the Market

The real world is one of mixed economies. The government intervenes in many markets, even highly competitive ones. This intervention can take a number of forms:

- **Fixing prices, either above or below the free-market equilibrium.**
- **Taxing the production or sale of various goods.**
- **Subsidising the production or sale of various goods.**
- **Producing goods or services directly (e.g. defence and health).**
- **Regulation. Various laws could be passed to regulate the behaviour of firms. For example, various activities, such as the dumping of toxic waste, could be made illegal; or licences or official permission might have to be obtained to produce certain goods; or a regulatory body could supervise the activities of various firms and prevent any that it felt to be against the public interest (e.g. the production of unsafe toys).**

Supply and demand analysis is a useful tool for examining the effects of government intervention. First we apply the analysis to two types of intervention: price control and taxation. Then we examine what could happen if a government seeks to do away with a market system of allocation: either by providing things free to consumers, or by banning certain harmful activities.

The final section is an extended case study which examines government intervention in agriculture – a sector that has received massive government support in many countries of the world. We look at the economic arguments for such intervention and then examine the specific measures that governments have taken.

CHAPTER MAP

3.1 THE CONTROL OF PRICES

TC 7 p 26

At the equilibrium price, there will be no shortage or surplus. The equilibrium price, however, may not be the most desirable price. The government, therefore, may prefer to keep prices above or below the equilibrium price.

If the government sets a ***minimum price*** above the equilibrium (a price floor), there will be a surplus: $Q_s - Q_d$ in Figure 3.1. Price will not be allowed to fall to eliminate this surplus.

If the government sets a ***maximum price*** below the equilibrium (a price ceiling), there will be a shortage: $Q_d - Q_s$ in Figure 3.2. Price will not be allowed to rise to eliminate this shortage.

Setting a minimum (high) price

The government sets minimum prices to prevent them from falling below a certain level. It may do this for various reasons:

- To protect producers' incomes. If the industry is subject to supply fluctuations (e.g. crops, due to fluctuations in weather) and if industry demand is price inelastic, prices are likely to fluctuate severely. Minimum prices will prevent the fall in producers' incomes that would accompany periods of low prices (see section 3.4).
- To create a surplus (e.g. of grains) – particularly in periods of glut – which can be stored in preparation for possible future shortages.
- In the case of wages (the price of labour), minimum wage legislation can be used to prevent workers' wage rates from falling below a certain level (see Box 10.3).

?

Draw a supply and demand diagram with the price of labour (the wage rate) on the vertical axis and the quantity of labour (the number of workers) on the horizontal axis. What will happen to employment if the government raises wages from the equilibrium to some minimum wage above the equilibrium?

The government can use various methods to deal with the surpluses associated with minimum prices.

- The government could buy the surplus and store it, destroy it or sell it abroad in other markets.
- Supply could be artificially lowered by restricting producers to particular quotas. In Figure 3.1, supply could therefore be reduced to Q_d.
- Demand could be raised by advertising, by finding alternative uses for the good, or by reducing consumption of substitute goods (e.g. by imposing taxes or quotas on substitutes, such as imports).

One of the problems with minimum prices is that firms with surpluses on their hands may try to evade the price control and cut their prices.

Another problem is that high prices may cushion inefficiency. Firms may feel less need to find more efficient methods of production and to cut their costs if their profits are being protected by the high price. Also the high price may discourage firms from producing alternative goods which they could produce more efficiently or which are in higher demand, but which nevertheless have a lower (free-market) price. TC 3 p 21

Figure 3.1 Minimum price: price floor

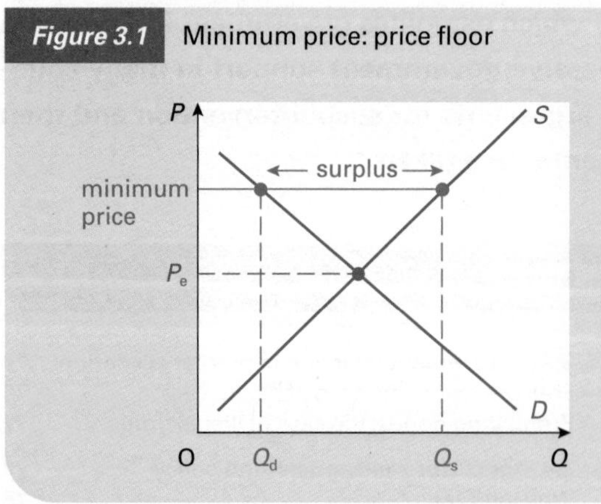

Figure 3.2 Maximum price: price ceiling

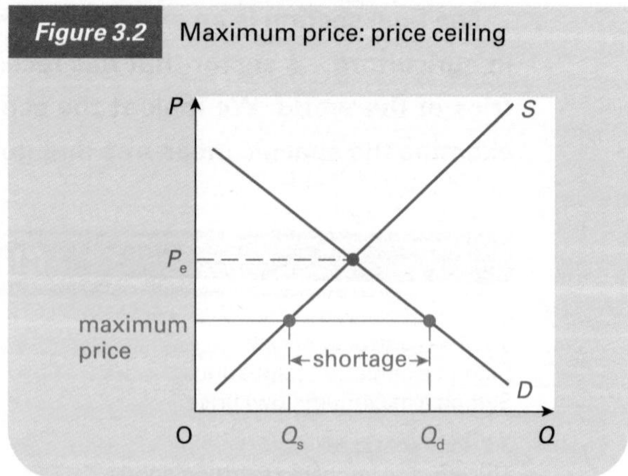

Definitions

Minimum price A price floor set by the government or some other agency. The price is not allowed to fall below this level (although it is allowed to rise above it).

Maximum price A price ceiling set by the government or some other agency. The price is not allowed to rise above this level (although it is allowed to fall below it).

CASE STUDIES AND APPLICATIONS **BOX 3.1**

RENT CONTROL

Cheap housing for all?

The purpose of rent control is to protect tenants from paying high rent, as well as to provide cheap housing for the very poor. In practice, however, many economists argue that such rent controls only succeed in making a larger part of the population worse off. How is this so?

Referring to the diagram, assume that the rent for a particular type of accommodation is initially at the equilibrium level, R_0, where $D = S$. Now assume that legislation is passed that sets a rent ceiling of R_1. Despite this reduction in rent, the supply of rental accommodation will fall only slightly in the short run, as landlords cannot quickly transfer their accommodation to other uses. In the diagram this is shown by a movement from point *a* to point *b* on the relatively inelastic supply curve *S*.

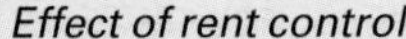

Effect of rent control

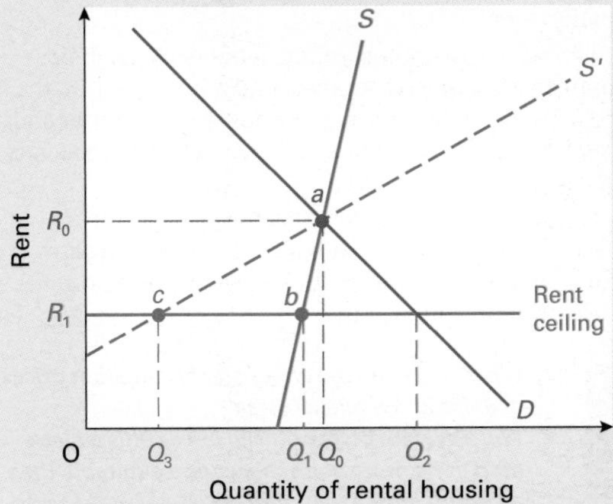

With the rent set below equilibrium there will be a shortage of rented property. In the short run, this will be relatively small (i.e. $Q_2 - Q_1$), and hence only a relatively small number of people will be unable to find accommodation. The remainder will benefit from the lower rents.

In the long run, however, many landlords will respond to the lower rent by putting their accommodation to other uses. The supply curve will become more elastic (curve *S'*) and the supply of rented property will fall to Q_3 (point *c*). Shortages now increase (to $Q_2 - Q_3$) as less rental housing is available. More people become homeless – more, perhaps, than in an unregulated market.

Rent controls may have further adverse effects. First, on equity grounds it is somewhat arbitrary as to who gets and who does not get housing at the lower rent. Second, in the long run, those landlords who still keep their property available for rent may cut maintenance costs and let their property fall into disrepair.

Those in favour of rent controls counter these arguments by claiming that the demand and supply curves of rented accommodation are very inelastic.

Take the case of the demand curve. People have got to live somewhere. If rent control is abolished, people will just have to pay the higher rent or become homeless: and given that people will only sacrifice their home as a last resort, demand remains inelastic and rents could rise to a very high level.

?

1. ***How could housing supplied by the public sector be made to rectify some of the problems we have identified above? (What would it do to the supply curve?)***
2. ***If the government gives poor people rent allowances (i.e. grants), how will this affect the level of rents in an uncontrolled market? What determines the size of this effect?***
3. ***The case for and against rent controls depends to a large extent on the long-run elasticity of supply. Do you think it will be relatively elastic or inelastic? Give reasons.***

Setting a maximum (low) price

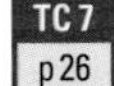
TC 7 p26

The government may set maximum prices to prevent them from rising above a certain level. This will normally be done for reasons of fairness. In wartime, or times of famine, the government may set maximum prices for basic goods so that poor people can afford to buy them.

The resulting shortages, however, create further problems. If the government merely sets prices and does not intervene further, the shortages will lead to the following:

- Allocation on a 'first come, first served' basis. This is likely to lead to queues developing, or firms adopting waiting lists. Queues were a common feature of life in the former communist east European countries where governments kept prices below the level necessary to equate demand and supply. In recent years, as part of their economic reforms, they have allowed prices to rise. This has had the obvious benefit of reducing or eliminating queues, but at the same time it has made life very hard for those on low incomes.
- Firms deciding which customers should be allowed to buy: for example, giving preference to regular customers.

Neither of the above may be considered fair. Certain needy people may be forced to go without. Therefore, the government may adopt a system of ***rationing***. People could

KI 4 p11

Definition

Rationing Where the government restricts the amount of a good that people are allowed to buy.

CASE STUDIES AND APPLICATIONS BOX 3.2

BLACK MARKETS

A consequence of low fixed prices

When the government sets maximum prices, a *black market* is likely to result. A black market is one where sellers ignore the government's price restrictions. But why is it in their interest to do so, given that they probably run the risk of fines or even imprisonment?

Take the case of wartime price controls. The government set maximum prices for many essential items that were in short supply. This is illustrated in the diagram.

Effect of price control on black-market prices

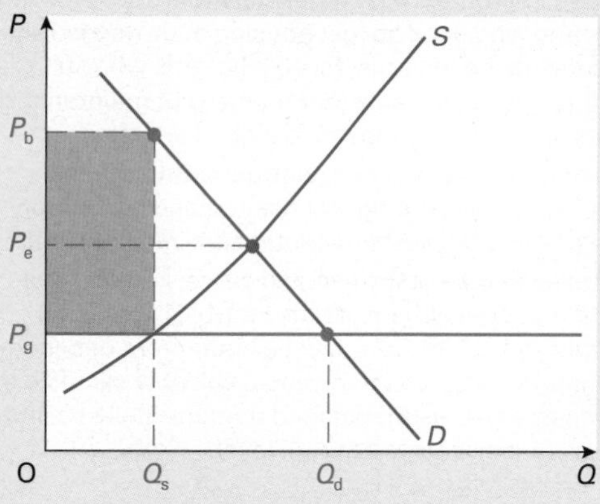

The unacceptably high equilibrium price is P_e. The price fixed by the government is P_g. But at P_g there is a shortage of $Q_d - Q_s$. To deal with the shortage, either the government will have to accept queues, or shops selling only to 'regular' customers; or alternatively a system of rationing will have to be introduced.

But whichever system is adopted, one thing is clear: many consumers would be prepared to pay a price considerably above P_g in order to get hold of the good. The demand curve shows this: the less the supply, the higher up the demand curve will the equilibrium price be.

This is where black marketeers come in. Provided they can get supplies (maybe by some shady dealing), provided they can have access to consumers, provided consumers are willing to break the law, and provided they can escape detection, black marketeers can charge a price considerably above P_g. But what price can they charge?

Take the extreme case. Assume that the black marketeers buy up *all* the supply (Q_s) from the producers at the official price and then sell it at a price that clears the market. The black-market price will be P_b: at that price, demand is equal to Q_s. The black marketeers gain the extra revenue shown by the shaded area.

In practice, of course, many people will get their supplies from official sources, and pay only P_g. On the other hand, if black marketeers are few in number and have only limited supplies, they could sell them at very high prices: above P_b even.

During the Second World War, 'spivs' (as these black marketeers were called) could often charge extortionately high prices for such items as nylon stockings and coffee.

1. ***What would be the effect on black-market prices of a rise in the official price?***
2. ***Will a system of low official prices plus a black market be more equitable or less equitable than a system of free markets?***

be issued with a set number of coupons for each item rationed.

A major problem with maximum prices is likely to be the emergence of ***black markets***, where customers, unable to buy enough in legal markets, may well be prepared to pay very high prices: prices above P_e in Figure 3.2 (see Box 3.2).

Another problem is that the maximum prices reduce the quantity produced of an already scarce commodity. For example, artificially low prices in a famine are likely to reduce food supplies: if not immediately, then at the next harvest, because of less being sown. In many developing countries, governments control the price of basic foodstuffs in order to help the urban poor. The effect, however, is to reduce incomes for farmers, who are then encouraged to leave the land and flock into the ever-growing towns and cities.

To minimise these types of problem the government may attempt to reduce the shortage by encouraging supply: by drawing on stores, by direct government production, or by giving subsidies or tax relief to firms. Alternatively, it may attempt to reduce demand: by the production of more alternative goods (e.g. homegrown vegetables in times of war) or by controlling people's incomes.

?

Think of some examples where the price of a good or service is kept below the equilibrium (e.g. rent controls). In each case, consider the advantages and disadvantages of the policy.

Definition

Black markets Where people ignore the government's price and/or quantity controls and sell illegally at whatever price equates illegal demand and supply.

Section summary

1. There are several ways in which the government intervenes in the operation of markets. It can fix prices, tax or subsidise products, regulate production, or produce goods directly itself.
2. The government may fix minimum or maximum prices. If a minimum price is set above the equilibrium, a surplus will result. If a maximum price is set below the equilibrium price, a shortage will result.
3. Minimum prices are set as a means of protecting the incomes of suppliers or creating a surplus for storage in case of future reductions in supply. If the government is not deliberately trying to create a surplus, it must decide what to do with it.
4. Maximum prices are set as a means of keeping prices down for the consumer. The resulting shortage will cause queues, waiting lists or the restriction of sales by firms to favoured customers. Alternatively, the government could introduce a system of rationing. With maximum prices, black markets are likely to arise. This is where goods are sold illegally above the maximum price.

3.2 INDIRECT TAXES

The effect of imposing taxes on goods

Another example of government intervention in markets is the imposition of taxes on goods. These ***indirect taxes***, as they are called, include taxes such as value added tax (VAT) and excise duties on cigarettes, petrol and alcoholic drinks.

These taxes can be a fixed amount per unit sold – a ***specific tax***. An example is the tax per litre of petrol. Alternatively, they can be a percentage of the price or value added at each stage of production – an ***ad valorem tax***. An example is VAT.

When a tax is levied on a good, this has the effect of shifting the supply curve upwards by the amount of the tax (see Figure 3.3). In the case of a specific tax, it will be a parallel shift, since the amount of the tax is the same at all prices. In the case of an ad valorem tax, the curve will *swing* upwards. At a zero price there would be no tax and hence no shift in the supply curve. As price rises, so the gap between the original and new supply curves will widen, since a given *percentage* tax will be a larger *absolute* amount the higher the price.

But why does the supply curve shift upwards by the amount of the tax? This is illustrated in Figure 3.4. To be persuaded to produce the same quantity as before the imposition of the tax (i.e. Q_1), firms must now receive a price which allows them fully to recoup the tax they have to pay (i.e. P_1 + tax).

Figure 3.3 Effect of a tax on the supply curve

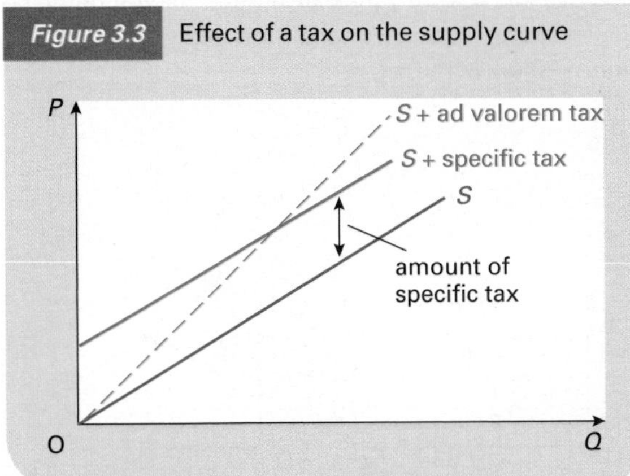

Figure 3.4 Effect of a tax on price and quantity

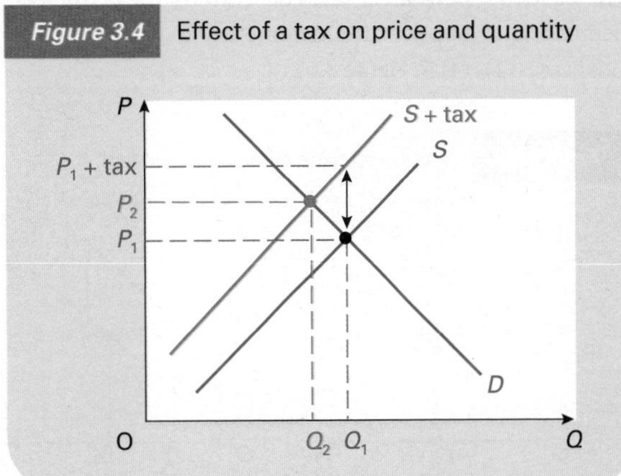

Definitions

Indirect tax A tax on the expenditure on goods. Indirect taxes include value added tax (VAT) and duties on tobacco, alcoholic drinks and petrol. These taxes are not paid directly by the consumer, but indirectly via the sellers of the good. Indirect taxes contrast with direct taxes (such as income tax) which are paid directly out of people's incomes.

Specific tax An indirect tax of a fixed sum per unit sold.

Ad valorem tax An indirect tax of a certain percentage of the price of the good.

*LOOKING AT THE MATHS

Assume that a specific tax per unit of t is imposed on producers of a good. This is then added to the pre-tax price of P_1. The price paid by consumers is thus $P_1 + t$.

Assuming linear demand and supply equations (see page 45), these can be written as:

$$Q_D = a - b(P_1 + t) \quad (1)$$

$$Q_S = c + dP_1 \quad (2)$$

In equilibrium, $Q_D = Q_S$. Thus:

$$a - b(P_1 + t) = c + dP_1$$

We can rearrange this equation to give:

$$bP_1 + dP_1 = a - c - bt$$

Thus:

$$P_1 = \frac{a - c - bt}{b + d} \quad (3)$$

Take the following example. If the demand and supply equations were:

$$Q_D = 120 - 10(P_1 + t) \quad (4)$$

$$\text{and } Q_S = 10 + 5P_1 \quad (5)$$

and $t = 2$, then from equation (3):

$$P_1 = \frac{120 - 10 - (10 \times 2)}{10 + 5} = 6$$

and from equations (4) and (5):

$$Q_D = 120 - 80 = Q_S = 10 + 30 = 40$$

The market price will be:

$$P_1 + t = 6 + 2 = 8$$

? ***Assuming that the pre-tax equations were:***

$Q_D = 120 - 10P$ and $Q_S = 10 + 5P$

what is (a) the consumer share of the tax and (b) the producer share?

KI 5 p21 The effect of the tax is to raise price and reduce quantity. Price will not rise by the full amount of the tax, however, because the demand curve is downward sloping. In Figure 3.4, price rises only to P_2. Thus the burden or ***incidence*** of such taxes is distributed between consumers and producers. Consumers pay to the extent that price rises. Producers pay to the extent that this rise in price is not sufficient to cover the tax.

Elasticity and the incidence of taxation

KI 9 p58 The incidence of indirect taxes depends on the elasticity of demand and supply of the commodity in question. Consider cases (1)–(4) in Figure 3.5.

In each of the diagrams (which are all drawn to the same scale), the size of the tax is the same: the supply curve shifts upwards by the same amount. Price rises to P_2 in each case and quantity falls to Q_2; but as you can see, the size of this increase in price and decrease in quantity differs in each case, depending on the price elasticity of demand and supply.

The total tax revenue is given by the amount of tax per unit (the vertical difference between the two supply curves) multiplied by the new amount sold (Q_2). This is shown as the total shaded area in each case in Figure 3.5.

The rise in price from P_1 to P_2 multiplied by the number of goods sold (Q_2) (the pink area) is the amount of the tax passed on to consumers and thus represents the ***consumers' share*** of the tax.

Figure 3.5 The incidence of an indirect tax

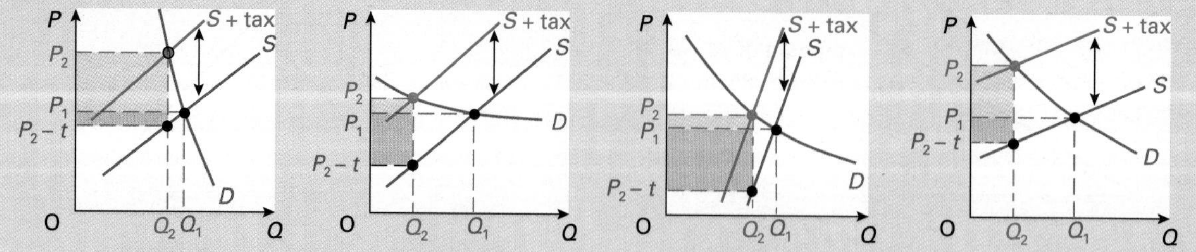

Case (1) Inelastic demand

Case (2) Elastic demand

Case (3) Inelastic supply

Case (4) Elastic supply

Definitions

Incidence of tax The distribution of the burden of tax between sellers and buyers.

Consumers' share of a tax on a good The proportion of the revenue from a tax on a good that arises from an increase in the price of the good.

CASE STUDIES AND APPLICATIONS

BOX 3.3

ASHES TO ASHES?

A moral dilemma of tobacco taxes

Consider the following dilemma. Cigarettes have a fairly price-inelastic demand (approximately −0.6), and thus placing a tax on them is an effective means of generating revenue. In the UK in 2004/5, tobacco duties raised £8.1 billion or 1.9 per cent of total tax revenue. This compares with 5.5 per cent for fuel duties and 1.8 per cent for alcohol duties.

Clearly, then, tobacco duties are a major source of revenue for the government. The less people can be put off smoking by the tax, the more revenue will be raised. In fact, if the government were to encourage people to smoke, it could thereby raise more revenue! The dilemma is that there is strong pressure on governments around the world to discourage people from smoking. The more governments succeed in this, the less will be their tax revenue.

But would a reduction in smoking represent a cost to the government? Clearly it would represent a cut in tax revenue, but it would also reduce spending on smoking-related diseases. The amount spent by the National Health Service on smoking-related illness is around £1.7 billion per year. This, however, is considerably less than the revenue raised from tobacco taxes. Clearly smokers more than pay for their own treatment. Indeed, the state and the NHS may acquire further financial benefit from smokers. The benefits stem from the fact that smokers die younger. The NHS gains from avoiding many of the high-cost treatments required by elderly patients. The state gains from having to pay out less in pensions and other benefits.

The costs of smoking, however, are not limited to healthcare costs and other costs to the exchequer. There are also costs in terms of lost output as a result of smoking-related illnesses. According to the Chief Medical Officer[1], banning smoking in workplaces and public places, such as shops, bars and restaurants, would save up to £2.7 billion from a more healthy workforce. Then there are savings in human costs from reduced suffering and deaths. Smoking kills over 100 000 people per year in the UK, with an additional 3000 or more killed by the effects of passive smoking. More than 17 000 children each year are admitted to hospital because of the effects of passive smoking.

So perhaps raising tobacco taxes would be doubly beneficial. Not only would it raise revenue, but also it would help to back up other anti-smoking measures. There are, however, two problems with this.

The first concerns smuggling and tobacco-related crime. Smuggled cigarettes account for over 20 per cent of the UK market. Not only is the high price differential between tobacco prices in the UK and abroad encouraging criminality, but smuggled tobacco products are losing the government over £2 billion each year in tax revenue.

The other issue concerns the poorest households. The poorer people are, the larger the proportion of their income is spent on tobacco (and hence tobacco taxes). The poorest 10 per cent of the population spend approximately 15 per cent of their disposable income on tobacco. This compares with a figure of just 2 per cent for the population as a whole. As such, the higher the tax on tobacco, the more it redistributes incomes from the poor to the rich.

?

1. ***If raising the tax rate on cigarettes both raises more revenue* and *reduces smoking, is there any conflict between the health and revenue objectives of the government?***
2. ***You are a government minister. What arguments might you put forward in favour of maximising the revenue from cigarette taxation?***
3. ***You are a doctor. Why might you suggest that smoking should be severely restricted? What methods would you advocate?***

[1] Annual Report of the Chief Medical Officer 2003 (http://www.publications.doh.gov.uk/cmo/annualreport2003/smokefree.htm)

The remainder (the green area) is the ***producers' share***. This is the amount by which the producers' net price ($P_2 - t$) is below the original price (P_1) multiplied by Q_2.

From these diagrams the following conclusions can be drawn:

- Quantity will fall less, and hence tax revenue for the government will be greater, the less elastic are demand and supply (cases (1) and (3)).
- Price will rise more, and hence the consumers' share of the tax will be larger, the less elastic is demand and the more elastic is supply (cases (1) and (4)).
- Price will rise less, and hence the producers' share will be larger, the more elastic is demand and the less elastic is supply (cases (2) and (3)).

Cigarettes, petrol and alcohol have been major targets for indirect taxes. Demand for each of them is high and fairly inelastic. Thus the tax will not curb demand greatly. They are good sources, therefore, of tax revenue to the government (see Box 3.3).

?

Supply tends to be more elastic in the long run than in the short run. Assume that a tax is imposed on a good that was previously untaxed. How will the incidence of this tax change as time passes? How will the incidence be affected if demand too becomes more elastic over time?

Definition

Producers' share of a tax on a good The proportion of the revenue from a tax on a good that arises from a reduction in the price to the producer (after the payment of the tax).

Section summary

1. If the government imposes a tax on a good, this will cause its price to rise to the consumers, but it will also cause the revenue to producers (after the tax has been paid) to fall.
2. The 'incidence of tax' will depend on the price elasticity of demand and supply of the good.
3. The consumers' burden will be higher and the producers' burden correspondingly lower, the less elastic the demand and the more elastic the supply of the good. The total tax revenue for the government will be higher the less elastic are both demand and supply.

3.3 GOVERNMENT REJECTION OF MARKET ALLOCATION

TC 7 p26

Sometimes the government may consider that certain products or services are best not allocated through the market at all. This section examines two extreme cases. The first is goods or services that are provided free at the point of delivery, such as treatment in National Health Service hospitals and education in state schools. The second is goods and services whose sale is banned, such as certain drugs, weapons and pornography.

Providing goods and services free at the point of delivery: the case of hospital treatment

When the government provides goods and services free to consumers, this is often reflecting the public's view that they have a *right* to such things. Most people believe that it would be wrong to charge parents for their children's schooling or for having treatment in a hospital, certainly emergency treatment.

KI 4 p11

But what are the consequences of not charging for a service such as health? The analysis is similar to that of a maximum price, only here the maximum price is zero! Figure 3.6 illustrates the situation. It shows a demand and a supply curve for a specific type of treatment in a given hospital.

The demand curve is assumed to be downward sloping. If people had to pay, the amount of treatment demanded would fall as the price went up – partly because some people would feel that they could not afford it (the income effect), and partly because people would turn to alternative treatments, such as prescription drugs. The fewer the alternatives, and the less close they are to hospital treatment, the less elastic would be the demand curve.

KI 9 p58

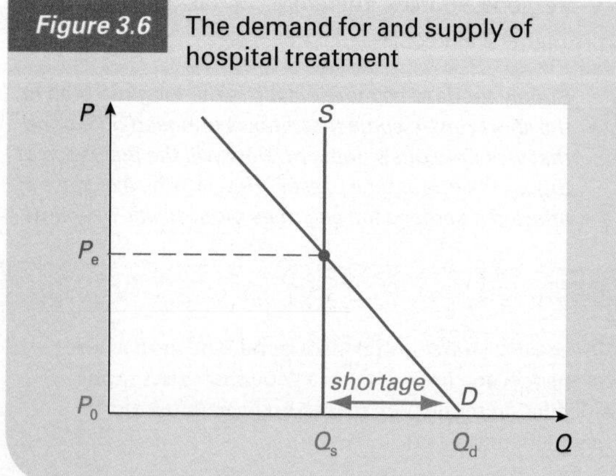

Figure 3.6 The demand for and supply of hospital treatment

The supply curve is assumed to be totally inelastic, at least in the short run, given current space and equipment. In the longer run, the supply curve may be upward sloping, but only if any charges made could be used to employ extra staff and buy more equipment, and even build extra wards and theatres, rather than the money simply going to the government.

At a price of zero, there is a shortage of $Q_d - Q_s$. Only at the equilibrium price of P_e will demand equal supply.

The shortage will have to be dealt with. One way would be to have a waiting list system. Most hospitals in the UK have waiting lists for treatment. The trouble with this 'solution', however, is that waiting lists will continue to lengthen unless the shortage is reduced. There is also the problem that some people on the waiting list may require urgent treatment. For this reason, medical professionals will normally rank patients according to the urgency of their condition. Urgent cases will get faster treatment than non-urgent cases, and emergency cases will probably get immediate treatment. A consequence, however, is that non-urgent cases, such as those waiting for hip replacements or the treatment of varicose veins, may have to wait a very long time.

Changes in demand and supply

One of the problems for the provision of health care is that the demand has grown more rapidly than people's incomes. Unless an increasing proportion of a nation's income is devoted to health care, shortages are likely to get worse. The demand curve in Figure 3.6 will shift to the right faster than the supply curve.

But why has demand grown so rapidly? There are two main reasons. The first has to do with demography. People in developed countries are living longer and the average age of the population is rising. But elderly people require a larger amount of medical treatment than younger people. The second has to do with advances in medical science and technology. More and more medical conditions are now treatable, so there is now a demand for such treatment where none existed before.

What is the solution? The answer for most people would be to increase supply, while keeping treatment free. Partly this can be done by increases in efficiency, and, indeed, various initiatives have been taken by government and health managers to try to reduce costs. Often, however, such measures are highly controversial, such as reducing the length of time people are allowed to stay in hospital after an operation, or moving patients to hospitals, often at a distance, where operations can be done more cheaply. The only other way of increasing supply is to allocate more funds to health care, and this means either increasing taxes or diverting resources from other forms of public expenditure, such as education or social security. But scarcity involves choices!

TC 1 p8

? *Schooling is free in state schools in most countries. If parents are given a choice of schools for their children, there will be a shortage of places at popular schools (the analysis will be the same as in Figure 3.6, with the number of places in a given school measured on the horizontal axis). What methods could be used for dealing with this shortage? What are their relative merits?*

Prohibiting the sale of certain goods and services: the case of illegal drugs

It is illegal to sell certain goods and services, and yet many of these goods have flourishing markets. Billions of pounds change hands worldwide in the illegal drugs, arms and pornography trades. What, then, is the impact of making certain products illegal? How would the effect compare with other policies, such as taxing these products?

KI 6 p29

Note that as economists we can examine the effects of such policies and hence help to inform public debate: we cannot, however, *as economists* make judgements as to whether such policies are *morally* right or wrong (see page 28 on the distinction between positive and normative statements).

The market for illegal products

Figure 3.7 illustrates the market for a product, such as a drug. If it were not illegal, the demand and supply curves would look something like D_{legal} and S_{legal}. The equilibrium price and quantity would be P_{legal} and Q_{legal}.

Now assume that the drug is made illegal. The effect will be to reduce supply and demand (i.e. shift both curves to the left), as both suppliers and users of the drug fear being caught and paying the penalty (fines or imprisonment). Also some people will stop supplying or using the drug simply because it is illegal and irrespective of any penalty. The harsher the penalties for supplier or user, and the more likely they are to get caught, and also the more law abiding

Figure 3.7 The market for an illegal drug

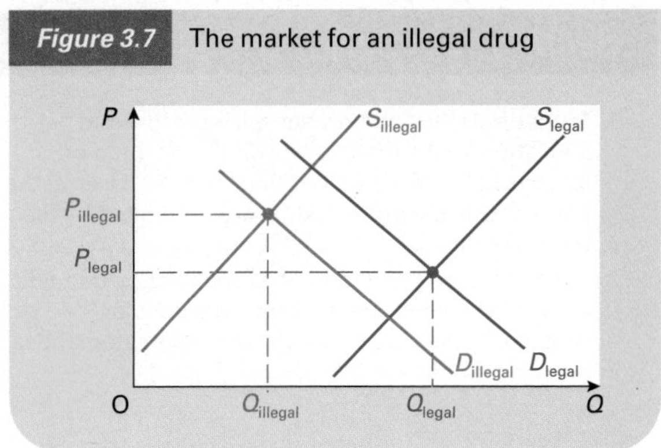

people are, the bigger will be the leftward shift in the respective supply or demand curve.

In Figure 3.7, the supply curve shifts to $S_{illegal}$ and the demand curve shifts to $D_{illegal}$. The quantity sold will fall to $Q_{illegal}$ and the price will rise to $P_{illegal}$. It is assumed that there will be a bigger shift in the supply curve (and hence a rise in price) as the penalties for supplying drugs are usually higher than those for merely possessing them.

Under what circumstances would making a product illegal (a) cause a fall in its price; (b) cause the quantity sold to fall to zero?

A comparison of prohibition with taxing the product

Cocaine is illegal. Other drugs, such as tobacco and alcohol, are taxed. But the effect in both cases is to reduce consumption. So are there any differences in the results of using taxation and prohibition?

A *tax* on a product, like making a product illegal, will have the effect of shifting the supply curve upwards to the left (as we saw in Figure 3.4). Unlike making the product illegal, however, a tax will not shift the demand curve. A bigger shift in the supply curve would therefore be needed than in Figure 3.7 for a tax to have the same effect as prohibition on the level of consumption. It would also result in a higher price for any given level of consumption.

So why not simply use taxes rather than making goods illegal? Those in favour of legalising various drugs argue that this would avoid the associated criminal activity that goes with illegal products (such as drugs gangs, violence and money laundering) and the resulting costs of law enforcement. It would also bring in tax revenue for the government.

The reason given by governments for keeping drugs illegal is that it sends out important messages to society and reflects what the majority wants. Taxing something, by contrast, implies that the product is acceptable. Also, if taxes were to be set high enough to reduce legal consumption to a politically acceptable level, there would then develop a large illegal market in the drugs as people sought to evade the tax.

What are the arguments for and against making the sale of alcoholic drinks illegal? To what extent can an economist help to resolve the issue?

Section summary

1. Sometimes the government will want to avoid allocation by the market for a particular good or service. Examples include things provided free at the point of use and products that are prohibited by the government.
2. If products are provided free to consumers, demand is likely to exceed supply. This is a particular problem in the case of health care, where demand is growing rapidly.
3. If products such as drugs are prohibited, an illegal market is likely to develop. Demand and supply would be less than in a free market. The price could be either higher or lower, depending on who faces the harshest penalties and the greatest likelihood of being caught – suppliers or users.
4. A similar reduction in consumption could be achieved by using taxation. Other effects, however, such as on the price, on allied crime and on public perceptions of the acceptability of the product, will be different.

3.4 AGRICULTURE AND AGRICULTURAL POLICY

TC 4 p 22

If markets for agricultural products were free from government intervention, they would be about as close as one could get to perfect competition in the real world. There are thousands of farmers, each insignificantly small relative to the total market. As a result, farmers are price takers.

Yet despite this high degree of competition, there is more government intervention in agriculture throughout the world than in virtually any other industry. For example, nearly half of the EU budget is spent on agricultural support. This amounted to over €4700 per person employed in agriculture in 2004, or €110 per head of population. Agricultural markets therefore pose something of a paradox. If they are so perfect, why is there so much government intervention?

TC 7 p 26

Why intervene?

The following are the most commonly cited problems of a free market in agricultural products.

Agricultural prices are subject to considerable fluctuations. This has a number of effects:

- Fluctuating prices cause fluctuating farm incomes. In some years, farm incomes may be very low.
- In other years, the consumer will suffer by having to pay very high prices.

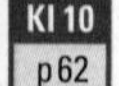

- Fluctuating prices make the prediction of future prices very difficult. This in turn makes rational economic decision making very difficult. How is a farmer to choose which of two or more crops to plant if their prices cannot be predicted?

- This uncertainty may discourage farmers from making long-term investment plans. A farmer may be reluctant to invest in, say, a new milking parlour, if in a couple of years it might be more profitable to switch to sheep rearing or arable farming. A lack of investment by farmers will reduce the growth of efficiency in agriculture.

Low incomes for those in farming. Over the years, farm incomes are likely to decline relative to those in other sectors of the economy. What is more, farmers have very little market power. A particular complaint of farmers is that they have to buy their inputs (tractors, fertilisers, etc.) from non-competitive suppliers who charge high prices. Then they often have to sell their produce at very low prices to food processors, packers, distributors and supermarkets. Farmers thus feel squeezed from both directions. KI 4 p 11

Traditional rural ways of life may be destroyed. The pressure on farm incomes may cause unemployment and bankruptcies; smaller farms may be taken over by larger ones; and generally, as the rural population declines, village life may be threatened – with the break-up of communities and the closure of schools, shops and other amenities.

Competition from abroad. Farming may well be threatened by cheap food imports from abroad. This may drive farmers out of business.

Against all these arguments must be set the argument that intervention involves economic costs. These may be costs to the taxpayer in providing financial support to farmers, or costs to the consumer in higher prices of foodstuffs, or costs to the economy as a whole by keeping resources locked into agriculture that could have been more efficiently used elsewhere.

Causes of short-term price fluctuations

Supply problems. A field is not like a machine. It cannot produce a precisely predictable amount of output according to the inputs fed in. The harvest is affected by a number of unpredictable factors such as the weather, pests and diseases. Fluctuating harvests mean that farmers' incomes will fluctuate.

CASE STUDIES AND APPLICATIONS — BOX 3.4

ELASTICITIES OF DEMAND FOR VARIOUS FOODSTUFFS

The table below shows the price and income elasticities of demand in the UK for various foodstuffs.

With the exception of lamb, all the foodstuffs have a price inelastic demand. The lower the price elasticity of demand, the more the price is likely to fluctuate with any change in supply, and hence the greater will be the variability of farmers' and other food producers' incomes.

All the foodstuffs have an income-inelastic demand. The lower the income elasticity of demand, the less will demand rise as national income rises, and hence the more slowly will farmers' and other food producers' incomes rise over time.

1. ***The income elasticity of demand for milk is negative (an 'inferior' good). What is the implication of this for milk producers?***
2. ***Why do pork and lamb have relatively high price elasticities of demand compared with the other foodstuffs in the table? What are the implications of this for the relative stability or instability of the prices of pork and lamb compared with other foodstuffs?***

Foodstuff	Price elasticity of demand (1988–2000)	Income elasticity of demand (1998–2000)
Bread	−0.40	0.12
Milk	−0.17	−0.17
Cheese	−0.35	0.23
Lamb	−1.29	0.15
Pork	−0.82	0.13
Fresh fish	−0.80	0.31
Eggs	−0.28	−0.01
Fresh potatoes	−0.12	0.09
Fresh green vegetables	−0.66	0.27
Frozen peas	−0.68	0.06
Bananas	−0.32	0.12
Cakes and biscuits	−0.56	0.13
All foods	n.a.	0.20

Source: *National Food Survey 2000* (National Statistics, 2001), extracted from Tables 6.1, 6.3, 6.4 and 6.5.

Demand problems. Food, being a basic necessity of life, has no substitute. If the price of food in general goes up, people cannot switch to an alternative: they have either to pay the higher price or to consume less food. They might consume a bit less, but not much! The price elasticity for food in general, therefore, is very low (see Box 3.4).

KI 9 p58

It is not quite so low for individual foodstuffs because if the price of one goes up, people can always switch to an alternative. If beef goes up in price, people can buy pork or lamb instead. Nevertheless, certain foodstuffs still have a low price elasticity, especially if they are considered to be basic foods rather than luxuries; there are no close substitutes; or they account for a relatively small portion of consumers' income.

With an inelastic demand curve, any fluctuations in supply will cause large fluctuations in price. This is illustrated in Figure 3.8.

? *Why is the supply curve drawn as a vertical straight line in Figure 3.8?*

Causes of declining farm incomes

Demand problems. There is a limit to the amount people wish to eat. As people get richer, they might buy better cuts of meat, or more convenience foods, but they will spend very little extra on basic foodstuffs. Their income elasticity of demand for basic foods is very low (see Box 3.4).

? *Why don't farmers benefit from a high income elasticity of demand for convenience foods?*

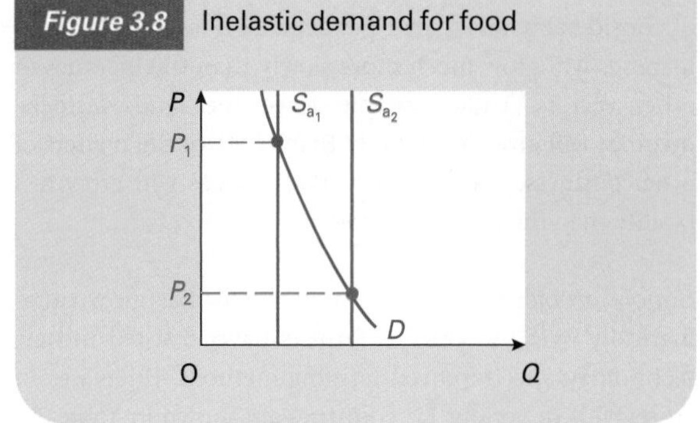

Figure 3.8 Inelastic demand for food

EXPLORING ECONOMICS — BOX 3.5

THE FALLACY OF COMPOSITION

Or when good is bad

Ask farmers whether they would like a good crop of potatoes this year, or whether they would rather their fields be ravaged by pests and disease, and the answer is obvious. After all, who would wish disaster upon themselves!

And yet, what applies to an individual farmer does not apply to farmers as a whole. Disaster for all may turn out not to be disaster at all.

Why should this be? The answer has to do with price elasticity. The demand for food is highly price inelastic. A fall in supply, due to a poor harvest, will therefore cause a proportionately larger rise in price. Farmers' incomes will therefore rise, not fall.

Look at diagram (a). Farmer Giles is a price taker. If he alone has a bad harvest, price will not change. He simply sells less (Q_2) and thus earns less. His revenue falls by the amount of the shaded area. But if *all* farmers have a bad harvest the picture is quite different, as shown in diagram (b). Supply falls from Q_1 to Q_2, and consequently price rises from P_1 to P_2. Revenue thus *rises* from areas (1 + 2) to areas (1 + 3).

And so what applies to a single farmer in isolation (a fall in revenue) does not apply to farmers in general. This is known as the 'fallacy of composition'.

(a) *Farmer Giles* **(b)** *All farmers*

Key Idea 12 ***The fallacy of composition.*** What applies in one case will not necessarily apply when repeated in all cases.

?

1. ***Can you think of any other (non-farming) examples of the fallacy of composition?***
2. ***Would the above arguments apply in the case of foodstuffs that can be imported as well as being produced at home?***

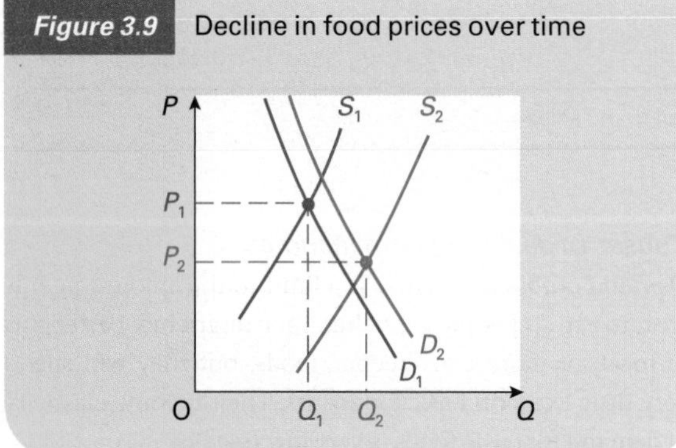

Figure 3.9 Decline in food prices over time

This very low income elasticity of demand has a crucial effect on farm incomes. It means that a rise in national income of 1 per cent leads to a rise in food consumption of considerably less than 1 per cent. As a result, total farm incomes will grow much more slowly than the incomes of other sectors. Unless people leave the land, farmers' incomes will grow less rapidly than those of the owners of other businesses, and farm workers' wages will grow less rapidly than those of other workers.

KI 9 p58

Supply problems. Farming productivity has grown dramatically over the years as farmers have invested in new technology and improved farming methods. (Increases in crop yields in various EU countries are shown in Table 3.1 on page 83.) But, given the price-inelastic demand for food, increased supply will have the effect of driving down agricultural prices, thus largely offsetting any reduction in costs. And given the income-inelastic demand for food, the long-term rise in demand will be less than the long-term rise in supply.

Figure 3.9 shows a basic foodstuff like potatoes or other vegetables. Rising productivity leads to an increase in supply from S_1 to S_2. But given that demand is price inelastic and shifts only slightly to the right over time, from D_1 to D_2, price falls from P_1 to P_2.

Government intervention

There are five main types of government intervention that can be used to ease the problems examined above.

Buffer stocks

Buffer stocks involve the government buying food and placing it in store when harvests are good, and then

Definition

Buffer stocks Stocks of a product used to stabilise its price. In years of abundance, the stocks are built up. In years of low supply, stocks are released on to the market.

Figure 3.10 Buffer stocks to stabilise prices

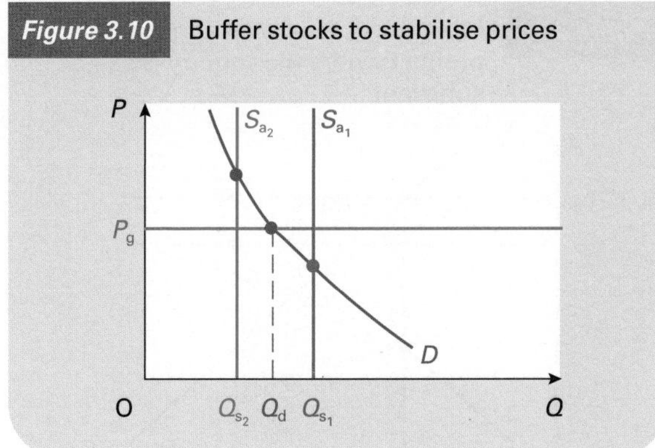

releasing the food back on to the market when harvests are bad. They can thus only be used with food that can be stored: i.e. non-perishable foods, such as grain, wine or milk powder; or food that can be put into frozen storage, such as butter and meat. The idea of buffer stocks is a very ancient one, as Web Case 3.2, *Seven years of plenty and seven years of famine*, demonstrates.

What the government does is to fix a price. Assume that this is P_g in Figure 3.10. At this price demand is Q_d. If there is a good harvest (S_{a_1}), the government buys up the surplus, $Q_{s_1} - Q_d$, and puts it into store. If there is a bad harvest (S_{a_2}), it releases $Q_d - Q_{s_2}$ from the store on to the market.

This system clearly stabilises price, at P_g. At this price, however, farm incomes will still fluctuate with the size of the harvest. It is possible, however, to have a buffer stock system that stabilises *incomes*. Such a system is examined in Web Case 3.3, *Buffer stocks to stabilise farm incomes*.

To prevent stores mounting over time, the government price will have to be the one that balances demand and supply over the years. Surpluses in good years will have to match shortages in bad years. Buffer stocks, therefore, can only *stabilise* prices or incomes; they do not *increase* farm incomes over the long term.

Subsidies

The government can pay subsidies or grant tax relief to farmers to compensate for low market prices. Subsidies can be used to increase farm incomes as well as to stabilise them. The simplest form of subsidy is one known as ***direct income support*** or ***direct aid***. Here farmers are paid a fixed sum of money irrespective of output. Given that such subsidies are unrelated to output, they do not provide an incentive to produce more.

An alternative system is to pay a subsidy *per unit of output*. This, of course, will encourage farmers to produce more, which in turn will depress the market price.

Definition

Direct income support or **direct aid** A fixed grant to farmers that does not vary with current output. It may be based on acreage, number of livestock or past output.

Figure 3.11 Effect of subsidies on agricultural products in which the country is self-sufficient

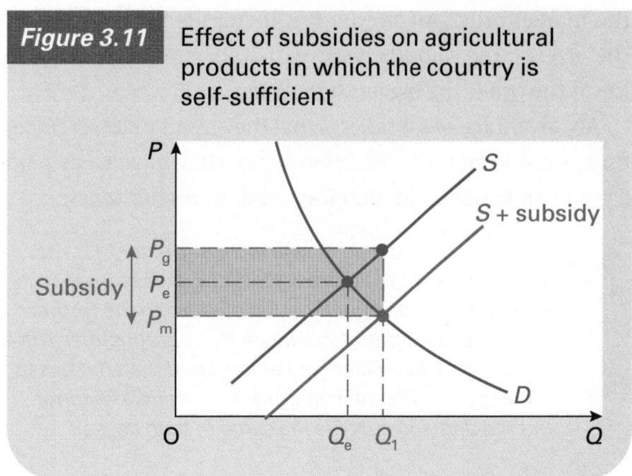

Figure 3.11 illustrates the case of an agricultural product where the country is self-sufficient. Without a subsidy the market price would be P_e, where supply equals demand.

Assume now that the government wishes farmers to receive a price of P_g. If farmers do receive this price, they will plan to increase production to Q_1, which will push the market price down to P_m. The size of the subsidy that the government must pay, therefore, will be $P_g - P_m$. The total amount of taxpayers' money spent will be the shaded area. The effect of the subsidy is to shift the effective supply curve downwards by the amount of the subsidy, to S + subsidy.

When some of the product is imported, the effect is slightly different. Let us assume, for simplicity, that a country is a price taker in world markets. It will face a horizontal world supply curve of the product at the world price. In other words, consumers can buy all they want at the world price. In Figure 3.12 the world price is P_w. Without a subsidy, domestic supply is Q_{s_1}. Domestic demand is Q_d. Imports are therefore the difference: $Q_d - Q_{s_1}$.

Assume now that the government wants farmers to receive a price of P_g. At that price, domestic supply increases to Q_{s_2}, but the price paid by the consumer does not fall. It remains at P_w. The subsidy paid per unit is $P_g - P_w$. The cost to the taxpayer is again shown by the shaded area.

A problem with subsidies of a fixed amount per unit is that the price the farmer receives will fluctuate along with

Figure 3.12 Effect of subsidies on agricultural products which are partly imported

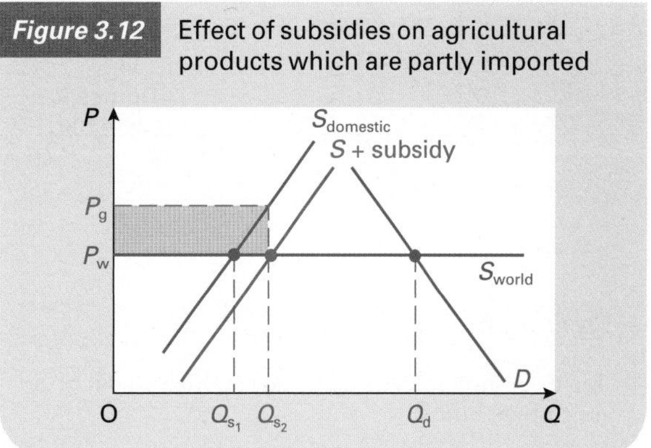

the market price. An alternative, therefore, would be to let the size of the subsidy vary with the market price. The lower the price, the bigger the subsidy.

An advantage of subsidies is that they result in lower prices for the consumer. On the other hand, they have to be paid from tax revenues and therefore result in higher taxes.

? *The total amount paid in subsidies is greater in Figure 3.11 than in Figure 3.12. Will it always be the case that, for a given after-subsidy price to the farmer (P_g), a greater amount will be paid out in subsidies if the country is self-sufficient in the foodstuff than if it has to import part of the total amount consumed? (Assume that the demand curve is the same in both cases.)*

High minimum prices

If the government considers agricultural prices to be too low, it can set a minimum price for each product above the free-market level. This was the traditional approach adopted in the EU. In recent years, however, forms of intervention in the EU have become more diverse.

The effect of high minimum prices will vary between products, depending on whether the country is a net importer or self-sufficient. Let us consider each case in turn.

Agricultural products where the country is a net importer. Assuming that the minimum price is above the world price, the government will need to impose customs duties (known alternatively as ***tariffs*** or ***import levies***) on imported products to bring them up to the required price. Given that the world price will fluctuate, these import levies would need to be variable.

The effects of this system are illustrated in Figure 3.13. If trade took place freely at the world price P_w, Q_{d_1} would be demanded and Q_{s_1} supplied domestically. The difference ($Q_{d_1} - Q_{s_1}$) would be imported.

Figure 3.13 Minimum price where some of the product is imported

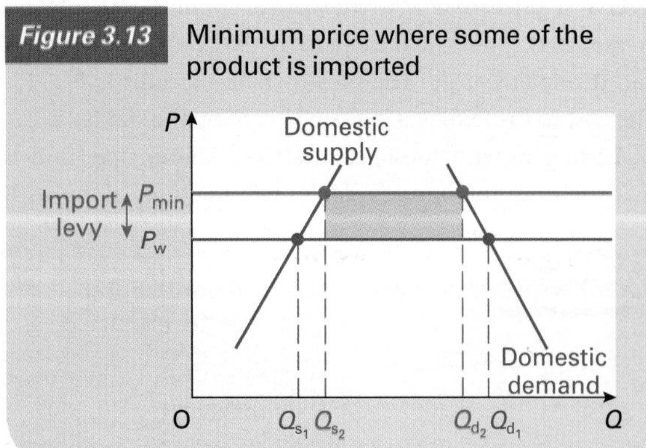

Definition

Tariffs or import levies Taxes on imported products: i.e. customs duties.

Figure 3.14 Minimum price for an agricultural product where the country is self-sufficient

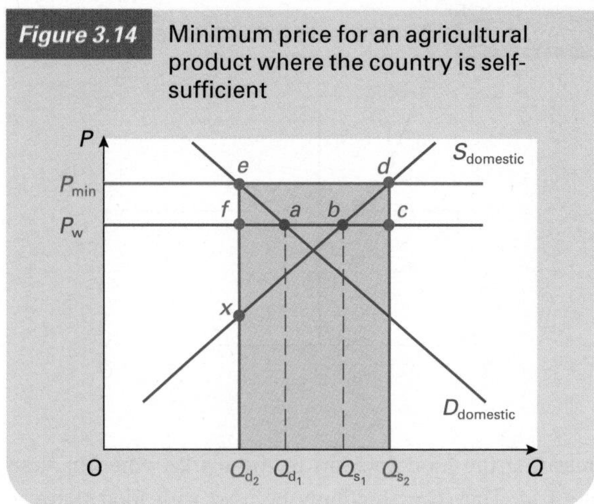

If a minimum price P_{min} is now set and a levy imposed on imports to raise their price to P_{min}, domestic prices will also rise to this level. Demand will fall to Q_{d_2}. Domestic supply will rise to Q_{s_2}. Imports will fall to $Q_{d_2} - Q_{s_2}$. The amount paid in import levies is shown by the shaded area.

Agricultural products where the country is self-sufficient. The effects of a minimum price in this situation are illustrated in Figure 3.14. Assume that the world price is P_w. This will be the equilibrium price, since any domestic surplus at P_w (i.e. $b - a$) will be exported at that price.

Now assume that the government sets a minimum price of P_{min}. Given that this is above the equilibrium (world) price, there will be an unsold surplus of $d - e$ (i.e. $Q_{s_2} - Q_{d_2}$).

But what will happen to this surplus? If farmers are to be helped, and not merely find that they cannot sell all they produce, the government will have to buy up this surplus. This is what happens in the EU. 'Intervention Boards' buy up the surpluses and in most cases (e.g. grains, milk powder and beef) put them into storage. In Figure 3.14, the cost to the government of buying the surplus is shown by the total shaded area ($edQ_{s_2}Q_{d_2}$). Unless the food is thrown away or otherwise disposed of, there will obviously then be the additional costs of storing this food: costs that could be very high over time, especially if the food has to be frozen.

An alternative to storing the food is for the government to sell the surpluses on the world market. In this case, the net cost would only be area *edcf*.

? *What will be the amount paid in Figure 3.14 if instead of the government buying the surpluses, export subsidies were given to farmers so as to guarantee them a price (plus subsidy) of P_{min}?*

Reductions in supply

An alternative approach would be to find some way of reducing supply. This would lead to a higher market price and could avoid the cost to the taxpayer of buying surpluses or paying subsidies.

In open markets, however, a reduction in domestic supply could simply lead to an increase in imports, with the result that the price would not rise to the desired level. In such a case, a combination of a reduction in domestic supply and import levies (or other import restrictions) would be required. This can be illustrated using Figure 3.14. First, by the use of various restrictions on output, the domestic supply curve could be shifted to the left, so that it intersected the demand curve at point *e*. Second, an import levy of $P_{min} - P_w$ would need to be imposed to bring the price up to the desired level.

But how could supply be reduced to Q_{d_2}? The simplest way would be to give farmers a quota of how much each was allowed to produce. The effect would be to make the domestic supply curve vertical above point *x*. Milk quotas, which have be in force in the EU since 1984, are an example of this system.

Alternatively, farmers could be required to limit the amount of *land* they used for a particular product. The problem with this is that supply, and hence price, would still vary according to the yield. Another alternative would be to require farmers to withdraw a certain percentage of their land from agricultural use. This would shift supply curves for food to the left generally, but they would still be upward sloping because farmers could still switch from one product to another on their remaining land, according to which products gave the best price.

? *Compare the relative merits of (a) quotas on output, (b) limits to the amount of land used for a particular product and (c) farmers being required to take land out of food production.*

Structural policies

The government could provide retraining or financial help for people to leave agriculture. It could provide grants or other incentives for farmers to diversify into forestry, tourism, rural industry or different types of food, such as organically grown crops, or other foods with a high income elasticity of demand.

The Common Agricultural Policy of the EU

Imagine public reaction if the government decided that the car industry needed protection from foreign competition and as a result decided to fix car prices some 20 per cent above current levels, and also agreed to buy up any unsold cars and put them into giant car parks, selling some of them off later on world markets at a knock-down price. There would be public uproar. And yet this is very similar to the type of support that has, until relatively recently, been the main one given to farmers under the EU's Common Agricultural Policy (CAP).

It involves setting an intervention price for each product above the free-market equilibrium, with any surpluses being bought by Intervention Boards and then either stored or sold on world markets. If products are exported, then export subsidies are paid to make up the difference between export prices and the intervention price. In addition to high minimum prices, the CAP has involved various subsidies, primarily in the beef and sheep sectors but also in the arable sector.

The objectives of the CAP were set out in 1957 in Article 39 of the Treaty of Rome. They included the following:

- Assured supplies of food.
- A fair standard of living for those working in agriculture.
- A growth in agricultural productivity.
- Stable prices.
- Reasonable prices for consumers.

How successful has the CAP been in meeting these objectives? It has certainly helped to increase the self-sufficiency of the EU in many agricultural products, which could be valuable if world food prices were to rise. Also, by fixing prices that do not fluctuate with demand and supply, stable prices are guaranteed – at least for a year. It has also directly increased farm incomes. Indeed, some larger farmers have benefited greatly from the CAP. Nevertheless, average incomes in farming have continued to lag behind those of other sectors of the economy, and many farmers face periodic losses.

Agricultural productivity has grown rapidly, as illustrated by Table 3.1. This has been in large part the result of technological improvements and a greater use of chemicals. It is difficult, however, to judge the extent to which this has resulted directly from higher food prices rather than the simple availability of new techniques, or competition from other farmers.

What of the final objective: 'reasonable prices for consumers'? In the short run, a policy of high prices is inconsistent with reasonable prices for consumers (if 'reasonable' is defined as 'low' or at any rate 'not high'). In the long run, however, it can be argued that, if prices above the market equilibrium encourage investment and productivity increases, then after a number of years they will end up lower than they would have been without the policy.

Table 3.1 Yields of selected crops (100 kg/hectare)

	Year	Wheat	Barley	Potatoes
Belgium	1970	39.0	31.0	293
	2003	84.9	66.4	425
France	1970	34.5	27.8	223
	2003	64.2	56.0	404
Germany	1970	37.9	32.2	272
	2003	65.0	51.1	345
Netherlands	1970	45.0	31.9	354
	2003	87.4	63.6	408
UK	1970	42.0	33.6	276
	2003	76.8	59.1	407

Source: data from selected tables in *Agriculture in the European Union* (EU DG for Agriculture and Rural Development, 2005).

Criticisms of the CAP

If the arguments in favour of the CAP's system of price support are questionable, the arguments against are substantial.

Agricultural surpluses (not sold on world markets)

The costs of the surpluses are borne by consumers and taxpayers. They can be illustrated by referring back to Figure 3.14. Assume that the intervention is P_{min}.

- The cost to the taxpayer is shown by the shaded area.
- The cost to the consumer arises from having to pay the higher price P_{min}.
- There will be a gain to farmers, however, from the extra profits resulting from the rise in price.

The costs and benefits of this system of high minimum prices are compared with those of a system of per-unit subsidies in Web Case 3.4.

Over the longer term, surpluses are likely to increase. The reason is that higher prices encourage more investment in farming and therefore greater increases in long-run supply. The attendant costs to taxpayers, not only from purchasing the surpluses each year, but also from storing previous years' surpluses, will therefore tend to rise over time.

By the early 1990s, European butter, grain and beef 'mountains' and wine 'lakes' had become symbols of a failed policy.

When surpluses are bought by the Intervention Boards, the money comes from the Guarantee section of the European Agricultural Guarantee and Guidance Fund (EAGGF).[2] Table 3.2 shows the EAGGF's Guarantee expenditure, and hence the cost to the EU taxpayer of supporting farm incomes.

Table 3.2 The cost of price and other market support for agriculture in the EU

Year	EAGGF Guarantee expenditure		
	Total (€ m)	% of total EU budget	% of total EU GDP
1977	6830	76.5	0.43
1980	11 315	69.4	0.50
1984	18 346	67.4	0.59
1988	27 687	67.3	0.68
1992	32 108	54.6	0.59
1996	39 108	48.6	0.58
2000	40 467	52.0	0.48
2004*	44 760	44.5	0.44

Note: The figures before 1999 are in millions of European Currency Units (ECUs). The ECU was the EU unit of account before the birth of the euro. The euro was introduced at a rate of 1 euro = 1 ECU.
* Planned.
Source: *Agriculture in the European Union* (Commission of the EU).

Inequitable

The system of high support prices as it has operated in the EU is inequitable at three levels.

Increases inequalities in agriculture. The bigger the farm, the bigger its output, and therefore the bigger the benefit the farmer receives from high prices. Also, the degree of price support has varied enormously from one product to another and has tended to favour farmers in the richer northern countries of the EU. Thus producers of arable crops have received a disproportionately large amount of price support.

Increases inequalities generally. Poor people spend a larger proportion of their income on food than the rich, but pay a lower proportion of their income in taxes than the rich. A system of high prices for food therefore directly penalises the poor and reduces the burden on taxpayers. It thus increases inequality.

A system of subsidies, on the other hand, leads to lower prices for the consumer, the cost being borne entirely by the taxpayer. It therefore leads to greater equality.

Inequitable between member countries of the EU. Countries that import the most food from outside the EU – countries like the UK – have paid the most in import levies into the EAGGF. The countries with the greatest food surpluses have drawn most from the EAGGF.

Harmful effects on the environment

By encouraging increased output, the CAP has encouraged the destruction of hedgerows, and the increased use of chemical fertilisers and pesticides. Many of these chemicals have caused pollution. For example, nitrates are now the biggest single cause of river pollution in the UK, especially in the east. This issue is examined in Web Case 3.5.

Effects on the rest of the world

The CAP has had a very damaging effect on agriculture in non-EU countries in two ways.

Import levies. Levies on imported food substantially reduce the amount of food that other countries have been able to export to the EU. For example, Australia, a low-cost producer of butter, and once a major exporter to the UK, has found it impossible to export any butter at all to the EU.

'Dumping' surpluses on world markets. Export subsidies have allowed EU surpluses to be sold at very low prices on world markets. This has a doubly damaging effect on

[2] The EAGGF also provides 'Guidance' support for farm modernisation and help for rural communities. This, however, accounts for only some 5 per cent of EAGGF expenditure.

agriculture in developing countries: (a) exporters of foodstuffs find it very difficult to compete with subsidised EU exports; (b) farmers in developing countries who are producing for their domestic market find that they cannot compete with cheap imports of food.

Agriculture in the developing world thus declines. Farmers' incomes are too low to invest in the land. Many migrate to the overcrowded cities and become slum dwellers in shanty towns, with little or no paid employment (see Chapter 26). The neglect of agriculture can then lead to famines if there is poor rainfall in any year. Calls are then made for European (and North American) food surpluses to be used for emergency aid: the same food surpluses that contributed to the problem in the first place!

Reforming the CAP

Proposals for reforming the CAP have been debated within the EU for a number of years. Most have focused on the growing problem of food surpluses and on the resulting demands made on the EU budget. Reforms can be grouped into two broad categories: those that seek to lower prices and those that seek to reduce supply.

Early reforms

Early reforms focused on reductions in supply. There were two main reforms.

Production quotas. These were introduced in the mid-1980s for sugar and milk. They involve imposing limits (or 'quotas') on the amount that farmers are permitted to produce. It is not practical, however, to have a quota system for grains and vegetables where yields fluctuate with the harvest, and where it would thus be difficult to monitor the system. But if quotas are applied only to a limited range of products, this merely encourages farmers to switch to other products which may already be in surplus.

Dairy farmers have been bitterly opposed to quotas, seeing them as a barrier against expansion, efficiency and increased profit. There is, however, a trade in quotas, with farmers buying and selling their right to produce milk. This does, at least, allow individual farmers to expand their dairy business, although the amount they are permitted to expand is restricted.

Acreage controls (set-aside). Another way of reducing cereal production has been to reduce the area cultivated. Subsidies are paid to farmers to leave their land fallow. Under this ***set-aside*** scheme, which was introduced in 1988, farmers are required to withdraw part of their arable land from production, and in return are paid compensation. From 2000/1 farmers have been required to set aside 10 per cent of their land. This land, however, can be used for products not intended for human or animal consumption (e.g. timber or cultivated flowers).

> **Definition**
>
> **Set-aside** A system in the EU of paying farmers not to use a certain proportion of their land.

A problem with set-aside is that farmers tend to set aside their least productive land, thereby making little difference to total output. Another problem is that farmers tend to put in extra effort on the remaining land, again hoping to maintain total output. If they are successful, supply will not be reduced and the problem of surpluses will remain. To increase yields they would probably use more chemicals with the attendant problems of pollution.

The MacSharry reforms

In 1992 a major reform package was introduced. These 'MacSharry reforms' (named after the EU agriculture commissioner) included the following:

- A substantial cut in intervention prices (including a 29 per cent cut in cereal prices) phased in over three years. There was also a corresponding cut in export subsidies. (Intervention prices were still somewhat above world prices.)
- Farmers were then paid compensation for their resulting loss of income. Since this income support (or 'direct aid', as it is known) is based on average historical yields in each farming region, it is independent of any changes in production by individual farmers. It thus provides no direct incentive to increase production.
- In order to receive direct aid, all except small farmers had to abide by the set-aside system (which at that time was set at 15 per cent of their land).
- Incentives were paid for farmers to switch to less intensive farming methods, with less use of chemical pesticides and fertilisers, and fewer livestock per hectare.

The effect of these measures was to reduce farm surpluses. This is illustrated in Figure 3.15. At the old intervention price of P_1, and with demand and supply

Figure 3.15 Effect of the MacSharry reforms on cereal surpluses

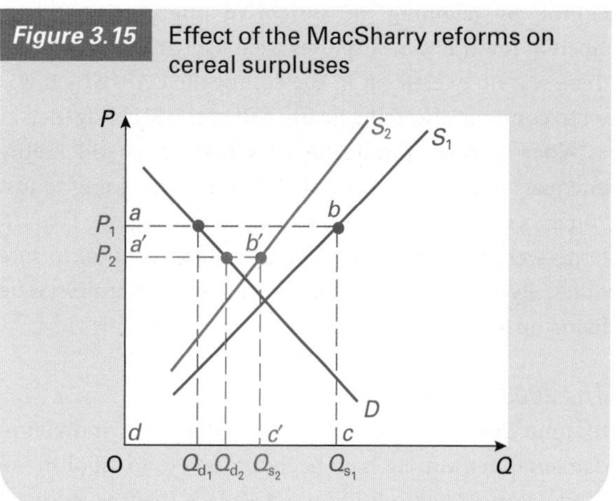

curves of D and S_1, the surplus was $Q_{s_1} - Q_{d_1}$. Farmers' revenues were *abcd*. The effect of the increased set-aside has been to shift the supply curve of cereals to the left, shown by S_2. This, plus a reduction in the intervention price to P_2, has reduced the surplus to $Q_{s_2} - Q_{d_2}$. Farmers' revenues have been reduced to *a'b'c'd*, but the CAP pays compensation payments for the loss in profits.

In the first three years after these reforms, annual cereal output fell from 180 million tonnes to 160 million tonnes, and intervention stocks all but disappeared. Set-aside land had increased by 30 per cent, and, contrary to the predictions of some analysts, yields had not increased (partly the result of poor weather). In response to this success, land required to be set aside was reduced to 10 per cent in 1995 and, temporarily, to 5 per cent in 1996.

? *Does the requirement to set aside x per cent of land reduce output by x per cent?*

But with crop yields subsequently increasing again, the problem of cereal surpluses had not been completely solved. Also, there was the worry among farmers that the level of direct aid would not keep pace with inflation. Large farmers might be able to compensate for this by increases in efficiency. Small farmers, however, often growing crops on more marginal lands and unable to afford the same level of investment per hectare as large farmers, might find it hard to survive. In fact, parts of farming have been in crisis in recent years. In the UK, with problems such as BSE and foot and mouth disease, many farmers have been forced into bankruptcy.

Agenda 2000

In July 1997, as part of its proposed plans for expansion of the EU to include various eastern European countries, the European Commission published a document entitled *Agenda 2000*. In response to this document, it was agreed to cut intervention prices for cereals by 15 per cent, for beef by 20 per cent and, in 2005/6, for butter and skimmed milk powder by 15 per cent. It was also agreed to provide more support for rural development and the environment.

Critics claimed that the agreement was not sufficiently radical. By retaining the system of intervention prices, albeit at lower levels, surpluses were likely to remain. Also, there was no overall cut in the cost of the CAP, which was set to continue absorbing nearly half of the EU budget.

What is more, the degree of support was still highly unequal. Some 70 per cent of CAP funds was going to just KI 4 p11 20 per cent of Europe's farms (mainly the largest). Five UK farms were receiving more than £1 million per year in subsidies. By contrast, over 70 per cent of EU farmers were living on less than £5000 a year.

The 2003 reforms

In June 2003, EU farm ministers adopted a more fundamental reform. It had been proposed to abolish all production-related subsidies and replace them with direct aid, but in the end a compromise deal was reached. This allowed countries to retain up to 25 per cent of support linked to production for cereals, 50 per cent for sheep and 100 per cent for beef.

Most countries, however, have moved to a system of direct aid. This involves making annual 'single farm payments'. The UK adopted this system in January 2005. It has the following features:

- Annual payments to each farm based on the average of the EU funds it received over the three years from 2000 to 2002.
- Payments conditional on farmers making environmental improvements to their land.
- Payments to large farms (those that receive more than €5000 a year from the CAP), gradually reduced, with 80 per cent of the money saved in each country being diverted to rural development.

Despite the plan to decouple subsidies for farmers from levels of production, intervention prices for cereals were not reduced (although the monthly increases in such prices were reduced by 50 per cent). Dairy intervention prices, however, have been cut. Skimmed milk prices have been reduced by 15 per cent and butter prices by 25 per cent. Then in 2005 it was announced that intervention prices for sugar beet would be cut by 42 per cent over three years. In all the above cases, the resulting loss in farm incomes has been offset wholly or partly by the introduction of the single farm payments.

The 10 per cent set-aside requirement has been retained, but with greater flexibility to trade set-aside entitlements (along with their corresponding payments).

Despite the obvious advantages to many developing countries from the cuts in intervention prices, not all have gained. Take the case of sugar. Some sugar producers in Africa and the Caribbean had been given preferential access to European markets and were able to sell at the high guaranteed prices. They would clearly lose from the fall in prices. The EU offered some support to such countries, but not enough to prevent a fall in their income.

Conclusions

The gradual shift from price support to direct aid reduces food prices and hence helps EU consumers, benefiting low-income families relatively more than high-income ones. Taxpayers have to finance the direct aid to farmers, but, with less incentive to expand production, this should be less of a burden than that of paying high intervention prices for large food surpluses.

Over the years there has been a shift in emphasis towards viewing agriculture as part of the whole rural environment. This has involved increasing the grants available for setting up alternative rural industries and 'environmentally friendly' farm activities. In other words, there has been a shift towards *discretionary* payments and away from automatic support based on output.

Section summary

1. Despite the fact that a free market in agricultural produce would be highly competitive, there is large-scale government intervention in agriculture throughout the world. The aims of intervention include preventing or reducing price fluctuations, encouraging greater national self-sufficiency, increasing farm incomes, encouraging farm investment, and protecting traditional rural ways of life and the rural environment generally.
2. Price fluctuations are the result of fluctuating supply combined with a price-inelastic demand. The supply fluctuations are due to fluctuations in the harvest.
3. The demand for food is generally income inelastic and thus grows only slowly over time. Supply, on the other hand, has generally grown rapidly as a result of new technology and new farm methods. This puts downward pressure on prices – a problem made worse for farmers by the price inelasticity of demand for food.
4. Government intervention can be in the form of buffer stocks, subsidies, price support, quotas and other ways of reducing supply, and structural policies.
5. Buffer stocks can be used to stabilise prices. They cannot be used to increase farm incomes over time.
6. Subsidies will increase farm incomes but will lower consumer prices to the world price level (or to the point where the market clears).
7. In the EU prices have been kept high to both farmer and consumer. In the case of partly imported foodstuffs, this is achieved by imposing variable import levies. In cases where the EU is self-sufficient, surpluses are purchased at an intervention price.
8. The CAP system of high intervention prices has been justified as providing assured supplies of food, a fair standard of living for farmers, incentives to increase productivity, stable prices, and, in the *long* term, possibly lower prices for consumers.
9. The CAP has been criticised, however, on a number of counts: it leads to food surpluses, the static costs of which are greater than those of subsidies; price support has been unequal as between foodstuffs, with a resulting misallocation of resources; it has aggravated inequalities within agriculture; it has been inequitable between member countries; it has encouraged environmental damage; import levies and the surpluses 'dumped' on world markets have had a damaging effect on the agricultural sector of non-EU countries.
10. Reforms have included the following: reductions in intervention prices and, in return, paying farmers compensation *unrelated* to output; acreage controls; increasing expenditure on rural diversification and restructuring; encouraging the use of less intensive farming methods.

END OF CHAPTER QUESTIONS

1. Assume that the (weekly) market demand and supply of tomatoes are given by the following figures:

Price (£ per kilo)	4.00	3.50	3.00	2.50	2.00	1.50	1.00
Q_d *(000 kilos)*	30	35	40	45	50	55	60
Q_s *(000 kilos)*	80	68	62	55	50	45	38

   (a) What are the equilibrium price and quantity?
   (b) What will be the effect of the government fixing a *minimum* price of (i) £3 per kilo; (ii) £1.50 per kilo?
   (c) Suppose that the government paid tomato producers a subsidy of £1 per kilo. (i) Give the new supply schedule. (ii) What will be the new equilibrium price? (iii) How much will this cost the government?
   (d) Alternatively, suppose that the government guaranteed tomato producers a price of £2.50 per kilo. (i) How many tomatoes would it have to buy in order to ensure that all the tomatoes produced were sold? (ii) How much would this cost the government?
   (e) Alternatively, suppose it bought *all* the tomatoes produced at £2.50. (i) At what single price would it have to sell them in order to dispose of the lot? (ii) What would be the net cost of this action?
2. Think of two things that are provided free. In each case, identify when and in what form a shortage might occur. In what ways are/could these shortages be dealt with? Are they the best solution to the shortages?
3. If the government increases the tax on wine by 10p, what will determine the amount by which the price of wine will go up as a result of this tax increase?
4. Illustrate on four separate diagrams (as in Figure 3.5) the effect of different elasticities of demand and supply on the incidence of a *subsidy*.
5. Why are agricultural prices subject to greater fluctuations than those of manufactured products?
6. Compare the relative benefits of subsidies and high minimum prices (as under the CAP) to (a) the consumer; (b) the farmer.
7. The EU is more than self-sufficient in a number of commodities. Does this mean that the objectives of the CAP have been achieved? What has been the cost of achieving this success? What do you think would have happened in the absence of the CAP?
8. In what ways have the reforms of recent years solved the problems experienced under the CAP?

Additional case studies on the book's website (www.pearsoned.co.uk/sloman)

3.1 **Rationing.** A case study in the use of rationing as an alternative to the price mechanism. In particular, it looks at the use of rationing in the UK during the Second World War.

3.2 **Seven years of plenty and seven years of famine.** This looks at how buffer stocks were used by Joseph in biblical Egypt.

3.3 **Buffer stocks to stabilise farm incomes.** This theoretical case shows how the careful use of buffer stocks combined with changes in set prices can be used to stabilise farm incomes.

3.4 **Agricultural subsidies.** This considers who gains and who loses from the use of subsidies on the production of agricultural products.

3.5 **The CAP and the environment.** This case shows how the system of high intervention prices had damaging environmental effects. It also examines the more recent measures the EU has adopted to reverse the effects.

WEBSITES RELEVANT TO THIS CHAPTER

Numbers and sections refer to websites listed in the Web Appendix and hotlinked from this book's website at www.pearsoned.co.uk/sloman.

- For news articles relevant to this chapter, see the *Economics News Articles* link from the book's website.
- For general news on markets and market intervention, see websites in section A, and particularly A1–5, 7–9, 18, 24, 25, 26, 33, 36. See also A38 and 39 for links to newspapers worldwide; and A42 for links to economics news articles from newspapers worldwide.
- For information on taxes in the UK, see sites 30 and 36.
- For information on agriculture and the Common Agricultural Policy, see sites E14 and G9.
- For sites favouring the free market, see C17 and E34.
- For student resources relevant to this chapter, see sites C1–7, 9, 10, 19.
- For a simulation of running a farm, see site D3.
- For a range of classroom games and simulations of markets and market intervention, see sites C24 (computer based) and C20 (non-computer based).

Part C: Microeconomics

We now examine in more detail how economies function at a micro level. In doing so, we will look at some of the big questions of our time. Why do some firms make such large profits? Why is there such a gap between the rich and the poor? Why, if everyone wants a better environment, are we plagued with problems of pollution and congestion?

Chapters 4 and 5 examine demand and supply in more detail. Then in Chapters 6 to 8 we look at how the degree of competition a firm faces affects its prices and profits. The following two chapters look at the distribution of income: why some are rich while others are poor. Finally, in Chapters 11 and 12, we ask how well a market economy functions and what policies can be adopted to tackle market failures.

Chapter 4
Background to Demand

In this chapter we take a more detailed look at consumer demand. If we had unlimited income (and unlimited time too!), we could consume as much as we wanted. We would not have to be careful with our money. In the real world, however, given limited incomes and the problem of scarcity, we have to make choices about what to buy. You may have to choose between that new economics textbook you feel you ought to buy and going to a rock concert, between a new pair of jeans and a meal out, between saving up for a car and having more money to spend on everyday items, and so on.

We will be assuming in this chapter that consumers behave 'rationally'. Remember from Chapter 1 how we defined rational choices. It is the weighing up of the costs and benefits of our actions. As far as consumption is concerned, rational action involves considering the relative costs and benefits to us of the alternatives we could spend our money on. We do this in order to gain the maximum satisfaction possible from our limited incomes.

This does not mean that you get a calculator out every time you go shopping! When you go round the supermarket, you are hardly likely to look at every item on the shelf and weigh up the satisfaction you think you would get from it against the price on the label. Nevertheless, you have probably learned over time the sort of things you like and what they cost. You can probably make out a 'rational' shopping list quite quickly.

There are two main approaches to analysing consumer behaviour: the marginal utility approach and the indifference approach. We examine both of them in this chapter. We also look at the problem of making rational choices when we have only limited information.

CHAPTER MAP

TC1 p8

As we are going to be examining the ***rational consumer***, it is important to understand what we mean by the term. It means a person who attempts to get the best value for money from his or her purchases. Given that we have limited income, we do not want to waste our money. Thus most of the time, we try to ensure that the benefits of what we are buying are worth the expense to us.

Sometimes we may act 'irrationally'. We may purchase goods impetuously or out of habit, with little thought to their price or quality. In general, however, it is reasonable to assume that people behave rationally.

1. *Do you ever purchase things irrationally? If so, what are they and why is your behaviour irrational?*
2. *If you buy something in the shop on the corner when you know that the same item could have been bought more cheaply two miles up the road in the supermarket, is your behaviour irrational? Explain.*

Two words of warning before we go on. First, don't confuse irrationality and ignorance. We are going to assume that consumers behave rationally, but that does not mean that they have perfect information. How often have you been disappointed after buying something when you find that it is not as good as you had been led to believe by advertisements or by its packaging, or when you find later that you could have bought an alternative more cheaply? Take the case of a foreign holiday. It may not turn out to be nearly as good as the brochure led you to believe. This is a problem of ignorance. You probably nevertheless behaved rationally in the first place, believing (albeit wrongly) that you were getting value for money.

Second, the term 'rational' does not imply any moral approval. It is simply referring to behaviour that is consistent with your own particular goals, behaviour directed to getting the most out of your limited income. People may well disapprove of the things that others buy – their clothes, their records, their cigarettes, their cans of lager – but that is making a judgement about their goals: their tastes or morality. As economists we cannot make judgements about what people's goals should be. We can, however, look at the implications of people behaving rationally in pursuit of those goals. This is what we are doing when we examine rational consumer behaviour: we are looking at its implications for consumer demand. KI6 p29

4.1 MARGINAL UTILITY THEORY

Total and marginal utility

People buy goods and services because they get satisfaction from them. Economists call this satisfaction 'utility'.

An important distinction must be made between *total utility* and *marginal utility*.

Total utility (*TU*) is the total satisfaction a person gains from all those units of a commodity consumed within a given time period. Thus if Tracey drank 10 cups of tea a day, her daily total utility from tea would be the satisfaction derived from those 10 cups.

Marginal utility (*MU*) is the additional satisfaction gained from consuming one *extra* unit within a given period of time. Thus we might refer to the marginal utility that Tracey gains from her third cup of tea of the day or her eleventh cup.

A difficulty arises immediately with the utility approach to explaining demand: how do you measure utility? Utility is subjective. There is no way of knowing what another person's experiences are really like. Just how satisfying does Brian find his first cup of tea in the morning? How does his utility compare with Tracey's? We do not have utility meters that can answer these questions!

For the moment, we will ignore this problem and assume that a person's utility can be measured in ***utils***, where a util is one unit of satisfaction.

Diminishing marginal utility

Up to a point, the more of a commodity you consume, the greater will be your total utility. However, as you become more satisfied, each *extra* unit that you consume will probably give you less additional utility than previous units. In other words, your marginal utility falls, the more you consume. This is known as the ***principle of diminishing marginal utility***.

Definitions

Rational consumer A person who weighs up the costs and benefits to him or her of each additional unit of a good purchased.

Total utility The total satisfaction a consumer gets from the consumption of all the units of a good consumed within a given time period.

Marginal utility The extra satisfaction gained from consuming one extra unit of a good within a given time period.

Util An imaginary unit of satisfaction from the consumption of a good.

Principle of diminishing marginal utility As more units of a good are consumed, additional units will provide less additional satisfaction than previous units.

Key Idea 13 ***The principle of diminishing marginal utility.*** The more of a product a person consumes, the less will be the additional utility gained from one more unit.

For example, the second cup of tea in the morning gives you less additional satisfaction than the first cup. The third cup gives less satisfaction still.

At some level of consumption, your total utility will be at a maximum. No extra satisfaction can be gained by the consumption of further units within that period of time. Thus marginal utility will be zero. Your desire for tea may be fully satisfied at 12 cups per day. A thirteenth cup will yield no extra utility. It may even give you displeasure (i.e. negative marginal utility).

Are there any goods or services where consumers do not experience diminishing marginal utility?

Total and marginal utility curves

If we could measure utility, we could construct a table showing how much total and marginal utility a person would gain at different levels of consumption of a particular commodity. This information could then be transferred to a graph. Table 4.1 and Figure 4.1 do just this. They show the imaginary utility that Darren gets from consuming packets of crisps.

Referring first to the table, if Darren consumes no crisps, he obviously gets no satisfaction from crisps: his total utility is zero. If he now consumes 1 packet a day, he gets 7 utils of satisfaction. (Sorry if this sounds silly, but we will tackle this question of measurement later.) His total utility is 7, and his marginal utility is also 7. They must be equal if only 1 unit is consumed.

If he now consumes a second packet, he gains an extra 4 utils (*MU*), giving him a total utility of 11 utils (i.e. 7 + 4). His marginal utility has fallen because, having already eaten 1 packet, he has less craving for a second. A third packet gives him less extra utility still: marginal utility has fallen to 2 utils, giving a total utility of 13 utils (i.e. 11 + 2).

Table 4.1 Darren's utility from consuming crisps (daily)

Packets of crisps consumed	*TU* in utils	*MU* in utils
0	0	–
1	7	7
2	11	4
3	13	2
4	14	1
5	14	0
6	13	−1

By the time he has eaten 5 packets, he would rather not eat any more. A sixth actually reduces his utility (from 14 utils to 13): its marginal utility is negative.

The information in Table 4.1 is plotted in Figure 4.1. Notice the following points about the two curves:

- The *MU* curve slopes downwards. This is simply illustrating the principle of diminishing marginal utility.
- The *TU* curve starts at the origin. Zero consumption yields zero utility.
- It reaches a peak when marginal utility is zero. When marginal utility is zero (at 5 packets of crisps), there is no addition to total utility. Total utility must be at the maximum – the peak of the curve.
- Marginal utility can be derived from the *TU* curve. It is the slope of the line joining two adjacent quantities on the curve. For example, the marginal utility of the third packet of crisps is the slope of the line joining points *a* and *b*. The slope of such a line is given by the formula:

Figure 4.1 Darren's utility from consuming crisps (daily)

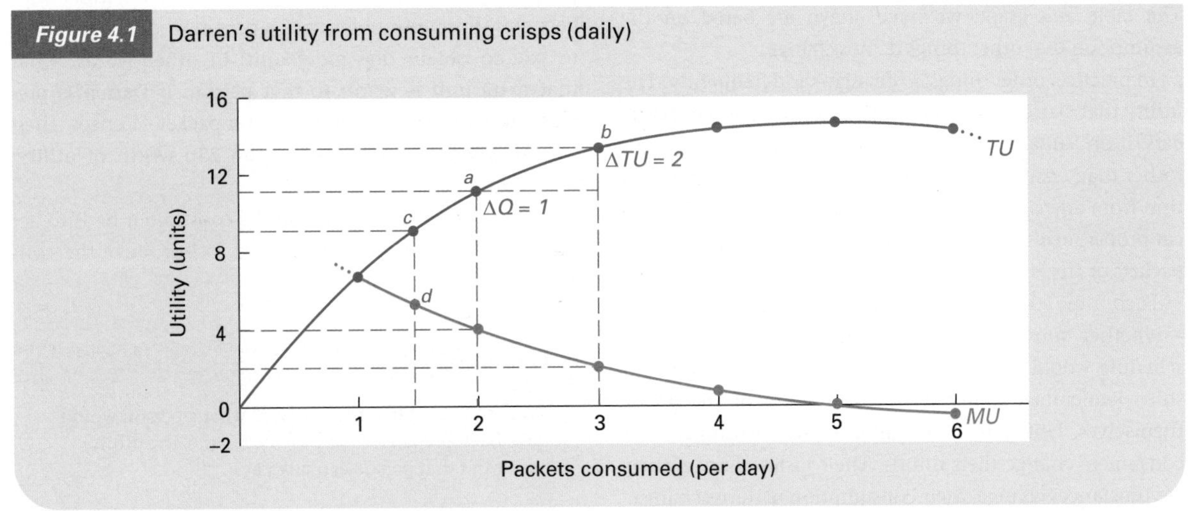

EXPLORING ECONOMICS *BOX 4.1

USING CALCULUS TO DERIVE A MARGINAL UTILITY FUNCTION

The relationship between total utility and marginal utility can be shown using calculus. If you are not familiar with the rules of calculus, ignore this box (or see Appendix 1, pp. A:9–12).

A consumer's typical utility function for a good might be of the form:

$$TU = 60Q - 4Q^2$$

where Q is the quantity of the good consumed.

This would give the figures shown in the following table.

Q	$60Q$	$-4Q^2$	=	TU
1	60	−4	=	56
2	120	−16	=	104
3	180	−36	=	144
4	240	−64	=	176
.	.	.		.

Complete this table to the level of consumption at which TU is at a maximum.

Marginal utility is the first derivative of total utility. In other words, it is the rate of *change* of total utility. Differentiating the *TU* function gives:

$$MU = \frac{dTU}{dQ} = 60 - 8Q$$

This gives the figures shown in the following table.

Q	60	$-8Q$	=	MU
1	60	−8	=	52
2	60	−16	=	44
3	60	−24	=	36
4	60	−32	=	28
.	.	.		.

Note that the marginal utility diminishes.

The *MU* function we have derived is a straight-line function. If, however, the *TU* function contained a cubed term (Q^3), the *MU* function would be a curve.

Derive the MU function from the following TU function:

$$TU = 200Q - 25Q^2 + Q^3$$

From this MU function, draw up a table (like the one above) up to the level of Q where MU becomes negative. Graph these figures.

$$\frac{\Delta TU}{\Delta Q} \quad (= MU)$$

In our example $\Delta TU = 2$ (total utility has risen from 11 to 13 utils), and $\Delta Q = 1$ (one more packet of crisps has been consumed). Thus $MU = 2$.

If Darren were to consume more and more crisps, would this total utility ever (a) fall to zero; (b) become negative? Explain.

The ceteris paribus *assumption*

The table and graph we have drawn are based on the assumption that other things do not change.

In practice, other things *do* change – and frequently. The utility that Darren gets from crisps depends on what else he eats. If on Saturday he has a lot to eat, and nibbles snacks (other than crisps) between meals, he will get little satisfaction from crisps. If on Monday, however, he is too busy to eat proper meals, he would probably welcome one or more packets of crisps.

Each time the consumption of *other* goods changed – whether substitutes or complements – a new utility schedule would have to be drawn up. The curves would shift. Remember, utility is not a property of the goods themselves. Utility is in the mind of the consumer, and consumers change their minds. Their tastes change; their circumstances change; their consumption patterns change.

The optimum level of consumption: the simplest case – one commodity

Just how much of a good should people consume if they are to make the best use of their limited income? To answer this question we must tackle the problem of how to measure utility, given that in practice we cannot measure 'utils'.

One solution to the problem is to measure utility with money. In this case, utility becomes the value that people place on their consumption. Marginal utility thus becomes the amount of money a person would be prepared to pay to obtain one more unit: in other words, what that extra unit is worth to that person. If Darren is prepared to pay 25p to obtain an extra packet of crisps, then we can say that packet yields him 25p worth of utility: $MU = 25\text{p}$.

So how many packets should he consume if he is to act rationally? To answer this we need to introduce the concept of ***consumer surplus***.

Definition

Consumer surplus The excess of what a person would have been prepared to pay for a good (i.e. the utility) over what that person actually pays.

Marginal consumer surplus

Marginal consumer surplus (*MCS*) is the difference between what you are willing to pay for one more unit of a good and what you are actually charged. If Darren were willing to pay 25p for another packet of crisps which in fact only cost him 20p, he would be getting a marginal consumer surplus of 5p.

$$MCS = MU - P$$

Total consumer surplus

Total consumer surplus (*TCS*) is the sum of all the marginal consumer surpluses that you have obtained from all the units of a good you have consumed. It is the difference between the total utility from all the units and your expenditure on them. If Darren consumes four packets of crisps, and if he would have been prepared to spend £1.20 on them and only had to spend 80p, then his total consumer surplus is 40p.

$$TCS = TU - TE$$

where *TE* is the total expenditure on a good: i.e. $P \times Q$.

TC 2 p10

Let us define ***rational consumer behaviour*** as the attempt to maximise consumer surplus. How do people set about doing this?

People will go on purchasing additional units as long as they gain additional consumer surplus: in other words, as long as the price they are prepared to pay exceeds the price they are charged ($MU > P$). But as more units are purchased, so they will experience diminishing marginal utility. They will be prepared to pay less and less for each additional unit. Their marginal utility will go on falling until $MU = P$: i.e. until no further consumer surplus can be gained. At that point, they will stop purchasing additional units. Their optimum level of consumption has been reached: consumer surplus has been maximised. If they continue to purchase beyond this point, *MU* would be less than *P*, and thus they would be paying more for the last units than they were worth to them.

The process of maximising consumer surplus can be shown graphically. Let us take the case of Tina's annual purchases of petrol. Tina has her own car, but as an alternative she can use public transport or walk. To keep the analysis simple, let us assume that Tina's parents bought her the car and pay the licence duty, and that Tina does not have the option of selling the car. She does, however, have to buy the petrol. The current price is 80p per litre. Figure 4.2 shows her consumer surplus.

Figure 4.2 Tina's consumer surplus from petrol

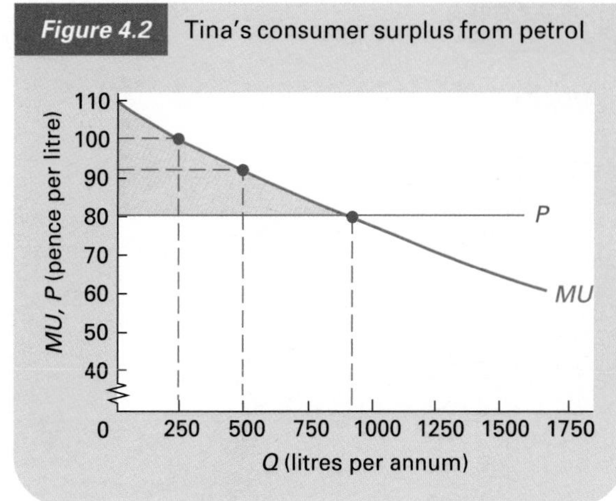

If she were to use just a few litres per year, she would use them for very important journeys for which no convenient alternative exists. For such trips she may be prepared to pay up to £1.10 per litre. For the first few litres, then, she is getting a marginal utility of around £1.10 per litre, and hence a marginal consumer surplus of around 30p (i.e. £1.10 − 80p).

By the time her annual purchase is around 250 litres, she would be prepared to pay only around £1 for additional litres. The additional journeys, although still important, would be less vital. Perhaps these are journeys where she could have taken public transport, albeit at some inconvenience. Her marginal consumer surplus at 250 litres is 20p (i.e. £1.00p − 80p).

Gradually, additional litres give less and less additional utility as less and less important journeys are undertaken. The 500th litre yields 91p worth of extra utility. Marginal consumer surplus is now 11p (i.e. 91p − 80p).

KI 13 p93

By the time she gets to the 900th litre, Tina's marginal utility has fallen to 80p. There is no additional consumer surplus to be gained. Her total consumer surplus is at a maximum. She thus buys 900 litres, where $P = MU$.

Her total consumer surplus is the sum of all the marginal consumer surpluses: the sum of all the 900 vertical lines between the price and the *MU* curve. This is shown by the total *area* between *P* and *MU* up to 900 litres (i.e. the pink shaded area in Figure 4.2).

This analysis can be expressed in general terms. In Figure 4.3, if the price of a commodity is P_1, the consumer will consume Q_1. The person's total expenditure (*TE*) is P_1Q_1, shown by area 1. Total utility (*TU*) is the area under the

Definitions

Marginal consumer surplus The excess of utility from the consumption of one more unit of a good (*MU*) over the price paid: $MCS = MU - P$.

Total consumer surplus The excess of a person's total utility from the consumption of a good (*TU*) over the total amount that person spends on it (*TE*): $TCS = TU - TE$.

Rational consumer behaviour The attempt to maximise total consumer surplus.

Figure 4.3 Consumer surplus

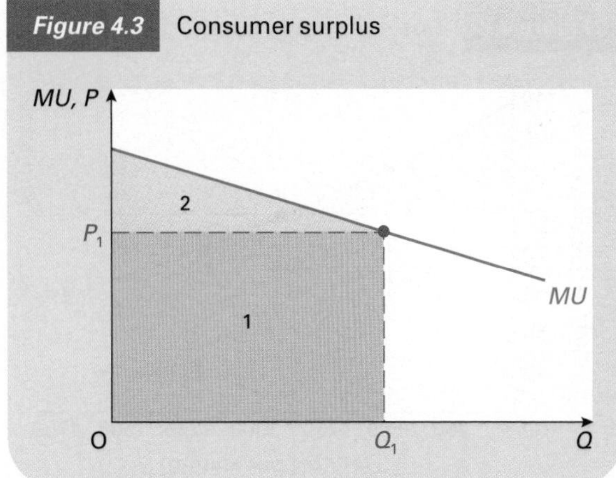

Figure 4.4 An individual person's demand curve

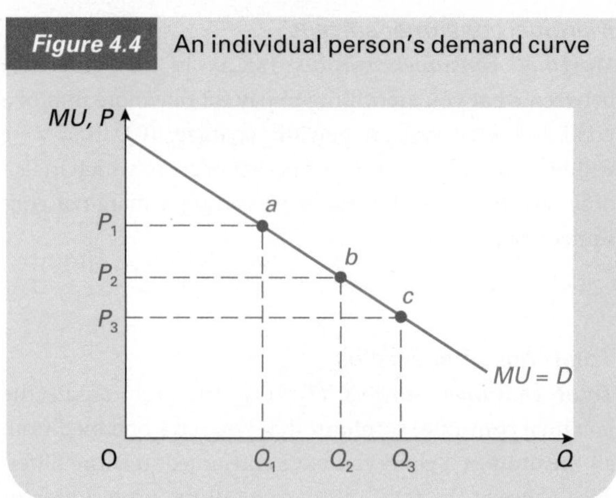

marginal utility curve: i.e. areas 1 + 2. Total consumer surplus ($TU - TE$) is shown by area 2.

? *If a good were free, why would total consumer surplus equal total utility? What would be the level of marginal utility at the equilibrium level of consumption?*

Marginal utility and the demand curve for a good

An individual's demand curve

Individual people's demand curve for any good will be the same as their marginal utility curve for that good, where utility is measured in money.

This is demonstrated in Figure 4.4, which shows the marginal utility curve for a particular person and a particular good. If the price of the good were P_1, the person would consume Q_1: where $MU = P$. Thus point *a* would be one point on that person's demand curve. If the price fell to P_2, consumption would rise to Q_2, since this is where $MU = P_2$. Thus point *b* is a second point on the demand curve. Likewise if price fell to P_3, Q_3 would be consumed. Point *c* is a third point on the demand curve.

Thus as long as individuals seek to maximise consumer surplus and hence consume where $P = MU$, their demand curve will be along the same line as their marginal utility curve.

The market demand curve

The market demand curve will simply be the (horizontal) sum of all individuals' demand curves and hence *MU* curves.

The shape of the demand curve. The price elasticity of demand will reflect the rate at which *MU* diminishes. If there are close substitutes for a good, it is likely to have an elastic demand, and its *MU* will diminish slowly as consumption increases. The reason is that increased consumption of this product will be accompanied by *decreased* consumption of the alternative product(s). Since total consumption of this product *plus* the alternatives has increased only slightly (if at all), the marginal utility will fall only slowly.

For example, the demand for a certain brand of petrol is likely to have a fairly high price elasticity, since other brands are substitutes. If there is a cut in the price of Texaco petrol (assuming the prices of other brands stay constant), consumption of Texaco will increase a lot. The *MU* of Texaco petrol will fall slowly, since people consume less of other brands. Petrol consumption *in total* may be only slightly greater, and hence the *MU* of petrol only slightly lower.

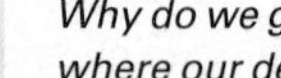

? *Why do we get less total consumer surplus from goods where our demand is relatively elastic?*

Shifts in the demand curve. How do *shifts* in demand relate to marginal utility? For example, how would the marginal utility of (and hence demand for) margarine be affected by a rise in the price of butter? The higher price of butter would cause less butter to be consumed. This would increase the marginal utility of margarine, since if people are using less butter, their desire for margarine is higher. The *MU* curve (and hence the demand curve) for margarine thus shifts to the right.

? *How would marginal utility and market demand be affected by a rise in the price of a complementary good?*

Weaknesses of the one-commodity version of marginal utility theory

A change in the consumption of one good will affect the marginal utility of substitute and complementary goods. It will also affect the amount of income left over to be spent on other goods. Thus a more satisfactory explanation of demand would involve an analysis of choices between goods, rather than looking at one good in isolation.

What is more, deriving a demand curve from a marginal utility curve measured in money assumes that money itself has a constant marginal utility. The trouble is that it does not. If people have a rise in income, they will consume more. Other things being equal, the marginal utility of the goods that they consume will diminish. Thus an extra £1 of

EXPLORING ECONOMICS

BOX 4.2

THE MARGINAL UTILITY REVOLUTION: JEVONS, MENGER, WALRAS

Solving the diamonds–water paradox

What determines the market value of a good? We already know the answer: demand and supply. So if we find out what determines the position of the demand and supply curves, we will at the same time be finding out what determines a good's market value.

This might seem obvious. Yet for years economists puzzled over just what determines a good's value.

Some economists like Karl Marx and David Ricardo concentrated on the supply side. For them, value depended on the amount of resources used in producing a good. This could be further reduced to the amount of *labour* time embodied in the good. Thus, according to the *labour theory of value*, the more labour that was directly involved in producing the good, or indirectly in producing the capital equipment used to make the good, the more valuable would the good be.

Other economists looked at the demand side. But here they came across a paradox.

Adam Smith in the 1760s gave the example of water and diamonds. 'How is it', he asked, 'that water which is so essential to human life, and thus has such a high "value-in-use", has such a low market value (or "value-in-exchange")? And how is it that diamonds which are relatively so trivial have such a high market value?' The answer to this paradox had to wait over a hundred years until the marginal utility revolution of the 1870s. William Stanley Jevons (1835–82) in England, Carl Menger (1840–1921) in Austria, and Leon Walras (1834–1910) in Switzerland all independently claimed that the source of the market value of a good was its *marginal* utility, not its *total* utility.

This was the solution to the diamonds–water paradox. Water, being so essential, has a high total utility: a high 'value in use'. But for most of us, given that we consume so much already, it has a very low marginal utility. Do you leave the cold tap running when you clean your teeth? If you do, it shows just how trivial water is to you *at the margin*. Diamonds, on the other hand, although they have a much lower total utility, have a much higher marginal utility. There are so few diamonds in the world, and thus people have so few of them, that they are very valuable at the margin. If, however, a new technique were to be discovered of producing diamonds cheaply from coal, their market value would fall rapidly. As people had more of them, so their marginal utility would rapidly diminish.

KI 13 p93

Marginal utility still only gives the demand side of the story. The reason why the marginal utility of water is so low is that *supply* is so plentiful. Water is very expensive in Saudi Arabia! In other words, the full explanation of value must take into account both demand *and* supply.

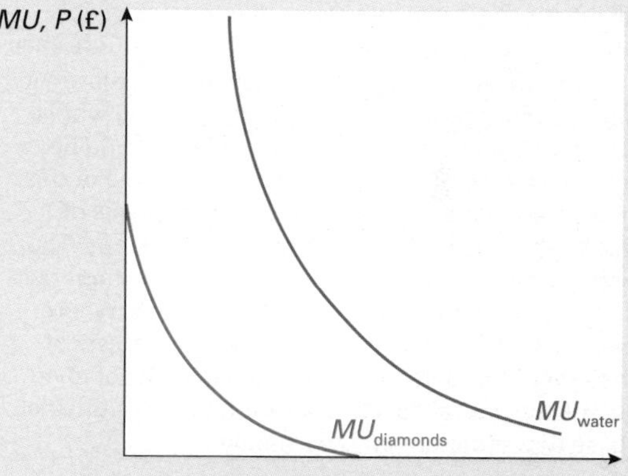

?

The diagram illustrates a person's MU curves of water and diamonds. Assume that diamonds are more expensive than water. Show how the MU of diamonds will be greater than the MU of water. Show also how the TU of diamonds will be less than the TU of water. (Remember: TU is the area under the MU curve.)

consumption will bring less satisfaction than previously. In other words, it is likely that the *marginal utility of money diminishes as income rises*.

Unless a good occupies only a tiny fraction of people's expenditure, a fall in its price will mean that their real income has increased: i.e. they can afford to purchase more goods in general. As they do so, the marginal utility of their money will fall. We cannot, therefore, legitimately use money to measure utility in an absolute sense. We can, however, still talk about the relative utility that we get from various goods for a given increase in expenditure.

The following sections thus look at the choice between goods, and how it relates to marginal utility.

The optimum combination of goods consumed

We can use marginal utility analysis to show how a rational person decides what combination of goods to buy. Given that we have limited incomes, we have to make choices. It is not just a question of choosing between two obvious substitutes (like carrots and peas or a holiday in Greece and one in Spain), but about allocating our incomes between all the goods and services we might like to consume. If you have, say, an income of £10 000 per year, what is the optimum 'bundle' of goods and services for you to spend it on?

CASE STUDIES AND APPLICATIONS

CHOICES WITHIN THE HOUSEHOLD

Is what's best for the individual best for the family?

Many of the choices we make are not made as individuals purely for ourselves. If you are a member of a family or living with friends, many of your 'consumption' decisions will affect the other members of the household and many of their decisions will affect you.

Some things will be decided jointly: what to have for dinner, what colour to paint the hall, whether to have a party. Put this another way: when you gain utility, the other members of the household will often gain too (e.g. from things 'jointly' consumed, such as central heating).

Sometimes, however, it is the other way round. When things are jointly purchased, such as food, then one person's consumption will often be at the *expense* of other members of the household. 'Who's finished all the milk?' 'I want to watch a different television programme.' 'Why are you sitting in my favourite chair?'

What we are saying is that when individuals are in a group, such as a family, a club or an outing with a group of friends, their behaviour will affect and be affected by the other members of the group. For this reason, we have to amend our simple analysis of 'rational' choice. Let us consider two situations. The first is where people are trying to maximise their own self-interest within the group. The second is where people are genuinely motivated by the interests of the other members – whether from feelings of love, friendship, moral duty or whatever. We will consider these two situations within a family.

Self-interested behaviour

If you do not consider the other members of the family, this could rebound on you. For example, if you do not clean out the bath after you, or do not do your share of the washing up, or if you eat things that were bought for other family members, then you may have to 'pay the price'. Other family members may get cross with you, behave equally selfishly themselves or take sanctions against you (e.g. parents punishing their children for inconsiderate behaviour).

When considering doing things for their own benefit, therefore, the 'rational' person would at the very least consider the reactions of the other members of the family. We could still use the concept of marginal utility, however, to examine such behaviour. If marginal utility were greater than the price ($MU > P$), it would be 'rational' to do more of any given activity. Here, though, marginal utility would include utility not only from directly consuming goods or services within the household, but also from the favourable reactions to you from other family members. Likewise, marginal utility would be reduced if there were any unfavourable reaction from other family members. The 'price' (i.e. the marginal cost to you) would include not only the monetary costs to you of consuming something, but also any other sacrifice you make in order to consume it. In other words, the price would be the full opportunity cost.

Take first the case of goods or services jointly consumed, such as a family meal. Do you offer to cook dinner? If you were motivated purely by self-interest, you would do so if the marginal benefit (i.e. marginal utility) to you exceeded the marginal cost to you. The marginal benefit would include the benefit to you of consuming the meal, plus any pleasure you got from the approval of other family members, plus any entitlement to being let off other chores. The marginal cost to you would include any monetary costs to you

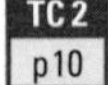

The rule for rational consumer behaviour is known as the ***equi-marginal principle***. This states that a consumer will get the highest utility from a given level of income when the ratio of the marginal utilities is equal to the ratio of the prices. Algebraically, this is when, for any pair of goods, A and B, that are consumed:

$$\frac{MU_A}{MU_B} = \frac{P_A}{P_B} \qquad (1)$$

> **Definition**
>
> **Equi-marginal principle (in consumption)** Consumers will maximise total utility from their incomes by consuming that combination of goods where:
>
> $$\frac{MU_A}{MU_B} = \frac{P_A}{P_B}$$

To see the sense of this, say that the last unit of good A you consumed gave three times as much utility as the last unit of B. Yet good A only cost twice as much as good B. You would obviously gain by increasing your consumption of A and cutting your purchases of B. But as you KI 13 p93 switched from B to A, the marginal utility of A would fall due to diminishing marginal utility, and conversely the marginal utility of B would rise. To maximise utility you would continue this substitution of A for B until the ratios of the marginal utilities (MU_A/MU_B) equalled the ratio of the prices of the two goods (P_A/P_B). At this point, no further gain can be made by switching from one good to another. This is the optimum combination of goods to consume.

Equation (1) is a specific example of the general equi-marginal principle in economics, which applies to all rational choices between two alternatives, whether in production, consumption, employment or whatever:

BOX 4.3

(e.g. of purchasing the ingredients) and the sacrifice of any alternative pleasurable activities that you had to forgo (such as watching television). Whether the actual preparation of the meal was regarded as a marginal benefit or a marginal cost would depend on whether the individual saw it as a pleasure or a chore.

Clearly, these benefits and costs are highly subjective: they are as you perceive them. But the principle is simple: if you were behaving purely out of self-interest, you would cook the meal if you felt that you would gain more from doing so than it cost you.

Now take the case of consuming something individually where it deprives another household member of consuming it (such as taking the last yoghurt from the fridge). Again, if you were behaving purely out of self-interest, you would have to weigh up the pleasure from that yoghurt against the cost to you of incurring the wrath of other family members (plus what they might do to you in return!).

Behaviour in the interests of the family as a whole

Most people are not totally selfish, especially when it comes to relating to other members of the family. Of course, there will be occasions when even the most caring of families will have to find ways of reconciling conflicting interests (such as what to watch on television), but on many occasions, consumption decisions are taken jointly by the family members in the interests of the family as a whole. In fact, family members are often willing to make personal sacrifices or put in considerable effort (e.g. with household chores or child rearing) for the sake of other family members, without being motivated by what they individually can get out of it.

In such cases, consumption decisions can be examined at two levels: that of the individual and that of the whole family.

As far as individuals are concerned, analysis in terms of their own marginal benefit and marginal cost would be too simplistic. Often it is a more accurate picture to see household members, rather than behaving selfishly, instead behaving in the self-interest of the whole household. So a decision about what food to buy for the family at the supermarket, if taken by an individual member, is likely to take into account the likes and dislikes of other family members, and the costs to the whole household budget. In other words, it is the whole family's marginal benefits and marginal costs that the individual family member is considering.

Then there is the question of one family member providing 'services' to other members: e.g. mothers caring for young children at home. The mother may make considerable personal *sacrifices* for the sake of the child. One family member's gain is another's cost. Here again, analysis in terms of marginal costs and marginal benefits is too simplistic. Rather than self-interest, parents are likely to be motivated by love and caring.

Imagine that you are going out for the evening with a group of friends. How would you decide where to go? Would this decision-making process be described as 'rational' behaviour?

Key Idea 14

The equi-marginal principle. The optimum amount of two alternatives consumed (or produced) will be where the marginal benefit ratios of the two alternatives are equal to their marginal cost ratios:

$$\frac{MB_A}{MB_B} = \frac{MC_A}{MC_B}$$

The multi-commodity version of marginal utility and the demand curve

How can we derive a demand curve from the above analysis?

Let us simply reinterpret equation (1) so that it relates the *MU* and *P* of good A to the *MU* and *P* of *any* other good. In other words, the equation would be the same for goods B, C, D, E and any other good. For any given income, and given prices for good A and all other goods, the quantity a person will demand of good A will be that which satisfies equation (1). One point on the individual's demand curve for good A has been determined.

If the price of good A now falls, such that:

$$\frac{MU_A}{MU_B} > \frac{P_A}{P_B} \text{ (and similarly for goods C, D, E, etc.)}$$

the person would buy more of good A and less of all other goods (B, C, D, E, etc.), until equation (1) is once more satisfied. A second point on the individual's demand curve for good A has been determined.

Further changes in the price of good A would bring further changes in the quantity demanded, in order to satisfy equation (1). Further points on the individual's demand curve would thereby be derived.

If the price of *another* good changed, or if the marginal utility of any good changed (including good A), then again the quantity demanded of good A (and other goods) would change, until again equation (1) were satisfied. These changes in demand will be represented by a *shift* in the demand curve for good A.

CASE STUDIES AND APPLICATIONS

BOX 4.4

TAKING ACCOUNT OF TIME

Can I spare the time to enjoy myself?

Do you take a taxi or go by bus? How long do you spend soaking in the bath? Do you go to the bother of cooking a meal or will you get a take-away?

We have argued that such decisions, if they are to be rational, should involve weighing up the relative marginal utilities of these activities against their relative marginal costs.

One crucial dimension we have ignored up to now is the *time* dimension. One of the opportunity costs of doing any activity is the sacrifice of time.

A take-away meal may be more expensive than a home-cooked one, but it saves you time. Part of the cost of the home-cooked meal, therefore, is the sacrifice of time involved. The full cost is therefore not just the cost of the ingredients and the fuel used, but also the opportunity cost of the alternative activities you have sacrificed while you were cooking.

Given the high-pressured lives many people lead in affluent countries, a high value is often put on time saved. Fast-food restaurants and supersonic jet travel are symptoms of this lifestyle.

Even pleasurable activities involve a time cost. The longer you spend doing pleasurable activity 'a', the less time you will have for doing pleasurable activity 'b'. The longer you laze in the bath, the less TV will you be able to watch (unless you have a TV in the bathroom!).

Section summary

1. The satisfaction people get from consuming a good is called 'utility'. Total utility is the satisfaction gained from the total consumption of a particular good over a given period of time. Marginal utility is the *extra* satisfaction gained from consuming *one more* unit of the good.
2. The marginal utility tends to fall the more that people consume. This is known as the 'principle of diminishing marginal utility'.
3. The utility that people get from consuming a good will depend on the amount of other goods they consume. A change in the amount of other goods consumed, whether substitutes or complements, will shift the total and marginal utility curves.
4. 'Rational' consumers will attempt to maximise their consumer surplus. Consumer surplus is the excess of people's utility (measured in money terms) over their expenditure on the good. This will be maximised by purchasing at the point where the *MU* of a good is equal to its price.
5. In the simple case where the price and consumption of other goods is held constant, a person's *MU* curve will lie along the same line as that person's demand curve.
6. The market demand curve is merely the horizontal sum of the demand curves of all the individual consumers. The elasticity of the market demand curve will depend on the rate at which marginal utility diminishes as more is consumed. This in turn depends on the number and closeness of substitute goods. If there are close substitutes, people will readily switch to this good if its price falls, and thus marginal utility will fall only slowly. The demand will be elastic.
7. Measuring the marginal utility of a good in money avoids the problem of using some imaginary unit such as utils, but it assumes that money has a constant utility. In reality, the marginal utility of money is likely to decrease as income rises.
8. A more satisfactory way of analysing the demand for goods is to look at people's choices between goods. A consumer will maximise utility from a given income by consuming according to the 'equi-marginal principle'. This states that goods should be consumed in that combination which equates the *MU*/*P* ratio for each good.

4.2 DEMAND UNDER CONDITIONS OF RISK AND UNCERTAINTY

The problem of imperfect information

So far we have assumed that when people buy goods and services, they know exactly what price they will pay and how much utility they will gain. In many cases this is a reasonable assumption. When you buy a bar of chocolate, you clearly do know how much you are paying for it and have a very good idea how much you will like it. But what about a video recorder, or a car, or a washing machine, or any other ***consumer durable***? In each of these cases you are buying something that will last you a long time, and the further

> **Definition**
>
> **Consumer durable** A consumer good that lasts a period of time, during which the consumer can continue gaining utility from it.

THINKING LIKE AN ECONOMIST — *THRESHOLD CONCEPT 9*

PEOPLE'S ACTIONS DEPEND ON THEIR EXPECTATIONS

Many, if not most, economic actions are taken *before* the benefits are enjoyed. Thus, you work first and get paid later – at the end of the week or month, or whatever. Similarly, you buy something in a shop today, and consume it later. In the case of a product like a food item from the supermarket, you will probably consume it fairly soon and pretty well all at once. In the case of many 'consumer durables', such as cars, furniture or electrical goods, you enjoy them over a much longer period.

It is the same with firms. What they produce today will be sold at some point in the future. In other words, firms typically incur costs first and receive revenues later. In the case of investing in new buildings or equipment, it may be a very long time before the firm starts earning money from the investment.

In each of these cases, then, the decision is made to do something now *in anticipation* of what will happen in the future. The *threshold concept* here is that decision making is only as good as the information on which it is based. If your expectations turn out to be wrong, a seemingly good decision may turn out disastrously – as many failed businesses bear witness! Part of what we do as economists is to examine how people get information and on what basis they form their expectations. Part of what we do is to forecast the future.

Whenever information about the future is imperfect, as it nearly always will be, then there are risks involved in basing decisions on such information. Businesses constantly have to live with risk: risk that market prices will decline, that costs will rise, that supplies will not arrive, that machinery will break down, that competitors will launch new and better products, and so on. But in our everyday lives, we too face risks because of poor information about the future. Do you spend money on a holiday in this country and risk having a wet week? Do you go to the cinema to see a film, only to find out that you don't enjoy it?

Sometimes you lack information simply because you have not taken the time or paid the money to acquire it. This could apply to the specifications of a product. A little research could give you the information you require. Sometimes, however, the information is simply not available – at least not in the form that will give you certainty. A firm may do market research to find out what consumers want, but until a product is launched, it will not be certain how much will be sold. A market analyst may give you a forecast of what will happen to stock market prices or to the dollar/euro exchange rate, but analysts frequently get it wrong.

1. ***What risks are involved in buying a house?***
2. ***Give some examples of ways in which it is possible to buy better information. Your answer should suggest that there is profitable business to be made in supplying information.***

into the future you look, the less certain you will be of its costs and benefits to you.

Take the case of a washing machine costing you £400. If you pay cash, your immediate outlay involves no uncertainty: it is £400. But washing machines can break down. In two years' time you could find yourself with a repair bill of £100. This cannot be predicted and yet it is a price you will have to pay, just like the original £400. In other words, when you buy the washing machine, you are uncertain as to the full 'price' it will entail over its lifetime.

If the costs of the washing machine are uncertain, so too are the benefits. You might have been attracted to buy it in the first place by the manufacturer's glossy brochure, or by the look of it, or by adverts on TV, in magazines, etc. When you have used it for a while, however, you might discover things you had not anticipated. Perhaps the spin dryer does not get your clothes as dry as you had hoped; it is noisy; it leaks; the door sticks; and so on.

Buying consumer durables thus involves uncertainty. So too does the purchase of assets, whether a physical asset such as a house or financial assets such as shares. In the case of assets, the uncertainty is over their future *price*. If you buy shares in a company, what will happen to their price? Will it shoot up, thus enabling you to sell them at a large profit, or will it fall? You cannot know for certain.

Key Idea 15 ***Good decision making requires good information.*** Where information is poor, decisions and their outcomes may be poor.

The problems surrounding making decisions today based on expectations of the future are explored in Threshold Concept 9.

TC 9 p101

Attitudes towards risk and uncertainty

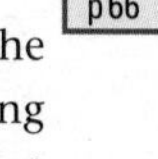

KI 11 p66

So how will uncertainty affect people's behaviour? The answer is that it depends on their attitudes towards taking a gamble. To examine these attitudes let us assume that a person does at least know the *odds* of the gamble. In other words, the person is operating under conditions of *risk* rather than *uncertainty*.

Define 'risk' and 'uncertainty' (see pages 64–6).

To illustrate different attitudes towards risk, consider the case of gambling that a particular number will come up on the throw of a dice. There is a one in six chance of this happening. Would you gamble? It depends on what odds you were offered and on your attitude to risk.

Odds can be of three types. They can be *favourable* odds. This is where on average you will gain. If, for example, you were offered odds of 10 to 1 on the throw of a dice, then for a £1 bet you would get nothing if you lost, but you would get £10 (plus your £1 stake) if your number came up. Since your number should come up on average one time in every six, on average you will gain. The longer you go on playing, the more money you are likely to win. If the odds were 5 to 1 (i.e. you win £5 plus get your £1 stake back), they would be *fair* odds. On average you would break even. If, however, they were less than 5 to 1, they would be described as *unfavourable*. On average you would lose.

? *Give some examples of gambling (or risk taking in general) where the odds are (a) unfavourable; (b) fair; (c) favourable.*

There are three possible categories of attitude towards risk.

Risk neutral. This is where a person will take a gamble if the odds are favourable; not take a gamble if the odds are unfavourable; and be indifferent about taking a gamble if the odds are fair.

Risk loving. Such a person is prepared to take a gamble even if the odds are unfavourable. The more risk loving a person is, the worse the odds he or she will be prepared to accept.

Risk averse. Such a person may not be prepared to take a gamble even if the odds are favourable. The more risk averse people are, the better the odds would have to be to entice them to take a gamble. Few people are *totally risk averse* and thus totally unwilling to take a gamble. If I offered people a bet on the toss of a coin such that tails they pay me 10p and heads I pay them £100, few would refuse (unless on moral grounds).

Diminishing marginal utility of income and attitudes towards risk taking

Avid gamblers may be risk lovers. People who spend hours in the betting shop or at the race track may enjoy the risks, knowing that there is always the chance that they might win. On average, however, such people will lose. After all, the bookies have to take their cut and thus the odds are generally unfavourable.

Most people, however, for most of the time are risk averse. We prefer to avoid insecurity. But why? Is there a simple reason for this? Economists use marginal utility analysis to explain why.

They argue that the gain in utility to people from an extra £100 is less than the loss of utility from forgoing £100. Imagine your own position. You have probably adjusted your standard of living to your income (or are trying to!). If you unexpectedly gained £100, that would be very nice: you could buy some new clothes or have a weekend away. But if you lost £100, it could be very hard indeed. You might have very serious difficulties in making ends meet. Thus if you were offered the gamble of a 50:50 chance of winning or losing £100, you would probably decline the gamble.

? *Which gamble would you be more likely to accept, a 60:40 chance of gaining or losing £10 000, or a 40:60 chance of gaining or losing £1? Explain why.*

This risk-averting behaviour accords with the principle of *diminishing marginal utility*. Up to now in this chapter we have been focusing on the utility from the consumption of individual goods: Tracey and her cups of tea; Darren and his packets of crisps. In the case of each individual good, the more we consume, the less satisfaction we gain from each additional unit: the marginal utility falls. But the same principle applies if we look at our *total* consumption. The higher our level of total consumption, the less additional satisfaction will be gained from each additional £1 spent. What we are saying here is that there is a ***diminishing marginal utility of income***. The more you earn, the lower will be the utility gained from each *extra* £1. If people on low incomes earn an extra £100, they will feel a lot better off: their marginal utility from that income will be very high. If rich people earn an extra £100, however, their gain in utility will be less.

? *Do you think that this provides a moral argument for redistributing income from the rich to the poor? Does it prove that income should be so redistributed?*

Why, then, does a diminishing marginal utility of income make us risk averse? The answer is illustrated in Figure 4.5, which shows the *total* utility you get from your income.

The slope of this curve gives the *marginal* utility of your income. As the marginal utility of income diminishes, so the curve gets flatter. A rise in income from £5000 to £10 000 will cause a movement along the curve from point *a* to point *b*. Total utility rises from U_1 to U_2. A similar rise in income from £10 000 to £15 000, however, will lead to a move from point *b* to point *c*, and hence a *smaller* rise in total utility from U_2 to U_3.

Now assume that your income is £10 000 and you are offered a chance of gambling £5000 of it. You are offered the fair odds of a 50:50 chance of gaining an extra £5000 (i.e. doubling it) or losing it. Effectively, then, you have an equal chance of your income rising to £15 000 or falling to £5000.

Definition

Diminishing marginal utility of income Where each additional pound earned yields less additional utility.

Figure 4.5 The total utility of income given diminishing marginal utility

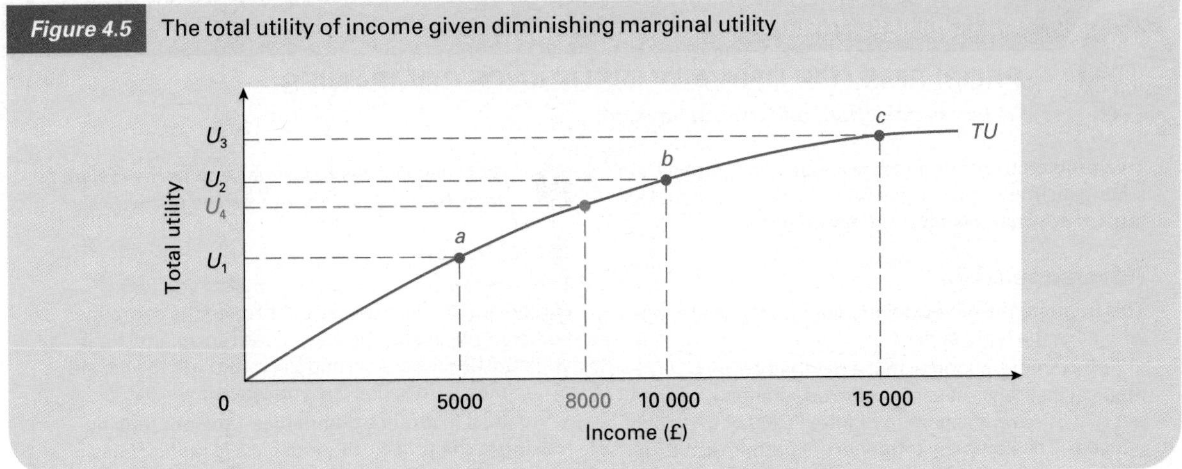

At an income of £10 000, your total utility is U_2. If your gamble pays off and raises your income to £15 000, your total utility will rise to U_3. If it does not pay off, you will be left with only £5000 and a utility of U_1. Given that you have a 50:50 chance of winning, your *average* expected utility will be midway between U_1 and U_3 (i.e. $\frac{(U_1 + U_3)}{2}$) = U_4. But this is the utility that would be gained from an income of £8000. Given that you would prefer U_2 to U_4 you will choose not to take the gamble.

TC 2 p10 Thus risk aversion is part of rational utility-maximising behaviour.

If people are generally risk averse, why do so many around the world take part in national lotteries?

On most occasions we do know the odds of taking a gamble. In other words, we will be operating under conditions of *uncertainty*. This could make us very cautious indeed. The more pessimistic we are, the more cautious we are.

KI 11 p66

Insurance: a way of removing risks

Insurance is the opposite of gambling. It takes the risk away. If, for example, you risk losing your job if you are injured, you can remove the risk of loss of income by taking out an appropriate insurance policy.

Since people are risk averse, they will be prepared to pay the premiums even though they give them 'unfair odds'. The total premiums paid to an insurance company will be *more* than the amount it pays out: that is how such companies make a profit.

But does this mean that an insurance company is less risk averse than its customers? Why is it prepared to shoulder the risks that its customers were not? The answer is that the insurance company is able to ***spread its risks***.

The spreading of risks

Suppose that each year there is a one in a hundred chance of your house burning down. Although this is only a small chance, it would be so disastrous that you are simply not prepared to take the risk. You thus take out house insurance and are prepared to pay a premium of *more than* 1 per cent (one in a hundred).

The insurance company, however, is not just insuring you. It is insuring thousands of others at the same time. If your house burns down, there will be approximately 99 others that do not. The premiums the insurance company has collected will be more than enough to cover its payments. The more houses it insures, the smaller will be the variation in the proportion that actually burn down each year.

This is an application of the ***law of large numbers***. What is unpredictable for an individual becomes highly predictable in the mass. The more people the insurance company insures, the more predictable is the total outcome.

What is more, the insurance company is in a position to estimate just what the risks are. It can thus work out what

Definitions

Spreading risks (for an insurance company) The more policies an insurance company issues and the more independent the risks of claims from these policies are, the more predictable will be the number of claims.

Law of large numbers The larger the number of events of a particular type, the more predictable will be their average outcome.

EXPLORING ECONOMICS

BOX 4.5

PROBLEMS FOR UNWARY INSURANCE COMPANIES

'Adverse selection' and 'moral hazard'

Two problems encountered by insurance companies in setting insurance premiums (the price of insurance) are termed ***adverse selection*** and ***moral hazard***.

Adverse selection

This is where the people taking out insurance are those who have the highest risk.

For example, suppose that a company offers medical insurance. It surveys the population and works out that the average person requires £200 of treatment per year. The company thus sets the premium at £250 (the extra £50 to cover its costs and provide a profit). But it is likely that the people most likely to take out the insurance are those most likely to fall sick: those who have been ill before, those whose families have a history of illness, those in jobs that are hazardous to health, etc. These people on average may require £500 of treatment per year. The insurance company would soon make a loss.

But cannot the company then simply raise premiums to £550 or £600? It can, but the problem is that it will thereby be depriving the person of *average* health of reasonably priced insurance.

The answer is for the company to discriminate more carefully between people. You may have to fill out a questionnaire so that the company can assess your own particular risk and set an appropriate premium. There may need to be legal penalties for people caught lying!

What details does an insurance company require to know before it will insure a person to drive a car?

Moral hazard

This is where having insurance makes you less careful and thus increases your risk to the company. For example, if your bicycle is insured against theft, you may be less concerned to go through the hassle of chaining it up each time you leave it.

Again, if insurance companies work out risks by looking at the *total* number of bicycle thefts, these figures will understate the risks to the company because they will include thefts from *uninsured* people who are likely to be more careful.

?

How will the following reduce moral hazard?

(a) A no-claims bonus.

(b) You having to pay the first so many pounds of any claim.

(c) Offering lower premiums to those less likely to claim (e.g. lower house contents premiums for those with burglar alarms).

The problem of moral hazard occurs in many other walks of life. A good example is that of debt. If someone else is willing to pay your debts (e.g. your parents) it is likely to make you less careful in your spending! This argument has been used by some rich countries for not cancelling the debts of poor countries (see section 26.4).

premiums it must charge in order to make a profit. With individuals, however, the precise risk is rarely known. Do you know your chances of living to 70? Almost certainly you do not. But a life assurance company has the statistical data to work out precisely the chances of a person of your age, sex and occupation living to 70! It can convert your *uncertainty* into the company's *risk*.

The spreading of risks does not just require a large number of policies. It also requires the risks to be ***independent***. If an insurance company insured 1000 houses *all in the same neighbourhood*, and then there were a major fire in the area, the claims would be enormous. The risks of fire were not independent. The company would, in fact, have been taking a gamble on a single event. If, however, it provides fire insurance for houses scattered all over the country, the risks *are* independent.

1. *Why are insurance companies unwilling to provide insurance against losses arising from war or 'civil insurrection'?*
2. *Name some other events where it would be impossible to obtain insurance.*

Another way in which insurance companies can spread their risks is by ***diversification***. The more types of insurance a company offers (car, house, life, health, etc.), the greater is likely to be the independence of the risks.

Definitions

Adverse selection The tendency of those who are at greatest risk to take out insurance.

Moral hazard The temptation to take more risk when you know that other people (e.g. insurers) will cover the risks.

Independent risks Where two risky events are unconnected. The occurrence of one will not affect the likelihood of the occurrence of the other.

Diversification Where a firm expands into new types of business.

Section summary

1. When people buy consumer durables, they may be uncertain of their benefits and any additional repair and maintenance costs. When they buy financial assets, they may be uncertain of what will happen to their price in the future. Buying under these conditions of imperfect knowledge is therefore a form of gambling. When we take such gambles, if we know the odds we are said to be operating under conditions of *risk*. If we do not know the odds, we are said to be operating under conditions of *uncertainty*.
2. People can be divided into risk lovers, those who are risk averse and those who are risk neutral. Because of the diminishing marginal utility of income, it is rational for people to be risk averse (unless gambling is itself pleasurable).
3. Insurance is a way of eliminating risks for policy holders. Being risk averse, people are prepared to pay premiums in order to obtain insurance. Insurance companies, on the other hand, are prepared to take on these risks because they can spread them over a large number of policies. According to the law of large numbers, what is unpredictable for a single policy holder becomes highly predictable for a large number of them provided that their risks are independent of each other.

*4.3 INDIFFERENCE ANALYSIS

The limitations of the marginal utility approach to demand

Even though the multi-commodity version of marginal utility theory is useful in demonstrating the underlying logic of consumer choice, it still has a major weakness. Utility cannot be measured in any absolute sense. We cannot really say, therefore, by *how much* the marginal utility of one good exceeds another.

An alternative approach is to use *indifference analysis*. This does not involve measuring the *amount* of utility a person gains, but merely *ranking* various combinations of goods in order of preference. In other words, it assumes that consumers can decide whether they prefer one combination of goods to another. For example, if you were asked to choose between two baskets of fruit, one containing 4 oranges and 3 pears and the other containing 2 oranges and 5 pears, you could say which you prefer or whether you are indifferent between them. It does not assume that you can decide just *how much* you prefer one basket to another or just how much you like either.

The aim of indifference analysis, then, is to analyse, *without having to measure utility*, how a rational consumer chooses between two goods. As we shall see, it can be used to show the effect on this choice of (a) a change in the consumer's income and (b) a change in the price of one or both goods. It can also be used to analyse the income and substitution effects of a change in price.

Indifference analysis involves the use of *indifference curves* and *budget lines*.

Indifference curves

An ***indifference curve*** shows all the various combinations of two goods that give an equal amount of satisfaction or utility to a consumer.

To show how one can be constructed, consider the following example. Imagine that a supermarket is conducting a survey about the preferences of its customers for different types of fruit. One of the respondents is Clive, a student who likes a healthy diet and regularly buys fresh fruit. He is asked his views about various combinations of oranges and pears. Starting with the combination of 10 pears and 13 oranges, he is asked what other combinations he would like the same as this one. From his answers a table is constructed (Table 4.2). What we are saying here is that Clive would be equally happy to have any one of the combinations shown in the table.

This table is known as an ***indifference set***. It shows alternative combinations of two goods that yield the same level

Table 4.2 Combinations of pears and oranges that Clive likes the same amount as 10 pears and 13 oranges

Pears	Oranges	Point in Figure 4.6
30	6	*a*
24	7	*b*
20	8	*c*
14	10	*d*
10	13	*e*
8	15	*f*
6	20	*g*

Definitions

Indifference curve A line showing all those combinations of two goods between which a consumer is indifferent: i.e. those combinations that give the same level of utility.

Indifference set A table showing the same information as an indifference curve.

Figure 4.6 An indifference curve

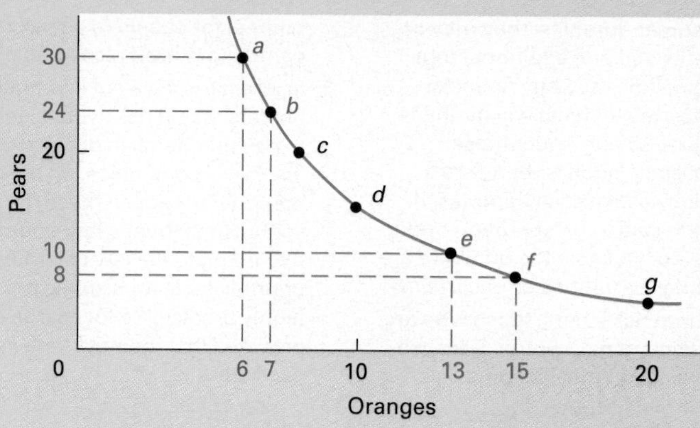

of satisfaction. From this we can plot an indifference curve. We measure units of one good on one axis and units of the other good on the other axis. Thus in Figure 4.6, which is based on Table 4.2, pears and oranges are measured on the two axes. The curve shows that Clive is indifferent as to whether he consumes 30 pears and 6 oranges (point *a*) or 24 pears and 7 oranges (point *b*) or any other combination of pears and oranges along the curve.

Notice that we are not saying *how much* Clive likes pears and oranges, merely that he likes all the combinations along the indifference curve the same amount. All the combinations thus yield the same (unspecified) utility.

The shape of the indifference curve

As you can see, the indifference curve we have drawn is not a straight line. It is bowed in towards the origin. In other words, its slope gets shallower as we move down the curve. Indifference curves are normally drawn this shape. But why?

Let us see what the slope of the curve shows us. It shows the rate at which the consumer is willing to exchange one good for the other, holding his or her level of satisfaction the same. For example, consider the move from point *a* to point *b* in Figure 4.6. Clive gives up 6 units of pears and requires 1 orange to compensate for the loss. The slope of the indifference curve is thus $-6/1 = -6$. Ignoring the negative sign, the slope of the indifference curve (that is, the rate at which the consumer is willing to substitute one good for the other) is known as the ***marginal rate of substitution*** (*MRS*). In this case, therefore, the $MRS = 6$.

Note that as we move down the curve, the marginal rate of substitution diminishes as the slope of the curve gets less. For example, look at the move from point *e* to point *f*. Here the consumer gives up 2 pears and requires 2 oranges to compensate. Thus along this section of the curve, the slope is $-2/2 = -1$ (and hence the $MRS = 1$).

The reason for a ***diminishing marginal rate of substitution*** is related to the *principle of diminishing marginal utility* KI 13 p93 that we looked at in section 4.1. This stated that individuals will gain less and less additional satisfaction the more of a good that they consume. This principle, however, is based on the assumption that the consumption of other goods is held *constant*. In the case of an indifference curve, this is not true. As we move down the curve, more of one good is consumed but *less* of the other. Nevertheless the effect on consumer satisfaction is similar. As Clive consumes more pears and fewer oranges, his marginal utility from pears will diminish, while that from oranges will increase. He will thus be prepared to give up fewer and fewer pears for each additional orange. *MRS* diminishes.

The relationship between the marginal rate of substitution and marginal utility

In Figure 4.6, consumption at point *a* yields equal satisfaction with consumption at point *b*. Thus the utility sacrificed by giving up 6 pears must be equal to the utility gained by consuming one more orange. In other words, the marginal utility of an orange must be six times as great as that of a pear. Therefore, $MU_{\text{oranges}}/MU_{\text{pears}} = 6$. But this is the same as the marginal rate of substitution. With X measured on the horizontal axis and Y on the vertical axis, then:

$$MRS = \frac{MU_X}{MU_Y} = \frac{\text{slope of indifference curve}}{\text{(ignoring negative sign)}}$$

Definitions

Marginal rate of substitution (between two goods in consumption) The amount of one good (Y) that a consumer is prepared to give up in order to obtain one extra unit of another good (X): i.e. $\Delta Y/\Delta X$.

Diminishing marginal rate of substitution The more a person consumes of good X and the less of good Y, the less additional Y will that person be prepared to give up in order to obtain an extra unit of X: i.e. $\Delta Y/\Delta X$ diminishes.

?

Although indifference curves will normally be bowed in towards the origin, on odd occasions they might not be. Which of the following diagrams correspond to which of the following?

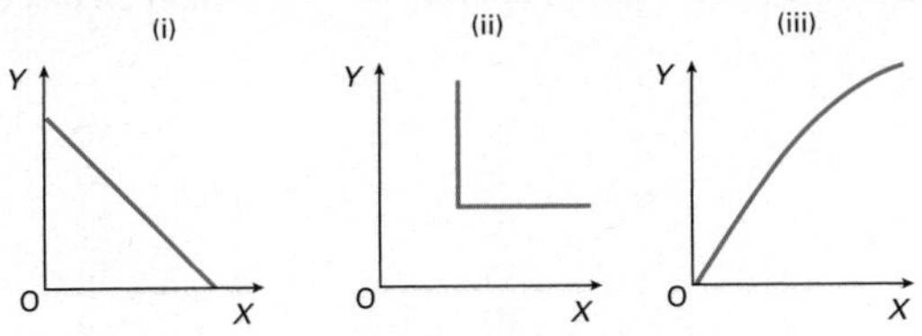

(a) X and Y are left shoes and right shoes.
(b) X and Y are two brands of the same product, and the consumer cannot tell them apart.
(c) X is a good but Y is a 'bad' – like household refuse.

An indifference map

More than one indifference curve can be drawn. For example, referring back to Table 4.2, Clive could give another set of combinations of pears and oranges that all give him a higher (but equal) level of utility than the set shown in the table. This could then be plotted in Figure 4.6 as another indifference curve.

Although the actual amount of utility corresponding to each curve is not specified, indifference curves further out to the right would show combinations of the two goods that yield a higher utility, and curves further in to the left would show combinations yielding a lower utility.

In fact, a whole ***indifference map*** can be drawn, with each successive indifference curve showing a higher level of utility. Combinations of goods along I_2 in Figure 4.7 give a higher utility to the consumer than those along I_1. Those along I_3 give a higher utility than those along I_2, and so on.

The term 'map' is appropriate here, because the indifference curves are rather like contours on a real map. Just as a contour joins all those points of a particular height, so an indifference curve shows all those combinations yielding a particular level of utility.

?

Draw another two indifference curves on Figure 4.6, one outward from and one inward from the original curve. Read off various combinations of pears and oranges along these two new curves and enter them on a table like Table 4.2.

The budget line

We turn now to the ***budget line***. This is the other important element in the analysis of consumer behaviour. Whereas indifference maps illustrate people's preferences, the *actual* choices they make will depend on their *incomes*. The budget line shows what combinations of two goods you are *able* to buy, given (a) your income available to spend on them and (b) their prices.

Just as we did with an indifference curve, we can construct a budget line from a table. The first two columns of Table 4.3 show various combinations of two goods X and Y that can be purchased assuming that (a) the price of X is £2 and the price of Y is £1 and (b) the consumer has a budget of £30 to be divided between the two goods.

In Figure 4.8, then, if you are limited to a budget of £30, you can consume any combination of X and Y along the line (or inside it). You cannot, however, afford to buy combinations that lie outside it: i.e. in the darker shaded area. This area is known as the *infeasible region* for the given budget.

Figure 4.7 An indifference map

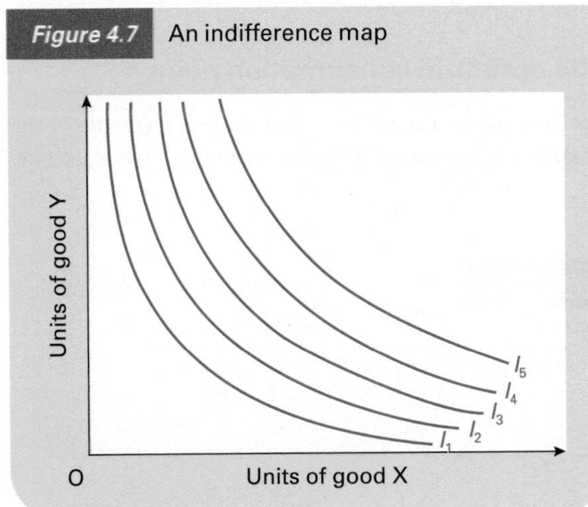

Figure 4.8 A budget line (budget of £30)

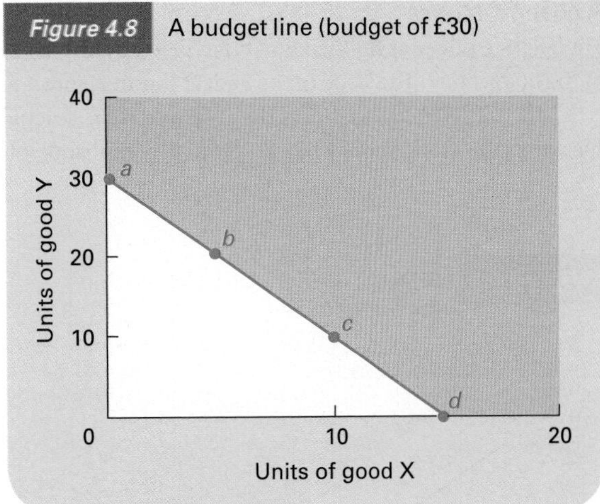

Definitions

Indifference map A graph showing a whole set of indifference curves. The further away a particular curve is from the origin, the higher the level of satisfaction it represents.

Budget line A graph showing all the possible combinations of two goods that can be purchased at given prices and for a given budget.

Table 4.3 Consumption possibilities for budgets of £30 and £40

Budget of £30			Budget of £40	
Units of good X	Units of good Y	Point on budget line in Figure 4.8	Units of good X	Units of good Y
0	30	*a*	0	40
5	20	*b*	5	30
10	10	*c*	10	20
15	0	*d*	15	10
			20	0

Note: It is assumed that $P_X = £2$, $P_Y = £1$.

We have said that the amount people can afford to buy will depend on (a) their budget and (b) the prices of the two goods. We can show how a change in either of these two determinants will affect the budget line.

A change in income

If the consumer's income (and hence budget) increases, the budget line will shift outwards, parallel to the old one. This is illustrated in the last two columns of Table 4.3 and in Figure 4.9, which show the effect of a rise in the consumer's budget from £30 to £40. (Note that there is no change in the prices of X and Y, which remain at £2 and £1 respectively.)

More can now be purchased. For example, if the consumer was originally purchasing 7 units of X and 16 units of Y (point *m*), this could be increased with the new budget of £40, to 10 units of X and 20 units of Y (point *n*) or any other combination of X and Y along the new higher budget line.

A change in price

The relative prices of the two goods are given by the *slope* of the budget line. The slope of the budget line in Figure 4.8 is 30/15 = 2. (We are ignoring the negative sign: strictly speaking, the slope should be –2.) Similarly, the slope of the new higher budget line in Figure 4.9 is 40/20 = 2. But in each case this is simply the ratio of the *price* of X (£2) to the *price* of Y (£1). Thus the slope of the budget line equals P_X/P_Y.

If the price of either good changes, the slope of the budget line will change. This is illustrated in Figure 4.10 which, like Figure 4.8, assumes a budget of £30 and an initial price of X of £2 and a price of Y of £1. The initial budget line is B_1.

Now let us assume that the price of X falls to £1 but that the price of Y remains the same (£1). The new budget line will join 30 on the Y axis with 30 on the X axis. In other words, the line pivots outwards on point *a*. If, instead, the price of Y changed, the line would pivot on point *b*.

?

1. *Assume that the budget remains at £30 and the price of X stays at £2, but that Y rises in price to £3. Draw the new budget line.*
2. *What will happen to the budget line if the consumer's income doubles and the prices of both X and Y double?*

The optimum consumption point

We are now in a position to put the two elements of the analysis together: the indifference map and a budget line.

Figure 4.9 Effect of an increase in income on the budget line

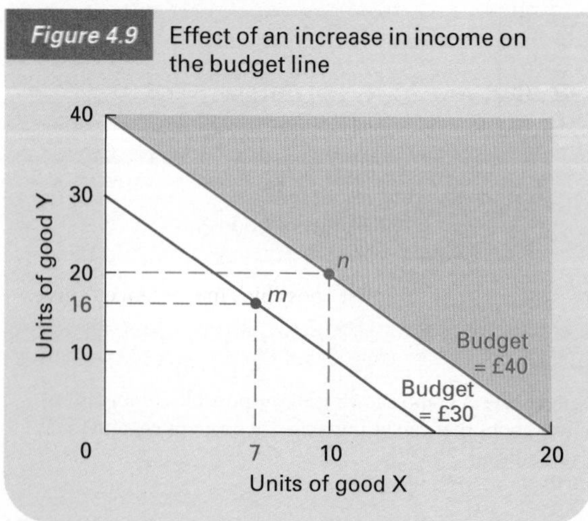

Figure 4.10 Effect on the budget line of a fall in the price of good X

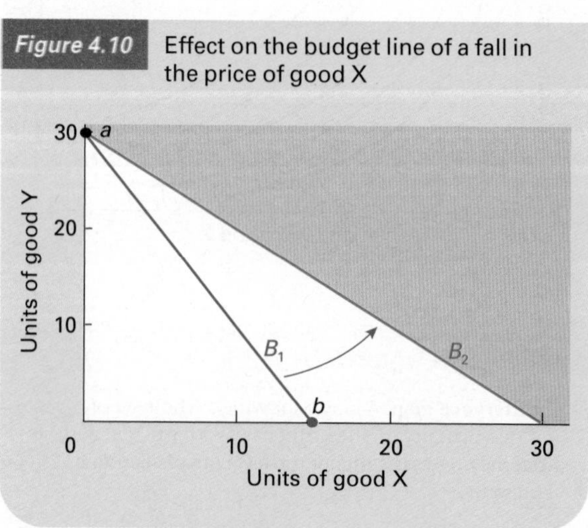

Figure 4.11 The optimum consumption point

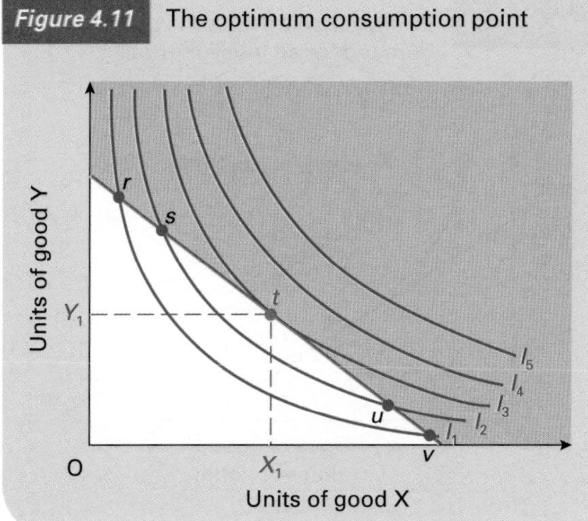

This will enable us to show how much of each of the two goods the 'rational' consumer will buy from a given budget. Let us examine Figure 4.11.

The consumer would like to consume along the highest possible indifference curve. This is curve I_3 at point *t*. Higher indifference curves, such as I_4 and I_5, although representing higher utility than curve I_3, are in the infeasible region: they represent combinations of X and Y that cannot be afforded with the current budget. The consumer *could* consume along curves I_1 and I_2, between points *r* and *v*, and *s* and *u* respectively, but they give a lower level of utility than consuming at point *t*.

TC 2 p10

The optimum consumption point for the consumer, then, is where the budget line touches (is 'tangential to') the highest possible indifference curve. At any other point along the budget line, the consumer would get a lower level of utility.

If the budget line is tangential to an indifference curve, they will have the same slope. (The slope of a curve is the slope of the tangent to it at the point in question.) But as we have seen:

$$\text{the slope of the budget line} = \frac{P_X}{P_Y}$$

$$\text{and the slope of the indifference curve} = MRS = \frac{MU_X}{MU_Y}$$

Therefore, at the optimum consumption point:

$$\frac{P_X}{P_Y} = \frac{MU_X}{MU_Y}$$

KI 14 p99

But this is the *equi-marginal principle* that we established in the first part of this chapter: only this time, using the indifference curve approach, there has been no need to measure utility. All we have needed to do is to observe, for any two combinations of goods, whether the consumer preferred one to the other or was indifferent between them.

***LOOKING AT THE MATHS**

We can express the optimum consumption point algebraically. With a limited budget of *B*, the objective is to maximise utility subject to this budget constraint. This can be expressed as:

$$\text{Max } TU(X,Y) \qquad (1)$$

subject to the budget constraint that:

$$P_X X + P_Y Y = B \qquad (2)$$

Equation (1) is known as the 'objective function' and says that the objective is to maximise utility, which depends on the consumption of two goods, X and Y. For example, assume that the utility function is:

$$TU = X^{3/4}Y^{1/4}$$

This is known as a 'Cobb–Douglas utility function' and will give smooth convex indifference curves. Assume also that the price of *X* is 4, the price of *Y* is 2 and the budget is 64. Thus:

$$4X + 2Y = 64$$

Rearranging this constraint to express *X* in terms of *Y* gives:

$$X = 16 - \frac{Y}{2}$$

By first substituting this value of *X* into the utility function (so that it is expressed purely in terms of *Y*) and then differentiating the resulting equation and setting it equal to zero, we can solve for the value of *Y* and then *X* that yields the maximum utility for the given budget. The answer is:

$$X = 12 \text{ and } Y = 8$$

The workings of this are given in Maths Case 4.1 on the book's website.

An alternative method, which is slightly longer but is likely to involve simpler calculations, involves the use of 'Lagrangian multipliers'. This method is explained, along with a worked example, in Maths Case 4.2.

The effect of changes in income

As we have seen, an increase in income is represented by a parallel shift outwards of the budget line (assuming no change in the price of X and Y). This will then lead to a new optimum consumption point on a higher indifference curve. A different consumption point will be found for each different level of income.

In Figure 4.12 a series of budget lines are drawn representing different levels of consumer income. The corresponding optimum consumption points (*r*, *s*, *t*, *u*) are shown. Each point is where the new higher budget line just touches the highest possible indifference curve.[1]

[1] We can always draw in an indifference curve that will be tangential to a given budget line. Just because we only draw a few indifference curves on a diagram, it does not mean that there are only a few *possible* ones. We could draw as many as we liked. Again it is rather like the contours on a real map. They may be drawn at, say, 10 metre intervals. We could, however, if we liked, draw them at 1 metre or even 1 cm intervals, or at whatever height was suitable to our purpose. For example, if the maximum height of a lake were 32.45 metres above sea level, it might be useful to draw a contour at that height to show what land might be liable to flooding.

Figure 4.12 Effect on consumption of a change in income

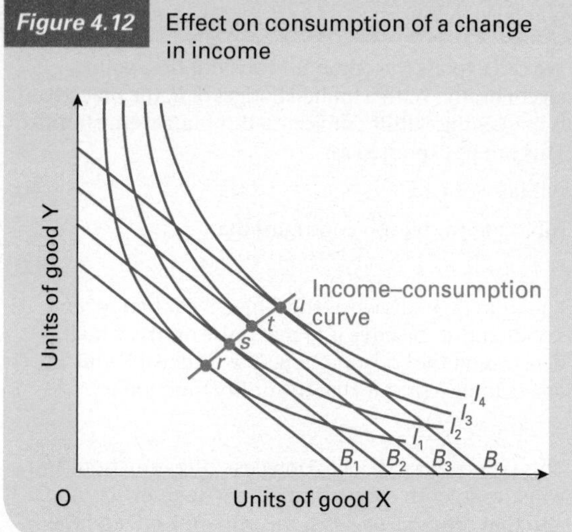

Figure 4.13 Effect of a rise in income on the demand for an inferior good

The line joining these points is known as the ***income–consumption curve***.

If your money income goes up and the price of goods does not change, we say that your ***real income*** has risen. In other words, you can buy more than you did before. But your real income can also rise even if you do not earn any more money. This will happen if prices fall. For the same amount of money, you can buy more goods than previously. We analyse the effect of a rise in real income caused by a fall in prices in just the same way as we did when money income rose and prices stayed the same. Provided the *relative* prices of the two goods stay the same (i.e. provided they fall by the same percentage), the budget line will shift outwards parallel to the old one.

Income elasticity of demand and the income–consumption curve

The income–consumption curve in Figure 4.12 shows that the demand for both goods rises as income rises. Thus both goods have a positive income elasticity of demand: they are both normal goods.

KI 9 p 58

Now let us focus just on good X. If the income–consumption curve became flatter at higher levels of income, it would show an increasing proportion of income being spent on X. The flatter it became, the higher would be the income elasticity of demand for X.

If, by contrast, X were an inferior good, such as cheap margarine, its demand would fall as income rose; its income elasticity of demand would be negative. This is illustrated in Figure 4.13. Point *b* is to the left of point *a*, showing that at the higher income B_2, less X is purchased.

?

1. *The income–consumption curve in Figure 4.13 is drawn as positively sloped at low levels of income. Why?*
2. *Show the effect of a rise in income on the demand for X and Y, where this time Y is the inferior good and X is the normal good. Is the income–consumption curve positively or negatively sloped?*

The effect of changes in price

If either X or Y changes in price, the budget line will 'pivot'. Take the case of a reduction in the price of X (but no change in the price of Y). If this happens, the budget line will swing outwards. We saw this effect in Figure 4.10 (on page 108). These same budget lines are reproduced in Figure 4.14, but this time we have added indifference curves.

The old optimum consumption point was at *j*. After the reduction in the price of good X, a new optimum consumption point is found at *k*.

?

Illustrate on an indifference diagram the effects of the following:

(a) A rise in the price of good X (assuming no change in the price of Y).

(b) A fall in the price of good Y (assuming no change in the price of X).

A series of budget lines could be drawn, all pivoting round point *a* in Figure 4.14. Each one represents a different price of good X, but with money income and the price of Y held constant. The flatter the curve, the lower the price of X. At each price, there will be an optimum consumption

Definitions

Income–consumption curve A line showing how a person's optimum level of consumption of two goods changes as income changes (assuming the prices of the goods remain constant).

Real income Income measured in terms of how much it can buy. If your *money* income rises by 10 per cent, but prices rise by 8 per cent, you can buy only 2 per cent more goods than before. Your *real* income has risen by 2 per cent.

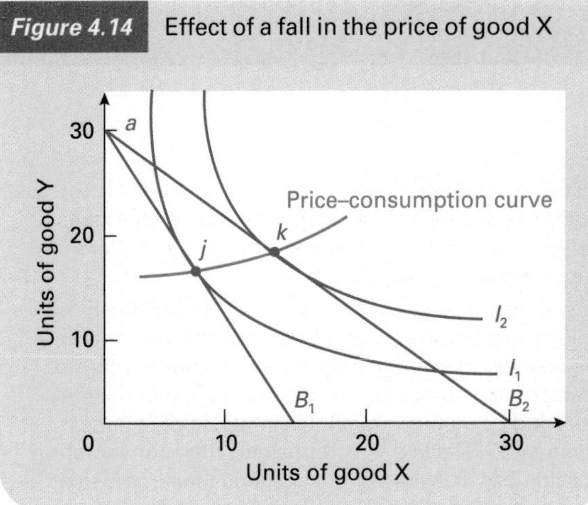

Figure 4.14 Effect of a fall in the price of good X

point. The line that connects these points is known as the ***price–consumption curve***.

Deriving the individual's demand curve

We can use the analysis of price changes to show how in theory a person's demand curve for a product can be derived. To do this we need to modify the diagram slightly.

Let us assume that we want to derive a person's demand curve for good X. What we need to show is the effect on the consumption of X of a change in the price of X assuming the prices of all other goods are held constant. To do this we need to redefine good Y. Instead of being a *single* good, Y becomes the total of *all other* goods. But what units are we to put on the vertical axis? Each of these other goods will be in different units: litres of petrol, loaves of bread, kilograms of cheese, numbers of haircuts, etc. We cannot add them all up unless we first convert them to a common unit. The answer is to measure them as the total amount of money spent on them: i.e. what is *not* spent on good X.

With expenditure on all other goods plotted on the vertical axis and with income, tastes and the price of all other goods held constant, we can now derive the demand curve for X. This is demonstrated in Figure 4.15.

We illustrate the changes in the price of X by pivoting the budget line on the point where it intersects the vertical axis. It is then possible, by drawing a price–consumption line, to show the amount of X demanded at each price. It is then a simple matter of transferring these price–quantity relationships on to a demand curve. In Figure 4.15, each of the points *a*, *b*, *c* and *d* on the demand curve in the lower

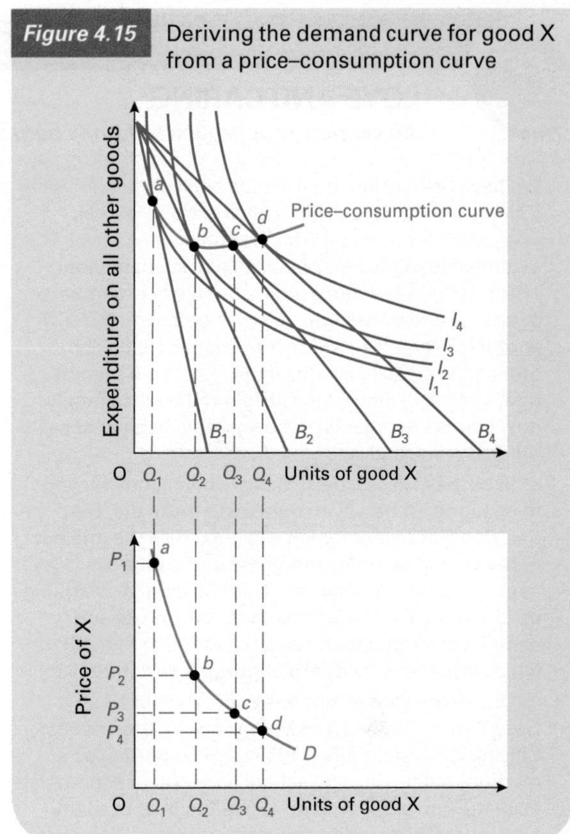

Figure 4.15 Deriving the demand curve for good X from a price–consumption curve

part of the diagram corresponds to one of the four points on the price–consumption curve. (Note that P_2 is half of P_1, P_3 is one-third of P_1 and P_4 is one-quarter of P_1.)

? *As quantity demanded increases from Q_1 to Q_2 in Figure 4.15, the expenditure on all other goods decreases. (Point b is lower than point a.) This means, therefore, that the person's total expenditure on X has correspondingly increased. What, then, can we say about the person's price elasticity of demand for X between points a and b? What can we say about the price elasticity of demand between points b and c, and between points c and d?*

The income and substitution effects of a price change

In Chapter 2 we argued that when the price of a good rises, consumers will purchase less of it for two reasons:

- They cannot afford to buy so much. This is the ***income effect***.

Definitions

Price–consumption curve A line showing how a person's optimum level of consumption of two goods changes as the price of one of the two goods changes (assuming that income and the price of the other good remain constant).

Income effect of a price change That portion of the change in quantity demanded that results from the change in real income.

CASE STUDIES AND APPLICATIONS

LOVE AND CARING

An economic approach to family behaviour

We have been using indifference analysis to analyse a single individual's choices between two goods. The principles of rational choice, however, can be extended to many other fields of human behaviour. These include situations where people are members of groups and where one person's behaviour affects another. Examples include how friends treat each other, how sexual partners interrelate, how parents treat children, how chores are shared out in a family, how teams are organised, how people behave to each other at work, and so on.

In all these cases, decisions are constantly having to be made. Generally people try to make the 'best' decisions, decisions which will maximise the interests of the individual or the members of the group, decisions that are 'rational'. This will involve weighing up (consciously or subconsciously) the costs and benefits of alternative courses of action to find out which is in the individual's or group's best interests.

One of the pioneers of this approach has been Gary Becker (1930–). Becker has been a professor at Chicago University since 1970 and is regarded as a member of the 'Chicago school', a group of economists from the university who advocate the market as the best means of solving economic problems. He is also a member of the free-market pressure group called the Mont Pelerin Society (see Box 11.6).

Gary Becker has attempted to apply simple economic principles of rational choice to a whole range of human activities: from racial and sexual discrimination, to competition in politics, to the study of criminal behaviour. Much of his work, however, has focused on the family, a field previously thought to be the domain of sociologists, anthropologists and psychologists. Even when family members are behaving lovingly and unselfishly, they nevertheless, according to Becker, tend to behave 'rationally' in the economists' sense of trying to maximise their interests, only in this case their 'interests' include the welfare of the other members of their family.

A simple illustration of this approach is given in the following diagram. It assumes, for simplicity, that there are just two members of the family: Judy and Warren. Warren's consumption is measured on the horizontal axis; Judy's on the vertical. Their total joint income is given by Y_T. The line Y_TY_T represents their consumption possibilities. If Warren were to spend their entire joint income on himself, he would consume at point *g*.

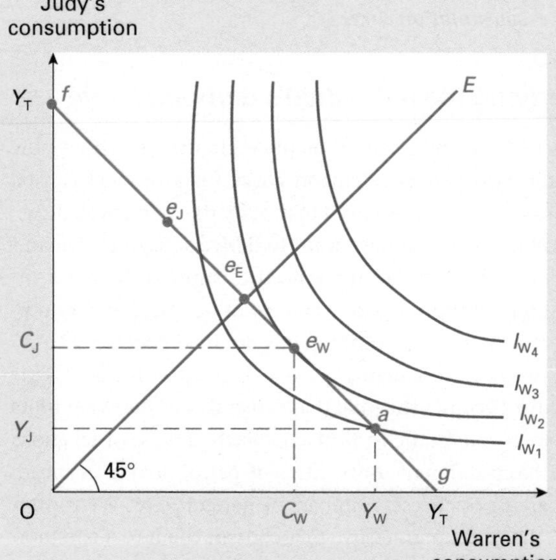

- The good is now more expensive relative to other goods. Therefore consumers substitute alternatives for it. This is the ***substitution effect***.

We can extend our arguments of Chapter 2 by demonstrating the income and substitution effects with the use of indifference analysis. Let us start with the case of a normal good and show what happens when its price changes.

A normal good

In Figure 4.16 the price of ***normal good*** X has *risen* and the budget line has pivoted *inwards* from B_1 to B_2. The consumption point has moved from point *f* to point *h*. Part of this shift in consumption is due to the substitution effect and part is due to the income effect.

The substitution effect. To separate these two effects a new budget line is drawn, parallel to B_2 but tangential to the original indifference curve I_1. This is the line B_{1a}. Being parallel to B_2, it represents the new price ratio (i.e. the higher price of X). Being tangential to I_1, however, it enables the consumer to obtain the *same utility* as before: in other words, there is no loss in *real* income to the consumer. By focusing on B_{1a}, then, which represents no change in real income, we have excluded the income effect. The movement from point *f* to point *g* is due *purely* to a change in the relative prices of X and Y. The movement from Q_{X_1} to Q_{X_2} is the *substitution* effect.

Definitions

Substitution effect of a price change That portion of the change in quantity demanded that results from the change in the relative price of the good.

Normal good A good whose demand increases as income increases.

*BOX 4.6

If Judy were to spend their entire joint income on herself, she would consume at point *f*.

Let us assume that Warren works full time and Judy works part time. As a result Warren earns more than Judy. He earns Y_W; she earns Y_J. If each spent their own incomes on themselves alone, they would consume at point *a*.

But now let us assume that Warren loves Judy, and that he would prefer to consume less than Y_W to allow her to consume more than Y_J. His preferences are shown by the indifference curves. Each curve shows all the various combinations of consumption between Warren and Judy that give Warren equal satisfaction. (Note that because he loves Judy, he gets satisfaction from her consumption: her happiness gives him pleasure.)

Warren's optimum distribution of consumption between himself and Judy is at point e_W. This is the highest of his indifference curves that can be reached with a joint income of Y_T. At this point he consumes C_W; she consumes C_J.

If he loved Judy 'as himself' and wanted to share their income out equally, then the indifference curves would be shallower. The tangency point to the highest indifference curve would be on the 45° line *OE*. Consumption would be at point e_E.

Similar indifference curves could be drawn for Judy. Her optimum consumption point might be at point e_J. But if she loved Warren 'as herself', her optimum point would then be at point e_E.

Some interesting conclusions can be drawn from this analysis:

- Income redistribution (i.e. consumption redistribution) within the family can be to the benefit of all the members. In the case we have been considering, both Warren and Judy gain from a redistribution of income from point *a* to point e_W. The only area of contention is between points e_W and e_J. Here negotiation would have to take place. This might be in return for some favour. 'If you'll let me have the money I need for that new coat, I'll do the washing up for a whole month.'
- In the case of each one loving the other as him- or herself, there is no area of contention. They are both happiest with consumption at point e_E.
- In the case of 'extreme love', where each partner would prefer the other to have more than him- or herself, point e_W would be above point e_E, and point e_J would be below point e_E. In this case, each would be trying to persuade the other to have more than he or she wanted. Here a different type of negotiation would be needed. 'I'll only let you buy me that coat if you let me do the washing up for a whole month.'
- Some forms of consumption benefit *both* partners. Household furniture or a new car would be cases in point. Any such purchases would have the effect of shifting the consumption point out beyond line Y_TY_T, and could lead to both partners consuming on a higher indifference curve. This shows the 'economic' advantages of the collective consumption that can be experienced in households or other groups (such as clubs).

?

1. ***If Judy earned more than Warren, show how much income she would redistribute to him if (a) she cared somewhat for him; (b) she loved him 'as herself'. Draw her indifference curves in each of these two cases.***
2. ***In the case where they both love each other 'as themselves', will their two sets of indifference curves be identical?***

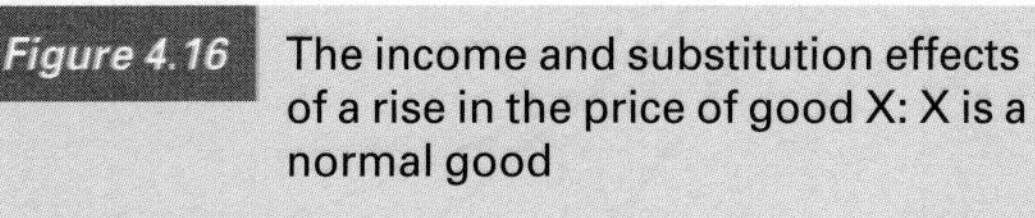

Figure 4.16 The income and substitution effects of a rise in the price of good X: X is a normal good

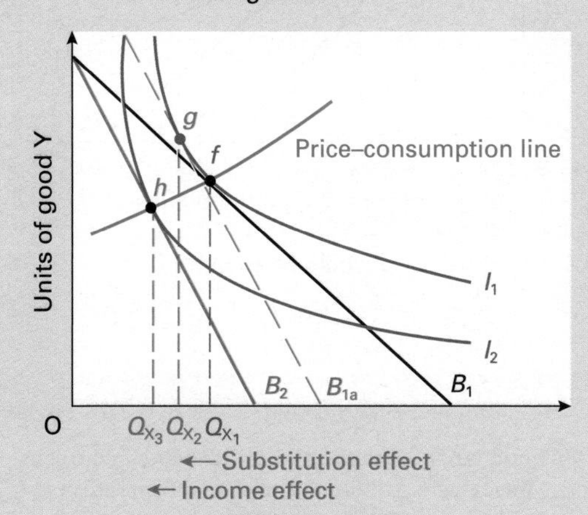

The income effect. In reality, the budget line has shifted to B_2 and the consumer is forced to consume on a lower indifference curve I_2: real income has fallen. Thus the movement from Q_{X_2} to Q_{X_3} is the *income* effect.

In the case of a normal good, therefore, the income and substitution effects of a price change reinforce each other. They are both negative: they *both* involve a *reduction* in the quantity demanded as price *rises* (and vice versa).[2]

The bigger the income and substitution effects, the higher will be the price elasticity of demand for good X.

[2] It is important not to confuse the income effect of a *price* change from the simple effect on demand of an increase in income. In the latter case, a *rise* in income will cause a *rise* in demand for a normal good – a positive effect (and hence there will be a positive income elasticity of demand). In the case of a price reduction, although for a normal good the resulting rise in real income will still cause a rise in demand, it is in the *opposite* direction from the change in price – a negative effect *with respect to price* (and hence there will be a negative price elasticity of demand).

?

Illustrate on two separate indifference diagrams the income and substitution effects of the following:
(a) A decrease in the price of good X (and no change in the price of good Y).
(b) An increase in the price of good Y (and no change in the price of good X).

An inferior good

As we saw above, when people's incomes rise, they will buy less of ***inferior goods*** such as poor-quality margarine and cheap powdered instant coffee, since they will now be able to afford better-quality goods instead. Conversely, when income falls, they will now have to reduce their living standards: their consumption of inferior goods will thus rise.

The substitution effect. If the *price* of an inferior good (good X) rises, the substitution effect will be in the same direction as for a normal good: i.e. it will be negative. People will consume less X relative to Y, since X is now more expensive relative to Y. For example, if the price of inferior-quality margarine (good X) went up, people would tend to use better-quality margarine or butter (good Y) instead. This is illustrated in Figure 4.17 by a movement along the original indifference curve (I_1) from point *f* to point *g*. The quantity of X demanded falls from Q_{X_1} to Q_{X_2}.

The income effect. The income effect of the price rise, however, will be the opposite of that for a normal good: it will be *positive*. The reduction in real income from the rise in price of X will tend to *increase* the consumption of X, since with a fall in real income *more* inferior goods will now be purchased – including more X. Thus point *h* is to the *right* of point *g*: the income effect increases quantity back from Q_{X_2} to Q_{X_3}.

A Giffen good: a particular type of inferior good

If the inferior good were to account for a very large proportion of a consumer's expenditure, a change in its price would have a significant effect on the consumer's real income, resulting in a large income effect. It is conceivable, therefore, that this large abnormal income effect could outweigh the normal substitution effect. In such a case, a rise in the price of X would lead to *more* X being consumed!

This is illustrated in Figure 4.18, where point *h* is to the *right* of point *f*. In other words, the fall in consumption (Q_{X_1} to Q_{X_2}) as a result of the substitution effect is more than offset by the rise in consumption (Q_{X_2} to Q_{X_3}) as a result of the large positive income effect.

Such a good is known as a ***Giffen good***, after Sir Robert Giffen (1837–1910), who is alleged to have claimed that the consumption of bread by the poor rose when its price rose. Bread formed such a large proportion of poor people's consumption that, if its price went up, the poor could not afford to buy so much meat, vegetables, etc. and had to buy more bread instead. It is possible that in very low income countries in Africa today, staple foods such as manioc and maize are Giffen goods. Naturally, such cases must be very rare indeed.

Figure 4.17 The income and substitution effects of a rise in the price of good X: X is an inferior (non-Giffen) good

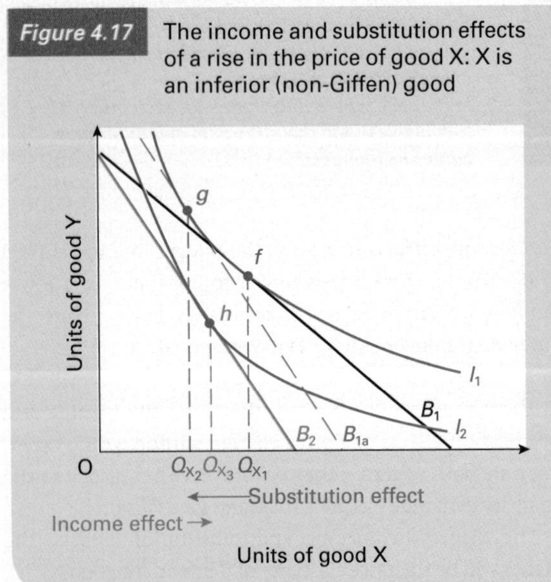

Figure 4.18 The income and substitution effects of a rise in the price of good X: X is a Giffen good

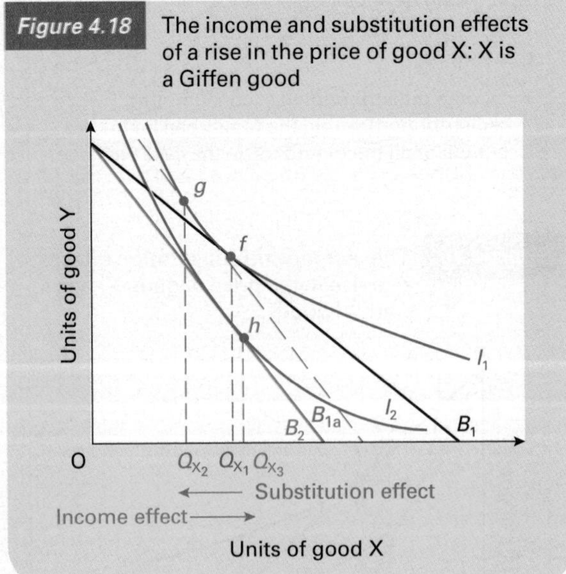

Definitions

Inferior good A good whose demand decreases as income increases.

Giffen good An inferior good whose demand increases as its price increases as a result of a positive income effect larger than the normal negative substitution effect.

EXPLORING ECONOMICS

*BOX 4.7

CONSUMER THEORY: A FURTHER APPROACH

Characteristics theory

Characteristics theory was developed in the mid-1960s by Kelvin Lancaster. He argued that people demand goods not for their own sake, but for the *characteristics* they possess.

Take cars, for example. When choosing between the different makes, consumers do not just consider their relative prices, they also consider their attributes: comfort, style, performance, durability, reliability, fuel consumption, etc. It is these *characteristics* that give rise to utility.

Characteristics theory, then, is based on four crucial assumptions:

- All goods possess various characteristics.
- Different brands possess them in different proportions.
- The characteristics are measurable: they are 'objective'.
- The characteristics (along with price and income) determine consumer choice.

Let us assume that you are choosing between three different goods or brands of a good (e.g. a foodstuff). Each one has a different combination of two characteristics (e.g. protein and calories). Your choices can be shown graphically.

The choice between brands of a product: each brand has different characteristics

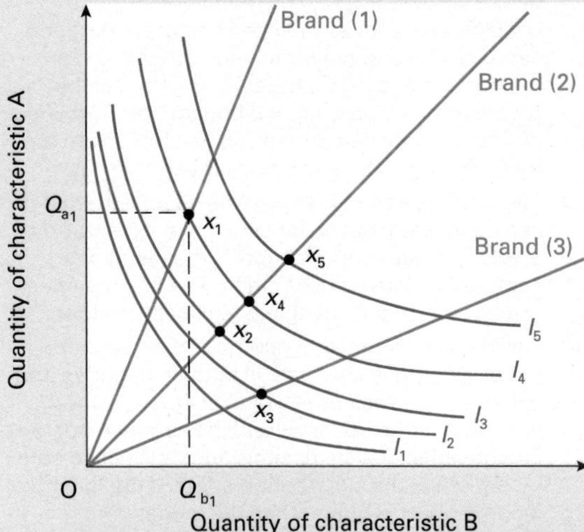

The levels of two characteristics are shown on the two axes. An indifference map can be constructed, showing the different combinations of the two characteristics that yield given levels of utility. Thus any combination of the two characteristics along indifference curve I_4 in the diagram gives a higher level of utility than those along I_3, and so on. The shape of the indifference curves (bowed in) illustrates a diminishing marginal rate of substitution between the two characteristics.

The amounts of the two characteristics given by the three brands are shown by the three rays. The more that is consumed of each brand, the further up the respective ray will the consumer be. Thus at x_1, the consumer is gaining Q_{a_1} of characteristic A and Q_{b_1} of characteristic B.

Assume that, for the same money, the consumer could consume at x_1 with brand (1), x_2 with brand (2) and x_3 with brand (3). The consumer will consume brand (1): x_1 is on a higher indifference curve than x_2 or x_3.

Now assume that the price of brand (2) falls. For a given expenditure, the consumer can now move up the brand (2) ray. But not until the price has fallen enough to allow consumption at point x_4 will the consumer consider switching from brand (1). If price falls enough for consumption to be at point x_5, clearly the consumer will switch.

The characteristics approach has a number of advantages over conventional indifference curve analysis in explaining consumer behaviour.

- It helps to explain brand loyalty. When price changes, people will not necessarily gradually move from one brand to another. Rather they will stick with a brand until a critical price is reached. Then they will switch brands all at once.
- It allows the choice between *several* goods to be shown on the same diagram. Each good or brand has its own ray.
- It helps to explain the nature of substitute goods. The closer substitutes are, the more similar will be their characteristics and hence the closer will be their rays. The closer the rays, the more likely it is that there will be a shift in consumption to one good when the price of the other good changes.
- A change in the quality of a good can be shown by rotating its ray.

There are weaknesses with the approach, however:

- Some characteristics cannot be measured. Such characteristics as beauty, taste and entertainment value are subjective: they are in the mind of the consumer.
- Only two characteristics can be plotted. Most goods have several characteristics.

?

1. ***Make a list of the characteristics of shoes. Which are 'objective' and which are 'subjective'?***
2. ***If two houses had identical characteristics, except that one was near a noisy airport and the other was in a quiet location, and if the market price of the first house were £80 000 and of the second were £100 000, how would that help us to put a value on the characteristic of peace and quiet?***

Characteristics theory is examined in more detail in Web Case 4.6.

? *Are there any Giffen goods that you consume? If not, could you conceive of any circumstances in which one or more items of your expenditure would become Giffen goods?*

The usefulness of indifference analysis

Indifference analysis has made it possible to demonstrate the logic of 'rational' consumer choice, the derivation of the individual's demand curve, and the income and substitution effects of a price change. All this has been done without having to measure utility.

Nevertheless there are limitations to the usefulness of indifference analysis:

- In practice it is virtually impossible to derive indifference curves, since it would involve a consumer having to imagine a whole series of different combinations of goods and deciding in each case whether a given combination gave more, equal or less satisfaction than other combinations.
- Consumers may not behave 'rationally', and hence may not give careful consideration to the satisfaction they believe they will gain from consuming goods. They may behave impetuously.
- Indifference curves are based on the satisfaction that consumers *believe* they will gain from a good. This belief may well be influenced by advertising. Consumers may be disappointed or pleasantly surprised, however, when they actually consume the good. In other words, consumers are not perfectly knowledgeable. Thus the 'optimum consumption' point may not in practice give consumers maximum satisfaction for their money. TC 9 p101
- Certain goods are purchased only now and again, and then only one at a time. Examples would include consumer durables such as cars, televisions and washing machines. Indifference curves are based on the assumption that marginal increases in one good can be traded off against marginal decreases in another. This will not be the case with consumer durables.

Section summary

1. The indifference approach to analysing consumer demand avoids having to measure utility.
2. An indifference curve shows all those combinations of two goods that give an equal amount of satisfaction to a consumer. An indifference map can be drawn with indifference curves further to the north-east representing higher (but still unspecified) levels of satisfaction.
3. Indifference curves are usually drawn convex to the origin. This is because of a diminishing marginal rate of substitution between the two goods. As more of one good is purchased, the consumer is willing to give up less and less of the other for each additional unit of the first. The marginal rate of substitution is given by the slope of the indifference curve, which equals MU_X/MU_Y.
4. A budget line can be drawn on an indifference diagram. A budget line shows all those combinations of the two goods that can be purchased for a given amount of money, assuming a constant price of the two goods. The slope of the budget line depends on the relative price of the two goods. The slope is equal to P_X/P_Y.
5. The consumer will achieve the maximum level of satisfaction for a given income (budget) by consuming at the point where the budget line just touches the highest possible indifference curve. At this point of tangency, the budget line and the indifference curve have the same slope. Thus $MU_X/MU_Y = P_X/P_Y$, which is the 'equi-marginal principle' for maximising utility from a given income that was established in section 4.1.
6. If the consumer's real income (and hence budget) rises, there will be a parallel outward shift of the budget line. The 'rational' consumer will move to the point of tangency of this new budget line with the highest indifference curve. The line that traces out these optimum positions for different levels of income is known as the 'income–consumption curve'.
7. If the price of one of the two goods changes, the budget line will pivot on the axis of the other good. An outward pivot represents a fall in price; an inward pivot represents an increase in price. The line that traces the tangency points of these budget lines with the appropriate indifference curves is called a 'price–consumption curve'.
8. By measuring the expenditure on all other goods on the vertical axis and by holding their price constant and money income constant, a demand curve can be derived for the good measured on the horizontal axis. Changes in its price can be represented by pivoting the budget line. The effect on the quantity demanded can be found from the resulting price–consumption curve.
9. The effect of a change in price on quantity demanded can be divided into an income and a substitution effect. The substitution effect is the result of a change in relative prices alone. The income effect is the result of the change in real income alone.
10. For a normal good, the income and substitution effects of a price change will both be negative and will reinforce each other. With an inferior good, the substitution effect will still be negative but the income effect will be positive and thus will to some extent offset the substitution effect. If the (positive) income effect is bigger than the (negative) substitution effect, the good is called a Giffen good. A rise in the price of a Giffen good will thus cause a *rise* in the quantity demanded.
11. Indifference analysis, although avoiding having to measure utility, nevertheless has limitations. Indifference curves are difficult to derive in practice; consumers may not behave rationally; the 'optimum' consumption point may not be optimum if the consumer lacks knowledge of the good; indifference curves will not be smooth for items where single units each account for a large proportion of income.

END OF CHAPTER QUESTIONS

1. Imagine that you had £10 per month to allocate between two goods a and b. Imagine that good a cost £2 per unit and good b cost £1 per unit. Imagine also that the utilities of the two goods are those set out in the table below. (Note that the two goods are not substitutes for each other, so that the consumption of one does not affect the utility gained from the other.)
   (a) What would be the marginal utility ratio (MU_a/MU_b) for the following combinations of the two goods: (i) 1a, 8b; (ii) 2a, 6b; (iii) 3a, 4b; (iv) 4a, 2b? (Each combination would cost £10.)
   (b) Show that where the marginal utility ratio (MU_a/MU_b) equals the price ratio (P_a/P_b), total utility is maximised.
   (c) If the two goods were substitutes for each other, why would it not be possible to construct a table like the one given here?

The utility gained by a person from various quantities of two goods: a and b

Good a			Good b		
Units per month	*MU* (utils)	*TU* (utils)	Units per month	*MU* (utils)	*TU* (utils)
0	–	0.0	0	–	0.0
1	11.0	11.0	1	8.0	8.0
2	8.0	19.0	2	7.0	15.0
3	6.0	25.0	3	6.5	21.5
4	4.5	29.5	4	5.0	26.5
5	3.0	32.5	5	4.5	31.0
			6	4.0	35.0
			7	3.5	38.5
			8	3.0	41.5
			9	2.6	44.1
			10	2.3	46.4

2. Is it reasonable to assume that people seek to equate the marginal utility/price ratios of the goods that they purchase, if (a) they have never heard of 'utility', let alone 'marginal utility'; (b) marginal utility cannot be measured in any absolute way?
3. Consider situations where you might consider swapping items with someone. Why are such situations relatively rare?
4. Explain why the price of a good is no reflection of the *total* value that consumers put on it.
5. A country's central bank (e.g. the Bank of England or the US Federal Reserve Bank) has a key role in ensuring the stability of the banking system. In many countries the central bank is prepared to bail banks out which find themselves in financial difficulties. Although this has the benefit of reducing the chance of banks going bankrupt and depositors losing their money, it can create a moral hazard. Explain why.

*6. Sketch a person's indifference map for two goods X and Y. Mark the optimum consumption point. Now illustrate the following (you might need to draw a separate diagram for each):
   (a) A rise in the price of good X, but no change in the price of good Y.
   (b) A shift in the person's tastes from good Y to good X.
   (c) A fall in the person's income and a fall in the price of good Y, with the result that the consumption of Y remains constant (but that of X falls).

*7. Distinguish between a normal good, an inferior good and a Giffen good. Use indifference curves to illustrate your answer.

*8. Assume that commuters regard bus journeys as an inferior good and car journeys as a normal good. Using indifference curves, show how (a) a rise in incomes and (b) a fall in bus fares will affect the use of these two modes of transport. How could people's tastes be altered so that bus journeys were no longer regarded as an inferior good? If tastes *were* altered in this way, what effect would it have on the indifference curves?

Additional case studies on the book's website (www.pearsoned.co.uk/sloman)

4.1 **Bentham and the philosophy of utilitarianism.** This looks at the historical and philosophical underpinning of the ideas of utility maximisation.

4.2 **Utility under attack.** This looks at the birth of indifference analysis, which was seen as a means of overcoming the shortcomings of marginal utility analysis.

4.3 **Applying indifference curve analysis to taxes on goods.** Assume that the government wants to raise extra revenue from an expenditure tax? Should it put a relatively small extra tax on *all* goods, or a relatively large one on just certain *selected* goods?

4.4 **Income and substitution effects: the Slutsky approach.** This looks at an alternative way of using indifference analysis to analyse income and substitution effects.

4.5 **Deriving an Engel curve.** Income elasticity of demand and the income–consumption curve.

4.6 **The characteristics approach to analysing consumer demand.** This is an extension of the analysis of Box 4.7.

WEBSITES RELEVANT TO THIS CHAPTER

Numbers and sections refer to websites listed in the Web Appendix and hotlinked from this book's website at www.pearsoned.co.uk/sloman.

- For news articles relevant to this chapter, see the *Economics News Articles* link from the book's website.
- For general news on demand and consumers, see websites in section A, and particularly A2, 3, 4, 8, 9, 11, 12, 23, 25, 36. See also site A41 for links to economics news articles on particular search topics (e.g. consumer demand and advertising).
- For data, information and sites on products and marketing, see sites B2, 10; I7, 11, 13, 17.
- For student resources relevant to Part C, see sites C1–7, 19.

Chapter 5

Background to Supply

So far we have assumed that supply curves are upward sloping: that a higher price will encourage firms to supply more. But just how much will firms choose to supply at each price? It depends largely on the amount of profit they will make. If a firm can increase its profits by producing more, it will normally do so.

Profit is made by firms earning more from the sale of goods than they cost to produce. A firm's total profit ($T\Pi$) is thus the difference between its total sales revenue (TR) and its total costs of production (TC):

$$T\Pi = TR - TC$$

In order then to discover how a firm can maximise its profit or even get a sufficient level of profit, we must first consider what determines costs and revenue.

The first four sections build up a theory of short-run and long-run costs. They show how output depends on the inputs used, and how costs depend on the amount of output produced. Section 5.5 then looks at revenue. Finally, in section 5.6, we bring cost and revenue together to see how profit is determined. In particular, we shall see how profit varies with output and how the point of maximum profit is found.

CHAPTER MAP

Chapter 4 went behind the demand curve. It saw how the 'rational' consumer weighs up the *benefits* (utility) of consuming various amounts of goods or combinations of goods against their *costs* (their price).

We now need to go behind the supply curve and find out just how the ***rational producer*** (or 'firm' as we call all producers) will behave.

In this case, we shall be looking at the benefits and costs to the firm of producing various quantities of goods and using various alternative methods of production. We shall be asking:

- How much will be produced?
- What combination of inputs will be used?
- How much profit will be made?

Profit and the aims of a firm

The traditional theory of supply, or ***theory of the firm***, assumes that firms aim to *maximise profit*: a realistic assumption in many cases. The traditional profit-maximising theory of the firm is examined in this and the following two chapters. First we examine the general principles that govern how much a firm supplies. Then, in Chapters 6 and 7, we look at how supply is affected by the amount of competition a firm faces.

In some circumstances, however, firms may not seek to maximise profits. Instead they may seek to maximise sales, or the rate of growth of sales. Alternatively, they may have no *single* aim, but rather a series of potentially conflicting aims held by different managers in different departments of the firm. Not surprisingly, a firm's behaviour will depend on just what its aims are. Chapter 8 looks at various ***alternative theories*** to profit maximisation, each theory depending on the particular aims of the firm.

5.1 THE SHORT-RUN THEORY OF PRODUCTION

The cost of producing any level of output will depend on the amount of inputs (or 'factors of production') used and the price the firm must pay for them. Let us first focus on the quantity of factors used.

Key Idea 16

Output depends on the amount of resources and how they are used. Different amounts and combinations of inputs will lead to different amounts of output. If output is to be produced efficiently, then inputs should be combined in the optimum proportions.

Short-run and long-run changes in production

If a firm wants to increase production, it will take time to acquire a greater quantity of certain inputs. For example, a manufacturer can use more electricity by turning on switches, but it might take a long time to obtain and install more machines, and longer still to build a second or third factory.

If, then, the firm wants to increase output in a hurry, it will only be able to increase the quantity of certain inputs. It can use more raw materials, more fuel, more tools and possibly more labour (by hiring extra workers or offering overtime to its existing workforce). But it will have to make do with its existing buildings and most of its machinery.

The distinction we are making here is between ***fixed factors*** and ***variable factors***. A *fixed* factor is an input that cannot be increased within a given time period (e.g. buildings). A *variable* factor is one that can.

The distinction between fixed and variable factors allows us to distinguish between the ***short run*** and the ***long run***.

The short run is a time period during which at least one factor of production is fixed. In the short run, then, output can be increased only by using more variable factors. For

Definitions

Rational producer behaviour When a firm weighs up the costs and benefits of alternative courses of action and then seeks to maximise its net benefit.

Traditional theory of the firm The analysis of pricing and output decisions of the firm under various market conditions, assuming that the firm wishes to maximise profit.

Alternative theories of the firm Theories of the firm based on the assumption that firms have aims other than profit maximisation.

Fixed factor An input that cannot be increased in supply within a given time period.

Variable factor An input that can be increased in supply within a given time period.

Short run The period of time over which at least one factor is fixed.

Long run The period of time long enough for *all* factors to be varied.

example, if a shipping line wanted to carry more passengers in response to a rise in demand, it could possibly accommodate more passengers on existing sailings if there was space. It could possibly increase the number of sailings with its existing fleet, by hiring more crew and using more fuel. But in the short run it could not buy more ships: there would not be time for them to be built.

The long run is a time period long enough for all inputs to be varied. Given long enough, a firm can build a second factory and install new machines.

The actual length of the short run will differ from firm to firm. It is not a fixed period of time. Thus if it takes a farmer a year to obtain new land, buildings and equipment, the short run is any time period up to a year and the long run is any time period longer than a year. If it takes a shipping company three years to obtain an extra ship, the short run is any period up to three years and the long run is any period longer than three years.

?

1. How will the length of the short run for the shipping company depend on the state of the shipbuilding industry?
2. Up to roughly how long is the short run in the following cases?
(a) A mobile disco firm. (b) Electricity power generation. (c) A small grocery retailing business. (d) 'Superstore Hypermarkets Ltd'. In each case specify your assumptions.

For the remainder of this section we will concentrate on *short-run* production.

Production in the short run: the law of diminishing returns

Production in the short run is subject to *diminishing returns*. You may well have heard of 'the law of diminishing returns': it is one of the most famous of all 'laws' of economics. To illustrate how this law underlies short-run production let us take the simplest possible case where there are just two factors: one fixed and one variable.

Take the case of a farm. Assume the fixed factor is land and the variable factor is labour. Since the land is fixed in supply, output per period of time can be increased only by increasing the amount of workers employed. But imagine what would happen as more and more workers crowd on to a fixed area of land. The land cannot go on yielding more and more output indefinitely. After a point the additions to output from each extra worker will begin to diminish.

We can now state the ***law of diminishing (marginal) returns***.

Key Idea 17

The law of diminishing marginal returns. When increasing amounts of a variable factor are used with a given amount of a fixed factor, there will come a point when each extra unit of the variable factor will produce less extra output than the previous unit.

A good example of the law of diminishing returns is given in Web Case 5.1 on the book's website. It looks at diminishing returns to the application of nitrogen fertiliser on farmland.

The short-run production function: total product

KI 16 p120

Let us now see how the law of diminishing returns affects total output or ***total physical product*** (*TPP*) as it is sometimes called.

The relationship between inputs and output is shown in a ***production function***. In the simple case of the farm with only two factors – namely, a fixed supply of land ($\bar{L}n$) and a variable supply of farm workers (*Lb*) – the production function would be:

$$TPP = f(\bar{L}n, Lb)$$

This states that total physical product (i.e. the output of the farm) over a given period of time is a function of (i.e. depends on) the quantity of land and labour employed. We could express the precise relationship using an equation (an example is given in Box 5.4).

Alternatively, the production function could be expressed in the form of a table or a graph. Table 5.1 and Figure 5.1 show a hypothetical production function for a farm producing wheat. The first two columns of Table 5.1 and the top diagram in Figure 5.1 show how total wheat output per year varies as extra workers are employed on a fixed amount of land.

With nobody working on the land, output will be zero (point *a*). As the first farm workers are taken on, wheat output initially rises more and more rapidly. The assumption behind this is that with only one or two workers efficiency

Definitions

Law of diminishing (marginal) returns When one or more factors are held fixed, there will come a point beyond which the extra output from additional units of the variable factor will diminish.

Total physical product The total output of a product per period of time that is obtained from a given amount of inputs.

Production function The mathematical relationship between the output of a good and the inputs used to produce it. It shows how output will be affected by changes in the quantity of one or more of the inputs.

EXPLORING ECONOMICS — BOX 5.1

MALTHUS AND THE DISMAL SCIENCE OF ECONOMICS

Population growth + diminishing returns = starvation

KI 20 p182

The law of diminishing returns has potentially cataclysmic implications for the future populations of the world.

If the population of the world grows rapidly, then food output may not keep pace with it. There will be diminishing returns to labour as more and more people crowd on to the limited amount of land available.

This is already a problem in some of the poorest countries of the world, especially in sub-Saharan Africa. The land is barely able to support current population levels. Only one or two bad harvests are needed to cause mass starvation – witness the appalling famines in recent years in Ethiopia and the Sudan.

The relationship between population and food output was analysed as long ago as 1798 by the Reverend Thomas Robert Malthus (1766–1834) in his *Essay on the Principle of Population*. This book was a bestseller and made Robert Malthus perhaps the best known of all social scientists of his day.

Malthus argued as follows:

> I say that the power of population is indefinitely greater than the power in the earth to produce subsistence for man.
>
> Population when unchecked, increases in a geometrical ratio. Subsistence increases only in an arithmetical ratio. A slight acquaintance with numbers will show the immensity of the first power in comparison with the second.[1]

What Malthus was saying is that world population tends to double about every 25 years or so if unchecked. It grows geometrically, like the series: 1, 2, 4, 8, 16, 32, 64, etc. But food output, because of diminishing returns, cannot keep pace with this. It is likely to grow at only an arithmetical rate, like the series: 1, 2, 3, 4, 5, 6, 7, etc. It is clear that population, if unchecked, will soon outstrip food supply.

So what is the check on population growth? According to Malthus, it is starvation. As population grows, so food output per head will fall until, with more and more people starving, the death rate will rise. Only then will population growth stabilise at the rate of growth of food output.

Have Malthus' gloomy predictions been borne out by events? Two factors have mitigated the forces that Malthus described:

- The rate of population growth tends to slow down as countries become more developed. Although improved health prolongs life, this tends to be more than offset by a decline in the birth rate as people choose to have smaller families.
- Technological improvements in farming have greatly increased food output per hectare. (See Web Case 5.1 for a relatively recent example.)

The growth in food output has thus exceeded the rate of population growth in advanced countries.

The picture is much more gloomy, however, in developing countries. There *have* been advances in agriculture. The 'green revolution', whereby new high-yielding crop varieties have been developed (especially in the cases of wheat and rice), has led to food output growth outstripping population growth in many developing countries. India, for example, now exports grain.

Nevertheless, the Malthusian spectre is very real for some of the poorest developing countries, which are simply unable to feed their populations satisfactorily. It is these poorest countries of the world which have some of the highest rates of population growth. Many African countries have population growth rates of around 3 per cent per annum.

?

1. ***Why might it be possible for there to be a zero marginal productivity of labour on many family farms in poor countries and yet just enough food for all the members of the family to survive? (Illustrate using MPP and APP curves.)***
2. ***The figures in the following table are based on the assumption that birth rates will fall faster than death rates. Under what circumstances might these forecasts underestimate the rate of growth of world population?***

World population levels and growth: actual and projected

Year	World population (billions)	Average annual rate of increase (%)		
		World	More developed regions	Less developed regions
1950	2.6			
		1.7	1.2	2.1
1960	3.0			
		2.0	1.0	2.4
1970	3.7			
		1.8	0.7	2.2
1980	4.5			
		1.7	0.6	2.1
1990	5.3			
		1.4	0.3	1.8
2000	6.1			
		1.2	0.2	1.5
2010	6.8			
		1.0	0.2	1.2
2020	7.5			
		0.8	0.1	1.1
2030	8.1			

Source: various.

[1] T. R. Malthus, *First Essay on Population* (Macmillan, 1926), pp. 13–14.

Table 5.1 Wheat production per year from a particular farm

	Number of workers (*Lb*)	*TPP*	*APP* (= *TPP*/*Lb*)	*MPP* (= Δ*TPP*/Δ*Lb*)
a	0	0	–	
	1	3	3	3
	2	10	5	7
b	3	24	8	14
	4	36	9	12
c	5	40	8	4
	6	42	7	2
d	7	42	6	0
	8	40	5	−2

is low, since the workers are spread too thinly. With more workers, however, they can work together – each, perhaps, doing some specialist job – and thus they can use the land more efficiently. In Table 5.1, output rises more and more rapidly up to the employment of the third worker (point *b*). In Figure 5.1 the *TPP* curve gets steeper up to point *b*.

After point *b*, however, diminishing marginal returns set in: output rises less and less rapidly, and the *TPP* curve correspondingly becomes less steeply sloped.

When point *d* is reached, wheat output is at a maximum: the land is yielding as much as it can. Any more workers employed after that are likely to get in each other's way. Thus beyond point *d*, output is likely to fall again: eight workers produce less than seven workers.

The short-run production function: average and marginal product

In addition to total physical product, two other important concepts are illustrated by a production function: namely, ***average physical product*** (*APP*) and ***marginal physical product*** (*MPP*).

Average physical product

This is output (*TPP*) per unit of the variable factor (Q_v). In the case of the farm, it is the output of wheat per worker.

Figure 5.1 Wheat production per year (tonnes)

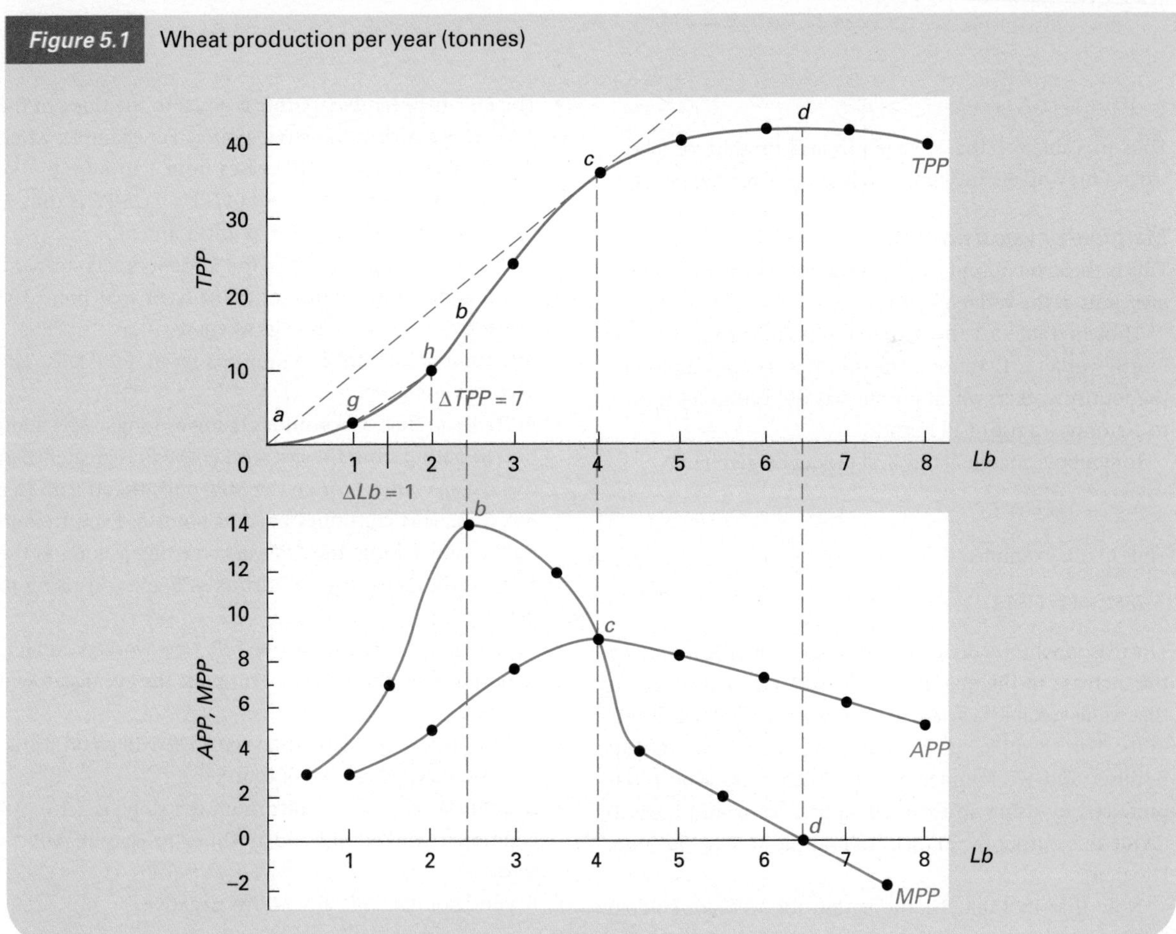

Definitions

Average physical product Total output (TPP) per unit of the variable factor in question: $APP = TPP/Q_v$.

Marginal physical product The extra output gained by the employment of one more unit of the variable factor: $MPP = \Delta TPP/\Delta Q_v$.

CASE STUDIES AND APPLICATIONS — BOX 5.2

DIMINISHING RETURNS IN THE BREAD SHOP

Is the baker using his loaf?

Just up the road from where I live is a bread shop. Like many others, I buy my bread there on a Saturday morning. Not surprisingly, Saturday morning is the busiest time of the week for the shop and as a result it takes on extra assistants.

KI 17 p121 During the week only one assistant serves the customers, but on a Saturday morning there used to be five serving. But could they serve five times as many customers? No, they could not. There were diminishing returns to labour.

The trouble is that certain factors of production in the shop are fixed:

- The shop is a fixed size. It gets very crowded on Saturday morning. Assistants sometimes had to wait while customers squeezed past each other to get to the counter, and with five serving, the assistants themselves used to get in each other's way.
- There is only one cash till. Assistants frequently had to wait while other assistants used it.
- There is only one pile of tissue paper for wrapping the bread. Again the assistants often had to wait.

The fifth and maybe even the fourth assistant ended up serving very few extra customers.

I am still going to the same bread shop and they still have only one till and one pile of tissue paper. But now only three assistants are employed on a Saturday! The shop, however, is just as busy.

? ***How would you advise the baker as to whether he should (a) employ four assistants on a Saturday; (b) extend his shop, thereby allowing more customers to be served on a Saturday morning?***

$APP = TPP/Q_v$

Thus in Table 5.1 the average physical product of labour when four workers are employed is 36/4 = 9 tonnes per year.

Marginal physical product

This is the *extra* output (ΔTPP) produced by employing *one more* unit of the variable factor.

Thus in Table 5.1 the marginal physical product of the fourth worker is 12 tonnes. The reason is that by employing the fourth worker, wheat output has risen from 24 tonnes to 36 tonnes: a rise of 12 tonnes.

In symbols, marginal physical product is given by:

$MPP = \Delta TPP/\Delta Q_v$

Thus in our example:

$MPP = 12/1 = 12$

The reason why we divide the increase in output (ΔTPP) by the increase in the quantity of the variable factor (ΔQ_v) is that some variable factors can be increased only in multiple units. For example, if we wanted to know the *MPP* of fertiliser and we found out how much extra wheat was produced by using an extra 20 kg bag, we would have to divide this output by 20 (ΔQ_v) to find the *MPP* of *one* more kilogram.

Note that in Table 5.1 the figures for *MPP* are entered in the spaces between the other figures. The reason is that *MPP* can be seen as the *difference* in output *between* one level of input and another. Thus in the table the difference in output between five and six workers is 2 tonnes.

The figures for *APP* and *MPP* are plotted in the lower diagram of Figure 5.1. We can draw a number of conclusions from these diagrams:

- The *MPP* between two points is equal to the slope of the *TPP* curve between those two points. For example, when the number of workers increases from 1 to 2 ($\Delta Lb = 1$), *TPP* rises from 3 to 10 tonnes ($\Delta TPP = 7$). *MPP* is thus 7: the slope of the line between points *g* and *h*.
- *MPP* rises at first: the slope of the *TPP* curve gets steeper.
- *MPP* reaches a maximum at point *b*. At that point the slope of the *TPP* curve is at its steepest.
- After point *b*, diminishing returns set in. *MPP* falls. *TPP* becomes less steep. KI 17 p121
- *APP* rises at first. It continues rising as long as the addition to output from the last worker (*MPP*) is greater than the average output (*APP*): the *MPP* pulls the *APP* up (see Box 5.3). This continues beyond point *b*. Even though *MPP* is now falling, the *APP goes on* rising as long as the *MPP* is still above the *APP*. Thus *APP* goes on rising to point *c*.
- Beyond point *c*, *MPP* is below *APP*. New workers add less to output than the average. This pulls the average down: *APP* falls.
- As long as *MPP* is greater than zero, *TPP* will go on rising: new workers add to total output.
- At point *d*, *TPP* is at a maximum (its slope is zero). An additional worker will add nothing to output: *MPP* is zero.
- Beyond point *d*, *TPP* falls. *MPP* is negative.

?

1. *What is the significance of the slope of the line* ac *in the top part of Figure 5.1?*
2. *Given that there is a fixed supply of land in the world, what implications can you draw from Figure 5.1 about the effects of an increase in world population for food output per head? (See Box 5.1.)*

EXPLORING ECONOMICS BOX 5.3

THE RELATIONSHIP BETWEEN AVERAGES AND MARGINALS

In this chapter we have just examined the concepts of *average* and *marginal* physical product. We shall be coming across several other average and marginal concepts later on. It is useful at this stage to examine the general relationship between averages and marginals. In all cases there are three simple rules that relate them.

To illustrate these rules, consider the following example.

Imagine a room with ten people in it. Assume that the *average* age of those present is 20.

Now if a 20-year-old enters the room (the *marginal* age), this will not affect the average age. It will remain at 20. If a 56-year-old now comes in, the average age will rise: not to 56, of course, but to 23. This is found by dividing the sum of everyone's ages (276) by the number of people (12). If then a child of 10 were to enter the room, this would pull the average age down.

From this example we can derive the three universal rules about averages and marginals:

- If the marginal equals the average, the average will not change.
- If the marginal is above the average, the average will rise.
- If the marginal is below the average, the average will fall.

A cricketer scores the following number of runs in five successive innings:

Innings:	*1*	*2*	*3*	*4*	*5*
Runs:	*20*	*20*	*50*	*10*	*0*

These can be seen as the marginal number of runs from each innings. Calculate the total and average number of runs after each innings. Show how the average and marginal scores illustrate the three rules above.

EXPLORING ECONOMICS *BOX 5.4

THE RELATIONSHIP BETWEEN TPP, MPP AND APP

Using calculus again

The total physical product of a variable factor (e.g. fertiliser) can be expressed as an equation. For example:

$$TPP = 100 + 32Q_f + 10Q_f^2 - Q_f^3 \qquad (1)$$

where *TPP* is the output of grain in tonnes per hectare, and Q_f is the quantity of fertiliser applied in kilograms per hectare.

From this we can derive the *APP* function. *APP* is simply TPP/Q_f: i.e. output per kilogram of fertiliser. Thus:

$$APP = \frac{100}{Q_f} + 32 + 10Q_f - Q_f^2 \qquad (2)$$

We can also derive the *MPP* function. *MPP* is the rate of increase in *TPP* as additional fertiliser is applied. It is thus the first derivative of *TPP*: $dTPP/dQ_f$. Thus:

$$MPP = 32 + 20Q_f - 3Q_f^2 \qquad (3)$$

From these three equations we can derive the table shown.

Check out some figures by substituting values of Q_f into each of the three equations.

Maximum output (484 tonnes) is achieved with 8 kg of fertiliser per hectare. At that level, *MPP* is zero: no additional output can be gained.

Q_f	*TPP*	*APP*	*MPP*
1	141	141	49
2	196	98	60
3	259	86	65
4	324	81	64
5	385	77	57
6	436	72	44
7	471	67	25
8	484	60	0
9	469	52	−31

This maximum level of *TPP* can be discovered from the equations by using a simple technique. If *MPP* is zero at this level, then simply find the value of Q_f where:

$$MPP = 32 + 20Q_f - 3Q_f^2 = 0 \qquad (4)$$

Solving this equation[2] gives $Q_f = 8$.

[2] By applying the second derivative test (see Appendix 1) you can verify that $Q_f = 8$ gives the *maximum TPP* rather than the *minimum*. (Both the maximum *and* the minimum point of a curve have a slope equal to zero.)

Section summary

1. A production function shows the relationship between the amount of inputs used and the amount of output produced from them (per period of time).
2. In the short run it is assumed that one or more factors (inputs) are fixed in supply. The actual length of the short run will vary from industry to industry.
3. Production in the short run is subject to diminishing returns. As greater quantities of the variable factor(s) are used, so each additional unit of the variable factor will add less to output than previous units: marginal physical product will diminish and total physical product will rise less and less rapidly.
4. As long as marginal physical product is above average physical product, average physical product will rise. Once *MPP* has fallen below *APP*, however, *APP* will fall.

5.2 COSTS IN THE SHORT RUN

We have seen how output changes as inputs are varied in the short run. We now use this information to show how costs vary with the amount a firm produces. Obviously, before deciding how much to produce, it has to know the precise level of costs for each level of output.

But first we must be clear on just what we mean by the word 'costs'. The term is used differently by economists and accountants.

Measuring costs of production

When measuring costs, economists always use the concept of ***opportunity cost***. Remember from Chapter 1 how we defined opportunity cost. It is the cost of any activity measured in terms of the *sacrifice* made in doing it: in other words, the cost measured in terms of the opportunities forgone.

How do we apply this principle of opportunity cost to a firm? First we must discover what factors of production it is using. Then we must measure the sacrifice involved. To do this it is necessary to put factors into two categories.

Factors not owned by the firm: explicit costs

The opportunity cost of using factors not already owned by the firm is simply the price that the firm has to pay for them. Thus if the firm uses £100 worth of electricity, the opportunity cost is £100. The firm has sacrificed £100 which could have been spent on something else. These costs are called ***explicit costs*** because they involve direct payment of money by firms.

Factors already owned by the firm: implicit costs

When the firm already owns factors (e.g. machinery), it does not as a rule have to pay out money to use them. Their opportunity costs are thus ***implicit costs***. They are equal to what the factors could earn for the firm in some alternative use, either within the firm or hired out to some other firm.

Here are some examples of implicit costs:

- A firm owns some buildings. The opportunity cost of using them is the rent it could have received by letting them out to another firm.
- A firm draws £100 000 from the bank out of its savings in order to invest in new plant and equipment. The opportunity cost of this investment is not just the £100 000 (an explicit cost), but also the interest it thereby forgoes (an implicit cost).
- The owner of the firm could have earned £20 000 per annum by working for someone else. This £20 000 then is the opportunity cost of the owner's time.

If there is no alternative use for a factor of production, as in the case of a machine designed to produce a specific product, and if it has no scrap value, the opportunity cost of using it is *zero*. In such a case, if the output from the machine is worth more than the cost of all the *other* inputs involved, the firm might as well use the machine rather than let it stand idle.

What the firm paid for the machine – its ***historic cost*** – is irrelevant. Not using the machine will not bring that money back. It has been spent. These are sometimes referred to as 'sunk costs'.

The 'bygones' principle states that sunk (fixed) costs should be ignored when deciding whether to produce or sell more or less of a product. Only variable costs should be taken into account.

Definitions

Opportunity cost Cost measured in terms of the next best alternative forgone.

Explicit costs The payments to outside suppliers of inputs.

Implicit costs Costs that do not involve a direct payment of money to a third party, but which nevertheless involve a sacrifice of some alternative.

Historic costs The original amount the firm paid for factors it now owns.

EXPLORING ECONOMICS BOX 5.5

THE FALLACY OF USING HISTORIC COSTS

Or there's no point crying over spilt milk

If you fall over and break your leg, there is little point in saying, 'If only I hadn't done that I could have gone on that skiing holiday; I could have taken part in that race; I could have done so many other things (sigh).' Wishing things were different won't change history. You have to manage as well as you can *with* your broken leg.

It is the same for a firm. Once it has purchased some inputs, it is no good then wishing it hadn't. It has to accept that it has now got them, and make the best decisions about what to do with them.

Take a simple example. The local greengrocer in early December decides to buy 100 Christmas trees for £10 each. At the time of purchase, this represents an opportunity cost of £10 each, since the £10 could have been spent on something else. The greengrocer estimates that there is enough local demand to sell all 100 trees at £20 each, thereby making a reasonable profit.

But the estimate turns out to be wrong. On 23 December there are still 50 trees unsold. What should be done? At this stage the £10 that was paid for the trees is irrelevant. It is a historic cost. It cannot be recouped: the trees cannot be sold back to the wholesaler!

In fact, the opportunity cost is now zero. It might even be negative if the greengrocer has to pay to dispose of any unsold trees. It might, therefore, be worth selling the trees at £10, £5 or even £1. Last thing on Christmas Eve it might even be worth giving away any unsold trees.

Why is the correct price to charge (for the unsold trees) the one at which the price elasticity of demand equals −1? (Assume no disposal costs.)

Likewise the ***replacement cost*** is irrelevant. That should be taken into account only when the firm is considering replacing the machine.

Costs and inputs

A firm's costs of production will depend on the factors of production it uses. The more factors it uses, the greater will its costs be. More precisely, this relationship depends on two elements:

- The productivity of the factors. The greater their physical productivity, the smaller will be the quantity of them required to produce a given level of output, and hence the lower will be the cost of that output. In other words, there is a direct link between *TPP*, *APP* and *MPP* and the costs of production.
- The price of the factors. The higher their price, the higher will be the costs of production.

In the short run, some factors are fixed in supply. Their total costs, therefore, are fixed, in the sense that they do not vary with output. Rent on land is a ***fixed cost***. It is the same whether the firm produces a lot or a little.

The total cost of using variable factors, however, does vary with output. The cost of raw materials is a ***variable cost***. The more that is produced, the more raw materials are used and therefore the higher is their total cost.

? *The following are some costs incurred by a shoe manufacturer. Decide whether each one is a fixed cost or a variable cost or has some element of both. (a) The cost of leather. (b) The fee paid to an advertising agency. (c) Wear and tear on machinery (d) Business rates on the factory. (e) Electricity for heating and lighting. (f) Electricity for running the machines. (g) Basic minimum wages agreed with the union. (h) Overtime pay. (i) Depreciation of machines as a result purely of their age (irrespective of their condition).*

Total cost

The ***total cost*** (*TC*) of production is the sum of the *total variable costs* (*TVC*) and the *total fixed costs* (*TFC*) of production:

$$TC = TVC + TFC$$

Consider Table 5.2 and Figure 5.2. They show the total costs for firm X of producing different levels of output (Q). Let us examine each of the three cost curves in turn.

Definitions

Replacement costs What the firm would have to pay to replace factors it currently owns.

Fixed costs Total costs that do not vary with the amount of output produced.

Variable costs Total costs that do vary with the amount of output produced.

Total cost The sum of total fixed costs and total variable costs: $TC = TFC + TVC$.

Table 5.2 Total costs for firm X

Output (Q)	TFC (£)	TVC (£)	TC (£)
0	12	0	12
1	12	10	22
2	12	16	28
3	12	21	33
4	12	28	40
5	12	40	52
6	12	60	72
7	12	91	103
.	.	.	.

Total fixed cost (TFC)

In our example, total fixed cost is assumed to be £12. Since this does not vary with output, it is shown by a horizontal straight line.

Total variable cost (TVC)

With a zero output, no variable factors will be used. Thus $TVC = 0$. The TVC curve, therefore, starts from the origin.

The shape of the TVC curve follows from the law of diminishing returns. Initially, *before* diminishing returns set in, TVC rises less and less rapidly as more variable factors are added. Take the case of a factory with a fixed supply of machinery: initially as more workers are taken on the workers can do increasingly specialist tasks and make a fuller use of the capital equipment. This corresponds to the portion of the TPP curve that rises more rapidly (up to point b in Figure 5.1 on p. 123).

As output is increased beyond point m in Figure 5.2, diminishing returns set in. Since extra workers (the extra variable factors) are producing less and less extra output, the extra units of output they do produce will cost more and more in terms of wage costs. Thus TVC rises more and more rapidly. The TVC curve gets steeper. This corresponds to the portion of the TPP curve that rises less rapidly (between points b and d in Figure 5.1).

Total cost (TC)

Since $TC = TVC + TFC$, the TC curve is simply the TVC curve shifted vertically upwards by £12.

Average and marginal costs

Average cost (AC) is cost per unit of production:

$$AC = TC/Q$$

Thus if it cost a firm £2000 to produce 100 units of a product, the average cost would be £20 for each unit (£2000/100).

Like total cost, average cost can be divided into the two components, fixed and variable. In other words, average cost equals ***average fixed cost*** ($AFC = TFC/Q$) plus ***average variable cost*** ($AVC = TVC/Q$):

$$AC = AFC + AVC$$

Marginal cost (MC) is the *extra* cost of producing *one more unit*: that is, the rise in total cost per one unit rise in output:

$$MC = \frac{\Delta TC}{\Delta Q}$$

Figure 5.2 Total costs for firm X

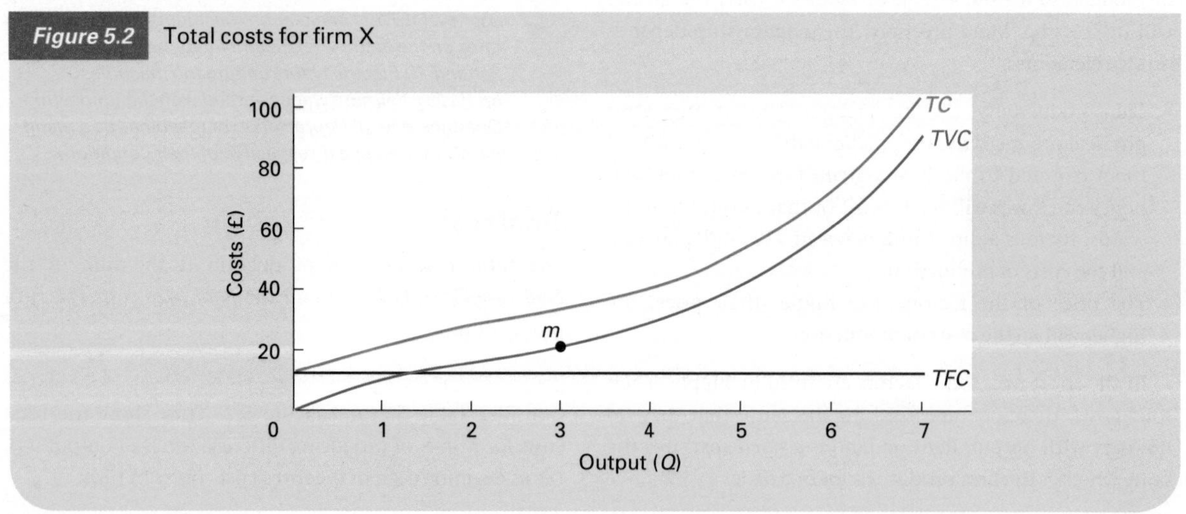

Definitions

Average (total) cost Total cost (fixed plus variable) per unit of output: $AC = TC/Q = AFC + AVC$.

Average fixed cost Total fixed cost per unit of output: $AFC = TFC/Q$.

Average variable cost Total variable cost per unit of output: $AVC = TVC/Q$.

Marginal cost The cost of producing one more unit of output: $MC = \Delta TC/\Delta Q$.

Table 5.3 Total, average and marginal costs for firm X

Output (Q) (units)	TFC (£)	AFC (TFC/Q) (£)	TVC (£)	AVC (TVC/Q) (£)	TC (TFC + TVC) (£)	AC (TC/Q) (£)	MC (ΔTC/ΔQ) (£)
0	12	–	0	–	12	–	
1	12	12	10	10	22	22	10
2	12	6	16	...	28	14	...
3	...	...	21	7	...	...	5
4	...	3	28	...	40	...	7
5	...	2.4	...	8	52	10.4	12
6	...	...	...	10	...	12	...
7	...	1.7	91	13	103	14.7	31

For example, assume that a firm is currently producing 1 000 000 boxes of matches a month. It now increases output by 1000 boxes (another batch): $\Delta Q = 1000$. As a result, its total costs rise by £30: $\Delta TC = £30$. What is the cost of producing one more box of matches? It is:

$$\frac{\Delta TC}{\Delta Q} = \frac{£30}{1000} = 3\text{p}$$

(Note that all marginal costs are variable, since, by definition, there can be no extra fixed costs as output rises.)

Given the *TFC*, *TVC* and *TC* for each output, it is possible to derive the *AFC*, *AVC*, *AC* and *MC* for each output using the above definitions.

For example, using the data of Table 5.2, Table 5.3 can be constructed.

? *Fill in the missing figures in Table 5.3. (Note that the figures for MC come in the spaces between each level of output.)*

What will be the shapes of the *MC*, *AFC*, *AVC* and *AC* curves? These follow from the nature of the *MPP* and *APP* curves that we looked at in section 5.1 above. You may recall that the typical shapes of the *APP* and *MPP* curves are like those illustrated in Figure 5.3.

Marginal cost (MC)

KI 17 p121

The shape of the *MC* curve follows directly from the law of diminishing returns. Initially, in Figure 5.4, as more of the variable factor is used, extra units of output cost less than previous units. *MC* falls. This corresponds to the rising portion of the *MPP* curve in Figure 5.3 and the portion of the *TVC* curve in Figure 5.2 to the left of point *m*.

Beyond a certain level of output, diminishing returns set in. This is shown as point *x* in Figure 5.4 and corresponds to point *b* in Figure 5.3 (and point *m* in Figure 5.2). Thereafter *MC* rises as *MPP* falls. Additional units of output cost more and more to produce, since they require ever-increasing amounts of the variable factor.

Average fixed cost (AFC)

This falls continuously as output rises, since *total* fixed costs are being spread over a greater and greater output.

Average variable cost (AVC)

The shape of the *AVC* curve depends on the shape of the *APP* curve. As the average product of workers rises (up to point *c* in Figure 5.3), the average labour cost per unit of output (the *AVC*) falls: as far as point *y* in Figure 5.4. Thereafter, as *APP* falls, *AVC* must rise.

Figure 5.3 Average and marginal physical product

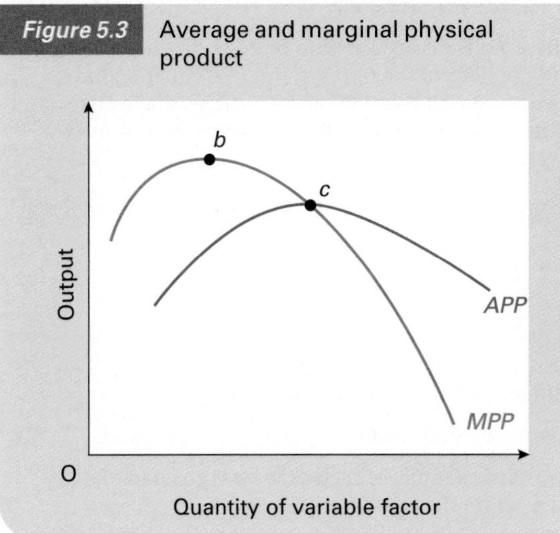

Figure 5.4 Average and marginal costs

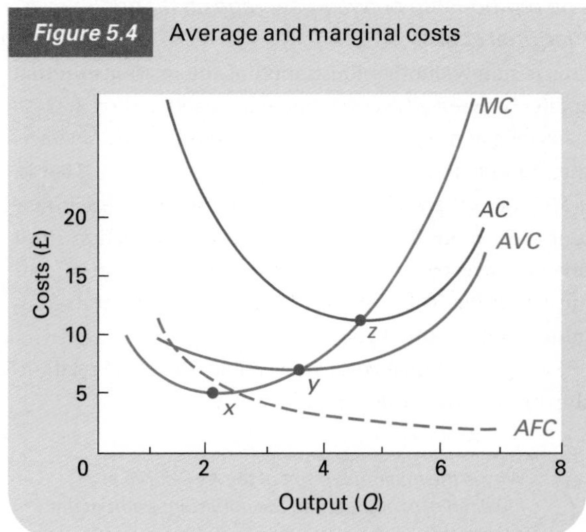

EXPLORING ECONOMICS **BOX 5.6**

COST CURVES IN PRACTICE

When fixed factors are divisible

Are cost curves always the shape depicted in this chapter? The answer is no. Sometimes, rather than being U-shaped, the *AVC* and *MC* curves are flat bottomed, like the curves in the diagram. Indeed, they may be constant (and equal to each other) over a *substantial* range of output.

The reason for this is that fixed factors may sometimes not have to be in full use all the time. Take the case of a firm with 100 identical machines, each one requiring one person to operate it. Although the firm cannot use *more* than the 100 machines, it could use fewer: in other words, some of the machines could be left idle. Assume, for example, that instead of using 100 machines, the firm uses only 90. It would need only 90 operatives and 90 per cent of the raw materials.

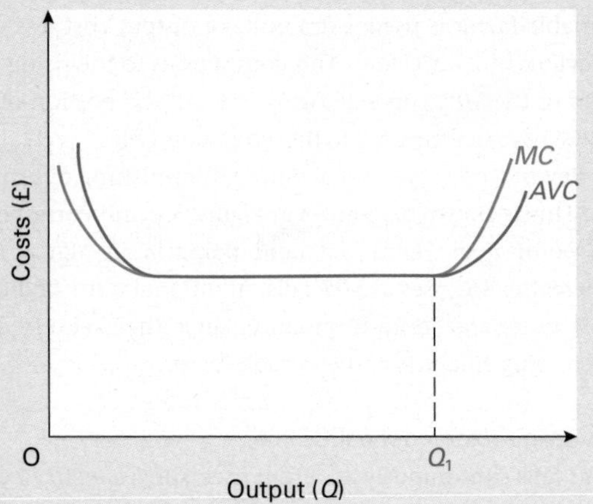

Similarly, if it used only 20 machines, its total variable costs (labour and raw materials) would be only 20 per cent. What we are saying here is that *average* variable cost remains constant – and over a very large range of output, using anything from 1 machine to 100 machines.

The reason for the constant *AVC* (and *MC*) is that by varying the amount of fixed capital used, the *proportions* used of capital, labour and raw materials can be kept the same and hence the average and marginal productivity of labour and raw materials will remain constant.

Only when all machines are in use (at Q_1) will *AVC* start to rise if output is further expanded. Machines may then have to work beyond their optimal speed, using more raw materials per unit of output (diminishing returns to raw materials), or workers may have to work longer shifts with higher (overtime) pay.

1. ***Assume that a firm has 5 identical machines, each operating independently. Assume that with all 5 machines operating normally, 100 units of output are produced each day. Below what level of output will AVC and MC rise?***
2. ***Manufacturing firms like the one we have been describing will have other fixed costs (such as rent and managerial overheads). Does the existence of these affect the argument that the AVC curve will be flat bottomed?***

Average (total) cost (AC)

This is simply the vertical sum of the *AFC* and *AVC* curves. Note that as *AFC* gets less, the gap between *AVC* and *AC* narrows.

The relationship between average cost and marginal cost

This is simply another illustration of the relationship that applies between *all* averages and marginals (see Box 5.3).

As long as new units of output cost less than the average, their production must pull the average cost down. That is, if *MC* is less than *AC*, *AC* must be falling. Likewise, if new units cost more than the average, their production must drive the average up. That is, if *MC* is greater than *AC*, *AC* must be rising. Therefore, the *MC* crosses the *AC* at its minimum point (point *z* in Figure 5.4).

Since all marginal costs are variable, the same relationship holds between *MC* and *AVC*.

? *Why is the minimum point of the AVC curve at a lower level of output than the minimum point of the AC curve?*

*LOOKING AT THE MATHS

The total, average and marginal cost functions can be expressed algebraically as follows:

$$TFC = a \quad (1)$$

$$TVC = bQ - cQ^2 + dQ^3 \quad (2)$$

$$TC = a + bQ - cQ^2 + dQ^3 \quad (3)$$

where *a* is the constant term representing fixed costs, and the signs of the terms in the *TVC* equation have been chosen to give *TVC* and *TC* curves shaped like those in Figure 5.2. Dividing each of the above by Q gives:

$$AFC = \frac{a}{Q} \quad (4)$$

$$AVC = b - cQ + dQ^2 \quad (5)$$

$$AC = \frac{a}{Q} + b - cQ + dQ^2 \quad (6)$$

Differentiating equation (3) or (2) gives:

$$MC = b - 2cQ + 3dQ^2 \quad (7)$$

A worked example of each of these is given in Maths Case 5.1 on the book's website.

Section summary

1. When measuring costs of production, we should be careful to use the concept of opportunity cost. In the case of factors not owned by the firm, the opportunity cost is simply the explicit cost of purchasing or hiring them. It is the price paid for them. In the case of factors already owned by the firm, it is the implicit cost of what the factor could have earned for the firm in its next best alternative use.
2. In the short run, some factors are fixed in supply. Their total costs are thus fixed with respect to output. In the case of variable factors, their total cost will increase as more output is produced and hence as more of the variable factor is used.
3. Total cost can be divided into total fixed and total variable costs. Total variable cost will tend to increase less rapidly at first as more is produced, but then when diminishing returns set in, it will increase more and more rapidly.
4. Marginal cost is the cost of producing one more unit of output. It will probably fall at first (corresponding to the part of the *TVC* curve where the slope is getting shallower), but will start to rise as soon as diminishing returns set in.
5. Average cost, like total cost, can be divided into fixed and variable costs. Average fixed cost will decline as more output is produced. The reason is that the total fixed cost is being spread over a greater and greater number of units of output. Average variable cost will tend to decline at first, but once the marginal cost has risen above it, it must then rise.

5.3 THE LONG-RUN THEORY OF PRODUCTION

KI 16 p120 In the long run, *all* factors of production are variable. There is time for the firm to build a new factory (maybe in a different part of the country), to install new machines, to use different techniques of production, and in general to combine its inputs in whatever proportion and in whatever quantities it chooses.

In the long run, then, there are several decisions that a firm has to make: decisions about the scale and location of its operations and what techniques of production it should use. These decisions affect the costs of production. It is important, therefore, to get them right.

Table 5.4 Short-run and long-run increases in output

Short run			Long run		
Input 1	Input 2	Output	Input 1	Input 2	Output
3	1	25	1	1	15
3	2	45	2	2	35
3	3	60	3	3	60
3	4	70	4	4	90
3	5	75	5	5	125

The scale of production

If a firm were to double all of its inputs – something it could do in the long run – would it double its output? Or will output more than double or less than double? We can distinguish three possible situations:

Constant returns to scale. This is where a given percentage increase in inputs will lead to the *same* percentage increase in output.

Increasing returns to scale. This is where a given percentage increase in inputs will lead to a *larger* percentage increase in output.

Decreasing returns to scale. This is where a given percentage increase in inputs will lead to a *smaller* percentage increase in output.

Notice the terminology here. The words 'to scale' mean that *all* inputs increase by the same proportion. Decreasing returns *to scale* are therefore quite different from diminishing *marginal* returns (where only the *variable* factor increases). The differences between marginal returns to a variable factor and returns to scale are illustrated in Table 5.4.

In the short run, input 1 is assumed to be fixed in supply (at 3 units). Output can be increased only by using more of the variable factor (input 2). In the long run, however, both input 1 and input 2 are variable.

Referring still to Table 5.4, are there diminishing or increasing marginal returns, and are there decreasing or increasing returns to scale?

Economies of scale

The concept of increasing returns to scale is closely linked to that of ***economies of scale***. A firm experiences economies of scale if costs per unit of output fall as the scale of

Definition

Economies of scale When increasing the scale of production leads to a lower cost per unit of output.

production increases. Clearly, if a firm is getting increasing returns to scale from its factors of production, then as it produces more it will be using smaller and smaller amounts of factors per unit of output. Other things being equal, this means that it will be producing at a lower unit cost.

There are several reasons why firms are likely to experience economies of scale. Some are due to increasing returns to scale; some are not.

Specialisation and division of labour. In large-scale plants workers can do more simple, repetitive jobs. With this ***specialisation and division of labour*** less training is needed; workers can become highly efficient in their particular job, especially with long production runs; there is less time lost in workers switching from one operation to another; and supervision is easier. Workers and managers can be employed who have specific skills in specific areas.

Indivisibilities. Some inputs are of a minimum size: they are indivisible. The most obvious example is machinery. Take the case of a combine harvester. A small-scale farmer could not make full use of one. They only become economical to use, therefore, on farms above a certain size. The problem of ***indivisibilities*** is made worse when different machines, each of which is part of the production process, are of a different size. For example, if there are two types of machine, one producing 6 units a day, and the other packaging 4 units a day, a minimum of 12 units would have to be produced, involving two production machines and three packaging machines, if all machines are to be fully utilised.

The 'container principle'. Any capital equipment that contains things (blast furnaces, oil tankers, pipes, vats, etc.) tends to cost less per unit of output the larger its size. The reason has to do with the relationship between a container's volume and its *surface area*. A container's cost depends largely on the materials used to build it and hence roughly on its surface area. Its output depends largely on its *volume*. Large containers have a bigger volume relative to surface area than do small containers. For example, a container with a bottom, top and four sides, with each side measuring 1 metre, has a volume of 1 cubic metre and a surface area of 6 square metres (six surfaces of 1 square metre each). If each side were now to be doubled in length to 2 metres, the volume would be 8 cubic metres and the surface area 24 square metres (six surfaces of 4 square metres each). Thus an eightfold increase in capacity has been gained at only a fourfold increase in the container's surface area, and hence an approximate fourfold increase in cost.

Greater efficiency of large machines. Large machines may be more efficient in the sense that more output can be gained for a given amount of inputs. For example, only one worker may be required to operate a machine whether it be large or small. Also, a large machine may make more efficient use of raw materials.

By-products. With production on a large scale, there may be sufficient waste products to enable them to make some by-product.

Multi-stage production. A large factory may be able to take a product through several stages in its manufacture. This saves time and cost in moving the semi-finished product from one firm or factory to another. For example, a large cardboard-manufacturing firm may be able to convert trees or waste paper into cardboard and then into cardboard boxes in a continuous sequence.

All the above are examples of ***plant economies of scale***. They are due to an individual factory or workplace or machine being large. There are other economies of scale, however, that are associated with the *firm* being large – perhaps with many factories.

Organisational economies. With a large firm, individual plants can specialise in particular functions. There can also be centralised administration of the firm. Often, after a merger between two firms, savings can be made by ***rationalising*** their activities in this way.

Spreading overheads. Some expenditures are economic only when the *firm* is large: for example, research and development – only a large firm can afford to set up a research laboratory. This is another example of indivisibilities, only this time at the level of the firm rather than the plant. The greater the firm's output, the more these ***overhead*** costs are spread.

Definitions

Specialisation and division of labour Where production is broken down into a number of simpler, more specialised tasks, thus allowing workers to acquire a high degree of efficiency.

Indivisibilities The impossibility of dividing a factor into smaller units.

Plant economies of scale Economies of scale that arise because of the large size of the factory.

Rationalisation The reorganising of production (often after a merger) so as to cut out waste and duplication and generally to reduce costs.

Overheads Costs arising from the general running of an organisation, and only indirectly related to the level of output.

Financial economies. Large firms may be able to obtain finance at lower interest rates than small firms. They may be able to obtain certain inputs cheaper by buying in bulk.

Economies of scope. Often a firm is large because it produces a range of products. This can result in each individual product being produced more cheaply than if it was produced in a single-product firm. The reason for these ***economies of scope*** is that various overhead costs and financial and organisational economies can be shared among the products. For example, a firm that produces a whole range of CD players, amplifiers and tuners can benefit from shared marketing and distribution costs and the bulk purchase of electronic components.

1. *Which of the economies of scale we have considered are due to increasing returns to scale and which are due to other factors?*
2. *What economies of scale is a large department store likely to experience?*

Diseconomies of scale

When firms get beyond a certain size, costs per unit of output may start to increase. There are several reasons for such ***diseconomies of scale***:

- Management problems of co-ordination may increase as the firm becomes larger and more complex, and as lines of communication get longer. There may be a lack of personal involvement by management.
- Workers may feel 'alienated' if their jobs are boring and repetitive, and if they feel an insignificantly small part of a large organisation. Poor motivation may lead to shoddy work.
- Industrial relations may deteriorate as a result of these factors and also as a result of the more complex interrelationships between different categories of worker.
- Production-line processes and the complex interdependencies of mass production can lead to great disruption if there are hold-ups in any one part of the firm.

Whether firms experience economies or diseconomies of scale will depend on the conditions applying in each individual firm.

Why are firms likely to experience economies of scale up to a certain size and then diseconomies of scale after some point beyond that?

Location

In the long run, a firm can move to a different location. The location will affect the cost of production since locations differ in terms of the availability and cost of raw materials, suitable land and power supply, the qualifications, skills and experience of the labour force, wage rates, transport and communications networks, the cost of local services, and banking and financial facilities. In short, locations differ in terms of the availability, suitability and cost of the factors of production.

Transport costs will be an important influence on a firm's location. Ideally, a firm will wish to be as near as possible to both its raw materials and the market for its finished product. When market and raw materials are in different locations, the firm will minimise its transport costs by locating somewhere between the two. In general, if the raw materials are more expensive to transport than the finished product, the firm should be located as near as possible to the raw materials. This will normally apply to firms whose raw materials are heavier or more bulky than the finished product. Thus heavy industry, which uses large quantities of coal and various ores, tends to be concentrated near the coal fields or near the ports. If, on the other hand, the finished product is more expensive to transport (e.g. bread and beer), the firm will probably be located as near as possible to its market.

When raw materials or markets are in many different locations, transport costs will be minimised at the 'centre of gravity'. This location will be nearer to those raw materials and markets whose transport costs are greater per mile.

How is the opening-up of trade and investment between eastern and western Europe likely to affect the location of industries within Europe that have (a) substantial economies of scale; (b) little or no economies of scale?

The size of the whole industry

As an *industry* grows in size, this can lead to ***external economies of scale*** for its member firms. This is where a firm, whatever its own individual size, benefits from the *whole industry* being large. For example, the firm may benefit from having access to specialist raw material or component suppliers, labour with specific skills, firms that specialise in marketing the finished product, and banks and other financial institutions with experience of the industry's requirements. What we are referring to here is the ***industry's infrastructure***: the facilities, support services, skills and experience that can be shared by its members.

Definitions

Economies of scope When increasing the range of products produced by a firm reduces the cost of producing each one.

Diseconomies of scale Where costs per unit of output increase as the scale of production increases.

External economies of scale Where a firm's costs per unit of output decrease as the size of the whole industry grows.

Industry's infrastructure The network of supply agents, communications, skills, training facilities, distribution channels, specialised financial services, etc. that supports a particular industry.

?

1. Name some industries where external economies of scale are gained. What are the specific external economies in each case?

2. Would you expect external economies to be associated with the concentration of an industry in a particular region?

The member firms of a particular industry might experience ***external diseconomies of scale***. For example, as an industry grows larger, this may create a growing shortage of specific raw materials or skilled labour. This will push up their prices, and hence the firms' costs.

The optimum combination of factors: the marginal product approach

In the long run, all factors can be varied. The firm can thus choose what techniques of production to use: what design of factory to build, what types of machine to buy, how to organise the factory, whether to use highly automated processes or more labour-intensive techniques. It must be very careful in making these decisions. Once it has built its factory and installed the machinery, these then become fixed factors of production, maybe for many years: the subsequent 'short-run' time period may in practice last a very long time!

For any given scale, how should the firm decide what technique to use? How should it decide the optimum 'mix' of factors of production?

The profit-maximising firm will obviously want to use the least costly combination of factors to produce any given output. It will therefore substitute factors, one for another, if by so doing it can reduce the cost of a given output. What then is the optimum combination of factors?

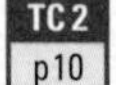

The simple two-factor case

Take first the simplest case where a firm uses just two factors: labour (L) and capital (K). The least-cost combination of the two will be where:

$$\frac{MPP_L}{P_L} = \frac{MPP_K}{P_K}$$

in other words, where the extra product (MPP) from the last pound spent on each factor is equal. But why should this be so? The easiest way to answer this is to consider what would happen if they were not equal.

If they were not equal, it would be possible to reduce cost per unit of output, by using a different combination of labour and capital. For example, if:

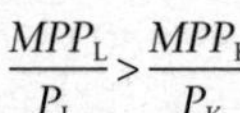

$$\frac{MPP_L}{P_L} > \frac{MPP_K}{P_K}$$

more labour should be used relative to capital, since the firm is getting a greater physical return for its money from extra workers than from extra capital. As more labour is used per unit of capital, however, diminishing returns to labour set in. Thus MPP_L will fall. Likewise, as less capital is used per unit of labour, MPP_K will rise. This will continue until:

$$\frac{MPP_L}{P_L} = \frac{MPP_K}{P_K}$$

At this point, the firm will stop substituting labour for capital.

Since no further gain can be made by substituting one factor for another, this combination of factors or 'choice of technique' can be said to be the most efficient. It is the least-cost way of combining factors for any given output. Efficiency in this sense of using the optimum factor proportions is known as ***productive efficiency***.

The multi-factor case

Where a firm uses many different factors, the least-cost combination of factors will be where:

$$\frac{MPP_a}{P_a} = \frac{MPP_b}{P_b} = \frac{MPP_c}{P_c} \ldots = \frac{MPP_n}{P_n}$$

where a . . . n are different factors. This is a variant of the equi-marginal principle that we examined on page 99.

The reasons are the same as in the two-factor case. If any inequality exists between the MPP/P ratios, a firm will be able to reduce its costs by using more of those factors with a high MPP/P ratio and less of those with a low MPP/P ratio until they all become equal.

A major problem for a firm in choosing the least-cost technique is in predicting future factor price changes.

If the price of a factor were to change, the MPP/P ratios would cease to be equal. The firm, to minimise costs, would then like to alter its factor combinations until the MPP/P ratios once more became equal. The trouble is that, once it has committed itself to a particular technique, it may be several years before it can switch to an alternative one. Thus if a firm invests in labour-intensive methods of production and is then faced with an unexpected wage rise, it may regret not having chosen a more capital-intensive technique.

If factor X costs twice as much as factor Y ($P_X/P_Y = 2$), what can be said about the relationship between the MPPs of the two factors if the optimum combination of factors is used?

Definitions

External diseconomies of scale Where a firm's costs per unit of output increase as the size of the whole industry increases.

Productive efficiency The least-cost combination of factors for a given output.

*LOOKING AT THE MATHS

We can express the long-run production function algebraically. In the simple two-factor model, where capital (K) and labour (L) are the two factors, the production function is:

$$TPP = f(K,L)$$

A simple and widely used production function is the ***Cobb–Douglas production function***. This takes the form:

$$TPP = AK^{\alpha}L^{\beta}$$

Box 5.7 demonstrates that where $\alpha + \beta = 1$, there are constant returns to scale; where $\alpha + \beta > 1$, there are increasing returns to scale; and where $\alpha + \beta < 1$, there are decreasing returns to scale.

A multiple-factor Cobb–Douglas production function would take the form:

$$TPP = AF_1^{\alpha}F_2^{\beta}F_3^{\gamma} \ldots F_n^{\omega}$$

where $F_1, F_2, F_3 \ldots F_n$ are all the factors. For example, if there were 6 factors, n would be factor 6. Again, it can be shown that where $\alpha + \beta + \gamma + \ldots + \omega = 1$, there are constant returns to scale; where $\alpha + \beta + \gamma + \ldots + \omega > 1$, there are increasing returns to scale; and where $\alpha + \beta + \gamma + \ldots + \omega < 1$, there are decreasing returns to scale.

KI 16 p120

*The optimum combination of factors: the isoquant/isocost approach

This section is optional. You can skip straight to page 139 without loss of continuity.

A firm's choice of optimum technique can be shown graphically. This graphical analysis takes the simplest case of just two variable factors – for example, labour and capital. The amount of labour used is measured on one axis and the amount of capital used is measured on the other.

The graph involves the construction of *isoquants* and *isocosts*.

Isoquants

Imagine that a firm wants to produce a certain level of output: say, 5000 units per year. Let us assume that it estimates all the possible combinations of labour and capital that could produce that level of output. Some of these estimates are shown in Table 5.5.

Technique *a* is a capital-intensive technique, using 40 units of capital and only 5 workers. As we move towards technique *e*, labour is substituted for capital. The techniques become more labour intensive.

These alternative techniques for producing a given level of output can be plotted on a graph. The points are joined to form an ***isoquant***. Figure 5.5 shows the 5000 unit isoquant corresponding to Table 5.5.

Table 5.5 Various capital and labour combinations to produce 5000 units of output per year

	a	b	c	d	e
Units of capital (K)	40	20	10	6	4
Number of workers (L)	5	12	20	30	50

Figure 5.5 An isoquant

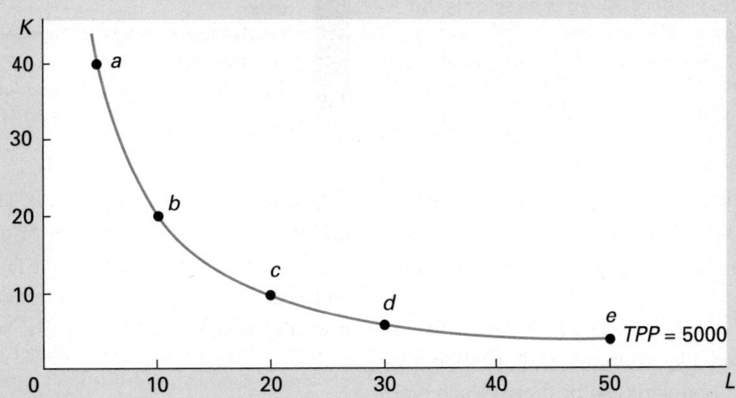

Definitions

Cobb–Douglas production function Like other production functions, it shows how output (TPP) varies with inputs of various factors (F_1, F_2, F_3, etc.). In the simple two-factor case it takes the following form:

$$TPP = f(F_1,F_2) = AF_1^{\alpha}F_2^{\beta}$$

If $\alpha + \beta = 1$, there are constant returns to scale; if $\alpha + \beta > 1$, there are increasing returns to scale; if $\alpha + \beta < 1$, there are decreasing returns to scale.

Isoquant A line showing all the alternative combinations of two factors that can produce a given level of output.

EXPLORING ECONOMICS *BOX 5.7

THE COBB–DOUGLAS PRODUCTION FUNCTION

Exploring its properties

Let us take the simple Cobb–Douglas production function:

$$TPP = AK^{\alpha}L^{\beta} \quad (1)$$

Returns to scale and the Cobb–Douglas production function

What would happen if you were to double the amount of both K and L used (in other words, the scale of production doubles)? If output doubles, there are constant returns to scale. If output more than doubles, there are *increasing* returns to scale; if it less than doubles, there are *decreasing* returns to scale. Let us see what happens when we double the amount of K and L in equation (1).

$$\begin{aligned} TPP &= A(2K^{\alpha})(2L^{\beta}) \\ &= A2^{\alpha}K^{\alpha}2^{\beta}L^{\beta} \\ &= A2^{\alpha+\beta}K^{\alpha}L^{\beta} \end{aligned}$$

If $\alpha + \beta = 1$, then $2^{\alpha+\beta} = 2$. Thus:

$$TPP = 2AK^{\alpha}L^{\beta}$$

In other words, doubling the amount of K and L used has doubled output: there are constant returns to scale.

If $\alpha + \beta > 1$, then $2^{\alpha+\beta} > 2$. In this case, doubling inputs will more than double output: there are increasing returns to scale. Similarly, if $\alpha + \beta < 1$, then $2^{\alpha+\beta} < 2$ and there are decreasing returns to scale.

Finding the marginal physical products of labour and capital

The marginal physical product (MPP) of a factor is the additional output obtained by employing one more unit of that factor, while holding other factors constant. The MPP of either factor in the above Cobb–Douglas production function can be found by differentiating the function with respect to that factor (see page A:12 for the rules of partial differentiation). Thus:

$$MPP_K = \frac{\partial(TPP)}{\partial K} = \alpha AK^{\alpha-1}L^{\beta} \quad (2)$$

$$\text{and} \quad MPP_L = \frac{\partial(TPP)}{\partial L} = \beta AK^{\alpha}L^{\beta-1} \quad (3)$$

For example, if the production function were:

$$TPP = 4K^{3/4}L^{1/2} \quad (4)$$

and if $K = 81$ and $L = 36$, then, from equations (2) and (4):

$$\begin{aligned} MPP_K &= \alpha AK^{\alpha-1}L^{\beta} \\ &= \frac{3}{4} \times 4(81^{-1/4})(36^{1/2}) \\ &= 3 \times \frac{1}{3} \times 6 = 6 \end{aligned}$$

$$\begin{aligned} MPP_L &= \beta AK^{\alpha}L^{\beta-1} \\ \text{and} \quad &= \frac{1}{2} \times 4(81^{3/4})(36^{-1/2}) \\ &= 2 \times 27 \times \frac{1}{6} = 9 \end{aligned}$$

In other words, an additional unit of capital will produce an extra 6 units of output and an additional unit of labour will produce an extra 9 units of output.

?

Assume that the production function is given by:

$$TPP = 36K^{1/3}L^{1/2}R^{1/4}$$

where R is the quantity of a particular raw material used.

(a) Are there constant, increasing or decreasing returns to scale?

(b) What is the marginal productivity of the raw material if K = 8, L = 16 and R = 81?

The isoquant shows the whole *range* of alternative ways of producing a given output. Thus Figure 5.5 shows not only points *a* to *e* from the table, but all the intermediate points too.

Like an indifference curve, an isoquant is rather like a contour on a map. And like contours and indifference curves, a whole series of isoquants can be drawn, each one representing a different level of output (*TPP*). The higher the output, the further out to the right will the isoquant be. Thus in Figure 5.6, isoquant I_5 represents a higher level of output than I_4, and I_4 a higher output than I_3, and so on.

?

1. Could isoquants ever cross?

2. Could they ever slope upwards to the right? Explain your answers.

KI 17 p121 *The shape of the isoquant.* Why is the isoquant 'bowed in' towards the origin? This illustrates a diminishing ***marginal rate of factor substitution*** (*MRS*). This, as we shall see in a minute, is due to the law of diminishing returns.

The *MRS*[3] is the amount of one factor (e.g. *K*) that can be replaced by a 1 unit increase in the other factor (e.g. *L*), if output is to be held constant. So if 2 units of capital

[3] Note that we use the same letters *MRS* to refer to the marginal rate of *factor* substitution as we did in the previous chapter to refer to the marginal rate of substitution *in consumption*. Sometimes we use the same words too – just 'marginal rate of substitution' rather than the longer title. In this case we must rely on the context in order to tell which is being referred to.

Definition

Marginal rate of factor substitution The rate at which one factor can be substituted by another while holding the level of output constant:

$$MRS = \Delta F_1 / \Delta F_2 = MPP_{F_2} / MPP_{F_1}$$

Figure 5.6 An isoquant map

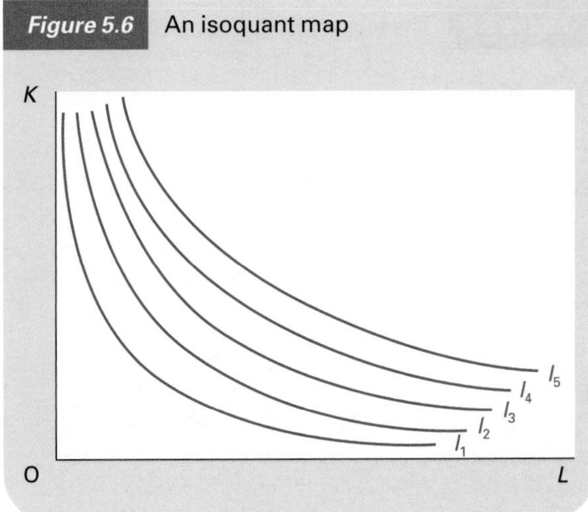

Figure 5.7 Diminishing marginal rate of factor substitution

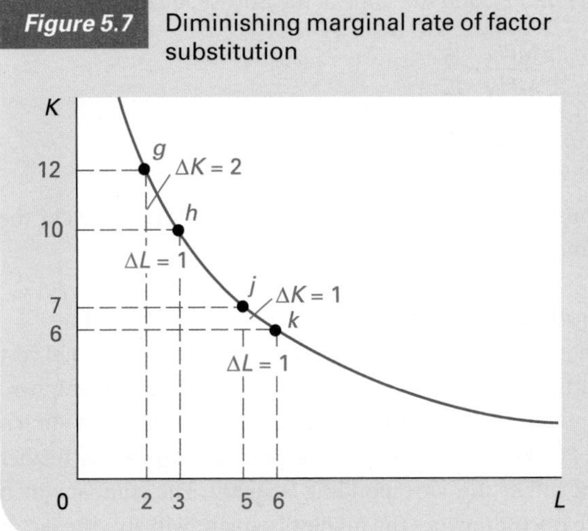

($\Delta K = 2$) could be replaced by 1 unit of labour ($\Delta L = 1$) the *MRS* would be 2. Thus:

$$MRS = \frac{\Delta K}{\Delta L} = \frac{2}{1} = 2$$

The *MRS* between two points on the isoquant will equal the slope of the line joining those two points. Thus in Figure 5.7, the *MRS* between points *g* and *h* is 2 ($\Delta K/\Delta L = 2/1$). But this is merely the slope of the line joining points *g* and *h* (ignoring the negative sign).

When the isoquant is bowed in towards the origin, the slope of the isoquant will diminish as one moves down the curve, and so too, therefore, will the *MRS* diminish. Referring again to Figure 5.7, between points *g* and *h* the *MRS* = 2. Lower down the curve between points *j* and *k*, it has fallen to 1.

? *Calculate the MRS moving up the curve in Figure 5.5 between each of the points: e–d, d–c, c–b and b–a. Does the MRS diminish moving in this direction?*

The relationship between MRS and MPP. As one moves down the isoquant, total output, by definition, will remain the same. Thus the loss in output due to less capital being used (i.e. $MPP_K \times \Delta K$) must be exactly offset by the gain in output due to more labour being used (i.e. $MPP_L \times \Delta L$). Thus:

$$MPP_L \times \Delta L = MPP_K \times \Delta K$$

This equation can be rearranged as follows:

$$\frac{MPP_L}{MPP_K} = \frac{\Delta K}{\Delta L} \quad (= MRS)$$

Thus the *MRS* is equal to the inverse of the marginal productivity ratios of the two factors.

Diminishing MRS and the law of diminishing returns. The principle of diminishing *MRS* is related to the law of diminishing returns. As one moves down the isoquant, increasing amounts of labour are being used relative to capital. This, given diminishing returns, would lead the *MPP* of labour to fall relative to the *MPP* of capital. But since $MRS = MPP_L/MPP_K$, if MPP_L/MPP_K diminishes, then, by definition, so must *MRS*.

The less substitutable factors are for each other, the faster *MRS* will diminish, and therefore the more bowed in will be the isoquant.

Isocosts

We have seen how factors combine to produce different levels of output, but how do we choose the level of output? This will involve taking costs into account.

Assume that factor prices are fixed. A table can be constructed showing the various combinations of factors that a firm can use for a particular sum of money.

For example, assuming that P_K is £20 000 per unit per year and P_L is £10 000 per worker per year, Table 5.6 shows various combinations of capital and labour that would cost the firm £300 000 per year.

These figures are plotted in Figure 5.8. The line joining the points is called an ***isocost***. It shows all the combinations of labour and capital that cost £300 000.

As with isoquants, a series of isocosts can be drawn. Each one represents a particular cost to the firm. The higher the cost, the further out to the right will the isocost be.

Table 5.6 Combinations of capital and labour costing the firm £300 000 per year

Units of capital (at £20 000 per unit)	0	5	10	15
No. of workers (at a wage of £10 000)	30	20	10	0

Definition

Isocost A line showing all the combinations of two factors that cost the same to employ.

Figure 5.8 An isocost

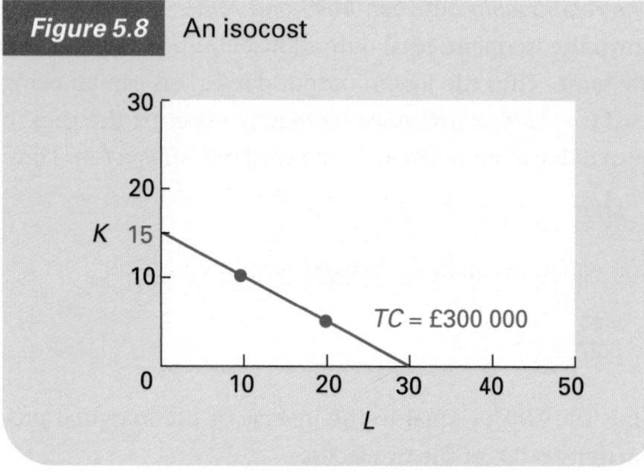

Figure 5.9 The least-cost method of production

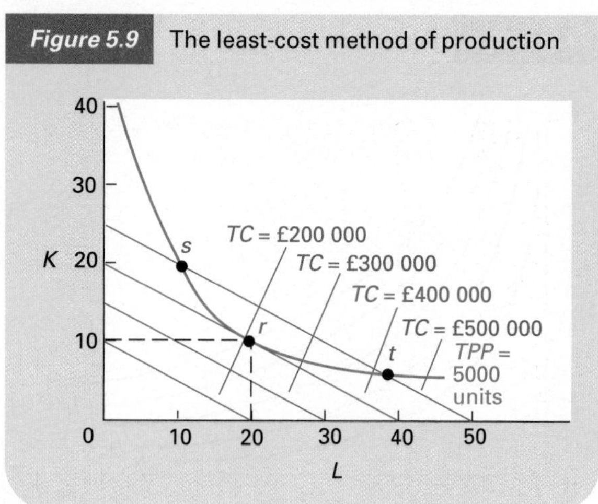

1. What will happen to an isocost if the prices of both factors rise by the same percentage?
2. What will happen to the isocost in Figure 5.8 if the wage rate rises to £15 000?

The slope of the isocost equals:

$$\frac{P_L}{P_K}$$

This can be shown in the above example. The slope of the isocost in Figure 5.8 is 15/30 = $^1/_2$. But this is P_L/P_K (i.e. £10 000/£20 000).

Isoquants and isocosts can now be put on the same diagram. The diagram can be used to answer either of two questions: (a) What is the least-cost way of producing a particular level of output? (b) What is the highest output that can be achieved for a given cost of production?

These two questions are examined in turn.

TC 2 p10

The least-cost combination of factors to produce a given level of output

First the isoquant is drawn for the level of output in question: for example, the 5000 unit isoquant in Figure 5.5. This is reproduced in Figure 5.9.

Then a series of isocosts are drawn representing different levels of total cost. The higher the level of total cost, the further out will be the isocosts.

KI 3 p10

The least-cost combination of labour and capital is shown at point *r*, where *TC* = £400 000. This is where the isoquant just touches the lowest possible isocost. Any other point on the isoquant (e.g. *s* or *t*) would be on a higher isocost.

Comparison with the marginal productivity approach. We showed earlier that the least-cost combination of labour and capital was where:

$$\frac{MPP_L}{P_L} = \frac{MPP_K}{P_K}$$

In this section it has just been shown that the least-cost combination is where the isoquant is tangential to an isocost (i.e. point *r* in Figure 5.9). Thus their slope is the same. The slope of the isoquant equals *MRS*, which equals MPP_L/MPP_K; and the slope of the isocost equals P_L/P_K.

KI 14 p99

$$\therefore \quad \frac{MPP_L}{MPP_K} = \frac{P_L}{P_K}$$

$$\therefore \quad \frac{MPP_L}{P_L} = \frac{MPP_K}{P_K}$$

Thus, as one would expect, the two approaches yield the same result.

Highest output for a given cost of production

An isocost can be drawn for the particular level of total cost outlay in question. Then a series of isoquants can be drawn, representing different levels of output (*TPP*). This is shown in Figure 5.10. The higher the level of output, the further out will lie the corresponding isoquant. The point at which the isocost touches the highest isoquant will give the factor combination yielding the highest output for that level of cost. This will be at point *h* in Figure 5.10.

Again this will be where the slopes of the isocost and isoquant are the same: where $P_L/P_K = MRS$.

Figure 5.10 Maximising output for a given total cost

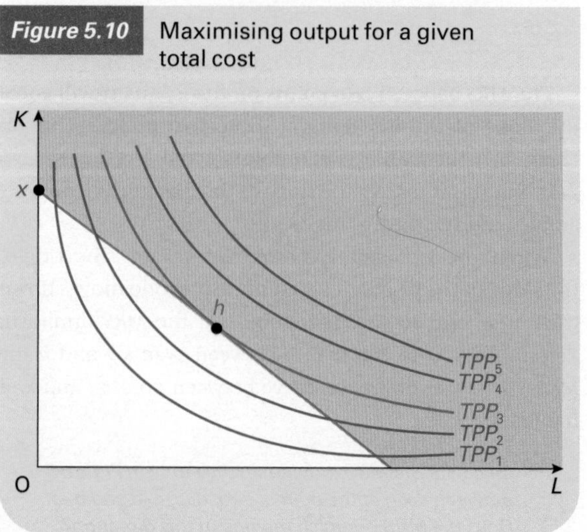

If the prices of factors change, new isocosts will have to be drawn. Thus in Figure 5.10, if the wage rate goes up, less labour can be used for a given sum of money. The isocost will swing inwards round point *x*. The isocost will get steeper. Less labour will now be used relative to capital.

*LOOKING AT THE MATHS

We can express the optimum production point algebraically. This can be done in either of two ways, corresponding to Figures 5.9 or 5.10. The method is similar to that used for finding the optimum consumption point that we examined on page 109.

(a) Corresponding to Figure 5.9. The first way involves finding the least-cost method of producing a given output (Q). This can be expressed as:

$$\text{Min } P_K K + P_L L \qquad (1)$$

subject to the output constraint that:

$$Q = Q(K,L) \qquad (2)$$

In other words, the objective is to find the lowest isocost (equation 1) to produce on a given isoquant (equation 2).

(b) Corresponding to Figure 5.10. The second involves finding the highest output that can be produced for a given cost. This can be expressed as:

$$\text{Max } Q(K,L) \qquad (3)$$

subject to the cost constraint that:

$$P_K K + P_L L = C \qquad (4)$$

In other words, the objective is to find the highest isoquant (equation 3) that can be reached along a given isocost (equation 4).

There are two methods of solving (a) and (b) for any given value of P_K, P_L and either Q (in the case of (a)) or C (in the case of (b)). The first involves substituting the constraint equation into the objective function (to express K in terms of L) and then finding the value of L and then K that minimises the objective function in the case of (a) or maximises it in the case of (b). This involves differentiating the objective function and setting it equal to zero. A worked example of this method is given in Maths Case 5.2 on the book's website.

The second method, which is slightly longer but is likely to involve simpler calculations, involves the use of 'Lagrangian multipliers'. This method is explained, along with a worked example, in Maths Case 5.3. It is the same method as we used in Maths Case 4.2 when finding the optimal level of consumption of two products.

Postscript: Decision making in different time periods

We have distinguished between the short run and the long run. Let us introduce two more time periods to complete the picture. The complete list then reads as follows.

Very short run (immediate run). All factors are fixed. Output is fixed. The supply curve is vertical. On a day-to-day basis, a firm may not be able to vary output at all. For example, a flower seller, once the day's flowers have been purchased from the wholesaler, cannot alter the amount of flowers available for sale on that day. In the very short run, all that may remain for a producer to do is to sell an already produced good.

Why are Christmas trees and fresh foods often sold cheaply on Christmas Eve? (See Box 5.5.)

Short run. At least one factor is fixed in supply. More can be produced, but the firm will come up against the law of diminishing returns as it tries to do so.

Long run. All factors are variable. The firm may experience constant, increasing or decreasing returns to scale. But although all factors can be increased or decreased, they are of a fixed *quality*.

Very long run. All factors are variable, *and* their quality and hence productivity can change. Labour productivity can increase as a result of education, training, experience and social factors. The productivity of capital can increase as a result of new inventions (new discoveries) and innovation (putting inventions into practice).

Improvements in factor quality will increase the output they produce: *TPP*, *APP* and *MPP* will rise. These curves will shift vertically upwards.

Just how long the 'very long run' is will vary from firm to firm. It will depend on how long it takes to develop new techniques, new skills or new work practices.

It is important to realise that decisions *for* all four time periods can be made *at* the same time. Firms do not make short-run decisions *in* the short run and long-run decisions *in* the long run. They can make both short-run and long-run decisions today. For example, assume that a firm experiences an increase in consumer demand and anticipates that it will continue into the foreseeable future. It thus wants to increase output. Consequently, it makes the following four decisions *today*.

- (*Very short run*) It accepts that for a few days it will not be able to increase output. It informs its customers that they will have to wait. It may temporarily raise prices to choke off some of the demand.
- (*Short run*) It negotiates with labour to introduce overtime working as soon as possible, to tide it over the next few weeks. It orders extra raw materials from its suppliers. It launches a recruitment drive for new labour so as to avoid paying overtime longer than is necessary.
- (*Long run*) It starts proceedings to build a new factory. The first step may be to discuss requirements with a firm of consultants.
- (*Very long run*) It institutes a programme of research and development and/or training in an attempt to increase productivity.

?

1. *Could the long run and the very long run ever be the* same *length of time?*
2. *What will the long-run and very-long-run market supply curves for a product look like? How will the shape of the long-run curve depend on returns to scale?*
*3. *In the very long run, new isoquants will have to be drawn as factor productivity changes. An increase in productivity will shift the isoquants inwards towards the origin: less capital and labour will be required to produce any given level of output. Will this be a* parallel *inward shift of the isoquants? Explain.*

Although we distinguish these four time periods, it is the middle two we are primarily concerned with. The reason for this is that there is very little the firm can do in the *very* short run. And in the *very* long run, although the firm will obviously want to increase the productivity of its inputs, it will not be in a position to make precise calculations of how to do it. It will not know precisely what inventions will be made, or just what will be the results of its own research and development.

Section summary

1. In the long run, a firm is able to vary the quantity it uses of all factors of production. There are no fixed factors.
2. If it increases all factors by the same proportion, it may experience constant, increasing or decreasing returns to scale.
3. Economies of scale occur when costs per unit of output fall as the scale of production increases. This can be due to a number of factors, some of which result directly from increasing (physical) returns to scale. These include the benefits of specialisation and division of labour, the use of larger and more efficient machines, and the ability to have a more integrated system of production. Other economies of scale arise from the financial and administrative benefits of large-scale organisations.
4. Long-run costs are also influenced by a firm's location. The firm will have to balance the needs to be as near as possible both to the supply of its raw materials and to its market. The optimum balance will depend on the relative costs of transporting the inputs and the finished product.
5. To minimise costs per unit of output, a firm should choose that combination of factors which gives an equal marginal product for each factor relative to its price: i.e. $MPP_a/P_a = MPP_b/P_b = MPP_c/P_c$, etc. (where a, b and c are different factors). If the MPP/P ratio for one factor is greater than for another, more of the first should be used relative to the second.

*6. An isoquant shows the various combinations of two factors to produce a given output. A whole map of such isoquants can be drawn with each isoquant representing a different level of output. The slope of the isoquant ($\Delta K/\Delta L$) gives the marginal rate of factor substitution (MPP_L/MPP_K). The bowed-in shape of isoquants illustrates a diminishing marginal rate of factor substitution, which in turn arises because of diminishing marginal returns.

*7. An isocost shows the various combinations of two factors that cost a given amount to employ. It will be a straight line. Its slope is equal to the price ratio of the two factors (P_L/P_K).

*8. The tangency point of an isocost with an isoquant represents the optimum factor combination. It is the point where MPP_L/MPP_K (the slope of the isoquant) = P_L/P_K (the slope of the isocost). By drawing a single isoquant touching the lowest possible isocost, we can show the least-cost combination of factors for producing a given output. By drawing a single isocost touching the highest possible isoquant, we can show the highest output obtainable for a given cost of production.

9. Four distinct time periods can be distinguished. In addition to the short- and long-run periods, we can also distinguish the very-short- and very-long-run periods. The very short run is when all factors are fixed. The very long run is where not only the quantity of factors but also their quality is variable (as a result of changing technology, etc.).

5.4 COSTS IN THE LONG RUN

We turn now to *long-run* cost curves. Since there are no fixed factors in the long run, there are no long-run fixed costs. For example, the firm may rent more land in order to expand its operations. Its rent bill therefore goes up as it expands its output. All costs, then, in the long run are variable costs.

Long-run average costs

Long-run average cost (LRAC) curves can take various shapes, but a typical one is shown in Figure 5.11.

It is often assumed that as a firm expands, it will initially experience economies of scale and thus face a downward-sloping *LRAC* curve. After a point, however, all such economies will have been achieved and thus the curve will

Definition

Long-run average cost curve A curve that shows how average cost varies with output on the assumption that *all* factors are variable. (It is assumed that the least-cost method of production will be chosen for each output.)

Figure 5.11 A typical long-run average cost curve

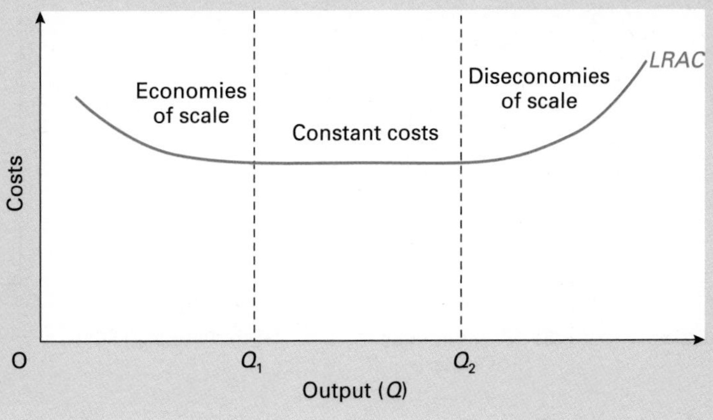

flatten out. Then (possibly after a period of constant *LRAC*) the firm will get so large that it will start experiencing diseconomies of scale and thus a rising *LRAC*. At this stage, production and financial economies will begin to be offset by the managerial problems of running a giant organisation.

Given the LRAC curve in Figure 5.11, what would the firm's long-run total cost curve look like?

Assumptions behind the long-run average cost curve

We make three key assumptions when constructing long-run average cost curves.

Factor prices are given. At each level of output, it is assumed that a firm will be faced with a given set of factor prices. If factor prices *change*, therefore, both short- and long-run cost curves will shift. Thus an increase in nationally negotiated wage rates would shift the curves upwards.

However, factor prices might be different at *different* levels of output. For example, one of the economies of scale that many firms enjoy is the ability to obtain bulk discount on raw materials and other supplies. In such cases, the curve does *not* shift. The different factor prices are merely experienced at different points along the curve, and are reflected in the shape of the curve. Factor prices are still given for any particular level of output.

The state of technology and factor quality are given. These are assumed to change only in the *very* long run. If a firm gains economies of scale, it is because it is being able to exploit *existing* technologies and make better use of the existing availability of factors of production.

Firms choose the least-cost combination of factors for each output. The assumption here is that firms operate efficiently: that they choose the cheapest possible way of producing any level of output. In other words, at every point along the *LRAC* curve, the firm will adhere to the cost-minimising formula (see page 134):

$$\frac{MPP_a}{P_a} = \frac{MPP_b}{P_b} = \frac{MPP_c}{P_c} \ldots = \frac{MPP_n}{P_n}$$

KI 14 p99

where a . . . *n* are the various factors the firm uses.

If the firm did not choose the optimum factor combination, it would be producing at a point above the *LRAC* curve.

Long-run marginal costs

The relationship between long-run average and ***long-run marginal cost*** curves is just like that between any other averages and marginals (see Box 5.3). This is illustrated in Figure 5.12.

If there are economies of scale (diagram (a)), additional units of output will add less to costs than the average. The *LRMC* curve must be below the *LRAC* curve and thus pulling the average down as output increases. If there are diseconomies of scale (diagram (b)), additional units of output will cost more than the average. The *LRMC* curve must be above the *LRAC* curve, pulling it up. If there are no economies or diseconomies of scale, so that the *LRAC* curve is horizontal, any additional units of output will cost the same as the average and thus leave the average unaffected (diagram (c)).

1. *Explain the shape of the LRMC curve in diagram (d).*
2. *What would the LRMC curve look like if the LRAC curve were 'flat bottomed', as in Figure 5.11?*

Definition

Long-run marginal cost The extra cost of producing one more unit of output assuming that all factors are variable. (It is assumed that the least-cost method of production will be chosen for this extra output.)

Figure 5.12 The relationship between long-run average and marginal costs

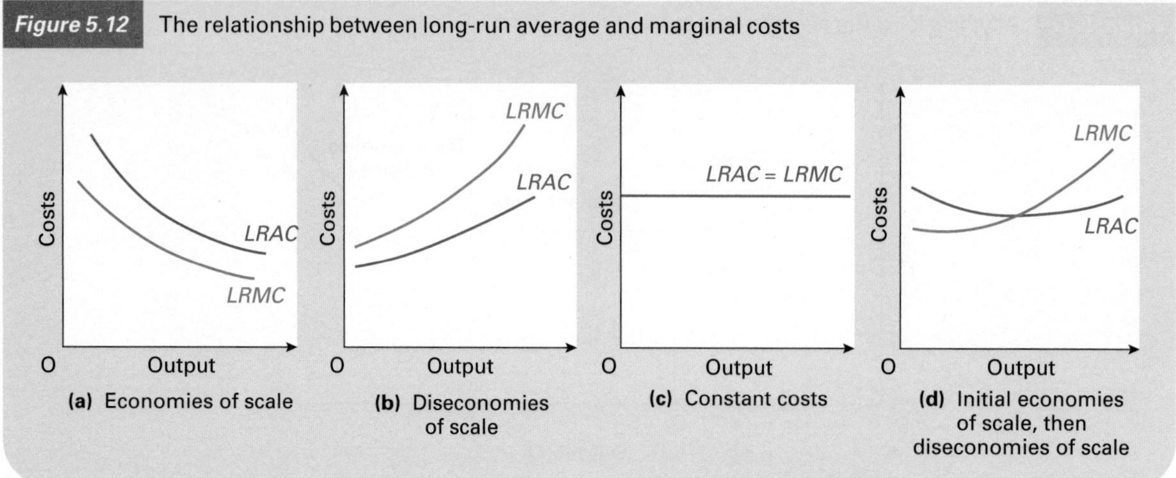

The relationship between long-run and short-run average cost curves

Take the case of a firm which has just one factory and faces a short-run average cost curve illustrated by $SRAC_1$ in Figure 5.13.

In the long run, it can build more factories. If it thereby experiences economies of scale (due, say, to savings on administration), each successive factory will allow it to produce with a new lower *SRAC* curve. Thus with two factories it will face $SRAC_2$; with three factories $SRAC_3$, and so on. Each *SRAC* curve corresponds to a particular amount of the factor that is fixed in the short run: in this case, the factory. (There are many more *SRAC* curves that could be drawn between the ones shown, since factories of different sizes could be built or existing ones could be expanded.)

From this succession of short-run average cost curves we can construct a long-run average cost curve, as shown in Figure 5.13. This is known as the ***envelope curve***, since it envelopes the short-run curves.

? *Will the envelope curve be tangential to the bottom of each of the short-run average cost curves? Explain why it should or should not be.*

Long-run cost curves in practice

Firms do experience economies of scale. Some experience continuously falling *LRAC* curves, as in Figure 5.12(a). Others experience economies of scale up to a certain output and thereafter constant returns to scale.

Evidence is inconclusive on the question of diseconomies of scale. There is little evidence to suggest the existence of *technical* diseconomies, but the possibility of diseconomies due to managerial and industrial relations problems cannot be ruled out.

Some evidence on economies of scale in the UK is considered in Box 5.8 (on pages 144–5).

Definition

Envelope curve A long-run average cost curve drawn as the tangency points of a series of short-run average cost curves.

Figure 5.13 Constructing long-run average cost curves from short-run average cost curves

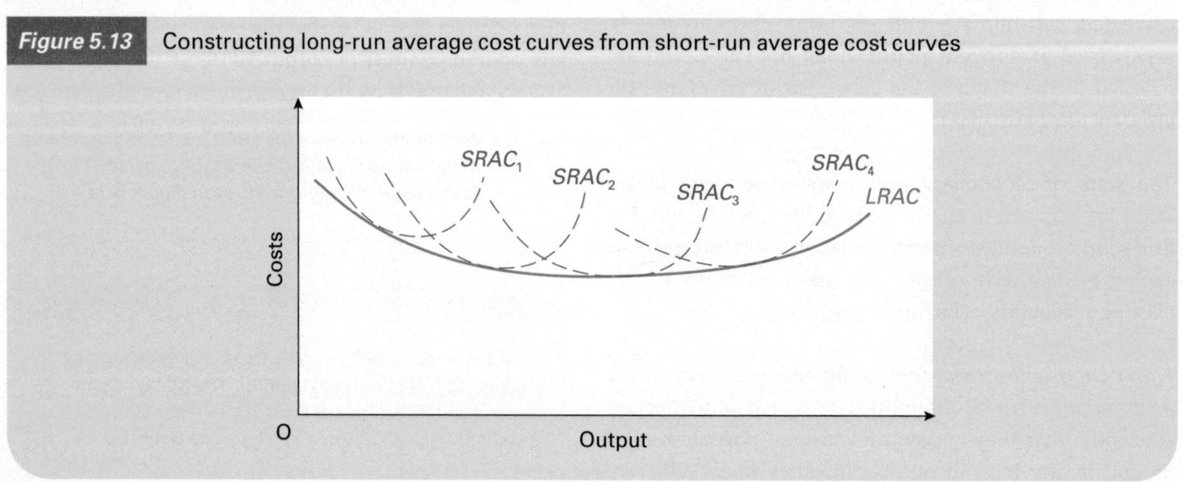

Figure 5.14 Deriving an *LRAC* curve from an isoquant map

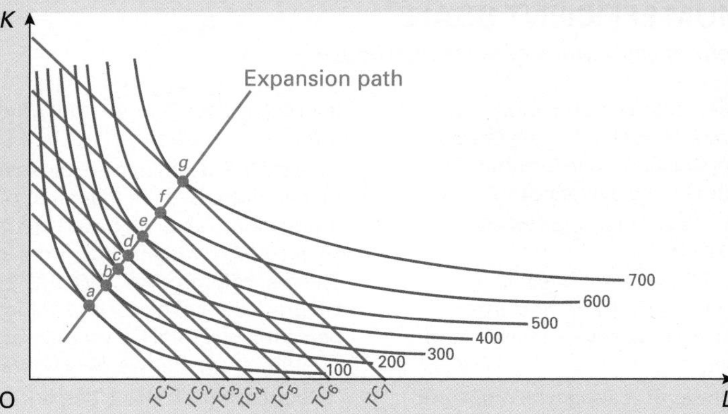

*Derivation of long-run costs from an isoquant map[4]

Cost curves are drawn on the assumption that, for any output, the least-cost combination of factors is used: that is, that production will take place at the tangency point of the isoquant and an isocost, where $MPP_L/MPP_K = P_L/P_K$: i.e. where $MPP_L/P_L = MPP_K/P_K$. By drawing a series of isoquants and isocosts, long-run costs can be derived for each output.

In Figure 5.14, isoquants are drawn for some hypothetical firm at 100 unit intervals. Up to 400 units of output, the isoquants are getting closer together. Thereafter, the gap between the isoquants widens again.

The line from *a* to *g* is known as the ***expansion path***. It traces the tangency points of the isoquants and isocosts, and thus shows the minimum-cost combinations of labour and capital to produce each output: the (long-run) total cost being given by the isocost.

Up to point *d*, less and less *extra* capital (*K*) and labour (*L*) are required to produce each extra 100 units of output. Thus long-run marginal cost is falling. Above point *d*, more and more extra *K* and *L* are required and thus *LRMC* rises.

Thus the *isoquant* map of Figure 5.14 gives an *LRMC* curve that is ⌣-shaped. The *LRAC* curve will therefore also be ⌣-shaped (only shallower) with the *LRMC* coming up through the bottom of the *LRAC*.

What would the isoquant map look like if there were (a) continuously increasing returns to scale; (b) continuously decreasing returns to scale?

Definition

Expansion path The line on an isoquant map that traces the minimum-cost combinations of two factors as output increases. It is drawn on the assumption that both factors can be varied. It is thus a long-run path.

[4] This optional section is based on the material in the optional section on pages 135–9.

Section summary

1. In the long run, all factors are variable. There are thus no long-run fixed costs.
2. When constructing long-run cost curves, it is assumed that factor prices are given, that the state of technology is given and that firms will choose the least-cost combination of factors for each given output.
3. The *LRAC* curve can be downward sloping, upward sloping or horizontal, depending in turn on whether there are economies of scale, diseconomies of scale or neither. Typically, *LRAC* curves are drawn saucer-shaped or ⌣-shaped. As output expands, initially there are economies of scale. When these are exhausted, the curve will become flat. When the firm becomes very large, it may begin to experience diseconomies of scale. If this happens, the *LRAC* curve will begin to slope upwards, again.
4. The long-run marginal cost curve will be below the *LRAC* curve when *LRAC* is falling, above it when *LRAC* is rising and equal to it when *LRAC* is neither rising nor falling.
5. An envelope curve can be drawn which shows the relationship between short-run and long-run average cost curves. The *LRAC* curve envelops the short-run *LRAC* curves: it is tangential to them.

*6. Costs can be derived from an isoquant map. Long-run total costs are found from the expansion path, which shows the least-cost combination of factors to produce any given output. It traces out the tangency points of the isocosts and isoquants.

CASE STUDIES AND APPLICATIONS

MINIMUM EFFICIENT SCALE

The extent of economies of scale in practice

Two of the most important studies of economies of scale are those made by C. F. Pratten[5] in the late 1980s and by a group advising the European Commission[6] in 1997. Both studies found strong evidence that many firms, especially in manufacturing, experienced substantial economies of scale.

In a few cases, long-run average costs fell continuously as output increased. For most firms, however, they fell up to a certain level of output and then remained constant.

The extent of economies of scale can be measured by looking at a firm's *minimum efficient scale (MES)*. The *MES* is the size beyond which no significant additional economies of scale can be achieved: in other words, the point where the *LRAC* curve flattens off. In Pratten's studies, he defined this level as the minimum scale above which any possible doubling in scale would reduce average costs by less than 5 per cent (i.e. virtually the bottom of the *LRAC* curve). In the diagram, *MES* is shown at point *a*.

The *MES* can be expressed in terms either of an individual factory or of the whole firm. Where it refers to the minimum efficient scale of an individual factory, the *MES* is known as the *minimum efficient plant size (MEPS)*.

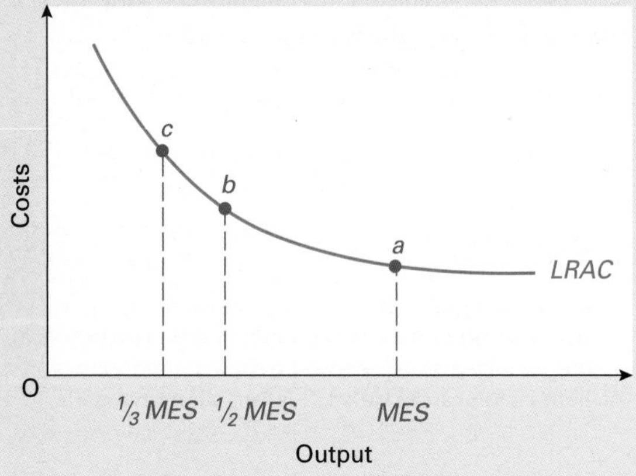

The *MES* can then be expressed as a percentage of the total size of the market or of total domestic production. Table (a), based on the Pratten study, shows *MES* for plants and firms in various industries. The first column shows *MES* as a percentage of total UK production. The second column shows *MES* as a percentage of total EU production. Table (b), based on the 1997 study, shows *MES* for various plants.

Expressing *MES* as a percentage of total output gives an indication of how competitive the industry could be. In some industries (such as footwear and carpets), economies of scale were exhausted (i.e. *MES* was reached) with plants or firms that were still small relative to total UK production and even smaller relative to total EU production. In such industries, there would be room for many firms and thus scope for considerable competition.

In other industries, however, even if a single plant or firm were large enough to produce the whole output of the industry in the UK, it would still not be large enough to experience the full potential economies of scale: the *MES* is greater than 100 per cent. Examples from Table (a) include factories producing cellulose fibres, and car manufacturers. In these industries, there is no possibility of competition from within the country. In fact, as long as the *MES* exceeds 50 per cent, there will not be room for more than one firm large enough to gain full economies of scale (unless they export). In this case, the industry is said to be a *natural monopoly*.

As we shall see in the next few chapters, when competition is lacking, consumers may suffer by firms charging prices considerably above costs.

A second way of measuring the extent of economies of scale is to see how much costs would increase if production were reduced to a certain fraction of *MES*. The normal fractions used are ½ or ⅓ *MES*. This is illustrated in the diagram. Point *b*

5.5 REVENUE

Remember that we defined a firm's total profit as its total revenue minus its total costs of production. So far in this chapter we have examined costs. We now turn to revenue.

As with costs, we distinguish between three revenue concepts: total revenue (*TR*), average revenue (*AR*) and marginal revenue (*MR*).

Total, average and marginal revenue

Total revenue (TR)

Total revenue is the firm's total earnings per period of time from the sale of a particular amount of output (*Q*). For example, if a firm sells 1000 units (*Q*) per month at a price of £5 each (*P*), then its monthly total revenue will be £5000: in other words, £5 × 1000 ($P \times Q$). Thus:

$$TR = P \times Q$$

Definition

Total revenue A firm's total earnings from a specified level of sales within a specified period: $TR = P \times Q$.

BOX 5.8

Table (a)

Product	MES as % of production UK	MES as % of production EU	% additional cost at ½ MES
Individual plants			
Cellulose fibres	125	16	3
Rolled aluminium semi-manufactures	114	15	15
Refrigerators	85	11	4
Steel	72	10	6
Electric motors	60	6	15
TV sets	40	9	9
Cigarettes	24	6	1.4
Ball-bearings	20	2	6
Beer	12	3	7
Nylon	4	1	12
Bricks	1	0.2	25
Carpets	0.3	0.04	10
Footwear	0.3	0.03	1
Firms			
Cars	200	20	9
Lorries	104	21	7.5
Mainframe computers	> 100	n.a.	5
Aircraft	100	n.a.	5
Tractors	98	19	6

Source: see footnote 4 below.

corresponds to ½ *MES*; point to *C* ⅓ *MES*. The greater the percentage by which *LRAC* at point *b* or *c* is higher than at point *a*, the greater will be the economies of scale to be gained by producing at *MES* rather than at ½ *MES* or ⅓ *MES*. For example, in Table (a) there are greater economies of scale to be gained from moving from ½ *MES* to *MES* in the production of electric motors than in cigarettes.

Table (b)

Plants	MES as % of total EU production
Aerospace	12.19
Agricultural machinery	6.57
Electric lighting	3.76
Steel tubes	2.42
Shipbuilding	1.63
Rubber	1.06
Radio and TV	0.69
Footwear	0.08
Carpets	0.03

Source: see footnote 5 below.

The main purpose of the studies was to determine whether the single EU market is big enough to allow both economies of scale and competition. The tables suggest that in all cases, other things being equal, the EU market is indeed large enough for this to occur. The second study also found that 47 of the 53 manufacturing sectors analysed had scope for further exploitation of economies of scale.

1. ***Why might a firm operating with one plant achieve MEPS and yet not be large enough to achieve MES? (Clue: are all economies of scale achieved at plant level?)***
2. ***Why might a firm producing bricks have an MES which is only 0.2 per cent of total EU production and yet face little effective competition from other EU countries?***

[5] C. F. Pratten, 'A survey of the economies of scale', in *Research on the 'Costs of Non-Europe'*, vol. 2 (Office for Official Publications of the European Communities, 1988).

[6] European Commission/Economists Advisory Group Ltd, 'Economies of Scale', *The Single Market Review, Subseries V, Volume 4,* Office for Official Publications of the European Communities, Luxembourg, 1997

Average revenue (AR)

Average revenue is the amount the firm earns per unit sold. Thus:

$AR = TR/Q$

So if the firm earns £5000 (*TR*) from selling 1000 units (*Q*), it will earn £5 per unit. But this is simply the price! Thus:

$AR = P$

(The only exception to this is when the firm is selling its products at different prices to different consumers. In this case, *AR* is simply the (weighted) average price.)

Marginal revenue (MR)

Marginal revenue is the extra total revenue gained by selling one more unit (per time period). So if a firm sells an extra 20 units this month compared with what it expected to sell, and in the process earns an extra £100, then it is getting an extra £5 for each extra unit sold: *MR* = £5. Thus:

$MR = \Delta TR/\Delta Q$

Definitions

Average revenue Total revenue per unit of output. When all output is sold at the same price, average revenue will be the same as price: $AR = TR/Q = P$.

Marginal revenue The extra revenue gained by selling one more unit per period of time: $MR = \Delta TR/\Delta Q$.

Figure 5.15 Deriving a firm's *AR* and *MR*: price-taking firm

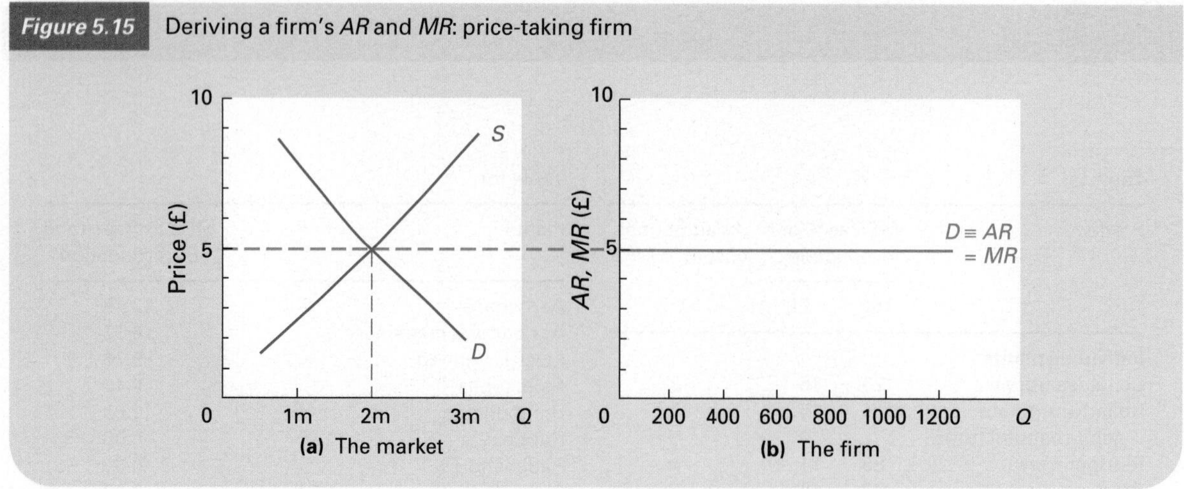

We now need to see how each of these three revenue concepts (*TR*, *AR* and *MR*) varies with output. We can show this graphically in the same way as we did with costs.

The relationships will depend on the market conditions under which a firm operates. A firm that is too small to be able to affect market price will have different-shaped revenue curves from a firm that is able to choose the price it charges. Let us examine each of these two situations in turn.

Revenue curves when price is not affected by the firm's output

Average revenue

If a firm is very small relative to the whole market, it is likely to be a ***price taker***. That is, it has to accept the price given by the intersection of demand and supply in the whole market. But, being so small, it can sell as much as it is capable of producing at that price. This is illustrated in Figure 5.15.

The left-hand part of the diagram shows market demand and supply. Equilibrium price is £5. The right-hand part of the diagram looks at the demand for an individual firm that is tiny relative to the whole market. (Look at the differences in the scale of the horizontal axes in the two parts of the diagram.)

Being so small, any change in its output will be too insignificant to affect the market price. It thus faces a horizontal demand 'curve' at the price. It can sell 200 units, 600 units, 1200 units or whatever without affecting this £5 price.

Definition

Price taker A firm that is too small to be able to influence the market price.

Average revenue is thus constant at £5. The firm's average revenue curve must therefore lie along exactly the same line as its demand curve.

Marginal revenue

In the case of a horizontal demand curve, the marginal revenue curve will be the same as the average revenue curve, since selling one more unit at a constant price (*AR*) merely adds that amount to total revenue. If an extra unit is sold at a constant price of £5, an extra £5 is earned.

Total revenue

Table 5.7 shows the effect on total revenue of different levels of sales with a constant price of £5 per unit. As price is constant, total revenue will rise at a constant rate as more is sold. The *TR* 'curve' will therefore be a straight line through the origin, as in Figure 5.16.

? *What would happen to the* TR *curve if the market price rose to £10? Try drawing it.*

Table 5.7 Deriving total revenue: the firm is a price taker

Quantity (units)	Price ≡ *AR* = *MR* (£)	*TR* (£)
0	5	0
200	5	1000
400	5	2000
600	5	3000
800	5	4000
1000	5	5000
1200	5	6000
.	.	.

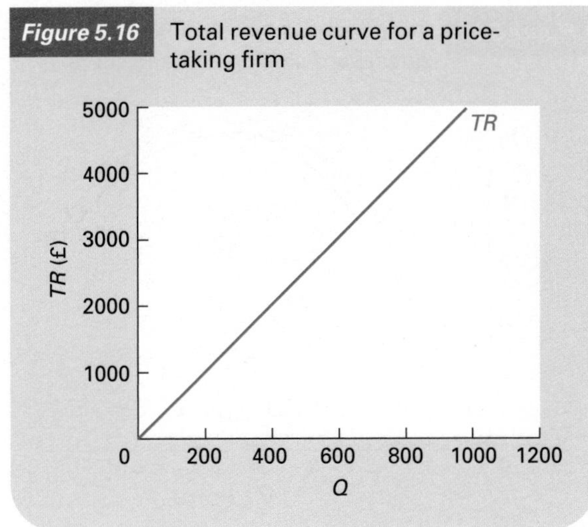

Figure 5.16 Total revenue curve for a price-taking firm

Revenue curves when price varies with output

The three curves (*TR*, *AR* and *MR*) look quite different when price does vary with the firm's output. If a firm has a relatively large share of the market, it will face a downward-sloping demand curve. This means that if it is to sell more, it must lower the price. It could also choose to raise its price. If it does so, however, it will have to accept a fall in sales.

Average revenue

Remember that average revenue equals price. If, therefore, price has to be lowered to sell more output, average revenue will fall as output increases.

Table 5.8 gives an example of a firm facing a downward-sloping demand curve. The demand curve (which shows how much is sold at each price) is given by the first two columns.

Note that, as in the case of a price-taking firm, the demand curve and the *AR* curve lie along exactly the same line. The reason for this is simple: $AR = P$, and thus the curve relating price to quantity (the demand curve) must be the same as that relating average revenue to quantity (the *AR* curve).

Table 5.8 Revenues for a firm facing a downward-sloping demand curve

Q (units)	*P* = *AR* (£)	*TR* (£)	*MR* (£)
1	8	8	6
2	7	14	4
3	6	18	2
4	5	20	0
5	4	20	–2
6	3	18	–4
7	2	14	
.	.	.	.

Marginal revenue

When a firm faces a downward-sloping demand curve, marginal revenue will be less than average revenue, and may even be negative. But why?

If a firm is to sell more per time period, it must lower its price (assuming it does not advertise). This will mean lowering the price not just for the extra units it hopes to sell, but also for those units it would have sold had it not lowered the price.

Thus the marginal revenue is the price at which it sells the last unit, *minus* the loss in revenue it has incurred by reducing the price on those units it could otherwise have sold at the higher price. This can be illustrated with Table 5.8.

Assume that the price is currently £7. Two units are thus sold. The firm now wishes to sell an extra unit. It lowers the price to £6. It thus gains £6 from the sale of the third unit, but loses £2 by having to reduce the price by £1 on the two units it could otherwise have sold at £7. Its net gain is therefore £6 – £2 = £4. This is the marginal revenue: it is the extra revenue gained by the firm from selling one more unit. (Notice that in Table 5.8 the figures for *MR* are entered in the spaces between the figures for the other three columns.)

There is a simple relationship between marginal revenue and *price elasticity of demand*. Remember from Chapter 2 (p. 50) that if demand is price elastic, a *decrease* in price will lead to a proportionately larger increase in the quantity demanded and hence an *increase* in revenue. Marginal revenue will thus be positive. If, however, demand is inelastic, a decrease in price will lead to a proportionately smaller increase in sales. In this case, the price reduction will more than offset the increase in sales and as a result revenue will fall. Marginal revenue will be negative.

KI 9 p58

If, then, at a particular quantity sold marginal revenue is a positive figure (i.e. if sales per time period are 4 units or less in Figure 5.17), the demand curve will be elastic at that quantity, since a rise in quantity sold (as a result of a reduction in price) would lead to a rise in total revenue. If, on the other hand, marginal revenue is negative (i.e. at a level of sales of 5 or more units in Figure 5.17), the demand curve

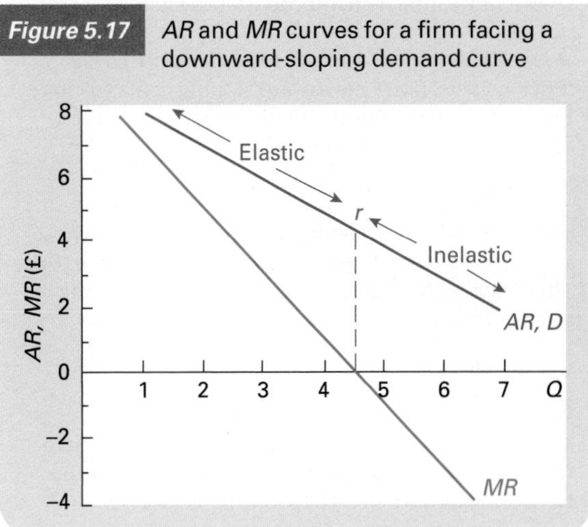

Figure 5.17 *AR* and *MR* curves for a firm facing a downward-sloping demand curve

will be inelastic at that quantity, since a rise in quantity sold would lead to a *fall* in total revenue.

Thus the demand (*AR*) curve in Figure 5.17 is elastic to the left of point *r* and inelastic to the right.

Total revenue

Total revenue equals price times quantity. This is illustrated in Table 5.8. The *TR* column from Table 5.8 is plotted in Figure 5.18.

Unlike the case of a price-taking firm, the *TR* curve is not a straight line. It is a curve that rises at first and then falls. But why? As long as marginal revenue is positive (and hence demand is price elastic), a rise in output will raise total revenue. However, once marginal revenue becomes negative (and hence demand is inelastic), total revenue will fall. The peak of the *TR* curve will be where $MR = 0$. At this point, the price elasticity of demand will be equal to −1.

Figure 5.18 Total revenue for a firm facing a downward-sloping demand curve

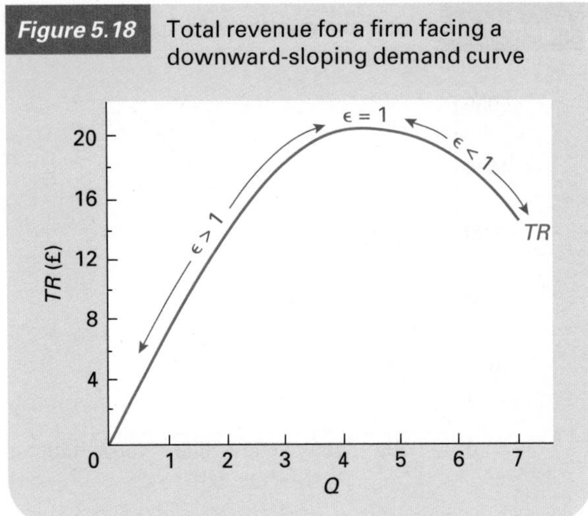

*LOOKING AT THE MATHS

As with cost curves (see page 130), we can express revenue curves algebraically.

Price-taking firms. Let us take *TR*, *AR* and *MR* in turn. They will take the following forms:

$$TR = bQ \tag{1}$$

This equation will give an upward-sloping straight-line *TR* 'curve', with a slope of *b*. Note that the absence of a constant (*a*) term means that the line passes through the origin. This is obviously the case, given that if sales (*Q*) are zero, total revenue will be zero.

$$AP = \frac{TR}{Q} = b \tag{2}$$

This will give a horizontal *AR* curve at an *AR* (i.e. price) of *b*.

$$MR = \frac{d(TR)}{dQ} = b \tag{3}$$

Differentiating the *TR* function gives a value of *b*. As we have seen, $AR = MR$ when the firm is a price taker and faces a horizontal demand curve (at the market price).

Price-making firms: a straight-line demand 'curve'. 'Price-makers' face a downward-sloping demand curve. If this is a straight-line demand curve, the revenue equations will be as follows:

$$TR = bQ - cQ^2 \tag{4}$$

The negative cQ^2 term will give a revenue curve whose slope gets less until a peak is reached (see Figure 5.18). Thereafter, as the cQ^2 term becomes bigger than the bQ term, *TR* will fall.

$$AR = \frac{TR}{Q} = b - cQ \tag{5}$$

This gives a straight-line downward-sloping *AR* curve (demand curve) with a slope of $-c$, which crosses the horizontal axis when cQ becomes bigger than *b*.

$$MR = \frac{d(TR)}{dQ} = b - 2cQ \tag{6}$$

This again gives a straight downward-sloping line, this time with a slope of $-2c$. Note that this means that the slope of the *MR* curve is twice that of the *AR* curve.

But what if the demand curve is actually curved? What will the three revenue equations be then? We explore this in Maths Case 5.4 on the book's website and relate the equations to the relevant diagrams.

The relationship between marginal revenue and price elasticity of demand. You can see from Figure 5.17 how price elasticity of demand and marginal revenue are related. We can express this relationship algebraically as follows:

$$MR = P(1 + (1/P\epsilon_D)) \tag{7}$$

or

$$P = \frac{MR}{1 + (1/P\epsilon_D)}$$

Proof of this relationship is given in Maths Case 6.2, but for now we can see how equation (7) relates to Figure 5.17. The *P* term must be positive. If demand is elastic, then $P\epsilon_D$ must have a value less than −1 (i.e. the figure for elasticity, ignoring the negative sign, must be greater than 1). Thus the term $1/P\epsilon_D$ must have a negative value between 0 and −1. This means, therefore, that the term $(1 + (1/P\epsilon_D))$ must be positive, and hence *MR* must be positive.

If, however, demand is inelastic, then $P\epsilon_D$ must have a value between −1 and zero. Thus the term $1/P\epsilon_D$ must have a negative value less than −1 (i.e. an absolute value, ignoring the negative sign, that is greater than 1). This means, therefore, that the term $(1 + (1/P\epsilon_D))$ must be negative, and hence *MR* must be negative.

Finally, if demand is unit elastic, then the term $1/P\epsilon_D$ must have a value of −1 and hence the term $(1 + (1/P\epsilon_D))$ must have a value of zero. *MR* must be zero.

Shifts in revenue curves

We saw in Chapter 2 that a change in *price* will cause a movement along a demand curve. It is similar with revenue curves, except that here the causal connection is in the other direction. Here we ask what happens to revenue when there is a change in the firm's *output*. Again the effect is shown by a movement along the curves.

A change in any *other* determinant of demand, such as tastes, income or the price of other goods, will shift the demand curve. By affecting the price at which each level of output can be sold, there will be a shift in all three revenue curves. An increase in revenue is shown by a shift upwards; a decrease by a shift downwards.

Copy Figures 5.17 and 5.18 (which are based on Table 5.8). Now assume that incomes have risen and that, as a result, two more units per time period can be sold at each price. Draw a new table and plot the resulting new AR, MR and TR curves on your diagrams. Are the new curves parallel to the old ones? Explain.

Section summary

1. Total revenue (*TR*) is the total amount a firm earns from its sales in a given time period. It is simply price times quantity: $TR = P \times Q$.
2. Average revenue (*AR*) is total revenue per unit: $AR = TR/Q$. In other words, $AR = P$.
3. Marginal revenue is the extra revenue earned from the sale of one more unit per time period.
4. The *AR* curve will be the same as the demand curve for the firm's product. In the case of a price taker, the demand curve and hence the *AR* curve will be a horizontal straight line and will also be the same as the *MR* curve. The *TR* curve will be an upward-sloping straight line from the origin.
5. A firm that faces a downward-sloping demand curve must obviously also face the same downward-sloping *AR* curve. The *MR* curve will also slope downwards, but will be below the *AR* curve and steeper than it. The *TR* curve will be an arch shape starting from the origin.
6. When demand is price elastic, marginal revenue will be positive and the *TR* curve will be upward sloping. When demand is price inelastic, marginal revenue will be negative and the *TR* curve will be downward sloping.
7. A change in output is represented by a movement along the revenue curves. A change in any other determinant of revenue will shift the curves up or down.

5.6 PROFIT MAXIMISATION

We are now in a position to put costs and revenue together to find the output at which profit is maximised, and also to find out how much that profit will be.

There are two ways of doing this. The first and simpler method is to use total cost and total revenue curves. The second method is to use marginal and average cost and marginal and average revenue curves. Although this method is a little more complicated (but only a little!), it is more useful when we come to compare profit maximising under different market conditions.

We will look at each method in turn. In both cases, we will concentrate on the short run: namely, that period in which one or more factors are fixed in supply. In both cases, we take the instance of a firm facing a downward-sloping demand curve.

Short-run profit maximisation: using total curves

Table 5.9 shows the total revenue figures from Table 5.8. It also shows figures for total cost. These figures have been chosen so as to produce a *TC* curve of a typical shape.

Total profit ($T\Pi$) is found by subtracting *TC* from *TR*. Check this out by examining the table. Where $T\Pi$ is negative, the firm is making a loss. Total profit is maximised at an output of 3 units: namely, where there is the greatest gap between total revenue and total costs. At this output, total profit is £4 (£18 – £14).

Table 5.9 Total revenue, total cost and total profit

Q (units)	*TR* (£)	*TC* (£)	$T\Pi$ (£)
0	0	6	–6
1	8	10	–2
2	14	12	2
3	18	14	4
4	20	18	2
5	20	25	–5
6	18	36	–18
7	14	56	–42
.	.	.	.

The *TR*, *TC* and $T\Pi$ curves are plotted in Figure 5.19. The size of the maximum profit is shown by the arrows.

What can we say about the slope of the TR and TC curves at the maximum profit point? What does this tell us about marginal revenue and marginal cost?

Table 5.10 Revenue, cost and profit

Q (units)	P = AR (£)	TR (£)	MR (£)	TC (£)	AC (£)	MC (£)	TΠ (£)	AΠ (£)
0	9	0		6	–		–6	–
			8			4		
1	8	8		10	10		...	–2
			...			2		
2	7	14		12	...		2	1
			4			2		
3	6	18		14	$4^2/_3$		4	$1^1/_3$
			2			4		
4	5	20		18	$4^1/_2$		2	$^1/_2$
			0			7		
5	4	20		25	5		–5	–1
			–2			...		
6	3	18		36	...		...	...
			...			20		
7	2	14		56	8		–42	–6
.	.	.	.	.	.	.	.	.

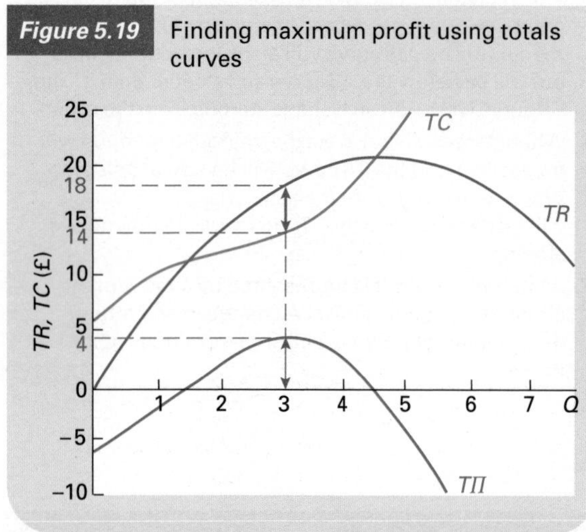

Figure 5.19 Finding maximum profit using totals curves

Figure 5.20 Finding the profit-maximising output using marginal curves

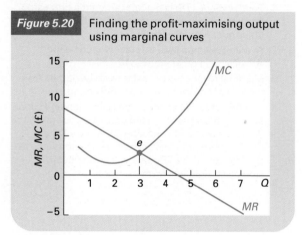

Short-run profit maximisation: using average and marginal curves

Table 5.10 is based on the figures in Table 5.9.

1. *Fill in the missing figures (without referring to Table 5.8 or 5.9).*
2. *Why are the figures for MR and MC entered in the spaces between the lines in Table 5.10?*

Finding the maximum profit that a firm can make is a two-stage process. The first stage is to find the profit-maximising output. To do this we use the *MC* and *MR* curves. The second stage is to find out just how much profit is at this output. To do this we use the *AR* and *AC* curves.

Stage 1: Using marginal curves to arrive at the profit-maximising output

There is a very simple ***profit-maximising rule***: if profits are to be maximised, *MR must equal MC*. From Table 5.10 it can be seen that *MR* = *MC* at an output of 3. This is shown as point *e* in Figure 5.20.

But why are profits maximised when *MR* = *MC*? The simplest way of answering this is to see what the position would be if *MR* did not equal *MC*.

Referring to Figure 5.20, at a level of output below 3, *MR* exceeds *MC*. This means that by producing more units there will be a bigger addition to revenue (*MR*) than to cost (*MC*). Total profit will *increase. As long as MR exceeds MC, profit can be increased by increasing production.*

At a level of output above 3, *MC* exceeds *MR*. All levels of output above 3 thus add more to cost than to revenue and hence *reduce* profit. *As long as MC exceeds MR, profit can be increased by cutting back on production.*

Profits are thus maximised where *MC* = *MR*: at an output of 3. This can be confirmed by reference to the *TΠ* column in Table 5.10.

Students worry sometimes about the argument that profits are maximised when *MR* = *MC*. Surely, they say, if the last unit is making no profit, how can profit be at a *maximum*? The answer is very simple. If you cannot *add* anything more to a total, the total must be at the maximum. Take the simple analogy of going up a hill. When you cannot go any higher, you must be at the top.

Definition

Profit-maximising rule Profit is maximised where marginal revenue equals marginal cost.

***LOOKING AT THE MATHS**

As we have seen, the rule for profit maximisation is that firms should produce where $MC = MR$. This can be derived algebraically as follows. Profit is defined as:

$$T\Pi = TR - TC \quad (1)$$

Profit is maximised at the point where an additional unit of output will add no more to profit – that is, where:

$$\frac{\Delta T\Pi}{\Delta Q} = M\Pi = 0 \quad (2)$$

or, from (1), where:

$$\frac{\Delta TR}{\Delta Q} - \frac{\Delta TC}{\Delta Q} = 0 \quad (3)$$

or

$$\frac{\Delta TR}{\Delta Q} = \frac{\Delta TC}{\Delta Q} \quad (4)$$

i.e. where $MR = MC$.

Equation (2) can be related to Figure 5.19. Profits are maximised at the highest point of the $T\Pi$ curve. At the top of any curve (or bottom for that matter), its slope is zero. Thus $\Delta T\Pi/Q = M\Pi = 0$. Put another way, the tangent to the top of the $T\Pi$ curve is horizontal.

Stage 2: Using average curves to measure the size of the profit

Once the profit-maximising output has been discovered, we use the average curves to measure the *amount* of profit at the maximum. Both marginal and average curves corresponding to the data in Table 5.10 are plotted in Figure 5.21.

First, average profit ($A\Pi$) is found. This is simply $AR - AC$. At the profit-maximising output of 3, this gives a figure for $A\Pi$ of £6 – £4 $^2/_3$ = £1$^1/_3$. Then total profit is obtained by multiplying average profit by output:

$$T\Pi = A\Pi \times Q$$

This is shown as the shaded area. It equals £1$^1/_3$ × 3 = £4. This can again be confirmed by reference to the $T\Pi$ column in Table 5.10.

?

From the information for a firm given in the table below, construct a table like 5.10.

Q	0	1	2	3	4	5	6	7
P	12	11	10	9	8	7	6	5
TC	2	6	9	12	16	21	28	38

Use your table to draw diagrams like Figures 5.19 and 5.21. Use these two diagrams to show the profit-maximising output and the level of maximum profit. Confirm your findings by reference to the table you have constructed.

Figure 5.21 Measuring the maximum profit using average curves

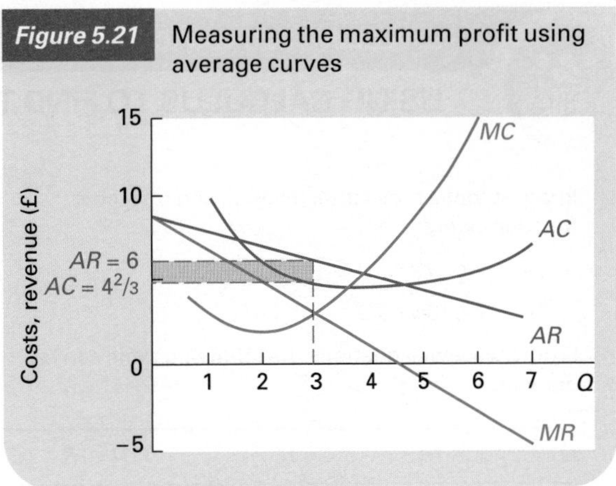

Some qualifications

Long-run profit maximisation

Assuming that the *AR* and *MR* curves are the same in the long run as in the short run, long-run profits will be maximised at the output where *MR* equals the *long-run MC*. The reasoning is the same as with the short-run case.

The meaning of 'profit'

One element of cost is the opportunity cost to the owners of the firm of being in business. This is the minimum return the owners must make on their capital in order to prevent them from eventually deciding to close down and perhaps move into some alternative business. It is a *cost* because, just as with wages, rent, etc., it has to be covered if the firm is to continue producing. This opportunity cost to the owners is sometimes known as ***normal profit***, and is *included in the cost curves*. KI 2 p8

What determines this normal rate of profit? It has two components. First, someone setting up in business invests capital in it. There is thus an opportunity cost. This is the interest that could have been earned by lending it in some riskless form (e.g. by putting it in a savings account in a bank). Nobody would set up a business unless they expected to earn at least this rate of profit. Running a business is far from riskless, however, and hence a second element is a return to compensate for risk. Thus:

Normal profit (%) = Rate of interest on a riskless loan + A risk premium

The risk premium varies according to the line of business. In those with fairly predictable patterns, such as

Definition

Normal profit The opportunity cost of being in business: the profit that could have been earned in the next best alternative business. It is counted as a cost of production.

EXPLORING ECONOMICS *BOX 5.9

USING CALCULUS TO FIND THE MAXIMUM PROFIT OUTPUT

Imagine that a firm's total revenue and total cost functions were:

$$TR = 48Q - Q^2$$

$$TC = 12 + 16Q + 3Q^2$$

From these two equations the following table can be derived.

Q	TR	TC	$T\Pi (= TR - TC)$
0	0	12	−12
1	47	31	16
2	92	56	36
3	135	87	48
4	176	124	52
5	215	167	48
6	252	216	36
7	287	271	16
.	.	.	.

1. ***How much is total fixed cost?***
2. ***Continue the table for $Q = 8$ and $Q = 9$.***
3. ***Plot TR, TC and $T\Pi$ on a diagram like Figure 5.19.***

It can clearly be seen from the table that profit is maximised at an output of 4, where $T\Pi = 52$.

This profit-maximising output and the level of profit can be calculated without drawing up a table. The calculation involves calculus. There are two methods that can be used.

Finding where $MR = MC$

Marginal revenue can be found by differentiating the total revenue function.

$$MR = dTR/dQ$$

The reason is that marginal revenue is the rate of change of total revenue. Differentiating a function gives its rate of change.

Similarly, marginal cost can be found by differentiating the total cost function:

$$MC = dTC/dQ$$

Differentiating TR and TC gives:

$$dTR/dQ = 48 - 2Q = MR$$

$$dTC/dQ = 16 + 6Q = MC$$

Profit is maximised where $MR = MC$: in other words, where:

$$48 - 2Q = 16 + 6Q$$

Solving this for Q gives:

$$32 = 8Q$$

$$\therefore Q = 4$$

The equation for total profit ($T\Pi$) is:

$$T\Pi = TR - TC$$

$$= 48Q - Q^2 - (12 + 16Q + 3Q^2)$$

$$= -12 + 32Q - 4Q^2$$

Substituting $Q = 4$ into this equation gives:

$$T\Pi = -12 + (32 \times 4) - (4 \times 4^2)$$

$$\therefore T\Pi = 52$$

These figures can be confirmed from the table.

Maximising the total profit equation

To maximise an equation we want to find the point where the slope of the curve derived from it is zero. In other words, we want to find the top of the $T\Pi$ curve.

The slope of a curve gives its rate of change and is found by differentiating the curve's equation. Thus to find maximum $T\Pi$ we differentiate it (to find the slope) and set it equal to zero (to find the top).

$$T\Pi = -12 + 32Q - 4Q^2 \text{ (see above)}$$

$$\therefore dT\Pi/dQ = 32 - 8Q$$

Setting this equal to zero gives:

$$32 - 8Q = 0$$

$$\therefore 8Q = 32$$

$$\therefore Q = 4$$

This is the same result as was found by the first method. Again $Q = 4$ can be substituted into the $T\Pi$ equation to give:

$$T\Pi = 52$$

Given the following equations:

$$TR = 72Q - 2Q^2; \quad TC = 10 + 12Q + 4Q^2$$

calculate the maximum profit output and the amount of profit at that output using both methods.

food retailing, it is relatively low. Where outcomes are very uncertain, such as mineral exploration or the manufacture of fashion garments, it is relatively high.

Thus if owners of a business earn normal profit, they will (just) be content to remain in that industry. If they earn more than normal profit, they will also (obviously) prefer to stay in this business. If they earn less than normal profit, then after a time they will consider leaving and using their capital for some other purpose.

?

Will the size of 'normal profit' vary with the general state of the economy?

Figure 5.22 Loss-minimising output

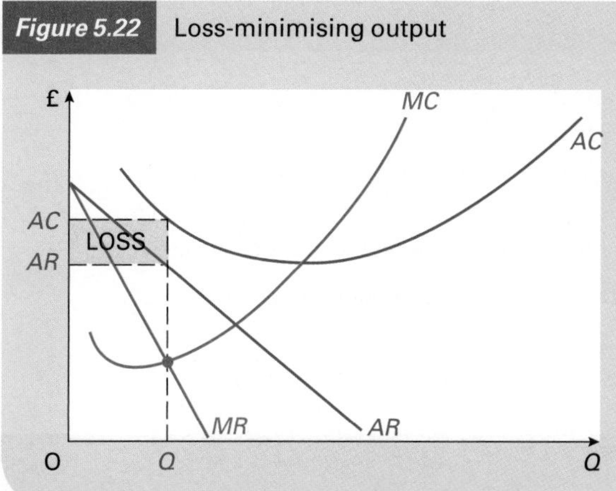

Figure 5.23 The short-run shut-down point

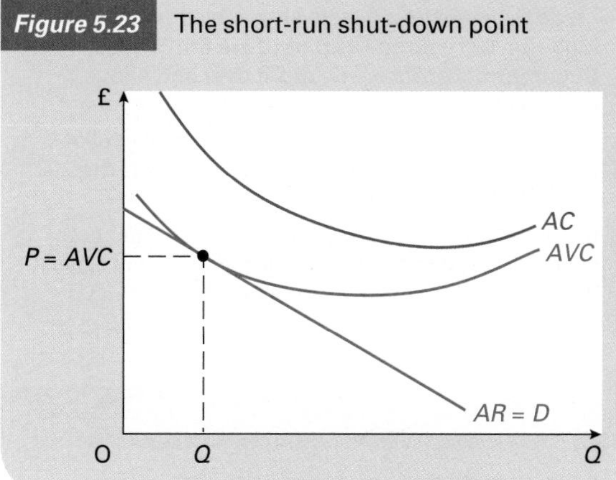

Given that normal profits are included in costs, any profit that is shown diagrammatically (e.g. the shaded area in Figure 5.21) must therefore be over and above normal profit. It is known by several alternative names: ***supernormal profit, pure profit, economic profit*** or sometimes simply ***profit***. They all mean the same thing: the excess of total profit over normal profit.

Loss minimising

It may be that there is no output at which the firm can make a profit. Such a situation is illustrated in Figure 5.22: the *AC* curve is above the *AR* curve at all levels of output.

In this case, the output where $MR = MC$ will be the loss-minimising output. The amount of loss at the point where $MR = MC$ is shown by the shaded area in Figure 5.22.

Whether or not to produce at all

The short run. Fixed costs have to be paid even if the firm is producing nothing at all. Rent and business rates have to be paid, etc. Providing, therefore, that the firm is more than covering its *variable* costs, it can go some way to paying off these fixed costs and therefore will continue to produce. **KI 18** p126

It will shut down if it cannot cover its variable costs: that is, if the *AVC* curve is above, or the *AR* curve below, the position illustrated in Figure 5.23. This situation is known as the ***short-run shut-down point***.

The long run. All costs are variable in the long run. If, therefore, the firm cannot cover its long-run average costs (which include normal profit), it will close down. The ***long-run shut-down point*** will be where the *AR* curve is tangential to the *LRAC* curve.

Definitions

Supernormal profit (also known as **pure profit, economic profit** or simply **profit**) The excess of total profit above normal profit.

Short-run shut-down point Where the AR curve is tangential to the AVC curve. The firm can only just cover its variable costs. Any fall in revenue below this level will cause a profit-maximising firm to shut down immediately.

Long-run shut-down point Where the AR curve is tangential to the LRAC curve. The firm can just make normal profits. Any fall in revenue below this level will cause a profit-maximising firm to shut down once all costs have become variable.

*LOOKING AT THE MATHS

We can state the short- and long-run shut-down points algebraically. Remember that total profit ($T\Pi$) is defined as:

$$T\Pi = TR - TC = TR - (TFC + TVC) \quad (1)$$

A negative value for $T\Pi$ means that the firm makes a loss. This will occur when:

$$TR - (TFC + TVC) < 0$$

$$\text{or } TR < (TFC + TVC)$$

But when should the firm shut down?

Short-run shut-down point. If the firm shuts down, *TR* and *TVC* will be zero, but in the short run it will still incur total fixed costs (*TFC*) and thus:

$$T\Pi = -TFC \quad (2)$$

In other words, it will make a loss equal to total fixed costs. From this it can be seen that the firm should close in the short run only if:

$$T\Pi < -TFC$$

$$\text{i.e. } (TR - TFC - TVC) < -TFC \quad (3)$$

In other words, the loss should not exceed fixed costs. Put another way (i.e. by re-arranging (3)), it should continue in production as long as:

$$TR \geq TVC \quad (4)$$

or, dividing both sides of (4) by quantity, where:

$$AR \geq AVC \quad (5)$$

The firm, therefore, should shut down if:

$$AR < AVC$$

This is shown in Figure 5.23.

***LOOKING AT THE MATHS (continued)**

Long-run shut-down point. In the long run, there are no fixed costs. Thus:

$$T\Pi = TR - TVC = TR - TC \quad (6)$$

If the firm shuts down, it will earn no revenue, but incur no costs. Thus:

$$T\Pi = TR - TC = 0 - 0 = 0$$

The firm should therefore continue in production as long as:

$$(TR - TC) \geq 0$$

i.e. $TR \geq TC$

or, dividing both sides by quantity, as long as:

$AR \geq AC$
(where AC in this case is long-run average cost)

The firm, therefore, should shut down if:

$$AR < AC$$

Section summary

1. Total profit equals total revenue minus total cost. By definition, then, a firm's profits will be maximised at the point where there is the greatest gap between total revenue and total cost.
2. Another way of finding the maximum profit point is to find the output where marginal revenue equals marginal cost. Having found this output, the level of maximum profit can be found by finding the average profit (*AR* – *AC*) and then multiplying it by the level of output.
3. Normal profit is the minimum profit that must be made to persuade a firm to stay in business in the long run. It is counted as part of the firm's cost. Supernormal profit is any profit over and above normal profit.
4. For a firm that cannot make a profit at any level of output, the point where *MR* = *MC* represents the loss-minimising output.
5. In the short run, a firm will close down if it cannot cover its variable costs. In the long run, it will close down if it cannot make normal profits.

END OF CHAPTER QUESTIONS

1. The following table shows the average cost and average revenue (price) for a firm at each level of output.

Output	1	2	3	4	5	6	7	8	9	10
AC (£)	7.00	5.00	4.00	3.30	3.00	3.10	3.50	4.20	5.00	6.00
AR (£)	10.00	9.50	9.00	8.50	8.00	7.50	7.00	6.50	6.00	5.50

   (a) Construct a table to show *TC*, *MC*, *TR* and *MR* at each level of output (put the figures for *MC* and *MR* mid-way between the output figures).
   (b) Using *MC* and *MR* figures, find the profit-maximising output.
   (c) Using *TC* and *TR* figures, check your answer to (b).
   (d) Plot the *AC*, *MC*, *AR* and *MR* figures on a graph.
   (e) Mark the profit-maximising output and the *AR* and *AC* at this output.
   (f) Shade in an area to represent the level of profits at this output.

*2. Draw the isoquant corresponding to the following table, which shows the alternative combinations of labour and capital required to produce 100 units of output per day of good X.

K	16	20	$26^2/_3$	40	60	80	100
L	200	160	120	80	$53^1/_3$	40	32

   (a) Assuming that capital costs are £20 per day and the wage rate is £10 per day, what is the least-cost method of producing 100 units? What will the daily total cost be? (Draw in a series of isocosts.)
   (b) Now assume that the wage rate rises to £20 per day. Draw a new set of isocosts. What will be the least-cost method of producing 100 units now? How much labour and capital will be used?

3. Choose a particular industry. Identify factors used in that industry that in the short run are (a) fixed; (b) variable.
4. Taking the same industry, identify as many economies of scale as you can.
5. 'Both short-run and long-run average cost curves may be ◡-shaped, but the explanations for their respective shapes are quite different.' Explain this statement.
6. Why do marginal cost curves intersect both the average variable cost curve and the average cost curve at their lowest point?
7. Draw a diagram like that in Figure 5.21. Now illustrate the effect of a rise in demand for the product. Mark the new profit-maximising price and output. Will the profit-maximising output, price, average cost and profit necessarily be higher than before?
8. Why might it make sense for a firm which cannot sell its output at a profit to continue in production for the time being?

Additional case studies on the book's website (www.pearsoned.co.uk/sloman)

5.1 **Diminishing returns to nitrogen fertiliser.** This case study provides a good illustration of diminishing returns in practice by showing the effects on grass yields of the application of increasing amounts of nitrogen fertiliser.

5.2 **Deriving cost curves from total physical product information.** This shows how total, average and marginal costs can be derived from total product information and the price of inputs.

5.3 **Division of labour in a pin factory.** This is the famous example of division of labour given by Adam Smith in his *Wealth of Nations* (1776).

5.4 **Followers of fashion.** This case study examines the effects of costs on prices of fashion-sensitive goods.

5.5 **Putting on a duplicate.** This examines the effects on marginal costs of additional passengers on a coach journey.

5.6 **Comparing the behaviour of long-run and short-run costs.** This is an application of isoquant analysis.

WEBSITES RELEVANT TO THIS CHAPTER

Numbers and sections refer to websites listed in the Web Appendix and hotlinked from this book's website at www.pearsoned.co.uk/sloman.

- For news articles relevant to this chapter, see the *Economics News Articles* link from the book's website.
- For student resources relevant to this chapter, see sites C1–7, 9, 10, 14, 19, 20.
- For a case study examining costs, see site D2.
- For sites that look at companies, their scale of operation and market share, see B2 (third link); E4, 10; G7, 8.
- For links to sites on various aspects of production and costs, see section *Microeconomics > Production* in sites I7 and 11.

Chapter 6

Profit Maximising under Perfect Competition and Monopoly

As we saw in Chapter 5, a firm's profits are maximised where its marginal cost equals its marginal revenue: *MC* = *MR*. But we will want to know more than this.

- **What determines the *amount* of profit that a firm will make? Will profits be large, or just enough for the firm to survive, or so low that it will be forced out of business?**
- **Will the firm produce a high level of output or a low level?**
- **Will it be producing efficiently?**
- **Will the price charged to the consumer be high or low?**
- **More generally, will the consumer benefit from the decisions a firm makes? This is, of course, a normative question (see section 1.3). Nevertheless, economists can still identify and analyse the effects these decisions have on consumers.**

The answers to these questions depend on the amount of *competition* that a firm faces. A firm in a highly competitive environment will behave quite differently from a firm facing little or no competition. In particular, a firm facing competition from many other firms will be forced to keep its prices down and be as efficient as possible, simply to survive. If, however, the firm faces little or no competition (like the local water company or a major pharmaceutical company), it may have considerable power over prices, and we may end up paying considerably more as a result.

In this chapter and the next, we consider different types of market structure. Here we focus on the extremes: perfect competition (very many firms competing) and monopoly (only one firm in the industry).

CHAPTER MAP

6.1 ALTERNATIVE MARKET STRUCTURES

It is traditional to divide industries into categories according to the degree of competition that exists between the firms within the industry. There are four such categories.

At one extreme is ***perfect competition***, where there are very many firms competing. Each firm is so small relative to the whole industry that it has no power to influence price. It is a price taker. At the other extreme is ***monopoly***, where there is just one firm in the industry, and hence no competition from within the industry. In the middle come ***monopolistic competition***, which involves quite a lot of firms competing and where there is freedom for new firms to enter the industry, and ***oligopoly***, which involves only a few firms and where entry of new firms is restricted.

To distinguish more precisely between these four categories, the following must be considered:

- How freely can firms enter the industry. Is entry free or restricted? If it is restricted, just how great are the barriers to the entry of new firms?
- The nature of the product. Do all firms produce an identical product, or do firms produce their own particular brand or model or variety?
- The firm's degree of control over price. Is the firm a price taker or can it choose its price, and if so, how will changing its price affect its profits? What we are talking about here is the nature of the demand curve it faces. How elastic is it? If the firm puts up its price, will it lose (a) all its sales (a horizontal demand curve), or (b) a large proportion of its sales (a relatively elastic demand curve), or (c) just a small proportion of its sales (a relatively inelastic demand curve)?

KI 9 p58

Key Idea 19

Market power. When firms have market power over prices, they can use this to raise prices and profits above the perfectly competitive level. Other things being equal, the firm will gain at the expense of the consumer. Similarly, if consumers or workers have market power, they can use this to their own benefit.

Table 6.1 shows the differences between the four categories.

1. *Give one more example in each category.*
2. *Would you expect builders and restaurateurs to have the same degree of control over price?*

Table 6.1 Features of the four market structures

Type of market	Number of firms	Freedom of entry	Nature of product	Examples	Implication for demand curve for firm
Perfect competition	Very many	Unrestricted	Homogeneous (undifferentiated)	Cabbages, carrots (these approximate to perfect competition)	Horizontal. The firm is a price taker
Monopolistic competition	Many/several	Unrestricted	Differentiated	Builders, restaurants	Downward sloping, but relatively elastic. The firm has some control over price
Oligopoly	Few	Restricted	1. Undifferentiated or 2. Differentiated	1. Cement 2. Cars, electrical appliances	Downward sloping, relatively inelastic but depends on reactions of rivals to a price change
Monopoly	One	Restricted or completely blocked	Unique	Many prescription drugs, local water company	Downward sloping, more inelastic than oligopoly. The firm has considerable control over price

Definitions

Perfect competition A market structure where there are many firms; where there is freedom of entry into the industry; where all firms produce an identical product; and where all firms are price takers.

Monopoly A market structure where there is only one firm in the industry.

Monopolistic competition A market structure where, like perfect competition, there are many firms and freedom of entry into the industry, but where each firm produces a differentiated product and thus has some control over its price.

Oligopoly A market structure where there are few enough firms to enable barriers to be erected against the entry of new firms.

TC 3 p21 The market structure under which a firm operates will determine its behaviour. Firms under perfect competition will behave quite differently from firms which are monopolists, which will behave differently again from firms under oligopoly or monopolistic competition.

This behaviour (or 'conduct') will in turn affect the firm's performance: its prices, profits, efficiency, etc. In many cases, it will also affect other firms' performance: *their* prices, profits, efficiency, etc. The collective conduct of all the firms in the industry will affect the whole industry's performance.

Economists thus see a causal chain running from market structure to the performance of that industry.

Structure → Conduct → Performance

First we shall look at the two extreme market structures: perfect competition and monopoly. Then we shall look at the two intermediate cases of monopolistic competition and oligopoly (Chapter 7).

The two intermediate cases are sometimes referred to collectively as ***imperfect competition***. The vast majority of firms in the real world operate under imperfect competition. It is still worth studying the two extreme cases, however, because they provide a framework within which to understand the real world. Some industries tend more to the competitive extreme, and thus their performance corresponds to some extent to perfect competition. Other industries tend more to the other extreme: for example, when there is one dominant firm and a few much smaller firms. In such cases, their performance corresponds more to monopoly.

Chapters 6 and 7 assume that firms, under whatever market structure, are attempting to maximise profits. Chapter 8 questions this assumption. It looks at alternative theories of the firm: theories based on assumptions *other* than profit maximising.

6.2 PERFECT COMPETITION

Assumptions of perfect competition

The model of perfect competition is built on four assumptions:

- Firms are *price takers*. There are so many firms in the industry that each one produces an insignificantly small portion of total industry supply, and therefore has no power whatsoever to affect the price of the product. It faces a horizontal demand 'curve' at the market price: the price determined by the interaction of demand and supply in the whole market.
- There is complete *freedom of entry* into the industry for new firms. Existing firms are unable to stop new firms setting up in business. Setting up a business takes time, however. Freedom of entry, therefore, applies in the long run.
- All firms produce an *identical product*. (The product is 'homogeneous'.) There is therefore no branding or advertising.
- TC 9 p101 Producers and consumers have *perfect knowledge* of the market. That is, producers are fully aware of prices, costs and market opportunities. Consumers are fully aware of the price, quality and availability of the product.

These assumptions are very strict. Few, if any, industries in the real world meet these conditions. Certain agricultural markets are perhaps closest to perfect competition. The market for fresh vegetables is an example.

Nevertheless, despite the lack of real-world cases, the model of perfect competition plays a very important role in economic analysis and policy. Its major relevance is as an 'ideal type'. Many on the political right argue that perfect competition would bring a number of important advantages. The model can thus be used as a standard against which to judge the shortcomings of real-world industries. It can help governments to formulate policies towards industry.

1. It is sometimes claimed that the market for various stocks and shares is perfectly competitive, or nearly so. Take the case of the market for shares in a large company like Ford. Go through each of the four assumptions above and see if they apply in this case. (Don't be misled by the first assumption. The 'firm' in this case is not Ford itself.)

2. Is the market for gold perfectly competitive?

The short run and the long run

Before we can examine what price, output and profits will be, we must first distinguish between the short run and the long run as they apply to perfect competition.

In the ***short run***, the number of firms is fixed. Depending on its costs and revenue, a firm might be making large profits, small profits, no profits or a loss; and in the short run, it may continue to do so.

Definitions

Imperfect competition The collective name for monopolistic competition and oligopoly.

The short run under perfect competition The period during which there is too little time for new firms to enter the industry.

EXPLORING ECONOMICS BOX 6.1

CONCENTRATION RATIOS

Measuring the degree of competition

We can get some indication of how competitive a market is by observing the number of firms: the more the firms, the more competitive the market would seem to be. However, this does not tell us anything about how *concentrated* the market might be. There may be *many* firms (suggesting a situation of perfect competition or monopolistic competition), but the largest two firms might produce 95 per cent of total output. This would make these two firms more like oligopolists.

Thus, even though a large number of producers may make the market *seem* highly competitive, this could be deceiving. Another approach, therefore, to measuring the degree of competition is to focus on the level of concentration of firms.

The simplest measure of industrial concentration involves adding together the market share of the largest so many firms: e.g. the largest three or the largest five. This would give what is known as the '3-firm' or '5-firm concentration ratio'.

The table below shows the 5-firm concentration ratios of selected industries in the UK. As you can see, there is an enormous variation in the degree of concentration from one industry to another.

One of the main reasons for this is differences in the percentage of total industry output at which economies of scale are exhausted. If this occurs at a low level of output, there will be room for several firms in the industry which are all benefiting from the maximum economies of scale.

The degree of concentration will also depend on the barriers to entry of other firms into the industry (see page 166) and on various factors such as transport costs and historical accident. It will also depend on how varied the products are within any one industrial category. For example, in categories as large as frozen foods there is room for many firms, each producing a specialised range of products. Within each sub-category, e.g. frozen Indian meals, there may be relatively few firms producing (see table).

So is the degree of concentration a good guide to the degree of competitiveness of the industry? The answer is that it is *some* guide, but on its own it can be misleading. In particular, it ignores the degree of competition from abroad. Thus the five largest book publishers in the UK may produce 37.6 per cent of the UK's books, but these manufacturers face considerable competition from books published overseas that are imported into the country.

1. ***What are the advantages and disadvantages of using a 5-firm concentration ratio rather than a 10-firm, a 3-firm or even a 1-firm ratio?***
2. ***Why are some industries like bread baking and brewing relatively concentrated, in that a few firms produce a large proportion of total output (see Box 7.3 and Web Case 7.5), and yet there are also many small producers?***

Concentration ratios in selected industries (2001)

Industry	5-firm ratio	Industry	5-firm ratio
Chilled Indian ready meals	89.3	Bottled water (still)	58.0
Frozen Indian ready meals	75.0	Bottled water (sparkling)	35.0
Record companies	73.9	Frozen foods	34.4
Batteries	70.9		
Skin care products	64.4		3-firm ratio
Jeans retail	39.0	Chocolate manufacturers	76.0
Book publishing	37.6	Breakfast cereals	69.0

Source: Various Keynote reports.

In the ***long run***, however, the level of profits affects entry and exit from the industry. If supernormal profits are made (see page 153), new firms will be attracted into the industry, whereas if losses are being made, firms will leave.

Note that although we shall be talking about the *level* of profit (since that makes our analysis of pricing and output decisions simpler to understand), in practice it is usually the *rate* of profit that determines whether a firm stays in the industry or leaves. The ***rate of profit*** (r) is the level of profit ($T\Pi$) as *a proportion of the level of capital (K) employed:* $r = T\Pi/K$. As you would expect, larger firms will require to make a larger *total* profit to persuade them to stay in an industry. Total normal profit is thus larger for them than

Definitions

The long run under perfect competition The period of time that is long enough for new firms to enter the industry.

Rate of profit Total profit ($T\Pi$) as a proportion of the capital employed (K): $r = T\Pi/K$.

EXPLORING ECONOMICS

BOX 6.2

IS PERFECT BEST?

Be careful of the word 'perfect'.

'Perfect' competition refers to competition that is total. Perhaps 'total' competition would be a better term. There is a total absence of power, a total absence of entry barriers, a total absence of product differentiation between producers, and total information for producers and consumers on the market. It is thus useful for understanding the effects of power, barriers, product differentiation and lack of information.

Perfect does not mean 'best', however.

Just because it is at the extreme end of the competition spectrum, it does not follow that perfect competition is desirable. You could have a perfect bomb – i.e. one that kills everyone in the world. You could have a perfect killer virus – i.e. one that is totally immune to drugs, and against which humans have no natural protection at all. Such things, though perfect, are hardly desirable!

To say that perfect competition is desirable and that it is a goal towards which government policy should be directed are normative statements. Economists, in their role as economists, cannot make such statements.

This does not mean, of course, that economists cannot identify the effects of perfect competition, but whether these effects are *desirable* or not is an ethical question.

The danger is that by using perfect competition as a yardstick, and by using the word 'perfect' rather than 'total', economists may be surreptitiously persuading their audience that perfect competition is a goal we *ought* to be striving to achieve.

for a small firm. The *rate* of normal profit, however, will probably be similar.

?

1. *Why do economists treat normal profit as a cost of production?*
2. *What determines (a) the level and (b) the rate of normal profit for a particular firm?*

Thus whether the industry expands or contracts in the long run will depend on the rate of profit. Naturally, since the time a firm takes to set up in business varies from industry to industry, the length of time before the long run is reached also varies from industry to industry.

The short-run equilibrium of the firm

TC 4 p22

The determination of price, output and profit in the short run under perfect competition can best be shown in a diagram.

Figure 6.1 shows a short-run equilibrium for both industry and a firm under perfect competition. Both parts of the diagram have the same scale for the vertical axis. The horizontal axes have totally different scales, however. For example, if the horizontal axis for the firm were measured in, say, thousands of units, the horizontal axis for the whole industry might be measured in millions or tens of millions of units, depending on the number of firms in the industry.

Let us examine the determination of price, output and profit in turn.

Price

The price is determined in the industry by the intersection of demand and supply. The firm faces a horizontal demand (or average revenue) 'curve' at this price. It can sell all it can produce at the market price (P_e), but nothing at a price above P_e.

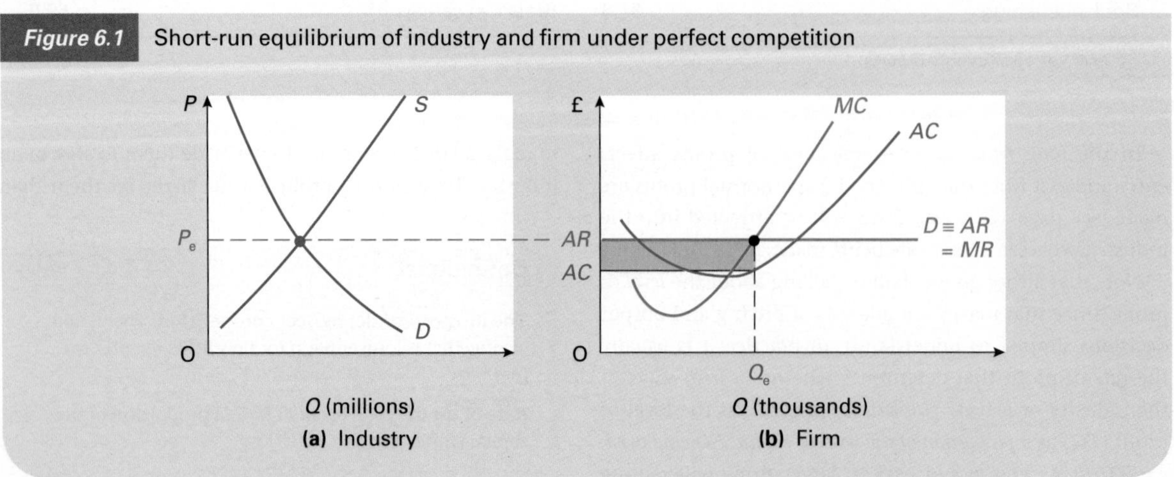

Figure 6.1 Short-run equilibrium of industry and firm under perfect competition

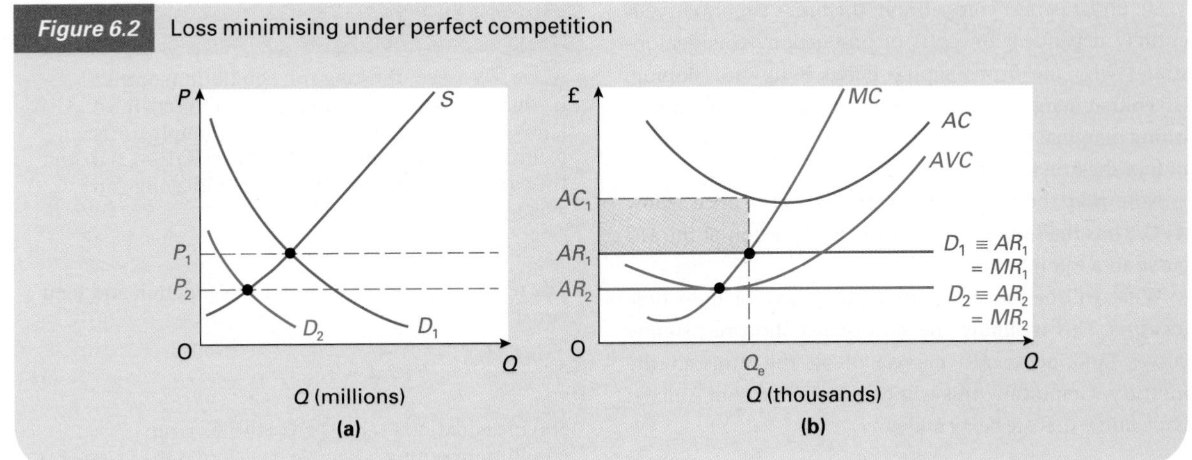

Figure 6.2 Loss minimising under perfect competition

Output

TC 2 p146 The firm will maximise profit where marginal cost equals marginal revenue ($MR = MC$), at an output of Q_e. Note that, since the price is not affected by the firm's output, marginal revenue will equal price (see page 146 and Figure 5.15).

Profit

If the average cost (AC) curve (which includes normal profit) dips below the average revenue (AR) 'curve', the firm will earn supernormal profit. Supernormal profit *per unit* at Q_e is the vertical difference between AR and AC at Q_e. *Total* supernormal profit is the shaded rectangle in Figure 6.1.

What happens if the firm cannot make a profit at *any* level of output? This situation would occur if the AC curve were above the AR curve at all points. This is illustrated in Figure 6.2, where the market price is P_1. In this case, the point where $MC = MR$ represents the *loss-minimising* point (where loss is defined as anything less than normal profit). The amount of the loss is represented by the shaded rectangle.

As we saw in section 5.6, whether the firm is prepared to continue making a loss in the short run or whether it will close down immediately depends on whether it can cover its *variable* costs.

Provided price is above average variable cost (AVC), the firm will still continue producing in the short run: it can pay its variable costs and go some way to paying its fixed costs. It will shut down in the short run only if the market price falls below P_2 in Figure 6.2.

The short-run supply curve

The *firm's* short-run supply curve will be its (short-run) marginal cost curve.

A supply curve shows how much will be supplied at each price: it relates quantity to price. The marginal cost curve relates quantity to marginal cost. But under perfect competition, given that $P = MR$, and $MR = MC$, P must equal MC. Thus the supply curve and the MC curve will follow the same line.

For example, in Figure 6.3(b), if price were P_1, profits would be maximised at Q_1 where $P_1 = MC$. Thus point *a* is one point on the supply curve. At a price of P_2, Q_2 would be produced. Thus point *b* is another point on the supply curve, and so on.

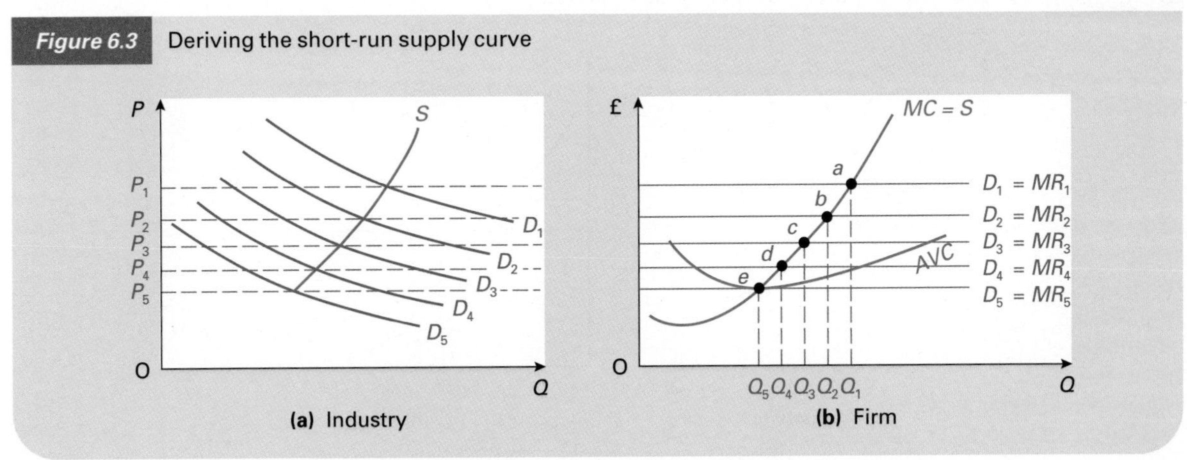

Figure 6.3 Deriving the short-run supply curve

So, under perfect competition, the firm's supply curve is entirely dependent on costs of production. This demonstrates why the firm's supply curve is upward sloping. Given that marginal costs rise as output rises (due to diminishing marginal returns), a higher price will be necessary to induce the firm to increase its output.

Note that the firm will not produce at a price below *AVC*. Thus the supply curve is only that portion of the *MC* curve above point *e*.

What will be the short-run supply curve of the whole *industry*? This is simply the sum of the short-run supply curves (and hence *MC* curves) of all the firms in the industry. Graphically this will be a *horizontal* sum, since it is *quantities* that are being added.

? *Will the industry supply be zero below a price of P_5 in Figure 6.3?*

TC 3 p21

The long-run equilibrium of the firm

In the long run, if typical firms are making supernormal profits, new firms will be attracted into the industry. Likewise, if established firms can make supernormal profits by increasing the scale of their operations, they will do so, since all factors of production are variable in the long run.

KI 5 p21

The effect of the entry of new firms and/or the expansion of existing firms is to increase industry supply. This is illustrated in Figure 6.4. At a price of P_1 supernormal profits are earned. This causes industry supply to expand (the industry supply curve shifts to the right). This in turn leads to a fall in price. Supply will go on increasing and price falling until firms are making only normal profits. This will be when price has fallen to the point where the demand 'curve' for the firm just touches the bottom of its long-run average cost curve. Q_L is thus the long-run equilibrium output of the firm, with P_L the long-run equilibrium price.

? *Illustrate on a diagram similar to Figure 6.4 what would happen in the long run if price were initially below P_L.*

*LOOKING AT THE MATHS

As we have seen, the long-run equilibrium output is where long-run average cost is minimised. If we know the equation for *LRAC*, we can simply use the techniques of minimisation (see pages A:10–12) to find the equilibrium output. Assume that the long-run average cost function is:

$$LRAC = a - bQ + cQ^2$$

The technique is to differentiate this function and set it equal to zero, i.e.:

$$\frac{d(LRAC)}{dQ} = -b + 2cQ = 0 \qquad (1)$$

Solving equation (1) for *Q* gives the long-run equilibrium output. Once we have found the value of *Q*, we can substitute it back into equation (1) to find the value of *LRAC* and hence the equilibrium price (since $P = LRAC$).

We can then use the second derivative test (see page A:10) to check that this indeed does represent a minimum, not a maximum, *LRAC*. An example of this is given in Maths Case 6.1 on the book's website.

Since the *LRAC* curve is tangential to all possible short-run *AC* curves (see section 5.4), the full long-run equilibrium will be as shown in Figure 6.5 where:

$$LRAC = AC = MC = MR = AR$$

The long-run industry supply curve

If industry demand increased, what would happen to industry price and output in the long run? The long-run supply curve gives the answer.

Each of the diagrams in Figure 6.6 shows an increase in demand. The demand curve shifts from D_1 to D_2. Equilibrium in the short run moves from point *a* to point *b*, where D_2 and S_1 intersect. After the initial rise in price, the resulting supernormal profit attracts new firms into

Figure 6.4 Long-run equilibrium under perfect competition

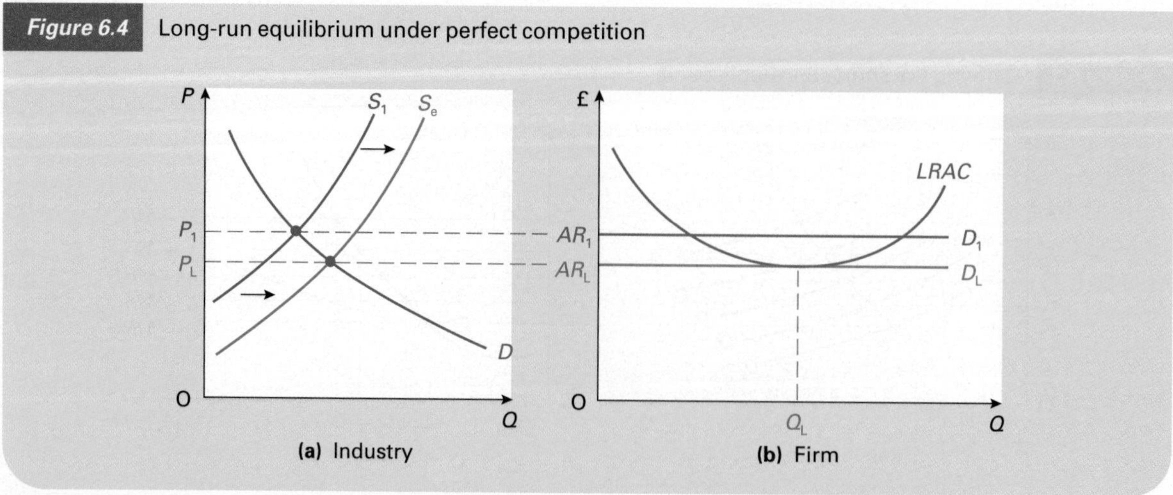

Figure 6.5 Long-run equilibrium of the firm under perfect competition

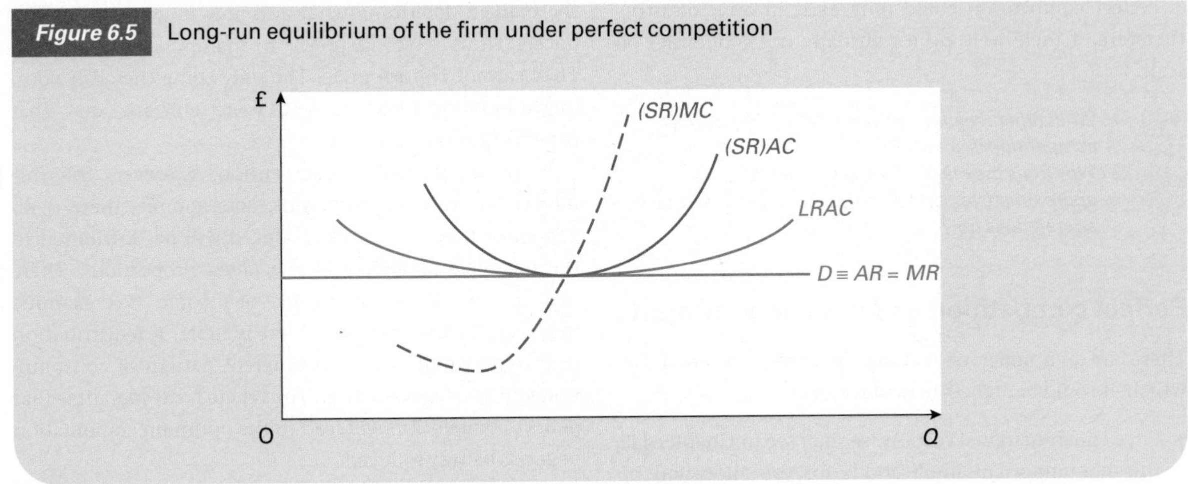

Figure 6.6 Various long-run industry supply curves under perfect competition

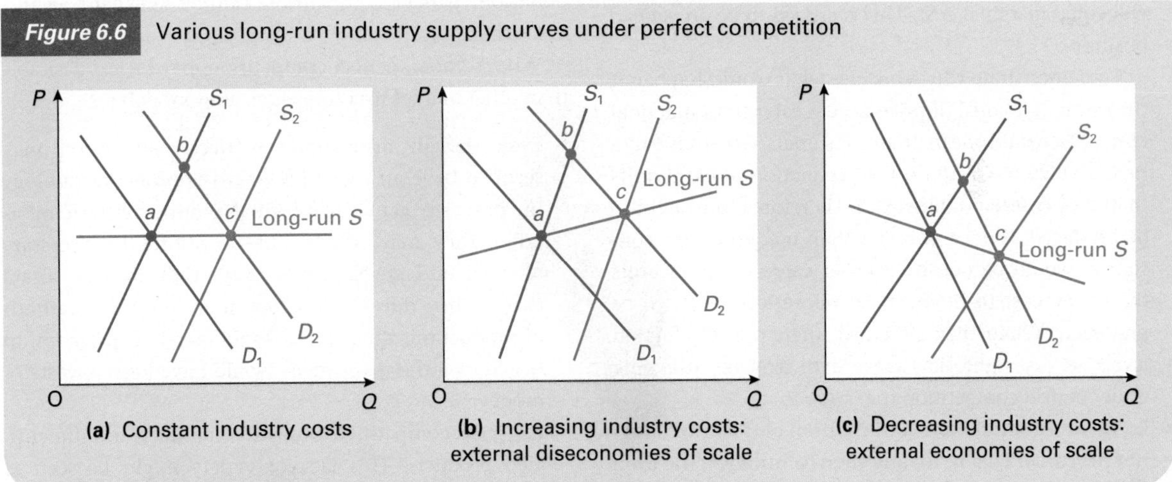

(a) Constant industry costs

(b) Increasing industry costs: external diseconomies of scale

(c) Decreasing industry costs: external economies of scale

the industry. The short-run supply curve shifts to S_2 and equilibrium moves to point *c*. Thus the long-run effect of the increase in demand has been to move the equilibrium from point *a* to point *c*. This means, therefore, that the *long-run* supply curve will pass through points *a* and *c*. This is illustrated in each of the three diagrams.

If price falls back to its original level (i.e. points *a* and *c* are at the *same* price) the *long-run* supply curve will be horizontal (see diagram (a)). This would occur if there were no change in firms' average cost curves. Price would simply return to the bottom of firms' *LRAC* curve.

If, however, the entry of new firms creates a shortage of factors of production, this will bid up factor prices. Firms' *LRAC* curve will shift vertically upwards, and so the long-run equilibrium price will be higher. The long-run supply curve of the industry, therefore, will slope upwards, as in diagram (b). This is the case of *increasing industry costs* or *external diseconomies of scale*: i.e. diseconomies external to the firm (see section 5.3).

If the expansion of the industry lowers firms' *LRAC* curve, due, say, to the building-up of an industrial infrastructure (distribution channels, specialist suppliers, banks, communications, etc.), the long-run supply curve will slope downwards, as in diagram (c). This is the case of *decreasing industry costs* or *external economies of scale*.

The incompatibility of perfect competition and substantial economies of scale

Why is perfect competition so rare in the real world – if it even exists at all? One important reason for this has to do with economies of scale.

In many industries, firms may have to be quite large if they are to experience the full potential economies of scale. But perfect competition requires there to be *many* firms. Firms must therefore be small under perfect competition: too small in most cases for economies of scale.

Once a firm expands sufficiently to achieve economies of scale, it will usually gain market power. It will be able to undercut the prices of smaller firms, which will thus be driven out of business. Perfect competition is destroyed.

Perfect competition could only exist in any industry, therefore, if there were no (or virtually no) economies of scale.

> ?
> 1. *What other reasons can you think of why perfect competition is so rare?*
> 2. *Why does the market for fresh vegetables approximate to perfect competition, whereas that for aircraft does not?*

Perfect competition and the public interest

There are a number of features of perfect competition which, it could be argued, benefit society:

KI3 p10

- Price equals marginal cost. As we shall see in Chapter 11, this has important implications for the allocation of resources between alternative products. Given that price equals marginal utility (see Chapter 4), marginal utility will equal marginal cost. This is argued to be an *optimal* position.

  To demonstrate why, consider what would happen if they were not equal. If price were greater than marginal cost, this would mean that consumers were putting a higher value ($P = MU$) on the production of extra units than they cost to produce (MC). Therefore more ought to be produced. If price were less than marginal cost, consumers would be putting a lower value on extra units than they cost to produce. Therefore less ought to be produced. When they are equal, therefore, production levels are just right. But, as we shall see later, it is only under perfect competition that $MC = P$.
- Long-run equilibrium is at the bottom of the firm's long-run AC curve. That is, for any *given* technology, the firm, in the long run, will produce at the least-cost output.

- Perfect competition is a case of 'survival of the fittest'. Inefficient firms will be driven out of business, since they will not be able to make even normal profits. This encourages firms to be as efficient as possible and, where possible, to invest in new improved technology.
- The combination of (long-run) production being at minimum average cost and the firm making only normal profit keeps prices at a minimum.
- If consumer tastes change, the resulting price change will lead firms to respond (purely out of self-interest). An increased consumer demand will call forth extra supply with only a short-run increase in profit.

Because of these last two points, perfect competition is said to lead to ***consumer sovereignty***. Consumers, through the market, determine what and how much is to be produced. Firms have no power to manipulate the market. They cannot control price. The only thing they can do to increase profit is to become more efficient, and that benefits the consumer too.

TC6 p26

Even under perfect competition, however, the free market has various limitations. For example, there is no guarantee that the goods produced will be distributed to the members of society in the *fairest* proportions. There may be considerable inequality of income. (We examine this issue in Chapter 10.) What is more, a redistribution of income would lead to a different pattern of consumption and hence production. Thus there is no guarantee that perfect competition will lead to the optimum combination of goods being produced.

Another limitation is that the production of certain goods may lead to various undesirable side-effects, such as pollution. Perfect competition cannot safeguard against this either.

What is more, perfect competition may be less desirable than other market structures such as monopoly:

- Even though firms under perfect competition may seem to have an incentive to develop new technology (in order to gain supernormal profits, albeit temporarily), they may not be able to afford the necessary research and development. Also, they may be afraid that if they did develop new more efficient methods of production, their rivals would merely copy them, in which case the investment would have been a waste of money.
- Perfectly competitive industries produce undifferentiated products. This lack of variety might be seen as a disadvantage to the consumer. Under monopolistic competition and oligopoly there is often intense competition over the quality and design of the product. This can lead to pressure on firms to improve their products. This pressure will not exist under perfect competition.

The issue of the efficiency or otherwise of perfect markets and the various failings of real-world markets is examined in more detail in Chapter 11.

At this stage, however, it is important to emphasise that the whole question of advantages and disadvantages is a normative one, and as such it is a question to which the economist cannot give a definitive answer. After all, people have very different views as to what constitutes 'good' or 'bad'.

Definitions

Consumer sovereignty A situation where firms respond to changes in consumer demand without being in a position in the long run to charge a price above average cost.

CASE STUDIES AND APPLICATIONS

BOX 6.3

E-COMMERCE AND PERFECT COMPETITION

A return of power to the people?

The relentless drive towards big business in recent decades has seen many markets become more concentrated and increasingly dominated by large producers. And yet forces are at work that are undermining this dominance and bringing more competition to markets. One of these forces is *e-commerce*.

In this case study, we will consider just how far e-commerce is returning 'power to the people'.

Moving markets back towards perfect competition?

To see the extent to which e-commerce is making markets more competitive, let's look at the assumptions of perfect competition.

Large number of firms. The growth of e-commerce has led to many new firms starting up in business. It's not just large firms like Amazon.com that are providing increased competition for established firms, but the thousands of small online companies that are being established every day. Many of these firms are selling directly to us as consumers. This is known as 'B2C' e-commerce (business-to-consumers). But many more are selling to other firms ('B2B'). More and more companies, from the biggest to the smallest, are transferring their purchasing to the Web and are keen to get value for money.

The reach of the Web is global. This means that firms, whether conventional or web-based, are having to keep an eye on the prices and products of competitors in the rest of the world, not just in the local neighbourhood. Firms' demand curves are thus becoming very price elastic. This is especially so for goods that are cheap to transport, or for services such as insurance and banking.

Perfect knowledge. There are various ways in which e-commerce is adding to the consumer's knowledge. There is greater price transparency, with consumers able to compare prices online. Online shopping agents, such as Kelkoo, DealTime and Froogle, can quickly locate a list of alternative suppliers. There is greater information on product availability and quality. Virtual shopping malls, full of e-retailers, place the high street retailer under intense competitive pressure.

The pressure is even greater in the market for intermediate products. Many firms are constantly searching for cheaper sources of supply, and the Internet provides a cheap and easy means of conducting such searches.

Freedom of entry. Internet companies often have lower start-up costs than their conventional rivals. Their premises are generally much smaller, with no 'shop-front' costs and lower levels of stockholding. Marketing costs can also be relatively low, especially given the ease with which companies can be located with search engines. Internet companies are often smaller and more specialist, relying on Internet 'outsourcing' (buying parts, equipment and other supplies through the Internet), rather than making everything themselves. They are also more likely to use delivery firms rather than having their own transport fleet. All this makes it relatively cheap for new firms to set up and begin trading over the Internet.

In fact, the distinction between firms and consumers is becoming increasingly blurred. With the rise of eBay, more and more people are finding going into business incredibly easy. Suddenly people are finding a market for all the junk they've collected over the years! As the eBay TV advertisement says, 'someone wants everything'. There are over 100 million registered eBay users worldwide, and hundreds of thousands of people make a full-time living from buying and selling on eBay. Annual sales on eBay are worth over £8 billion.

Not only do these factors make markets more price competitive, they also bring other benefits. Costs are driven down, as firms economise on stockholding, rely more on outsourcing and develop more efficient relationships with suppliers. 'Procurement hubs', online exchanges and trading communities are now well established in many industries. The competition also encourages innovation, which improves quality and the range of products.

Is there a limit to e-commerce?

In 20 years, will we be doing all our shopping on the Internet? Will the only shopping malls be virtual ones? Although e-commerce is revolutionising some markets, it is unlikely that things will go anything like that far.

The benefits of 'shop shopping' are that you get to see the good, touch it and use it. You can buy the good there and then, and take instant possession of it: you don't have to wait. Shopping is also an enjoyable experience. Many people like wandering round the shops, meeting friends, seeing what takes their fancy, trying on clothes, browsing through CDs and so on. 'Retail therapy' for many is an important means of 'de-stressing'.

Online shopping is limited by the screen; Internet access may be slow and frustrating; 'surfing' may instead become 'wading'; you have to wait for goods to be delivered; and what if deliveries are late or fail completely?

Also costs might not be as low as expected. How efficient is it to have many small deliveries of goods? How significant are the lost cost savings from economies of scale that larger producers or retailers are likely to generate?

Nevertheless, e-commerce has made many markets, both retail and B2B, more competitive. This is especially so for services and for goods whose quality is easy to identify online. Many firms are being forced to face up to having their prices determined by the market.

?

1. ***Why may the Internet work better for replacement buys than for new purchases?***
2. ***Give three examples of products that are particularly suitable for selling over the Internet and three that are not. Explain your answer.***

Section summary

1. The assumptions of perfect competition are: a very large number of firms, complete freedom of entry, a homogeneous product and perfect knowledge of the good and its market by both producers and consumers.
2. In the short run, there is not time for new firms to enter the market, and thus supernormal profits can persist. In the long run, however, any supernormal profits will be competed away by the entry of new firms.
3. The short-run equilibrium for the firm will be where the price, as determined by demand and supply in the market, is equal to marginal cost. At this output, the firm will be maximising profit. The firm's short-run supply curve is the same as its marginal cost curve (that portion of it above the *AVC* curve).
4. The long-run equilibrium will be where the market price is just equal to firms' long-run average cost. The long-run industry supply curve will thus depend on what happens to firms' *LRAC* curves as industry output expands. If their *LRAC* curves shift upwards (due to external diseconomies of scale), the long-run industry supply curve will slope upwards. If their *LRAC* curves shift downwards (due to external economies of scale), the long-run industry supply curve will slope downwards.
5. There are no substantial (internal) economies of scale to be gained by perfectly competitive firms. If there were, the industry would cease to be perfectly competitive as the large, low-cost firms drove the small, high-cost ones out of business.
6. Under perfect competition, production will be at the point where $P = MC$. This can be argued to be optimal. Perfect competition can act as a spur to efficiency and bring benefits to the consumer in terms of low costs and low prices.
7. On the other hand, perfectly competitive firms may be unwilling to invest in research and development or may have insufficient funds to do so. They may also produce a lack of variety of goods. Finally, perfect competition does not necessarily lead to a fair distribution of income or guarantee an absence of harmful side-effects of production.

6.3 MONOPOLY

What is a monopoly?

This may seem a strange question because the answer seems obvious. A monopoly exists when there is only one firm in the industry.

But whether an industry can be classed as a monopoly is not always clear. It depends how narrowly the industry is defined. For example, a textile company may have a monopoly on certain types of fabric, but it does not have a monopoly on fabrics in general. The consumer can buy alternative fabrics to those supplied by the company. A pharmaceutical company may have a monopoly of a certain drug, but there may be alternative drugs for treating a particular illness.

To some extent, the boundaries of an industry are arbitrary. What is more important for a firm is the amount of monopoly *power* it has, and that depends on the closeness of substitutes produced by rival industries. The Post Office in the UK has a monopoly over the delivery of letters under a certain weight, but it faces competition in communications from phones, faxes and e-mail.

?

As an illustration of the difficulty in identifying monopolies, try to decide which of the following are monopolies: British Telecom; your local evening newspaper; the village post office; a rail company; Interflora; the London Underground; ice creams in the cinema; Guinness; food sold in a university refectory; the board game 'Monopoly'. (As you will quickly realise in each case, it depends how you define the industry.)

Barriers to entry

For a firm to maintain its monopoly position, there must be ***barriers to entry*** of new firms. Barriers also exist under oligopoly, but in the case of monopoly they must be high enough to block the entry of new firms. Barriers can be of various forms.

Economies of scale. If a monopoly experiences substantial economies of scale, the industry may not be able to support more than one producer. In Figure 6.7, D_1 represents the industry demand curve, and hence the demand curve for the firm under monopoly. The monopolist can gain supernormal profit at any output between points *a* and *b*. If there were two firms, however, each charging the same price and supplying half the industry output, they would both face the demand curve D_2. There is no price that would allow them to cover costs.

This case is known as ***natural monopoly***. It is particularly likely if the market is small. For example, two bus

Definitions

Barrier to entry Anything that prevents or impedes the entry of firms into an industry and thereby limits the amount of competition faced by existing firms.

Natural monopoly A situation where long-run average costs would be lower if an industry were under monopoly than if it were shared between two or more competitors.

Figure 6.7 Natural monopoly

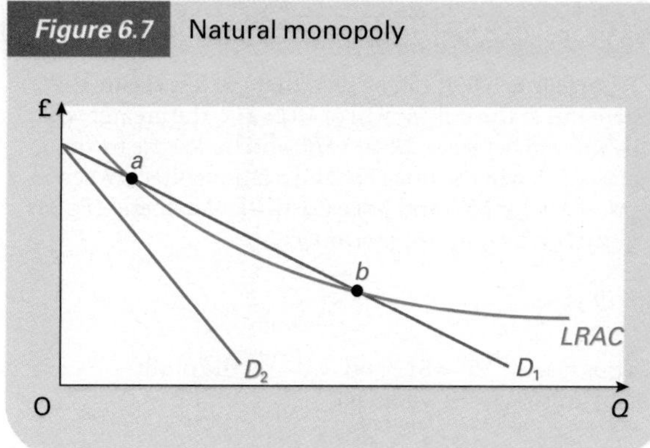

companies might find it unprofitable to serve the same routes, each running with perhaps only half-full buses, whereas one company with a monopoly of the routes could make a profit. Electricity transmission via a national grid is another example of a natural monopoly.

Even if a market could support more than one firm, a new entrant is unlikely to be able to start up on a very large scale. Thus a monopolist already experiencing economies of scale can charge a price below the cost of the new entrant and drive it out of business. If, however, the new entrant is a firm already established in another industry, it may be able to survive this competition.

Network economies. When a product or service is used by everyone in the market, there are benefits to all users from having access to other users. Thus eBay, by providing such large ***network economies*** makes it very difficult for other online auction houses to compete. Similar network economies apply to Microsoft's Windows (see Box 6.4), Adobe's *Acrobat* (for pdf files) and airlines operating interconnecting routes (see Box 6.6).

Economies of scope. A firm that produces a range of products is also likely to experience a lower average cost of production. For example, a large pharmaceutical company producing a range of drugs and toiletries can use shared research, marketing, storage and transport facilities across its range of products. These lower costs make it difficult for a new single-product entrant to the market, since the large firm will be able to undercut its price and drive it out of the market.

Product differentiation and brand loyalty. If a firm produces a clearly differentiated product, where the consumer associates the product with the brand, it will be very difficult for a new firm to break into that market. Rank Xerox invented, and patented, the plain paper photocopier. After this legal monopoly (see below) ran out, people still associated photocopiers with Rank Xerox. It is still not unusual to hear someone say that they are going to 'Xerox the article' or, for that matter, 'Hoover their carpet'. Other examples of strong brand image include Guinness, Kellogg's Cornflakes, Coca-Cola, Nescafé and Sellotape. In most cases, such loyalty would not be enough to *block* entry, but it might well reinforce other barriers.

Definition

Network economies The benefits to consumers of having a network of other people using the same product or service.

Lower costs for an established firm. An established monopoly is likely to have developed specialised production and marketing skills. It is more likely to be aware of the most efficient techniques and the most reliable and/or cheapest suppliers. It is likely to have access to cheaper finance. It is thus operating on a lower cost curve. New firms would therefore find it hard to compete and would be likely to lose any price war.

Ownership of, or control over, key inputs. If a firm governs the supply of vital inputs (say, by owning the sole supplier of some component part), it can deny access to these inputs to potential rivals. On a world scale, the de Beers company has a monopoly in fine diamonds because all diamond producers market their diamonds through de Beers.

Ownership of, or control over, wholesale or retail outlets. Similarly, if a firm controls the outlets through which the product must be sold, it can prevent potential rivals from gaining access to consumers. For example, Birds Eye Wall's used to supply freezers free to shops on the condition that they stocked only Wall's ice cream in them.

Legal protection. The firm's monopoly position may be protected by patents on essential processes, by copyright, by various forms of licensing (allowing, say, only one firm to operate in a particular area) and by tariffs (i.e. customs duties) and other trade restrictions to keep out foreign competitors. Examples of monopolies protected by patents include most new medicines developed by pharmaceutical companies (e.g. anti-AIDS drugs), Microsoft's Windows operating systems and agro-chemical companies, such as Monsanto, with various genetically modified plant varieties and pesticides.

Mergers and takeovers. The monopolist can put in a takeover bid for any new entrant. The sheer threat of takeovers may discourage new entrants.

Aggressive tactics. An established monopolist can probably sustain losses for longer than a new entrant. Thus it can start a price war, mount massive advertising campaigns, offer an attractive after-sales service, introduce new brands to compete with new entrants, and so on.

Intimidation. The monopolist may resort to various forms of harassment, legal or illegal, to drive a new entrant out of business.

Figure 6.8 Profit maximising under monopoly

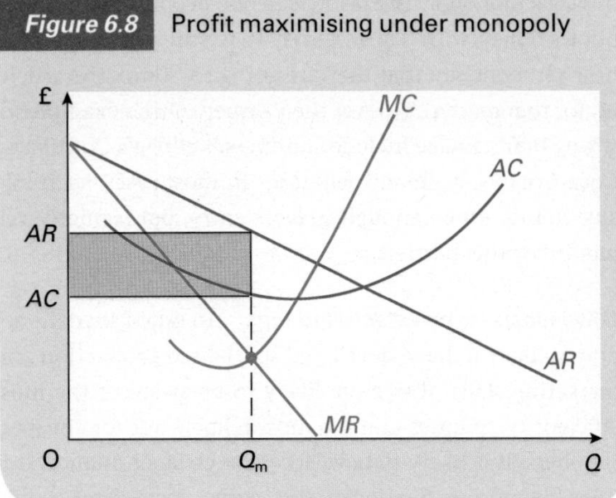

*LOOKING AT THE MATHS

From Figure 6.8, it can be seen that the less elastic the demand at the output where $MC = MR$, the greater will be the gap between AR and MR, and hence the further above MR will the price be. The relationship between price, MR (or MC) and price elasticity of demand ($P\epsilon_D$) is given by the following formula:

$$P = \frac{MR}{1 + (1/P\epsilon_D)}$$

Thus if $MR = MC = £12$ and $P\epsilon_D = -4$, the profit-maximising price would be:

$$\frac{£12}{1 + (1/-4)} = \frac{£12}{1 - 1/4} = \frac{£12}{0.75} = £16$$

Proof of this rule is given in Maths Case 6.2 on the book's website. You can see simply by examining the formula, however, that the lower the elasticity, the greater will be the price relative to MR or MC.[1]

? ***What is the profit-maximising price if $MR = MC = £12$ and $P\epsilon_D = -2$?***

[1] Note that this formula works only if demand is elastic, as it must be if MR is positive (which it will be, since MC must be positive).

Equilibrium price and output

Since there is, by definition, only one firm in the industry, the firm's demand curve is also the industry demand curve.

Compared with other market structures, demand under monopoly will be relatively inelastic at each price. The monopolist can raise its price and consumers have no alternative firm in the industry to turn to. They either pay the higher price or go without the good altogether.

TC 8 p59

Unlike the firm under perfect competition, the monopoly firm is a 'price maker'. It can choose what price to charge. Nevertheless, it is still constrained by its demand curve. A rise in price will lower the quantity demanded.

As with firms in other market structures, a monopolist will maximise profit where $MR = MC$. In Figure 6.8, profit is maximised at Q_m. The supernormal profit obtained is shown by the shaded area.

These profits will tend to be larger the less elastic is the demand curve (and hence the steeper is the MR curve), and thus the bigger is the gap between MR and price (AR). The actual elasticity will depend on whether reasonably close substitutes are available in *other* industries. The demand for a rail service will be much less elastic (and the potential for profit greater) if there is no bus service to the same destination.

Since there are barriers to the entry of new firms, these supernormal profits will not be competed away in the long run. The only difference, therefore, between short-run and long-run equilibrium is that in the long run the firm will produce where MR = *long-run MC*.

? *Try this brain teaser. A monopoly would be expected to face an inelastic demand. After all, there are no direct substitutes. And yet, if it produces where MR = MC, MR must be positive and demand must therefore be* elastic. *Therefore the monopolist must face an elastic demand! Can you solve this conundrum?*

Limit pricing

If the barriers to the entry of new firms are not total, and if the monopolist is making very large supernormal profits, there may be a danger in the long run of potential rivals breaking into the industry. In such cases, the monopolist may keep its price down and thereby deliberately restrict the size of its profits so as not to attract new entrants. This practice is known as ***limit pricing***.

In Figure 6.9, two AC curves are drawn: one for the monopolist and one for a potential entrant. The monopolist, being established, has a lower AC curve. The new entrant, if it is to compete successfully with the monopolist, must charge the same price or a lower one. Thus, provided the monopolist does not raise price above P_L, the

Figure 6.9 Limit pricing

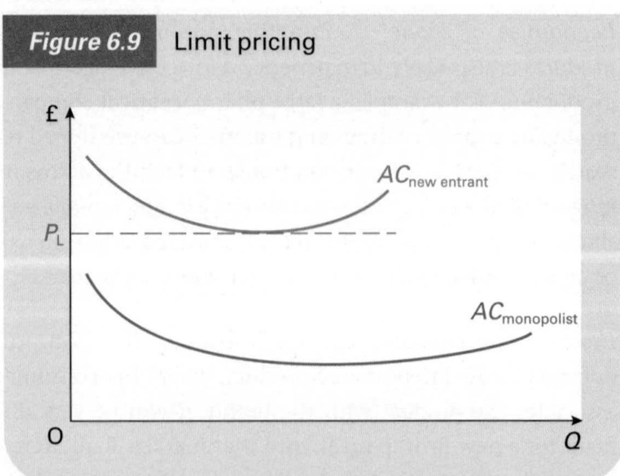

Definition

Limit pricing Where a monopolist (or oligopolist) charges a price below the short-run profit maximising level in order to deter new entrants.

other firm, unable to make supernormal profit, will not be attracted into the industry.

P_L may well be below the monopolist's short-run profit-maximising price, but the monopolist may prefer to limit its price to P_L to protect its long-run profits from damage by competition.

TC 3 p21 Fear of government intervention to curb the monopolist's practices (e.g. the Office of Fair Trading referring the firm to the Competition Commission: see section 12.3) may have a similar restraining effect on the price that the monopolist charges.

1. *On a diagram like Figure 6.9, by drawing in MR and MC curves, demonstrate that P_L could be below the short-run profit-maximising price.*
2. *What does this analysis assume about the price elasticity of demand for the new entrant (a) above P_L; (b) below P_L?*

Monopoly and the public interest

TC 6 p26

Disadvantages of monopoly

There are several reasons why monopolies may be against the public interest. As we shall see in sections 12.3 and 12.4, these have given rise to legislation to regulate monopoly power and/or behaviour.

Higher price and lower output than under perfect competition (short run). Figure 6.10 compares the profit-maximising position for an industry under monopoly with that under perfect competition. The monopolist will produce Q_1 at a price of P_1. This is where $MC = MR$.

If the same industry operated under perfect competition, however, it would produce at Q_2 and P_2 – a higher output and a lower price. This is where industry supply under perfect competition equals industry demand. (Remember, we showed in section 6.2 that the firm's supply curve under perfect competition is its *MC* curve and thus the industry's supply curve is simply the *industry MC* curve: the *MC* curve shown in Figure 6.10.)

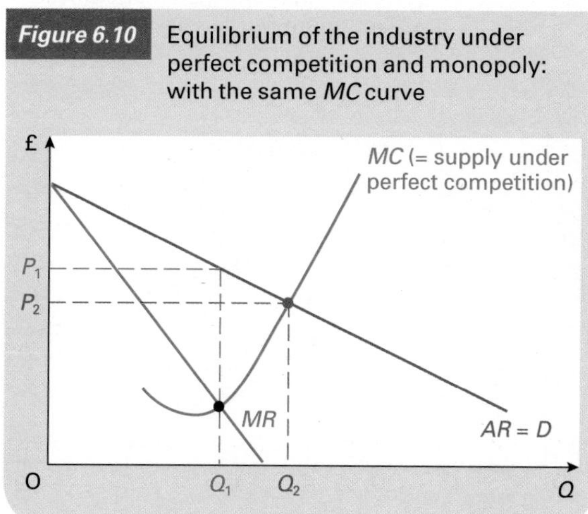

Figure 6.10 Equilibrium of the industry under perfect competition and monopoly: with the same *MC* curve

This analysis is based on the assumption that the industry has the *same AC* and *MC* curves whether under perfect competition or run as a monopoly. For example, suppose some potato farmers initially operate under perfect competition. The market price is P_2 in Figure 6.10. Then they set up a marketing agency through which they all sell their potatoes. The agency therefore acts as a monopoly supplier to the market and charges a price of P_1. Since it is the same farmers before and after, production costs are unlikely to have changed much. But as we shall see below, even if an industry has *lower AC* and *MC* curves under monopoly than under perfect competition, it is still likely to charge a higher price and produce a lower output.

When we were looking at the advantages of perfect competition, we said that where $P = MC$ could be argued to be the *optimum* level of production. Clearly, if a monopolist is producing below this level (at only Q_1 in Figure 6.10 – where $P > MC$), the monopolist can be argued to be producing at *less* than optimal output. Consumers would be prepared to pay more for additional units than they cost to produce.

Higher price and lower output than under perfect competition (long run). Under perfect competition, freedom of entry eliminates supernormal profit and forces firms to produce at the bottom of their *LRAC* curve. The effect, therefore, is to keep long-run prices down. Under monopoly, however, barriers to entry allow profits to remain supernormal in the long run. The monopolist is not forced to operate at the bottom of the *AC* curve. Thus, other things being equal, long-run prices will tend to be higher, and hence output lower, under monopoly.

Possibility of higher cost curves due to lack of competition. The sheer survival of a firm in the long run under perfect competition requires that it uses the most efficient known technique, and develops new techniques wherever possible. The monopolist, however, sheltered by barriers to entry, can still make large profits even if it is not using the most efficient technique. It has less incentive, therefore, to be efficient (see Box 6.4).

On the other hand, if it can lower its costs by using and developing more efficient techniques, it can gain extra supernormal profits which will not be competed away.

Unequal distribution of income. The high profits of monopolists may be considered as unfair, especially by competitive firms, or anyone on low incomes for that matter. The scale of this problem obviously depends on the size of the monopoly and the degree of its power. The monopoly profits of the village store may seem of little consequence when compared to the profits of a giant national or international company.

?

If the shares in a monopoly (such as a water company) were very widely distributed among the population, would the shareholders necessarily want the firm to use its monopoly power to make larger profits?

CASE STUDIES AND APPLICATIONS

WINDOWS CLEANING!

Microsoft, the Internet and the US Justice Department

On 18 May 1998, the US government initiated its biggest competition case for 20 years: it sued Microsoft, the world's largest software company. It accused Microsoft of abusing its market power and seeking to crush its rivals.

KI 19 p157

By controlling the *Windows* operating software, Microsoft could force its own Internet browser, *Internet Explorer*, on to consumers and computer manufacturers.

The case against Microsoft had been building for many years, but it was with the release of *Windows 98* that the US Justice Department decided to act. It alleged that Microsoft had committed the following anti-competitive actions:

- Back in May 1995, Microsoft attempted to collude with Netscape Communications to divide the Internet browser market. Netscape Communications refused.
- Microsoft had forced personal computer manufacturers to install *Internet Explorer* in order to obtain a *Windows 95* operating licence.
- Microsoft insisted that PC manufacturers conformed to a Microsoft front screen for Windows. This included specified icons, one of which was Microsoft's *Internet Explorer*.
- It had set up reciprocal advertising arrangements with the USA's largest Internet service providers, such as America Online. Here Microsoft would promote America Online via Windows. In return, America Online would not promote Netscape's browsers.

Microsoft, in its defence, argued that the integration of its own browser into the Windows system was a natural part of the process of product innovation and development. Microsoft officials claimed that accusations of unfair trading practices were not founded: it was simply attempting to improve the quality of its product. It argued that if it was to do nothing with its Windows product, it would, over time, lose its dominant market position and be replaced by a more innovative and superior product manufactured by a rival software producer.

In this respect, Microsoft could be seen to be operating in the consumer's interest. The argument is that, in an environment where technology is changing rapidly, Microsoft's control over standards gives the user a measure of stability, knowing that any new products and applications will be compatible with existing ones. In other words, new software can be incorporated into existing systems.

Network effects

The key issue in respect to Microsoft, then, was not so much the browser war, but far more fundamentally to do with the operating system, and how Microsoft used its ownership of this system to extend its leverage into other related high-technology markets.

> An operating system attracts software developed around that operating system, thereby discouraging new competition since any alternative faces not only the challenge of creating a better operating system but competing against a whole array of already existing software applications. Businesses train employees in one technology and are reluctant to abandon that investment in training, while the existence of a pool of people trained in that technology encourages other businesses to adopt that technology. . . . These so-called 'network effects' give an incredible anti-competitive edge to

In addition to these problems, monopolies may lack the incentive to introduce new product varieties, and large monopolies may be able to exert political pressure and thereby get favourable treatment from governments.

Advantages of monopoly

Despite these arguments, monopolies can have some advantages.

Economies of scale. The monopoly may be able to achieve substantial economies of scale due to larger plant, centralised administration and the avoidance of unnecessary duplication (e.g. a monopoly water company would eliminate the need for several sets of rival water mains under each street). If this results in an *MC* curve substantially below that of the same industry under perfect competition, the monopoly will produce a *higher* output at a *lower* price. In Figure 6.11, the monopoly produces Q_1 at a price of P_1,

Figure 6.11 Equilibrium of the industry under perfect competition and monopoly: with different *MC* curves

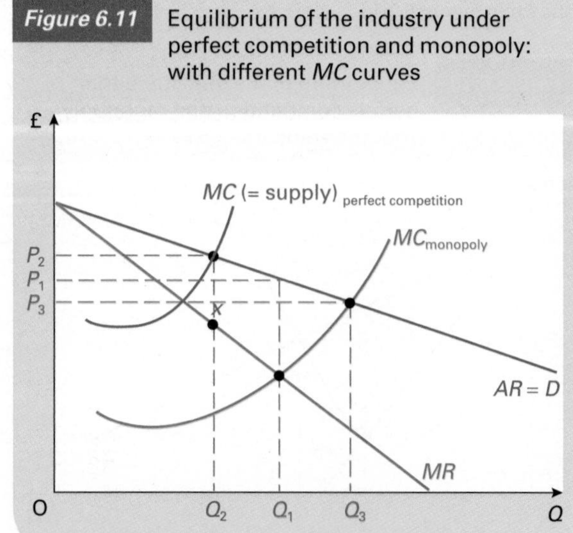

BOX 6.4

companies like Microsoft that control so many different parts of the network.[2]

Network effects arise when consumers of a product benefit from it being used by *other* consumers. The more people that use it, the greater the benefit to each individual user. The problem for the consumer in such a scenario is that these network effects can lead to the establishment of a monopoly producer and hence to higher prices. There is also the problem of whether the best product is being produced by the monopolist. In such an instance, the consumer may be 'locked in' to using an inferior product or technology, with limited opportunity (if any) to change.

Microsoft had been able to use consumer lock-in to drive competitors from the market. Where choice does exist – for example, in Internet browsers – Microsoft was using its operating system dominance to promote its own product.

Court findings

A verdict was reached on 7 June 2000, when Federal Judge Thomas Penfield Jackson ruled that Microsoft be split in two to prevent it operating as a monopoly. One company would produce and market the *Windows* operating system; the other would produce and market the applications software, such as *Microsoft Office* and *Internet Explorer*.

Microsoft appealed against the judgment to the US Federal Appeals Court, which in June 2001 overturned the ruling and referred the case to a different judge for reconsideration. Judge Colleen Kollar-Kotelly urged both sides (Microsoft and the US Justice Department) to try to reach a settlement and in November 2001 they did just that. They agreed that Microsoft would provide technical information about *Windows* to other companies to enable them to write software that would compete with Microsoft's own software. Also Microsoft would not be allowed to retaliate against computer manufacturers that installed rival products or removed icons for Microsoft applications.

Nine states, however, refused to sign up to the agreement and a further year went past before Judge Kollar-Kotelly gave her final ruling. Whilst she agreed with many of Judge Jackson's original findings, she did not require that Microsoft be split into two companies. Instead, she upheld the November 2001 agreement.

Legal action against Microsoft was not confined to the USA. In March 2004, the European Commission fined Microsoft a record €497 million for abusing its monopoly position. In addition, Microsoft was ordered to issue a version of *Windows XP* without *Windows Media Player* (*WMP*). The argument was similar to the earlier ones used in the USA over browsers. This time it was claimed that by bundling *WMP* with *XP*, Microsoft was gaining an unfair advantage over competitor media players, such as *RealPlayer* and Apple's *QuickTime*.

?

1. ***In what respects might Microsoft's behaviour be deemed to be: (a) against the public interest; (b) in the public interest?***
2. ***Being locked in to a product or technology is a problem only if such a product can be clearly shown to be inferior to an alternative. What difficulties might there be in establishing such a case?***

[2] N. Newman, *From Microsoft Word to Microsoft World: How Microsoft is Building a Global Monopoly* (1997) www.netaction.org/msoft/world.

whereas the perfectly competitive industry produces Q_2 at the higher price P_2.

Note that this result follows only if the monopoly MC curve is below point x in Figure 6.11. Note also that an industry cannot exist under perfect competition if substantial economies of scale can be gained. It is thus somewhat hypothetical to compare a monopoly with an alternative situation that could not exist. What is more, were the monopolist to follow the $P = MC$ rule observed by perfectly competitive firms, it would charge an even lower price (P_3) and produce an even higher output (Q_3).

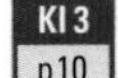

Possibility of lower cost curves due to more research and development and more investment. Although the monopolist's sheer survival does not depend on its finding ever more efficient methods of production, it can use part of its supernormal profits for research and development and investment. It thus has a greater ability to become efficient than has the small firm with limited funds.

Competition for corporate control. Although a monopoly faces no competition in the goods market, it may face an alternative form of competition in financial markets. A monopoly, with potentially low costs, which is currently run inefficiently, is likely to be subject to a takeover bid from another company. This ***competition for corporate control*** may thus force the monopoly to be efficient in order to avoid being taken over. KI 10 p62

Innovation and new products. The promise of supernormal profits, protected perhaps by patents, may encourage the development of new (monopoly) industries producing new products.

Definition

Competition for corporate control The competition for the control of companies through takeovers.

EXPLORING ECONOMICS

BOX 6.5

X INEFFICIENCY

The cost of a quiet life

KI 3 p10

The major criticism of monopoly has traditionally been that of the monopoly's power in selling the good. The firm charges a price above *MC* (see Figure 6.10). This is seen as *allocatively inefficient* because at the margin consumers are willing to pay more than it is costing to produce ($P > MC$); and yet the monopolist is deliberately holding back, so as to keep its profits up. Allocative inefficiency is examined in detail in section 11.1.

Monopolies may also be inefficient for another reason: they may have higher costs. But why?

Higher costs may be the result of *X inefficiency*[3] (sometimes known as *technical inefficiency*). Without competitive pressure on profit margins, cost controls may become lax. The result may be overstaffing and spending on prestige buildings and equipment, as well as less effort to keep technologically up to date, scrap old plant, research new products, or develop new domestic and export markets.

Thus the more comfortable the situation, the less may be the effort which is expended to improve it. The effect of this X inefficiency is to make the *AC* and *MC* curves higher than they would otherwise be.

During the early 1980s, there were significant reductions in X inefficiency in many countries. With a world-wide recession, and a fall in both sales and profits, many firms embarked on cost-cutting programmes. Much out-of-date plant was closed down, and employment was reduced. Those firms that survived the recession (and many did not) tended to emerge both more competitive and more efficient.

Another factor causing a reduction in X inefficiency has been the growth in international competition. As markets have increasingly become global in scale, and as customs duties and other barriers to trade have been reduced (see section 23.2), so many companies are facing fiercer competition from abroad.

1. ***How might you measure X inefficiency?***
2. ***Another type of inefficiency is productive inefficiency. What do you think this is? (Clue: it has to do with the proportions in which factors are used.)***

[3] This term was coined by Harvey Leibenstein, 'Allocative efficiency or X efficiency', *American Economic Review*, June 1966.

Section summary

1. A monopoly is where there is only one firm in an industry. In practice, it is difficult to determine that a monopoly exists because it depends on how narrowly an industry is defined.
2. Barriers to the entry of new firms are usually necessary to protect a monopoly from competition. Such barriers include economies of scale (making the firm a natural monopoly or at least giving it a cost advantage over new (small) competitors), control over supplies of inputs or over outlets, patents or copyright, and tactics to eliminate competition (such as takeovers or aggressive advertising).
3. Profits for the monopolist (as for other firms) will be maximised where $MC = MR$. In the case of monopoly, this will probably be at a higher price relative to marginal cost than for other firms, due to the less elastic nature of its demand at any given price.
4. Monopolies may be against the public interest to the extent that they charge a higher price relative to cost than do competitive firms; if they cause a less desirable distribution of income; if a lack of competition removes the incentive to be efficient and innovative; and if they exert undesirable political pressures on governments.
5. On the other hand, any economies of scale will in part be passed on to consumers in lower prices, and the monopolist's high profits may be used for research and development and investment, which in turn may lead to better products at possibly lower prices.

6.4 THE THEORY OF CONTESTABLE MARKETS

Potential competition or monopoly?

In recent years, economists have developed the theory of contestable markets. This theory argues that what is crucial in determining price and output is not whether an industry is *actually* a monopoly or competitive, but whether there is the real *threat* of competition.

If a monopoly is protected by high barriers to entry – say that it owns all the raw materials – then it will be able to make supernormal profits with no fear of competition.

If, however, another firm *could* take over from it with little difficulty, it will behave much more like a competitive firm. The threat of competition has a similar effect to actual competition.

As an example, consider a catering company engaged by a factory to run its canteen. The catering company has a monopoly over the supply of food to the workers in that factory. If, however, it starts charging high prices or providing a poor service, the factory could offer the running of the canteen to an alternative catering company. This threat may force the original catering company to charge 'reasonable' prices and offer a good service.

Perfectly contestable markets

A market is ***perfectly contestable*** when the costs of entry and exit by potential rivals are zero, and when such entry can be made very rapidly. In such cases, the moment it becomes possible to earn supernormal profits, new firms will enter, thus driving profits down to a normal level. The sheer threat of this happening, so the theory goes, will ensure that the firm already in the market will (a) keep its prices down, so that it just makes normal profits, and (b) produce as efficiently as possible, taking advantage of any economies of scale and any new technology. If it did not do this, rivals would enter, and potential competition would become actual competition.

KI 10 p62

This is illustrated in Figure 6.12. Assume that there is only one firm in the industry, which faces a long-run average cost curve given by *LRAC*. Assume that profits are maximised at a price of P_1, with supernormal profits being shown by the shaded area. If entry and exit costs are high, the price will remain at this level. If entry and exit costs are low, however, rival firms may be tempted to enter and take over the monopoly. To avert this, the existing firm will have to lower its price. In the case of zero entry and exit costs, the monopolist will have to lower its price to P_2, where price equals *LRAC*, and where, therefore, profits are normal and would not attract rival firms to enter. At the same time, the monopolist will have to ensure that its *LRAC* curve is as low as possible (i.e. that it avoids any X inefficiency (see Box 6.5)).

Figure 6.12 A contestable monopoly

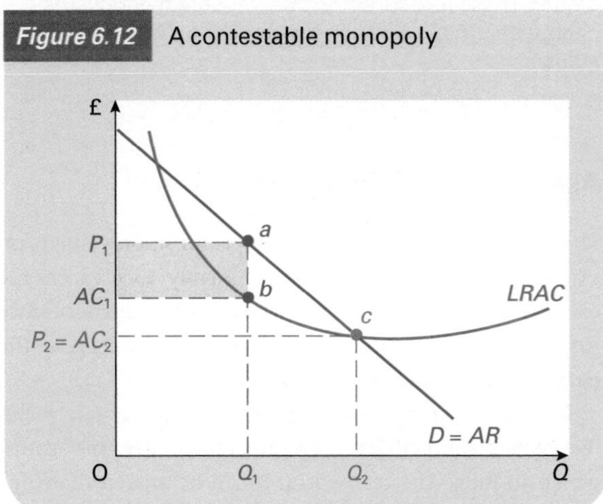

Contestable markets and natural monopolies

So why in such cases are the markets not *actually* perfectly competitive? Why do they remain monopolies?

The most likely reason has to do with economies of scale and the size of the market. To operate on a minimum efficient scale, the firm may have to be so large relative to the market that there is only room for one such firm in the industry. If a new firm does come into the market, then one or other of the two firms will not survive the competition. The market is simply not big enough for both of them. This is the case in Figure 6.12. The industry is a natural monopoly, given that the *LRAC* curve is downward sloping even at output *c*.

If, however, there are no entry or exit costs, new firms will be perfectly willing to enter even though there is only room for one firm, provided they believe that they are more efficient than the established firm. The established firm, knowing this, will be forced to produce as efficiently as possible and with only normal profit.

The importance of costless exit

Setting up in a new business usually involves large expenditures on plant and machinery. Once this money has been spent, it becomes fixed costs. If these fixed costs are no higher than those of the existing firm, then the new firm could win the battle. But, of course, there is always the risk that it might lose.

But does losing the battle really matter? Can the firm not simply move to another market?

It does matter if there are substantial costs of exit. This will be the case if the capital equipment cannot be transferred to other uses (e.g. a power station). In this case, these fixed costs are known as ***sunk costs***. The losing firm is left with capital equipment that it cannot use. The firm may therefore be put off entering in the first place. The market is not perfectly contestable, and the established firm can make supernormal profit.

If, however, the capital equipment can be transferred, the exit costs will be zero (or at least very low), and new firms will be more willing to take the risks of entry. For example, a rival coach company may open up a service on a route previously operated by only one company, and where there is still only room for one operator. If the new firm loses the resulting battle, it can still use the coaches it has purchased. It simply uses them for a different route. The cost of the coaches is not a sunk cost.

KI 11 p66

Definitions

Perfectly contestable market A market where there is free and costless entry and exit.

Sunk costs Costs that cannot be recouped (e.g. by transferring assets to other uses).

CASE STUDIES AND APPLICATIONS

AIRLINE DEREGULATION IN THE USA AND EUROPE

A case study of contestable markets

If a market is highly contestable, the mere threat of competition may be successful in keeping prices and profits down. Of course, established firms would not like this! They would be keen to erect barriers to entry and to make exit more costly for any firm that did enter.

Governments around the world are generally in favour of increased competition and frown on the erection of entry barriers (see section 12.3). This means that they generally prefer not to intervene if markets are competitive or highly contestable, but may attempt to regulate the prices, profits or behaviour of firms where competition or contestability is limited. Conversely, if markets have been regulated and yet are potentially competitive, many governments have then deregulated them (i.e. removed regulations).

A good case study of deregulation and contestability (or lack of it) is the airline industry.

The USA

The airline industry in the United States has been deregulated since 1978. Prior to this, air routes were allocated by the government, with the result that many airlines operated as monopolies or shared the route with just one other airline. Now there exists a policy of 'open skies'.

Initially the consequences were dramatic, with lower fares and, over many routes, a greater choice of airlines. The Brookings Institute calculated that, in the first ten years of deregulation, the lower fares saved consumers some $100 billion. One consequence of the increased competition was that many US airlines went out of business. Gone are famous names such as Eastern and PanAm. In the depth of the 1992 recession, 32 American carriers went out of business.

Even where routes continued to be operated by just one or two airlines, fares still fell if the route was *contestable*: if the entry and exit costs remained low. In 1992, despite the bankruptcies, 23 new carriers were established in North America, and many routes were taken over by existing carriers.

But deregulation did not make all routes more contestable. In some cases the reverse happened. In a situation of rising costs and falling revenues, there were mergers and takeovers of the vulnerable airlines. By 2000 just seven airlines accounted for over 90 per cent of American domestic air travel, compared with fifteen in 1984, and merger talks continue between various pairs from the seven. With this move towards greater monopolisation, some airlines managed to make their routes *less* contestable. The result was that airfares over the 1990s rose faster than prices in general.

A key ingredient in making routes less contestable was the development of a system of air routes radiating out from about 30 key or 'hub' airports. With waves of flights scheduled to arrive and depart within a short space of time, passengers can make easy connections at these hub airports.

The problem is that several of these hub airports became dominated by single airlines which, through economies of scale and the ownership or control of various airport facilities, such as boarding gates or check-in areas, could effectively keep out potential entrants. The problem was worse in congested airports where room for a new entrant could only be made if existing airlines cut back their flights: something they will obviously resist. By 2002, at 15 of the hub airports, including some of the busiest, the dominant airline had a market share in excess of 70 per cent.

The airlines have also used measures to increase 'customer loyalty' and thereby make entry barriers higher. These measures include frequent flier rewards, deals with travel agents and code sharing with 'partner' airlines.

Costless exit, therefore, encourages firms to enter an industry, knowing that, if unsuccessful, they can always transfer their capital elsewhere.

TC 3 p21 The lower the exit costs, the more contestable the market. This implies that firms already established in other similar markets may provide more effective competition against monopolists, since they can simply transfer capital from one market to another. For example, studies of airlines in the USA show that entry to a particular route may be much easier for an established airline, which can simply transfer planes from one route to another (see Box 6.6).

? *In which of the following industries are exit costs likely to be low: (a) steel production; (b) market gardening; (c) nuclear power generation; (d) specialist financial advisory services; (e) production of a new drug; (f) mobile discos; (g) car ferry operators? Do these exit costs depend on how narrowly the industry is defined?*

Assessment of the theory

The theory of contestable markets is an improvement on simple monopoly theory, which merely focuses on the existing structure of the industry and makes no allowance for potential competition: no allowance for the size of the barriers to entry and the costs of exit.

Perfectly contestable markets may exist only rarely. But like perfect competition they provide an *ideal type* against which to judge the real world. It can be argued that they provide a more useful ideal type than perfect competition, since the extent of divergence from this ideal provides a better means of predicting firms' price and output behaviour than does the simple portion of the market currently supplied by the existing firm.

One criticism of the theory, however, is that it does not take sufficient account of the possible reactions of the

BOX 6.6

In the 2000s, however, the domestic US airlines market has become more competitive again, thanks to the growth of low-cost carriers (LCCs). These accounted for just 7 per cent of US domestic passengers in 1990. By 2005 this had risen to nearly 25 per cent. With operating costs some 25 to 50 per cent lower than the large hub-and-spoke carriers, they have become a highly effective competitive force on routes between various city pairs. The competition has forced the major carriers to cut their own prices on these routes.

A danger here is that big airlines may undercut the prices of small new entrants so as to drive them out of the market. Such 'predatory pricing' (see page 201), however, is illegal and the Department of Justice has begun investigating several cases.

Europe

Until the early 1990s, the European air transport industry was highly regulated, with governments controlling routes. National routes were often licensed to the national airline and international routes to the two respective national airlines. Since 1993, the industry has been progressively deregulated and competition has increased, with a growing availability of discount fares. Now, within the EU, airlines are free to charge whatever they like, and any EU airline can fly on any route it wants, providing it can get the slots at the airports at either end.

As in the USA, however, whilst increased competition has benefited passengers, many of the airlines have tried to make their routes less contestable by erecting entry barriers. Predatory pricing has occurred, as the established airlines have tried to drive out new competitors. What is more, the proliferation of fare categories has made it hard for consumers to compare prices, and established carriers' highly publicised fares often have many restrictions, with most people having to pay considerably higher fares. As in the USA, code sharing and airline alliances have reduced competition. Finally, at busy airports, such as Heathrow, the shortage of check-in and boarding gates, runways and airspace has provided a major barrier to new entrants.

Nevertheless, new low-cost airlines, such as easyJet, Ryanair and FlyBE, are increasingly providing effective competition for the established national and short-haul international carriers, which have been forced to cut fares on routes where they directly compete. Low-cost airlines have been able to enter the market by using other airports, such as Stansted and Luton in the case of London, and various regional airports throughout Europe. The question is whether the middle-sized national carriers, with relatively high fixed costs, will be able to survive the competition. The filing for bankruptcy and subsequent baling out of Swissair and Sabena (the Belgian airline) following the September 2001 attack on the World Trade Center in New York, illustrates the vulnerability of such airlines. It is likely that several of the medium-sized carriers will have to merge or be taken over by a big carrier.

?

1. ***Make a list of those factors that determine the contestability of a particular air route.***
2. ***In the UK, train operators compete for franchises to run services on a particular route. The franchises are normally for 7, 10, 12 or 15 years. The franchise specifies prices and minimum levels of services (frequency, timing and quality). Would this be a good system to adopt in the airline market over particular routes? How is the airline market similar to/different from the rail market in this regard?***

established firm. There may be no cost barriers to entry or exit (i.e. a perfectly contestable market), but the established firm may let it be known that any firm that dares to enter will face all-out war! This may act as a deterrent to entry. In the meantime, the established firm may charge high prices and make supernormal profits.

Contestable markets and the public interest

If a monopoly operates in a perfectly contestable market, it might bring the 'best of both worlds'. Not only will it be able to achieve low costs through economies of scale, but also the potential competition will keep profits and hence prices down.

For this reason, the theory has been seized on by politicians on the political right to justify a policy of *laissez-faire* (non-intervention) and deregulation (e.g. coach and air routes). They argue that the theory vindicates the free market. There are two points in reply to this:

- Few markets are *perfectly* contestable. If entry and exit are not costless, a monopoly can still make supernormal profits in the long run.
- There are other possible failings of the market beside monopoly power (e.g. inequality, pollution). These failings are examined in Chapters 10 and 11.

Nevertheless the theory of contestable markets has highlighted the importance of entry barriers in determining monopoly behaviour. The size of the barriers has therefore become the focus of attention of many politicians and academics when considering anti-monopoly policy.

Section summary

1. Potential competition may be as important as actual competition in determining a firm's price and output strategy.
2. The threat of this competition increases as entry and exit costs to and from the industry diminish. If the entry and exit costs are zero, the market is said to be *perfectly* contestable. Under such circumstances, an existing monopolist will be forced to keep its profits down to the normal level if it is to resist entry by new firms. Exit costs will be lower, the lower are the sunk costs of the firm.
3. The theory of contestable markets provides a more realistic analysis of firms' behaviour than theories based simply on the *existing* number of firms in the industry.

END OF CHAPTER QUESTIONS

1. A perfectly competitive firm faces a price of £14 per unit. It has the following short-run cost schedule:

Output	0	1	2	3	4	5	6	7	8
TC (£)	10	18	24	30	38	50	66	91	120

   (a) Copy the table and put in additional rows for average cost and marginal cost at each level of output. (Enter the figures for marginal cost in the space between each column.)
   (b) Plot *AC*, *MC* and *MR* on a diagram.
   (c) Mark the profit-maximising output.
   (d) How much (supernormal) profit is made at this output?
   (e) What would happen to the price in the long run if this firm were typical of others in the industry? Why would we need to know information about long-run average cost in order to give a precise answer to this question?
2. If the industry under perfect competition faces a downward-sloping demand curve, why does an individual firm face a horizontal demand curve?
3. If supernormal profits are competed away under perfect competition, why will firms have an incentive to become more efficient?
4. Is it a valid criticism of perfect competition to argue that it is incompatible with economies of scale?
5. On a diagram similar to Figure 6.4, show the long-run equilibrium for both firm and industry under perfect competition. Now assume that the demand for the product falls. Show the short-run and long-run effects.
6. Why is the profit-maximising price under monopoly greater than marginal cost? In what way can this be seen as inefficient?
7. On three diagrams like Figure 6.8, illustrate the effect on price, quantity and profit of each of the following: (a) a rise in demand; (b) a rise in fixed costs; (c) a rise in variable costs. In each case, show only the *AR*, *MR*, *AC* and *MC* curves.
8. Think of three examples of monopolies (local or national) and consider how contestable their markets are.

Additional case studies on the book's website (www.pearsoned.co.uk/sloman)

6.1 B2B electronic marketplaces. This case study examines the growth of firms trading with each other over the Internet (business to business or 'B2B') and considers the effects on competition.

6.2 Measuring monopoly power. An examination of how the degree of monopoly power possessed by a firm can be measured.

6.3 Competition in the pipeline? Monopoly in the supply of gas.

WEBSITES RELEVANT TO THIS CHAPTER

See sites listed at the end of Chapter 7 on page 203.

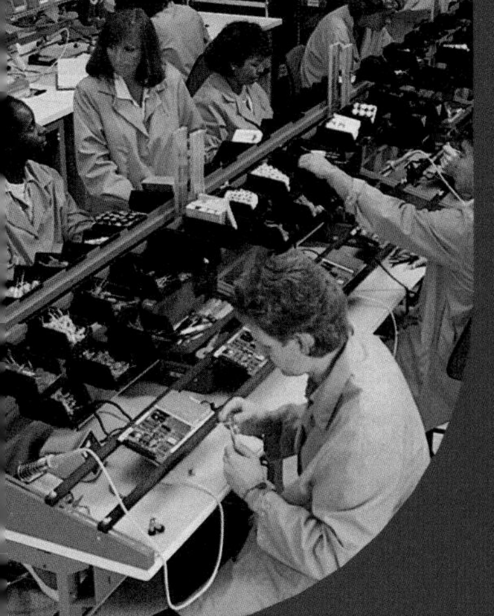

Chapter 7

Profit Maximising under Imperfect Competition

Very few markets in practice can be classified as perfectly competitive or as a pure monopoly. The vast majority of firms do compete with other firms, often quite aggressively, and yet they are not price-takers: they do have some degree of market power. Most markets, therefore, lie between the two extremes of monopoly and perfect competition, in the realm of 'imperfect competition'.

There are two types of imperfect competition: namely, monopolistic competition and oligopoly.

Under monopolistic competition, there will normally be quite a large number of relatively small firms. Think of the large number of car repair garages, builders, double glazing companies, restaurants and other small traders that you get in any large town or city. They are in fierce competition with each other, and yet competition is not perfect. They are all trying to produce a product that is different from their rivals.

Under oligopoly, there will be only a few firms competing. Most of the best-known companies, such as Ford, Coca-Cola, Nike, BP, Monsanto and IBM, are oligopolists. Sometimes oligopolists will attempt to collude with each other to keep prices up. On other occasions, competition will be intense, with rival firms trying to undercut each other's prices, or developing new or better products in order to gain a larger share of the market. We will examine both collusion and competition between oligopolists and show when each is more likely to occur.

CHAPTER MAP

7.1 MONOPOLISTIC COMPETITION

We will start by looking at monopolistic competition. This was a theory developed in the 1930s by the American economist Edward Chamberlin. Monopolistic competition is nearer to the competitive end of the spectrum. It can best be understood as a situation where there are a lot of firms competing, but where each firm does nevertheless have some degree of market power (hence the term 'monopolistic' competition): each firm has some choice over what price to charge for its products.

Assumptions of monopolistic competition

- There are *quite a large number of firms*. As a result, each firm has an insignificantly small share of the market, and therefore its actions are unlikely to affect its rivals to any great extent. This means that when each firm makes its decisions it does not have to worry how its rivals will react. It assumes that what its rivals choose to do will *not* be influenced by what it does.

  This is known as the assumption of ***independence***. (As we shall see later, this is not the case under oligopoly. There we assume that firms believe that their decisions *do* affect their rivals, and that their rivals' decisions will affect them. Under oligopoly, we assume that firms are *inter*dependent.)
- There is *freedom of entry* of new firms into the industry. If any firm wants to set up in business in this market, it is free to do so.

In these two respects, therefore, monopolistic competition is like perfect competition.

KI 9 p58

- Unlike perfect competition, however, each firm produces a product or provides a service in some way different from its rivals. As a result, it can raise its price without losing all its customers. Thus its demand curve is downward sloping, albeit relatively elastic given the large number of competitors to whom customers can turn. This is known as the assumption of ***product differentiation***.

Petrol stations, restaurants, hairdressers and builders are all examples of monopolistic competition.

?

Give some other examples of monopolistic competition. (Try looking through the Yellow Pages *if you are stuck.)*

A typical feature of monopolistic competition is that, although there are many firms in the industry, there is only one firm in a particular location. This applies particularly in retailing. There may be many hairdressers in a town, but only one in a particular street. In a sense, therefore, it has a local monopoly. People may be prepared to pay higher prices for their haircuts there to avoid having to go elsewhere.

Equilibrium of the firm

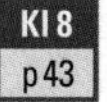

Short run

As with other market structures, profits are maximised at the output where $MC = MR$. The diagram will be the same as for the monopolist, except that the AR and MR curves will be more elastic. This is illustrated in Figure 7.1(a). As with perfect competition, it is possible for the monopolistically competitive firm to make supernormal profit in the short run. This is shown as the shaded area.

TC 2 p10

Just how much profit the firm will make in the short run depends on the strength of demand: the position and elasticity of the demand curve. The further to the right the demand curve is relative to the average cost curve, and the less elastic the demand curve is, the greater will be the firm's short-run profit. Thus a firm facing little competition and whose product is considerably differentiated from that of its rivals may be able to earn considerable short-run profits.

1. *Why may a food shop charge higher prices than supermarkets for 'essential items' and yet very similar prices for delicatessen items?*
2. *Which of these two items is a petrol station more likely to sell at a discount: (a) oil; (b) sweets? Why?*

Long run

If typical firms are earning supernormal profit, new firms will enter the industry in the long run. As they do, they will take some of the customers away from established firms. The demand for the established firms will therefore fall. Their demand (AR) curve will shift to the left, and will continue doing so as long as supernormal profits remain and thus new firms continue entering.

Long-run equilibrium is reached when only normal profits remain: when there is no further incentive for new firms to enter. This is illustrated in Figure 7.1(b). The firm's demand curve settles at D_L, where it is tangential to the

Definitions

Independence (of firms in a market) Where the decisions of one firm in a market will not have any significant effect on the demand curves of its rivals.

Product differentiation Where one firm's product is sufficiently different from its rivals' to allow it to raise the price of the product without customers all switching to the rivals' products. A situation where a firm faces a downward-sloping demand curve.

Figure 7.1 Equilibrium of the firm under monopolistic competition

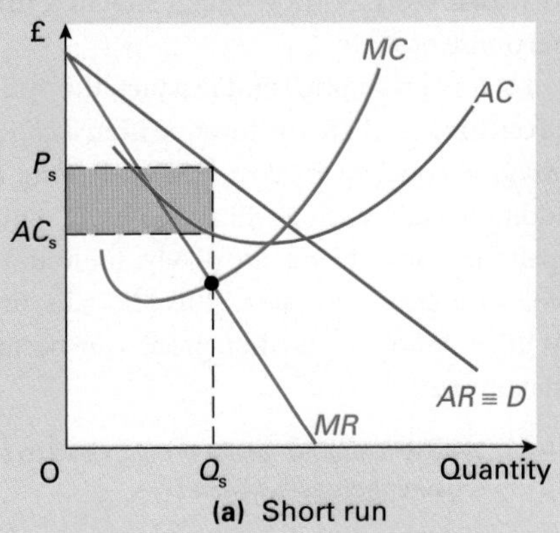

(a) Short run

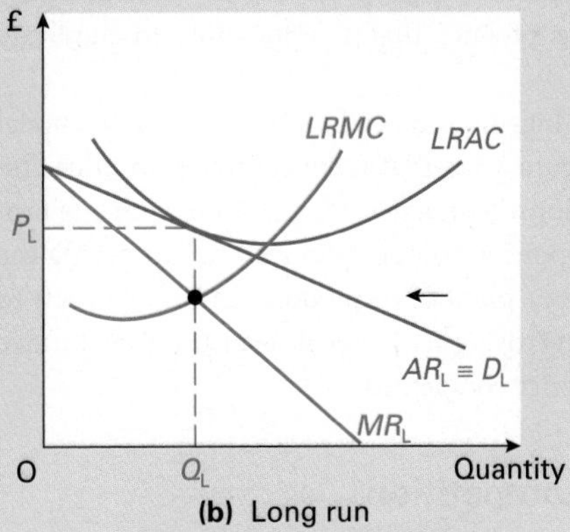

(b) Long run

firm's *LRAC* curve. Output will be Q_L: where $AR_L = LRAC$. (At any other output, *LRAC* is greater than *AR* and thus less than normal profit would be made.)

1. Why does the LRMC curve cross the MR_L curve directly below the tangency point of the LRAC and AR_L curves?
2. Assuming that supernormal profits can be made in the short run, will there be any difference in the long-run and short-run elasticity of demand? Explain.

Limitations of the model

There are various problems in applying the model of monopolistic competition to the real world:

- Information may be imperfect. Firms will not enter an industry if they are unaware of what supernormal profits are being made, or if they underestimate the demand for the particular product they are considering selling. TC9 p101
- Given that the firms in the industry produce different products, it is difficult if not impossible to derive a demand curve for the industry as a whole. Thus the analysis has to be confined to the level of the firm.
- Firms are likely to differ from each other not only in the product they produce or the service they offer, but also in their size and cost structure. What is more, entry may not be *completely* unrestricted. Two petrol stations could not set up in exactly the same place – on a busy crossroads, say. Thus although the typical

CASE STUDIES AND APPLICATIONS **BOX 7.1**

SELLING ICE CREAM WHEN I WAS A STUDENT

My own experience of monopolistic competition

When I was a student, my parents lived in Exeter in Devon, and at that time, the city's by-pass became completely jammed on a summer Saturday as holidaymakers made their way to the coast. Traffic queues were several miles long.

For a summer job, I drove a small ice-cream van. Early on, I had the idea of selling ice cream from a tray to the people queuing in their cars. I made more money on a Saturday than the rest of the week put together. I thought I was on to a good thing.

But news of this lucrative market soon spread, and each week new ice-cream sellers appeared – each one reducing my earnings! By the middle of August there were over 30 ice-cream sellers from five different ice-cream companies. Most tried to get to the beginning of the queue, to get ahead of their rivals.

Imagine the scene. A family driving to the coast rounds a bend and is suddenly met by a traffic jam and several ice-cream sellers all jostling to sell them an ice cream. It was quite surreal. Not surprisingly, many of the potential customers refused to buy, feeling somewhat intimidated by the spectacle. It was not long before most of us realised that it was best to disperse and find a section of the road where there were no other sellers.

But with so many ice-cream sellers, no one made much money. My supernormal earnings had been reduced to a normal level. I made about the same on Saturday to people stuck in queues as I would have done if I had driven my van around the streets.

1. Was there totally free entry to this market?
2. What forms of product differentiation were there?

or 'representative' firm may earn only normal profit in the long run, other firms may be able to earn long-run supernormal profit. They may have some cost advantage or produce a product that is impossible to duplicate perfectly.

- One of the biggest problems with the simple model shown in Figure 7.1 is that it concentrates on price and output decisions. In practice, the profit-maximising firm under monopolistic competition also has to decide the exact variety of product to produce and how much to spend on advertising it. This will lead the firm to take part in non-price competition.

Non-price competition

Non-price competition involves two major elements: product development and advertising.

The major aims of *product development* are to produce a product that will sell well (i.e. one in high or potentially high demand) and that is different from rivals' products (i.e. has a relatively inelastic demand due to lack of close substitutes). For shops or other firms providing a service, 'product development' takes the form of attempting to provide a service which is better than, or at least different from, that of rivals: personal service, late opening, certain lines stocked and so on.

TC 8 p59

The major aim of *advertising* is to sell the product. This can be achieved not only by informing the consumer of the product's existence and availability, but also by deliberately trying to persuade consumers to purchase the good. Like product development, successful advertising will not only increase demand, but also make the firm's demand curve less elastic since it stresses the specific qualities of this firm's product over its rivals' (see Box 2.3).

Definition

Non-price competition Competition in terms of product promotion (advertising, packaging, etc.) or product development.

Product development and advertising not only increase a firm's demand and hence revenue, they also involve increased costs. So how much should a firm advertise, to maximise profits?

For any given price and product, the optimal amount of advertising is where the revenue from *additional* advertising (MR_A) is equal to its cost (MC_A). As long as $MR_A > MC_A$, additional advertising will add to profit. But extra amounts spent on advertising are likely to lead to smaller and smaller increases in sales. Thus MR_A falls, until $MR_A = MC_A$. At that point, no further profit can be made. It is at a maximum.

Why will additional advertising lead to smaller and smaller increases in sales?

Two problems arise with this analysis:

- The effect of product development and advertising on demand will be difficult for a firm to forecast.
- Product development and advertising are likely to have different effects at different prices. Profit maximisation, therefore, will involve the more complex choice of the optimum combination of price, type of product, and level and variety of advertising.

Monopolistic competition and the public interest

Comparison with perfect competition

It is often argued that monopolistic competition leads to a less efficient allocation of resources than perfect competition.

Figure 7.2 compares the long-run equilibrium positions for two firms. One firm is under perfect competition and thus faces a horizontal demand curve. It will produce an output of Q_1 at a price of P_1. The other is under monopolistic competition and thus faces a downward-sloping demand curve. It will produce the lower output of Q_2 at the higher price of P_2. A crucial assumption here is that a firm would have the *same* long-run average cost (*LRAC*) curve in both cases. Given this assumption, monopolistic competition has the following disadvantages:

Figure 7.2 Long-run equilibrium of the firm under perfect and monopolistic competition

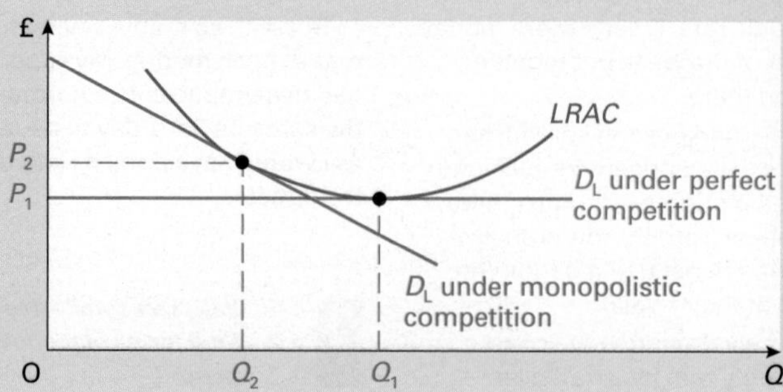

- Less will be sold and at a higher price.
- Firms will not be producing at the least-cost point.

By producing more, firms would move to a lower point on their *LRAC* curve. Thus firms under monopolistic competition are said to have ***excess capacity***. In Figure 7.2 this excess capacity is shown as $Q_1 - Q_2$. In other words, monopolistic competition is typified by quite a large number of firms (e.g. petrol stations), all operating at an output less than that necessary to achieve minimum cost, and thus being forced to charge a price above that which they could charge if they had a bigger turnover. How often have you been to a petrol station and had to queue for the pumps?

?

Does this imply that if, say, half of the petrol stations were closed down, the consumer would benefit? (Clue: what would happen to the demand curves of the remaining stations?)

On the other hand, it is often argued that these wastes of monopolistic competition may be insignificant. In the first place, although the firm's demand curve is downward sloping, it is still likely to be highly elastic due to the large number of substitutes. In the second place, although the firm under monopolistic competition will not be operating quite at the bottom of its *LRAC* curve, the nature of the industry may allow some economies of scale to be gained. The *LRAC* curve would thus be lower than in the case of the larger number of smaller firms that would be necessary to keep the industry perfectly competitive. The size of the economies of scale, if any, will obviously vary from industry to industry.

Furthermore, the consumer may benefit from monopolistic competition by having a greater variety of products to choose from. Each firm may satisfy some particular requirement of particular consumers.

?

Which would you rather have: five restaurants to choose from, each with very different menus and each having spare tables so that you could always guarantee getting one; or just two restaurants to choose from, charging a bit less but with less choice and making it necessary to book well in advance?

Comparison with monopoly

The arguments here are very similar to those when comparing perfect competition and monopoly.

On the one hand, freedom of entry for new firms and hence the lack of long-run supernormal profits under monopolistic competition are likely to help keep prices down for the consumer and encourage cost saving. On the other hand, monopolies are likely to achieve greater economies of scale and have more funds for investment and research and development.

> **Definition**
>
> **Excess capacity (under monopolistic competition)** In the long run, firms under monopolistic competition will produce at an output below their minimum-cost point.

Section summary

1. Monopolistic competition occurs where there is free entry to the industry and quite a large number of firms operating independently of each other, but where each firm has some market power by producing differentiated products or services.
2. In the short run, firms can make supernormal profits. In the long run, however, freedom of entry will drive profits down to the normal level. The long-run equilibrium of the firm is where the (downward-sloping) demand curve is tangential to the long-run average cost curve.
3. The long-run equilibrium is one of excess capacity. Given that the demand curve is downward sloping, its tangency point with the *LRAC* curve will not be at the bottom of the *LRAC* curve. Increased production would thus be possible at *lower* average cost.
4. In practice, supernormal profits may persist into the long run: firms have imperfect information; entry may not be completely unrestricted; firms may use non-price competition to maintain an advantage over their rivals.
5. Non-price competition may take the form of product development or product promotion (advertising, etc.).
6. Monopolistically competitive firms, because of excess capacity, may have higher costs than perfectly competitive firms, but consumers may gain from a greater diversity of products.
7. Monopolistically competitive firms may have fewer economies of scale than monopolies and conduct less research and development, but the competition may keep prices lower than under monopoly.

7.2 OLIGOPOLY

Oligopoly occurs when just a few firms between them share a large proportion of the industry.

There are, however, significant differences in the structure of industries under oligopoly and similarly significant differences in the behaviour of firms. The firms may produce a virtually identical product (e.g. metals, chemicals, sugar, petrol). Most oligopolists, however, produce differentiated products (e.g. cars, soap powder, soft drinks, electrical appliances). Much of the competition between such oligopolists is in terms of the marketing of their particular brand. Marketing practices may differ considerably from one industry to another.

The two key features of oligopoly

Despite the differences between oligopolies, two crucial features distinguish oligopoly from other market structures.

Barriers to entry

Unlike firms under monopolistic competition, there are various barriers to the entry of new firms. These are similar to those under monopoly (see pages 166–72). The size of the barriers, however, varies from industry to industry. In some cases entry is relatively easy, whereas in others it is virtually impossible.

Interdependence of the firms

Because there are only a few firms under oligopoly, each has to take account of the others. This means that they are mutually dependent: they are ***interdependent***. Each firm is affected by its rivals' actions. If a firm changes the price or specification of its product, for example, or the amount of its advertising, the sales of its rivals will be affected. The rivals may then respond by changing their price, specification or advertising. No firm can afford to ignore the actions and reactions of other firms in the industry.

Key Idea 20

People often think and behave strategically. How you think others will respond to your actions is likely to influence your own behaviour. Firms, for example, when considering a price or product change will often take into account the likely reactions of their rivals.

KI 10 p62 It is impossible, therefore, to predict the effect on a firm's sales of, say, a change in its price without first making some assumption about the reactions of other firms. Different assumptions yield different predictions. For this reason there is no one single theory of oligopoly. Firms may react differently and unpredictably.

Competition and collusion

Oligopolists are pulled in two different directions:

- The interdependence of firms may make them wish to *collude* with each other. If they could club together and act as if they were a monopoly, they could jointly maximise industry profits. TC 3 p21
- On the other hand, they will be tempted to *compete* with their rivals to gain a bigger share of industry profits for themselves.

These two policies are incompatible. The more fiercely firms compete to gain a bigger share of industry profits, the smaller these industry profits will become! For example, price competition will drive down the average industry price, while competition through advertising will raise industry costs. Either way, industry profits will fall.

Sometimes firms collude, sometimes not. The following sections examine first ***collusive oligopoly*** (both open and tacit), and then ***non-collusive oligopoly***.

The equilibrium of the industry under collusive oligopoly

When firms under oligopoly engage in collusion, they may agree on prices, market share, advertising expenditure, etc. Such collusion reduces the uncertainty they face. It reduces the fear of engaging in competitive price cutting or retaliatory advertising, both of which could reduce total industry profits. KI 19 p157

A formal collusive agreement is called a ***cartel***. The cartel will maximise profits if it acts like a monopoly: if the members behave as if they were a single firm. This is illustrated in Figure 7.3 on page 184.

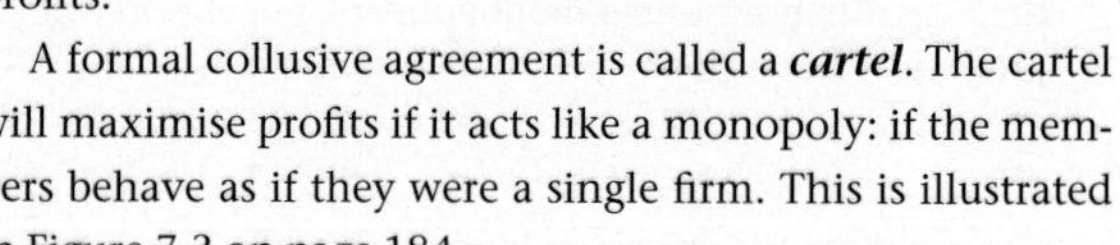

The total market demand curve is shown with the corresponding market *MR* curve. The cartel's *MC* curve is the *horizontal* sum of the *MC* curves of its members (since we are adding the *output* of each of the cartel members at each level of marginal cost). Profits are maximised at Q_1 where $MC = MR$. The cartel must therefore set a price of P_1 (at which Q_1 will be demanded). TC 2 p10

Having agreed on the cartel price, the members may then compete against each other using *non-price competition*, to gain as big a share of resulting sales (Q_1) as they can.

How will advertising affect the cartel's MC and AR curves? How will this affect the profit-maximising output? Is there any problem here for the cartel in fixing the price?

Definitions

Interdependence (under oligopoly) One of the two key features of oligopoly. Each firm will be affected by its rivals' decisions. Likewise its decisions will affect its rivals. Firms recognise this interdependence. This recognition will affect their decisions.

Collusive oligopoly Where oligopolists agree (formally or informally) to limit competition between themselves. They may set output quotas, fix prices, limit product promotion or development, or agree not to 'poach' each other's markets.

Non-collusive oligopoly Where oligopolists have no agreement between themselves, formal, informal or tacit.

Cartel A formal collusive agreement.

CASE STUDIES AND APPLICATIONS — BOX 7.2

IS BEER BECOMING MORE CONCENTRATED?

Oligopoly in the brewing industry

At first glance, the UK brewing industry might appear to be highly competitive, with many pubs in close proximity to one another and with many brands of beer and lager offered for sale. However, in reality most pubs are owned by the major brewers. These 'tied houses' sell only a limited range of the beers and lagers that are available. Consumer choice is clearly constrained.

The oligopolistic nature of the brewing industry can be seen when we consider the market shares of the leading brewers (see table). In 1985 the three largest brewers held 47 per cent of the market. By 2001 this had grown to 73 per cent. What is also significant is that small independent brewers, which generally operate within a local or regional market, have seen a dramatic fall in their market share. With this huge growth in the market power of the major brewers have come large rises in the price of beer (even after taking inflation and tax increases into account). Prices in the UK have risen faster than anywhere else in Europe.

In 1987, the Monopolies and Mergers Commission, the forerunner to the Competition Commission (see section 12.3), investigated the brewing industry and in 1989 issued the 'Beer Orders', requiring the large brewers to sell many of their pubs. The objective was to increase competition as smaller brewers and other companies and individuals bought these pubs and then stocked a range of beers.

However, the hopes were ill-founded. The pubs that were sold were the least profitable, and many have since closed. There is thus now less competition between pubs. Also, about 40 per cent of UK pubs are now owned by large pub chains.

The Beer Orders also required that over 10 000 pubs owned by the big breweries should stock 'guest beers' from rival breweries. But the big breweries responded by selling most of these pubs. In pubs not owned by the big breweries, and where there is the threat of genuine competition, the big breweries often supply their beers at lower prices, thus making it impossible for the smaller breweries to compete.

The brewers, finding a reduction in their scope for achieving economies of scale from *vertical* integration (owning both breweries and pubs), have sought to gain economies of scale from *horizontal* integration (having a larger share of total brewing). Mergers and takeovers in the brewing industry have been common. For example, in May 2000 Interbrew (the Belgian brewer and owners of the Stella Artois brand) acquired Whitbread, the UK's third largest brewer, and a month later acquired Bass, the second largest. This gave Interbrew nearly one-third of the market. The acquisitions were referred to the Competition Commission (see page 352), which recommended a break-up of the new giant: a recommendation accepted by the government. In response, at the end of 2001 Interbrew (now called !nBev) sold most of the Whitbread division, including brands such as Carling, Caffrey's and Worthington, to the US brewer Coors.

In the light of this splitting of Interbrew, and feeling that this proved that competition policy was effective (see section 12.3), the government in 2002 decided to scrap the Beer Orders. This was greeted with dismay by small independent brewers, which were already reluctant to expand, faced with the power of such massive competitors in both production and retail, with heavily advertised brands gaining larger and larger shares of the market.

1. ***What are the barriers to entry in (a) brewing; (b) opening new pubs?***
2. ***Do small independent brewers have any market advantages?***

Market shares of the largest brewers

	1985 (%)		2005 (%)
Bass	22	Scottish-Courage	27
Allied Lyons (Carlsberg)	13	Coors (Carling, Worthington)	20
Grand Met (Watneys)	12	!nBev (Bass, Beck's, Stella)	19
Whitbread	11	Carlsberg UK (Tetley's)	13
Scottish and Newcastle	10	Diageo (Guinness)	6
		Anheuser-Busch (Budweiser)	2
Courage	9	Others	13
Others	23		
	100		100
3-firm concentration ratio	47		66
5-firm concentration ratio	68		85

Source: Various newspaper articles.

Figure 7.3 Profit-maximising cartel

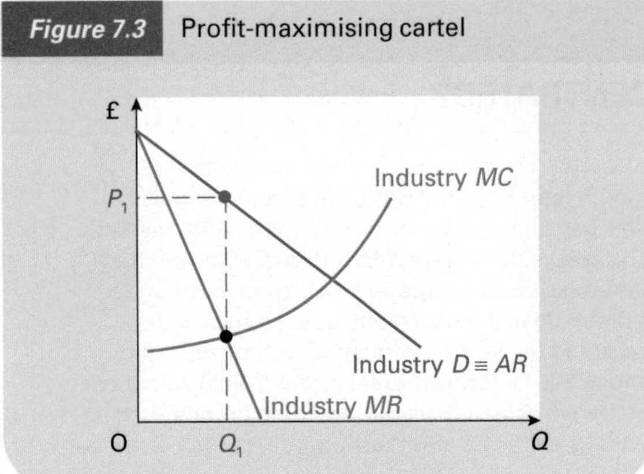

Alternatively, the cartel members may somehow agree to divide the market between them. Each member would be given a ***quota***. The sum of all the quotas must add up to Q_1. If the quotas exceeded Q_1, either there would be output unsold if price remained fixed at P_1, or the price would fall.

But if quotas are to be set by the cartel, how will it decide the level of each individual member's quota? The most likely method is for the cartel to divide the market between the members according to their current market share. This is the solution most likely to be accepted as 'fair'.

? *If this 'fair' solution were adopted, what effect would it have on the industry MC curve in Figure 7.3?*

In many countries, cartels are illegal – being seen by the government as a means of driving up prices and profits, and thereby as being against the public interest (see section 12.3). Where open collusion is illegal, however, firms may simply break the law, or get round it. Alternatively, firms may stay within the law, but still *tacitly* collude by watching each other's prices and keeping theirs similar. Firms may tacitly 'agree' to avoid price wars or aggressive advertising campaigns.

Tacit collusion: price leadership

One form of ***tacit collusion*** is where firms keep to the price set by an established leader. The leader may be the largest firm: the one dominating the industry. This is known as ***dominant firm price leadership***. Alternatively, the price leader may simply be the one that has proved to be the most reliable one to follow: the one that is the best barometer of market conditions. This is known as ***barometric firm price leadership***. Let us examine each of these two types of price leadership in turn.

Dominant firm price leadership

How in theory does the leader set the price? The leader will maximise profits where its marginal revenue is equal to its marginal cost. Figure 7.4(a) shows the total market demand curve and the supply curve of all followers. These firms, like perfectly competitive firms, accept the price as given, only

Figure 7.4 Dominant firm price leadership

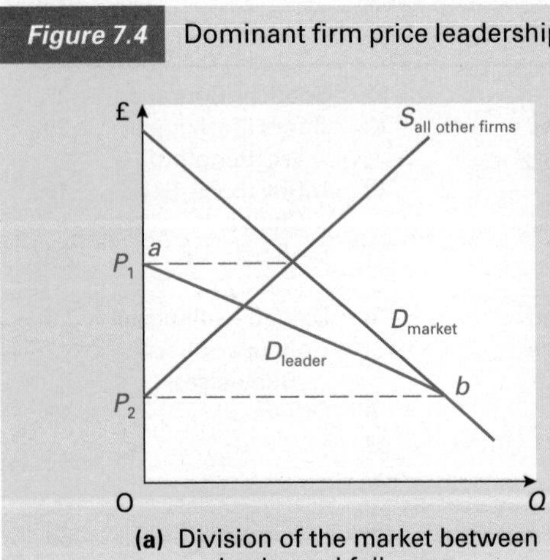

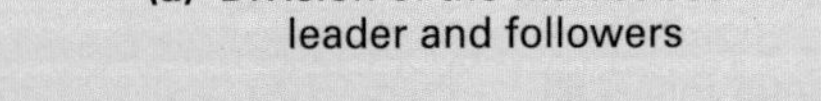
(a) Division of the market between leader and followers

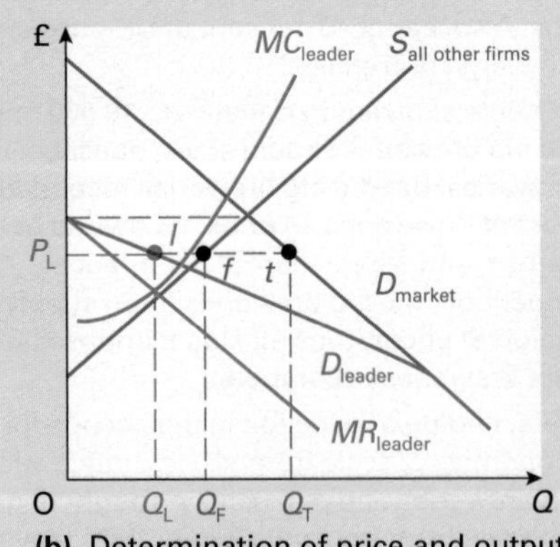

(b) Determination of price and output

Definitions

Quota (set by a cartel) The output that a given member of a cartel is allowed to produce (production quota) or sell (sales quota).

Tacit collusion Where oligopolists take care not to engage in price cutting, excessive advertising or other forms of competition. There may be unwritten 'rules' of collusive behaviour such as price leadership.

Dominant firm price leadership Where firms (the followers) choose the same price as that set by a dominant firm in the industry (the leader).

Barometric firm price leadership Where the price leader is the one whose prices are believed to reflect market conditions in the most satisfactory way.

in this case it is the price set by the leader, and thus their joint supply curve is simply the sum of their *MC* curves – the same as under perfect competition.

The leader's demand curve can be seen as that portion of market demand unfilled by the other firms. In other words, it is market demand minus other firms' supply. At P_1 the whole of market demand is satisfied by the other firms, and so the demand for the leader is zero (point *a*). At P_2 the other firms' supply is zero, and so the leader faces the full market demand (point *b*). The leader's demand curve thus connects points *a* and *b*.

The leader's profit will be maximised where its marginal cost equals its marginal revenue. This is shown in Figure 7.4(b). The diagram is the same as Figure 7.4(a) but with the addition of *MC* and *MR* curves for the leader. The leader's marginal cost equals its marginal revenue at an output of Q_L (giving a point *l* on its demand curve). The leader thus sets a price of P_L, which the other firms then duly follow. They supply Q_F (i.e. at point *f* on their supply curve). Total market demand at P_L is Q_T (i.e. point *t* on the market demand curve), which must add up to the output of both leader and followers (i.e. $Q_L + Q_F$).

? *Draw a pair of diagrams like those in Figure 7.4. Illustrate what would happen if market demand rose but the costs of neither leader nor followers rose. Would there be an equal percentage increase in the output of both leader and followers?*

In practice, however, it is very difficult for the leader to apply this theory. The leader's demand and *MR* curves depend on the followers' supply curve – something the leader will find virtually impossible to estimate with any degree of accuracy. The leader will thus have to make a rough estimate of what its profit-maximising price and output will be, and simply choose that. That is the best it can do!

A simpler model is where the leader assumes that it will maintain a constant *market share* (say, 50 per cent). It makes this assumption because it also assumes that all other firms will follow its price up and down. This is illustrated in Figure 7.5. It knows its current position on its demand curve (say, point *a*). It then estimates how responsive its demand will be to industry-wide price changes and thus constructs its demand and *MR* curves accordingly. It then chooses to produce Q_L at a price of P_L: at point *l* on its demand curve (where $MC = MR$). Other firms then follow that price. Total market demand will be Q_T, with followers supplying that portion of the market not supplied by the leader, namely $Q_T - Q_L$.

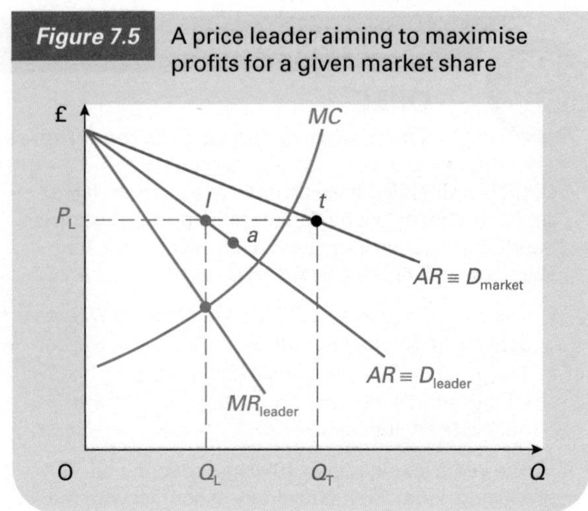

Figure 7.5 A price leader aiming to maximise profits for a given market share

There is one problem with this model: the assumption that the followers will want to maintain a constant market share. If the leader raises its price, the followers may want to supply more, given that the new price (= *MR* for a price-taking follower) may well be above their marginal cost. On the other hand, the followers may decide merely to maintain their market share for fear of retaliation from the leader, in the form of price cuts or an aggressive advertising campaign.

Barometric firm price leadership

A similar exercise can be conducted by a barometric firm. Although such a firm does not dominate the industry, its price will be followed by the others. It merely tries to estimate its demand and *MR* curves – assuming, again, a constant market share – and then produces where $MR = MC$ and sets price accordingly.

In practice, which firm is taken as the barometer may frequently change. Whether we are talking about oil companies, car producers or banks, any firm may take the initiative in raising prices. Then, if the other firms are merely waiting for someone to take the lead – say, because costs have risen – they will all quickly follow suit. For example, if one of the banks raises its mortgage rates by 1 per cent, then this is likely to stimulate the others to follow suit.

*LOOKING AT THE MATHS

In Figure 7.4, the various curves can be represented by equations and this would allow us to solve for P_L, Q_L, Q_F and Q_T. An example of this is given in Maths Case 7.1 on the book's website.

Note that we derived all the curves in Figure 7.4 from just three: the market demand curve, the followers' supply curve and the leader's *MC* curve. It follows that, if we know the functions for these three curves, we can derive the functions for the remainder.

Tacit collusion: rules of thumb

An alternative to following an established leader is to follow an established set of simple 'rules of thumb'. These rules do not involve setting *MC* equal to *MR*, and thus may involve an immediate loss of profit. They do, however, help to prevent an outbreak of competition, and thus help to maintain profits into the longer term.

CASE STUDIES AND APPLICATIONS

OPEC

The history of the world's most famous cartel

OPEC is probably the best known of all cartels. It was set up in 1960 by the five major oil-exporting countries: Saudi Arabia, Iran, Iraq, Kuwait and Venezuela. Its stated objectives were as follows:

- The co-ordination and unification of the petroleum policies of member countries.
- The organisation of means to ensure the stabilisation of prices, eliminating harmful and unnecessary fluctuations.

The years leading up to 1960 had seen the oil-producing countries increasingly in conflict with the international oil companies, which extracted oil under 'concessionary agreement'. Under this scheme, oil companies were given the right to extract oil in return for royalties. This meant that the oil-producing countries had little say over output and price levels.

Despite the formation of OPEC in 1960, it was not until 1973 that control of oil production was effectively transferred from the oil companies to the oil countries, with OPEC making the decisions on how much oil to produce and thereby determining its oil revenue. By this time OPEC consisted of thirteen members.

OPEC's pricing policy over the 1970s consisted of setting a market price for Saudi Arabian crude (the market leader), and leaving other OPEC members to set their prices in line with this: a form of dominant 'firm' price leadership.

As long as demand remained buoyant, and was price inelastic, this policy allowed large price increases with consequent large revenue increases. In 1973/4, after the Arab–Israeli war, OPEC raised the price of oil from around \$3 per barrel to over \$12. The price was kept at roughly this level until 1979. And yet the sales of oil did not fall significantly.

Illustrate what was happening here on a demand and supply diagram. Remember that demand was highly inelastic and was increasing over time.

After 1979, however, following a further increase in the price of oil from around \$15 to \$40 per barrel, demand did fall. This was largely due to the recession of the early 1980s (although, as we shall see later on when we look at macroeconomics, this recession was in turn largely caused by governments' responses to the oil price increases).

Faced by declining demand, OPEC after 1982 agreed to limit output and allocate production quotas in an attempt to keep the price up. A production ceiling of 16 million barrels per day was agreed in 1984.

The cartel was beginning to break down, however, due to the following:

- The world recession and the resulting fall in the demand for oil.
- Growing output from non-OPEC members.
- 'Cheating' by some OPEC members who exceeded their quota limits.

With a glut of oil, OPEC could no longer maintain the price. The 'spot' price of oil (the day-to-day price at which oil was trading on the open market) was falling, as the graph shows.

The trend of lower oil prices was reversed in the late 1980s. With the world economy booming, the demand for oil rose and along with it the price. Then in 1990 Iraq invaded Kuwait and the Gulf War ensued. With the cutting-off of supplies from Kuwait and Iraq, the supply of oil fell and there was a sharp rise in its price.

But with the ending of the war and the recession of the early 1990s, the price rapidly fell again and only recovered slowly as the world economy started expanding once more.

On the demand side, the development of energy-saving technology plus increases in fuel taxes led to a relatively slow growth in consumption. On the supply side, the growing proportion of output supplied by non-OPEC members, plus the adoption in 1994 of a relatively high OPEC production ceiling of 24½ million barrels per day, meant that supply more than kept pace with demand.

The situation for OPEC deteriorated further in the late 1990s, following the recession in the Far East. Oil demand fell by some 2 million barrels per day. By early 1999, the price had fallen to around \$10 per barrel – a mere \$2.70 in 1973 prices! In response, OPEC members agreed to cut production by 4.3 million barrels per day. The objective was to push the price back up to around \$18–20 per barrel. But, with the Asian economy recovering and the world generally experiencing more rapid economic growth, the price rose rapidly and soon overshot the \$20 mark. By early 2000 it had reached \$30: a tripling in price in just 12 months. With the world economy then slowing down, however, the price rapidly fell back, reaching \$18 in November 2001.

However, in late 2001 the relationship between OPEC and non-OPEC oil producers changed. The ten members of the OPEC cartel decided to cut production by 1.5 million barrels a day. This followed an agreement with five of the major oil producers *outside* of the cartel to reduce their output too, the aim

One example of a rule of thumb is ***average cost pricing***. Here, producers simply add a certain percentage for profit on top of average costs. Thus, if average costs rise by 10 per cent, prices will automatically be raised by 10 per cent. This is a particularly useful rule of thumb in times of inflation, when all firms will be experiencing similar cost increases.

> **Definition**
>
> **Average cost pricing** Where a firm sets its price by adding a certain percentage for (average) profit on top of average cost.

BOX 7.3

being to push oil prices upwards and then stabilise them at around $25 per barrel. The alliance between OPEC and non-OPEC oil producers is the first such instance of its kind in the oil industry. As a result, it seemed that OPEC might now once again be able to control the market for oil.

But how successfully could this cope with crisis? With worries over an impending war with Iraq and a strike in Venezuela, the price rose again in late 2002, passing the $30 mark in early 2003. OPEC claimed that it could maintain supply and keep prices from surging even with an Iraq war, but with prices rising rapidly above $30, many doubted that it could. In 2004 the situation worsened with supply concerns related to the situation in Iraq, Saudi Arabia, Russia and Nigeria, and the oil price rose to peak at over $50 in October 2004. OPEC tried to relax the quotas, but found it difficult to adjust supply sufficiently quickly to make any real difference to the price.

The recent history of OPEC illustrates the difficulty of using supply quotas to achieve a particular price. With demand being price inelastic but income elastic (responsive to changes in world income, such as rising demand frm China), and with considerable speculative movements in demand, the equilibrium price for a given supply quota can fluctuate wildly.

?

1. ***What conditions facilitate the formation of a cartel? Which of these conditions were to be found in the oil market in (a) the early 1970s; (b) the mid-1980s; (c) the early 2000s?***
2. ***Could OPEC have done anything to prevent the long-term decline in real oil prices since 1981?***
3. ***Many oil analysts are predicting a rapid decline in world oil output in 10 to 20 years as world reserves are depleted. What effect is this likely to have on OPEC's behaviour?***

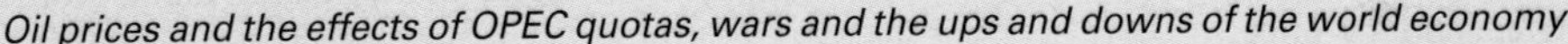

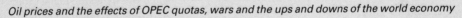

Oil prices and the effects of OPEC quotas, wars and the ups and downs of the world economy

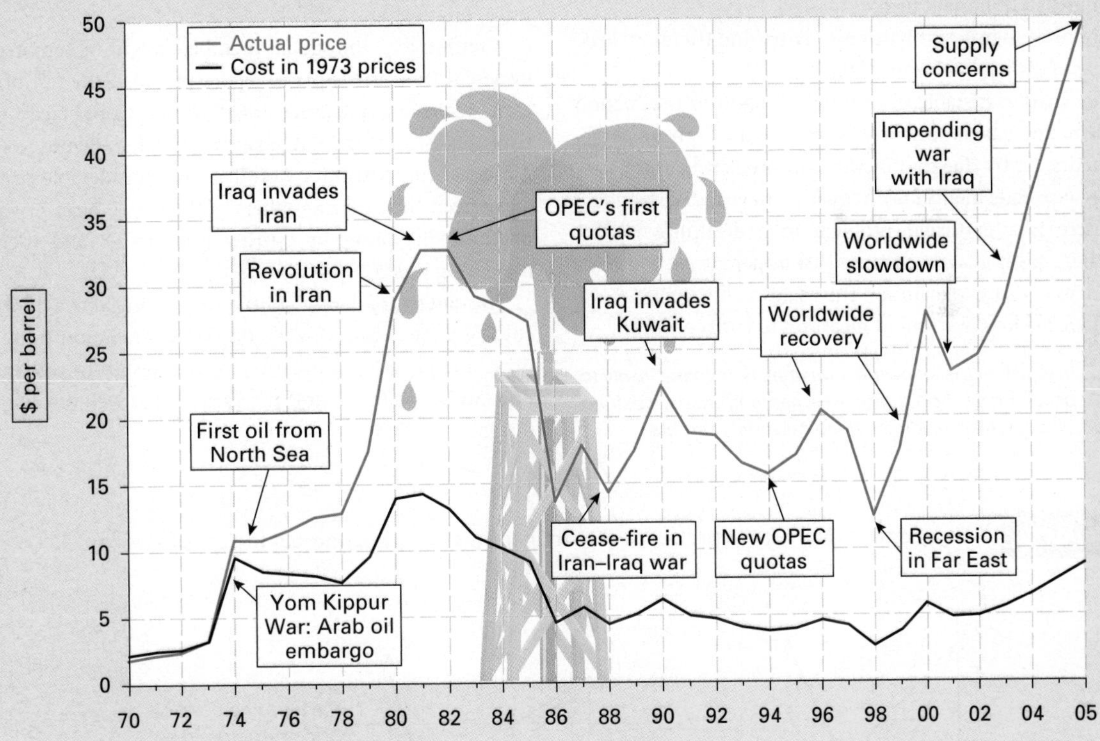

Source: *Annual Statistical Bulletin 2004* (OPEC, 2005).

?

If a firm has a typically shaped average cost curve and sets prices 10 per cent above average cost, what will its supply curve look like?

Another rule of thumb is to have certain ***price benchmarks***. Thus clothes may sell for £9.95, £14.95 or £19.95 (but not £12.31 or £16.42). If costs rise, then firms simply

Definition

Price benchmark A price that is typically used. Firms, when raising a price, will usually raise it from one benchmark to another.

raise their price to the next benchmark, knowing that other firms will do the same.

Rules of thumb can also be applied to advertising (e.g. you do not criticise other firms' products, only praise your own); or to the design of the product (e.g. lighting manufacturers tacitly agreeing not to bring out an everlasting light bulb).

Factors favouring collusion

Collusion between firms, whether formal or tacit, is more likely when firms can clearly identify with each other or some leader and when they trust each other not to break agreements. It will be easier for firms to collude if the following conditions apply:

- There are only very few firms all well known to each other.
- They are not secretive with each other about costs and production methods.
- They have similar production methods and average costs, and are thus likely to want to change prices at the same time and by the same percentage.
- They produce similar products and can thus more easily reach agreements on price.
- There is a dominant firm.
- There are significant barriers to entry and therefore little fear of disruption by new firms.
- The market is stable. If industry demand or production costs fluctuate wildly, it will be difficult to make agreements, partly due to difficulties in predicting and partly because agreements may frequently have to be amended. There is a particular problem in a declining market where firms may be tempted to undercut each other's prices in order to maintain their sales.
- There are no government measures to curb collusion.

? *In which of the following industries is collusion likely to occur: bricks, beer, margarine, cement, crisps, washing powder, blank audio or video cassettes, carpets?*

Non-collusive oligopoly: the breakdown of collusion

In some oligopolies, there may only be a few (if any) factors favouring collusion. In such cases, the likelihood of price competition is greater.

Even if there is collusion, there will always be the temptation for individual oligopolists to 'cheat', by cutting prices or by selling more than their allotted quota.

Let us take the case of a cartel consisting of five equal-sized firms. The whole cartel is illustrated in Figure 7.6(a). Assume that the cartel sets the industry profit-maximising price of £10. This will give an industry output of 1000 units, which the cartel divides equally between its five members: i.e. each member is assigned a quota of 200 units.

Now consider Figure 7.6(b). This shows the position for one of the members of the cartel, firm A. Provided the cartel's price remains fixed at £10, then £10 would also be the marginal revenue for the individual firm. This will create an incentive for cartel members to cheat: to sell more than their allotted quota. Firm A would maximise its own profits by selling 600 units, where $MC = P$ (= MR), provided it could do this by taking market share off the other members, and thus leaving total industry output (and hence price) unaffected.

Alternatively, individual members might be tempted to undercut the cartel's price. Again, provided the rest of the cartel maintained its price at £10, firm A would face a relatively elastic demand curve (shown by *AR* in Figure 7.6(b)). A modest cut in its price would attract considerable custom away from the other members of the cartel. Firm A would maximise its profit by cutting price to £8 and thereby increasing its sales to 400 units.

The danger, of course, with either selling above quota or cutting price is that this would invite retaliation from the other members of the cartel, with a resulting price war. Price would then fall and the cartel could well break up in disarray.

Figure 7.6 The incentive for a firm to produce more than its quota, or to undercut the cartel's price

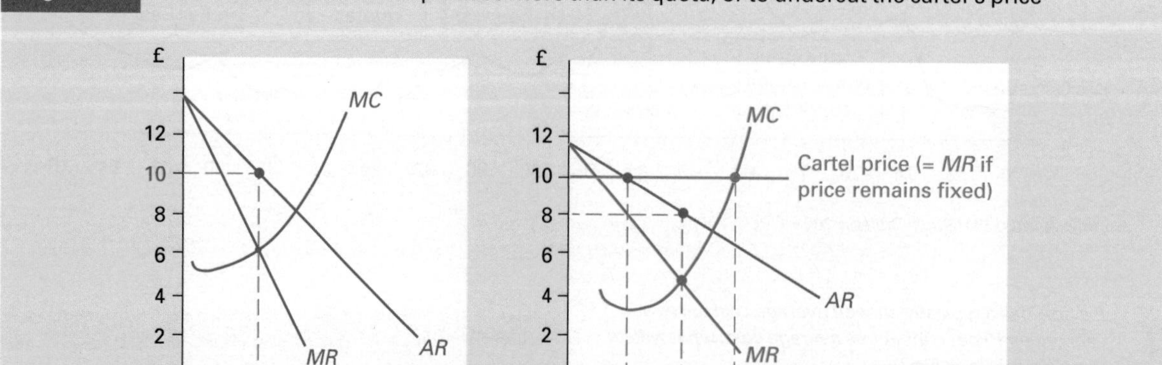

Figure 7.7 The Cournot model

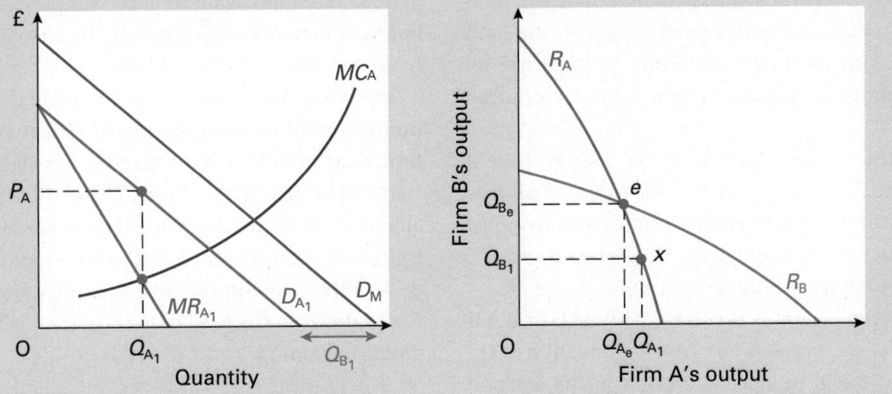

(a) Firm A's profit-maximising position

(b) The two firms' reaction functions

When considering whether to break a collusive agreement, even if only a tacit one, a firm will ask: (1) 'How much can we get away with without inviting retaliation?' and (2) 'If a price war does result, will we be the winners? Will we succeed in driving some or all of our rivals out of business and yet survive ourselves, and thereby gain greater market power?'

The position of rival firms, therefore, is rather like that of the generals of opposing armies or the players in a game. It is a question of choosing the appropriate *strategy*: the strategy that will best succeed in outwitting your opponents.

The strategy that a firm adopts will, of course, be concerned not just with price but also with advertising and product development.

Non-collusive oligopoly: assumptions about rivals' behaviour

Even though oligopolists might not collude, they will still need to take account of rivals' likely behaviour when deciding their own strategy. In doing so, they will probably look at rivals' past behaviour and make assumptions based on it. There are three well-known models, each based on a different set of assumptions.

Assumption that rivals produce a given quantity: the Cournot model

One assumption is that rivals will produce a particular *quantity*. This is most likely when the market is stable and the rivals have been producing a relatively constant quantity for some time. The task, then, for the individual oligopolist is to decide its own price and quantity given the presumed output of its competitors.

The earliest model based on this assumption was developed by the French economist Augustin Cournot[1] in 1838.

The ***Cournot model*** takes the simple case of just two firms (a ***duopoly***) producing an identical product: for example, two electricity generating companies supplying the whole country.

This is illustrated in Figure 7.7(a), which shows the profit-maximising price and output for firm A. The total market demand curve is shown as D_M. Assume that firm A believes that its rival, firm B, will produce Q_{B_1} units. Thus firm A perceives its own demand curve (D_{A_1}) to be Q_{B_1} units less than total market demand. In other words, the horizontal gap between D_M and D_{A_1} is Q_{B_1} units. Given its perceived demand curve of D_{A_1}, its marginal revenue curve will be MR_{A_1} and the profit-maximising output will be Q_{A_1}, where $MR_{A_1} = MC_A$. The profit-maximising price will be P_{A_1}.

If firm A believed that firm B would produce *more* than Q_{B_1}, its perceived demand and *MR* curves would be further to the left and the profit-maximising quantity and price would both be lower.

Figure 7.7(b) illustrates the ***reaction functions*** of firm A and firm B. Each curve shows the amount of output the respective firm will produce in the light of how much it perceives the other firm will produce. Take the reaction curve for firm A. If it assumes that firm B will produce Q_{B_1} (as in Figure 7.7(a)) it will choose to produce Q_{A_1}: i.e. at point *x* on its reaction curve.

Definitions

Cournot model A model of duopoly where each firm makes its price and output decisions on the assumption that its rival will produce a particular quantity.

Duopoly An oligopoly where there are just two firms in the market.

Reaction function (or curve) This shows how a firm's optimal output varies according to the output chosen by its rival (or rivals).

[1] See http://cepa.newschool.edu/het/profiles/cournot.htm for a profile of Cournot and his work.

We can now conduct a similar analysis for firm B, again using a diagram like Figure 7.7(a). If it assumes that firm A will produce a particular level of output, it will then decide its profit-maximising price and output in the light of this. Firm B's reaction curve in Figure 7.7(b) shows all the profit-maximising outputs for firm B for each output of firm A.

What will the market equilibrium be? This will be at point *e* in Figure 7.7(b). It is known as the ***Cournot equilibrium***. Only at this point will neither firm choose to adjust its output. How will the equilibrium be reached if production is currently *not* at equilibrium?

Assume that production is at point *x*. Although firm A is on its reaction curve, firm B is not. Given production of Q_{A_1} by firm A, firm B will produce at a point on its reaction curve vertically above this (i.e. an output *greater* than Q_{B_1}). This will cause firm A to move up its reaction curve. The process will continue until point *e* is reached.

Profits in the Cournot model. Industry profits will be *less* than under a monopoly or a cartel. The reason is that price will be lower than the monopoly price. This can be seen from Figure 7.7(a). If this were a monopoly, then to find the profit-maximising output, we would need to construct an *MR* curve corresponding to the market demand curve (D_M). This would intersect with the *MC* curve at a higher output than Q_{A_1} and a *higher* price (given by D_M).

Nevertheless, profits in the Cournot model will be higher than under perfect competition, since price is still above marginal cost.

Maths Case 7.2 on the book's website shows how the Cournot equilibrium can be derived algebraically from the market demand function and the cost functions of the two firms.

Assumption that rivals set a particular price: the Bertrand model

An alternative assumption is that rival firms set a particular price and stick to it. This scenario is more realistic when firms do not want to upset customers by frequent price changes or want to produce catalogues which specify prices. The task, then, for a given oligopolist is to choose its own price and quantity in the light of the prices set by rivals.

The most famous model based on this assumption was developed by a another French economist, Joseph Bertrand in 1883. Bertrand again took the simple case of a duopoly, but its conclusions apply equally to oligopolies with three or more firms.

The outcome is one of price cutting until all supernormal profits are competed away. The reason is simple. If firm A assumes that its rival, firm B, will hold price constant, then firm A should undercut this price by a small amount and as a result gain a large share of the market. At this point, firm B will be forced to respond by cutting its price. What we end up with is a price war until price is forced down to the level of average cost, with only normal profits remaining.

Nash equilibrium. The equilibrium outcome in either the Cournot or Bertrand models is not in the *joint* interests of the firms. In each case, total profits are less than under a monopoly or cartel. But, in the absence of collusion, the outcome is the result of each firm doing the best it can, given its assumptions about what its rivals are doing. The resulting equilibrium is known as a ***Nash equilibrium***, after John Nash, a US mathematician (and subject of the film *A Beautiful Mind*) who introduced the concept in 1951.

In practice, when competition is intense, as in the Bertrand model, the firms may seek to collude long before profits have been reduced to a normal level. Alternatively firms may put in a ***takeover bid*** for their rival(s).

The kinked demand-curve assumption

In 1939 a theory of non-collusive oligopoly was developed simultaneously on both sides of the Atlantic: in the USA by Paul Sweezy and in Britain by R. L. Hall and C. J. Hitch. This ***kinked demand theory*** has since become perhaps the most famous of all theories of oligopoly. The model seeks to explain how it is that, even when there is no collusion at all between oligopolists, prices can nevertheless remain stable.

The theory is based on two asymmetrical assumptions:

- If an oligopolist cuts its price, its rivals will feel forced to follow suit and cut theirs, to prevent losing customers to the first firm.
- If an oligopolist raises its price, however, its rivals will *not* follow suit since, by keeping their prices the same, they will thereby gain customers from the first firm.

Definitions

Cournot equilibrium Where the outputs chosen by each firm are consistent with each other: where the two firms' reaction curves cross.

Nash equilibrium The position resulting from everyone making their optimal decision based on their assumptions about their rivals' decisions. Without collusion, there is no incentive for any firm to move from this position.

Takeover bid Where one firm attempts to purchase another by offering to buy the shares of that company from its shareholders.

Kinked demand theory The theory that oligopolists face a demand curve that is kinked at the current price, demand being significantly more elastic above the current price than below. The effect of this is to create a situation of price stability.

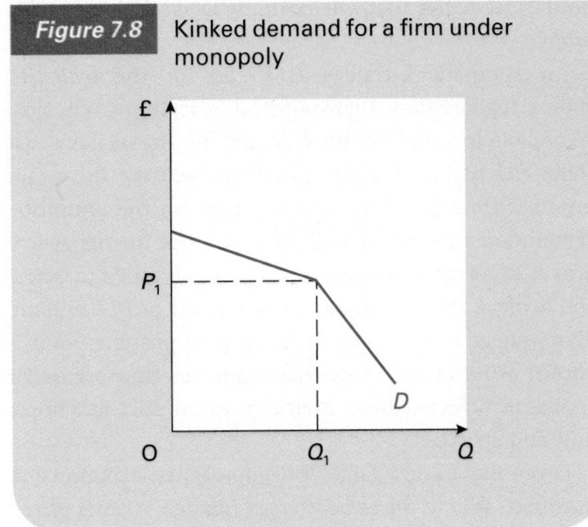

Figure 7.8 Kinked demand for a firm under monopoly

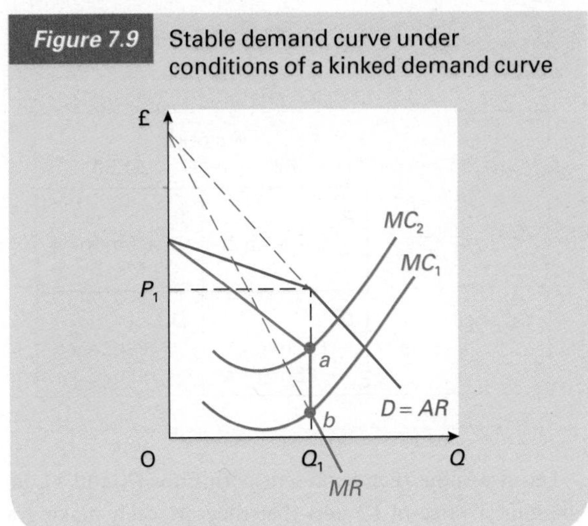

Figure 7.9 Stable demand curve under conditions of a kinked demand curve

On these assumptions, each oligopolist will face a demand curve that is *kinked* at the current price and output (see Figure 7.8). A rise in price will lead to a large fall in sales as customers switch to the now relatively lower-priced rivals. KI 9 p58 The firm will thus be reluctant to raise its price. Demand is relatively elastic above the kink. On the other hand, a fall in price will bring only a modest increase in sales, since rivals lower their prices too and therefore customers do not switch. The firm will thus also be reluctant to lower its price. Demand is relatively inelastic below the kink. Thus oligopolists will be reluctant to change prices at all.

This price stability can be shown formally by drawing in the firm's marginal revenue curve, as in Figure 7.9.

To see how this is done, imagine dividing the diagram into two parts either side of Q_1. At quantities less than Q_1 (the left-hand part of the diagram), the *MR* curve will correspond to the shallow part of the *AR* curve. At quantities greater than Q_1 (the right-hand part), the *MR* curve will correspond to the steep part of the *AR* curve. To see how this part of the *MR* curve is constructed, imagine extending the steep part of the *AR* curve back to the vertical axis. This and the corresponding *MR* curve are shown by the dotted lines in Figure 7.9.

As you can see, there will be a gap between points *a* and *b*. In other words, there is a vertical section of the *MR* curve between these two points.

Profits are maximised where $MC = MR$. Thus, if the *MC* curve lies anywhere between MC_1 and MC_2 (i.e. between points *a* and *b*), the profit-maximising price and output will be P_1 and Q_1. Thus prices will remain stable *even with a considerable change in costs*.

Despite its simple demonstration of the real-world phenomenon of price stability, the model does have two major limitations:

- Price stability may be due to *other* factors. Firms may not want to change prices too frequently as this involves modifying price lists, working out new revenue predictions and revaluing stocks of finished goods, and it may upset customers. Price stability, therefore, is not proof of the accuracy of the model.
- Although the model can help to explain price stability, it does not explain how prices are set in the first place. To do this, some other model would be required. This is a serious limitation in times of inflation, when oligopolists, like other firms, raise prices in response to higher costs and higher demand. What the model does predict, however, is that the price will be raised only after marginal cost has risen above MC_2 in Figure 7.9, and that once it has been raised, a new kink will form at that price. Price will then remain fixed at that level until higher costs once more force a further price rise.

Non-collusive oligopoly: game theory

As we have seen, the behaviour of a firm under non-collusive oligopoly will depend on how it thinks its rivals will react to its policies.

Economists use ***game theory*** to examine the best strategy a firm can adopt for each assumption about its rivals'  KI 20 p182 behaviour.

Simple dominant strategy games

The simplest case is where there are just two firms with identical costs, products and demand. They are both considering which of two alternative prices to charge. Table 7.1 shows typical profits they could each make.

> **Definition**
>
> **Game theory (or the theory of games)** The study of alternative strategies that oligopolists may choose to adopt, depending on their assumptions about their rivals' behaviour.

Table 7.1 Profits for firms X and Y at different prices

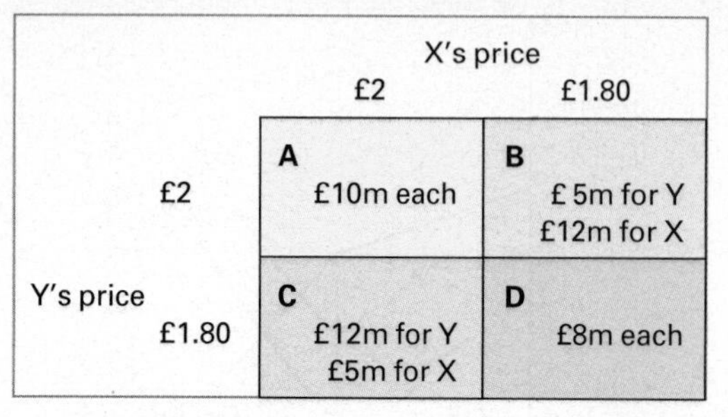

		X's price £2	X's price £1.80
Y's price	£2	A £10m each	B £5m for Y £12m for X
	£1.80	C £12m for Y £5m for X	D £8m each

Let us assume that at present both firms (X and Y) are charging a price of £2 and that they are each making a profit of £10 million, giving a total industry profit of £20 million. This is shown in cell A in Table 7.1.

TC 9 p101 Now assume they are both (independently) considering reducing their price to £1.80. First they must take into account what their rival might do, and how this will affect them. Let us consider X's position. In our simple example, we assume that there are just two things that its rival, firm Y, might do. Either Y could cut its price to £1.80, or it could leave its price at £2. What should X do?

KI 11 p66 One alternative is to go for the *cautious* approach and think of the worst thing that its rival could do. If X kept its price at £2, the worst thing for X would be if its rival Y cut its price. This is shown by cell C: X's profit falls to £5 million. If, however, X cut its price to £1.80, the worst outcome would again be for Y to cut its price, but this time X's profit only falls to £8 million. In this case, then, if X is cautious, it will *cut its price to £1.80*. Note that Y will argue along similar lines, and if it is cautious it too will cut its price to £1.80. This policy of adopting the safer strategy is known as ***maximin***. Following a maximin strategy, the firm will opt for the alternative that will *maxi*mise its *mini*mum possible profit.

An alternative strategy is to go for the *optimistic* approach and assume that your rivals react in the way most favourable to you. Here the firm goes for the strategy that yields the highest possible profit. In X's case, this again means cutting its price, only this time on the optimistic assumption that firm Y will leave its price unchanged. If firm X is correct in its assumption, it will move to box B and achieve the maximum possible profit of £12 million. This strategy of going for the maximum possible profit is known as ***maximax***. Note that again the same argument applies to Y. Its maximax strategy is to cut price and hopefully end up in cell C.

Given that in this 'game' *both* approaches, maximin and maximax, lead to the *same* strategy (namely cutting price), this is known as a ***dominant strategy game***.

As we saw above, the equilibrium outcome of a game where there is no collusion between the players is known as a *Nash equilibrium*. The Nash equilibrium in this game is cell D.

But, given that both X and Y will be tempted to lower prices, they will both end up earning a lower profit (£8 million profit each in cell D) than if they had charged the higher price (£10 million profit each in cell A). Thus collusion, rather than a price war, would have benefited both, and yet both would be tempted to cheat and cut prices. This is known as the ***prisoners' dilemma*** (see Box 7.4).

More complex games with no dominant strategy

More complex 'games' can be devised with more than two firms, many alternative prices, differentiated products and various forms of non-price competition (e.g. advertising). Table 7.2 illustrates a more complex game.

It shows the profits that will result from three alternative strategies that firm X can pursue (e.g. price cut, advertising

Table 7.2 Profit possibilities for firm X (£m)

		Other firms' responses a	b	c	d	e	f	
Strategies for firm X	1	100	60	−20	10	30	80	(Maximax – a)
	2	40	50	20	30	25	60	(Maximin – c)
	3	90	15	30	25	20	50	(Best compromise)

Definitions

Maximin The strategy of choosing the policy whose worst possible outcome is the least bad.

Maximax The strategy of choosing the policy that has the best possible outcome.

Dominant strategy game Where the same policy is suggested by different strategies.

Prisoners' dilemma Where two or more firms (or people), by attempting independently to choose the best strategy for whatever the other(s) are likely to do, end up in a worse position than if they had co-operated in the first place.

CASE STUDIES AND APPLICATIONS

BOX 7.4

THE PRISONERS' DILEMMA

KI 20 p182

Game theory is not just relevant to economics. A famous non-economic example is the prisoners' dilemma.

Nigel and Amanda have been arrested for a joint crime of serious fraud. Each is interviewed separately and given the following alternatives:

- First, if they say nothing, the court has enough evidence to sentence both to a year's imprisonment.
- Second, if either Nigel or Amanda *alone* confesses, he or she is likely to get only a three-month sentence but the partner could get up to ten years.
- Third, if both confess, they are likely to get three years each.

What should Nigel and Amanda do?

		Amanda's alternatives: Not confess	Amanda's alternatives: Confess
Nigel's alternatives	Not confess	**A** Each gets 1 year	**C** Nigel gets 10 years; Amanda gets 3 months
	Confess	**B** Nigel gets 3 months; Amanda gets 10 years	**D** Each gets 3 years

Let us consider Nigel's dilemma. Should he confess in order to get the short sentence (the maximax strategy)? This is better than the year he would get for not confessing. There is, however, an even better reason for confessing. Suppose Nigel doesn't confess but, unknown to him, Amanda does confess. Then Nigel ends up with the long sentence. Better than this is to confess and to get no more than three years: this is the safest (maximin) strategy.

Amanda is in the same dilemma. The result is simple. When both prisoners act selfishly by confessing, they both end up in position D with relatively long prison terms. Only when they collude will they end up in position A with relatively short prison terms, the best combined solution.

Of course, the police know this and will do their best to prevent any collusion. They will keep Nigel and Amanda in separate cells and try to persuade each of them that the other is bound to confess.

Thus the choice of strategy depends on:

- Nigel's and Amanda's risk attitudes: i.e. are they 'risk lovers' or 'risk averse'?
- Nigel's and Amanda's estimates of how likely the other is to own up.

1. Why is this a dominant strategy 'game'?

2. How would Nigel's choice of strategy be affected if he had instead been involved in a joint crime with Jeremy, Pauline, Diana and Dave, and they had all been caught?

The prisoners' dilemma is a good illustration of *the fallacy of composition* that we examined in Box 3.5 (see page 80). What applies at the level of the individual does not apply to the group as a whole. It might be in the individual's interests to confess. It is clearly *not* in the interests of both, however, for both to confess.

Let us now look at two real-world examples of the prisoners' dilemma.

Standing at concerts. When people go to some public event, such as a concert or a match, they often stand in order to get a better view. But once people start standing, everyone is likely to do so: after all, if they stayed sitting, they would not see at all. In this Nash equilibrium, most people are worse off, since, except for tall people, their view is likely to be worse and they lose the comfort of sitting down.

Too much advertising. Why do firms spend so much on advertising? If they are aggressive, they do so to get ahead of their rivals (the maximax approach). If they are cautious, they do so in case their rivals increase their advertising (the maximin approach). Although in both cases it may be in the individual firm's best interests to increase advertising, the resulting Nash equilibrium is likely to be one of excessive advertising: the total spent on advertising (by all firms) is not recouped in additional sales.

Give some other non-economic examples of the prisoners' dilemma.

campaign, new model) and six possible responses from rivals (e.g. all rivals cutting price, some cutting price, all increasing advertising). It is assumed that firm X can calculate the effects on its profits of these various reactions.

Which strategy will X choose? It may go for the safe strategy – *maximin*. Here it will choose strategy 2. The worst outcome from strategy 2 (response c) will still give a profit of £20 million, whereas the worst outcome from strategy 3 (response b) is a profit of only £15 million, and the worst outcome from strategy 1 (response c) is a loss of £20 million.

Alternatively, firm X may go for a high-risk strategy: the one with highest maximum profit – *maximax*. Here it would choose strategy 1. This has a potential maximum profit of £100 million (response a), whereas the best outcome from strategy 3 is only £90 million (response a), and for strategy 2 only £60 million (response f).

Alternatively, it may go for a ***compromise strategy*** and choose strategy 3. The best outcome from strategy 3 (response a) is only slightly lower than strategy 1 (response a) – £90 million compared with £100 million. The worst outcome (response b) is only slightly lower than strategy 2 (response c) – £15 million compared with £20 million.

It is also likely to weigh up the *likelihood* of each outcome occurring. For example, in Table 7.2, firm X is much more likely to adopt the maximax solution if the chances of response *a* occurring are very high and the chances of outcome *c* occurring are very low.

The importance of threats and promises

In many situations, an oligopolist will make a threat or promise that it will act in a certain way. As long as the threat or promise is ***credible*** (i.e. its competitors believe it), the firm can gain and it will influence its rivals' behaviour.

Take the simple situation where a large oil company, such as Esso, states that it will match the price charged by any competitor within a given radius. Assume that competitors believe this 'price promise' but also that Esso will not try to *undercut* their price. In the simple situation where there is only one other filling station in the area, what price should it charge? Clearly it should charge the price that would maximise its profits, assuming that Esso will charge the *same* price. In the absence of other filling stations in the area, this is likely to be a relatively high price.

Now assume that there are several filling stations in the area. What should the company do now? Its best bet is probably to charge the same price as Esso and hope that no other company charges a lower price and forces Esso to cut its price. Assuming that Esso's threat is credible, other companies are likely to reason in a similar way.

Assume that there are two major oil companies operating filling stations in an area. The first promises to match the other's prices. The other promises always to sell at 1p per litre cheaper than the first. Describe the likely sequence of events in this 'game' and the likely eventual outcome. Could the promise of the second company be seen as credible?

The importance of timing

Most decisions by oligopolists are made by one firm at a time rather than simultaneously by all firms. Sometimes a firm will take the initiative. At other times it will respond to decisions taken by other firms.

Take the case of a new generation of large passenger aircraft that can fly further without refuelling. Assume that there is a market for a 500-seater version of this type of aircraft and a 400-seater version, but that the market for each sized aircraft is not big enough for the two manufacturers, Boeing and Airbus, to share it profitably. Let us also assume that the 400-seater market would give an annual profit of £50 million to a single manufacturer and the 500-seater would give an annual profit of £30 million, but that if both manufacturers produced the same version, they would each make an annual loss of £10 million.

Assume that Boeing announces that it is building the 400-seater plane. What should Airbus do? The choice is illustrated in Figure 7.10. This diagram is called a ***decision tree*** and shows the sequence of events. The small square at the left of the diagram is Boeing's decision point (point A). If it decided to build the 500-seater plane, we would move up the top branch. Airbus would now have to make a decision (point B_1). If it too built the 500-seater plane, we would move to outcome 1: a loss of £10 million for both manufacturers. Clearly, with Boeing building a 500-seater plane, Airbus would choose the 400-seater plane: we would move to outcome 2, with Boeing making a profit of £30 million and Airbus a profit of £50 million. Airbus would be very pleased!

Boeing's best strategy at point A, however, would be to build the 400-seater plane. We would then move to Airbus's decision point B_2. In this case, it is in Airbus's interests to build the 500-seater plane. Its profit would be only £30 million (outcome 3), but this is better than a £10 million loss if it too built the 400-seater plane (outcome 4). With Boeing deciding first, the Nash equilibrium will thus be outcome 3.

There is clearly a ***first-mover advantage*** here. Once Boeing has decided to build the more profitable version of the plane, Airbus is forced to build the less profitable one. Naturally, Airbus would like to build the more profitable one and be the first mover. Which company succeeds in going first depends on how advanced they are in their research and development and in their production capacity.

More complex decision trees. The aircraft example is the simplest version of a decision tree, with just two companies and each one making only one key decision. In many

Definitions

Compromise strategy A strategy whose worst outcome is better than under the maximax strategy and whose best outcome is better than under the maximin strategy.

Credible threat (or promise) One that is believable to rivals because it is in the threatener's interests to carry it out.

Decision tree (or game tree) A diagram showing the sequence of possible decisions by competitor firms and the outcome of each combination of decisions.

First-mover advantage When a firm gains from being the first one to take action.

Figure 7.10 A decision tree

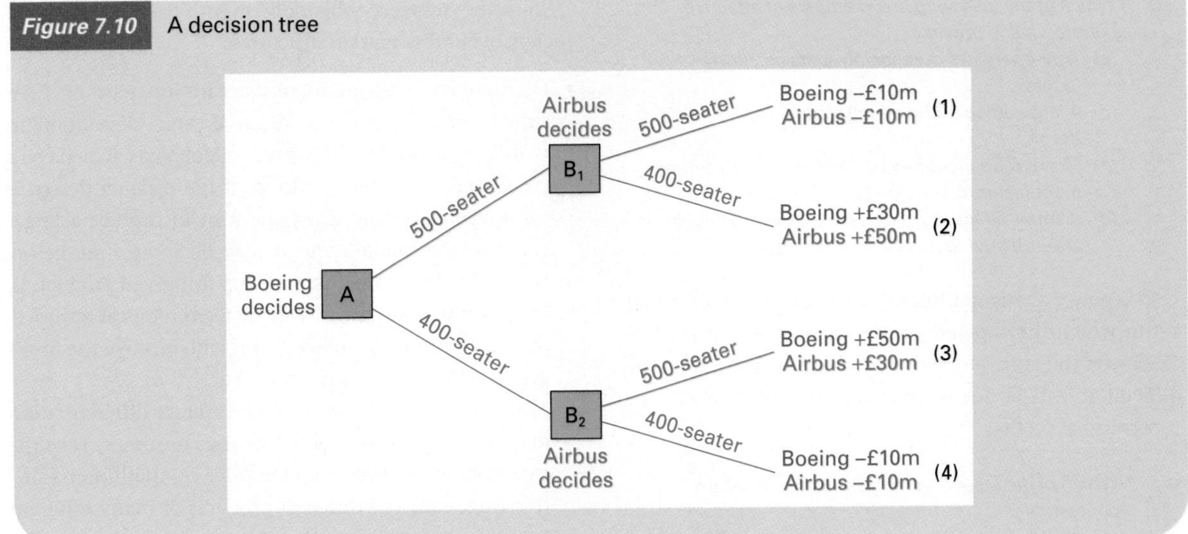

business situations, much more complex trees could be constructed. The 'game' would be more like one of chess, with many moves and several options on each move. If there were more than two companies, the decision tree would be more complex still.

? *Give an example of decisions that two firms could make in sequence, each one affecting the other's next decision.*

Assessing the theory of games

The advantage of the game theory approach is that the firm does not need to know which response its rivals will make. However, it must be able to measure the effect of each possible response. This will be virtually impossible to do with many firms competing and many different possible responses. The approach is useful, therefore, only in relatively simple cases, and even here the estimates of profit from each outcome may amount to no more than a rough guess.

It is thus difficult for an economist to predict with any accuracy what price, output and level of advertising the firm will choose. This problem is compounded by the difficulty in predicting the type of strategy – safe, high risk, compromise – that the firm will adopt.

In some cases, firms may compete hard for a time (in price or non-price terms) and then realise that maybe no one is winning. Firms may then start to collude and jointly raise prices and reduce advertising. Later, after a period of tacit collusion, competition may break out again. This may be sparked off by the entry of a new firm, by the development of a new product design, by a change in market demand, or simply by one or more firms no longer being able to resist the temptation to 'cheat'. In short, the behaviour of particular oligopolists may change quite radically over time.

Finally, we have been assuming that people behave selfishly. In reality, people's actions are likely to be influenced by their moral values. Businesspeople will often be unwilling to behave ruthlessly or dishonestly, or to undertake profitable activities that they regard as unfair. In Chapter 8 we examine some of the consequences of pursuing goals other than ruthless profit maximisation.

Oligopoly and the public interest

If oligopolists act collusively and jointly maximise industry profits, they will in effect be acting together as a monopoly. In such cases, the disadvantages to society experienced under monopoly will also be experienced under oligopoly (see section 6.3). KI 19 p157

Furthermore, in two respects, oligopoly may be more disadvantageous than monopoly: 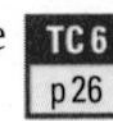 TC 6 p26

- Depending on the size of the individual oligopolists, there may be less scope for economies of scale to mitigate the effects of market power.
- Oligopolists are likely to engage in much more extensive advertising than a monopolist (see Web Case 7.8).

These problems will be less, however, if oligopolists do not collude, if there is some degree of price competition and if barriers to entry are weak.

Also, the power of oligopolists in certain markets may to some extent be offset if they sell their product to other powerful firms. Thus oligopolistic producers of baked beans sell a large proportion of their output to giant supermarket chains, which can use their market power to keep down the price at which they purchase the beans. This phenomenon is known as ***countervailing power***.

Definition

Countervailing power Where the power of a monopolistic/oligopolistic seller is offset by powerful buyers who can prevent the price from being pushed up.

?

Which of the following are examples of effective countervailing power?

(a) Tour operators purchasing seats on charter flights.

(b) A large office hiring a photocopier from Rank Xerox.

(c) Marks & Spencer buying clothes from a garment manufacturer.

(d) A small village store (but the only one for miles around) buying food from a wholesaler.

The power of oligopolists will also be reduced if the market in which they operate is contestable (see section 6.4). The lower the entry and exit costs for new firms, the more difficult it will be for oligopolists to collude and make supernormal profits.

?

Which of the following markets do you think are contestable:

(a) credit cards;

(b) brewing;

(c) petrol retailing;

(d) insurance services;

(e) compact discs?

In some respects, oligopoly may have *advantages* to society over other market structures:

- Oligopolists, like monopolists, can use part of their supernormal profit for research and development. Unlike monopolists, however, oligopolists will have a considerable *incentive* to do so. If the product design is improved, this may allow the firm to capture a larger share of the market, and it may be some time before rivals can respond with a similarly improved product. If, in addition, costs are lowered by technological improvement, the resulting higher profits will improve the firm's capacity to withstand any price war.
- Non-price competition through product differentiation may result in greater choice for the consumer. Take the case of stereo equipment. Non-price competition has led to a huge range of different products of many different specifications, each meeting the specific requirements of different consumers.

It is difficult, however, to draw any general conclusions, since oligopolies differ so much in their performance.

Section summary

1. An oligopoly is where there are just a few firms in the industry with barriers to the entry of new firms. Firms recognise their mutual dependence.
2. Oligopolists will want to maximise their joint profits. This will tend to make them collude to keep prices high. On the other hand, they will want the biggest share of industry profits for themselves. This will tend to make them compete.
3. They are more likely to collude if there are few of them; if they are open with each other; if they have similar products and cost structures; if there is a dominant firm; if there are significant entry barriers; if the market is stable; and if there is no government legislation to prevent collusion.
4. Collusion can be open or tacit.
5. A formal collusive agreement is called a 'cartel'. A cartel aims to act as a monopoly. It can set price and leave the members to compete for market share, or it can assign quotas. There is always a temptation for cartel members to 'cheat' by undercutting the cartel price if they think they can get away with it and not trigger a price war.
6. Tacit collusion can take the form of price leadership. This is where firms follow the price set by either a dominant firm in the industry or a firm seen as a reliable 'barometer' of market conditions. Alternatively, tacit collusion can simply involve following various rules of thumb such as average cost pricing and benchmark pricing.
7. Even when firms do not collude, they will still have to take into account their rivals' behaviour. In the Cournot model, firms assume that their rivals' output is given and then choose the profit-maximising price and output in the light of this assumption. The resulting price and profit are lower than under monopoly, but still higher than under perfect competition. In the Bertrand model, firms assume that their rivals' price is given. This will result in prices being competed down until only normal profits remain. In the kinked-demand curve model, firms are likely to keep their prices stable unless there is a large shift in costs or demand.
8. Non-collusive oligopolists will have to work out a price strategy. Game theory examines various strategies that firms can adopt when the outcome of each is not certain. They can adopt a low-risk 'maximin' strategy of choosing the policy that has the least-bad worst outcome, or a high-risk 'maximax' strategy of choosing the policy with the best possible outcome, or some compromise.
9. An oligopolist is likely to be more profitable if its rivals take its threats seriously. It is important here that its threats are credible.
10. Timing can be vitally important for the success of an oligopolist. There is often a 'first-mover advantage' for the company that beats its rivals to the market with a new product.
11. Whether oligopoly behaviour is in the public interest depends on the particular oligopoly and how competitive it is; whether there is any countervailing power; whether the firms engage in extensive advertising and of what type; whether product differentiation results in a wide range of choice for the consumer; how much of the profits are ploughed back into research and development; and how contestable the market is. Since these conditions vary substantially from oligopoly to oligopoly, it is impossible to state just how well or how badly oligopoly in general serves the public interest.

7.3 PRICE DISCRIMINATION

Up to now we have assumed that a firm will sell its output at a single price. Sometimes, however, firms may practise ***price discrimination***. This is where a firm sells the same product to different consumers at different prices *even though production costs are the same*. There are three major varieties of price discrimination:

- ***First-degree price discrimination*** is where the firm charges each consumer the maximum price he or she is prepared to pay for each unit. For example, stallholders in a bazaar will attempt to do this when bartering with their customers.
- ***Second-degree price discrimination*** is where the firm charges customers different prices according to how much they purchase. It may charge a high price for the first so many units, a lower price for the next so many units, a lower price again for the next, and so on. For example, electricity companies in some countries charge a high price for the first so many kilowatts. This is the amount of electricity that would typically be used for lighting and running appliances: in other words, the uses for which there is no substitute fuel. Additional kilowatts are charged at a much lower rate. This is electricity that is typically used for heating and cooking, where there are alternative fuels.
- ***Third-degree price discrimination*** is where consumers are grouped into two or more independent markets and a separate price is charged in each market. Examples include different bus fares for adults and children, and different prices charged by a firm for the same product in different countries. Third-degree price discrimination is much more common than first- or second-degree discrimination.

Conditions necessary for price discrimination to operate

As we shall see, a firm will be able to increase its profits if it can engage in price discrimination. But under what circumstances will it be able to charge discriminatory prices? There are three conditions that must be met:

CASE STUDIES AND APPLICATIONS **BOX 7.5**

WHAT'S THE TRAIN FARE TO LONDON?

Price discrimination on the trains

Ask the question, 'What's the fare to London?' at ticket enquiries, and you may receive any of the following replies:

- Do you want 1st or standard class?
- Do you want single or return?
- How old are you?
- Do you have a railcard (family, young person's, disabled adult or child, senior citizen's)?
- Do you want a 'supersaver', a 'saver' or an open return?
- Will you be travelling back on a Friday?
- Will you be travelling out before 10 a.m.?
- Will you be leaving London between 4 p.m. and 6 p.m.?
- Do you want an 'APEX' or 'super advance' ticket (one booked in advance)?
- Do you want to take advantage of our special low-priced winter Saturday fare?

?

1. ***Look at each of the above questions. In each case, decide whether price discrimination is being practised. If it is, is it sensible for train operators to do so? Is it discriminating between people with different price elasticities of demand?***
2. ***Are these various forms of price discrimination in the traveller's interest?***

You can check out the range of ticket types and prices by going to the National Rail website at www.nationalrail.co.uk/planmyjourney and selecting a journey.

Definitions

Price discrimination Where a firm sells the same product at different prices.

First-degree price discrimination Where a firm charges each consumer for each unit the maximum price which that consumer is willing to pay for that unit.

Second-degree price discrimination Where a firm charges a consumer so much for the first so many units purchased, a different price for the next so many units purchased, and so on.

Third-degree price discrimination Where a firm divides consumers into different groups and charges a different price to consumers in different groups, but the same price to all the consumers within a group.

EXPLORING ECONOMICS **BOX 7.6**

PEAK-LOAD PRICING

Charging more when it costs more to produce

A common form of price discrimination is ***peak-load pricing***. This is where people are charged more at times of peak demand and less at off-peak times. Take the case of a holiday. If you look through the brochures, you will see that high-season prices are often considerably higher than low-season prices. Similarly, call charges for telephones are often much higher during weekdays than in the evenings and weekends. Other examples of peak-load (or 'peak-period') pricing are rail and air fares, prices in cinemas and restaurants (higher in the evenings) and charges made by health and sports clubs (higher at weekends and in the evenings).

The reason for the higher prices charged at peak times has partly to do with elasticity of demand. Demand is less elastic at peak times. For example, many commuters have little option but to pay higher rail fares at peak times. This is genuine price discrimination.

But often the higher charges also have to do with higher marginal costs incurred at peak times and, as such, are not true price discrimination. With various fixed factors (such as plant and equipment), marginal costs are likely to rise as output expands to meet higher demand. This could be due to diminishing returns to the variable factors; or it could be due to having to use additional equipment with higher operating costs.

Take the case of electricity. At off-peak times, the power stations with the lowest operating costs will be used. These are normally the nuclear and coal-fired stations. At periods of peak demand, however, the stations with higher operating costs will have to be brought on line, such as oil-fired stations. (Oil-fired stations are relatively cheap to build, but have higher running costs.) As a result, the marginal cost of generating electricity is higher at peak times than at off-peak times.

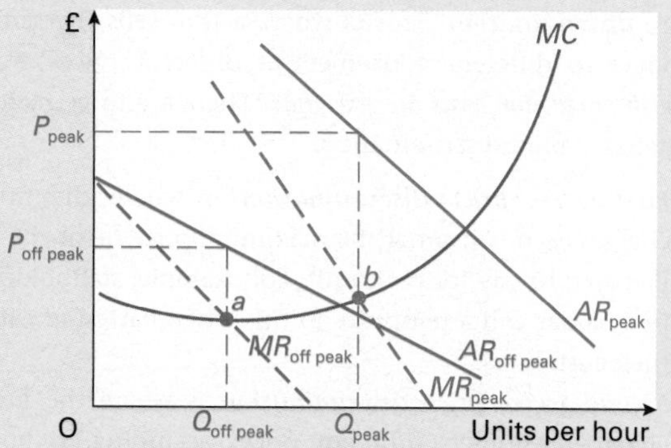

But what are the profit-maximising peak and off-peak prices? These are illustrated in the diagram, which shows units per hour (e.g. of electricity). There are two demand (*AR*) curves – peak and off peak – and their corresponding marginal revenue (*MR*) curves. Profit is maximised in either period at the output where $MR = MC$ (points *a* and *b* respectively). In the peak period, this will be at the higher price P_{peak}. There are two reasons why the price is higher. First, demand is less elastic. This is demonstrated by the fact that price is a higher percentage above *MR* in the peak period than in the off-peak period. Second, marginal cost is higher in the peak period.

?

1. ***If, over time, consumers are encouraged to switch their consumption to off-peak periods, what will happen to peak and off-peak prices?***
2. ***To what extent is peak-load pricing in the interests of consumers?***
3. ***Is total consumption likely to be higher or lower with a system of peak and off-peak prices as opposed to a uniform price at all times?***

- The firm must be able to set its price. Thus price discrimination will be impossible under perfect competition, where firms are price takers.
- The markets must be separate. Consumers in the low-priced market must not be able to resell the product in the high-priced market. For example, children must not be able to resell a half-priced child's cinema ticket for use by an adult.
- Demand elasticity must differ in each market. The firm will charge the higher price in the market where demand is less elastic, and thus less sensitive to a price rise.

KI 9 p58

Advantages to the firm

Price discrimination allows the firm to earn a higher revenue from any given level of sales. Let us examine the case of third-degree price discrimination.

Figure 7.11 represents a firm's demand curve. If it is to sell 200 units without price discrimination, it must charge a price of P_1. The total revenue it earns is shown by the green area. If, however, it can practise third-degree price discrimination by selling 150 of those 200 units at the higher price of P_2, it will gain the pink area in addition to the green area in Figure 7.11.

Explain why, if the firm can practise first-degree price *discrimination by selling every unit at the maximum price each consumer is prepared to pay, its revenue from selling 200 units will be the grey area plus the pink area in Figure 7.12.*

Definition

Peak-load pricing Price discrimination (second or third degree) where a higher price is charged in peak periods and a lower price in off-peak periods.

Figure 7.11 Third-degree price discrimination

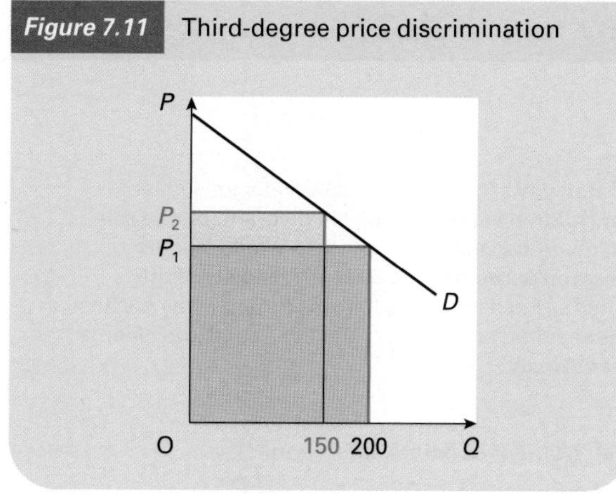

Figure 7.12 First-degree price discrimination

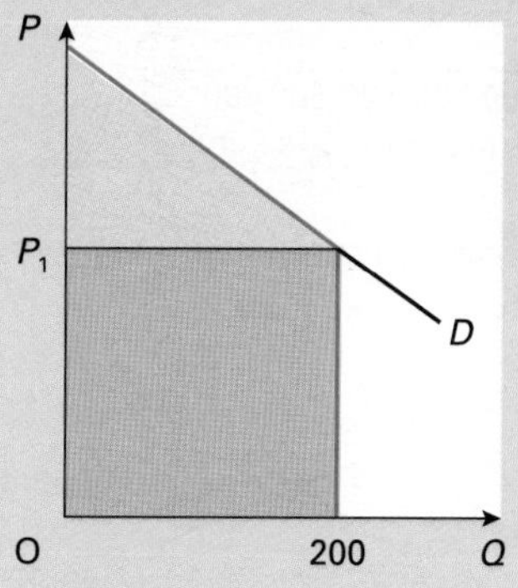

Another advantage to the firm of price discrimination is that it may be able to use it to drive competitors out of business. If a firm has a monopoly in one market (e.g. the home market), it may be able to charge a high price due to relatively inelastic demand, and thus make high profits. If it is under oligopoly in another market (e.g. the export market), it may use the high profits in the first market to subsidise a very low price in the oligopolistic market, thus forcing its competitors out of business.

Profit-maximising prices and output

Assuming that the firm wishes to maximise profits, what discriminatory prices should it charge and how much should it produce? Let us first consider the case of first-degree price discrimination.

First-degree price discrimination

Since an increase in sales does not involve lowering the price for any unit save the *extra* one sold, the extra revenue gained from the last unit (*MR*) will be its price. Thus profit is maximised at Q_1 in Figure 7.13, where $MC = MR$ (= P of the *last* unit).

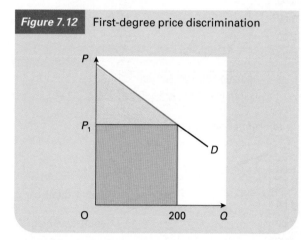

Third-degree price discrimination

Assume that a firm sells an identical product in two separate markets X and Y with demand and *MR* curves as shown in Figure 7.14.

Figure 7.13 Profit-maximising output under first-degree price discrimination

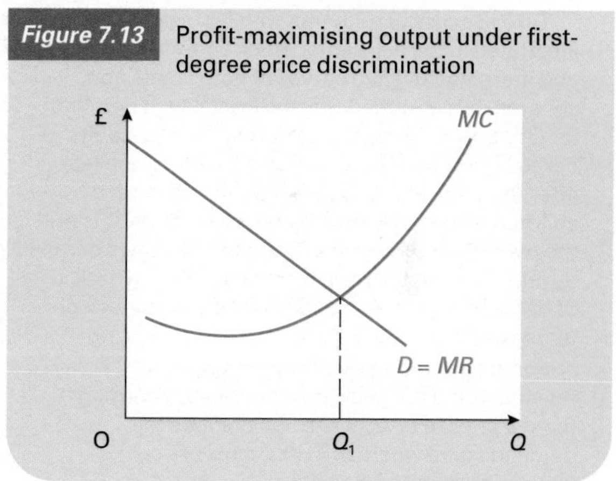

Figure 7.14 Profit-maximising output under third-degree price discrimination

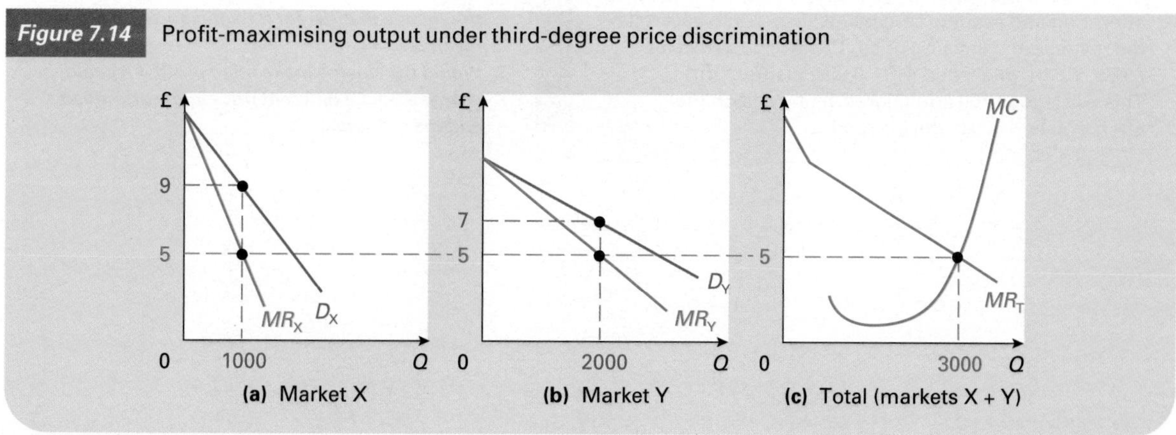

CASE STUDIES AND APPLICATIONS — BOX 7.7

JUST THE TICKET?

Price discrimination in the cinema

One of the commonest forms of price discrimination is where children are charged a lower price than adults, whether on public transport or for public entertainment. Take the case of cinema tickets. In most cinemas, children pay less than adults during the day. In the evening, however, many cinemas charge both adults and children the same price.

But why do cinemas charge children less during the day? After all, the child is seeing the same film as the adult and occupying a whole seat. In other words, there is no difference in the 'product' that they are 'consuming'. And why are children charged the higher price in the evenings, given that the seat and the film are the same as during the day?

The answer has to do with revenue maximisation and the price elasticity of demand. Once a cinema has decided to show a film, the marginal costs of an additional customer are zero. There are no additional staffing, film-hire, electricity or other costs. With marginal costs equal to zero, profits will be maximised where marginal revenue is also equal to zero: in other words, where total revenue is maximised.

Take the case of a cinema with 500 seats. This is illustrated in the diagrams, which show the demand and marginal revenue curves of both adults and children. It is assumed that the elasticity of demand for children's tickets is greater than that for adults' tickets. Diagram (a) shows demand during the late afternoon (i.e. after school). Here the demand by children is relatively high compared with adults, but the overall demand is low. Diagram (b) shows demand during the evening. Here there is a higher overall level of demand,especially by adults, many of whom work during the day.

For the afternoon screening (diagram (a)), revenue is maximised from children by charging them a price of £2.00, i.e. at the point on the demand curve where $MR = 0$. At this price, 200 child tickets will be sold.

Assuming that the same adult price is charged in both the afternoon and the evening, we need to look at the *total* demand for full-priced tickets (i.e. for both afternoon and evening screenings) in order to ascertain the revenue-maximising price. This will be a price of £3.50, where total adult $MR = 0$ (see diagram (b)). This will lead to 100 adult tickets being sold in the afternoon and 500 in the evening.

But why are reduced-price tickets not available for children in the evening? In diagram (b), the sale of low-priced tickets for children would lead to demand exceeding the 500 seat capacity of the cinema. Each time an adult was turned away because the seat had already been sold to a child, the cinema would lose.

(a) *Number of tickets (afternoon)*

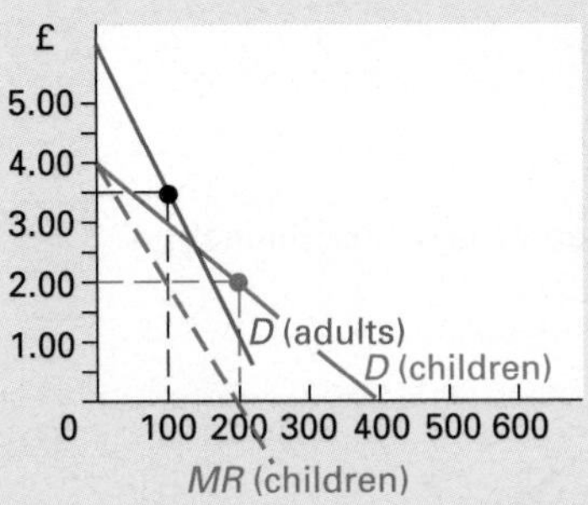

(b) *Number of tickets (evening and total)*

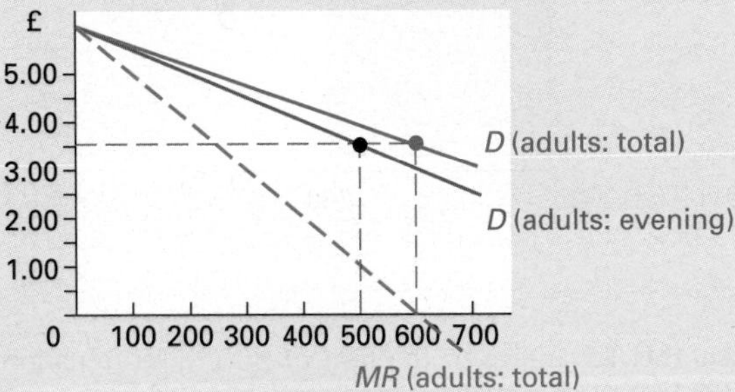

?

1. ***Which type of price discrimination is the cinema pursuing: first, second or third degree? Could it pursue either of the other two types?***
2. ***If all cinema seats could be sold to adults in the evenings at the end of the week, but only a few on Mondays and Tuesdays, what price discrimination policy would you recommend to the cinema in order for it to maximise its weekly revenue?***
3. ***Would the cinema make more profit if it could charge adults a different price in the afternoon and the evenings?***

TC 2 p10

Diagram (c) shows the MC and MR curves for the firm as a whole. This MR curve is found by adding the amounts sold in the two markets at each level of MR (in other words, the horizontal addition of the two MR curves). Thus, for example, with output of 1000 units in market X and 2000 in market Y, making 3000 in total, revenue would increase by £5 if one extra unit were sold, whether in market X or Y.

Total profit is maximised where $MC = MR$: i.e. at an output of 3000 units in total. This output must then be divided between the two markets so that MC is equal to MR in each market: i.e. $MC = MR = £5$ in each market. MR must be the same in both markets, otherwise revenue could be increased by switching output to the market with the higher MR.

TC 8 p59

The profit-maximising price in each market is given by the relevant demand curve. Thus, in market X, 1000 units will be sold at £9 each, and in market Y, 2000 units will be sold at £7 each. Note that the higher price is charged in the market with the less elastic demand curve.

?

How would profit-maximising output and price be determined under third-degree price discrimination if there were three separate markets? Draw a diagram to illustrate your answer.

*LOOKING AT THE MATHS

We can use calculus to work out the profit-maximising prices and outputs in each of the two markets X and Y in Figure 7.14. If we know the demand functions in each of the two markets, X and Y, we can derive the total revenue functions in each market (TR_X and TR_Y) and hence the two markets together ($TR = TR_X + TR_Y$). Total profit is given by:

$$T\Pi = TR_X + TR_Y - TC$$

To find the maximum-profit output in each market, we (partially) differentiate the total profit equation with respect to output in each of X and Y and set each equal to zero and solve for Q_X and Q_Y (see page A:10 for how calculus is used to find a maximum value). We can then substitute these values of Q_X and Q_Y in the respective demand functions to work out P_X and P_Y.

Maths Case 7.2 on the book's website shows how this is done by using a worked example.

Price discrimination and the public interest

No clear-cut decision can be made over the social desirability of price discrimination. Some people benefit from it; others lose. This can be illustrated by considering the effects of price discrimination on the following aspects of the market. TC 6 p26

Distribution

Those paying the higher price will probably feel that price discrimination is unfair to them. On the other hand, those charged the lower price may thereby be able to obtain a good or service they could not otherwise afford: for example, concessionary bus fares for pensioners. Price discrimination is likely to increase output and make the good or service available to more people. KI 4 p11

Competition

As explained above, a firm may use price discrimination to drive competitors out of business. This is known as ***predatory pricing***. For example, in many towns, large bus companies have used profits they make in *other* towns where they have a monopoly to subsidise their bus fares and thereby drive competitors out of business, only then to raise prices above those that the competitors had been charging. On the other hand, a firm might use the profits from its high-priced market to break into another market and withstand a possible price war. Competition is thereby increased.

Profits

Price discrimination raises a firm's profits. This could be seen as an undesirable redistribution of income in society, especially if the average price of the product is raised. On the other hand, the higher profits may be reinvested and lead to lower costs in the future.

Definition

Predatory pricing Where a firm sets its prices below average cost in order to drive competitors out of business.

Section summary

1. Price discrimination is where a firm sells the same product at different prices even though costs are the same. It can be first-degree, second-degree or third-degree price discrimination.
2. Price discrimination allows the firm to earn a higher revenue from a given level of sales.
3. Under first-degree price discrimination, the profit-maximising output is where $MC = P$. Under third-degree price discrimination, profit-maximising output is where the firm's MC is equal to the overall MR (found by adding horizontally the MR curves in each of the separate markets). This is then divided between the markets by selling that amount in each market where $MC = MR$, at a price given by the demand curve in each market.
4. Some people will gain from price discrimination; others will lose.

END OF CHAPTER QUESTIONS

1. Assume that firm X is considering four possible strategies: 1, 2, 3 and 4. Assume that firm X estimates that there are five possible responses (a, b, c, d and e) that its rivals might make to its actions. It estimates the effects on its profits in the case of each of these five responses to each of its four strategies. Its estimates are given in the following table.

Profit possibilities for firm X (£m)

		Rivals' responses				
		a	b	c	d	e
	1	30	20	80	−10	100
Alternative	2	−5	105	40	100	30
strategies	3	90	0	50	45	60
for firm X	4	30	15	10	20	25

(a) Which of the strategies (1, 2, 3 or 4) should it adopt if it is hoping to make the maximum possible profit (maximax)?

(b) Which of the strategies should it adopt if it is very cautious and decides to assume that the worst will happen (maximin)?

(c) Which of the strategies might be the best compromise between these two extreme positions? Explain.

2. Assume that a monopolistically competitive industry is in long-run equilibrium. On a diagram like Figure 7.1(b), show the effect of a fall in demand on a firm's price and profit in (a) the short run and (b) the long run.
3. In what ways is a monopolistically competitive firm likely to be less efficient than one under perfect competition?
4. Are there any shops in your area that stay open later than others? If so, are their prices similar? Why, do you think, are their prices similar/different?
5. Give three examples of oligopolistic industries. In what ways do the firms in each of these industries compete? Why do they choose to compete in the way that they do?
6. Why, under oligopoly, might a particular industry be collusive at one time and yet highly price competitive at another?
7. What is meant by the *prisoners' dilemma game* when applied to the behaviour of oligopolists? What will determine the outcome of the game?
8. Think of two examples of price discrimination. In what ways do the consumers gain or lose? What information would you need to be certain in your answer?

Additional case studies on the book's website (www.pearsoned.co.uk/sloman)

7.1 **The motor vehicle repair and servicing industry.** A case study of monopolistic competition.

7.2 **The corner shop and the hypermarket.** A case study in non-price competition: how the corner shop can survive competition from the big supermarkets.

7.3 **Curry wars.** Monopolistic competition in the take-away food market.

7.4 **Bakeries: oligopoly or monopolistic competition.** A case study on the bread industry, showing that small-scale local bakeries can exist alongside giant national bakeries.

7.5 **'Rip-off Britain'.** This examines the evidence for oligopolistic collusion in the car, supermarket and banking industries.

7.6 **Fair wars in the skies?** The effect of the entry of low-cost airlines on air fares.

7.7 **A product's life cycle.** How market conditions vary at different stages in a product's life.

7.8 **Advertising and the public interest.** Does the consumer benefit from advertising?

WEBSITES RELEVANT TO CHAPTERS 6 AND 7

Numbers and sections refer to websites listed in the Web Appendix and hotlinked from this book's website at www.pearsoned.co.uk/sloman.

- For news articles relevant to this and the previous chapter, see the *Economics News Articles* link from the book's website.
- For general news on companies and markets, see websites in section A, and particularly A2, 3, 4, 5, 8, 9, 18, 24, 25, 26, 36. See also A38, 39, 40, 43 and 44 for links to newspapers worldwide; and A41 and 42 for links to economics news articles from newspapers worldwide.
- For sites that look at competition and market power, see B2 (third link); E4, 10, 18; G7, 8. See also links in I7, 11, 14 and 17.
- For information on OPEC (Box 7.3), see site H6.
- For a site on game theory, see A40 including its home page. See also D4; C20; I17 and 4 (in the EconDirectory section).
- For a site that contains a number of open-access computer-based games on oligopoly and game theory that can be played between students, see site C24.
- For a simulation of running a farm (under perfect competition), see site D12.
- For a simulation on third-degree price discrimination, see site D3.

Chapter 8
Alternative Theories of the Firm

The traditional theories of the firm that we have been looking at in the previous three chapters assume that firms aim to maximise profits. Although this is an accurate assumption for many firms, for many it is not.

Some firms would *like* to maximise profits, but have insufficient information to enable them to do so. Others do not even want to maximise profits, if that means sacrificing achieving some other aim, such as rapid growth or increased market share.

In this chapter, we first examine some of the weaknesses of traditional theory. We then turn to look at various aims that firms might pursue as an alternative to maximum profits: aims such as maximum sales revenue or maximum growth. We also examine the implications of pursuing alternative aims for the profitability of the firm and for the prices paid by the consumer.

Many firms, especially larger ones, are complex organisations, with different individuals and departments pursuing their own agenda. What happens when these various goals come into conflict? How does conflict get resolved? What are the implications for consumers and other 'stakeholders'? We examine these issues in section 8.3.

Finally we ask how prices get determined in practice. If firms do not use marginal revenue and marginal cost concepts in setting their prices, or if they are not aiming to achieve maximum profits, how do they choose the price to charge? As we shall see, firms often base their prices on average cost.

CHAPTER MAP

8.1 PROBLEMS WITH TRADITIONAL THEORY

The traditional profit-maximising theories of the firm have been criticised for being unrealistic. The criticisms are mainly of two sorts: (a) that firms wish to maximise profits but for some reason are unable to do so; or (b) that firms have aims other than profit maximisation. Let us examine each in turn.

Difficulties in maximising profit

One criticism of traditional theory sometimes put forward is that firms do not use *MR* and *MC* concepts. This may be true, but firms could still arrive at maximum profit by trial and error adjustments of price, or by finding the output where *TR* and *TC* are furthest apart. Provided they end up maximising profits, they will be equating *MC* and *MR*, even if they do not know it! In this case, traditional models will still be useful in predicting price and output.

TC 9 p101

Lack of information

The main difficulty in trying to maximise profits is a *lack of information*.

Firms may well use accountants' cost concepts not based on opportunity cost. If it were thereby impossible to measure true profit, a firm would not be able to maximise profit except by chance.

What cost concepts are there other than those based on opportunity cost? Would the use of these concepts be likely to lead to an output greater or less than the profit-maximising one?

More importantly, firms are unlikely to know precisely (or even approximately) their demand curves and hence their *MR* curves. Even though (presumably) they will know how much they are selling at the moment, this only gives them one point on their demand curve and no point at all on their *MR* curve. In order to make even an informed guess of marginal revenue, they must have some idea of how responsive demand will be to a change in price. But how are they to estimate this price elasticity? Market research may help. But even this is frequently very unreliable.

The biggest problem in estimating the firm's demand curve is in estimating the actions and reactions of *other* firms and their effects. Collusion between oligopolists or price leadership would help, but there will still be a considerable area of uncertainty, especially if the firm faces competition from abroad or from other industries.

Game theory may help a firm decide its price and output strategy: it may choose to sacrifice the chance of getting the absolute maximum profit (the high-risk, maximax option), and instead go for the safe strategy of getting probably at least reasonable profits (maximin). But even this assumes that it knows the consequences for its profits of each of the possible reactions of its rivals. In reality, it will not even have this information to any degree of certainty, because it simply will not be able to predict just how consumers will respond to each of its rivals' alternative reactions.

Time period

Finally there is the problem of deciding the *time period* over which the firm should be seeking to maximise profits. Firms operate in a changing environment. Demand curves shift; supply curves shift. Some of these shifts occur as a result of factors outside the firm's control, such as changes in competitors' prices and products, or changes in technology. Some, however, change as a direct result of a firm's policies, such as an advertising campaign, the development of a new improved product, or the installation of new equipment. The firm is not, therefore, faced with static cost and revenue curves from which it can read off its profit-maximising price and output. Instead it is faced with a changing (and often highly unpredictable) set of curves. If it chooses a price and output that maximises profits *this* year, it may as a result jeopardise profits in the future.

Take a simple example. The firm may be considering whether to invest in new expensive equipment. If it does, its costs will rise in the short run and thus short-run profits will fall. On the other hand, if the quality of the product thereby increases, demand is likely to increase over the longer run. Also, variable costs are likely to decrease if the new equipment is more efficient. In other words, long-run profit is likely to increase, but probably by a highly uncertain amount.

Given these extreme problems in deciding profit-maximising price and output, firms may fall back on simple rules of thumb for pricing (see page 185).

Alternative aims

An even more fundamental attack on the traditional theory of the firm is that firms do not even *aim* to maximise profits (even if they could).

The traditional theory of the firm assumes that it is the *owners* of the firm who make price and output decisions. It is reasonable to assume that owners *will* want to maximise profits: this much most of the critics of the traditional theory accept. The question is, however, whether the owners do in fact make the decisions.

In ***public limited companies*** the shareholders are the owners and presumably will want the firm to maximise

Definition

Public limited company A company owned by its shareholders. Shareholders' liability is limited to the value of their shares. Shares may be bought and sold publicly – on the Stock Exchange.

CASE STUDIES AND APPLICATIONS

INSIDE THE FIRM

The organisational structure of firms

KI 21 p 207

The internal operating structure of firms is frequently governed by their size. Small firms tend to be centrally managed, with decision making operating through a clear managerial hierarchy. In large firms, however, the organisational structure tends to be more complex, although technological change is forcing many organisations to reassess the most suitable organisational structure for their business.

U-form

Medium-sized firms are often broken up into separate departments, such as marketing, finance and production. The managers of each department are normally directly responsible to a chief executive, whose function is to co-ordinate their activities, relaying the firm's overall strategy to them and being responsible for inter-departmental communication. We call this type of structure ***U (unitary) form*** (see figure (a)).

When firms expand beyond a certain size, however, a U-form structure is likely to become inefficient. This inefficiency arises from difficulties in communication, co-ordination and control. It becomes too difficult to manage the whole organisation from the centre.

M-form

To overcome these organisational problems, the firm can adopt an ***M (multi-divisional) form*** of managerial structure (see figure (b)).

This suits larger firms. The firm is divided into a number of 'divisions'. Each division could be responsible for a particular product or group of products, or a particular market (e.g. a specific country). The day-to-day running and even certain long-term decisions of each division would be the responsibility of the divisional manager(s).

(a) *U-form business organisation*

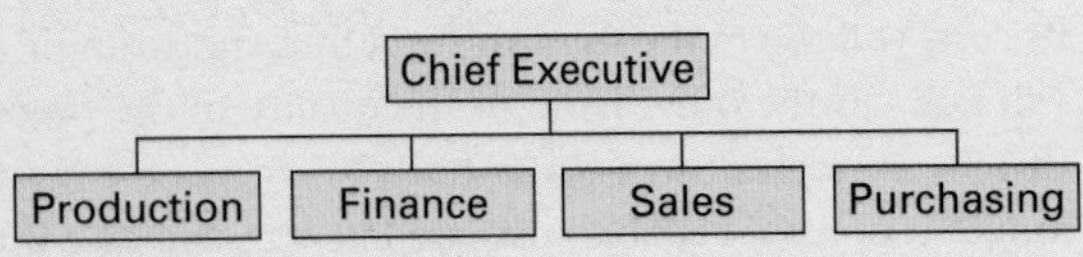

(b) *M-form business organisation*

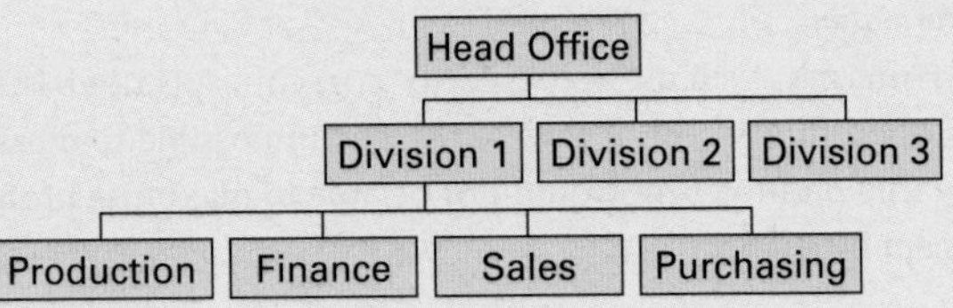

profits so as to increase their dividends and the value of their shares. Shareholders elect directors. Directors in turn employ professional managers who are often given considerable discretion in making decisions. There is therefore a *separation between the ownership and control* of a firm. (See Web Case 8.1 for an examination of the legal structure of firms.)

But what are the objectives of managers? Will *they* want to maximise profits, or will they have some other aim?

Managers may be assumed to want to *maximise their own utility*. This may well involve pursuits that conflict with profit maximisation. They may, for example, pursue higher salaries, greater power or prestige, better working conditions, greater sales, etc. Different managers in the same firm may well pursue different aims.

Managers will still have to ensure that *sufficient* profits are made to keep shareholders happy, but that may be very different from *maximising* profits.

Alternative theories of the firm to those of profit maximisation, therefore, tend to assume that large firms are ***profit satisficers***. That is, managers strive hard for a minimum target level of profit, but are less interested in profits above this level.

Such theories fall into two categories: first, those theories that assume that firms attempt to maximise some other aim, provided that sufficient profits are achieved (these are examined in section 8.2); and second, those theories that assume that firms pursue a number of potentially conflicting aims, of which sufficient profit is merely one (these are examined in section 8.3).

Definitions

U-form (unitary form) of corporate organisation Where the managers of the various departments of a firm are directly responsible to head office, normally to a chief executive.

M-form (multi-divisional form) of corporate organisation Where the firm is split into a number of separate divisions (e.g. different products or countries), with each division then split into a number of departments.

Profit satisficing Where decision makers in a firm aim for a target level of profit rather than the absolute maximum level.

BOX 8.1

There are a number of benefits:

- Reduced length of information flows.
- The chief executive being able to concentrate on overall strategic planning.
- An enhanced level of control by managers, with each division being run as a mini 'firm', each competing with other divisions for the limited amount of company resources available.

One of the major problems with M-form organisations is that they can become very bureaucratic with many layers of management. Managers might pursue goals that conflict with those of shareholders or head office (see the section on the principal–agent problem below). As a result, some companies in recent years have moved back towards simpler structures. These ***flat organisations***, as they are called, dispense with various layers of middle management. Recent technological innovations, especially in respect to computer systems such as e-mail and management information systems, have enabled senior managers to communicate easily and directly with those lower in the organisational structure.

In many respects, the flat organisation represents a return to the U-form structure. It is yet to be seen whether we also have a return to the problems associated with this type of organisation.

H-form

As many businesses have expanded their operations, often on a global scale, so further more complex forms of business organisation have evolved. One such organisation is the ***H-form*** or ***holding company***. A holding company (or parent company) is one that owns a controlling interest in other subsidiary companies. These subsidiaries, in turn, may also have controlling interests in other companies. There may thus be a complex web of interlocking holdings.

While the parent company has ultimate control over its various subsidiaries, it is likely that both tactical and strategic decision making is left to the individual companies within the organisation. Many multinationals are organised along the lines of an international holding company, where overseas subsidiaries pursue their own independent strategy.

As the organisational structures of companies and their forms of governance become more complex, so it becomes increasingly difficult to identify simple company aims. Different managers or departments may have different objectives. What predictions, then, can we make about firms' behaviour? We will examine this question throughout this chapter.

What advantages might the consumer gain from a large M- or H-form company?

Key Idea 21

The nature of institutions and organisations is likely to influence behaviour. There are various forces influencing people's decisions in complex organisations. Assumptions that an organisation will follow one simple objective (e.g. short-run profit maximisation) is thus too simplistic in many cases.

Make a list of six possible aims that a manager of a high street department store might have. Identify some conflicts that might arise between these aims.

The principal–agent problem

Can the owners of a firm ever be sure that their managers will pursue the business strategy most appropriate to achieving the owners' goals (i.e. maximisation of profit)? This is an example of what is known in economics as the ***principal–agent problem***. One of the features of a complex modern economy is that people (principals) have to employ others (agents) to carry out their wishes. If you want to go on holiday, it is easier to go to a travel agent to sort out the arrangements than to do it all yourself. Likewise, if you want to buy a house, it is more convenient to go to an estate agent. The point is that these agents have specialist knowledge and can save you, the principal, a great deal of time and effort. It is merely an example of the benefits of the specialisation and division of labour.

It is the same with firms. They employ people with specialist knowledge and skills to carry out specific tasks. Companies frequently employ consultants to give them advice or engage the services of specialist firms such as an advertising agency. It is the same with the employees of the company. They can be seen as 'agents' of their employer.

Definitions

Flat organisation Where the senior management communicate directly with those lower in the organisational structure, bypassing middle management.

H-form organisation (holding company) Where the parent company holds interests in a number of subsidiary companies.

Principal–agent problem Where people (principals), as a result of lack of knowledge, cannot ensure that their best interests are served by their agents.

CASE STUDIES AND APPLICATIONS — BOX 8.2

WHAT DO YOU MAXIMISE?

Or managers are only human too

You are a student studying economics. So what do you maximise?

Do you attempt to maximise the examination marks you will get? If so, you will probably have to spend most of each week studying. Obviously you will have to have breaks for food and sleep, and you will need some recreation, but you will probably still spend a lot more time studying than you do now!

What is more likely is that you will, in some rather vaguely defined way, try to maximise your happiness. Getting a good mark in your exams is just one element contributing to your happiness, and you will have to weigh it against the opportunity cost of studying – namely, time not spent out with friends, watching television, pursuing your hobby, etc.

To argue that managers seek to maximise profits to the exclusion of everything else is rather like arguing that you seek to maximise your exam marks. Managers' happiness (or utility) will depend on their salaries, the pleasantness of their job, their power, their respect, the friendship of their colleagues, etc.

Achieving profits may be an important aim (after all, it does contribute to a manager's utility), but the effort required to make extra profits involves an opportunity cost to the manager. For example, the manager may have to work longer hours! Managers are only human too.

?

1. ***When are increased profits in the manager's personal interest?***
2. ***Do you carefully allocate your time between study and leisure? If not, why not?***

In the case of workers, they can be seen as the agents of management. Junior managers are the agents of senior management. Senior managers are the agents of the directors, who are themselves agents of the shareholders. Thus in large firms there is often a complex chain of principal–agent relationships.

TC 9 p101 But these relationships have an inherent danger for the principal: there is ***asymmetric information*** between the two sides. The agent knows more about the situation than the principal – in fact this is part of the reason why the principal employs the agent in the first place. The danger is that the agent may well not act in the principal's best interests, and may be able to get away with it because of the principal's imperfect knowledge. The estate agent may try to convince the vendor that it is necessary to accept a lower price, while the real reason is to save the agent time, effort and expense.

In firms too, agents frequently do not act in the best interests of their principals. For example, workers may be able to get away with not working very hard, preferring instead a quiet life. Similarly, given the divorce between the ownership and control of a company, managers (agents) may pursue goals different from those of shareholders (principals). Thus *X inefficiency* is likely to occur (see Box 6.5).

The principal–agent problem. Where people (principals), as a result of a lack of knowledge, cannot ensure that their best interests are served by their agents. Agents may take advantage of this situation to the disadvantage of the principals.

So how can principals tackle the problem? There are two elements in the solution:

- The principals must have some way of *monitoring* the performance of their agents. Thus a company might employ efficiency experts to examine the operation of its management. 
- There must be *incentives* for agents to behave in the principals' interests. Thus managers' salaries could be closely linked to the firm's profitability. 

Alternative theories of the firm therefore place considerable emphasis on incentive mechanisms in explaining the behaviour of managers and the resulting performance of their companies.

In a competitive market, managers' and shareholders' interests are more likely to coincide. Managers have to ensure that the company remains efficient or it may not survive the competition and they might lose their jobs. In monopolies and oligopolies, however, where supernormal profits can often be relatively easily earned, the interests of shareholders and managers are likely to diverge. Here it will be in shareholders' interests to institute incentive mechanisms that ensure that their agents, the managers, are motivated to strive for profitability.

Survival and attitudes towards risk

Aiming for profits, sales, salaries, power, etc. will be useless if the firm does not survive! Trying to *maximise* any of the various objectives may be risky. For example, if a firm tries to maximise its market share by aggressive advertising or

Definition

Asymmetric information Where one party in an economic relationship (e.g. an agent) has more information than another (e.g. the principal).

price cutting, it might invoke a strong response from its rivals. The resulting war may drive it out of business. Concern with survival, therefore, may make firms cautious.

KI 11 p66

Not all firms, however, make survival the top priority. Some are adventurous and are prepared to take risks. Adventurous firms are most likely to be those dominated by a powerful and ambitious individual – an individual prepared to take gambles.

KI 21 p207

The more dispersed the decision-making power is in the firm, however, and the more worried managers are about their own survival, the more cautious are their policies likely to be: preferring collusion to competition, preferring to stick with products that have proved to be popular, and preferring to expand slowly and steadily. If a firm is too cautious, however, it may not after all survive. It may find that it loses markets to more aggressive competitors.

Section summary

1. There are two major types of criticism of the traditional profit-maximising theory: (a) firms may not have the information to maximise profits; (b) they may not even want to maximise profits.
2. Lack of information on demand and costs and on the actions and reactions of rivals, and a lack of use of opportunity cost concepts, may mean that firms adopt simple 'rules of thumb' for pricing.
3. In large companies, there is likely to be a divorce between ownership and control. The shareholders (the owners) may want maximum profits, but it is the managers who make the decisions and managers are likely to aim to maximise their own utility rather than that of the shareholders. This leads to profit 'satisficing'.
4. The problem of managers not pursuing the same goals as the owners is an example of the *principal–agent problem*. Agents (in this case, the managers) may not always carry out the wishes of their principals (in this case, the owners). Because of asymmetric information, managers are able to pursue their own aims, just so long as they produce results that will satisfy the owners. The solution for owners is to monitor the performance of managers, and create incentives for managers to behave in the owners' interests.
5. Some alternative theories assume that there is a single alternative aim that firms seek to maximise. Others assume that managers have a series of (possibly conflicting) aims.

8.2 ALTERNATIVE MAXIMISING THEORIES

Long-run profit maximisation

The traditional theory of the firm is based on the assumption of *short-run* profit maximisation. Many actions of firms may be seen to conflict with this aim and yet could be consistent with the aim of ***long-run profit maximisation***. For example, policies to increase the size of the firm or the firm's share of the market may involve heavy advertising or low prices to the detriment of short-run profits. But if this results in the firm becoming larger, with a bigger share of the market, the resulting economic power may enable the firm to make larger profits in the long run.

At first sight, a theory of long-run profit maximisation would seem to be a realistic alternative to the traditional short-run profit-maximisation theory. In practice, however, the theory is not a very useful predictor of firms' behaviour and is very difficult to test.

Definition

Long-run profit maximisation An alternative theory which assumes that managers aim to shift cost and revenue curves so as to maximise profits over some longer time period.

A claim by managers that they were attempting to maximise long-run profits could be an excuse for virtually any policy. When challenged as to why the firms had, say, undertaken expensive research or high-cost investment, or had engaged in a damaging price war, the managers could reply, 'Ah, yes, but in the long run it will pay off.' This is very difficult to refute (until it is too late!).

Even if long-run profit maximisation *is* the prime aim, the means of achieving it are extremely complex. The firm will need a plan of action for prices, output, investment, etc., stretching from now into the future. But today's pricing and marketing decisions affect tomorrow's demand. Therefore, future demand curves cannot be taken as given. Today's investment decisions will affect tomorrow's costs. Therefore, future cost curves cannot be taken as given either. These shifts in demand and cost curves will be very difficult to estimate with any precision. Quite apart from this, the actions of competitors, suppliers, unions and so on are difficult to predict. Thus the picture of firms making precise calculations of long-run profit-maximising prices and outputs is a false one.

It may be useful, however, simply to observe that firms, when making current price, output and investment decisions, try to judge the approximate effect on new entrants,

EXPLORING ECONOMICS BOX 8.3

WHEN IS A THEORY NOT A THEORY?

Have you heard the joke about the man sitting in a railway carriage who was throwing pieces of paper out of the window? A fellow traveller was curious and asked him why he kept doing this.

'It keeps the elephants down,' was the reply.

'But,' said the other man, 'there are no elephants around here.'

'I know,' said the first man. 'Effective, isn't it?'

Let's reformulate this joke.

Once upon a time there was this boss of a company who kept doing strange things. First he would spend a massive amount of money on advertising, and then stop. Then he would pay a huge wage increase 'to keep his workforce happy'. Then he would close the factory for two months to give everyone a break. Then he would move the business, lock, stock and barrel, to a new location.

One day he was talking to an accountant friend, who asked, 'Why do you keep doing these strange things?'

'I have to do them to make the business profitable,' was the reply.

'But your business *is* profitable,' said the accountant.

'I know. It just goes to show how effective my policies are.'

1. ***Why might it be difficult to refute a theory of long-run profit maximisation?***
2. ***If a theory cannot* in principle *be refuted, is it a useful theory?***

consumer demand, future costs, etc., and try to avoid decisions that would appear to conflict with long-run profits. Often this will simply involve avoiding making decisions (e.g. cutting price) that may stimulate an unfavourable result from rivals (e.g. rivals cutting their price).

Managerial utility maximisation

One of the most influential of the alternative theories of the firm has been that developed by O. E. Williamson[1] in the 1960s. Williamson argued that, provided satisfactory levels of profit are achieved, managers often have the discretion to choose what policies to pursue. In other words, they are free to pursue their *own* interests. And what are the managers' interests? To maximise their own utility, argued Williamson.

Williamson identified a number of factors that affect a manager's utility. The four main ones were salary, job security, dominance (including status, power and prestige) and professional excellence.

Of these only salary is *directly* measurable. The rest have to be measured indirectly. One way of doing this is to examine managers' expenditure on various items, and in particular on *staff*, on *perks* (such as a company car and a plush office) and on *discretionary investment*. The greater is the level of expenditure by managers on these items, the greater is likely to be their status, power, prestige, professional excellence and job security, and hence utility.

Having identified the factors that influence a manager's utility, Williamson developed several models in which managers seek to maximise their utility. He used these models to predict managerial behaviour under various conditions and argued that they performed better than traditional profit-maximising theory.

[1] *The Economics of Discretionary Behaviour* (Prentice Hall, 1964), p. 3.

One important conclusion was that average costs are likely to be higher when managers have the discretion to pursue their own utility. For example, perks and unnecessarily high staffing levels add to costs. On the other hand, the resulting 'slack' allows managers to rein in these costs in times of low demand (see page 220). This enables them to maintain their profit levels. To support these claims he conducted a number of case studies. These did indeed show that staff and perks were cut during recessions and expanded during booms, and that new managers were frequently able to cut staff without influencing the productivity of firms.

Sales revenue maximisation (short run)

Perhaps the most famous of all alternative theories of the firm is that developed by William Baumol in the late 1950s. This is the theory of ***sales revenue maximisation***. Unlike the theories of long-run profit maximisation and managerial utility maximisation, it is easy to identify the price and output that meet this aim – at least in the short run.

So why should managers want to maximise their firm's sales revenue? The answer is that the success of managers, and in particular sales managers, may be judged according to the level of the firm's sales. Sales figures are an obvious barometer of the firm's health. Managers' salaries, power and prestige may depend directly on sales revenue. The firm's sales representatives may be paid commission on

KI 21 p207

Definition

Sales revenue maximisation An alternative theory which assumes that managers aim to maximise the firm's short-run total revenue.

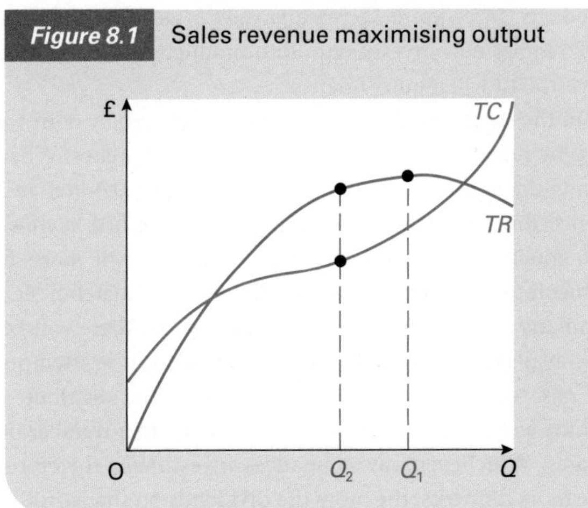

Figure 8.1 Sales revenue maximising output

their sales. Thus sales revenue maximisation may be a more dominant aim in the firm than profit maximisation, particularly if it has a dominant sales department.

Sales revenue will be maximised at the top of the *TR* curve at output Q_1 in Figure 8.1. Profits, by contrast, would be maximised at Q_2. Thus, for given total revenue and total cost curves, sales revenue maximisation will tend to lead to a higher output and a lower price than profit maximisation.

? *Draw a diagram with MC and MR curves. Mark the output (a) at which profits are maximised; (b) at which sales revenue is maximised.*

The firm will still have to make sufficient profits, however, to keep the shareholders happy. Thus firms can be seen to be operating with a profit constraint. They are *profit satisficers*.

The effect of this profit constraint is illustrated in Figure 8.2. The diagram shows a total profit ($T\Pi$) curve. (This is found by simply taking the difference between *TR* and *TC* at each output.) Assume that the minimum acceptable profit is Π (whatever the output). Any output greater than Q_3 will give a profit less than Π. Thus the sales revenue maximiser who is also a profit satisficer will produce Q_3 not Q_1. Note, however, that this output is still greater than the profit-maximising output Q_2.

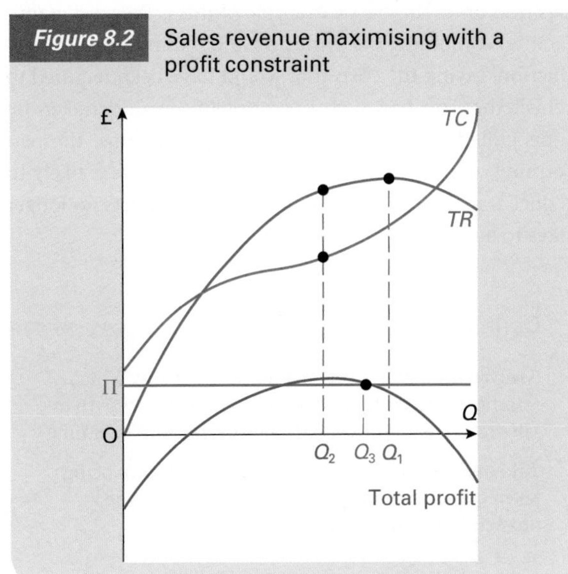

Figure 8.2 Sales revenue maximising with a profit constraint

If the firm could maximise sales revenue and still make more than the minimum acceptable profit, it would probably spend this surplus profit on advertising to increase revenue further. This would have the effect of shifting the

*LOOKING AT THE MATHS

We can express sales revenue maximisation algebraically. We start with the situation with no profit constraint.

Unconstrained sales revenue maximisation. Assume that the total revenue function is given by:

$$TR = bQ - cQ^2 \quad (1)$$

This will give a straight-line *MR* function given by:

$$MR = \frac{dTR}{dQ} = b - 2cQ$$

Total revenue is maximised where $MR = 0$, since, when total revenue is maximised, any increase in output will give a zero rise in total revenue. In other words, at the top of the total revenue curve in Figures 8.1 and 8.2, the slope of the curve is zero (the tangent to the curve is horizontal). Thus:

$$MR = b - 2cQ = 0$$

$$\text{i.e. } 2cQ = b$$

$$\text{i.e. } Q = \frac{b}{2c} \quad (2)$$

Thus, if the total revenue function were:

$$TR = 120Q - 3Q^2$$

then, from equation (2), total revenue would be maximised at an output (Q), where:

$$Q = \frac{b}{2c} = \frac{120}{2 \times 3} = 20$$

Constrained sales revenue maximisation. If there is a profit constraint, we can write the objective function as:

$$\text{Max } TR, \text{ subject to } TR - TC \geq T\Pi^*$$

where $T\Pi^*$ is the minimum profit that must be achieved. Assume that the *TR* and *TC* functions are given by:

$$TR = bQ - cQ^2$$

$$\text{and } TC = a + dQ - eQ^2 + gQ^3$$

Note that these two equations match the shapes of the *TR* and *TC* curves in Figures 8.1 and 8.2. The constraint can now be written:

$$TR - TC = -a + (b - d)Q + (e - c)Q^2 - gQ^3 \geq T\Pi^*$$

We can use this to solve for Q. An example of this is given in Maths Case 8.1 on the book's website.

TR curve upwards and also the *TC* curve (since advertising costs money).

Sales revenue maximisation will tend to involve more advertising than profit maximisation. Ideally the profit-maximising firm will advertise up to the point where the marginal revenue of advertising equals the marginal cost of advertising (assuming diminishing returns to advertising). The firm aiming to maximise sales revenue will go beyond this, since further advertising, although costing more than it earns the firm, will still add to total revenue. The firm will continue advertising until surplus profits above the minimum have been used up.

? *Since advertising increases a firm's costs, will prices necessarily be lower with sales revenue maximisation than with profit maximisation?*

Growth maximisation

Rather than aiming to maximise *short-run* revenue, managers may take a longer-term perspective and aim for ***growth maximisation*** in the size of the firm. They may directly gain utility from being part of a rapidly growing 'dynamic' organisation; promotion prospects are greater in an expanding organisation since new posts tend to be created; larger firms may pay higher salaries; managers may obtain greater power in a larger firm.

Growth is probably best measured in terms of a growth in sales revenue, since sales revenue (or 'turnover') is the simplest way of measuring the size of a business. An alternative would be to measure the capital value of a firm, but this will depend on the ups and downs of the stock market and is thus a rather unreliable method.

If a firm is to maximise growth, it needs to be clear about the time period over which it is setting itself this objective. For example, maximum growth over the next two or three years might be obtained by running factories to absolute maximum capacity, cramming in as many machines and workers as possible, and backing this up with massive advertising campaigns and price cuts. Such policies, however, may not be sustainable in the longer run. The firm may simply not be able to finance them. A longer-term perspective (say, 5–10 years) may require the firm to 'pace' itself, and perhaps to direct resources away from current production and sales into the development of new products that have a potentially high and growing long-term demand.

Growth may be achieved either by internal expansion or by merger.

Growth by internal expansion

Internal growth requires an increase in sales, which in turn requires an increase in the firm's productive capacity. In order to increase its *sales*, the firm is likely to engage in extensive product promotion and to try to launch new products. In order to increase *productive capacity*, the firm will require new investment. Both product promotion and investment will require finance.

In the short run, the firm can finance growth by borrowing, by retaining profits or by a new issue of shares. What limits the amount of finance that a firm can acquire, and hence the rate at which it can grow? If the firm *borrows* too much, the interest payments it incurs will make it difficult to maintain the level of dividends to shareholders. Similarly, if the firm *retains* too much *profit*, there will be less available to pay out in dividends. Also, if it attempts to raise capital by a *new issue of shares*, the distributed profits will have to be divided between a larger number of shares. Whichever way it finances investment, therefore, the more it invests, the more the dividends on shares in the short run will probably fall.

TC1 p8

This could lead shareholders to sell their shares, unless they are confident that *long-run* profits and hence dividends will rise again, thus causing the share price to remain high in the long run. If shareholders do sell their shares, this will cause share prices to fall. If they fall too far, the firm runs the risk of being taken over and of certain managers losing their jobs. The ***takeover constraint*** therefore requires that the growth-maximising firm distribute sufficient profits to avoid being taken over.

In the long run, a rapidly growing firm may find its profits increasing, especially if it can achieve economies of scale and a bigger share of the market. These profits can then be used to finance further growth.

Growth through vertical integration

If market conditions make growth through increased sales difficult, then a firm may choose to grow through vertical integration. This has a number of advantages.

Economies of scale. These can occur by the business performing *complementary* stages of production within a single business unit. The classic example of this is the steel manufacturer combining the furnacing and milling stages of production, saving the costs that would have been required to reheat the iron had such operations been undertaken by independent businesses. Clearly, for most firms, the performing of more than one stage on a single site is likely to reduce transport costs, as semi-finished products no longer have to be moved from one plant to another.

Definitions

Growth maximisation An alternative theory which assumes that managers seek to maximise the growth in sales revenue (or the capital value of the firm) over time.

Takeover constraint The effect that the fear of being taken over has on a firm's willingness to undertake projects that reduce distributed profits.

Reduced uncertainty. A business that is not vertically integrated may find itself subject to various uncertainties in the marketplace. Examples include uncertainty over future price movements, supply reliability or access to markets.

Barriers to entry. Vertical integration may give the firm greater power in the market by enabling it to erect entry barriers to potential competitors. For example, a firm that undertakes backward vertical integration and acquires a key input resource can effectively close the market to potential new entrants, either by simply refusing to supply a competitor, or by charging a very high price for the input, such that new firms face an absolute cost disadvantage.

See if you can identify two companies that are vertically integrated and what advantages they gain from such integration.

The major problem with vertical integration is that it may reduce the firm's ability to respond to changing market demands. A business that integrates may find itself tied to its own supply source. If, by contrast, it were free to choose between suppliers, inputs might be obtained at a lower price than the firm could achieve by supplying itself.

Many firms are finding that it is better *not* to be vertically integrated but to focus on their core business and to outsource their supplies, their marketing and many other functions. That way they put alternative suppliers and distributors in competition with each other.

Growth through diversification

An alternative internal growth strategy to vertical integration is that of diversification. A good example of a highly diversified company is Virgin. Its interests include planes, trains, cars, finance, music, mobile phones, holidays, wine, cinemas, radio, cosmetics, publishing and even space travel.

If the current market is saturated, stagnant or in decline, diversification might be the only avenue open to the business if it wishes to maintain a high growth performance. In other words, it is not only the level of profits that may be limited in the current market, but also the growth of sales.

Diversification also has the advantage of spreading risks. So long as a business produces a single product in a single market, it is vulnerable to changes in that market's conditions. If a farmer produces nothing but potatoes and the potato harvest fails, the farmer is ruined. If, however, the farmer produces a whole range of vegetable products, or even diversifies into livestock, then he or she is less subject to the forces of nature and the unpredictability of the market.

Growth by merger

A merger may be the result of the mutual agreement of two firms to come together. Alternatively, one firm may put in a takeover bid for another. This involves the first firm offering to buy the shares of the second for cash, to swap them for shares in the acquiring company, or to issue fixed-interest securities (debentures). The shareholders of the second firm then vote on whether to accept the offer. (Technically this is an 'acquisition' or 'takeover' rather than a merger, but the term 'merger' is generally used to include both mutual agreements and acquisitions.)

There are three types of merger:

- A ***horizontal merger*** is where firms in the same industry and at the same stage of production merge: e.g. two car manufacturers.
- A ***vertical merger*** is where firms in the same industry but at different stages in the production of a good merge: e.g. a car manufacturer with a car component parts producer.
- A ***conglomerate merger*** is where firms in different industries merge: e.g. when British Aerospace acquired Austin Rover.

Motives for merger

But why do firms want to take over others? Economists have identified a number of possible motives.

Merger for growth. Mergers provide a much quicker means to growth than does internal expansion. Not only does the firm acquire new capacity, it also acquires additional consumer demand. There is a danger for growth-maximising firms, however, from being taken over themselves. If they are growing rapidly and yet have a relatively low profit and a low stock market value, they will be attractive to predators.

Merger for economies of scale. Once the merger has taken place, the constituent parts can be reorganised through a process of 'rationalisation'. The result can be a reduction in costs. For example, only one head office will now be needed. Reduced costs are a way of increasing profits and thereby of increasing the rate of growth.

In fact the evidence suggests that most mergers result in few if any cost savings: either potential economies of scale are not exploited due to a lack of rationalisation, or diseconomies result from the disruptions of reorganisation. New managers installed by the parent company are often seen as unsympathetic, and morale may go down.

Definitions

Horizontal merger Where two firms in the same industry at the same stage in the production process merge.

Vertical merger Where two firms in the same industry at different stages in the production process merge.

Conglomerate merger Where two firms in different industries merge.

Merger for monopoly power. Here the motive is to reduce competition and thereby gain greater market power and larger profits. With less competition, the firm will face a less elastic demand and will be able to charge a higher percentage above marginal cost. This obviously fits well with the traditional theory of the firm.

Which of the three types of merger (horizontal, vertical and conglomerate) are most likely to lead to (a) reductions in average costs; (b) increased market power?

Merger for increased market valuation. A merger can benefit shareholders of *both* firms by leading to a potential increase in the stock market valuation of the merged firm. If both sets of shareholders believe that they will make a capital gain, then they are more likely to give the go-ahead to the merger.

In practice, however, there is little evidence to suggest that mergers lead to a capital gain. One possible reason for this is the increases in costs referred to above. In fact, a survey by *BusinessWeek* in 2002 showed that 61 per cent of mergers undertaken in the USA during the merger boom in spring 1998 actually *reduced* shareholder value.

Merger to reduce uncertainty. There are two major sources of uncertainty for firms. The first is the behaviour of rivals. Mergers, by reducing the number of rivals, can correspondingly reduce uncertainty. At the same time they can reduce the costs of competition (e.g. by reducing advertising). The second source of uncertainty is the economic environment. In a period of rapid change, such as often accompanies a boom, firms may seek to protect themselves by merging with others.

Merger due to opportunity. Sometimes mergers occur simply as a consequence of opportunities that suddenly and unexpectedly arise. Such mergers are largely unplanned and thus virtually impossible to predict. Dynamic business organisations are constantly on the lookout for such opportunities.

Other motives. Other motives for mergers include:

- Getting bigger so as to become less likely to be taken over oneself.
- Merging with another firm to prevent it being taken over by an unwanted predator (the 'White Knight' strategy).
- Asset stripping. This is where a firm buys another and then breaks it up, selling off the profitable bits and probably closing down the remainder.
- Empire building. This is where owners or managers like the power or prestige of owning or controlling several (preferably well-known) companies.
- Broadening the geographical base of the company by merging with a firm in a different part of the country or the world.

Most of these theories are in need of greater empirical investigation and support.

1. *Which of the above theories overlap and in what way?*
2. *Why, do you think, is it difficult to find adequate empirical support for any of them?*

Mergers and the relationship between growth and profit

In order for a firm to be successful in a takeover bid, it must be sufficiently profitable to finance the takeover. Thus the faster it tries to grow and the more takeovers it attempts, the higher must be its profitability.

In addition to being an obvious means to the growth of the firm, mergers may be a means of increasing profits, since mergers can lead to both lower average costs through economies of scale and higher average revenue through increased market power over prices. These profits in turn may be seen as a means of financing further growth.

It can therefore be seen that, whichever way it is financed, growth is closely linked to profits. High profits can help a firm grow. Rapid growth can lead to a rapid growth in profits.

These are not inevitable links, however. For example, long-run profits may not increase if a firm, as part of its growth policy, invests in risky projects or projects with a low rate of return. Expansion alone is no guarantee of profits. Also, high profits will not necessarily lead to growth if a large proportion is distributed to shareholders and only a small proportion is reinvested. High profits may help growth, but they do not guarantee it.

Growth through strategic alliances

One means of achieving growth is through the formation of ***strategic alliances*** with other firms. They are a means whereby business operations can be expanded relatively quickly and at relatively low cost, and are a common way in which firms can deepen their involvement in global markets.

There are many types of strategic alliance between businesses, covering a wide range of alternative collaborative arrangements.

Joint ventures. A ***joint venture*** is where two or more firms decide to create, and jointly own, a new independent

Definitions

Strategic alliance Where two firms work together, formally or informally, to achieve a mutually desirable goal.

Joint venture Where two or more firms set up and jointly own a new independent firm.

organisation. The creation of Cellnet by BT and Securicor is an example of such a strategy.

Consortia. In recent years, many consortia have been created. Camelot, the company that runs the UK National Lottery, and Trans Manche Link, the company that built the Channel Tunnel, are two examples. A ***consortium*** is usually created for very specific projects, such as a large civil engineering work. As such they have a very focused objective, and once the project is completed, the consortium is usually dissolved.

Franchising. A less formal strategic alliance is where a business agrees to ***franchise*** its operations to third parties. McDonald's and Coca-Cola are good examples of businesses that use a franchise network. In such a relationship,

CASE STUDIES AND APPLICATIONS ***BOX 8.4***

ENRON

A cautionary tale of business growth

Not many companies come bigger than Enron, and none bigger has ever filed for bankruptcy, as Enron did on 1 December 2001.

Enron seemed to have everything going for it, being the largest energy trader in the USA with 25 per cent of the market. In 2000, Enron earned $100 billion in revenue and turned a profit of $1 billion. But by the time it filed for bankruptcy, the seventh largest company in the USA had seen its market value collapse from $80 billion to less than $400 million. Its shares fell from a high of $89.50 in the previous year to a meagre 26 cents. How did it all go so wrong so quickly?

Enron was created in 1986, following the merger of two gas pipeline companies, Houston Natural Gas and InterNorth. As US energy and utility markets were deregulated, Enron diversified rapidly into alternative sources of energy supply such as electricity, and established interests in areas such as water. This diversification in Enron's interests was not restricted to the US market. Enron embarked upon a global growth strategy, which involved it acquiring interests in utilities throughout the world.

As Enron grew, it also shifted its business focus. It gradually reduced its role in gas and oil production, its traditional core business activities, and moved into the new world of online energy trading. This appeared to have been a wise move, as by November 1999 it had traded more than $1 trillion of electricity and gas online. Enron was, at this time, the largest business on the Internet. So what went wrong?

The weakness in Enron's growth strategy lay in both the speed of its expansion and, most crucially, in how its growth was financed. On declaring bankruptcy in December 2001, the scale of Enron's debts was revealed to be both massive and global. Creditors were estimated to be owed some $18.7 billion.

Clearly, Enron had financed an overwhelming part of its growth through borrowing. As a source of finance for business growth, this only becomes a problem if revenue begins to fall and you are unable to meet the payments on the money owed. Given the public picture presented by Enron, and its apparent success, revenue and profits seemed to be guaranteed. The business was a clear winner. Such a picture would certainly have helped Enron to attract significant amounts of capital to fund its expansion plans.

However, everything was not as it seemed. Enron's financial position was precarious. In October 2001, Enron announced unexpected losses, which led it to reduce capital by $1.2 billion. A series of bad investments overseas were held to be the main reason for this decision. The announcement of losses was swiftly followed by the revelation that Enron was to be investigated by the US Securities and Exchange Commission for financial irregularities. It was subsequently revealed that through some accounting loophole Enron had been overstating its earnings since 1997 to the value of some $600 million. Predictably many of Enron's trading partners had by this stage begun to lose confidence in the business and started to pull out of deals.

At this point Dynegy, one of Enron's smaller rivals, agreed to buy the company for $9 billion in stock. However, as more losses were disclosed, and the need to get regulatory approval for the acquisition was established, Dynegy pulled out of the deal. Shareholder confidence had by this point totally collapsed and Enron's credit rating plummeted.

Enron's rise and fall reveals a tale of unsustainable growth and expansion that was bought on debt. It reveals not only the folly of such a strategy, but the need to have a strong system of financial regulation to ensure that a business's true financial position is reflected in its balance sheet.

1. ***Why might a business favour borrowing, as a means of financing growth, over other sources of finance?***
2. ***What are the strengths and weaknesses of diversification as a business growth strategy?***

Definitions

Consortium Where two or more firms work together on a specific project and create a separate company to run the project.

Franchise A formal agreement whereby a company uses another company to produce or sell some or all of its product.

CASE STUDIES AND APPLICATIONS

MERGER ACTIVITY

A worldwide perspective

What have been the trends, patterns and driving factors in mergers and acquisitions[2] (M&A) around the world over the past ten years? An overview is given in figure (a). The 1990s saw a rapid growth in M&A as the world economy boomed. Then with a slowing down in economic growth after 2000, M&A activity declined, both in value and in the number of deals.

The 1990s

The early 1990s saw relatively low M&A activity as the world was in recession, but as world economic growth picked up, so worldwide M&A activity increased. Economic growth was particularly rapid in the USA, which became the major target for acquisitions.

There was also an acceleration in the process of 'globalisation'. With the dismantling of trade barriers around the world and increasing financial deregulation, international competition increased. Companies felt the need to become bigger in order to compete more effectively.

In Europe, M&A activity was boosted by the development of the Single Market, which came into being in January 1993. Companies took advantage of the abolition of trade barriers in the EU, which made it easier for them to operate on an EU-wide basis. As 1999 approached, and with it the arrival of the euro, so European merger activity reached fever pitch, stimulated also by the strong economic growth experienced throughout the EU.

By the end of the 1990s, annual worldwide M&A activity was three times the level of the beginning of the decade. At this time there were some very large mergers indeed. These included a €29.4 billion marriage of pharmaceutical companies Zeneca of the UK and Astra of Sweden in 1998, a €205 billion takeover of telecoms giant Mannesmann of Germany by Vodafone of the UK in 1999 and a €50.8 billion takeover of Orange of the UK by France Telecom in 2000.

Other sectors in which merger activity was rife included financial services and the privatised utilities sector. In the UK, in particular, most of the privatised water and electricity companies were taken over, with buyers attracted by the sector's monopoly profits. French and US buyers were prominent.

The early 2000s

Then, with a worldwide economic slowdown after 2000, there was a fall in both the number and value of mergers throughout most of the world. What is more, the worldwide pattern of M&A activity was changing. Increasingly, both European and US companies were

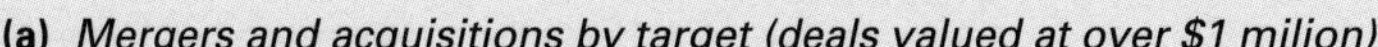

(a) *Mergers and acquisitions by target (deals valued at over $1 milion)*

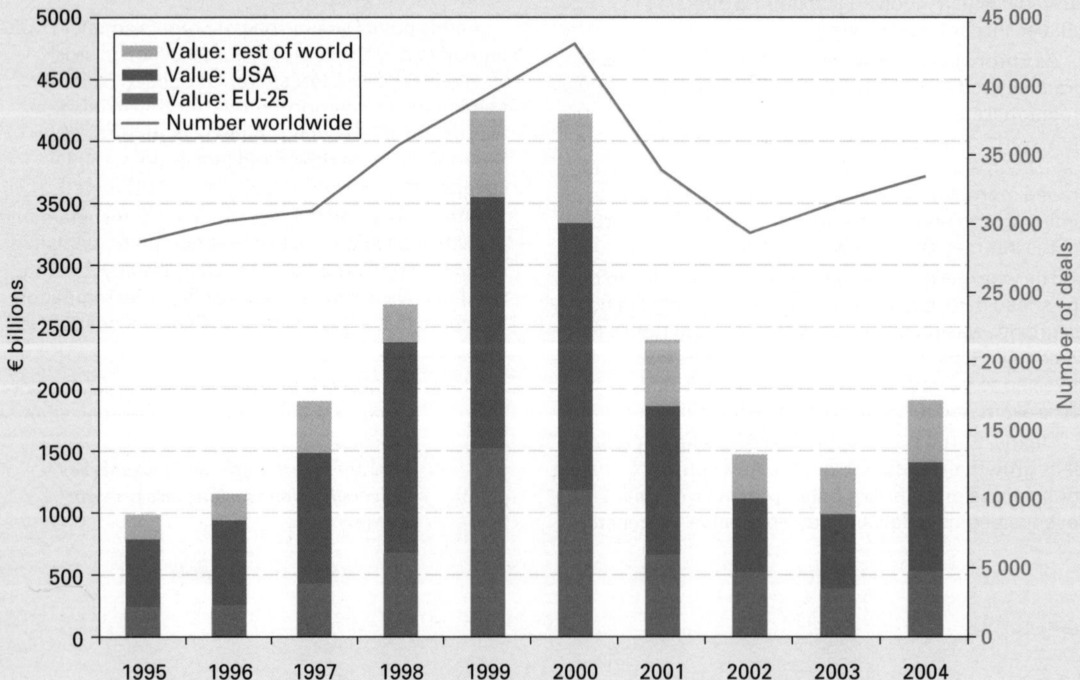

Source: *Mergers & Acquisitions Note* (European Commission, DG ECFIN, June 2005).

BOX 8.5

looking to other parts of the world to expand their activities. This is illustrated in figure (b).

The two major target regions have been (a) the rest of Europe, especially the ten countries joining the EU in 2004 plus Russia, and (b) Asian countries, especially India and China. These new markets have the twin attractions of rapidly growing demand and low costs, including cheap skilled labour and low tax rates.

Companies from the EU-15 countries have focused especially on the rest of Europe, taking a 65 per cent share of inward M&A between 2000 and 2003. By contrast, the EU-15 countries had only a 17 per cent share of inward M&A in Asia, compared with a 29 per cent share taken by North America and a 47 per cent share by Asia itself.

The small share of inward investment in Asia by EU companies is worrying for EU ministers, given that China and India are the world's two fastest-growing markets. Those companies which have already invested in these countries are likely to have gained a 'first-mover' advantage through establishing sources of supply and building relationships.

Types of M&A activity

Many M&A deals are 'hostile'. In other words, the company being taken over does not want to be. The deals are often concluded after prolonged boardroom battles, with bosses of the acquiring company seeking opportunities to build empires, and bosses of the target company attempting all sorts of manoeuvres to avoid being taken over. This may involve them seeking deals with alternative, more 'friendly' companies. Generally companies are increasingly using the services of investment banks to help them in the process of making or warding off deals.

Despite the growing number of horizontal mergers, there has also been a tendency for companies to become more focused, by selling off parts of their business that are not seen as 'core activities'. For example, Volvo, after unsuccessfully attempting to merge with Renault in 1993, subsequently divested itself of several companies that it owned in a variety of industries, ranging from banking and finance to food, matches and pharmaceuticals.

This trend of horizontal mergers and conglomerate and vertical de-mergers has allowed companies to increase their market power in those specific sectors where they have expertise. Consumers may gain from lower costs, but the motives of the companies are largely to gain increased market power – something of dubious benefit to consumers.

Are the motives for merger likely to be different in a recession from in a period of rapid economic growth?

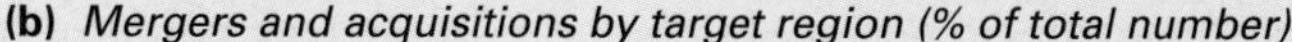

[2] By 'acquisitions' we mean takeovers or the acquiring of at least 5 per cent of a company's shares.

(b) *Mergers and acquisitions by target region (% of total number)*

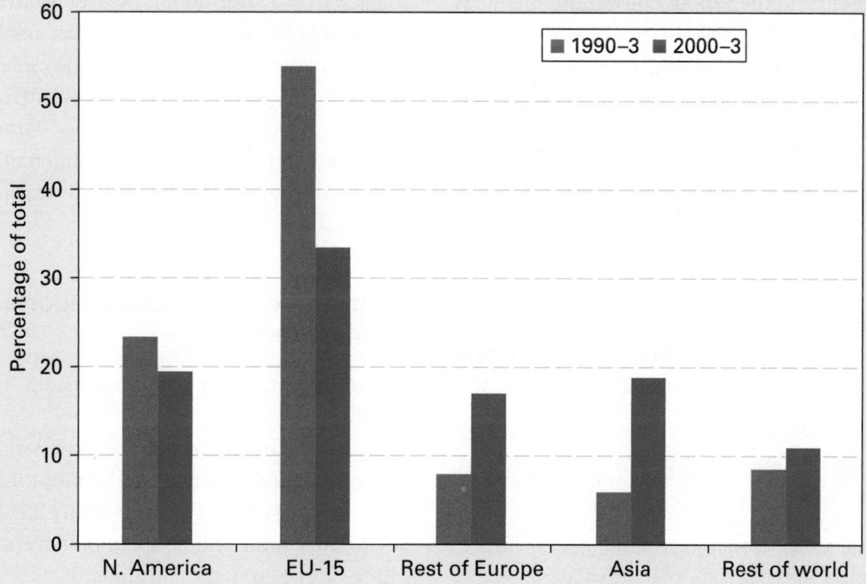

Source: *Mergers & Acquisitions Note* (European Commission, DG ECFIN, October 2004).

the franchisee is responsible for manufacturing and/or selling, and the franchiser retains responsibility for branding and marketing.

Subcontracting. Like franchising, ***subcontracting*** is a less formal source of strategic alliance, where companies maintain their independence. When a business subcontracts, it employs an independent business to manufacture or supply some service rather conduct the activity itself. Car manufacturers are major subcontractors. Given the multitude and complexity of components that are required to manufacture a car, the use of subcontractors to supply specialist items, such as brakes and lights, seems a logical way to organise the business.

Networks. ***Networks*** are less formal than any of the above alliances. A network is where two or more businesses work collaboratively but without any formal relationship binding one to the other. Such a form of collaboration is highly prevalent in Japan. Rather than a formal contract regulating the behaviour of the partners to the agreement, their relationship is based upon an understanding of trust and loyalty.

Why form strategic alliances?

As a business expands, possibly internationally, it may well be advantageous to join with an existing player in the market. Such a business would have local knowledge and an established network of suppliers and distributors.

In addition, strategic alliances allow firms to share risk. The Channel Tunnel and the consortium of firms that built it is one such example. The construction of the Channel Tunnel was a massive undertaking and far too risky for any single firm to embark upon. With the creation of a consortium, risk was spread and the various consortium members were able to specialise in their areas of expertise.

They also allow firms to pool capital. Projects that might have prohibitively high start-up costs, or running costs, may become feasible if firms co-operate and pool their capital. In addition, an alliance of firms, with their combined assets and credibility, may find it easier to generate finance, whether from investors in the stock market or from the banking sector.

The past 20 years have seen a flourishing of strategic alliances. They have become a key growth strategy for business both domestically and internationally. They are seen as a way of expanding business operations quickly without the difficulties associated with the more aggressive approach of acquisition or the more lengthy process of merger.

> **Definitions**
>
> **Subcontracting** Where a firm employs another firm to produce part of its output or some of its input(s).
>
> **Network** An informal arrangement between businesses to work together towards some common goal.

Growth through going global

In many respects, a firm's global strategy is simply an extension of its strategy within its own domestic market. However, opening up to global markets can provide an obvious means for a business to expand its markets and spread its risks. It is also a means of reducing costs, whether through economies of scale or from accessing cheap sources of supply or low-wage production facilities.

A firm's global growth strategy may involve simply exporting or opening up factories abroad, or it may involve merging with businesses abroad or forming strategic alliances. As barriers to trade and the international flow of capital have come down, so more and more businesses have sought to become multinational. The result is that the global business environment has tended to become more and more competitive.

Equilibrium for a growth-maximising firm

What will a growth-maximising firm's price and output be? Unfortunately there is no simple formula for predicting this.

In the short run, the firm may choose the profit-maximising price and output – so as to provide the greatest funds for investment. On the other hand, it may be prepared to sacrifice some short-term profits in order to mount an advertising campaign. It all depends on the strategy it considers most suitable to achieve growth.

In the long run, prediction is more difficult still. The policies that a firm adopts will depend crucially on the assessments of market opportunities made by managers. But this involves judgement, not fine calculation. Different managers will judge a situation differently.

One prediction can be made. Growth-maximising firms are likely to diversify into different products, especially as they approach the limits to expansion in existing markets.

Alternative maximising theories and the public interest

It is difficult to draw firm conclusions about the public interest.

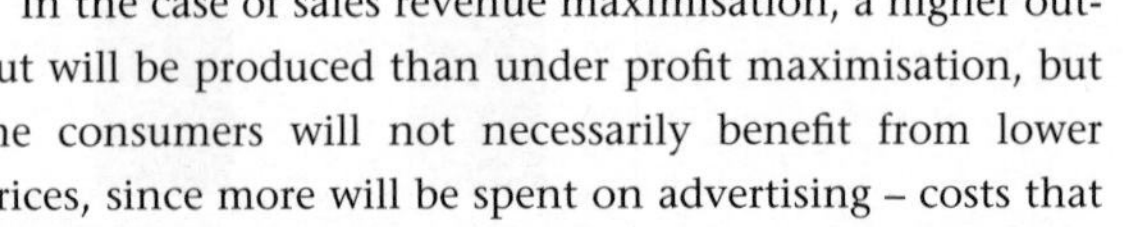

In the case of sales revenue maximisation, a higher output will be produced than under profit maximisation, but the consumers will not necessarily benefit from lower prices, since more will be spent on advertising – costs that will be passed on to the consumer.

In the case of growth and long-run profit maximisation, there are many possible policies that a firm could pursue. To the extent that a concern for the long run encourages firms to look to improved products, new products and new techniques, the consumer may benefit from such a concern. To the extent, however, that growth encourages a greater level of industrial concentration through merger, the consumer may lose from the resulting greater level of monopoly power.

KI 19 p157

As with the traditional theory of the firm, the degree of competition a firm faces is a crucial factor in determining just how responsive it will be to the wishes of the consumer.

? *How will competition between growth-maximising firms benefit the consumer?*

Section summary

1. Rather than seeking to maximise short-run profits, a firm may take a longer-term perspective. It is very difficult, however, to predict the behaviour of a long-run profit-maximising firm, since (a) different managers are likely to make different judgements about how to achieve maximum profits and (b) demand and cost curves may shift unpredictably both in response to the firm's own policies and as a result of external factors.
2. Managers may seek to maximise their own utility, which, in turn, will depend on factors such as salary, job security, power within the organisation and the achieving of professional excellence. Given, however, that managerial utility depends on a range of variables, it is difficult to use the theory to make general predictions of firms' behaviour.
3. Managers may gain utility from maximising sales revenue. They will still have to ensure that a satisfactory level of profit is achieved, however. The output of a firm which seeks to maximise sales revenue will be higher than that for a profit-maximising firm. Its level of advertising will also tend to be higher. Whether price will be higher or lower depends on the relative effects on demand and cost of the additional advertising.
4. Many managers aim for maximum growth of their organisation, believing that this will help their salaries, power, prestige, etc.
5. Growth may be by internal expansion. This can be financed by ploughing back profits, by share issue or by borrowing. Whichever method a firm uses, it will require sufficient profits, if it is to avoid becoming vulnerable to a takeover.
6. Vertical integration can reduce a firm's costs through various economies of scale. It can also help to reduce uncertainty, as the vertically integrated business can hopefully secure supply routes and/or retail outlets.
7. Growth may be by merger. Mergers can be horizontal, vertical or conglomerate. Merger activity tends to occur in waves. Various motives have been suggested for mergers, including growth, economies of scale, market power, increased share values, reduction in uncertainty, and simply taking advantage of opportunities as they occur.
8. One means of achieving growth is through the formation of strategic alliances with other firms. They have the advantage of allowing easier access to new markets, risk sharing and capital pooling.
9. Most firms' growth strategy includes expansion abroad.
10. As with long-run profit-maximising theories, it is difficult to predict the price and output strategies of a growth-maximising firm. Much depends on the judgements of particular managers about growth opportunities.
11. Alternative aims will benefit the consumer to the extent that they encourage firms to develop new products and to find more efficient methods of production. They may be against the consumer's interest to the extent that they lead firms to engage in extensive advertising or to merge with a resulting increased concentration of market power.

8.3 MULTIPLE AIMS

KI 21 p 207

Satisficing and the setting of targets

Large firms are often complex institutions with several departments (sales, production, design, purchasing, personnel, finance, etc.). Each department is likely to have its own specific set of aims and objectives, which may come into conflict with those of other departments. These aims in turn will be constrained by the interests of shareholders, workers, customers and creditors (collectively known as ***stakeholders***), who will need to be kept sufficiently happy.

Definition

Stakeholders (in a company) People who are affected by a company's activities and/or performance (customers, employees, owners, creditors, people living in the neighbourhood, etc.). They may or may not be in a position to take decisions, or influence decision taking, in the firm.

CASE STUDIES AND APPLICATIONS — BOX 8.6

STAKEHOLDER POWER?

Who governs the firm?

The concept of the 'stakeholder economy' became fashionable in the late 1990s. Rather than the economy being governed by big business, and rather than businesses being governed in the interests of shareholders (many of whom are big institutions, such as insurance companies and pension funds), the economy should serve the interests of everyone. But what does this mean for the governance of firms?

KI 21 p 207

The stakeholders of a firm include customers, employees (from senior managers to the lowest-paid workers), shareholders, suppliers, lenders and the local and national communities.

The supporters of a stakeholding economy argue that *all* these interest groups ought to have a say in the decisions of the firm. Trade unions or workers' councils ought to be included in decisions affecting the workforce, or indeed all company decisions. They could be represented on decision-making bodies and perhaps have seats on the board of directors. Alternatively, the workforce might be given the power to elect managers.

Banks or other institutions lending to firms ought to be included in investment decisions. In Germany, where banks finance a large proportion of investment, banks are represented on the boards of most large companies.

Local communities ought to have a say in any projects (such as new buildings or the discharge of effluent) that affect the local environment. Customers ought to have more say in the quality of products being produced: for example, by being given legal protection against the production of shoddy or unsafe goods. Where interest groups cannot be directly represented in decision making, companies ought to be regulated by the government in order to protect the interests of the various groups. For example, if farmers and other suppliers to supermarkets are paid very low prices, then the purchasing behaviour of the supermarkets could be regulated by some government agency.

But is this vision of a stakeholder economy likely to become reality? Trends in the international economy suggest that the opposite might be occurring. The growth of multinational corporations, with their ability to move finance and production to wherever it is most profitable, has weakened the power of employees, local interest groups and even national governments.

Employees in one part of the multinational may have little in the way of common interests with employees in another. In fact, they may vie with each other: for example, over which plant should be expanded or closed down. What is more, many firms are employing a larger and larger proportion of casual, part-time, temporary or agency workers. With these new 'flexible labour markets', such employees have far less say in the company than permanent members of staff: they are 'outsiders' to decision making within the firm (see Box 9.8).

Also, the widespread introduction of share incentive schemes for managers (whereby managers are rewarded with shares) has increasingly made profits their driving goal. Finally, the policies of opening up markets and deregulation – policies that have been adopted by many governments round the world in recent years – have again weakened the power of many stakeholders.

Nevertheless, many firms in recent years have put greater emphasis on 'corporate social responsibility' (CSR), seeing it as important to have an ethical dimension to their business practices. Whether this is a genuine commitment to the interests of society, or simply an attempt to win a larger market by gaining a good public image, clearly varies from firm to firm. CSR and business ethics are explored in Web Case 8.3.

Are customers' interests best served by profit-maximising firms, answerable primarily to shareholders, or by firms where various stakeholder groups are represented in decision taking?

In many firms, targets will be set for production, sales, profit, stockholding, etc. If, in practice, target levels are not achieved, a 'search' procedure will be started to find what went wrong and how to rectify it. If the problem cannot be rectified, managers will probably adjust the target downwards. If, on the other hand, targets are easily achieved, managers may adjust them upwards. Thus the targets to which managers aspire depend to a large extent on the success in achieving *previous* targets. Targets are also influenced by expectations of demand and costs, by the achievements of competitors and by expectations of competitors' future behaviour. For example, if it is expected that the economy is likely to move into recession, sales and profit targets may be adjusted downwards.

TC 9 p 101

If targets conflict, the conflict will be settled by a bargaining process between managers. The outcome of the bargaining, however, will depend on the power and ability of the individual managers concerned. Thus a similar set of conflicting targets may be resolved differently in different firms.

Organisational slack

Since changing targets often involves search procedures and bargaining processes and is therefore time consuming, and since many managers prefer to avoid conflict, targets tend to be changed fairly infrequently. Business conditions, however, often change rapidly. To avoid the need to change targets, therefore, managers will tend to be fairly conservative in their aspirations. This leads to the phenomenon known as ***organisational slack***.

When the firm does better than planned, it will allow slack to develop. This slack can then be taken up if the firm does worse than planned. For example, if the firm produces more than it planned, it will build stocks of finished goods and draw on them if subsequently production falls. It would not, in the meantime, increase its sales target or reduce its production target. If it did, and production then fell below target, the production department might not be able to supply the sales department with its full requirement.

Thus keeping targets fairly low and allowing slack to develop allows all targets to be met with minimum conflict.

Organisational slack, however, adds to a firm's costs. If firms are operating in a competitive environment, they may be forced to cut slack in order to survive. In the 1970s, many Japanese firms succeeded in cutting slack by using ***just-in-time*** methods of production. These involve keeping stocks to a minimum and ensuring that inputs are delivered as required. Clearly, this requires that production is tightly controlled and that suppliers are reliable. Many firms today have successfully cut their warehouse costs by using such methods. These methods are examined in Box 9.8.

Multiple goals: some predictions of behaviour

Conservatism

Some firms may be wary of unnecessary change. Change is risky. They may prefer to stick with tried and tested practices. 'If it works, stick with it.' This could apply to pricing policies, marketing techniques, product design and range, internal organisation of the firm, etc.

If something does not work, managers will probably change it, but again they may be conservative and only try a cautious change: perhaps imitating successful competitors.

This safe, satisficing approach makes prediction of any given firm's behaviour relatively easy. You simply examine its past behaviour. Making generalisations about all such cautious firms, however, is more difficult. Different firms are likely to have established different rules of behaviour depending on their own particular experiences of their market.

Comparison with other firms

Managers may judge their success by comparing their firm's performance with that of rival firms. For example, growing market share may be seen as a more important indicator of 'success' than simple growth in sales. Similarly, they may compare their profits, their product design, their technology or their industrial relations with those of rivals. To many managers it is *relative* performance that matters, rather than absolute performance.

What predictions can be made if this is how managers behave? The answer is that it depends on the nature of competition in the industry. The more profitable, innovative and efficient are the competitors, the more profitable, innovative and efficient will managers try to make their particular firm.

The further ahead of their rivals that firms try to stay, the more likely it is that there will be a 'snowballing' effect, with each firm trying to outdo the other.

? *Will this type of behaviour tend to lead to profit maximisation?*

Satisficing and the public interest

Firms with multiple goals will be satisficers. The greater the number of goals of the different managers, the greater is the chance of conflict, and the more likely it is that organisational slack will develop. Satisficing firms are therefore likely to be less responsive to changes in consumer demand and changes in costs than profit-maximising firms. They may thus be less efficient.

On the other hand, such firms may be less eager to exploit their economic power by charging high prices, or to use aggressive advertising, or to pay low wages.

The extent to which satisficing firms do act in the public interest will, as in the case of other types of firm, depend to a large extent on the amount and type of competition they face, and their attitudes towards this competition. Firms that compare their performance with that of their rivals are more likely to be responsive to consumer wishes than firms that prefer to stick to well-established practices. On the other hand, they may be more concerned to 'manipulate' consumer tastes than the more traditional firm.

? *Are satisficing firms more likely to suffer from X inefficiency (see Box 6.5) than firms which seek to maximise profit or sales revenue?*

Definitions

Organisational slack Where managers allow spare capacity to exist, thereby enabling them to respond more easily to changed circumstances.

Just-in-time methods Where a firm purchases supplies and produces both components and finished products as they are required. This minimises stock holding and its associated costs.

Section summary

1. In large firms, decisions are taken by or influenced by a number of different people, including various managers, shareholders, workers, customers, suppliers and creditors. If these different people have different aims, a conflict between them is likely to arise. A firm cannot maximise more than one of these conflicting aims. The alternative is to seek to achieve a satisfactory target level of a number of aims.
2. If targets were easily achieved last year, they are likely to be made more ambitious next year. If they were not achieved, a search procedure will be conducted to identify how to rectify the problem. This may mean adjusting targets downwards, in which case there will be some form of bargaining process between managers.
3. Life is made easier for managers if conflict can be avoided. This will be possible if slack is allowed to develop in various parts of the firm. If targets are not being met, the slack can then be taken up without requiring adjustments in other targets.
4. Satisficing firms may be less innovative, less aggressive and less willing to initiate change. If they do change, it is more likely to be in response to changes made by their competitors. Managers may judge their performance by comparing it with that of rivals.
5. Satisficing firms may be less aggressive in exploiting a position of market power. On the other hand, they may suffer from greater X inefficiency.

8.4 PRICING IN PRACTICE

What is the typical procedure by which firms set prices? Do they construct marginal cost and marginal revenue curves (or equations) and find the output where they are equal? Do they then use an average revenue curve (or equation) to work out the price at that output?

TC 9 p101

As we saw in section 8.1, firms often do not have the information to do so, even if they wanted to. In practice, firms look for rules of pricing that are relatively simple to apply.

Cost-based pricing

One approach is ***average cost*** or ***mark-up pricing***. Here producers work out the price by simply adding a certain percentage (mark-up) for profit on top of average costs (average fixed costs plus average variable costs).

$P = AFC + AVC + \text{profit mark-up}$

Choosing the mark-up

The level of profit mark-up on top of average cost will depend on the firm's aims: whether it is aiming for high or even maximum profits, or merely a target based on previous profit. It will also depend on the likely actions of rivals and their responses to changes in this firm's price and how these responses will affect demand.

If a firm could estimate its demand curve, it could then set its output and profit mark-up at levels to avoid a shortage or surplus. Thus in Figure 8.3 it could choose a lower output (Q_1) with a higher mark-up (*fg*) or a higher output (Q_2) with a lower mark-up (*hj*), depending on its aims. If the firm could not estimate its demand curve, it could adjust its mark-up and output over time by a process of trial and error, according to its success in meeting profit and sales aims.

Figure 8.3 Choosing the output and profit mark-up

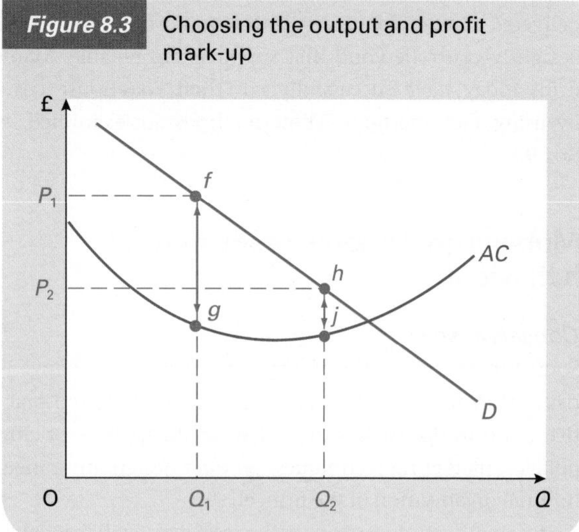

> **Definition**
>
> **Average cost** or **mark-up pricing** Where firms set the price by adding a profit mark-up to average cost.

The equilibrium price and output

Is it possible to identify an equilibrium price and output for the firm that sets its prices by adding a mark-up to average cost? To answer this we can identify a supply curve for the firm.

If a firm is aiming for a particular profit *per unit* of output and does not adjust this target, the firm's supply curve is

CASE STUDIES AND APPLICATIONS

BOX 8.7

HOW DO UK COMPANIES SET PRICES?

In 1995 the Bank of England conducted a survey of price-setting behaviour in 654 UK companies.[3] Among other things, the survey sought to establish what factors influenced companies' pricing decisions. The results are given table (a).

> Companies were asked to rank alternative methods of pricing of their main product . . . The most popular response was that prices were set with respect to market conditions. The top preference[4] for almost 40 per cent of respondents was that prices were set at the highest level that the market could bear. An additional 25 per cent of respondents stated that they set prices in relation to their competitors – this was the second choice most popular among companies.
>
> KI 21 p207
>
> . . . The survey also confirmed the importance of company-specific factors. The first preference of about 20 per cent of respondents was that price was made up of a direct cost per unit plus a variable percentage mark-up . . . A further 17 per cent of companies, particularly retailing companies, stated that they priced on the basis of costs plus a fixed percentage mark-up.
>
> Cost plus mark-ups tended to be more important for small companies, which cannot afford expensive market research.

The survey also sought to establish those factors which could cause prices to change – either up or down.

> The survey asked companies to rank those factors most likely to push prices up or down. It found that there were substantial differences between the factors that influenced price increases and those that influenced price decreases. First, many more companies said that cost rises were likely to push prices up than said that cost reductions were likely to push prices down. Second, a rise in demand seemed less likely to lead to a price increase than a fall in demand was to lead to a price cut.
>
> KI 20 p182
>
> . . . The importance of strategic interaction with competitors suggests that when contemplating a price cut, companies need to consider the chance of sparking off a price war . . . The finding that companies were much more likely to match rival price falls than they are to follow rival price rises appears to support the importance of strategic behaviour.

?

1. ***Which of the following is more likely to be consistent with the aim of maximising profits: pricing on the basis of (a) cost per unit plus a variable percentage mark-up; (b) cost per unit plus a fixed percentage mark-up?***
2. ***Explain the differences between the importance attached to the different factors leading to price increases and those leading to price reductions.***

[3] Simon Hall, Mark Walsh and Tony Yates, 'How do UK companies set prices?', *Bank of England Quarterly Bulletin*, May 1996.

[4] Companies were able to show more than one response as their top preference. This means the total percentage of companies expressing first preferences for all of the explanations of price determination exceeds 100%.

(a) How are prices determined?

	1st	%	2nd	%	3rd	%
Market level	257	39	140	21	78	12
Competitors' prices	161	25	229	35	100	15
Direct cost plus variable mark-up	131	20	115	18	88	14
Direct cost plus fixed mark-up	108	17	49	8	42	6
Customer set	33	5	52	8	47	7
Regulatory agency	11	2	3	1	5	1

Source: *Bank of England Quarterly Bulletin*, May 1996.

(b) Factors leading to a rise or fall in price

Rise	Number[a]	%	Fall	Number[a]	%
Increase in material costs	421	64	Decrease in material costs	186	28
Rival price rise	105	16	Rival price fall	235	36
Rise in demand	101	15	Fall in demand	146	22
Prices never rise	26	4	Prices never fall	75	12
Increase in interest rates	18	3	Decrease in interest rates	8	1
Higher market share	14	2	Lower market share	69	11
Fall in productivity	5	1	Rise in productivity	22	3

[a] Numbers citing a scenario as most important.
Note: Top preferences only.

Source: *Bank of England Quarterly Bulletin*, May 1996.

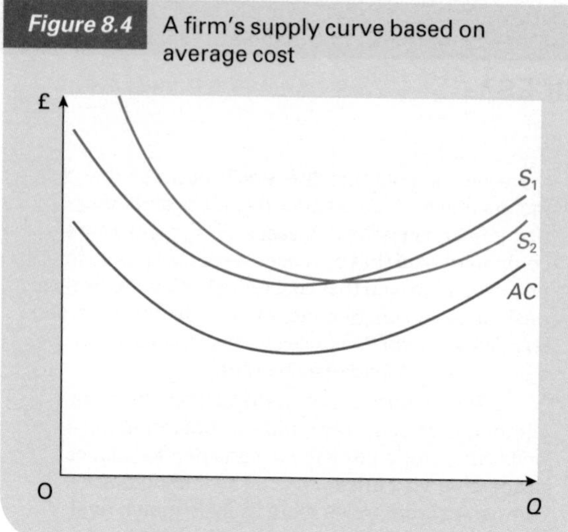

Figure 8.4 A firm's supply curve based on average cost

derived by adding the mark-up to the *AC* curve. This is shown by curve S_1 in Figure 8.4. If, however, a firm is aiming for a particular level of *total* profit, and does not adjust this target, its supply curve will be like curve S_2. The greater the output, the less the profit per unit needs to be (and hence the less the mark-up) to give a particular level of total profit.

In either case, price and quantity can be derived from the intersection of demand and supply. Price and output will change if the demand or cost (and hence supply) curve shifts.

The main problem here is in predicting the demand curve, since it depends not only on consumer tastes but on the prices and behaviour of competitors. In practice, firms will usually base their assumptions about future sales on current figures, add a certain percentage to allow for growth in demand and then finally adjust this up or down if they decide to change the mark-up.

Variations in the mark-up

In most firms, the mark-up is not rigid. In expanding markets, or markets where firms have monopoly/oligopoly power, the size of the mark-up is likely to be greater. In contracting markets, or under conditions of rising costs and constant demand, a firm may well be forced to accept lower profits and thus reduce the mark-up.

Multi-product firms often have different mark-ups for their different products depending on their various market conditions. Such firms will often distribute their overhead costs unequally between their products. The potentially most profitable products, often those with the least elastic demands, will probably be required to make the greatest contribution to overheads.

The firm is likely to take account of the actions and possible reactions of its competitors. It may well be unwilling to change prices when costs or demand change, for fear of the reactions of competitors (see the kinked demand curve theory on pages 190–1). If prices are kept constant and yet costs change, either due to a movement along the *AC* curve in response to a change in demand, or due to a shift in the *AC* curve, the firm must necessarily change the size of the mark-up.

All this suggests that, whereas the mark-up may well be based on a target profit, firms are often prepared to change their target and hence their mark-up, according to market conditions.

?

1. *If the firm adjusts the size of its mark-up according to changes in demand and the actions of competitors, could its actions approximate to setting price and output where MC = MR?*
2. *Some firms set their prices by adding a mark-up to average variable cost (the mark-up would be larger to include an element to cover fixed cost). Why might this make pricing easier for the firm? (See Box 5.6.)*

*LOOKING AT THE MATHS

Using a mark-up approach to find the profit-maximising price. Could the firm use a mark-up approach to set the *profit-maximising* price? It could, provided it bases its mark-up on marginal cost (*MC*), rather than average cost, and provided it knows the price elasticity of demand ($P\epsilon_D$) for its product. The rule is:

$$P = \frac{MC}{1 + (1/P\epsilon_D)}$$

This is simply the formula for profit-maximising price that we derived in section 6.3 (see page 168), except that we have used *MC* rather than *MR* (where profits are maximised, *MC* = *MR*). Proof of this formula is given in Maths Case 6.2 on the book's website.

Thus if $MC = £10$ and $P\epsilon_D = -5$, the firm should charge a price of:

$$\frac{£10}{1 + (1/-5)} = \frac{£10}{1 - 1/5} = \frac{£10}{0.8} = £12.50$$

The weakness of this pricing rule is that it applies only at the profit-maximising output. If the firm is currently a long way from that output, *MC* and $P\epsilon_D$ may diverge considerably from the values that the firm should use in its calculation. If, however, the firm is producing relatively near to its profit-maximising output, the rule can give a price that is a close approximation to the profit-maximising price.

Section summary

1. Many firms set prices by adding a profit mark-up to average cost. This cost-plus pricing is most likely when firms are profit satisficers or when they do not have the information to find the price that will equate marginal cost and marginal revenue.
2. The mark-up could be based on achieving a target level of either *total* profit or profit per unit. In either case, a supply curve can be derived by adding the corresponding mark-up to the average cost curve.
3. For firms keen to increase profit, the size of the mark-up can be varied as market conditions permit the target profit to be increased.

END OF CHAPTER QUESTIONS

1. Assume that a firm faces a downward-sloping demand curve. Draw a diagram showing the firm's *AR*, *MR*, *AC* and *MC* curves. (Draw them in such a way that the firm can make supernormal profits.) Mark the following on the diagram:
   (a) The firm's profit-maximising output and price.
   (b) Its sales-revenue-maximising output and price.
   (c) Its sales-maximising output and price (subject to earning at least normal profit).

   Could the answer to (a) and (b) ever be the same? Could the answer to (b) and (c) ever be the same?
2. Would it be possible for firms to calculate their maximum-profit output if they did not use marginal cost and marginal revenue concepts?
3. What is meant by the principal–agent problem? Give two examples of this problem that you have come across in your own experience.
4. 'A firm will always prefer to make more profit rather than less.' Do you agree with this statement? Is it compatible with alternatives to the profit-maximising theory of the firm?
5. A firm under monopoly or oligopoly that aims to maximise sales revenue will tend to produce more than a firm that aims to maximise profits. Does this conclusion also apply under (a) perfect competition and (b) monopolistic competition, given that there is freedom of entry?
6. What are the potential costs and benefits of mergers to (a) shareholders; (b) managers; (c) customers?
7. Why is it difficult to test the assumption that firms seek to maximise *long-run* profits?
8. Do behavioural theories of the firm allow us to make any predictions about firms' prices and output?
9. Is mark-up pricing likely to benefit consumers?

Additional case studies on the book's website (www.pearsoned.co.uk/sloman)

8.1 **The legal structure of firms.** A study of the different types of legal identity that a firm can take – from the sole proprietor to the partnership to the limited company.

8.2 **The Body Shop.** A case study of 'alternative business values'.

8.3 **Corporate social responsibility.** An examination of social responsibility as a goal of firms and its effect on business performance.

8.4 **The global information economy and strategic alliances.** The way forward for companies such as America Online?

8.5 **Downsizing and business organisation.** The case of IBM.

WEBSITES RELEVANT TO THIS CHAPTER

Numbers and sections refer to websites listed in the Web Appendix and hotlinked from this book's website at www.pearsoned.co.uk/sloman.

- For news articles relevant to this chapter, see the *Economics News Articles* link from the book's website.
- For general news relevant to alternative strategies, see websites in section A, and particularly A2, 3, 8, 9, 23, 24, 25, 26, 35, 36. See also A38, 39, 43 and 44 for links to newspapers worldwide; and A42 and 43 for links to economics news articles on particular search topics from newspapers worldwide.
- For student resources relevant to this chapter, see sites C1–7, 9, 10, 19.
- For information on mergers, see sites E4, 10, 18, 20.
- For data on small and medium-sized enterprises, see the database in B3 or E10.
- For information on pricing, see site E10 and the sites of the regulators of the privatised industries: E16, 19, 21, 22, 25.
- Sites I7 and 11 in the Business section contain links to *Business > Management > Organisational Management.*
- Site D3 has a simulation on sales revenue versus profit maximisation.

Chapter 9
The Theory of Distribution of Income

Why do pop stars, footballers and stockbrokers earn such large incomes? Why, on the other hand, do cleaners, hospital porters and workers in clothing factories earn very low incomes? These are the types of question that the theory of distribution seeks to answer. It attempts to explain why some people are rich and others poor.

The explanation for differences in wages lies in the working of labour markets. In sections 9.1 and 9.2, we will consider how labour markets operate. In particular, we will focus on the determination of wage rates in different types of market: ones where employers are wage takers, ones where they can choose the wage rate, and ones where wage rates are determined by a process of collective bargaining. In the final two sections, we turn to capital and land and ask what determines the rewards that their owners receive.

This chapter examines the *theory* of income distribution by showing how the rewards to factors of production (labour, capital and land) depend on market conditions. Chapter 10, on the other hand, looks at income distribution in practice. It looks at inequality and poverty and at government policies to tackle the problem.

CHAPTER MAP

9.1 WAGE DETERMINATION UNDER PERFECT COMPETITION

Perfect labour markets

When looking at the market for labour, it is useful to make a similar distinction to that made in the theory of the firm: the distinction between perfect and imperfect markets. Although in practice few labour markets are totally perfect, many do at least approximate to it.

The assumptions of perfect labour markets are similar to those of perfect goods markets. The main one is that everyone is a ***wage taker***. In other words, neither employers nor employees have any economic power to affect wage rates. This situation is not uncommon. Small employers are likely to have to pay the 'going wage rate' to their employees, especially when the employee is of a clearly defined type, such as an electrician, a bar worker, a secretary or a porter. As far as employees are concerned, being a wage taker means not being a member of a union and therefore not being able to use collective bargaining to push up the wage rate.

The other assumptions of a perfect labour market are as follows:

Freedom of entry. There are no restrictions on the movement of labour. For example, workers are free to move to alternative jobs or to areas of the country where wage rates are higher. There are no barriers erected by, say, unions, professional associations or the government. Of course, it takes time for workers to change jobs and maybe to retrain. This assumption therefore applies only in the long run.

Definition

Wage taker An employer or employee who has no power to influence the market wage rate.

Perfect knowledge. Workers are fully aware of what jobs are available at what wages and with what conditions of employment. Likewise employers know what labour is available and how productive that labour is.

Homogeneous labour. It is usually assumed that, in perfect markets, workers of a given category are identical in terms of productivity. For example, it would be assumed that all bricklayers are equally skilled and motivated.

? *Which of the above assumptions do you think would be correct in each of the following cases?*
(a) Supermarket checkout operators. (b) Agricultural workers. (c) Crane operators. (d) Economics teachers. (e) Call-centre workers.

Wage rates and employment under perfect competition are determined by the interaction of the market demand and supply of labour. This is illustrated in Figure 9.1(b). TC 4 p22

Generally it would be expected that the supply and demand curves slope the same way as in goods markets. The higher the wage paid for a certain type of job, the more workers will want to do that job. This gives an upward-sloping supply curve of labour. On the other hand, the higher the wage that employers have to pay, the less labour they will want to employ. Either they will simply produce less output, or they will substitute other factors of production, like machinery, for labour. Thus the demand curve for labour slopes downwards.

Diagram (a) shows how an individual employer has to accept this wage. The supply of labour to that employer is infinitely elastic. In other words, at the market wage W_m, there is no limit to the number of workers available to that employer (but no workers at all will be available below it: they will all be working elsewhere). At the market wage W_m, the employer will employ Q_1 hours of labour.

Figure 9.1 A perfectly competitive labour market

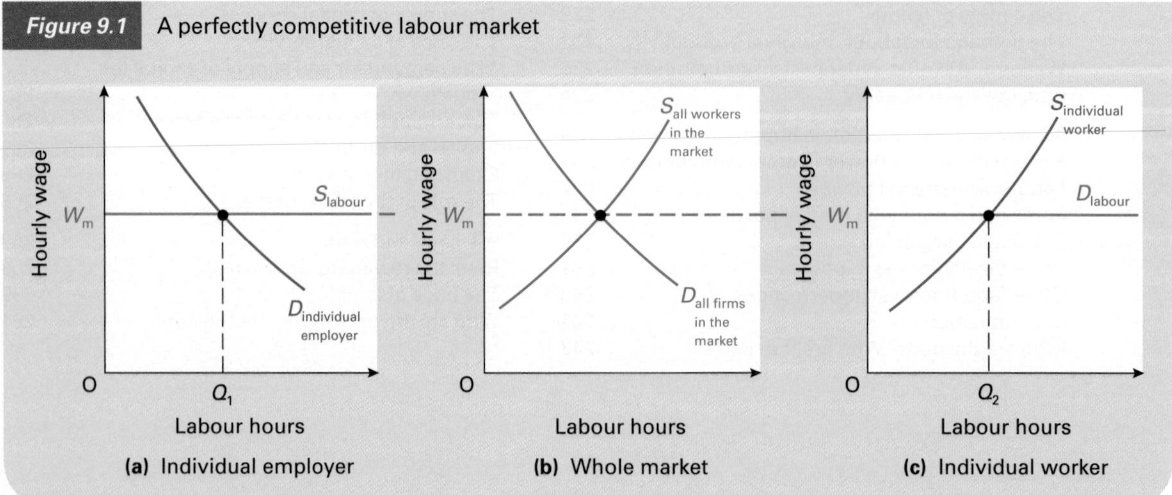

EXPLORING ECONOMICS BOX 9.1

LABOUR AS A FACTOR OF PRODUCTION

Is this any way to treat a worker?

The theory that wages depend on demand and supply is often referred to as the 'neo-classical' theory of wages. Treated as pure theory it is value free and does not involve moral judgements. It does not say, for example, whether the resulting distribution of income is fair or just.

In practice, however, the neo-classical theory is often used in such a way as to imply moral judgements. It is a theory that tends to be associated with the political right and centre: those who are generally in favour of markets and the capitalist system. Many on the political left are critical of its implied morality. They make the following points:

- By treating labour as a 'factor of production', it demeans labour. Labour is not the same as a piece of land or a machine.
- It somehow legitimises the capitalist system, where some people own land and capital whereas others have only their own labour. It seems to imply that people have a right to the incomes from their property even if that property is highly unequally distributed among the population.
- It implies that labour has no rights to the goods that it produces. These goods are entirely the property of the employer, even though it is the workers who made them.

Karl Marx (1818–83) was highly critical of these values and the way that the capitalist system led to extremes of wealth and poverty. He argued that labour was the only true source of value. After all, it is labour that makes machines, labour that tills the land and makes it yield, labour that mines coal and other natural resources. Property, he argued, is therefore a form of theft. When capitalists extract profits from their enterprises, he continued, they are stealing part of the value produced by labour.

Neo-classical economists defend their position against the Marxist 'labour theory of value' by arguing the following:

- They are merely describing the world. If people want to draw pro-capitalist conclusions from their theory, then that is up to them.
- If the labour theory of value is used in any practical way to evaluate costs and output, it will lead to a misallocation of resources. Labour is not the only scarce resource. Land, for example, is also scarce and needs to be included in calculations of costs, otherwise it will be used wastefully.

Assume that it is agreed by everyone that it is morally wrong to treat labour as a mere 'factor of production', with no rights over the goods produced. Does this make the neo-classical theory wrong?

Diagram (c) shows how an individual worker also has to accept this wage. In this case it is the demand curve for that worker that is infinitely elastic. In other words, there is as much work as the worker cares to do at this wage (but none at all above it).

We now turn to look at the supply and demand for labour in more detail.

The supply of labour

We can look at the supply of labour at three levels: the supply of hours by an individual worker, the supply of workers to an individual employer and the total market supply of a given category of labour. Let us examine each in turn.

The supply of hours by an individual worker

Work involves two major costs (or 'disutilities') to the worker:

- When people work they sacrifice leisure.
- The work itself may be unpleasant.

Each extra hour worked will involve additional disutility. This ***marginal disutility of work*** (*MDU*) will tend to *increase* as people work more hours. There are two reasons for this. First, the less the leisure they have left, the greater is the disutility they experience in sacrificing a further hour of leisure. Second, any unpleasantness they experience in doing the job tends to increase due to boredom or tiredness.

This increasing marginal disutility (see Figure 9.2(a)) will tend to give an upward-sloping supply curve of hours by an individual worker (see Figure 9.2(b)). The reason is that, in order to persuade people to work more hours, a higher hourly wage must be paid to compensate for the higher marginal disutility incurred. This helps to explain why overtime rates are higher than standard rates.

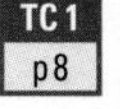

Under certain circumstances, however, the supply of hours curve might bend backwards (see Figure 9.3). The reason is that when wage rates go up, two opposing forces operate on the individual's labour supply.

On the one hand, with higher wage rates people tend to work more hours, since time taken in leisure now involves

Definition

Marginal disutility of work The extra sacrifice/hardship to a worker of working an extra unit of time in any given time period (e.g. an extra hour per day).

Figure 9.2 Marginal disutility of work and an individual's supply of labour

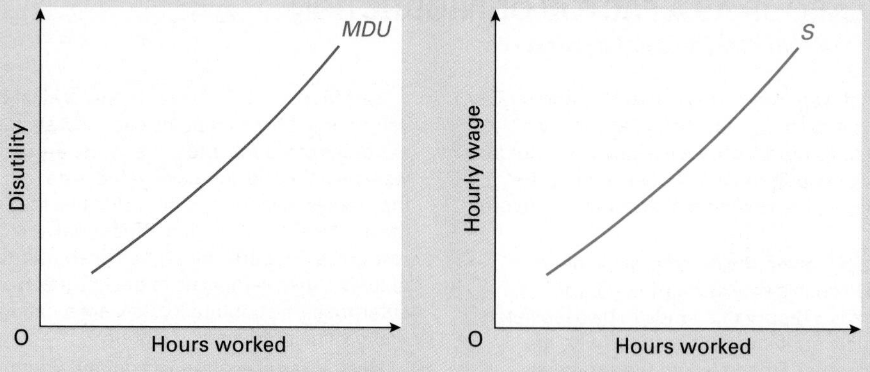

MDU
Disutility
O
Hours worked

(a) The marginal disutility of hours worked

S
Hourly wage
O
Hours worked

(b) The supply of hours worked

Figure 9.3 Backward-bending supply curve of labour

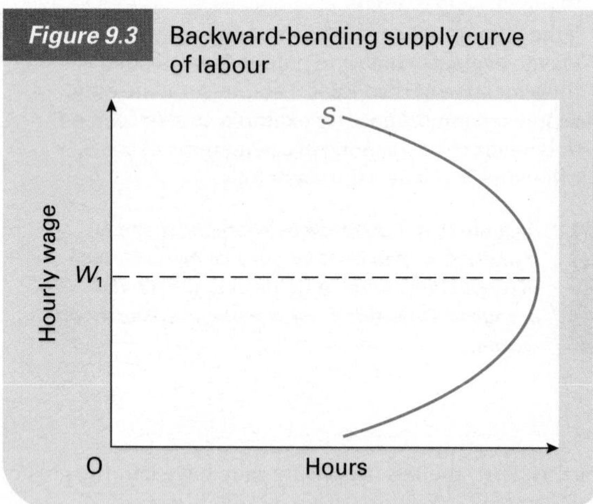

KI 7 p35

a greater sacrifice of income and hence consumption. They substitute income (i.e. work) for leisure. This is called the ***substitution effect*** of the increase in wage rates.

On the other hand, people may feel that with higher wage rates they can afford to work less and have more leisure. This is called the ***income effect***.

The relative magnitude of these two effects determines the slope of the individual's supply curve. It is normally assumed that the substitution effect outweighs the income effect, especially at lower wage rates. A rise in the wage rate acts as an incentive: it encourages a person to work more hours. It is possible, however, that the income effect might outweigh the substitution effect. Particularly at very high wage rates people say, 'There's not so much point now in doing overtime. I can afford to spend more time at home.'

If the wage rate becomes high enough for the income effect to dominate, the supply curve will begin to slope backwards. This occurs above a wage rate of W_1 in Figure 9.3.

These considerations are particularly important for a government considering tax cuts. The Conservative governments of the 1980s argued that cuts in income taxes are like giving people a pay rise, and thus provide an incentive for people to work harder. This analysis is only correct, however, if the substitution effect dominates. If the income effect dominates, people will work *less* after the tax cut. These questions are examined in Chapter 10.

The supply of labour to an individual employer

Under perfect competition, the supply of labour to a particular firm will be perfectly elastic, as in Figure 9.1(a). The firm is a 'wage taker' and thus has no power to influence wages. Take the case of a small firm that wishes to employ a temporary typist via a secretarial agency. It has to pay the 'going rate', and presumably will be able to employ as many typists as it likes (within reason) at that wage rate.

The market supply of a given type of labour

This will typically be upward sloping, as in Figure 9.1(b). The higher the wage rate offered in a particular type of job, the more people will want to do that job.

The *position* of the market supply curve of labour depends on the number of people willing and able to do

Definitions

Substitution effect of a rise in wage rates Workers will tend to substitute income for leisure as leisure now has a higher opportunity cost. This effect leads to *more* hours being worked as wage rates rise.

Income effect of a rise in wage rates Workers get a higher income for a given number of hours worked and may thus feel they need to work *fewer* hours as wage rates rise.

EXPLORING ECONOMICS

*BOX 9.2

USING INDIFFERENCE CURVE ANALYSIS TO DERIVE THE INDIVIDUAL'S SUPPLY CURVE OF LABOUR

Indifference curve analysis (see section 4.3) can be used to derive the individual's supply curve of labour. The analysis can show why the supply curve may be backward bending.

Assume that an individual can choose the number of hours to work and has 12 hours a day to divide between work and leisure (the remaining 12 being for sleep, shopping, travelling, etc.). In the diagram, with an hourly wage rate of £5, budget line B_1 shows all the possible combinations of daily income and leisure hours. For example, at point *x* the individual has an
TC1 p8 income of £40 by working 8 hours and taking 4 hours off as leisure.

At an hourly wage of £10, the budget line becomes B_2, and of £12.50, B_3.

The diagram also shows three indifference curves. Each indifference curve shows all those combinations of income and leisure that give the individual a particular level of utility. The curves are bowed in towards the origin, showing that increasingly higher incomes are necessary to compensate for each hour of leisure sacrificed. Curve I_3 shows a higher level of utility than I_2, and I_2 a higher level than I_1.

At a wage rate of £5 per hour, the individual can move along budget line B_1. Point *x* shows the highest level of utility that can be achieved. The individual thus supplies 8 hours of labour (and takes 4 off in leisure).

At the higher wage rate of £10 per hour, the individual is now on budget line B_2 and maximises utility at point *y* by working 9 hours. Thus the higher wage has encouraged the individual to work one more hour. So far, then, the individual's supply curve would be upward sloping: a higher wage rate leading to more labour hours supplied.

The choice of hours worked at different wage rates

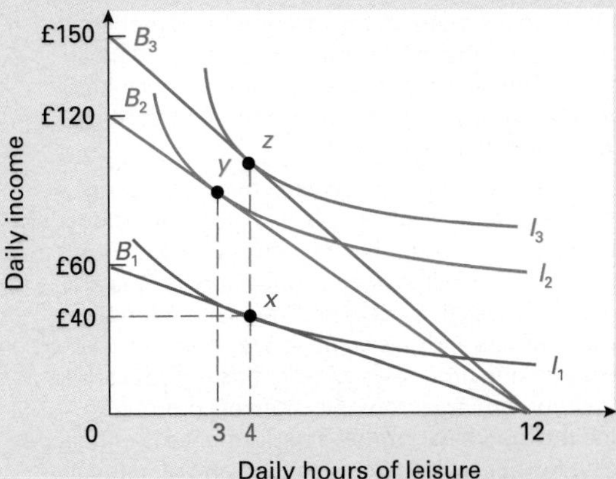

At the higher wage rate still of £12.50 per hour, the individual is on budget line B_3, and now maximises utility at point *z*. But this means that only 8 hours are now worked. The supply curve has begun to bend backwards. In other words, the individual is now in a position to be able to afford to take more time off in leisure. The income effect has begun to offset the substitution effect. KI7 p35

?

1. ***Using the analysis developed in Chapter 4, try to show the size of the income and substitution effects when moving from point x to point y and from point y to point z.***
2. ***Illustrate on an indifference diagram the effect on the hours a person works of (a) a cut in the rate of income tax; (b) an increase in child benefit (assuming the person has children).***

the job at each given wage rate. This depends on three things:

- The number of qualified people.
- TC1 p8 The non-wage benefits or costs of the job, such as the pleasantness or otherwise of the working environment, job satisfaction or dissatisfaction, status, power, the degree of job security, holidays, perks and other fringe benefits.
- The wages and non-wage benefits in alternative jobs.

A change in the wage rate will cause a movement along the supply curve. A change in any of these other three determinants will shift the whole curve.

? *Which way will the supply curve shift if the wage rates in alternative jobs rise?*

TC8 p59 *The elasticity of the market supply of labour*

How responsive will the supply of labour be to a change in the wage rate? If the market wage rate goes up, will a lot more labour become available or only a little? This responsiveness (elasticity) depends on (a) the difficulties and costs of changing jobs and (b) the time period.

Another way of looking at the elasticity of supply of labour is in terms of the ***mobility of labour***: the willingness and ability of labour to move to another job, whether in a different location (geographical mobility) or in a different industry (occupational mobility). The mobility of labour (and hence the elasticity supply of labour) will be higher when there are alternative jobs in the same location, when alternative jobs require similar skills and when people have good information about these jobs. It is also much higher in the long run, when people have the time to acquire new skills and when the education system has time to adapt to the changing demands of industry.

Definition

Mobility of labour The willingness and ability of labour to move to another job.

CASE STUDIES AND APPLICATIONS — BOX 9.3

'TELECOMMUTERS'

The electronic cottage

The increasing sophistication of information technology, with direct computer linking, broadband access to the Internet, fax machines and mobile phones, has meant that many people can work at home. The number of these 'telecommuters' has grown steadily since the information technology revolution of the early 1980s.

It has been found that where 'telecommuting networks' have been established, gains in productivity levels have been significant, when compared with comparable office workers. Most studies indicate rises in productivity of over 35 per cent. With fewer interruptions and less chatting with fellow workers, less working time is lost. Add to this the stress-free environment, free from the strain of commuting, and the individual worker's performance is enhanced. With further savings in the renting and maintenance of offices (often in high-cost inner-city locations) and in heating and lighting costs, the economic arguments in favour of telecommuting seem very persuasive.

These technological developments have been the equivalent of an increase in labour mobility. Work can be taken to the workers rather than the workers coming to the work. The effect will be to reduce the premium that needs to be paid to workers in commercial centres, such as the City of London.

Then there are the broader gains to society. Telecommuting opens up the labour market to a wider group of workers who might find it difficult to leave the home – groups such as single parents and the disabled. Also, with fewer commuters, there are benefits from reduced traffic congestion and pollution.

But do such employees feel isolated? For many people, work is an important part of their social environment, providing them with an opportunity to meet others and to work as a team. For those who are unable to leave the home, however, telecommuting may be the *only* means of earning a living: the choice of travelling to work may simply not be open to them.

There is no reason, of course, why telecommuters cannot work in different countries. Some American companies have a lot of their data-processing work undertaken in low-wage countries. Delta Airlines, for example, employs telecommuters in the Caribbean.

However, telecommuters can be exploited. The Low Pay Commission has found that many homeworkers in the UK are paid well below the hourly national minimum wage. This is because employers typically pay by the amount of work done and underestimate the amount of time it takes to complete work.

?

1. ***What effects are such developments likely to have on (a) trade union membership; (b) trade union power?***
2. ***How is a growth in telecommuting likely to affect relative house prices between capital cities and the regions?***
3. ***Is the outsourcing of call-centre work to India an example of telecommuting?***

?

1. *Assume that there is a growing demand for computer programmers. As a result more people train to become programmers. Does this represent a rightward shift in the supply curve of programmers, or merely the supply curve becoming more elastic in the long run, or both? Explain.*
2. *Which is likely to be more elastic, the supply of coal miners or the supply of shop assistants? Explain.*

If the demand for a particular category of worker increases, the wage rate will rise. The less elastic the supply of labour, the higher will the rise be. Workers already employed in that industry will get the benefit of that rise, even though they are doing the same job as before. They are now earning a premium above the wage that was necessary to attract them into the industry in the first place. This premium is called ***economic rent***. Web Case 9.1 on the book's website explores this concept and its relationship with the elasticity of supply of labour.

The demand for labour: the marginal productivity theory

The traditional 'neo-classical' theory of the firm assumes that firms aim to maximise profits. The same assumption is made in the neo-classical theory of labour demand. This theory is generally known as the ***marginal productivity theory***.

The profit-maximising approach

How many workers will a profit-maximising firm want to employ? The firm will answer this question by weighing up

KI 16 p120

Definitions

Economic rent The excess that a factor of production is paid over the amount necessary to keep it in its current employment.

Marginal productivity theory The theory that the demand for a factor depends on its marginal revenue product.

TC 2 p10 the costs of employing extra labour against the benefits. It will use exactly the same principles as in deciding how much output to produce.

In the goods market, the firm will maximise profits where the marginal cost of an extra unit of *goods* produced equals the marginal revenue from selling it: $MC = MR$.

In the labour market, the firm will maximise profits where the marginal cost of employing an extra *worker* equals the marginal revenue that the worker's output earns for the firm: *MC* of labour = *MR* of labour. The reasoning is simple. If an extra worker adds more to a firm's revenue than to its costs, the firm's profits will increase. It will be worth employing that worker. But as more workers are KI 17 p121 employed, diminishing returns to labour will set in (see page 121). Each extra worker will produce less than the previous one, and thus earn less revenue for the firm. Eventually the marginal revenue from extra workers will fall to the level of their marginal cost. At that point, the firm will stop employing extra workers. There are no additional profits to be gained. Profits are at a maximum.

Measuring the marginal cost and revenue of labour

Marginal cost of labour (MC_L). This is the extra cost of employing one more worker. Under perfect competition, the firm is too small to affect the market wage. It faces a horizontal supply curve (see Figure 9.1(a) on page 228). Thus the additional cost of employing one more person will simply be the wage: $MC_L = W$.

Marginal revenue of labour (MRP_L). The marginal revenue that the firm gains from employing one more worker is called the ***marginal revenue product*** of labour. The MRP_L is found by multiplying two elements – the *marginal physical product* of labour (MPP_L) and the marginal revenue gained by selling one more unit of output (*MR*):

$$MRP_L = MPP_L \times MR$$

The MPP_L is the extra output produced by the last worker. Thus if the last worker produces 100 tonnes of output per week (MPP_L), and if the firm earns an extra £2 for each additional tonne sold (*MR*), then the worker's *MRP* is £200. This extra worker is adding £200 to the firm's revenue.

The profit-maximising level of employment for a firm

The MPP_L curve was illustrated in Figure 5.3 (see page 129). As more workers are employed, there will come a point when diminishing returns set in (point *b*). The MPP_L curve thus slopes down after this point. The MRP_L curve will be a similar shape to the MPP_L curve, since it is merely being multiplied by a constant figure, *MR*. (Under perfect competition $MR = P$ and does not vary with output.) The MRP_L curve is illustrated in Figure 9.4, along with the MC_L 'curve'.

Figure 9.4 The profit-maximising level of employment

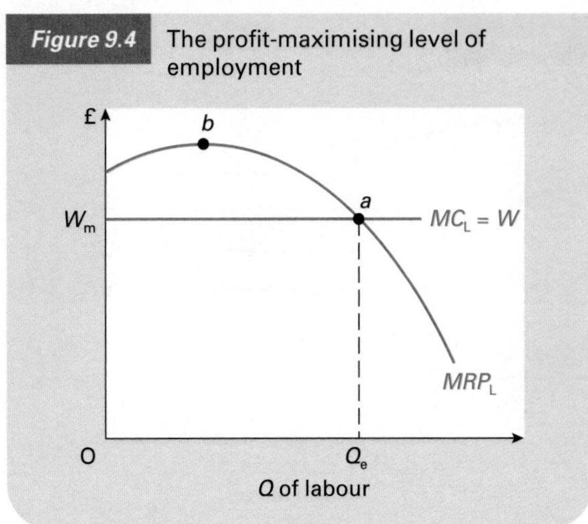

? *Why is the MC_L curve horizontal?*

Definition

Marginal revenue product (of a factor) The extra revenue that a firm earns from employing one more unit of a variable factor: $MRP_{factor} = MPP_{factor} \times MR_{good}$.

***LOOKING AT THE MATHS**

The marginal product of labour can be expressed using calculus. It is the rate of increase in output of good *X* with respect to changes in the quantity of labour:

$$MPP_L = \frac{\partial X}{\partial L}$$

The marginal revenue product of labour is thus given by:

$$MRP_L = MR\frac{\partial X}{\partial L}$$

Profits are maximised at the level of employmet (*L*), where $W = MRP_L$: i.e. where:

$$W = MR\frac{\partial X}{\partial L} \quad (1)$$

We can easily move from this to the level of profit-maximising *output* of good *X* (where $MC = MR$). Rearranging equation (1), we get:

$$\frac{W}{\partial X/\partial L} = MR \quad (2)$$

But, assuming that labour is the only variable factor, marginal cost (of output) is the extra cost of employing labour (the only extra cost) *per unit of output*. In other words:

$$MC = \frac{W}{\partial X/\partial L} \quad (3)$$

i.e. $MC = MR$

Thus, not surprisingly, the profit-maximising employment of labour (where $W = MRP_L$) will yield the profit-maximising output (where $MC = MR$).

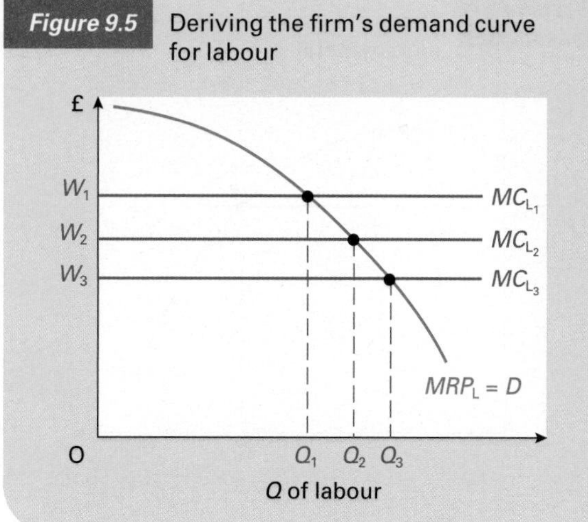

Figure 9.5 Deriving the firm's demand curve for labour

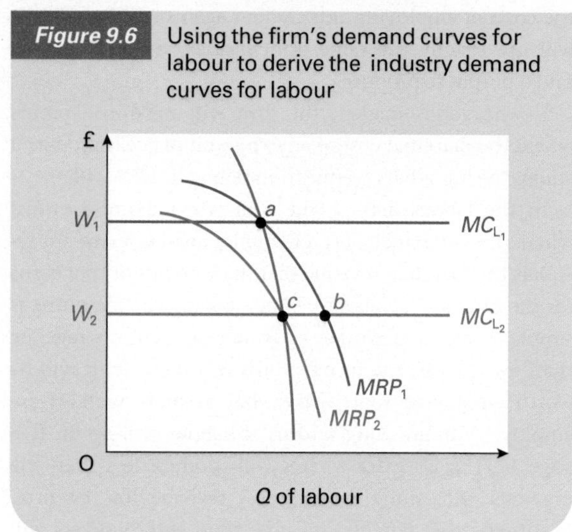

Figure 9.6 Using the firm's demand curves for labour to derive the industry demand curves for labour

Profits will be maximised at an employment level of Q_e, where MC_L (i.e. W) = MRP_L. Why? At levels of employment below Q_e, MRP_L exceeds MC_L. The firm will increase profits by employing more labour. At levels of employment above Q_e, MC_L exceeds MRP_L. In this case, the firm will increase profits by reducing employment.

Derivation of the firm's demand curve for labour

No matter what the wage rate, the quantity of labour demanded will be found from the intersection of W and MRP_L (see Figure 9.5). At a wage rate of W_1, Q_1 labour is demanded; at W_2, Q_2 is demanded; at W_3, Q_3 is demanded.

Thus the MRP_L curve will show the quantity of labour employed at each wage rate. But this is just what the demand curve for labour shows. Thus the MRP_L curve is the demand curve for labour.

There are three determinants of the demand for labour:

- The wage rate. This determines the position *on* the demand curve. (Strictly speaking, we should refer here to the wage rate determining the 'quantity demanded' rather than the 'demand'.)
- The productivity of labour (MPP_L). This determines the position *of* the demand curve.
- The demand for the good. The higher the market demand for the good, the higher will be its market price, and hence the higher will be the *MR*, and thus the MRP_L. This too determines the position of the demand curve. It shows how the demand for labour (and other factors) is a ***derived demand***: i.e. one derived from the demand for the good. For example, the higher the demand for houses, and hence the higher their price, the higher will be the demand for bricklayers.

Definition

Derived demand The demand for a factor of production depends on the demand for the good that uses it.

A change in the wage rate is represented by a movement *along* the demand curve for labour. A change in the productivity of labour or the demand for the good *shifts* the curve.

Derivation of the industry demand curve for labour

This is not simply the sum of the demand curves of the individual firms. The firm's demand curve is based on a constant *P* and *MR*, no matter how many workers the firm employs (this is one of the assumptions of perfect competition). In Figure 9.6, when the wage rate falls from W_1 to W_2 the firm will employ more labour by moving from *a* to *b* along its demand curve MRP_1.

The trouble with this analysis is that when the wage rate falls, it will affect *all* employers. They will all want to employ more labour. But when they do, the total industry output will increase, and hence *P* (and *MR*) will be pushed down. This will shift the firm's *MRP* curve to the left and lead to a lower level of employment at point *c*. Therefore, when we allow for the effect of lower wages on the market price of the good, the firm's demand curve for labour will be the *green* line passing through points *a* and *c*.

Thus the *industry* demand curve for labour is the (horizontal) sum of the *green* lines for each firm, and is therefore less elastic than the firm's *MRP* curve.

What will determine the elasticity of this curve?

The elasticity of demand for labour

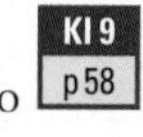

The elasticity of demand for labour (with respect to changes in the wage rate) will be greater:

- The greater the price elasticity of demand for the good. A fall in *W* leads to higher employment and more output. This will drive *P* down. If the market demand for the good is elastic, this fall in *P* will lead to a lot more being sold and hence to a lot more people being employed.
- The easier it is to substitute labour for other factors and vice versa. If labour can be readily substituted for other

factors, then a reduction in W will lead to a large increase in labour used to replace these other factors.

- The greater the elasticity of supply of complementary factors. If the wage rate falls, a lot more labour will be demanded if plenty of complementary factors can be obtained at little increase in their price.
- The greater the elasticity of supply of substitute factors. If the wage rate falls and more labour is used, less substitute factors will be demanded and their price will fall. If their supply is elastic, a lot less will be supplied and therefore a lot more labour will be used instead.
- The greater the wage cost as a proportion of total costs. If wages are a large proportion of total costs and the wage rate falls, total costs will fall significantly; therefore production will increase significantly, and so too will the demand for labour.
- The longer the time period. Given sufficient time, firms can respond to a fall in wage rates by reorganising their production processes to make use of the now relatively cheap labour.

?

For each of the following jobs, check through the above list of determinants (excluding the last), and try to decide whether demand would be relatively elastic or inelastic: firefighters; typists; carpenters; bus drivers; Punch and Judy operators; farm workers; car workers.

Wages and profits under perfect competition

The wage rate (W) is determined by the interaction of demand and supply in the labour market. It will be equal to the value of the output that the last person produces (MRP_L).

Profits to the individual firm arise from the fact that the MRP_L curve slopes downwards (diminishing returns). Thus the last worker adds less to the revenue of firms than was added previously by workers already employed.

If *all* workers in the firm receive a wage equal to the *MRP* of the *last* worker, everyone but the last worker will receive a wage less than their *MRP*. This excess of MRP_L over W of previous workers provides a surplus to the firm over its wages bill (see Figure 9.7). Part of this will be required for paying non-wage costs; part will be profits for the firm.

Perfect competition between firms ensures that profits are kept down to *normal* profits. If the surplus over wages is such that *supernormal* profits are made, new firms will enter the industry. The price of the good (and hence MRP_L) will fall, and the wage rate will be bid up, until only normal profits remain.

Equality and inequality under perfect competition

The mythical world of perfect wage equality

Under certain very strict assumptions, a perfectly competitive market will lead to perfect equality of wage rates. All workers will earn exactly the same. These strict assumptions are as follows:

Figure 9.7 Wages and profits

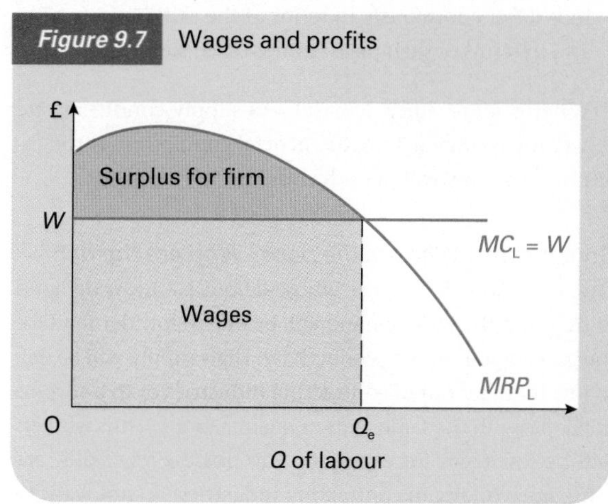

- All workers have identical abilities.
- There is perfect mobility of labour.
- All jobs are equally attractive to all workers.
- All workers and employers have perfect knowledge.
- Wages are determined entirely by demand and supply.

Given these assumptions, if consumer demand rose in any industry, the demand for labour would rise. As a result, wage rates would begin to rise. Immediately workers would flood into this industry, attracted by the higher wages. Very quickly, then, wage rates would be competed back down to the level in the rest of the economy. Likewise if wage rates began to fall in any industry, workers would leave, thereby eliminating any labour surplus and preventing the fall in wage rates.

TC 8 p59

Under these conditions, therefore, not only would the labour supply curve to a *firm* be infinitely elastic, but so too would the labour supply curve to each *industry* at the universal wage rate.

Of course, in the real world these conditions do not hold. Huge inequalities of wages exist. A financial dealer in the City can earn fifty times as much as a shop assistant. But even if markets *were* perfect, inequality would be expected to persist.

Causes of inequality under perfect competition

In the short run, inequality will exist under perfect competition because of the time it takes for changes in demand and supply conditions to bring new long-run equilibria. Thus expanding industries will tend to pay higher wage rates than contracting industries.

KI 4 p11

But even after enough time has elapsed for all adjustments to be made to changes in demand and supply, long-run wage differentials will still exist for the following reasons:

- Workers do not have identical abilities.
- Workers are not perfectly mobile, even in the long run. People have different preferences about where they want to live and the jobs they like to do.

- Jobs differ enormously in terms of the skills they require and in terms of their pleasantness or unpleasantness.

What is more, since demand and supply conditions are constantly changing, long-run general equilibrium throughout the economy will never be reached.

KI 4 p11

Conclusions: Who are the poor? Who are the rich?

The low paid will be those whose labour is in low demand or high supply. Low demand will be due to low demand for the good or low labour productivity. High supply will be due to low mobility out of contracting industries or to a surplus of people with the same skills or qualifications. Thus workers will be low paid, for example, who possess few skills, are unfit, are working in contracting industries, do not want to move from the area and will not or cannot retrain.

TC 6 p26

The highly paid will be those whose labour is in high demand or low supply. Thus workers who possess skills or talents that are in short supply, especially if those skills take a long time for others to acquire, and those who are working in expanding industries will tend to earn high wages.

Although the movement of labour from low-paid to high-paid jobs will tend to reduce wage differentials, considerable inequality will persist even under perfect competition. It is a fallacy, therefore, to believe that simply by 'freeing up' markets and encouraging workers to 'stand on their own feet' or 'get on their bikes', poverty and inequality will be eliminated.

What is more, in the real world there exist many market imperfections. These tend to make inequality greater. These imperfections are examined in the next section.

Finally, income inequality under capitalism will also be due to unequal distribution of the ownership of land and capital. Even under perfect competition, considerable inequality will therefore exist if wealth is concentrated in the hands of the few.

Section summary

1. Wages in a perfect market are determined by supply and demand.
2. The supply curve of hours by an individual worker reflects the increasing marginal disutility of work. Its shape depends on the relative sizes of the substitution and income effects of a wage change. The substitution effect is positive. A higher wage encourages people to work more by substituting wages for leisure. The income effect, however, is negative. A higher wage makes people feel that they can afford to work less. If the income effect is bigger than the substitution effect, the supply of hours curve will bend backwards.
3. The supply of labour to a particular employer under perfect competition is infinitely elastic.
4. The market supply is typically upward sloping. Its elasticity depends on labour mobility.
5. The demand for labour depends on a worker's marginal revenue product. This is the extra revenue that a firm will gain from the output of an extra worker. The profit-maximising firm will continue taking on extra workers until MRP_L is equal to MC_L (= W under perfect competition).
6. The elasticity of demand for labour depends on the elasticity of demand for the good, the ease of substituting labour for other factors and vice versa, the elasticity of supply of substitute and complementary factors, wages as a proportion of total costs, and the time period involved.
7. Although market forces will tend to lead to the elimination of differentials as workers move from low-paid to high-paid jobs, nevertheless inequality can persist even under perfect competition. People have different abilities and skills; people are not perfectly mobile; and jobs differ in their labour requirements.
8. Inequality is also caused by market imperfections and by unequal ownership of land and capital.

9.2 WAGE DETERMINATION IN IMPERFECT MARKETS

In the real world, firms and/or workers are likely to have the power to influence wage rates: they are not wage takers. This is one of the major types of labour market imperfection.

When a firm is the only employer of a certain type of labour, this situation is called a ***monopsony***. The Post Office is a monopsony employer of postal workers. A monopsony is more likely to occur in a local market. Thus a factory may be the only employer of certain types of labour in that district. When there are just a few employers, this is called ***oligopsony***.

Workers may have market power as members of unions. When a single union bargains on behalf of a certain type of labour, it is acting as a monopolist. When there is more than one union, they are oligopolists.

Definitions

Monopsony A market with a single buyer or employer.

Oligopsony A market with just a few buyers or employers.

Figure 9.8 Monopsony

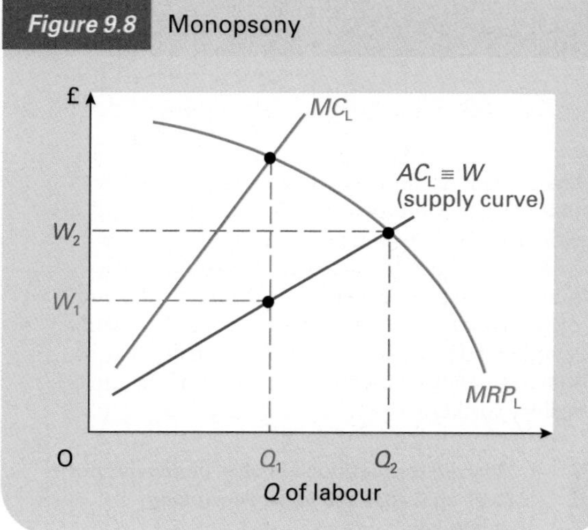

When a monopsonist employer faces a monopolist union, the situation is called ***bilateral monopoly***.

Firms with market power in employing labour (monopsony, etc.)

KI 19 p157 Monopsonists (and oligopsonists too) are 'wage setters' not 'wage takers'. A large employer in a small town, for example, may have considerable power to resist wage increases or even to force wage rates down.

Such firms face an upward-sloping supply curve of labour. This is illustrated in Figure 9.8. If the firm wants to take on more labour, it will have to pay a higher wage rate to attract workers away from other industries. But conversely, by employing less labour it can get away with paying a lower wage rate.

The supply curve shows the wage rate that must be paid to attract a given quantity of labour. The wage it pays is the *average cost* to the firm of employing labour (AC_L). The supply curve is also therefore the AC_L curve.

The *marginal cost* of employing one more worker (MC_L) will be above the wage (AC_L). The reason is that the wage rate has to be raised to attract extra workers. The MC_L will thus be the new higher wage paid to the new employee *plus* the small rise in the total wages bill for existing employees: after all, they will be paid the higher wage too.

The profit-maximising employment of labour would be at Q_1, where $MC_L = MRP_L$. The wage paid would thus be W_1.

If this had been a perfectly competitive labour market, employment would have been at the higher level Q_2, with the wage rate at the higher level W_2, where $W = MRP_L$. What in effect the monopsonist is doing, therefore, is forcing the wage rate down by restricting the number of workers employed.

Definition

Bilateral monopoly Where a monopsony buyer faces a monopoly seller.

?

1. *The following table shows data for a monopsonist employer. Fill in the missing figures. How many workers should the firm employ if it wishes to maximise profits?*

Number of workers	*Wage rate (£)*	*Total cost of labour (£)*	*Marginal cost of labour (£)*	*Marginal revenue product (£)*
1	100	100		
2	105	210	110	230
3	110	330	120	240
4	115	...	...	240
5	120	...	...	230
6	125	...	...	210
7	130	...	...	190
8	135	...	...	170
9	140	...	...	150

2. *Will a monopsony typically be a monopoly? Give examples of monopsonists that are not monopolists, and monopolists that are not monopsonists.*

Labour with market power (union monopoly or oligopoly)

The extent to which unions will succeed in pushing up wage rates depends on their power and militancy. It also depends on the power of firms to resist and on their ability to pay higher wages. In particular, the scope for unions to gain a better deal for their members depends on the sort of market in which the employers are producing.

If the employers are producing under perfect or monopolistic competition, unions can raise wage rates only at the expense of employment. Firms are earning only normal profit. Thus if unions force up wage rates, the marginal firms will go bankrupt and leave the industry. Fewer workers will be employed. The fall in output will lead to higher prices. This will enable the remaining firms to pay a higher wage rate.

Figure 9.9 illustrates these effects. If unions force the wage rate up from W_1 to W_2, employment will fall from Q_1

Figure 9.9 Monopoly union facing producers under perfect competition

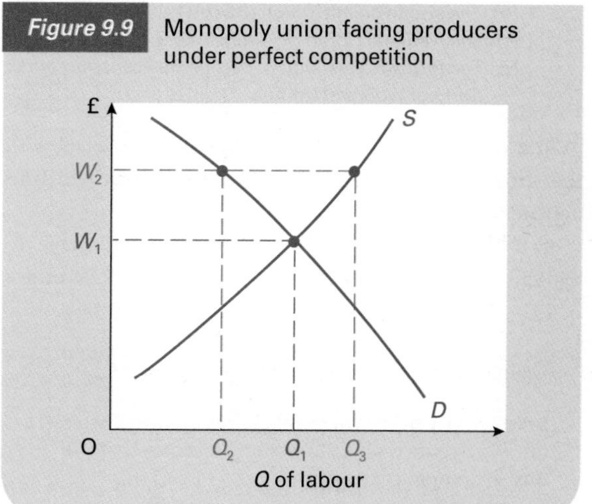

CASE STUDIES AND APPLICATIONS

BOX 9.4

LIFE AT THE MILL

Monopsony in Victorian times

KI 19 p157

A dramatic illustration of the effects of extreme monopsony power is that of the textile mill in nineteenth-century England. When a mill was the only employer in a small town, or when factory owners colluded as oligopsonists, and when there was no union to counterbalance the power of the employer, things could be very bad for the worker. Very low pay would be combined with often appalling working conditions.

Friedrich Engels described the life of the textile factory worker as follows:

> The factory worker is condemned to allow his physical and mental powers to become atrophied. From the age of eight he enters an occupation which bores him all day long. And there is no respite from this boredom. The machine works ceaselessly. Its wheels, belts and spindles hum and rattle ceaselessly in his ears, and if he thinks of taking even a moment's rest, the overlooker is always there to punish him with a fine. It is nothing less than torture of the severest kind to which the workers are subjected by being condemned to a life-sentence in the factory, in the service of a machine which never stops. It is not only the body of the worker which is stunted, but also his mind. It would indeed be difficult to find a better way of making a man slow-witted than to turn him into a factory worker.[1]

1. ***Why did competition between employers not force up wages and improve working conditions?***
2. ***Were the workers making a 'rational economic decision' when they chose to work in such factories?***

[1] F. Engels, *The Condition of the Working Class in England*, translated by W. O. Henderson and W. H. Chaloner (Basil Blackwell, 1971), pp. 199–200.

to Q_2. There will be a surplus of people ($Q_3 - Q_2$) wishing to work in this industry for whom no jobs are available.

The union is in a doubly weak position. Not only will jobs be lost as a result of forcing up the wage rate, but there is also a danger that these unemployed people might undercut the union wage, unless the union can prevent firms employing non-unionised labour.

Wage rates can be increased without a reduction in the level of employment only if, as part of the bargain, the productivity of labour is increased. This is called a ***productivity deal***. The *MRP* curve, and hence the demand curve in Figure 9.9, shifts to the right.

?

Which of the following unions find themselves in a weak bargaining position for the above reasons?

(a) The seafarers' part of the rail and maritime union RMT.
(b) The shopworkers' union (USDAW).
(c) The National Union of Mineworkers.
(d) The farmworkers' union (part of the Transport and General Workers' Union).

In a competitive market, then, the union is faced with the choice between wages and jobs. Its actions will thus depend on its objectives.

If it wants to *maximise employment*, it will have to content itself with a wage of W_1 in Figure 9.9, unless productivity deals can be negotiated. At W_1, Q_1 workers will be employed. Above W_1 fewer than Q_1 workers will be *demanded*. Below W_1 fewer than Q_1 workers will be *supplied*.

If the union is more concerned with securing a higher wage rate, it may be prepared to push for a wage rate above W_1 and accept some reduction in employment. This is more likely if the reduction can be achieved through ***natural wastage***. This is where people retire, or take voluntary redundancy, or simply leave for another job.

Firms and labour with market power (bilateral monopoly)

What happens when a union monopoly faces a monopsony employer? What will the wage rate be? What will the level of employment be? Unfortunately, economic theory cannot give a precise answer to these questions. There is no 'equilibrium' level as such. Ultimately, the wage rate and the level of employment will depend on the relative bargaining strengths and skills of unions and management.

Strange as it may seem, unions may well be in a stronger position to make substantial gains for their members when they are facing a powerful employer. There is often considerable scope for them to increase wage rates *without* this leading to a reduction in employment, or even for them to

Definitions

Productivity deal Where, in return for a wage increase, a union agrees to changes in working practices that will increase output per worker.

Natural wastage Where a firm wishing to reduce its workforce does so by not replacing those who leave or retire.

Figure 9.10 Bilateral monopoly

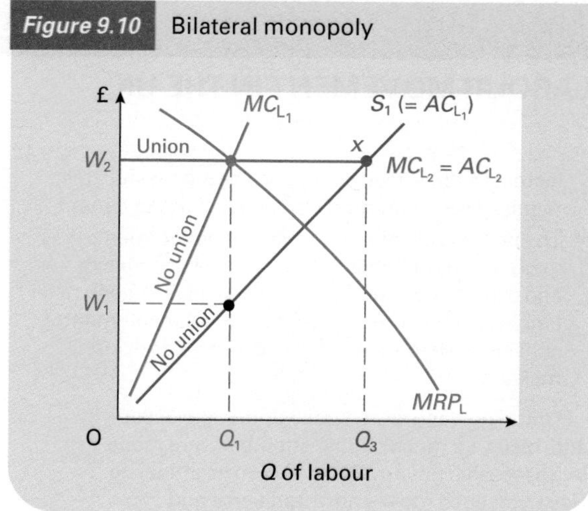

increase both the wage rate *and* employment. Figure 9.10 shows how this can be so.

Assume first that there is no union. The monopsonist will maximise profits by employing Q_1 workers at a wage rate of W_1. (Q_1 is where $MRP_L = MC_L$.)

What happens when a union is introduced into this situation? Wage rates will now be set by negotiation between unions and management. Once the wage rate has been agreed, the employer can no longer drive the wage rate down by employing fewer workers. If it tried to pay less than the agreed wage, it could well be faced by a strike, and thus have a zero supply of labour!

Similarly, if the employer decided to take on *more* workers, it would not have to *increase* the wage rate, as long as the negotiated wage were above the free-market wage: as long as the wage rate were above that given by the supply curve S_1.

The effect of this is to give a new supply curve that is horizontal up to the point where it meets the original supply curve. For example, let us assume that the union succeeds in negotiating a wage rate of W_2 in Figure 9.10. The supply curve will be horizontal at this level to the left of point *x*. To the right of this point it will follow the original supply curve S_1, since to acquire more than Q_3 workers the employer would have to raise the wage rate above W_2.

If the supply curve is horizontal to the left of point *x* at a level of W_2, so too will be the MC_L curve. The reason is simply that the extra cost to the employer of taking on an extra worker (up to Q_3) is merely the wage rate: no rise has to be given to existing employees. If MC_L is equal to the wage, the profit-maximising level of employment ($MC_L = MRP_L$) will now be where $W = MRP_L$. At a negotiated wage rate of W_2, the firm will therefore choose to employ Q_1 workers.

What this means is that the union can push the wage rate right up from W_1 to W_2 and the firm will still *want* to employ Q_1. In other words, a wage rise can be obtained *without* a reduction in employment.

If the negotiated wage rate were somewhere between W_1 and W_2, what would happen to employment?

The union could go further still. By threatening industrial action, it may be able to push the wage rate above W_2 and still insist that Q_1 workers are employed (i.e. no redundancies). The firm may be prepared to see profits drop right down to normal level rather than face a strike and risk losses. The absolute upper limit to wages will be that at which the firm is forced to close down.

Collective bargaining

Sometimes when unions and management negotiate, *both* sides can gain from the resulting agreement. For example, the introduction of new technology may allow higher wages, improved working conditions and higher profits. Usually, however, one side's gain is the other's loss. Higher wages mean lower profits. Either way, both sides will want to gain the maximum for themselves.

In collective bargaining, there are various threats or promises that either side can make. Union *threats* might include strike action, ***picketing***, ***working to rule*** or refusing to co-operate with management: for example, in the introduction of new technology. Alternatively, in return for higher wages or better working conditions, unions might *offer* no-strike agreements (or an informal promise not to take industrial action), increased productivity, reductions in the workforce, or long-term deals over pay.

In turn, employers might *threaten* employees with plant closure, ***lock-outs***, redundancies or the employment of non-union labour. Alternatively, they might *offer*, in return for lower wage increases, various 'perks', such as productivity bonuses, profit-sharing schemes, better working conditions, more overtime, better holidays or security of employment.

The outcome of negotiations. The success of a union in achieving its demands depends on its financial strength, the determination of its members and the level of support from other unions and the public in general. It also depends on the willingness of the firm to concede and on its profitability. Firms earning substantial supernormal profits are in a much better position to pay wage increases than firms operating in a highly competitive environment.

Definitions

Picketing Where people on strike gather at the entrance to the firm and attempt to dissuade workers or delivery vehicles from entering.

Working to rule Workers do the bare minimum they have to, as set out in their job descriptions.

Lock-outs Union members are temporarily laid off until they are prepared to agree to the firm's conditions.

CASE STUDIES AND APPLICATIONS

THE RISE AND DECLINE OF THE LABOUR MOVEMENT IN THE UK

Modern trade unionism had its birth with the industrial revolution of the eighteenth and nineteenth centuries. Unions were seen as a means of improving the lot of industrial workers, most of whom suffered low pay, long hours and poor working conditions. But with great hostility from employers and from the legal system, membership grew slowly. By the end of the nineteenth century, only just over 10 per cent of manual workers were in an effective union.

The big change came after the First World War. Many working men, on returning from France, began to demand that their sacrifice for their country should be rewarded. The trade union movement was seen as one way to improve wages and working conditions. Membership soared. By 1920, 45 per cent of the total labour force (8.3 million workers) were in trade unions.

But it was after the Second World War that the trade union movement in the UK really became established as a substantial economic and political force. This can be explained by three crucial trends:

- The growth in the public sector meant that government was itself becoming increasingly responsible for determining wages and conditions of service for many workers.
- In their attempt to control inflation in the 1960s and 1970s, governments sought to constrain wage increases ('incomes policy'). To be successful, this required acceptance by the trade union movement.
- The philosophy of many post-war governments was to govern by consent. Social contracts and pacts, and tripartite discussions between government, employers and unions, gave the union movement considerable influence over economic decision making.

Union power grew steadily during the 1950s and 1960s, so much so that attempts were made by successive governments to curb its influence. However, such moves attracted fierce and widespread opposition, and as a result legislation was in many cases abandoned or modified. The trade union movement had by the late 1970s become very powerful with over 13 million members (see diagram).

The election of the Conservative government in 1979 ushered in a new wave of trade union reform, eroding and removing many rights and privileges acquired by unions over the years. Trade union membership began to fall. Since 1979 it has fallen by over 5 million. This can be explained in part by the shift from a manufacturing to a service-based economy, a sector which is far less unionised than manufacturing. The main explanation, however, lies in the attitudes of new

The wage settlement may be higher if the union represents only ***core workers***. It may be able to secure a higher wage rate at the expense of non-members, who might lose their jobs or be replaced by part-time or temporary workers. The core workers can be seen as ***insiders***. Their union(s) can prevent the unemployed – the ***outsiders*** – from competing wages down.

Industrial action imposes costs on both unions and firms. Unions lose pay. Firms lose revenue. It is usually in both sides' interests, therefore, to settle by negotiation. Nevertheless, to gain the maximum advantage, each side must persuade the other that it will carry out its threats if pushed.

Definitions

Core workers Workers, normally with specific skills, who are employed on a permanent or long-term basis.

Insiders Those in employment who can use their privileged position (either as members of unions or because of specific skills) to secure pay rises despite an excess supply of labour (unemployment).

Outsiders Those out of work or employed on a casual, part-time or short-term basis, who have little or no power to influence wages or employment.

The approach described so far has essentially been one of confrontation. The alternative is for both sides to concentrate on increasing the total net income of the firm by co-operating on ways to increase efficiency or the quality of the product. This approach is more likely when unions and management have built up an atmosphere of trust over time.

Recall the various strategies that rival oligopolists can adopt. What parallels are there in union and management strategies?

The role of government in collective bargaining

The government can influence the outcome of collective bargaining in a number of ways. One is to try to set an example. It may take a tough line in resisting wage demands by public-sector workers, hoping thereby to persuade employers in the private sector to do likewise.

Alternatively, it could set up arbitration or conciliation machinery. For example, in the UK, the Advisory Conciliation and Arbitration Service (ACAS) conciliates in over 1000 disputes each year. It also provides, on request by both sides, an arbitration service, where its findings will be binding.

Another approach is to use legislation. The government could pass laws that restrict the behaviour of employers or unions. It could pass laws that set a minimum wage rate

BOX 9.5

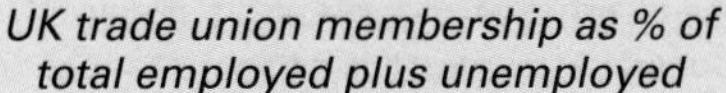
UK trade union membership as % of total employed plus unemployed

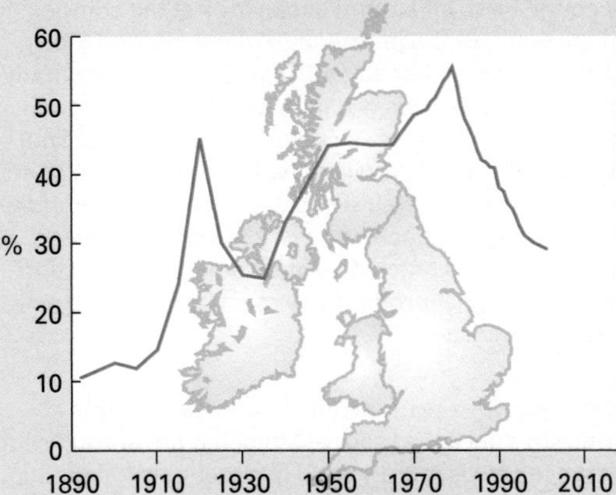

Sources: A. Marsh and B. Cox, *The Trade Union Movement in the UK 1992* (Malthouse Press); *Labour Market Trends* (National Statistics).

firms to union recognition, where in many cases a more aggressive management style and a highly competitive environment have made it virtually impossible for unions to gain bargaining rights.

With continued privatisation and the introduction of private-sector management practices, local pay bargaining and contracted-out services into many of the remaining parts of the public sector, trade unionism is still further under threat.

The future of the union movement is unclear. The creation of mega-unions is one possibility, as groups of unions merge in an attempt to retain some form of power and influence. For example, in 1993 a new union, UNISON, was created by an amalgamation of various public-sector unions. It has some 1.3 million members. Many unions have adopted a 'new realism', accepting single-union agreements and supporting flexible working practices and individualised pay packets based on performance (see Box 9.8). Some commentators have suggested that unions may become little more than advisers to individual employees on questions of law and rights, their influence over pay bargaining simply withering away. Unions are being forced to reconsider their role, however uncertain it may appear to be.

? ***What factors, other than the ones identified above, could account for the decline in union membership in recent years?***

(see Box 10.3), or prevent discrimination against workers on various grounds. Similarly, it could pass laws that curtail the power of unions. The UK Conservative governments between 1979 and 1997 put considerable emphasis on reducing the power of trade unions and making labour markets more 'flexible'. Several Acts of Parliament were passed. These included the following measures:

- Employees were given the right to join any union. This effectively ended ***closed-shop*** agreements.
- Secret postal ballots of the union membership were made mandatory for the operation of a political fund, the election of senior union officials, and strikes and other official industrial action.
- Political strikes, sympathy action and action against other non-unionised companies were made illegal.
- Lawful action would be confined to that against workers' own direct employers, even to their own particular place of work. All ***secondary action*** was made unlawful.
- It was made unlawful for employers to penalise workers for choosing to join or refusing to join a trade union. It was also made unlawful for employers to deny employment on the grounds that an applicant does not belong to a union.

The effect of these measures was considerably to weaken the power of trade unions in the UK.

The efficiency wage hypothesis

We have seen that a union may be able to force an employer to pay a wage above the market-clearing rate. But wage rates above the equilibrium are not just the result of union power. It may well be in firms' interests to pay higher wage rates, even in non-unionised sectors.

One explanation for this phenomenon is the ***efficiency wage hypothesis***. This states that the productivity of workers rises as the wage rate rises. As a result, employers are frequently prepared to offer wage rates above the market-clearing level, attempting to balance increased wage costs against gains in productivity. But why may higher wage rates lead to higher productivity? There are three main explanations. KI 3 p10

Definitions

Closed shop Where a firm agrees to employ only union members.

Secondary action Industrial action taken against a company not directly involved in a dispute (e.g. a supplier of raw materials to a firm whose employees are on strike).

Efficiency wage hypothesis The hypothesis that the productivity of workers is affected by the wage rate that they receive.

EXPLORING ECONOMICS BOX 9.6

HOW USEFUL IS MARGINAL PRODUCTIVITY THEORY?

Reality or the fantasy world of economists?

The marginal productivity theory of income distribution has come in for a lot of criticisms. Are they justified?

To start with, you cannot criticise something unless you know precisely what it is you are criticising. Marginal productivity theory has been criticised for assuming perfect competition. It doesn't!

Marginal productivity theory merely states that to maximise profits an employer will employ workers up to the point where the worker's marginal cost equals the extra revenue added by that worker: $MC_L = MRP_L$. This applies equally under perfect competition, monopsony and oligopsony.

What it does say is that, if there is perfect competition, then the worker's *wage* will equal MRP_L. It certainly does not say that there will always be perfect competition, or that $W = MRP_L$ in other market structures.

A second criticism is that employers simply do not behave in this 'marginal way', weighing up each additional worker's costs and revenues for the firm. There are three possible reasons for this.

Ignorance of the theory of profit maximisation. The employer may use some rule of thumb, but nevertheless is attempting to maximise profits.

This is a criticism of the theory only if the theory is supposed to describe how employers actually behave. It does not. It merely states that, if firms are attempting to maximise profits, they will in fact be equating MC_L and MRP_L, whether they realise it or not!

A worker's marginal productivity cannot be calculated. When workers are part of a team, it is not usually possible to separate out the contribution to output of each individual. What is the marginal productivity of a cleaner, a porter, a secretary, a security guard, or even a member of a production line? Similarly, it may not be possible to separate the contribution of workers from that of their tools. A lathe operator is useless without a lathe, as is a lathe without a lathe operator.

This is a more fundamental criticism. Nevertheless it is possible to amend the theory to take this into account. First, an employer can look at the composition of the team, or the partnership of worker and tools, and decide whether any reorganisations or alternative production methods will increase the firm's profitability (i.e. increase revenue more than costs). Second, the employer can decide whether to expand or contract the overall size of the team, or the number of workers plus machines. Here the whole team or the worker plus machine is the 'factor of production' whose marginal productivity must be weighed against its costs.

Firms are not always profit maximisers. This is a criticism only if the theory states that firms are. As long as the theory is merely used to describe what would happen *if* firms maximised profits, there is no problem.

This criticism, then, is really one of how the theory is used. And even if it is used to predict what will actually happen in the real world, it is still relatively accurate in the large number of cases where firms' behaviour diverges only slightly from profit maximising. It is clearly wrong in other cases.

A final criticism is the moral one. If economists focus their attention exclusively on how to maximise profits, it might be concluded that they are putting their seal of approval on this sort of behaviour. Of course, economists will respond by saying that they are doing no such thing: they are confining themselves to positive economics. Nevertheless the criticism has some force. What an economist chooses to study is in part a normative decision.

Do any of the following contradict marginal productivity theory: (a) wage scales related to length of service (incremental scales); (b) nationally negotiated wage rates; (c) discrimination; (d) firms taking the lead from other firms in determining this year's pay increase?

Less 'shirking'. In many jobs it is difficult to monitor the effort individuals put into their work. Workers may thus get away with shirking or careless behaviour. This is an example of the principal–agent problem (see page 208). The worker, as an agent of the employer (the principal), is not necessarily going to act in the principal's interest.

KI 22 p208

The business could attempt to reduce shirking by imposing a series of sanctions, the most serious of which would be dismissal. The greater the wage rate currently received, the greater will be the cost to the individual of dismissal, and the less likely it is, therefore, that workers will shirk. The business will benefit not only from the additional output but also from a reduction in the costs of having to monitor workers' performance. As a consequence the ***efficiency wage rate*** for the business will lie above the market-determined wage rate.

Reduced labour turnover. If workers receive on-the-job training or retraining, then to lose a worker once the training has been completed is a significant cost to the business. Labour turnover, and hence its associated costs, can be

Definition

Efficiency wage rate The profit-maximising wage rate for the firm after taking into account the effects of wage rates on worker motivation, turnover and recruitment.

reduced by paying a wage above the market-clearing rate. By paying such a wage rate the business is seeking a degree of loyalty from its employees.

TC 3 p21

Morale. A simple reason for offering wage rates above the market-clearing level is to motivate the workforce – to create the feeling that the firm is a 'good' employer that cares about its employees. As a consequence, workers might be more industrious and more willing to accept the introduction of new technology (with the reorganisation that it involves).

The paying of efficiency wages above the market-clearing wage will depend upon the type of work involved. Workers who occupy skilled positions, especially where the business has invested time in their training (thus making them costly to replace) are likely to receive efficiency wages considerably above the market wage. By contrast, workers in unskilled positions, where shirking can be easily monitored, where little training takes place and where workers can be easily replaced, are unlikely to command an 'efficiency wage premium'. In such situations, rather than keeping wage rates high, the business will probably try to pay as little as possible.

Other labour market imperfections

The possession of power by unions and/or firms is not the only way in which real-world labour markets diverge from the perfectly competitive model:

- Workers or employers may have imperfect information.
- Wages may respond very slowly to changes in demand and supply, causing disequilibrium in labour markets to persist.
- Firms may not be profit maximisers. Likewise workers may not seek to maximise their 'worker surplus' – the excess of benefits from working (i.e. wages) over the disutility of working (displeasure in doing the job and lost leisure).

Some of the forms and effects of these three imperfections are examined in Web Case 9.2.

Discrimination

KI 4 p11

This can be another major factor in determining wages. Discrimination can take many forms: it can be by race, sex, age, class, dress, etc.; it can occur in many different aspects of society. This section is concerned with ***economic discrimination.*** This is defined as a situation where otherwise identical workers receive different pay for doing the same job, or are given different chances of employment or promotion.

Take the case of racial discrimination by employers. Figure 9.11 illustrates the wages and employment of both black and white workers by a firm with monopsony power which practises racial discrimination against black workers. Let us assume that there is no difference in the productivity of black and white workers. Let us also assume for simplicity that there is an equal number of black workers and white workers available at any given wage rate. Finally, let

> **Definition**
>
> **Economic discrimination** Where workers of identical *ability* are paid different wages or are otherwise discriminated against because of race, age, sex, etc.

Figure 9.11 The effect of racial discrimination by a monopsony employer

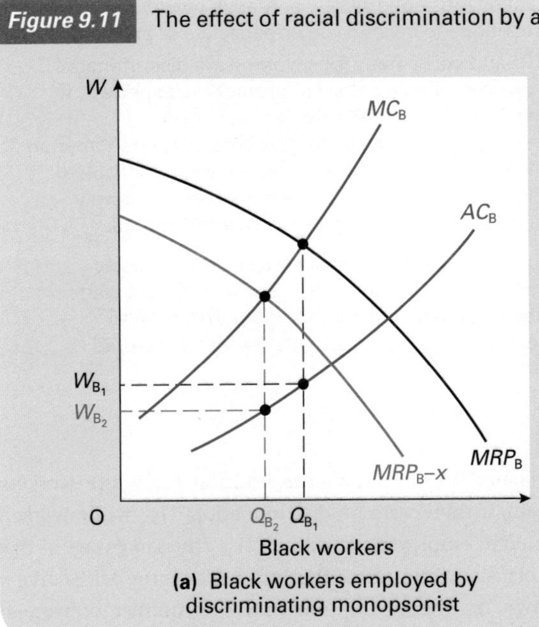

(a) Black workers employed by discriminating monopsonist

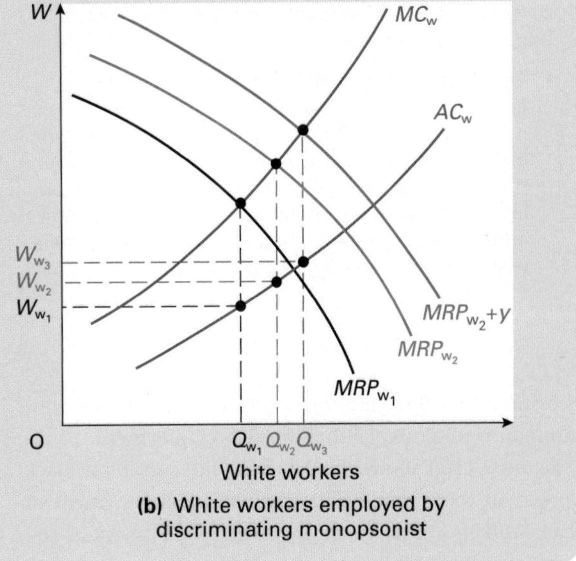

(b) White workers employed by discriminating monopsonist

CASE STUDIES AND APPLICATIONS

EQUAL PAY FOR EQUAL WORK?

(a) Average hourly pay, excluding overtime, for full-time UK employees, aged 18 and over, 1970–2004 (pence per hour)

	1970	1974	1978	1982	1986	1990	1994	1998	2000	2002	2004
Men	67	105	200	355	482	689	865	1065	1153	1292	1373
Women	42	71	148	262	358	528	688	839	920	1032	1121
Women's pay as a % of men's	63.1	67.4	73.9	73.9	74.3	76.6	79.5	78.8	79.8	79.9	81.6

Source: *Annual Survey of Hours and Earnings* (National Statistics).

Women earn less than men. How much less depends on how earnings are measured, but on the most widely used definition (see table (a)), women in the UK earn nearly 20 per cent less than men. The gender wage gap has narrowed over the years, however. In 1970, women earned 37 per cent less than men.

A similar picture can be seen throughout the EU. In 2000, women's average hourly pay was 75 per cent of men's. In Portugal it was as low as 67 per cent, whereas in Belgium, Denmark, Luxembourg and Sweden the pay gap was less than 15 per cent.

The inequality between male and female earnings can in part be explained by the fact that men and women are occupationally segregated. Seeing that women predominate in poorly paid occupations, the difference in earnings is somewhat to be expected. But if you consider table (b), you can see that quite substantial earnings differentials persist *within* particular occupations.

?

1. ***If we were to look at weekly rather than hourly pay and included the effects of overtime, what do you think would happen to the pay differentials in table (a)?***
2. ***In table (b), which of the occupations have a largely female workforce?***

So why has this inequality persisted? There are a number of possible reasons:

- The marginal productivity of labour in typically female occupations may be lower than in typically male occupations. This may in part be due to simple questions of physical strength. Very often, however, it is due to the fact that women tend to work in more labour-intensive occupations. If there is less capital equipment per female worker than there is per male worker, then it would be expected that the marginal product of a woman would be less than that of a man.
- Many women take career breaks to have children. For this reason, employers are sometimes more willing to invest money in training men (thereby increasing their marginal productivity), and more willing to promote men.
- Women tend to be less geographically mobile than men. If social norms are such that the man's job is seen as somehow more 'important' than the woman's, then a couple will often move if necessary for the man to get promotion. The woman, however, will have to settle for whatever job she can get in the same locality as her partner.
- A smaller proportion of women workers are members of unions than men. Even when they are members of unions, these are often in jobs where unions are weak (e.g. clothing industry workers, shop assistants and secretaries).
- Part-time workers (mainly women) have less bargaining power, less influence and less chance of obtaining promotion.
- Custom and practice. Despite equal pay legislation, many jobs done wholly or mainly by women continue to be low paid, irrespective of productivity.
- Prejudice. In many jobs women are discriminated against when it comes to promotion, especially to senior positions. Women are seriously underrepresented in boardrooms. This phenomenon is known as the 'glass ceiling'. It is very difficult to legislate against when the employer can simply claim that the 'better' person was promoted.

Which of the above reasons could be counted as economically 'irrational' (i.e. paying different wage rates to women and men for other than purely economic reasons)? Certainly the last two would

us assume that there are no laws to prevent the firm discriminating in terms of either wages or employment.

Figure 9.11(a) shows the *MC* and *MRP* curves for black workers. If there were no discrimination, employment of black workers would be at Q_{B_1}, where $MRP_B = MC_B$. The wage rate paid to black workers would be W_{B_1}.

Figure 9.11(b) shows the position for white workers. Again, if there were no discrimination, Q_{W_1} white workers would be employed at a wage of W_{W_1}: the same wage as that of black workers. (Note that in each case the *MRP* curve is drawn on the assumption that the number of workers employed from the other ethnic group is constant.)

BOX 9.7

classify. Paying different wage rates on these grounds would *not* be in the profit interests of the employer.

Some of the others, however, are more difficult to classify. The causes of the inequality in wage rates may be traced back beyond the workplace: perhaps to the educational system, or to a culture that discourages women from being so aggressive in seeking promotion or 'self-advertisement', or to more generous maternity than paternity leave.

Evidence from the EU as a whole suggests that occupational segregation is a significant factor in explaining pay differences. Also, pay inequality rises with educational attainment, suggesting that promotion prospects to senior positions for educated women are less favourable than those for educated men. Women with a university education earn on average 32 per cent less than men with a similar educational background. The gap between men and women with no qualifications, however, is only 22 per cent.

?

1. ***If employers were forced to give genuinely equal pay for equal work, how would this affect the employment of women and men? What would determine the magnitude of these effects?***
2. ***What measures could a government introduce to increase the number of women getting higher-paid jobs?***

(b) Average hourly pay, excluding overtime, for selected occupations, full-time UK employees on adult rates, 2004

Occupation	Men (£ per hour)	Women (£ per hour)	Women's pay as a % of men's
Social workers	13.10	13.37	102.1
Nurses	12.79	12.48	97.6
Bar staff	5.52	5.32	96.4
Telephonists	8.59	7.98	92.9
Police officers (sergeant and below)	14.34	13.01	90.7
Chefs, cooks	7.30	6.62	90.7
Secondary school teachers	20.24	18.10	89.4
Laboratory technicians	11.38	10.09	88.7
Solicitors, lawyers and judges	27.28	23.62	86.6
Sales and retail assistants	7.27	6.23	85.7
Medical practitioners	31.25	26.61	85.2
Librarians	14.09	11.86	84.2
Personnel managers	24.09	19.60	81.4
Hairdressers, barbers	7.83	6.30	80.5
Directors/chief executives of major organisations	55.86	44.23	79.2
Assemblers and routine operatives	8.96	6.85	76.5
Management consultants and economists	26.13	18.48	70.7
All occupations	13.73	11.21	81.6
Average *gross weekly* pay (incl. overtime)	558.60	422.30	75.6
Average weekly hours worked (incl. overtime)	40.8	37.5	
Average weekly overtime	2.2	0.8	

Source: *Annual Survey of Hours and Earnings* (National Statistics, 2004).

If the firm now discriminates against black workers, it will employ workers along a lower curve, $MRP_B - x$ (where x can be seen as the discriminatory factor). Employment of black workers will thus be at the lower level of Q_{B_2} and the wage they receive will be at the lower level of W_{B_2}.

How will discrimination against black workers affect wages and employment of white workers? Let us consider two cases.

In the first case, assume that the employer practises economic discrimination purely in the negative sense: i.e. it discriminates against black workers but employs white

CASE STUDIES AND APPLICATIONS

FLEXIBLE LABOUR MARKETS AND THE FLEXIBLE FIRM

New work practices for old?

KI 21 p207

The past 25 years have seen sweeping changes in the ways that firms organise their workforce. Two world recessions combined with rapid changes in technology have led many firms to question the wisdom of appointing workers on a permanent basis to specific jobs. Instead, they want to have the greatest flexibility possible to respond to new situations. If demand falls, they want to be able to 'shed' labour without facing large redundancy costs. If demand rises, they want rapid access to additional labour supplies. If technology changes (say, with the introduction of new computerised processes), they want to have the flexibility to move workers around, or to take on new workers in some areas and lose workers in others.

What many firms seek, therefore, is flexibility in employing and allocating labour. What countries are experiencing is an increasingly flexible labour market, as workers and employment agencies respond to the new 'flexible firm'.

There are three main types of flexibility in the use of labour:

- ***Functional flexibility***. This is where an employer is able to transfer labour between different tasks within the production process. It contrasts with traditional forms of organisation where people were employed to do a specific job, and then stuck to it. A functionally flexible labour force will tend to be multiskilled and relatively highly trained.
- ***Numerical flexibility***. This is where the firm is able to adjust the size and composition of its workforce according to changing market conditions. To achieve this, the firm is likely to employ a large proportion of its labour on a part-time or casual basis, or even sub-contract out specialist requirements, rather than employing such labour skills itself.
- ***Financial flexibility***. This is where the firm has flexibility in its wage costs. In large part it is a result of functional and numerical flexibility. Financial flexibility can be achieved by rewarding individual effort and productivity rather than paying a given rate for a particular job. Such rates of pay are increasingly negotiated at the local level rather than being nationally set. The result is not only a widening of pay differentials between skilled and unskilled workers, but also growing differentials in pay between workers within the same industry but in different parts of the country.

The flexible firm

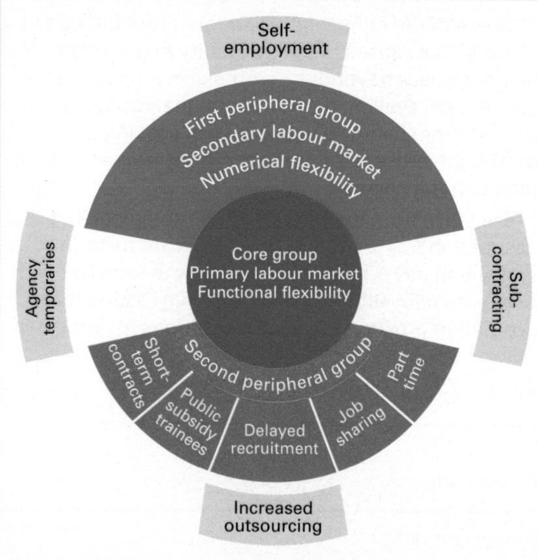

Source: *The Flexible Firm* (Institute of Manpower Studies, 1984).

The diagram shows how these three forms of flexibility are reflected in the organisation of a ***flexible firm***, an organisation quite different from that of the traditional firm. The most significant difference is that the labour force is segmented. The core group, drawn from the ***primary labour market***, will be composed of functionally flexible workers, who have relatively

workers on profit-maximising principles. Thus white workers would be employed up to that point where their *MC* equals their *MRP*. But the fact that fewer black workers are now being employed will mean that for any given quantity of white workers there will be fewer workers employed in total, and therefore the *MRP* of white workers will have increased. In Figure 9.11(b) the white workers' *MRP* curve has shifted to MRP_{W_2}. This has the effect of

Definitions

Functional flexibility Where employers can switch workers from job to job as requirements change.

Numerical flexibility Where employers can change the size of their workforce as their labour requirements change.

Financial flexibility Where employers can vary their wage costs by changing the composition of their workforce or the terms on which workers are employed.

Flexible firm A firm that has the flexibility to respond to changing market conditions by changing the composition of its workforce.

Primary labour market The market for permanent full-time core workers.

BOX 9.8

secure employment and are generally on full-time permanent contracts. Such workers will be relatively well paid and receive wages reflecting their scarce skills.

The periphery, drawn from the ***secondary labour market***, is more fragmented than the core, and can be sub-divided into a first and a second peripheral group. The first peripheral group is composed of workers with a lower level of skill than those in the core, skills that tend to be general rather than firm specific. Thus workers in the first peripheral group can usually be drawn from the external labour market, often through agencies. Such workers may be employed on full-time contracts, but they will generally face less secure employment than those workers in the core.

The business gains a greater level of numerical flexibility by drawing labour from the second peripheral group. Here workers are employed on a variety of short-term, part-time contracts, often again through agencies. Some of these workers may be working from home, or online from another country, such as India, where wage rates are much lower. Workers in the second peripheral group have little job security.

As well as supplementing labour in the first peripheral group, the second periphery can also provide high-level specialist skills. In this instance the business can sub-contract or hire self-employed labour, minimising its commitment to such workers. The business thereby gains both functional and numerical flexibility simultaneously.

The Japanese model

The application of new flexible working patterns is becoming more prevalent in businesses in the UK and elsewhere in Europe and North America. In Japan, flexibility has been part of the business way of life for many years and was crucial in shaping the country's economic success in the 1970s and 1980s. In fact we now talk of a Japanese model of business organisation, which many of its competitors seek to emulate.

The model is based around four principles:

- *Total quality management (TQM).* This involves all employees working towards continuously improving all aspects of quality, both of the finished product and of methods of production.
- *Elimination of waste.* According to the 'just-in-time' (JIT) principle, businesses should take delivery of just sufficient quantities of raw materials and parts, at the right time and place. Stocks are kept to a minimum and hence the whole system of production runs with little, if any, slack. For example, supermarkets today have smaller storerooms relative to the total shopping area than they did in the past, and take more frequent deliveries.
- *A belief in the superiority of team work.* Collective effort is a vital element in Japanese working practices. Team work is seen not only to enhance individual performance, but also to involve the individual in the running of the business and thus to create a sense of commitment.
- *Functional and numerical flexibility.* Both are seen as vital components in maintaining high levels of productivity.

The principles of this model are now widely accepted as being important in creating and maintaining a competitive business in a competitive marketplace.

Within the EU, the UK has been one of the most successful in cutting unemployment and creating jobs. Much of this has been attributed to increased labour market flexibility. As a result, other EU countries, such as Italy and Germany, are seeking to emulate many of the measures the UK has adopted.

1. Is a flexible firm more likely or less likely to employ workers up to the point where their $MRP = MC_L$?

2. How is the advent of flexible firms likely to alter the gender balance of employment and unemployment?

raising employment of white workers to Q_{W_2} and the wage rate to W_{W_2}.

Firms may, however, also practise economic discrimination *in favour* of certain groups. Figure 9.11(b) also illustrates this second case, where the employer practises economic discrimination in favour of white workers. Here the firm will employ workers along a higher curve, $MRP_{W_2} + y$, where y is the discriminatory factor. The effect is further to increase the wage rate and level of employment of white workers, to W_{W_3} and Q_{W_3} respectively.

? *What effect will the discrimination by the firm have on the wages and employment of black workers in other firms in the area if (a) these other firms discriminate against black workers; (b) they do not discriminate?*

If the government now insists on equal pay for equal work, then employers that discriminate will respond by further cutting back on black workers. The answer to *this* problem would seem to be for the government to pass laws that insist not only that black workers be paid the same as white for doing the same job, but also that they be treated

Definition

Secondary labour market The market for peripheral workers, usually employed on a temporary or part-time basis, or a less secure 'permanent' basis.

equally when applying for jobs. The problem here is that an employer which wants to continue discrimination can always claim that the black applicants were less well qualified than the white applicant who got the job. Such laws are therefore difficult to enforce.

The type of discrimination considered so far can be seen as 'irrational' if the firm wants to maximise profits. After all, to produce a given amount of output, it would be paying out more in wages to employ white workers than black workers. In a competitive market environment, such firms may be forced to end discrimination simply to survive the competition from non-discriminating rivals. If, however, the firm has market power, it will probably be making sufficient profits to allow it to continue discriminating. The main pressure here to end discrimination is likely to come from unions, customers, shareholders or race relations organisations.

Other examples of non-economic discrimination stem from unequal educational opportunities. If the educational system discriminates against black children, they are likely to end up with poorer qualifications. They have less ***human capital*** invested in them. Under these circumstances, employers, preferring to employ the best-qualified applicants, are likely to choose white people. This is particularly so in the more highly paid jobs that require a higher level of educational attainment. Tackling this problem at source means tackling weaknesses in the education system or problems of inner-city deprivation.

> **Definition**
>
> **Human capital** The qualifications, skills and expertise that contribute to a worker's productivity.

Conclusions: Who are the poor? Who are the rich?

To the list we made at the end of section 9.1 we can now add the following factors that will tend to make people poor:

- Lack of economic power, not belonging to a union or belonging to a union with only weak bargaining power.
- Ignorance of better job opportunities.
- Lack of will to search for a better job.
- Discrimination against them by employers or fellow workers.

Thus before the advent of the minimum wage many people of Asian origin, especially women, working in the garment industry in back-street 'sweatshops' earned pitifully low wages.

Conversely, belonging to a powerful union, working for a profitable employer which nevertheless is not a ruthless profit maximiser, being aware of new job opportunities and having the 'get up and go' to apply for better jobs, and being white, male and middle class are all factors that help to contribute to people earning high wages.

Section summary

1. If a firm is a monopsony employer, it will employ workers to the point where $MRP_L = MC_L$. Since the wage is below MC_L, the monopsonist, other things being equal, will employ fewer workers at a lower wage than would be employed in a perfectly competitive labour market.
2. If a union has monopoly power, its power to raise wage rates will be limited if the employer operates under perfect or monopolistic competition in the goods market. A rise in wage rates will force the employer to cut back on employment.
3. In a situation of bilateral monopoly (where a monopoly union faces a monopsony employer), the union may have considerable scope to raise the wage rate above the monopsony level, without the employer wishing to reduce the level of employment. There is no unique equilibrium wage. The wage will depend on the outcome of a process of collective bargaining between union and management.
4. Each side can make various threats or promises. The outcome of the bargaining will depend on the relative power, attitudes and bargaining skills of both sides, the firm's profitability and the information each side has about the other. The outcome also depends on the legal framework within which the negotiations take place.
5. Power is not the only factor that makes actual wage determination different from the perfectly competitive model. Firms and workers may have imperfect knowledge of the labour market; disequilibrium in labour markets may persist; firms may not be profit maximisers (see Web Case 9.2).
6. Firms may exercise discrimination (by race, sex, age, etc.) in their employment policy. By discriminating against a particular group, an employer with market power can drive down the wages of the members of that group. Unless firms are forced not to discriminate, equal pay legislation may well lead to a reduction in the employment of members of groups that are discriminated against.

9.3 CAPITAL AND PROFIT

The non-human factors of production

In the final two sections of the chapter, we consider the market for *other* factors of production. These can be divided into two broad groups.

Land. This includes all those productive resources supplied by nature: in other words, not only land itself, but also all natural resources. (We examine land in section 9.4.)

Capital. This includes all manufactured products that are used to produce goods and services. Thus capital includes such diverse items as a blast furnace, a bus, a cinema projector, a computer, a factory building and a screwdriver.

The capital goods described above are physical assets and are known as *physical* capital. The word 'capital' is also used to refer to various *paper* assets, such as shares and bonds. These are the means by which firms raise finance to purchase physical capital, and are known as *financial* capital. Being merely paper assets, however, they do not count as factors of production. Nevertheless, financial markets have an important role in determining the level of investment in physical capital, and we shall be examining these markets in the final part of section 9.3.

Factor prices versus the price of factor services

A feature of most non-human factors is that they last a period of time. A machine may last 10 years; a coal mine may last 50 years before it is exhausted; farmland will last for ever if properly looked after. We must therefore distinguish between the income the owner will get from *selling* the factor and that which the owner will get from *using* it or *hiring* it out:

- The income from selling the factor is the factor's *price*. It is a once-and-for-all payment. Thus a machine might sell for £10 000, or a hectare of land for £20 000.
- The income gained from using a factor is its *return*, and the income gained from hiring a factor out is its *rental*. This income represents the value or price of the factor's *services*, expressed per period of time. Thus a machine might earn a firm £1000 per year. A hectare of land might earn a landowner £2000 rent per year.

Obviously the price of a factor will be linked to the value of its services. The price that a hectare of land will fetch if sold will depend on the return or rent that can be earned on that land. If it is highly productive farmland, it will sell for a higher price than a piece of scrubby moorland.

When we were looking at wage rates, were we talking about the price of labour or the price of labour services? Is this distinction between the price of a factor and the price of factor services a useful one in the case of labour? Was it in Roman times?

The profit-maximising employment of land and capital

On the demand side, the same rules apply for land and capital as for labour, if a firm wishes to maximise profits. Namely, it should demand factors up to the point where the marginal cost of the factor equals its marginal revenue product: $MC_f = MRP_f$. This same rule applies whether the firm is buying the factor outright, or merely renting it. 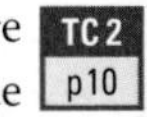

Figure 9.12 illustrates the two cases of perfect competition and monopsony. In both diagrams the *MRP* curve slopes downwards. This is another illustration of the law of diminishing returns, but this time applied to land or 

Figure 9.12 Profit-maximising employment of a factor

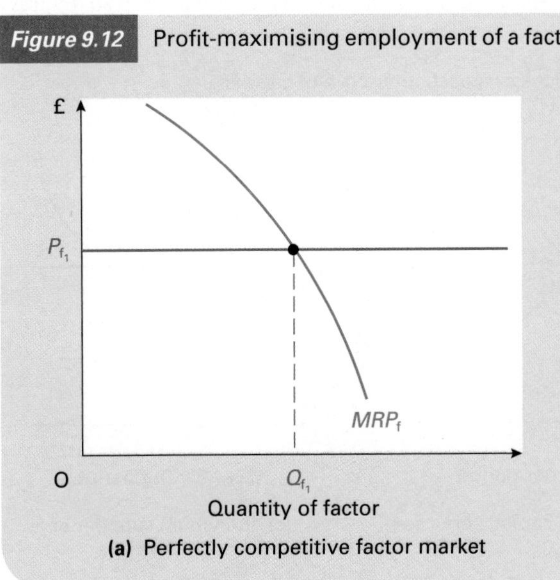

(a) Perfectly competitive factor market

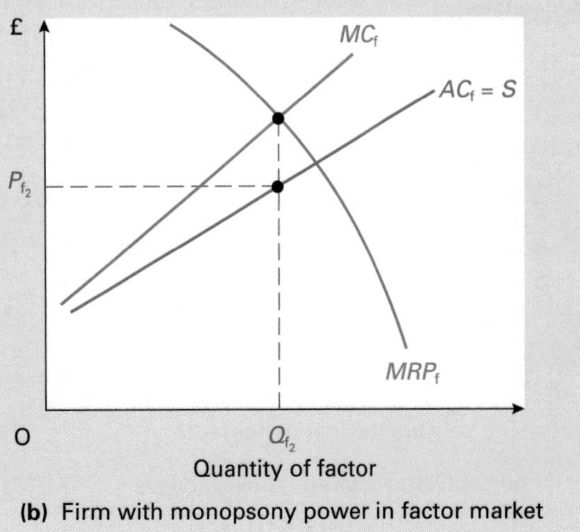

(b) Firm with monopsony power in factor market

capital. For example, if a farmer increases the amount of land farmed while *holding other factors constant*, diminishing returns to land will occur. If the same number of farm workers and the same amount of agricultural machinery and fertilisers are used but on a larger area, then returns per hectare will fall.

In diagram (a) the firm is a price taker. The factor price is given at P_{f_1}. Profits are maximised at Q_{f_1} where $MRP_f = P_f$ (since $P_f = MC_f$).

In diagram (b) the firm has monopsony power. The factor price will vary, therefore, with the amount that the firm uses. The firm will again use factors to the point where $MRP_f = MC_f$. In this case, it will mean using Q_{f_2} at a price of P_{f_2}.

What is the difference between buying a factor and renting it? Although the $MRP_f = MC_f$ rule remains the same, there are differences. As far as buying the factors is concerned, the MC_f is the extra outlay for the firm in *purchasing* one more unit of the factor; and the MRP_f is all the revenue produced by that factor over its *whole life* (but measured in terms of what this is worth when purchased: see pages 252–4). In the case of renting, MC_f is the extra outlay for the firm in rent *per period*, while MRP_f is the extra revenue earned from it *per period*.

The demand for capital services

What we are talking about in this section is the hiring of capital equipment for a period of time (as opposed to buying it outright). The analysis is virtually identical to that of the demand for labour. As with labour, we can distinguish between an individual firm's demand and the whole market demand.

Individual firm's demand

Take the case of a small painting and decorating firm thinking of hiring some scaffolding in order to complete a job. It could use ladders, but the job would take longer to complete. If it hires the scaffolding for one day, it can perhaps shorten the job by, say, two or three days. If it hires it for a second day, it can perhaps save another one or two days. Hiring it for additional days may save extra still. But diminishing returns are occurring: the longer the scaffolding is up, the less intensively it will be used, and the less additional time it will save. Perhaps for some of the time it will be used when ladders could have been used equally easily.

The time saved allows the firm to take on extra work. Thus each extra day the scaffolding is hired gives the firm extra revenue. This is the scaffolding's marginal revenue product of capital (MRP_K). Diminishing returns mean that it has the normal downward-sloping shape (see Figure 9.12).

Market demand

The market demand for capital services is derived in exactly the same way as the market demand for labour (see Figure 9.6 on page 234). It is the horizontal sum of the MRP_K curves of the individual firms, corrected for the fact that increased use of capital will increase output, drive down the price of the good and hence reduce *MRP*. This means that the market demand curve for capital is steeper than the horizontal sum of the demand curves (MRP_K) of all the firms in the market.

Under what circumstances would the market demand for renting a type of capital equipment be (a) elastic; (b) inelastic? (Clue: turn back to page 234 and see what determines the elasticity of demand for labour.)

The supply of capital services

It is necessary to distinguish (a) the supply *to* a single firm, (b) the supply *by* a single firm and (c) the market supply.

Supply to a single firm

This is illustrated in Figure 9.13(a). The small firm renting capital equipment is probably a price taker. If so, it faces a

Figure 9.13 Long-run equilibrium rental rate for the services of a particular type of capital

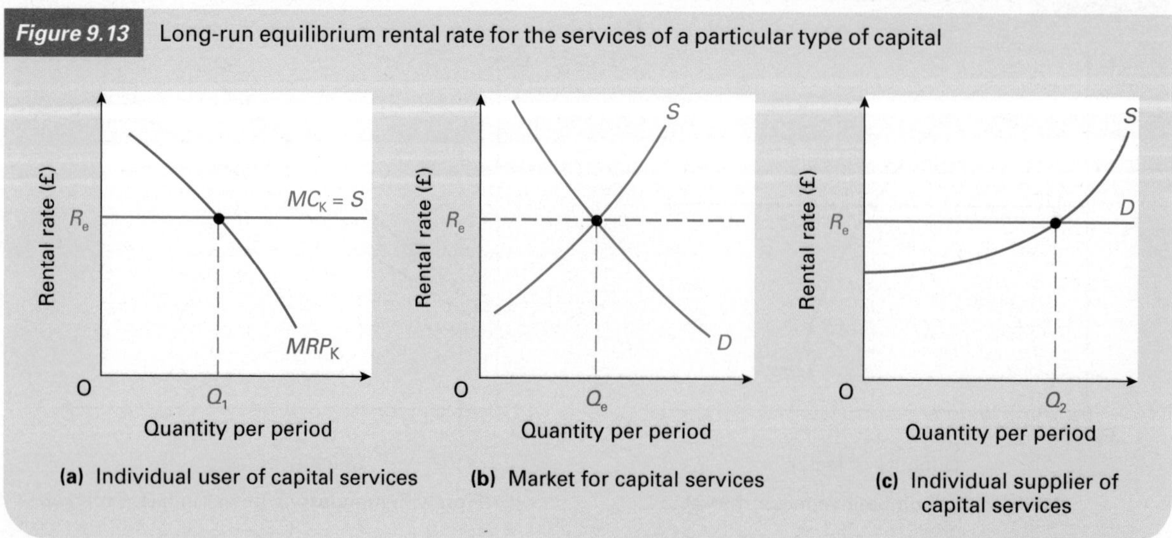

(a) Individual user of capital services **(b)** Market for capital services **(c)** Individual supplier of capital services

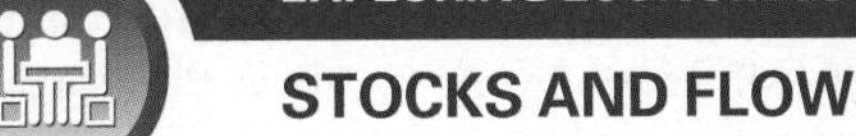

EXPLORING ECONOMICS — BOX 9.9

STOCKS AND FLOWS

The discussion of the rewards to capital and land leads to a very important distinction: that between stocks and flows.

A *stock* is a quantity of something held. A landowner may own 200 hectares. A farmer may have a barn with 500 tonnes of grain. You may have £1000 in a savings account. These are all stocks: they are all quantities held at a given point in time.

A *flow* is an increase or decrease in quantity over a specified period. The landowner may buy another 10 hectares during the year. The farmer may use 10 tonnes of grain from the barn each week as animal feed. You may save £10 per month.

Wages, rent and interest are all rewards to *flows*. Wages are the amount paid for the services of a person's labour for a week or month. Rent is the amount paid per period of time to use the services of land. Likewise interest is the reward paid to people per year for the use of their money.

If an asset is sold, its value is the value of the *stock*. It is a simple payment at a single point in time for the transfer of a whole asset. Thus the price of land and the price of capital are stock concepts.

An important example of stocks and flows arises with capital and investment. If a firm has 100 machines, that is a stock of capital. It may choose to build up its stock by investing. Investment is a flow concept. The firm may choose to invest in 10 new machines each year. This may not add 10 to the stock of machines, however, as some may be wearing out (a negative flow).

Key Idea 23

Stocks and flows. A stock is a quantity of something at a given point in time. A flow is an increase or decrease in something over a specified period of time. This is an important distinction and a common cause of confusion.

Which of the following are stocks and which are flows?
(a) Unemployment.
(b) Redundancies.
(c) Profits.
(d) A firm's stock market valuation.
(e) The value of property after a period of inflation.

horizontal supply curve at the going rental rate (R_e). If, however, it has monopsony power, it will face an upward-sloping supply curve as in Figure 9.12(b).

Supply by a single firm

This is illustrated in Figure 9.13(c). On the demand side, the firm is likely to be a price taker. It has to accept the going rental rate (R_e) established in the market. If it tries to charge more, then customers are likely to turn to rival suppliers.

But what will the individual supplier's *supply* curve look like? The theory here has a lot in common with perfect competition in the goods market (see page 161): the supply curve is the firm's *MC* curve, only here the *MC* is the extra cost of supplying one more unit of capital equipment for rent over a given time period.

The problem with working out the marginal cost of renting out capital equipment is that the piece of equipment probably cost a lot to buy in the first place, but lasts a long time. How then are these large costs to be apportioned to each new rental? The answer is that it depends on the time period under consideration.

The short run. In the short run, the hire company is not buying any new equipment: it is simply hiring out its existing stock of equipment. In the case of our scaffolding hire firm, the marginal costs of doing this will be as follows:

- Depreciation. Scaffolding has second-hand value. Each time the scaffolding is hired out it deteriorates, and thus its second-hand value falls. This loss in value is called 'depreciation'.
- Maintenance and handling. When equipment is hired out, it can get damaged and thus incur repair costs. The equipment might need servicing. Also, hiring out equipment involves labour time (e.g. in the office) and possibly transport costs.

These marginal costs are likely to rise relatively slowly. In other words, for each extra day a piece of equipment is hired out, the company will incur the same or only slightly higher additional costs. This gives a relatively flat supply curve of capital services in Figure 9.13(c) up to the hire company's maximum capacity. Once the scaffolding firm is hiring out all its scaffolding, the supply curve becomes vertical.

Assume now that the firm has monopoly power in hiring out equipment, and thus faces a downward-sloping demand curve. Draw in two such demand curves on a diagram like Figure 9.13(c), one crossing the MC curve in the horizontal section, and one in the vertical section. How much will the firm supply in each case and at what price? (You will need to draw in MR curves too.) Is the MC curve still the supply curve?

The long run. In the long run, the hire company will consider purchasing additional equipment. It can therefore supply as much as it likes in the long run. The supply curve will be relatively elastic, or if it is a price taker itself (i.e. if the scaffolding firm simply buys scaffolding at the market price), the supply curve will be horizontal. This long-run supply curve will be vertically higher than the short-run curve, since the long-run *MC* includes the cost of purchasing each additional piece of equipment.

Maths Case 9.1 on the book's website shows how this marginal cost can be calculated.

Market supply

This is illustrated in Figure 9.13(b). The market supply curve of a particular type of capital service is the sum of the quantities supplied by all the individual firms.

In the short run, the market supply will be relatively inelastic, given that it takes time to manufacture new equipment and that stocks of equipment currently held by manufacturers are likely to be relatively small. Also, capital is *heterogeneous*: i.e. one piece of capital equipment is not the same as another. If there is a shortage of scaffolding, you cannot use a cement mixer instead: people would fall off! Finally, hire companies may be unwilling to purchase (expensive) new equipment immediately there is a rise in demand: after all, the upsurge in demand may turn out to be short-lived.

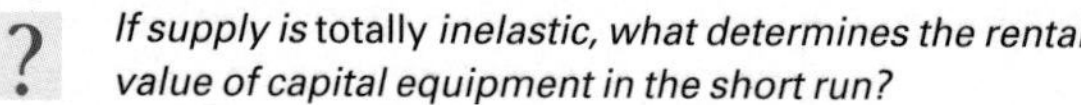

? *If supply is* totally *inelastic, what determines the rental value of capital equipment in the short run?*

In the *long run*, the supply curve of capital services will be more elastic because extra capital equipment can be produced. It will not be horizontal, however, but upward sloping. Its elasticity will depend on the elasticity of supply of capital equipment to the hire companies.

KI 8 p43

Determination of the price of capital services

As Figure 9.13(b) shows, in a perfect market the market rental rate for capital services will be determined by the interaction of market demand and supply. Note that the analysis here parallels that of the determination of the equilibrium wage in a given labour market (see Figure 9.1 on page 228).

? *What will happen to the demand for capital services and the equilibrium rental if the price of some other factor, say labour, changes? Assume that wage rates fall. Trace through the effects on a three-section diagram like Figure 9.13. (Clue: a fall in wages will reduce costs and hence the price of the product, so that more will be sold; and it will make labour cheaper relative to capital.)*

If there is monopsony power on the part of the users of hired capital, this will have the effect of depressing the rental rate below the MRP_K (see Figure 9.12(b)). If, on the other hand, there is monopoly power on the part of hire companies, the analysis is similar to that of monopoly in the goods market (see Figure 6.8 on page 168). The firm, by reducing the supply of capital for hire, can drive up the rental rate. It will maximise profit where the marginal revenue from hiring out the equipment is equal to the marginal cost of so doing: at a rental rate (price) *above* the marginal cost.

*The demand for and supply of capital for purchase

The alternative to hiring capital is to buy it outright. This section examines the demand and supply of capital for purchase.

The demand for capital: investment

How many computers will an engineering firm want to buy? Should a steelworks install another blast furnace? Should a removal firm buy another furniture lorry? These are all ***investment*** decisions. Investment involves purchasing of additional capital.

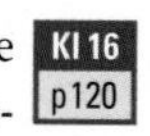

The demand for capital, or 'investment demand', by a profit-maximising firm is based on exactly the same principles as the demand for labour or the demand for capital services. The firm must weigh up the marginal revenue product of that investment (i.e. the money it will earn for the firm) against its marginal cost.

The problem is that capital is durable. It goes on producing goods, and hence yielding revenue for the firm, for a considerable period of time. Calculating these benefits therefore involves taking account of their timing.

There are two ways of approaching the problem: the *present value* approach and the *rate of return* approach. In both cases, the firm is comparing the marginal benefits with the marginal costs of the investment.

Present value approach. To work out the benefit of an investment (its *MRP*), the firm must estimate all the future earnings it will bring and then convert them to a ***present value***. It can then compare this with the cost of the investment. Let us take a simple example.

Assume that a firm is considering buying a machine. It will produce £1000 per year (net of operating costs) for four years and then wear out and sell for £1000 as scrap. What is the benefit of this machine to the firm? At first sight the answer would seem to be £5000. This, after all, is the total income earned from the machine. Unfortunately, it is not as simple as this. The reason is that money earned in the

Definitions

Investment The purchase by the firm of equipment or materials that will add to its stock of capital.

Present value approach to appraising investment This involves estimating the value *now* of a flow of future benefits (or costs).

future is less beneficial to the firm than having the same amount of money today: if the firm has the money today, it can earn interest on it by putting it in the bank or reinvesting it in some other project.

To illustrate this, assume that you have £100 today and can earn 10 per cent interest by putting it in a bank. In one year's time that £100 will have grown to £110, in two years' time to £121, in three years' time to £133.10 and so on. This process is known as ***compounding***.

It follows that if someone offered to give you £121 in two years' time, that would be no better than giving you £100 today, since, with interest, £100 would grow to £121 in two years. What we say, then, is that, with a 10 per cent interest rate, £121 in two years' time has a *present value* of £100.

The procedure of reducing future value back to a present value is known as ***discounting***.

Key Idea 24 ***The principle of discounting.*** People generally prefer to have benefits today rather than in the future. Thus future benefits have to be reduced (discounted) to give them a present value.

When we do discounting, the rate we use is called the ***rate of discount***: in this case, 10 per cent. The formula for discounting is as follows:

$$PV = \sum \frac{R_t}{(1+r)^t}$$

where PV is the present value
R_t is the revenue from the investment in year t
r is the rate of discount (expressed as a decimal: e.g. 10% = 0.1)
Σ is the sum of each of the years' discounted earnings.

So what is the present value of the investment in the machine that produced £1000 for four years and then is sold as scrap for £1000 at the end of the four years? According to the formula it is:

Year 1 Year 2 Year 3 Year 4

$$= \frac{£1000}{1.1} + \frac{£1000}{(1.1)^2} + \frac{£1000}{(1.1)^3} + \frac{£2000}{(1.1)^4}$$

$$= £909 + £826 + £751 + £1366$$

$$= £3852$$

Thus the present value of the investment (i.e. its *MRP*) is £3852, *not* £5000 as might seem at first sight. In other words, if the firm had £3852 today and deposited it in a bank at a 10 per cent interest rate, the firm would earn exactly the same as it would by investing in the machine.

So is the investment worthwhile? It is now simply a question of comparing the £3852 benefit with the cost of buying the machine. If the machine costs less than £3852, it will be worth buying. If it costs more, the firm would be better off keeping its money in the bank and earning the 10 per cent rate of interest.

The difference between the present value of the benefits (PV_b) of the investment and its cost (C) is known as the ***net present value*** (*NPV*):

$$NPV = PV_b - C$$

If the *NPV* is positive, the investment is worthwhile.

? *What is the present value of a machine that lasts three years, earns £100 in year 1, £200 in year 2 and £200 in year 3, and then has a scrap value of £100? Assume that the rate of discount is 5 per cent. If the machine costs £500, is the investment worthwhile? Would it be worthwhile if the rate of discount were 10 per cent?*

Rate of return approach. The alternative approach when estimating whether an investment is worthwhile is to calculate the investment's *rate of return*. This rate of return is known as the firm's ***marginal efficiency of capital*** (*MEC*) or ***internal rate of return*** (*IRR*). KI 24 p253

We use the same formula as for calculating present value:

$$PV = \sum \frac{R_t}{(1+r)^t}$$

and then calculate what value of r would make the PV equal to the cost of investment: in other words, the rate of discount that would make the investment just break even. Say this worked out at 20 per cent. What we would be saying is that the investment would just cover its costs if the current rate of interest (rate of discount) were 20 per cent. In other words, this investment is equivalent to receiving 20 per cent interest: it has a 20 per cent rate of return (*MEC*).

Details of how to calculate the internal rate of return, along with a worked example, are given in Maths Case 9.1 on the book's website.

Definitions

Compounding The process of adding interest each year to an initial capital sum.

Discounting The process of reducing the value of future flows to give them a present valuation.

Rate of discount The rate that is used to reduce future values to present values.

Net present value of an investment The discounted benefits of an investment minus the cost of the investment.

Marginal efficiency of capital or **internal rate of return** The rate of return of an investment: the discount rate that makes the net present value of an investment equal to zero.

So should the investment go ahead? Yes, if the actual rate of interest (i) is less than 20 per cent. The firm is better off investing its money in this project than keeping it in the bank: i.e. if $MEC > i$ the investment should proceed.

TC 2 p10

This is just one more application of the general rule that if $MRP_f > MC_f$ then more of the factor should be used: only in this case, MRP is expressed as a rate of return (MEC), and MC is expressed as a rate of interest (i).

KI 17 p121

The profit-maximising position is illustrated in Figure 9.14. As the firm invests more, and thus builds up its stock of capital, so MEC will fall due to diminishing returns. As long as MEC is greater than i, the firm should invest more. It should stop when the stock of capital has reached Q_1. Thereafter it should cut investment to a level just sufficient to replace worn-out machines, and thus keep the capital stock at Q_1.

KI 11 p66

The risks of investment. One of the problems with investment is that the future is uncertain. The return on an investment will depend on the value of the goods it produces, which will depend on the goods market. But future markets cannot be predicted with accuracy: they depend on consumer tastes, the actions of rivals and the whole state of the economy. Investment is thus risky.

Risk may also be incurred in terms of the output from an investment. Take the case of prospecting for oil. An oil company may be lucky and have a major strike, but it may simply drill dry well after dry well. If it does get a major strike, and hence earn a large return on its investment, these profits will not be competed away by competitors prospecting in other fields, because they too still run the risk of drilling dry holes.

How is this risk accounted for when calculating the benefits of an investment? The answer is to use a higher rate of discount. The higher the risk, the bigger the premium that must be added to the rate.

The supply of capital

It is necessary to distinguish the supply of *physical* capital from the supply of *finance* to be used by firms for the purchase of capital.

Supply of physical capital. The principles here are just the same as those in the goods market. It does not matter whether a firm is supplying lorries (capital) or cars (a consumer good): it will still produce up to the point where $MC = MR$ if it wishes to maximise profits.

Supply of finance. An economy will have a stock of financial capital (or 'loanable funds') held in banks and other financial institutions. These funds can be borrowed by firms for investment in new physical capital.

KI 23 p251

When people save, this will build up the stock of loanable funds. This flow of saving represents the resources released when people refrain from consumption. Among other things, saving depends on the rate of interest. This is illustrated in Figure 9.15. A rise in the interest rate will encourage people to save more, thereby increasing the supply (i.e. the stock) of loanable funds (a movement up along the supply curve).

This supply curve will be relatively inelastic in the short run, since the flow of saving over a short time period (say, a month) will have only a relatively small effect on the total stock of funds. Over a year, however, the effect would be twelve times bigger. The longer the time period, therefore, the more elastic the supply curve.

Saving also depends on the level of people's incomes, their expectations of future price changes, and their general level of 'thriftiness' (their willingness to forgo present consumption in order to be able to have more in the future). A change in any of these other determinants will shift the supply curve.

Figure 9.14 The profit-maximising stock of capital

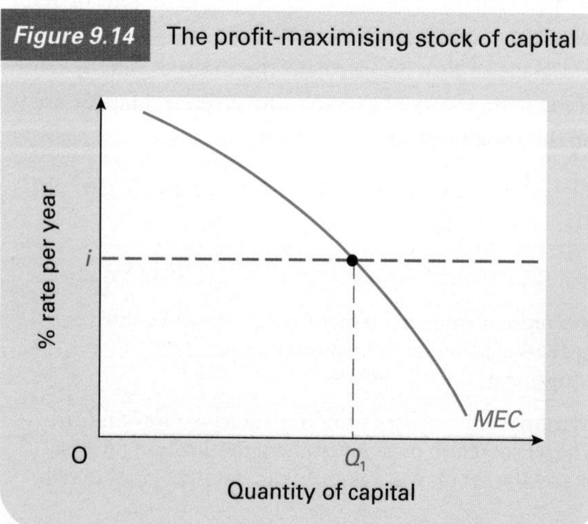

Figure 9.15 The market for loanable funds

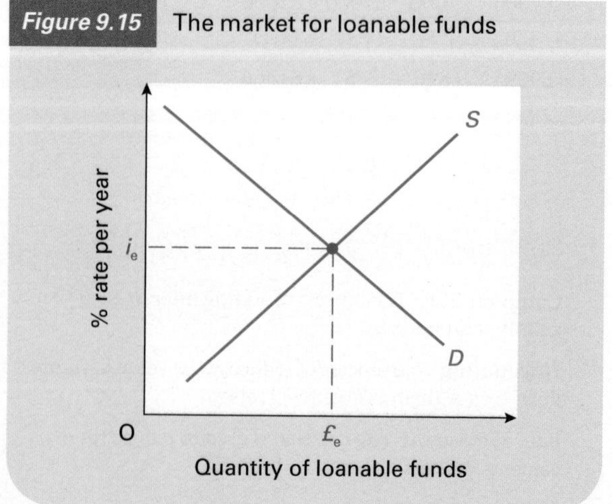

*Determination of the rate of interest

The rate of interest is determined by the interaction of supply and demand in the market for loanable funds. This is illustrated in Figure 9.15. As we have seen, supply represents accumulated savings.

The demand curve includes the demand by households for credit and the demand by firms for funds to finance their investment. The curve slopes downwards for two reasons. First, households will borrow more at lower rates of interest. It effectively makes goods cheaper for them to buy. Second, it reflects the falling rate of return on investment as investment increases. This is simply due to diminishing returns to investment. As rates of interest fall, it will become profitable for firms to invest in projects that have a lower rate of return: the quantity of loanable funds demanded thus rises.

Equilibrium will be achieved where demand equals supply at an interest rate of i_e and a quantity of loanable funds $£_e$.

How will this market adjust to a change in demand or supply? Assume that there is a rise in demand for capital equipment, due, say, to an improvement in technology that increases the productivity of capital. There is thus an increase in demand for loanable funds. The demand curve shifts to the right in Figure 9.15. The equilibrium rate of interest will rise and this will encourage more savings. The end result is that more money will be spent on capital equipment.

Capital and profit

What does the analysis so far tell us about the amount of profit that firms will earn? After all, profit is the reward that the owners of firms get from having and using capital.

Remember from Chapter 6 the distinction between normal and supernormal profit. In a perfectly competitive world, all supernormal profits will be competed away in the long run.

Another way of putting this is that a perfectly competitive firm in the long run will earn only a ***normal rate of return*** on capital. This means that the return on capital (after taking risk into account) will be just the same as if the owners of capital had simply deposited their money in a bank instead. If a firm's capital yields a higher rate of return than this normal level (i.e. supernormal returns), other firms will be attracted to invest in similar capital. The resulting increased level of capital will increase the supply of goods. This in turn will lower the price of the goods and hence lower the rate of return on capital until it has fallen back to the normal level.

? *Can a perfectly competitive firm earn a supernormal rate of return on capital if it* continuously *innovates?*

If, however, capital owners have monopoly/oligopoly power and can thus restrict the entry of new firms or the copying of innovations – for example, by having a patent on a particular process – they can continue to get a supernormal return on their capital.

Financing investment

Sources of business finance

A firm can finance capital investment in one of three major ways:

- Internal funds (i.e. retained profits).
- Borrowing from the banking sector.
- Issuing new shares (equities) or debentures (fixed-interest loan stock).

The largest source of finance for investment in the UK is firms' own internal funds (i.e. ploughed-back profits). Given, however, that business profitability depends in large part on the general state of the economy, internal funds as a source of business finance are likely to show considerable cyclical variation. When profits are squeezed in a recession, this source of investment will decline.

Other sources of finance, which include borrowing and the issue of shares and debentures, are known as 'external funds'. These are then categorised as short-term, medium-term or long-term sources of finance.

- Short-term finance is usually in the form of a short-term bank loan or overdraft facility, and is used by business as a form of working capital to aid it in its day-to-day business operations.
- Medium-term finance, again provided largely by banks, is usually in the form of a loan with set repayment targets. It is common for such loans to be made at a fixed rate of interest, with repayments being designed to fit in with the business's expected cash flow. Bank lending has been the most volatile source of business finance, and has been particularly sensitive to the state of the economy. While part of the reason is the lower demand for loans during a recession, part of the reason is the caution of banks in granting loans if prospects for the economy are poor.
- Long-term finance, especially in the UK, tends to be acquired through the stock market. It will usually be in the form of ***shares (or equities)***. This is where members of the public or institutions (such as pension funds) buy a part ownership in the company and, as a result, receive dividends on those shares. The dividends depend on

Definitions

Normal rate of return The rate of return (after taking risks into account) that could be earned elsewhere.

Shares (equities) A part ownership of a company. Companies' distributed profits are paid to shareholders in the form of dividends according to the number of shares held.

the amount of profit the company makes and distributes to shareholders. The proportion of business financing from this source clearly depends on the state of the stock market. In the late 1990s, with a buoyant stock market, the proportion of funds obtained through share issue increased. Then with a decline in stock market prices from 2000 to 2003, this proportion fell.

Alternatively, firms can issue ***debentures (or company bonds)***. These securities are fixed-interest loans to firms. Debenture holders have a prior claim on company shares. Their interest must be paid in full before shareholders can receive any dividends.

Despite the traditional reliance on the stock market for external long-term sources of finance, there has been a growing involvement of banks in recent years. Banks have become more willing to provide finance for business start-ups and for diversification. Nevertheless, there is a concern that banks are still relatively cautious. This results in a problem of 'short-termism', with bankers often demanding a quick return on their money or charging high interest rates, and being less concerned to finance long-term investment.

Comparison of the UK with other European countries. In other European countries, notably Germany and France, the attitude towards business funding is quite different from that in the UK. In these countries banks provide a significant amount of *long-term*, fixed-rate finance. This provides a much more stable source of finance and creates an environment where banks are much more committed to the long-run health of companies.

The role of the stock market

The London Stock Exchange operates as both a primary and secondary market in capital.

As a ***primary market***, it is where public limited companies (see Web Case 8.1) can raise finance by issuing new shares, whether to new shareholders or to existing ones. To raise finance on the Stock Exchange a business must be 'listed'. The Listing Agreement involves directors agreeing to abide by a strict set of rules governing behaviour and levels of reporting to shareholders. Companies must have at least three years' trading experience and make at least 25 per cent of their shares available to the public. In January 2005, there were 1460 UK and 349 international companies on the Official List. During 2004 £236.2 billion's worth of new capital was raised by selling equity (ordinary shares) and fixed-interest securities on the London Stock Exchange.

As well as those on the Official List, there are over 1000 companies on what is known as the Alternative Investment Market (AIM). Companies listed here tend to be young but with growth potential, and do not have to meet the strict criteria or pay such high costs as companies on the Official List.

As a ***secondary market***, the Stock Exchange enables investors to sell *existing* shares and debentures to one another. In 2004, on an average day's trading, £9.1 billion's worth of trading in UK equities took place.

The advantages and disadvantages of using the stock market to raise capital

As a market for raising capital, the stock market has a number of advantages:

- It brings together those that wish to invest and companies that seek investment, and does so in a relatively low-cost way. It thus represents a way that savings can be mobilised to generate output.
- Firms that are listed on the stock exchange are subject to strict regulations. This is likely to stimulate investor confidence, making it easier for business to raise finance.
- The process of merger and acquisition is facilitated by having a share system, which in turn increases competition for corporate control (see page 171).

The main weaknesses of the stock market for raising capital are:

- The cost to a business of getting listed can be immense, not only in a financial sense, but also in being open to public scrutiny. Directors' and senior managers' decisions will often be driven by how the market is likely to react, rather than by what they perceive to be in the business's best interests. They always have to think about the reactions of those large shareholders in the City that control a large proportion of their shares.
- In the UK, it is often claimed that the market suffers from ***short-termism***. Investors on the Stock Exchange

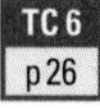

Definitions

Debentures (company bonds) Fixed-interest loans to firms. These assets can be traded on the stock market and their market price is determined by demand and supply.

Primary market in capital Where shares are sold by the issuer of the shares (i.e. the firm) and where, therefore, finance is channelled directly from the purchasers (i.e. the shareholders) to the firm.

Secondary market in capital Where shareholders sell shares to others. This is thus a market in 'second-hand' shares.

Short-termism Where firms and investors take decisions based on the likely short-term performance of a company, rather than on its long-term prospects. Firms may thus sacrifice long-term profits and growth for the sake of a quick return.

are more concerned with a company's short-term performance and its share value. In responding to this, the business might neglect its long-term performance and potential.

Is the stock market efficient?

One of the arguments made in favour of the stock market is that it acts as an arena within which share values can be accurately or efficiently priced. If new information comes on to the market concerning a business and its performance, this will be quickly and rationally transferred into the business's share value. This is known as the ***efficient market hypothesis***. So, for example, if an investment analyst found that, in terms of its actual and expected dividends, a particular share was under-priced and thus represented a 'bargain', the analyst would advise investors to buy. As people then bought the shares, their price would rise, pushing their value up to their full worth. So by attempting to gain from inefficiently priced securities, investors will encourage the market to become more efficient.

KI 3 p10

So how efficient is the stock market in pricing securities? Is information rationally and quickly conveyed into the share's price? Or are investors able to prosper from the stock market's inefficiencies?

We can identify three levels of efficiency.

The weak form of efficiency. Share prices often move in cycles that do not reflect the underlying performance of the firm. If information is imperfect, those with a better understanding of such cycles gain from buying shares at the trough and selling them at the peak of the cycles. They are taking advantage of the market's inefficiency.

The technical analysis used by investment analysts to track share cycles is a complex science, but more and more analysts are using the techniques. As they do so and knowledge becomes more perfect, so the market will become more efficient and the cycles will tend to disappear. But why?

As more people buy a company's shares as the price falls towards its trough, so this extra demand will prevent the price falling so far. Similarly, as people sell as the price rises towards its peak, so this extra supply will prevent the price rising so far. This is an example of stabilising speculation (see page 63). As more and more people react in this way, so the cycle all but disappears. When this happens, ***weak efficiency*** has been achieved.

The semi-strong form of efficiency. ***Semi-strong efficiency*** is when share prices adjust fully to publicly available information. In practice, not all investors will interpret such information correctly: their knowledge is imperfect. But as investors become more and more sophisticated, and as more and more advice is available to shareholders (through stockbrokers, newspapers, published accounts, etc.), and as many shares are purchased by professional fund managers, so the interpretation of public information becomes more and more perfect and the market becomes more and more efficient in the semi-strong sense.

If the market were efficient in the semi-strong sense, then no gain could be made from studying a company's performance and prospects, as any such information would *already* be included in the current share price. In selecting shares, you would do just as well by pinning the financial pages of a newspaper on the wall, throwing darts at them, and buying the shares the darts hit!

The strong form of efficiency. If the stock market showed the ***strong form of efficiency***, then share prices would fully reflect *all* available information – whether public or not. For this to be so, all 'inside' information would have to be reflected in the share price the moment the information became available.

If the market is *not* efficient at this level, then people who have access to privileged information will be able to make large returns from their investments by acting on such information. For example, directors of a company would know if the company was soon to announce better-than-expected profits. In the meantime, they could gain by buying shares in the company, knowing that the share price would rise when the information about the profits became public. Gains made from such 'insider dealing' are illegal. However, proving whether individuals are engaging in it is very difficult. Nevertheless, there are people in prison for insider dealing: so it does happen!

TC 3 p21

Given the penalties for insider dealing and the amount of private information that firms possess, it is unlikely that all such information will be reflected in share prices. Thus the strong form of stock market efficiency is unlikely to hold.

? *Would the stock market be more efficient if insider dealing were made legal?*

Definitions

Efficient (capital) market hypothesis The hypothesis that new information about a company's current or future performance will be quickly and accurately reflected in its share price.

Weak efficiency (of share markets) Where share dealing prevents cyclical movements in shares.

Semi-strong efficiency (of share markets) Where share prices adjust quickly, fully and accurately to publicly available information.

Strong efficiency (of share markets) Where share prices adjust quickly, fully and accurately to all available information, both public and that only available to insiders.

If stock markets were fully efficient, the expected returns from every share would be the same. The return is referred to as the ***yield***: this is measured as the dividends paid on the share as a percentage of the share's market price. For example, if you hold shares whose market price is £1 per share and you receive an annual dividend of 3p per share, then the yield on the shares is 3 per cent. But why should the expected returns on shares be the same? If any share was expected to yield a higher-than-average return, people would buy it; its price would rise and its yield would correspondingly fall.

It would only be unanticipated information, therefore, that would cause share prices to deviate from that which reflected expected average yields. Such information must, by its nature, be random, and as such would cause share prices to deviate randomly from their expected price, or follow what we call a ***random walk***. Evidence suggests that share prices do tend to follow random patterns.

Section summary

1. It is necessary to distinguish between buying the *services* of land (by renting) or capital (by hiring) from buying them outright.
2. The profit-maximising employment of land and capital services will be where the factor's *MRP* is equal to its price (under perfect competition) or its *MC* (where firms have monopsony power).
3. The demand for capital services will be equal to MRP_K. Due to diminishing returns, this will decline as more capital is used.
4. The supply of capital services *to* a firm will be horizontal or upward sloping depending on whether the firm is perfectly competitive or has monopsony power. The supply of capital services by a firm in the short run is likely to be relatively elastic up to its maximum use, and then totally inelastic. In the long run, the supplying firm can purchase additional capital equipment for hiring out. The long-run supply curve will therefore be very elastic, but at a higher rental rate than in the short run, given that the cost of purchasing the equipment must be taken into account in the rental rate.
5. The *market* supply of capital services is likely to be highly inelastic in the short run, given that capital equipment tends to have very specific uses and cannot normally be transferred from one use to another. In the long run, it will be more elastic.
6. The price of capital services is determined by the interaction of demand and supply.

*7. The demand for capital for purchase will depend on the return it earns for the firm. To calculate this return, all future earnings from the investment have to be reduced to a present value by discounting at a market rate of interest (discount). If the present value exceeds the cost of the investment, the investment is worthwhile. Alternatively, a rate of return from the investment can be calculated and then this can be compared with the return that the firm could have earned by investing elsewhere.

*8. The supply of finance for investment depends on the supply of loanable funds, which in turn depends on the rate of interest, on the general level of thriftiness and on expectations about future price levels and incomes.

*9. The rate of interest will be determined by the demand and supply of loanable funds. When deciding whether to make an investment, a firm will use this rate for discounting purposes. If, however, an investment involves risks, the firm will require a higher rate of return on the investment than current market interest rates.

10. Business finance can come from internal sources (ploughed-back profits) or from external ones. External sources of finance include borrowing and the issue of shares.
11. The stock market operates as both a primary and secondary market in capital. As a primary market it channels finance to companies as people purchase new shares and debentures. It is also a market for existing shares and debentures.
12. It helps to stimulate growth and investment by bringing together companies and people who want to invest in them. By regulating firms and by keeping transaction costs of investment low, it helps to ensure that investment is efficient.
13. It does impose costs on firms, however. It is expensive for firms to be listed and the public exposure may make them too keen to 'please' the market. It can also foster short-termism.
14. The stock market is relatively efficient. It achieves weak efficiency by reducing cyclical movements in share prices. It achieves semi-strong efficiency by allowing share prices to respond quickly and fully to publicly available information. Whether it achieves strong efficiency by adjusting quickly and fully to *all* information (both public or insider), however, is more doubtful.

Definitions

Yield on a share The dividend received per share expressed as a percentage of the current market price of the share.

Random walk Where fluctuations in the value of a share away from its 'correct' value are random: i.e. have no systematic pattern. When charted over time, these share price movements would appear like a 'random walk': like the path of someone staggering along drunk!

9.4 LAND AND RENT

Rent: the reward to landlords

We turn now to land. The income it earns for landowners is the *rent* charged to the users of the land. This rent, like the rewards to other factors, is determined by demand and supply.

What makes land different from other factors of production is that it has an inelastic supply. In one sense, this is obvious. The total supply of land in any area is fixed. It is in the very nature of land that it cannot be moved from one place to another!

In another sense, supply is not *totally* inelastic. Land can be improved. It can be cleared, levelled, drained, fertilised, etc. Thus the supply of a certain type of land can be increased by expending human effort on improving it. The question is whether *land* has thereby increased, or whether the improvements constitute *capital* invested in land, and if so whether the higher rents that such land can earn really amount to a return on the capital invested in it.

To keep the analysis simple, let us assume that land *is* fixed. Let us take the case of an area of 10 000 hectares surrounding the village of Oakleigh. This is shown as a vertical supply 'curve' in Figure 9.16. The demand curve for that land will be like the demand curve for other factors of production. It is the *MRP* curve and slopes down due to diminishing returns to land. The equilibrium rent is r_e, where demand and supply intersect.

Notice that the level of this rent depends entirely on *demand*. If a new housing development takes place in Oakleigh, due perhaps to a growth in employment in a nearby town, the demand curve will shift to D_1 and the equilibrium rent will rise to r_{e1}. But the supply of land remains fixed at 10 000 hectares. Landowners will earn more rent, but they themselves have done nothing: the higher rent is a pure windfall gain.

Figure 9.16 Determination of rent

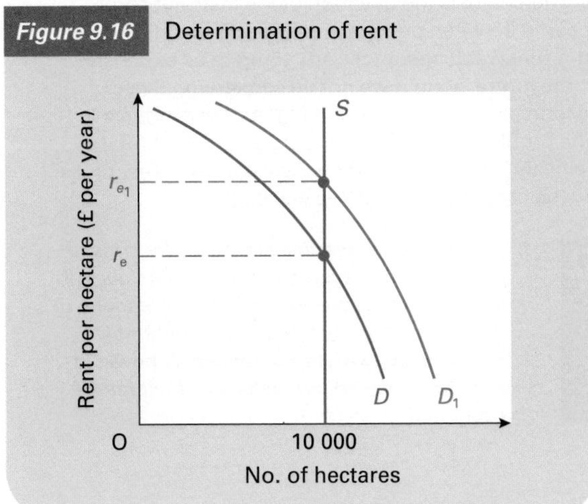

So why are rents in the centre of London many times higher per hectare than they are in the north of Scotland? The answer is that demand is very much higher in London.

Demand for land depends on its marginal revenue product. Thus it is differences in the *MRP* of land that explain the differences in rent from one area to another. There are two reasons for differences in *MRP*. Remember that *MRP* = *MPP* (marginal physical product of the factor) × *MR* (marginal revenue of the good produced by that factor).

Differences in MPP. Land differs in productivity. Fertile land will produce a higher output than deserts or moorland. Similarly, land near centres of population will be of much more use to industry than land in the middle of nowhere.

? *What other factors will determine the MPP of land for industry?*

Differences in MR. The higher the demand for a particular good, the higher its price and marginal revenue, and hence the higher the demand and rent for the land on which that good is produced. Thus if the demand for housing rises relative to the demand for food, the rent on land suitable for house building will rise relative to the rent on agricultural land.

To summarise: rents will be high on land that is physically productive (high *MPP*) and produces goods in high demand (high *MR*).

?
1. *We defined the factor of production 'land' to include raw materials. Does the analysis of rent that we have just been looking at apply to raw materials?*
2. *The supply of land in a particular area may be totally inelastic, but the supply of land in that area for a specific purpose (e.g. growing wheat) will be upward sloping: the higher the price of wheat and thus the higher the rent that wheat producers are prepared to pay, the more will be made available for wheat production. What will determine the elasticity of supply of land for any particular purpose?*

The price of land

Not all land is rented: much of it is bought and sold outright. Its price will depend on what the purchaser is prepared to pay, and this will depend on the land's rental value.

Let us say that a piece of land can earn £1000 per year. What would a person be prepared to pay for it? There is a simple formula for working this out:

$$P = \frac{R}{i} \qquad (1)$$

where *P* is the price of the land, *R* is the rent per year and *i* is the market rate of interest.

EXPLORING ECONOMICS **BOX 9.10**

THE ECONOMICS OF NON-RENEWABLE RESOURCES

What happens as stocks diminish?

As world population inexorably rises, so the demands on our planet's resources continue to grow. Some of these resources are *renewable*. Water resources are replenished by rain. The soil, if properly managed, can continue to grow crops. Felled forests can be replanted. Of course, if we use these resources more rapidly than they are replenished, stocks will run down. We are all aware of the problems of seas that are over fished, or rain forests that are cleared, or reservoirs that are inadequate to meet our growing demand for water.

But whereas these resources can be replenished, others cannot. These are known as *non-renewable resources*. What determines the price of such resources and their rate of depletion? Will we eventually run out of resources such as oil, coal, gas and various minerals? To answer these questions, we need to distinguish between the available *stock* of such resources, and their use (a *flow*). The greater their use, the faster the stocks will run down.

KI 23 p251

Price increases over time

As stocks run down, so the price of the resources will tend to increase. Thus we can all expect to pay more for fossil fuels as remaining reserves are depleted. Owners of the reserves (e.g. mineowners and owners of oil wells) will thus find the value of their assets increasing. But how quickly will prices rise? In a perfect market, they will rise at the market rate of return on *other* assets (of equivalent risk). This is known as the *Hotelling rule*, named after Harold Hotelling who developed the argument in the early 1930s.

To understand why this is so, consider what would happen if the price of oil rose more slowly than the rate of return on other assets. People who owned oil wells would find that the value of their oil reserves was increasing less rapidly than the value of other assets. They might as well sell more oil now and invest the money in other assets, thereby getting a higher return. The extra oil coming to the market would depress the *current* oil price, but also reduce reserves, thereby creating a bigger shortage for the future and hence a higher *future* price. This would cause oil prices to rise more quickly over time (from the new lower base). Once the rate of price increase has risen to equal the rate of return on other assets, equilibrium has occurred. There will no longer be an incentive for the oil to be extracted faster.

The current price

But what determines the current price *level* (as opposed to its rate of increase)? This will be determined by supply and demand for the extracted resource (its flow).

In the case of a resource used by households, demand will depend on consumer tastes, the price of other goods, income, etc. Thus the greater the desire for using private cars, the greater the demand for petrol. In the case of minerals used by firms, demand will depend on the marginal revenue product of the resources. In either case, a rise in demand will cause a rise in the resource's price.

Supply will depend on three things:

- The rate of interest on other assets. As we have seen, the higher the rate of interest, the faster will the resource be extracted, in order that the mineowners (or well owners) can reinvest their profits at these higher rates of interest.
- The stock of known reserves. As new reserves are discovered, this will push down the price.
- The costs of extraction. The lower the costs, the greater will be the amount extracted, and hence the lower will be the market price of the resource.

Are we extracting non-renewable resources at the optimum rate?

If there are limited reserves of fossil fuels and other minerals, are we in danger that they will soon run out? Should we be more concerned with conservation?

In fact, the market provides an incentive to conserve such resources. As reserves run down, so the price of non-renewable resources will rise. This will create an incentive to discover alternatives. For example, as fossil fuels become more expensive, so renewable sources of energy, such as solar power, wind and wave power, will become more economical. There will also be a greater incentive to discover new techniques of power generation and to conserve energy. TC 3 p21

Markets, however, are imperfect. As we shall see in Chapter 11, when we consume natural resources, we do not take into account the full costs. For example, the burning of fossil fuels creates harmful environmental effects in the form of acid rain and the greenhouse effect, but these 'external' costs are not included in the price we pay. TC 6 p26

Then there is the question of the distribution of income between present and future generations. If non-renewable resources are going to be expensive in the future, should we not be conserving these resources *today* in order to help our descendants? The problem is that consumers may well act totally selfishly, saying, 'Why should we conserve resources? By the time they run out, we will be dead.' KI 4 p11

?

1. ***Will the market provide incentives for firms to research into energy-conserving techniques, if energy prices at present are not high enough to make the use of such techniques profitable?***
2. ***How will the existence of monopoly power in the supply of resources influence their rate of depletion?***

Let us assume that the market rate of interest is 10 per cent (i.e. 0.1). Then according to the formula, a purchaser would be prepared to pay:

$$\frac{£1000}{0.1} = £10\,000$$

Why should this be so? If a person deposits £10 000 in the bank, with an interest rate of 10 per cent this will earn that person £1000 per year. Assuming our piece of land is guaranteed to earn a rent of £1000 per year, then provided it costs less than £10 000 to buy, it is a better investment than putting money in the bank. The competition between people to buy this land will drive its price up until it reaches £10 000.

This is just another example of equilibrium being where marginal cost equals marginal benefit. This can be demonstrated by rearranging equation (1) to give:

$$Pi = R$$

Remember that the equilibrium price of the land (P) is £10 000 and that the rate of interest (i) is 0.1. If you borrow the £10 000 to buy the land, it will cost you £1000 per year in interest payments (i.e. Pi). This is your annual marginal cost. The annual marginal benefit will be the rent (R) you will earn from the land.

?

1. *What price would the same piece of land sell for if it still earned £1000 rent per year, but if the rate of interest were now 5 per cent?*
2. *What does this tell us about the relationship between the price of an asset (like land) and the rate of interest?*

KI 4 p11

Conclusions: Who are the poor? Who are the rich?

We have been building up an answer to these questions as this chapter has progressed. The final part of the answer concerns the ownership of land and capital. Many people own no land or capital at all. These people will therefore earn no profit, rent or interest.

For those who are fortunate enough to own productive assets, their income from them will depend on (a) the quantity they own and (b) their rental value.

The quantity of assets owned

This will depend on the following:

- Inheritance. Some people have rich parents who leave them substantial amounts of land and capital.
- Past income and savings. If people have high incomes and save a large proportion of them, this helps them to build up a stock of assets.
- Skill in investment (entrepreneurial skill). The more skilful people are in investing and in organising production, the more rapidly will their stock of assets grow.
- Luck. When people open up a business, there are usually substantial risks. The business might flourish or fail.

The rental value

This is the income earned per unit of land and capital. It will depend on the following:

- The level of demand for the factor. This depends on the factor's *MRP*, which in turn depends on its physical productivity (*MPP*) and the demand for the good it produces and hence the good's *MR*.
- The elasticity of demand for the good. The greater the monopoly power that capital owners have in the goods market, the less elastic will be the demand for the product and the greater will be the supernormal returns they can earn on their capital. TC 8 p59
- The elasticity of supply of the factor. The less elastic its supply, the more factor owners can gain from a high demand. The high demand will simply push up the level of economic rent that the factor will earn.
- The total factor supply by other factor owners. The further to the left the total factor supply curve, the higher the level of economic rent that each unit of the factor can earn for any given level of demand.

Thus if you are lucky enough to have rich parents who leave you a lot of money when you are relatively young; if you are a skilful investor and save and reinvest a large proportion of your earnings; if you have luck in owning assets that few other people own, and which produce goods in high demand: then you may end up very rich.

If you have no assets, you will have no property income at all. If at the same time you are on a low wage or are unemployed, then you may be very poor indeed.

Section summary

1. Rent on land, like the price of other factor services, is determined by the interaction of demand and supply. Its supply is totally inelastic (or nearly so). Its demand curve is downward sloping and will equal the *MRP* of land.
2. The price of land depends on its potential rental value (its marginal benefit) and the repayment costs of borrowing to pay for the land (its marginal cost). Equilibrium is where the two are equal.
3. People's income depends not only on their wages but on whether they own any land or capital, and, if they do, the rental value of these assets. This is the final element in determining the distribution of income in the economy.

END OF CHAPTER QUESTIONS

1. The wage rate that a firm has to pay and the output it can produce vary with the number of workers as follows (all figures are hourly):

Number of workers	1	2	3	4	5	6	7	8
Wage rate (AC_L) (£)	3	4	5	6	7	8	9	10
Total output (TPP_L)	10	22	32	40	46	50	52	52

Assume that output sells at £2 per unit.

(a) Copy the table and add additional rows for TC_L, MC_L, TRP_L and MRP_L. Put the figures for MC_L and MRP_L in the spaces between the columns.

(b) How many workers will the firm employ in order to maximise profits?

(c) What will be its hourly wage bill at this level of employment?

(d) How much hourly revenue will it earn at this level of employment?

(e) Assuming that the firm faces other (fixed) costs of £30 per hour, how much hourly profit will it make?

(f) Assume that the workers now formed a union and that the firm agreed to pay the negotiated wage rate to all employees. What is the maximum to which the hourly wage rate could rise without causing the firm to try to reduce employment below that in (b) above? (See Figure 9.10.)

(g) What would be the firm's hourly profit now?

2. If a firm faces a shortage of workers with very specific skills, it may decide to undertake the necessary training itself. If, on the other hand, it faces a shortage of unskilled workers, it may well offer a small wage increase in order to obtain the extra labour. In the first case, it is responding to an increase in demand for labour by attempting to shift the supply curve. In the second case, it is merely allowing a movement along the supply curve. Use a demand and supply diagram to illustrate each case. Given that elasticity of supply is different in each case, do you think that these are the best policies for the firm to follow? What would happen to wages and economic rent if it used the second policy in the first case?

3. Why does the marginal revenue product differ between workers in different jobs?

4. For what reasons is the average gross weekly pay of women only 75.6 per cent of that of men in the UK?

5. Given the analysis of bilateral monopoly, if the passing of minimum wage legislation forces employers to pay higher wage rates to low-paid employees, will this necessarily cause a reduction in employment?

6. Using a diagram like Figure 9.13, demonstrate what will happen under perfect competition when there is an increase in the productivity of a particular type of capital. Consider the effects on the demand, price (rental rate) and quantity supplied of the services of this type of capital.

7. What factors could cause a rise in the market rate of interest?

8. How is the market price of land related to its productivity?

Additional case studies on the book's website (www.pearsoned.co.uk/sloman)

9.1 Economic rent and transfer earnings. This examines a way of classifying the earnings of a factor of production and shows how these earnings depend on the elasticity of supply of the factor.

9.2 Other labour market imperfections. This looks at the three imperfections identified on page 243: namely, imperfect information, persistent disequilibria in labour markets and non-maximising behaviour by firms or workers.

9.3 Ethnic minorities in the UK labour market. This case study looks at differences in income and employment between different ethnic groups in the UK.

9.4 Profit sharing. An examination of the case for and against profit sharing as a means of rewarding workers.

WEBSITES RELEVANT TO THIS CHAPTER

See sites listed at the end of Chapter 10 on page 290.

Chapter 10

Inequality, Poverty and Policies to Redistribute Incomes

In Chapter 9 we saw that there are considerable differences in wage rates, and that these depend on market conditions. Similarly, we saw that differences in rewards to owners of capital and land also depend on their respective markets.

But differences in factor rewards are only part of the explanation of inequality. In this chapter, we open out the analysis. We take a more general look at why some people are rich while others are poor, and consider the overall degree of inequality in our society: a society that includes the super rich, with their luxury yachts and their villas abroad, and people living in slum conditions, with not enough to feed and clothe themselves or their children properly: a society where people begging in the streets are an all too familiar sight. We will see how the gap between rich and poor has tended to widen over time.

We will show how inequality can be measured. We will also look at how incomes are distributed between particular groups, whether by occupation, age, sex, household composition or geographical area.

The second part of the chapter considers what can be done to reduce inequality. Is the solution to tax the rich very heavily, so that the money can be redistributed to the poor? Or might this discourage people from working so hard? Would it be better, then, to focus on benefits and increase the support for the poor? Or might this discourage people from taking on work for fear of losing their benefits?

We look at the attitudes of governments and at some of the debates taking place today over how to reduce inequality without discouraging effort or initiative.

CHAPTER MAP

10.1 INEQUALITY AND POVERTY

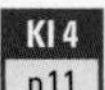

Inequality is one of the most contentious issues in the world of economics and politics. Some people have incomes far in excess of what they need to enjoy a comfortable, if not luxurious, lifestyle, while others struggle to purchase even the basic necessities.

The need for some redistribution from rich to poor is broadly accepted across the political spectrum. Thus the government taxes the rich more than the poor and then transfers some of the proceeds to the poor, either as cash benefits or in kind. Nevertheless there is considerable disagreement as to the appropriate *amount* of redistribution.

KI 6 p29

Whether the current distribution of income is desirable or not is a normative question. Economists therefore cannot settle the debate between politicians over how much the government should redistribute incomes from rich to poor. Nevertheless economists do have a major role to play in the analysis of inequality. They can do the following:

- Identify the extent of inequality and analyse how it has changed over time.
- Explain why a particular level of income distribution occurs and what causes inequality to grow or to lessen.
- Examine the relationship between equality and other economic objectives such as efficiency.
- Identify various government policies to deal with problems of inequality and poverty.
- Examine the effects of these policies, both on inequality itself and on other questions such as efficiency, inflation and unemployment.

Types of inequality

There are a number of different ways of looking at the distribution of income and wealth. Each way highlights a different aspect of inequality.

The distribution of income

There are three broad ways of examining the distribution of income. First we can look at how evenly incomes are distributed among the population. This is known as the ***size distribution of income***. It can be expressed between *households*, or between *individual earners*, or between *all individuals*. It can be expressed either *before* or *after* the deduction of taxes and the receipt of benefits. For example, we might want to know the proportion of pre-tax national income going to the richest 10 per cent of households.

Then there is the question of distribution between different *factors of production*. This is known as the ***functional distribution of income***. At the *broader* level, we could look at the distribution between the general factor categories: labour, land and capital. For example, there is the question of the relative shares of wages and profits in national income. At a *narrower* level, we could look at distribution within the factor categories. Why are some jobs well paid while others are badly paid? Why are rents higher in some areas than in others? This is the type of distribution we looked at in Chapter 9.

Finally there is the question of the ***distribution of income by class of recipient***. This can be by *class of person*: women, men, single people, married people, people within a particular age group or ethnic group, and so on. Alternatively, it can be by *geographical area*. Typically, this is expressed in terms of differences in incomes between officially defined regions within a country.

The distribution of wealth

Income is a *flow*. It measures the receipt of money per period of time (e.g. £10 000 per year). Wealth, by contrast, is a stock (see Box 9.9). It measures the value of a person's assets at a particular point in time. The distribution of wealth can be measured as a size distribution (how evenly it is distributed among the population); as a functional distribution (the proportion of wealth held in various forms, such as dwellings, land, company shares, bank deposits, etc.); or according to the holders of wealth, classified by age, sex, geographical area, etc.

Analysis of incomes below a certain level: the analysis of poverty

A major problem here is in defining just what is meant by poverty. The dividing line between who is poor and who is not is necessarily arbitrary. Someone who is classed as poor in the UK may seem comparatively rich to an Ethiopian. Where the line is drawn is important, however, to the extent that it determines who receives state benefits and who does not.

The extent and nature of poverty can be analysed in a number of ways:

Definitions

Size distribution of income Measurement of the distribution of income according to the levels of income received by individuals (irrespective of source).

Functional distribution of income Measurement of the distribution of income according to the source of income (e.g. from employment, from profit, from rent, etc.).

Distribution of income by class of recipient Measurement of the distribution of income between the classes of person who receive it (e.g. homeowners and non-homeowners or those in the north and those in the south).

Figure 10.1 Size distribution of UK income by quintile group of households: 2003/4

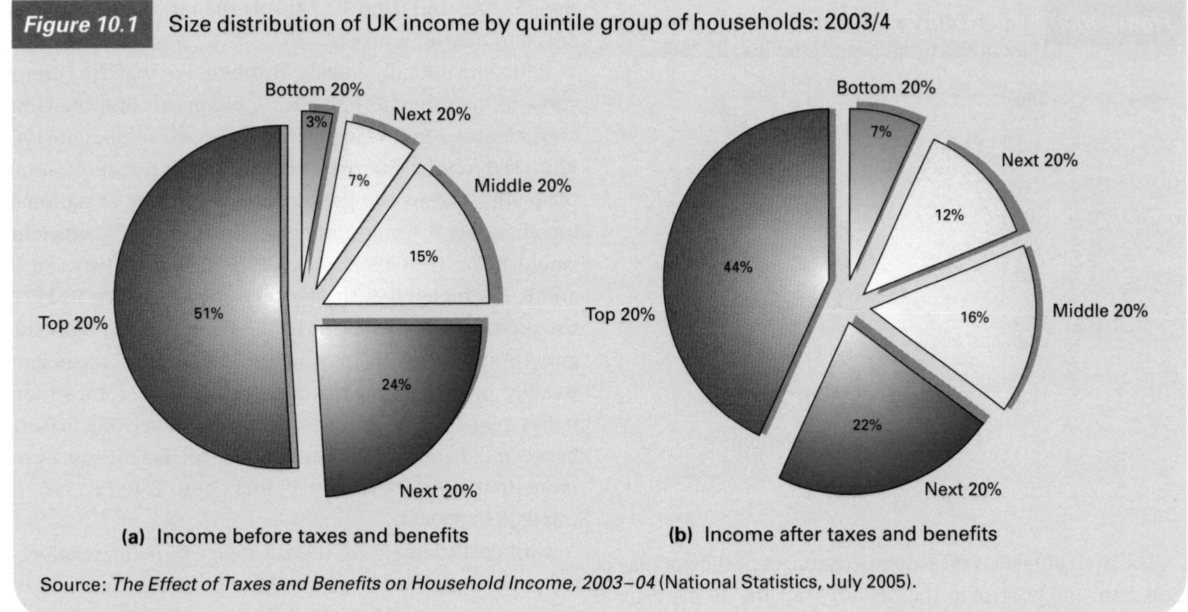

Source: *The Effect of Taxes and Benefits on Household Income, 2003–04* (National Statistics, July 2005).

- The number or proportion of people or households falling into the category.
- The occupational distribution of poverty.
- The geographical distribution of poverty.
- The distribution of poverty according to age, sex, ethnic origin, marital status, educational attainment, etc.

It is not possible in this chapter to look at all aspects of inequality in the UK. Nevertheless some of the more important facts are considered, along with questions of their measurement and interpretation.

The size distribution of income in the UK

Figure 10.1 shows the size distribution of income in the UK. It covers income from all sources. In each chart, households are grouped into five equal-sized groups or ***quintiles***, from the poorest 20 per cent of households up to the richest 20 per cent. The following points can be drawn from these statistics:

- In 2003/4 the richest 20 per cent of households earned 51 per cent of national income, and even after the deduction of taxes this was still 44 per cent.
- The poorest 20 per cent, by contrast, earned a mere 3 per cent of national income, and even after the receipt of benefits this had risen only to 7 per cent.

Inequality grew dramatically in the 1980s and did not begin to reduce again until 2000, and then only very slightly. Between 1977 and 2003/4 the post-tax-and benefits share of national income of the bottom 40 per cent of households fell from 23 per cent to 19 per cent; while the share of the top 20 per cent grew from 37 per cent to 44 per cent.

As we shall see in section 10.2, by taxing the rich proportionately more than the poor, taxes can be used as a means of reducing inequality. In the UK, however, taxes have the opposite effect. In 2003/4, taxes had the effect of increasing the share of the highest earning 10 per cent from 27.0 per cent to 27.3 per cent and reducing the share of the poorest 10 per cent from 2.5 per cent to only 2.2 per cent. The reason for this effect is that indirect taxes (e.g. on tobacco and alcohol) are paid proportionately more by the poor. This more than offsets the redistributive effect from income tax being paid proportionately more by the rich.

Redistribution of income in the UK, therefore, is achieved mainly through the benefits system.

Measuring the size distribution of income

Apart from tables and charts, two of the most widely used methods for measuring inequality are the *Lorenz curve* and the *Gini coefficient*.

Lorenz curve

Figure 10.2 shows the ***Lorenz curve*** for the UK based on pre-tax (but post-benefit) incomes.

Definitions

Quantiles Divisions of the population into equal-sized groups.

Quintiles Divisions of the population into five equal-sized groups (an example of a quantile).

Lorenz curve A curve showing the proportion of national income earned by any given percentage of the population (measured from the poorest upwards).

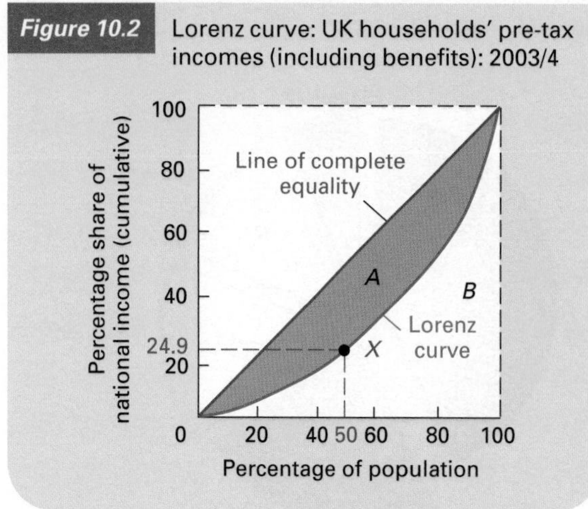

Figure 10.2 Lorenz curve: UK households' pre-tax incomes (including benefits): 2003/4

The horizontal axis measures percentages of the population from the poorest to the richest. Thus the 40 per cent point represents the poorest 40 per cent of the population. The vertical axis measures the percentage of national income they receive.

The curve starts at the origin: zero people earn zero incomes. If income were distributed totally equally, the Lorenz curve would be a straight 45° line. The 'poorest' 20 per cent of the population would earn 20 per cent of national income; the 'poorest' 60 per cent would earn 60 per cent, and so on. The curve ends up at the top right-hand corner, with 100 per cent of the population earning 100 per cent of national income.

In practice, the Lorenz curve will 'hang below' the 45° line. Point *x*, for example, shows that the poorest 50 per cent of UK households received only 24.9 per cent of national income. The further the curve drops below the 45° line, the greater will be the level of inequality.

The Lorenz curve is quite useful for showing the change in income distribution over time. From 1949 to 1979 the curve moved inwards towards the 45° line, suggesting a lessening of inequality. Then from 1979 to 1990 it moved downwards away from the 45° line, suggesting a deepening of inequality. Since 1990 it has remained approximately the same.

The problem with simply comparing Lorenz curves by eye is that it is imprecise. This problem is overcome by using Gini coefficients.

Gini coefficient

The ***Gini coefficient*** is a precise way of measuring the position of the Lorenz curve. It is the ratio of the area between the Lorenz curve and the 45° line to the whole area below the 45° line. In Figure 10.2 this is the ratio of the shaded area *A* to the whole area (*A* + *B*).

If income is totally equally distributed so that the Lorenz curve follows the 45° line, area *A* disappears and the Gini coefficient is zero. As inequality increases, so does area *A*. The Gini coefficient rises. In the extreme case of total inequality, where one person earns the whole of national income, area *B* would disappear and the Gini coefficient would be 1. Thus the Gini coefficient will be between 0 and 1. The higher it is, the greater is the inequality. In 1979 the pre-tax Gini coefficient in the UK was 0.30. With the growth in inequality during the 1980s, the coefficient steadily increased and stood at 0.38 in 1990. Since then it has remained at approximately that level (fluctuating between 0.36 and 0.39). The post-tax coefficient rose even more dramatically – from 0.29 in 1979 to 0.40 in 1990. It was 0.38 in 2003/4.

Gini coefficients have the advantage of being relatively simple to understand and use. They provide a clear way of comparing income distribution either in the same country at different times, or between different countries. They suffer two main drawbacks, however.

First, a single measure cannot take into account all the features of inequality. Take the case of the two countries illustrated in Figure 10.3. If area *X* is equal to area *Y*, they will have the same Gini coefficient, and yet the pattern of their income distribution is quite different.

> ? *In which country in Figure 10.3 would you expect to find the highest number of poor people? Describe how income is distributed in the two cases.*

Second, there is the problem of what statistics are used in the calculation. Are they pre-tax or post-tax; do they include benefits; do they include non-monetary incomes (such as food grown for own consumption: a major item in many developing countries); are they based on individuals, households or tax units? Unfortunately, different countries use different types of statistics. International comparisons of inequality are thus fraught with difficulties.

Figure 10.3 Lorenz curves for two countries with the same Gini coefficients

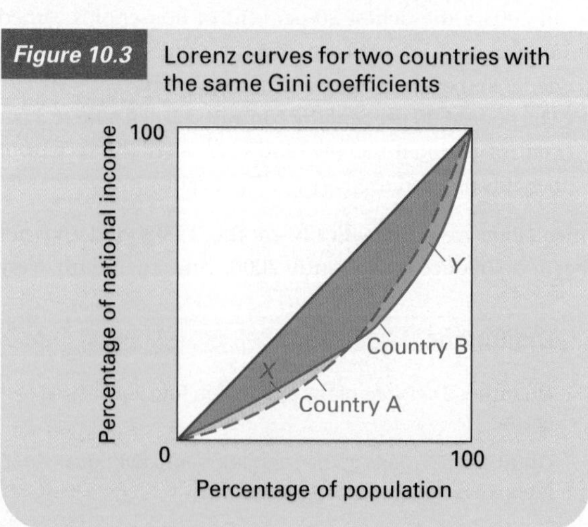

> **Definition**
>
> **Gini coefficient** The area between the Lorenz curve and the 45° line divided by the total area under the 45° line.

Figure 10.4 Ratio of income shares of bottom 40% to top 20% of households (after taxes and benefits)

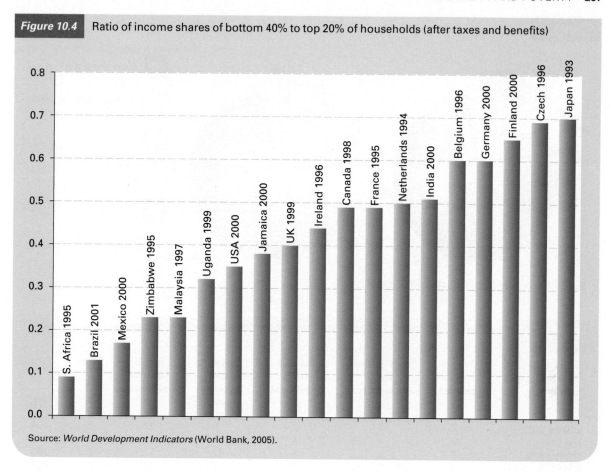

Source: *World Development Indicators* (World Bank, 2005).

Ratios of the shares in national income of two quantile groups

This is a very simple method of measuring income distribution. A ratio quite commonly used is that of the share of national income of the *bottom 40 per cent* of the population to that of the *top 20 per cent*. Thus if the bottom 40 per cent earned 15 per cent of national income and the top 20 per cent earned 50 per cent of national income, the ratio would be 15/50 = 0.3. The lower the ratio, therefore, the greater the inequality. Figure 10.4 gives some examples of this ratio from different countries.

1. *Why, do you think, are the ratios for developing countries lower than those for developed countries?*
2. *Make a list of reasons why the ratios in Figure 10.4 may not give an accurate account of relative levels of inequality between countries.*
3. *What would the ratio be if national income were absolutely equally distributed?*

The functional distribution of income in the UK

Distribution of income by source

Figure 10.5 shows the sources of household incomes in 1975 and 2003/4. Wages and salaries constitute by far the largest element. However, their share fell from 77 per cent to 67 per cent of national income between 1975 and 2003/4. Conversely, the share coming from social security benefits and pensions rose from 12 per cent to 20 per cent, reflecting the growing proportion of the population past retirement age.

In contrast to wages and salaries, investment income (dividends, interest and rent) accounts for a relatively small percentage of household income – a mere 3 per cent in 2003/4.

With the growth of small businesses and the increased numbers of people being 'employed' on a freelance basis, the proportion of incomes coming from self-employment has grown. It rose from 6 per cent in 1975 to 9 per cent in 2003/4.

The overall shares illustrated in Figure 10.5 hide the fact that the sources of income differ quite markedly between different income groups. These differences are shown in Table 10.1.

Column (1) shows that higher-income groups get a larger proportion of their income from wages and salaries than do lower-income groups. This can be largely explained by examining column (5). As would be expected, the poor tend to get a larger proportion of their incomes in social security benefits than do people further up the income scale.

It is interesting to note that the second poorest 20 per cent of households have a larger proportion of their income from pensions and annuities than any other group.

Figure 10.5 Sources of UK household income as a percentage of gross household income

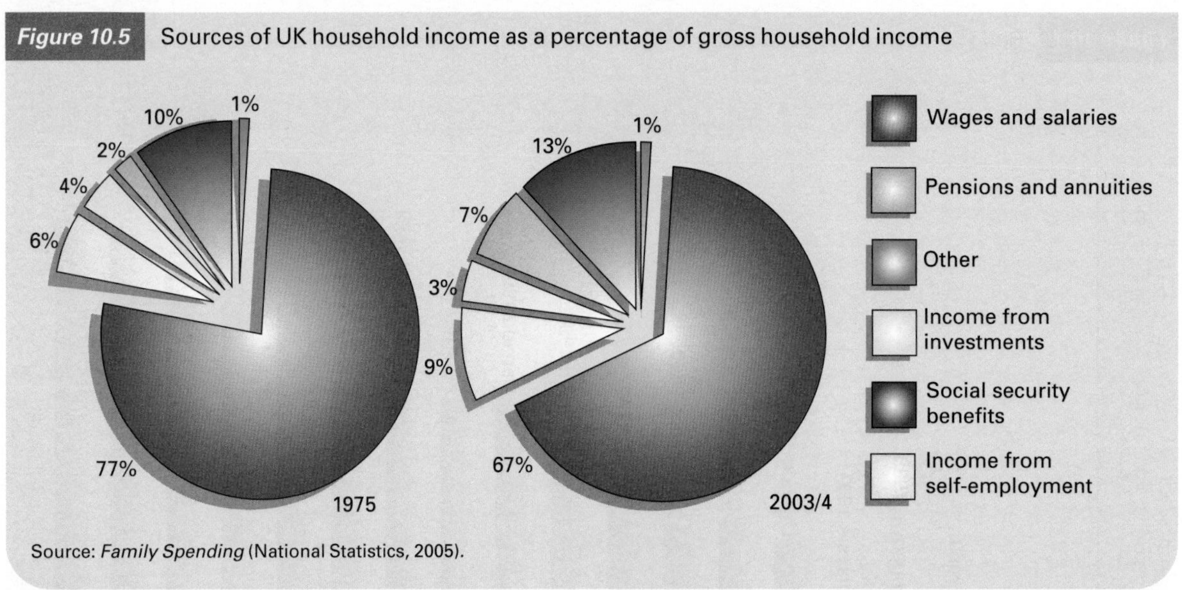

Source: *Family Spending* (National Statistics, 2005).

Table 10.1 Sources of UK household income as a percentage of total household income by quintile groups: 2003/4

Gross household weekly incomes (quintiles)	Wages and salaries (1)	Income from self-employment (2)	Income from investments (3)	Pensions and annuities (4)	Social security benefits (5)	Other (6)	Total (7)
Lowest 20%	7	2	3	8	77	2	100
Next 20%	30	4	4	17	44	2	100
Middle 20%	59	6	3	12	17	2	100
Next 20%	76	7	2	7	7	1	100
Highest 20%	79	12	3	3	2	1	100
All households	67	9	3	7	13	1	100

Source: *Family Spending* (National Statistics, 2005).

Pensioners are clustered in this group because they tend to be fairly poor (pensions being less than wages), but not as poor as the unemployed or families on low incomes.

One perhaps surprising feature to note is that the proportion of income coming from profits, rent and interest (column (3)) varies little between the income groups. In fact only for those people in the top 1 or 2 per cent is it significantly higher. The conclusion from this, plus the fact that investment incomes account for only 3 per cent of household incomes in total, is that incomes from capital and land are of only relatively minor significance in explaining income inequality.

The major cause of differences in incomes between individuals in employment is the differences in wages and salaries between different occupations.

Distribution of wages and salaries by occupation

Differences in full-time wages and salaries are illustrated in Figure 10.6. This shows the average gross weekly pay of full-time adult workers in selected occupations in 2004. As you can see, there are considerable differences in pay between different occupations. The causes of differences in wage rates from one occupation to another were examined in Chapter 9.

? *If fringe benefits (such as long holidays, company cars, free clothing/uniforms, travel allowances and health insurance) were included, do you think the level of inequality would increase or decrease? Explain why.*

Since the late 1970s, wage differentials have widened. Part of the explanation lies in a shift in the demand for labour. Many firms have adopted new techniques which require a more highly educated workforce. Wage rates in some of these skilled occupations have increased substantially.

At the same time, there has been a decline in the number of unskilled jobs in industry and, along with it, a decline in the power of unions to represent such people. Where low-skilled jobs remain, there will be intense pressure on employers to reduce wage costs if they are competing with companies based in developing countries, where wage rates are much lower.

As prospects for the unskilled decline in industry, so people with few qualifications increasingly compete for low-paid, service-sector jobs (e.g. in supermarkets and fast-food outlets). The growth in people seeking part-time work has also kept wage rates down in this sector.

Figure 10.6 Average gross weekly earnings of UK full-time adult employees (£): 2004

Directors/chief executives
Medical practitioners
Financial brokers
HE lecturers
Journalists
Primary teachers
Social workers
Nurses
Plumbers
Clergy
Farmers
Sales assistants
Hairdressers
Bar staff
0 200 400 600 800 1000 1200 1400 1600 1800 2000

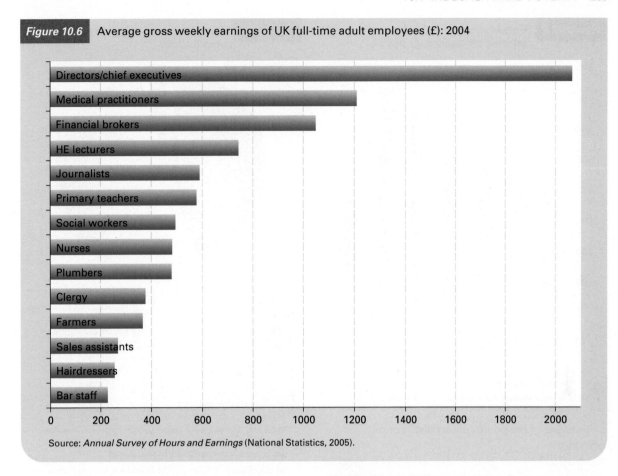

Source: *Annual Survey of Hours and Earnings* (National Statistics, 2005).

Other determinants of income inequality

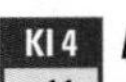

Differences in household composition

Other things being equal, the more dependants there are in a household, the lower the income will be *per member* of that household. Figure 10.7 gives an extreme example of this. It shows the average household income in the UK in 2003/4 of four different categories of household.

Households with two adults and four or more children had approximately the same income as households with only one man and one woman. This means that they had a very much lower income *per member* of the household.

There is a twin problem for many large households. Not only may there be relatively more children and old-age dependants, but also the total household income will be reduced if one of the adults stays at home to look after the family, or works only part time.

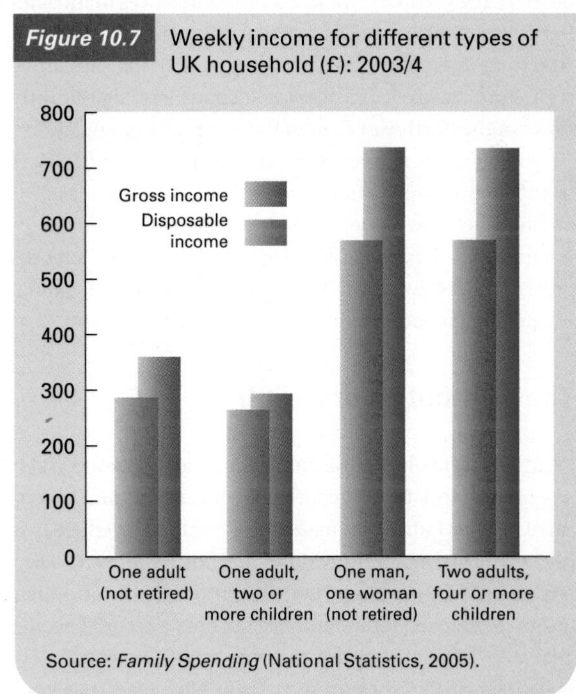

Figure 10.7 Weekly income for different types of UK household (£): 2003/4

Source: *Family Spending* (National Statistics, 2005).

Differences by sex

Box 9.7 on pages 244–5 looked at some of the aspects of income inequality between the sexes. In 2004, the average gross weekly pay for full-time female employees was £422.30. For male employees it was £588.60. There are three important factors to note:

- Women are paid less than men in the same occupations. You will see this if you compare some of the occupations in Table (b) in Box 9.7.
- Women tend to be employed in lower-paid occupations than men.
- Women do much less overtime than men (on average, 0.8 hours per week, compared with 2.2 for men).

Figure 10.8 Gross weekly household income, selected UK regions (£): 2003/4

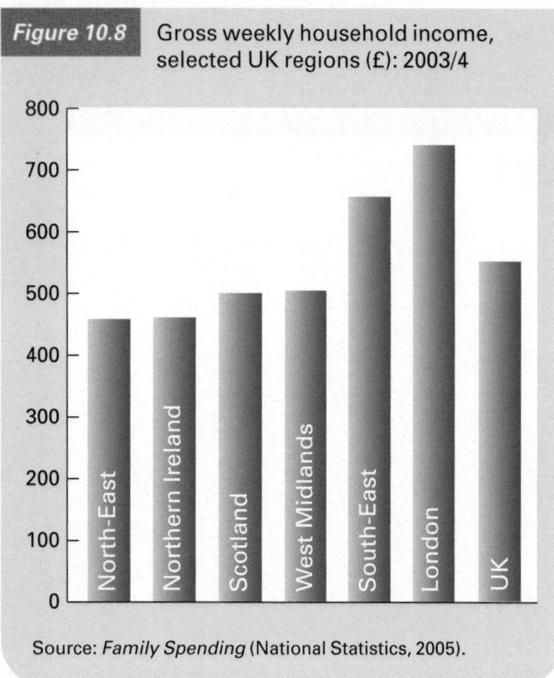

Source: *Family Spending* (National Statistics, 2005).

? *List the reasons for each of the three factors above. (Re-read section 9.2 and Box 9.7 if you need help.)*

Differences in the geographical distribution of income

Figure 10.8 shows the gross weekly household incomes in different regions of the UK in 2003/4. Differences in incomes between the regions reflect regional differences in industrial structure, unemployment and the cost of living. As can be seen from Figure 10.8, average incomes are significantly lower in the north-east than in the south-east of England.

On a more local level, there are considerable differences in incomes between affluent areas and deprived areas. It is at this level that some of the most extreme examples of inequality can be observed, with 'leafy' affluent suburbs only a mile or two away from run-down estates. Regional inequality and local inequality are explored in section 22.4.

The distribution of wealth

Wealth is difficult to measure. Being a *stock* of assets (such as a house, land, furniture, personal possessions and investments), it has an easily measurable value only when it is sold. What is more, individuals are not required to keep any record of their assets. Only when people die and their assets are assessed for inheritance tax does a record become available. Official statistics are thus based on Inland Revenue data of the assets of those who have died that year. These statistics are suspect for two reasons. First, the people who have died are unlikely to be a representative sample of the population. Second, many items are excluded, such as household and personal items, and items passed automatically to the surviving spouse.

Figure 10.9 Composition of UK gross personal wealth: 2002

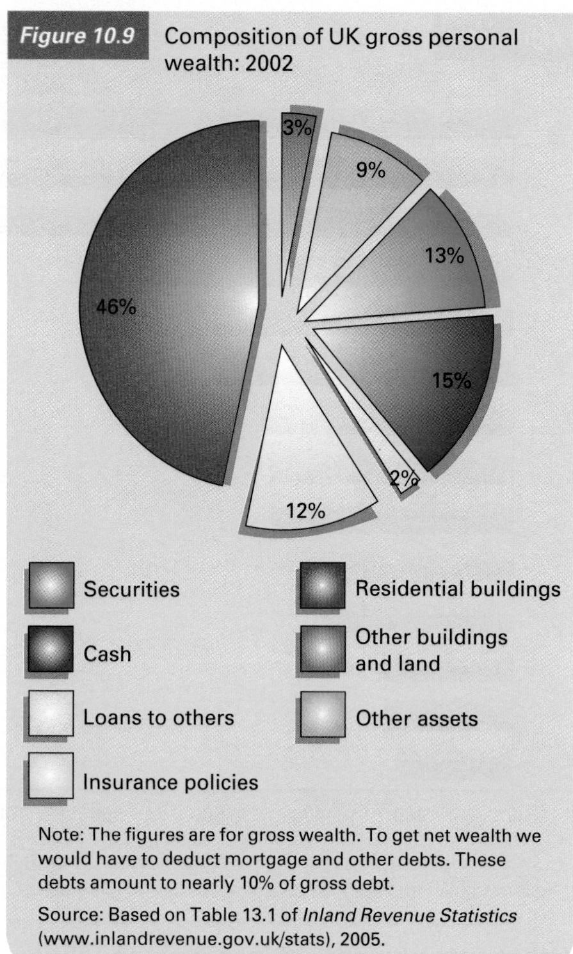

Note: The figures are for gross wealth. To get net wealth we would have to deduct mortgage and other debts. These debts amount to nearly 10% of gross debt.

Source: Based on Table 13.1 of *Inland Revenue Statistics* (www.inlandrevenue.gov.uk/stats), 2005.

Table 10.2 Size distribution of UK wealth

	Proportion of marketable wealth (%)			
	1971	1981	1991	2002
Wealthiest 1%	31	18	17	23
Wealthiest 5%	52	36	35	43
Wealthiest 10%	65	50	47	56
Wealthiest 25%	86	73	71	74
Wealthiest 50%	97	92	92	94
Gini coefficient	0.80	0.67	0.64	0.70

Source: Based on Table 13.5 of *Inland Revenue Statistics* (www.inlandrevenue.gov.uk/stats/), 2005.

Figure 10.9 and Table 10.2 give official statistics on the UK composition and distribution of wealth. As can be seen from Table 10.2, inequality of wealth is far greater than inequality of income. The wealthiest 1 per cent of the adult population owned 23 per cent of the marketable wealth in 2002, and the wealthiest 10 per cent owned 56 per cent. These figures do not include pension rights, which are much more equally distributed. The level and distribution of wealth tend to fluctuate somewhat in the short term with movements in share prices and house prices.

CASE STUDIES AND APPLICATIONS **BOX 10.1**

POVERTY IN THE PAST

Consider from the following passage whether it is reasonable or even possible to compare poverty today with poverty in the 1800s.

> Every great city has one or more slums, where the working class is crowded together. True, poverty often dwells in hidden alleys close to the palaces of the rich; but, in general, a separate territory has been assigned to it, where, removed from the sight of the happier classes, it may struggle along as it can.
>
> The houses are occupied from cellar to garret, filthy within and without, and their appearance is such that no human being could possibly wish to live in them . . . the filth and tottering ruin surpass all description. Scarcely a whole window-pane can be found, the walls are crumbling, doorposts and window-frames loose and broken, doors of old boards nailed together, or altogether wanting in this thieves' quarter, where no doors are needed, there being nothing to steal. Heaps of garbage and ashes lie in all directions, and the foul liquids emptied before the doors gather in stinking pools. Here the poorest of the poor, the worst-paid workers with thieves and the victims of prostitution indiscriminately huddled together . . . and those who have not yet sunk in the whirlpool of moral ruin which surrounds them, sinking daily deeper, losing daily more and more of their power to resist the demoralising influence of want, filth, and evil surroundings.[1]

?

1. ***If we were to measure poverty today and in the 1800s in* absolute terms*, in which would there be the greater number of poor?***
2. ***If we measure poverty in* relative terms*, must a society inevitably have a problem of poverty, however rich it is?***

[1] F. Engels, *The Condition of the Working Class in England* (Progress Publishers, 1973), pp. 166–7.

The four major causes of inequality in the distribution of wealth are as follows:

- Inheritance. This allows inequality to be perpetuated from one generation to another.
- Income inequality. People with higher incomes can save more.
- Different propensities to save. People who save a larger proportion of their income will build up a bigger stock of wealth.
- Entrepreneurial and investment talent/luck. Some people are successful in investing their wealth and making it grow rapidly.

Even though wealth is still highly concentrated, there was a significant reduction in inequality of wealth up to the early 1990s. From 1971 to 1991 the Gini coefficient of wealth fell a full sixteen percentage points from 0.80 to 0.64. A major reason for this was the increased taxation of inherited wealth. Since 1991, however, this reduction in inequality has been reversed somewhat. This can be explained by lower levels of inheritance tax and substantial rises in property prices and share values.

Causes of inequality

We turn now to identify the major causes of inequality. The problem has many dimensions and there are many factors that determine the pattern and depth of inequality. It is thus wrong to try to look for a single cause, or even the major one. What follows then is a list of the possible determinants of inequality:

- Inequality of wealth. People with wealth are able to obtain an income other than from their own labour. The greater the inequality of wealth, the greater is the inequality of income likely to be.
- Differences in ability. People differ in intelligence, strength, dexterity, etc. Some of these differences are innate and some are acquired through the process of 'socialisation' – education, home environment, peer group, etc.
- Differences in attitude. Some people are adventurous, willing to take risks, willing to move for better jobs, keen to push themselves forward. Others are much more cautious.  
- Differences in qualifications. These are reflections of a number of things: ability, attitudes towards study, access to educational establishments, the quality of tuition, attitudes and income of parents, etc.
- Differences in hours worked. Some people do a full-time job plus overtime, or a second job; others work only part time.
- Differences in job utility/disutility. Other things being equal, unpleasant, arduous or dangerous jobs will need to pay higher wages.
- Differences in power. Monopoly power in the supply of factors or goods, and monopsony power in the demand for factors, is unequally distributed in the economy. KI 19 p157
- Differences in the demand for goods. Factors employed in expanding industries will tend to have a higher marginal revenue product because their output has a higher market value.
- Differences in household composition. The greater the number of dependants relative to income earners, the poorer the average household member will be (other things being equal).

CASE STUDIES AND APPLICATIONS **BOX 10.2**

HOW TO REVERSE THE UK'S INCREASED INEQUALITY

Recommendations of the Rowntree Foundation

KI 4 p11

In February 1995 the Rowntree Foundation published the results of a comprehensive inquiry into the UK's growing inequality since 1979.[2] The findings made grim reading. Inequalities in income had widened further and faster than in any other period in history. The rich had got substantially richer, while the poor had become not only relatively poorer, but *absolutely* poorer.

TC 6 p26

This growing divide, the report argued, was threatening the whole fabric of society. There was a growing underclass of people with little hope of clawing their way out of their desperate poverty, frequently seeing crime as their only escape route. The poor include the long-term unemployed, pensioners, families dependent on state benefits and young people without the educational attainment to compete in the increasingly competitive labour market. And it is not just the poor who are affected by poverty. Do we want a society, asks the report, where the rich have to build fortresses to protect themselves?

The report recommended various remedies. The thrust of them was to encourage employment and improve the lot of low-paid workers. Suggested measures included increased government expenditure on training schemes, top-up benefits for those on low wages and tax cuts targeted at the poor. These were seen as much better alternatives than simply increasing unemployment benefits, which could well make people more reluctant to get a job.

Have such recommendations been heeded and is inequality in the UK now in decline?

Policies and their effects since 1997

After coming to office in 1997, the Labour government put the reduction of poverty, especially child and pensioner poverty, high on its agenda. It made a commitment to cutting child poverty by a quarter by 2004/5 and to halving it by 2010/11. It also gave substantial new resources to neighbourhood regeneration schemes.

A number of measures were taken, including making work more financially worthwhile for poor families by the use of tax credits (see Box 10.6) and increasing the benefits for poor families with children. The result has been a reduction in child poverty, although it still remains above the EU average. The government also extended means-tested benefits for pensioners, but there has been a problem of lack of take-up of some of these benefits.

> Simulation modelling shows that tax and benefit reforms have reduced child poverty quickly enough to give the government a good chance of hitting its 2004/5 targets. Pensioner poverty should be falling by 2004/5, and tax and benefit policies have at least stopped overall income inequality growing (as it would otherwise have done).[3]

As far as poor neighbourhoods are concerned, despite the setting up of a Social Exclusion Unit, with resources being channelled to deprived areas, only limited progress has been made. Substantial differences remain between poor areas and crime remains a major problem on some estates.

There were no targets, however, for alleviating poverty in other groups. For example, the working poor with no children have received considerably less support, and poverty among this group has reached record levels. As for asylum seekers, government policies have actively worsened their poverty and social exclusion.

Similarly, there has been no specific aim of reducing income inequality. The result is that it has remained roughly the same as in 1997.

> There are substantial differences between the policies pursued in the years since 1997 and those pursued previously. In some of the most important areas, the tide has turned and policy has contributed to turning that tide. This is no mean achievement. However, it does not follow that policy has already succeeded, or that Britain has yet become a more equal society. In some respects it has, but in virtually all of the areas discussed, there is still a very long way to go to reach an unambiguous picture of success. Sustained and imaginative effort will be needed to make further progress and to reach groups not touched by policy so far.[4]

Suggest a range of 'direct' policies that the government might pursue in order to reduce inequality and poverty within the UK.

[2] *Income and Wealth* (Joseph Rowntree Foundation, 1995).

[3] Policies towards poverty, inequality and exclusion since 1997, http://www.jrf.org.uk/knowledge/findings/socialpolicy/0015.asp. This report from the Joseph Rowntree Foundation summarises the findings of a book, *A More Equal Society? New Labour, Poverty, Inequality and Exclusion*, edited by John Hills and Kitty Stewart (The Policy Press, 2005).

[4] Ibid.

- Discrimination, whether by race, sex, age, social background, etc.
- Degree of government support. The greater the support for the poor, the less will be the level of inequality in the economy.
- Unemployment. When unemployment levels are high, this is one of the major causes of poverty.

? *Which of the above causes are reflected in differences in the marginal revenue product of factors?*

Government attitudes towards inequality

The political right sees little problem with inequality as such. In fact, inequality has an important economic function. Factor price differences are an essential part of a dynamic market economy. They are the price signals that encourage resources to move to sectors of the economy where demand is growing, and away from sectors where demand is declining. If the government interferes with this process by taxing high incomes and subsidising low incomes, working people will not have the same incentive to gain better qualifications, to seek promotion, to do overtime, or to move for better jobs. Similarly, owners of capital will not have the same incentive to invest.

If inequality is to be reduced, claims the political right, it is better done by encouraging greater factor mobility. If factor supply curves are more elastic (greater mobility), then any shifts in demand will cause smaller changes in factor prices and thus less inequality. But how is greater mobility to be encouraged? The answer, they say, is to create a culture of self-help: where people are not too reliant on state support; where they will 'get on their bikes' and look for higher incomes. At the same time, they argue that the monopoly power of unions to interfere in labour markets should be curtailed. The net effect of these two policies, they claim, would be to create a more competitive labour market which would help to reduce inequality as well as promoting economic growth and efficiency.

TC3 p21

State support, say those on the right, should be confined to the relief of 'genuine' poverty. Benefits should be simply a minimum safety net for those who cannot work (e.g. the sick or disabled), or on a temporary basis for those who, through no fault of their own, have lost their jobs. Even at this basic level, however, the right argues that state support can discourage people from making more effort.

Although many on the political left accept that there is some possibility of a trade-off between equality and efficiency, they see it as a far less serious problem. Questions of efficiency and growth, claims the left, are best dealt with by encouraging investment. This, they argue, is best achieved by creating an environment of industrial democracy where workers participate in investment decisions. This common purpose is in turn best achieved in a more equal and less individualistically competitive society. The left also sees a major role for government in providing support for investment: for example, through government-sponsored research, by investment grants, by encouraging firms to get together and plan a co-ordinated strategy, or by maintaining low interest rates that make borrowing cheaper for investment.

These policies to achieve growth and efficiency, claims the left, will leave the government freer to pursue a much more active policy on redistribution.

Section summary

1. Inequality can be examined by looking at the size distribution of income, the functional distribution of income (whether by broad factor categories, narrow factor categories, occupation or other individual factor reward), the distribution of income by recipient (whether by class of person or geographical area), the distribution of wealth, or the extent and nature of poverty.
2. An analysis of the size distribution of income in the UK shows that inequality has grown.
3. The size distribution of income can be illustrated by means of a Lorenz curve. The greater the inequality, the more bowed the curve will be towards the bottom right-hand corner.
4. Size distribution can also be measured by a Gini coefficient. This will give a figure between 0 (total equality) and 1 (total inequality). Income distribution can also be measured as the ratio of the share of national income of a given lower income quantile to that of a higher income quantile.
5. Wages and salaries constitute by far the largest source of income, and thus inequality can be explained mainly in terms of differences in wages and salaries. Nevertheless state benefits are an important moderating influence on inequality and constitute the largest source of income for the poorest 20 per cent of households. Investment earnings are only a minor determinant of income except for the richest 1 or 2 per cent.
6. Other determinants of income inequality include differences in household composition, sex and where people live.
7. The distribution of wealth is less equal than the distribution of income.
8. Attitudes towards government redistribution of income vary among political parties. The political right stresses the danger that redistributive policies may destroy incentives. The best approach to inequality, according to the right, is to 'free up' markets so as to encourage greater mobility. The left, by contrast, sees fewer dangers in reducing incentives and stresses the moral and social importance of redistribution from rich to poor.

CASE STUDIES AND APPLICATIONS

MINIMUM WAGE LEGISLATION

A way of helping the poor?

The Labour government introduced a statutory UK minimum wage in April 1999. The rate was £3.60 per hour for those aged 22 and over, and £3.00 for those between 18 and 21. The rates have been increased every year and in 1995/6 were £5.05 and £4.25.

The call for a minimum wage had grown stronger during the 1990s as the number of low-paid workers within the UK increased. There were many people working as cleaners, kitchen hands, garment workers, security guards and shop assistants, who were receiving pittance rates of pay, sometimes less than £2 per hour. There were several factors explaining the growth in the size of the low-pay sector.

- *Unemployment.* Very high rates of unemployment since the early 1980s had shifted the balance of power from workers to employers. Employers were able to force many wage rates downwards, especially those of unskilled and semi-skilled workers.
- *Growth in part-time employment.* Changes in the structure of the UK economy, particularly the growth in the service sector and the growing proportion of women seeking work, had led to an increase in part-time employment, with many part-time workers not receiving the same rights, privileges and hourly pay as their full-time equivalents.
- *Changes in labour laws.* The abolition of 'wages councils' in 1993, which had set legally enforceable minimum hourly rates in various low-paid industries, and the introduction of various new laws to reduce the power of labour (see pages 240–1) had taken away what little protection there was for low-paid workers.

Assessing the arguments

The principal argument against imposing a national minimum wage concerns its impact on employment. If you raise wage rates above the equilibrium level, there will be surplus labour: i.e. unemployment (see Figure 9.9 on page 237). However, the impact of a national minimum wage on employment is not so simple.

In the case of a firm operating in *competitive* labour and goods markets, the demand for low-skilled workers is relatively wage sensitive. Any rise in wage rates, and hence prices, by this firm alone would lead to a large fall in sales and hence to employment. But given that *all* firms face the minimum wage, individual employers are more able to pass on higher wages in higher prices, knowing that their competitors are doing the same.

When employers have a degree of *monopsony* power, however, it is not even certain that they would want to reduce employment. Remember what we argued in Figure 9.10 (on page 239) when we were examining the effects of unions driving up wages. The argument is the same with a minimum wage. The minimum wage can be as high as W_2 and the firm will still want to employ as many workers as at W_1. The point is that the firm can no longer drive down the wage rate by employing fewer workers, so the incentive to cut its workforce has been removed!

10.2 TAXES, BENEFITS AND THE REDISTRIBUTION OF INCOME

In this section, we will look at policies to redistribute incomes more equally, and in particular we will focus on the use of government expenditure and taxation. Redistribution is just one of three major roles for government expenditure and taxation. The second is to compensate for the failure of the market to allocate resources efficiently. We examine this role in the next two chapters. The third is to influence the overall level of activity in the economy. Adjusting government expenditure and/or taxation for this purpose is known as *fiscal policy* and is examined in Chapter 19.

The use of taxation and government expenditure to redistribute income

Taxation. By taxing the rich proportionately more than the poor, the post-tax distribution of income will be more equal than the pre-tax distribution.

Subsidies. These are of two broad types. First, *cash benefits* can be seen as subsidies to people's incomes. They include such things as child benefit and old-age pensions. Second, *benefits in kind* provide subsidised goods and services, which may be provided free (e.g. education and health care) or at a reduced price (e.g. concessionary bus fares for the elderly). Subsidies will lessen inequality if they account for a larger proportion of a poor person's income than a rich person's.

Although we shall focus mainly on the use of taxes and benefits, there are two other types of redistributive policy.

Legislation. Examples include minimum wage legislation (see Box 10.3) and anti-discrimination legislation.

Structural. This encompasses a wide range of policies where the government tries to alter those institutions and

BOX 10.3

Indeed, if the minimum wage rate were above W_1 but below W_2, the firm would now want to employ *more* workers (where the minimum wage rate (= MC_L) is equal to the MRP_L). What is effectively happening is that the minimum wage is redistributing the firm's income from profits to wages.

In the long run, the effect on unemployment will depend on the extent to which the higher wages are compensated by higher labour productivity.

Evidence from the USA and other countries suggests that modest increases in the minimum wage have had a neutral effect upon employment. Similarly in the UK, there is little evidence to suggest that employers have responded by employing fewer workers. In fact, unemployment rates have fallen. This, however, can be explained by a buoyant economy and increasing labour market flexibility (see Box 9.8).

Whether there would continue to be little effect if the minimum wage were to rise substantially is another matter! The issue, then, seems to be how *high* can the minimum wage be set before unemployment begins to rise.

Impact of the minimum wage in the UK

Some 1.3 million workers benefit from the minimum wage. The main beneficiaries have been women, the majority of whom work part time and many of whom are lone parents, and people from ethnic minorities. Even the Conservative Party, previously a staunch opponent of a minimum wage, has dropped its opposition.

The biggest weakness of a minimum wage as a means of relieving poverty is that it only affects the employed. One of the main causes of poverty is unemployment. Clearly the unemployed would not benefit from a minimum wage.

Another cause of poverty is a large number of dependants in a family. If there is only one income earner, he or she may be paid above the minimum wage rate and yet the family could be very poor. By contrast, many of those who would be helped by a minimum wage are second income earners in a family.

These are not arguments against minimum wage legislation. They merely suggest that a minimum wage rate cannot be the sole answer to poverty.

?

1. ***If an increase in wage rates for the low paid leads to their being more motivated, how would this affect the marginal revenue product and the demand for such workers? What implications does your answer have for the effect on employment in such cases? (See page 241 on the efficiency wage hypothesis.)***
2. ***If a rise in the minimum wage encourages employers to substitute machines for workers, will this necessarily lead to higher long-term unemployment in (a) that industry and (b) the economy in general?***

attitudes of society that increase or at least perpetuate inequalities. Examples of such policies include attacking privileges, encouraging widening participation in higher education, promoting worker share ownership, encouraging industries to move to areas of high unemployment and encouraging the provision of crèche facilities at work.

Before we turn to look at the use of taxation and government expenditure to redistribute incomes, we must first look at what taxes are available to a government and what are the requirements of a good tax system.

The requirements of a good tax system

Whatever the purpose of taxation, when it comes to devising and administering particular taxes there are various principles that many people argue should be observed.

Horizontal equity. According to ***horizontal equity***, people in the *same circumstances* should be taxed equally. In other words, taxes should be levied impartially. For example, people earning the same level of income and with the same personal circumstances (e.g. number and type of dependants, size of mortgage, etc.) should pay the same level of income tax.

KI 4 p11

? *Is it horizontally equitable for smokers and drinkers to pay more tax than non-smokers and non-drinkers?*

Vertical equity. According to ***vertical equity***, taxes should be 'fairly' apportioned between rich and poor. What constitutes fairness here is highly controversial. No one likes paying taxes and thus a rich person's concept of a fair tax is unlikely to be the same as a poor person's. This whole question of using taxes as a means of redistributing incomes will be examined in detail below.

Definitions

Horizontal equity The equal treatment of people in the same situation.

Vertical equity The redistribution from the better off to the worse off. In the case of taxes, this means the rich paying proportionately more taxes than the poor.

Equity between recipients of benefits. Under the ***benefit principle***, it is argued that those who receive the most benefits from government expenditure ought to pay the most in taxes. For example, it can be argued that roads should be paid for from fuel tax. That way those who use the roads the most will pay the most towards their construction and maintenance.

?

1. *Does the benefit principle conflict with either vertical or horizontal equity?*
2. *Would this be a good principle to apply in the case of health care?*

In most cases, the benefits principle would be difficult to put into practice. There are two reasons why. First, a specific tax would have to be devised for each particular good and service provided by the state. Second, in the case of many goods and services provided by the state, it would be difficult to identify the amount of benefit received by each individual. Just how much benefit (in money terms) do you derive from street lighting, from the police, from the navy, from clean air, etc.?

Cheap to collect. Taxes cost money to collect. These costs should be kept to a minimum relative to the revenue they yield.

Difficult to evade. If it is desirable to have a given tax, people should not be able to escape paying. A distinction here is made between ***tax evasion*** and ***tax avoidance***:

- Tax evasion is illegal. This is where, for example, people do not declare income to the tax authorities.
- Tax avoidance is legal, albeit from the government's point of view undesirable. This is where people try to find ways of managing their affairs so as to reduce their tax liability. They may employ an accountant to help them.

Non-distortionary. Taxes alter market signals: taxes on goods and services alter market prices; taxes on income alter wages. They should not do this in an undesirable direction.

If prices are not distorted in the first place, it is best to use taxes that have the same percentage effect on prices of all goods and services. That way *relative* prices remain the same. For example, VAT in the UK is levied on virtually all goods and services at a single rate of $17\frac{1}{2}$ per cent. If goods were taxed at different rates, this would create distortions, switching consumption and production from goods with high taxes to goods with low taxes.

If, however, the government feels that market prices *are* distorted in the first place, taxes can be used to alter price signals in the desired direction.

How can the market distortions argument be used to justify putting excise duties on specific goods such as petrol, alcohol and tobacco? Is this the only reason why excise duties are put on these particular products?

Convenient to the taxpayer. Taxes should be *certain* and *clearly understood* by taxpayers so that they can calculate their tax liabilities. The method of payment should be *straightforward.*

Convenient to the government. Governments use tax changes as an instrument for managing the economy. Tax rates should thus be *simple to adjust.* Also, the government will need to be able to *calculate* as accurately as possible the effects of tax changes, both on the total tax yield and on the distribution of the burden between taxpayers.

Minimal disincentive effects. Taxes may discourage people from working longer or harder, from saving, from investing or from taking initiative. For example, a high rate of income tax may discourage people from seeking promotion or from doing overtime. 'What is the point,' they may say, 'if a large proportion of my extra income is taken away in taxes?' It is desirable that these disincentives should be kept to a minimum. TC 3 p21

Of course, not all these requirements can be met at the same time. There is no perfect tax. The government thus has to seek a compromise when there is a conflict between any of the requirements. One of the most serious conflicts is between vertical equity and the need to keep disincentives to a minimum. The more steeply the rich are taxed, it is argued, the more serious are the disincentive effects on them likely to be. This particular conflict is examined below.

Types of tax

Taxes can be divided into two broad categories. ***Direct taxes*** are paid directly by the taxpayer to the tax authorities. Such taxes include personal income tax, tax on companies' income and tax on capital and wealth. ***Indirect***

Definitions

Benefit principle of taxation The principle that people ought to pay taxes in proportion to the amount that they use government services.

Tax evasion The illegal non-payment of taxes (e.g. by not declaring income earned).

Tax avoidance The rearrangement of one's affairs so as to reduce one's tax liability.

Direct taxes Taxes on income and wealth. Paid directly to the tax authorities on that income or wealth.

Table 10.3 UK marginal income tax and national insurance contribution rates: 2005/6

Income per annum (£)	Marginal income tax rate (%)	Marginal NIC rate (%)	Marginal income tax plus NIC rate (%)
0–4895	0	0	0
4896–6985	10	11	21
6986–32 760	22	11	33
32 761–37 295	22	1	23
Above 37 295	40	1	41

taxes, on the other hand, are paid via a middle person. For example, value added tax (VAT) is designed to be a tax on consumption. But you the consumer do not pay it to the authorities: it is paid by firms, which then pass it on to consumers in higher prices (see section 3.2). You are thus taxed indirectly when you buy goods and services.

Direct taxes

Personal income tax. All types of income are included – wages, salaries, interest, dividends and rent. In most countries, people can earn a certain amount of income free of tax: this is known as their ***personal tax allowance***. In many countries, employees' income tax is paid directly on their behalf by their employers. In the UK this is known as the pay-as-you-earn scheme (PAYE).

The marginal rate of income tax is the rate that people pay on additional income. In most countries, the marginal rate increases in bands as people earn more. In many countries, there is a main marginal rate of tax that most people pay. This is known as the ***basic*** or ***standard rate of tax***.

The *average* rate is a person's total income tax as a fraction of total income. This will always be less than the marginal rate, since part of a person's income will be tax free; and for higher tax rate payers, part will be taxed at lower rates.

Individuals' social security contributions. In the UK these are known as national insurance contributions (NICs). These are like income taxes in that they are generally charged as a percentage of a person's income, the marginal rate varying with income. Unlike other taxes, which are paid into a common fund to finance government expenditure, they are used to finance *specific* expenditure: namely, pensions and social security. Although they do not officially count as 'taxes', to all intents and purposes they are so.

Table 10.3 and Figure 10.10 show the marginal and average rates of income tax and social security contributions in the UK (in 2005/6). Notice the effect of the marginal national insurance rate falling to a mere 1 per cent on incomes above £32 760.

Employers' social security contributions. Employers also have to pay social security contributions on behalf of their employees. These are paid per employee. In some countries, small firms pay reduced rates.

Figure 10.10 UK average and marginal rates of income tax plus NIC: 2005/6

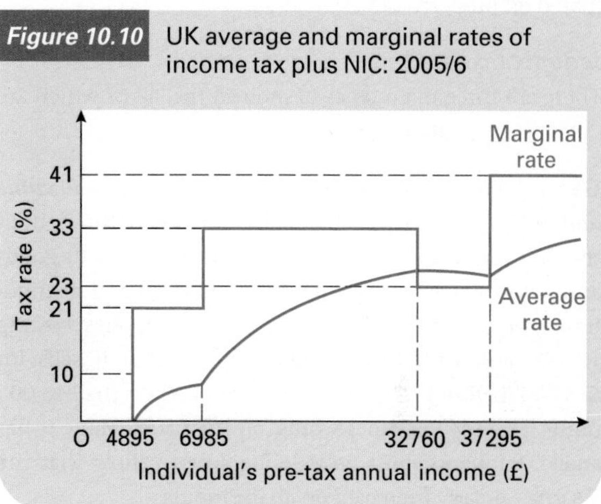

Tax on corporate income. In the UK this is known as corporation tax. It is a tax on the profits of limited companies. In most countries, there are lower rates for small companies. Profits can usually be offset against capital expenditure and interest payments when working out the tax liability. This effectively means that profits that are reinvested are not taxed.

Taxes on capital gains. This is a tax payable when a person sells assets, such as property or shares. It is payable on the gain in value of these assets since a set date in the past, or since they were purchased if this was after the set date.

Taxes on wealth. These are taxes on assets held or acquired by individuals. One form of wealth tax in most countries is that on inherited assets or assets transferred before a person's death. Another is taxes based on the value

Definitions

Indirect taxes Taxes on expenditure. Paid to the tax authorities not by the consumer, but indirectly by the suppliers of the goods or services.

Tax allowance An amount of income that can be earned tax free. Tax allowances vary according to a person's circumstances.

Basic rate of tax The main marginal rate of tax, applying to most people's incomes.

of a person's property. This is a particularly common form of local taxation (the others being local income tax, local business tax and local sales tax).

Poll taxes. These are fixed-sum charges per head of the population, irrespective of the person's income. Very few countries use such taxes as they are regarded as grossly unfair. A poll tax (or 'community charge') was introduced in Scotland in 1989 and in England and Wales in 1990 as the new form of local tax. But it was massively unpopular with the electorate and was replaced by the 'council tax' (based on property values) in 1993.

Indirect taxes

There are three main types of indirect tax, all of which are taxes on *expenditure*.

General expenditure taxes. An example of this is ***value added tax*** (VAT). This is the main indirect tax throughout the EU. VAT is paid on the value that firms add to goods and services at each stage of their production and distribution. For example, if a firm purchases supplies costing 10 000 and with them produces goods that it sells for £15 000 (before VAT), it is liable to pay VAT on the £15 000 minus £10 000: in other words, on the £5000 value it has added. Suppliers must provide invoices to show that the VAT has already been paid on all the inputs.

The example in Table 10.4 can be used to show how the tax eventually gets passed on to the consumer. For simplicity's sake, assume that the rate of VAT is 10 per cent and that each firm uses only one supplier.

The value added at each stage plus VAT adds up to the total amount paid by the consumer: £44 000 in this case. The total VAT paid, therefore, amounts to a tax on the consumer. In the example, the £4000 VAT is 10 per cent of the (pre-tax) consumer price of £40 000.

The rates of VAT in the various EU countries are shown in the table in Box 23.9 on page 663. Each country has a standard rate and up to two lower rates for basic goods and services.

Many other countries levy general expenditure taxes at a *single* stage (either wholesale or retail). These taxes are called *purchase taxes* and will normally be a percentage of the price of the good at that stage.

Excise duties. These are taxes on particular goods and services: for example, petrol and diesel, alcoholic drinks, tobacco products and gambling. They are a single-stage tax levied on the manufacturer. They are paid in addition to VAT.

VAT is an ***ad valorem tax***. This means that the tax is levied at a *percentage* of the value of the good. The higher the value of the good, the higher the tax paid. Excise duties, by contrast, are a ***specific tax***. This means that they are levied at a *fixed amount*, irrespective of the value of the good. Thus the duty on a litre of unleaded petrol is the same for a cut-price filling station as for a full-price one.

Customs duties. Economists normally refer to these as ***tariffs***. They are duties on goods imported from outside the country.

To what extent do (a) income tax, (b) VAT and (c) a poll tax meet the various requirements for a good tax system on pages 275–6 above? (Some of the answers to this question are given below.)

Table 10.4 Calculating VAT: an example where the rate of VAT is 10%

	Value added (1)		VAT (2)		Value added plus VAT (3)	Price sold to next stage (4)
Firm A sells raw materials to firm B for £11 000	£10 000		£1000		£11 000	£11 000
Firm B processes them and sells them to a manufacturer, firm C, for £19 800	£8000		£800		£8800	£19 800
Firm C sells the manufactured goods to a wholesaler, firm D, for £27 500	£7000		£700		£7700	£27 500
Firm D sells them to a retailer, firm E, for £33 000	£5000		£500		£5500	£33 000
Firm E sells them to consumers for £44 000	£10 000		£1000		£11 000	£44 000
	£40 000	+	**£4000**	=	**£44 000**	

Definitions

Value added tax (VAT) A tax on goods and services, charged at each stage of production as a percentage of the value added at that stage.

Ad valorem tax A tax on a good levied as a percentage of its value. It can be a single-stage tax or a multi-stage tax (such as VAT).

Specific tax A tax on a good levied at a fixed amount per unit of the good, irrespective of the price of that unit.

Tariff A tax on imported goods.

Table 10.5 Balance of taxation in selected countries (2003)

Types of tax as % of total tax[a]	France	Germany	Sweden	UK	USA
Personal income	17.8	23.2	30.8	28.1	34.9
Social security	40.8	44.9	30.5	21.3	27.3
Corporate taxes	7.3	4.6	10.0	8.1	7.8
Property and wealth	9.6	1.9	3.1	4.9	12.0
Expenditure	24.6	25.4	25.6	37.6	18.0
Total taxes[a] as % of GDP	45.3	41.4	48.7	36.6	25.9

[a] 'Taxes' in this table include social security contributions.

Source: Extracted from various tables in *Government Finance Statistics* (IMF).

Details of tax rates in the UK are given in Web Case 10.3 on the book's website. This case study also examines how progressive or regressive the various types of tax are.

The balance of taxation

Table 10.5 shows the balance of the different types of tax in selected countries. Some striking differences can be seen between the countries. In France, income taxes account for only 17.8 per cent of tax revenue, whereas in the USA they account for nearly 35 per cent. In the UK, social security contributions (national insurance) are a much lower percentage of total taxes than in other countries, whereas indirect taxes are a much higher percentage. In all countries except the USA, taxes on property and wealth are a very small proportion of total taxation.

The table also shows total taxes as a percentage of gross domestic product or GDP. (GDP is a measure of the nation's income: we will be examining how it is measured in the appendix to Chapter 13.) In Sweden nearly half of the nation's income is paid in tax, whereas in the USA the figure is only just over a quarter.

Taxes as a means of redistributing income

If taxes are to be used as a means of achieving greater equality, the rich must be taxed proportionately more than the poor. The degree of redistribution will depend on the degree of 'progressiveness' of the tax. In this context, taxes may be classified as follows:

- ***Progressive tax***. As people's income (Y) rises, the percentage of their income paid in the tax (T) rises. In other words, the *average* rate of tax (T/Y) rises.
- ***Regressive tax***. As people's income rises, the percentage of their income paid in the tax falls: T/Y falls.
- ***Proportional tax***. As people's income rises, the percentage of their income paid in the tax stays the same: T/Y is constant.

In other words, progressiveness is defined in terms of what happens to the average rate of tax as incomes rise. (Note that it is not defined in terms of the *marginal* rate of tax.)

?

1. *If a person earning £5000 per year pays £500 in a given tax and a person earning £10 000 per year pays £800, is the tax progressive or regressive?*
2. *A proportional tax will leave the distribution of income unaffected. Why should this be so, given that a rich person will pay a larger absolute amount than a poor person?*

An extreme form of regressive tax is a lump-sum tax (e.g. a poll tax). This is levied at a fixed *amount* (not rate) irrespective of income.

Figure 10.11 illustrates these different categories of tax. Diagram (a) shows the total amount of tax that a person pays. With a progressive tax, the curve gets progressively steeper, showing that the average rate of tax (T/Y) rises. The marginal rate of tax ($\Delta T/\Delta Y$) is given by the slope. Thus between points x and y the marginal tax rate is 40 per cent.

Diagram (b) shows the average rates. With a proportional tax, a person pays the same amount of tax on each pound earned. With a progressive tax, a larger proportion is paid by a rich person than by a poor person, and vice versa with a regressive tax.

The more steeply upward sloping the average tax curve, the more progressive is the tax, and the more equal will be the post-tax incomes of the population.

Problems with using taxes to redistribute incomes

How successfully can taxes redistribute income, and at what economic cost?

Problems in achieving redistribution

How to help the very poor. Taxation takes away income. It can thus reduce the incomes of the rich. But no taxes,

Definitions

Progressive tax A tax whose average rate with respect to income rises as income rises.

Regressive tax A tax whose average rate with respect to income falls as income rises.

Proportional tax A tax whose average rate with respect to income stays the same as income rises.

Figure 10.11 Different categories of tax

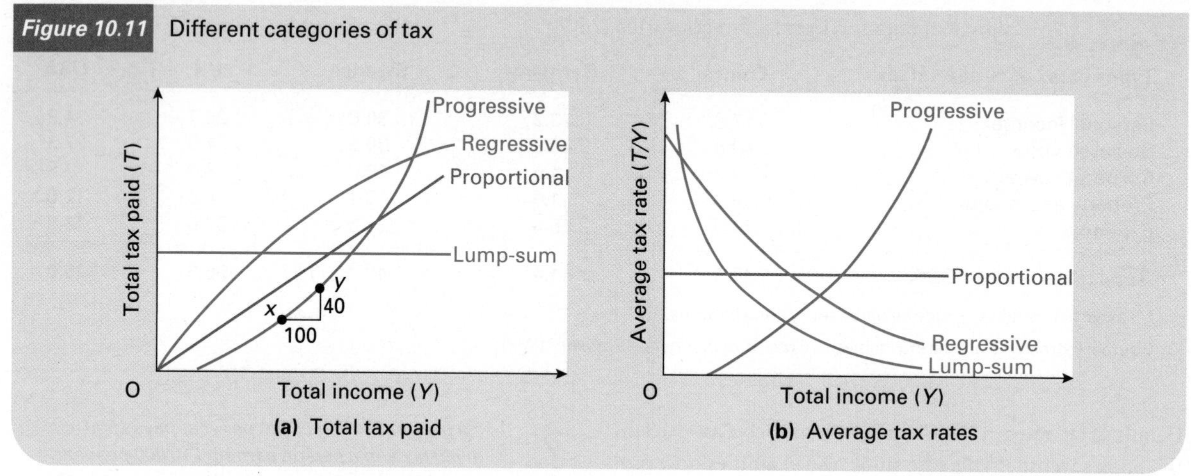

however progressive, can *increase* the incomes of the poor. This will require subsidies (i.e. benefits).

But what about tax cuts? Can bigger tax cuts not be given to the poor? This is possible only if the poor are already paying taxes in the first place. Take the two cases of income tax and taxes on goods and services.

- Income tax. If the government cuts income tax, then anyone currently paying it will benefit. A cut in tax *rates* will give proportionately more to the rich, since they have a larger proportion of taxable income relative to total income. An increase in personal *allowances*, on the other hand, will give the same *absolute* amounts to everyone above the new tax threshold. This will therefore represent a smaller proportionate gain to the rich. In either case, however, there will be no gain at all to those people below the tax threshold. They paid no income tax in the first place. These poorest of all people therefore gain nothing at all from income tax cuts.
- Taxes on goods and services. Since these taxes are generally regressive, any cut in their rate will benefit the poor proportionately more than the rich. A more dramatic effect would be obtained by cutting the rate most on those goods consumed relatively more by the poor.

The government may not wish to cut the overall level of taxation, given its expenditure commitments. In this case, it can switch the burden from regressive to progressive taxes. That way at least some benefit is gained by the very poor.

TC 3 p21

Tax evasion and tax avoidance. The higher the rates of tax, the more likely are people to try to escape paying some of their taxes.

People who are subject to higher rates of income tax will be more tempted not to declare all their income. This tax *evasion* will be much easier for people not paying all their taxes through a pay-as-you-earn (PAYE) scheme. This will include the self-employed and people doing casual work on top of their normal job ('moonlighting'). Furthermore, richer people can often reduce their tax liability – *tax avoidance* – by a careful use of various legal devices such as trusts and tax loopholes such as being allowed to offset 'business expenses' against income.

Part of the government's justification for abolishing income tax rates above 40 per cent in 1988 was that many people escaped paying these higher taxes.

?

Why may a steeply progressive income tax which is designed to achieve greater vertical *equity lead to a reduction in* horizontal *equity?*

Undesired incidence of tax. High rates of income tax on high wage earners may simply encourage employers to pay them higher wages. At the other end of the scale, tax cuts for low-paid workers may simply allow employers to cut wages. In other words, part of the incidence of income taxes will be borne by the employer and only part by the employee. Thus attempting to make taxes more 'progressive' will fail if employers simply adjust wages to compensate.

KI 9 p58

The incidence of income tax is determined by the elasticity of supply and demand for labour. In Figure 10.12, the initial supply and demand curves for labour (before the imposition of the tax) intersect at point (1), giving Q_1 labour employed at a wage of W_1. Now an income tax is imposed. This shifts the labour supply curve vertically upwards by the amount of the tax, giving the new labour supply curve, S + tax. The new equilibrium is reached at point (2) with Q_2 labour employed at a (gross) wage of W_2.

The incidence of the tax is as follows:

- The total tax revenue for the government is shown by the total shaded area.
- Workers' take-home pay is cut from W_1 to W_2 – tax. Their share of the tax is thus area A.
- Employers have to pay workers a rise of $W_2 - W_1$. They pay area B.

If the supply curve of labour of well-paid workers is relatively elastic, as shown in Figure 10.12, there will only

Figure 10.12 The incidence of an income tax: elastic supply of labour

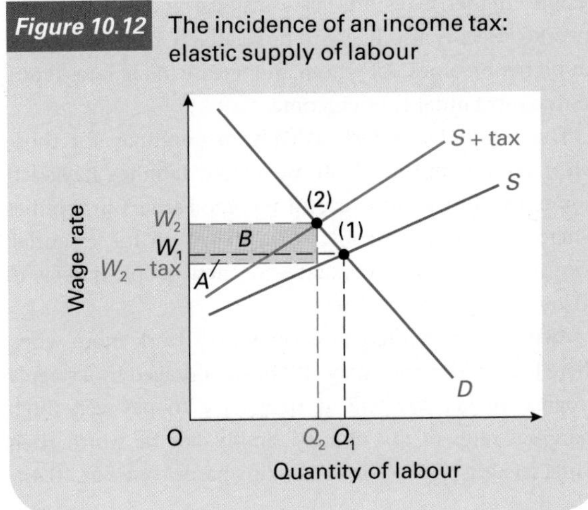

Figure 10.13 Indirect tax applied to good X

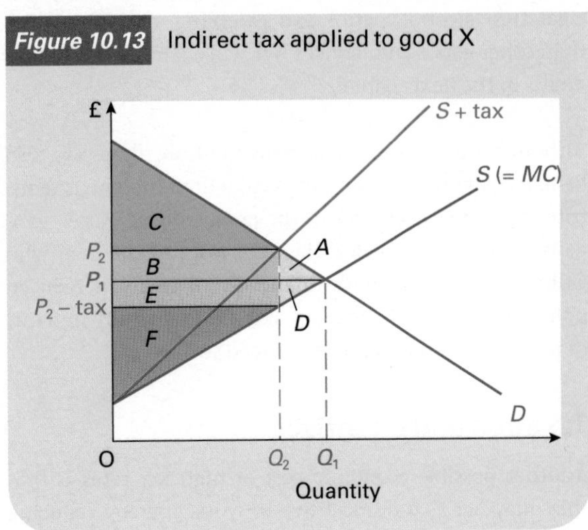

be a relatively slight fall in take-home pay (the workers' share of the tax is relatively small). The tax will, therefore, have only a relatively slight redistributive effect away from this group of workers.

?

1. *Do poor people gain more from a cut in income tax with an elastic or an inelastic supply of labour? Is the supply of unskilled workers likely to be elastic or inelastic?*
2. *Draw two diagrams like Figure 10.12, one with a steep demand curve and one with a shallow demand curve. How does the elasticity of demand affect the incidence of the income tax?*

Of course, income taxes are not imposed on workers in one industry alone. People, therefore, cannot move to another industry to avoid paying taxes. This fact will cause a relatively inelastic supply response to any rise in income tax, since the only alternative to paying the income tax is to work less. The less elastic this response, the more will the burden of the tax fall on the taxpayer and the more effectively can income taxes be used to redistribute incomes.

The economic costs of redistribution

KI 3 p11

If redistribution is to be achieved through *indirect* taxes, this can lead to market distortions.

Take first the case of an indirect tax applied to one good only. Assume for simplicity that there is universal perfect competition. Raising the price of this good relative to other goods will introduce a market distortion. Consumption will shift away from this good towards other goods that people preferred less at the original prices. What is more, the loss to consumers and producers (other things being equal) will be greater than the gain to the community from the tax revenue. This is illustrated in Figure 10.13.

With no tax, price will be at P_1 and output at Q_1, where demand equals supply. By imposing a tax on the good, the supply curve shifts upwards to S + tax. Price rises to P_2 and output falls to Q_2. Producers are left with P_2 – tax. What are the various losses and gains?

Consumers, by having to pay a higher price, lose consumer surplus (see section 4.1). Originally their consumer surplus was areas $A + B + C$. With the price now at P_2, the consumer surplus falls to area C alone. The loss to consumers is areas $A + B$.

Producers, by receiving a lower price after tax and selling fewer units, lose profits. In the simple case where there are no fixed costs of production, total profits are simply the sum of all the marginal profits (P (= MR) – MC) on each of the units sold. Thus before the tax is imposed, firms receive total profits of areas $D + E + F$. After the tax is imposed, they receive a profit of area F alone. The loss in profits to producers is therefore areas $D + E$.

The total loss to consumers and producers is areas $A + B + D + E$. The gain to the government in tax revenue is areas $B + E$: the tax rate times the number of units sold (Q_2). There is thus a net loss to the community of areas $A + D$. This is known as the ***deadweight loss of the tax***.

However, if the money raised from the tax is redistributed to the poor, their gain in welfare is likely to exceed the loss in welfare from the higher tax. The reason is that a pound sacrificed by the average consumer is probably of less value to him or her than a pound gained by a poor person.

What is more, if the tax is applied at a uniform rate to *all* goods, there is no distortion resulting from reallocation between goods. This is one of the major justifications for having a single rate of VAT.

Of course, in the real world, markets are highly imperfect and there is no reason why taxes will necessarily make these imperfections worse. In fact, it might be desirable on efficiency grounds to tax certain goods and services, such as

Definition

Deadweight loss of an indirect tax The net loss of consumer plus producer surplus (after adding in the tax revenue) from the imposition of an indirect tax.

cigarettes, alcohol, petrol and gambling, at higher rates than other goods and services. We will examine these arguments in the next chapter.

Although there are costs of redistribution, there are also benefits extending beyond those to whom income is redistributed. If redistribution to the poor reduces crime, vandalism and urban squalor, then it is not just the poor who gain: it is everyone, both financially in terms of reduced policing and social work costs, and more generally in terms of living in a happier and less divided society.

Taxation and incentives

Another possible economic cost of high tax rates is that they may act as a disincentive to work, thereby reducing national output and consumption. This whole question of incentives is highly charged politically. According to the political right, there is a trade-off between output and equity. High and progressive income taxes can lead to a more equal distribution of income, but a smaller national output. Alternatively, by cutting taxes there will be a bigger national output, but less equally divided. If many on the left are correct, however, we can have both a more equal society *and* a bigger national output: there is no trade-off.

KI 7 p35

The key to analysing these arguments is to distinguish between the *income effect* and the *substitution effect* of a tax rise. Raising taxes does two things:

- It reduces incomes. People may therefore work *more* in an attempt to maintain their consumption of goods and services. This is the ***income effect***.
- It reduces the opportunity cost of leisure. An extra hour taken in leisure now involves a smaller sacrifice in consumption, since each hour less worked involves less sacrifice in after-tax income. Thus people may substitute leisure for consumption, and work *less*. This is the ***substitution effect***.

The relative size of the income and substitution effects is likely to differ for different types of people and different types of tax change.

Different types of people

The *income* effect is likely to dominate for people with long-term commitments: for example, those with families, with mortgages and other debts. They may feel forced to work *more* to maintain their disposable income. Clearly for such people, higher taxes are *not* a disincentive to work. The income effect is also likely to be relatively large for people on higher incomes, for whom an increase in tax rates represents a substantial cut in income.

The *substitution* effect is likely to dominate for those with few commitments: those whose families have left home, the single, and second income earners in families where that second income is not relied on for 'essential' consumption. A rise in tax rates for these people is likely to encourage them to work less.

Although high income earners may work more when there is a tax *rise*, they may still be discouraged by a steeply progressive tax *structure*. If they have to pay very high marginal rates of tax, it may simply not be worth their while seeking promotion or working harder (see Box 10.4).

1. *Who is likely to work harder as a result of a cut in income tax rates, a rich person or a poor person? Why? Would your answer be different if personal allowances were zero?*
2. *How will tax cuts affect the willingness of women to return to employment after having brought up a family?*

Different types of tax

If the government wishes to raise income taxes in order to redistribute incomes, there are three main ways it can do it: raising the higher rates of tax; raising the basic rate; and reducing tax allowances.

Raising the higher rates of tax. This may seem the most effective way of redistributing incomes: after all, it is only the rich who will suffer. There are, however, serious problems:

- The income effect will be relatively small, since it is only that part of incomes subject to the higher rates that will be affected. The substitution effect, however, could be relatively high. Rich people are likely to put a higher premium on leisure, and may well feel that it is not worth working so hard if a larger proportion of any increase in income is taken in taxes.
- It may discourage risk taking by business people. 
- The rich may be more mobile internationally, so there may be a 'brain drain'.

Raising the basic rate of tax. As we have seen, the income effect is likely to be relatively large for those with higher incomes, especially if they have substantial commitments like a large mortgage. For such people, a rise in tax rates is likely to act as an incentive.

For those just above the tax threshold, there will be very little extra to pay on *existing* income, since most of it is tax free. However, each *extra* pound earned will be taxed at the new higher rate. The substitution effect, therefore, is likely to outweigh the income effect. For these people, a rise in tax rates will act as a disincentive.

For those below the tax threshold, the marginal rate remains at zero. A rise in the basic rate might nevertheless

Definitions

Income effect of a tax rise Tax increases reduce people's incomes and thus encourage people to work more.

Substitution effect of a tax rise Tax increases reduce the opportunity cost of leisure and thus encourage people to work less.

EXPLORING ECONOMICS

BOX 10.4

THE LAFFER CURVE

Having your cake and eating it

Professor Art Laffer was one of President Reagan's advisers during his first administration (1981–4). He was a strong advocate of income tax cuts, arguing that substantial increases in output would result.

He went further than this. He argued that tax cuts would actually *increase* the amount of tax revenue that the government earned.

Total tax revenue

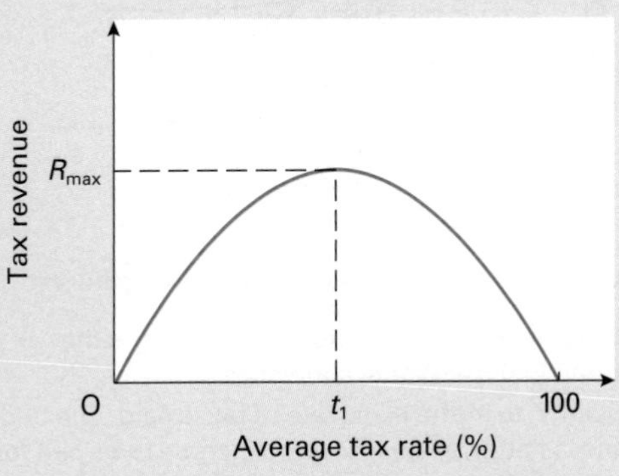

If tax cuts cause income to rise (due to incentives) proportionately more than the tax rate has fallen, then tax revenues will increase. These effects are illustrated by the now famous 'Laffer' curve.

If the average tax rate were zero, no revenue would be raised. As the tax rate is raised above zero, tax revenues will increase. The curve will be upward sloping. Eventually, however, the curve will peak (at tax rate t_1). Thereafter tax rates become so high that the resulting fall in output more than offsets the rise in tax rate. When the tax rate reaches 100 per cent, the revenue will once more fall to zero, since no one will bother to work.

The curve may not be symmetrical. It may peak at a 40 per cent, 50 per cent, 60 per cent or even 90 per cent rate. Nevertheless, Laffer and others on the political right argued that tax rates were above t_1. In fact most evidence suggests that tax rates in most countries were well below t_1 in the 1980s and certainly are now, given the cuts in income tax rates that have been made around the world over the past 20 years.

?

1. ***What is the elasticity of supply of output with respect to changes in tax rates at a tax rate of t_1? What is it below t_1? What is it above t_1?***
2. ***If the substitution effect of a tax cut outweighs the income effect, does this necessarily mean that the economy is to the right of point t_1?***

deter them from undertaking training in order to get a better wage.

For those people who are not employed, a rise in tax rates may make them feel that it is no longer worth looking for a job.

Reducing tax allowances. For all those above the old tax threshold, there is no *substitution* effect at all. The rate of tax has not changed. However, there is an *income* effect. The effect is like a lump-sum tax. Everyone's take-home pay is cut by a fixed sum, and people will need to work harder to make up some of the shortfall. This type of tax change, however, is highly regressive. If everyone pays the same *amount* of extra tax, this represents a bigger percentage for poorer people than richer people. In other words, there may be no negative incentive effects, but it is not suitable as part of a policy to redistribute incomes more equally!

The conclusion from the theoretical arguments is that tax changes will have very different effects depending on (a) whom they affect and (b) the nature of the change.

?

1. *Go through each of the above types of tax change and consider the effects of a tax cut.*
2. *What tax changes (whether up or down) will have a positive incentive effect and also redistribute incomes more equally?*

One final point should be stressed. For many people, there is no choice in the amount they work. The job they do dictates the number of hours worked, irrespective of changes in taxation.

Evidence

All the available evidence suggests that the effects of tax changes on output are relatively small. Labour supply curves seem highly inelastic to tax changes.

Benefits

Benefits can be either cash benefits or benefits in kind.

Cash benefits

Means-tested benefits. ***Means-tested benefits*** are available only to those whose income (and savings in some instances) fall below a certain level. To obtain such benefits, therefore, people must apply for them and declare their personal circumstances to the authorities.

Definition

Means-tested benefits Benefits whose amount depends on the recipient's income or assets.

EXPLORING ECONOMICS

TAX CUTS AND INCENTIVES

***An application of indifference curve analysis*[5]**

Will tax cuts provide an incentive for people to work more? This question can be analysed using indifference curves (see section 4.3). The analysis is similar to that developed in Box 9.2. It is assumed that individuals can choose how many hours a day to work.

The position with no income tax

Diagram (a) shows the situation without income tax.

(a) *Without income tax*

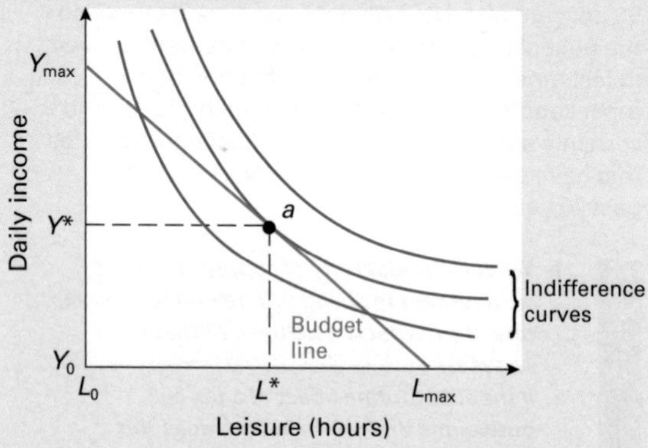

The budget line shows the various combinations of leisure and income open to an individual at a given wage rate.

? ***Why is the budget line straight? What would it look like if overtime were paid at higher rates per hour?***

The indifference curves show all the combinations of income and leisure that give the person equal satisfaction. The optimum combination of income and leisure is at Y^* and L^* where the individual is on the highest possible indifference curve: point *a*.

The position with income tax

Now let us introduce a system of income taxes. This is illustrated in diagram (b).

(b) *With income tax*

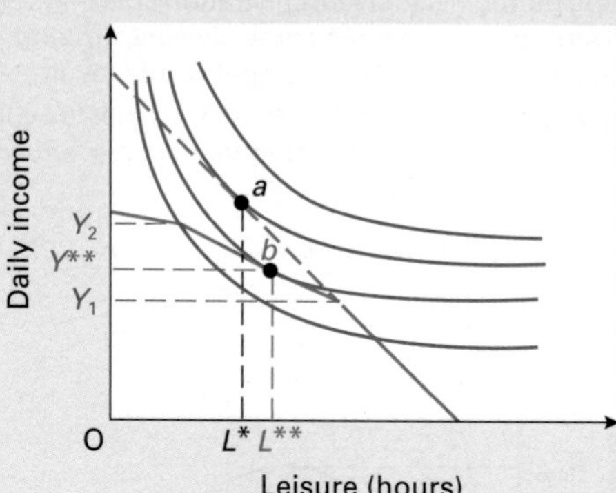

Assume that the tax has the following features:

- Up to an income of Y_1 no tax is paid: Y_1 is the individual's personal allowance.
- From Y_1 to Y_2 the basic rate of tax is paid. The budget line is flatter, since less extra income is earned for each extra hour of leisure sacrificed.
- Above Y_2 the higher rate of tax is paid. The budget line becomes flatter still.

The individual illustrated in the diagram will now choose to earn a take-home pay of Y^{**} and have L^{**} hours of leisure: point *b*. Note that this is more leisure than in the no-tax situation (point *a*). In this diagram, then, the tax has acted as a disincentive. The substitution effect has outweighed the income effect.

Redraw diagram (b), but in such a way that the income effect outweighs the substitution effect.

A cut in the basic tax rate

We can now analyse the effects of tax cuts. A cut in the basic rate is shown in diagram (c).

The tax cut makes the budget line steeper above point *q* (the tax threshold).

The benefits could be given as grants or merely as loans. They could be provided as general income support or for the meeting of specific needs, such as rents, fuel bills and household items.

Universal benefits. ***Universal benefits*** are those that everyone is entitled to, irrespective of their income, if they fall into a certain category. Examples include state pensions, and unemployment, sickness and invalidity benefits.

Benefits in kind

Individuals receive other forms of benefit from the state, not as direct monetary payments, but in the form of the provision of free or subsidised goods or services. These are known as ***benefits in kind***. The two largest items in most countries are health care and education. They are

Definitions

Universal benefits Benefits paid to everyone in a certain category irrespective of their income or assets.

Benefits in kind Goods or services that the state provides directly to the recipient at no charge or at a subsidised price. Alternatively, the state can subsidise the private sector to provide them.

*BOX 10.5

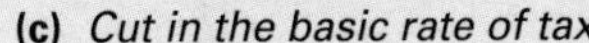

(c) *Cut in the basic rate of tax*

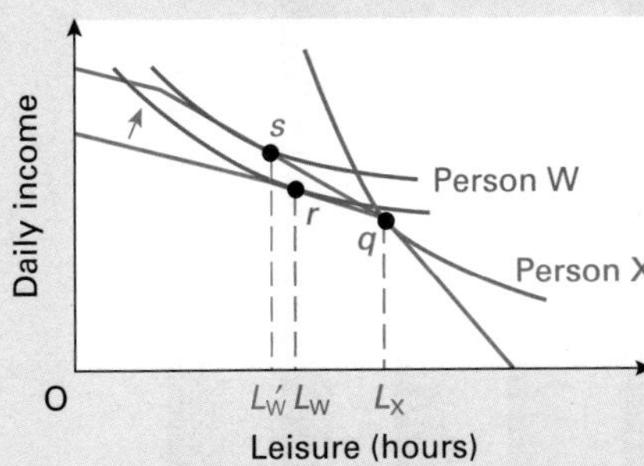

(d) *Increase in the tax threshold*

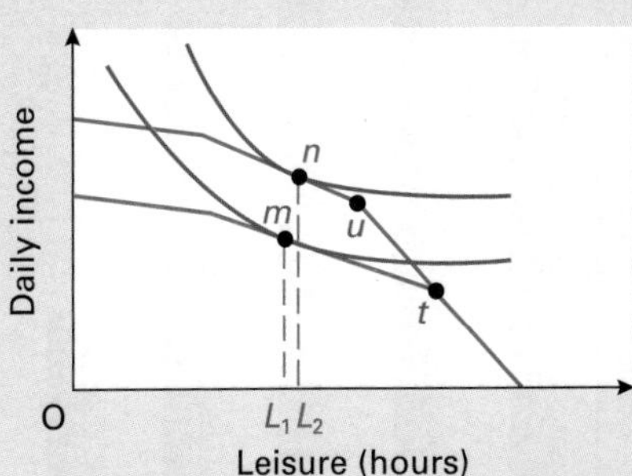

For people on the tax threshold – like person X – the cut in the basic rate makes no difference. Person X was originally taking L_X hours of leisure (point *q*) and will continue to do so.

For people above the tax threshold – like person W – the tax cut will enable them to move to a higher indifference curve. Person W will move from point *r* to point *s*. The way this diagram is drawn, point *s* is to the left of point *r*. This means that person W will work more: the substitution effect is greater than the income effect.

? ***Try drawing two or three diagrams like diagram (c), with the tangency point at different points along the budget line to the left of q. You will find that the further to the left you move, the* less *likely is the substitution effect to outweigh the income effect: i.e. the more likely are people to work* less *when given a tax cut.***

A rise in the tax threshold

Diagram (d) shows a rise in personal allowances while the tax rates stay the same.

The point at which people start paying taxes rises from point *t* to point *u*. The *slope* of the budget line remains the same, however, since the tax *rates* have not changed.

For people paying taxes, the increase in allowances represents a lump-sum increase in income: there will thus be an income effect. But since tax *rates* have not changed, there is no substitution effect. People therefore work less. The person in the diagram moves from point *m* to point *n*, taking L_2 rather than L_1 hours in leisure.

Will people actually on the old tax threshold (i.e. those whose indifference curve/budget line tangency point is at t) work more or less? Try drawing it.

A cut in the higher rate of tax

It is likely that the income effect of this will be quite small except for those on very high incomes. The substitution effect is therefore likely to outweigh the income effect, causing people to work more.

All the above analysis assumes that taxes will not affect people's* gross *wage rates. If part of the incidence of taxes is borne by the employer, so that gross wages fall, after-tax wages will fall less. There will therefore be a smaller shift in the budget line. How will this affect the argument for tax cuts?

[5] This box is based on D. Ulph, 'Tax cuts: will they work?', *Economic Review*, March 1987.

distributed very unevenly, however, largely due to the age factor. Old people use a large proportion of health services, but virtually no education services.

Benefits in kind tend to be consumed roughly equally by the different income groups. Nevertheless they still have some equalising effect, since they represent a much larger proportion of poor people's income than rich people's. They still have a far smaller redistributive effect, however, than cash benefits.

Figure 10.14 shows the expenditure on social protection benefits in selected European countries. These include unemployment, sickness, invalidity, maternity, family, survivors' and housing benefits and state pensions. They are mainly cash benefits, but do include some benefits in kind. They exclude health and education. As you can see, the benefits vary significantly from one country to another. Part of the reason for this is that countries differ in their rates of unemployment and in the age structure of their population. Thus Ireland has the lowest percentage of people over 65 in the EU and the smallest share of benefits devoted to pensions. Despite this, however, the generosity and coverage of benefits varies considerably from country to country, reflecting, in part, the level of income per head.

The system of benefits in the UK and their redistributive effects are examined in Web Case 10.5 on the book's website.

Figure 10.14 Social protection benefits in various European countries

9000
8000
7000
6000
5000
4000
3000
2000
1000
0
€ per head
2002
Belgium
Denmark
France
Germany
Greece
Ireland
Italy
Netherlands
Portugal
Spain
Sweden
UK
EU15

(a) € per head[a]

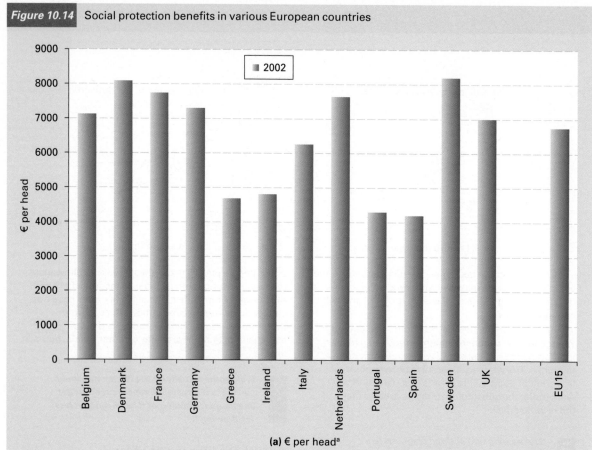

[a] Figures have been corrected to take account of differences in the purchasing power of a euro in the different countries.

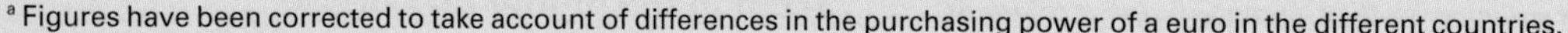

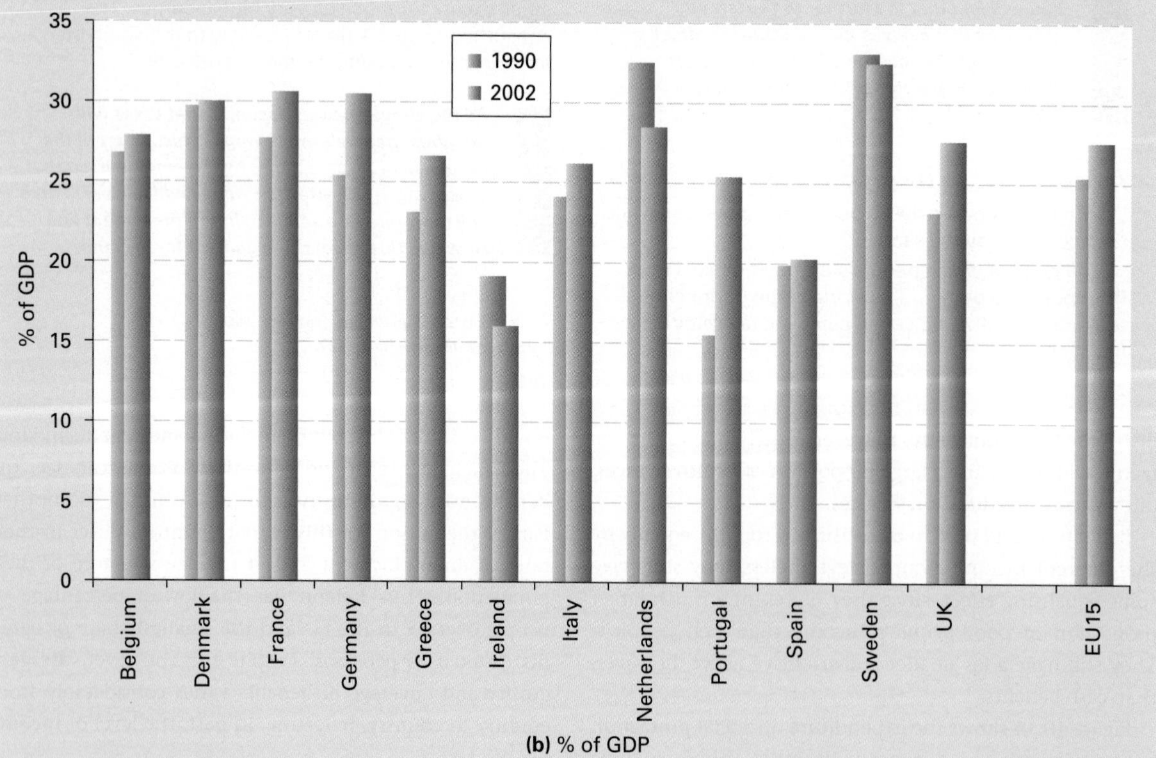

(b) % of GDP

Source: Eurostat, 2005.

KI 4 p11

Benefits and the redistribution of income

It might seem that means-tested benefits are a much more efficient system for redistributing income from the rich to the poor: the money is directed to those most in need. With universal benefits, by contrast, many people may receive them who have little need for them. Do families with very high incomes need child benefit? Would it not be better for the government to redirect the money to those who are genuinely in need?

There are, however, serious problems in attempting to redistribute incomes by the use of means-tested benefits:

- Not everyone entitled to means-tested benefits applies for them, whether from ignorance of what is available, from the complexities of claiming or from reluctance to reveal personal circumstances. Thus some of the poorest families receive no support.
- The level of income above which people become ineligible for benefits may be set too low. Even if it were raised, there will always be some people just above the level who will still find difficulties.
- Means tests based purely on *income* (or even universal benefits based on broad categories) ignore the very special needs of many poor people. A person earning £80 a week and living in a small, well-appointed flat with a low rent will have less need of assistance than another person who also earns £80 per week but lives in a cold, draughty and damp house with large bills to meet. If means tests are to be fair, *all* of a person's circumstances need to be taken into account.

The tax/benefit system and the problem of disincentives: the poverty trap

When means-tested benefits are combined with a progressive income tax system, there can be a serious problem of disincentives. As poor people earn more money, so not only will they start paying income taxes and national insurance, but also they will begin losing means-tested benefits. Theoretically, it is possible to have a marginal tax-plus-lost-benefit rate in excess of 100 per cent. In other words, for every extra £1 earned, taxes and lost benefits add up to more than £1. High marginal tax-plus-lost-benefit rates obviously act as a serious disincentive. What is the point of getting a job or trying to earn more money, if you end up earning little more or even losing money?

This situation is known as the ***poverty trap***. People are trapped on low incomes with no realistic means of bettering their position.

The problem of the poverty trap would be overcome by switching to a system of universal benefits unrelated to income. For example, *everyone* could receive a flat payment from the state fixed at a sufficiently high level to cover their basic needs. There would still be *some* disincentive, but this would be confined to an income effect: people would not have the same need to work if the state provided a basic income. But there would no longer be the disincentive to work caused by a resulting *loss* of benefits (a substitution effect).

The big drawback with universal benefits, however, is their cost. If they were given to everyone and were large enough to help the poor, their cost would be enormous. Thus although the benefits themselves would not create much disincentive effect, the necessary taxation to fund them probably would.

There is no ideal solution to this conundrum. On the one hand, the more narrowly benefits are targeted on the poor, the greater is the problem of the poverty trap. On the other hand, the more widely they are spread, the greater is the cost of providing any given level of support to individuals. A compromise proposal is that of a ***negative income tax***. This is examined in Web Case 10.6. Box 10.6 examines the use of tax credits – a form of negative income tax – in the UK.

Conclusions

Redistribution is not costless. Whether it takes place through taxes or benefits or both, it can pose a problem of disincentives. Nevertheless the size of the disincentive problem varies enormously from one tax to another and from one benefit to another, and in some cases there may even be an *in*centive effect: for example, when the income effect of a tax outweighs the substitution effect. It is therefore important to estimate the particular effects of each type of proposal not only on income distribution itself, but also on economic efficiency.

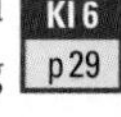

Ultimately, the questions of how much income should be redistributed and whether the costs are worth bearing are normative questions, and ones therefore that an economist cannot answer. They are moral and political questions. It would be nice if the 'utility' gained by the

Definitions

Poverty trap Where poor people are discouraged from working or getting a better job because any extra income they earn will be largely taken away in taxes and lost benefits.

Negative income tax A combined system of tax and benefits. As people earn more, they gradually lose their benefits until beyond a certain level they begin paying taxes.

CASE STUDIES AND APPLICATIONS

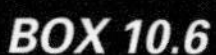

BOX 10.6

UK TAX CREDITS

An escape from the poverty trap?

Tax credits (negative income taxes) were introduced in the UK in 1999 in the form of working families tax credit, which was replaced in 2003 by working tax credit (WTC) and child tax credit (CTC). These credits are paid either as tax relief or as a cash benefit.

Working tax credit is designed for working people on low incomes. To be eligible for the basic amount (see the table), people without children must be aged 25 or over and work at least 30 hours per week. People with children must work at least 16 hours per week. Couples and lone parents receive an additional amount. There is a further addition for anyone with children who works at least 30 hours per week, or for couples who *jointly* work at least 30 hours per week. This is designed as an incentive for people to move from part-time to full-time work. Recipients of WTC also get paid 70 per cent of eligible childcare costs (80 per cent from 2006/7) up to £175 per week for one child and £300 for two or more children. For each pound earned above a threshold amount, relief is reduced by 37p.

Child tax credit provides support to families with children, whether or not anyone in the family works. It is paid in addition to WTC and child benefit. There is a basic rate and an additional amount per child. Relief tapers off for incomes over a threshold amount. (See table for rates of WTC and CTC.)

WTC and CTC rates (£ annual): 2005/6

Working tax credit (WTC)	
Basic element	1620
Addition for couples and lone parents	1595
Addition for those working 30 hours or more	660
Income threshold (above which WTC is reduced)	5220
Child tax credit (CTC)	
Basic element	545
Additional amount per child	1690
Income threshold (above which CTC is reduced)	13 910

Source: Inland Revenue.

Apart from targeting support at poorer families, these tax credits are intended to improve incentives to work, by reducing the poverty trap (see page 287). In other words, the aim is to reduce the financial penalties for parents working by tapering off more slowly the rate at which benefits are lost. With a lost-benefit rate of 37 per cent, the combined marginal tax-plus-lost-benefit rate (the 'marginal deduction rate') is typically around 58 to 70 per cent, depending on a person's marginal rate of tax and other means-tested benefits received.

Although the introduction of these tax credits has reduced the typical marginal deduction rate for poor families, the rate is still very high. For many poor parents, therefore, the incentive to work is still relatively low.

There is another effect from reducing the rate at which benefit tapers off. Some benefit will now be available to slightly less poor families. Although this is good in terms of providing support for them, there is now more of a disincentive for parents in such families to work extra hours, or to take a better job, since the marginal deduction rate is now higher. In other words, although they are better off, they will take home less for each extra hour worked.

WTC and CTC illustrate the general problem of providing support to poor people which is affordable for taxpayers without creating disincentives to work. The more gently the support tapers off (and hence the less the disincentive to earn extra money), the more costly it is to finance. The problems with using negative income taxes are explored in Web Case 10.6.

Economists sometimes refer to an 'unemployment trap'. People are discouraged from taking work in the first place. Explain how such a 'trap' arises. Does the working tax credit create an unemployment trap? What are the best ways of eliminating, or at least reducing, the unemployment trap?

poor and lost by the rich could be quantified so that any net gain from redistribution could be weighed up against lost output. But such 'interpersonal comparisons of utility' are not possible. For example, the benefit that a person receives from a cooker or an electric fire cannot be measured in 'utils' or any other 'psychic unit'. What people are prepared to pay for the items is no guide either, since a poor person obviously cannot afford to pay nearly as much as a rich person, and yet will probably get the same if not more personal benefit from them.

Yet decisions have to be made!

Section summary

1. Government intervention in the economy through taxation and government expenditure has a number of purposes including redistribution, the correction of market distortions and macroeconomic stabilisation.
2. There are various requirements of a good tax system, including horizontal and vertical equity, payment according to the amount of benefit received, being cheap to collect, difficult to evade, non-distortionary and convenient to the taxpayer and the government, and having the minimum disincentive effects.
3. Taxes can be divided into those paid directly to the authorities (direct taxes: e.g. income tax) and those paid via a middle person (indirect taxes: e.g. VAT).
4. Taxes can be categorised as progressive, regressive or proportional. Progressive taxes have the effect of reducing inequality. The more steeply progressive they are, the bigger is the reduction in inequality.
5. There are various limitations to using taxes to redistribute incomes. First, they cannot on their own increase the incomes of the poor. (Cutting taxes, however, can help the poor if the cuts are carefully targeted.) Second, high taxes on the rich may encourage evasion or avoidance. Third, higher income taxes on the rich will probably lead to their employers paying higher (gross) wages.
6. Using indirect taxes to redistribute incomes involves costs of resource reallocation.
7. Raising taxes has two effects on the amount that people wish to work. On the one hand, people will be encouraged to work more in order to maintain their incomes. This is the income effect. On the other hand, they will be encouraged to substitute leisure for income (i.e. to work less), since an hour's leisure now costs less in forgone income. This is the substitution effect. The relative size of the income and substitution effects will depend on the nature of the tax change. The substitution effect of a tax rise is more likely to outweigh the income effect for those with few commitments, for people just above the tax threshold and in cases where the highest rates of tax are increased.
8. Benefits can be cash benefits or benefits in kind. Means-tested cash benefits include support for poor families and the low paid. Universal benefits include state pensions, unemployment benefits, and child benefit. Benefits in kind include health care, education and free school meals.
9. Means-tested benefits can be specifically targeted to those in need and are thus more 'cost-effective'. However, there can be serious problems with such benefits, including: limited take-up, some relatively needy people falling just outside the qualifying limit and inadequate account taken of *all* relevant circumstances affecting a person's needs.
10. The poverty trap occurs when the combination of increased taxes and reduced benefits removes the incentive for poor people to earn more. The more steeply progressive this combined system is at low incomes, the bigger is the disincentive effect.

END OF CHAPTER QUESTIONS

1. Using the data shown on the pie charts in Figure 10.1, construct two Lorenz curves (on the same diagram), corresponding to the before- and after-tax income figures. Interpret and comment on the diagram you have drawn.
2. Can taxes be used to relieve poverty?
3. In what ways might the views of different politicians on what constitutes a 'good' tax system conflict?
4. Distinguish between proportional, progressive and regressive taxation. Could a progressive tax have a constant marginal rate?
5. Consider the cases for and against a poll tax.
6. Under what circumstances would a rise in income tax act as (a) a disincentive and (b) an incentive to effort?
7. What is meant by the *poverty trap*? Would a system of *universal* benefits be the best solution to the problem of the poverty trap?
8. How would you go about deciding whether person A or person B gets more personal benefit from each of the following: (a) an electric fire; (b) a clothing allowance of £ *x*; (c) draught-proofing materials; (d) child benefit? Do your answers help you in deciding how best to allocate benefits?

Additional case studies on the book's website (www.pearsoned.co.uk/sloman)

10.1 How can we define poverty? This examines different definitions of poverty and, in particular, distinguishes between absolute and relative measures of poverty.

10.2 Adam Smith's maxims of taxation. This looks at the principles of a good tax system as identified by Adam Smith.

10.3 Taxation in the UK. This case study looks at the various types of tax in the UK. It gives the current tax rates and considers how progressive the system is.

10.4 The poll tax. This case charts the introduction of the infamous poll tax (or 'community charge') in the UK and its subsequent demise.

10.5 The system of benefits in the UK. A description of the various benefits used in the UK and their redistributive effects.

10.6 Negative income tax and redistribution. How effectively can a negative income tax redistribute income without causing adverse incentive effects?

WEBSITES RELEVANT TO CHAPTERS 9 AND 10

Numbers and sections refer to websites listed in the Web Appendix and hotlinked from this book's website at www.pearsoned.co.uk/sloman.

- For news articles relevant to this and the previous chapter, see the *Economics News Articles* link from the book's website.
- For general news on labour markets, see websites in section A, and particularly A1, 2, 4, 5 and 7. See also A41 and 42 for links to economics news articles from newspapers worldwide.
- For data on labour markets, see links in B1 or 2, especially to *Labour Market Trends* on the National Statistics site. Also see B9 and links in B19. Also see the labour topic in B33 and the *resources > statistics* links in H3. For international data on labour markets, see the ILO datasets in the ESDS International site (B35) (you will need an Athens password, available free to all students in UK higher education).
- For information on international labour standards and employment rights, see site H3.
- Sites I7 and 11 contain links to *Labour economics, Labour force and markets* and *Labour unions* in the *Microeconomics* section and to *Distribution of income and wealth* in the *Macroeconomics* section. Site I4 has links in the *Directory* section to *Labor* and *Labor Economics.* Site I17 in the *Labor Economics* section has links to various topics, such as *Labor Unions, Minimum Wage, Poverty* and *Work.*
- Links to the TUC and Confederation of British Industry sites can be found at E32 and 33.
- For information and poverty and inequality, see sites B18; E9, 13.
- For information on taxes, benefits and the redistribution of income, see E9, 30, 36; G5, 13. See also *The Virtual Economy* at D1.
- For student resources relevant to these two chapters, see sites C1–7, 9, 10, 19.
- For simulations on *Labour market reforms* and *Tackling child poverty*, see site D3.

Chapter 11

Markets, Efficiency and the Public Interest

In Chapter 10 we examined the problem of inequality. In this chapter we turn to examine another major area of concern. This is the question of the *efficiency* (or inefficiency) of markets in allocating resources.

First we show how a *perfect* market economy could under certain conditions lead to 'social efficiency'. In section 11.2 we examine the *real* world and show how markets in practice fail to meet social goals. These failures provide the major arguments in favour of government intervention in a market economy. We then turn to discuss the alternative ways in which a government can intervene to correct these various market failings.

If the government is to replace the market and provide goods and services directly, it will need some way of establishing their costs and benefits. Section 11.4 looks at 'cost–benefit analysis'. This is a means of establishing the desirability of a public project such as a new motorway or a new hospital. Finally, in section 11.5, we look at the case for restricting government intervention. We examine the advantages of real-world markets and the drawbacks of government intervention.

CHAPTER MAP

11.1 EFFICIENCY UNDER PERFECT COMPETITION

Perfect competition has been used by many economists and policy makers as an ideal against which to compare the benefits and shortcomings of real-world markets.

As was shown in Chapter 6, perfect competition has various advantages for society. Under perfect competition, firms' supernormal profits are competed away in the long run by the entry of new competitors. As a result, firms are forced to produce at the bottom of their average cost curves. What is more, the fear of being driven out of business by the entry of new firms forces existing firms to try to find lower-cost methods of production, thus shifting their *AC* curves downwards.

KI 3 p10

Perhaps the most wide-reaching claim for perfect competition is that under certain conditions it will lead to a *socially efficient* use of a nation's resources.

Social efficiency: 'Pareto optimality'

If it were possible to make changes in the economy – changes in the combination of goods produced or consumed, or changes in the combination of inputs used – and if such changes benefited some people without anyone else being made worse off, economists would describe this as an ***improvement in social efficiency***, or a ***Pareto improvement***, after Vilfredo Pareto, the Italian social scientist (see Person Profile on the book's website).

> ? *Do you agree that, if some people gain and if no one loses, then this constitutes an 'improvement' in the well-being of society? Would it be possible to improve the well-being of society without a Pareto improvement?*

When all Pareto improvements have been made – in other words, when any additional changes in the economy would benefit some people only by making others worse off – the economy is said to be ***socially efficient***, or Pareto optimal. What we shall show is that under certain conditions a perfect market will lead to ***Pareto optimality***.

But a word of caution. Just because social *efficiency* is achieved in a particular market environment, it does not necessarily make that environment *ideal*. It may be a *necessary* condition for an ideal allocation of resources that all Pareto improvements are made. It is not *sufficient*, however. If, for example, the government redistributed income from the rich to the poor, there would be no Pareto improvement, since the rich would lose. Thus both an equal and a highly unequal distribution of income could be Pareto optimal, and yet it could be argued that a more equal distribution is socially more desirable. For the moment, however, we will ignore questions of fairness and just focus on social efficiency.

KI 4 p11

So why may a perfect market lead to social efficiency? The following sections explain.

The simple analysis of social efficiency: marginal benefit and marginal cost

Remember how we defined 'rational' choices. A rational person will choose to do an activity if the gain from so doing exceeds any sacrifice involved. In other words, whether as a producer, a consumer or a worker, a person will gain by expanding any activity whose marginal benefit (*MB*) exceeds its marginal cost (*MC*) and by contracting any activity whose marginal cost exceeds its marginal benefit. Remember that when economists use the term 'cost', they are referring to 'opportunity cost': in other words, the *sacrifice* of alternatives. Thus when we say that the marginal benefit of an activity is greater than its marginal cost, we mean that the additional benefit gained exceeds any sacrifice in terms of alternatives forgone.

KI 2 p8

TC 2 p10

Thus the economist's rule for ***rational economic behaviour*** is that a person should expand or contract the level of any activity until its marginal benefit is equal to its marginal cost. At that point, the person will be acting efficiently in his or her own private interest. Only when $MB = MC$ can no further gain be made. This is known as a situation of ***private efficiency***.

By analogy, *social* efficiency will be achieved where, for any activity, the marginal benefit to *society* (*MSB*) is equal to the marginal (opportunity) cost to *society* (*MSC*).

$$MSB = MSC$$

Definitions

An improvement in social efficiency A Pareto improvement.

Pareto improvement Where changes in production or consumption can make at least one person better off without making anyone worse off.

Social efficiency A situation of Pareto optimality.

Pareto optimality Where all possible Pareto improvements have been made: where, therefore, it is impossible to make anyone better off without making someone else worse off.

Rational economic behaviour Doing more of those activities whose marginal benefit exceeds their marginal cost and doing less of those activities whose marginal cost exceeds their marginal benefit.

Private efficiency Where a person's marginal benefit from a given activity equals the marginal cost.

Key Idea 25

Allocative efficiency (simple formulation) in any activity is achieved where marginal benefit equals marginal cost. Private efficiency is achieved where marginal private benefit equals marginal private cost ($MB = MC$). Social efficiency is achieved where marginal social benefit equals marginal social cost ($MSB = MSC$).

But why is social efficiency (i.e. Pareto optimality) achieved at this point? If *MSB* were greater than *MSC*, there would be a Pareto improvement if there were an increase in the activity. For example, if the benefits to consumers from additional production of a good exceed the cost to producers, the consumers could fully meet the cost of production in the price they pay, and so no producer loses, and yet there would still be a net gain to consumers. Thus society has gained. Likewise if *MSC* were greater than *MSB*, society would gain from a decrease in production.

Economists argue that under certain circumstances the achievement of *private* efficiency will result in *social* efficiency also. Two major conditions have to be fulfilled, however:

- There must be *perfect competition* throughout the economy. This is examined in the following sections.
- There must be *no* ***externalities***. Externalities are additional costs or benefits to society, *over and above* those experienced by the individual producer or consumer. Pollution is an example. It is a cost that society experiences from production, but it is not a cost that the individual producer has to pay. In the *absence* of externalities, the only costs or benefits to society are the ones that the individual producer or consumer experiences: i.e. marginal social benefit (*MSB*) is the same as marginal private benefit (*MB*), and marginal social cost (*MSC*) is the same as marginal private cost (*MC*).

To understand just how social efficiency is achieved, we must look at how people maximise their interests through the market.

Achieving social efficiency through the market

Consumption: $MU = P$

The marginal benefit to a consumer from the consumption of any good is its marginal utility. The marginal cost is the price the consumer has to pay.

As demonstrated in section 4.1, the 'rational' consumer will maximise consumer surplus where $MU = P$: in other words, where the marginal benefit from consumption is equal to the marginal cost of consumption. Do you remember the case of Tina and her purchases of petrol? (See page 95.) She goes on making additional journeys and hence buying extra petrol as long as she feels that the journeys are worth the money she has to spend: in other words, as long as the marginal benefit she gets from buying extra petrol (its marginal utility to her) exceeds its marginal cost (its price). She will stop buying extra petrol when its marginal utility has fallen (the law of diminishing marginal utility) to equal its price. At that point, her consumer surplus is maximised: she has an 'efficient' level of consumption. KI 2 p93

Definition

Externalities Costs or benefits of production or consumption experienced by society but not by the producers or consumers themselves. Sometimes referred to as 'spillover' or 'third-party' costs or benefits.

? *Assume that the price of the good falls. How will an 'efficient' level of consumption be restored?*

As we have seen, an individual's consumer surplus is maximised at the output where $MU = P$. With all consumers doing this, and all facing the same market price, their collective consumer surplus will be maximised. This is illustrated in Figure 11.1. Consumers' total utility is given by the area under the demand (*MU*) curve (areas $A + B + C$). Consumers' total expenditure is $P \times Q$ (areas $B + C$). Consumer surplus is the difference between total utility and total expenditure: in other words, the area between the price and the demand curve (area *A*).

Production: $P = MC$

The marginal benefit to a producer from the production of any good is its marginal revenue (which under perfect competition will be the same as the price of the good). As demonstrated in Chapter 6, the 'rational' firm will maximise its profit where its marginal revenue (i.e. the price under conditions of perfect competition) is equal to its marginal cost of production. This is the same thing as saying that it will produce where the marginal benefit from production is equal to the marginal cost from production.

Figure 11.1 Maximum total surplus under perfect competition

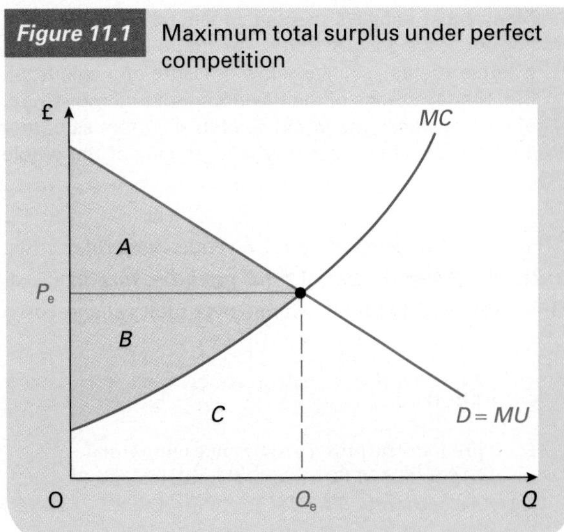

THINKING LIKE AN ECONOMIST

THRESHOLD CONCEPT 10

GENERAL EQUILIBRIUM: WHEN ALL MARKETS ARE IN BALANCE

In previous chapters we have been looking at individual markets: goods markets and factor markets. But any change in one market is likely to have repercussions in other markets. And changes in these other markets will probably affect other markets, and so on.

The point about a market economy is that it is like an interconnected web. Understanding these connections helps us understand the concept of an 'economy'.

If we started with an economy where all markets were in equilibrium, we would have a state of ***general equilibrium***. Then let's assume that a change occurs in just one market – say a rise in oil prices resulting from increased demand from China, India and other rapidly growing newly industrialised countries. This will have knock-on effects throughout the economy. Costs, and hence prices, will rise in oil-consuming industries. Consumption will fall for the products of these industries and rise for substitute products which do not use oil, or use less of it. Some motorists will be encouraged to use public transport or cycle. This could have knock-on effects on the demand for houses, with people choosing to live nearer to their work. This could then have effects on the various parts of the construction industry. You can work out some of these effects for yourself.

You will quickly see that a single change in one industry can set off a chain reaction throughout the economy. If there is just the one initial change, things will settle to a new general equilibrium where all markets are back in balance with demand equal to supply. In practice, of course, economic 'shocks' are occurring all the time and thus the economy is in a constant state of flux with no stable general equilibrium.

The concept of general equilibrium is a *threshold concept* because it gives us an insight into how market forces apply to a *whole* economy, and not just to its individual parts. It is about seeing how the whole jigsaw fits together and how changes ripple throughout the economy.

Many other subjects use the concept of general equilibrium. Take meteorology. We could study a single weather system, such as a low pressure or a cold front. But, to make sense of the development and movement of such systems, we would need to see them as part of a bigger picture. In other words, as part of the whole world's weather system, which at any time is moving towards a general equilibrium in response to various changes.

For instance, in the short term, we can see how weather systems respond to the changing seasons: for example, how pressure systems move northwards in the northern hemisphere summer. In the longer term we could model how world weather systems will respond to global warming. Will the resulting general equilibrium be one where sea levels rise; where the Gulf Stream is turned off, with much of north-western Europe becoming colder; where the deserts of north Africa spread to southern Europe; and so on?

The human body is another example of general equilibrium. Another is the operation of various ecosystems, such as a jungle or the tundra. Various natural events or human intervention can profoundly affect such ecosystems and result in a new general equilibrium. For example, cutting down rain forests can affect a vast range of plant and animal life, let alone the climate.

But in economics, understanding general equilibrium is not just about understanding and predicting the output of the various industries that make up the economy. It can help us make value judgements and formulate policy. As we shall see in Threshold Concept 11 (see page 297), under certain conditions, general equilibrium can be seen as *socially efficient*. These conditions are (a) perfect competition and (b) an absence of externalities.

If social efficiency is seen as desirable, then one policy implication might be to try to make markets as perfect as possible and to 'internalise' externalities. In this chapter we examine whether such policies should be adopted and, if so, what form should they take?

1. ***If general equilibrium is achieved when all markets have responded to a change and its knock-on effects, and if such changes are constantly occurring, will general equilibrium actually be achieved? Does your answer have any implications for policy?***
2. ***If social efficiency is seen as desirable (a normative issue), should policy necessarily be geared to achieving this?***

Profit is the excess of total revenue over total costs. A related concept is that of ***total producer surplus*** (*TPS*). This is the excess of total revenue over total *variable* costs: $TPS = TR - TVC$. In other words, total producer surplus is total profit plus fixed costs: $TPS = T\Pi + TFC$. But since there are no marginal fixed costs (by definition), both producer surplus and profit will be maximised at the same output.

Total producer surplus for all firms in the market is shown in Figure 11.1. Total revenue (i.e. total expenditure) is $P \times Q$ (areas $B + C$). Total variable cost is the area under the *MC* curve (area *C*): i.e. it is the sum of all the marginal costs of each unit produced. Producer surplus is thus the area between the price and the *MC* curve (area *B*).

Definition

Total producer surplus Total revenue minus total variable costs ($TR - TVC$): in other words, total profit plus total fixed costs ($T\Pi + TFC$).

KI 25 p293

Private efficiency in the market: MU = MC

In Figure 11.1, both consumer surplus and producer surplus are maximised at output Q_e. This is the equilibrium output under perfect competition. Thus, under perfect competition, the market will ensure that ***total surplus*** (areas $A + B$), sometimes called *total private surplus*, is maximised. At this output, $MU = P = MC$.

At any output other than Q_e total surplus will be less. If output were below Q_e, then MU would be above MC: total surplus would be increased by producing more. If output were above Q_e, then MU would be below MC: total surplus would be increased by producing less.

Social efficiency in the market: MSB = MSC

Provided the two conditions of (a) perfect competition and (b) the absence of externalities are fulfilled, Pareto optimality (i.e. social efficiency) will be achieved. Let us take each condition in turn.

Perfect competition. Perfect competition will ensure that private efficiency is achieved:

$MU = MC$ (for all producers and all consumers)

No externalities. In the absence of externalities, $MSB = MU$ (i.e. the benefits of consumption within society are confined to the direct consumers) and $MSC = MC$ (i.e. the costs of production to society are simply the costs paid by the producers). Thus:

$$MSB = MU = P = MC = MSC$$

i.e. $MSB = MSC$

With no externalities, the total surplus shown in Figure 11.1 will represent ***total social surplus***.

Inefficiency would arise if (a) competition were not perfect and hence if marginal revenue were *not* equal to price and as a result marginal cost were not equal to price; or (b) there were externalities and hence either marginal social benefit were different from marginal utility (i.e. marginal *private* benefit) or marginal social cost were different from marginal (private) cost. We examine such 'market failures' in section 11.2.

1. *If monopoly power existed in an industry, would production be above or below the socially efficient level (assuming no externalities)? Which would be greater, MSB or P?*
2. *Assuming perfect competition and no externalities, social efficiency will also be achieved in factor markets. Demonstrate that this will be where:*

   $MSB_f = MRP_f = P_f = MDU_f = MSC_f$

   (where MRP is the marginal revenue product of a factor, MDU is the marginal disutility of supplying it, and f is any factor – see section 9.1).
3. *Why will marginal social benefit not equal marginal social costs in the labour market if there exists (a) union monopoly power and/or (b) firms with monopsony power?*

Interdependence, efficiency and the 'invisible hand': the simple analysis of general equilibrium

If there is perfect competition and an absence of externalities throughout the economy, then the whole economy, when in equilibrium, will be socially efficient. A state of general Pareto optimality will exist.

No economy, however, is static. Conditions of demand and supply are constantly changing. Fashions change, technology changes and so on. Thus old patterns of consumption and production will cease to be Pareto optimal. Nevertheless, provided there is perfect competition and no externalities, forces will come into play to restore Pareto optimality.

In this perfect market economy, Pareto optimality is restored not by government action, but rather by the individual actions of producers, consumers and factor owners all seeking their own self-interest. It is as if an 'invisible hand' were working to guide the economy towards social efficiency (see Box 1.6).

KI 5 p21

The economic system will respond to any change in demand or supply by a whole series of subsequent changes in various interdependent markets. Social efficiency will thereby be restored. The whole process can be illustrated with a circular flow of income diagram (see Figure 11.2).

Assume, for example, that tastes change such that the marginal utility of a particular good rises. This is illustrated on the right-hand side of the diagram by a shift in the MU curve (i.e. the demand curve) from MU_1 to MU_2 (i.e. D_1 to D_2). This will lead to the following sequence of events, which you can follow round the diagram in an anti-clockwise direction.

Consumer demand

The rise in marginal utility (i.e. the rise in marginal social benefit of the good, MSB_g) leads to increased consumption. The resulting shortage will drive up the market price.

Producer supply

The rise in the market price will mean that price is now above the marginal (social) cost of production. It will thus be profitable for firms to increase their production. This in turn will lead to an increase in marginal cost (a movement up along the marginal cost curve) due to diminishing returns. There is a movement up along the supply curve from point a. Price will continue to rise until equilibrium is reached at P_2Q_2 (point b), where $MSB_{g_2} = MSC_g$.

Definitions

Total (private) surplus Total consumer surplus ($TU - TE$) plus total producer surplus ($TR - TVC$).

Total social surplus Total benefits to society from consuming a good minus total costs to society from producing it. In the absence of externalities, total social surplus is the same as total (private) surplus.

Figure 11.2 The interdependence of goods and factor markets

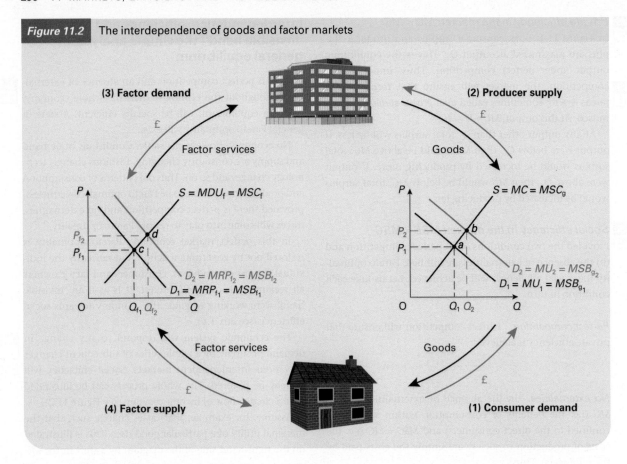

Factor demand

The rise in the price of the good will lead to an increase in the marginal revenue product of factors that are employed in producing the good. The reason for this is that the marginal *revenue* product of a factor is its marginal *physical* product multiplied by the *price* of the good (see section 9.1). But since the price of the good has now gone up, the output of factors will be worth correspondingly more. The following takes just one factor (f) as an example.

A rise in the value of the factor's output (due to the higher price of the good) will make its marginal revenue product higher than its marginal cost to the firm. This will increase the demand for the factor. Factor demand shifts to D_2 ($= MRP_{f_2} = MSB_{f_2}$). This in turn will drive up the price of the factor.

Factor supply

The rise in the price of the factor will raise the marginal benefit of supplying it (and hence the marginal social benefit). This will mean that the marginal benefit now exceeds the marginal cost (the marginal disutility, MDU_f) of supplying the factor. There is thus a movement up along the factor supply curve from point c as more units of the factor are supplied. The price of the factor will continue to rise until equilibrium is reached at $P_{f_2}Q_{f_2}$ (point d), where $MSB_{f_2} = MSC_f$.

The process of adjustment does not end here. If supernormal profits are made, new firms will enter. Similarly, if factor rewards are supernormal, new factors will be attracted from other industries. This in turn will affect prices and hence quantities in *other* industries in both goods and factor markets.

In other words, a single change in tastes will create a ripple effect throughout the economy, through a whole series of interdependent markets. Eventually, long-run equilibrium will be restored with $MSB = MSC$ in all markets. The economy has returned to a position of Pareto optimality. And all this has taken place with no government intervention. It is the 'invisible hand' of the market that has achieved this state of social efficiency.

These arguments form a central part of the neo-classical case for *laissez-faire*: the philosophy of non-intervention by the government. Under ideal conditions, it is argued, the free pursuit of individual self-interest will lead to the social good.

?

Trace through the effects in both factor and goods markets of the following:

(a) An increase in the productivity of a particular type of labour.

(b) An increase in the supply of a particular factor.

Show in each case how social efficiency will initially be destroyed and then how market adjustments will restore social efficiency.

THINKING LIKE AN ECONOMIST — THRESHOLD CONCEPT 11

ALLOCATIVE EFFICIENCY: PRIVATE AND SOCIAL

Economics is concerned with the allocation of scarce resources. Whenever choices are made, whether by consumers, firms, the government or any other agency, a choice is being made about the allocation of resources.

When you buy a CD costing £10, you are choosing to allocate £10 of your money to the purchase – £10 that could have been spent on something else. But have you allocated your money in the best way?

Similarly, when a firm chooses to produce one product rather than another, or to use technique A rather than some alternative technique, it is choosing to allocate its resources in particular ways. But are these the best ways?

The question is whether the resources have been allocated *efficiently*. We define an efficient allocation of resources as one which brings the maximum benefit for that level of costs. In other words, no gain would be made by reallocating resources in some alternative way. Thus your decision to spend £10 on a CD is an efficient allocation of your resources, if it brings you more benefit (i.e. utility) for the £10 than could any other purchase. The firm's decision to use technique A is an efficient one if it leads to a higher rate of profit: if the marginal benefit (i.e. marginal revenue) relative to the marginal cost is greater than for any other technique.

KI 14 p99

What we are talking about here is 'allocative efficiency'. It is a *threshold concept* because to understand it is to understand how to make the most of scarce resources: and scarcity is the core problem of economics for all of us. It is obvious that poor people on very limited incomes will want to spend their money as efficiently as possible. But even exceedingly rich people, who can buy anything they want, are still likely to have limited time or opportunities. They too will probably want to use their time efficiently so that they can make best use of their wealth!

Allocative efficiency is a threshold concept for another reason. We need to see how it relates to *social* objectives. If people all individually achieve their own *private efficiency*, does this mean that society will have an efficient allocation of resources? The answer is no. The reason is that our decisions often have consequences for *other* people: our actions have external costs and/or benefits. These externalities mean that private efficiency and *social efficiency* diverge. We need to understand how and why, and how social efficiency can be achieved.

Then there is the question of equity. Just because everyone is allocating their resources in the best possible way for them, and even if there were no externalities, it does not follow that the allocation of resources is *fair*. However efficiently rich people spend their money, most people would still argue that it is socially desirable to redistribute part of rich people's income to the poor through the tax and benefit system.

KI 4 p11

1. ***Why might consumers* not *always make efficient consumption decisions?***
2. ***Explain the meaning of social efficiency using the concept of Pareto improvements.***

The following pages examine social efficiency in more detail. You may omit these and skip straight to section 11.2 (page 300) if you want to.

*The intermediate analysis of social efficiency: marginal benefit and marginal cost ratios

In practice, consumers do not consider just one good in isolation. They make choices between goods. Likewise firms make choices as to which goods to produce and which factors to employ. A more satisfactory analysis of social efficiency, therefore, considers the choices that firms and households make.

TC 11 p297

Whether as a producer, consumer or worker, a person will gain by expanding activity X relative to activity Y if:

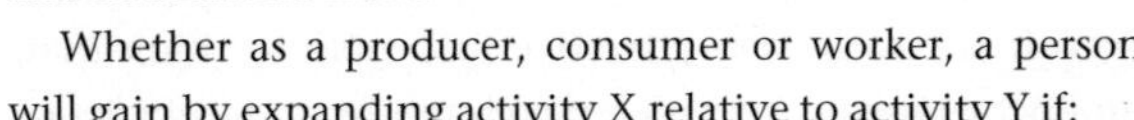

$$\frac{MB_X}{MB_Y} > \frac{MC_X}{MC_Y}$$

The reason is straightforward. Activity X is giving a greater benefit relative to its cost than is activity Y. Only when:

$$\frac{MB_X}{MB_Y} = \frac{MC_X}{MC_Y}$$

KI 14 p99

can no further gain be made by switching from the one activity to the other. At this point, people will be acting efficiently in their own private interest.

By analogy,

Key Idea 26

Social efficiency (equi-marginal formulation) is achieved where the marginal social benefit ratios are equal to the marginal social cost ratios for any two alternatives. In the case of two alternatives X and Y, this will be where:

$$\frac{MSB_X}{MSB_Y} = \frac{MSC_X}{MSC_Y}$$

As with the simple analysis of social efficiency, it can be shown that, provided there is perfect competition and no externalities, the achievement of private efficiency will result in social efficiency also. This will be demonstrated in the following sections.

TC 11 p297

*Efficiency in the goods market (intermediate analysis)

Private efficiency under perfect competition

Consumption. The optimum combination of two goods X and Y consumed for any consumer is where:

$$\frac{MU_X}{MU_Y} \text{ (i.e. } MRS) = \frac{P_X}{P_Y}$$

The *marginal rate of substitution in consumption (MRS)* (see page 106) is the amount of good Y that a consumer would be willing to sacrifice for an increase in consumption of good X (i.e. $\Delta Y/\Delta X$). $MRS = MU_X/MU_Y$ since, if X gave twice the marginal utility of Y, the consumer would be prepared to give up two of Y to obtain one of X (i.e. $MRS = 2/1$).

If MU_X/MU_Y were greater than P_X/P_Y, how would consumers behave? What would bring consumption back to equilibrium where $MU_X/MU_Y = P_X/P_Y$?

Production. The optimum combination of two goods X and Y produced for any producer is where:

$$\frac{MC_X}{MC_Y} \text{ (i.e. } MRT) = \frac{P_X}{P_Y}$$

The *marginal rate of transformation in production (MRT)* is the amount of good Y that the producer will have to give up producing for an increase in production of good X (i.e. $\Delta Y/\Delta X$) if total costs of production are to remain unchanged. $MRT = MC_X/MC_Y$ since, if the marginal cost of good X were twice that of Y, the firm's costs would remain constant if it gave up producing two of Y in order to produce an extra X (i.e. $MRT = 2/1$).

If MC_X/MC_Y were greater than P_X/P_Y, how would firms behave? What would bring production back into equilibrium where $MC_X/MC_Y = P_X/P_Y$?

Social efficiency under perfect competition

In each of the following three cases, it will be assumed that there are no externalities.

Social efficiency between consumers. If MU_X/MU_Y for person a is greater than MU_X/MU_Y for person b, *both* people would gain if person a gave person b some of good Y in exchange for some of good X. There would be a Pareto improvement. The Pareto optimal distribution of consumption will therefore be where:

$$\frac{MU_X}{MU_Y}_{\text{person a}} = \frac{MU_X}{MU_Y}_{\text{person b}} = \frac{MU_X}{MU_Y}_{\text{person c}} \ldots \text{etc.}$$

i.e. *MRS* is the same for all consumers.

But this will be achieved *automatically* under perfect competition, since each consumer will consume that combination of goods where $MU_X/MU_Y = P_X/P_Y$ and all consumers face the *same* (market) prices and hence the *same* P_X/P_Y.

Social efficiency between producers. If MC_X/MC_Y for producer g is greater than MC_X/MC_Y for producer h, then if producer g produced relatively more Y and producer h produced relatively more X, the same output could be produced at a lower total cost (i.e. with less resources). There would be a Pareto improvement. The Pareto optimal distribution of production between firms is therefore where:

$$\frac{MC_X}{MC_Y}_{\text{producer g}} = \frac{MC_X}{MC_Y}_{\text{producer h}} = \frac{MC_X}{MC_Y}_{\text{producer i}} \ldots \text{etc.}$$

i.e. *MRT* is the same for all producers.

This too will be achieved *automatically* under perfect competition, since each producer will maximise profits where $MC_X/MC_Y = P_X/P_Y$ and all producers face the *same* (market) prices and hence the *same* P_X/P_Y.

Social efficiency in exchange. If MU_X/MU_Y (i.e. *MRS*) for all consumers is greater than MC_X/MC_Y (i.e. *MRT*) for all producers, then there would be a Pareto improvement if resources were reallocated to produce relatively more X and less Y.

Assume the *MRS* (i.e. $\Delta Y/\Delta X$) = 3/1 and the *MRT* (i.e. $\Delta Y/\Delta X$) = 2/1. Consumers will be prepared to give up 3 units of Y to obtain 1 unit of X, and yet producers only have to sacrifice producing 2 units of Y to produce 1 unit of X. Thus consumers can pay producers in full for extra units of X they produce and there will still be a net gain to consumers. There has been a Pareto improvement.

The Pareto optimal allocation of resources is where:

$$\text{Social } MRS\ (SMRS) = \text{Social } MRT\ (SMRT)$$

Assuming no externalities, this will be achieved automatically under perfect competition, since (a) with no externalities, social and private marginal rates of substitution will be the same, and similarly social and private marginal rates of transformation will be the same, and (b) P_X/P_Y is the same for all producers and consumers. In other words:

$$SMRS = MRS_{\text{all consumers}} = \frac{MU_X}{MU_Y}_{\text{all consumers}} = \frac{P_X}{P_Y}$$

and $$SMRT = MRT_{\text{all producers}} = \frac{MC_X}{MC_Y}_{\text{all producers}} = \frac{P_X}{P_Y}$$

i.e. $SMRS = SMRT$

Thus the pursuit of *private* gain, it is argued, has led to the achieving of *social* efficiency. This is a momentous conclusion. It is clearly very attractive to people to think that, simply by looking after their own interests, *social* efficiency will thereby be achieved!

This is illustrated graphically in Figure 11.3. A production possibility curve (the red line) shows the various combinations of two goods X and Y that can be produced (see

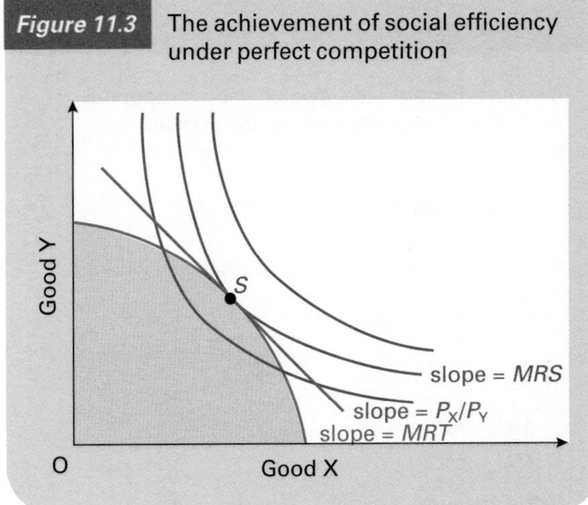

Figure 11.3 The achievement of social efficiency under perfect competition

page 12). Its slope is given by $\Delta Y/\Delta X$ and shows how much Y must be given up to produce 1 more of X. Its slope, therefore, is the marginal rate of transformation (*MRT*).

Social indifference curves can be drawn showing the various combinations of X and Y that give particular levels of satisfaction to consumers as a whole. Their slope is given by $\Delta Y/\Delta X$ and shows how much Y consumers are prepared to give up to obtain 1 more unit of X. Their slope, therefore, is the marginal rate of substitution in consumption (*MRS*).

The Pareto optimal combination of goods is at point *S*, where the production possibility curve is tangential to the highest possible indifference curve. At any other point on the production possibility curve, a lower level of consumer satisfaction is achieved. The slope of the tangent at *S* is equal to both *MRT* and *MRS*, and hence also to P_X/P_Y.

If production were at a point on the production possibility curve below point S, describe the process whereby market forces would return the economy to point S.

TC 11 p297

*Efficiency in the factor market (intermediate analysis)

A similar analysis can be applied to factor markets, showing that perfect competition and the absence of externalities will lead to efficiency in the use of factors between firms. Assume that there are two factors: labour (*L*) and capital (*K*).

If MPP_L/MPP_K for firm g is greater than MPP_L/MPP_K for firm h, then if firm g were to use relatively more labour and firm h relatively more capital, more could be produced for the same total input. There would be a Pareto improvement.

The Pareto optimum distribution of factors between firms will therefore be where:

$$\frac{MPP_L}{MPP_K}_{\text{firm g}} = \frac{MPP_L}{MPP_K}_{\text{firm h}} = \frac{MPP_L}{MPP_K}_{\text{firm i}} \ldots \text{etc.}$$

But this will be achieved automatically under perfect competition since, as we saw in section 5.3, each producer will be producing where $MPP_L/MPP_K = P_L/P_K$ and each producer will face the same factor prices and hence P_L/P_K.

Provided there are no externalities, the marginal private benefit of labour to a firm (MPP_L) will equal the marginal social benefit of labour (MSB_L). The same applies to capital. Thus $MPP_L/MPP_K = MSB_L/MSB_K = P_L/P_K$. Similarly on the cost side, if there are no externalities, then $MC_L/MC_K = MSC_L/MSC_K = P_L/P_K$. Therefore:

KI 26 p297

$$\frac{MSB_L}{MSB_K} = \frac{MSC_L}{MSC_K}$$

TC 10 p294

*The intermediate analysis of general equilibrium

General equilibrium is where equilibrium exists in all markets. Under perfect competition and in the absence of externalities, general equilibrium will give Pareto optimality.

KI 5 p21

If any change in the conditions of demand or supply occurs, this disequilibrium will automatically create a whole series of interdependent reactions in various markets.

Assume, for example, that tastes change such that MU_X rises and MU_Y falls. This will lead to the following sequence of events in the goods market.

MU_X/MU_Y will now be greater than P_X/P_Y. Thus consumers buy more X relative to Y. This causes MU_X/MU_Y to fall (due to diminishing marginal utility) and P_X/P_Y to rise (due to a relative shortage of X and a surplus of Y), helping to restore equilibrium where $MU_X/MU_Y = P_X/P_Y$. The rise in P_X/P_Y causes P_X/P_Y to be greater than MC_X/MC_Y. Thus firms produce more X relative to Y. This causes MC_X/MC_Y to rise (due to diminishing returns), helping to restore equilibrium where $P_X/P_Y = MC_X/MC_Y$. This process of price and quantity adjustment thus continues until once more:

KI 14 p99

$$\frac{MU_X}{MU_Y} = \frac{P_X}{P_Y} = \frac{MC_X}{MC_Y}$$

Similar adjustments will take place in the factor market. The price of those factors used in producing good X will be bid up and those used in producing Y will be bid down. This will encourage factors to move from industry Y and into industry X. The whole process of adjustment continues until equilibrium and Pareto optimality are restored in all goods and factor markets.

Definition

General equilibrium Where all the millions of markets throughout the economy are in a simultaneous state of equilibrium.

Section summary

1. Social efficiency (Pareto optimality) will be achieved when it is not possible to make anyone better off without making someone else worse off. This will be achieved if people behave 'rationally' under perfect competition providing there are no externalities.
2. Rational behaviour involves doing more of any activity whose marginal benefit (*MB*) exceeds its marginal cost (*MC*) and less of any activity whose marginal cost exceeds its marginal benefit. The optimum level of consumption or production for the individual consumer or firm will be where *MB* = *MC*. This is called a situation of 'private efficiency'.
3. In a perfectly competitive goods market, the consumer will achieve private efficiency where *MU* = *P*; and the producer where *P* = *MC*. Thus *MU* = *MC*. In the absence of externalities, private benefits and costs will equal social benefits and costs. Thus *MU* = *MSB* and *MC* = *MSC*. Thus *MSB* = *MSC*: a situation of social efficiency (Pareto optimality).
4. Given perfect competition and an absence of externalities, if the equality of marginal benefit and marginal cost is destroyed in any market (by shifts in demand or supply), price adjustments will take place until general equilibrium is restored where *MSB* = *MSC* in all markets: a situation of general Pareto optimality.

*5. The rational producer or consumer will choose the combination of any two pairs of goods where their marginal benefit ratio is equal to their marginal cost ratio. Consumers will achieve private efficiency where:

$$\frac{MU_X}{MU_Y} \text{ (i.e. } MRS) = \frac{P_X}{P_Y}$$

Producers will achieve private efficiency where:

$$\frac{P_X}{P_Y} = \frac{MC_X}{MC_Y} \text{ (i.e. } MRT)$$

Thus:

$$\frac{MU_X}{MU_Y} = \frac{MC_X}{MC_Y}$$

In the absence of externalities, this will give a situation of social efficiency where:

$$\frac{MSB_X}{MSB_Y} = \frac{MSC_X}{MSC_Y}$$

*6. Similarly, in factor markets, social efficiency will be achieved if there is perfect competition and an absence of externalities. This will be where the *MSB* ratio for any two factors is equal to their *MSC* ratio.

*7. Again assuming perfect competition and an absence of externalities, general equilibrium will be achieved where there is a socially efficient level of production, consumption and exchange in all markets: where the *MSB* ratio for any pair of goods or factors is equal to the *MSC* ratio.

11.2 THE CASE FOR GOVERNMENT INTERVENTION

In the real world, markets fail to achieve social efficiency. Part of the problem is the existence of externalities, part is a lack of perfect competition and part is the fact that markets may take a long time to adjust to any disequilibrium given the often considerable short-run immobility of factors. What is more, social efficiency (i.e. Pareto optimality) is not the only economic goal of society. Markets may also fail to the extent that they fail to achieve other objectives such as greater equality and faster growth. In this section we explore the various categories of market failure.

Markets generally fail to achieve social efficiency. There are various types of market failure. Market failures provide one of the major justifications for government intervention in the economy.

Externalities

The market will not lead to social efficiency if the actions of producers or consumers affect people other than themselves: in other words, when there are *externalities* (side-effects).

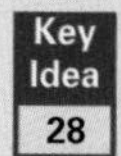

Externalities are spillover costs or benefits. Where these exist, even an otherwise perfect market will fail to achieve social efficiency.

Whenever other people are affected beneficially, there are said to be ***external benefits***. Whenever other people are affected adversely, there are said to be ***external costs***.

Definitions

External benefits Benefits from production (or consumption) experienced by people *other* than the producer (or consumer).

External costs Costs of production (or consumption) borne by people *other* than the producer (or consumer).

Figure 11.4 External costs and benefits in production

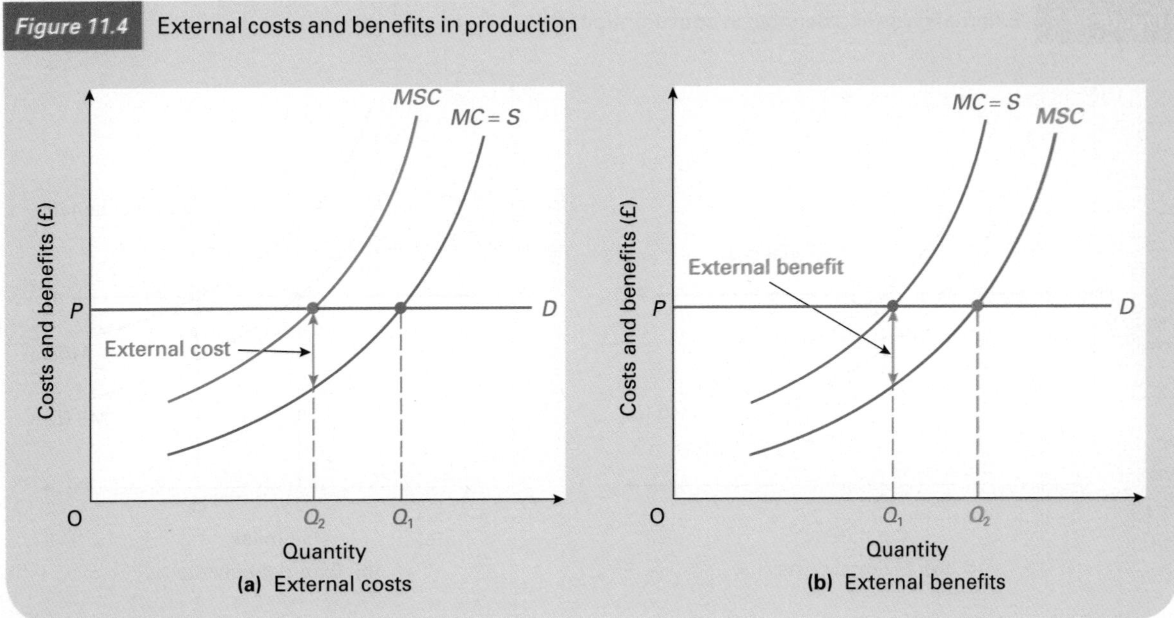

Thus the full cost to society (the ***social cost***) of the production of any good is the private cost faced by firms plus any externalities of production. Likewise the full benefit to society (the ***social benefit***) from the consumption of any good is the private benefit enjoyed by consumers plus any externalities of consumption.

There are four major types of externality. (In each case, we will assume that the market is in other respects perfect.)

External costs of production (MSC > MC)

When a chemical firm dumps waste in a river or pollutes the air, the community bears costs additional to those borne by the firm. The marginal *social* cost (*MSC*) of chemical production exceeds the marginal private cost (*MC*). Diagrammatically, the *MSC* curve is above the *MC* curve. This is shown in Figure 11.4(a), which assumes that the firm in other respects is operating in a perfect market, and is therefore a price taker (i.e. faces a horizontal demand curve).

The *socially* optimal output would be Q_2, where $P = MSC$. The firm, however, produces Q_1, which is more than the optimum. Thus external costs lead to overproduction from society's point of view.

The problem of external costs arises in a free-market economy because no one has legal ownership of the air or rivers and can prevent or charge for their use as a dump for waste. Such a 'market' is missing. Control must, therefore, be left to the government or local authorities.

Definitions

Social cost Private cost plus externalities in production.

Social benefit Private benefit plus externalities in consumption.

Other examples are extensive farming that destroys hedgerows and wildlife, and global warming caused by CO_2 emissions from power stations.

External benefits of production (MSC < MC)

If a forestry company plants new woodlands, there is a benefit not only to the company itself, but also to the world through a reduction of CO_2 in the atmosphere (forests are a carbon sink). The marginal *social* cost of providing timber, therefore, is less than the marginal *private* cost.

In Figure 11.4(b), the *MSC* curve is *below* the *MC* curve. The level of output provided by the forestry company is Q_1, where $P = MC$, a *lower* level than the social optimum, Q_2, where $P = MSC$.

Another example of external benefits in production is that of research and development. If other firms have access to the results of the research, then clearly the benefits extend beyond the firm that finances it. Since the firm receives only the private benefits, it will conduct a less than optimal amount of research.

External costs of consumption (MSB < MB)

When people use their cars, other people suffer from their exhaust, the added congestion, the noise, etc. These 'negative externalities' make the marginal social benefit of using cars less than the marginal private benefit (i.e. marginal utility).

Figure 11.5(a) shows the marginal utility and price to a consumer of using a car. The distance travelled by this motorist will be Q_1 miles: i.e. where $MU = P$ (where price is the cost of petrol, oil, wear and tear, etc. per mile). The *social* optimum, however, would be less than this, namely Q_2, where $MSB = P$.

Figure 11.5 External costs and benefits in consumption

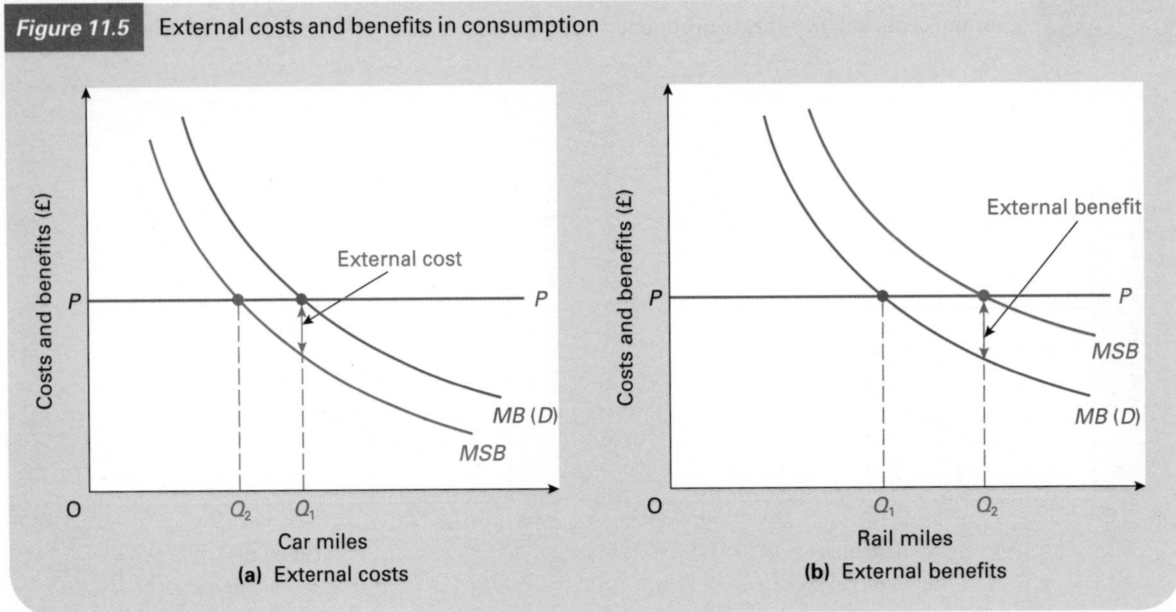

Other examples are noisy radios in public places, the smoke from cigarettes, and litter.

? *Is it likely that the MSB curve will be parallel to the MU curve? Explain your reasoning.*

External benefits of consumption (MSB > MB)

When people travel by train rather than by car, other people benefit by there being less congestion and exhaust and fewer accidents on the roads. Thus the marginal social benefit of rail travel is *greater* than the marginal private benefit (i.e. marginal utility). There are external benefits from rail travel. In Figure 11.5(b), the *MSB* curve is *above* the private *MB* curve. The actual level of consumption (Q_1) is thus below the socially optimal level of consumption (Q_2).

Other examples include the beneficial effects for other people of deodorants, vaccinations and attractive clothing. To summarise: whenever there are external benefits, there will be too little produced or consumed. Whenever there are external costs, there will be too much produced or consumed. The market will not equate *MSB* and *MSC*.

1. *Give other examples of each of the four types of externality.*
2. *Redraw Figures 11.4(a) and 11.5(a), only this time assume that the producer (in the first diagram) or the consumer (in the second) has economic power and is thus* not *a price taker. How does the existence of power affect the relationship between the private and the social optimum positions?*

Public goods

KI 27 p300

There is a category of goods where the positive externalities are so great that the free market, whether perfect or imperfect, may not produce at all. They are called ***public goods***. Examples include lighthouses, pavements, flood-control dams, public drainage, public services such as the police and even government itself.

Public goods have two important characteristics: *non-rivalry* and *non-excludability*.

- If I consume a bar of chocolate, it cannot then be consumed by someone else. If, however, I walk along a pavement or enjoy the benefits of street lighting, it does not prevent you or anyone else doing the same. There is thus what we call ***non-rivalry*** in the consumption of such goods. These goods have large external benefits relative to private benefits. This makes them socially desirable, but privately unprofitable. No one person alone would pay to have a pavement built along his or her street. The private benefit would be too small relative to the cost. And yet the social benefit to all the other people using the pavement may far outweigh the cost.

? *Which of the following have the property of non-rivalry: (a) a can of drink; (b) public transport; (c) a commercial radio broadcast; (d) the sight of flowers in a public park?*

- If I spend money erecting a flood control dam to protect my house, my neighbours will also be protected by the dam. I cannot prevent them enjoying the benefits of my

Definitions

Public good A good or service that has the features of non-rivalry and non-excludability and as a result would not be provided by the free market.

Non-rivalry Where the consumption of a good or service by one person will not prevent others from enjoying it.

CASE STUDIES AND APPLICATIONS — BOX 11.1

THE POLICE AS A PUBLIC SERVICE

Could policing be provided privately?

A good example of a public good or service is that of the police. Take the case of police officers on the beat. They are providing a general service to the community by deterring and detecting crime.

If individuals had to employ privately their own police officers, this would create considerable external benefits relative to private benefits. One police officer can provide protection to *many* individuals. But for most people it would be out of the question to employ their own police officer: the private cost would hugely exceed the private benefit. Also, once such privately employed police were on duty catching and deterring criminals, people who did not employ their own police officers could not be excluded from these benefits. There would be a 'free-rider' problem.

KI 29 p303

It obviously makes sense, therefore, that policing should be provided as a public service.

But do all aspects of policing come into this category? The answer is no. When there is a *specific* task of guarding specific property, policing could be provided by the market. This is in fact done by security firms. Security guards are employed by banks, shops, factories, etc. to prevent theft or criminal damage to their property. In these cases, the private benefits are perceived to exceed the private costs.

Should such security services be provided privately or are they better provided by the police? Since the *private* benefits in such cases are large, there is a strong argument for charging the recipient. But why should the service be provided by private security firms? Could the police not charge firms for specific guard duties? The problem here is that, if private security firms were not allowed to operate, the police would have a monopoly and could charge very high prices unless the prices were regulated by the government. Also, the quality of the service might be poorer than that provided by private security companies which were competing against each other for business.

On the other hand, the police are likely to bring greater expertise to the job. There are also economies of scale to be gained: for example, the police may have knowledge of criminal activities in other parts of the area which may pose a threat to the particular property in question. Finally, there is the problem that private security guards may not show the same level of courtesy as the police in dealing with the public (or criminals for that matter).

?

1. ***The police charge football clubs for policing inside football grounds. Do you think this is a good idea?***
2. ***Some roads could be regarded as a public good, but some could be provided by the market. Which types of road could be provided by the market? Why? Would it be a good idea?***

expenditure. This feature of ***non-excludability*** means that they would get the benefits free, and would therefore have no incentive to pay themselves. This is known as the ***free-rider problem***.

Key Idea 29

The free-rider problem. People are often unwilling to pay for things if they can make use of things other people have bought. This problem can lead to people not purchasing things that would be to the benefit of them and other members of society to have.

When goods have these two features the free market will simply not provide them. Thus these public goods can be provided only by the government or by the government subsidising private firms. (Note that not all goods produced by the public sector are public goods.)

?

1. *Give some other examples of public goods. Does the provider of these goods (the government or local authority) charge for their use? If so, is the method of charging based on the amount of the good that people use? Is it a good method of charging? Could you suggest a better method?*
2. *Name some goods or services provided by the government or local authorities that are not public goods.*

Definitions

Non-excludability Where it is not possible to provide a good or service to one person without it thereby being available for others to enjoy.

Free-rider problem When it is not possible to exclude other people from consuming a good that someone has bought.

Common resources

Common resources are not owned but are available free of charge to anyone. Examples include the air we breathe and the oceans for fishing. Like public goods, they are non-excludable. For example, fishing boats can take as many fish as they are able from the open seas. There is no 'owner' of the fish to stop them. As long as there are plentiful stocks of fish, there is no problem.

But as more people fish the seas, so fish stocks are likely to run down. This is where common resources differ from public goods. There *is* rivalry. One person's use of a common resource diminishes the amount available for others. This result is an overuse of common resources. This is why fish stocks in many parts of the world are severely depleted, why virgin forests are disappearing (cut down for timber or firewood), why many roads are so congested and why the atmosphere is becoming so polluted (being used as a common 'dump' for emissions). In each case, a resource that is freely available is overused.

KI 28 p300 How can we analyse the overuse of common resources? The simplest way is in terms of externalities. When I use a common resource, I am reducing the amount available for others. I am imposing a cost on other people: an external cost. If I am motivated purely by self-interest, I will not take these external costs into account. In terms of Figure 11.4(a), I will produce Q_1, which is above the socially optimal amount, Q_2. Overuse of the resource thus occurs.

KI 2 p8 Another way of analysing it is to examine the effect of one person's use of a resource on other people's output. Take the case of fishing grounds. In Figure 11.6 the horizontal axis measures the use of this common resource, say in terms of the number of fishing boats per day. The average cost of operating a boat (e.g. the wages of the crew and the fuel) is taken to be constant and is thus equal to the marginal cost. For the sake of simplicity, the price of fish is also assumed to be constant.

As the number of boats increases and fish stocks decline, so each extra boat entering will add less and less to the total catch. The revenue added by each extra boat – the marginal revenue product (*MRP*) – thus declines. Eventually, at point B_2, no more fish can be caught: $MRP = 0$. The catch is at the maximum. The average revenue product (*ARP*) is the revenue earned per boat: i.e. the total value of the catch divided by the number of boats.

The average and marginal revenue product curves have to be interpreted with care. Say one additional boat enters the fishing ground. The *MRP* curve shows the extra revenue accruing to the boat operators collectively. It does *not* show the revenue actually earned by the additional boat. The extra boat gets an average catch (which has been reduced somewhat because of the additional boat) and hence gains the average revenue product of all the boats.

What will be the equilibrium? Note first that the optimal number of boats for the boat operators collectively is B_1, where the marginal cost of an extra boat equals its marginal revenue product. In other words, this maximises the collective profit. At point B_1, however, there will be an incentive for extra boats to enter the fishery because the average revenue product (that is, the return that an additional boat gets) is greater than the cost of operating the boat.

More boats will enter as long as the value earned by each boat (*ARP*) is greater than the cost of operating it: as long as the *ARP* curve is above the $AC = MC$ line. Equilibrium is reached with B_3 boats: considerably above the collective profit-maximising number. Note also that the way the diagram is drawn, marginal revenue product is negative. The last boat has *decreased* the total value of the catch.

In many parts of the world, fish stocks have become so severely depleted that governments, individually or collectively, have had to act. Measures have included quotas on catches or the number of boats, minimum net mesh sizes (to allow young fish to escape), or banning fishing altogether in certain areas.

Market power

Lack of Pareto optimality

Whenever markets are imperfect, whether as pure monopoly or monopsony or as some form of imperfect competition, the market will fail to equate *MSB* and *MSC*. Pareto optimality will not be achieved. KI 19 p157

This is illustrated in Figure 11.7, which shows revenue and cost curves for a monopolist. It assumes no externalities. The socially efficient (Pareto optimal) output is Q_2, where $MSB = MSC$. The monopolist, however, produces the lower output Q_1, where $MR = MC$.

Figure 11.6 Fishing in open-access fishing grounds

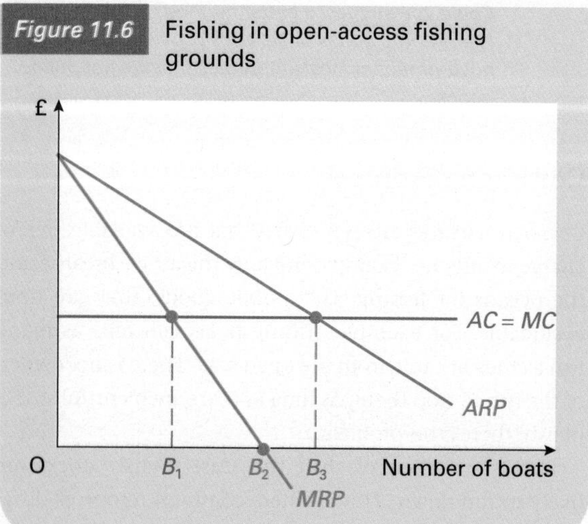

Figure 11.7 The monopolist producing less than the Pareto optimum

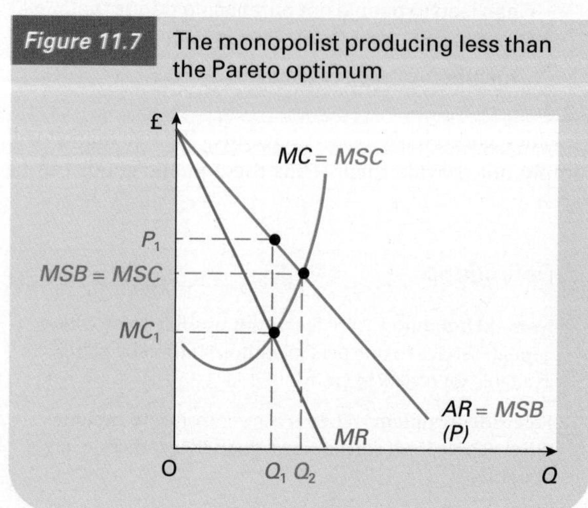

Figure 11.8 Deadweight loss from a monopoly

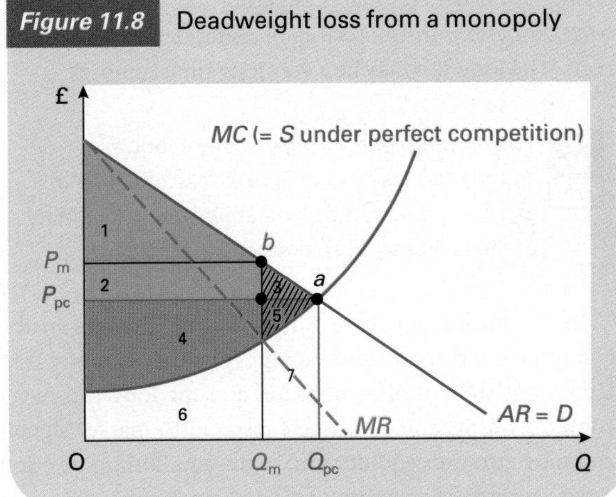

?
Referring back to Figure 9.8 on page 237, and assuming that the MRP_L curve represents the marginal social benefit from the employment of a factor, and that the price of the factor represents its marginal social cost (i.e. assuming no externalities), show that a monopsony will employ less than the Pareto optimal amount of factors.

Deadweight loss under monopoly

Another way of analysing the welfare loss that occurs under monopoly is to use the concepts of *consumer* and *producer surplus*. The two concepts are illustrated in Figure 11.8, which is similar to Figure 11.7. The diagram shows an industry that is initially under perfect competition and then becomes a monopoly (but faces the same revenue and cost curves).

Under *perfect competition* the industry will produce an output of Q_{pc} at a price of P_{pc}, where $MC (= S) = P (= AR)$: i.e. at point *a*. Consumer surplus is shown by areas 1 + 2 + 3, and producer surplus by areas 4 + 5. Total surplus (i.e. consumer plus producer surplus) is maximised at this output (see Figure 11.1 on page 293).

What happens when the industry is under *monopoly*? The firm will produce where $MC = MR$, at an output of Q_m and a price of P_m (at point *b* on the demand curve). Total revenue is $P_m \times Q_m$ (areas 2 + 4 + 6). Total cost is the area under the *MC* curve (area 6). Thus the producer surplus is areas 2 + 4. This is clearly a *larger* surplus than under perfect competition (since area 2 is larger than area 5). The consumer surplus, however, will fall dramatically. With consumption at Q_m, total utility is given by areas 1 + 2 + 4 + 6, whereas consumer expenditure is given by areas 2 + 4 + 6. Consumer surplus, then, is simply area 1. (Note that area 2 has been transformed from consumer surplus to producer surplus.)

Total surplus under monopoly is therefore areas 1 + 2 + 4: a smaller surplus than under perfect competition. 'Monopolisation' of the industry has resulted in a loss of total surplus of areas 3 + 5. The producers' gain has been more than offset by the consumers' loss. This loss of surplus is known as the ***deadweight welfare loss*** of monopoly.

KI 27 p300

***LOOKING AT THE MATHS**

Total consumer surplus (*TCS*) equals total utility minus total expenditure (i.e. total revenue). Total producer surplus (*TPS*) equals total revenue minus total variable cost. Thus total surplus (*TS*) is given by:

$$TS = TCS + TPS$$
$$= (TU - TR) + (TR - TVC)$$
$$= TU - TVC$$

Assuming that the demand curve traces out the marginal utility curve (see page 96), this allows us to derive the total utility function. To do this, you would need to use the technique of integration. Assuming that the total utility function is:

$$TU = bQ - cQ^2$$

and that the total variable cost function is:

$$TVC = jQ - kQ^2 + lQ^3$$

this will give a total surplus function of:

$$TS = (bQ - cQ^2) - (jQ - kQ^2 + lQ^3) \quad (1)$$

To find the level of deadweight welfare loss, we would then subtract total surplus under perfect competition from that under monopoly. To do this, we would solve equation (1) first for Q_{pc} and then for Q_m and then subtract the second from the first. A worked example of this is given in Maths Case 11.1 on the book's website.

Conclusions

The firm with market power uses fewer factors and produces less output than the Pareto optimum. It also causes deadweight welfare loss. To the extent, however, that the firm seeks aims *other* than profit maximisation and thus may produce more than the profit-maximising output, so these criticisms must be relaxed.

As was shown in Chapter 6, there are possible social *advantages* from powerful firms: advantages such as economies of scale and more research and development. These advantages may outweigh the lack of Pareto optimality. It can be argued that an ideal situation would be where firms are large enough to gain economies of scale and yet are somehow persuaded or compelled to produce where $P = MC$ (assuming no externalities).

With oligopoly and monopolistic competition, further wastes may occur because of possibly substantial resources involved in non-price competition. Advertising is the major example. It is difficult to predict just how much oligopolists will diverge from the Pareto optimum, since

Definition

Deadweight welfare loss The loss of consumer plus producer surplus in imperfect markets (when compared with perfect competition).

their pricing and output depends on their interpretation of the activities of their rivals.

> ? *Why will Pareto optimality not be achieved in markets where there are substantial economies of scale in production?*

Other market failures

Ignorance and uncertainty

Perfect competition assumes that consumers, firms and factor suppliers have perfect knowledge of costs and benefits. In the real world, there is often a great deal of ignorance and uncertainty. Thus people are unable to equate marginal benefit with marginal cost.

Consumers purchase many goods only once or a few times in a lifetime. Cars, washing machines, televisions and other consumer durables fall into this category. Consumers may not be aware of the quality of such goods until they have purchased them, by which time it is too late. Advertising may contribute to people's ignorance by misleading them as to the benefits of a good.

Firms are often ignorant of market opportunities, prices, costs, the productivity of factors (especially white-collar workers), the activity of rivals, etc.

Many economic decisions are based on expected future conditions. Since the future can never be known for certain, many decisions may turn out to be wrong.

In some cases, it may be possible to obtain the information through the market. There may be an agency that will sell you the information or a newspaper or magazine that contains the information. In this case, you will have to decide whether the cost to you of buying the information is worth the benefit it will provide you. A problem here is that you may not have sufficient information to judge how reliable the information is that you are buying!

> ?
> 1. *Assume that you wanted the following information. In which cases might you (i) buy perfect information, (ii) buy imperfect information, (iii) be able to obtain information without paying for it, (iv) not be able to obtain information?*
>   *(a) Which washing machine is the most reliable?*
>   *(b) Which of two vacant jobs is more satisfying?*
>   *(c) Which builder will repair my roof most cheaply?*
>   *(d) Which builder is best value for money?*
>   *(e) How big a mortgage would it be wise for me to take out?*
>   *(f) What course of higher education should I follow?*
>   *(g) What brand of washing powder washes whiter?*
> 2. *Make a list of pieces of information that a firm might want to know, and consider whether it could buy the information and how reliable that information might be.*

Immobility of factors and time lags in response

Even under conditions of perfect competition, factors may be very slow to respond to changes in demand or supply. Labour, for example, may be highly immobile both occupationally and geographically. This can lead to large price changes and hence to large supernormal profits and high wages for those in the sectors of rising demand or falling costs. The long run may be a very long time coming!

> **Key Idea 30** ***The problem of time lags.*** Many economic actions can take a long time to take effect. This can cause problems of instability and an inability of the economy to achieve social efficiency.

In the meantime, there will be further changes in the conditions of demand and supply. Thus the economy is in a constant state of disequilibrium and the long run never comes. As firms and consumers respond to market signals and move towards equilibrium, so the equilibrium position moves and the social optimum is never achieved.

Whenever monopoly/monopsony power exists, the problem is made worse as firms or unions put up barriers to the entry of new firms or factors of production.

Protecting people's interests

Dependants. People do not always make their own economic decisions. They are often dependent on decisions made by others. Parents make decisions on behalf of their children; partners on each other's behalf; younger adults on behalf of old people; managers on behalf of shareholders; etc. This is the principal–agent issue that we looked at in section 8.1. KI 22 p208

A free market will respond to these decisions, however good or bad they may be, and whether or not they are in the interests of the dependant. Thus the government may feel it necessary to protect dependants.

> ? *Give examples of how the government intervenes to protect the interests of dependants from bad economic decisions taken on their behalf.*

Poor economic decision making by individuals on their own behalf. The government may feel that people need protecting from poor economic decisions that they make on their *own* behalf. It may feel that, in a free market, people will consume too many harmful things. Thus if the government wants to discourage smoking and drinking, it can put taxes on tobacco and alcohol. In more extreme cases, it could make various activities illegal: activities such as prostitution, certain types of gambling, and the sale and consumption of drugs.

On the other hand, the government may feel that people consume too little of things that are good for them: things such as education, preventative health care and sports facilities. Such goods are known as ***merit goods***. The

> **Definition**
>
> **Merit goods** Goods that the government feels people will underconsume and which therefore ought to be subsidised or provided free.

government could either provide them free or subsidise their production.

? *How do merit goods differ from public goods?*

Other objectives

As we saw in Chapter 10, one of the major criticisms of the free market is the problem of *inequality*. The Pareto criterion gives no guidance, however, as to the most desirable distribution of income. A redistribution of income will benefit some and make others worse off. Thus Pareto optimality can be achieved for *any* distribution of income. Pareto optimality merely represents the efficient allocation of resources for any *given* distribution of income.

In addition to social efficiency and greater equality, we can identify other social goals: goals such as moral behaviour (however defined), enlightenment, social consciousness, co-operation, the development of more refined tastes, fulfilment, freedom from exploitation, and freedom to own, purchase and inherit property. The unfettered free market may not be very successful in achieving social efficiency. It may be even less successful in achieving many other social goals.

Finally, the free market is unlikely to achieve simultaneously the *macroeconomic objectives* of rapid economic growth, full employment, stable prices and a balance of international payments. These problems and the methods of government intervention to deal with them are examined in later chapters.

Conclusions

KI 6 p29

It is not within the scope of economics to make judgements as to the relative importance of social goals. Economics can only consider means to achieving stated goals. First, therefore, the goals have to be clearly stated by the policy makers. Second, they have to be quantifiable so that different policies can be compared as to their relative effectiveness in achieving the particular goal. Certain goals, such as growth in national income, changes in the distribution of income and greater efficiency, are relatively easy to quantify. Others, such as enlightenment, are virtually impossible to quantify. For this reason, economics tends to concentrate on the means to achieving a relatively narrow range of goals. The danger is that, by concentrating on a limited number of goals, economists may well influence the policy makers – the government, local authorities, various pressure groups, etc. – into doing the same, and thus into neglecting other perhaps important social goals.

Different objectives are likely to conflict. For example, economic growth may conflict with greater equality. In the case of such 'trade-offs', all the economist can do is to demonstrate the effects of a given policy, and leave the policy makers to decide whether the benefits in terms of one goal outweigh the costs in terms of another goal.

? *Summarise the economic policies of the major political parties. (If it is near an election, you could refer to their manifestos.) How far can an economist go in assessing these policies?*

Section summary

1. Real-world markets will fail to achieve Pareto optimality. What is more, there are objectives other than social efficiency, and real-world markets may fail to achieve these too.
2. Externalities are spillover costs or benefits. Whenever there are external costs, the market will (other things being equal) lead to a level of production and consumption *above* the socially efficient level. Whenever there are external benefits, the market will (other things being equal) lead to a level of production and consumption *below* the socially efficient level.
3. Public goods will be underprovided by the market. The problem is that they have large external benefits relative to private benefits, and without government intervention it would not be possible to prevent people having a 'free ride' and thereby escape contributing to their cost of production.
4. Common resources are likely to be overused, since people do not take into account the effect of their use of such resources on other people.
5. Monopoly power will (other things being equal) lead to a level of output below the socially efficient level. It will lead to a deadweight welfare loss: a loss of consumer plus producer surplus.
6. Ignorance and uncertainty may prevent people from consuming or producing at the levels they would otherwise choose. Information, however, may sometimes be provided (at a price) by the market.
7. Markets may respond sluggishly to changes in demand and supply. The time lags in adjustment can lead to a permanent state of disequilibrium and to problems of instability.
8. In a free market there may be inadequate provision for dependants and an inadequate output of merit goods; there are likely to be macroeconomic problems and problems of inequality and poverty; finally, there may be a whole series of social, moral, attitudinal and aesthetic problems arising from a market system.
9. These being normative questions, the economist cannot make ultimate pronouncements on the rights and wrongs of the market. The economist can, however, point out the consequences of the market and of various government policies, and also the trade-offs that exist between different objectives.

CASE STUDIES AND APPLICATIONS

SHOULD HEALTH CARE PROVISION BE LEFT TO THE MARKET?

A case of multiple market failures

In the UK, the National Health Service provides free hospital treatment, a free general practitioner service and free prescriptions for certain categories of people (such as pensioners and children). Their marginal cost to the patient is thus zero. Of course, these services use resources and they thus have to be paid for out of taxes.

TC 6 p 26

But why are these services not sold directly to the patient, thereby saving the taxpayer money? There are, in fact, a number of reasons why the market would fail to provide the optimum amount of health care.

People may not be able to afford treatment

KI 4 p 11

This is a problem connected with the distribution of income. Because income is unequally distributed, some people will be able to afford better treatment than others, and the poorest people may not be able to afford treatment at all. On grounds of equity, therefore, it is argued that health care should be provided free – at least for poor people.

The concept of equity that is usually applied to health care is that of treatment according to medical need rather than according to the ability to pay.

? ***Does this argument also apply to food and other basic goods?***

Difficulty for people in predicting their future medical needs

If you were suddenly taken ill and required a major operation, it could be very expensive indeed for you if you had to pay. On the other hand, you may go through life requiring very little if any medical treatment. In other words, there is great uncertainty about your future medical needs. As a result it would be very difficult to plan your finances and budget for possible future medical expenses if you had to pay for treatment. Medical insurance is a possible solution to this problem, but there is still a problem of equity. Would the chronically sick or very old be able to obtain cover, and if so, would they be able to afford the premiums?

Externalities

KI 28 p 300

Health care generates a number of benefits *external* to the patient. If you are cured of an infectious disease, for example, it is not just you who benefits but also others, since you will not infect them. In addition your family and friends benefit from seeing you well; and if you have a job you will be able to get back to work, thus reducing the disruption there. These external benefits of health care could be quite large.

If the sick had to pay the cost of their treatment, they may decide not to be treated – especially if they are poor. They may not take into account the effect that their illness has on other people. The market, by equating *private* benefits and costs, would produce too little health care.

KI 22 p 208

Patient ignorance

Markets only function well to serve consumer wishes if the consumer has the information to make informed

11.3 FORMS OF GOVERNMENT INTERVENTION

Faced with all the problems of the free market, what is a government to do?

There are several policy instruments that the government can use. At one extreme, it can totally replace the market by providing goods and services itself. At the other extreme, it can merely seek to persuade producers, consumers or workers to act differently. Between the two extremes, the government has a number of instruments that it can use to change the way markets operate. These include taxes, subsidies, laws and regulatory bodies.

Before looking at different forms of government intervention and their relative merits, it is first necessary to look at a general problem concerned with all forms of intervention. This is known as the ***problem of the second best***.

In an ideal free market, where there are no market failures of any sort (the 'first-best' world), there would be no need for government intervention at all. If in this world there did then arise just one failure, in theory its correction would be simple. Say a monopoly arose, or some externality (e.g. pollution) was produced by a particular firm, with the result that the marginal social cost was no longer equal to the marginal social benefit. In theory, the government should simply intervene to restore production

Definition

Problem of the second best The difficulty of working out the best way of correcting a specific market distortion if distortions in other parts of the market continue to exist.

BOX 11.2

decisions. For many products that we buy, we have a pretty good idea how much we will like them. In the case of health care, however, 'consumers' (i.e. patients) may have very poor knowledge. If you have a pain in your chest, it may be simple muscular strain, or it may be a symptom of heart disease. You rely on the doctor (the *supplier* of the treatment) to give you the information: to diagnose your condition. Two problems could arise here with a market system of allocating health care.

The first is that unscrupulous doctors might advise more expensive treatment than is necessary, or drugs companies might try to persuade you to buy an expensive branded product rather than an identical cheaper version.

The second is that patients suffering from the early stages of a serious disease might not consult their doctor until the symptoms become acute, by which time it might be too late to treat the disease, or very expensive to do so. With a free health service, however, a person is likely to receive an earlier diagnosis of serious conditions. On the other hand, some patients may consult their doctors over trivial complaints.

Oligopoly

If doctors and hospitals operated in the free market as profit maximisers, it is unlikely that competition would drive down their prices. Instead they might collude to fix standard prices for treatment, so as to protect their incomes.

Even if doctors did compete openly, it is unlikely that consumers would have enough information to enable them to 'shop around' for the best value. Doctor A may charge less than doctor B, but is the quality of service the same? Simple bedside manner – the thing that may most influence a patient's choice – may be a poor indicator of the doctor's skill and judgement.

To argue that the market system will fail to provide an optimal allocation of health-care resources does not in itself prove that *free provision* is the best alternative. In the USA there is much more reliance on *private medical insurance*. Only the very poor get free treatment. Alternatively, the government may simply *subsidise* health care, so as to make it cheaper rather than free. This is the case with prescriptions and dental treatment in the UK, where many people have to pay part of the cost of treatment. Also the government can *regulate* the behaviour of the providers of health care, to prevent exploitation of the patient. Thus only people with certain qualifications are allowed to operate as doctors, nurses, pharmacists, etc.

?

1. ***If health care is provided free, the demand is likely to be high. How is this high demand dealt with? Is this a good way of dealing with it?***
2. ***Go through each of the market failings identified in this box. In each case, consider what alternative policies are open to a government to tackle them. What are the advantages and disadvantages of these alternatives?***

to the point where $MSC = MSB$. This is known as the ***first-best solution***.

Of course, the real world is not like this. It is riddled with imperfections. What this means is that, if one imperfection is 'corrected' (i.e. by making $MSB = MSC$), it might aggravate problems elsewhere. For example, if an airport like Gatwick banned night-time flights so as not to disturb the sleep of local residents, the airlines might simply use Heathrow instead. This simply passes the buck. It now imposes an additional cost on those people living near Heathrow.

?

Give some examples of how correcting problems in one part of the economy will create problems elsewhere.

As the first-best solution of a perfectly efficient, distortion-free world is obviously not possible, the ***second-best solution*** needs to be adopted. Essentially this involves seeking the best compromises. This means attempting to minimise the *overall* distortionary effects of the policy measure. Some second-best *rules* can be applied in certain cases. We will examine these in the following sections as we look at specific policy measures.

Taxes and subsidies

A policy instrument particularly favoured by many economists is that of taxes and subsidies. They can be used

Definitions

First-best solution The solution of correcting a specific market distortion by ensuring that the whole economy operates under conditions of social efficiency (Pareto optimality).

Second-best solution The solution to a specific market distortion that recognises distortions elsewhere and seeks to minimise the overall distortionary effects to the economy of tackling this specific distortion.

for two main microeconomic purposes: (a) to promote greater social efficiency by altering the composition of production and consumption: and (b) to redistribute incomes. We examined their use for the second purpose in Chapter 10. Here we examine their use to achieve greater social efficiency.

When there are imperfections in the market (such as externalities or monopoly power), Pareto optimality will not be achieved. Taxes and subsidies can be used to correct these imperfections. Essentially the approach is to tax those goods or activities where the market produces too much, and subsidise those where the market produces too little.

Taxes and subsidies to correct externalities

KI 28 p300 Assume that a chemical works emits smoke from a chimney and thus pollutes the atmosphere. This creates external costs for the people who breathe in the smoke. The marginal social cost of producing the chemicals thus exceeds the marginal private cost to the firm: $MSC > MC$.

The first-best world. In Figure 11.9, the firm is producing in an otherwise perfect world. It produces Q_1 where $P = MC$ (its profit-maximising output), but in doing so takes no account of the external pollution costs it imposes on society. If the government imposes a tax on production equal to the marginal pollution cost, it will effectively 'internalise' the externality. The firm will have to pay an amount equal to the external cost it creates. It will therefore now maximise profits at Q_2, which is the socially optimum KI 25 p293 output where $MSB = MSC$. In the first-best world, then, the optimum tax is equal to the marginal external cost.

By analogy, if a firm produced an external benefit, then in the first-best world it ought to be given a subsidy equal to that marginal external benefit.

Note that a tax or subsidy ought to be directed as closely as possible to the source of the externality. For example, if a firm trains labour, and that creates a benefit to society, then ideally it ought to be given a subsidy for each person trained, rather than a general output subsidy. After all, an output subsidy not only encourages the firm to train more people (the desired effect), but also encourages it to use more capital and raw materials (an undesired side-effect). This is a general maxim of welfare economics: *a distortion should be corrected at source if side-effect problems are to be avoided.*

Second-best tax and subsidy policies. In reality, the KI 27 p300 government must tackle imperfections in a world that has many other imperfections. Figure 11.10 shows a firm that both produces an external cost ($MSC > MC$) and *also* has monopoly power. It will maximise profits at Q_1 where $MC = MR$ (point x).

The socially efficient level of output in this case is Q_2, KI 25 p293 where MSB equals MSC. To persuade the monopolist to produce at this level, a tax of $a - b$ must be imposed (since at point a, $MR = MC$ + tax). This tax is *less* than the full amount of the externality because of the problem of monopoly power. Were the monopolist to be charged a tax *equal* to the externality (so that its MC + tax curve was equal to the MSC curve), it would maximise profits at point y, at a price of P_3 and an output of Q_3. This would not be socially efficient, since MSB would now be *above* MSC.

Taxes to correct for monopoly

So far we have considered the use of taxes to correct for externalities. Taxes can also be used to regulate the behaviour of monopolies and oligopolies.

If the government wishes to tackle the problem of excessive monopoly profits, it can impose a *lump-sum* tax on the monopolist. The 'windfall tax', imposed in the UK in 1997 by the incoming Labour government on the profits of various privatised utilities, is an example of such a tax. The use of a lump-sum tax is illustrated in Figure 11.11.

Being of a fixed amount, a lump-sum tax is a fixed cost to the firm. It does not affect the firm's marginal cost. It shifts the AC curve upwards.

Profits continue to be maximised where $MC = MR$, at an output of Q_1 and a price of P_1. But profits are reduced from areas 1 + 2 to area 1 alone. Area 2 now represents the

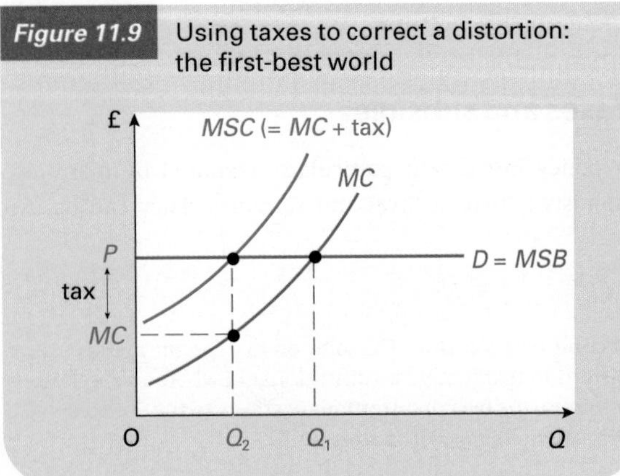

Figure 11.9 Using taxes to correct a distortion: the first-best world

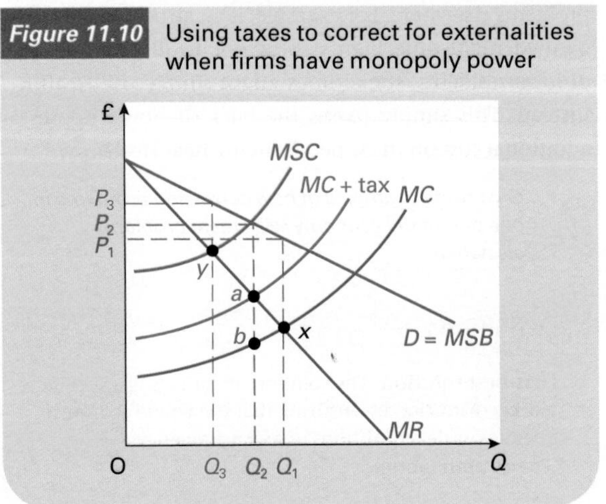

Figure 11.10 Using taxes to correct for externalities when firms have monopoly power

EXPLORING ECONOMICS

BOX 11.3

DEADWEIGHT LOSS FROM TAXES ON GOODS AND SERVICES

The excess burden of taxes

Taxation can be used to correct market failures, but taxes can have adverse effects themselves. One such effect is the deadweight loss that results when taxes are imposed on goods and services (see page 281).

The diagram shows the demand and supply of a particular good. Equilibrium is initially at a price of P_1 and a level of sales of Q_1 (i.e. where $D = S$). Now an excise tax is imposed on the good. The supply curve shifts upwards by the amount of the tax, to $S + \text{tax}$. Equilibrium price rises to P_2 and equilibrium quantity falls to Q_2. Producers receive an after-tax price of $P_2 - \text{tax}$.

Deadweight loss from an indirect tax

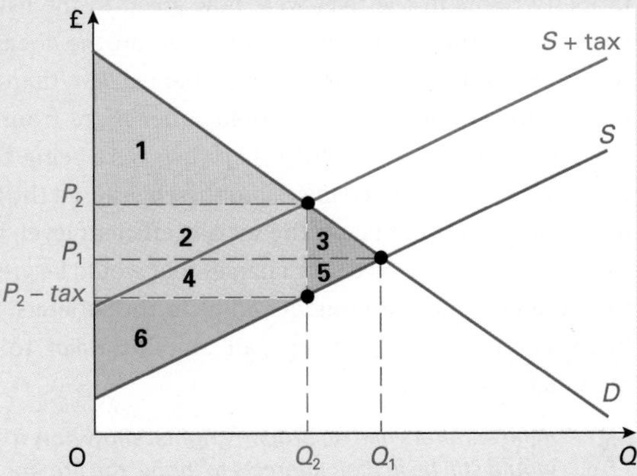

Consumer surplus falls from areas 1 + 2 + 3, to area 1 (the green area). Producer surplus falls from areas 4 + 5 + 6 to area 6 (the blue area). Does this mean, therefore, that total surplus falls by areas 2 + 3 + 4 + 5? The answer is no, because there is a gain to the government from the tax revenue (and hence a gain to the population from the resulting government expenditure). The revenue from the tax is known as the ***government surplus***. It is given by areas 2 + 4 (the pink area).

But, even after including government surplus, there is still a fall in total surplus of areas 3 + 5. This is the deadweight loss of the tax. It is sometimes known as the ***excess burden***.

Does this loss of total surplus from taxation imply that taxes on goods are always a 'bad thing'? The answer is no. This conclusion would follow only in a 'first-best' world where there were no market failures: where competition was perfect, where there were no externalities and where income distribution was optimum. In such a world, the loss of surplus from imposing a tax on a good would represent a reduction in welfare.

In the real world of imperfect markets and inequality, taxes can do more good than harm. As we have shown in this section, they can help to correct for externalities; and as we showed in the previous chapter, they can be used as a means of redistributing incomes. Nevertheless, the excess burden of taxes is something that ideally ought to be considered when weighing up the desirability of imposing taxes on goods and services, or of increasing their rate.

1. ***How far can an economist contribute to this normative debate over the desirability of an excise tax?***
2. ***What is the excess burden of a lump-sum tax? (For a clue, see Figure 11.11.)***

Figure 11.11 Using a lump-sum tax to reduce monopoly profits

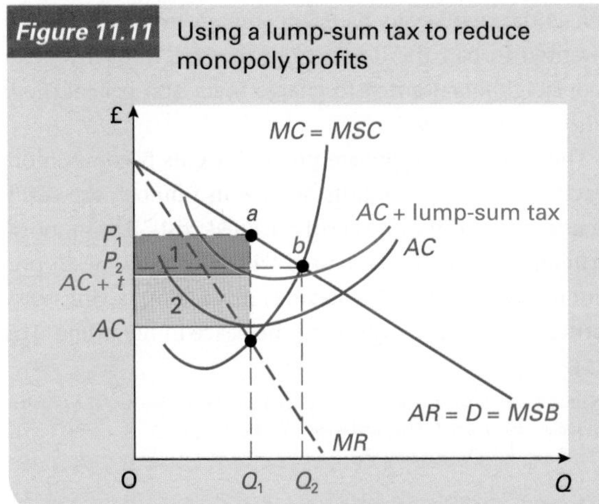

amount of tax paid to the government. If the lump-sum tax were large enough to make the *AC* + lump-sum tax curve cross the demand curve at point *a*, *all* the supernormal profits would be taken as tax.

If the government also wants to increase the monopolist's output to the socially efficient level of Q_2, and wants it to charge a price of P_2, it could do this with a careful combination of a per-unit subsidy (which will shift both the *AC* and the *MC* curves downwards) and a lump-sum tax. The required level of subsidy will be that which shifts the *MC* curve downwards to the point where it intersects *MR* at output Q_2. Then a lump-sum tax would be imposed that would be big enough to shift the *AC* curve back up again so that it crosses the demand curve at point *b*.

Definitions

Government surplus (from a tax on a good) The total tax revenue earned by the government from sales of a good.

Excess burden (of a tax on a good) The amount by which the loss in consumer plus producer surplus exceeds the government surplus.

? *What could we say about the necessary subsidy if the MR curve crossed the horizontal axis to the left of point b?*

Advantages of taxes and subsidies

Many economists favour the tax/subsidy solution to market imperfections (especially the problem of externalities) because it still allows the market to operate. It forces firms to take on board the full social costs and benefits of their actions. It is also adjustable according to the magnitude of the problem.

Moreover, if firms are taxed for polluting, they are encouraged to find cleaner ways of producing. The tax acts as an incentive over the longer run to reduce pollution. Likewise, by subsidising *good* practices, firms are given the incentive to adopt more good practices.

The most suitable situation for imposing a pollution tax is when there is a clearly measurable emission, like a particular chemical waste. The government can then impose a tax per litre or per tonne of that waste.

Disadvantages of taxes and subsidies

Infeasible to use different tax and subsidy rates. Each firm produces different levels and types of externality and operates under different degrees of imperfect competition. It would be administratively very difficult and expensive to charge every offending firm its own particular tax rate (or grant every relevant firm its own particular rate of subsidy). Even in the case of pollution where it is possible to measure a firm's emissions, there would still have to be a different tax rate for each pollutant and even for each environment, depending on its ability to absorb the pollutant.

KI 15 p101

Lack of knowledge. Even if a government did decide to charge a tax equal to each offending firm's marginal external costs, it would still have the problem of measuring those costs and apportioning blame. The damage to lakes and forests from acid rain has been a major concern since the beginning of the 1980s. But just how serious is that damage? What is its current monetary cost? How long lasting is the damage? Just what and who are to blame? These questions cannot be answered precisely. It is thus impossible to fix the 'correct' pollution tax on, say, a particular coal-fired power station.

1. *Why is it easier to use taxes and subsidies to tackle the problem of car exhaust pollution than to tackle the problem of peak-time traffic congestion in cities?*
2. *If the precise environmental costs of CFCs in fridges were known, would the tax solution be a suitable remedy for the problem?*

Changes in property rights

One cause of market failure is the limited nature of property rights. If someone dumps a load of rubble in your garden, you can insist that it is removed. If, however, someone dumps a load of rubble in their *own* garden, which is next door to yours, what can you do? You can still see it from your window. It is still an eyesore. But you have no property rights over the next-door garden.

Property rights define who owns property, to what uses it can be put, the rights other people have over it and how it may be transferred. By *extending* these rights, individuals may be able to prevent other people from imposing costs on them or charge them for doing so.

KI 25 p293

The socially efficient level of charge would be one that was equal to the marginal external cost (and would have the same effect as the government charging a tax on the firm of that amount: see Figure 11.9). The ***Coase theorem***[1] states that in an otherwise perfectly competitive market, the socially efficient charge *will* be levied. But why?

Let us take the case of river pollution by a chemical works that imposes a cost on people fishing in the river. If property rights to the river were now given to the fishing community, they could impose a charge on the chemical works per unit of output. If they charged *less* than the marginal external cost, they would suffer more from the last unit (in terms of lost fish) than they were being compensated. If they charged *more*, and thereby caused the firm to cut back its output below the socially efficient level, they would be sacrificing receiving charges that would be greater than the marginal suffering. It will be in the sufferers' best interests, therefore, to charge an amount *equal* to the marginal externality.

? *If the sufferers had no property rights, show how it would still be in their interests to 'bribe' the firm to produce the socially efficient level of output.*

In most instances, however, this type of solution is totally impractical. It is impractical when *many* people are *slightly* inconvenienced, especially if there are many culprits imposing the costs. For example, if I were disturbed by noisy lorries passing by my house, it would not be practical to negotiate with every haulage company involved. What if I wanted to ban the lorries from the street but my next-door neighbour wanted to charge them 10p per journey? Who gets their way?

The extension of private property rights becomes more practical where the culprits are few in number, are easily identifiable and impose clearly defined costs. Thus a noise abatement Act could be passed which allowed me to prevent my neighbours from playing noisy radios, having noisy parties or otherwise disturbing the peace in my home. The

[1] Named after Ronald Coase, who developed the theory. See his 'The problem of social cost', *Journal of Law and Economics* (1960).

Definition

Coase theorem By sufferers from externalities doing deals with perpetrators (by levying charges or offering bribes), the externality will be 'internalised' and the socially efficient level of output will be achieved.

onus would be on me to report them. Or I could agree not to report them if they paid me adequate compensation.

But even in cases where only a few people are involved, there may still be the problem of litigation. Justice may not be free, and thus there is a conflict with equity. The rich can afford 'better' justice. They can employ top lawyers. Thus even if I have a right to sue a large company for dumping toxic waste near me, I may not have the legal muscle to win.

KI 4 p11

Finally, the extension of private property rights may favour the rich (who tend to have more property) at the expense of the poor. Ramblers may get great pleasure from strolling across a great country estate, along public rights of way. If the owner's property rights were now extended to exclude the ramblers, would this be a social gain?

Of course, equity considerations can also be dealt with by altering property rights, but in a different way. *Public* property, like parks, open spaces, libraries and historic buildings, could be extended. Also, the property of the rich could be redistributed to the poor. Here it is less a question of the rights that ownership confers, and more a question of altering the ownership itself.

?

1. *To what extent could property rights (either public or private) be successfully extended and invoked to curb the problem of industrial pollution (a) of the atmosphere; (b) of rivers; (c) by the dumping of toxic waste; (d) by the erection of ugly buildings; (e) by the creation of high levels of noise?*
2. *What protection do private property rights in the real world give to sufferers of noise (a) from neighbours; (b) from traffic; (c) from transistor radios at the seaside?*

Laws prohibiting or regulating undesirable structures or behaviour

Laws are frequently used to correct market imperfections. This section examines three of the most common cases.

Laws prohibiting or regulating behaviour that imposes external costs

Laws can be applied both to individuals and to firms. In the case of individuals, it is illegal to drive when drunk. Drunk driving imposes costs on others in the form of accidents and death. Another example is the banning of smoking in public places.

In the case of firms, various polluting activities can be banned or restricted; safety standards can be imposed in the place of work; building houses or factories may be prohibited in green-belt areas.

In the case of common resources, restrictions can be placed on their use. For example, in the case of fishing grounds, governments can limit the size of fleets, impose quotas on catches or specify the types of net to be used. In extreme cases, they could ban fishing altogether for a period of time to allow fish stocks to recover. In order to be able to enforce restrictions, many governments have extended their 'territorial waters' to 200 miles from their coast.

Advantages of legal restrictions

- They are simple and clear to understand and are often relatively easy to administer. Inspectors or the police can conduct spot checks to see that the law is being obeyed.
- When the danger is very great, it might be much safer to ban various practices altogether rather than to rely on taxes or on individuals attempting to assert their property rights through the civil courts.
- When a decision needs to be taken quickly, it might be possible to invoke emergency action. For example, in a city like Athens or Los Angeles it would be simpler to ban or restrict the use of private cars during a chemical smog emergency than to tax their use (see Box 12.3).

Disadvantages of legal restrictions. The main problem is that legal restrictions tend to be a rather blunt weapon. If, for example, a firm were required to reduce the effluent of a toxic chemical to 20 tonnes per week, it would have no incentive to reduce it further. With a tax on the effluent, however, the more the firm reduced the effluent, the less tax it would pay. Thus with a system of taxes there is a *continuing* incentive to cut pollution.

TC 3 p21

Laws to prevent or regulate monopolies and oligopolies

Laws affecting structure. Various mergers or takeovers could be made illegal. The criterion would probably have to be the level of market concentration that results. For example, the law could set a limit of 60 per cent of the market to be controlled by the five largest firms. Or it could require that merging firms have less than a certain percentage share of the market.

Laws affecting behaviour. Firms could be prohibited from engaging in various types of oligopolistic collusion, or various monopolistic practices. For example, manufacturers could be prevented from fixing the prices that retailers must charge, or from refusing to supply certain retailers.

Use of the law to regulate monopolies and oligopolies in the UK and the EU is examined in section 12.3.

?

How suitable are legal restrictions in the following cases?
(a) Ensuring adequate vehicle safety.
(b) Reducing traffic congestion.
(c) Preventing the abuse of monopoly power.
(d) Ensuring that mergers are in the public interest.
(e) Ensuring that firms charge a price equal to marginal cost.

Laws to prevent firms from exploiting people's ignorance

Given that consumers have imperfect information, consumer protection laws can make it illegal for firms to sell shoddy or dangerous goods, or to make false or misleading claims about their products.

The problem is that the firms most likely to exploit the consumer are often the ones that are most elusive when it comes to prosecuting them.

Regulatory bodies

A more subtle approach than banning or restricting various activities involves the use of regulatory bodies.

Having identified possible cases where action might be required (e.g. potential cases of pollution or the abuse of monopoly power), the regulatory body would probably conduct an investigation and then prepare a report containing its findings and recommendations. It might also have the power to enforce its decisions, or this might be up to some higher authority.

An example of such a body is the Competition Commission, the work of which is examined in section 12.3. Other examples are the bodies set up to regulate the privatised utilities: e.g. OFWAT, the Office of Water Services. These are examined in section 12.4.

The advantage of this approach is that a case-by-case method can be used and, as a result, the most appropriate solution adopted. However, investigations may be expensive and time consuming, only a few cases may be examined, and offending firms may make various promises of good behaviour which, owing to a lack of follow-up by the regulatory body, may not in fact be carried out.

? *What other forms of intervention are likely to be necessary to back up the work of regulatory bodies?*

Price controls

Price controls could be used to prevent a monopoly or oligopoly from charging excessive prices. Currently, sections of various privatised industries such as telecommunications, water and electricity are not allowed to raise their prices by more than a certain percentage below the rate of inflation (see section 12.4).

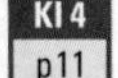

Price controls could also be used with the objective of redistributing incomes. Prices could be fixed either above or below equilibrium. Thus (high) minimum farm prices can be used to protect the incomes of farmers, and minimum wage legislation can help those on low incomes. On the consumption side, (low) maximum rents can help poor people afford housing, and price ceilings on food or other essentials during a war or other emergency can allow poor people to afford such items. However, as was argued in section 3.1, the problem with price controls is that they cause shortages (in the case of low prices) or surpluses (high prices).

Provision of information

When ignorance is a reason for market failure, the direct provision of information by the government or one of its agencies may help to correct that failure. An example is the information on jobs provided by job centres to those looking for work. They thus help the labour market to work better and increase the elasticity of supply of labour.

Another example is the provision of consumer information – for example, on the effects of smoking, or of eating certain foodstuffs. Another is the provision of government statistics on prices, costs, employment, sales trends, etc. This enables firms to plan with greater certainty.

? *Information may not be provided by the private sector if it can be used by those who do not pay: if it is a public good (service). Do all the examples above come into the category of public goods? Give some other examples of information that is a public good. (Clue: do not confuse a public good with something merely provided by the government, which* could *also be provided by the private sector.)*

The direct provision of goods and services

In the case of public goods and services, such as streets, pavements, seaside illumination and national defence, the market may completely fail to provide. In this case, the government must take over the role of provision. Central government, local government or some other public agency could provide these goods and services directly. Alternatively, they could pay private firms to do so.

But just what quantity of the public good should be provided? How can the level of public demand or public 'need' be identified? Should any charge at all be made to consumers for each unit consumed?

With a pure public good, once it is provided the marginal cost of supplying one more consumer is zero. Take the case of a lighthouse. Once it is constructed and in operation, there is no extra cost of providing the service to additional passing ships. Even if it were *possible* to charge ships each time they make use of it, it would not be socially desirable. Assuming no external costs, *MSC* is zero. Thus *MSB* = *MSC* at a price of zero. Zero is thus the socially efficient price.

But what about the construction of a new public good, like a new road or a new lighthouse? How can a rational decision be made by the government as to whether it should go ahead? This time the marginal cost is not zero: extra roads and lighthouses cost money to build. The solution is to identify all the costs and benefits to society from the project, and to weigh them up. This is where cost–benefit analysis comes in – the subject of section 11.4.

The government could also provide goods and services directly which are *not* public goods. Examples include health and education. There are four reasons why such things are provided free or at well below cost.

Social justice. Society may feel that these things should not be provided according to ability to pay. Rather, as *merit goods*, they should be provided according to need.

Large positive externalities. People other than the consumer may benefit substantially. If a person decides to get treatment for an infectious disease, other people benefit

by not being infected. A free health service thus helps to combat the spread of disease.

KI 22 p208

Dependants. If education were not free, and if the quality of education depended on the amount spent, and if parents could choose how much or little to buy, then the quality of children's education would depend not just on their parents' income, but also on how much they cared. A government may choose to provide such things free in order to protect children from 'bad' parents. A similar argument is used for providing free prescriptions and dental treatment for all children.

KI 15 p101

Ignorance. Consumers may not realise how much they will benefit. If they had to pay, they might choose (unwisely) to go without. Providing health care free may persuade people to consult their doctors before a complaint becomes serious.

Public ownership

This is different from direct provision, in that the goods and services produced by publicly owned (nationalised) industries are sold in the market. The costs and benefits of public ownership are examined in detail in section 12.4.

Section summary

1. If there were a distortion in just one part of the economy, the 'first-best' solution would be possible. This would be to correct that one distortion. In the real world, where there are many distortions, the first-best solution will not be possible. The second-best solution will be to seek the best compromise that minimises the *relative* distortions between the industry in question and other parts of the economy.
2. Taxes and subsidies are one means of correcting market distortions. In the first-best world, externalities can be corrected by imposing tax rates equal to the size of marginal external costs, and granting rates of subsidy equal to marginal external benefits. In the second-best world, taxes and subsidies can be used to correct externalities that create *relative* distortions between this industry and others, or externalities that exist along with other distortions within this industry.
3. Taxes and subsidies can also be used to affect monopoly price, output and profit. Subsidies can be used to persuade a monopolist to increase output to the competitive level. Lump-sum taxes can be used to reduce monopoly profits without affecting price or output.
4. Taxes and subsidies have the advantages of 'internalising' externalities and of providing incentives to reduce external costs. On the other hand, they may be impractical to use when different rates are required for each case, or when it is impossible to know the full effects of the activities that the taxes or subsidies are being used to correct.
5. An extension of property rights may allow individuals to prevent others from imposing costs on them. This is not practical, however, when many people are affected to a small degree, or where several people are affected but differ in their attitudes towards what they want doing about the 'problem'.
6. Laws can be used to tackle various market failures. Legal controls are often simpler and easier to operate than taxes, and are safer when the danger is potentially great. However, they tend to be rather a blunt weapon.
7. Regulatory bodies can be set up to monitor and control activities that are against the public interest (e.g. anti-competitive behaviour of oligopolists).
8. The government may provide information in cases where the private sector fails to provide an adequate level. It may also provide goods and services directly. These could be either public goods or other goods where the government feels that provision by the market is inadequate.

*11.4 COST–BENEFIT ANALYSIS

Cost–benefit analysis (CBA) is a technique used to help governments decide whether to go ahead with various projects such as a new motorway, a bypass, an underground line, a hospital, a health-care programme, a dam, and so on. The analysis seeks to establish whether the benefits to society from the project outweigh the costs, in which case the project should go ahead; or whether the costs outweigh the benefits, in which case it should not.

TC 1 p8

Definition

Cost–benefit analysis The identification, measurement and weighing-up of the costs and benefits of a project in order to decide whether or not it should go ahead.

TC 7 p26

CBAs are usually commissioned either by a government department or by a local authority. Unlike the techniques of project evaluation used by private firms, which take into account only *private monetary* costs and benefits, CBA takes into account *externalities* and private *non-monetary* costs and benefits as well. Thus a cost–benefit study of a proposed new road might attempt to assess the external costs of noise to local residents and destruction of wildlife as well as the direct costs and benefits to the travellers.

The procedure

The procedure at first sight seems fairly straightforward.

- All costs and benefits are identified. These include all private monetary and non-monetary costs and benefits and all externalities.
- A monetary value is assigned to each cost and benefit. This is essential if costs and benefits are to be added up: a common unit of measurement must be used. As might be expected, assigning monetary values to externalities like noise, pollution and the quality of life is fraught with difficulties! KI 28 p300
- Account is taken of the likelihood of a cost or benefit occurring. The simplest way of doing this is to multiply the monetary value of a cost or benefit by the probability of its occurrence. So if there were a 60 per cent chance of a cost of £100 occurring, it would be valued at £60.
- Account is taken of the timing of the costs and benefits. £100 of benefits received today would be regarded as more desirable than having to wait, say, ten years to receive the £100. Likewise it is a greater sacrifice to pay £100 today than being able to wait ten years to pay it. Thus future costs and benefits must be reduced in value to take this into account. Discounting techniques (similar to those we examined in section 9.3: see pages 252–4) are used for this purpose. KI 24 p253
- Some account may also be taken of the distribution of the costs and benefits. Is it considered fair that, although some people will gain from the project, others will lose? Will the losers be compensated in any way? KI 4 p11
- A recommendation is then made by weighing up the costs and benefits. In simplest terms, if the benefits exceed the costs, it will be recommended that the project goes ahead.

Each of these stages involves a number of difficulties. These are examined in the following sections.

Identifying the costs and benefits

Identifying costs and benefits is relatively easy, although there are some problems in predicting what types of external effect are likely to occur.

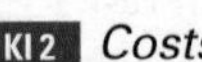

Costs

Direct (private) monetary costs. These include all the construction costs and the operating and maintenance costs.

External costs. These fall into two categories:

- *Monetary costs*, such as the loss of profits to competitors. Thus in the case of a CBA of a tunnel under a river, external monetary costs would include the loss of profits to ferry operators.

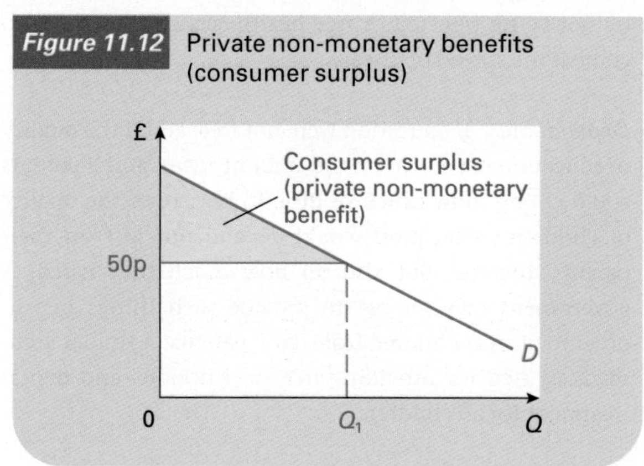

Figure 11.12 Private non-monetary benefits (consumer surplus)

- *Non-monetary costs*, such as pollution, spoiling the landscape, noise and various other forms of inconvenience to local residents. In some projects like a tunnel, these costs will be largely confined to the construction phase. With other projects, however, like a new airport, there may be considerable externalities resulting from its operation (e.g. noise). These non-monetary externalities are usually the most difficult costs to identify.

Benefits

Direct (private) monetary benefits. These are also easy to identify. They consist of the revenues received from the users of the project. The direct monetary benefits of a toll bridge, for example, are the tolls paid.

Private non-monetary benefits. These are the benefits to consumers over and above what they actually pay: in other words, the consumer surplus. For example, if a bridge had a toll of 50p, and yet a person was prepared to pay £2 if necessary to avoid the long trip round the estuary, then the person's consumer surplus is £1.50. Total consumer surplus is thus the area between the demand curve (which shows what people are willing to pay) and the price charged. This is illustrated in Figure 11.12.

External benefits. These are the benefits to the non-users of the project. For example, the Victoria Underground line CBA identified external benefits to road users in central London. The roads would become less congested as people used the new Underground line. Usually these benefits are non-monetary benefits, but sometimes they may result in direct financial gain (e.g. higher profits to companies from reduced transport costs on less crowded roads). 

Measuring the costs and benefits

Identifying costs and benefits may be relatively easy: measuring them is another matter. Difficulties in measurement depend on the type of cost and benefit. There are four types.

Direct private monetary costs and benefits

These would seem to be the simplest to measure. Normally the simple financial costs and revenues are used. In the

EXPLORING ECONOMICS *BOX 11.4

WHAT PRICE A HUMAN LIFE?

A difficult question for cost–benefit analysis

Many projects involve saving lives, whether they be new hospitals or new transport systems. This is obviously a major benefit, but how is a life to be evaluated?

TC1 p8

Some people argue, 'You can't put a price on a human life: life is priceless.' But just what are they saying here? Are they saying that life has an *infinite* value? If so, this project must be carried out *whatever* the costs, and even if other benefits from it were zero! Clearly, when evaluating lives saved from the project, a value less than infinity must be given.

Other people might argue that human life cannot be treated like other costs and benefits and put into mathematical calculations. But what are these people saying? That the question of lives saved should be excluded from the cost–benefit study? If so, the implication is that life has a *zero* value! Again this is clearly not the case.

So if a value somewhere between zero and infinity should be used, what should it be?

Some economists have suggested that a life be valued in terms of a person's future earning potential. But this implies that the only value of a person is as a factor of production! Would the life of a disabled person, for example, who is unable to work and draws state benefit be given a *negative* value? Again this is clearly not the solution.

Can any inferences be drawn from people's behaviour?

How much are people prepared to spend on safety: on making their car roadworthy, on buying crash helmets, etc? This approach too has serious drawbacks. People are wishful thinkers. They obviously do not want to be killed, but simply believe that accidents happen to other people, not to them.

Then again, there are the problems of estimating the effects on other people: on family and friends. Can the amount that people are willing to spend on life assurance be a guide here? Again people are wishful thinkers. Also, it is not the family and friends who buy the assurance; it is the victim, who may not take the effect on others fully into account.

In 2004, the UK Department of the Environment, Transport and the Regions (DETR) put a value of £1 377 742 on a life saved from a road safety project. This was based partly on the (discounted) average value of individuals' output for the rest of their lives (£473 620), partly on saved ambulance and hospital costs (£809) and partly on people's willingness to pay (if they had to) for the enjoyment of life over and above the consumption of goods and services (£903 313). It thus ignored benefits to family and friends, let alone the benefits from safer roads to people now being able to cycle or let their children walk to school, etc. If these are taken into account, it is easy to arrive at a value closer to £2 million.

?

1. ***Can you think of any other ways of getting a more 'rational' evaluation of human life? Would the person's age make any difference?***
2. ***If you had to decide whether more money from a hospital's budget were to be spent on hip replacements (which do not save lives, but do dramatically improve the quality of the patient's life), or on heart transplants (which do save lives, but are expensive), how would you set about making a rational decision?***

case of a new Underground line, for example, such costs would include excavation, construction and capital costs (such as new rolling stock) and the operating costs (such as labour, electricity and maintenance). Revenues would be the fares paid by travellers. There are two problems, nevertheless:

- What *will* these financial costs and revenues be? It is all very well using current prices, but prices rise over time, and at different and unpredictable rates. Also, it is difficult to forecast demand and hence revenues. There is thus a large element of *uncertainty*.
- The prices will often be distorted by the existence of monopoly power. Should this be taken into account? In an otherwise perfect world (the first-best situation), the answer would be yes. But in the real world, where price distortions exist throughout the economy, actual prices should normally be used. In the case of a proposed Undergound line, for example, it makes sense to use market prices, given that market prices are paid by car drivers and taxi and bus users (the alternatives to using the Underground). Thus the second-best solution is to use actual market prices *unless* there is a price distortion that applies *only* to the specific project.

? *What price should be used when there is such a distortion?*

Non-monetary private benefits: consumer surplus

Consumer surplus is a private benefit – it accrues to the users of the project – but is not part of the money earned from the project. There are two ways of estimating it.

The first way is to estimate the demand curve and then estimate the shaded area in Figure 11.12. Estimating demand is very difficult, since it depends on the price and availability of substitutes. The demand for the Channel Tunnel depends on the price, frequency and convenience of ferry crossings. It also depends on the overall level of activity in the economy and perhaps the world generally. Thus estimates of air traffic (an essential piece of information when deciding whether to build a new airport) have often been proved wrong as the world economy has grown more rapidly or less rapidly than previously forecast.

Another problem is that the consumer surplus gained from the project (e.g. the Channel Tunnel) may replace the albeit smaller consumer surplus from a competing service (e.g. cross-Channel ferries). In this case, the non-monetary private benefit is merely the *additional* consumer surplus of those who switch, but still the *full* consumer surplus of those who would not otherwise have crossed the Channel. This makes calculation less straightforward.

An alternative approach is to focus on specific non-monetary benefits to consumers. This approach is more useful when the service is to be provided free and thus no estimate of a demand curve can be made. Assume that a new motorway saves 20 000 hours of travelling time per week. (This, of course, will first have to be estimated, and again a prediction will have to be made of the number of people using the motorway.) How is this 20 000 hours to be evaluated? In the case of business people and lorry drivers, the average hourly wage rate will be used to estimate the value of each labour hour saved. In the case of leisure time, there is less agreement on how to value an hour saved. Usually it is simply assumed to be some fraction of the average hourly wage. This method is somewhat arbitrary, however, and a better approach, though probably impractical, would be to attempt to measure how the travellers themselves evaluate their time.

Another way of measuring time saved would be to see how much money people would be prepared to spend to save travelling time. For example, how much extra would people be prepared to pay for a taxi that saved, say, ten minutes over the bus journey? This method, however, has to take account of the fact that taxis may be more desirable for other reasons too, such as comfort.

? *How would you attempt to value time that you yourself save (a) getting to work; (b) going on holiday; (c) going out in the evening?*

Monetary externalities

These would normally be counted at face value. Thus the external monetary costs of a new Underground would include the loss of profits to taxi and bus companies. The external monetary benefits of a new motorway would include the profits to be made by the owners of the motorway service stations.

Non-monetary externalities

These are likely to be the hardest to measure. The general principle employed is to try to find out how much people would be prepared to pay to obtain the benefits or avoid the costs, if they were able to do so. There are two approaches here.

Ask people (questionnaires). Take the case of noise from an airport or motorway. People could be asked how much they would need to be compensated. There are two problems with this:

- Ignorance. People will not know just how much they will suffer *until* the airport or motorway is built.
- Dishonesty. People will tend to exaggerate the compensation they would need. After all, if compensation is actually going to be paid, people will want to get as much as possible. But even if it is not, the more people exaggerate the costs to themselves, the more likely it is that they can get the project stopped.

These problems can be lessened if people are questioned who have already experienced a similar project elsewhere. They have less to gain from being dishonest.

Make inferences from people's behaviour. Take the case of noise again. In similar projects elsewhere, how have people actually reacted? How much have they spent on double glazing or other noise insulation? How much financial loss have they been prepared to suffer to move somewhere quieter? What needs to be measured, however, is not just the financial cost, but also the loss of consumer surplus. The Roskill Commission in 1968 examined the siting of a third London airport. It attempted to evaluate noise costs, and looked at the difference in value of house prices round Gatwick compared with elsewhere. A problem with this approach is in finding cases elsewhere that are directly comparable. Were the four potential sites for the third London airport directly comparable with Gatwick?

Another example of externalities would be a reduction in accidents from a safer road. How is this to be measured? Obviously there are the monetary benefits from reduced medical expenditures. But how would you value a life saved? This question is examined in Box 11.4.

How would you evaluate (a) the external effects of building a reservoir in an area of outstanding natural beauty; (b) the external effects of acid rain pollution from a power station?

Risk and uncertainty

Taking account of *risk* is relatively straightforward. The value of a cost or benefit is simply multiplied by the probability of its occurrence.

The problem is that *risk* is less frequent than *uncertainty*. As was explained in section 4.2, in the case of uncertainty all that is known is that an outcome *might* occur. The likelihood of its occurring, however, is uncertain.

How then can uncertainty be taken into account? The best approach is to use ***sensitivity analysis***. Let us consider two cases.

Definition

Sensitivity analysis Where a range of possible values of uncertain costs and benefits are given to see whether the project's desirability is sensitive to these different values.

Table 11.1 Effect of different estimates of the costs of production on the viability of a project

	Total costs other than pollution (£m)	Total pollution cost (£m)	Total benefits (£m)	Net benefits (total benefits – total costs) (£m)
	100	10	200	90
Case A	100	20	200	80
	100	50	200	50
	140	10	160	10
Case B	140	20	160	0
	140	50	160	–30

Individual uncertain outcomes

A range of possible values can be given to an uncertain item in the CBA: for example, damage from pollution. Table 11.1 illustrates two possible cases.

The lowest estimate for pollution damage is £10 million; the highest is £50 million. In case A, given a very high margin of benefits over *other* costs, the project's desirability is *not* sensitive to different values for pollution damage. Even with the highest value (£50 million), the project still yields a net benefit.

In case B, however, the project's desirability *is* sensitive to pollution damage. If the damage exceeds £20 million, the project becomes undesirable. In this case, the government will have to decide whether it is prepared to take the gamble.

A number of uncertain outcomes

When there are several uncertain outcomes the typical approach is to do three cost–benefit calculations: the most optimistic (where all the best possible outcomes are estimated), the most pessimistic (where all the worst possible outcomes are estimated), and the most likely (where all the middle-of-the-range outcomes are estimated). This approach can give a good guide to just how 'borderline' the project is.

Discounting future costs and benefits

As we saw in section 9.3, discounting is a procedure for giving a present value to costs and benefits that will not occur until some time in the future.

KI 24 p253

Discounting in cost–benefit analysis

The procedure is as follows:

- Work out the costs and benefits for each year of the life of the project.
- Subtract the costs from the benefits for each year, to give a net benefit for each year.
- Discount each year's net benefit to give it a present value.
- Add up all of these present values. This gives a *net present value (NPV)*.
- If the *NPV* is greater than zero, the benefits exceed the costs: the project is worthwhile.

Maths Case 11.2 on the book's website gives a worked example.

Choosing the discount rate

Apart from the problems of measuring the costs and benefits, there is the problem of choosing the rate of interest/discount.

If it were a private-sector project, the firm would probably choose the market rate of interest as its rate of discount. This is the rate that it would have to pay to borrow money to finance the project.

In the case of CBA, however, it is argued that the government ought to use a ***social rate of discount***. This rate should reflect society's preference for present benefits over future benefits. But just what is this rate? If a high rate is chosen, then future net benefits will be discounted more, and projects with a long life will appear less attractive than projects yielding a quick return. Since the government has a responsibility to future generations and not just to the present one, it is argued that a relatively low discount rate should be chosen.

?

Imagine that a specific public project yields a return of 13 per cent (after taking into account all social costs and benefits), whereas a 15 per cent private return could typically be earned by projects in the private sector. How would you justify diverting resources from the private sector to this project?

Inevitably, the choice of discount rate is arbitrary. As a result, the analysis will normally be conducted using two or three alternative discount rates to see whether the outcome is sensitive to the choice of discount rate. If it is, then again the project will be seen as borderline.

CBA and the distribution of costs and benefits

Virtually all projects involve gainers and losers. For example, the majority may gain from the construction of a new motorway, but not those whose homes lie alongside it. So how is the distribution of costs and benefits to be taken into account?

Definition

Social rate of discount A rate of discount that reflects society's preferences for present benefits over future ones.

CASE STUDIES AND APPLICATIONS

MEETING THE KYOTO PROTOCOL

The costs and benefits of lowering the sulphur content of petrol and diesel

In signing up to the Kyoto Protocol environmental treaty (see Box 12.2), the EU committed itself to reducing carbon dioxide emissions and other greenhouse gases by up to 8 per cent of 1990 levels by 2012. How best might such reductions be achieved? What strategy would achieve the benefits from lower carbon dioxide emissions at least cost?

One investigation conducted for the EU to assess such questions[2] aimed to evaluate the costs and benefits of lowering the sulphur content of petrol and diesel to less than 10 parts per million (ppm) from its level at the time of 50 ppm. By reducing sulphur levels in petrol, reductions would be achieved in emissions of carbon dioxide, nitrogen oxides and volatile organic compounds, with resulting improvements in environmental quality. In addition, cars designed to run on low-sulphur fuels (all new cars coming into the EU market from 2006) are more fuel efficient and thus consume less fuel. Offsetting such gains in environmental quality and fuel efficiency is the fact that producing sulphur-free fuel requires more energy and hence the generation of more carbon dioxide, the very thing the policy is seeking to reduce! In addition, existing refineries had to be adapted to process such fuel. This has resulted in additional investment costs. Operating costs too tend to be higher.

In order to evaluate these costs and benefits, the study identified five alternative scenarios for reducing sulphur content. These varied in terms of time period and type of vehicle:

1. Main scenario 2005: 2005, introduction of sulphur-free petrol[3] and diesel to new vehicles. 2011, 100 per cent sulphur-free fuel made compulsory.
2. Main scenario 2007: identical to scenario 1, only sulphur-free fuel introduced two years later.
3. Phased-in scenario 2007: sulphur-free fuel introduced for new vehicles alone (since only new vehicle types will be able to derive an improvement in fuel efficiency from sulphur-free fuels).
4. 100 per cent switch for cars in 2007: sulphur-free fuel compulsory for all cars in 2007.
5. Phased-in for cars from 2007: sulphur-free fuel introduced for cars alone at a rate determined by new car growth.

Emission reductions. Although precise emissions reductions were not identified, it was estimated that enhanced fuel efficiency, and hence reduced fuel consumption, would see vehicle emissions fall by an average of 3 per cent. Diesel vehicle emissions would fall by an estimated 2 per cent.

Additional refinery emissions and costs. As the production of sulphur-free fuel is more energy intensive, additional carbon dioxide emissions are inevitable. The report concluded that if all fuel was refined to 10 ppm, the additional emissions from refineries would increase by 4.6 million tonnes of carbon dioxide.

The additional investment and running costs of the refineries were estimated at 0.2 euro cents per litre (0.25 euro cents for EU south)[4] for petrol, and 0.45 euro cents per litre (0.65 euro cents for EU south) for diesel. This would represent a 1–2 per cent increase in costs. However, given the fact that approximately 75 per cent of the price of fuel to the consumer is made up of tax, the price increase borne by the consumer was likely to be very small.

The findings. For all the scenarios considered, the benefits (financial and air quality) were greater than the costs, and hence there would be a positive effect on reducing carbon dioxide emissions (see Table (a)).

Comparing the main scenarios from 2005 and 2007, the 2005 scenario produces a far more desirable outcome. The earlier start for gaining fuel cost savings and the higher number of vehicles benefiting from the use of sulphur-free fuel explain the higher *NPV* and the larger reduction in carbon dioxide emissions found in the 2005 scenario (see Tables (b) and (c)).

However, when the use of sulphur-free fuel is phased in as new vehicles are sold, the 2007 scenarios

Table (a) Summary results of the scenarios

	Reduction of CO_2 during 2008–12		Reduction in CO_2 2013–20		Net present value (4%) € billion
	Total Mt CO_2	Per annum Mt CO_2	Total Mt CO_2	Per annum Mt CO_2	
Main scenario; introduction in 2005	12.9	2.6	50.8	6.3	2.7
Main scenario; introduction in 2007	9.2	1.8	44.5	5.6	1.1
Phased-in scenario (all vehicles) from 2007	15.8	3.2	58.8	7.3	2.8
Cars-only scenario in 2007	7.8	1.6	63.1	7.9	2.6
Phased-in scenario (cars only) from 2007	11.4	2.3	41.9	5.2	3.0

Note: Net present values (calculated using a 4% real discount rate) include net financial and air quality benefits.

Source: *The costs and benefits of lowering the sulphur content of petrol and diesel to less than 10 ppm* (EU Directorate-General Environment, 2001), Table 9.

*BOX 11.5

become a lot more favourable (scenarios 3 and 5). As drivers swap to new vehicles using sulphur-free fuel, the gain from fuel efficiency consistently outweighs the increase in refining costs.

The use of cost–benefit analysis thus demonstrated the best strategy for introducing low-sulphur fuel. A phased-in use of sulphur-free fuel would generate a higher *NPV* than the compulsory introduction of the fuel for all vehicles at a specified point in time.

? ***Why is this type of cost–benefit analysis simpler to conduct than ones assessing the desirability of a new road or airport?***

[2] *The costs and benefits of lowering the sulphur content of petrol and diesel to less than 10 ppm* (EU Directorate-General Environment, 2001).

[3] The term 'sulphur-free fuel' in the report refers to low-sulphur fuel with less than 10 ppm of sulphur.

[4] The differences in costs between north and south Europe are due to the quality of fuel used in refining and its sulphur content.

Table (b) 'Main scenario 2005' – costs, benefits and emissions reductions

	2005	2012	2020
CO_2 emissions changes			
Change in CO_2 emissions in refineries, (kT)	215.7	5348.3	5404.3
CO_2 change from cars (3% petrol 2% diesel), (kT)	−562.8	−8241.6	−14 960.5
Net change (− = decrease in CO_2 emissions)	−347.1	−2893.2	−9556.2
Costs and benefits, € million			
Increase in refining costs (average per year)	−39.0	−816.9	−831.4
Savings due to lower fuel consumption (average)	54.1	795.5	1441.2
Benefits from better air quality	0.0	221.1	3.7
Net benefits (– depicts net costs)	15.1	199.7	613.5
Net present value (4%), € million	2673.5		
Changes in air-related emissions			
NOx, kilotonnes	0	−28.5	−0.5
VOC, kilotonnes	0	−10.6	−0.2
CO, kilotonnes	0	−135.9	−4.7
PM, tonnes	0	−280.8	−8.0

Note: All costs are without VAT or excise duties. For emissions, negative signs indicate reductions; for benefits, negative signs indicate net costs. The above analysis has assumed a phased introduction of zero-sulphur fuels in 2005.

Source: Ibid., Table 4.

Table (c) 'Main scenario 2007' – costs, benefits and emissions reductions

	2007	2012	2020
CO_2 emissions changes			
Change in CO_2 emissions in refineries, (kT)	407.0	5348.3	5404.3
CO_2 change from cars (3% petrol 2% diesel), (kT)	−1245.9	−6850.0	−13 574.9
Net change (− = decrease in CO_2 emissions)	−838.9	−1501.7	−8170.6
Costs and benefits, € million			
Increase in refining costs (average per year)	−75.4	−995.0	−1019.0
Savings due to lower fuel consumption (average)	120.5	661.6	1309.1
Benefits from better air quality	0.0	304.1	18.3
Net benefits (– depicts net costs)	45.2	−29.3	308.4
Net present value (4%), € million	1061.2		
Changes in air-related emissions			
NOx, kilotonnes	0	−39.0	−2.5
VOC, kilotonnes	0	−14.4	−0.9
CO, kilotonnes	0	−176.8	−9.9
PM, tonnes	0	−366.7	−11.8

Note: All costs are without VAT or excise duties. For emissions, negative signs indicate reductions; for benefits, negative signs indicate net costs. The above analysis has assumed a phased introduction of zero-sulphur fuels from 1 January 2007.

Source: Ibid., Table 5.

The strict Pareto criterion

According to the strict Pareto criterion, a project is unequivocally desirable only if there are some gains and *no one* is made worse off. According to this, then, a project would be accepted only if the gainers *fully* compensated the losers, with the gainers still being better off after doing so.

In practice, this never happens. Often compensation is simply not paid. Even when it is, the recipients rarely feel as well off as before, and there will still be many who do not get compensation. Also, the compensation is usually paid not by the project users, but by the general taxpayer (who will thus be *worse* off).

The Hicks–Kaldor criterion

To get round this problem, J. R. Hicks and N. Kaldor suggested an alternative criterion. This states that a project is desirable if it leads to a *potential* Pareto improvement: in other words, if the gainers could *in principle* fully compensate the losers and still have a net gain, even though in practice they do not pay any compensation at all.

This criterion is what lies behind conventional CBA. If the benefits of a project are greater than the costs, then in principle the losers could be fully compensated with some net benefits left over.

But what is the justification for using this test? The losers, after all, will still lose. Its advocates argue that questions of *efficiency* should be kept separate from questions of *equity*.
KI 3 p10 Projects, they argue, should be judged on efficiency grounds. They are efficient if their benefits exceed their costs. Questions
KI 4 p11 of fairness in distribution, on the other hand, should be dealt with through the general system of taxation and welfare.

This is a 'useful' argument because it lets the proponents of the project off the hook. Nevertheless the problem still remains that some people will lose. People do not like living near a new motorway, airport or power station. These people cannot expect to receive special welfare benefits from general taxation.

Thus other economists have argued that a more specific account should be taken of distributional effects when *measuring* costs and benefits.

Taking specific account of distributional consequences

One way this could be done would be to give a higher weighting to the costs of individual, as opposed to corporate, losers. The justification is simple. The pain for one person of losing £10 000 is greater than the collective pain of 10 000 people losing just £1 each. Just how much higher this weighting should be, however, is a matter of judgement, not of precise calculation.

Another way distribution can be taken into account is to give a higher weighting to the costs incurred by poor people than to those incurred by rich people. For example, assume that a new airport is built. As a result, house prices nearby fall by 10 per cent. A rich person's house falls from £400 000 to £360 000 – a loss of £40 000. A poor person's house falls from £50 000 to £45 000 – a loss of £5000. Is the loss to the rich person eight times as painful as that to the poor person? Probably not. It is argued, therefore, that the poorer people are, the higher the weighting that should be given to each £1 lost. Just what this weighting should be, however, is controversial.

Section summary

1. Cost–benefit analysis (CBA) can help a government decide whether or not to go ahead with a particular public project, or which of alternative projects to choose. CBA involves a number of stages.
2. All costs and benefits must be identified. These include the direct costs of constructing and operating the project, the direct monetary benefits to the operators and the consumer surplus of the users. They also include external costs and benefits to non-users.
3. Direct monetary costs and benefits are relatively easy to measure. Nevertheless there is still uncertainty about their *future* values. Also, there is a problem if prices are distorted.
4. Non-monetary private benefit (consumer surplus) is difficult to estimate because of the difficulty of estimating the shape and position of the demand curve. The alternative approach is to focus on specific non-monetary benefits, such as journey time saved, and then to evaluate how much people would be prepared to pay for them if they could.
5. Monetary externalities would normally be counted at face value. Non-monetary externalities are much more difficult to estimate. The approach is to try to estimate the value that consumers would put on them in a market environment. Questionnaire techniques could be used, or inferences could be drawn from people's actual behaviour elsewhere.
6. Figures would then have to be adjusted for risk and uncertainty.
7. Discounting techniques would then have to be used to reduce future benefits and costs to a present value.
8. The study may also take distributional questions into account. The Hicks–Kaldor criterion suggests a compensation test for deciding whether a project is desirable. But given that in practice full compensation would be unlikely, the distributional questions may need to be taken into account more specifically.
9. Having adjusted the costs and benefits for risk and uncertainty, timing and distributional effects, a recommendation to go ahead with the project will probably be given if its net present value (*NPV*) is positive: in other words, if the discounted social benefits exceed the discounted social costs.

11.5 GOVERNMENT FAILURE AND THE CASE FOR THE MARKET

TC 7 p26 Government intervention in the market can itself lead to problems. The case for non-intervention (*laissez-faire*) or very limited intervention is not that the market is the *perfect* means of achieving given social goals, but rather that the problems created by intervention are greater than the problems overcome by that intervention.

Drawbacks of government intervention

Shortages and surpluses. If the government intervenes by fixing prices at levels other than the equilibrium, this will create either shortages or surpluses (see section 3.1).

If the price is fixed *below* the equilibrium, there will be a shortage. For example, if the rent of council houses is fixed below the equilibrium in order to provide cheap housing for poor people, demand will exceed supply. In the case of such shortages the government will have to adopt a system of waiting lists, or rationing, or giving certain people preferential treatment. Alternatively it will have to allow allocation to be on a first-come, first-served basis or allow queues to develop. Black markets are also likely to develop (see page 72 and Box 3.2).

If the price is fixed *above* the equilibrium price, there will be a surplus. Such surpluses are obviously wasteful. High prices may protect inefficient producers. (The problem of food surpluses in the EU was examined in section 3.4.)

?

What are the possible arguments in favour of fixing prices (a) below and (b) above the equilibrium? Are there any means of achieving the same social goals without fixing prices?

KI 15 p101 *Poor information.* The government may not know the full costs and benefits of its policies. It may genuinely wish to pursue the interests of consumers or any other group, and yet may be unaware of people's wishes or misinterpret their behaviour.

Bureaucracy and inefficiency. Government intervention involves administrative costs. The more wide reaching and detailed the intervention, the greater the number of people and material resources that will be involved. These resources may be used wastefully.

Lack of market incentives. If government intervention removes market forces or cushions their effect (by the use of subsidies, welfare provisions, guaranteed prices or wages, etc.), it may remove certain useful incentives. Subsidies may allow inefficient firms to survive. Welfare payments may discourage effort. The market may be imperfect, but it does tend to encourage efficiency by allowing the efficient to receive greater rewards.

Shifts in government policy. The economic efficiency of industry may suffer if government intervention changes too frequently. It makes it difficult for firms to plan if they cannot predict tax rates, subsidies, price and wage controls, etc.

Lack of freedom for the individual. Government intervention may involve a loss of freedom for individuals to make economic choices. The argument is not just that the pursuit of individual gain is seen to lead to the social good, but that it is desirable in itself that individuals should be as free as possible to pursue their own interests with the minimum of government interference: that minimum being largely confined to the maintenance of laws consistent with the protection of life, liberty and property.

Go through the above arguments and give a reply to the criticisms made of government intervention.

Advantages of the free market

Although markets in the real world are not perfect, even imperfect markets can be argued to have positive advantages over government provision or even government regulation.

Automatic adjustments. Government intervention requires administration. A free-market economy, on the other hand, leads to the automatic, albeit imperfect, adjustment to demand and supply changes. TC 4 p22

Even under oligopoly, it is claimed, the competition between firms will be enough to encourage firms to produce goods that are desirable to consumers and at not excessively high prices, and will encourage more efficient production methods. Cases of pure monopoly with total barriers to entry are extremely rare.

Dynamic advantages of the free market. The chances of making high monopoly/oligopoly profits will encourage capitalists to invest in new products and new techniques. Prices may be high initially, but new firms will sooner or later break into the market and competition will ensue. If the government tries to correct the misallocation of resources under monopoly/oligopoly either by regulating monopoly power or by nationalisation, any resulting benefits could be outweighed by a loss in innovation and growth. This is one of the major arguments put forward by the neo-Austrian libertarian school – a school that passionately advocates the free market (see Box 11.6).

Are there any features of free-market capitalism that would discourage *innovation?*

A high degree of competition even under monopoly/oligopoly. Even though an industry at first sight may seem to be highly monopolistic, competitive forces may still work for the following reasons.

EXPLORING ECONOMICS

MISES, HAYEK AND THE MONT PELERIN SOCIETY

The birth of post-war libertarianism

After the Second World War, governments in the western world were anxious to avoid a return to the high levels of unemployment and poverty experienced in the 1930s. The free market was seen to have failed. Governments, it was therefore argued, should take on the responsibility for correcting or counteracting these failings. This would involve various measures such as planning, nationalisation, the restriction of monopoly power, controls on prices, the macroeconomic management of the economy and the provision of a welfare state.

But this new spirit of intervention deeply troubled a group of economists and other social scientists who saw it leading to an erosion of freedom. In 1947 this group met in an hotel in the Swiss Alps. There they formed the Mont Pelerin Society: a society pledged to warn against the dangers of socialism and to advocate the freedom for individuals to make their own economic choices.

Two of the most influential figures in the society were the Austrians Ludwig von Mises (1881–1973) and Friedrich von Hayek (1899–1992). They were the intellectual descendants of the nineteenth-century 'Austrian school'. Carl Menger, the originator of the school, had (along with Jevons and Walras (see Box 4.2)) emphasised the importance of individuals' marginal utility as the basis of demand. The Austrian school of economists was famous for its stress on individual choice as the basis for rational economic calculation and also for its advocacy of the free market.

Mises and Hayek (the 'neo-Austrians' as they became known) provided both a critique of socialism and an advocacy of the free market. There were two main strands to their arguments.

The impossibility of rational calculation under socialism

In his famous book *Socialism* (1922), Mises argued that centrally planned socialism was logically incapable of achieving a rational allocation of resources. Given that scarcity is the fundamental economic problem, all societies, whether capitalist or socialist, will have to make choices. But rational choices must involve weighing up the costs and benefits of alternatives. Mises argued that this cannot be done in a centrally planned economy. The reason is that costs and benefits can be measured only in terms of money prices, prices which reflect demand and supply. But such prices can be established only in a market economy.

In a centrally planned economy, prices will be set by the state and no state will have sufficient information on demand and supply to set rational prices. Prices under centrally planned socialism will thus inevitably be arbitrary. Also, with no market for land or capital these factors may not be given a price at all. The use of land and capital, therefore, may be highly wasteful.

Many democratic socialists criticised Mises' arguments that rational prices *logically* cannot be established under socialism. In a centrally planned economy, the state can in theory, if it chooses, set prices so as to balance supply and demand. It can, if it chooses, set an interest rate for capital and a rent for land, even if capital and land are owned by the state. And certainly in a mixed-market socialist economy, prices will merely reflect the forces of demand and supply that have been modified by the state in accordance with its various social goals.

Hayek modified Mises' arguments somewhat. He conceded that some imperfect form of pricing system could be established under socialism, even under centrally planned socialism. Hayek's point was that such a system would inevitably be inferior to capitalism. The problem was one of imperfect information under socialism.

Calculation of costs and benefits requires knowledge. But that knowledge is dispersed amongst the millions of consumers and producers throughout the economy. Each consumer possesses unique information about his or her own tastes; each manager or worker possesses unique information about his or her own job. No government could hope to have this

- A fear that excessively high profits might encourage firms to attempt to break into the industry (assuming that the market is contestable).
- Competition from closely related industries (e.g. coach services for rail services, or electricity for gas).
- The threat of foreign competition. Additional competition was one of the main purposes behind the Single European Act which led to the abolition of trade barriers within the EU in 1993 (see section 23.4).
- Countervailing powers. Large powerful producers often sell to large powerful buyers. For example, the power of detergent manufacturers to drive up the price of washing powder is countered by the power of supermarket chains to drive down the price at which they purchase it. Thus power is to some extent neutralised.
- The competition for corporate control (see page 171).

Should there be more or less intervention in the market?

No firm conclusions can be drawn in the debate between those who favour more and those who favour less government intervention, for the following reasons:

- Many normative issues are involved that cannot be settled by economic analysis. For example, it could be argued that freedom to set up in business and freedom KI 6 p29

BOX 11.6

knowledge. Planning will inevitably, therefore, be based on highly imperfect information.

The market, by contrast, is a way of co-ordinating this dispersed information: it co-ordinates all the individual decisions of suppliers and demanders, decisions based on individuals' own information. And it does it all without the need for an army of bureaucrats.

> The economic problem of society is thus not merely a problem of how to allocate 'given' resources – if 'given' is taken to mean given to a single mind which deliberately solves the problem set by these 'data'. It is rather a problem of how to secure the best use of resources known to any of the members of society, for ends whose relative importance only these individuals know. Or, to put it briefly, it is a problem of the utilization of knowledge not given to anyone in its totality.[5]

TC 3 p21

Lack of dynamic incentives under socialism

A planned socialist economy will, according to Mises and Hayek, lack the incentives for people to take risks. Even a 'market socialist' society, where prices are set so as to equate demand and supply, will still lack the crucial motivating force of the possibility of large personal economic gains. Under capitalism, by contrast, a firm that becomes more efficient or launches a new or improved product can gain huge profits. The prospect of such profits is a powerful motivator.

> Without the striving of entrepreneurs (including the shareholders) for profit, of the landlords for rent, of the capitalists for interest and the labourers for wages, the successful functioning of the whole mechanism is not to be thought of. It is only the prospect of profit which directs production into those channels in which the demands of the consumer are best satisfied at least cost. If the prospect of profit disappears the mechanism of the market loses its mainspring, for it is only this prospect which sets it in motion and maintains it in operation. The market is thus the focal point of the capitalist order of society; it is the essence of capitalism. Only under capitalism, therefore, is it possible; it cannot be 'artificially' imitated under socialism.[6]

In addition to these economic criticisms of socialism, Mises and Hayek saw government intervention as leading down the road towards totalitarianism. The more governments intervened to correct the 'failings' of the market, the more this tended to erode people's liberties. But the more people saw the government intervening to help one group of people, the more help they would demand from the government for themselves. Thus inexorably the role of the state would grow and grow, and with it the size of the state bureaucracy.

In the early years after the war, the Mont Pelerin Society had little influence on government policy. Government intervention and the welfare state were politically popular.

In the late 1970s, however, the society, along with other similar libertarian groups, gained increasing influence as a new breed of politicians emerged who were wedded to the free market and were looking for an intellectual backing for their beliefs.

Libertarian thinkers such as Hayek and Milton Friedman (see Person Profiles on the book's website) had a profound effect on many right-wing politicians, and considerably influenced the economic programmes of the Thatcher, Reagan and both Bush (Snr and Jnr) administrations.

Do the arguments of Mises and Hayek necessarily infer that a free market is the most desirable alternative to centrally planned socialism?

[5] F. von Hayek, 'The price system as a mechanism for using knowledge', *American Economic Review*, September 1945, p. 519.

[6] L. von Mises, *Socialism: An economic and sociological analysis* (Jonathan Cape, 1936), p. 138.

from government regulation are desirable *for their own sake*. As a fundamental ethical point of view, this can be disputed, but not disproved.

- In principle, the issue of whether a government ought to intervene in any situation could be settled by weighing up the costs and benefits of that intervention. Such costs and benefits, however, even if they could be identified, are extremely difficult, if not impossible, to measure, especially when the costs are borne by different people from those who receive the benefits and when externalities are involved.
- Often the effect of more or less intervention simply cannot be predicted: there are too many uncertainties.

Nevertheless, economists can make a considerable contribution to analysing problems of the market and the effects of government intervention. Chapter 12 illustrates this by examining specific problem areas.

Section summary

1. Government intervention in the market may lead to shortages or surpluses; it may be based on poor information; it may be costly in terms of administration; it may stifle incentives; it may be disruptive if government policies change too frequently; it may remove certain liberties.
2. By contrast, a free market leads to automatic adjustments to changes in economic conditions; the prospect of monopoly/oligopoly profits may stimulate risk taking and hence research and development and innovation; there may still be a high degree of actual or potential competition under monopoly and oligopoly.
3. It is impossible to draw firm conclusions about the 'optimum' level of government intervention. This is partly due to the normative nature of the question, partly due to the difficulties of measuring costs and benefits of intervention/non-intervention, and partly due to the difficulties of predicting the effects of government policies, especially over the longer term.

END OF CHAPTER QUESTIONS

1. Assume that a firm discharges waste into a river. As a result, the marginal social costs (*MSC*) are greater than the firm's marginal (private) costs (*MC*). The following table shows how *MC, MSC, AR* and *MR* vary with output.

Output	1	2	3	4	5	6	7	8
MC (£)	23	21	23	25	27	30	35	42
MSC (£)	35	34	38	42	46	52	60	72
TR (£)	60	102	138	168	195	219	238	252
AR (£)	60	51	46	42	39	36.5	34	31.5
MR (£)	60	42	36	30	27	24	19	14

   (a) How much will the firm produce if it seeks to maximise profits?
   (b) What is the socially efficient level of output (assuming no externalities on the demand side)?
   (c) How much is the marginal external cost at this level of output?
   (d) What size tax would be necessary for the firm to reduce its output to the socially efficient level?
   (e) Why is the tax less than the marginal externality?
   (f) Why might it be equitable to impose a lump-sum tax on this firm?
   (g) Why will a lump-sum tax not affect the firm's output (assuming that in the long run the firm can still make at least normal profit)?
2. Why might it be argued that a redistribution of consumption, whilst not involving a Pareto improvement, could still be desirable?
3. Assume that a country had no state education at all. For what reasons might the private education system not provide the optimal allocation of resources to and within education?
4. Why might it be better to ban certain activities that cause environmental damage rather than to tax them?
5. Distinguish between publicly provided goods, public goods and merit goods.
6. Consider the advantages and disadvantages of extending property rights so that everyone would have the right to prevent people imposing any costs on them whatsoever (or charging them to do so).
7. Should all investment be subject to a social cost–benefit appraisal?
8. Make out a case for (a) increasing and (b) decreasing the role of the government in the allocation of resources.

Additional case studies on the book's website (www.pearsoned.co.uk/sloman)

11.1 **Can the market provide adequate protection for the environment?** This explains why markets generally fail to take into account environmental externalities.

11.2 **Catastrophic risk.** This examines how a cost–benefit study could put a monetary value on a remote chance of a catastrophe happening (such as an explosion at a nuclear power station).

11.3 **Evaluating the cost of aircraft noise.** This case study looks at the method used by the Roskill Commission, which in the 1960s investigated the siting of a third major London airport.

11.4 **CBA of the Glasgow canal project.** A cost–benefit study carried out in the late 1980s of the restoration of the Glasgow canal system.

11.5 **Public choice theory.** This examines how economists have attempted to extend their analysis of markets to the field of political decision making.

WEBSITES RELEVANT TO THIS CHAPTER

See sites listed at the end of Chapter 12 on page 364.

Chapter 12
Applied Microeconomics

Just how far should things be left to the market in practice? Just how much should a government intervene? These are clearly normative questions, and the answers to them will depend on a person's politics. Conservative politicians tend to favour the absolute minimum degree of intervention required to ensure the 'efficient' working of the market. Socialist politicians, on the other hand, prefer a much greater degree of intervention, to ensure not only that the inefficiencies of the market are corrected, but also that questions of 'fairness' and 'equality' are taken into account.

This chapter examines four topics that illustrate well the possible strengths and weaknesses of both the market and government intervention. In the first two sections we look at environmental issues and consider alternative policies for dealing with pollution and urban traffic congestion. In section 12.3 we look at the problem of market power and at various policies for preventing firms abusing a monopolistic or oligopolistic position. Finally we look at privatisation and the extent to which privatised industries should be regulated to prevent them abusing their market power. We also consider whether it is possible to introduce enough competition in these industries to make regulation unnecessary.

CHAPTER MAP

12.1 ECONOMICS OF THE ENVIRONMENT

Scarcely a day goes by without some or other environmental issue featuring in the news: another warning about global warming, a company fined for illegally dumping waste, a drought or flood blamed on pollution, a health scare about car exhausts, smog in tropical countries caused by forest fires.

Ask virtually anyone if they would like a cleaner and more attractive environment and the answer would be yes. Ask them, however, what we as taxpayers or consumers should be prepared to pay for such improvements and there would be much more disagreement. The point is that environmental improvement normally comes at a cost: whether that is a cost in cleaning up waste or pollution, or a cost in terms of the higher price we might need to pay for 'green' products, such as organic foods, low-emission cars and electricity from renewable sources.

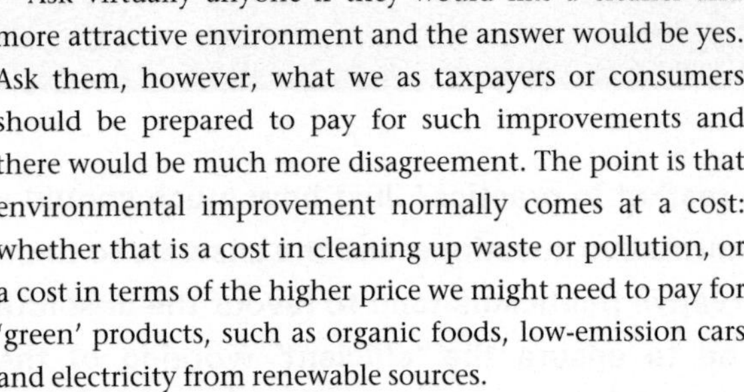

TC 2 p10

Economists are concerned with choices, and rational choices involve weighing up costs and benefits. Increasingly, people are recognising that such costs and benefits ought to include the effects on the environment: the effects on the planet we share.

The environmental problem

Why do people misuse the environment? To answer this we have to understand the nature of the economic relationship between humans and the natural world. We all benefit from the environment in three ways: as an amenity to be enjoyed, as a source of primary products (food, raw materials and other resources) and as a dump for waste.

The relationship between these uses of the environment and the rest of the economy is shown in Figure 12.1. These three uses, however, tend to conflict with each other.

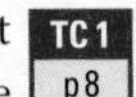

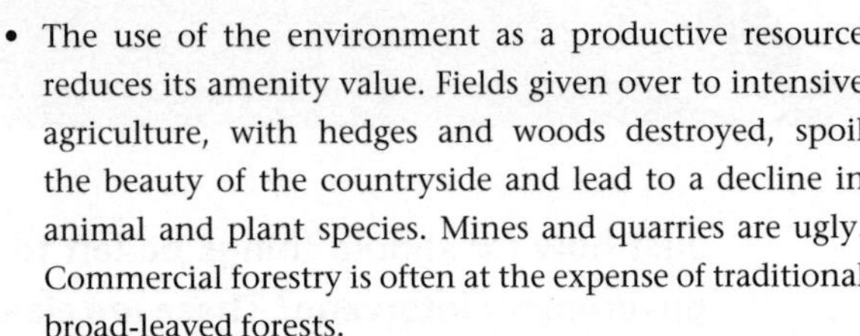

- The use of the environment as a productive resource reduces its amenity value. Fields given over to intensive agriculture, with hedges and woods destroyed, spoil the beauty of the countryside and lead to a decline in animal and plant species. Mines and quarries are ugly. Commercial forestry is often at the expense of traditional broad-leaved forests.
- Similarly, the use of the environment as a dump for waste reduces its amenity value. The environment becomes dirtier and uglier.

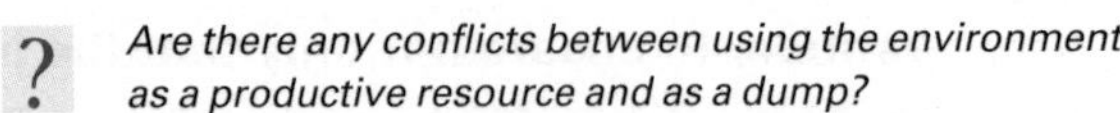

? *Are there any conflicts between using the environment as a productive resource and as a dump?*

But are these conflicts getting worse? Let us examine the arguments.

Population pressures and limited resources

As we saw in Box 5.1, as more and more people crowd on to the fixed supply of world land, so diminishing returns to labour will occur. If food output per head is to remain constant, let alone increase, land must be made to yield

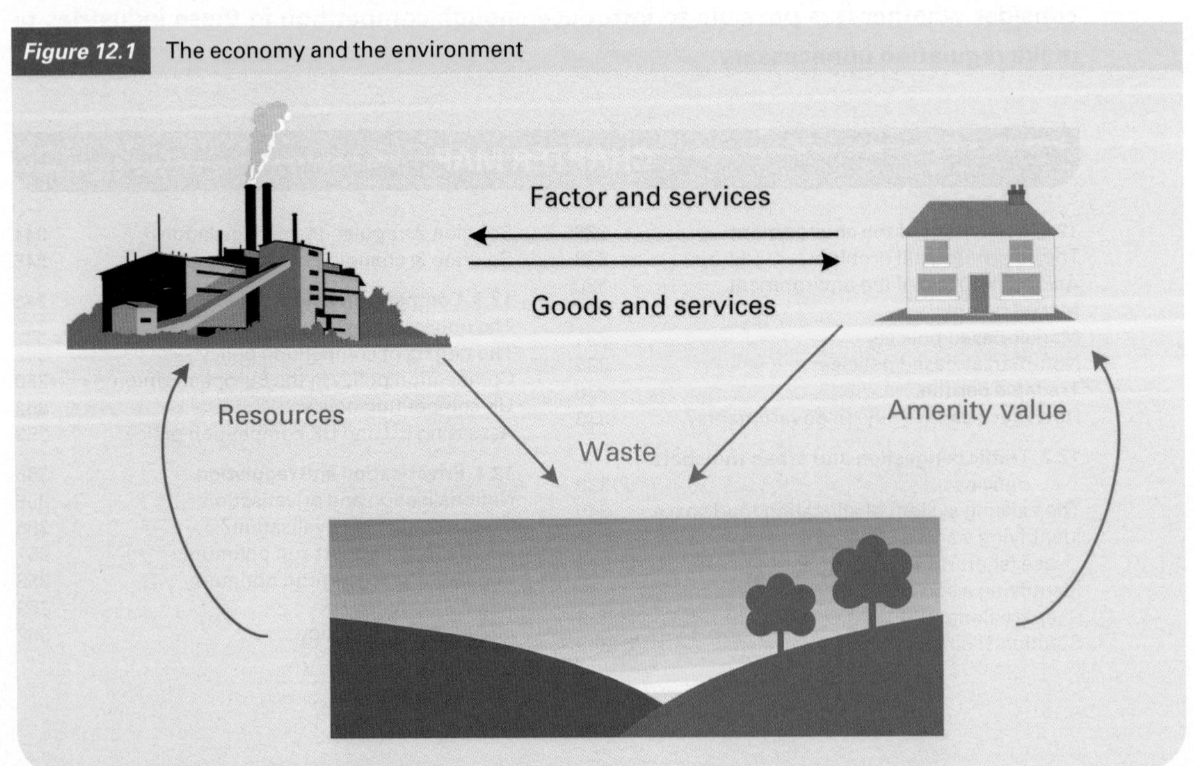

Figure 12.1 The economy and the environment

more and more. The answer has been to use increasing amounts of fertiliser and pesticides. Likewise, if the increasing world population is to have higher levels of material consumption, this will generate increased demands for natural resources, many of which are non-renewable, and generate more pollution.

The environment is able to absorb most types of waste up to certain levels of emission. Beyond such levels, however, environmental damage is likely to accelerate. Other things being equal, as population and waste grow, so environmental degradation is likely to grow at a faster rate.

Cause for optimism?

Despite population pressures, there are various factors that are helping to reduce environmental degradation.

Technological developments. Many newer industrial processes are cleaner and make a more efficient use of resources, leading to less waste and a slowdown in the rate of extraction of various minerals and fossil fuels. What is more, the production of less waste, or the recycling of waste, is often in the commercial interests of firms: it allows them to cut costs. For example, in 2004 companies in the UK spent some £250 million on energy efficiency. This produced cost savings of around £600 million. Firms thus have an incentive both to use such technology and also to research into cleaner and more resource-efficient techniques. Similarly, firms have an incentive to produce products that save consumers money, such as fuel-efficient cars, domestic boilers, fires, cookers and electrical appliances. TC3 p21

Increased price of non-renewable resources. As we saw in Box 9.10, as resources become scarcer, so their prices rise. This encourages people to use less of them, either by using more efficient technology or by switching to renewable alternatives.

Public opinion. As knowledge about environmental damage has grown, so too has pressure from public opinion to do something about it. Many firms gain commercially from having a 'green image' and governments see electoral advantage in policies to create a cleaner, greener environment.

Despite these developments, however, many aspects of environmental degradation continue to worsen.

The OECD *Environmental Outlook* has identified the main environmental issues for the next 20 years, and uses a traffic-light system to classify them as serious (red light), moderate (amber light) or satisfactory (green light): see Table 12.1.

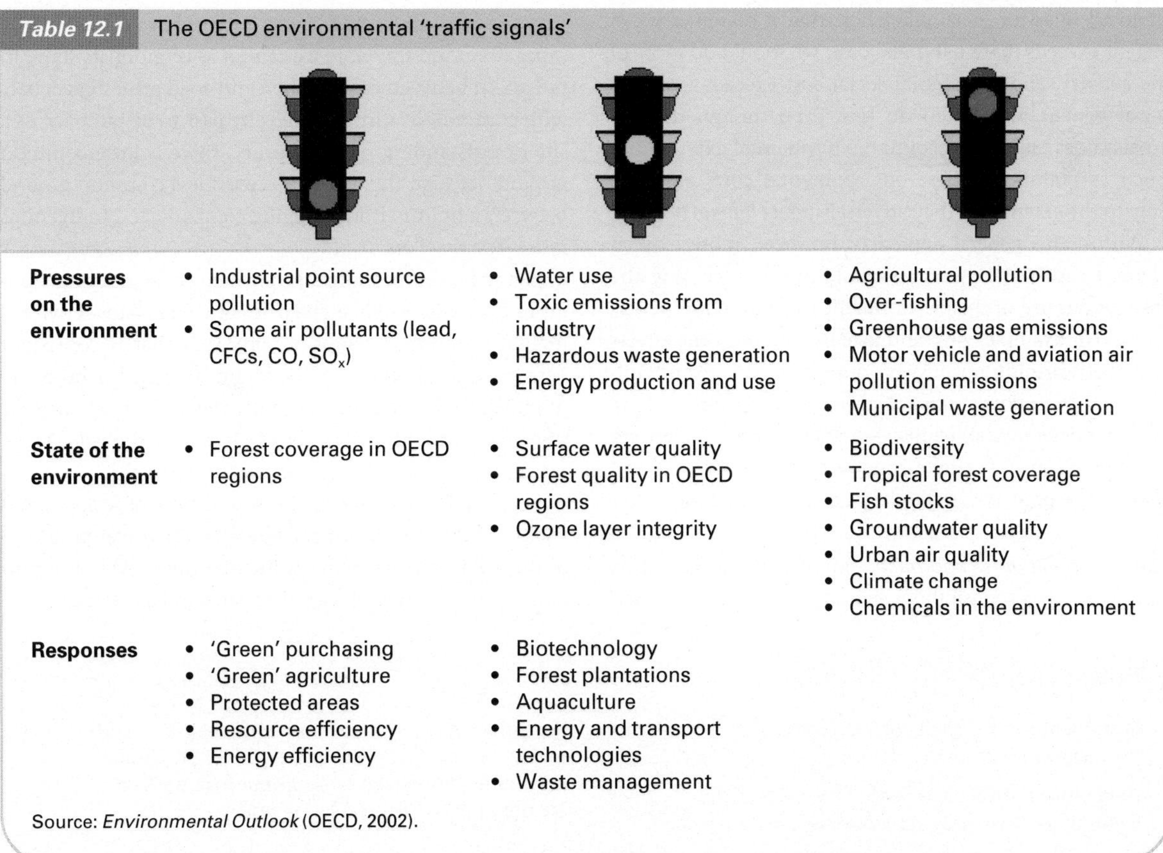

Table 12.1 The OECD environmental 'traffic signals'

Pressures on the environment	• Industrial point source pollution • Some air pollutants (lead, CFCs, CO, SO_x)	• Water use • Toxic emissions from industry • Hazardous waste generation • Energy production and use	• Agricultural pollution • Over-fishing • Greenhouse gas emissions • Motor vehicle and aviation air pollution emissions • Municipal waste generation
State of the environment	• Forest coverage in OECD regions	• Surface water quality • Forest quality in OECD regions • Ozone layer integrity	• Biodiversity • Tropical forest coverage • Fish stocks • Groundwater quality • Urban air quality • Climate change • Chemicals in the environment
Responses	• 'Green' purchasing • 'Green' agriculture • Protected areas • Resource efficiency • Energy efficiency	• Biotechnology • Forest plantations • Aquaculture • Energy and transport technologies • Waste management	

Source: *Environmental Outlook* (OECD, 2002).

An optimum use of the environment

If the current levels of pollution and environmental degradation are too high, then can we identify an optimum use of the environment? To do this, we have to go back to first principles, and look at the ethics of our relationship with the natural world and at our attitudes towards ***sustainability***.

Different approaches to sustainability

We can identify four different approaches to the environment and sustainability.

TC 4 p 22

The free-market approach. At the one extreme, we could regard the world as there purely for ourselves: a resource that belongs to individual property owners to do with as they choose, or a 'common asset', such as the air and seas, for individuals to use for their own benefit. In this view of the world, we are entitled simply to weigh up the marginal costs and benefits to ourselves of any activity. Sustainability is achieved in this free-market world only to the extent that resource prices rise as they become scarce and to the extent that environmentally friendly technologies are in firms' (or consumers') private interests.

The social efficiency approach. A somewhat less extreme version of this view is one that takes the social costs and benefits of using the environment into account: i.e. the costs and benefits not only to the direct producer or consumer, but to people in general. Here we would apply the standard rules for social efficiency: that if marginal social benefit exceeds marginal social cost, we should do more of the activity, and if marginal social cost exceeds marginal social benefit, we should do less. Even though this approach does take into account environmental externalities (such as pollution), these environmental costs are costs only to the extent that they adversely affect *human beings*.

Within this general approach, however, more explicit account can be taken of sustainability, by including the costs of our use of the environment today to *future* generations. For example, we could take into account the effects of global warming not just on ourselves, but on our children and their descendants. Depending on people's views on 'intergenerational' equity, a higher or lower weighting could be given to future (as opposed to present) costs and benefits (see page 319 on the choice of a social discount rate).

KI 24 p 253

The conservationist approach. Many environmentalists argue that our responsibilities should not be limited to each other, or even to future generations, but should include the environment for its own sake. Such a view would involve downplaying the relative importance of material consumption and economic growth, and putting greater emphasis on the maintenance of ecosystems. Growth in consumption would be ethically acceptable only if it led to no (or only very minor) environmental degradation. Maintenance of the environment is thus seen as an ethical *constraint* on human activity.

The Gaia approach. The strongest approach to sustainability involves a fundamentally different ethical standpoint. Here the Earth itself, and its various natural species of animals and plants, have moral rights. According to this ***Gaia philosophy***, people are seen as mere custodians of the planet: the planet does not belong to them, any more than a dog belongs to the fleas on its back! This view of the environment is similar to that held by indigenous peoples living in marginal areas, such as the Aborigines in Australia and the San (Bushmen) of the Kalahari, and to various other 'hunter-gatherer' peoples in developing countries. Their ethic is that the land they leave their descendants should be as good as, if not better than, the land they inherited from their ancestors. Conservation is a 'prime directive'. This approach to the environment has been dubbed the 'deep green' approach.

Making optimum decisions concerning the environment

Choice between these four approaches is essentially normative, and therefore we cannot as economists stand in judgment between them. When anti-road protesters debate with commuters wanting a new by-pass to be built across a site of outstanding natural beauty, there is little common ground between them. There is even less common ground between a multinational logging company and indigenous rain forest dwellers.

Nevertheless, economists can help in identifying optimum decisions *within* a given set of values. Most environmental economists adopt an approach that is consistent with the social efficiency view, and which can be easily modified to fit the conservationist view. The main area for disagreement within this approach is over the *value* to be put on specific environmental costs and benefits.

Let us take the case of the production of a good that yields benefits to consumers, but which involves pollution to the environment. What is the optimum level of output of the good? The choices are illustrated in Figure 12.2.

Definitions

Sustainability The ability of the environment to survive its use for economic activity.

Gaia philosophy The respect for the rights of the environment to remain unharmed by human activity. Humans should live in harmony with the planet and other species. We have a duty to be stewards of the natural environment, so that it can continue to be a self-maintaining and self-regulating system.

Figure 12.2 Optimum level of an activity that involves pollution

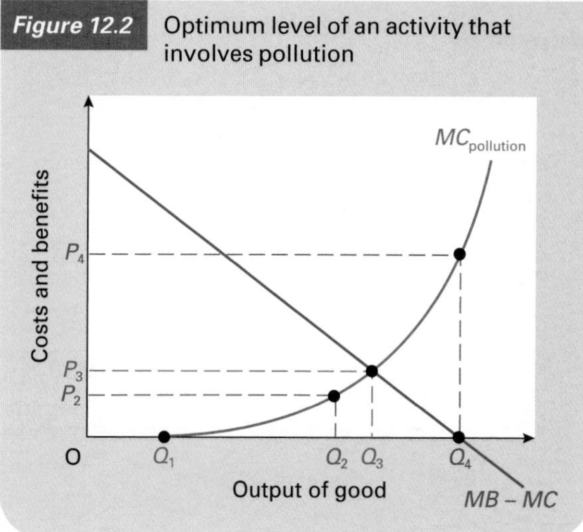

The line $MC_{pollution}$ shows the amount of pollution from each additional unit of the good. Up to level of activity Q_1 there is no pollution: the environment can cope with the waste generated. The curve gets steeper as output increases because the environment is increasingly unable to cope with the waste. The costs of pollution therefore accelerate.

The line *MB* – *MC* shows the net marginal private benefit from the good (i.e. its private profitability). The curve slopes downwards for two reasons: marginal benefit falls as more of the good is consumed (the principle of diminishing marginal utility); marginal cost rises (diminishing marginal returns). It is privately profitable to produce extra units of the good up to Q_4. Total private gain is maximised at this output.

An otherwise perfect free market will produce Q_4 units of output, with a pollution cost of P_4. The *socially* efficient level of output, however, is Q_3, with the lower pollution cost, P_3. (We are assuming that there are no other externalities.) Here the marginal net private benefit is equal to the marginal external cost of the pollution (i.e. where there is a zero net *social* benefit: where *MSB* = *MSC*). Identifying this socially efficient level of output is not easy in practice, since it re-
KI 25 p293 quires us to *measure* pollution costs, and that is fraught with problems. These problems were considered in section 11.4.

A more conservationist approach could be to set a maximum pollution cost of, say, P_2. This would reduce the optimum output to Q_2. A Gaian approach would be to restrict output to Q_1 in order to prevent any pollution. Of course, as we move towards 'greener' approaches, so it becomes more important to look for less polluting methods for producing this good (causing the $MC_{pollution}$ curve to shift downwards), and for alternative goods that involve less pollution (thus reducing the need to consume this good).

Market failures

KI 27 p300 What is clear from all the attitudes towards sustainability, other than the free-market one, is that the market system will fail to provide adequate protection for the environment. In fact, the market fails for various reasons.

The environment as a common resource. The air, the seas and many other parts of the environment are not privately owned. They are a global 'commons', and thus have the characteristic of 'non-excludability' (see page 303). Many of the 'services' provided by the environment do not have a price, so there is no economic incentive to economise on their use. Yet most environmental resources are *scarce*: there is 'rivalry' in their use. At a zero price, these resources will be overused. KI 1 p4

Externalities. One of the major problems of the environment being a public good is that of externalities. When people pollute the environment, the costs are borne mainly by others. The greater these external costs, the lower will be the socially efficient level of output (Q_3 in Figure 12.2). Because no one owns the environment, there is no one to enforce property rights over it. If a company pollutes the air that I breathe, I cannot stop it, because the air does not belong to me. KI 28 p300

Ignorance. There have been many cases of people causing environmental damage without realising it, especially when the effects build up over a long time. Take the case of aerosols. It was not until the 1980s that scientists connected their use to ozone depletion. Even when the problems are known to scientists, consumers may not appreciate the full environmental costs of their actions. So even if people would like to be more 'environmentally friendly' in their activities, they might not have the knowledge to be so. KI 15 p101

Inter-generational problems. The environmentally harmful effects of many activities are long term, whereas the benefits are immediate. Thus consumers and firms are frequently prepared to continue with various practices and leave future generations to worry about their environmental consequences. The problem, then, is a reflection of the importance that people attach to the present relative to the future. KI 24 p253

Look through the categories of possible market failings in section 11.2 on page 300. Are there any others, in addition to the four we have just identified, that will result in a socially inefficient use of the environment?

Policy alternatives: market-based policies

The policies that a government adopts to reduce pollution will depend on its attitudes towards sustainability: on how 'green' it is.

If governments adopt a social efficiency approach to sustainability, environmental problems are seen to be the result of prices not reflecting marginal social costs and benefits. In this section, we look at ways in which markets can be adjusted so that they do achieve social efficiency.

Extending private property rights

If those suffering from pollution are granted property rights, they can charge the polluters for the right to pollute. According to the Coase theorem (see page 312), this would result in the socially efficient level of output being achieved.

We can use Figure 12.2 to illustrate the Coase theorem. If output is initially less than Q_3, the marginal profit to the polluter will exceed the marginal pollution cost to the TC 5 p24 sufferer. In this case, if the sufferers impose a charge on the polluter that is greater than the sufferers' marginal pollution cost but less than the polluter's marginal profit, both sides will benefit from more of the good being produced. Such a situation can continue up to Q_3. Beyond Q_3, the marginal pollution cost exceeds the marginal profit. There is no charge that would compensate for the victim's suffering and leave enough over for the polluter to make a profit. Equilibrium output is therefore at Q_3, the socially efficient output.

Similarly, if the polluting *firm* is given the right to pollute, victims could offer a payment to persuade it not to pollute. The victims would be prepared to pay only up to the cost to them of the pollution. The firm would cut back production only provided the payment was at least as great as the loss in profit. This would be the case at levels of output above Q_3. Once output falls below Q_3, the maximum payment that the victim would be prepared to pay would be less than the minimum that the firm would be prepared to accept. Again, equilibrium would be at Q_3.

Extending private property rights in this way is normally impractical whenever there are many polluters and many victims. But the principle of the victims paying polluters to reduce pollution is sometimes followed by governments. Thus, under Article 11 of the 1997 Kyoto Protocol, the developed countries agreed to provide financial assistance to the developing countries to help them reduce greenhouse gas emissions.

In addition, there are sometimes direct environmental gains to be made from extending private property rights to individuals. In many developing countries, tenant farmers or squatters in urban slums have no incentive to invest in the land where they work or live. Give such people secure property rights, however, and they are more likely to take care of the property. For example, farmers are much more likely to plant trees if they know they have the right to the wood or fruit several years later.

Charging for use of the environment (as a resource or a dump)

One way of 'pricing the environment' is for the government to impose ***environmental charges*** on consumers or firms. Thus *emissions charges* could be levied on firms discharging waste. Another example is the use of *user charges* to households for sewage disposal or rubbish collection. If a social efficiency approach to sustainability is taken, the optimum level of environmental use would be where the marginal social benefits and costs of that use were equal. This is illustrated in Figure 12.3, which shows the emission of toxic waste into a river by a chemical plant.

Figure 12.3 An emissions charge

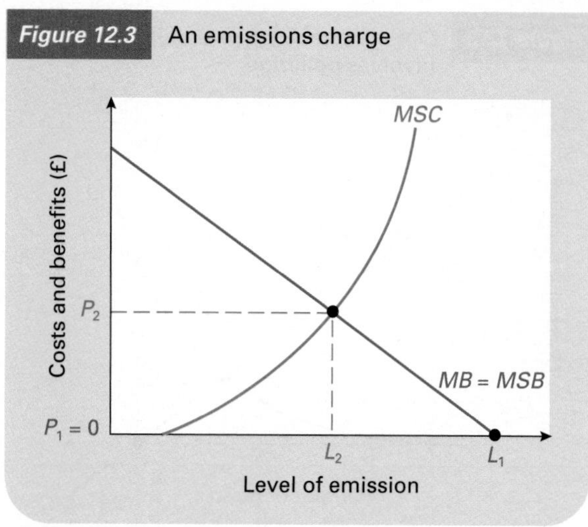

It is assumed that all the benefits from emitting the waste into the river accrue to the firm (i.e. there is no external benefit). Marginal private and marginal social benefits are thus the same ($MB = MSB$). The curve slopes downwards because, with a downward-sloping demand curve for the *good*, higher output will have a lower marginal benefit, and so too will the waste associated with it.

But what about the marginal costs? Without charges, the marginal private cost of using the river for emitting the waste is zero. The pollution of the river, however, imposes an external cost on those living by the river or using it for fishing or water supply. The marginal external cost rises as the river becomes less and less able to cope with increased levels of emission. As there is no private cost, the marginal social cost is the same as the marginal external cost.

Without a charge, the firm will emit L_1, since this is where its private marginal cost (= 0) equals its private marginal benefit. The socially efficient level of emission is L_2 and the socially efficient level of emission charge, therefore, is P_2.

If these charges are to achieve a reduction in pollution, they must be a charge *per unit* of emissions or resource use (as in Figure 12.3). *Fixed total* charges, by contrast, such as water rates or council tax, will *not* encourage households to cut back on water use or domestic refuse, since this will not save them any money: such charges have a *marginal* rate of zero. If the firm in Figure 12.3 were charged a fixed total pollution fee, it would still choose to emit L_1 waste.

Definition

Environmental charges Charges for using natural resources (e.g. water or national parks), or for using the environment as a dump for waste (e.g. factory emissions or sewage).

Environmental ('green') taxes and subsidies

Rather than charging for environmental use, a tax could be imposed on the output (or consumption) of a *good*, wherever external environmental costs are generated. These are known as ***green taxes***. In this case, the good already has a price: the tax has the effect of increasing the price. To achieve a socially efficient output, the rate of tax should be equal to the marginal external cost. The alternative is to subsidise activities that reduce pollution (such as the installation of loft insulation). Here the rate of subsidy should be equal to the marginal external benefit.

Figure 11.9 (on page 310) showed the optimum rate of pollution tax in an otherwise perfect market. In terms of Figure 12.2, this rate of tax would be P_3: i.e. equal to the marginal pollution cost at the socially optimum output Q_3. The tax, by adding to private costs, shifts the $MB - MC$ line downwards so that it crosses the horizontal axis at Q_3. Profit is maximised where $MB - MC = 0$: at Q_3.

Although green taxes and subsidies are theoretically a means of achieving social efficiency, they do have serious limitations (see Box 12.1).

?

Draw a diagram like Figure 12.2, only this time assume that the activity has the effect of reducing pollution, with the result that the $MC_{pollution}$ curve lies below the horizontal axis, sloping downwards. Identify the socially optimal level of the activity. What would be the level of subsidy required to achieve this level of activity?

Policy alternatives: non-market-based policies

Command-and-control systems (laws and regulations)

The traditional way of tackling pollution has been to set maximum permitted levels of emission or resource use, or minimum acceptable levels of environmental quality, and then to fine firms contravening these limits. Measures of this type are known as ***command-and-control (CAC) systems***. Clearly, there have to be inspectors to monitor the amount of pollution, and the fines have to be large enough to deter firms from exceeding the limit.

Virtually all countries have environmental regulations of one sort or another. For example, the EU has over 200 items of legislation covering areas such as air and water pollution, noise, the marketing and use of dangerous chemicals, waste management, the environmental impacts of new projects (such as power stations, roads and quarries), recycling, depletion of the ozone layer and global warming.

Typically, there are three approaches to devising CAC systems.[1]

- ***Technology-based standards***. The focus could be on the amount of pollution generated, irrespective of its environmental impact. As technology for reducing pollutants improves, so tougher standards could be imposed, based on the 'best available technology' (as long as the cost were not excessive). Thus car manufacturers could be required to ensure that new car engines meet lower CO_2 emission levels as the technology enabled them to do so.
- ***Ambient-based standards***. Here the focus is on the environmental impact. For example, standards could be set for air or water purity. Depending on the location and the number of polluters in that area, a given standard would be achieved with different levels of discharge. If the object is a cleaner environment, this approach is more efficient than technology-based standards.
- ***Social-impact standards***. Here the focus is on the effect on people. Thus tougher standards would be imposed in densely populated areas. Whether this approach is more efficient than that of ambient-based standards depends on the approach to sustainability. If the objective is to achieve social efficiency, human-impact standards are preferable. If the objective is to protect the environment for its own sake (a deeper green approach), ambient standards would be preferable.

Assessing CAC systems. Given the uncertainty over the environmental impacts of pollutants, especially over the longer term, it is often better to play safe and set tough emissions or ambient standards. These could always be relaxed at a later stage if the effects turn out not to be so damaging, but it might be too late to reverse damage if the effects turn out to be more serious. Taxes may be a more sophisticated means of reaching a socially efficient output, but CAC methods are usually more straightforward to devise, easier to understand by firms and easier to implement.

[1] See R. K. Turner, D. Pearce and I. Bateman, *Environmental Economics* (Harvester Wheatsheaf, 1994), page 198.

Definitions

Green tax A tax on output designed to charge for the adverse effects of production on the environment. The socially efficient level of a green tax is equal to the marginal environmental cost of production.

Command-and-control (CAC) systems The use of laws or regulations backed up by inspections and penalties (such as fines) for non-compliance.

Technology-based standards Pollution control that requires firms' emissions to reflect the levels that could be achieved from using the best available pollution control technology.

Ambient-based standards Pollution control that requires firms to meet minimum standards for the environment (e.g. air or water quality).

Social-impact standards Pollution control that focuses on the effects on people (e.g. on health or happiness).

CASE STUDIES AND APPLICATIONS

GREEN TAXES

Are they the perfect answer to the problem of pollution?

Increasingly countries are introducing 'green' taxes in order to discourage pollution as goods are produced, consumed or disposed of. The table shows the range of green taxes used around the world and the chart shows green tax revenues as a percentage of GDP in various countries. As can be seen, they are higher than average in Scandinavian countries, reflecting the strength of their environmental concerns. They are lowest in the USA. By far the largest green tax revenues come from fuel taxes. Fuel taxes are relatively high in the UK and so, therefore, are green tax revenues.

There are various problems, however, with using the tax weapon in the fight against pollution.

Identifying the socially efficient tax rate. It will be difficult to identify the $MC_{\text{pollution}}$ curve for each firm (see Figure 12.2), given that each one is likely to produce different amounts of pollutants for any given level of output. Even if two firms produce identical amounts of pollutants, the environmental damage might be quite different, because the ability of the environment to cope with it will differ between the two locations. Also, the number of people suffering will differ (a factor that is very important when considering the *human* impact of pollution). What is more, the harmful effects are likely to build up over time, and predicting these effects is fraught with difficulty.

Problems of demand inelasticity. The less elastic the demand for the product, the less effective will a tax be in cutting production and hence in cutting pollution. Thus taxes on petrol would have to be very high indeed to make significant reductions in the consumption of petrol and hence significant reductions in the exhaust gases that contribute towards global warming and acid rain.

Problems with international trade. If a country imposes pollution taxes on its industries, its products will become less competitive in world trade. To compensate for this, it may be necessary to give the industries tax rebates for exports. Also taxes would have to be imposed on imports of competitors' products from countries where there is no equivalent green tax.

Types of environmental taxes and charges

Motor fuels	*Other goods*	*Air transport*
Leaded/unleaded	Batteries	Noise charges
Diesel (quality differential)	Plastic carrier bags	Aviation fuels
Carbon/energy taxation	Glass containers	*Water*
Sulphur tax	Drink cans	Water charges
Other energy products	Tyres	Sewage charges
Carbon/energy tax	CFCs/halons	Water effluent charges
Sulphur tax or charge	Disposable razors/cameras	Manure charges
NO_2 charge	Lubricant oil charge	*Direct tax provisions*
Methane charge	Oil pollutant charge	Tax relief on green investment
Agricultural inputs	Solvents	Taxation on free company cars
Fertilisers	*Waste disposal*	Employer-paid commuting expenses taxable
Pesticides	Municipal waste charges	Employer-paid parking expenses taxable
Manure	Waste-disposal charges	Commuter use of public transport tax deductible
Vehicle-related taxation	Hazardous waste charges	
Sales tax depends on car size	Landfill tax or charges	
Road tax depends on car size	Duties on waste water	

Voluntary agreements

Rather than imposing laws and regulations, the government can seek to enter into voluntary agreements (VAs) with firms for them to cut pollution. Such agreements may involve a formal contract, and hence be legally binding, or they may be looser commitments by firms. VAs will be helped if (a) companies believe that this will improve their image with customers and hence improve sales; (b) there is an underlying threat by the government of introducing laws and regulations should voluntary agreements fail.

Firms often prefer VAs to regulations, because they can negotiate such agreements to suit their own particular circumstances and build them into their planning. The result is that the firms may be able to meet environmental objectives at lower cost. This clearly helps their competitive position.

BOX 12.1

Effects on employment. Reduced output in the industries affected by green taxes will lead to a reduction in employment. If, however, the effect was to encourage investment in new cleaner technology, employment might not fall. Furthermore, employment opportunities could be generated elsewhere, if the extra revenues from the green taxes were spent on alternative products (e.g. buses and trains rather than cars).

Redistributive effects. Some green taxes are regressive. The poor spend a higher proportion of their income on domestic fuel than the rich. A 'carbon tax' on such fuel therefore has the effect of redistributing incomes away from the poor. The poor also spend a larger proportion of their income on food than the rich do. Taxes on agriculture, designed to reduce the intensive use of fertilisers and pesticides, also tend to hit the poor proportionately more than the rich.

Not all green taxes, however, are regressive. The rich spend a higher proportion of their income on motoring than the poor (see Figure 12.4 on page 341). Thus petrol and other motoring taxes could have a progressive effect.

Despite these problems, such taxes can still move output closer to the socially efficient level. What is more, they do have the major advantage of providing a continuing incentive to firms to find cleaner methods of production and thereby save more on their tax bills.

Is it a good idea to use the revenues from green taxes to subsidise green alternatives (e.g. using petrol taxes for subsidising rail transport)?

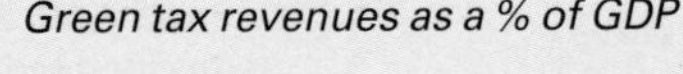

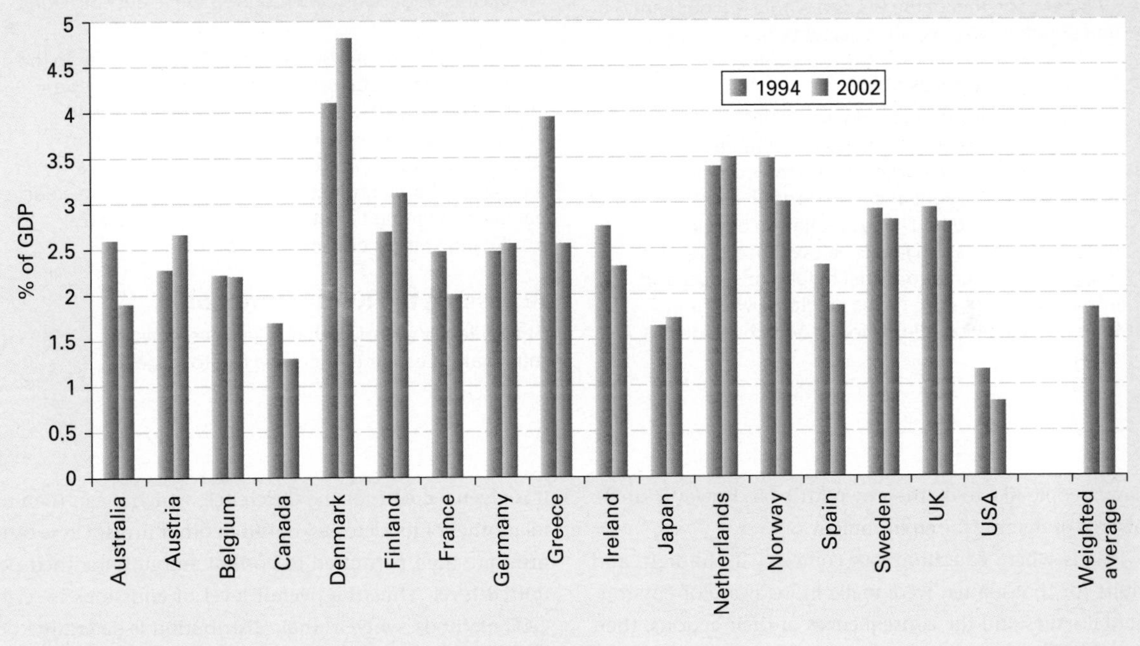

Source: *Environmentally Related Taxes Database* (OECD, 2005).

As far as the effectiveness of VAs is concerned, that depends on how tightly specified the agreements are and how easy they are for government inspectors to monitor. It also depends on the goodwill of firms. Without it, firms may well try to draw up agreements in a way that allows them to get around having to cut emissions as much as was intended by the government.

Education

People's attitudes are very important in determining the environmental consequences of their actions. Fortunately for the environment, people are not always out simply to maximise their own self-interest. If they were, then why do people often buy more expensive 'green' products, such as environmentally friendly detergents? The answer is that

CASE STUDIES AND APPLICATIONS

SELLING THE ENVIRONMENT

The market-led solution of the Kyoto Protocol

In 1997, a draft accord to reduce greenhouse gas emissions was agreed by most nations of the world at the UN international climate change conference in Kyoto, Japan. It was based on principles established in a framework convention signed in 1992. The 'Kyoto Protocol' is an agreement to reduce greenhouse gas emissions by an average of 5.2 per cent (based on 1990 levels) by the year 2012.

To become a legally binding treaty, it had to be signed by nations accounting for at least 55 per cent of greenhouse gas emissions from industrialised countries. Because the Bush administration decided to withdraw the USA from the agreement, and given that the USA accounts for some 36 per cent of such emissions, the 55 per cent target could be met only if Russia signed, which it eventually did in November 2004. The treaty came into force on 16 February 2005, having been ratified by 141 countries. Of these, 39 industrialised countries have agreed to emissions reductions.

Each of the 39 countries has its own agreed emissions reduction target. The UK's target is 12.5 per cent, that of the EU as a whole is 8 per cent and Japan's is 6 per cent, as is Canada's.

Market-based systems

The agreement, although not originally envisaged in this way, involves the climate being turned into a market, where the right to pollute can be bought and sold through a system of emissions credits. These credits can be earned by reducing emission levels below those agreed or by creating conditions that help to minimise the impact of greenhouse gases on global warming: for example, by planting a forest (which absorbs carbon).

Within the Kyoto Protocol there are three distinct market-based mechanisms:

- Emissions trading.
- Joint Implementation (JI).
- Clean Development Mechanism (CDM).

Emissions trading. The countries that have ratified the Kyoto Protocol will, by 2008, be allowed to trade amongst themselves rights to emit six greenhouse gases. If a country reduces emissions below its agreed limit, it will be able to sell the additional reduction as a credit. So if a country is finding it difficult to cut emissions, it will be able to buy these credits within some kind of marketplace. (As you will see on page 338, CO_2 emissions trading began within the EU in January 2005.)

Joint implementation. Under Article 6 of the protocol, an industrialised country can earn credits by investing in projects that reduce emissions in other industrialised countries (primarily former Soviet countries). These credits then reduce its own requirement to cut emissions.

Clean Development Mechanism. This is similar to the joint implementation process above, but involves a country or company from the industrialised world earning credit by investing in emissions reduction schemes in *developing* countries. For example, a typical CDM or JI project might involve installing solar panels or planting forests or investing in a factory producing energy-efficient light bulbs.

Assessing the Kyoto Protocol

But while the use of such market mechanisms may make it easier to meet the Kyoto targets,

many people like to do their own little bit, however small, towards protecting the environment.

This is where education can come in. If children, and adults for that matter, were made more aware of environmental issues and the consequences of their actions, then people's consumption habits could change and more pressure would be put on firms to improve their 'green credentials'.

Policy alternatives: tradable permits

A policy measure that has grown in popularity in recent years is that of ***tradable permits***. This is a combination of command-and-control and market-based systems.

A maximum permitted level of emission is set for a given pollutant for a given factory, and the firm is given a permit to emit up to this amount. If it emits less than this amount, it is given a credit for the difference, which it can then use in another of its factories, or sell to other firms. These other firms are then permitted to go that amount *over* their permitted level. Thus the overall level of emissions is set by CAC methods, whereas their distribution is determined by the market.

Take the example of firms A and B, which are currently producing 12 units of a pollutant each. Now assume that a standard is set permitting them to produce only 10 units

Definition

Tradable permits Each firm is given a permit to produce a given level of pollution. If less than the permitted amount is produced, the firm is given a credit. This can then be sold to another firm, allowing it to exceed its original limit.

BOX 12.2

many claim that the targets are much too low. The Intergovernmental Panel on Climate Change (a UN-appointed panel of 2500 of the world's leading scientists) estimates that a 60 to 80 per cent cut in greenhouse gas emissions from 1990 levels will ultimately be needed to avert serious climate disruption. In the light of this, a 5.2 per cent reduction, which will probably not be met anyway, seems minuscule.

There is also the danger that businesses, rather than cutting greenhouse gas emissions, will simply buy credits offered for sale on the open market, many of which will not be earned from reducing current emissions. For example, Russia has CO_2 emissions some 45 per cent below its 1990 level and as such has a massive emissions credit. However, such credit is not the result of Russian environmental policy, but rather the consequence of the collapse and closure of Russian industry! The EU has consistently argued that, to ensure some real gains are made, no more than 50 per cent of the emissions reduction should be achieved through these market-based mechanisms.

One of the biggest problems with the Kyoto treaty is that developing countries are not obliged to cut their emissions. As countries such as China and India continue with their rapid industrialisation, often using relatively dirty technology, emissions are likely to increase rapidly.

Finally, with the USA (and other countries, such as Australia) opting out of the Kyoto Protocol, this has clearly weakened the effectiveness of the treaty.

George W. Bush and the Kyoto Protocol

So did the Bush administration take any measures to cut greenhouse gases? In its 'clear skies and global climate change initiative', launched in February 2002, the USA stated that its aim was to cut the growth in greenhouse gas emissions relative to the growth in the economy. There would be tax incentives to encourage renewable energy schemes and fuel efficiency schemes, but corporations would not be obliged to meet any CO_2 targets. The effect would still be one of a *growth* in greenhouse gases. By 2012, US CO_2 emissions would be some 25 per cent above 1990 levels: not the 7 per cent below that the Clinton administration had agreed at Kyoto in 1997!

But while the Bush administration does little, elsewhere in the USA action is being taken.

> A group of major companies (including DuPont, International Paper, and IBM), have formed the Chicago Climate Exchange to trade carbon dioxide emission reductions on a spot market basis. Member companies have agreed to reduce their greenhouse emissions by 4% by 2006.
> . . . Meanwhile, nine eastern states (the six New England states plus Delaware, New Jersey, and New York) have formed the Regional Greenhouse Gas Initiative requiring large power plants to reduce carbon emissions through a cap-and-trade system. Auto-clogged California is even trying to force automakers to limit emissions.[2]

Explain who are likely to be the 'winners' and 'losers' as a result of the recent talks on carbon dioxide emissions. Use the concepts of game theory to illustrate your argument.

[2] *USA Today* (15/2/05).

each. If firm A managed to reduce the pollutant to 8 units, it would be given a credit for 2 units. It could then sell this to firm B, enabling B to continue emitting 12 units. The effect would still be a total reduction of 4 units between the two firms. However, the trade in pollution permits allows pollution reduction to be concentrated where it can be achieved at lowest cost. In our example, if it cost firm B more to reduce its pollution than firm A, the permits could be sold from A to B at a price that was profitable to both (i.e. at a price above the cost of emission reduction to A, but below the cost of emission reduction to B).

TC 5 p 24

The principle of tradable permits can be used as the basis of international agreements on pollution reduction. Each country could be required to achieve a certain percentage reduction in a pollutant (e.g. CO_2 or SO_2), but any country exceeding its reduction could sell its right to these emissions to other (presumably richer) countries.

A similar principle can be adopted for using natural resources. Thus fish quotas could be assigned to fishing boats or fleets or countries. Any parts of these quotas not used could then be sold.

How are the permitted pollution levels (or fish quotas) to be decided? The way that seems to be the most acceptable is to base them on firms' *current* levels, with any subsequent reduction in total permitted pollution being achieved by requiring firms to reduce their emissions by the *same* percentage. This approach is known as ***grandfathering***. The

Definition

Grandfathering Where each firm's emission permit is based on its current levels of emission (e.g. permitted levels for all firms could be 80 per cent of their current levels).

main problem with this approach is that it could be seen as unfair by those firms that are already using cleaner technology. Why should they be required to make the same reductions as firms using dirty technology?

The EU carbon trading system. In the EU, a carbon Emissions Trading Scheme (ETS) has been in place since January 2005 as part of the EU's approach to meeting its targets under the Kyoto Treaty (see Box 12.2). Under the scheme, some 12 000 industrial plants have been allocated CO_2 emissions allowances, or credits, by their respective governments. Companies that exceed their limits must purchase credits to cover the difference, while those that reduce their emissions can sell their surplus credits for a profit. Companies can trade directly with each other or via brokers operating throughout Europe.

TC 3 p21

Assessing the system of tradable permits. The main advantage of tradable permits is that they combine the simplicity of CAC methods with the benefits of achieving pollution reduction in the most efficient way. There is also the advantage that firms have a financial incentive to cut pollution. This might then make it easier for governments to impose tougher standards (i.e. impose lower permitted levels of emission).

There are, however, various problems with tradable permits. One is the possibility that trade will lead to pollution being concentrated in certain geographical areas. Another is that it may reduce the pressure on dirtier factories (or countries) to cut their emissions. Finally, the system will lead to significant cuts in pollution only if the permitted levels are low. Once the system is in place, the government might then feel that the pressure is off to *reduce* the permitted levels.

?

What determines the size of the administrative costs of a system of tradable permits? For what reasons might green taxes be cheaper to administer than a system of tradable permits?

How much can we rely on governments?

If governments are to be relied upon to set the optimum green taxes or regulations, several conditions must be met.

First, they must have the will to protect the environment. But governments are accountable to their electorates and must often appease various pressure groups, such as representatives of big business. In the USA, for example, there has been great resistance to cuts in greenhouse gases from the automobile, power and various other industries, many of which have powerful representation in Congress. So there must be the political will in a country if significant environmental improvements are to be made. One of the problems here is that many of the environmental effects of our actions today will be on future generations; but governments represent today's generation, and today's generation may not be prepared to make the necessary sacrifices. This brings us back to the importance of education.

Second, it must be possible to identify just what the optimum is. This requires a clear set of objectives towards sustainability and any conflicts between human and ecological objectives. It also requires a knowledge of just what the environmental effects are of various activities, such as the emission of CO_2 into the atmosphere, and that is something on which scientists disagree.

Finally, there is the problem that many environmental issues are global and not just local or national. Many require concerted action by governments around the world. The history of international agreements on environmental issues, however, is one plagued with difficulties between countries, which seem more concerned with their own national interests. To understand the difficulties of reaching international agreements, we can draw on game theory (see pages 191–5).

Game theory and international agreements

KI 20 p182

Assume that the world would benefit from a reduction in greenhouse gases and that these benefits would exceed the costs of having to cut back on activities (such as motoring or the generation of electricity) that release such gases into the atmosphere. What would be in the interests of an *individual* country, such as the USA? Its optimum solution would be for *other* countries to cut their emissions, while maintaining its own levels. This *maximax* approach would yield most of the benefits to the USA and none of the costs. However, when *all* countries refuse to cut emissions, no one gains! This is an example of the *prisoners' dilemma* (see page 193), and is illustrated in Table 12.2.

Assume that there is an international agreement (as at the Kyoto summit in December 1997) to cut emissions. If all countries stick to the agreement, the outcome is cell A: a moderate gain to all. What should Congress do? Whatever other countries do (all stick to the agreement, some stick to it, none stick to it), it will be in the USA's interests *not* to

Table 12.2 Outcomes for countries from strategies of pollution reduction

		Other countries' strategy		
		All cut pollution	**Some cut pollution**	**None cut pollution**
USA's strategy	Cut pollution	A **Moderate net gain for all**	B Small loss for USA; gain for countries not cutting pollution	C Large loss for USA; slight gain for other countries
	Don't cut pollution	D High gain for USA; small gain for other countries	E Fairly high gain for USA; loss for other countries	F **No gain for any country**

stick to it: this is the dominant strategy – a lesson that George W. Bush seemed quick to learn! Cell D is preferable to Cell A; E is preferable to B; F is preferable to C. But when *all* countries reason like this, the world ends up in Cell F, with no cut in pollution. Cell F is worse for all countries than Cell A!

Only if countries believe that the other countries will (a) ratify the agreement and (b) stick to it once it is ratified will the agreement be likely to succeed. This requires trust on all sides and the ability to monitor the outcomes.

KI 4 p11 The other major problem area concerns equity. Most countries will feel that they are being asked to do too much and that others are being asked to do too little. Developed countries will want to adopt a grandfathering approach. The starting point with this approach would be current levels of pollution. Every country would then be required to make the same percentage cut. Developing countries, on the other hand, will want the bulk of the cuts, if not all of them, to be made by the developed countries. After all, the rich countries produce much higher levels of pollutants per capita than do the poor countries.

? *How does an international negotiation 'game' differ from the prisoners' dilemma game?*

Section summary

1. The environment benefits humans in three ways: as an amenity, as a source of primary products and as a dump for waste.
2. Given the increasing population pressures and the demands for economic growth, the pressures on the environment are likely to grow. These pressures can be lessened, however, with the use of cleaner technology, a more efficient use of natural resources and 'greener' behaviour of consumers, firms and governments.
3. The concept of an 'optimum' use of the environment depends on people's attitudes towards sustainability. These attitudes vary from regarding the environment simply as a resource for human use at the one extreme to seeing the environment as having moral rights at the other.
4. Under the social efficiency approach to sustainability, the optimum output of a good is where the marginal external environmental cost is equal to the marginal net benefit to users (assuming no other externalities).
5. The market fails to achieve a socially efficient use of the environment because large parts of the environment are a common resource, because production or consumption often generates environmental externalities, because of ignorance of the environmental effects of our actions, and because of a lack of concern for future generations.
6. One approach to protecting the environment is to use the market. This can be done by extending private property rights. In many cases, however, this approach is impractical. Another way it can be done is to impose charges for using the environment or taxes per unit of output. The problem with these methods is in identifying the appropriate charges or tax rates, since these will vary according to the environmental impact.
7. Another approach is to use command-and-control systems, such as making certain practices illegal or putting limits on discharges. This is a less sophisticated alternative to taxes or charges, but it is safer when the environmental costs of certain actions are unknown. Other alternatives to market-based approaches include voluntary agreements and education.
8. Tradable permits are a mix of command-and-control and market-based systems. Firms are given permits to emit a certain level of pollution and then these can be traded. A firm that can relatively cheaply reduce its pollution below its permitted level can sell this credit to another firm that finds it more costly to do so. The system is an efficient and administratively cheap way of limiting pollution to a designated level. It can, however, lead to pollution being concentrated in certain areas and can reduce the pressure on firms to find cleaner methods of production.
9. Although governments can make a major contribution to reducing pollution, government action is unlikely to lead to the perfect outcome (however defined). Governments may be more concerned with short-run political considerations and will not have perfect information. What is more, given that many environmental effects spill over national borders, governments may 'play games' internationally to try to reduce the costs to their country of any international action to protect the environment.

12.2 TRAFFIC CONGESTION AND URBAN TRANSPORT POLICIES

Traffic congestion is a problem that faces all countries, especially in the large cities and at certain peak times: a problem that has grown at an alarming rate as our lives have become increasingly dominated by the motor car. Sitting in a traffic jam is both time wasting and frustrating. It adds considerably to the costs and the stress of modern living.

And it is not only the motorist that suffers. Congested streets make life less pleasant for the pedestrian, and increased traffic leads to increased accidents. What is more, the inexorable growth of traffic has led to significant problems of pollution. Traffic is noisy and car fumes are unpleasant and lead to substantial environmental damage.

Table 12.3 Passenger transport in Great Britain: percentage of passenger kilometres by road

Year	Cars	Motor cycles	Buses and coaches	Bicycles
1953	34.6	3.8	50.3	11.4
1963	67.5	2.9	26.7	2.9
1973	83.3	1.0	14.7	1.0
1983	86.7	1.9	10.1	1.3
1993	91.9	0.6	6.9	0.6
2003	92.1	0.8	6.4	0.7

Source: *Transport Statistics of Great Britain* (Dept for Transport).

Between 1970 and 2004 road traffic in Great Britain rose by 148 per cent, whereas the length of public roads rose by only 22 per cent (albeit some roads were widened). Most passenger and freight transport is by road. In 2004, 93 per cent of passenger kilometres and 62 per cent of freight tonnage kilometres in Great Britain were by road, whereas rail accounted for a mere 6 per cent of passenger traffic and 7 per cent of freight tonnage. Of road passenger kilometres, 92 per cent was by car in 2004, and, as Table 12.3 shows, this proportion has been growing. Motoring costs now amount to some 15 per cent of household expenditure.

But should the government do anything about the problem? Is traffic congestion a price worth paying for the benefits we gain from using cars? Or are there things that can be done to ease the problem without greatly inconveniencing the traveller?

We will look at various schemes later in this section and at their relative costs and benefits. But first it is necessary to examine the existing system of allocating road space to see the extent to which it meets or fails to meet society's transport objectives. This will enable us to identify the problems that the government must address. (Our discussion will focus on the motor car and passenger transport, but clearly lorries are another major source of congestion, and any comprehensive policy to deal with traffic congestion must also examine freight transport.)

The existing system of allocating road space

The allocation of road space depends on both demand and supply. Demand is by individuals who base their decisions on largely private considerations. Supply, by contrast, is usually by the central government or local authorities. Let us examine each in turn.

Demand for road space (by car users)

The demand for road space can be seen largely as a *derived* demand. What people want is not the car journey for its own sake, but to get to their destination. The greater the benefit they gain at their destination, the greater the benefit they gain from using their car to get there.

The demand for road space, like the demand for other goods and services, has a number of determinants. If congestion is to be reduced, it is important to know how responsive demand is to a change in any of these: it is important to consider the various elasticities of demand.

Price. This is the *marginal cost* to the motorist of a journey. It includes petrol, oil, maintenance, depreciation and any toll charges.

? *Are there any costs associated with motoring that would not be included as marginal costs? Explain why.*

The price elasticity of demand for motoring tends to be relatively low. There can be a substantial rise in the price of petrol, for example, and there will be only a modest fall in traffic.

Recent estimates of the short-run price elasticity of demand for road fuel in industrialised countries typically range from −0.15 to −0.28. Long-run elasticities are somewhat higher, but are still generally inelastic.[3]

TC 8 p59

The low price elasticity of demand suggests that schemes to tackle traffic congestion that merely involve raising the costs of motoring will have only limited success.

KI 2 p8

In addition to monetary costs, there are also the time costs of travel. The opportunity cost of sitting in your car is the next best alternative activity you could have been pursuing – relaxing, working, sleeping or whatever. Congestion, by increasing the duration of the journey, increases the opportunity cost.

Income. As incomes rise, car ownership and usage increase substantially. Demand for road space is elastic with respect to income.

Figure 12.4 shows motoring costs as a percentage of UK household expenditure by quintile groups of household income. The higher the household income, the higher the percentage of income spent on motoring. Clearly, the income elasticity of demand is significantly greater than 1.

This is also reflected in international statistics of car ownership. Figure 12.5 shows the growth of car ownership between 1980 and 2002 in selected countries. As national incomes have risen, so has the proportion of car ownership. People see car transport as a 'luxury good' compared with alternatives such as public transport, walking or cycling. Also, the growth of suburbs has meant that many people travel longer distances to work.

The implication of this is that, if countries continue to experience economic growth, car ownership and usage are likely to increase substantially: a conclusion in line with most forecasts.

[3] See: *Environmentally Related Taxes in OECD Countries: Issues and Strategies* (OECD, 2001), pages 99–103.

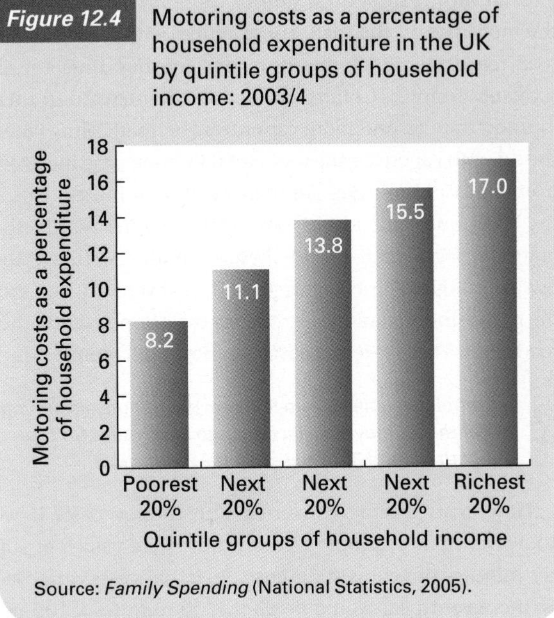

Figure 12.4 Motoring costs as a percentage of household expenditure in the UK by quintile groups of household income: 2003/4

Source: *Family Spending* (National Statistics, 2005).

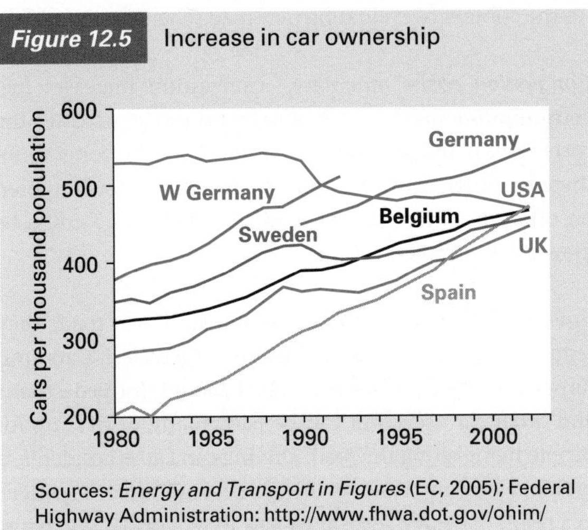

Figure 12.5 Increase in car ownership

Sources: *Energy and Transport in Figures* (EC, 2005); Federal Highway Administration: http://www.fhwa.dot.gov/ohim/qfvehicles.htm.

KI 9 p58

Price of substitutes. If bus and train fares came down, people might switch from travelling by car. The cross-price elasticity, however, is likely to be relatively low, given that most people regard these alternatives as a poor substitute for travelling in their own car. Cars are seen as more comfortable and convenient.

The 'price' of substitutes also includes the time taken to travel by these alternatives. The quicker a train journey is compared with a car journey, the lower will be its time cost to the traveller and thus the more people will switch from car to rail.

Price of complements. Demand for road space will depend on the price of cars. The higher the price of cars, the fewer people will own cars and thus the fewer cars there will be on the road.

? *Is the cross-price elasticity of demand for road space with respect to the price of cars likely to be high or low?*

Demand will also depend on the price of complementary services, such as parking. A rise in car parking charges will reduce the demand for car journeys. But here again the cross elasticity is likely to be relatively low. In most cases, the motorist will either pay the higher charge or park elsewhere, such as in side streets.

? *Go through each of the determinants we have identified so far and show how the respective elasticity of demand makes the problem of traffic congestion difficult to tackle.*

Tastes/utility. Another factor explaining the preference of many people for travelling by car is the pleasure they gain from it compared with alternative modes of transport. Car ownership is regarded by many people as highly desirable, and once accustomed to travelling in their own car, most people are highly reluctant to give it up.

One important feature of the demand for road space is that it fluctuates. There will be periods of peak demand, such as during the rush hour or at holiday weekends. At such times, roads can get totally jammed. At other times, however, the same roads may be virtually empty.

Supply of road space

The supply of road space can be examined in two contexts: the short run and the long run.

The short run. In the short run, as we have seen, the supply of road space is constant. When there is no congestion, supply is more than enough to satisfy demand. There is spare road capacity. At times of congestion, there is pressure on this fixed supply. Maximum supply for any given road is reached at the point where there is the maximum flow of vehicles per minute along the road.

The long run. In the long run, the authorities can build new roads or improve existing ones. This will require an assessment of the costs and benefits of such schemes.

Identifying a socially efficient level of road usage (short run)

The existing system of *government* provision of roads and *private* ownership of cars is unlikely to lead to an optimum allocation of road space. So how do we set about identifying just what the social optimum is?

In the short run, the supply of road space is fixed. The question of the short-run optimum allocation of road space, therefore, is one of the optimum *usage* of existing road space. It is a question of *consumption* rather than supply. For this reason we must focus on the road user, rather than on road provision.

A socially efficient level of consumption occurs where the marginal social benefit of consumption equals its marginal social cost ($MSB = MSC$). So what are the marginal social benefits and costs of using a car?

Marginal social benefit of road usage

Marginal social benefit equals marginal private benefit plus externalities. Marginal private benefit is the direct benefit to the car user and is reflected in the demand for car journeys, the determinants of which we examined above. External benefits are few. The one major exception occurs when drivers give lifts to other people.

Marginal social cost of road usage

Marginal social cost equals marginal private cost plus externalities. Marginal private costs to the motorist include the costs of petrol, wear and tear, tolls, etc. They also include the time costs of travel. There may also be substantial external costs. These include the following.

KI 28 p300

Congestion costs: time. When a person uses a car on a congested road, it will add to the congestion. This will therefore slow down the traffic even more and increase the journey time of other car users.

This is illustrated in Table 12.4 (which uses imaginary figures). Column (1) shows the number of cars travelling along a given road per minute. Column (2) shows the time taken for each car and thus can be seen as the marginal time cost to a motorist of making this journey. It is thus the *private* marginal time cost. With up to 3 cars per minute there is no congestion and therefore the traffic flows freely, each car taking 5 minutes to complete the journey. As traffic increases beyond this, however, the road becomes progressively more congested, and thus journey times increase. It is not just the additional cars that are forced to travel more slowly, but *all* the cars on the road. The extra cars thus impose a congestion cost on existing users of the road. By the time 7 cars per minute are entering the road, journey time has increased to 16 minutes.

Column (3) shows the sum of the journey times of all the motorists on the road. For example, with 6 cars on the road, each taking 11 minutes, total journey time for all six is 66 minutes. Column (4) shows the increase in total journey time as one more car enters the road. Thus when the seventh car enters the road, total journey time increases from 66 to 112 minutes: an increase of 46 minutes. This is the additional cost to *all* road users: in other words, the marginal *social* cost. But of these 46 minutes, 16 are the private marginal costs incurred by the extra motorist. Only the remaining 30 minutes are *external* costs imposed on other road users. These external costs are shown in column (5).

? *Complete Table 12.4 up to 9 cars per minute, assuming that the journey time increases to 24 minutes for the eighth car and 35 minutes for the ninth car.*

Time costs can be converted into money costs if we know the value of people's time. If time were valued at 10p per minute, the congestion costs (external costs) imposed by the seventh car would be £3 (i.e. 30 minutes × 10p per minute). Web Case 12.4 on the book's website examines the method used in the UK for estimating the value of time (in the context of evaluating new road schemes).

Congestion costs: monetary. Congestion increases fuel consumption, and the stopping and starting increases the costs of wear and tear. When a motorist adds to congestion, therefore, there will be additional monetary costs imposed on other motorists. A table similar to Table 12.3 could be drawn to illustrate this.

Environmental costs. When motorists use a road, they reduce the quality of the environment for others. Cars emit fumes and create noise. This is bad enough for pedestrians and other car users, but can be particularly distressing for people living along the road. Driving can cause accidents, a problem that increases as drivers become more impatient as a result of delays. Also, as we saw in section 12.1, exhaust gases contribute to global warming and acid rain.

Table 12.4 Time taken to travel between two points along a given road

Traffic density (cars entering road per minute) (1)	Journey time per car (marginal private time cost: in minutes) (2)	Total journey time for all cars (total time cost: in minutes) (3) = (1) × (2)	Extra total journey time as traffic increases by one more car (marginal social time cost: in minutes) (4) = Δ(3)	Additional time cost imposed on other road users by one more car (marginal external time cost: in minutes) (5) = (4) − (2)
1	5	5	5	0
2	5	10	5	0
3	5	15	5	0
4	6	24	9	3
5	8	40	16	8
6	11	66	26	15
7	16	112	46	30

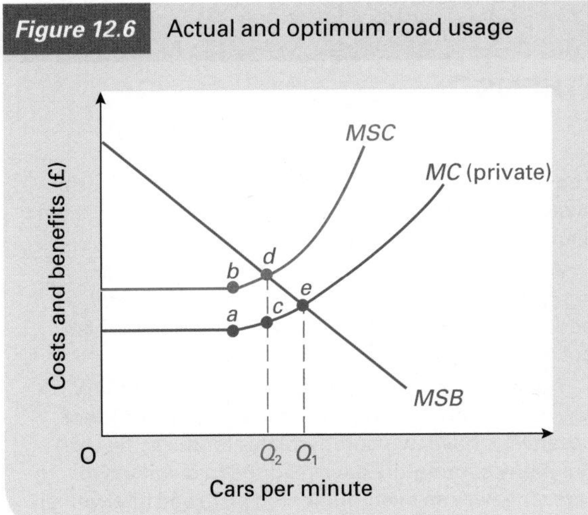

Figure 12.6 Actual and optimum road usage

The socially efficient level of road usage

KI 25 p293

The point where the marginal social benefit of car use is equal to the marginal social cost can be illustrated on a diagram. In Figure 12.6, costs and benefits are shown on the vertical axis and are measured in money terms. Thus any non-monetary costs or benefits (such as time costs) must be given a monetary value. The horizontal axis measures road usage in terms of cars per minute passing a specified point on the road.

For simplicity it is assumed that there are no external benefits from car use and that therefore marginal private and marginal social benefits are the same. The *MSB* curve is shown as downward sloping. The reason for this is that different road users put a different value on this particular journey. If the marginal (private) cost of making the journey were high, only those for whom the journey had a high marginal benefit would travel along the road. If the marginal cost of making the journey fell, more people would make the journey: people choosing to make the journey at the point at which the marginal cost of using their car had fallen to the level of their marginal benefit. Thus the greater the number of cars in any given time period, the lower the marginal benefit.

The marginal (private) cost curve (*MC*) is likely to be constant up to the level of traffic flow at which congestion begins to occur. This is shown as point *a* in Figure 12.6. Beyond this point, marginal cost is likely to rise as time costs increase and as fuel consumption rises.

KI 28 p300

The marginal *social* cost curve (*MSC*) is drawn above the marginal private cost curve. The vertical difference between the two represents the external costs. Up to point *b*, external costs are simply the environmental costs. Beyond point *b*, there are also external congestion costs, since additional road users slow down the journey of *other* road users. These external costs get progressively greater as the volume of traffic increases (as column (5) of Table 12.4 illustrated).

The actual level of traffic flow will be at Q_1, where marginal private costs and benefits are equal (point *e*). The socially efficient level of traffic flow, however, will be at the lower level of Q_2, where marginal social costs and benefits are equal (point *d*). In other words, the existing system of allocating road space is likely to lead to an excessive level of road usage.

Identifying a socially optimum level of road space (long run)

In the long run, the supply of road space is not fixed. The authorities must therefore assess what new road schemes (if any) to adopt. This will involve the use of some form of *cost–benefit analysis* (see section 11.4).

KI 25 p293

The socially efficient level of construction will be where the marginal social benefit from construction is equal to the marginal social cost. This means that schemes should be adopted as long as their marginal social benefit exceeds their marginal social cost.

But how are these costs and benefits assessed in practice? Web Case 12.4 on the book's website examines the procedure used in the UK.

We now turn to look at different solutions to traffic congestion. These can be grouped into three broad types.

Solution 1: direct provision (supply-side solutions)

The road solution

One obvious solution to traffic congestion is to build more roads. There are serious problems, however, with this approach.

The objective of equity. The first problem concerns *equity*. After all, social efficiency is not the only possible economic objective. For example, when an urban motorway is built, those living beside it will suffer from noise and fumes. Motorway users gain, but the local residents lose. The question is whether this is fair.

The more the government tries to appeal to the car user by building more and better roads, the fewer will be the people who use public transport, and thus the more will public transport decline. Those without cars lose, and these tend to be from the most vulnerable groups – the poor, the elderly, children and the disabled.

Building more roads may lead to a *potential* Pareto improvement: in other words, if the gainers had fully to compensate the losers (e.g. through taxes or tolls), they would still have a net gain. The problem is that such compensation is rarely if ever paid. There is thus no actual Pareto improvement.

Congestion may not be solved. Increasing the amount of road space may encourage more people to use cars.

A good example is the London orbital motorway, the M25. In planning the motorway, not only did the government underestimate the general rate of traffic growth, but

CASE STUDIES AND APPLICATIONS — BOX 12.3

RESTRICTING CAR ACCESS TO ATHENS

A solution to local atmospheric pollution?

Athens lies in a bowl-shaped valley. When there are light winds, a humid atmosphere and sunshine, the levels of atmospheric pollution can soar to dangerous heights. The major cause of this chemical smog (the '*néfos*') is the emission of exhaust fumes.

The solution that the Greeks have adopted is one of restricting the use of vehicles in the city. The restrictions are of two levels of severity. The more severe ones apply on Mondays to Fridays when there is a chemical smog emergency, typically two or three times a month; the less severe ones apply on all other Mondays to Fridays.

The city is divided into an inner zone and an outer zone. The levels of various pollutants (such as nitrogen dioxide and ozone) are constantly monitored by the city authorities, and when they reach certain critical levels a smog emergency is declared on radio, on television and in the press.

During an emergency, all cars and half the taxis are banned from use in the inner zone. On even-numbered dates, only taxis with an even-numbered registration can operate in the inner zone; on odd-numbered dates, only those with an odd-numbered registration can operate. In the outer zone, all taxis can operate, with the odd/even number plate system applying to cars.

The police check on cars entering the zones and turn away those not allowed. The drivers of cars being used illegally in the zones are fined.

When an emergency is not in force, restrictions apply only to the inner zone. The even-numbered/odd-numbered registration restrictions apply to cars, but not to taxis.

The measures are successful in one respect: very few cars are driven illegally in the zones (and it is not possible to have two numberplates for the same car!). But many commuters have resorted to owning two cars: one with an even-numbered plate and one with an odd-numbered one. The authorities even help in this by allowing people to request an even- or odd-numbered registration!

? ***Compare the relative advantages and disadvantages of these measures with those of charging people to come into the zones.***

In recent years, stimulated by hosting the Olympics in 2004, public transport has improved, with a large expansion of the metro system. Only with a more integrated transport system and tougher controls on emissions can Athens' serious pollution be significantly reduced.

it also underestimated the direct effect it would have on encouraging people to use the motorway rather than some alternative route, or some alternative means of transport, or even not to make the journey at all. It also underestimated the effect it would have on encouraging people to live further from their place of work and to commute along the motorway. The result is that there is now serious congestion on the motorway.

Thus new roads may simply generate extra traffic, with little overall effect on congestion.

The environmental impact of new roads. New roads lead to the loss of agricultural land, the destruction of many natural habitats, noise, the splitting of communities and disruption to local residents. To the extent that they encourage a growth in traffic, they add to atmospheric pollution and a depletion of oil reserves. It is thus important to take account of these costs when assessing new road schemes. The problem, however, is that these environmental costs are frequently ignored, or only considered as an afterthought and not taken seriously. Part of the problem is that they are difficult to assess, and part is that there is often a strong road lobby which persuades politicians to ignore or play down environmental considerations.

Government or local authority provision of public transport

An alternative supply-side solution is to increase the provision of public transport. If, for example, a local authority ran a local bus service and decided to invest in additional buses, open up new routes and operate a low fare policy, these services might encourage people to switch from using their cars.

To be effective, this would have to be an attractive alternative. Many people would switch only if the buses were frequent, cheap, comfortable and reliable, and if there were enough routes to take people close to where they wanted to go.

? *What other types of transport could be directly provided by the government or a local authority?*

A policy that has proved popular with many local authorities is to adopt park-and-ride schemes. Here the authority provides free or cheap out-of-town parking and cheap bus services from the car park to the town centre.

Solution 2: regulation and legislation

An alternative strategy is to restrict car use by various forms of regulation and legislation.

Restricting car access

One approach involves reducing car access to areas that are subject to high levels of congestion. The following measures are widely used: bus and cycle lanes, 'high occupancy vehicle lanes' (confined to cars with two or more occupants), pedestrian-only areas and no entry to side streets from main roads.

There is a serious problem, however, with these measures. They tend not to solve the problem of congestion, but merely to divert it. Bus lanes tend to make the car lanes more congested; no entry to side streets tends to make the main roads more congested; and pedestrian-only areas often make the roads round these areas more congested.

Parking restrictions

An alternative to restricting road access is to restrict parking. If cars are not allowed to park along congested streets, this will improve the traffic flow. Also, if parking is difficult, this will discourage people from using their cars to come into city centres.

Apart from being unpopular with people who want to park, there are some serious drawbacks with parking restrictions:

- People may well 'park in orbit', driving round and round looking for a parking space, and in the meantime adding to congestion.
- People may park illegally. This may add to rather than reduce congestion, and may create a safety hazard.
- People may feel forced to park down side streets in residential areas, thereby causing a nuisance for residents.

Solution 3: changing market signals

The solution favoured by many economists is to use the price mechanism. As we have seen, one of the causes of traffic congestion is that road users do not pay the full marginal social costs of using the roads. If they could be forced to do so, a social optimum usage of road space could be achieved.

In Figure 12.6 (page 343) this would involve imposing a charge on motorists of d–c. By 'internalising' the congestion and environmental externalities in this way, traffic flow will be reduced to the social optimum of Q_2.

So how can these external costs be charged to the motorist? There are several possible ways.

Extending existing taxes

Three major types of tax are levied on the motorist: fuel tax, taxes on new cars and car licences. Could increasing these taxes lead to the optimum level of road use being achieved?

Increasing the rates of new car tax and car licences may have *some* effect on reducing the total level of car ownership, but will probably have little effect on car use. The problem is that these taxes do not increase the *marginal* cost of car use. They are fixed costs. Once you have paid these taxes, there is no extra to pay for each extra journey you make. They do not discourage you from using your car.

Unlike the other two, fuel taxes are a marginal cost of car use. The more you use your car, the more fuel you use and the more fuel tax you pay. They are also mildly related to the level of congestion, since fuel consumption tends to increase as congestion increases. Nevertheless, they are not ideal. The problem is that *all* motorists would pay an increase in fuel tax, even those travelling on uncongested roads. To have a significant effect on congestion, there would have to be a very large increase in fuel taxes and this would be very unfair on those who are not causing congestion, especially those who have to travel long distances. Also, as the fuel protests in recent years have shown, increasing fuel taxes could make the government very unpopular.

Would a tax on car tyres be a good way of restricting car usage?

Introducing new taxes

An alternative to extending existing taxes is to introduce new ones. One that has received much attention in recent times has been the taxing of car parking spaces, particularly those provided by businesses for their employees. The problem with taxing car parking, however, is similar to that of restricting car parking places: people may simply try to park on neighbouring streets, and may spend longer driving around trying to find a space (thereby adding to congestion in the process).

Road pricing

Taxes are inevitably an indirect means of tackling congestion. Charging people for using roads, on the other hand, where the size of the charge reflects the marginal social cost, is a direct means of achieving an efficient use of road space. The higher the congestion, the higher should be the charge. This would encourage people not only to look for alternative means of transport, but also to travel, wherever possible, at off-peak times. TC 3 p21

Variable tolls. Tolls are used in many countries, and could be adapted to reflect marginal social costs.

One obvious problem, however, is that, even with automatic tolls, there can be considerable tail-backs from the booths at peak times. Another problem is that they may simply encourage people to use minor roads into cities, thereby causing congestion on these roads. Cities have networks of streets and thus in most cases it is not difficult to avoid the tolls. Finally, if the tolls are charged to people *entering* the city, they will not affect *local* commuters. But it is these short-distance commuters *within* the city who are most likely to be able to find some alternative means of transport (including walking!), and who thus could make a substantial contribution to reducing congestion.

CASE STUDIES AND APPLICATIONS — BOX 12.4

ROAD PRICING IN SINGAPORE

Part of an integrated transport policy

It takes only one hour to drive from one end of Singapore to the other. Yet the average Singaporean driver travels an estimated 18 600 km per year, more than the average US driver, and over 50 per cent more than the average Japanese driver. But despite very high levels of traffic density, Singapore suffers much less than many of its neighbours from traffic congestion. Part of the reason is that it has an integrated transport policy. This includes the following:

- Restricting the number of new car licences, and allowing their price to rise to the corresponding equilibrium. This makes cars in Singapore among the most expensive in the world.
- A 111-kilometre long mass rail transit (MRT) system with subsidised fares. Trains are comfortable, clean and frequent. Stations are air-conditioned.
- A programme of building new estates near MRT stations.
- Cheap, frequent buses, serving all parts of the island.
- A modest expansion of expressways.

But it is in respect to road usage that the Singaporean authorities have been most innovative.

The first innovation came in 1975. The city centre was made a restricted zone. Motorists who wished to enter this zone had to buy a ticket (an 'area licence') at any one of 33 entry points. Police were stationed at these entry points to check that cars had paid and displayed.

Then in 1990 a quota system for new cars was established. The government decides the total number of cars that the country should have, and issues just enough licences each month to maintain that total. These licences (or 'Certificates of Entitlement') are for 10 years and are offered at auction. Their market price varies from around £10 000 to £30 000.

A problem with the licences is that they are a once-and-for-all payment, which does not vary with the amount that people use their car. In other words, their marginal cost (for additional miles driven) is zero. Many people feel that, having paid such a high price for their licence, they ought to use their car as much as possible in order to get value for money!

With traffic congestion steadily worsening, it was recognised that something more had to be done. Either the Area Licensing Scheme had to be widened, or some other form of charging had to be adopted. The decision was taken to introduce electronic road pricing (ERP). This alternative would not only save on police labour costs, but enable charge rates to be varied according to levels of congestion, times of the day, and locality.

Since 1998 all vehicles in Singapore have been fitted with an in-vehicle unit (IU). Every journey made requires the driver to insert a smart card containing pre-paid units into the IU. On specified roads, overhead gantries read the IU and deduct the appropriate charge from the card. If a car does not have sufficient funds on its smart card, the car's details are relayed to a control centre and a fine is imposed. The system has the benefit of operating on three-lane highways and does not require traffic to slow down.

The ERP system operates on Mondays to Fridays from 7.30 a.m. to 7.00 p.m. in the central area and from 7.30 to 9.30 a.m. on the expressways and outer ring roads. Charges vary every 5, 20 or 30 minutes within these times. Rates are published in advance but are reviewed every three months. The system is thus very flexible to allow traffic to be kept at the desired level.

The system was expensive to set up, however. Cheaper schemes have been adopted elsewhere, such as Norway and parts of the USA. These operate by funnelling traffic into a single lane in order to register the car, but they have the disadvantage of slowing the traffic down.

One message is clear from the Singapore solution. Road pricing alone is not enough. Unless there are fast, comfortable and affordable public transport alternatives, the demand for cars will be highly price inelastic. People have to get to work!

Explain how, by varying the charge debited from the smart card according to the time of day or level of congestion, a socially optimal level of road use can be achieved.

Area charges. One simple and practical means of charging people to use congested streets is the area charge. People would have to pay (normally by the day) for using their car in a city centre. Earlier versions of this scheme involved people having to purchase and display a ticket on their car, rather like a 'pay-and-display' parking system.

More recently, electronic versions have been developed. The London Congestion Charge is an example. Car drivers must pay £8 per day to enter the inner London area (or 'congestion zone') any time between 7.00 and 18.30, Monday to Friday. Payment can be made by various means, including post, Internet, telephone, mobile phone SMS text message and at various shops and petrol stations. Payment can be in advance or up to 22.00 on the day of travel, or up to midnight for an extra £2. Cars entering the congestion zone have their number plate recorded by camera and a computer check then leads to a fine of £100 being sent to those who have not paid.

The London congestion charging system has reduced traffic in the zone by nearly 20 per cent and has significantly increased the rate of traffic flow. The charge is not a marginal one, however, in the sense that it does not vary with the degree of congestion or the amount of time spent or distance travelled by a motorist within the zone. This is an intrinsic problem of area charges. Nevertheless, their simplicity makes the system easy to understand and relatively cheap to operate.

Variable electronic road pricing. The scheme most favoured by many economists and traffic planners is that of variable electronic road pricing. It is the scheme that can most directly relate the price that the motorist is charged to the specific level of marginal social cost. The greater the congestion, the greater the charge imposed on the motorist. Ideally, the charge would be equal to the marginal congestion cost plus any marginal environmental costs additional to those created on non-charged roads.

Various systems have been adopted in various parts of the world, or are under consideration. One involves devices in the road which record the number plates of cars as they pass. Alternatively, cars must be fitted with sensors. A charge is registered to that car on a central computer. The car owner then receives a bill at periodic intervals, in much the same way as a telephone bill. Several cities around the world are already operating such schemes, including Barcelona, Dallas, Orlando, Lisbon, Oklahoma City and Oslo.

Another system involves having a device installed in the car into which a 'smart card' (like a telephone or photocopying card) is inserted. The cards have to be purchased and contain a certain number of units. Beacons or overhead gantries automatically deduct units from the smart cards at times of congestion. If the card is empty, the number of the car is recorded and the driver fined. Such a system was introduced in 1997 on Stockholm's ring road, and in 1998 in Singapore (see Box 12.4).

With both these types, the rate can easily be varied electronically according to the level of congestion (and pollution too). The rates could be in bands and the current bands displayed by the roadside and/or broadcast on local radio so that motorists knew what they were being charged.

The most sophisticated scheme, still under development, involves equipping all vehicles with a receiver. Their position is located by satellites, which then send this information to a dashboard unit, which deducts charges according to location, distance travelled, time of day and type of vehicle. The charges can operate through either smart cards or central computerised billing. It is likely that such schemes would initially be confined to lorries.

Despite the enthusiasm for such schemes amongst economists, there are nevertheless various problems associated with them:

- Estimates of the level of external costs are difficult to make.
- Motorists will have to be informed *in advance* what the charges will be, so that they can plan the timing of their journeys.
- There may be political resistance. Politicians may therefore be reluctant to introduce road pricing for fear of losing popular support.
- If demand is relatively inelastic, the charges might have to be very high to have a significant effect on congestion.
- The costs of installing road-pricing equipment could be very high.
- A new industry in electronic evasion may spring up!

Subsidising alternative means of transport

An alternative to charging for the use of cars is to subsidise the price of alternatives, such as buses and trains. But cheaper fares alone may not be enough. The government may also have to invest directly in or subsidise an *improved* public transport service: more frequent services, more routes, more comfortable buses and trains.

Subsidising public transport need not be seen as an alternative to road pricing: it can be seen as complementary. If road pricing is to persuade people not to travel by car, the alternatives must be attractive. Unless public transport is seen by the traveller as a close substitute for cars, the elasticity of demand for car use is likely to remain low. This problem is recognised by the UK government, which in the 2000 Transport Act encourages local authorities to use various forms of road pricing and charges on businesses for employee car parking spaces (the Workplace Parking Levy) on condition that the revenues generated are ploughed back into improved public transport. All local authorities have had to produce five-year Local Transport Plans covering all forms of transport. These include targets for traffic reduction and increases in the use of public transport.

Subsidising public transport can also be justified on grounds of equity. It benefits poorer members of society who cannot afford to travel by car.

Which is preferable: general subsidies for public transport, or cheap fare policies for specific groups (such as children, students and pensioners)?

Conclusions

It is unlikely that any one policy can provide the complete solution. Certain policies or mixes of policies are better suited to some situations than others. It is important for governments to learn from experiences both within their own country and in others, in order to find the optimum solution to each specific problem.

Section summary

1. Increased car ownership and car usage have led to a growing problem of traffic congestion.
2. The allocation of road space depends on demand and supply. Demand depends on the price to motorists of using their cars, incomes, the cost of alternative means of transport, the price of cars and complementary services (such as parking), and the comfort and convenience of car transport. The price and cross-price elasticities of demand for car usage tend to be low: many people are unwilling to switch to alternative modes of transport. The income elasticity, on the other hand, is high. The demand for cars and car usage grows rapidly as incomes grow.
3. The short-run supply of road space is fixed. The long-run supply depends on government road construction programmes.
4. The existing system of government provision of roads and private ownership of cars is unlikely to lead to the optimum allocation of road space.
5. In the short run, with road space fixed, allocation depends on the private decisions of motorists. The problem is that motorists create two types of external cost: pollution costs and congestion costs. Thus $MSC > MC$. Because of these externalities, the actual use of road space (where $MB = MC$) is likely to be greater than the optimum (where $MSB = MSC$).
6. In the long run, the socially efficient amount of road space will be where $LRMSB = LRMSC$. New road schemes should be adopted as long as their $LRMSB > LRMSC$. Governments must therefore conduct some form of cost–benefit analysis in order to estimate these costs and benefits.
7. There are various types of solution to traffic congestion. These include direct provision by the government or local authorities (of additional road space or better public transport); regulation and legislation (such as restricting car access – by the use of bus and cycle lanes, no entry to side streets and pedestrian-only areas – and various forms of parking restrictions); changing market signals (by the use of taxes, by road pricing, and by subsidising alternative means of transport).
8. Problems associated with building additional roads include the decline of public transport, attracting additional traffic on to the roads and environmental costs.
9. The main problem with restricting car access is that it tends merely to divert congestion elsewhere. The main problem with parking restrictions is that they may actually increase congestion.
10. Increasing taxes is effective in reducing congestion only if it increases the *marginal* cost of motoring. Even when it does, as in the case of additional fuel tax, the additional cost is only indirectly related to congestion costs, since it applies to all motorists and not just those causing congestion.
11. Road pricing is the preferred solution of many economists. By the use of electronic devices, motorists can be charged whenever they add to congestion. This should encourage less essential road users to travel at off-peak times or to use alternative modes of transport, while those who gain a high utility from car transport can still use their cars, but at a price. Variable tolls and area charges are alternative forms of congestion pricing, but are generally less effective than the use of variable electronic road pricing.
12. If road pricing is to be effective, there must be attractive substitutes available. A comprehensive policy, therefore, should include subsidising efficient public transport. The revenues required for this could be obtained from road pricing.

12.3 COMPETITION POLICY

Competition, monopoly and the public interest

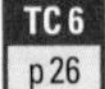
TC 6 p26

Most markets in the real world are imperfect, with firms having varying degrees of market power. But will this power be against the public interest? This question has been addressed by successive governments in framing legislation to deal with monopolies and oligopolies.

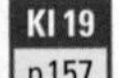
KI 19 p157

It might be thought that market power is always 'a bad thing', certainly as far as the consumer is concerned. After all, it enables firms to make supernormal profit, thereby 'exploiting' the consumer. The greater the firm's power, the higher will prices be relative to the costs of production. Also, a lack of competition removes the incentive to become more efficient.

But market power is not necessarily a bad thing. Firms may not fully exploit their position of power – perhaps for fear that very high profits would eventually lead to other firms overcoming entry barriers, or perhaps because they are not aggressive profit maximisers. Even if they do make large supernormal profits, they may still charge a lower price than more competitive sectors of the industry because of their economies of scale. Finally, they may use their profits for research and development and for capital investment. The consumer might then benefit from improved products at lower prices.

Competition policy could seek to ban various *structures*. For example, it could ban mergers leading to market share of more than a certain amount. Most countries, however, prefer to focus on whether the *practices* of particular monopolists or oligopolists are anti-competitive. Some of these practices may be made illegal, such as price fixing by oligopolists; others may be assessed on a case-by-case approach to determine whether or not they should be permitted. Such an approach does not presume that the mere *possession* of power is against the public interest, but rather that certain uses of that power may be.

 *Try to formulate a definition of 'the public interest'.*

The targets of competition policy

There are three possible targets of competition policy.

Abuse of the existing power of monopolies and oligopolies: monopoly policy

KI 19 p157

Monopoly policy seeks to prevent firms from abusing their economic power. Although it is referred to as 'monopoly' policy, it also applies to many larger oligopolists acting on their own. The approach has been to weigh up the gains and losses to the public of individual firms' behaviour.

As we saw in Figure 6.10 (on page 169), faced with the same cost curves as an industry under perfect competition, a monopoly will charge a higher price, produce a lower output and make a larger profit. On the other hand, a monopolist may achieve substantial economies of scale, with the result that its price is *below* the competitive price (see Figure 6.11 on page 170). It may also use a proportion of its profits for investment and for research and development (R&D). This may result in better products and/or lower prices.

Thus the government (or regulatory authority, if separate from the government) has to work out, if it insisted on a reduction in price, whether R&D and other investment would thereby suffer, and whether the consumer would lose in the long run.

The growth of power through mergers and acquisitions: merger policy

The aim of merger policy is to monitor mergers and prevent those that are considered to be against the public interest. The gains and losses to the public must be weighed up, and the authorities must then decide whether or not a prospective merger should be allowed to proceed.

On the plus side, the merged firms may be able to *rationalise*. Horizontal mergers particularly may allow economies of scale to be gained. Production may be able to be concentrated on fewer sites, with a more intensive utilisation of capital and labour. Also, a more efficient use may be made of transport fleets, with distribution in greater bulk. Savings may be made in warehousing costs too.

There may also be some scope for rationalisation with vertical mergers. Various stages in the production process may be able to be concentrated on one site, with consequent savings in transport and handling costs.

Then there are cost savings that apply to all types of merger: horizontal, vertical and conglomerate. One of the two head offices may be closed down. Greater financial strength may allow the merged firm to drive down the prices charged by its suppliers. The combined profits may allow larger-scale investment and R & D. Finally, if two relatively small firms merge, their increased market power may allow them to compete more effectively against large firms.

On the negative side, mergers lead to a greater concentration of economic power, which could be used against the consumer's interests. This is particularly true of horizontal mergers, which will result in fewer firms for the consumer to choose from. But even conglomerate mergers can lead to certain anti-competitive activities. In particular, a conglomerate can use large profits gained in one market where it already has monopoly power to ***cross-subsidise*** prices in a competitive market, thereby driving out competitors.

? *What are the possible disadvantages of* vertical *mergers?*

What is more, rationalisation may lead to redundancies. While this may be a potential Pareto gain, it is unlikely that the redundant will be fully compensated by the gainers.

In deciding how tough to be with mergers, the government must consider how this will affect firms' behaviour. If the government has a liberal policy towards mergers, the competition for ownership and control of other companies may force firms to be more efficient. If the managers of a firm are afraid that it will be taken over, they will need to ensure that the firm is economically strong and that it is perceived by shareholders to be more profitable than it would be under alternative ownership. This competition for corporate control (see page 171) may lead to lower costs and thereby benefit the consumer. It may, however, make firms even more keen to exploit any monopoly power they have, either in their battle for other firms, or in the battle to persuade shareholders not to vote for being taken over. TC 3 p21

Government policy towards this market for corporate control will need to ensure that mergers and the possibility of mergers encourage competition rather than reducing it.

Oligopolistic collusion: restrictive practice policy

In most countries, the approach towards cases of oligopolistic collusion, or ***restrictive practices*** as they are known, tends to be tougher. After all, the firms are combining to exploit their joint power to make bigger profits. They could do this by jointly trying to keep out new entrants; or they could agree to keep prices high and/or restrict output; or they could divide up the market between them, agreeing

Definitions

Cross-subsidise To use profits in one market to subsidise prices in another.

Restrictive practice Where two or more firms agree to adopt common practices to restrict competition.

not to 'poach' on each other's territory. For example, two or more supermarket chains could agree to open only one supermarket in each district.

Banning formal cartels is easy. Preventing tacit collusion is another matter. It may be very difficult to prove that firms are making informal agreements behind closed doors.

Competition policy in the European Union

EU legislation is contained in Articles 81 and 82 of the Amsterdam Treaty and in additional regulations covering mergers, which came into force in 1990 and were amended in 2004.

Article 81 is concerned with restrictive practices and Article 82 with the abuse of market power. The articles are largely confined to firms trading between EU members and thus do not cover monopolies or oligopolies operating solely within a member country. The policy is implemented by the European Commission. If any firm appears to be breaking the provisions of either article, the Commission can refer it to the European Court of Justice.

EU restrictive practices policy

Article 81 covers *agreements* between firms, *joint decisions*, and concerted *practices* that prevent, restrict or distort competition. In other words, it covers all types of oligopolistic collusion that are against the interests of consumers.

Article 81 is designed to prevent not oligopolistic *structures* (i.e. the simple existence of co-operation between firms), but rather collusive *behaviour*. No matter what form collusion takes, if the European Commission finds that firms are committing anti-competitive *practices*, they will be banned from doing so and possibly fined (up to 10 per cent of annual turnover), although firms do have the right of appeal to the European Court of Justice.

Practices considered anti-competitive include firms colluding to do any of the following:

- Fix prices (i.e. above competitive levels).
- Limit production, markets, technical development or investment.
- Share out markets or sources of supply.
- Charge discriminatory prices or operate discriminatory trading conditions, such as to benefit the colluding parties and disadvantage others.
- Make other firms that sign contracts with any of the colluding firms accept unfavourable obligations which, by their nature, have no connection with the subject of such contracts.

In recent years, the Commission has adopted a tough stance and has fined many firms.

EU monopoly policy

Article 82 relates to the abuse of market power and has also been extended to cover mergers. As with Article 81, it is the *behaviour* of firms that is the target of the legislation. The following are cited as examples of the abuse of market power. As you can see, they are very similar to those in Article 81.

- Charging unfairly high prices to consumers, or paying unfairly low prices to suppliers.
- Limiting production, markets or technical developments to the detriment of consumers.
- Using price discrimination or other discriminatory practices to the detriment of certain parties.
- Making other firms that sign contracts with it accept unfavourable obligations which, by their nature, have no connection with the subject of such contracts.

Under Article 82, such practices can be banned and firms can be fined where they are found to have abused a dominant position. A firm need not have some specified minimum market share before Article 82 can be invoked. Instead, if firms are able to conduct anti-competitive practices, it is simply assumed that they must be in a position of market power. This approach is sensible, given the difficulties of identifying the boundaries of a market, either in terms of geography or in terms of type of product.

EU merger policy

The 1990 merger control measures tightened up the legislation in Article 82. They cover mergers where combined worldwide annual sales exceed €5 billion; where EU sales of at least two of the companies exceed €250 million; and where at least one of the companies conducts no more than two-thirds of its EU-wide business in a single member state.

Relevant mergers must be notified to the Commission, which must then conduct preliminary investigations (Phase 1). A decision must then be made, normally within 25 working days, whether to conduct a formal investigation (Phase 2) or to let the merger proceed. A formal investigation must normally be completed within a further 90 working days (or 110 days in complex cases).

The process of EU merger control is thus very rapid and administratively inexpensive. The regulations are also potentially quite tough. Mergers are disallowed if they result in 'a concentration which would significantly impede effective competition, in particular by the creation or strengthening of a dominant position'.

But the regulations are also flexible, since they recognise that mergers *may* be in the interests of consumers if they result in cost reductions. In such cases they are permitted.

The merger investigation process is now overseen by a Chief Competition Economist and a panel to scrutinise the investigating team's conclusions. One concern of this panel is that the Commission, in being willing to show flexibility, is not too easily persuaded by firms and, as a result, imposes conditions that are too lax and that rely too much on the firms' co-operation. Indeed, in the first 15 years of the merger control measures, 2648 mergers were notified, but only 141 proceeded to Phase 2 and only

CASE STUDIES AND APPLICATIONS

BOX 12.5

TAKING YOUR VITAMINS – AT A PRICE

The global vitamin cartel

In a report on world-wide cartels published in 2000, the OECD found that:

> Actions against price fixing and other such 'hard core' cartels have halted billions of dollars in secret overcharges to individual consumers and business purchasers. The lesson of these successful cases is that such cartels are much more prevalent and harmful to the global economy than previously believed.[4]

The report cited the following cases:

- A global citric acid cartel, which raised prices by over 30 per cent and collected $1.5 billion in overcharges.
- A graphite electrode cartel, which raised prices by over 50 per cent and made monopoly profits from world-wide sales estimated at some $7 billion over a five-year period.
- A global lysine cartel, which doubled world prices. Over the time of the cartel $1.4 billion worth of sales were affected, leading to estimated overcharges of $140 million.

In the United States, it is estimated that recently exposed cartels have affected over $10 billion worth of commerce, with overcharges in the US market alone standing at $1 billion. Globally the impact would be many billions of dollars. It has also been estimated in the United States that the average gain from price fixing is about 10 per cent of the selling price. However, when taking into account the waste and inefficiency generated by such cartels, the cost to society may be as high as 20 per cent.

The case of vitamins

In November 2001, the EU announced that it would be imposing fines on companies colluding in a world-wide vitamin cartel. This cartel was shown to be one of the most sophisticated and well organised so far discovered. Mario Monti, the EU Competition Commissioner, referred to the cartel as the 'most damaging' the Commission had ever had to investigate. Not only was the cartel extensive, covering 12 different vitamins, but as Monti remarked:

> It is particularly unacceptable that this illegal behaviour concerned substances which are vital elements for nutrition and essential for normal growth and maintenance of life.[5]

Vitamins are added both to animal foodstuffs and human food products, such as cereals. They are used in cosmetics and form an important part of skin and health-care products. The Competition Commission estimated that in the EU, in 1998, the market covered by vitamin products was worth over €800 million.

The EU investigation revealed that a series of 12 global vitamin cartels had been established, the earliest in 1989, the most recent in 1993. Thirteen companies were involved in these cartels, but only Hoffman La-Roche, the world's largest vitamin producer, was present in all of them. BASF was present in 10 out of the 12. In each of the cartels, prices were fixed for different vitamin products; companies had allocated sales quotas; and they agreed upon and implemented price increases. In addition, they set up a system to monitor and enforce the agreements, which involved regular meetings between the cartel members. These meetings detailed the cartel's operations, which involved the exchange of sales values, volumes of sales and pricing information. As the EU report into the cartel remarks: 'The arrangements were part of a strategic plan conceived at the highest levels to control the world market in vitamins by illegal means.'[6]

Given the severity of the collusion and the long length of time over which the cartel had been operating, the EU imposed record fines on the cartel members, totalling €855.2 million. Because Swiss firm Hoffman La-Roche was not only present in all 12 cartels, but was also seen as one of the prime instigators of these cartels, it received the heaviest fine, totalling some €462 million. Such fines might have been far larger had not the conspirators aided the EU's investigation. As a result of doing so, they received a reduction in their fines of 50 per cent.

As well as facing financial penalties in the EU, the global vitamin cartel has been prosecuted in the United States, Canada and Australia. In the USA, fines have totalled over $1 billion, and two Hoffman La-Roche executives, as well as paying individual fines, have received prison sentences for their parts in the cartel's activities.

In the face of such abuses of market power, the OECD is attempting to toughen anti-competitive legislation in its members' countries. It is also, given the global scale of such cartels, seeking to co-ordinate the activities of different countries' investigations into such cartels. The problem is clearly a global one, which requires a global solution to be truly effective.

Why might global cartels be harder to identify and eradicate than cartels solely located within the domestic economy? What problems does this raise for competition policy?

[4] *Hard Core Cartels* (OECD, 2000).

[5] 'Commission imposes fines on vitamin cartels' (EU press release, 21/11/2001).

[6] Ibid.

19 were prohibited. In many cases (too many, claim critics), the Commission accepted the undertakings of firms.

There is considerable disagreement in the EU between those who want to encourage competition *within* the EU and those who want to see European companies being world leaders. For them, the ability to compete in *world* markets normally requires that companies are large, which may well imply having monopoly power within the EU.

To what extent is Article 82 consistent with both *these points of view?*

UK competition policy

There have been substantial changes to UK competition policy since the first legislation was introduced in 1948. The current approach is based on the 1998 Competition Act and the 2002 Enterprise Act.

The Competition Act brought UK policy in line with EU policy, detailed above. The Act has two key sets (or 'chapters') of prohibitions. Chapter I prohibits various restrictive practices, and mirrors Article 81. Chapter II prohibits various abuses of monopoly power, and mirrors Article 82. The Enterprise Act strengthened the Competition Act and introduced new measures for the control of mergers.

Under the two Acts, the body charged with ensuring that the prohibitions are carried out is the Office of Fair Trading (OFT). The OFT can investigate any firms suspected of engaging in one or more of the prohibited practices. Its officers have the power to enter and search premises, and can require the production and explanation of documents. Where the OFT decides that an infringement of one of the prohibitions has occurred, it can direct the offending firms to modify their behaviour or cease their practices altogether. Companies in breach of a prohibition are liable to fines of up to 10 per cent of their annual UK turnover. Third parties adversely affected by such breaches can seek compensation through the courts.

The Competition Act also set up a Competition Commission (CC) to which the OFT can refer cases for further investigation. The CC is charged with determining whether the structure of an industry or the practices of firms within it are detrimental to competition.

If a case is referred to the Competition Commission, it will carry out an investigation to establish whether competition is adversely affected. If it finds that it is, it will decide on the appropriate remedies, such as prohibiting various practices.

UK restrictive practices policy

Under the 2002 Enterprise Act, it is a *criminal* offence to engage in cartel agreements (i.e. horizontal, rather than vertical, collusive agreements between firms), irrespective of whether there are appreciable effects on competition. Convicted offenders may receive a prison sentence of up to five years and/or an unlimited fine. Prosecutions may be brought by the Serious Fraud Office or the OFT. Under the Act, the OFT can enter premises, seize documents and require people to answer questions or provide information.

But what practices constitute 'cartel agreements'? These involve one or more of the following agreements by firms: price fixing; limiting supply, perhaps by each firm agreeing to an output quota; sharing out markets by geographical area, type or size of customer or nature of outlet (e.g. bus companies agreeing not to run services in each other's areas); ***collusive tendering*** for a contract, where two or more firms put in a tender at secretly agreed (high) prices; or agreements between purchasers (e.g. supermarkets) to keep down prices paid to suppliers (e.g. farmers).

Are all such agreements necessarily against the interests of consumers?

In the case of other types of agreement, the OFT has the discretion to decide, on a case-by-case basis, whether or not competition is appreciably restricted, and whether, therefore, they should be terminated or the firms should be exempted. Such cases include the following:

- Vertical price-fixing agreements. These are price agreements between purchasing firms and their suppliers. An example of this is ***resale price maintenance***. This is where a manufacturer or distributor sets the price for retailers to charge. It may well distribute a price list to retailers (e.g. a car manufacturer may distribute a price list to car showrooms). Resale price maintenance is a way of preventing competition between retailers driving down retail prices and ultimately the price they pay to the manufacturer. Both manufacturers and retailers, therefore, are likely to gain from resale price maintenance.
- Agreements to exchange information that could have the effect of reducing competition. For example, if producers exchange information on their price intentions, it is a way of allowing price leadership, a form of tacit collusion, to continue.

?

What problems are likely to arise in identifying which firms' practices are anti-competitive? Should the OFT take firms' assurances into account when deciding whether to grant an exemption?

UK monopoly policy

Under the Chapter II prohibition of the 1998 Competition Act, it is illegal for a dominant firm to exercise its market power in such a way as to reduce competition. Any suspected

Definitions

Collusive tendering Where two or more firms secretly agree on the prices they will tender for a contract. These prices will be above those that would be put in under a genuinely competitive tendering process.

Resale (or retail) price maintenance Where the manufacturer of a product (legally) insists that the product should be sold at a specified retail price.

case is investigated by the OFT, which uses a two-stage process in deciding whether an abuse has taken place.

The first stage is to establish whether a firm has a position of dominance. The firm does not literally have to be a monopoly. Rather 'dominance' normally involves the firm having at least a 40 per cent share of the market (national or local, whichever is appropriate), although this figure will vary from industry to industry. Also, dominance depends on the barriers to entry to new competitors. The higher the barriers to the entry of new firms, the less contestable will be the market (see pages 172–4), and the more dominant a firm is likely to be for any given current market share.

If the firm *is* deemed to be dominant, the second stage involves the OFT deciding whether the firm's practices constitute an abuse of its position. As with restrictive practices, Chapter II follows EU legislation. It specifies the same four types of market abuse as does Article 82 (see above). Within these four categories, the OFT identifies the following practices as being overtly anti-competitive:

- Charging excessively high prices. These are prices above those that the firm would charge if it faced effective competition. One sign of excessively high prices is abnormally high rates of profit.
- Price discrimination. This is regarded as an abuse only to the extent that the higher prices are excessive or the lower prices are used to exclude competitors.
- Predatory pricing. This is where prices are set at loss-making levels, so as to drive competitors out of business (see page 201). The test is to look at the dominant firm's price in relation to its average costs. If its price is below average variable cost, predation would be assumed. If its price is above average variable cost, but below average total cost, then the Director-General would need to establish whether the reason was to eliminate a competitor.
- ***Vertical restraints.*** This is where a supplying firm imposes conditions on a purchasing firm (or vice versa). For example, a manufacturer may impose rules on retailers about displaying the product or the provision of after-sales service, or it may refuse to supply certain outlets (e.g. perfume manufacturers refusing to supply discount chains, such as Superdrug). Another example is ***tie-in sales***. This is where a firm controlling the supply of a first product insists that its customers buy a second product from it rather than from its rivals.

The simple *existence* of any of these practices may not constitute an abuse. The OFT has to decide whether their *effect* is to restrict competition. If the case is not straightforward, the OFT can refer it to the Competition Commission (CC). The CC will then carry out a detailed investigation to establish whether competition is restricted or distorted. If it is, the CC will rule what actions must be taken to remedy the situation.

Definitions

Vertical restraints Conditions imposed by one firm on another which is either its supplier or its customer.

Tie-in sales Where a firm is only prepared to sell a first product on the condition that its customers buy a second product from it.

UK merger policy

Merger policy is covered by the 2002 Enterprise Act. It seeks to prevent mergers that are likely to result in a substantial lessening of competition.

A merger or takeover will be investigated by the OFT if the target company has a turnover of £70 million or more, or if the merger results in the new company having a market share of 25 per cent or more. The OFT conducts a preliminary investigation to see whether competition is likely to be threatened. If it is, and if there are unlikely to be any substantial compensating benefit to consumers, the OFT refers the case to the Competition Commission.

If reference is made to the CC, it conducts a detailed investigation to establish whether the merger is likely to lead to a significant reduction in competition. If so, it can prohibit the merger. Alternatively, it can require the merged firm to behave in certain ways in order to protect consumers' interests. In such cases, the OFT then monitors the firm to ensure that it is abiding by the CC's conditions. CC investigations must normally be completed within 24 weeks.

The 2002 Act tightened up merger legislation. In the past, the vast majority of mergers were not referred to the CC (or its predecessor, the Monopolies and Mergers Commission). Yet studies had shown that mergers were generally *not* in the public interest. Mergers had contributed to a growing degree of market concentration in the UK and few benefits from cost reduction and research had occurred. The 2002 Act sought to rectify this problem.

If anti-monopoly legislation is effective enough, is there ever any need to prevent mergers from going ahead?

Assessment of competition policy

With UK competition legislation having been brought in line with EU legislation, it is possible to consider the two together.

It is generally agreed by commentators that the policy is correct to concentrate on anti-competitive *practices* and their *effects* rather than simply on the existence of agreements or on the size of a firm's market share. After all, economic power is a problem only when it is abused. When, by contrast, it enables firms to achieve economies of scale, or more finance for investment, the result can be of benefit to consumers. In other words, the assumption that structure determines conduct and performance (see page 158) is not necessarily true, and certainly it is not necessarily true that market power is always bad and competitive industries are always good.

CASE STUDIES AND APPLICATION

WHAT PRICE FOR PEACE OF MIND?

Exploiting monopoly power in the sale of extended warranties on electrical goods

If you go into Dixons, Comet, PC World or virtually any other High Street retailer to buy an electrical good, such as a DVD player, a fridge or PC, the sales assistant will probably be very keen to sell you an extended warranty (EW). These EWs are typically for three to five years and sometimes merely extend the product's guarantee against breakdown beyond its normal one- or two-year expiry date. Sometimes they go further and provide cover against other risks, such as accidental damage or theft.

There EWs are highly profitable for the retailer. In 2002 they accounted for approximately 40 per cent of Dixon's profits and 80 per cent of Comet's. It's hardly surprising that retailers are very keen to sell them to you!

In 2002 the Office of Fair Trading (OFT) published a report on EWs and concluded that 'there is insufficient competition and information to ensure that consumers get good value, and that many electrical retailers may make considerable profits on the sale of EWs'.

> Research conducted by the OFT indicates that customers can feel pressurised to rush to a decision to buy an extended warranty when they buy their new appliance. A high percentage of consumers had not thought about buying an extended warranty before they arrive at the store.
>
> Buyers should think whether extended warranties offer them value for money. OFT research found that the average washing machine repair costs between £45 to £65. So if a five-year extended warranty costs £150 on a £300 washing machine, it would need to break down four times for a consumer to benefit.
>
> A recent *Which?* report highlights that modern domestic appliances are generally reliable. It found that 81 per cent of washing machines didn't break down at all in the first six years.
>
> . . . Some sales staff are paid commission on each extended warranty they sell, so may be keen for a customer to sign on the dotted line.[7]

The OFT was concerned that retailers were using their market power at the point of sale and benefiting from consumers' ignorance. It decided, therefore, to refer the case to the Competition Commission (CC), which published its report in December 2003.

The CC report found that there was a 'complex monopoly'[8] in the market, worth £900 million per year, which was working against the public interest. It

Secondly, most commentators favour the system of certain practices being *prohibited*, with fines applicable to the first offence. This acts as an important deterrent to anti-competitive behaviour.

A problem with any policy to deal with collusion is the difficulty in rooting it out. When firms do all their deals 'behind closed doors' and are careful not to keep records or give clues, then collusion can be very hard to spot. The cases that have come to light, such as that of collusive tendering between firms supplying ready-mixed concrete, may be just the tip of an iceberg.

If two or more firms were charging similar prices, what types of evidence would you look for to prove that this was collusion rather than coincidence?

Section summary

1. Competition policy in most countries recognises that monopolies, mergers and restrictive practices can bring both costs and benefits to the consumer. Generally, though, restrictive practices tend to be more damaging to consumers' interests than simple monopoly power or mergers.
2. European Union legislation applies to firms trading between EU countries. Article 81 applies to restrictive practices. Article 82 applies to dominant firms. There are also separate merger control provisions.
3. UK legislation is covered largely by the 1998 Competition Act and 2002 Enterprise Act. The Chapter I prohibition of the 1998 Act applies to restrictive practices and is similar to Article 81. The Chapter II prohibition applies to dominant firms and is similar to Article 82. The 2002 Act made certain cartel agreements a criminal offence and required mergers over a certain size to be investigated by the Office of Fair Trading, with possible reference to the Competition Commission. Both the OFT and CC were made independent of government.
4. The focus of both EU and UK legislation is on anti-competitive practices rather than on the simple existence of agreements between firms or market dominance. Practices that are found after investigation to be detrimental to competition are prohibited and heavy fines can be imposed, even for a first offence.

BOX 12.6

concluded that there had been an abuse of monopoly power, stating that:

> Were this market fully competitive such that the top five EW retailers' returns were no greater than their cost of capital,[9] we estimate that EW prices would have been, on average, up to one-third lower.
>
> . . . Many of the practices that we have identified during the course of our investigation operate or may be expected to operate against the public interest. They result in lack of choice, excessive prices, insufficient information, insufficient competition at point of sale, limited but not insignificant sales pressure, some terms which could be disadvantageous, and lack of information about the scope of protection under service-backed schemes.[10]

Despite these findings, the Competition Commission did not recommend banning shops from bundling warranties with electrical goods at the point of sale, despite many of the EWs being 'unfair and uncompetitive'. Instead, it recommended that retailers should display prices for EWs alongside the price of the goods, both in shops and in advertisements. It also recommended that the shops should provide information about customers' rights and that customers should get a full refund on the EW if they cancelled within 45 days.

The government minister, the Secretary of State for Trade and Industry, Patricia Hewitt, accepted these findings and ruled that they should be implemented.

1. ***What features of the market for EWs distort competition?***
2. ***To what extent will the ruling by the government make the market for EWs competitive?***

[7] OFT News Release, PN 68/02, October 2002.

[8] A complex monopoly is where several companies separately (i.e. not collusively) are in a position to exploit a particular market advantage to the detriment of the consumer.

[9] A measure of 'normal profit'.

[10] Summary to *Extended Warranties on Domestic Electrical Goods: A Report on the Supply of Extended Warranties on Domestic Electrical Goods within the UK*, Competition Commission, Dec. 2003 (http://www.competition-commission.org.uk/rep_pub/reports/2003/485xwars.htm#summary).

12.4 PRIVATISATION AND REGULATION

Nationalisation and privatisation

One solution to market failure, advocated by some on the political left, is nationalisation. If industries are not being run in the public interest by the private sector, then bring them into public ownership. This way, so the argument goes, the market failures can be corrected. Problems of monopoly power, externalities, inequality, etc. can be dealt with directly if these industries are run with the public interest, rather than private gain, at heart.

Most nationalisation in the UK took place during the Labour government of 1945–51, when coal, railways, gas and steel were nationalised. The Labour Party at the time saw nationalisation not just as a means of correcting market failures, but as something that was morally desirable. It was seen to be much fairer and less divisive to have a society based on common ownership of the means of production than one where people were divided into separate classes: workers and capitalists.

From the early 1980s, however, the Conservative governments under Margaret Thatcher and John Major engaged in an extensive programme of 'privatisation', returning virtually all of the ***nationalised industries***, including telecommunications, gas, water, steel, electricity and the railways, to the private sector. By 1997, the year when the Conservatives left office, the only nationalised industry remaining in the UK was the Post Office.

Other countries have followed similar programmes of privatisation in what has become a worldwide phenomenon. Privatisation has been seen by many governments as a means of revitalising inefficient industries and as a golden opportunity to raise revenues to ease budgetary problems.

How desirable is privatisation?

Arguments for privatisation

Market forces. The first argument is that privatisation will expose these industries to market forces, from which will flow the benefits of greater efficiency, faster growth and greater responsiveness to the wishes of the consumer. There are three parts to this argument.

Definition

Nationalised industries State-owned industries that produce goods or services that are sold in the market.

- Greater competition in the goods market. If privatisation involves splitting an industry into competing parts (for example, separate power stations competing to sell electricity to different electricity distribution companies), the resulting competition may drive costs and prices down.
- Greater competition for finance. After privatisation a company has to finance investment through the market: it must issue shares or borrow from financial institutions. In doing so, it will be competing for funds with other companies, and thus must be seen as capable of using these funds profitably.
- Accountability to shareholders. Shareholders want a good return on their shares and will thus put pressure on the privatised company to perform well. If the company does not make sufficient profits, shareholders will sell their shares. The share price will fall and the company will be in danger of being taken over. The market for corporate control thus provides incentives for private firms to be efficient. There has been considerable takeover activity in the water and electricity industries, with most of the 12 regional electricity companies and several of the water companies being taken over, often by non-UK companies.

Reduced government interference. In nationalised industries, managers may frequently be required to adjust their targets for political reasons. At one time they may have to keep prices low as part of a government drive against inflation. At another they may have to raise their prices substantially in order to raise extra revenue for the government and help finance tax cuts. At another they may find their investment programmes cut as part of a government economy drive.

Privatisation frees the company from these constraints and allows it to make more rational economic decisions and plan future investments with greater certainty.

Financing tax cuts. The privatisation issue of shares directly earns money for the government and thus reduces the amount it needs to borrow. Effectively, then, the government can use the proceeds of privatisation to finance tax cuts.

There is a danger here, however, that in order to raise the maximum revenue the government will want to make the industries as potentially profitable as possible. This may involve selling them as monopolies. But this, of course, would probably be against the interests of the consumer.

Potential problems with privatisation

The markets in which privatised industries operate are unlikely to be perfect. What is more, the process of privatisation itself can create problems.

Natural monopolies. The market forces argument for privatisation largely breaks down if a public monopoly is simply replaced by a private monopoly, as in the case of the water companies. Critics of privatisation argue that at least a public-sector monopoly is not out to maximise profits and thereby exploit the consumer.

KI 19 p157

Some industries have such great economies of scale that there is only room for one firm in the industry. They are natural monopolies. The best examples of *natural monopolies* are the various grids that exist in the privatised utilities: the national electricity grid, the national gas pipe network, the network of railway lines. These grids account for a relatively high proportion of the total costs of these industries. The more intensively the electricity and gas grids are used, however, the lower their cost will become per unit of fuel supplied. Similarly with railways: the relatively high costs of providing track and signalling, etc. will become smaller per passenger, the more passengers use the railway.

In the short run, these costs are fixed. Average fixed costs must necessarily decline as more is produced: overheads are being spread over a greater output.

In the long run, when new (electricity, gas, railway) lines can be built, these costs become variable. It is still likely, however, that they will decline per unit of output, the higher the output becomes. A pylon carrying ten lines does not cost five times as much as one carrying two. This means that long-run average costs fall as more is produced.

In Figure 12.7, assume that the total industry output is Q_1. With just one company in the industry, long-run average cost is therefore $LRAC_1$. Now assume that the industry is split into two equal-sized companies, each with its own grid. If total output remains at Q_1, the two firms will produce Q_2 each at the higher long-run average cost of $LRAC_2$.

It is potentially more efficient therefore to have a single monopoly supplier whenever there is a natural monopoly. It avoids wasteful duplication.

The problem is that the monopoly producer in a free market could use its power to drive up prices. The long-run profit-maximising position is illustrated in Figure 12.8. The monopolist produces Q_m at a price P_m and at a cost of $LRAC_m$. There is a misallocation of resources.

Figure 12.7 Natural monopoly

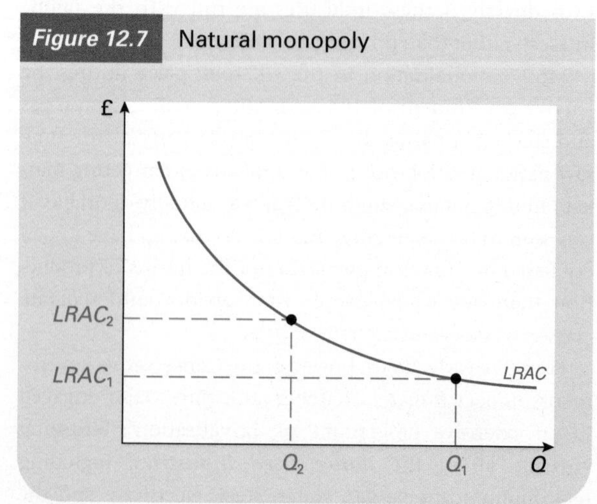

Figure 12.8 Profit maximising natural monopoly

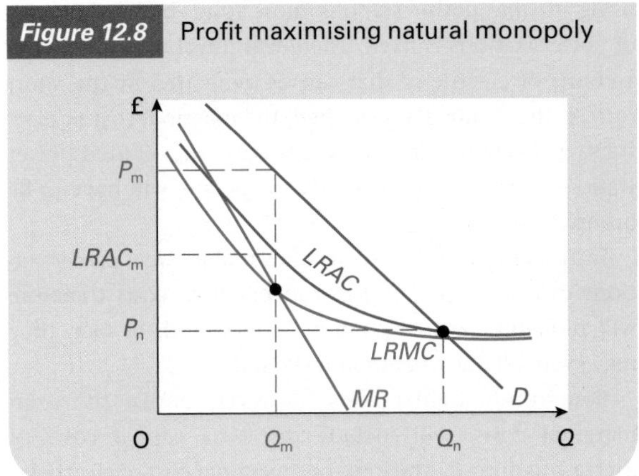

If, however, the industry remained nationalised, or if it was privatised but regulated, it could be run as a monopoly and thus achieve the full economies of scale. And yet it could be directed to set a price that just covered costs (including normal profits), and thus make no more profit than a highly competitive industry. In Figure 12.8, it would produce Q_n at a price of P_n. We examine regulation later in this section.

Planning and the co-ordination of industry. Road use and road construction affect the demand for railways and vice versa. Decisions in the coal, electricity, gas and oil industries (and to a large extent in the steel industry) all affect each other. If these industries were nationalised, it should make their decisions easier to co-ordinate in the public interest. It could help the sensible planning of the nation's infrastructure. If these industries were under private enterprise, however, either there would be little co-ordination, or alternatively co-ordination might degenerate into oligopolistic collusion, with the consumer losing out. In the extreme case, the same company may have a monopoly in more than one industry. For example, in some regions of the UK, one company runs both buses and trains.

KI 28 p300 *Problems of externalities and inequality.* Various industries may create substantial external benefits and yet may be privately unprofitable. A railway or an underground line, for example, may considerably ease congestion on the roads, thus benefiting road as well as rail users. Other industries may cause substantial external costs. Nuclear power stations may produce nuclear waste that is costly to dispose of safely, and/or provides hazards for future generations. Coal-fired power stations may pollute the atmosphere and cause acid rain.

For reasons of equity, it can be argued that various transport services should be subsidised in order to keep them going and/or to keep their prices down. For instance, it can be argued that rural bus services should be kept operating at subsidised prices and that certain needy people (e.g. pensioners) should be charged lower prices.

Will such externalities and issues of equity be ignored under privatisation? The advocates of privatisation argue that externalities are a relatively minor problem, and anyway can be dealt with by appropriate taxes, subsidies and regulations even if the industry is privatised. Likewise questions of fairness and social justice can be dealt with by subsidies or regulations. A loss-making bus service can be subsidised so that it can be run profitably by a private bus company.

Critics argue that only the most glaring examples of externalities and injustice can be taken into account, given that the whole ethos of a private company is different (KI 21 p207) from a nationalised one: private profit rather than public service is the goal. Externalities, they argue, are extremely widespread and need to be taken into account by the industry itself and not just by an occasionally intervening government.

In assessing these arguments, a lot depends on the toughness of government legislation and the attitudes and powers of regulatory agencies after privatisation.

To what extent can the problems with privatisation be seen as arguments in favour of nationalisation?

Regulation: identifying the short-run optimum price and output

Privatised industries, if left free to operate in the market, will have monopoly power; they will create externalities; and they will be unlikely to take into account questions of fairness. An answer to these problems is for the government or some independent agency to regulate their behaviour so that they produce at the socially optimum price and output.

Exactly what this optimum is depends on what problems need to be taken into account. Take three cases. In the first, the privatised industry is a monopoly (perhaps it is a natural monopoly), but there are no other problems. In the second case, there are also externalities to be considered, and in the third, questions of fairness too.

The privatised industry is a monopoly

The 'first-best' situation: $P = MC$. Assume that all other firms in the economy are operating under perfect competition, and thus producing where $P = MC$. This is the imaginary 'first-best' situation. If this were so, the privatised  company should be required to follow the same pricing rule: $P = MC$. As we saw in section 11.1, this will give the Pareto optimal output, where total consumer plus producer surplus is maximised (see page 293).

The theory of the 'second best': $P = MC + Z$. Now let us drop the assumption that the rest of the economy operates under perfect competition. If other industries on average are charging a price, say, 10 per cent above MC, then the theory of the second best suggests that the privatised company should also charge a price 10 per cent above *MC*. At least that way it will not cause a diversion of consumption away from relatively low-cost industries (at the margin) to a relatively high-cost one. The second-best rule is therefore to set $P = MC + Z$, where Z in this case is 10 per cent.

The privatised industry produces externalities

In the first-best situation the privatised industry should produce where price equals marginal *social* (not private) cost: $P = MSC$. The second-best solution is to produce where $P = MSC + Z$ (where Z is the average of other industries' price above their *MSC*).

The difficulty for the regulator in applying these rules in practice is to identify and measure the externalities: not an easy task! (See section 11.4.)

The behaviour of the privatised industry involves questions of fairness

If the government wishes the regulator to insist on a price below *MC* because it wishes to help certain groups (e.g. pensioners, children, rural dwellers, those below certain incomes), what should this price be?

In practice, one of two simple rules could be followed. Either the industry could be required to charge uniform prices, despite higher costs for supplying certain categories of people (this could apply, for example, to rural customers of a privatised postal service); or a simple formula could be used (e.g. half price for pensioners and children). These are often the only practical solutions given the impossibility of identifying the specific needs of individual consumers.

Two further questions arise:

- Should the lower price be subsidised by central or local *government*, or by the privatised company and hence by *other users* of the service (i.e. by them paying *higher* prices)? Justice would suggest that support should come from the community as a whole – the taxpayer – and not just from other users of the service.
- If people require help, should they not be given *general* tax relief or benefits, rather than specifically subsidised services? For example, should pensioners not be paid better pensions, rather than be charged reduced fares on buses?

1. *In the case of buses, subsidies are often paid by local authorities to support various loss-making routes. Is this the best way of supporting these services?*
2. *In the case of postal services, profitable parts of the service cross-subsidise the unprofitable parts. Should this continue if the industry is privatised?*

Regulation: identifying the long-run optimum price and output

In the short run, certain factors of production are fixed in supply. For example, electricity output can be increased by using *existing* power stations more fully, but the *number* of power stations is fixed. There will thus be a limit to the amount of electricity that can be generated in the short run. As that limit is approached, the marginal cost of electricity is likely to rise rapidly. For example, oil-fired power stations, which are more costly to operate, will have to be brought on line.

In the long run, all factors are variable. New power stations can be built. The *long*-run marginal costs therefore will probably not rise as more is produced. In fact, they may even fall due to economies of scale.

Long-run marginal costs, however, unlike short-run marginal costs, will include the extra capital costs of increasing output. The long-run marginal cost of electricity will thus be all the extra costs of producing one more unit: namely, the extra operating costs (fuel, labour, etc.) *plus* the extra capital costs (power stations, pylons, etc.).

The rule for the optimum long-run price and output is simple. The regulator should require the industry to produce where price equals *long-run* marginal social cost (*LRMSC*). This is illustrated in Figure 12.9.

In the short run, optimum price and output are P_S and Q_S: where $P =$ (short-run) *MSC*. This might mean that production is at quite a high cost: existing capital equipment is being stretched and diminishing returns have become serious.

In the long run, then, it will be desirable to increase capacity if $LRMSC < MSC$. Optimum long-run price and output are thus at P_L and Q_L: where $P = LRMSC$.

This is the rule for the first-best situation. In the second-best situation, the industry should produce where $P = LRMSC + Z$ (where Z is the average of other industries' price above their *LRMSC*).

?

If the regulator imposed such rules, would they cause the firm to make a loss if it faced a downward-sloping LRMSC curve? (Clues: Where would the LRAC curve be relative to the LRMC curve? What would be the effect of externalities and the addition of the Z factor on the price?)

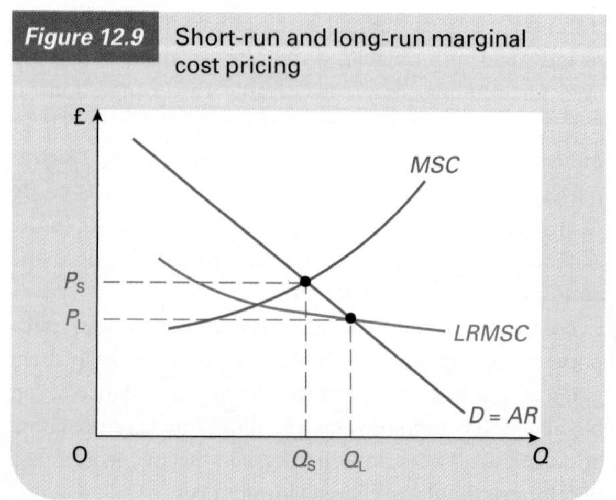

Figure 12.9 Short-run and long-run marginal cost pricing

Regulation in the UK

To some extent the behaviour of privatised industries may be governed by general monopoly and restrictive practice legislation. For example, in the UK, privatised firms can be investigated by the Office of Fair Trading and if necessary referred to the Competition Commission.

In addition to this, there is a separate regulatory office to oversee the structure and behaviour of each of the privatised utilities. These regulators are as follows: the Office for Gas and Electricity Markets (Ofgem), the Office of Communications (Ofcom) (for telecommunications and broadcasting), the Office of Rail Regulation (ORR) and the Office of Water Services (Ofwat). The regulators set terms under which the industries have to operate. For example, ORR sets the terms under which rail companies have access to the track and stations. The terms set by the regulator can be reviewed by negotiation between the regulator and the industry. If agreement cannot be reached, the Competition Commission acts as an appeal court and its decision is binding.

The regulator for each industry also sets limits to the prices that certain parts of the industry can charge (see Web Case 12.6). These parts are those where there is little or no competition: for example, the charges made to electricity and gas retailers by National Grid Transco, the owner of the electricity grid and major gas pipelines.

The price-setting formulae are essentially of the '*RPI* minus *X*' variety. What this means is that the industries can raise their prices by the rate of increase in the retail price index (*RPI*) (i.e. by the rate of inflation) *minus* a certain percentage (X) to take account of expected increases in efficiency. Thus if the rate of inflation were 6 per cent, and if the regulator considered that the industry (or firm) could be expected to reduce its costs by 2 per cent ($X = 2\%$), then price rises would be capped at 4 per cent. The $RPI - X$ system is thus an example of ***price-cap regulation***. The idea of this system of regulation is that it will force the industry to pass cost savings on to the consumer.

Whether this will result in marginal cost pricing depends on what the price was in the first place. If the price was equal to marginal cost, and if the X factor is the amount by which the regulator expects the *MC* curve to shift downwards (after taking inflation into account), then the formula could result in marginal cost pricing.

? *Why might it equally result in average cost pricing?*

Assessing the system of regulation in the UK

The system that has evolved in the UK has various advantages over that employed in the USA and elsewhere, where regulation often focuses on the level of profits (see Web Case 12.7):

- It is a *discretionary* system, with the regulator able to judge individual examples of the behaviour of the industry on their own merits. The regulator has a detailed knowledge of the industry which would not be available to government ministers or other bodies such as the Office of Fair Trading. The regulator could thus be argued to be the best person to decide on whether the industry is acting in the public interest.
- The system is *flexible*, since it allows for the licence and price formula to be changed as circumstances change.
- The '*RPI* minus *X*' formula provides an *incentive* for the privatised firms to be as efficient as possible. If they can lower their costs by more than X, they will, in theory, be able to make larger profits and keep them. If, on the other hand, they do not succeed in reducing costs sufficiently, they will make a loss. There is thus a continuing pressure on them to cut costs. (In the US system, where *profits* rather than *prices* are regulated, there is little incentive to increase efficiency, since any cost reductions must be passed on to the consumer in lower prices, and do not, therefore, result in higher profits.) TC 3 p21

There are, however, some inherent problems with the way in which regulation operates in the UK:

- The '*RPI* minus *X*' formula was designed to provide an incentive for the firms to cut costs. But if X is too low, the firm might make excessive profits. Frequently, regulators have underestimated the scope for cost reductions resulting from new technology and reorganisation, and have thus initially set X too low. As a result, instead of X remaining constant for five years, as intended, new higher values for X have been set after only one or two years. Alternatively, one-off price cuts have been ordered, as happened when the water companies were required by Ofwat to cut prices by an average of 10 per cent in 2000. In either case, this can then lead to the same problem as with the US system. The incentive for the industry to cut costs will be removed. What is the point of being more efficient if the regulator is merely going to take away the extra profits?
- Regulation is becoming increasingly complex. This makes it difficult for the industries to plan and may lead to a growth of 'short-termism'. One of the claimed advantages of privatisation was to give greater independence to the industries from short-term government interference and allow them to plan for the longer term. In practice, one type of interference may have been replaced by another.
- As regulation becomes more detailed and complex, and as the regulator becomes more and more involved in the detailed running of the industry, so managers and regulators will become increasingly involved in a game of strategy: each trying to outwit the other. Information

Definition

Price-cap regulation Where the regulator puts a ceiling on the amount by which a firm can raise its price.

CASE STUDIES AND APPLICATIONS

SELLING POWER TO THE PEOPLE

Attempts to introduce competition into the electricity industry

The electricity industry in England and Wales

Generation
Transmission
Distribution
Supply

Generation
NGC
Distributor
Supplier
Customer
Use-of-system charges
Payment for electricity
Wholesale electricity market
Retail electricity market

Source: R. Green, '*Electricity supply: reorganisation and privatisation*' (*The Economic Review*, March 1991).

Competition is generally seen as better than regulation as a means of protecting consumers' interests. The electricity industry provides a good case study of ways to introduce competition into a privatised industry.

The industry before privatisation

Under nationalisation, the industry in England and Wales was organised as a monopoly with the Central Electricity Generating Board (CEGB) supplying 99 per cent of all electricity. It operated the power stations and transmitted the electricity round the country via the national grid. However, the CEGB did not sell electricity directly to the consumer; rather it sold it to 12 regional boards, which in turn supplied it to the consumer.

Privatisation of the industry

Non-nuclear generation in England and Wales was privatised in 1990 as two companies: National Power (with just over 50 per cent of capacity) and PowerGen (with nearly 30 per cent). It was not until 1996, however, that nuclear power stations were privatised.

The 12 regional boards were privatised in 1991 as separate regional electricity companies (RECs), which were responsible for local distribution and supply to consumers. They would also be permitted to build their own power stations if they chose. The RECs jointly owned the national grid, but it was run independently. This was eventually sold as a separate company in 1996.

The diagram shows the structure of the industry. Electricity is produced by the *generators* (the power stations). The electricity is *transmitted* along the power lines of the National Grid Company plc (NGC) to different parts of the country. It is then transmitted locally by the *distributors* (the 12 distribution companies), which initially were also the *suppliers* of electricity to the customers (homes, local authorities and businesses).

An Office of Electricity Regulation (Offer) was set up to control prices in parts of the industry where there was no competition. This has been of the *RPI* – *X* variety (see page 359). For example, the charges paid by the generators and the suppliers to the transmission company are regulated. Offer was later merged with the gas regulator to become the Office of Gas and Electricity Markets (Ofgem).

It was hoped, however, that the new structure would allow a growth in competition, thereby making regulation increasingly unnecessary. So what was the nature of this competition? After all, National Power had over half of the generating capacity; the National Grid Company had a natural monopoly of electricity transmission; and the 12 RECs had a natural monopoly of distribution in each of their areas.

Competition was possible at two levels: at the *wholesale* level, with generators competing with each other to sell to suppliers; and at the *retail* level, with

BOX 12.7

suppliers competing to sell to customers. Let us examine each of these markets in turn.

Competition in the wholesale market for electricity: NETA and BETTA

Since 2001 in England and Wales electricity has been traded in the wholesale market under the New Electricity Trading Arrangements (NETA). In April 2005, this system was extended to Scotland and renamed the British Electricity Trading and Transmission Arrangements (BETTA). Participants in the market include generators, suppliers, large commercial consumers of electricity and traders (i.e. dealers).

In this market, bulk electricity is traded 'forward' in bilateral contracts between individual buyers and sellers. A forward contract means that a price is agreed today for an amount of electricity to be traded over a particular period in the future, which could be as soon as the next day or three or more years hence. The long forward contracts are to allow generators to plan to build extra capacity.

Of course, the future price will be based on anticipated demand, and demand in practice may not turn out as anticipated. To allow for this, NGC operates 'central balancing mechanisms'. This is a system of buying and selling additional electricity where necessary to ensure that demand actually balances supply second by second. It is also a system to sort out who owes what to whom when there is a surplus. In practice, only about 2 per cent of electricity has to be traded under the balancing mechanisms; the remainder is traded in the forward contracts.

With more than 200 participants in BETTA, the system is highly competitive. In the first few months of NETA's operation, wholesale prices fell by some 20–25 per cent.

Competition in the retail market for electricity

All customers, whether domestic or business, can choose their supplier, thereby putting suppliers into competition. This competition was introduced in stages, with larger consumers being the first to be able to 'shop around'. It was not until 1999, however, that the choice of their supplier was open to all customers.

But how are consumers able to choose? Suppliers purchase electricity through NETA. The local distribution company is then obliged to transmit this electricity on behalf of suppliers at the same (regulated) price that it charges itself as a supplier. Thus any supplier can use the same cables. There have been several new entrants into the supplier market, including various gas companies diversifying into electricity supply.

By 2001, 38 per cent of customers had switched suppliers at least once and the former regional monopoly suppliers now had only 70 per cent of the market. In the light of this, and the fact that switching was seen as easy by 80 per cent of customers, Ofgem announced that competition was sufficiently developed to allow all regulation of the retail market to be removed by April 2002. Indeed, by 2005, 51 per cent of customers had switched at least once and the former suppliers' market share had been reduced to 57 per cent.

Competition between suppliers is likely to go further still, thanks to the development of new technology. 'Smart meters' could eventually be installed in homes to allow customers automatically to switch between suppliers depending on which one was offering the lowest price! The meters would read price information that was transmitted down the electricity cable.

What of the future?

The electricity industry, like other privatised utilities, is complex. Parts are a natural monopoly, such as the national grid and distribution through local cables. Here regulation is essential. But other parts are potentially competitive, such as generation and supply. Is it right for these parts to be deregulated?

A danger for competition lies in mergers. These mergers may be horizontal. Generators could merge. So far, however, the number of generators has continued to increase, thanks partly to the regulator requiring National Power and PowerGen to sell power stations. Suppliers could merge. Indeed, it is predicted that, over the next few years, the number of suppliers could be reduced to four or five. Clearly, if the number of firms at any level of the industry is too low, there is a severe danger of collusion or a simple abuse of market power. Here the regulator would have to behave like the OFT and prevent anti-competitive behaviour.

Mergers could be vertical. Generators could merge with distributors or suppliers. In 1998, PowerGen acquired East Midlands Electricity, the third largest supplier. A similar threat comes from the fact that the new gas-fired power stations are mainly owned by the regional electricity companies, which might buy electricity from themselves at inflated prices, which are then passed on to their customers. The regulator warned that a vertically integrated industry would be much harder to control – if contracts between separate companies were replaced by internal arrangements within a single company.

Does vertical integration matter if consumers still have a choice of suppliers and if generators are still competing with each other?

will become distorted and time and energy will be wasted in playing this game of cat and mouse.

- Alternatively, there is the danger of ***regulatory capture***. As regulators become more and more involved in their industry and get to know the senior managers at a personal level, so they are increasingly likely to see the managers' point of view and will thus become less tough. This, it is argued, has happened in the USA. Commentators do not believe that it has happened yet in the UK: the regulators are generally independently minded. But it remains a potential danger.
- The regulators could instead be 'captured' by the government. Rather than being totally independent, there to serve the interests of the consumer, they might bend to pressures from the government to do things that might help the government win the next election.

One way in which the dangers of ineffective or over-intrusive regulation can be avoided is to replace regulation with competition wherever this is possible. Indeed, one of the major concerns of the regulators has been to do just this. (See Box 12.7 for ways in which competition has been increased in the electricity industry.)

Increasing competition in the privatised industries

KI 19 p157

Where natural monopoly exists, competition is impossible in a free market. Of course, the industry *could* be broken up by the government, with firms prohibited from owning more than a certain percentage of the industry. But this would lead to higher costs of production. Firms would be operating further back up a downward-sloping long-run average cost curve.

But many parts of the privatised industries are *not* natural monopolies. Generally, it is only the *grid* that is a natural monopoly. In the case of gas and water, it is the pipelines. It would be wasteful to duplicate these. In the case of electricity, it is the power lines: the national grid and the local power lines. In the case of the railways, it is the track.

Other parts of these industries, however, have generally been opened up to competition (with the exception of water). Thus there are now many producers and sellers of electricity and gas. This is possible because they are given access, by law, to the national and local electricity grids and gas pipelines. The telecommunications market too has become more competitive with the growth of mobile phones and lines supplied by cable operators.

To help the opening up of competition, regulators have sometimes restricted the behaviour of the established firms (like BT or British Gas), to prevent them using their dominance in the market as a barrier to entry of new firms. For example, British Gas since 1995 has had to limit its share of the industrial gas market to 40 per cent.

As competition has been introduced into these industries, so price-cap regulation has been progressively abandoned. The intention is ultimately to confine price regulation to the operation of the grids: the parts that are natural monopolies.

Even for the parts where there *is* a natural monopoly, they could be made *contestable* monopolies. One way of doing this is by granting operators a licence for a specific period of time. This is known as ***franchising***. This has been the approach used for the railways (see Web Case 12.8). Once a company has been granted a franchise, it has the monopoly of passenger rail services over specific routes. But the awarding of the franchise can be highly competitive, with rival companies putting in competitive bids, in terms of both price (or, in the case of many of the train operating companies, the level of government subsidy required) and the quality of service.

Another approach is to give all companies equal access to the relevant grid. For example, regional electricity companies have to charge the same price for using their local power lines to both rival companies and themselves.

But despite attempts to introduce competition into the privatised industries, they are still dominated by giant companies. Even if they are no longer strictly monopolies, they still have considerable market power. Competition is far from being perfect! The scope for price leadership or other forms of oligopolistic collusion is great. Thus although regulation through the price formula has been progressively abandoned as elements of competition have been introduced, the regulators have retained a role similar to that of the OFT: namely, to prevent collusion and the abuse of monopoly power. The companies, however, do have the right of appeal to the Competition Commission.

Definitions

Regulatory capture Where the regulator is persuaded to operate in the industry's interests rather than those of the consumer.

Franchising Where a firm is granted the licence to operate a given part of an industry for a specified length of time.

Section summary

1. From around 1983 the Conservative government in the UK embarked on a large programme of privatisation. Many other countries have followed suit.
2. The economic arguments for privatisation include: greater competition, not only in the goods market but in the market for finance and for corporate control; reduced government interference; and raising revenue to finance tax cuts.
3. The economic arguments against privatisation of utilities include the following: the firms are likely to have monopoly power because their grids are natural monopolies; it makes overall planning and co-ordination of the transport and power sectors more difficult; and the industries produce substantial externalities and raise questions of fairness in distribution.
4. Regulators could require firms to charge the socially efficient price. In the first-best world, this will be where price equals marginal social cost. In the real world, this is not the case given that prices elsewhere are not equal to marginal social costs. Ideally, prices should still *reflect* marginal social costs, but there are difficulties in identifying and measuring social costs.
5. In the long run, the optimum price and output will be where price equals long-run marginal social cost. If *LRMSC* < *MSC*, it will be desirable to invest in additional capacity.
6. Regulation in the UK has involved setting up regulatory offices for the major privatised utilities. These generally operate informally, using negotiation and bargaining to persuade the industries to behave in the public interest. They also set the terms under which firms can operate (e.g. access rights to the respective grid).
7. As far as prices are concerned, the industries are required to abide by an '*RPI* minus *X*' formula. This forces them to pass potential cost reductions on to the consumer. At the same time, they are allowed to retain any additional profits gained from cost reductions greater than *X*. This provides them with an incentive to achieve even greater increases in efficiency.
8. Many parts of the privatised industries are not natural monopolies. In these parts, competition may be a more effective means of pursuing the public interest. Various attempts have been made to make the privatised industries more competitive, often at the instigation of the regulator. Nevertheless, considerable market power remains in the hands of many privatised firms, and thus regulators need to be able to retain the ability to prevent the abuse of monopoly power.

END OF CHAPTER QUESTIONS

1. Assume that as traffic density increases along a given stretch of road, there comes a point when traffic begins to slow down. The following table gives the times taken for a car to travel the stretch of road (in minutes) according to the number of cars entering the road per minute.

Cars entering the road	5	6	7	8	9	10	11
Journey time	10	10	11	13	16	22	30

   (a) Copy out the table and add the following rows: (i) total journey time for all cars; (ii) extra journey time as traffic increases by one more car (marginal social time cost); (iii) additional time cost imposed on other road users for each additional car entering the road (marginal external time cost). (See Table 12.4.)
   (b) Assume that time is valued at 1p per minute. On a graph, plot the marginal private time cost (journey time) and the marginal social time cost.
   (c) Assume that electronic road pricing is introduced. What charge should be levied when traffic density reaches (i) 6 cars per minute; (ii) 8 cars per minute; (iii) 11 cars per minute?
   (d) What additional information would you need in order to work out the socially efficient traffic density on this particular stretch of road?
2. Assume that there are several chemical firms in an industry, each one producing different levels of an effluent, whose damage to the environment depends on the location of the firm. Compare the relative merits of using green taxes, tradable permits and controls as means of achieving the socially optimum levels of effluent from these firms.
3. Make out a case from a deep green perspective for rejecting the 'social efficiency' approach to the environment.
4. Compare the relative merits of increased road fuel taxes, electronic road pricing and tolls as means of reducing urban traffic congestion. Why is the price inelasticity of demand for private car transport a problem here, whichever of the three policies is adopted? What could be done to increase the price elasticity of demand?
5. How would you set about measuring the external costs of road transport?
6. Should governments or regulators always attempt to eliminate the supernormal profits of monopolists/ oligopolists?
7. Compare the relative merits of banning certain types of market *structure* with banning certain types of market *behaviour*.
8. Consider the argument that whether an industry is in the public sector or private sector has far less bearing on its performance than the degree of competition it faces.
9. Should regulators of utilities that have been privatised into several separate companies allow (a) horizontal mergers (within the industry); (b) vertical mergers; (c) mergers with firms in other industries?
10. If an industry regulator adopts an *RPI* – *X* formula for price regulation, is it desirable that the value of *X* should be adjusted as soon as cost conditions change?

Additional case studies on the book's website (www.pearsoned.co.uk/sloman)

12.1 Perverse subsidies. An examination of the use of subsidies around the world that are harmful to the environment.

12.2 Selling the environment. This looks at the proposals made at international climate conferences to use market-based solutions to global warming.

12.3 Environmental auditing. Are businesses becoming greener? A growing number of firms are subjecting themselves to an 'environmental audit' to judge just how 'green' they are.

12.4 Evaluating new road schemes. The system used in the UK of assessing the costs and benefits of proposed new roads.

12.5 Cartels set in concrete, steel and cardboard. This examines some of the best-known Europe-wide cartels of recent years.

12.6 Price-cap regulation in the UK. How *RPI* – *X* regulation has been applied to the various privatised industries.

12.7 Regulation US-style. This examines rate-of-return regulation: an alternative to price-cap regulation.

12.8 The right track to reform? How successful has rail privatisation been in the UK?

12.9 Privatisation in transition economies. This extended case study examines state ownership under former communist countries of the USSR and how the transition of these countries to market economies involved a process of privatisation.

12.10 Forms of privatisation in transition countries. This focuses on how different types of privatisation are likely to affect the way industries are run.

WEBSITES RELEVANT TO CHAPTERS 11 AND 12

Numbers and sections refer to websites listed in the Web Appendix and hotlinked from this book's website at www.pearsoned.co.uk/sloman.

- For news articles relevant to this and the previous chapter, see the *Economics News Articles* link from the book's website.
- For general news on market failures and government intervention, see websites in section A, and particularly A1–5, 18, 19, 24, 31. See also links to newspapers in A38, 39, 43 and 44; and see A41 and 42 for links to economics news articles from newspapers worldwide.
- Sites I7 and 11 contain links to *Competition and monopoly, Policy and regulation* and *Transport* in the *Microeconomics* section; they also have an *Industry and commerce* section. Site I4 has links to *Environmental* and *Environmental Economics* in the *EconDirectory* section. Site I17 has several sections of links in the *Issues in Society* section.
- UK and EU departments relevant to competition policy can be found at sites E10; G7, 8.
- UK regulatory bodies can be found at sites E4, 11, 15, 16, 18, 19, 22, 25, 29.
- For information on taxes and subsidies, see E30, 36; G13. For use of green taxes (Box 12.1), see H5; G11; E2, 14, 30.
- For information on health and the economics of health care (Box 11.2), see E8; H9. See also links in I8 and 17.
- For sites favouring the free market, see C17; D34. See also C18 for the development of ideas on the market and government intervention.
- For the economics of the environment, see links in I4, 7, 11, 17. For policy on the environment and transport, see E2, 7, 11, 14, 21, 29; G10, 11. See also H11.
- For student resources relevant to these two chapters, see sites C1–7, 9, 10, 19.
- For a simulation on tackling traffic congestion, see site D3.

Part D: Foundations of Macroeconomics

Why do economies sometimes grow rapidly, while at other times they suffer from recession? Why, if people want to work, do they sometimes find themselves unemployed? Why do economies experience inflation (rising prices), and does it matter if they do? Why do exchange rates change and what will be the impact of such changes on imports and exports? These *macroeconomic* issues affect all countries, and economists are called on to try to find explanations and solutions.

In the next three chapters we will be looking at these issues and giving you a preliminary insight into the causes of these problems and what governments can do to tackle them.

Chapter 13

The National Economy

We turn now to *macroeconomics*. This will be the subject for the second half of the book. As we have already seen, *microeconomics* focuses on *individual* markets. It studies the demand for and supply of oranges, videos, petrol and haircuts; of bricklayers, doctors, office accommodation and computers. It examines the choices people make *between* goods, and what determines their relative prices and the relative quantities produced.

In macroeconomics we take a much loftier view. We examine the economy as a whole. We still examine demand and supply, but now it is the *total* level of spending in the economy and the *total* level of production. In other words, we examine *aggregate demand* and *aggregate supply*.

We still examine output, employment and prices, but now it is *national* output and its rate of growth, *national* employment and unemployment, and the *general* level of prices and their rate of increase (i.e. the rate of inflation).

In this chapter, we identify the major macroeconomic objectives and have a preliminary look at how they are related. Then we focus on national income and output. We look at how they are measured and what causes them to grow over time.

CHAPTER MAP

13.1 THE SCOPE OF MACROECONOMICS

The major macroeconomic issues

Economic growth

KI 1 p4 Governments try to achieve high ***rates of economic growth*** over the long term: in other words, growth that is sustained over the years and is not just a temporary phenomenon. To this end, governments also try to achieve *stable* growth, avoiding both recessions and excessive short-term growth that cannot be sustained (governments are nevertheless sometimes happy to give the economy an excessive boost as an election draws near!).

Key Idea 31 ***Economies suffer from inherent instability.*** As a result, economic growth and other macroeconomic indicators tend to fluctuate.

Table 13.1 shows the average annual growth in output between 1960 and 2005 for selected countries. As you can see, the differences between countries are quite substantial. 'Newly industrialised countries', such as Malaysia and Singapore, have experienced particularly rapid rates of economic growth.

There are also big differences between the growth rates of individual countries in different periods. Look, for example, at the figures for Japan. From being an 'economic miracle' in the 1960s, Japan by the 1990s had become a laggard, with a growth rate well below the OECD average.

Unemployment

Reducing unemployment is another major macroeconomic aim of governments, not only for the sake of the unemployed themselves, but also because it represents a waste of human resources and because unemployment benefits are a drain on government revenues. KI 1 p4

Unemployment in the 1980s and early 1990s was significantly higher than in the 1950s, 1960s and 1970s (see Table 13.1). Then, in the late 1990s and early 2000s, it fell in some countries, such as the UK and USA. In others, such as Germany and France, it remained stubbornly high.

We take a preliminary look at the nature and causes of unemployment in Chapter 14.

Inflation

By inflation we mean a general rise in prices throughout the economy. Government policy here is to keep inflation both low and stable. One of the most important reasons for this is that it will aid the process of economic decision making. For example, businesses will be able to set prices and wage rates, and make investment decisions with far more confidence.

Definition

Rate of economic growth The percentage increase in national output over a 12-month period.

Table 13.1 Economic growth (average % per annum), unemployment (average %) and inflation (average % per annum)

	France	Germany	Italy	Japan	UK	USA	EU (15)	OECD[a]	Brazil	Malaysia	Singapore
Growth											
1960–9	7.5	4.4	5.3	10.9	2.9	4.3	3.5	4.6	5.4	6.5	8.8
1970–9	3.2	2.6	3.8	4.3	2.0	2.8	3.2	3.6	8.1	7.9	8.3
1980–9	2.2	1.8	2.4	4.0	2.4	2.5	2.2	2.6	3.0	5.8	6.1
1990–9	1.7	2.2	1.5	1.7	2.1	3.0	2.1	2.6	1.8	6.9	7.7
2000–5	2.0	1.0	1.5	1.9	2.7	2.9	2.0	2.6	2.8	5.2	4.6
Unemployment											
1960–9	1.5	0.9	5.1	1.3	2.2	4.1	2.5	2.5	n.a.	n.a.	n.a.
1970–9	3.7	2.3	6.4	1.7	4.5	6.1	4.0	4.3	n.a.	n.a.	3.6
1980–9	9.0	5.9	9.5	2.5	10.0	7.2	9.3	7.3	n.a.	6.2	3.6
1990–9	10.6	7.7	10.4	3.7	8.1	5.8	9.2	6.9	9.3	3.4	2.8
2000–5	9.2	8.9	9.0	5.0	5.1	5.3	7.9	6.7	10.5	3.5	3.8
Inflation											
1960–9	4.2	3.2	4.4	4.9	4.1	2.8	3.7	3.1	46.1	−0.3	1.1
1970–9	9.4	5.0	13.9	9.0	13.0	6.8	10.3	9.2	30.6	7.3	5.9
1980–9	7.3	2.9	11.2	2.5	7.4	5.5	7.4	8.9	332.2	2.2	2.5
1990–9	2.0	2.2	4.7	0.8	3.9	2.4	3.3	4.4	847.0	3.6	1.9
2000–5	1.8	1.4	2.7	−1.3	1.8	2.2	2.1	2.3	7.1	1.6	1.0

[a] The Organisation for Economic Co-operation and Development: the 30 major industrialised countries (excluding Russia, but including Korea, Mexico and Turkey).

Today we are used to ***inflation rates*** of around 2 or 3 per cent, but it was not long ago that inflation in most developed countries was in double figures. In 1975, UK inflation reached 24 per cent.

In most developed countries, governments have a particular target for the rate of inflation. In the UK the target is 2 per cent. The Bank of England then adjusts interest rates to try to keep inflation on target (we see how this works in Chapter 19).

The balance of payments and the exchange rate

The final issue has to do with the country's foreign trade and its economic relationships with other countries.

A country's ***balance of payments account*** records all transactions between the residents of that country and the rest of the world. These transactions enter as either debit items or credit items. The debit items include all payments *to* other countries: these include the country's purchases of imports, the investments it makes abroad and the interest and dividends paid to people abroad who have invested in the country. The credit items include all receipts *from* other countries: these include the sales of exports, inflows of investment into the country and earnings of interest and dividends from abroad.

The sale of exports and any other receipts earn foreign currency. The purchase of imports or any other payments abroad use up foreign currency. If we start to spend more foreign currency than we earn, one of two things must happen. Both are likely to be a problem.

- The balance of payments will go into deficit. In other words, there will be a shortfall of foreign currencies. The government will therefore have to borrow money from abroad, or draw on its foreign currency reserves to make up the shortfall. This is a problem because, if it goes on too long, overseas debts will mount, along with the interest that must be paid; and/or reserves will begin to run low.
- The exchange rate will fall. The ***exchange rate*** is the rate at which one currency exchanges for another. For example, the exchange rate of the pound into the dollar might be £1 = $1.60.

  If the government does nothing to correct the balance of payments deficit, then the exchange rate must fall. (We will show just why this is so in section 14.4.) A falling exchange rate is a problem because it pushes up the price of imports and may fuel inflation. Also, if the exchange rate fluctuates, this can cause great uncertainty for traders and can damage international trade and economic growth.

What are the underlying causes of balance of payments problems? How do the balance of payments and the exchange rate relate to the other macroeconomic issues? What are the best policies for governments to adopt? We take an initial look at these questions in Chapter 15 and then examine them in more detail in Chapters 24 and 25.

Government macroeconomic policy

From the above four issues we can identify four macroeconomic policy objectives that governments typically pursue:

- High and stable economic growth.
- Low unemployment.
- Low inflation.
- The avoidance of balance of payments deficits and excessive exchange rate fluctuations.

Unfortunately, these policy objectives may conflict. For example, a policy designed to accelerate the rate of economic growth may result in a higher rate of inflation and a balance of payments deficit. Governments are thus often faced with awkward policy choices.

Societies face trade-offs between economic objectives. For example, the goal of faster growth may conflict with that of greater equality; the goal of lower unemployment may conflict with that of lower inflation (at least in the short run). This is an example of opportunity cost: the cost of achieving one objective may be achieving less of another. The existence of trade-offs means that policy-makers must make choices.

Definitions

Rate of inflation The percentage increase in prices over a 12-month period.

Balance of payments account A record of the country's transactions with the rest of the world. It shows the country's payments to or deposits in other countries (debits) and its receipts or deposits from other countries (credits). It also shows the balance between these debits and credits under various headings.

Exchange rate The rate at which one national currency exchanges for another. The rate is expressed as the amount of one currency that is necessary to purchase *one unit* of another currency (e.g. €1.40 = £1).

Section summary

1. Macroeconomics, like microeconomics, looks at issues such as output, employment and prices; but it looks at them in the context of the whole economy.
2. The four main macroeconomic goals that are generally of most concern to governments are economic growth, reducing unemployment, reducing inflation, and avoiding balance of payments and exchange rate problems.
3. Unfortunately, these goals are likely to conflict. Governments may thus be faced with difficult policy choices.

13.2 THE CIRCULAR FLOW OF INCOME

One way in which the four objectives are linked is through their relationship with ***aggregate demand*** (*AD*). This is the total spending on goods and services made within the country ('domestically produced goods and services'). This spending consists of four elements. The first is ***consumer spending on domestically produced goods and services*** (C_d), (i.e. total consumer expenditure on all products (C) minus expenditure on imports (M)). The other three elements are: investment expenditure by firms (I), government spending (G) and the expenditure by residents abroad on this country's exports (X). Thus:[1]

$$AD = C_d + I + G + X$$

or, put another way:

$$AD = C + I + G + X - M$$

To show how the four objectives are related to aggregate demand, we can use a simple model of the economy. This is the circular flow of income, and is shown in Figure 13.1. It is an extension of the model that we looked at back in Chapter 1 (pages 15–16).

In the diagram, the economy is divided into two major groups: *firms* and *households*. Each group has two roles. Firms are producers of goods and services; they are also the employers of labour and other factors of production. Households (which include all individuals) are the consumers of goods and services; they are also the suppliers of labour and various other factors of production. In the diagram there is an inner flow and various outer flows of incomes between these two groups.

Before we look at the various parts of the diagram, a word of warning. Do not confuse *money* and *income*. Money is a stock concept. At any given time, there is a certain quantity of money in the economy (e.g. £1 billion). But that does not tell us the level of national *income*. Income is a flow concept (as is expenditure). It is measured as so much *per period of time*. The relationship between money and income depends on how rapidly the money *circulates*: its 'velocity of circulation'. (We will examine this concept in detail later on.) If there is £1 billion of money in the economy and each £1 on average is paid out as income five times per year, then annual national income will be £5 billion.

[1] We assume, for simplicity, in this first equation that all investment, government expenditure and export expenditure is on domestic products. If, however, any part of these three went on imports, we would have to subtract this imported element (as we did with consumption). We would then have to write $AD = C_d + I_d + G_d + X_d$.

The inner flow, withdrawals and injections

The inner flow

Firms pay money to households in the form of wages and salaries, dividends on shares, interest and rent. These payments are in return for the services of the factors of production – labour, capital and land – that are supplied by households. Thus on the left-hand side of the diagram, money flows directly from firms to households as 'factor payments'.

Households, in turn, pay money to domestic firms when they consume domestically produced goods and services (C_d). This is shown on the right-hand side of the inner flow. There is thus a circular flow of payments from firms to households to firms and so on.

If households spend *all* their incomes on buying domestic goods and services, and if firms pay out *all* this income they receive as factor payments to domestic households, and if the velocity of circulation does not change, the flow will continue at the same level indefinitely. The money just goes round and round at the same speed and incomes remain unchanged.

? *Would this argument still hold if prices rose?*

In the real world, of course, it is not as simple as this. Not all income gets passed on round the inner flow; some is *withdrawn*. At the same time, incomes are injected into the flow from outside. Let us examine these withdrawals and injections.

Withdrawals (W)

Only part of the incomes received by households will be spent on the goods and services of domestic firms. The remainder will be withdrawn from the inner flow. Likewise only part of the incomes generated by firms will be paid to UK households. The remainder of this will also be withdrawn. There are three forms of ***withdrawals*** (or 'leakages' as they are sometimes called).

Definitions

Aggregate demand Total spending on goods and services produced in the economy. It consists of four elements, consumer expenditure (C), investment (I), government expenditure (G) and the expenditure on exports (X), less any expenditure on foreign goods and services (M). Thus $AD = C + X + G + X - M$, or $C_d + I + G + X$.

The consumption of domestically produced goods and services (C_d) The direct flow of money payments from households to firms.

Withdrawals (W) (or leakages) Incomes of households or firms that are not passed on round the inner flow. Withdrawals equal net saving (S) plus net taxes (T) plus import expenditure (M): $W = S + T + M$.

Figure 13.1 The circular flow of income

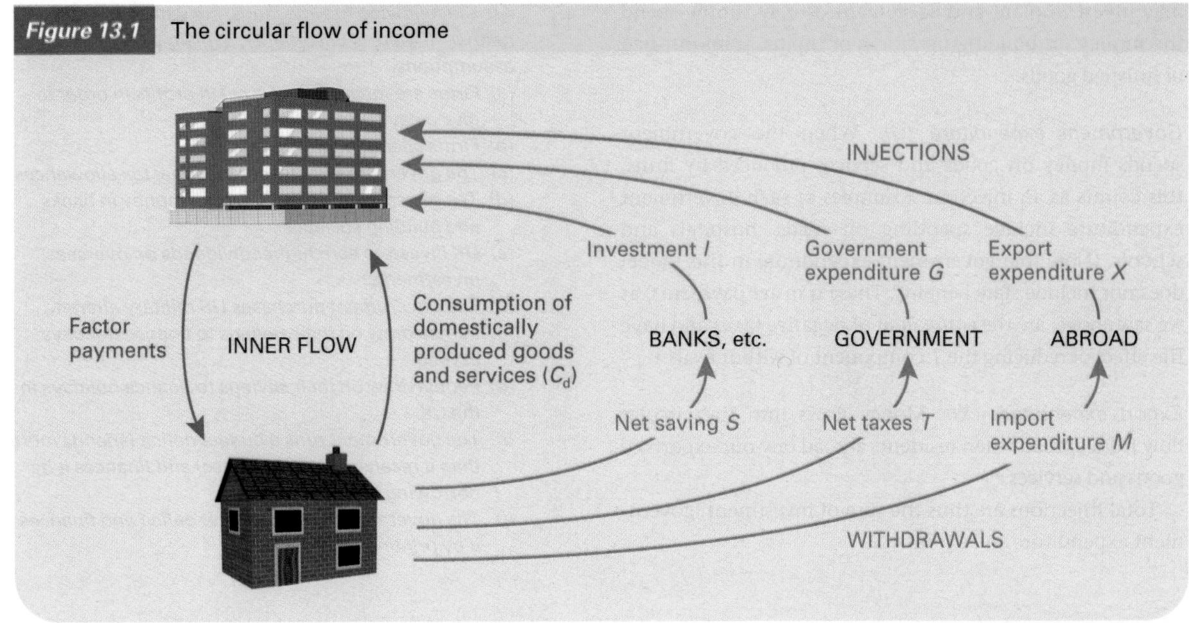

Net saving (S). Saving is income that households choose not to spend but to put aside for the future. Savings are normally deposited in financial institutions such as banks and building societies. This is shown in the bottom centre of the diagram. Money flows from households to 'banks, etc.'. What we are seeking to measure here, however, is the net flow from households to the banking sector. We therefore have to subtract from saving any borrowing or drawing on past savings by households to arrive at the *net* saving flow. Of course, if household borrowing exceeded saving, the net flow would be in the other direction: it would be negative.

Net taxes (T). When people pay taxes (to either central or local government), this represents a withdrawal of money from the inner flow in much the same way as saving: only in this case, people have no choice. Some taxes, such as income tax and employees' national insurance contributions, are paid out of household incomes. Others, such as VAT and excise duties, are paid out of consumer expenditure. Others, such as corporation tax, are paid out of firms' incomes before being received by households as dividends on shares. (For simplicity, however, taxes are shown in Figure 13.1 as leaving the circular flow at just one point.)

When, however, people receive *benefits* from the government, such as unemployment benefits, child benefit and pensions, the money flows the other way. Benefits are thus equivalent to a 'negative tax'. These benefits are known as ***transfer payments***. They transfer money from one group of people (taxpayers) to others (the recipients).

In the model, 'net taxes' (T) represent the *net* flow to the government from households and firms. It consists of total taxes minus benefits.

Import expenditure (M). Not all consumption is of totally home-produced goods. Households spend some of their incomes on imported goods and services, or on goods and services using imported components. Although the money that consumers spend on such goods initially flows to domestic retailers, it will eventually find its way abroad, either when the retailers or wholesalers themselves import them, or when domestic manufacturers purchase imported inputs to make their products. This expenditure on imports constitutes the third withdrawal from the inner flow. This money flows abroad.

Total withdrawals are simply the sum of net saving, net taxes and the expenditure on imports:

$$W = S + T + M$$

Injections (J)

Only part of the demand for firms' output arises from consumers' expenditure. The remainder comes from other sources outside the inner flow. These additional components of aggregate demand are known as ***injections** (J)*. There are three types of injection.

Investment (I). This is the money that firms spend after obtaining it from various financial institutions – either past savings or loans, or through a new issue of shares. They

Definitions

Transfer payments Moneys transferred from one person or group to another (e.g. from the government to individuals) without production taking place.

Injections (*J*) Expenditure on the production of domestic firms coming from outside the inner flow of the circular flow of income. Injections equal investment (I) plus government expenditure (G) plus expenditure on exports (X).

may invest in plant and equipment or may simply spend the money on building up stocks of inputs, semi-finished or finished goods.

Government expenditure (G). When the government spends money on goods and services produced by firms, this counts as an injection. Examples of such government expenditure include spending on roads, hospitals and schools. (Note that government expenditure in this model does not include state benefits. These transfer payments, as we saw above, are the equivalent of negative taxes and have the effect of reducing the T component of withdrawals.)

Export expenditure (X). Money flows into the circular flow from abroad when residents abroad buy our exports of goods and services.[2]

Total injections are thus the sum of investment, government expenditure and exports:

$$J = I + G + X$$

The relationship between withdrawals and injections

There are indirect links between saving and investment, taxation and government expenditure, and imports and exports, via financial institutions, the government (central and local) and foreign countries respectively. If more money is saved, there will be more available for banks and other financial institutions to lend out. If tax receipts are higher, the government may be more keen to increase its expenditure. Finally, if imports increase, incomes of people abroad will increase, which will enable them to purchase more of our exports.

These links, however, do not guarantee that $S = I$ or $G = T$ or $M = X$. Firms may wish to invest (I) more or less than people wish to save (S); governments can spend (G) more than they receive in taxes (T) or vice versa; and exports (X) can exceed imports (M) or vice versa.

A major point here is that the decisions to save and invest are made by different people, and thus they plan to save and invest different amounts. Likewise the demand for imports may not equal the demand for exports. As far as the government is concerned, it may choose not to make $T = G$. It may choose not to spend all its tax revenues: to run a 'budget surplus' ($T > G$). Or it may choose to spend more than it receives in taxes – to run a budget deficit ($G > T$) – by borrowing or printing money to make up the difference.

Thus planned injections (J) may not equal planned withdrawals (W).

[2] Note that X would not include investment in the UK by foreign companies (i.e. credits on the financial account of the balance of payments). Foreign 'investment' involves the acquisition of assets in the UK and thus represents an income to the previous owners of these assets. It therefore represents an inflow from abroad to the household sector and thus has the effect of reducing M.

?

Are the following net injections, net withdrawals or neither? If there is uncertainty, explain your assumptions.

(a) Firms are forced to take a cut in profits in order to give a pay rise.
(b) Firms spend money on research.
(c) The government increases personal tax allowances.
(d) The general public invests more money in banks and building societies.
(e) UK investors earn higher dividends on overseas investments.
(f) The government purchases US military aircraft.
(g) People draw on their savings to finance holidays abroad.
(h) People draw on their savings to finance holidays in the UK.
(i) The government runs a budget deficit (spends more than it receives in tax revenues) and finances it by borrowing from the public.
(j) The government runs a budget deficit and finances it by printing more money.

The circular flow of income and the four macroeconomic objectives

If planned injections are not equal to planned withdrawals, what will be the consequences? If, for example, injections exceed withdrawals, the level of expenditure will rise: there will be a rise in aggregate demand. This extra spending will increase firms' sales and thus encourage them to produce more. Total output in the economy will rise. Thus firms will pay out more in wages, salaries, profits, rent and interest. In other words, national income will rise.

The rise in aggregate demand will have the following effects upon the four macroeconomic objectives:  KI 32 p369

- There will be economic growth. The greater the initial excess of injections over withdrawals, the bigger will be the rise in national income.
- Unemployment will fall as firms take on more workers to meet the extra demand for output.
- Inflation will tend to rise. The greater the rise in aggregate demand relative to the capacity of firms to produce, the more will firms find it difficult to meet the extra demand, and the more likely they will be to raise prices.
- The exports and imports part of the balance of payments will tend to deteriorate. The higher demand sucks more imports into the country, and higher domestic inflation makes exports less competitive and imports relatively cheaper compared with home-produced goods. Thus imports will tend to rise and exports will tend to fall.

?

What effect will there be on the four objectives of an initial excess of withdrawals over injections?

Equilibrium in the circular flow

When injections do not equal withdrawals, a state of disequilibrium will exist. This will set in train a process to bring the economy back to a state of equilibrium where injections are equal to withdrawals.

To illustrate this, let us consider the situation again where injections exceed withdrawals. Perhaps there has been a rise in business confidence so that investment has risen. Or perhaps there has been a tax cut so that withdrawals have fallen. As we have seen, the excess of injections over withdrawals will lead to a rise in national income. But as national income rises, so households will not only spend more on domestic goods (C_d), but also save more (S), pay more taxes (T) and buy more imports (M). In other words, withdrawals will rise. This will continue until they have risen to equal injections. At that point, national income will stop rising, and so will withdrawals. Equilibrium has been reached.

Section summary

1. The circular flow of income model depicts the flows of money round the economy. The inner flow shows the direct flows between firms and households. Money flows from firms to households in the form of factor payments, and back again as consumer expenditure on domestically produced goods and services.
2. Not all incomes get passed on directly round the inner flow. Some is withdrawn in the form of saving, some is paid in taxes, and some goes abroad as expenditure on imports.
3. Likewise not all expenditure on domestic firms is by domestic consumers. Some is injected from outside the inner flow in the form of investment expenditure, government expenditure and expenditure on the country's exports.
4. Planned injections and withdrawals are unlikely to be the same.
5. If injections exceed withdrawals, national income will rise, unemployment will tend to fall, inflation will tend to rise, imports will tend to rise and exports fall. The reverse will happen if withdrawals exceed injections.
6. If injections exceed withdrawals, the rise in national income will lead to a rise in withdrawals. This will continue until $W = J$. At this point, the circular flow will be in equilibrium.

13.3 MEASURING NATIONAL INCOME AND OUTPUT

The circular flow of income is very useful as a model for understanding the working of an economy. It shows how national income can increase or decrease as a result of changes in the various flows. But just how do we measure national income or output? The measure we use is called ***gross domestic product*** (GDP).

This section shows how GDP is calculated. It also looks at difficulties in interpreting GDP statistics. Can the figures be meaningfully used to compare one country's standard of living with another? The appendix to this chapter goes into more detail on the precise way in which the statistics for GDP are derived.

The three ways of measuring GDP

GDP can be calculated in three different ways, which should all result in the same figure. These three methods are illustrated in the simplified circular flow of income shown in Figure 13.2.

Definition

Gross domestic product (GDP) The value of output produced within the country over a 12-month period.

Figure 13.2 The circular flow of national income and expenditure

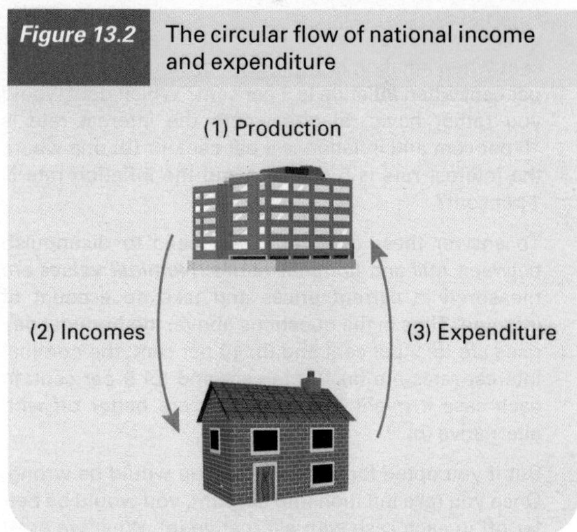

The first method of measuring GDP is to add up the value of all the goods and services produced in the country, industry by industry. In other words, we focus on firms and add up all their production. This first method is known as the *product method*.

The production of goods and services generates incomes for households in the form of wages and salaries, profits, rent and interest. The second method of measuring GDP, therefore, is to add up all these incomes. This is known as the *income method*.

The third method focuses on the expenditures necessary to purchase the nation's production. In this simple model of the circular flow of income, with no injections or withdrawals, whatever is produced is sold. The value of what is sold must therefore be the value of what is produced. The *expenditure method* measures this sales value.

Because of the way the calculations are made, the three methods of calculating GDP *must* yield the same result. In other words:

$$\text{National product} \equiv \text{National income} \equiv \text{National expenditure}$$

In the appendix to this chapter, we look at each of the three methods in turn, and examine the various factors that have to be taken into account to ensure that the figures are accurate.

Taking account of inflation

If we are to make a sensible comparison of one year's national income with another, we must take inflation into account. For example, if this year national income is 10 per cent higher than last year, but at the same time prices are also 10 per cent higher, then the average person will be no better off at all. There has been no *real* increase in income (see discussion in Appendix 1 at the end of the book on page A:6).

An important distinction here is between ***nominal GDP*** and ***real GDP***. *Nominal* GDP, sometimes called 'money GDP', measures GDP in the prices ruling at the time and thus takes no account of inflation. *Real* GDP, however, measures GDP in the prices that ruled in some particular year – the *base year*. Thus we could measure each year's GDP in, say, 1990 prices. This would enable us to see how much *real* GDP had changed from one year to another. In other words, it would eliminate increases in money GDP that were merely due to an increase in prices. TC 12 p374

The official statistics give both nominal and real figures. Web Case 13.1 on the book's website shows in more detail how real GDP figures are calculated.

Definitions

Nominal GDP GDP measured at current prices.

Real GDP GDP after allowing for inflation: i.e. GDP measured in constant prices: i.e. in terms of the prices ruling in some base year.

THINKING LIKE AN ECONOMIST — *THRESHOLD CONCEPT 12*

THE DISTINCTION BETWEEN REAL AND NOMINAL VALUES

Which would you rather have: (a) a pay rise of 5 per cent when inflation is 2 per cent, or (b) a pay rise of 10 per cent when inflation is 9 per cent? Which debt would you rather have: (a) one where the interest rate is 10 per cent and inflation is 8 per cent, or (b) one where the interest rate is 5 per cent and the inflation rate is 1 per cent?

To answer these questions, you need to distinguish between *real* and *nominal* values. ***Nominal values*** are measured in current prices and take no account of inflation. Thus in the questions above, the nominal pay rises are (a) 5 per cent and (b) 10 per cent; the nominal interest rates are (a) 10 per cent and (b) 5 per cent. In each case it might seem that you are better off with alternative (b).

But if you opted for answers (b), you would be wrong. Once you take inflation into account, you would be better off in each case with alternative (a). What we need to do is to use ***real values***. Real values take account of inflation. Thus in the first question, although the nominal pay rise in alternative (a) is 5 per cent, the *real* pay rise is only 3 per cent, since 2 of the 5 per cent is absorbed by higher prices. You are only 3 per cent better off in terms of what you can buy. In alternative (b) the real pay rise is only 1 per cent, since 9 of the 10 per cent is absorbed by higher prices. Thus in real terms, alternative (a) is better.

In the second question, although in alternative (a) you are paying 10 per cent in nominal terms, your debt is being reduced in real terms by 8 per cent and thus you are paying a real rate of interest of only 2 per cent. In alternative (b), although the nominal rate of interest is only 5 per cent, your debt is being eroded by inflation by only 1 per cent. The real rate of interest is thus 4 per cent. Again, in real terms, you are better off with alternative (a).

The distinction between real and nominal values is a *threshold concept*, as understanding the distinction is fundamental to assessing statistics about the economy. Often politicians will switch between real and nominal values depending on which are most favourable to them. Thus a government wishing to show how strong economic growth has been will tend to use nominal growth figures. On the other hand, the opposition will tend to refer to real growth figures, as these will be lower (assuming a positive inflation rate).

It's easy to make the mistake of using nominal figures when we should really be using real ones. This is known as 'money illusion': the belief that a rise in money terms represents a real rise.

When comparing two countries' GDP growth rates, does it matter if we use nominal figures, provided we use them for both countries?

Taking account of population: the use of per-capita measures

The figures we have been looking at up to now are *total* GDP figures. Although they are useful for showing how big the total output or income of one country is compared with another, we are often more interested in output or income *per head*. Luxembourg obviously has a much lower total national income than the UK, but it has a higher GDP per head.

Other per-capita measures are sometimes useful. For example, measuring GDP per head of the *employed* population allows us to compare how much the average worker produces. A country may have a relatively high GDP per head of population, but also have a large proportion of people at work. Its output per worker will therefore not be so high.

? *By what would we need to divide GDP in order to get a measure of labour productivity per hour?*

Taking account of exchange rates: the use of PPP measures

There is a big problem with comparing GDP figures of different countries. They are measured in the local currency and thus have to be converted into a common currency (e.g. dollars or euros) at the current exchange rate. But the exchange rate may be a poor indicator of the purchasing power of the currency at home. For example, £1 may exchange for, say, 200 yen. But will £1 in the UK buy the same amount of goods as ¥200 in Japan? The answer is almost certainly no.

To compensate for this, GDP can be converted into a common currency at a ***purchasing-power parity rate***. This is a rate of exchange that would allow a given amount of money in one country to buy the same amount of goods in another country after exchanging it into the currency of the other country. The European Commission publishes PPP rates against the euro for all EU currencies and for the US dollar and Japanese yen. The OECD also publishes PPP rates against the US dollar for all OECD currencies. Using such rates to measure GDP gives the ***purchasing-power standard (PPS) GDP***.

Box 13.1 compares GDP with PPS GDP for various countries.

Definitions

Purchasing-power parity (PPP) exchange rate An exchange rate corrected to take into account the purchasing power of a currency. $1 would buy the same in each country after conversion into its currency at the PPP rate.

Purchasing-power standard (PPS) GDP GDP measured at a country's PPP exchange rate.

CASE STUDIES AND APPLICATIONS — BOX 13.1

WHICH COUNTRY IS BETTER OFF?

Comparing national income statistics

Using PPS GDP figures can give a quite different picture of the relative incomes in different countries than using simple GDP figures. The table shows the GDP per head and PPS GDP per head in various countries. The figures are expressed as a percentage of the average of the EU-15 countries (i.e. those that were members prior to the entry of 10 new members in May 2004).

Thus in 2004, Denmark had a GDP per head 42.7 per cent higher than the EU-15 average. But, because of higher Danish prices, the average person in Denmark could buy only 12 per cent more goods and services. By contrast, GDP per head in the Czech Republic was only 33.2 per cent of the EU-15 average, but because of lower Czech prices the average person there could buy 64.6 per cent as much as the average citizen of the EU-15 countries.

GDP per head as a percentage of the EU-15 average: 2004

	GDP per head	GDP (PPS) per head
Luxembourg	220.5	196.9
Denmark	142.7	112.0
Ireland	141.7	127.1
USA	127.3	142.5
Sweden	122.5	106.7
Japan	116.0	107.1
UK	112.6	109.1
Netherlands	112.0	108.1
Germany	104.1	98.5
France	103.6	104.4
Italy	92.0	97.5
Spain	76.0	87.4
Greece	58.6	74.4
Portugal	50.3	67.7
Czech Republic	33.2	64.6
Poland	20.0	44.6

? ***Referring to the figures in the table, which countries' actual exchange rates would seem to understate the purchasing power of their currency?***

Do GDP statistics give a good indication of a country's standard of living?

If we take into account both inflation and the size of the population, and use figures for *real* per-capita PPS GDP, will this give us a good indication of a country's standard of living? The figures *do* give quite a good indication of the level of production of goods and the incomes generated from it, provided we are clear about the distinctions between the different measures. But when we come to ask the more general question of whether the figures give a good indication of the welfare or happiness of the country's citizens, then there are serious problems in relying exclusively on GDP statistics.

Problems of measuring national output

The main problem here is that the output of some goods and services goes unrecorded and thus the GDP figures will understate the nation's output. There are two reasons why these items are not recorded.

Non-marketed items. If you employ a decorator to paint your living room, this will be recorded in the GDP statistics. If, however, you paint the room yourself, it will not. Similarly, if a nanny is employed by parents to look after their children, this child care will form part of GDP. If, however, a parent stays at home to look after the children, it will not. The exclusion of these 'do-it-yourself' and other home-based activities means that the GDP statistics understate the true level of production in the economy. If over time there is an *increase* in the amount of do-it-yourself activities that people perform, the figures will also understate the *rate of growth* of national output. On the other hand, if in more and more families both partners go out to work and employ people to do the housework, this will overstate the rate of growth in output. The housework that was previously unrecorded now enters into the GDP statistics.

?

If we were trying to get a 'true' measure of national production, which of the following activities would you include: (a) washing-up; (b) planting flowers in the garden; (c) playing an educational game with children in the family; (d) playing any game with children in the family; (e) cooking your own supper; (f) cooking the supper for the whole family; (g) reading a novel for pleasure; (h) reading a textbook as part of studying; (i) studying holiday brochures?

Is there a measurement problem if you get pleasure from the do-it-yourself activity itself as well as from its outcome?

The 'underground' economy. The underground economy consists of illegal and hence undeclared transactions. These could be transactions where the goods and services are themselves illegal, such as drugs and prostitution. Alternatively, they could be transactions that are illegal only in that they are not declared for tax purposes. For example, to avoid paying VAT, a garage may be prepared to repair your car slightly more cheaply if you pay cash. Another example is that of 'moonlighting', where people do extra work outside their normal job and do not declare the income for tax purposes. For example, an electrician employed by a building contractor during the day may rewire people's houses in the evenings, again for cash. Unemployed people may do

CASE STUDIES AND APPLICATIONS — BOX 13.2

HOW BIG IS THE UNDERGROUND ECONOMY?

The factors that determine its size

Estimates for the size of the underground economy vary enormously from country to country. Clearly it is impossible to get precise estimates because, by their very nature, the details are largely hidden from the authorities. Nevertheless economists have tried to identify the factors that determine the size of the underground economy.

The first determinant is the level of taxes and regulations. The greater their level, the greater the incentive for people to evade the system and 'go underground'.

The second is the determination of the authorities to catch up with evaders, and the severity of the punishments for those found out.

A third is the size of the service sector relative to the manufacturing sector. It is harder for the authorities to detect the illicit activities of motor mechanics, builders and window cleaners than the output of cars, bricks and soap.

Another determinant is the proportion of the population that is self-employed. It is much easier for the self-employed to evade taxes than it is for people receiving a wage where taxes are deducted at source.

Some indication of the size of the underground economy is given by the demand for cash in the economy, since most underground transactions are conducted in cash. It was estimated that eurozone residents, prior to the adoption of euro notes and coins in January 2002, had over €180 billion in old-currency cash – equivalent to 2.6 per cent of eurozone GDP. In order to persuade people to put such money in legitimate accounts, France and Spain ruled that between December 2001 and June 2002 banks only had to report cash deposits of over €10 000.

1. ***Is the size of the underground economy likely to increase or decrease as the level of unemployment rises?***
2. ***If the amount of cash used in the economy falls, does this mean that the size of the underground economy must have fallen?***

casual jobs that again they do not declare, this time for fear of losing benefits.

Problems of using GDP statistics to measure welfare

GDP is essentially an indicator of a nation's *production*. But production may be a poor indicator of society's well-being for the following reasons.

Production does not equal consumption. Production is desirable only to the extent that it enables us to *consume* more. If GDP rises as a result of a rise in *investment*, this will not lead to an increase in *current* living standards. It will, of course, help to raise *future* consumption.

The same applies if GDP rises as a result of an increase in exports. Unless there is a resulting increase in imports, it will be consumers abroad that benefit, not domestic consumers.

KI 2 p8 *The human costs of production.* If production increases, this may be due to technological advance. If, however, it increases as a result of people having to work harder or longer hours, its net benefit will be less. Leisure is a desirable good, and so too are pleasant working conditions, but these items are not included in the GDP figures.

GDP ignores externalities. The rapid growth in industrial society is recorded in GDP statistics. What the statistics do not record are the environmental side-effects: the polluted air and rivers, the ozone depletion, the problem of global warming. If these external costs were taken into account, the *net* benefits of industrial production might be much less.

Name some external benefits that are not included in GDP statistics.

The production of certain 'bads' leads to an increase in GDP. Some of the undesirable effects of growth may actually *increase* GDP! Take the examples of crime, stress-related illness and environmental damage. Faster growth may lead to more of all three. But increased crime leads to more expenditure on security; increased stress leads to more expenditure on health care; and increased environmental damage leads to more expenditure on environmental clean-up. These expenditures *add* to GDP. Thus, rather than reducing GDP, crime, stress and environmental damage actually increase it!

Total GDP figures ignore the distribution of income. If some people gain and others lose, we cannot say that there has been an unambiguous increase in welfare. A typical feature of many rapidly growing countries is that some people grow very rich while others are left behind. The result is a growing inequality. If this is seen as undesirable, then clearly total GDP statistics are an inadequate measure of welfare. KI 4 p11

Conclusions

If a country's citizens put a high priority on a clean environment, a relaxed way of life, greater self-sufficiency, a less materialistic outlook, more giving rather than selling, and greater equality, then such a country will probably have a lower GDP than a similarly endowed country where the pursuit of wealth is given high priority. Clearly, we cannot conclude that the first country will have a lower level of well-being. However, this does not mean that we should reject GDP statistics as a means of judging economic performance. GDP statistics are not meant to be a measure of economic welfare. They are a measure of *output* or *income*, and should be seen in that context.

Section summary

1. National income is usually expressed in terms of gross domestic product. This is simply the value of domestic production over the course of the year. It can be measured by the product, expenditure or income methods.
2. *Real* national income takes account of inflation by being expressed in the prices of some base year.
3. In order to compare living standards of different countries, national income has to be expressed per capita and at purchasing-power parity exchange rates.
4. Even if it is, there are still problems in using national income statistics for comparative purposes. Certain items will not be included: items such as non-marketed products, services in the family and activities in the underground economy. Moreover, the statistics include certain 'bads' and ignore externalities, and they also ignore questions of the distribution of income.

13.4 SHORT-TERM ECONOMIC GROWTH AND THE BUSINESS CYCLE

The distinction between actual and potential growth

Before examining the causes of economic growth, it is essential to distinguish between *actual* and *potential* economic growth. People frequently confuse the two.

Actual growth is the percentage annual increase in national output: the rate of growth in actual output. When statistics on growth rates are published, it is actual growth they are referring to.

Definition

Actual growth The percentage annual increase in national output actually produced.

Potential growth is the speed at which the economy *could* grow. It is the percentage annual increase in the economy's *capacity* to produce: the rate of growth in ***potential output***. Two of the major factors contributing to potential economic growth are:

- An increase in resources – natural resources, labour or capital.
- An increase in the efficiency with which these resources are used, through advances in technology, improved labour skills or improved organisation.

If the potential growth rate exceeds the actual growth rate, there will be an increase in spare capacity and probably an increase in unemployment: there will be a growing gap between potential and actual output. To close this gap, the actual growth rate would temporarily have to exceed the potential growth rate. In the long run, however, the actual growth rate will be limited to the potential growth rate.

Definitions

Potential growth The percentage annual increase in the capacity of the economy to produce.

Potential output The output that could be produced in the economy if there were a full employment of resources (including labour).

CASE STUDIES AND APPLICATIONS

THE COSTS OF ECONOMIC GROWTH

Is more necessarily better?

For many developing countries, economic growth is a necessity if they are to remove mass poverty. When the majority of their population is underfed and poorly housed, with inadequate health care and little access to education, few would quarrel with the need for an increase in productive potential. The main query is whether the benefits of economic growth will flow to the mass of the population, or whether they will be confined to the few who are already relatively well off.

For developed countries, the case for economic growth is less clear cut. Economic growth is usually measured in terms of the growth in GDP. The problem is that there are many 'goods' and 'bads' that are not included in GDP (see Box 13.6). Economic growth, therefore, is not the same as growth in a nation's *welfare*.

So, what are the benefits and costs of economic growth?

The benefits of growth

Increased levels of consumption. Provided economic growth outstrips population growth, it will lead to higher real income per head. This can lead to higher levels of consumption of goods and services. If human welfare is related to the level of consumption, then growth provides an obvious gain to society.

It can help avoid other macroeconomic problems. People aspire to higher living standards. Without a growth in productive potential, people's demands for rising incomes are likely to lead to higher inflation, balance of payments crises (as more imports are purchased), industrial disputes, etc. Growth in productive potential helps to meet these aspirations and avoid macroeconomic crises.

It can make it easier to redistribute incomes to the poor. If incomes rise, the government can redistribute incomes from the rich to the poor *without the rich losing*. For example, as people's incomes rise, they automatically pay more taxes. These extra revenues for the government can be spent on programmes to alleviate poverty. Without a continuing rise in national income, the scope for helping the poor is much more limited.

Society may feel that it can afford to care more for the environment. As people grow richer, they may become less preoccupied with their own private consumption and more concerned to live in a clean environment. The regulation of pollution tends to be tougher in developed countries than in the developing world.

The costs of growth

In practice, more consumption may not make people happier; economies may be no less crisis riven; income may not be redistributed more equally; the environment may not be better protected. More than this, some people argue that growth may worsen these problems and create additional problems besides.

The current opportunity cost of growth. To achieve faster growth, firms will probably need to invest more. This will require financing. The finance can come from higher saving, higher retained profits or higher taxes. Either way, there must be a cut in consumption. In the short run, therefore, higher growth leads to *less* consumption, not more.

In the diagram, assume that consumption is currently at a level of C_1. Its growth over time is shown by the line out from C_1. Now assume that the government pursues a policy of higher growth. Consumption has to *fall* to finance the extra investment. Consumption falls to, say, C_2. The growth in consumption is now shown by the line out from C_2. Not until time t_1 is reached (which may be several years into the future) does consumption overtake the levels that it would have reached with the previous lower growth rate.

Growth may simply generate extra demands. 'The more people have, the more they want.' If this is so, more consumption may not increase people's utility at all. (Diagrammatically, indifference curves may move outwards as fast as, or even faster than, consumers' budget lines: see section 4.3.) It is often observed that rich people tend to be miserable!

There are thus two major policy issues concerned with economic growth: the short-run issue of ensuring that actual growth is such as to keep actual output as close as possible to potential output; and the long-run issue of what determines the rate of potential economic growth.

Economic growth and the business cycle

Although growth in potential output varies to some extent over the years – depending on the rate of advance of technology, the level of investment and the discovery of new raw materials – it nevertheless tends to be much more steady than the growth in actual output.

Actual growth tends to fluctuate. In some years, countries will experience high rates of economic growth: the country experiences a boom. In other years, economic growth is low or even negative: the country experiences a slowdown or recession.[3] This cycle of booms and recessions is known as the ***business cycle*** or ***trade cycle***.

KI 31 p368

[3] In official statistics, a recession is defined as when an economy experiences falling national output (negative growth) for two or more quarters.

Definition

Business cycle or **trade cycle** The periodic fluctuations of national output round its long-term trend.

BOX 13.3

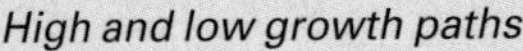

High and low growth paths

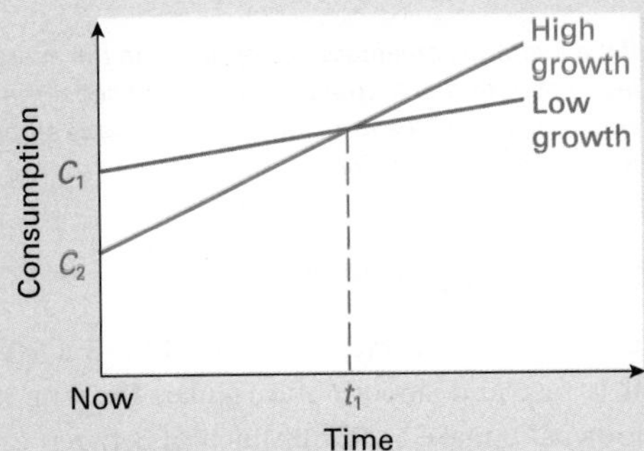

Social effects. Many people claim that an excessive pursuit of material growth by a country can lead to a more greedy, more selfish and less caring society. As society becomes more industrialised, violence, crime, loneliness, stress-related diseases, suicides, divorce and other social problems are likely to rise.

Environmental costs. A richer society may be more concerned for the environment, but it is also likely to do more damage to it. The higher the level of consumption, the higher is likely to be the level of pollution and waste. What is more, many of the environmental costs are likely to be underestimated due to a lack of scientific knowledge. Acid rain and the depletion of the ozone layer have been two examples.

Non-renewable resources. If growth involves using a greater amount of resources, rather than using the same amount of resources more efficiently, certain non-renewable resources will run out more rapidly. Unless viable alternatives can be found for various minerals and fossil fuels, present growth may lead to shortages for future generations (see Box 9.10).

Effects on the distribution of income. While some people may gain from a higher standard of living, others are likely to lose. If the means to higher growth are greater incentives (such as cuts in higher rates of income tax), then the rich might get richer, with little or no benefits 'trickling down' to the poor.

KI 4 p11

Growth involves changes in production: both in terms of the goods produced and in terms of the techniques used and the skills required. The more rapid the rate of growth, the more rapid the rate of change. People may find that their skills are no longer relevant. Their jobs may be replaced by machines. People may thus find themselves unemployed, or forced to take low-paid, unskilled work.

Conclusion

So should countries pursue growth? The answer depends on (a) just what costs and benefits are involved, (b) what weighting people attach to them, and (c) how opposing views are to be reconciled.

A problem is that the question of the desirability of economic growth is a normative one. It involves a judgement about what a 'desirable' society should look like.

KI 6 p29

A simpler point, however, is that the electorate seems to want economic growth. As long as that is so, governments will tend to pursue policies to achieve growth. That is why we need to study the causes of growth and the policies that governments can pursue.

One thing the government can do is to view the problem as one of *constrained optimisation.* It sets constraints: levels of environmental protection, minimum wages, maximum rates of depletion of non-renewable resources, etc. It then seeks policies that will maximise growth, while keeping within these constraints.

?

1. ***Is a constrained optimisation approach a practical solution to the possible costs of economic growth?***
2. ***Are worries about the consequences of economic growth a 'luxury' that only rich countries can afford?***

Figure 13.3 The business cycle

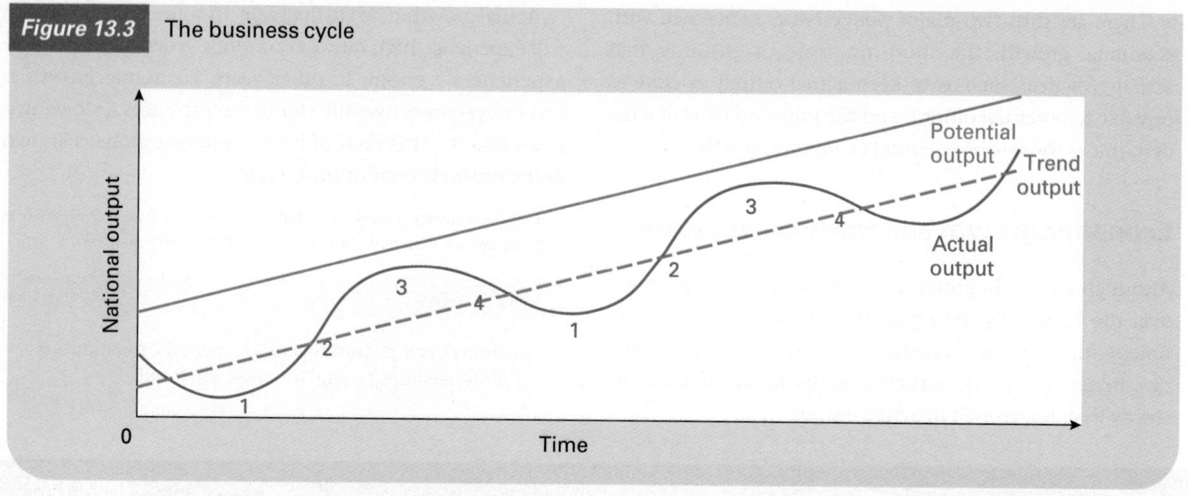

There are four 'phases' of the business cycle. They are illustrated in Figure 13.3.

1. *The upturn.* In this phase, a contracting or stagnant economy begins to recover, and growth in actual output resumes.
2. *The expansion.* During this phase, there is rapid economic growth: the economy is booming. A fuller use is made of resources, and the gap between actual and potential output narrows.
3. *The peaking out.* During this phase, growth slows down or even ceases.
4. *The slowdown, recession or slump.* During this phase, there is little or no growth or even a decline in output. Increasing slack develops in the economy.

A word of caution: do not confuse a high *level* of output with a high rate of *growth* in output. The level of output is highest in phase 3. The rate of growth in output is highest in phase 2 (i.e. where the curve is steepest).

? *Figure 13.3 shows a decline in actual output in recession. Redraw the diagram, only this time show a mere slowing down of growth in phase 4.*

Long-term output trend. A line can be drawn showing the trend of national output over time (i.e. ignoring the cyclical fluctuations around the trend). This is shown as the dashed line in Figure 13.3. If the average level of potential output that is unutilised stays constant from one cycle to another, the trend line will have the same slope as the potential output line. In other words, the trend rate of growth will be the same as the potential rate of growth. If, however, the level of unutilised potential changes from one cycle to another, then the trend line will have a different slope from the potential output line. For example, if unemployment and unused industrial capacity *rise* from one peak to another, or from one trough to another, the trend line will move further away from the potential output line (i.e. it will be less steep).

? *If the average* percentage *(as opposed to the average level) of potential output that was unutilised remained constant, would the trend line have the same slope as the potential output line?*

The business cycle in practice

The business cycle illustrated in Figure 13.3 is a 'stylised' cycle. It is nice and smooth and regular. Drawing it this way allows us to make a clear distinction between each of the four phases. In practice, however, business cycles are highly irregular. They are irregular in two ways.

The length of the phases. Some booms are short lived, lasting only a few months or so. Others are much longer, lasting perhaps three or four years. Likewise some recessions are short while others are long.

The magnitude of the phases. Sometimes in phase 2, there is a very high rate of economic growth, perhaps 5 per cent per annum or more. On other occasions in phase 2, growth is much gentler. Sometimes in phase 4 there is a recession, with an actual decline in output. On other occasions, phase 4 is merely a 'pause', with growth simply slowing down.

Nevertheless, despite the irregularity of the fluctuations, cycles are still clearly discernible, especially if we plot *growth* on the vertical axis rather than the *level* of output. This is done in Figure 13.4, which shows the business cycles in five major industrial countries from 1971 to 2006. As you can see, all five economies suffered a recession or slowdown in the mid-1970s, the early 1980s, the early 1990s and the early 2000s, and a boom in the early 1970s, the late 1970s, the late 1980s and, except in the case of Japan, the late 1990s.

THINKING LIKE AN ECONOMIST *THRESHOLD CONCEPT 13*

SHORT-TERM GROWTH IN A COUNTRY'S OUTPUT TENDS TO FLUCTUATE

Countries rarely experience stable economic growth. Instead they experience business cycles. Periods of rapid economic growth are followed by periods of low growth or even a fall in output (negative growth).

Sometimes these cycles can be the result of government policy: raising taxes in a recession in order to compensate for falling tax revenues caused by lower incomes and lower expenditure. The higher taxation dampens consumer demand and causes firms to cut back on production to match the fall in sales.

Usually, however, economic fluctuations are simply the result of the workings of a market system. Some economists see the problem as rooted in fluctuations in aggregate demand. Consumer spending fluctuates; firms' investment fluctuates; export sales fluctuate. What is more, these various elements interact with each other. A rise in consumer expenditure can stimulate firms to invest in order to build up capacity to meet the extra demand. This, in turn, generates more employment in the capital goods industries and extra incomes for their employees. This further stimulates consumer demand. We examine these explanations in section 17.4.

Some economists see the problem as rooted in fluctuations in aggregate supply. These 'real business cycle' economists argue that technological changes can boost output and employment and that these changes often come in waves. We look at these explanations in section 21.3.

But whatever the cause, it is vital to recognise the fundamental instability in market economies. This is what makes the business cycle a *threshold concept*. Analysing the causes and paths of business cycles occupies many macroeconomists. Their analysis leads to various policy conclusions. Some argue that it is best for the government or central bank to try to stabilise the cycle by active intervention: boosting aggregate demand (e.g. by cutting taxes, raising government expenditure or cutting interest rates) when the economy is experiencing low or negative growth, and dampening aggregate demand when the economy is experiencing unsustainably high growth. Others argue that it is best not to intervene, but to ride out the fluctuations, arguing that attempting to manage aggregate demand often makes things worse.

1. ***If people believe that the economy is about to go into recession (i.e. that real GDP will fall), how may their actions aggravate the problem?***
2. ***Why will some people suffer more than others from a recession?***

Figure 13.4 Growth rates in selected industrial countries

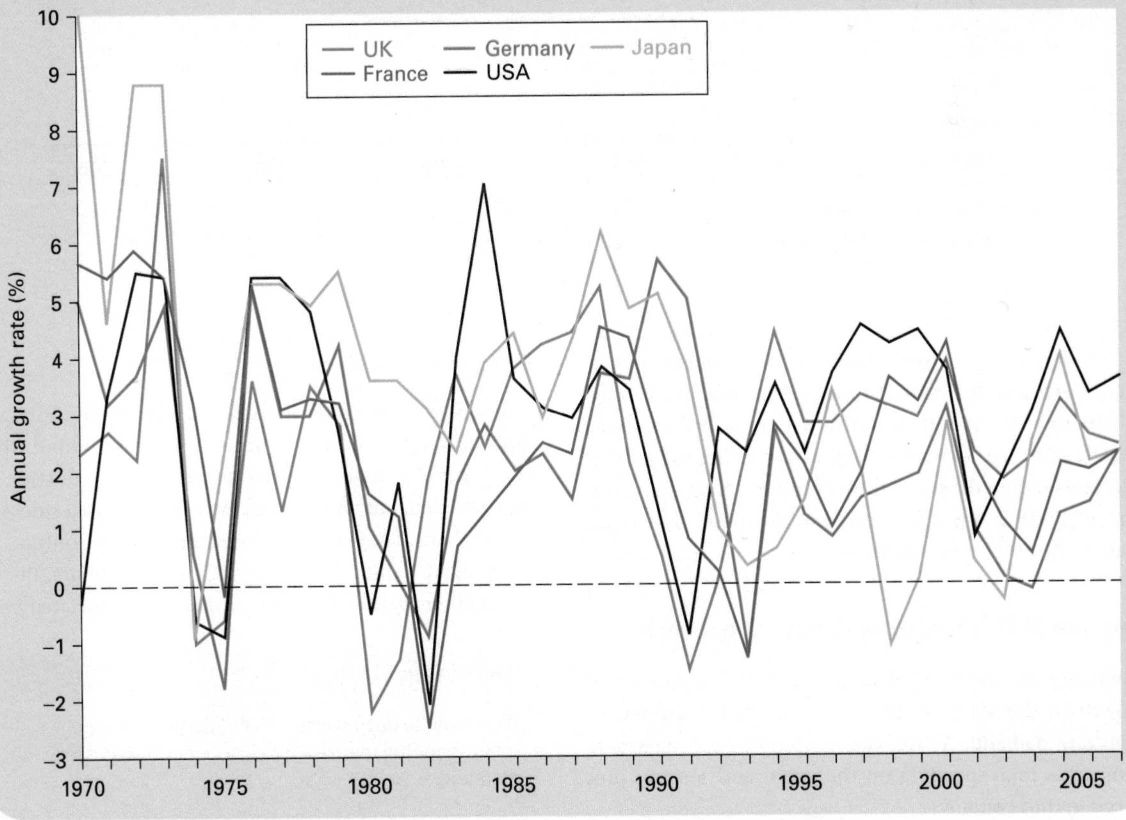

EXPLORING ECONOMICS

OUTPUT GAPS

An alternative measure of excess or deficient demand

If the economy grows, how fast and for how long can it grow before it runs into inflationary problems? What level of growth might be sustainable over the longer term?

To answer this question, economists have developed the concept of 'output gaps'.[4] The output gap is the difference between actual output and *sustainable* output. ***Sustainable output***[5] is the level of output corresponding to stable inflation. If output is below this level (the gap is negative), there will be a deficiency of demand and hence demand-deficient unemployment, but a fall in inflation. If output is above

Output gaps in selected countries: 1980–2006

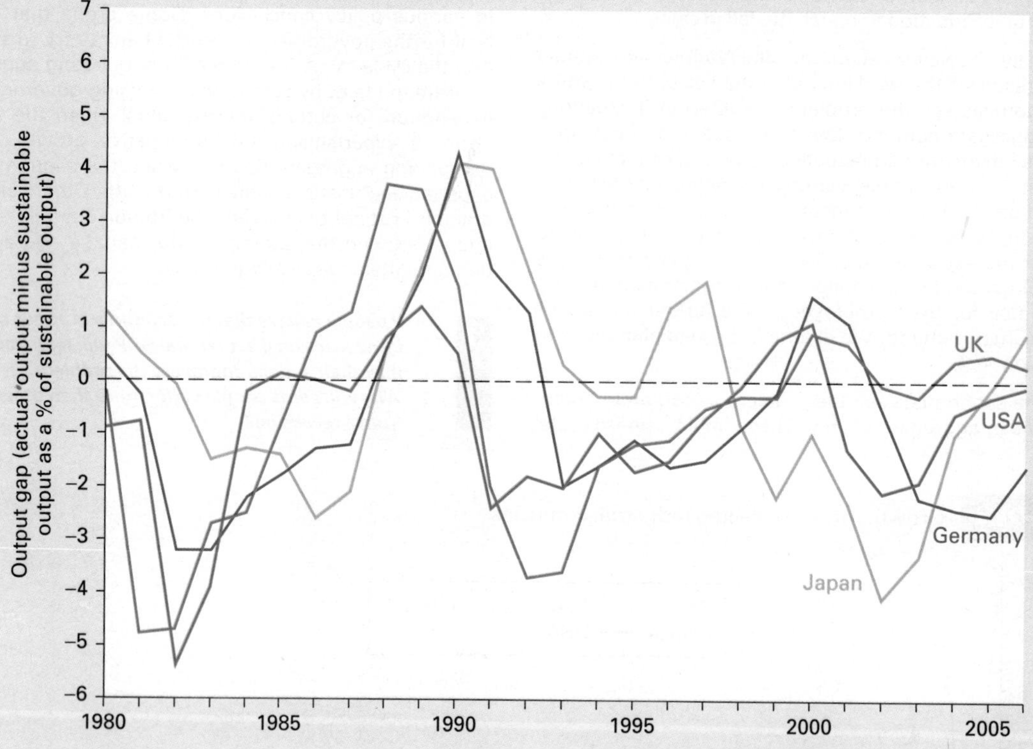

Note: 2005 and 2006 forecasts.

Source: Based on data in *Economic Outlook* (OECD, various years).

But despite this broad similarity in their experience, there were nevertheless significant differences in the magnitude and timing of their individual cycles. For example, the UK and the USA went into recession in the early 1990s two years before the other three countries. Also, the recession of 2001–2 was more severe in Germany and Japan than in the other three countries.

Causes of fluctuations in actual growth

The major determinants of variations in the rate of actual growth in the *short run* are variations in the growth of aggregate demand. As we saw in section 13.2, aggregate demand is total spending on the goods and services produced in the economy:

$$AD = C + I + G + X - M$$

A rapid rise in aggregate demand will create shortages. This will tend to stimulate firms to increase output, thus reducing slack in the economy. Likewise, a reduction in aggregate demand will leave firms with increased stocks of unsold goods. They will therefore tend to reduce output.

Aggregate demand and actual output, therefore, fluctuate together in the short run. A boom is associated with

Definition

Sustainable output The level of national output corresponding to no excess or deciency of aggregate demand.

BOX 13.4

this level (the gap is positive), there will be excess demand and a rise in inflation. Generally, output will be below this level in a recession and above it in a boom. In other words, output gaps follow the course of the business cycle.

The diagram shows output gaps for four countries from 1980 to 2006. As you can see, there was a large positive output gap in the UK in the late 1980s. This corresponded to a rapid rise in output and inflation and a fall in unemployment. You will also see that there was a large negative output gap in Japan in the early 2000s. This corresponded to a deep recession, high unemployment and inflation just below zero (i.e. a slight decline in prices).

Over the *long* term, the rate of economic growth will be approximately the same as the rate of growth of sustainable output. In other words, over the years, the average output gap will tend towards zero.

But how do we measure the output gap? There are two possible methods.

Measuring trend growth. The simplest way of calculating the output gap is by measuring the trend growth rate of the economy (i.e. the average growth rate over the course of the business cycle: see Figure 13.3) and then seeing how much actual output differs from trend output. The assumption here is that the sustainable level of output grows steadily. This is, in fact, a major weakness of this method. Technological innovations tend to come in waves, generating surges in an economy's sustainable output. Rates of innovation, in turn, depend upon how flexible the economy is in adapting to such new technologies and how much investment takes place in equipment using this technology and in training labour in the necessary skills.

Business surveys. An alternative way to measure the output gap is to ask businesses directly. However, survey-based evidence can provide only a broad guide to rates of capacity utilisation and whether there is deficient or excess demand. Survey evidence tends to focus on specific sectors, which might, or might not, be indicative of the capacity position of the economy as a whole.

Evidence for the UK. The trend growth rate in the UK was just over $2^1/_2$ per cent per year over the full economic cycle to 2002 (i.e. from 1992: the equivalent point in the previous cycle). But whereas the economy in 1992 was suffering quite a severe recession, with negative growth for six of the eight quarters from 1990 quarter 3, in 2002 the economy was experiencing a relatively mild slowdown (economic growth was 1.8 per cent). This reflects the fact that cyclical fluctuations in the UK have become less severe in recent years.

The question is whether the greater stability in the UK economy is encouraging a climate that will lead to a long-term increase in investment and hence a long-term increase in sustainable growth.

Under what circumstances would sustainable output (i.e. a zero output gap) move further away from the potential output ceiling shown in Figure 13.3?

[4] See Giorno *et al.*, 'Potential output, output gaps and structural budget balances', *OECD Economic Studies*, no. 24, 1995: 1.

[5] The level of sustainable output is sometimes referred to as the level of 'potential output'. This, however, is confusing, as the term 'potential output' is used elsewhere (including this book) to refer to full-capacity output. Full-capacity output, however, would not normally be sustainable over the longer term because of the upward pressure on inflation caused by various bottlenecks in the economy. Thus sustainable output is *below* the level of potential output in the sense that we are using the term 'potential output' (e.g. as in Figure 13.3).

a rapid rise in aggregate demand: the faster the rise in aggregate demand, the higher the short-run growth rate. A recession, by contrast, is associated with a reduction in aggregate demand.

A rapid rise in aggregate demand, however, is not enough to ensure a continuing high level of growth over a *number* of years. Without an expansion of potential output too, rises in actual output must eventually come to an end. Once spare capacity has been used up, once there is full employment of labour and other resources, the rate of growth of actual output will be restricted to the rate of growth of potential output. This is illustrated in Figure 13.3 (page 380). As long as actual output is below potential output, the actual output curve can slope upwards more steeply than the potential output curve. But once the gap between the two curves has been closed, the actual output curve can only slope as steeply as the potential output curve: the two curves cannot cross – actual output cannot be above potential output.[6]

[6] This statement depends on precisely how 'potential output' is defined, and unfortunately there is no simple universally agreed definition. If it is defined as the maximum output that is achievable (the way we have defined it), then clearly actual output cannot exceed potential output. If, however, it is defined as the output that can be achieved when factors are employed to a 'normal' level – i.e. allowing for some unemployment as people move from job to job and firms have a planned degree of spare capacity to meet unexpected demand – then actual output could temporarily exceed potential output if factors were used at a higher than normal rate. This is the definition that is commonly used when describing the size of 'output gaps' (i.e. over-capacity). We explore this in Box 13.4.

Section summary

1. Actual growth must be distinguished from potential growth. The actual growth rate is the percentage annual increase in the output that is actually produced, whereas potential growth is the percentage annual increase in the capacity of the economy to produce (whether or not it is actually produced).
2. Actual growth will fluctuate with the course of the business cycle. The cycle can be broken down into four phases: the upturn, the expansion, the peaking out, and the slowdown or recession. In practice, the length and magnitude of these phases will vary: the cycle is thus irregular.
3. Actual growth is determined by potential growth and by the level of aggregate demand. If actual output is below potential output, actual growth can temporarily exceed potential growth, if aggregate demand is rising sufficiently. In the long term, however, actual output can grow only as fast as potential output will permit.

13.5 LONG-TERM ECONOMIC GROWTH

For growth to be sustained over the long term, there must be an increase in *potential* output. In other words, the country's capacity to produce must increase. In this section we see what determines this capacity and why some countries grow faster than others over the long term. What we are concerned with here, therefore, is the *supply* side of the economy, rather than the level of aggregate demand.

Causes of long-term growth

KI 16 p120 There are two main determinants of potential output: (a) the amount of resources available and (b) their productivity. If supply potential is to grow, then either (a) or (b) or both must grow.

Increases in the quantity of resources: capital, labour, land and raw materials

Capital. The nation's output depends on its stock of capital (K). An increase in this stock will increase output. If we ignore the problem of machines wearing out or becoming obsolete and needing replacing, then the stock of capital will increase by the amount of investment: $\Delta K = I$.

But by how much will this investment raise output? This depends on the productivity of this new capital: on the *marginal efficiency of capital* (see page 253). Let us define the nation's marginal efficiency of capital (MEC) as the annual extra income (ΔY) yielded by an increase in the capital stock, relative to the cost of that extra capital (ΔK).

$$MEC = \frac{\Delta Y}{\Delta K} = \frac{\Delta Y}{I}$$

Thus if £100 million of extra capital yielded an annual income of £25 million, the marginal efficiency of capital would be £25 million/£100 million = $^1/_4$.

The rate of growth will depend on the fraction (i) of national income devoted to new investment (i.e. investment over and above what is necessary to replace worn-out equipment). The higher this rate of new investment, the higher will be the potential growth rate.

The relationship between the investment rate and the potential growth rate (g_p) is given by the simple formula:

$$g_p = i \times MEC$$

Thus if 20 per cent of national income went in new investment (i), and if each £1 of new investment yielded 25p of extra income per year ($MEC = ^1/_4$), then the growth rate would be 5 per cent. A simple example will demonstrate this. If national income is £100 billion, then £20 billion will be invested (i = 20 per cent). This will lead to extra annual output of £5 billion ($MEC = ^1/_4$). Thus national income grows to £105 billion: a growth of 5 per cent.

But what determines the rate of investment? There are a number of determinants. These include the confidence of business people about the future demand for their products, the profitability of business, the tax regime, the rate of growth in the economy and the rate of interest. We will examine these determinants in section 16.1.

Over the long term, if investment is to increase, then people must *save* more in order to finance that extra investment. Put another way, people must be prepared to consume less in order to allow more resources to be diverted into producing capital goods: factories, machines, etc.

Labour. If there is an increase in the working population, there will be an increase in potential output. This increase in working population may result from a higher 'participation rate': a larger proportion of the total population in work or seeking work. For example, if a greater proportion of women with children decide to join the labour market, the working population will rise.

Alternatively, a rise in the working population may be the result of an increase in total population. There is a problem here. If a rise in total population does not result in a greater *proportion* of the population working, output *per head* of population may not rise at all. In practice, many developed countries are faced with a growing proportion of their population above retirement age, and thus a potential *fall* in output per head of population.

THINKING LIKE AN ECONOMIST

LONG-TERM GROWTH IN A COUNTRY'S OUTPUT DEPENDS ON A GROWTH IN THE QUANTITY AND/OR PRODUCTIVITY OF ITS RESOURCES

In the short term, economic growth is likely to be influenced by changes in aggregate demand. If the economy is in recession, an expansion in aggregate demand will help to bring the economy out of recession and move it closer to full employment.

Actual output, however, cannot continue growing faster than potential output over the longer term. Firms will start reaching capacity and actual growth will then have to slow. The rate of potential growth thus places a limit to the rate of actual growth over the longer term.

What then determines the rate of growth in potential output? The answer lies on the supply side. It depends on the rate of growth of factors of production. There are two key elements here. The first is growth in the simple quantity of factors: growth in the size of the workforce, of the available land and raw materials, and of the stock of capital. The second is productivity growth. This involves elements such as growth in the educational attainments and skills of the workforce, growth in technology and growth in the efficiency with which resources are used.

To recognise the importance of resources and their productivity in determining long-term growth is a *threshold concept.* It helps in understanding the importance of designing appropriate *supply-side* policies: policies that focus on increasing aggregate supply rather than managing aggregate demand. It is easy to worry too much about the short term.

This is not to say that the short term should be neglected. John Maynard Keynes, the famous economist, argued that it was fundamentally important to focus on aggregate demand and the short term to avoid severe economic fluctuations, with the twin problems of high unemployment in recessions and high inflation in periods of unsustainably high growth. He used the famous phrase 'In the long term we're all dead.'

But although we all have to die some time, we may have many years left to reap the benefits of appropriate *supply-side* policy. And even if we don't, our children will.

1. ***Give some examples of supply-side policy (see Chapter 22 for some ideas if you are stuck).***
2. ***If there is an increase in aggregate supply, will this result in an increase in potential growth?***

Land and raw materials. The scope for generating growth here is usually very limited. Land is virtually fixed in quantity. Land reclamation schemes and the opening up of marginal land can add only tiny amounts to national output. Even if new raw materials are discovered (e.g. oil), this will result only in *short-term* growth: i.e. while the rate of extraction is building up. Once the rate of extraction is at a maximum, economic growth will cease. Output will simply remain at the new higher level, until eventually the raw materials begin to run out. Output will then fall back again.

The problem of diminishing returns. If a single factor of production increases in supply while others remain fixed, diminishing returns will set in. For example, if the quantity of capital increases with no increase in other factors of production, diminishing returns to capital will set in. The rate of return on capital will fall.

Unless *all* factors of production increase, therefore, the rate of growth is likely to slow down. It is not enough that labour and capital increase if there is a limited supply of land and raw materials. This was the worry of the classical economists of the nineteenth century, who were pessimistic about the future prospects for growth (see Box 13.5).

Then there is the problem of the environment. If a rise in labour and capital leads to a more *intensive* use of land and natural resources, the resulting growth in output may be environmentally unsustainable.

The solution to the problem of diminishing returns is an increase in the *productivity* of resources.

Increases in the productivity of resources

TC 14
p385

Technological improvements can increase the marginal productivity of capital. Much of the investment in new machines is not just in extra machines, but in superior machines producing a higher rate of return. Consider the microchip revolution of recent years. Modern computers can do the work of many people and have replaced many machines that were cumbersome and expensive to build. Improved methods of transport have reduced the costs of moving goods and materials. Improved communications (such as e-mail and the Internet) have reduced the costs of transmitting information. The high-tech world of today would seem a wonderland to a person of 100 years ago.

As a result of technical progress, the productivity of capital has tended to increase, not decrease, over time. Similarly, as a result of new skills, improved education and training, and better health, the productivity of labour has also tended to increase over time.

But technical progress on its own is not enough. There must also be the institutions and attitudes that encourage *innovation*. In other words, the inventions must be exploited.

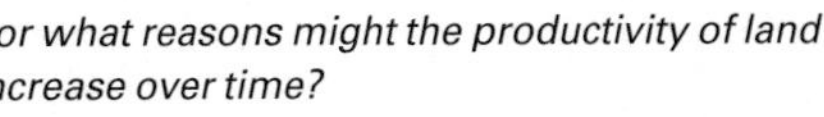

For what reasons might the productivity of land increase over time?

EXPLORING ECONOMICS — BOX 13.5

THEORIES OF GROWTH

From dismal economics to the economics of optimism

The classical theory of growth

The classical economists of the nineteenth century were very pessimistic about the prospects for economic growth. They saw the rate of growth petering out as diminishing returns to both labour and capital led to low wages and a falling rate of profit. The only gainers would be landlords, who, given the fixed supply of land, would receive higher and higher rents as the demand for scarce land rose.

Long-run stationary state in the classical model

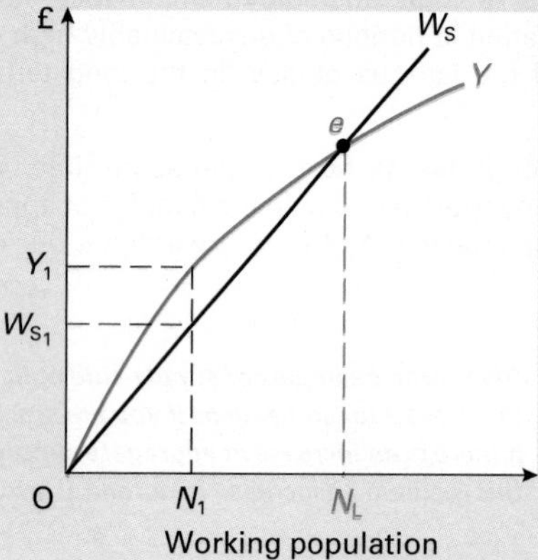

The classical position can be shown graphically. The size of the working population is plotted on the horizontal axis. If it is assumed that there is a basic minimum 'subsistence' wage that workers must earn in order to survive, then the line W_S traces out the total subsistence wage bill. It is a straight line because a doubling in the number of workers would lead to a doubling of the subsistence wage bill.

The line Y shows the total level of income that will be generated as more workers are employed, after subtracting rents to landlords. In other words, it is total wages plus profits. It gets less and less steep due to diminishing returns to labour and capital given the fixed supply of land.

As long as Y is above W_S (say, at a population of N_1), firms can make a profit. They will try to expand and will thus take on more labour.

Initially this will bid up the wage and will thus erode the level of profits. But the higher wages will encourage the population to expand. This increased supply of labour will compete wages back down to the subsistence level and will thus allow *some* recovery in profits. But profits will not be as high as they were before because, with an increase in workers, the gap between Y and W_S will have narrowed.

Firms will continue to expand and the population will continue to grow until point e is reached. At that point, even with wages at bare subsistence level, no profit can be made. Growth will cease. The economy will be in a long-run stationary state.

No wonder economics became dubbed 'the dismal science'.

New growth theory

Economists today are more optimistic about the prospects for economic growth. This is partly based on a simple appeal to the evidence. Despite a rapid growth in world population, most countries have experienced sustained economic growth. Over the last hundred years the industrialised countries have seen per-capita growth rates averaging from just over 1 per cent to nearly 3 per cent per annum. This has resulted in per-capita real incomes many times higher than in the nineteenth century.

This worldwide experience of economic growth has stimulated the development of new growth theories. These stress two features:

- The development and spread of new technology. The rapid advances in science and technology have massively increased the productivity of factors of production. What is more, new inventions and innovations stimulate other people, often in other countries, to copy, adapt and improve on them in order to stay competitive. Growth through technical progress stimulates more growth.
- The positive externalities of investment. If one KI 28 p300
firm invests in training in order to raise labour productivity, other firms will benefit from the improved stock of 'human capital'. There will be better-trained labour that can now be hired by *other* firms. Similarly, if one firm invests in research and development, the benefits can spill over to other firms (once any patents have expired). These spillover benefits to other firms can be seen as the *positive externalities* of investment.

New growth theories seek to analyse the process of the spread of technology and how it can be influenced.

Given that technological progress allows the spectre of diminishing returns to be banished, or at least indefinitely postponed, it is no wonder that many economists are more optimistic about growth. Nevertheless, there are still serious grounds for concern.

- If the benefits of investment spill over to other firms (i.e. if there are positive externalities), the free market will lead to too little investment: firms considering investing will take into account only the benefits to themselves, not those to *other* firms. There is thus an important role for governments to encourage or provide training, research and capital investment. (We consider such policies in Chapter 22.)
- Potential growth may not translate into actual growth. A *potentially* growing economy may be languishing in a deep recession.
- There may be serious costs of economic growth: see Box 13.3.

Can growth go on for ever, given that certain resources are finite in supply?

*LOOKING AT THE MATHS

Assuming that the quantity of land is fixed, economic growth (g) results from three main sources: the rate of growth in the labour force ($\Delta L/L$), the rate of growth in the stock of capital ($\Delta K/K$) and the rate of growth in overall productivity in the economy or 'total factor productivity' ($\Delta TFP/TFP$). Thus:

$$g = \frac{\Delta Y}{Y} = a\frac{\Delta L}{L} + b\frac{\Delta K}{K} + \frac{\Delta TFP}{TFP} \quad (1)$$

where a is the elasticity of national income (Y) with respect to labour. In other words, a is the percentage increase in national income that would result from a 1 per cent increase in the labour force. Similarly, b is the elasticity of national income with respect to capital: i.e. the percentage increase in national income from a 1 per cent increase in the capital stock.[7] If there are constant returns to scale, then:

$$a + b = 1$$

In other words, an increase in both labour and capital of x per cent would lead to an x per cent increase in national income.

If the capital stock is held constant and the labour force increases, there will be diminishing returns to labour. This implies that:

$$a < 1$$

and that the value of a gets less as the ratio of labour to capital increases. Similarly, if capital per head of the labour force increases, there will be diminishing returns to capital. This implies that:

$$b < 1$$

and that the value of b gets less as capital/labour ratio increases. In industrialised countries in the early 2000s the value of b is typically between 0.2 and 0.4, implying that a 10 per cent increase in the capital stock will increase national income by between 2 and 4 per cent. The value of a is typically between 0.6 and 0.8.

What about total factor productivity? Note that there is no 'c' term attached to $\Delta TFP/TFP$. What this means is that a total factor productivity increase of y per cent will lead to an increase in national income of y per cent for any given quantity of labour and capital. If we know the value of g, a, $\Delta L/L$, b and $\Delta K/K$, we can work out the rate of growth in total factor productivity. Rearranging equation (1) gives:

$$\frac{\Delta TFP}{TFP} = g - \left(a\frac{\Delta L}{L} + b\frac{\Delta K}{K}\right) \quad (2)$$

Web Case 13.4 examines how equation (1) can be used for growth accounting: a system of measuring the contribution of increases in factor inputs to economic growth. It also looks at the evidence for the UK.

[7] The term b is the elasticity of Y with respect to changes in K: i.e.

$$b = \frac{\Delta Y}{\Delta K} \cdot \frac{K}{Y} = MEC \cdot \frac{K}{Y}$$

But, from equation (1), growth from a rise in capital alone is given by:

$$g = b\frac{\Delta K}{K} = MEC \cdot \frac{K}{Y} \cdot \frac{\Delta K}{K}$$

Cancelling out the K terms gives:

$$g = \frac{\Delta K}{Y} \times MEC = i \times MEC$$

which is the formula for the growth rate that we established on page 384.

The effects of actual growth on potential growth

Some economists argue that potential growth is not influenced by actual growth. It depends largely on growth in factor productivity, and that in turn depends on scientific and technical advance. Such advances, they argue, are independent of the state of the economy.

Other economists, however, argue that actual growth *stimulates* investment and the development of new technology. For these economists, therefore, it is vital for the achievement of high long-term growth rates that the economy experiences continuous and stable growth in actual output. Recessions breed pessimism and a lack of investment, a lack of research and a lack of innovation.

Policies to achieve growth

How can governments increase a country's growth rate? Policies differ in two ways.

First, they may focus on the demand side or the supply side of the economy. In other words, they may attempt to create sufficient *aggregate demand* to ensure that firms wish to invest and that potential output is realised. Alternatively they may seek to increase *aggregate supply* by concentrating on measures to increase potential output: measures to encourage research and development, innovation and training.

Second, they may be market-orientated or interventionist policies. Many economists and politicians, especially those on the political right, believe that the best environment for encouraging economic growth is one where private enterprise is allowed to flourish: where entrepreneurs are able to reap substantial rewards from investment in new techniques and new products. Such economists, therefore, advocate policies designed to free up the market. Others, however, argue that a free market will be subject to considerable cyclical fluctuations. The resulting uncertainty will discourage investment. These economists, therefore, tend to advocate active intervention by the government to reduce these fluctuations.

We focus on demand-side policies in Chapter 19 and on supply-side policies in Chapter 22. In each case we look at both interventionist and market-orientated policies.

Postscript: the role of investment

Investment plays a twin role in economic growth. It is a component of aggregate demand and thus helps determine the level of actual output. It is also probably the major determinant of potential output, since investment both increases the capital stock and also leads to the development of new technology. It is important, therefore, that when investment rises, the resulting rise in aggregate demand matches the resulting rise in aggregate supply.

Section summary

1. Growth in potential output is determined by the rate of increase in the *quantity* of resources: capital, labour, land and raw materials; and by the *productivity* of resources. The productivity of capital can be increased by technological improvements and a more efficient use of the capital stock; the productivity of labour can be increased by better education, training, motivation and organisation.
2. Whether governments can best achieve rapid growth through market-orientated or interventionist policies is highly controversial.
3. Investment plays a key role in determining growth, since it affects both aggregate demand and aggregate supply.

APPENDIX: CALCULATING GDP

As explained in section 13.3, there are three ways of estimating GDP. In this appendix, we discuss each method in more detail. We also look at some alternative measures of national income.

The product method of measuring GDP

This approach simply involves adding up the value of everything produced in the country during the year: the output of cars, timber, lollipops, shirts, etc.; and all the myriad of services such as football matches, haircuts, bus rides and insurance services. In the national accounts these figures are grouped together into broad categories such as manufacturing, construction and distribution. The figures for the UK economy for 2004 are shown in Figure A13.1.

When we add up the output of various firms, we must be careful to avoid *double counting*. For example, if a manufacturer sells a television to a retailer for £200 and the retailer sells it to the consumer for £300, how much has this television contributed to GDP? The answer is *not* £500. We do not add the £200 received by the manufacturer to the £300 received by the retailer: that would be double counting. Instead we either just count the final value (£300) or the *value added* at each stage (£200 by the manufacturer + £100 by the retailer).

The sum of all the values added at each of the stages of production by all the various industries in the economy is known as ***gross value added at basic prices (GVA)***.

Some qualifications

Stocks (or inventories). We must be careful only to include the values added in the *particular year in question*. A problem

Definition

Gross value added at basic prices (GVA) The sum of all the values added by all industries in the economy over a year. The figures exclude taxes on products (such as VAT) and include subsidies on products.

Figure A13.1 UK GDP product-based measure: 2004

	Percentage of GVA
Agriculture, forestry and fishing £9381 m	0.9
Mining, energy and water supply £46 171 m	4.5
Manufacturing £154 636 m	15.0
Construction £67 619 m	6.5
Wholesale and retail trade; repairs £128 382 m	12.4
Hotels and restaurants £33 757 m	3.3
Transport and communication £78 279 m	7.6
Financial intermediation (Banking, finance, insurance etc.) £20 794 m	2.0
Letting of property (business and dwellings) £254 669 m	24.6
Public administration and defence £53 483 m	5.2
Education, health and social work £131 918 m	12.8
Other services £54 236 m	5.2
Gross value added (GVA) at basic prices £1033 324 m	100.0

Taxes on products	£138 639 m
Less subsidies on products	£7542 m

Total GDP (at market prices) £1 164 439 m

Source: *UK National Income and Expenditure* (National Statistics, 2005).

here is that some goods start being produced *before* the year begins. Thus when we come to work out GDP, we must ignore the values that had previously been added to stocks of raw materials and goods. Similarly, other goods are only sold to the consumer *after* the end of the year. Nevertheless we must still count the values that have been added during *this* year to these stocks of partially finished goods.

A final problem concerned with stocks is that they may increase in value simply due to increased prices. This is known as ***stock (or inventory) appreciation***. Since there has been no real increase in output, stock appreciation must be deducted from value added.

Government services. The output of private industry is sold on the market and can thus be easily valued. This is not the case with most of the services provided by the government. Such services (e.g. health and education) should be valued in terms of what they cost to provide.

Ownership of dwellings. When a landlord rents out a flat, this service is valued as the rent that the tenant pays. But owner occupiers living in their own property do not pay rent and yet they are 'consuming' a similar 'service'. Here a rental value for owner occupation is 'imputed'. In other words, a figure corresponding to a rent is included in the GDP statistics under the 'letting of property' heading.

Taxes and subsidies on products. Taxes paid on goods and services (such as VAT) and any subsidies on products are *excluded* from gross value added (GVA), since they are not part of the value added in production. Nevertheless the way GDP is measured throughout the EU is at *market prices*: i.e. at the prices actually paid at each stage of production. Thus ***GDP at market prices*** (sometimes referred to simply as GDP) is GVA *plus* taxes on products *minus* subsidies on products.

The income method of measuring GDP

The second approach focuses on the incomes generated from the production of goods and services. This must be the same as the sum of all values added, since value added is simply the difference between a firm's revenue from sales and the costs of its purchases from other firms. This difference is made up of wages and salaries, rent, interest and profit: the incomes earned by those involved in the production process.

Definitions

Stock (or inventory) appreciation The increase in monetary value of stocks due to increased prices. Since this does not represent increased output, it is not included in GDP.

GDP (at market prices) The value of output (or income or expenditure) in terms of the prices actually paid. GDP = GVA + Taxes on products – Subsidies on products.

Since GDP is the sum of all values added, it must also be the sum of all incomes generated: the sum of wages and salaries, rent, interest and profit.

?

If a retailer buys a product from a wholesaler for £80 and sells it to a consumer for £100, then the £20 of value that has been added will go partly in wages, partly in rent and partly in profits. Thus £20 of income has been generated at the retail stage. But the good actually contributes a total of £100 to GDP. Where, then, is the remaining £80 worth of income recorded?

Figure A13.2 shows how these incomes are grouped together in the official statistics. By far the largest category is 'compensation of employees': in other words, wages and salaries. As you can see, the total in Figure A13.2 is the same as in Figure A13.1, although the components are quite different. In other words, GDP is the same whether calculated by the product or the income method.

Figure A13.2 UK GDP by category of income: 2004

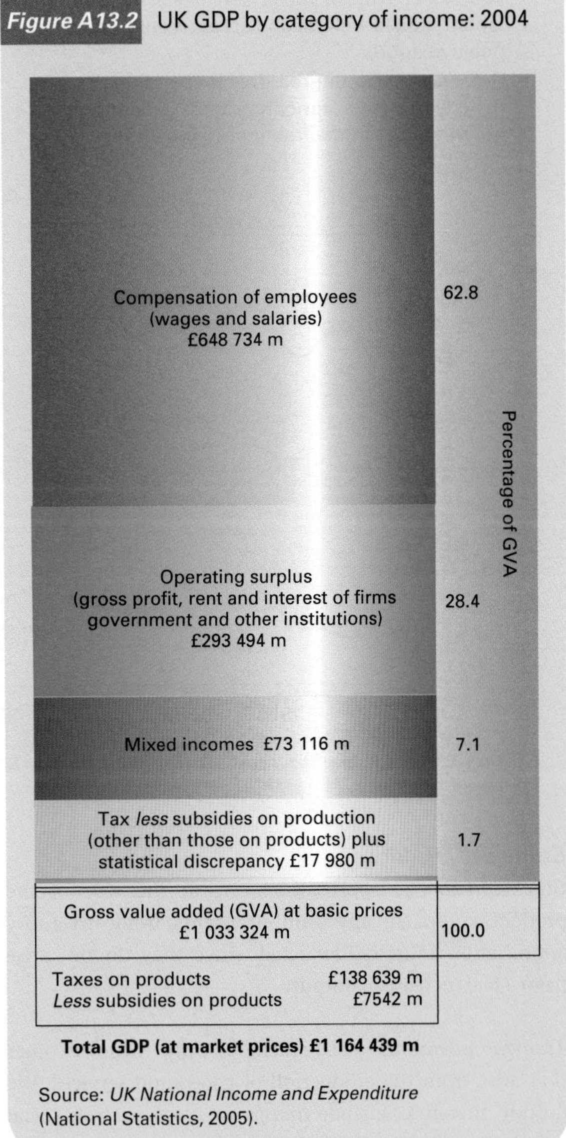

Source: *UK National Income and Expenditure* (National Statistics, 2005).

EXPLORING ECONOMICS

WHEN HIGHER GDP CAN LEAD TO LOWER WELFARE

The use of ISEW: the index of sustainable economic welfare

GDP is not a complete measure of economic welfare: nor is it meant to be. So is there any alternative that takes other factors into account and gives a more complete picture of the level of human well-being?

One measure that is popular among environmental groups is the *index of sustainable economic welfare* (ISEW).[8] This starts with consumption, as measured in GDP, and then makes various adjustments to account for factors that GDP ignores. These include:

- Inequality: the greater the inequality, the more the figure for consumption is reduced. This is based on the assumption of a diminishing marginal utility of income, such that an additional pound is worth less to a rich person than to a poor person.
- Household production (such as child care, care for the elderly or infirm, housework and various do-it-yourself activities). These 'services of household labour' add to welfare and are thus entered as a positive figure.
- Defensive expenditures. This is spending to offset the adverse environmental effects of economic growth (e.g. asthma treatment for sufferers whose condition arises from air pollution). Such expenditures are taken out of the calculations.
- 'Bads' (such as commuting costs). The monetary expense entailed is entered as a negative figure (to cancel out its measurement in GDP as a positive figure) and then an additional negative element is included for the stress incurred.
- Environmental costs. Pollution is entered as a negative figure.
- Resource depletion and damage. This too is given a negative figure, in just the same way that depreciation of capital is given a negative figure when working out net national income.

The table shows the calculation of ISEW for the UK for three years: 1950, 1973 and 1996. As you can see, household labour makes a substantial addition to GDP, but this is more than offset by inequality and various adverse environmental effects, especially the depletion of resources and long-term environmental damage.

The net effect is to make the UK's 1996 ISEW per capita only just over a quarter of GDP per capita (at constant prices). What is of perhaps more concern is

ISEW 1950–96 (maximum = 100)

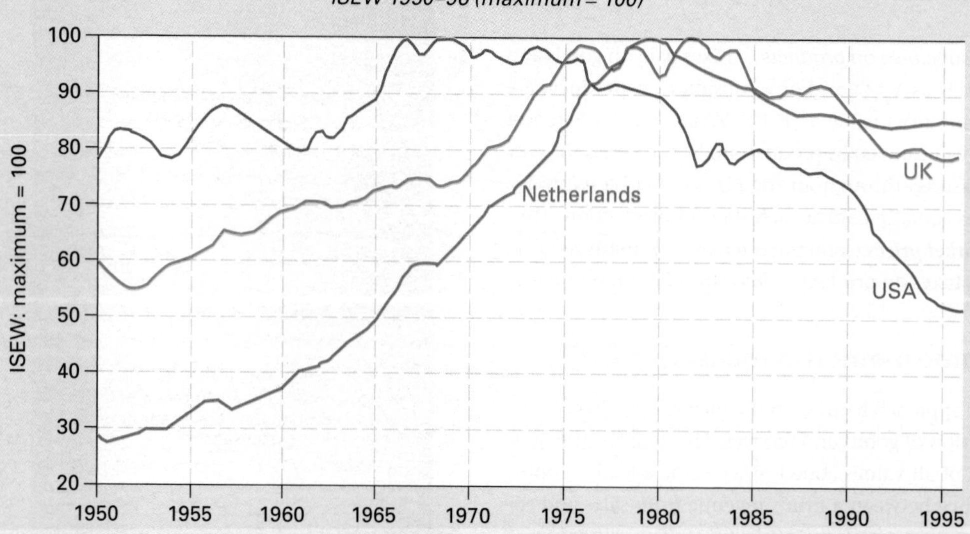

Source: E. Mayo, A. MacGillivray and D. McLaren, *Quality of Life Briefing* (New Economics Foundation/Friends of the Earth, 1998).

Some qualifications

Stock (inventory) appreciation. As in the case of the product approach, any gain in profits from inventory appreciation must be deducted, since they do not arise from a real increase in output.

Transfer payments. GDP includes only those incomes that arise from the production of goods and services. We do not, therefore, include *transfer payments* such as social security benefits, pensions and gifts.

Direct taxes. We count people's income *before* the payment of income and corporation taxes, since it is this *gross* (pre-tax) income that arises from the production of goods and services.

Taxes and subsidies on products. As with the product approach, if we are working out GVA, we measure incomes before the payment of taxes on products or the receipt of subsidies on products, since it is these pre-tax-and-subsidy incomes that arise from the value added by production.

BOX 13.6

Contributions to the index of sustainable economic welfare (ISEW) (£ per capita, 1990 prices)

	1950	1973	1996
Consumer expenditure	2435	4067	6402
Adjustment for inequality	−201	−316	−917
Services of household labour	948	1470	2368
Public expenditure on health and education	89	192	365
Difference between consumer expenditure on and services from goods	−206	−446	−1160
Defensive private expenditures on health and education	−14	−25	−109
Costs of commuting	−52	−127	−206
Costs of personal pollution control	–	−8	−58
Costs of car accidents	−30	−43	−36
Costs of water and air pollution	−504	−537	−376
Costs of noise pollution	−36	−36	−39
Costs of loss of habitat and farmlands	−35	−28	−88
Depletion of non-renewable resources	−332	−920	−1812
Long-term environmental damage	−292	−718	−1321
Ozone depletion costs	−8	−209	−621
Net capital growth	–	382	1
Change in net international position	37	52	−41
Per capita ISEW	***1799***	***2713***	***2349***
Per capita GDP	***3507***	***6151***	***8890***

Source: T. Jackson, N. Marks, J. Ralls and S. Stymne, *An Index of Sustainable Economic Welfare for the UK 1950–96*. (Centre for Environmental Strategy, University of Surrey).

that, while GDP per capita rose by nearly 50 per cent between 1973 and 1996, ISEW per capita actually fell (by 13.4 per cent). We may be materially richer, but if our lives are more stressful, if our environment is more polluted and if the gap between rich and poor has widened, it is easy to see how we could, in a real sense, be worse off than in the 1970s.

According to the 'threshold hypothesis', economic growth leads to a real improvement in the quality of life up to a certain point. Beyond that, however, further growth actually reduces the quality of life. The diagram shows this effect for three countries: the UK, the USA and the Netherlands. In each case, the maximum achieved ISEW is given a value of 100. Welfare peaked for the USA in the late 1960s, and for the UK and the Netherlands in about 1980.

Not surprisingly, ISEW has come in for considerable criticism. The most important one concerns the measurement of environmental effects, especially the long-term ones. For example, there is considerable debate as to the precise amount of global warming that results from the burning of fossil fuels, and the precise damage caused by a given amount of global warming. But as the advocates of the use of ISEW point out, *not* to count environmental effects is to give them a precise value: namely, zero! Surely, as Herman Daly argues, it is better to be roughly right than precisely wrong.

Make out a case against using ISEW. How would an advocate of he use of ISEW reply to your points?

[8] This measure was developed in the USA by Herman Daly, John Cobb and Clifford Cobb. See J. Daly and J. Cobb, *For the Common Good* (Beacon Press, Boston, MA, 1989).

When working out GDP, however, we add in these taxes and subtract these subsidies to arrive at a *market price* valuation.

The expenditure method of measuring GDP

The final approach to calculating GDP is to add up all expenditure on final output (which will be at market prices). This will include the following:

- Consumer expenditure (*C*). This includes all expenditure on goods and services by households and by non-profit institutions serving households (NPISH) (e.g. clubs and societies).
- Government expenditure (*G*). This includes central and local government expenditure on final goods and services. Note that it includes non-marketed services (such as health and education), but excludes transfer payments, such as pensions and social security payments.

Table A13.1 UK GDP at market prices by category of expenditure: 2004

	£ million	% of GDP
Consumption expenditure of households and NPISH (*C*)	760 678	65.3
Government final consumption (*G*)	246 810	21.2
Gross capital formation (*I*)	194 798	16.7
Exports of goods and services (*X*)	289 959	24.9
Imports of goods and services (*M*)	−328 384	−28.2
Statistical discrepancy	578	0.0
GDP at market prices	1 164 439	100.0

Source: *UK National Income and Expenditure* (National Statistics, 2005).

- Investment expenditure (I). This includes investment in capital, such as buildings and machinery. It also includes the value of any increase (+) or decrease (−) in inventories, whether of raw materials, semi-finished goods or finished goods.
- Exports of goods and services (X).

We then have to *subtract* imports of goods and services (M) from the total in order to leave just the expenditure on *domestic* product. In other words, we subtract the part of consumer expenditure, government expenditure and investment that goes on imports. We also subtract the imported component (e.g. raw materials) from exports.

$$\text{GDP (at market prices)} = C + G + I + X - M$$

Table A13.1 shows the calculation of the 2004 UK GDP by the expenditure approach.

From GDP to national income

Gross national income. Some of the incomes earned in this country will go abroad. These include wages, interest, profit and rent earned in this country by foreign residents and remitted abroad, and taxes on production paid to foreign governments and institutions (e.g. the EU). On the other hand, some of the incomes earned by domestic residents will come from abroad. Again, these can be in the form of wages, interest, profit or rent, or in the form of subsidies received from governments or institutions abroad. Gross *domestic* product, however, is concerned only with incomes generated *within* the country, irrespective of ownership. If, then, we are to take 'net income from abroad' into account (i.e. these inflows minus outflows), we need a new measure. This is ***gross national income (GNY)***.[9] It is defined as follows:

$$\text{GNY at market prices} = \text{GDP at market prices} + \text{Net income from abroad}$$

Table A13.2 UK GDP, GNY and NNY at market prices: 2004

	£ million
Gross domestic product (GDP)	**1 164 439**
Plus net income from abroad	25 184
Gross national income (GNY)	**1 189 623**
Less capital consumption (depreciation)	− 121 577
Net national income (NNY)	**1 068 046**

Source: *UK National Income and Expenditure* (National Statistics, 2005).

Thus GDP focuses on the value of domestic production, whereas GNY focuses on the value of incomes earned by domestic residents.

Net national income. The measures we have used so far ignore the fact that each year some of the country's capital equipment wears out or becomes obsolete: in other words, they ignore capital depreciation. If we subtract from gross national income an allowance for ***depreciation*** (or 'capital consumption' as it is called in the official statistics), we get ***net national income (NNY)***.

$$\text{NNY at market prices} = \text{GNY at market prices} - \text{Depreciation}$$

Table A13.2 shows the 2004 GDP, GNY and NNY figures for the UK.

Although NNY gives a truer picture of a nation's income than GNY, economists tend to use the gross figures because depreciation is hard to estimate accurately.

Households' disposable income

Finally, we come to a measure that is useful for analysing consumer behaviour. This is called ***households' disposable income***. It measures the income that people have available for spending (or saving): i.e. after any deductions for income tax, national insurance, etc. have been made. It is the best measure to use if we want to see how changes in household income affect consumption.

[9] In the official statistics, this is referred to as *GNI*. We use *Y* to stand for income, however, to avoid confusion with investment.

Definitions

Gross national income (GNY) GDP plus net income from abroad.

Depreciation The decline in value of capital equipment due to age or wear and tear.

Net national income (NNY) GNY minus depreciation.

Households' disposable income The income available for households to spend: i.e. personal incomes after deducting taxes on incomes and adding benefits.

How do we get from GNY at market prices to households' disposable income? As GNY measures the incomes that firms receive from production[10] (plus net income from abroad), we must deduct that part of their income that is *not* distributed to households. This means that we must deduct taxes that firms pay – taxes on goods and services (such as VAT), taxes on profits (such as corporation tax) and any other taxes – and add in any subsidies they receive. We must then subtract allowances for depreciation and any undistributed profits. This gives us the gross income that households receive from firms in the form of wages, salaries, rent, interest and distributed profits.

[10] We also include income from any public-sector production of goods or services (e.g. health and education) and production by non-profit institutions serving households.

To get from this to what is available for households to spend, we must subtract the money that households pay in income taxes and national insurance contributions, but add all benefits to households, such as pensions and child benefit: in other words, we must *include* transfer payments.

Households' disposable income =
GNY at market prices – Taxes paid by firms + Subsidies received by firms – Depreciation – Undistributed profits – Personal taxes + Benefits

Section summary

1. The product method measures the values added in all parts of the economy. Care must be taken in the evaluation of stocks, government services and the ownership of dwellings.
2. The income method measures all the incomes generated from domestic production: wages and salaries, rent, interest and profit. Transfer payments are not included, nor is stock appreciation.
3. The expenditure method adds up all the categories of expenditure: consumer expenditure, government expenditure, investment and exports. We then have to deduct the element of each that goes on imports in order to arrive at expenditure on *domestic* products. Thus GDP = $C + G + I + X - M$.
4. GDP at *market prices* measures what consumers pay for output (including taxes and subsidies on what they buy). Gross value added (GVA) measures what factors of production actually receive. GVA, therefore, is GDP at market prices minus taxes on products plus subsidies on products.
5. Gross *national* income (GNY) takes account of incomes earned from abroad (+) and incomes earned by people abroad from this country (–). Thus GNY = GDP plus net income from abroad.
6. Net national income (NNY) takes account of depreciation of capital. Thus NNY = GNY – Depreciation.
7. Personal disposable income is a measure of household income after the deduction of income taxes and the addition of benefits.

END OF CHAPTER QUESTIONS

1. The following table shows index numbers for real GDP (national output) for various countries (2000 = 100).

	2000	2001	2002	2003	2004	2005
USA	100.0	100.8	102.7	105.8	110.5	114.1
Japan	100.0	100.4	100.1	102.6	106.7	108.9
Germany	100.0	101.0	101.1	101.0	102.2	103.6
France	100.0	102.1	103.2	103.7	105.9	108.0
UK	100.0	102.3	104.1	106.4	109.8	112.7

Sources: Various.

(a) Work out the growth rate for each country for each year from 2001 to 2005.

(b) Plot the figures on a graph. Describe the pattern that emerges.

2. Explain how equilibrium would be restored in the circular flow of income if there were a fall in investment.
3. Explain the circumstances under which an increase in pensions and child benefit would (a) increase national income; (b) leave national income unaffected; (c) decrease national income.
4. For what reasons might GDP be a poor indicator of (i) the level of development of a country; (ii) its rate of economic development?
5. Will the rate of actual growth have any effect on the rate of potential growth?
6. For what possible reasons may one country experience a persistently faster rate of economic growth than another?
7. Why will investment affect both actual (short-term) growth and the long-term growth in potential output? What will be the implications if these two effects differ in magnitude?
8. Explain how you would derive a figure for households' disposable income if you were starting from a figure for GDP.

Additional case studies on the book's website (www.pearsoned.co.uk/sloman)

13.1 The GDP deflator. An examination of how GDP figures are corrected to take inflation into account.

13.2 Taking into account the redistributive effects of growth. This case shows how figures for economic growth can be adjusted to allow for the fact that poor people's income growth would otherwise count for far less than rich people's.

13.3 Simon Kuznets and the system of national income accounting. This looks at the work of Simon Kuznets, who devised the system of national income accounting that is used around the world. It describes some of the patterns of economic growth that he identified.

WEBSITES RELEVANT TO THIS CHAPTER

See sites listed at the end of Chapter 14 on page 428.

Chapter 14

Macroeconomic Issues and Analysis: an Overview

In the previous chapter we examined economic growth. In this chapter we turn to the other three key macroeconomic issues of unemployment, inflation and the balance of payments. We give an overview of these problems: how they are measured and their effects on society. We also have a first look at the causes of these problems. This helps prepare the ground for the analysis of later chapters.

We saw in Chapter 13 that macroeconomics deals with economic problems in the aggregate (i.e. for the whole economy). An important tool for analysing these aggregate problems is *aggregate demand and supply analysis*. We look at this analysis in section 14.2. This is then the basis for our analysis of inflation in section 14.3.

Part D has been laying the foundations of macroeconomics. The final section of this chapter brings the threads together. It examines the relationship between the four macroeconomic objectives in both the short run and the long run: something that will be explored in more detail in Part E.

CHAPTER MAP

14.1 UNEMPLOYMENT

TC 13 p381

Unemployment fluctuates with the business cycle. In recessions, such as those experienced by most countries in the early 1980s, early 1990s and early 2000s, unemployment tends to rise. In boom years, such as the late 1980s and late 1990s, it tends to fall. Figure 14.1 shows these cyclical movements in unemployment for selected countries.

As well as experiencing fluctuations in unemployment, most countries have experienced long-term changes in average unemployment rates. This is illustrated in Table 14.1, which shows average unemployment in the UK, the EU and the USA for four unemployment cycles (minimum to minimum). Average unemployment rates in the 1980s and 1990s were higher than in the 1970s, and average rates in the 1970s were, in turn, higher than in the 1950s and 1960s. In certain countries, such as the UK and USA, the late 1990s and early 2000s have seen a long-term fall in unemployment.

This section gives an overview of the problem of unemployment: how it is measured and what its costs are. Then we look at the range of possible causes of unemployment. We explore these causes and the policies for tackling unemployment in more detail as the book progresses.

Table 14.1 Average unemployment for given cycles (%)

Period	UK	EU	USA
1964–73	3.0	2.7	4.6
1974–9	5.0	4.7	5.8
1980–90	9.4	8.7	7.1
1991–2001	8.4	9.3	6.1

The meaning of 'unemployment'

Unemployment can be expressed either as a number (e.g. 1.6 million) or as a percentage (e.g. 6 per cent). But just who should be included in the statistics? Should it be everyone without a job? The answer is clearly no, since we would not want to include children and pensioners. We would probably also want to exclude those who were not looking for work, such as parents choosing to stay at home to look after children.

The most usual definition that economists use for the ***number unemployed*** is: *those of working age who are without work, but who are available for work at current wage rates.* If the figure is to be expressed as a percentage, then it is a percentage of the total ***labour force***. The labour force is defined as: *those in employment plus those unemployed.* Thus if 25 million people were employed and 1.5 million people were unemployed, the ***unemployment rate*** would be:

$$\frac{1.5}{25 + 1.5} \times 100 = 5.7\%$$

Definitions

Number unemployed (economist's definition) Those of working age who are without work, but who are available for work at current wage rates.

Labour force The number employed plus the number unemployed.

Unemployment rate The number unemployed expressed as a percentage of the labour force.

Figure 14.1 Unemployment rates in selected industrial countries: 1970–2006

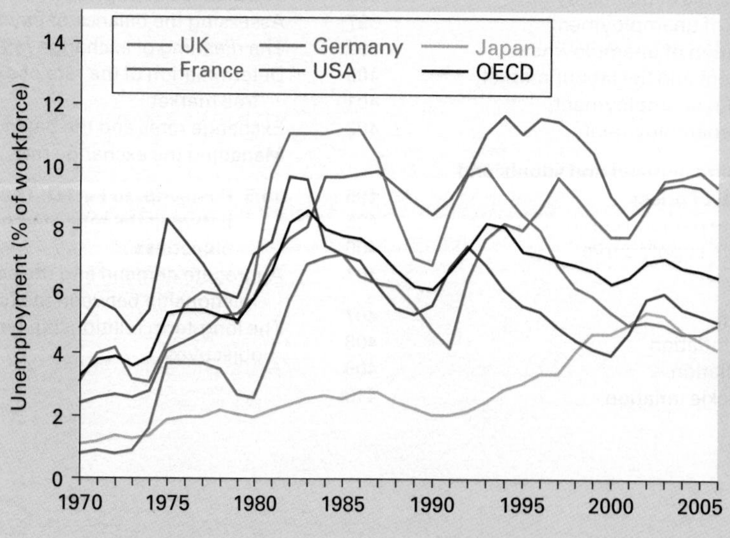

Source: *Thomson Financial.*

Official measures of unemployment

Claimant unemployment

Two common measures of unemployment are used in official statistics. The first is ***claimant unemployment***. This is simply a measure of all those in receipt of unemployment-related benefits. In the UK claimants receive the 'jobseeker's allowance'.

Claimant statistics have the advantage of being very easy to collect. However, they exclude all those of working age who are available for work at current wage rates, but who are *not* eligible for benefits. If the government changes the eligibility conditions so that fewer people are now eligible, this will reduce the number of claimants and hence the official number unemployed, even if there has been no change in the numbers with or without work.

The following categories of people are ineligible for benefits and are thus not included in claimant unemployment:

- People returning to the workforce (e.g. after raising children).
- Those who are on government training schemes (e.g. school leavers without jobs).
- People over 55. If such people are out of work, the benefit they receive is not regarded as 'unemployment related'.
- The temporarily unemployed.
- People seeking part-time work, rather than full-time work.

The claimant statistics in the UK thus understate the true level of unemployment.

Standardised unemployment rates

Recognising the weaknesses of the claimant statistics, the UK government since 1998 has used the ***standardised unemployment rate*** as the main measure of unemployment. In this measure, the unemployed are defined as people of working age who are without work, available to start work within two weeks and *actively seeking employment* or waiting to take up an appointment.

This is the measure used by the International Labour Organisation (ILO) and the Organisation for Economic Cooperation and Development (OECD), two international organisations that publish unemployment statistics for many countries. The figures are compiled from the results of national labour force *surveys*. A representative cross-section of the population is asked whether they are employed, unemployed (using the above definition) or economically inactive. From their replies, national rates of unemployment can be extrapolated. In the UK, the Labour Force Survey is conducted quarterly.

But is the standardised unemployment rate likely to be higher or lower than the claimant unemployment rate? The standardised rate is likely to be higher to the extent that it includes people seeking work who are nevertheless not entitled to claim benefits, but lower to the extent that it excludes those who are claiming benefits and yet who are not actively seeking work. Clearly, the tougher the benefit regulations, the lower the claimant rate will be relative to the standardised rate.

> ? *How does the ILO/OECD definition differ from the economist's definition? What is the significance of the phrase 'available for work at current wage rates' in the economist's definition?*

Definitions

Claimant unemployment Those in receipt of unemployment-related benefits.

Standardised unemployment rate The measure of the unemployment rate used by the ILO and OECD. The unemployed are defined as persons of working age who are without work, are available to start work within two weeks and either have actively looked for work in the last four weeks or are waiting to take up an appointment.

The duration of unemployment

A few of the unemployed may never have had a job and maybe never will. For most, however, unemployment lasts only a certain period. For some it may be just a few days while they are between jobs. For others it may be a few months. For others – the long-term unemployed – it could be several years. Table 14.2 shows the composition of standardised unemployment by duration.

What determines the average duration of unemployment? There are three important factors here.

The number unemployed (the size of the stock of unemployment). Unemployment is a 'stock' concept (see Box 9.9). It measures a *quantity* (i.e. the number unemployed) at a particular *point in time*. The higher the stock of unemployment, the longer will tend to be the duration of unemployment. There will be more people competing for vacant jobs.

The rate of inflow and outflow from the stock of unemployment. The people making up the unemployment total are constantly changing. Each week some people are made redundant or quit their jobs. They represent an inflow to the stock of unemployment. Other people find jobs and thus represent an outflow from the stock of unemployment. The various inflows and outflows are shown in Figure 14.2. 
KI 23 p251

Unemployment is often referred to as 'the pool of unemployment'. This is quite a good analogy. If the water flowing into a pool exceeds the water flowing out, the level of water in the pool will rise. Similarly, if the inflow of people into unemployment exceeds the outflow, the level of unemployment will rise.

Table 14.2 UK unemployment (ILO) by duration: Spring quarters (Mar–May)

	Up to 6 months	Over 6 and up to 12 months	Over 12 months	Total
1993 (thousands)	1156	576	1267	2999
(per cent)	*(38.6)*	*(19.2)*	*(42.2)*	*(100.0)*
1999 (thousands)	1025	269	503	1797
(per cent)	*(57.0)*	*(15.0)*	*(28.0)*	*(100.0)*
2004 (thousands)	915	232	291	1438
(per cent)	*(63.6)*	*(16.1)*	*(20.2)*	*(100.0)*

Source: *Labour Market Trends* (National Statistics).

Figure 14.2 Flows into and out of unemployment

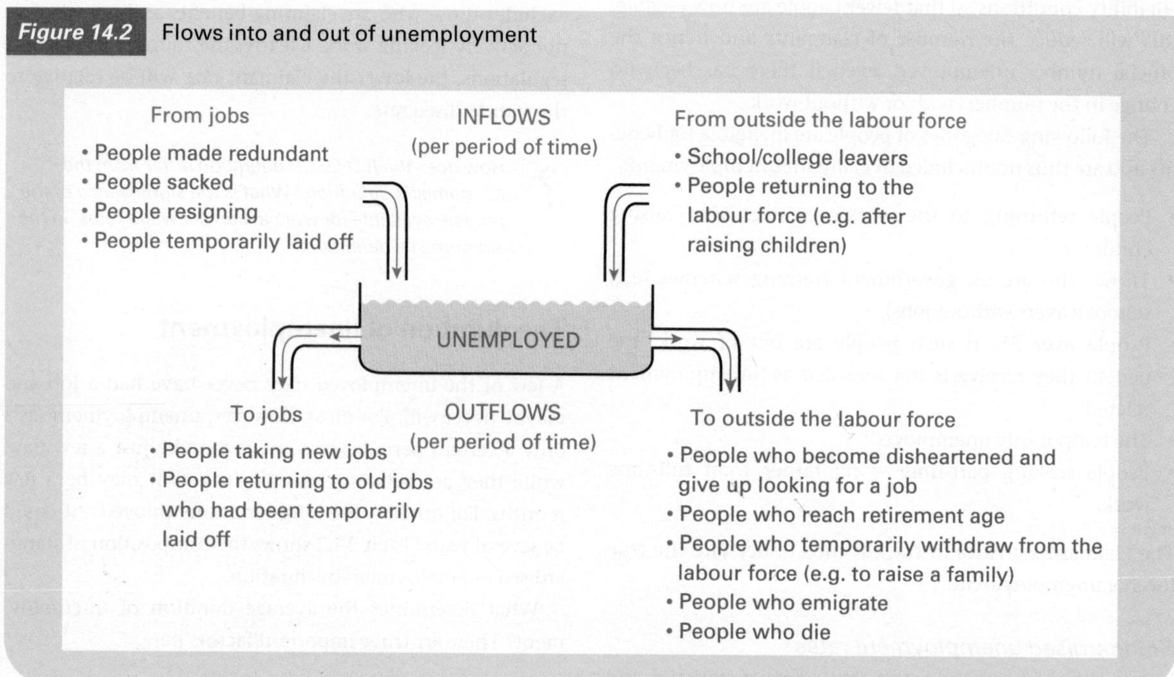

The duration of unemployment will depend on the *rate* of inflow and outflow. The rate is expressed as the number of people per period of time. Table 14.3 shows the inflows and outflows in selected years.

Note the magnitude of the flows. In each of the years, the outflows (and inflows) exceed the total number unemployed. The bigger the flows are relative to the total number unemployed, the less will be the average duration of unemployment. This is because people move into and out of the pool more quickly, and hence their average stay will be shorter.

?

1. *If the number unemployed exceeded the total annual outflow, what could we conclude about the average duration of unemployment?*
2. *Make a list of the various inflows to and outflows from employment from and to (a) unemployment; (b) outside the workforce.*

The phase of the business cycle. The duration of unemployment will also depend on the phase of the business cycle. At the onset of a recession, unemployment will rise, but as yet the average length of unemployment is likely to have been relatively short. Once a recession has lasted for a period of time, however, people on average will have been out of work longer, and this long-term unemployment is likely to persist even when the economy is pulling out of recession.

***LOOKING AT THE MATHS**

The duration of unemployment (D_U) will equal the stock of unemployment (U) as a proportion of the outflow (F) from unemployment.

$$D_u = \frac{U}{F}$$

Thus the bigger the stock of unemployment relative to the outflow from it, the longer will unemployment last. Taking the figures for 1992:

$$D_u = \frac{2.74}{4.09} = 0.67$$

Thus the average duration of unemployment was 0.67 years or 245 days. By contrast, in 2000, the average duration was 1.09/2.99 = 0.36 years or 133 days.

Table 14.3 UK (claimant) unemployment flows (millions)

	1980	1984	1986	1990	1992	1995	1998	2000	2002	2004
Inflow	3.85	4.50	4.49	3.51	4.51	3.62	3.08	2.85	2.74	2.42
Outflow	3.21	4.40	4.88	3.31	4.09	3.84	3.17	2.99	2.76	2.50
Total level of unemployment	1.66	3.16	3.29	1.65	2.74	2.29	1.35	1.09	0.95	0.85

Source: *Labour Market Trends* (National Statistics).

The composition of unemployment

Unemployment rates vary enormously between countries and between different groups within countries.

Geographical differences. Table 14.4 illustrates the considerable differences in unemployment rates between countries. Compare the unemployment rates in Ireland and Spain! Countries have very different labour markets, very different policies on unemployment, training schemes, redundancy, etc., and very different attitudes of firms towards their workers. Also, countries may not be at precisely the same phase of their respective business cycles.

Unemployment also varies substantially within a country from one area to another. Most countries have some regions that are more prosperous than others. In the UK, unemployment in the north of England, Scotland and Northern Ireland is higher than in the south of England. For example, in the fourth quarter of 2004, unemployment was 6.3 per cent in the north-east of England and only 3.2 per cent in the south-west.

But geographical differences in unemployment are not just a regional problem. In many countries, inner-city unemployment is very much higher than suburban or rural unemployment, and, as a result, most developed countries have schemes to attract employment to the inner cities. In 2002, unemployment in Tower Hamlets in London was 13.4 per cent, whereas in north Somerset it was 2.1 per cent.

Differences in unemployment rates between women and men. In many countries, female unemployment has traditionally been higher than male unemployment. Causes have included differences in education and training, discrimination by employers, more casual or seasonally-related employment among women and other social factors. In many countries, however, the position has changed in recent years. As you can see, in five of the countries in Table 14.4 male unemployment rates are higher than female. The main reason is the decline in many of the older industries, such as coal and steel, which employed mainly men.

Differences in unemployment rates between different age groups. Table 14.4 also shows that unemployment rates in the under-25 age group are higher than the average, and substantially so in many countries. There are various explanations for this, including the suitability (or unsuitability) of the qualifications of school leavers, the attitudes of employers to young people and the greater willingness of young people to spend time unemployed looking for a better job or waiting to start a further or higher education course. The only exception in the table is Germany, which has a well-established apprenticeship system.

Differences in unemployment rates between different ethnic groups. In many countries, members of ethnic minorities suffer from higher unemployment rates than

Table 14.4 Standardised unemployment rates in different sections of the labour market: 2004 (Q1)

Country	Total (all ages)	Women (all ages)	Men (all ages)	Total under 25 years old	Women under 25 years old	Men under 25 years old
Belgium	8.4	8.7	8.2	21.8	20.0	23.1
Germany	10.4	9.6	11.0	11.6	8.5	14.4
France	9.7	10.5	8.9	21.2	21.6	20.8
Ireland	4.6	4.1	4.9	8.1	7.2	9.1
Japan	5.0	4.7	5.2	10.5	9.1	11.8
Netherlands	4.8	5.0	4.7	9.4	8.5	10.2
Spain	11.4	15.7	8.4	23.1	27.6	19.7
UK	4.7	4.1	5.2	11.4	9.7	12.9
USA	6.1	5.6	6.5	12.4	11.1	13.6
EU-15	8.4	9.1	7.8	16.2	15.8	16.6

Source: *Eurostatistics* (Eurostat).

EXPLORING ECONOMICS **BOX 14.1**

THE COSTS OF UNEMPLOYMENT

Who loses and by how much?

The most obvious cost of unemployment is to the *unemployed themselves*. There is the direct financial cost of the loss in their earnings. Then there are the personal costs of being unemployed. The longer people are unemployed, the more dispirited they may become. Their self-esteem is likely to fall, and they are more likely to succumb to stress-related illness.

Then there are the costs to the *family and friends* of the unemployed. Personal relations can become strained, and there may be an increase in domestic violence and the number of families splitting up.

Then there are the *broader costs to the economy*. Unemployment represents a loss of output. In other words, actual output is below potential output. Apart from the lack of income to the unemployed themselves, this underutilisation of resources leads to lower incomes for other people too:

- The government loses tax revenues, since the unemployed pay no income tax and national insurance, and, given that the unemployed spend less, they pay less VAT and excise duties. The government also incurs administrative costs associated with the running of benefit offices. It may also have to spend extra on health care, the social services and the police.
- Firms lose the profits that could have been made, had there been full employment.
- Other workers lose any additional wages they could have earned from higher national output.

What is more, the longer people remain unemployed, the more deskilled they tend to become, thereby reducing *potential* as well as actual income.

Why have the costs to the government of unemployment benefits not been included as a cost to the economy?

Finally, there is some evidence that higher unemployment leads to increased *crime and vandalism*. This obviously imposes a cost on the sufferers.

The costs of unemployment are to some extent offset by benefits. If workers voluntarily quit their jobs to look for a better one, then they must reckon that the benefits of a better job more than compensate for their temporary loss of income. From the nation's point of view, a workforce that is prepared to quit jobs and spend a short time unemployed will be a more adaptable, more mobile workforce – one that is responsive to changing economic circumstances. Such a workforce will lead to greater allocative efficiency in the short run and more rapid economic growth over the longer run.

Long-term involuntary unemployment is quite another matter. The costs clearly outweigh any benefits, both for the individuals involved and for the economy as a whole. A demotivated, deskilled pool of long-term unemployed is a serious economic and social problem.

the average. In the UK, the unemployment rate for Afro-Caribbeans is $2^1/_2$ times greater than that for whites. For those of Pakistani and Bangladeshi origin, it is three times greater. Explanations are complex, but include differences in educational opportunities, a higher proportion of younger people, a greater sense of alienation among the unemployed, and the attitudes and prejudices of employers.

Unemployment and the labour market

We now turn to the causes of unemployment. These causes fall into two broad categories: *equilibrium* unemployment and *disequilibrium* unemployment. To make clear the distinction between the two, it is necessary to look at how the labour market works.

Figure 14.3 shows the ***aggregate demand*** for labour and ***aggregate supply*** of labour: that is, the total demand and supply of labour in the whole economy. The *real* average wage rate is plotted on the vertical axis. This is the average wage rate expressed in terms of its purchasing power: in other words, after taking prices into account.

The aggregate supply of labour curve (AS_L) shows the number of workers *willing to accept jobs* at each wage rate.

Figure 14.3 Disequilibrium unemployment

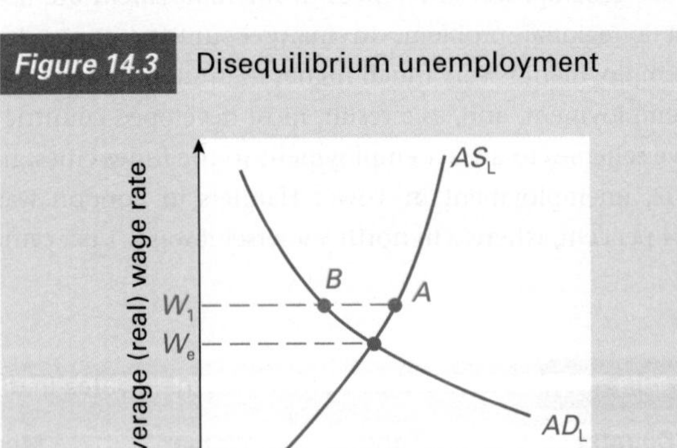

Definitions

Aggregate demand for labour curve A curve showing the total demand for labour in the economy at different average real wage rates.

Aggregate supply of labour curve A curve showing the total number of people willing and able to work at different average real wage rates.

KI 9 p 58 This curve is relatively inelastic, since the size of the labour force at any one time cannot change significantly. Nevertheless it is not totally inelastic because (a) a higher wage rate will encourage some people to enter the labour market (e.g. parents raising children), and (b) the unemployed will be more willing to accept job offers rather than continuing to search for a better-paid job.

The aggregate demand for labour curve (AD_L) slopes downwards. The higher the wage rate, the more will firms attempt to economise on labour and to substitute other factors of production for labour.

The labour market is in equilibrium at a wage of W_e – where the demand for labour equals the supply.

If the wage rate were above W_e, the labour market would be in a state of disequilibrium. At a wage rate of W_1, there is an excess supply of labour of $A - B$. This is called ***disequilibrium unemployment***.

For disequilibrium unemployment to occur, two conditions must hold:

- The aggregate supply of labour must exceed the aggregate demand.
- There must be a 'stickiness' in wages. In other words, the wage rate must not immediately fall to W_e.

Even when the labour market *is* in equilibrium, however, not everyone looking for work will be employed. Some people will hold out, hoping to find a better job. This is illustrated in Figure 14.4.

The curve N shows the total number in the labour force. The horizontal difference between it and the aggregate supply of labour curve (AS_L) represents the excess of people looking for work over those actually willing to accept jobs. Q_e represents the equilibrium level of employment and the distance $D - E$ represents the ***equilibrium level of unemployment***. This is sometimes known as the *natural level of unemployment*. KI 8 p 43

Note that the AS_L curve gets closer to the N curve at higher wages. The reason for this is that the unemployed will be more willing to accept jobs, the higher the wages they are offered.

Figure 14.4 Equilibrium unemployment

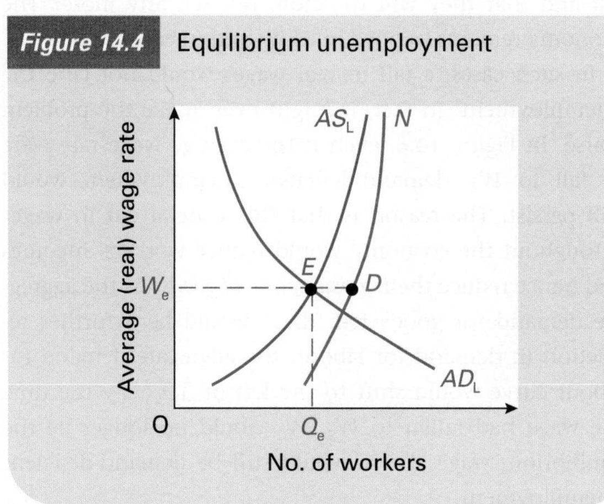

Figure 14.5 Equilibrium and disequilibrium unemployment

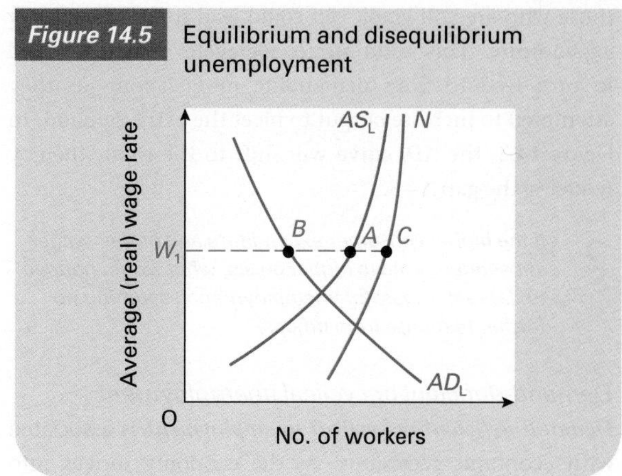

Figure 14.5 shows both equilibrium *and* disequilibrium unemployment. At a wage of W_1, disequilibrium unemployment is $A - B$; equilibrium unemployment is $C - A$; thus total unemployment is $C - B$.

But what are the causes of disequilibrium unemployment? What are the causes of equilibrium unemployment? We will examine each in turn.

Disequilibrium unemployment

There are three possible causes of disequilibrium unemployment.

Real-wage unemployment

Real-wage unemployment occurs when trade unions use their monopoly power to drive wages above the market-clearing level. It could also be caused by the government setting the national minimum wage too high. In Figure 14.3, the wage rate is driven up above W_e.

Excessive real wage rates were blamed by the Thatcher and Major governments for the high unemployment of the 1980s and 1990s. The possibility of higher real-wage unemployment was also one of the reasons for their rejection of a national minimum wage.

One effect of high real wage rates, however, may help to reduce real-wage unemployment. The extra wages paid to

Definitions

Disequilibrium unemployment Unemployment resulting from real wage rates in the economy being above the equilibrium level.

Equilibrium ('natural') unemployment The difference between those who would like employment at the current wage rate and those willing and able to take a job.

Real-wage unemployment Disequilibrium unemployment caused by real wages being driven up above the market-clearing level.

those who are still employed could lead to extra *consumer* expenditure. This addition to aggregate demand would in turn lead to firms demanding more labour, as they attempted to increase output to meet the extra demand. In Figure 14.3, the AD_L curve will shift to the right, thereby reducing the gap $A - B$.

? *If the higher consumer expenditure and higher wages subsequently led to higher* prices, *what would happen to: (a) real wages; (b) unemployment (assuming no further response from unions)?*

TC 13 p381

Demand-deficient or cyclical unemployment

Demand-deficient or ***cyclical unemployment*** is associated with economic recessions. As the economy moves into recession, consumer demand falls. Firms find that they are unable to sell their current level of output. For a time they may be prepared to build up stocks of unsold goods, but sooner or later they will start to cut back on production and cut back on the amount of labour they employ. The deeper the recession becomes and the longer it lasts, the higher will demand-deficient unemployment become.

As the economy recovers and begins to grow again, so demand-deficient unemployment will start to fall again. Because demand-deficient unemployment fluctuates with the business cycle, it is sometimes referred to as 'cyclical unemployment'. Figure 14.1 (on page 396) showed the fluctuations in unemployment in various industrial countries and for the OECD as a whole. If you compare this figure with the figure in Box 13.4 (on page 382), you can see how unemployment tends to rise in recessions and fall in booms.

Demand-deficient unemployment is also referred to as 'Keynesian unemployment', after John Maynard Keynes (see Person Profile on the book's website), who saw a deficiency of aggregate demand as the cause of the high unemployment between the two world wars. Today, many economists are known as 'Keynesian'. Although there are many strands of Keynesian thinking, these economists all see aggregate demand as important in determining a nation's output and employment.

Demand-deficient unemployment is illustrated in Figure 14.6. Assume initially that the economy is at the peak of the business cycle. The aggregate demand for and supply of labour are equal at the current wage rate of W_1. There is no disequilibrium unemployment. Now assume that the economy moves into recession. Consumer demand falls and as a result firms demand less labour. The demand for labour shifts to AD_{L_2}. If there is a resistance to wage cuts, such that the real wage rate remains fixed at W_1, there will now be disequilibrium unemployment of $Q_1 - Q_2$.

Figure 14.6 Demand-deficient unemployment

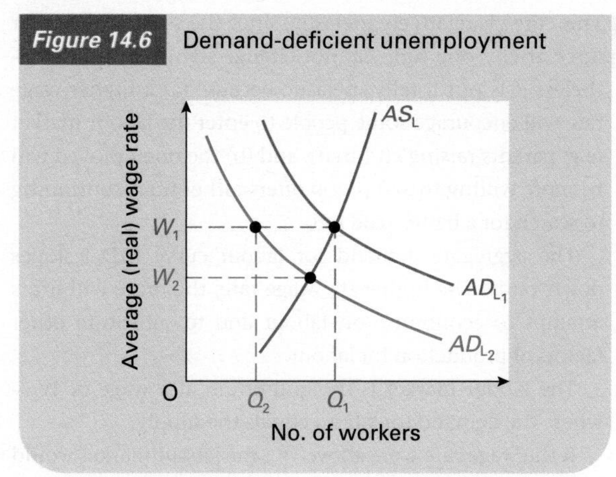

Some Keynesians specifically focus on the reluctance of real wage rates to fall from W_1 to W_2. This downward 'stickiness' in real wage rates may be the result of unions seeking to protect the living standards of their members (even though there are non-union members out of work), or of firms worried about the demotivating effects of cutting the real wages of their workers. For such economists, the problem of demand-deficient unemployment would be solved if there could somehow be a fall in real wage rates.

For other Keynesian economists, however, the problem is much more fundamental than a downward stickiness in real wages. For them the problem is that the low level of aggregate demand causes an *equilibrium* in the *goods* market at an output that is too low to generate full employment. Firms' supply is low (below the full-employment level of supply) because aggregate demand is low.

This low-level equilibrium in the goods market, and the corresponding disequilibrium in the labour market, may *persist*. This is the result of a lack of confidence on the part of firms. After all, why should firms produce more and take on more workers, if they believe that the recession will persist and that they will therefore not sell any more? The economy remains trapped in a low-output equilibrium.

In such cases, a fall in real wages would not cure the unemployment. In fact, it might even make the problem worse. In Figure 14.6, even if the average wage rate were to fall to W_2, demand-deficient unemployment would still persist. The reason is that this general cut in wages throughout the economy would reduce workers' incomes and hence reduce their *consumption of goods*. As the aggregate demand for goods fell, there would be a further reduction in demand for labour: the aggregate demand for labour curve would shift to the left of AD_{L_2}. By the time the wage had fallen to W_2, W_2 would no longer be the equilibrium wage. There would still be demand-deficient unemployment.

Definition

Demand-deficient or cyclical unemployment Disequilibrium unemployment caused by a fall in aggregate demand with no corresponding fall in the real wage rate.

? *If this analysis is correct, namely that a reduction in wages will reduce the aggregate demand for goods, what assumption must we make about the relative proportions of wages and profits that are spent (given that a reduction in real wage rates will lead to a corresponding increase in rates of profit)?*

Growth in the labour supply

If labour supply rises with no corresponding increase in the demand for labour, the equilibrium real wage rate will fall. If the real wage rate is 'sticky' downwards, disequilibrium unemployment will occur.

? *On a diagram similar to Figure 14.6, illustrate how a growth in labour supply can cause disequilibrium unemployment.*

This tends not to be such a serious cause of unemployment as demand deficiency, since the supply of labour changes relatively slowly. Nevertheless there is a problem of providing jobs for school leavers each year with the sudden influx of new workers on to the labour market.

Equilibrium unemployment (or natural unemployment)

Although there may be overall *macro*economic equilibrium, with the *aggregate* demand for labour equal to the *aggregate* supply, and thus no disequilibrium unemployment, at a *micro*economic level supply and demand may not match. There may be excess demand for labour (vacancies) in some markets and excess supply (unemployment) in others. There may be vacancies for computer technicians and unemployment in the steel industry, but unemployed steel workers cannot immediately become computer technicians. This is when equilibrium unemployment will occur.

There are various types of equilibrium unemployment.

Frictional (search) unemployment

KI 15 p101 ***Frictional (search) unemployment*** occurs when people leave their jobs, either voluntarily or because they are sacked or made redundant, and are unemployed for a period of time while they are looking for a new job. They may not get the first job they apply for, despite a vacancy existing.

The problem is that information is imperfect. Employers are not fully informed about what labour is available; workers are not fully informed about what jobs are available and what they entail. Both employers and workers, therefore, have to search: employers searching for the right labour and workers searching for the right jobs.

Figure 14.7 Average duration of unemployment

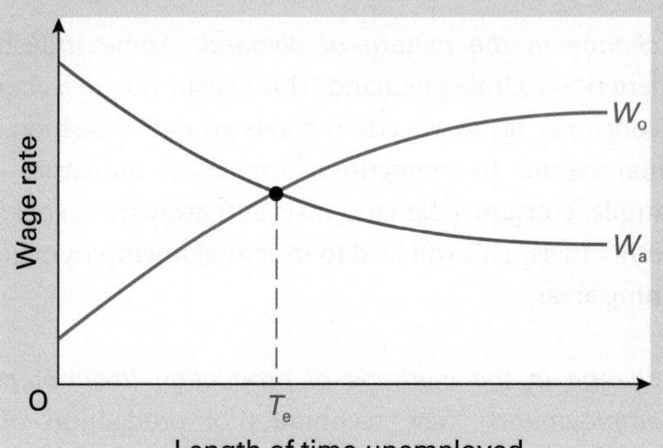

The longer people search for a job, the better the wage offers they are likely to be made. This is illustrated in Figure 14.7 by the curve W_o. It shows the highest wage offer that the typical worker will have received since being unemployed.

When they first start looking for a job, people may have high expectations of getting a good wage. The longer they are unemployed, however, the more anxious they are likely to be to get a job, and therefore the lower will be the wage they are prepared to accept. The curve W_a shows the wage that is acceptable to the typical worker. TC 9 p101

? *Why are W_o and W_a drawn as curves rather than straight lines?*

The average duration of unemployment will be T_e. That is, workers will remain unemployed until they find a job at an acceptable wage.

One obvious remedy for frictional unemployment is to provide better job information through government job centres, private employment agencies, or local and national newspapers. This would have the effect of making the curve W_o reach its peak earlier, and thus of shifting the intersection of W_o and W_a to the left.

Another much more controversial remedy is for the government to reduce the level of unemployment benefit. This will make the unemployed more desperate to get a job and thus prepared to accept a lower wage. It will therefore have the effect of shifting the W_a curve downwards and again of shifting the intersection of W_o and W_a to the left.

Structural unemployment

Structural unemployment occurs where the structure of the economy changes. Employment in some industries

Definitions

Frictional (search) unemployment Unemployment that occurs as a result of imperfect information in the labour market. It often takes time for workers to find jobs (even though there are vacancies) and in the meantime they are unemployed.

Structural unemployment Unemploymet that arises from changes in the pattern of demand or supply in the economy. People made redundant in one part of the economy cannot immediately take up jobs in other parts (even though there are vacancies).

may expand while in others it contracts. There are two main reasons for this.

A change in the pattern of demand. Some industries experience declining demand. This may be due to a change in consumer tastes as certain goods go out of fashion. Or it may be due to competition from other industries. For example, consumer demand may shift away from coal and to other fuels. This will lead to structural unemployment in mining areas.

A change in the methods of production (technological unemployment). New techniques of production often allow the same level of output to be produced with fewer workers (see Web Case 14.2). This is known as 'labour-saving technical progress'. Unless output expands sufficiently to absorb the surplus labour, people will be made redundant. This creates ***technological unemployment***. An example is the job losses in the banking industry caused by the increase in the number of cash machines and by the development of telephone and Internet banking.

Structural unemployment often occurs in particular regions of the country. When it does, it is referred to as ***regional unemployment***. Regional unemployment is due to the concentration of particular industries in particular areas. For example, the collapse in the South Wales coal-mining industry led to high unemployment in the Welsh valleys.

The level of structural unemployment will depend on three factors:

- The degree of regional concentration of industry. The more that industries are concentrated in particular regions, the greater will be the level of structural unemployment if particular industries decline.
- The speed of change of demand and supply in the economy. The more rapid the rate of technological change or the shift in consumer tastes, the more rapid will be the rate of redundancies.
- The immobility of labour. The less able or willing workers are to move to a new job, the higher will be the level of structural unemployment. Remember from Chapter 9 the distinction we made between geographical and occupational immobility. Geographical immobility is a particular problem with regional unemployment. Occupational immobility is a particular problem with technological unemployment where old skills are no longer required.

There are two broad approaches to tackling structural unemployment: *market orientated* and *interventionist*.

A market-orientated approach involves encouraging people to look more actively for jobs, if necessary in other parts of the country. It involves encouraging people to adopt a more willing attitude towards retraining, and if necessary to accept some reduction in wages.

An interventionist approach involves direct government action to match jobs to the unemployed. Two examples are providing grants to firms to set up in areas of high unemployment (regional policy), and government-funded training schemes.

Policies to tackle structural unemployment are examined in detail in sections 22.2–22.4.

Seasonal unemployment

Seasonal unemployment occurs when the demand for certain types of labour fluctuates with the seasons of the year. This problem is particularly severe in holiday areas, such as Cornwall, where unemployment can reach very high levels in the winter months. Policies for tackling seasonal unemployment are similar to those for structural unemployment.

Definitions

Technological unemployment Structural unemployment that occurs as a result of the introduction of labour-saving technology.

Regional unemployment Structural unemployment occurring in specific regions of the country.

Seasonal unemployment Unemployment associated with industries or regions where the demand for labour is lower at certain times of the year.

Section summary

1. Who should be counted as 'unemployed' is a matter for some disagreement. The two most common measures of unemployment are claimant unemployment (those claiming unemployment-related benefits) and ILO/OECD standardised unemployment (those available for work and actively seeking work or waiting to take up an appointment).
2. The 'stock' of unemployment will grow if the inflow of people into unemployment exceeds the outflow (to jobs or out of the labour market altogether). The more rapid these flows, the shorter the average duration of unemployment.
3. In most countries, unemployment is unevenly distributed across geographical regions, between women and men, between age groups and between different ethnic groups.
4. The costs of unemployment include the financial and other personal costs to the unemployed person,

continued

the costs to relatives and friends, and the costs to society at large in terms of lost tax revenues, lost profits and lost wages to other workers, and in terms of social disruption.

5. Unemployment can be divided into disequilibrium and equilibrium unemployment.
6. Disequilibrium unemployment occurs when real wage rates are above the level that will equate the aggregate demand and supply of labour. It can be caused by unions or government pushing up wages (real-wage unemployment), by a fall in aggregate demand but a downward 'stickiness' in real wages (demand-deficient unemployment), or by an increase in the supply of labour with again a downward stickiness in wages.
7. In the case of demand-deficient unemployment, the disequilibrium in the labour market may correspond to a low-output *equilibrium* in the goods market. A fall in real wage rates may be insufficient to remove the deficiency of demand in the labour market.
8. Equilibrium unemployment occurs when there are people unable or unwilling to fill job vacancies. This may be due to poor information in the labour market and hence a time lag before people find suitable jobs (frictional unemployment), to a changing pattern of demand or supply in the economy and hence a mismatching of labour with jobs (structural unemployment – specific types being technological and regional unemployment), or to seasonal fluctuations in the demand for labour.

14.2 AGGREGATE DEMAND AND SUPPLY AND THE LEVEL OF PRICES

Before we examine the causes of inflation (the rate of increase in prices), we need to look at how the *level* of prices in the economy is determined. It is determined by the interaction of aggregate demand and aggregate supply. The analysis is similar to that of demand and supply in individual markets, although as we shall see in later chapters there are some crucial differences. Figure 14.8 shows an aggregate demand and an aggregate supply curve. As with demand and supply curves for individual goods, we plot price on the vertical axis, except that now it is the *general* price level; and we plot quantity on the horizontal axis, except that now it is the *total quantity of national output* (GDP).

Let us examine each curve in turn.

The aggregate demand curve

Remember what we said about aggregate demand in Chapter 13. It is the total level of spending in the economy

Figure 14.8 Aggregate demand and aggregate supply

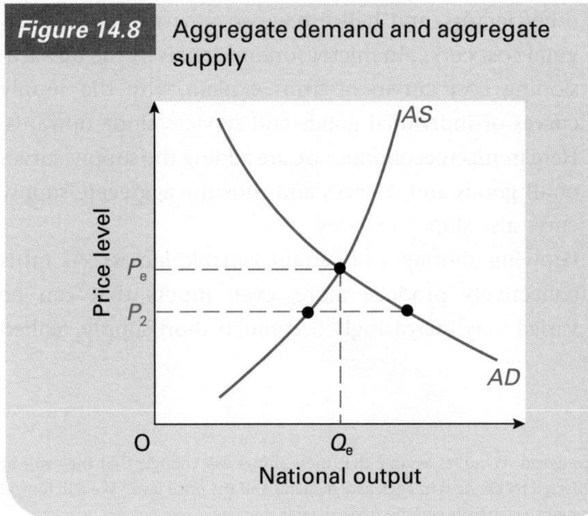

and consists of four elements: consumer spending (C), private investment (I), government expenditure on goods and services (G) and expenditure on exports (X) less expenditure on imports (M). Thus:

$$AD = C + I + G + X - M$$

The aggregate demand curve shows how much national output (GDP) will be demanded at each level of prices. But why does the *AD* curve slope downwards? Why will people demand fewer products as prices rise? There are two effects that can cause this: income effects and substitution effects. KI 7 p35

Income effects. For many people, when prices rise, their wages will not rise in line, at least not in the short run. There will therefore tend to be a redistribution of income away from wage earners (and hence consumers) and to those charging the higher prices – namely, firms. Thus for consumers there has been an *income effect* of the higher prices. The rise in prices leads to a cut in real incomes and thus people will spend less. Aggregate demand will fall. The *AD* curve will be downward sloping, as in Figure 14.8.

To some extent this will be offset by a rise in profits, but it is unlikely that much of these additional profits will be spent by firms on investment, especially if they see consumer expenditure falling; and any increase in dividends to shareholders will take a time before it is paid, and then may simply be saved rather than spent. To summarise: if prices rise more than wages, the redistribution from wages to profits is likely to lead to a fall in aggregate demand.

Clearly, this income effect will not operate if wages rise in line with prices. Real incomes of wage earners will be unaffected. In practice, as we shall see at several places in this book, in the short run wages do lag behind prices.

An income effect is also likely to occur as a result of progressive taxes. As prices and incomes rise, so people will find that they are paying a larger proportion of their incomes in taxes. As a result, they cannot afford to buy so much.

Substitution effects. In the *micro*economic situation, if the price of one good rises, people will switch to alternative goods. This is the substitution effect of that price rise and helps to explain why the demand curve for a particular good will be downward sloping. But how can there be a substitution effect at a *macro*economic level? If prices in general go up, what can people substitute for spending? There are in fact three ways in which people can switch to alternatives.

The first, and most obvious, concerns *imports and exports*. Higher prices for our country's goods will discourage foreign residents from buying our exports (which are part of aggregate demand) and encourage domestic residents to buy imports (which are *not* part of aggregate demand). Thus higher domestic prices will lead to a fall in aggregate demand (i.e. cause the *AD* curve to be downward sloping).

The second is known as the ***real balance effect***. If prices rise, the value (i.e. the purchasing power) of people's balances in their bank and building society accounts will fall. But many people will be reluctant to reduce the real value of their balances too much, and will thus probably cut back on their spending also. This desire by people to protect the real value of their balances will thus also cause aggregate demand to fall.

The third reason why people may switch away from spending concerns changes in *interest rates*. With higher prices to pay by consumers, and higher wages to pay by firms, there will tend to be a greater demand for *money*. With a given supply of money in the economy, there will now be a shortage of money. As a result, banks will tend to raise interest rates (we examine this process in Chapter 19). These higher rates of interest will have a dampening effect on spending: after all, the higher the interest rates people have to pay, the more expensive it is to buy things on credit. Again aggregate demand is likely to fall.

The shape of the aggregate demand curve

We have seen that both the income and substitution effects of a rise in the general price level will cause the aggregate demand for goods and services to fall. Thus the *AD* curve is downward sloping. The bigger the income and substitution effects, the more elastic will the curve be.

> **Definition**
>
> **Real balance effect** As the price level rises, so the value of people's money balances will fall. They will therefore spend less in order to increase their money balances and go some way to protecting their real value.

Shifts in the aggregate demand curve

The aggregate demand curve can shift inwards (to the right) or outwards (to the left), in exactly the same way as the demand curve for an individual good. A rightward shift represents an increase in aggregate demand, whatever the price level; a leftward shift represents a decrease in aggregate demand, whatever the price level.

A shift in the aggregate demand curve will occur if, for any given price level, there is a change in any of its components – consumption, investment, government expenditure or exports minus imports. Thus if the government decides to spend more, or if consumers spend more as a result of lower taxes, or if business confidence increases so that firms decide to invest more, the *AD* curve will shift to the right.

The aggregate supply curve

The aggregate supply (*AS*) curve shows the amount of goods and services that firms are willing to supply at each level of prices. To keep things simple, let us focus on the short-run *AS* curve. When constructing this curve, we assume that various other things remain constant. These include: wage rates and other input prices, technology and the total supply of factors of production (labour, land and capital).[1]

The short-run aggregate supply curve slopes upwards, as shown in Figure 14.8. In other words, the higher the level of prices, the more will be produced. The reason is simple. Because we are holding wages and other input prices fixed, then as the prices of their products rise, firms' profitability at each level of output will be higher than before. This will encourage them to produce more.

But what *limits* the increase in aggregate supply in response to an increase in prices? In other words, why is the aggregate supply curve not horizontal? There are two main reasons:

- Diminishing returns. With some factors of production fixed in supply, notably capital equipment, firms experience a diminishing marginal physical product from their other factors, and hence have an upward-sloping marginal cost curve. In microeconomic analysis the upward-sloping cost curves of firms explain why the supply curves of individual goods and services slope upwards. Here in macroeconomics we are adding the supply curves of all goods and services and thus the aggregate supply curve also slopes upwards.  KI 17 p121
- Growing shortages of certain variable factors. As firms collectively produce more, even inputs that can be varied may increasingly become in short supply. Skilled

[1] Long-run *AS* curves assume that these things *will* change: that they will be affected by changes in aggregate demand and the price level. We will look at long-run aggregate supply curves in later chapters.

labour may be harder to find, and certain raw materials may be harder to obtain.

Thus rising costs explain the upward-sloping aggregate supply curve. The more steeply costs rise as production increases, the less elastic will the aggregate supply curve be. It is likely that, as the level of national output increases and firms reach full-capacity working, the aggregate supply curve will tend to get steeper (as shown in Figure 14.8).

Shifts in the aggregate supply curve

The aggregate supply curve will shift if there is a change in any of the variables that are held constant when we plot the curve. Several of these variables, notably technology, the labour force and the stock of capital, change only slowly – normally shifting the curve gradually to the right. This represents an increase in potential output.

By contrast, wage rates and other input prices can change significantly in the short run, and are thus the major causes of shifts in the short-run supply curve. For example, a general rise in wage rates throughout the economy reduces the amount that firms wish to produce at any level of prices. The aggregate supply curve shifts to the left. A similar effect will occur if other costs increase, such as oil prices or indirect taxes.

Equilibrium

TC 4 p22

Equilibrium in the macroeconomy occurs when aggregate demand and aggregate supply are equal. To demonstrate this, consider what would happen if aggregate demand exceeded aggregate supply: for example, at P_2 in Figure 14.8. The resulting shortages throughout the economy would drive up prices. This would encourage firms to produce more: there would be a movement up *along* the *AS* curve. At the same time, the increase in prices would reduce the level of aggregate demand: that is, there would also be a movement back up *along* the *AD* curve. The shortage would be eliminated when price had risen to P_e.

Shifts in the AD or AS curves

If the *AD* or *AS* curve shifts, there will be a movement along the other curve to the new point of equilibrium. For example, if there is a cut in income taxes and a corresponding increase in consumer demand, the *AD* curve will shift to the right. This will result in a movement up along the *AS* curve to the new equilibrium point: in other words, to a new higher level of national output and a higher price level. The more elastic the *AS* curve, the more will output rise relative to prices. We will consider the shape of the *AS* curve in more detail in later chapters, and especially Chapter 20.

Section summary

1. An aggregate demand curve shows the relationship between aggregate demand ($C+I+G+X-M$) and the price level. The curve is downward sloping because of income and substitution effects.
2. If a rise in the price level causes wage rises to lag behind or causes a rise in the proportion of income paid in income tax, then consumers will respond to the resulting fall in their real incomes by cutting consumption. This is the income effect.
3. If a rise in the price level causes (a) imports to rise or exports to fall, or (b) people to spend less in order to maintain the value of their bank balances, or (c) people to spend less and save more because of a rise in interest rates, these too will result in a fall in the level of aggregate demand. These are all substitution effects.
4. If the determinant of any component of aggregate demand (other than the price level) changes, the aggregate demand will shift.
5. The (short-run) aggregate supply curve is upward sloping. This reflects the fact that at higher prices, firms will find it profitable to supply more. The curve will be more elastic, the less rapidly diminishing returns set in and the more elastic the supply of variable factors.
6. The aggregate supply curve will shift to the left (upwards) if wage rates or other costs rise independently of a rise in aggregate demand.
7. Equilibrium in the economy occurs when aggregate demand equals aggregate supply. A rise in the price level will occur if there is a rightward shift in the aggregate demand curve or a leftward shift in the aggregate supply curve.

14.3 INFLATION

The rate of inflation measures the annual percentage increase in prices. The most usual measure is that of *consumer* prices: i.e. retail prices. The UK government publishes a consumer prices index (CPI) each month, and the rate of inflation is the percentage increase in that index over the previous 12 months. This index is used throughout the EU, where it generally goes under its full title of the harmonised index of consumer prices (HICP). The HICP covers virtually 100 per cent of consumer spending (including cross-border spending) and uses sophisticated weights for each item.

Figure 14.9 shows the rates of inflation for the USA, Japan, France, the UK and the OECD. As you can see,

Figure 14.9 Inflation rates in selected industrial countries: 1965–2006

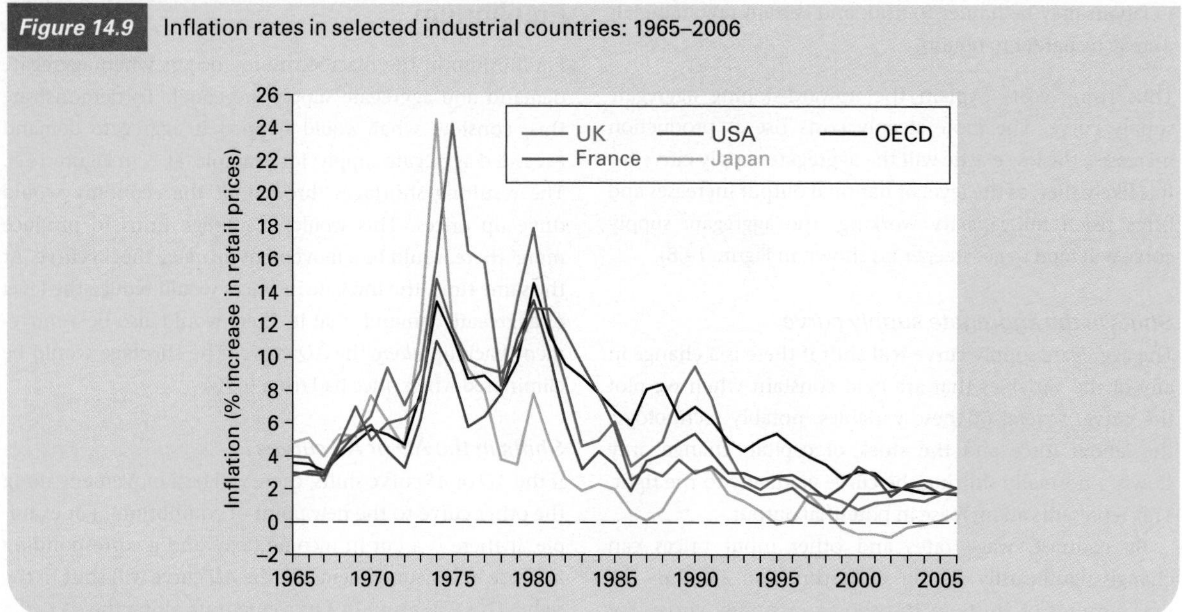

***LOOKING AT THE MATHS**

The inflation rate (π) is calculated from the following formula:

$$\pi_t = \frac{P_t - P_{t-1}}{P_{t-1}} \times 100$$

where P_t is the price index for year t and P_{t-1} is the price index for the previous year. Thus if the price index for year 1 is 149.1 and for year 2 is 149.0, then inflation in year 2 is:

$$\pi = \frac{149.1 - 140.0}{140.0} \times 100 = 6.5\%$$

inflation was particularly severe between 1973 and 1983, and relatively low in the mid-1980s and since the mid-1990s. Although most countries have followed a similar pattern over time, the average rates of inflation have differed substantially from one country to another. These differences, however, have tended to narrow in recent years as barriers to international trade and capital movements have been reduced and as increasing numbers of countries have directed their macroeconomic policy towards achieving target rates of inflation of around 2 per cent (see Table 14.5).

It is also possible to give the rates of inflation for other prices. For example, indices are published for commodity prices, for food prices, for house prices, for import prices, for prices after taking taxes into account and so on. Their respective rates of inflation are simply their annual percentage increases. Likewise it is possible to give the rate of inflation of wage rates ('wage inflation').

Before we proceed, a word of caution: be careful not to confuse a rise or fall in *inflation* with a rise or fall in *prices*.

Table 14.5 Inflation rates for selected countries (average % per annum)

Country	1971–80	1981–90	1991–2000	2001–06
Belgium	7.1	4.2	1.9	1.9
France	9.8	6.3	1.8	1.8
Germany	5.1	2.5	2.3	1.3
Italy	14.6	10.0	4.3	2.5
Japan	8.8	2.2	0.4	−1.2
Netherlands	7.3	2.4	2.4	2.2
Spain	15.0	9.2	4.2	3.0
Sweden	9.6	8.0	3.0	2.0
UK	13.2	6.2	3.3	1.9
USA	7.0	4.5	2.2	2.1
EU-15	10.0	6.2	3.0	2.0

Source: based on data in *European Economy Statistical Annex* (European Commission).

A rise in inflation means a *faster* increase in prices. A fall in inflation means a *slower* increase in prices (but still an increase as long as inflation is positive). (See Box A1.1 on page A:11.)

The costs of inflation

A lack of growth is obviously a problem if people want higher living standards. Unemployment is obviously a problem, both for the unemployed themselves and also for society, which suffers a loss in output and has to support the unemployed. But why is inflation a problem? If prices go up by 10 per cent, does it really matter? Provided your wages kept up with prices, you would have no cut in your living standards.

If people could correctly anticipate the rate of inflation and fully adjust prices and incomes to take account of it, then the costs of inflation would indeed be relatively small. For us as consumers, they would simply be the relatively minor inconvenience of having to adjust our notions of what a 'fair' price is for each item when we go shopping. For firms, they would again be the relatively minor costs of having to change price labels, or prices in catalogues or on menus, or adjust slot machines. These are known as ***menu costs***.

In reality, people frequently make mistakes when predicting the rate of inflation and are not able to adapt fully to it. This leads to the following problems, which are likely to be more serious the higher the rate of inflation becomes and the more the rate fluctuates.

KI 4 p11

Redistribution. Inflation redistributes income away from those on fixed incomes and those in a weak bargaining position, to those who can use their economic power to gain large pay, rent or profit increases. It redistributes wealth to those with assets (e.g. property) that rise in value particularly rapidly during periods of inflation, and away from those with types of savings that pay rates of interest below the rate of inflation and hence whose value is eroded by inflation. Pensioners may be particularly badly hit by rapid inflation.

1. *Do you personally gain or lose from inflation? Why?*
2. *Make a list of those who are most likely to gain and those who are most likely to lose from inflation.*

Uncertainty and lack of investment. Inflation tends to cause uncertainty among the business community, especially when the rate of inflation fluctuates. (Generally, the higher the rate of inflation, the more it fluctuates.) If it is difficult for firms to predict their costs and revenues, they may be discouraged from investing. This will reduce the rate of economic growth. On the other hand, as will be explained below, policies to reduce the rate of inflation may themselves reduce the rate of economic growth, especially in the short run. This may then provide the government with a policy dilemma.

Balance of payments. Inflation is likely to worsen the balance of payments. If a country suffers from relatively high inflation, its exports will become less competitive in world markets. At the same time, imports will become relatively cheaper than home-produced goods. Thus exports will fall and imports will rise. As a result, the balance of payments will deteriorate and/or the exchange rate will fall. Both of these effects can cause problems. This is examined in more detail in section 14.4.

Resources. Extra resources are likely to be used to cope with the effects of inflation. Accountants and other financial experts may have to be employed by companies to help them cope with the uncertainties caused by inflation.

The costs of inflation may be relatively mild if inflation is kept to single figures. They can be very serious, however, if inflation gets out of hand. If inflation develops into 'hyperinflation', with prices rising perhaps by several hundred per cent or even thousands per cent per year, the whole basis of the market economy will be undermined. Firms constantly raise prices in an attempt to cover their soaring costs. Workers demand huge pay increases in an attempt to stay ahead of the rocketing cost of living. Thus prices and wages chase each other in an ever-rising inflationary spiral. People will no longer want to save money. Instead they will spend it as quickly as possible before its value falls any further. People may even resort to barter in an attempt to avoid using money altogether.

Box 14.2 looks at perhaps the most severe case of hyperinflation ever: that of Germany in the early 1920s.

Causes of inflation

Demand-pull inflation

Demand-pull inflation is caused by continuing rises in aggregate demand. In Figure 14.10, the *AD* curve shifts to the right (and continues doing so). Firms will respond to a rise in demand partly by raising prices and partly by

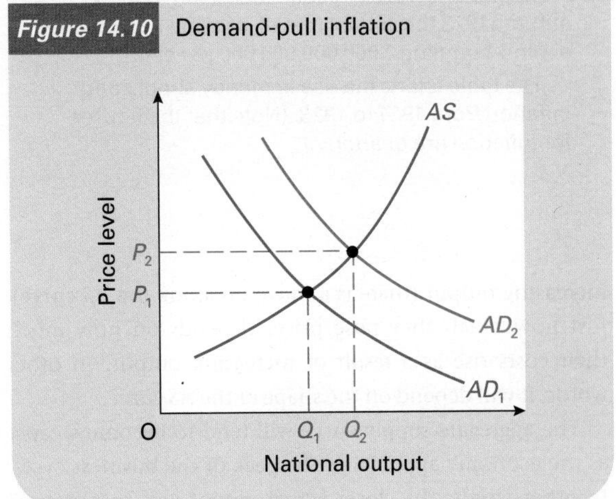

Figure 14.10 Demand-pull inflation

Definitions

Menu costs of inflation The costs associated with having to adjust price lists or labels.

Demand-pull inflation Inflation caused by persistent rises in aggregate demand.

CASE STUDIES AND APPLICATIONS

BOX 14.2

HYPERINFLATION IN GERMANY: 1923

When prices went crazy

In recent years in the UK we have come to expect relatively stable prices. If the rate of inflation were to rise to anywhere near the levels reached in the mid-1970s (24 per cent) or the early 1980s (18 per cent), it would be looked upon as a clear sign of economic failure.

But such rates are mild compared with those experienced by many other countries in the past, or in some cases relatively recently. Inflation in Brazil peaked at 1200 per cent in 1993, in Russia at 2500 per cent in 1992 and in Ukraine at 10 000 per cent in 1993. But even these cases of hyperinflation are mild compared with those experienced by several countries in the early 1920s!

In Austria and Hungary prices were several thousand times their pre-war level. In Poland they were over 2 million times higher, and in the USSR several billion times higher. But even these staggering rates of inflation seem insignificant beside those of Germany.

Following the chaos of the First World War, the German government resorted to printing money, not only to meet its domestic spending requirements in rebuilding a war-ravaged economy, but also to finance the crippling war reparations imposed on it by the allies in the Treaty of Versailles.

In 1919 the currency in circulation increased by a massive 80 per cent and prices increased by 91 per cent. At the end of 1919, however, a new socialist government attempted to slow this inflationary spiral. New taxes were imposed and government revenues increased. But public debt continued to grow, and by mid-1921 the government once more resorted to the printing presses to finance its expenditure.

Inflation now really began to take off, and by autumn 1923 the annual rate of inflation had reached a mind-boggling 7 000 000 000 000 per cent!

The table charts the rise in money supply and inflation from 1921 to 1923. (Note that the figures for inflation are *quarterly*.)

		Currency[a]	Prices[a]	Unemployment[b]	Real wages[c]
1921	I	−1.5	−7.1		
	II	5.6	2.1	2.8	18.1
	III	11.8	51.3		
	IV	29.5	68.7		
1922	I	14.3	55.8		
	II	28.6	29.4	1.5	−53.6
	III	84.0	308.3		
	IV	289.5	413.9		
1923	I	331.1	231.1		
	II	213.8	297.0	10.2	49.3
	III	1622.9	1234.4		
	IV	17 580.7	52 678.8		

[a] Percentage change from previous quarter.
[b] Percentage of the labour force.
[c] Percentage annual rate of change.

Source: A. Sommariva and G. Tullio, *German Macroeconomic History 1880–1979* (Macmillan, 1987).

As price increases accelerated, people became reluctant to accept money: before they knew it, the money would be worthless. People thus rushed to spend their money as quickly as possible. But this in turn further drove up prices.

For many Germans the effect was devastating. People's life savings were wiped out. Others whose wages were not quickly adjusted found their real incomes plummeting. Many were thrown out of work as businesses, especially those with *money* assets, went bankrupt. Poverty and destitution were widespread.

By the end of 1923 the German currency was literally worthless. In 1924, therefore, it was replaced by a new currency – one whose supply was kept tightly controlled by the government.

increasing output (there is a move up along the *AS* curve). Just how much they raise prices depends on how much their costs rise as a result of increasing output. In other words, it will depend on the shape of the *AS* curve.

The aggregate supply curve will tend to become steeper as the economy approaches the peak of the business cycle. In other words, the closer actual output gets to potential output, and the less slack there is in the economy, the more will firms respond to a rise in demand by raising their prices.

What we have illustrated so far is a *single* increase in demand (or a 'demand shock'). This could be due, for example, to an increased level of government expenditure. The effect is to give a *single* rise in the price level. Although this causes inflation in the short run, once the effect has taken place inflation will fall back to zero. For inflation to persist there must be *continuing* rightward shifts in the *AD* curve, and thus continuing rises in the price level. If *inflation* is to rise, these rightward shifts must get *faster*.

Demand-pull inflation is typically associated with a booming economy. Many economists therefore argue that it is the counterpart of demand-deficient unemployment. When the economy is in recession, demand-deficient unemployment is high, but demand-pull inflation is low. When, on the other hand, the economy is near the peak of the business cycle, demand-pull inflation is high, but demand-deficient unemployment is low.

Figure 14.11 Cost-push inflation

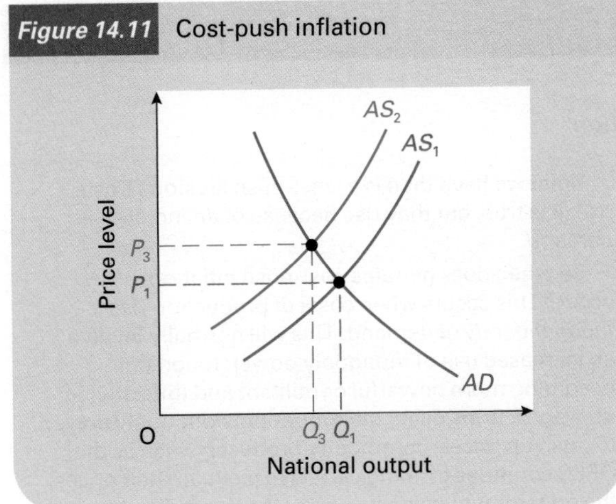

Cost-push inflation

Cost-push inflation is associated with continuing rises in costs and hence continuing leftward (upward) shifts in the *AS* curve. Such shifts occur when costs of production rise *independently* of aggregate demand.

If firms face a rise in costs, they will respond partly by raising prices and passing the costs on to the consumer, and partly by cutting back on production. This is illustrated in Figure 14.11. There is a leftward shift in the aggregate supply curve: from AS_1 to AS_2. This causes the price level to rise to P_3 and the level of output to *fall* to Q_3.

Just how much firms raise prices and cut back on production depends on the shape of the aggregate demand curve. The less elastic the *AD* curve, the less will sales fall as a result of any price rise, and hence the more will firms be able to pass on the rise in their costs to consumers as higher prices.

Note that the effect on output and employment is the opposite of demand-pull inflation. With demand-pull inflation, output and hence employment tends to rise. With cost-push inflation, however, output and employment tends to fall.

As with demand-pull inflation, we must distinguish between *single* shifts in the aggregate supply curve (known as 'supply shocks') and *continuing* shifts. If there is a single leftward shift in aggregate supply, there will be a single rise in the price level. For example, if the government raises the excise duty on oil, there will be a single rise in oil prices and hence in industry's fuel costs. This will cause *temporary* inflation while the price rise is passed on through the economy. Once this has occurred, prices will stabilise at the new level and the rate of inflation will fall back to zero again. If cost-push inflation is to continue over a number of years, therefore, the aggregate supply curve must *continually* shift to the left. If cost-push inflation is to *rise*, these shifts must get *faster*.

Rises in costs may originate from a number of different sources. As a result, we can distinguish various types of cost-push inflation:

- Wage-push inflation. This is where trade unions push up wages independently of the demand for labour.
- Profit-push inflation. This is where firms use their monopoly power to make bigger profits by pushing up prices independently of consumer demand.
- Import-price-push inflation. This is where import prices rise independently of the level of aggregate demand. An example is when OPEC quadrupled the price of oil in 1973/4.

In all these cases, inflation occurs because one or more groups are exercising economic power. The problem is likely to get worse, therefore, if there is an increasing concentration of economic power over time (for example, if firms or unions get bigger and bigger, and more monopolistic) or if groups become more militant. KI 19 p157

These causes are likely to interact. Firms and unions may compete with each other for a larger share of national income. This can lead to wages and prices chasing each other upwards.

Additional causes of cost-push inflation include the following:

- Tax-push inflation. This is where increased taxation adds to the cost of living. For example, when VAT in the UK was raised from 8 per cent to 15 per cent in 1979, prices rose as a result.
- The exhaustion of natural resources. If major natural resources become depleted, the *AS* curve will shift to the left. Examples include the gradual running-down of North Sea oil, pollution of the seas and hence a decline in incomes for nations with large fishing industries, and, perhaps the most devastating of all, the problem of 'desertification' in sub-Saharan Africa. Temporary inflationary problems could also arise due to short-run supply problems, such as a bad harvest.

The interaction of demand-pull and cost-push inflation

Demand-pull and cost-push inflation can occur together, since wage and price rises can be caused both by increases in aggregate demand and by independent causes pushing up costs. Even when an inflationary process *starts* as either demand-pull or cost-push, it is often difficult to separate the two. An initial cost-push inflation may encourage the government to expand aggregate demand to offset rises in unemployment. Alternatively, an initial demand-pull inflation may strengthen the power of certain groups, which then use this power to drive up costs.

Definition

Cost-push inflation Inflation caused by persistent rises in costs of production (independently of demand).

EXPLORING ECONOMICS

BOX 14.3

COST-PUSH ILLUSION

When rising costs are not cost-push inflation

It is easy to get confused between demand-pull and cost-push inflation.

Frequently, inflationary pressures *seem* to come from the cost side. Shopkeepers blame their price rises on the rise in their costs – the wholesale prices they have to pay. The wholesalers blame their price rises on a rise in *their* costs – the prices they are charged by the various manufacturers. The manufacturers in turn blame rising raw material costs, rising wage rates, rising rents and so on. Everyone blames their price rises on the rise in their costs.

But why have these costs risen?

It could well be due to a rise in aggregate *demand*! Wages may go up because of falling unemployment and a shortage of labour. Firms *have* to pay higher wages in order to recruit or maintain enough labour. Rents may rise because of the upsurge in demand. So too with raw materials: higher demand may pull up their prices too.

What we have then is a 'cost-push illusion'. Costs rise, it is true, but they rise because of an increase in *demand*.

So when does genuine cost-push inflation occur? This occurs when costs of production rise *independently* of demand. This will normally involve an increased use of monopoly power: unions becoming more powerful or militant and thus driving up wages; firms using their monopoly/oligopoly power to push up prices; commodity producers such as the OPEC countries forming cartels to push up their prices; the government using its power to raise indirect taxes (such as VAT).

?

If consumer demand rises and firms respond by raising prices, is this necessarily an example of demand-pull inflation? Could there be such a thing as demand-pull illusion? (Clue: why might consumer demand have risen?)

The interaction of the two causes is illustrated in Figure 14.12. Assume that powerful groups are constantly pushing up the costs of production. The *AS* curve is constantly shifting to the left. At the same time, assume that the government, in order to prevent a rise in unemployment, is constantly boosting the level of aggregate demand (say, by cutting taxes). The *AD* curve is constantly shifting to the right. The net effect on output and employment may be very small, but prices may rise substantially.

Structural (demand-shift) inflation

When the *pattern* of demand (or supply) changes in the economy, certain industries will experience increased demand and others decreased demand. If prices and wage rates are inflexible downwards in the contracting industries, and prices and wage rates rise in the expanding industries, the overall price and wage level will rise. The problem will be made worse, the less elastic is supply to these shifts.

Figure 14.12 The interaction of demand-pull and cost-push inflation

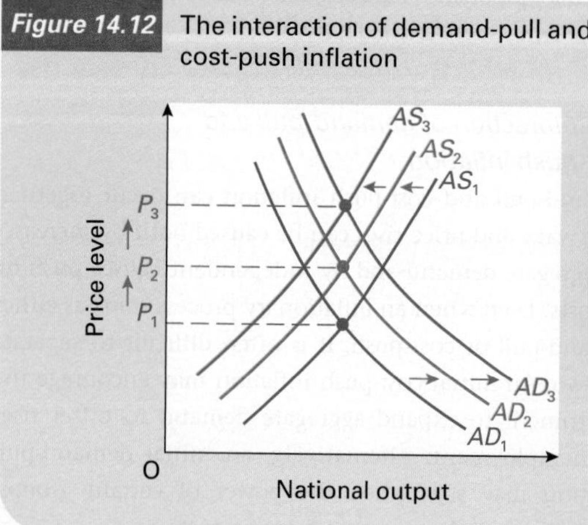

Thus a more rapid structural change in the economy can lead to both increased structural unemployment and increased structural inflation. An example of this problem was the so-called north–south divide in the UK during the boom of the second half of the 1980s. The north experienced high structural unemployment as old industries declined, while the south experienced excess demand. This excess demand in the south, among other things, led to rapid house price inflation, and rapid increases in incomes for various groups of workers and firms. With many prices and wages being set *nationally*, the inflation in the south then 'spilt over' into the north.

Expectations and inflation

TC 9 p101

Workers and firms take account of the *expected* rate of inflation when making decisions.

Imagine that a union and an employer are negotiating a wage increase. Let us assume that both sides expect a rate of inflation of 5 per cent. The union will be happy to receive a wage rise somewhat above 5 per cent. That way the members would be getting a *real* rise in incomes. The employers will be happy to pay a wage rise somewhat below 5 per cent. After all, they can put their price up by 5 per cent, knowing that their rivals will do approximately the same. The actual wage rise that the two sides agree on will thus be somewhere around 5 per cent.

Now let us assume that the expected rate of inflation is 10 per cent. Both sides will now negotiate around this benchmark, with the outcome being somewhere round about 10 per cent.

EXPLORING ECONOMICS

BOX 14.4

IS INFLATION DEAD?

No, just kept under control

'What's the big fuss about inflation?' That might seem to be a justified question today, when inflation rates in developed countries are typically below 3 per cent (see Figure 14.9).

Indeed, having some inflation, provided that it is relatively modest, could even be seen to be an advantage. This is because wages and prices are often 'sticky' downwards: unions are not prepared to accept wage cuts; firms are often unwilling to cut prices. Having a modest amount of inflation allows *relative* prices and wages in different parts of the economy to be adjusted up *and* down, in line with changes in demand and supply. Where demand has risen (or supply fallen), prices and wages can rise. Where demand has fallen (or supply risen), prices and wages can be held steady. There will be an overall rise in prices and wages in the economy (a modest inflation) and yet *relative* prices and wages will have adjusted.

So why be concerned about inflation, given that it is so low and, at such levels, can be useful? The reason *why* it is so low is that it has been made the main target of macroeconomic policy in many countries. For example, in the UK, the Bank of England tries to keep inflation at 2 per cent, as does the European Central Bank (ECB) in the euro area. In both cases, interest rates are adjusted up or down to keep inflation on target. If inflation is predicted to go above its target level, interest rates are raised. The resulting higher cost of borrowing dampens consumer expenditure and investment by firms. The resulting lower aggregate demand leads to a fall in demand-pull inflation.

If controlling inflation was *not* the main target of macroeconomic policy, then it could well rise, causing the problems we have been considering in this section. Although inflation is not a problem at present, this is only because keeping it low has been given such a high priority.

But has targeting inflation meant giving a lower priority to raising growth and reducing unemployment? Could we have higher growth and lower unemployment if we were prepared to accept a higher rate of inflation? Or is low inflation a means to achieving these other goals? We shall consider these questions in the following chapters.

How is the policy of targeting inflation likely to affect the expected rate of inflation?

Thus the higher the expected rate of inflation, the higher will be the level of pay settlements and price rises, and hence the higher will be the resulting actual rate of inflation.

Just how expectations impact on inflation depends on how they are formed. We examine some models of expectations in Chapter 20.

Policies to tackle inflation

We will be examining a number of different anti-inflationary policies in later chapters. These policies can be directed towards the control of either aggregate demand or aggregate supply, and hence are referred to as ***demand-side*** and ***supply-side*** policies respectively.

Demand-side policies

There are two types of demand-side policy:

Fiscal policy. ***Fiscal policy*** involves altering government expenditure and/or taxation. Aggregate demand can be reduced by cutting government expenditure (one of the four elements in aggregate demand) or by raising taxes and hence reducing consumer expenditure. These are both examples of ***contractionary (or deflationary)*** fiscal policy.

(Fiscal policy could also be used to *boost* aggregate demand if there were a problem of demand-deficient unemployment. In this case, the government would raise government expenditure and/or cut taxes. This is called ***expansionary (or reflationary)*** fiscal policy.)

Monetary policy. ***Monetary policy*** involves altering the supply of money in the economy or manipulating the rate of interest. The government or central bank (the Bank of England in the UK) can reduce aggregate demand (a *contractionary* monetary policy) by reducing the money

Definitions

Demand-side policies Policies designed to affect aggregate demand: fiscal policy and monetary policy.

Supply-side policies Policies designed to affect aggregate supply: policies to affect costs or productivity.

Fiscal policy Policy to affect aggregate demand by altering the balance between government expenditure and taxation.

Contractionary (or deflationary) policy Fiscal or monetary policy designed to reduce the rate of growth of aggregate demand.

Expansionary (or reflationary) policy Fiscal or monetary policy designed to increase the rate of growth of aggregate demand.

Monetary policy Policy to affect aggregate demand by altering the supply or cost of money (rate of interest).

EXPLORING ECONOMICS

THE PHILLIPS CURVE

Is higher inflation the price for lower unemployment?

If inflation tends to be higher when the economy is booming and if unemployment tends to be higher in recessions, does this mean that there is a 'trade-off' between inflation and unemployment: that lower unemployment tends to be associated with higher inflation, and lower inflation with higher unemployment? Such a trade-off was observed by the New Zealand economist, Bill Phillips (see Person Profile on the book's website), and was illustrated by the famous ***Phillips curve***.

The original Phillips curve

In 1958, Phillips showed the statistical relationship between wage inflation and unemployment in the UK from 1861 to 1957. With wage inflation (ω) on the vertical axis and the unemployment rate (U) on the horizontal axis, a scatter of points was obtained. Each point represented the observation for a particular year. The curve that best fitted the scatter has become known as the 'Phillips curve'. It is illustrated in the Figure (a) and shows an inverse relationship between inflation and unemployment.[2]

Given that wage increases over the period were approximately 2 per cent above price increases (made possible because of increases in labour productivity),

(a) *The Phillips curve*

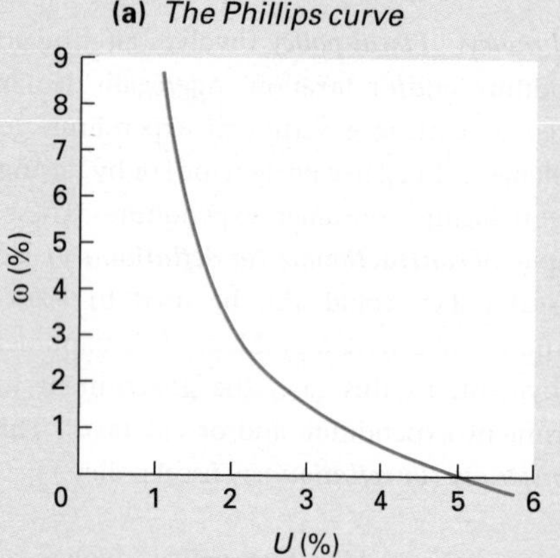

a similar-shaped, but lower curve could be plotted showing the relationship between *price* inflation and unemployment.

The curve has often been used to illustrate the effects of changes in aggregate demand. When aggregate demand rose (relative to potential output), inflation rose and unemployment fell: there was an upward movement along the curve. When aggregate demand fell, there was a downward movement along the curve.

There was also a second reason given for the inverse relationship. If wages rose, the unemployed might have believed that the higher wages they were offered represented a *real* wage increase. That is, they might not have realised that the higher wages would be 'eaten up' by price increases: they might have suffered from ***money illusion***. They would thus have accepted jobs more readily. The average duration of unemployment therefore fell. This is a reduction in *frictional* unemployment and is illustrated by an upward shift in the W_o curve in Figure 14.7 (on page 403).

TC 12 p374

The Phillips curve was bowed in to the origin. The usual explanation for this is that, as aggregate demand expanded, at first there would be plenty of surplus labour, which could meet the extra demand without the need to raise wages very much. But as labour became increasingly scarce, firms would find they had to offer increasingly higher wages to obtain the labour they required, and the position of trade unions would be increasingly strengthened.

The *position* of the Phillips curve depended on *non*-demand factors causing inflation and unemployment: frictional and structural unemployment; and cost-push, structural and expectations-generated inflation. If any of these non-demand factors changed so as to raise inflation or unemployment, the curve would shift outwards to the right. The relative stability of the curve over the 100 years or so observed by Phillips suggested that these non-demand factors had changed little.

The Phillips curve seemed to present governments with a simple policy choice. They could trade off inflation against unemployment. Lower

KI 32 p369

supply, thereby making less money available for spending, or by putting up interest rates and thus making borrowing more expensive. If people borrow less, they will spend less.

Supply-side policies

The aim here is to reduce the rate of increase in costs. This will help reduce leftward shifts in the aggregate supply curve. This can be done either (1) by restraining monopoly influences on prices and incomes (e.g. by policies to restrict the activities of trade unions, or policies to restrict mergers and takeovers), or (2) by designing policies to increase productivity (e.g. giving various tax incentives, encouraging various types of research and development, giving grants to firms to invest in up-to-date equipment or in the training of labour).

We will examine all these various policies as the book progresses. As we shall see, just as economists sometimes disagree on the precise causes of inflation, so too they sometimes disagree on the most appropriate cures.

Definitions

Phillips curve A curve showing the relationship between (price) inflation and unemployment. The original Phillips curve plotted wage inflation against unemployment for the years 1861–1957.

Money illusion When people believe that a money wage or price increase represents a real increase: in other words, they ignore or underestimate inflation.

BOX 14.5

(b) *The breakdown of the Phillips curve*

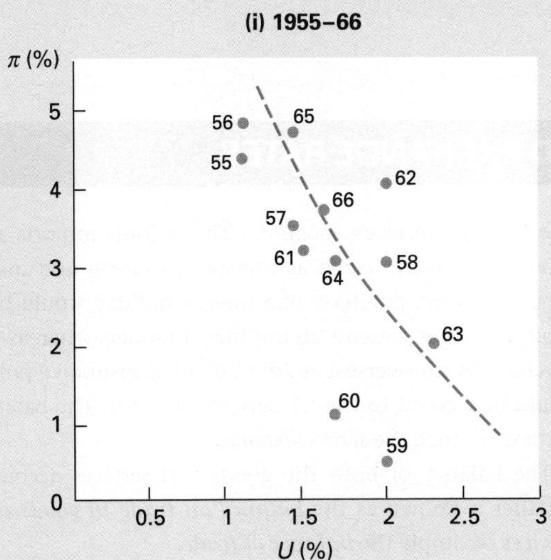

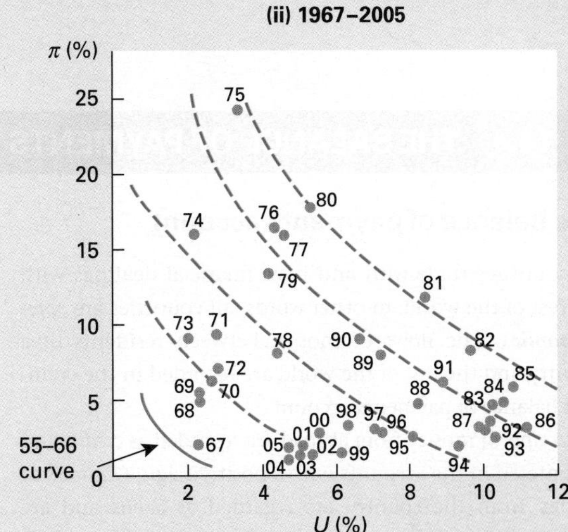

unemployment could be bought at the cost of higher inflation, and vice versa. Unfortunately, the experience since the late 1960s has suggested that no such simple relationship exists beyond the short run.

The breakdown of the Phillips curve

From about 1966 the Phillips curve relationship seemed to break down. The UK, and many other countries in the western world too, began to experience growing unemployment *and* higher rates of inflation as well.

Figure (b) shows price inflation (π) and (standardised) unemployment in the UK from 1955 to 2005. From 1955 to 1966 a curve similar to the Phillips curve can be fitted through the data (diagram (i)). From 1967 to the early 1990s, however, no simple picture emerges. Certainly the original Phillips curve could no longer fit the data; but whether the curve shifted to the right and then back again somewhat (the broken green lines), or whether the relationship broke down completely, or whether there was some quite different relationship between inflation and unemployment, is not clear. In fact, in recent years, as inflation has been targeted, the 'curve' would seem to have become a virtually horizontal straight line!

Over the years, there has been much debate among economists about the relationship between inflation and unemployment. The controversy will be examined in later chapters and particularly in Chapter 20. One thing does seem clear, however: the relationship is different in the short run and the long run.

Assume that there is a trade-off between unemployment and inflation, traced out by a 'Phillips curve'. What could cause a leftward shift in this curve?

[2] Phillips' estimated equation was $\omega = -0.9 + 9.638U^{-1.394}$.

Section summary

1. Inflation redistributes incomes from the economically weak to the economically powerful; it causes uncertainty in the business community and as a result reduces investment; it tends to lead to balance of payments problems and/or a fall in the exchange rate; it leads to resources being used to offset its effects. The costs of inflation can be very great indeed in the case of hyperinflation.
2. Demand-pull inflation occurs as a result of increases in aggregate demand. This can be due to monetary or non-monetary causes.
3. Cost-push inflation occurs when there are increases in the costs of production independent of rises in aggregate demand. Cost-push inflation can be of a number of different varieties: wage-push, profit-push, import-price-push, tax-push or that stemming from reductions in potential output.

continued

4. Cost-push and demand-pull inflation can interact to form spiralling inflation.
5. Inflation can also be caused by shifts in the pattern of demand in the economy, with prices rising in sectors of increasing demand but being reluctant to fall in sectors of declining demand.
6. Expectations play a crucial role in determining the level of inflation. The higher people expect inflation to be, the higher it will be.
7. Policies to tackle inflation can be either demand-side policies (fiscal or monetary) or supply-side policies (to reduce monopoly power or increase productivity).

14.4 THE BALANCE OF PAYMENTS AND EXCHANGE RATES

The balance of payments account

All countries trade with and have financial dealings with the rest of the world. In other words, all countries are ***open economies***. The flows of money between residents of a country and the rest of the world are recorded in the country's balance of payments account.

Receipts of money from abroad are regarded as *credits* and are entered in the accounts with a positive sign. *Outflows* of money from the country are regarded as *debits* and are entered with a negative sign.

There are three main parts of the balance of payments account: the *current account*, the *capital account* and the *financial account*. Each part is then subdivided. We shall look at each part in turn, and take the UK as an example. Table 14.6 gives a summary of the UK balance of payments for 1997 and 2004.

The current account

The ***current account*** records payments for imports and exports of goods and services, plus incomes flowing into and out of the country, plus net transfers of money into and out of the country. It is normally divided into four subdivisions.

The trade in goods account. This records imports and exports of physical goods (previously known as 'visibles'). Exports result in an inflow of money and are therefore a credit item. Imports result in an outflow of money and are therefore a debit item. The balance of these is called the ***balance on trade in goods*** or ***balance of visible trade*** or ***merchandise balance***. A *surplus* is when exports exceed imports. A *deficit* is when imports exceed exports.

The trade in services account. This records imports and exports of services (such as transport, tourism and insurance). Thus the purchase of a foreign holiday would be a debit, since it represents an outflow of money, whereas the purchase by an overseas resident of a UK insurance policy would be a credit to the UK services account. The balance of these is called the *services balance*.

The balance of both the goods and services accounts together is known as the ***balance on trade in goods and services*** or simply the ***balance of trade***.

Income flows. These consist of wages, interest and profits flowing into and out of the country. For example, dividends earned by a foreign resident from shares in a UK company would be an outflow of money (a debit item).

Current transfers of money. These include government contributions to and receipts from the EU and international organisations, and international transfers of money by private individuals and firms. Transfers out of the country are debits. Transfers into the country (e.g. money sent from Greece to a Greek student studying in the UK) would be a credit item.

The ***current account balance*** is the overall balance of all the above four subdivisions. A *current account surplus* is where credits exceed debits. A *current account deficit* is where debits exceed credits. Figure 14.13 shows the current account balances of the UK, the USA and Japan as a proportion of their GDP (national output).

? *Why is the US current balance approximately a 'mirror image' of the Japanese current balance?*

Definitions

Open economy One that trades with and has financial dealings with other countries.

Current account of the balance of payments The record of a country's imports and exports of goods and services, plus incomes and transfers of money to and from abroad.

Balance on trade in goods or **balance of visible trade** or **merchandise balance** Exports of goods minus imports of goods.

Balance on trade in goods and services or **balance of trade** Exports of goods and services minus imports of goods and services.

Balance of payments on current account The balance on trade in goods and services plus net investment incomes and current transfers.

Table 14.6 UK balance of payments (£ millions)

	1997		2004	
CURRENT ACCOUNT				
1. Trade in goods				
a) Exports of goods	+171 923		+190 688	
b) Imports of goods	−184 265		−248 632	
Balance on trade in goods	−12 342		−57 944	
2. Trade in services				
a) Exports of services	+61 104		+95 872	
b) Imports of services	−47 686		−76 754	
Balance on trade in services	+13 418		+19 118	
Balance on trade in goods and services		+1 076		−38 826
3. Net income flows (wages and investment income)		+3 905		+24 004
4. Net current transfers (government and private)		−5 918		−10 860
Current account balance		**−937**		**−25 682**
CAPITAL ACCOUNT				
5. Net capital transfers, etc:		+982		+2 073
Capital account balance		**+982**		**+2 073**
FINANCIAL ACCOUNT				
6. Investment (direct and portfolio)				
a) Net investment in UK from abroad	+49 609		+126 599	
b) Net UK investment abroad	−90 246		−183 078	
Balance of direct and portfolio investment		−40 637		−56 479
7. Other financial flows (mainly short-term)				
a) Net deposits in UK from abroad and borrowing from abroad by UK residents	+200 352		+407 526	
b) Net deposits abroad by UK residents and UK lending to overseas residents	−167 151		−323 826	
Balance of other financial flows		+33 201		+83 700
8. Reserves (drawing on + adding to −)		+2 380		−193
Financial account balance		**−5 056**		**+27 028**
TOTAL OF ALL THREE ACCOUNTS		−5 011		+3 419
9. Net errors and omissions		+5 011		−3 419
		0		**0**

Sources: *UK Economic Accounts* (National Statistics, 2005).

The capital account

The ***capital account*** records the flows of funds, into the country (credits) and out of the country (debits), associated with the acquisition or disposal of fixed assets (e.g. land), the transfer of funds by migrants, and the payment of grants by the government for overseas projects and the receipt of EU money for capital projects (e.g. from the Agricultural Guidance Fund).

The financial account[3]

The ***financial account*** of the balance of payments records cross-border changes in the holding of shares, property, bank deposits and loans, government securities, etc. In other words, unlike the current account which is concerned with money incomes, the financial account is concerned with the purchase and sale of assets.

Investment (direct and portfolio). This account covers primarily long-term investment.

[3] Prior to October 1998, this account was called the 'capital account'. The account that is *now* called the capital account used to be included in the transfers section of the current account. This potentially confusing change of names was adopted in order to bring the UK accounts in line with the system used by the International Monetary Fund (IMF), the EU and most individual countries.

Definitions

Capital account of the balance of payments The record of the transfers of capital to and from abroad.

Financial account of the balance of payments The record of the flows of money into and out of the country for the purposes of investment or as deposits in banks and other financial institutions.

Figure 14.13 Current account balance as a percentage of GDP in selected countries: 1970–2006

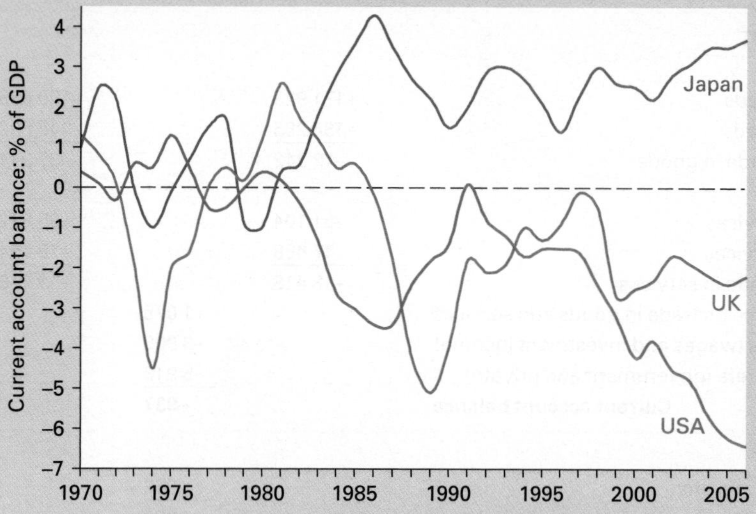

Source: based on data in *OECD Economic Outlook* (various years).

- Direct investment. If a foreign company invests money from abroad in one of its branches or associated companies in the UK, this represents an inflow of money when the investment is made and is thus a credit item. (Any subsequent profit from this investment that flows abroad will be recorded as an *investment income outflow* on the current account.) Investment abroad by UK companies represents an outflow of money when the investment is made. It is thus a debit item.

  Note that what we are talking about here is the acquisition or sale of assets: e.g. a factory or farm, or the takeover of a whole firm, not the imports or exports of equipment.
- Portfolio investment. This is changes in the holding of paper assets, such as company shares. Thus if a UK resident buys shares in an overseas company, this is an outflow of funds and is hence a debit item.

Other financial flows. These consist primarily of various types of short-term monetary movement between the UK and the rest of the world. Deposits by overseas residents in banks in the UK and loans to the UK from abroad are credit items, since they represent an inflow of money. Deposits by UK residents in overseas banks and loans by UK banks to overseas residents are debit items. They represent an outflow of money.

Short-term monetary flows are common between international financial centres to take advantage of differences in countries' interest rates and changes in exchange rates.

?

1. *Why may inflows of short-term deposits create a problem?*
2. *Where would interest payments on short-term foreign deposits in UK banks be entered on the balance of payments account?*

Note that in the financial account, credits and debits are recorded *net*. For example, UK investment abroad consists of the net acquisition of assets abroad (i.e. the purchase less the sale of assets abroad). Similarly, foreign investment in the UK consists of the purchase less the sale of UK assets by foreign residents. Note that in either case the flow could be in the opposite direction. For example, if UK residents purchased less assets abroad than they sold, this item would be a net credit, not a debit (there would be a net return of money to the UK). This was the case in 1994.

By recording financial account items net, the flows seem misleadingly modest. For example, if UK residents deposited an extra £100bn in banks abroad but drew out £99bn, this would be recorded as a mere £1bn net outflow on the other financial flows account. In fact, *total* financial account flows vastly exceed current plus capital account flows.

Flows to and from the reserves. The UK, like all other countries, holds reserves of gold and foreign currencies. From time to time the Bank of England (acting as the government's agent) will sell some of these reserves to purchase sterling on the foreign exchange market. It does this normally as a means of supporting the rate of exchange (see below). Drawing on reserves represents a *credit* item in the balance of payments accounts: money drawn from the reserves represents an *inflow* to the balance of payments (albeit an outflow from the reserves account). The reserves can thus be used to support a deficit elsewhere in the balance of payments.

Conversely, if there is a surplus elsewhere in the balance of payments, the Bank of England can use it to build up the reserves. Building up the reserves counts as a debit item in the balance of payments, since it represents an outflow from it (to the reserves).

When all the components of the balance of payments account are taken together, the balance of payments should exactly balance: credits should equal debits. As we shall see below, if they were not equal, the rate of exchange would have to adjust until they were, or the government would have to intervene to make them equal.

When the statistics are compiled, however, a number of errors are likely to occur. As a result, there will not be a balance. To 'correct' for this, a *net errors and omissions* item is included in the accounts. This ensures that there will be an exact balance. The main reason for the errors is that the statistics are obtained from a number of sources, and there are often delays before items are recorded and sometimes omissions too.

Assessing the balance of payments figures

It is often regarded as being undesirable for the combined current, capital and investment accounts to be in deficit. If they were in deficit, this would have to be covered by borrowing from abroad or attracting deposits from abroad. This might necessitate paying high rates of interest. It also leads to the danger that people abroad might at some time in the future suddenly withdraw their money from the UK and cause a 'run on the pound'. An alternative would be to draw on reserves. But this too causes problems. If the reserves are run down too rapidly, it may cause a crisis of confidence, and again a run on the pound. Also, of course, reserves are limited and hence there is a limit to which they can be used to pay for a balance of payments deficit.

It is also often regarded as undesirable for a country to have a *current account* deficit, even if it is matched by a surplus on the other two accounts. Although this will bring the short-term benefit of a greater level of consumption through imports, and hence a temporarily higher living standard, the excess of imports over exports is being financed by foreign investment in the UK. This will lead to greater outflows of interest and dividends in the future. On the other hand, inward investment may lead to increased production and hence possibly increased incomes for UK residents.

? *With reference to the above, provide an assessment of the UK balance of payments in each of the years illustrated in Table 14.6.*

What causes deficits to occur on the various parts of the balance of payments? The answer has to do with the demand for and supply of sterling on the foreign exchange market. Thus before we can answer the question, we must examine this market and in particular the role of the rate of exchange.

Exchange rates

An exchange rate is the rate at which one currency trades for another on the foreign exchange market.

If you want to go abroad, you will need to exchange your pounds into euros, dollars, Swiss francs or whatever. To do this, you will go to a bank. The bank will quote you that day's exchange rates: for example, €1.40 to the pound, or $1.75 to the pound. It is similar for firms. If an importer wants to buy, say, some machinery from Japan, it will require yen to pay the Japanese supplier. It will thus ask the foreign exchange section of a bank to quote it a rate of exchange of the pound into yen. Similarly, if you want to buy some foreign stocks and shares, or if companies based in the UK want to invest abroad, sterling will have to be exchanged into the appropriate foreign currency.

Likewise, if Americans want to come on holiday to the UK or to buy UK assets, or American firms want to import UK goods or to invest in the UK, they will require sterling. They will be quoted an exchange rate for the pound in the USA: say, £1 = $1.75. This means that they will have to pay $1.75 to obtain £1 worth of UK goods or assets.

Exchange rates are quoted between each of the major currencies of the world. These exchange rates are constantly changing. Minute by minute, dealers in the foreign exchange dealing rooms of the banks are adjusting the rates of exchange. They charge commission when they exchange currencies. It is important for them, therefore, to ensure that they are not left with a large amount of any currency unsold. What they need to do is to balance the supply and demand of each currency: to balance the amount they purchase to the amount they sell. To do this, they will need to adjust the price of each currency, namely the exchange rate, in line with changes in supply and demand.

Not only are there day-to-day fluctuations in exchange rates, but also there are long-term changes in them. Table 14.7 shows the average exchange rate between the pound and various currencies for selected years from 1960 to 2005.

One of the problems in assessing what is happening to a particular currency is that its rate of exchange may rise against some currencies (weak currencies) and fall against others (strong currencies). In order to gain an overall picture of its fluctuations, therefore, it is best to look at a weighted average exchange rate against all other currencies. This is known as the ***exchange rate index***. The last column in Table 14.7 shows the sterling exchange rate index based on 1990 = 100.

The weight given to each currency in the index depends on the proportion of trade done with that country. Table 14.8 gives the current weights of the various currencies that make up the sterling index. These weights have existed

Definition

Exchange rate index A weighted average exchange rate expressed as an index, where the value of the index is 100 in a given base year. The weights of the different currencies in the index add up to 1.

Table 14.7 Sterling exchange rates: 1960–2005

	US dollar	Japanese yen	French franc	German mark	Italian lira	Euro[a]	Sterling exchange rate index (1990 = 100)
1960	2.80	1008	13.82	11.76	1747	–	–
1970	2.40	858	13.33	8.78	1500	–	–
1975	2.22	658	9.50	5.45	1447	(1.70)	129.6
1980	2.33	526	9.83	4.23	1992	(1.62)	124.4
1985	1.30	307	11.55	3.78	2463	(1.71)	111.3
1990	1.79	257	9.69	2.88	2133	(1.37)	100.0
1992	1.77	224	9.32	2.75	2163	(1.33)	96.9
1994	1.53	156	8.49	2.48	2467	(1.27)	89.2
1996	1.56	170	7.99	2.35	2408	(1.21)	86.3
1998	1.66	217	9.77	2.91	2876	(1.49)	103.9
1999	1.62	184	(9.96)	(2.97)	(2941)	1.52	103.8
2000	1.52	163	(10.77)	(3.21)	(3180)	1.64	107.5
2001	1.44	175	(10.55)	(3.15)	(3115)	1.61	105.8
2002	1.50	188	–	–	–	1.59	106.0
2003	1.63	189	–	–	–	1.45	100.2
2004	1.83	198	–	–	–	1.47	104.1
2005 (Q1)	1.89	198	–	–	–	1.44	102.9

[a] The euro was introduced in 1999, with notes and coins circulating from 2001. The 'dummy' euro exchange rate figures prior to 1999 are projections backwards in time based on the weighted average exchange rates of the currencies that made up the euro.

Source: *Monetary and Financial Statistics Interactive database* (Bank of England).

Table 14.8 The weights of foreign currencies in the sterling exchange rate index

Country	Weight	Country	Weight
Euro	0.6513	(Ireland)	(0.0308)
(Germany)	(0.2249)	(Finland)	(0.0141)
USA	0.1649	Canada	0.0138
(France)	(0.1259)	Denmark	0.0138
(Italy)	(0.0827)	Norway	0.0119
Japan	0.0700	(Austria)	(0.0119)
(Netherlands)	(0.0571)	(Portugal)	(0.0084)
(Belgium)	(0.0539)	Australia	0.0048
(Spain)	(0.0385)	(Greece)	(0.0031)
Sweden	0.0345	New Zealand	0.0021
Switzerland	0.0327		

since 1995 and are based on trade solely in manufactured products during the period 1989–91. The Bank of England plans to change these weights every year to reflect changing patterns of trade, not only in manufactured products, but also in services. It also plans to incorporate a wider set of countries, including China and South Korea.

Note that all the exchange rates must be consistent with each other. For example, if £1 exchanged for $1.50 or 165 yen, then $1.50 would have to exchange for 165 yen directly (i.e. $1 = 110 yen), otherwise people could make money by moving around in a circle between the three currencies in a process known as ***arbitrage***.

?

How did the pound 'fare' compared with the dollar, the lira and the yen from 1960 to 2005? What conclusions can be drawn about the relative movements of these three currencies?

The determination of the rate of exchange in a free market

In a free foreign exchange market, the rate of exchange is determined by demand and supply. This is known as a ***floating exchange rate***, and is illustrated in Figure 14.14. 

TC 4 p22

For simplicity, assume that there are just two countries: the UK and the USA. When UK importers wish to buy goods from the USA, or when UK residents wish to invest in the USA, they will *supply* pounds on the foreign exchange market in order to obtain dollars. The higher the exchange rate, the more dollars they will obtain for their pounds. This will effectively make American goods cheaper to buy, and investment more profitable. Thus the *higher* the exchange rate, the *more* pounds will be supplied. The supply curve of pounds, therefore, typically slopes upwards.

When US residents wish to purchase UK goods or to invest in the UK, they will require pounds. They *demand* pounds by selling dollars on the foreign exchange market. The lower the $ price of the pound (the exchange rate), the cheaper it will be for them to obtain UK goods and assets, and hence the more pounds they are likely to demand.

Definitions

Arbitrage Buying an asset in a market where it has a lower price and selling it again in another market where it has a higher price and thereby making a profit.

Floating exchange rate When the government does not intervene in the foreign exchange markets, but simply allows the exchange rate to be freely determined by demand and supply.

Figure 14.14 Determination of the rate of exchange

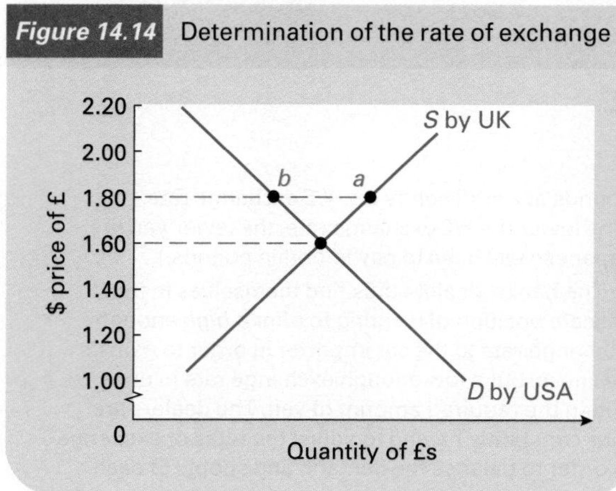

Figure 14.15 Floating exchange rates: movement to a new equilibrium

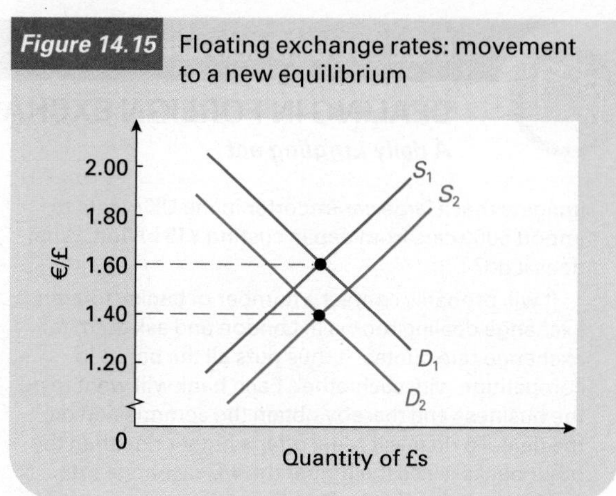

The demand curve for pounds, therefore, typically slopes downwards.

KI 8 p43 The equilibrium exchange rate is where the demand for pounds equals the supply. In Figure 14.14 this is at an exchange rate of £1 = $1.60. But what is the mechanism that equates demand and supply?

If the current exchange rate were above the equilibrium, the supply of pounds being offered to the banks would exceed the demand. For example, in Figure 14.14 if the exchange rate were $1.80, there would be an excess supply of pounds of *a* – *b*. The banks, wishing to make money by *exchanging* currency, would have to lower the exchange rate in order to encourage a greater demand for pounds and reduce the excessive supply. They would continue lowering the rate until demand equalled supply.

Similarly, if the rate were below the equilibrium, say at $1.40, there would be a shortage of pounds. The banks would find themselves with too few pounds to meet all the demand. At the same time, they would have an excess supply of dollars. The banks would thus raise the exchange rate until demand equalled supply.

In practice, the process of reaching equilibrium is extremely rapid. The foreign exchange dealers in the banks are continually adjusting the rate as new customers make new demands for currencies. What is more, the banks have to watch each other closely since they are constantly in competition with each other and thus have to keep their rates in line. The dealers receive minute-by-minute updates on their computer screens of the rates being offered round the world.

Shifts in the currency demand and supply curves

Any shift in the demand or supply curves will cause the exchange rate to change. This is illustrated in Figure 14.15, which this time shows the euro/sterling exchange rate. If the demand and supply curves shift from D_1 and S_1 to D_2 and S_2 respectively, the exchange rate will fall from €1.60 to €1.40. A fall in the exchange rate is called a ***depreciation***. A rise in the exchange rate is called an ***appreciation***.

But why should the demand and supply curves shift? The following are the major possible causes of a depreciation:

- A fall in domestic interest rates. UK rates would now be less competitive for savers and other depositors. More UK residents would be likely to deposit their money abroad (the supply of sterling would rise), and fewer people abroad would deposit their money in the UK (the demand for sterling would fall).
- Higher inflation in the domestic economy than abroad. UK exports will become less competitive. The demand for sterling will fall. At the same time, imports will become relatively cheaper for UK consumers. The supply of sterling will rise.
- A rise in domestic incomes relative to incomes abroad. If UK incomes rise, the demand for imports, and hence the supply of sterling, will rise. If incomes in other countries fall, the demand for UK exports, and hence the demand for sterling, will fall.
- Relative investment prospects improving abroad. If investment prospects become brighter abroad than in the UK, perhaps because of better incentives abroad, or because of worries about an impending recession in the UK, again the demand for sterling will fall and the supply of sterling will rise.
- Speculation that the exchange rate will fall. If businesses involved in importing and exporting, and also banks and other foreign exchange dealers, think that the exchange rate is about to fall, they will sell pounds *now* before the rate does fall. The supply of sterling will thus rise.

Definitions

Depreciation A fall in the free-market exchange rate of the domestic currency with foreign currencies.

Appreciation A rise in the free-market exchange rate of the domestic currency with foreign currencies.

CASE STUDIES AND APPLICATIONS

BOX 14.6

DEALING IN FOREIGN EXCHANGE

A daily juggling act

Imagine that a large car importer in the UK wants to import 5000 cars from Japan costing ¥15 billion. What does it do?

It will probably contact a number of banks' foreign exchange dealing rooms in London and ask them for exchange rate quotes. It thus puts all the banks in competition with each other. Each bank will want to get the business and thereby obtain the commission on the deal. To do this it must offer a higher rate than the other banks, since the higher the ¥/£ exchange rate, the more yen the firm will get for its money. (For an importer a rate of, say, ¥200 to £1 is better than a rate of, say, ¥180.)

Now it is highly unlikely that any of the banks will have a spare ¥15 billion. But a bank cannot say to the importer 'Sorry, you will have to wait before we can agree to sell them to you.' Instead the bank will offer a deal and then, if the firm agrees, the bank will have to set about obtaining the ¥15 billion. To do this, it must offer Japanese who are *supplying* yen to obtain pounds at a sufficiently *low* ¥/£ exchange rate. (The lower the ¥/£ exchange rate, the fewer yen the Japanese will have to pay to obtain pounds.)

KI 8 p43 The banks' dealers thus find themselves in the delicate position of wanting to offer a *high* enough exchange rate to the car importer in order to gain its business, but a *low* enough exchange rate in order to obtain the required amount of yen. The dealers are thus constantly having to adjust the rates of exchange in order to balance the demand and supply of each currency.

In general, the more of any foreign currency that dealers are asked to supply (by being offered sterling), the lower will be the exchange rate they will offer. In other words, a higher supply of sterling pushes down the foreign currency price of sterling.

Assume that an American firm wants to import Scotch whisky from the UK. Describe how foreign exchange dealers will respond.

- Longer-term changes in international trading patterns. Over time the pattern of imports and exports is likely to change as (a) consumer tastes change, (b) the nature and quality of goods change and (c) the costs of production change. If, as a result, UK goods become less competitive than, say, German or Japanese goods, the demand for sterling will fall and the supply will rise. These shifts, of course, are gradual, taking place over many years.

? *Go through each of the above reasons for shifts in the demand for and supply of sterling and consider what would cause an* appreciation *of the pound.*

Exchange rates and the balance of payments

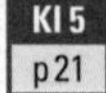

KI 5 p21 In a free foreign exchange market, the balance of payments will *automatically* balance. But why?

The credit side of the balance of payments constitutes the demand for sterling. For example, when people abroad buy UK exports or assets, they will demand sterling in order to pay for them. The debit side constitutes the supply of sterling. For example, when UK residents buy foreign goods or assets, the importers of them will require foreign currency to pay for them. They will thus supply pounds. A floating exchange rate ensures that the demand for pounds always equals the supply. It thus also ensures that the credits on the balance of payments are equal to the debits: that the balance of payments balances.

This does not mean that each part of the balance of payments account will separately balance, but simply that any current account deficit must be matched by a capital plus financial account surplus and vice versa.

For example, suppose initially that each part of the balance of payments *did* separately balance. Then let us assume that interest rates rise. This will encourage larger short-term financial inflows as people abroad are attracted to deposit money in the UK: the demand for sterling would shift to the right (e.g. from D_2 to D_1 in Figure 14.15). It will also cause smaller short-term financial outflows as UK residents keep more of their money in the country: the supply of sterling shifts to the left (e.g. from S_2 to S_1 in Figure 14.15). The financial account will go into surplus. The exchange rate will appreciate.

As the exchange rate rises, this will cause imports to be cheaper and exports to be more expensive. The current account will move into deficit. There is a movement up along the new demand and supply curves until a new equilibrium is reached. At this point, any financial account surplus is matched by an equal current (plus capital) account deficit.

Managing the exchange rate

The government may be unwilling to let the country's currency float freely. Frequent shifts in the demand and supply curves would cause frequent changes in the exchange rate. This, in turn, might cause uncertainty for businesses, which might curtail their trade and investment.

The government may thus ask the central bank (the Bank of England in the case of the UK) to intervene in the foreign exchange market. But what can it do? The answer to this will depend on the government's objectives. It may simply want to reduce the day-to-day fluctuations in the exchange rate, or it may want to prevent longer-term, more fundamental shifts in the rate.

Reducing short-term fluctuations

Assume, for example, that the government believes that an exchange rate of €1.60 to the pound is approximately the long-term equilibrium rate. Short-term leftward shifts in the demand for sterling and rightward shifts in the supply, however, are causing the exchange rate to fall below this level (see Figure 14.15). What can be done? There are three possibilities.

Using reserves. The Bank of England can sell gold and foreign currencies from the reserves to buy pounds. This will shift the demand for sterling back to the right.

Borrowing from abroad. In extreme circumstances, the government could negotiate a foreign currency loan from other countries or from an international agency such as the International Monetary Fund. The Bank of England can then use these moneys to buy pounds on the foreign exchange market, thus again shifting the demand for sterling back to the right.

Raising interest rates. If the Bank of England raises interest rates, it will encourage people to deposit money in the UK and encourage UK residents to keep their money in the country. The demand for sterling will increase and the supply of sterling will decrease.

Maintaining a fixed rate of exchange over the longer term

Governments may choose to maintain a fixed rate over a number of months or even years. Indeed, from 1945 to 1972 the whole world operated under such a system. Countries used to 'peg' (i.e. fix) their currencies against the US dollar. This meant, therefore, that every currency was fixed with respect to every other currency (see pages 690–2).

But how can a government maintain an exchange rate that is persistently above the equilibrium? How can it resist the downward pressure on the exchange rate? After all, it cannot *order* dealers to keep the rate up: the dealers would run out of foreign currency. It cannot go on and on using its reserves to support the rate: the reserves would begin to run out. It will probably not want to go on borrowing from abroad and building up large international debts.

So what can it do? It must attempt to shift the demand and supply curves back again, so that they once more intersect at the fixed exchange rate. The following are possible methods it can use.

Deflation. This is where the government deliberately curtails aggregate demand by either fiscal policy or monetary policy or both.

Deflationary fiscal policy involves raising taxes and/or reducing government expenditure. Deflationary monetary policy involves reducing the supply of money and raising interest rates. Note that in this case we are not just talking about the temporary raising of interest rates to prevent a short-term outflow of money from the country, but the use of higher interest rates to reduce borrowing and hence dampen aggregate demand.

A reduction in aggregate demand works in two ways:

- It reduces the level of consumer spending. This directly cuts imports, since there is reduced spending on Japanese videos, German cars, Spanish holidays and so on. The supply of sterling coming on to the foreign exchange market thus decreases.
- It reduces the rate of inflation. This makes UK goods more competitive abroad, thus increasing the demand for sterling. It will also cut back on imports as UK consumers switch to the now more competitive home-produced goods. The supply of sterling falls.

Supply-side policies. This is where the government attempts to increase the long-term competitiveness of UK goods by encouraging reductions in the costs of production and/or improvements in the quality of UK goods. For example, the government may attempt to improve the quantity and quality of training and research and development (see Chapter 22).

Controls on imports and or foreign exchange dealing. This is where the government restricts the outflow of money, either by restricting people's access to foreign exchange, or by the use of tariffs and quotas. Tariffs are another word for customs duties. As taxes on imports, they raise their price and hence reduce their consumption. Quotas are quantitative restrictions on various imports.

? *What problems might arise if the government were to adopt this third method of maintaining a fixed exchange rate?*

Section summary

1. The balance of payments account records all payments to and receipts from foreign countries. The current account records payments for imports and exports, plus incomes and transfers of money to and from abroad. The capital account records all transfers of capital to and from abroad. The financial account records inflows and outflows of money for investment and as deposits in banks and other financial institutions; it also includes dealings in the country's foreign exchange reserves.
2. The whole account must balance, but surpluses or deficits can be recorded on any specific part of the account.
3. It is generally regarded as undesirable to have persistent current account deficits.
4. The rate of exchange is the rate at which one currency exchanges for another. Rates of exchange are determined by demand and supply in the foreign exchange market. Demand for the domestic currency consists of all the credit items in the balance of payments account. Supply consists of all the debit items.
5. The exchange rate will depreciate (fall) if the demand for the domestic currency falls or the supply increases. These shifts can be caused by increases in domestic prices or incomes relative to foreign ones, reductions in domestic interest rates relative to foreign ones, worsening investment prospects at home compared with abroad, or the belief by speculators that the exchange rate will fall. The opposite in each case would cause an appreciation (rise).
6. The government can attempt to prevent the rate of exchange from falling by central bank purchases of the domestic currency in the foreign exchange market, either by selling foreign currency reserves or by using foreign loans. Alternatively, the central bank can raise interest rates. The reverse actions can be taken to prevent the rate from rising.
7. In the longer term, the government can prevent the rate from falling by pursuing deflationary policies or supply-side policies to increase the competitiveness of the country's exports, or by imposing import controls.

14.5 POSTSCRIPT TO PART D: THE RELATIONSHIP BETWEEN THE FOUR MACROECONOMIC OBJECTIVES

Aggregate demand and the short-term relationship between the four objectives

TC 13 p381

In the short term (up to about two years), the four objectives of faster growth in output, lower unemployment, lower inflation and the avoidance of excessive current account balance of payments deficits are all related. They all depend on aggregate demand, and all vary with the course of the business cycle. This is illustrated in Figure 14.16.

In the expansionary phase of the business cycle (phase 2), aggregate demand grows rapidly. The gap between actual and potential output narrows. There is relatively rapid growth in output, and (demand-deficient) unemployment falls. Thus two of the problems are getting better. On the other hand, the other two problems become worse. The growing shortages lead to higher (demand-pull) inflation and larger current account balance of payments deficits as the extra demand 'sucks in' more imports and as higher

Figure 14.16 The business cycle and the four macroeconomic objectives

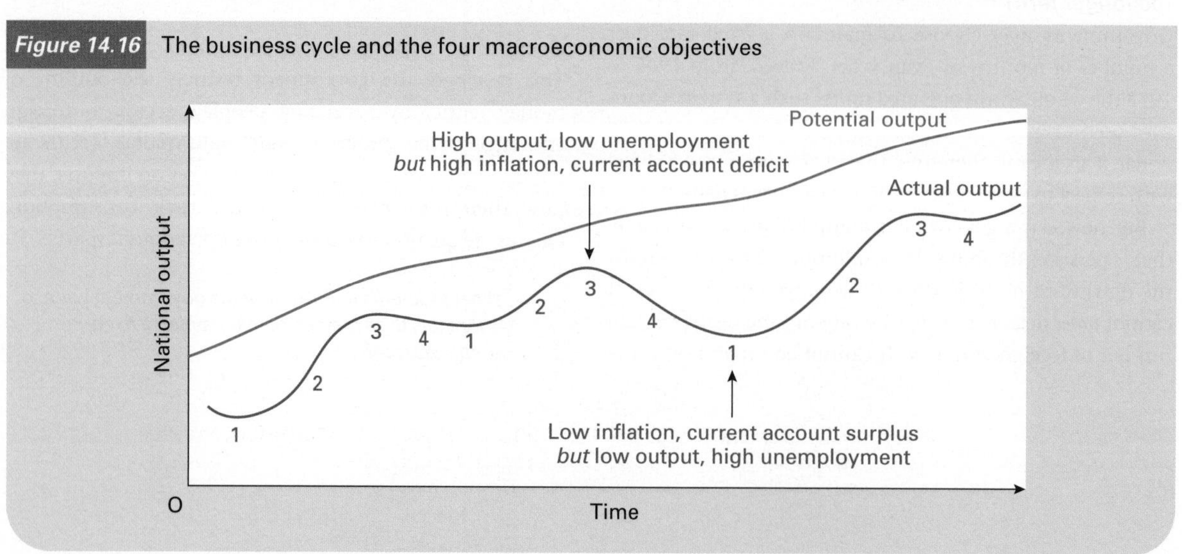

prices make UK goods less competitive internationally. As a result, unless there is a compensating rise in interest rates, the equilibrium exchange rate is likely to fall, which will raise the price of imports, thus further stoking up inflation. This will probably increase inflationary expectations.

At the peak of the cycle (phase 3), unemployment is probably at its lowest and output at its highest (for the time being). But growth has already ceased or at least slowed down. Inflation and balance of payments problems are probably acute.

As the economy moves into phase 4, the recession, the reverse happens to that of phase 2. Falling aggregate demand makes growth negative and demand-deficient unemployment higher, but inflation is likely to slow down and the current account balance of payments improves. These two improvements may take some time to occur, however.

Governments are thus faced with a dilemma. If they reflate the economy through fiscal and/or monetary policy, they will make two of the objectives better (growth and unemployment), but the other two worse (inflation and the current account of the balance of payments). If they deflate the economy, it is the other way round: inflation and the current account of the balance of payments will improve, but unemployment will rise and growth or even output will fall.

Is there any point in the business cycle where all four objectives are looking reasonable? If so, that would be the time when it would be wise for a government to call a general election! (See Box 14.7.)

?

What is likely to happen to the exchange rate during phase 2 if the government (a) seeks to maintain a stable rate of interest; (b) raises the rate of interest in order to dampen the growth in aggregate demand?

CASE STUDIES AND APPLICATIONS **BOX 14.7**

THE POLITICAL BUSINESS CYCLE (PART I)[4]

Getting things looking right on the night

Any government standing for re-election would like the economy to look as healthy as possible. It can then claim to the electorate that its economic policies have been a success.

Governments are able to engineer booms and recessions by the use of demand-side policies (fiscal and monetary). For example, by cutting taxes and/or increasing government expenditure, and by cutting interest rates, they can generate a period of economic expansion.

But how is this of any use politically, if the improvement in two of the objectives is at the cost of a deterioration in the other two? That would not help the government's election prospects.

The answer is that there is one point in the business cycle where *all four* objectives are likely to be looking good. This 'window of opportunity' for the government is in the middle of phase 2 – the period of rapid expansion. At this point, growth is at its highest and unemployment is *falling* most rapidly. In fact, falling unemployment is probably more popular with the electorate than simply a *low level* of unemployment. Three million unemployed but falling rapidly will probably win more votes than one million and rising rapidly!

But what about the other two objectives? Surely, in the middle of phase 2, inflation and the balance of payments will be deteriorating? The answer is that they will probably not yet have become a serious problem. Inflation takes a time to build up. It will probably only really start to rise rapidly as the peak of the business cycle is approached and shortages and bottlenecks occur. As far as the balance of payments is concerned, this tends to become a serious *political issue* only when the current account deficit gets really severe, or if the exchange rate starts to plummet. In the middle of phase 2, it is unlikely that this stage will yet have been reached.

By careful economic management, then, the government can get the four objectives to look good at the time of the election. Of course, economic management is not perfect and policies may take longer (or shorter) to work than the government had anticipated. Things are made easier for governments in countries like the UK, however, where the government can choose when to call an election. It is less easy in countries like the USA, where elections are at fixed times.

Once a government has won an election, it can then deflate the economy in order to remove inflationary pressures and improve the balance of payments. A recession is likely to follow. This will probably be highly unpopular with the electorate. But no matter: the government, having created sufficient slack in the economy, can then reflate the economy again in time for the next general election!

It is thus possible to observe *political* business cycles. Recessions in the past tended to follow elections. Rapid growth tended to precede elections.

Today, however, the likelihood of a political business cycle has been reduced. In 1997, the Labour government, as soon as it was elected, granted independence to the Bank of England in setting interest rates and gave it a clear mandate to achieve a target rate of inflation (see sections 19.4 and 19.5). This means that the government can no longer use monetary policy for political purposes.

The Labour Chancellor (Gordon Brown) also set limits for the size of government borrowing and hence for the balance between government expenditure and taxation (see Box 19.4). This made it much more difficult, although not impossible, to use fiscal policy for political purposes.

[4] See Box 20.4 on page 585 for part II.

Table 14.9 UK macroeconomic indicators: 1959–2006

	Inflation[a]	Unemployment[b]	Growth[c]	Current account balance[d]
1959–63	2.3	1.9	3.5	+0.1
1964–8	4.1	1.9	3.2	−0.7
1969–73	8.7	3.0	3.4	+0.4
1974–8	22.1	4.3	1.2	−1.5
1979–83	14.0	8.6	0.8	+1.3
1984–8	4.7	10.7	3.6	−0.8
1989–93	5.7	8.5	0.4	−2.5
1994–8	2.1	7.8	3.3	−0.8
1999–2003	1.2	5.3	2.6	−2.2
2004–6[e]	1.7	4.8	2.7	−2.3

[a] Average annual percentage increase in retail prices.
[b] Average percentage standardised unemployment.
[c] Average annual growth rate in real GDP at market prices.
[d] Average annual current account deficit (–) or surplus (+) as % of GDP.
[e] 2005 and 2006 figures based on forecasts.

Sources: Various.

The long-term relationship between the objectives

In the long run, the relationship between the objectives is much less straightforward. Over the long term, they can all get better or all get worse. Table 14.9 illustrates this. It looks at the four indicators in five-year periods.

1. *Was there any five-year period when all four indicators were better than in the previous five years?*
2. *Which macroeconomic problem(s) has/have generally been less severe since the early 1990s than in the 1980s?*
3. *Why could the world as a whole not experience the problem of a current account balance of payments deficit?*

TC 14 p385

Faster long-run economic growth will require a faster increase in the rate of growth of *potential* output, matched by a sufficient growth in aggregate demand. But how can such an increase be achieved? Is it enough to rely on supply-side policy, and if so, should the focus be on freeing up the market and relying on market incentives; or should the government be much more interventionist and spend more money, for example on training schemes or on the country's transport infrastructure by building more roads or improving the rail system? Or does the government also need to manage the level of aggregate demand so as to create a more stable economy, thereby encouraging more investment and hence an expansion of the economy's capacity to produce?

Then there is the question of unemployment. In the short run, as we have seen, it fluctuates with the business cycle. In the long run, however, to achieve lower unemployment it may not be enough merely to have a more rapidly growing economy. It may also be necessary to tackle underlying structural and frictional problems in the economy: to achieve a more flexible labour force, responsive to changes in the demand for products and skills. This may require government investment in education and training.

But will a reduction in unemployment in the long run also lead to higher inflation? Is there anything resembling a Phillips curve in the long run, and if so, can it be shifted to the left so as to permit both lower unemployment and lower inflation?

Finally there is the question of the balance of payments. Although the size of the current account deficit fluctuates with the business cycle, the underlying deficit may get larger or smaller over the long run. What determines long-run movements in the balance of payments? To what extent does it depend on the competitiveness of the country's exports, and to what extent does this depend on the exchange rate?

As the book progresses we will be looking at the relationship between the four objectives. Over the years there has been considerable debate among economists over these relationships. The next chapter gives an overview of these debates. It helps to put in context the current state of macroeconomics: where economists have reached agreement and where they still disagree.

Section summary

1. In the short run, the four macroeconomic objectives are related to aggregate demand and the business cycle. In the boom phase, growth is high and unemployment is falling, but inflation is rising and the current account of the balance of payments is moving into deficit. In the recession, the reverse is the case.
2. In the long run, the relationship between the four objectives is less straightforward. Nevertheless, improvements on the supply side of the economy can lead to improvements in all four objectives.

END OF CHAPTER QUESTIONS

1. The following table shows the UK consumer prices index (CPI) for the years 1999 to 2004, based on 1996 = 100.

Year	1999	2000	2001	2002	2003	2004
CPI	104.8	105.6	106.9	108.3	109.8	111.2

   Work out the rate of inflation for each of the years 2000 to 2004.
2. At what phase of the business cycle is the average *duration* of unemployment likely to be the highest? Explain.
3. Explain whether it would be desirable to have zero unemployment.
4. Consider the most appropriate policy for tackling each of the different types of unemployment.
5. Do any groups of people gain from inflation?
6. If everyone's incomes rose in line with inflation, would it matter if inflation were 100 per cent or even 1000 per cent per annum?
7. Imagine that you had to determine whether a particular period of inflation was demand pull, or cost push, or a combination of the two. What information would you require in order to conduct your analysis?
8. The following are the items in the UK's 2003 balance of payments.

	£ billions
Exports of goods	187.8
Imports of goods	235.1
Exports of services	89.7
Imports of services	75.1
Net income to/from abroad	+22.1
Net current transfers	–9.9
Capital transfers to the UK	2.7
Capital transfers from the UK	1.5
Overseas investment in UK	101.0
UK investment overseas	66.8
Other financial inflows	253.3
Other financial outflows	271.6
Reserves	+1.6

   Calculate the following: (a) the balance on trade in goods; (b) the balance of trade; (c) the balance of payments on current account; (d) the capital account balance; (e) the financial account balance; (f) the balancing item.
9. Explain how the current account of the balance of payments is likely to vary with the course of the business cycle.
10. The overall balance of payments must always balance. If this is the case, why might a deficit on one part of the balance of payments be seen as a problem?
11. List some factors that could cause an increase in the credit items of the balance of payments and a decrease in the debit items. What would be the effect on the exchange rate (assuming that it is freely floating)? What effect would these exchange rate movements have on the balance of payments?
12. What policy measures could the government adopt to prevent the exchange rate movements in question 11?

Additional case study on the book's website (www.pearsoned.co.uk/sloman)

14.1 **Do people volunteer to be unemployed?** Is it useful to make the distinction, often made, between voluntary and involuntary unemployment?

14.2 **Technology and employment.** Does technological progress create or destroy jobs?

14.3 **A high exchange rate.** This case looks at whether a high exchange rate is necessarily bad news for exporters.

14.4 **Disinflation.** The experience of Europe and Japan.

WEBSITES RELEVANT TO CHAPTERS 13 AND 14

Numbers and sections refer to websites listed in the Web Appendix and hotlinked from this book's website at www.pearsoned.co.uk/sloman.

- For news articles relevant to this and the previous chapter, see the *Economics News Articles* link from the book's website.
- For general news on macroeconomic issues, both national and international, see websites in section A, and particularly A1–5, 7–9, 20–25, 31. See also links to newspapers worldwide in A38, 39, 43 and 44, and the news search feature in Google at A41. See also A42 for links to economics news articles from newspapers worldwide.
- For macroeconomic data, see links in B1 or 2; also see B4 and 12. For UK data, see B3 and 34. For EU data, see G1 > *The Statistical Annex*. For US data, see *Current economic indicators* in B5 and the *Data* section of B17. For international data, see B15, 21, 24, 31, 33, 35 and especially 36. For links to data sets, see B28, 33 and 36; I14.
- For national income statistics for the UK (Appendix), see B1, *1. National Statistics* > the fourth link > *Economy* > *United Kingdom Economic Accounts* and *United Kingdom National Accounts – The Blue Book*.
- For data on UK unemployment, see B1, *1. National Statistics* > the fourth link > *Labour Market* > *Labour Market Trends*. For international data on unemployment, see G1; H3 and 5.
- For international data on balance of payments and exchange rates, see *World Economic Outlook* in H4 and *OECD Economic Outlook* in B21 (also in section 6 of B1). See also the trade topic in I14.
- For details of individual countries' balance of payments, see B32.
- For UK data on balance of payments, see B1, *1. National Statistics* > the fourth link > *Economy* > *United Kingdom Balance of Payments – the Pink Book*. See also B3, 34; F2. For EU data, see G1 > *The Statistical Annex* > *Foreign trade and current balance*.
- For exchange rates, see A3; B34; F2, 6, 8.
- For student resources relevant to Chapters 13 and 14, see sites C1–7, 9, 10, 19. See also the simulation: *The trade balance and the exchange rate* in site D3.

Part E: Macroeconomics

We now build on the foundations of the last three chapters. We will see why economies grow over the longer term but why they fluctuate in the short term and what governments can do to prevent these fluctuations.

In Chapter 15, to help understand the context of modern macroeconomics, we sketch out how the subject has developed over the past 100 years. In the following three chapters, we look at what determines the level of national income and the role that money plays in the process. Then, in Chapter 19, we look at government policy to stabilise the economy. In Chapter 20 we look at the relationship between inflation and unemployment. Finally, in Chapters 21 and 22, we turn to the long run and ask how economies can sustain faster growth.

Chapter 15
The Roots of Modern Macroeconomics

This chapter is optional. It looks at how the subject of macroeconomics has developed over the past 80 years. As the world economy has experienced various upheavals, such as the mass unemployment of the Great Depression of the 1930s, rapid inflation in the 1970s and recessions in the early 1980s and early 1990s, so economists have sought to analyse them and to provide solutions. Many 'battles' have been fought by opposing camps of economists, each seeking to provide the 'correct' analysis and each advocating particular policies to deal with the problems – policies that have ranged from highly interventionist to highly *laissez-faire*.

Although it is not necessary to have read this chapter to understand the following chapters, you will get a better feel for macroeconomic theories by understanding this historical context. After all, it was to help understand real problems, and to provide practical solutions to them, that many of the theories we shall be examining later in the book developed.

In this chapter we will be tracing events from the 1920s to the present day and seeing how economists wrestled with the problems. We shall also be seeing how politicians adopted the policies advocated by different schools of economic thought – with varying degrees of success. The unfolding of this story allows us to see how the different theories have developed. It also helps us to understand where there is now a general consensus among economists and where controversies remain.

CHAPTER MAP

Macroeconomics as a separate branch of economics had its birth with the mass unemployment experienced in the 1920s and 1930s. The old 'classical theories' of the time, which essentially said that free markets would provide a healthy economy with full employment, could not provide solutions to the problem. Their analysis seemed totally at odds with the facts.

A new analysis of the economy – one that *did* offer solutions to mass unemployment – was put forward by the economist John Maynard Keynes. His book *The General Theory of Employment, Interest and Money*, published in 1936, saw the dawn of 'Keynesian economics'. Keynes advocated active intervention by governments, in particular through the use of fiscal policy. By carefully managing aggregate demand, the government could prevent mass unemployment on the one hand, or an 'overheated' economy with unsustainable growth and high inflation on the other.

After the Second World War, governments around the world adopted Keynesian demand-management policies; and they seemed to be successful. The 1950s and 1960s were a period of low inflation, low unemployment and relatively high economic growth (see Table 14.9 on page 426). Macroeconomists were largely concerned with refining Keynesian economics.

In the 1970s, however, the macroeconomic consensus broke down as both inflation and unemployment rose and growth slowed down. Macroeconomics became highly controversial. Different 'schools of thought' had their own explanations of what was going wrong, and each had its own solutions to the problems.

Then, as the macroeconomic environment generally improved in the 1990s, so increasingly common ground re-emerged. Today there is broad agreement among many macroeconomists over the causes of macroeconomic problems and the appropriate policies to deal with them. There is not total agreement, however. We will be identifying the areas where disagreement remains.

15.1 SETTING THE SCENE: THREE KEY ISSUES

Most of the debate in macroeconomics has centred on the working of the market mechanism: just how well or how badly it achieves the various macroeconomic objectives. There have been three major areas of disagreement: (a) how flexible are wages and prices, (b) how flexible is aggregate supply and (c) what is the role of expectations? We examine each in turn.

Issue 1: The flexibility of prices and wages

Generally, the political right has tended to ally with those economists who argue that prices and wages are relatively flexible. Markets tend to clear, they say, and clear fairly quickly.

Disequilibrium unemployment is likely to be fairly small, according to their view, and normally only a temporary, short-run phenomenon. Any long-term unemployment, therefore, will be equilibrium (or 'natural') unemployment. To cure this, they argue, encouragement must be given to the free play of market forces: to a rapid response of both firms and labour to changes in market demand and supply, to a more rapid dissemination of information on job vacancies, and generally to greater labour mobility, both geographical and occupational.

There are some on the political right, however, who argue that in the short run wages may not be perfectly flexible. This occurs when unions attempt to keep wages above the equilibrium. In this case, disequilibrium unemployment may continue for a while. The solution here, they argue, is to curb the power of unions so that wage flexibility can be restored and disequilibrium unemployment cured.

The political centre and left have tended to ally with economists who reject the assumption of highly flexible wages and prices. If there is a deficiency of demand for labour in the economy, during a recession say, there will be a resistance from unions to cuts in real wages and certainly to cuts in money wages. Any cuts that do occur will be insufficient to eliminate the disequilibrium, and will anyway serve only to reduce aggregate demand further, so that workers have less money to spend. The demand curve in Figure 14.6 (see page 402) would shift further to the left.

The prices of goods may also be inflexible in response to changes in demand. As industry has become more concentrated and more monopolistic over the years, firms, it is argued, have become less likely to respond to a general fall in demand by cutting prices. Instead, they are likely to build up stocks if they think the recession is temporary, or cut production and hence employment if they think the recession will persist. It is also argued that firms typically use cost-plus methods of pricing. If wages are inflexible downwards, and if they form a major element of costs, prices will also be inflexible downwards.

Thus according to those who criticise the right, markets cannot be relied upon automatically to correct disequilibria and hence cure disequilibrium unemployment.

? *Why are* real *wages likely to be more flexible downwards than* money *wages?*

Issue 2: The flexibility of aggregate supply

The question here is, how responsive is national output (i.e. aggregate supply), and hence also employment, to a change in aggregate demand?

Figure 15.1 Different aggregate supply curves

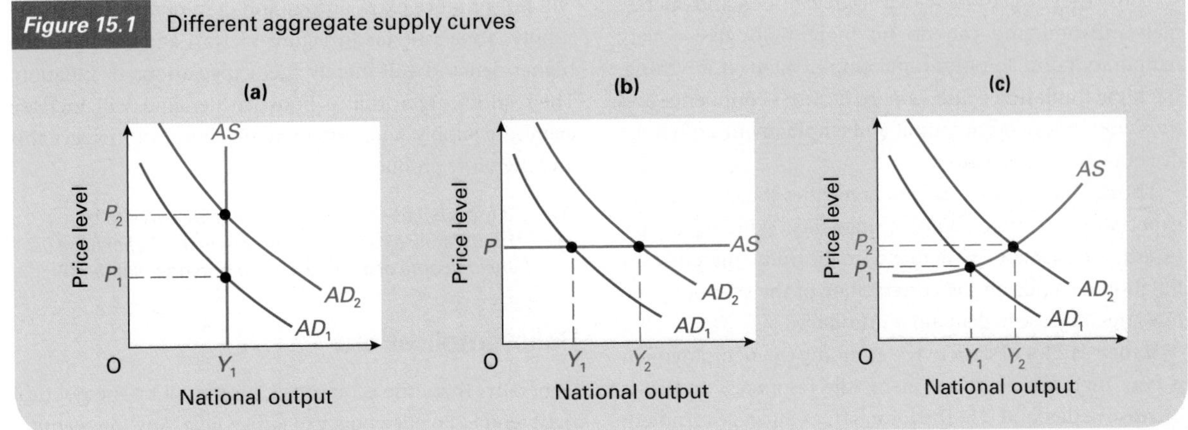

The arguments centre on the nature of the aggregate supply curve (*AS*). Three different *AS* curves are shown in Figure 15.1. In each of the three cases, it is assumed that the government now raises aggregate demand through the use of fiscal and/or monetary policy. Aggregate demand shifts from AD_1 to AD_2. The effect on prices and output will depend on the shape of the *AS* curve.

TC 8 p59

Some economists, generally supported by the political right, argue that output is not determined by aggregate demand (except perhaps in the very short run). Instead, the rise in aggregate demand will simply lead to a rise in prices. They therefore envisage an *AS* curve like that in diagram (a). If the government wants to expand aggregate supply and get more rapid economic growth, it is no good, they argue, concentrating on demand. Instead, governments should concentrate directly on supply by encouraging enterprise and competition, and generally by encouraging markets to operate more freely. For this reason, this approach is often labelled ***supply-side economics***.

Their critics, however, argue that a rise in aggregate demand will lead to a rise in output. In the extreme case where actual output is well below potential output, prices will not rise at all. In this case, the *AS* curve is like that in diagram (b). Output will rise to Y_2 with the price level remaining at *P*.

Others argue that both prices and output will rise. In this case, the short-term curve will be like that in diagram (c). If there is plenty of slack in the economy – idle machines, unemployed labour, etc. – output will rise a lot and prices only a little. But as slack is taken up, the *AS* curve becomes steeper. Firms, finding it increasingly difficult to raise output in the short run, simply respond to a rise in demand by raising prices.

Definition

Supply-side economics An approach that focuses directly on aggregate supply and how to shift the aggregate supply curve outwards.

In recent years, some consensus has emerged. Most economists now maintain that the short-run *AS* curve is similar to that in Figure 15.1(c), but that in the long run, given time for prices and wages to adjust, the curve is much steeper, if not vertical. Any increase in aggregate demand will simply result in higher prices.

There is not total agreement, however. Some Keynesian economists argue that the long-run effects of an increase in aggregate demand could be a higher level of investment and hence higher capacity and thus a higher aggregate supply. In such a case, the long-run *AS* curve would be much flatter.

? *Would it be possible for a short-run AS curve to be horizontal (as in diagram (b)) at* all *levels of output?*

Issue 3: The role of expectations in the working of the market

TC 9 p101

How quickly and how fully will individuals and firms anticipate changes in prices and changes in output? How are their expectations formed, and how accurate are they? What effect do these expectations have? This has been the third major controversial topic.

The political right has tended to ally with those economists who argue that people's expectations adjust rapidly and fully to changing economic circumstances. They emphasise the role of expectations of *price* changes.

If aggregate demand expands, they argue, people will expect higher prices. Workers will realise that the apparently higher wages they are offered are an illusion. The higher wages are 'eaten up' by higher prices. Thus workers are not encouraged to work longer hours, and unemployed workers are not encouraged to take on employment more readily. Likewise the higher prices that firms can charge are necessary to cover higher wages and other costs, and are not a reflection of higher real demand. Firms thus soon realise that any apparent increased demand for their products is an illusion. Their price rises will fully absorb the extra spending in money terms. There will be no increase in sales, and hence no increase in output and employment.

Thus, they argue, increased aggregate demand merely fuels inflation and can do no more than give a very temporary boost to output and employment. If anything, the higher inflation could damage business confidence and thus worsen long-term output and employment growth by discouraging investment.

Those who criticise this view argue that the formation of expectations is more complex than this. Whether people expect an increase in demand to be fully matched by inflation depends on the current state of the economy and how any increase in demand is introduced.

If there is a lot of slack in the economy (if unemployment is very high and there are many idle resources) and if an increase in demand is in the form, say, of direct government spending on production (on roads, hospitals, sewers and other infrastructure) then output and employment may quickly rise. Here the effect of expectations may be beneficial. Rather than expecting inflation from the increased demand, firms may expect faster growth and an expansion of markets. As a result, they may choose to invest, and this in turn will produce further growth in output and employment.

Views on expectations, therefore, parallel views on aggregate supply. The right argues that a boost to demand will not produce extra output and employment: aggregate supply is inelastic (as in Figure 15.1(a)) and therefore the higher demand will merely fuel expectations of inflation. Their critics argue that a boost to demand will increase aggregate supply and employment. Firms will expect this and therefore produce more.

If firms believe the aggregate supply curve to be moderately elastic, what effect will this belief have on the outcome of an increase in aggregate demand?

Policy implications

Generally, then, the economists supported by the political right tend to favour a policy of *laissez-faire*. Any intervention by government to boost demand will merely be inflationary and will thus damage long-term growth and employment. At most, governments should intervene to remove hindrances to the free and efficient operation of markets.

Economists supported by the political centre and left have tended to argue that disequilibrium unemployment may persist for several years and may be very great. The answer is to boost demand, thereby increasing aggregate supply and employment.

Section summary

1. There has been considerable debate among economists and politicians over the years about how the market mechanism works at a macroeconomic level.
2. The right argues (a) that prices and wages are relatively flexible, (b) that aggregate supply is determined independently of aggregate demand and (c) that people's price and wage expectations adjust rapidly to shifts in aggregate demand so as to wipe out any output effect.
3. The centre and left to varying degrees argue (a) that prices and wages are inflexible downwards, (b) that aggregate supply is relatively elastic when there is slack in the economy and (c) that positive expectations of output and employment can make investment and aggregate supply responsive to changes in aggregate demand.

15.2 CLASSICAL MACROECONOMICS

The classical economists of the early nineteenth century held a pessimistic view of the long-term prospects for economic growth (see Boxes 5.1 and 13.5). Population growth combined with the law of diminishing returns would undermine any benefits from improved technology or the discovery of new sources of raw materials. What is more, there was little the government could do to improve these prospects. In fact governments, they argued, by interfering with competition and the functioning of the market would be likely to make things worse. They therefore advocated a policy of *laissez-faire* and free trade.

KI 17 p121

The classical school continued into the twentieth century. By then, its predictions about economic growth had become less pessimistic. After all, the Victorian years had been ones of rapid industrialisation and growth, with a massive expansion of Britain's overseas trade. This growing optimism had, if anything, strengthened the advocacy of *laissez-faire*. In the early years of the twentieth century, then, most economists, most politicians and virtually all bankers and business people were relatively confident in the power of the free market to provide growing output and low unemployment.

The main role for the government was to provide 'sound finance' (i.e. not to print too much money), so as to maintain stable prices.

The classical analysis of output and employment

The classical theory predicted that, in the long run, equilibrium in the economy would be at virtually full employment. In the long run, any unemployment would be merely *frictional* unemployment: namely, people in the process of changing jobs.

There were two important elements in the classical theory.

KI5 p21

The free-market economy works to equate demand and supply in all markets

This element of classical theory assumes flexible prices: of goods and services, of labour (i.e. wage rates) and of money (i.e. the rate of interest).

The classical economists argued that flexible prices would ensure that saving equalled investment ($S = I$) and that imports equalled exports ($M = X$). From this it follows that, if the government were to 'balance its budget' and make taxation equal to government expenditure ($T = G$), then total withdrawals would equal total injections ($W = J$).[1]

$$\left.\begin{array}{l} S = I \\ M = X \\ T = G \end{array}\right\} \rightarrow W = J$$

But why should flexible prices ensure that $S = I$ and $M = X$? The reasoning of the classical economists was as follows.

$S = I$. This would be brought about by flexible rates of interest (r) in the ***market for loanable funds***. When firms want to invest in new plant and equipment, they will require finance. Investment demand, therefore, represents a demand for loanable funds from financial institutions. The higher the rate of interest, the more expensive will borrowing be, and hence the less will be the demand for investment. The investment schedule will therefore be downward sloping with respect to r. This is illustrated in Figure 15.2.

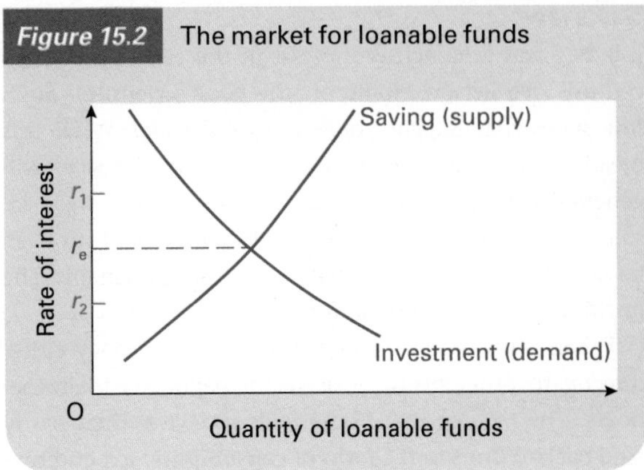

Figure 15.2 The market for loanable funds

Saving represents a supply of loanable funds. The saving schedule will be upward sloping. The higher the rate of interest, the more people will be attracted to save: that is, the more they will deposit in financial institutions.

Equilibrium will be at r_e, where $S = I$. If the rate of interest were above r_e, say at r_1, financial institutions would have surplus funds. They would have to lower the rate of interest to attract sufficient borrowers. If the rate of interest were below r_e, say at r_2, financial institutions would be short of funds. They would raise the rate of interest.

Assuming that rates of interest are initially above the equilibrium and that one particular financial institution chooses not *to reduce its rate of interest, what will happen? What will be the elasticity of supply of loanable funds to an* individual *institution?*

$M = X$. This would be brought about by flexible UK prices and wages. Before 1914, and from 1925 to 1931, the UK was on the ***gold standard***. This was a *fixed* exchange rate system in which each participating country's currency was valued at a certain fixed amount of gold.

If a country had a balance of payments deficit ($M > X$), this had to be paid in gold from its reserves. A country was then supposed to respond to this outflow of gold by reducing the amount of money in the economy and hence reducing total expenditure. This would create surpluses in the goods and labour markets, which would, in turn, lead to a fall in prices and wages. This fall in the prices of UK goods would increase the sale of exports and reduce the consumption of the now relatively expensive imports. This whole process would continue until the balance of payments deficit was eliminated: until $M = X$.

What would have happened if countries in deficit had not responded to an outflow of gold by reducing total expenditure?

(Note that, under a system of freely floating exchange rates, it is the flexibility in exchange rates, rather than the prices of goods and factors, that will ensure $M = X$.)

Provided the government balanced its budget ($T = G$), therefore, flexibility in the various markets would ensure that withdrawals equal injections.

[1] The classical economists did not use the terms 'withdrawals' and 'injections': these are modern terms. Nevertheless, their analysis implied an automatic equation of W and J if markets cleared and the government balanced its budget.

Definitions

Market for loanable funds The market for loans from and deposits into the banking system.

Gold standard The system whereby countries' exchange rates were fixed in terms of a certain amount of gold and whereby balance of payments deficits were paid in gold.

Say's law

J.-B. Say was a French economist of the early nineteenth century (see Person Profile on the book's website). ***Say's law*** states that: *supply creates its own demand*. What this means is that the production of goods and services will generate expenditures sufficient to ensure that they are sold. There will be no deficiency of demand and no need to lay off workers. There will be full employment. The justification for the law is as follows.

When firms produce goods, they pay out money either directly to other firms, or as factor payments to households. The income that households receive is then partly paid back to firms in the form of consumption expenditure (C_d): the inner flow of the circular flow of income.

But any withdrawals by firms or households are also fully paid back to firms in the form of injections, since $S = I$, $M = X$ and $T = G$. Thus all the incomes generated by firms' supply will be transformed into demand for their products, either directly in the form of consumption, or indirectly via withdrawals and then injections. There will thus be no deficiency of demand.

Of course, although aggregate demand might equal aggregate supply, consumers may shift their demand away from some industries in favour of others. Structural unemployment (a form of equilibrium unemployment) may then occur. But then wages would fall in the declining industries and rise in the expanding industries. This would help to eliminate the structural unemployment.

TC 8 p59

The reduction in structural unemployment will be quicker (a) the more flexible are wages and (b) the more willing and able are workers to move to industries and towns where jobs are available (labour mobility). In other words, the better markets work, the lower will be the level of equilibrium unemployment.

The classical analysis of prices and inflation

The classical economists based their analysis of inflation on the ***quantity theory of money***. In its simplest form, it states that the general level of prices (P) in the economy depends on the supply of money (M):[2]

$$P = f(M)$$

The greater the quantity of money, the higher the level of prices. Under this theory, inflation is simply caused by a rise in money supply.

To understand the reasoning behind the quantity theory of money, we need to examine the ***equation of exchange***. This comes in various versions (see Web Case 15.1), but the one most useful for our purposes is the simple identity between national expenditure and national income. This identity may be expressed as follows:

$$MV = PY$$

M, as we have already seen, is the supply of money in the economy. V is the ***velocity of circulation***. This is the number of times per year a pound is spent on buying goods and services that make up GDP. Suppose that each pound's worth of money is typically spent 5 times per year on such goods and services, and that money supply was £20 billion. This would mean that total expenditure on GDP ($M \times V$) was £100 billion.

P, again as we have already seen, is the general level of prices. Let us define it more precisely as the price index based on some specific year (e.g. 1995), where the index in the base year is assumed to be 1.00 (not 100) (see page A:7). Y is the real value of national income (i.e. GDP expressed in the prices of the base year). $P \times Y$, therefore, is simply the 'nominal' value of GDP (i.e. GDP expressed in *current* prices, rather than those of the base year). Thus if GDP in real terms (Y) (i.e. measured in base-year prices) were £80 billion and if the current price index (P) were 1.25, then nominal GDP ($P \times Y$) would be £100 billion.

Thus both MV and PY are equal to GDP and must, therefore, by definition be equal to each other.

The classical economists argued that both V and Y were determined independently of the money supply: i.e. a change in the money supply would *not* be expected to lead to a change in V or Y. The velocity of circulation (V), they claimed, was determined by the frequency with which people were paid (e.g. weekly or monthly), the nature of the banking system and other institutional arrangements for holding money. As far as Y was concerned, Say's law would ensure that the real value of output (Y) was maintained at the full-employment level.

With V and Y as 'constants' with respect to M, therefore, the quantity theory must hold:

$$P = f(M)$$

Increases in money supply simply lead to inflation.

[2] In the quantity theory of money the letter *M* is used to refer to money supply, whereas in the circular flow of income it is used to refer to the expenditure on imports. Naturally this is potentially confusing, but unfortunately it is normal practice to use the letter *M* in both ways. To avoid any such confusion we will always specify which is being referred to. Elsewhere, however, you will just have to judge from the context! (There is the same problem with the letter *P*, which can refer either to price or to product.)

Definitions

Say's law Supply creates its own demand. In other words, the production of goods will generate sufficient demand to ensure that they are sold.

Quantity theory of money The price level (P) is directly related to the quantity of money in the economy (M).

The equation of exchange MV = PY. The total level of spending on GDP (MV) equals the total value of goods and services produced (PY) that go to make up GDP.

Velocity of circulation The number of times annually that money on average is spent on goods and services that make up GDP.

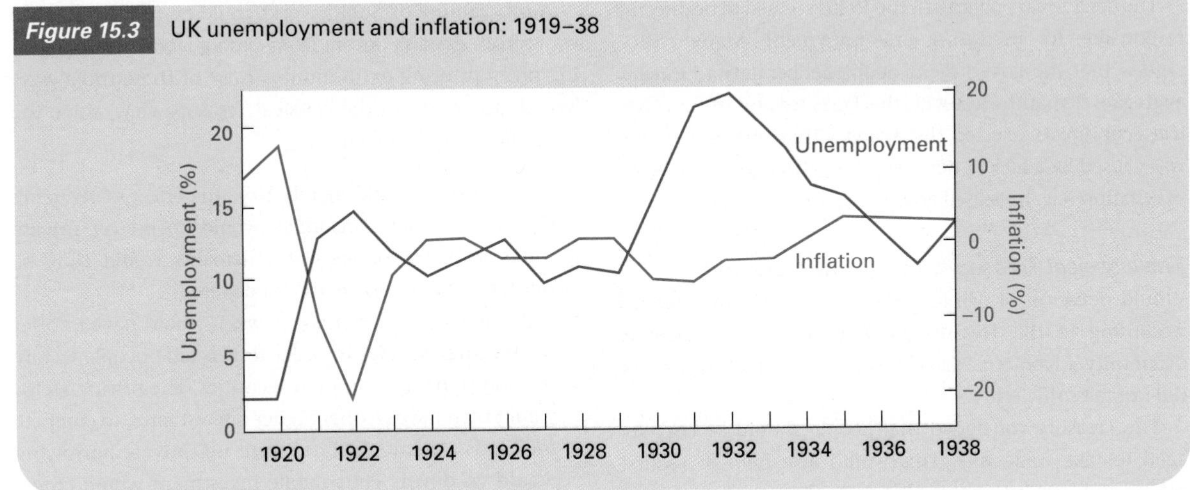

? *Assuming that Y rises each year as a result of increases in productivity, can money supply rise without causing inflation? Would this destroy the validity of the quantity theory?*

The classical response Great Depression

KI 31 p368

The classical economists had predicted that there would be virtual full employment. Any unemployment would simply be the frictional unemployment of people being 'between jobs'. Before the First World War their predictions were not far from the truth. Between the wars, however, Britain experienced a prolonged recession of unparalleled severity. Throughout this 'Great Depression' unemployment was very much higher than before the war, reaching over 22 per cent in the winter of 1932–3 with 3 million people unemployed. However, the depression eliminated inflation. In every year from 1921 to 1934 prices either were constant or fell (see Figure 15.3).

Part of the cause of the Depression was the decision in 1925 of Winston Churchill, the Chancellor of the Exchequer, to return to the gold standard at the pre-war rate of $4.86. But with many export markets lost in the war and a rapid rise in imports for rebuilding the economy, the balance of payments was in severe deficit. To correct this deficit required severely deflationary policies. The aim was to drive wage rates down, reduce costs and restore the competitiveness of exports. The result, however, was a severe recession.

But while in Britain output slumped and unemployment soared, most of the rest of the industrialised world initially experienced a boom. But in 1929, after a decade of rapid growth and a huge rise in share values, Wall Street crashed. This sent the US economy plunging into deep recession, with the rest of the world following suit. As the world economy slumped, so did international trade. With a collapse of its exports, Britain dived even deeper into depression. Eventually, in 1932, Britain was forced to leave the gold standard and allow the pound to depreciate. (Web Case 15.3 looks at the bitter experience of the return to the gold standard in 1925 and its aftermath.)

EXPLORING ECONOMICS — BOX 15.1

BALANCE THE BUDGET AT ALL COSTS

Fiscal policy in the early 1930s

The budget must be balanced. All government expenditure should be financed from taxation. This was orthodox opinion in the 1920s.

But as unemployment increased during the Great Depression, spending on unemployment benefits (the most rapidly growing item of government expenditure) threatened the balanced budget principle. Other spending had to be cut to restore balance. The result was more unemployment, and hence the payment of more unemployment benefits.

Treasury officials and classical economists called for cuts in unemployment benefits. The May Committee, set up to investigate the budgetary problem, recommended a 20 per cent reduction. Even the Labour government, elected on a mandate to tackle the unemployment problem, proposed a 10 per cent reduction in 1931. This contributed to its subsequent collapse.

Philip Snowdon, Labour's Chancellor of the Exchequer, remarked in 1931 how pensioners had returned their pension books and children sent in their savings to help the nation balance its budget. And yet, as Keynes argued, it was not saving that was necessary to cure the unemployment, but spending. Government deficits were *desirable*. Attempts to balance the budget merely deflated the economy further and deepened the problem of unemployment.

The deflationary policies of the 1920s seemed to be directly responsible for increasing unemployment. Many critics argued that the government ought deliberately to *expand* aggregate demand. However, the Treasury and other classical economists rejected the analysis that unemployment was caused by a lack of demand; they also rejected policies of reflation (e.g. increased government expenditure).

The classical Treasury view on unemployment

Would deflation of demand not lead to unemployment? According to the Treasury view, unemployment would occur only if labour markets *failed to clear*: if real wage costs did not fall sufficiently.

The Treasury concluded that people should be encouraged to take wage cuts. This would also help to reduce prices and restore export demand, thus correcting the balance of payments. People should also be encouraged to save. This would, via flexible interest rates, lead to more investment and hence a growth in output and demand for labour.

The classical Treasury view on public works

In the 1920s and 1930s, some politicians and economists argued that unemployment could be reduced if the government pursued a programme of public works: building roads, hospitals, houses, etc. The Treasury view was that this would not work and could have costly side-effects.

A programme of public works could be funded in three ways: from extra taxation, from extra government borrowing or by printing extra money. *None* of these three ways would, according to the classical Treasury view, solve the unemployment problem.

- *Extra taxation* would merely have the effect of reducing the money that consumers would spend on private industry. Extra public-sector demand would thus be offset by a fall in private-sector demand.
- If the government *borrowed more*, it would have to offer higher interest rates in order to persuade people to buy the additional government securities. The private sector would then have to offer higher interest rates, to compete for funds. As interest rates went up, private borrowing would go down. Thus public investment would ***crowd out*** private investment (see Box 15.2).
- According to the quantity theory of money, *printing extra money* would simply lead to inflation. The assumption here is that the aggregate supply 'curve' is vertical. In Figure 15.4 a rise in aggregate demand from AD_1 to AD_2 (as a result of the extra money supply) would simply

Definition

Crowding out Where increased public expenditure diverts money or resources away from the private sector.

EXPLORING ECONOMICS — BOX 15.2

THE CROWDING-OUT EFFECT

When public expenditure replaces private

Critics of the use of government expenditure to stimulate output and employment often refer to the problem of *crowding out*. In its starkest form, the argument goes like this.

There is no point in the government embarking on a programme of public works to bring the economy out of recession. If it attempts to spend more, it can do so only by reducing private expenditure. The effect on total spending will be zero. This crowding out can take two main forms.

Resource crowding out

This is when the government uses resources such as labour and raw materials that would otherwise be used by the private sector. If the economy is operating near full capacity, then if resources are used by the government, they cannot at the same time be used by private companies.

The argument is far less convincing, however, if there is slack in the economy. If the government merely mobilises otherwise *idle* resources, there need be no reduction in private-sector output. In fact, if private-sector firms have spare capacity, they will respond to the higher demand by producing more themselves: aggregate demand will stimulate extra production.

Financial crowding out

This occurs when extra government spending diverts *funds* from private-sector firms and thus deprives them of the finance necessary for investment.

If the government spends more (without raising taxes or printing more money), it will have to borrow more and will therefore have to offer higher rates of interest. Private companies will then have to offer higher rates of interest themselves in order to attract funds. Alternatively, if they borrow from banks, and banks have less funds, the banks will charge them higher interest rates. Higher interest rates will discourage firms from borrowing and hence discourage investment.

The weakness with this argument is that it assumes that the supply of money is fixed. If the government spends more but *increases* the amount of money in the economy, it need not deprive the private sector of finance. Interest rates will not be bid up.

But would that not be inflationary? Not if there are idle resources and hence the extra money can be spent on extra output. Only if *resource* crowding out takes place would it be inflationary.

Could resource crowding out take place at less than full employment?

Figure 15.4 The effect of printing extra money: the classical analysis

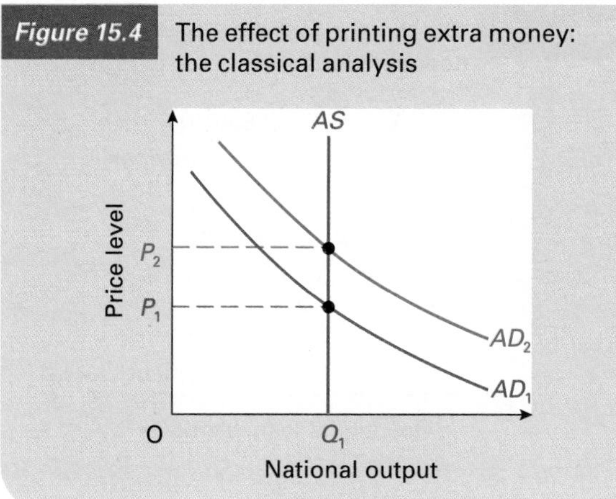

lead to a rise in the price level from P_1 to P_2. National output (and hence employment) would not increase. It would remain constant at Q_1. A re-emergence of inflation, which had been eliminated in the early 1920s, would further erode the competitiveness of British goods, jeopardising the return to the gold standard at the pre-war exchange rate.

Treasury orthodoxy insisted, therefore, that government should attempt to balance its budget, even if this meant cutting welfare benefits to the rising numbers of unemployed (see Box 15.1). The governments of the 1920s and early 1930s followed these classical recommendations. They attempted to balance their budgets and rejected policies of reflation. Yet mass unemployment persisted.

Section summary

1. The classical analysis of output and employment is based on the assumption that markets clear. More specifically, it assumes that there are flexible wages, flexible prices and flexible rates of interest. The result will be that demand and supply are equated in the labour market, in the goods market and in the market for loanable funds.
2. Given that markets will clear, Say's law will operate. This law states that supply creates its own demand. In other words, the production of goods and services will generate incomes for households, which in turn will generate consumption expenditure, ensuring that the goods are sold. If any incomes are not directly spent on domestic goods, flexible prices will help to ensure that any money withdrawn is reinjected. Flexible interest rates will ensure that investment equals saving, and flexible prices and wages will ensure that exports equal imports. Provided the government balances its budget, withdrawals will equal injections and Say's law will hold.
3. The classical economists based their analysis of prices on the quantity theory of money. This states that the level of prices is directly related to the quantity of money (M) in the economy. Their position can be demonstrated using the equation of exchange:

   $$MV = PY$$

   where V is the velocity of circulation, P is the price index and Y is real national income expressed in the prices of the base year. The classical economists assumed that V and Y were not affected by changes in the money supply and could thus be regarded as 'constants'. From this it follows that:

   $$P = f(M)$$

   Increases in the money supply simply lead to inflation.
4. In 1925 Britain returned to the gold standard system of fixed exchange rates at the pre-war rate. But given the massive balance of payments deficit at this rate, it had to pursue tough deflationary policies. The result was mass unemployment.
5. The classical economists saw the remedy to the problem to lie in reductions in wages and prices. According to the classical theory, this would allow Say's law to operate and full employment to be restored. They rejected public works as the solution, arguing that it would lead to crowding out if financed by borrowing, and to inflation if financed by printing money.

15.3 THE KEYNESIAN REVOLUTION

Keynes' rejection of classical macroeconomics

The main critic of classical macroeconomics was John Maynard Keynes (see Person Profile on the book's website). In his major work, *The General Theory of Employment, Interest and Money* (1936), he rejected the classical assumption that markets would clear. Disequilibrium could persist and mass unemployment could continue. There are two crucial markets in which disequilibrium could persist.

The labour market

Workers would resist wage cuts. Wages were thus 'sticky' downwards. In a recession, when the demand for labour is low, wages might not fall far or fast enough to clear the labour market.

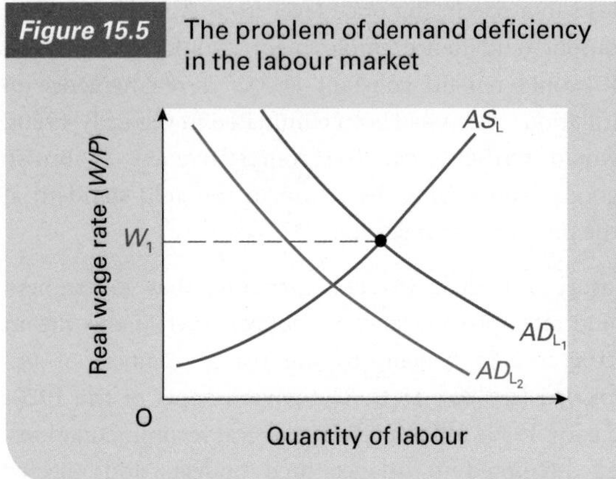

Figure 15.5 The problem of demand deficiency in the labour market

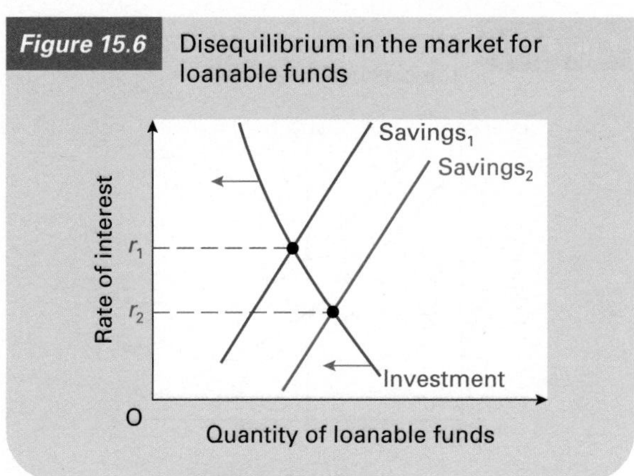

Figure 15.6 Disequilibrium in the market for loanable funds

In Figure 15.5 the recession has caused the aggregate demand for labour to shift to AD_{L_2}. If the real wage rate were to remain at W_1, the supply and demand for labour would no longer be in equilibrium. There would exist disequilibrium (demand-deficient) unemployment. But even if wage cuts could be introduced, as advocated by classical economists, Keynes rejected that as the solution to demand deficiency. Workers are also consumers. A cut in workers' wages would mean less consumer spending. Firms would respond to this by reducing their demand for labour. Thus a lowering of wage rates below W_1 would lead to a leftward shift in the AD_L curve, and this would more than offset the reduction in wages. Wage rates would not fall fast enough to clear the market. Disequilibrium would worsen. The recession would deepen.

Employers might well find that labour was cheaper to employ, but if demand for their product was falling, they would hardly be likely to take on more labour.

The market for loanable funds

Keynes also rejected the classical solution of increased saving as a means of stimulating investment and growth. Again the problem was one of market disequilibrium.

An increase in savings will cause a disequilibrium in the market for loanable funds. The rate of interest will fall from r_1 to r_2 in Figure 15.6. But an increase in saving means a fall in consumption. As a result, firms will sell less and will thus be discouraged from investing. The investment demand curve will shift to the left. The rate of interest will have to fall *below* r_2 to clear the market.

The demand for investment, according to Keynes, depends very much on business confidence in the future. A slide into recession could shatter such confidence. The resulting fall in investment would deepen the recession.

The problem of disequilibrium in the market for loanable funds is made worse, according to Keynes, because neither saving nor investment is very responsive to changes in interest rates, and thus very large changes in interest rates would be necessary if ever equilibrium were to be restored after any shift in the savings or investment curves.

Keynes also rejected the simple quantity theory of money. Increases in money supply will not necessarily lead merely to rises in prices. If there is a lot of slack in the economy, with high unemployment, idle machines and idle resources,

EXPLORING ECONOMICS — *BOX 15.3*

WILL WAGE CUTS CURE UNEMPLOYMENT?

Keynes' dismissal of the classical remedy

In *The General Theory of Employment, Interest and Money*, Keynes rejects the classical argument that unemployment is due to excessive wages. In Chapter 2 he argues:

> [T]he contention that the unemployment which characterises a depression is due to a refusal by labour to accept a reduction of money wages is not clearly supported by the facts. It is not very plausible to assert that unemployment in the United States in 1932 was due either to labour obstinately refusing to accept a reduction of money wages or to its obstinately demanding a real wage beyond what the productivity of the economic machine was capable of furnishing. Wide variations are experienced in the volume of employment without any apparent change either in the minimum real demands of labour or in its productivity. Labour is not more truculent in the depression than in the boom – far from it. Nor is its physical productivity less. These facts from experience are a *prima facie* ground for questioning the classical analysis.[3]

[3] J. M. Keynes, *The General Theory of Employment, Interest and Money* (Macmillan, 1967), p. 9.

an increased spending of money may lead to substantial increases in real income (Y) and leave prices (P) little affected.

? *Demonstrate this argument on an aggregate demand and supply diagram.*

If the government were to cut money supply in an attempt to reduce prices, the major effect might be to reduce output and employment instead. In terms of the quantity equation, a reduction in M may lead to a reduction in output and hence real income Y rather than a reduction in P.

All these arguments meant a rejection of Say's law. Far from supply creating demand and thus ensuring full employment, Keynes argued that it was *demand that created supply*. If aggregate demand rose, firms would respond to the extra demand by producing more and employing more people. But a fall in demand would lead to less output and rising unemployment.

Keynes' central point was that an unregulated market economy *could not ensure sufficient demand*. Governments should therefore abandon *laissez-faire*. Instead they should intervene to *control* aggregate demand.

Keynes' analysis of employment and inflation

Keynes' analysis of unemployment can be explained most simply in terms of the circular flow of income diagram (see Figure 15.7). Keynes himself did not use this exact model, but it clearly explains the essence of his argument.

If injections (J) do not equal withdrawals (W), a state of disequilibrium exists. What will bring them back into equilibrium, however, is not a change in prices (of labour or of loanable funds), but rather a change in *national income* and *employment*.

Start with a state of equilibrium, where injections equal withdrawals. If there is now a rise in injections – say, firms decide to invest more – aggregate demand ($C_d + J$) will be higher. Firms will respond to this increased demand by using more labour and other resources and thus paying out more incomes (Y) to households. Household consumption will rise and so firms will sell more.

Firms will respond by producing more, and thus using more labour and other resources. Household incomes will rise again. Consumption and hence production will rise again, and so on. There will thus be a multiplied rise in incomes and employment. This is known as the ***multiplier effect*** and is an example of the 'principle of cumulative causation'.

Key Idea 33 ***The principle of cumulative causation.*** An initial event can cause an ultimate effect that is much larger.

The process, however, does not go on for ever. Each time household incomes rise, households save more, pay more taxes and buy more imports. In other words, withdrawals rise. When withdrawals have risen to match the increased injections, equilibrium will be restored and national income and employment will stop rising. The process can be summarised as follows:

$$J > W \rightarrow Y\uparrow \rightarrow W\uparrow \text{ until } J = W$$

Similarly, an initial fall in injections (or rise in withdrawals) will lead to a multiplied fall in national income and employment:

$$J < W \rightarrow Y\downarrow \rightarrow W\downarrow \text{ until } J = W$$

Thus equilibrium in the circular flow of income can be at *any* level of output and employment.

If aggregate demand is too low, there will be a recession and high unemployment. In Figure 15.8 it is assumed that there is some potential level of national income and output

Definition

Multiplier effect An initial increase in aggregate demand of £xm leads to an eventual rise in national income that is greater than £xm.

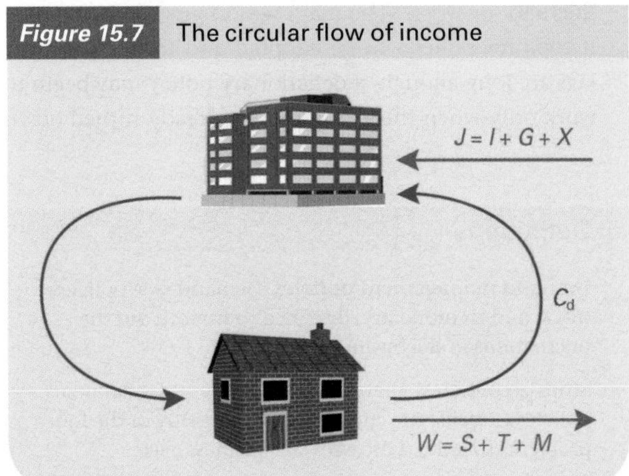

Figure 15.7 The circular flow of income

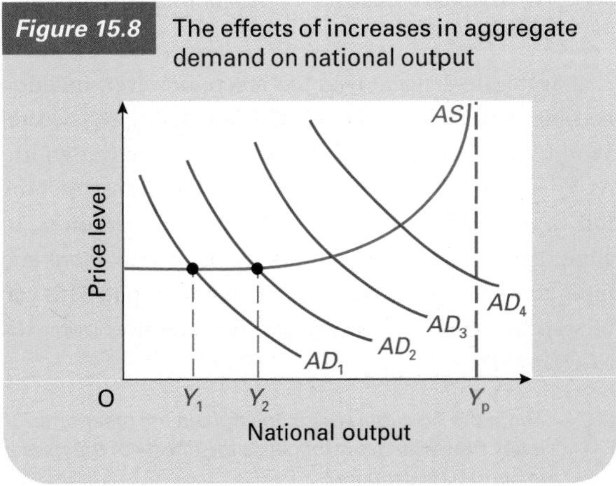

Figure 15.8 The effects of increases in aggregate demand on national output

(Y_p) at which there would be full employment of resources. This represents a limit to output. If aggregate demand were initially at AD_1, equilibrium would be at Y_1, considerably below the full-employment potential.

In this case, argued Keynes, governments should intervene to boost aggregate demand. There are two policy instruments that they can use.

Fiscal policy

Remember how we defined this in Chapter 14 (page 413). It is where the government alters the balance between government expenditure (G) and taxation (T), and thereby alters the balance between injections and withdrawals. In this way, it controls aggregate demand. Faced with a recession, it should raise G and/or lower T. In other words, the government should run a budget deficit rather than a balanced budget. There will then be a multiplier effect:

$$G\uparrow \text{ or } T\downarrow \rightarrow J > W \rightarrow Y\uparrow \rightarrow W\uparrow \text{ until } J = W$$

If the eventual rise in aggregate demand were to, say, AD_2 in Figure 15.8, output would rise to Y_2.

Monetary policy

This is where the central bank alters the supply of money in the economy or manipulates interest rates. If it were to raise money supply, there would be more available in the economy for spending, interest rates would fall and aggregate demand would rise. Keynes argued that this was a less reliable policy than fiscal policy, since some of the extra money could be used for speculating in paper assets rather than spending on real goods and services. The details of how money supply is controlled and the effects it has on the economy are examined in later chapters.

It is most effective if both policies are used simultaneously. For example, if the government undertook a programme of public works (fiscal policy) and financed it through increases in money supply (monetary policy), there would be no crowding out. There would be a significant rise in output and employment.

? *What would be the classical economists' criticisms of this argument?*

If aggregate demand rises too much, however, inflation becomes a problem. (This was the case during the Second World War, with the high expenditure on the war effort.) As Y_p is approached, with more and more firms reaching full capacity and with fewer and fewer idle resources, so additional increases in aggregate demand lead more and more to higher prices rather than higher output. This can be seen in Figure 15.8 as aggregate demand rises from AD_2 to AD_3 to AD_4.

? *Might the AS curve shift to the right in the meantime? If it did, how would this influence the effects of the rises in aggregate demand?*

Governments faced with the resulting demand-pull inflation should, according to Keynes, use *contractionary* fiscal and monetary policies to reduce demand. Contractionary fiscal policy would involve reducing government expenditure and/or raising taxes. Contractionary monetary policy would involve reducing the rate of growth of money supply. Keynes argued that here too fiscal policy was the more reliable, but again that the best solution was to combine both policies.

The Keynesian policies of the 1950s and 1960s

During the 1920s and 1930s, UK governments of all parties adopted the classical Treasury view of balanced budgets. By the end of the Second World War, the consensus had changed. From 1945 up to the mid-1970s, both Conservative and Labour governments pursued Keynesian ***demand management policies*** in an attempt to stabilise the economy and avoid excess or deficient demand.

When the economy began to grow too fast, with rising inflation and balance of payments deficits, the government adopted *deflationary* (contractionary) fiscal and monetary policies. When inflation and the balance of payments were sufficiently improved, but probably with recession looming, threatening rising unemployment and little or no growth, governments adopted *reflationary* (expansionary) fiscal and monetary policies (see Web Case 15.5). This succession of deflationary and reflationary policies to counteract the effect of the business cycle became known as ***stop–go policies***.

KI 31 p368

TC 13 p381

During the 1950s and 1960s, inflation in the UK averaged just 3.8 per cent and unemployment a mere 1.7 per cent (see Web Case 15.6). Similarly low rates of inflation and unemployment were experienced in other industrialised countries. Nevertheless, from the mid-1960s onwards there was increasing criticism of short-term demand management policies. Criticisms included the following:

- The policies were not very successful in stabilising the economy. Fluctuations still existed. Some economists even claimed that demand management policies made fluctuations worse. The main reason given was the time it took for policies to be adopted and to work. If time lags are long enough, a deflationary policy may begin to work only when the economy has already turned down

Definitions

Demand management policies Demand-side policies (fiscal and/or monetary) designed to smooth out the fluctuations in the business cycle.

Stop–go policies Alternate deflationary and reflationary policies to tackle the currently most pressing of the four problems that fluctuate with the business cycle.

into recession. Likewise a reflationary policy may begin to work only when the economy is already booming, thus further fuelling inflation.

- The UK's long-term growth at around 2.8 per cent per annum was appreciably lower than that of other industrialised countries. Some of the blame for this was attributed to an over-concentration on short-term policies of stabilisation, and a neglect of underlying structural problems in the economy.
- Persistent balance of payments problems meant that governments often had to pursue deflationary policies even when the economy was running below capacity and unemployment was rising.
- The simple Phillips curve relationship between inflation and unemployment was breaking down. If reflationary policies were the cure for unemployment and deflationary policies were the cure for inflation, what policies should be pursued when both inflation *and* unemployment were rising?
- The most fundamental criticism of all came from monetarists. They rejected Keynesianism as a whole, with its concentration on demand. They returned to the earlier classical analysis, with its concentration on supply, and extended it to take account of the increasingly important role of price expectations in explaining 'stagflation' (see the next section).

From the mid-1970s onwards, the Keynesian/monetarist split between economists was reflected in the political parties. The Conservative leadership embraced monetarism, whereas the other political parties continued to embrace variants of Keynesianism.

Section summary

1. Keynes rejected the classical assumption that all markets would clear. Disequilibrium could persist in the labour market. A fall in aggregate demand would not simply lead to a fall in wages and prices and a restoration of the full-employment equilibrium. Instead there would be demand-deficient unemployment: as demand fell, there would be less demand for labour.
2. Disequilibrium could also persist in the market for loanable funds. As aggregate demand fell, and with it business confidence, so the demand for loanable funds for investment would shrink. Reductions in interest rates would be insufficient to clear the market for loanable funds.
3. Keynes also rejected the simple quantity theory. If there is slack in the economy, an expansion of the money supply can lead to an increase in *output* rather than an increase in prices.
4. Keynes argued that there would be a multiplier effect from changes in injections or withdrawals. A rise in investment, for example, would cause a multiplied rise in national income, as additional expenditures flowed round and round the circular flow, stimulating more and more production and thus generating more and more real incomes.
5. If the economy is operating below full employment, the government can use fiscal and/or monetary policies to boost aggregate demand and thereby take up the slack in the economy. Excessive aggregate demand, however, causes inflation. Deflationary fiscal and monetary policies can be used to remove this excess demand.
6. Keynesianism became the orthodoxy of the 1950s and 1960s. Governments used fiscal (and to a lesser extent monetary) policies to manage the level of aggregate demand.
7. After the mid-1960s, however, there was growing criticism of Keynesian demand management. The economy still fluctuated and the various macroeconomic problems seemed to be getting worse.

15.4 THE MONETARIST–KEYNESIAN DEBATE

The monetarist counter-revolution

The most powerful criticisms of the Keynesian conventional wisdom came from monetarists, whose chief advocate was Milton Friedman, Professor of Economics at Chicago University (see Person Profile on the book's website). Monetarists returned to the old classical theory as the basis for their analysis, and extended it to take account of the growing problem of ***stagflation***.

At the heart of monetarism is the quantity theory of money. Friedman examined the historical relationship between money supply and prices, and concluded that inflation was 'always and everywhere a monetary phenomenon'. If money supply over the long run rises faster than the potential output of the economy, inflation will be the inevitable result.

Definition

Stagflation A term used in the 1970s to refer to the combination of stagnation (low growth and high unemployment) and high inflation.

Monetarists argued that over the long run, in the equation $MV = PY$, *both* V and Y are independently determined and are not, therefore, affected by changes in M. Any change in money supply (M), therefore, will only affect prices (P). Whether or not monetarists were correct in arguing that V and Y are not affected by changes in M will be examined in later chapters.

Monetarists drew two important conclusions from their analysis.

- The rising inflation from the mid-1960s onwards was entirely due to the growth in money supply increasingly outstripping the growth in output. If money supply rises, they argued, then the resulting rise in aggregate demand will lead not only to rising prices but also, for a few months, to higher output and employment. But soon people's expectations will adjust. Workers and firms come to expect higher wages and prices. Their actions then ensure that wages and prices *are* higher. Thus after 1–2 years the extra demand is fully taken up in inflation, and so output and employment fall back again. Then governments are tempted to raise money supply and aggregate demand again in a further attempt to get unemployment down. The effect of this over several years is for inflation simply to get higher and higher.
- Reducing the rate of growth of money supply will reduce inflation without leading to long-run increases in unemployment. It *will* lead to temporary increases in unemployment, they argued, as the demand for goods and labour fall. But once price and wage inflation have adjusted down to this new level of demand, disequilibrium unemployment will be eliminated. This process will be hindered and high unemployment is likely to persist if workers persist in demanding excessive wage increases, or if firms and workers continue to expect high inflation rates.

KI 10 p62

Monetarists argued that inflation is damaging to the economy because it creates uncertainty for business people and therefore reduces investment, and also because it reduces the country's competitiveness in international trade. They saw it as essential, therefore, for governments to keep a tight control over money supply and advocated the setting of money supply *targets*. Modest and well-publicised targets should help to reduce the *expected* rate of inflation. The UK government from the late 1970s to the mid-1980s set targets for the growth of money supply, and such targets were central to the Thatcher government's 'medium-term financial strategy'.

Apart from controlling the money supply, governments, according to monetarists, should intervene in the economy as little as possible, save to remove hindrances to the efficient functioning of the market (like various restrictive practices of unions). This way, they argued, aggregate supply would be encouraged to grow as firms and workers responded to market incentives. Monetarist 'supply-side policy', therefore, was essentially one of encouraging free enterprise.

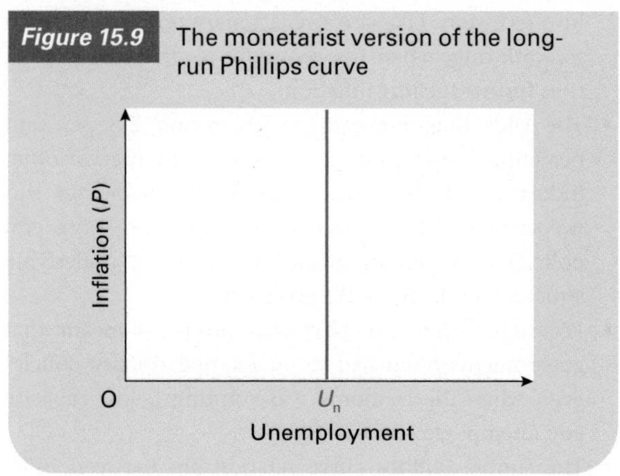

Figure 15.9 The monetarist version of the long-run Phillips curve

A vertical long-run Phillips curve

Monetarist analysis implied that the long-run Phillips curve (see Figure 15.9 and Box 14.5) is vertical at the equilibrium rate of unemployment (called the 'natural rate' by monetarists). In the *short run*, higher aggregate demand will reduce unemployment below the natural level, but in the long run, once expectations have adjusted, all the extra demand is absorbed in higher inflation. Unemployment thus rises back to the natural rate.

If unemployment is to be reduced in the long run, therefore, this vertical Phillips curve must be shifted to the left. This will be achieved by a reduction in the natural (equilibrium) rate of unemployment (U_n), *not* by an increase in demand. To reduce the natural rate, argued the monetarists, supply-side policies would be needed.

? *Give some examples of supply-side policies that would help to reduce the natural rate of unemployment.*

Government policies

Governments up to the late 1970s responded to rising unemployment by boosting aggregate demand (the balance of payments permitting). This, however, as the monetarists predicted, led only to more inflation, fuelled by rising expectations of inflation.

When governments eventually did curb the growth in aggregate demand, as the Thatcher government did after 1979, it took time for expectations to adjust downwards. In the meantime, there was a further temporary rise in unemployment due to wage rises being slow to moderate.

Nevertheless the pursuit of these policies did, according to monetarists, lead to a dramatic fall in the rate of inflation, and eventually the rise in unemployment was reversed.

The Keynesian response

Keynesians agreed with monetarists on one point. If demand is expanded too fast and for too long, inflation will result – and there will be a certain amount of unemployment of labour (and other resources too) that cannot be eliminated simply by expanding aggregate demand.

In other respects, Keynesians differed markedly from monetarists.

Inflation

Inflation was not just a problem of excess demand (caused by too much money). It was also caused by increased cost-push pressures: the increasing concentration of economic power in large multinational companies and large trade unions, and the large oil price increases of 1973/4 and 1978/9.

Also, workers had come to expect real wage increases each year, which could simply not be met from real increases in national income. The problem here for the long term was not so much the expectations of price increases, but rather the expectations of increases in real living standards.

Unemployment

Keynesians blamed a deficiency of aggregate demand for the massive rise in unemployment in the 1980s. Aggregate supply was highly elastic downwards in response to a reduction in aggregate demand. Firms responded to falling demand by producing less and employing fewer people. This was further aggravated by firms running down stocks to try to reduce costs and maintain profits.

Expectations are relevant here. But, when aggregate demand is reduced, it is not so much the expectation of lower inflation that reduces inflation (as monetarists claim); rather it is the expectation of lower sales that reduces production, investment and employment. The problem is not merely a short-term difficulty that markets will soon correct. Unless the government adopts a deliberate policy of reflation, the problem may continue. Business confidence may not return. Mass unemployment and recession may persist.

But why, when the world economy boomed in the late 1980s, did unemployment not return to the levels of the 1970s? In the late 1980s there was little or no deficiency of demand, and yet unemployment fell relatively slightly. Now the problem was not one of stagflation: a stagnant economy with high inflation. Now the problem was one of a booming economy but with persistently high unemployment. Keynesians typically offered two explanations of the persistence of unemployment.

Structural problems. The 1980s saw an acceleration in the decline of certain industries, a large-scale shift away from labour-intensive processes in manufacturing, an information technology revolution, a programme of privatisation, a more openly competitive world economy and campaigns by both governments and firms against overstaffing. The result was a large increase in equilibrium (structural) unemployment.

Hysteresis. The huge rise in unemployment in the early 1980s throughout the industrialised world, although largely caused by a lack of demand, could not simply be reversed by a rise in demand again. The recession had itself *caused* higher levels of unemployment to become embedded in the economy.

Many people had become deskilled and firms had become more cautious about taking on workers, preferring to manage with a smaller, more efficient workforce. What is more, people who remained employed (the ***insiders***) were often able, through their unions or close relationships with their employers, or because of the possession of specific skills, to secure wage increases for themselves, and prevent the unemployed (the ***outsiders***) from competing wages down. The insiders preferred to secure higher wages for themselves, rather than to have a larger number employed but with everyone on lower wages.

This continuation of high unemployment is known as ***hysteresis***. This term, used in physics, refers to the lagging or persistence of an effect, even when the initial cause has been removed. In our context, it refers to the persistence of unemployment even when the initial demand deficiency no longer exists.

Keynesian criticisms of monetarism

Keynesians criticised monetarists for putting too much reliance on markets. The problems of inflation, unemployment and industrial decline were much too deep seated and complex to be rectified by a simple reliance on controlling the money supply and then leaving private enterprise and labour to respond to unregulated market forces.

Free markets are often highly imperfect and will not lead to an optimum allocation of resources. What is more, markets frequently reflect short-term speculative movements of demand and supply, and do not give a clear indication of long-term costs and benefits. In particular,

Definitions

Insiders Those in employment who can use their privileged position (either as members of unions or because of specific skills) to secure pay rises despite an excess supply of labour (unemployment).

Outsiders Those out of work or employed on a casual, part-time or short-term basis, who have little or no power to influence wages or employment.

Hysteresis The persistence of an effect even when the initial cause has ceased to operate. In economics, it refers to the persistence of unemployment even when the demand deficiency that caused it no longer exists.

the stock market, the money market and the foreign exchange market can respond quite violently to short-term pressures. Such fluctuations can be very damaging to investment. For example, violent swings in exchange rates, as experienced between the euro and the dollar in the early 2000s (see Box 23.4), can dissuade firms from making long-term investment decisions to develop export markets. A sudden rise in exchange rates may make it impossible to compete abroad, even though at a lower exchange rate an exporter could have made a large profit.

KI 31 p368

The fluctuations inherent in free markets cause uncertainty about future demand, supply and prices. This uncertainty reduces investment and hence reduces growth. Government, therefore, should intervene much more to stimulate growth and investment.

Keynesian policy proposals

Keynesians generally favour a much more interventionist approach to policy than do monetarists. The following policies are typical of those favoured by Keynesians.

Maintaining a high and stable level of aggregate demand. A substantial increase in demand may be necessary initially if unemployment levels are very high. The best way of achieving this is for the government to increase its expenditure on public works such as roads and housing, since these projects have a relatively low import content and therefore increased expenditure does not lead to balance of payments problems. Thereafter the government should maintain a high and stable demand, by appropriate demand management policies. This should keep unemployment down and set the environment for long-term investment and growth.

Stabilising exchange rates. To reduce uncertainties, the central bank should intervene in foreign exchange markets to prevent excessive short-term fluctuations in exchange rates. This might involve international co-operation between central banks. More stable rates will encourage investment and growth.

Greater co-operation between government and industry. To promote long-term growth and to avoid the uncertainties of the market, the government should work much more closely with industry. This might involve the government helping to co-ordinate the plans of interdependent sectors of industry (such as the power and transport industries) and channelling finance to the more promising industries.

Structural policies. To reduce structural unemployment the government should pursue regional and urban policies to encourage firms to move to areas of high unemployment, and retraining policies to encourage greater occupational mobility of labour.

Section summary

1. Monetarists argued that there is a close correlation between the rate of growth of the money supply and the rate of inflation. Increases in money supply cause increases in aggregate demand, which in turn cause inflation. Along with the classical economists, they argued that output and employment are determined independently of money supply (at least in the long run). This means that a deflationary policy to cure inflation will *not* in the long run cause a fall in output or a rise in unemployment.
2. Monetarists thus argued that the long-run Phillips curve is vertical. Its position along the horizontal axis will depend on the level of equilibrium or 'natural' unemployment.
3. Keynesians rejected the notion of a totally vertical Phillips curve, but did accept that demand-side policies alone cannot cure unemployment completely. Keynesians blamed the combination of high inflation and high unemployment on a number of factors, each of which has the effect of shifting the Phillips curve to the right. These factors include cost-push and demand-shift pressures on inflation, and government attempts to cure inflation by continually pursuing deflationary policies.
4. Unemployment caused initially by a recession (a deficiency of demand) may persist even when the economy is recovering. This 'hysteresis' may be due to the deskilling of labour, a decline in firms' capacity, insiders preventing outsiders from bidding down the wage rate, or firms being cautious about taking on extra labour when the recovery does come.
5. Keynesians argued that markets do not clear rapidly and that in the meantime expectations of output and employment changes can have major effects on investment plans.
6. Whereas monetarists generally favoured policies of freeing up markets (within the framework of strict government control over money supply), Keynesians favoured a much more interventionist approach by the government. Central to this is the control of aggregate demand so as to retain actual income as close as possible to its potential level.

15.5 THE CURRENT POSITION: AN EMERGING CONSENSUS?

A range of views

From the monetarist–Keynesian debates of the 1970s and 1980s has emerged a degree of consensus among many economists that draws on insights from both schools. This is not to suggest, however, that all economists agree. In fact, a whole range of views can be identified.

One simple way of classifying these differing views is to see them falling along a spectrum. At the one end are those who see the free market as working well and who generally blame macroeconomic problems on excessive government intervention. At the other are those who see the free market as fundamentally flawed. Let us identify different views along this spectrum, starting with the pro-free market end.

KI 10 p62

The new classical/rational expectations school

The ***new classical school*** is like an extreme form of monetarism. New classicists maintain that markets clear very quickly and expectations adjust virtually instantaneously to new situations. These expectations are based on firms' and workers' rational assessment of what is happening in the economy and in their particular sector of it. They may be wrong, but they are as likely to overpredict as to underpredict the rate of inflation and hence the equilibrium price in their particular market. On average, they will guess it about right.

Expanding money supply will virtually instantaneously lead to higher expectations of inflation. Therefore it can only cause inflation; it cannot reduce unemployment. The short-run Phillips curve is vertical, as well as the long-run. Likewise tight monetary policy reduces inflation; it does not increase unemployment. Rising unemployment is entirely due to a rise in the natural rate of unemployment.

If changes in aggregate demand cannot affect output and employment, how do the new classical economists explain the business cycle of booms and recessions? The answer they give is that these cyclical changes in output and employment are the result of shifts in the aggregate *supply* curve. These in turn are the result of cycles in technological progress and labour productivity. The theory is therefore known as ***real business cycle theory***.

This school favours *laissez-faire* policies and is part of what is often called the 'radical right'.

Moderate monetarists/centre-right analysis

Many economists reject the new classical notion of a vertical short-run aggregate supply curve and vertical short-run Phillips curve, but still maintain that markets adjust fairly quickly – perhaps within one or two years.

TC 9 p101

A rise in money supply and hence aggregate demand will lead to a temporary reduction in unemployment, but as expectations of inflation (and hence of wage increases) adjust upwards, so eventually the whole of the rise in aggregate demand will be swallowed up in higher prices. *Real* aggregate demand falls back to its original level and hence the level of unemployment rises back to its original level too. Thus the short-run Phillips curve is downward sloping, but the long-run curve is vertical.

If the economy is faced with high inflation, a sudden tight monetary policy may temporarily lead to a recession. Thus sudden extreme policies should be avoided. Instead there should be a gradual reduction in the growth of the money supply.

Any temporary demand-deficient unemployment will be reduced if workers can be encouraged to take reductions in real wages. Ultimately, though, any policies to make long-term reductions in unemployment must be aimed at the supply side of the economy: reducing the natural rate of unemployment by increasing labour mobility and getting markets to work better.

Moderate Keynesians

Moderate Keynesians argue that economies will probably eventually pull out of recession even if governments do not boost demand. There will be a natural upturn in the business cycle. Firms' confidence will begin to return and investment will start to increase. Nevertheless a recession can be deep and long lived and the recovery slow and faltering. Thus moderate Keynesians argue for active intervention by government to boost demand.

Once the economy is back to near full employment, the government must continue to control aggregate demand to prevent fluctuations in output and employment. Keynesians generally advocate the use of anti-cyclical demand management policy.

Most moderate Keynesians blame the persistence of recessions on the reluctance of real wages to fall so as to

Definitions

New classical school A body of economists who believe that markets are highly competitive and clear very rapidly; any expansion of demand will feed through virtually instantaneously into higher prices, giving a vertical short-run as well as a vertical long-run Phillips curve.

Real business cycle theory The new classical theory which explains cyclical fluctuations in terms of shifts in aggregate supply, rather than aggregate demand.

clear the labour market and eliminate demand-deficient unemployment. In recent years ***new Keynesians***, as they are called, have attempted to discover the reasons for the downward stickiness in real wages during a recession. These include the following:

KI 3 p10

- The worry of employers about demotivating their workforce, and thus causing efficiency to suffer. This is known as the *efficiency wage theory*.
- The power of *insiders* to resist real wage cuts.
- The power of firms under *imperfect competition* to maintain their prices. Firms may prefer to respond to a fall in demand by cutting output rather than cutting (real) prices, especially if they believe that their rivals will do the same. In such cases, they are not under the same pressure to cut real wage rates.

Extreme Keynesians

Extreme Keynesians argue that there is no automatic mechanism to eliminate demand-deficient unemployment even in the long run.

Not only are real wage rates sticky downwards, but also any reductions in real wage rates that do take place will further reduce consumer demand. Money circulating will automatically fall as banks lend out less and less in response to falling demand. Firms are unlikely to borrow for investment, since they have no confidence in their market. Expectations are likely to remain pessimistic.

Under these circumstances, the government must intervene to expand demand. By raising government expenditure and cutting taxes, the nation must spend its way out of recession. It may be necessary to use import controls to prevent any resulting balance of payments problems.

After the economy has pulled out of recession, it is still important for the government to maintain a high level of demand. Not only will this maintain low unemployment and keep actual national income close to potential national income, but also it will provide the most favourable environment for research and development, innovations and investment generally. Thus *potential* national income will grow more rapidly.

Some Keynesians in this group are known as ***post-Keynesians***. They highlight some of the key features of Keynes' *General Theory* to explain why economies are not self-correcting. In particular, they stress the importance of what Keynes called 'animal spirits', or what is today known as business expectations or business confidence. The mood of the country's business community is fundamental in determining investment and output. Without appropriate demand management policy, this mood can remain depressed into the long term.

Post-Keynesians and other 'heterodox economists' also challenge most of the microeconomic assumptions on which other more 'mainstream' macroeconomic theories are based. Firms are not cold, rational profit maximisers, making calm calculations based on marginal analysis. Instead, firms make output decisions largely in response to anticipated demand, again based on their *confidence* of their market. The result is that anticipated demand changes are likely to lead to *output* and *employment* changes, not price changes.

Finally, post-Keynesians tend to focus on a country's *institutions* and *culture* to explain how firms and consumers respond to economic stimuli. In other words, they try to base their explanations and policies on real-world institutional and behavioural information rather than on abstract models.

The radical left

Some economists make a far more fundamental attack on the market economy. Most Keynesians, although they see a *free* market leading to serious problems, nevertheless argue that government intervention can rectify these problems. Those on the radical left disagree. They see the market economy as so flawed that mere intervention will not solve its problems. Instead the market economy needs to be *replaced* by an alternative system such as state planning and/or worker control of industry. Marxist economists see the problem of capitalism to be so severe that ultimately there will be a revolution and it will be overthrown.

The fact that there are so many different views as to how the macroeconomy functions makes it impossible to do justice to them all in an introductory book. Nevertheless it is hoped that you will get some insight into the major schools of thought and why they advocate the policies they do.

Two economists disagree over the best way of tackling the problem of unemployment. For what reasons might they disagree? Are these reasons positive or normative?

A mainstream consensus?

Although there are many areas of disagreement in macroeconomics, some general points of agreement have emerged in recent years, at least among the majority of economists.

- In the short run, changes in aggregate demand will have a major effect on output and employment. Only a few extreme new classical economists would disagree with this proposition.

Definitions

New Keynesians Economists who seek to explain the downward stickiness of real wages and the resulting persistence of unemployment.

Post-Keynesians Economists who stress the importance of institutional and behavioural factors, and the role of business confidence in explaining the state of the economy. They argue that firms are more likely to respond to changes in demand by changing output rather than prices.

- In the long run, changes in aggregate demand will have much less effect on output and employment and much more effect on prices. In fact, many economists say that there will be *no* effect at all on output and employment, and that the whole effect will be on prices. There is still a substantial body of Keynesians, however, especially post-Keynesians, who argue that changes in aggregate demand *will* have substantial effects on long-term output and employment via changes in investment and hence in potential output.
- There is no simple long-run trade-off between inflation and unemployment. There is still disagreement, however, as to whether there is no relationship between them at all (i.e. the long-run Phillips curve is vertical), or whether they are connected indirectly via the long-term effects of changes in aggregate demand on investment, etc.
- KI 10 p62 Expectations have an important effect on the economy. There is still disagreement, however, as to whether it is people's expectations of price changes or of output changes that are more important.
- Excessive growth in the money supply will lead to inflation. Some economists argue that the quantity theory of money holds in the long run (i.e. that inflation is *entirely* due to increases in the money supply). Others argue that the relationship is more general. Nevertheless, the consensus is that governments should avoid allowing the money supply to grow too rapidly.
- Controlling inflation through control of the money supply, however, is difficult, since money supply itself is not easy to control. Even if it were possible to control money supply, there is a time lag between changes in money supply and the resulting changes in inflation. This makes a precise control of inflation by this means very difficult. Most economists, therefore, argue that it is easier to control inflation by controlling interest rates, since this directly affects aggregate demand. Most central banks around the world today therefore use interest rate changes to achieve a target rate of inflation.
- Macroeconomic policy should not focus exclusively on the demand side. Long-term growth depends primarily on changes in supply (i.e. in potential output). It is important, therefore, for governments to develop an effective supply-side policy if they want to achieve faster economic growth. There is still disagreement, however, over the forms that supply-side policy should take: should it focus on freeing up the market, or should it focus on various forms of government intervention to compensate for market deficiencies? TC 14 p385
- Governments' ability to control their country's macroeconomic destiny is being increasingly eroded by the process of globalisation. As countries become more and more interdependent, and as capital moves more and more freely around the globe, so there is a growing need for co-ordinated policies between governments to tackle problems of global recessions or excessive exchange rate fluctuations.

It is perhaps too soon to say that there is now a macroeconomic consensus, but at least the areas of disagreement have been refined.

As the book progresses, we will be looking at the various areas of agreement and disagreement in more detail. We shall pull most of the arguments together in Chapter 20.

Section summary

1. There are many shades of opinion among the different groups of economists, from extreme new classical economists who advocate almost complete *laissez-faire* to the extreme left where economists advocate the virtual abandonment of markets. In between comes a whole spectrum of opinions and theories about the relative effectiveness of markets and the government in achieving the various macroeconomic goals.
2. Despite these disagreements, most economists would agree on the following points: changes in aggregate demand have a direct effect on output and employment in the short run, but either no effect or a far less certain effect in the long run; there is no simple long-run trade-off between inflation and unemployment; expectations have an important effect on the economy; excessive growth in the money supply causes inflation; it is easier to achieve inflation targets by controlling interest rates than by controlling money supply; changes on the supply side of the economy are the major determinant of long-term growth; globalisation reduces individual countries' ability to control their economies.

END OF CHAPTER QUESTIONS

1. In a given economy, the supply of money is £10 billion; the velocity of circulation of money (spent on final goods and services) is 3; and the price index is 2.00.
   (a) What is the level of real national income?
   (b) How much have prices risen (in percentage terms) since the base year?
   (c) Assume that money supply increases by 10 per cent and that the velocity of circulation remains constant. By what percentage will prices rise if
   (i) there is no increase in real national income;
   (ii) real national income increases by 10 per cent;
   (iii) real national income increases by 5 per cent?
2. In what way will the nature of aggregate supply influence the effect of a change in aggregate demand on prices and real national income?
3. Criticise the classical theory that higher government spending will necessarily crowd out private spending.
4. Criticise the use of increasing government expenditure as a means of reducing unemployment.
5. In what way may short-term demand management policies help to stabilise the economy? What problems occur in the use of such policies?
6. What explanations can you give for the increase in *both* unemployment and inflation in the 1970s?
7. What is meant by *hysteresis* when applied to unemployment? How do you account for this phenomenon in the 1980s?
8. What will cause people to expect higher rates of inflation? How will expectations of inflation affect the actual rate of inflation?

Additional case studies on the book's website (www.pearsoned.co.uk/sloman)

15.1 The equation of exchange. This examines two more versions that are commonly used: the Fisher version and the Cambridge version.

15.2 Money and inflation in ancient Rome. A very early case study of the quantity theory of money: how the minting of extra coins by the Romans caused prices to rise.

15.3 The Great Depression and the return to the gold standard. A time of great hardship and sacrifice.

15.4 Classical 'remedies' for unemployment. How the policies advocated by the classical economists to cure unemployment would, according to Keynes, make the problem worse.

15.5 A little bit less of this and a little bit more of that. Fine tuning in 1959 and 1960.

15.6 'You've never had it so good'. The claim in 1957 by Harold Macmillan, the British Conservative Prime Minister, that governments were now able to manage the economy so as to give growing prosperity.

WEBSITES RELEVANT TO THIS CHAPTER

See sites listed at the end of Chapter 16 on page 477.

Chapter 16

Short-run Macroeconomic Equilibrium

In this chapter we look at the determination of national income, employment and inflation in the short run: i.e. over a period of up to two years. The analysis is based on the model developed by Keynesians. Although many economists argue that this analysis is not appropriate for analysing the performance of the macroeconomy over the longer term, most agree that the analysis is essentially true over the short term.

The model assumes that aggregate demand determines the level of economic activity in the economy. In other words, the nation's production and employment depend on the amount of spending. Too little spending will lead to unemployment. More spending will stimulate firms to produce more and employ more people. Too much spending, however, will cause inflation. This chapter examines this relationship between aggregate demand and national income (GDP), employment and inflation.

One important simplifying assumption is made: *the rate of interest is fixed.* This allows us for the time being to ignore what is happening to the amount of *money* in the economy. A fixed interest rate effectively means that the supply of money will passively rise or fall as aggregate demand rises or falls. In other words, if spending rises and hence also the demand for money from the banking system, there will be a corresponding increase in the amount of money made available and hence no need for interest rates to rise. In subsequent chapters, we will drop this assumption and take specific notice of the role of money in the economy.

CHAPTER MAP

16.1 BACKGROUND TO THE THEORY

The relationship between aggregate demand and national income

This chapter explains what determines the level of national income (GDP) in the short run. It is based on the model developed by John Maynard Keynes, back in the 1930s.

TC 13 p381 The basic explanation is quite simple: the level of production in the economy depends on the level of aggregate demand. If people buy more, firms will produce more in response to this, providing they have spare capacity. If people buy less, firms will cut down their production and lay off workers. But just *how much* will national income rise or fall as aggregate demand changes? We will answer this as the chapter progresses.

First, let us return to the circular flow of income that we looked at in Chapter 13. This is illustrated in Figure 16.1. Looking at the bottom of the diagram, the consumption of domestically produced goods (C_d) and the three withdrawals (W) – net saving (S), net taxes (T) and spending on imports (M) – all depend on the level of national income (Y). In fact, in the model, national income must always equal consumption of domestic goods plus withdrawals: there is nothing else people can do with their incomes!

$$Y \equiv C_d + W$$

Moving now to the top part of Figure 16.1, total spending in the economy on the goods and services of domestic firms is what we have already defined as aggregate demand (AD). In the Keynesian model that we are examining in this chapter, it is normally referred to as ***aggregate expenditure*** (E). (This is useful to distinguish it from the AD and AS model that we looked at in Chapter 14.) Aggregate expenditure consists of C_d plus the three injections (J): investment in the domestic economy (I), government expenditure in the domestic economy (G) and expenditure from abroad on the country's exports (X).

$$AD \equiv E \equiv C_d + J$$

Figure 16.1 A simplified circular flow of income model

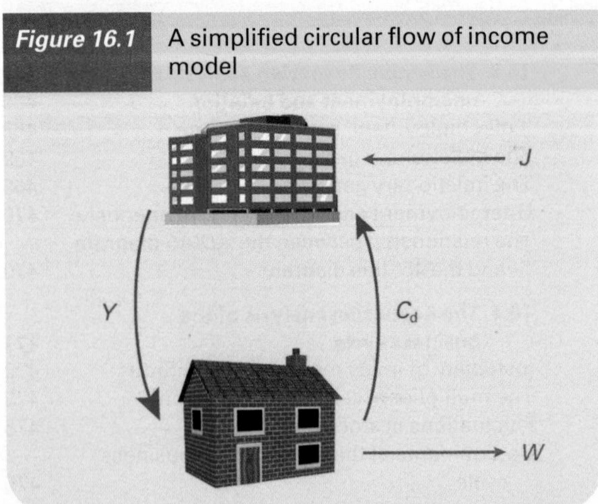

In equilibrium, withdrawals equal injections. (We demonstrated this in Chapter 13.) Since national income (Y) is simply withdrawals plus C_d, and aggregate expenditure (E) is simply injections plus C_d, it follows that in equilibrium national income must equal aggregate expenditure. To summarise:

$$W = J$$

$$\therefore C_d + W = C_d + J$$

$$\therefore Y = E\ (= AD)$$

Whenever aggregate expenditure ($C_d + J$) exceeds national income ($C_d + W$), injections will exceed withdrawals. Firms will respond to the extra demand by producing more and hence employing more factors of production. National income will thus rise. But as national income rises, so too will saving, imports and the amount paid in taxes: in other words, withdrawals will rise. Withdrawals will go on rising until they equal injections: until a new equilibrium has been reached. To summarise:

$$J > W \rightarrow Y\uparrow \rightarrow W\uparrow \text{ until } W = J$$

But *how much* will national income rise when aggregate demand (expenditure) rises? What will the new equilibrium level of national income be? To answer this question we must examine the relationship between national income and the component parts of the circular flow of income: consumption, withdrawals and injections. This relationship is shown in the Keynesian '45° line diagram'.

Introducing the Keynesian 45° line diagram

In this model, it is assumed that the levels of consumption and withdrawals are determined by the level of national income. Since national income is part of the model, we say that consumption and withdrawals are ***endogenous***. This means that they vary with one of the other components of the model (i.e. income). Injections, however, are assumed to be ***exogenous***: they are determined independently of what is going on in the model; they do *not* depend on the level of national income.

We will justify these assumptions later. First we must look at how the diagram is constructed, and at the significance of the 45° line, which is shown in Figure 16.2. We plot real national income (i.e. national income matched by

Definitions

Aggregate expenditure (E) Aggregate demand in the Keynesian model: i.e. $C_d + J$.

Endogenous variable A variable whose value is determined by the model of which it is part.

Exogenous variable A variable whose value is determined independently of the model of which it is part.

Figure 16.2 The 45° line

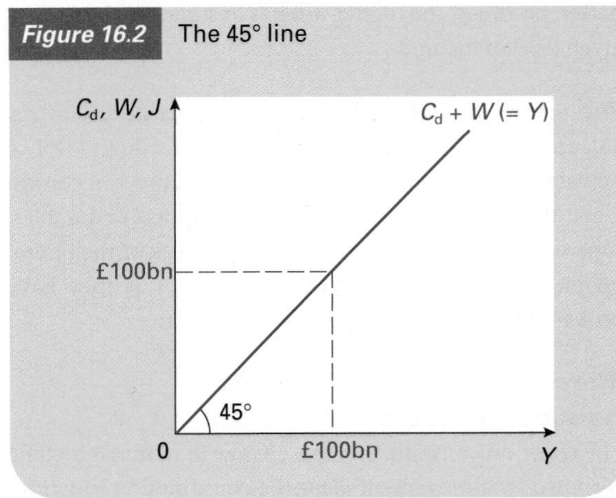

Figure 16.3 The consumption function

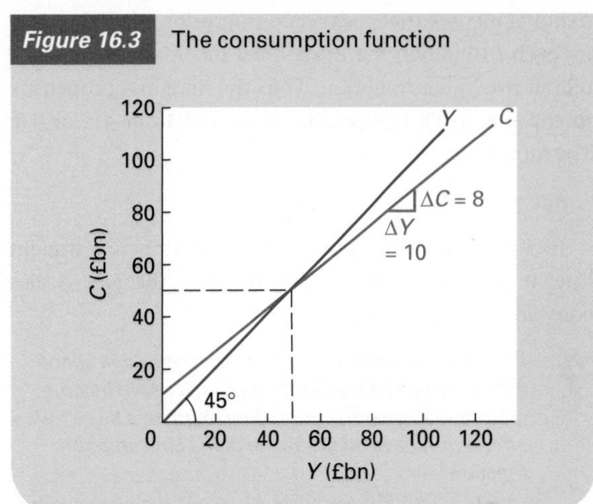

output) on the horizontal axis, and the various component parts of the circular flow (C_d, W and J) on the vertical axis. If the two axes are plotted to the same scale (which they are), then at every point on the 45° line the items on each axis are equal.

But what items on the vertical axis will always equal national income (Y), which is plotted on the horizontal axis? The answer is $C_d + W$, since, by definition, $Y = C_d + W$. For example, if Y were £100 billion, then $C_d + W$ must also be £100 billion (see Figure 16.2).

We turn now to look at each of the components of the circular flow and see how they fit into the 45° line diagram.

Table 16.1 $C = f(Y)$

National income (£bn)	Consumption (£bn)
0	10
10	18
20	26
30	34
40	42
50	50
60	58
70	66
80	74
90	82
100	90
110	98
.	.

Consumption

We will need to distinguish total consumption (C) from that part of consumption that goes purely on the output of domestically produced goods (C_d). C_d excludes expenditure taxes (e.g. VAT) and expenditure on imports. We start by looking at *total* consumption.

The consumption function

As national income increases, so does consumption. The reason is simple: if people earn more, they can afford to spend more. The relationship between consumption and income is expressed by the ***consumption function***:

$$C = f(Y)$$

It can be shown graphically on the 45° line diagram (see Figure 16.3 which is based on Table 16.1). The consumption function slopes upwards. This illustrates that, as national income rises, so does consumption. To keep the analysis simple, the consumption function is drawn as a straight line.

At very low levels of income, the consumption function will lie above the 45° line. When people are very poor, they may be forced to spend more than they earn merely to survive. They usually do this by borrowing or drawing on savings. Above a certain level of income, however (£50 billion in Figure 16.3), the consumption function will lie below the 45° line. People will spend less than they earn. The remainder will go on saving and taxes.

The higher the level of national income, the smaller the proportion that will be consumed: people can afford to save proportionately more, and will have to pay proportionately more in taxes. It follows that the slope of the consumption function is less than that of the 45° line.

The marginal propensity to consume. The slope of the consumption function is given by the ***marginal propensity to consume***. This is the proportion of any increase in

Definitions

Consumption function The relationship between consumption and national income. It can be expressed algebraically or graphically.

Marginal propensity to consume The proportion of a rise in national income that goes on consumption: $mpc = \Delta C/\Delta Y$.

national income that goes on consumption.[1] In Table 16.1 for each £10 billion rise in national income there is an £8 billion rise in consumption. Thus the marginal propensity to consume is £8 billion/£10 billion = 8/10 or 4/5 or 0.8. The formula is:

$$mpc = \Delta C/\Delta Y$$

In Figure 16.3, the consumption function is a straight line: it has a *constant* slope, and hence the *mpc* is also constant.

It is possible that as people get richer they will spend a smaller and smaller fraction of each rise in income (and save a larger fraction). Why might this be so? What effect will it have on the shape of the consumption function?

The other determinants of consumption

Of course, people's incomes are not the only determinants of the amount they consume. There are several other determinants.

Assets held. The more wealth people have, whether as savings, as shares or as property, the more they are likely to spend out of current income.

Taxation. The higher the level of income taxes, the less will people have left to spend out of their gross income: consumption depends on ***disposable income***.

KI 10 p62 *Expectations of future prices and incomes.* If people expect *prices* to rise, they tend to buy durable goods such as furniture and cars before this happens. Similarly, if people expect a rise in their *incomes*, they are likely to spend more now. If, on the other hand, they are uncertain about their future income prospects, or fear unemployment, they are likely to be cautious in their spending.

The distribution of income. The poor have a higher *mpc* than the rich, with very little left over to save. A redistribution of national income from the poor to the rich will therefore tend to reduce the total level of consumption in the economy.

Tastes and attitudes. If people have a 'buy now, pay later' mentality, or a craving for consumer goods, they are likely to have a higher level of consumption than if their tastes are more frugal. The more 'consumerist' and materialistic a nation becomes, the higher will its consumption be for any given level of income.

The age of durables. If people's car, carpets, clothes, etc. are getting old, they will tend to have a high level of 'replacement' consumption, particularly after a recession when they had cut back on their consumption of durables. Conversely, as the economy reaches the peak of the boom, people are likely to spend less on durables as they have probably already bought the items they want.

Movements along and shifts in the consumption function

The effect on consumption of a change in national income is shown by a movement *along* the consumption function. A change in any of the other determinants is shown by a *shift* in the consumption function.

What effect will the following have on the mpc: (a) a rise in the rate of income tax; (b) the economy begins to recover from recession; (c) people anticipate that the rate of inflation is about to rise; (d) the government redistributes income from the rich to the poor? In each case sketch what would happen to the consumption function.

Long-run and short-run consumption functions

The long-run consumption function is likely to be steeper than the short-run one (see Figure 16.4).

In the short run, people may be slow to respond to a rise in income. Perhaps they are cautious about whether their higher income will last, or are slow to change their consumption habits. In the short run, then, people may have a relatively low *mpc*. In the long run, however, people have time to adjust their consumption patterns.

Assuming that national income rises over time, the long-run consumption function will be intersected by a series of short-run ones. Each year's short-run function will be above the previous year's.

Which is likely to show the greater variation from one person to another at any given level of income: the short-run mpc or the long-run mpc?

Figure 16.4 Long-run and short-run consumption functions

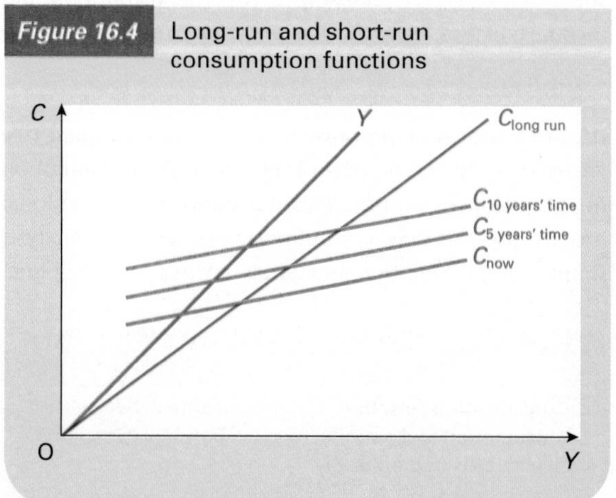

[1] The *mpc* is normally defined as the proportion of a rise in *disposable* national income that goes on consumption, where disposable income is income *after taxes*. By defining it the way we have done (i.e. as the proportion of *gross* income that goes in consumption), the analysis is simpler. The conclusions remain the same.

Definition

Disposable income Household income after the deduction of taxes and the addition of benefits.

Consumption of domestically produced goods (C_d)

The parts of consumption that go on imports and indirect taxes constitute withdrawals from the circular flow of income and thus do not contribute to aggregate demand. We shall concentrate on the part of consumption that *does*: namely, the consumption of domestic product (C_d). The C_d function lies below the C function, as in Figure 16.5. The gap between them constitutes imports of consumer goods and indirect taxes.

Figure 16.5 The consumption of domestic product

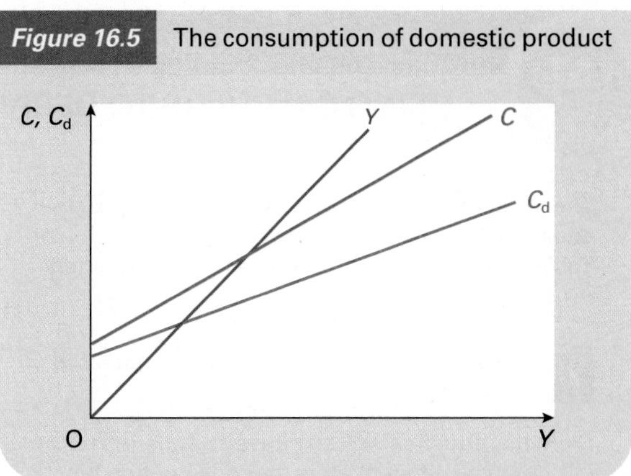

*LOOKING AT THE MATHS

Let us examine the relationship between C and C_d a bit more closely. When people make consumption decisions, this is largely based on their *disposable* income (Y_{dis}), where disposable income is income after the payment of income taxes and the receipt of benefits. We use the term 'net income taxes (T_Y)' to refer to income taxes minus benefits. Thus:

$$Y_{dis} = Y - T_Y$$

Also, people tend not to distinguish between domestic goods and imports when they make consumption decisions. Let us then focus on total consumption (C), not just the consumption of domestic products (C_d).

To get a better understanding of people's consumption behaviour, we could express the marginal propensity to consume *all products* (domestic and imported) relative to *disposable* income. Let us call this term mpc' (rather than mpc or mpc_d) where:

$$mpc' = \frac{\Delta C}{\Delta Y_{dis}} = \frac{\Delta C}{\Delta Y - \Delta T_Y} \quad (1)$$

Note that the consumption term C refers to consumers' total consumption expenditure, not the net amount received by domestic firms (C_d). To get from C to C_d, we would have to subtract the amount spent on imports (M) and the amount paid in indirect taxes, such as VAT and excise duties, (T_E). Thus:

$$C_d = C - M - T_E \text{ or } C = C_d + M + T_E$$

Thus:

$$\Delta C = \Delta C_d + \Delta M + \Delta T_E \quad (2)$$

Substituting equation (2) in equation (1) gives:

$$mpc' = \frac{\Delta C_d + \Delta T_E + \Delta M}{\Delta Y - \Delta T_Y} \quad (3)$$

Contrast this with the mpc_d, where:

$$mpc_d = \frac{\Delta C_d}{\Delta Y} \quad (4)$$

Withdrawals

All three withdrawals – net saving, net taxes and import expenditure – depend on the level of national income. They are thus all *endogenously* determined within the model.

Net saving

As with consumption, the major determinant of net saving (i.e. saving minus consumer borrowing and drawing on past savings) is income. As income increases, and a decreasing fraction of it goes on consumption, so an increasing fraction of it will be saved. The rich can afford to save a larger proportion of their income than the poor.

The proportion of an increase in national income that is saved is given by the ***marginal propensity to save*** (mps).

$$mps = \Delta S/\Delta Y$$

Other determinants of saving. To a large extent these are the same as the other determinants of consumption, since most things that encourage people to spend more will thereby encourage them to save less.

It might be easy to get the impression that saving is merely what is left over after consumption has taken place. In fact, for many people the decision to save is a very positive one. They might be saving up for something they are eager to buy but cannot afford at the moment, or saving for retirement. Indeed, people may be encouraged to save *more* by various factors, such as changes in pension provisions or new government-sponsored saving schemes.

? *Go through each of the determinants of consumption that were listed in the previous section and consider how they will affect saving. Are there any determinants of consumption that will* not *cause saving to rise if consumption is caused to fall?*

Net taxes

As national income increases, so the amount paid in tax will also increase. The ***marginal tax propensity*** (mpt) is the proportion of an increase in national income paid in taxes:[2]

$$mpt = \Delta T/\Delta Y$$

[2] We have defined net taxes as taxes minus benefits (i.e. the net flow from the household sector to the government). For our purposes, then, the *mpt* is the proportion of any rise in income going in taxes and reduced benefits.

Definitions

Marginal propensity to save The proportion of an increase in national income saved: $mps = \Delta S/\Delta Y$.

Marginal tax propensity The proportion of an increase in national income paid in tax: $mpt = \Delta T/\Delta Y$.

EXPLORING ECONOMICS *BOX 16.1

USING CALCULUS TO DERIVE THE *MPC*

The consumption function can be expressed as an equation. For example, the consumption function of Table 16.1 and Figure 16.3 is given by the equation:

$$C = 10 + 0.8Y \quad (1)$$

Try using this equation to derive the figures in Table 16.1.

From this equation we can derive an equation for *mpc*. It is found by differentiating the consumption function. Remember from previous calculus boxes what it is we are doing when we differentiate an equation. We are finding its rate of change. Thus by differentiating the consumption function, we are finding the rate of change of consumption with respect to income. But this is what we mean by the *mpc*.

The difference between using differentiation and the formula $\Delta C/\Delta Y$ is that with the former we are looking at the *mpc* at a single point on the consumption function. With the $\Delta C/\Delta Y$ formula we were looking at the *mpc* between two points.

Differentiating equation (1) gives:

$$mpc = dC/dY = 0.8 \quad (2)$$

Note that, since the consumption function is a straight line in this case, the *mpc* (which measures the slope of the consumption function) is constant.

What would we do to find the *mpc* of a non-linear (curved) consumption function? The procedure is the same.

Assume that the consumption function is given by the following equation:

$$C = 20 + 0.9Y - 0.001Y^2 \quad (3)$$

First of all, try constructing a table like Table 16.1 and then graph the consumption function that it gives. What is it about equation (3) that gives the graph its particular shape?

The *mpc* is given by dC/dY:

$$mpc = 0.9 - 0.002Y$$

1. ***What are the values of mpc at incomes of (a) 20; (b) 100?***
2. ***What happens to the value of mpc as national income increases? Is this what you would expect by examining the shape of the consumption function?***

The *mpt* depends on tax rates. In a simple world where there was only one type of tax, which was charged at a constant rate – for example, an income tax of 22 per cent – the *mpt* would be given directly by the tax rate. In this example, for each extra pound earned, 22p would be paid in income tax. The $mpt = \Delta T/\Delta Y = 22/100 = 0.22$. In practice, of course, there are many types of tax charged at many different rates, and thus working out the *mpt* is more complicated.

In most countries, the *mpt* rises as national income rises. This is because income tax is progressive. At higher incomes, people pay a higher marginal rate of income tax. In the UK and many other countries, however, income tax became much less progressive in the 1980s and 1990s, but the *mpt* remained roughly the same because of rises in indirect taxes.

Imports

The higher the level of national income, the higher will be the amount spent on imports. The ***marginal propensity to import*** (*mpm*) is the proportion of a rise in national income that goes on imports:

$$mpm = \Delta M/\Delta Y$$

Definition

Marginal propensity to import The proportion of an increase in national income that is spent on imports: $mpm = \Delta M/\Delta Y$.

Note that we only count that part of the expenditure on imports that actually goes abroad. Amounts retained by the retailer, the wholesaler and the importer, and amounts paid in indirect taxes are excluded.

Whether the *mpm* rises or falls as national income rises depends on the nature of a country's imports. If a country imports predominantly basic goods, which have a relatively low income elasticity of demand, the rate of increase in their consumption would tail off rapidly as incomes increase. The *mpm* for such a country would thus also rapidly decrease.

If, however, a country's imports were mainly of luxury goods, they would account for an increasing proportion of any rise in national income: the *mpm* would rise.

If a country imports a whole range of goods whose average income elasticity of demand is the same as for home-produced goods, will the mpm rise or fall as national income rises?

The determinants of the level of imports. Apart from national income, there are a number of other determinants of the level of imports:

- *Relative prices.* If the prices of home-produced goods go up relative to the prices of imports, the level of imports will rise. The rate of exchange is a major influence here. The higher the rate of exchange, the cheaper will imports be and hence the more will be spent on them.

CASE STUDIES AND APPLICATIONS **BOX 16.2**

CONSUMPTION AND SAVING IN PRACTICE

Consumer spending follows a regular cyclical pattern each year, reaching its peak in the fourth quarter as Christmas approaches. The graph shows the levels of UK personal disposable income and total consumer expenditure (i.e. consumption before indirect taxes and imports have been deducted) from 1995 Q1 to 2005 Q1. The annual cyclical pattern can clearly be seen, with consumption actually falling in quarter 1 of each year. The area between consumer expenditure and disposable income represents that fraction of disposable income that is saved.

As well as there being a clear annual pattern for consumption and saving, patterns can also be observed over the years. For example, saving ratios tend to fluctuate with the business cycle. In booms, especially if real interest rates are low and people are keen to spend, perhaps anticipating rising inflation, the saving ratio tends to fall. This can be seen in the late 1990s' boom.

The table also shows that there are marked differences in saving ratios between countries. This is partly a reflection of national attitudes towards saving and spending, and partly a reflection of the encouragement given to saving by government and financial institutions.

Some of the changes in saving ratios reflect long-term trends. For example, Italy's and the USA's saving ratios have shown a long-term decline, as traditional beliefs in the 'virtues' of saving have gradually been eroded. Other changes reflect changes in government policy. For example, Sweden after 1990 was concerned to prevent its exchange rate falling relative to EU currencies. This involved pursuing a policy of high interest rates, which had the effect of encouraging saving and discouraging borrowing (negative saving).

?

Comparing the saving ratios in France and New Zealand, what do the differences imply for the balance between government expenditure and taxation if both countries want to achieve similar rates of investment and want to maintain a balance between imports and exports?

Household saving (% of household disposable income)

	1987–91	1992–6	1997–2001	2001–6[a]
Australia	7.9	5.4	2.6	−1.6
Belgium	16.1	18.6	14.4	14.0
France	7.4	10.2	11.0	10.6
Germany	13.2	11.8	10.1	10.9
Italy	23.8	19.7	11.4	10.7
Japan	13.8	12.4	9.6	5.5
Netherlands	13.5	14.3	10.4	10.3
New Zealand	2.6	−1.8	−4.4	−6.6
Sweden	−0.1	9.4	4.1	8.3
UK	7.2	10.2	6.4	6.5
USA	7.1	5.4	2.9	1.2

[a] Forecast.

Source: based on data in *OECD Economic Outlook* (OECD, 2005).

UK personal disposable income and total consumer expenditure: 1995 Q1–2005 Q1

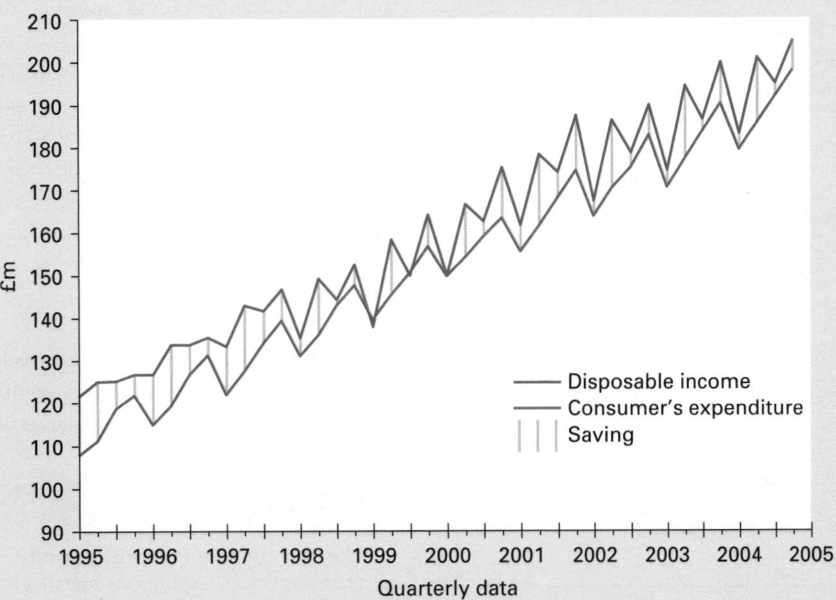

Source: *Financial Statistics* (National Statistics, 2005).

- *Tastes.* If consumer tastes shift towards foreign goods and services, imports will rise. For example, it might become more popular to go abroad for your holidays.
- *Relative quality.* If the quality of foreign goods and services increases relative to that of domestic goods and services, imports will rise.
- *The determinants of consumption.* Since imports of goods and services are part of *total* consumption (as opposed to C_d), the various determinants of consumption that we looked at on page 454 will also be determinants of imports.

The total withdrawals function

Remember that withdrawals consist of the three elements: net saving, net taxes and imports, all of which rise as national income rises. A withdrawals function along with the corresponding consumption of domestic goods function is shown in Figure 16.6.

Note the relationship between the C_d and W curves. The steeper the slope of the one, the flatter the slope of the other. The reason for this is that C_d and W add up to total national income (Y):

$$Y = C_d + W$$

Since the 45° line measures $C_d + W$, the distance between the C_d function and the 45° line must equal withdrawals. Thus at point x, where national income is £100 billion and C_d is £70 billion, W must be £30 billion – the gap between C_d and the 45° line.

The marginal propensity to withdraw

The formula for the ***marginal propensity to withdraw*** (*mpw*) is as we would expect:

$$mpw = \Delta W / \Delta Y$$

The *mpw* is the slope of the withdrawals function. Note that, since $W = S + T + M$, *mpw* must equal $mps + mpt + mpm$. For example, if for any rise in national income, 1/10 were saved, 2/10 paid in net taxes, and 2/10 spent on imports, then 5/10 must be withdrawn.

Note also that, since $C_d + W = Y$, $mpc_d + mpw$ must add up to 1. For example, if the country spends, say, 3/5 of any rise in income on domestically produced goods, the remaining 2/5 must go on withdrawals.

If the slope of the C_d function is 3/4, what is the slope of the W function?

Figure 16.6 The W and C_d functions

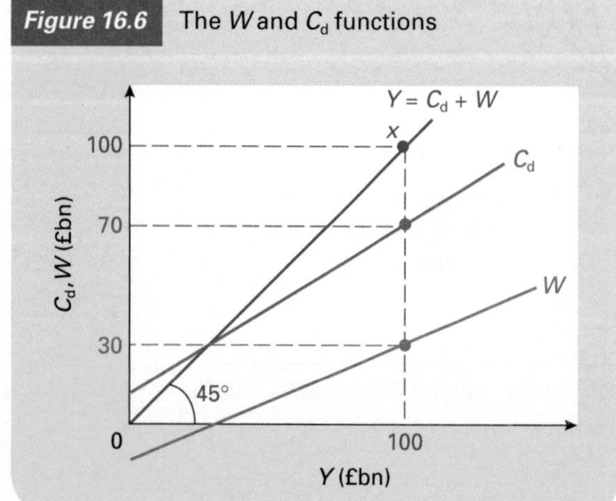

Injections

In simple Keynesian theory, injections are assumed not to depend on the level of national income: they are *exogenously* determined. This means that the injections function will be a horizontal straight line. Injections will be at a given level irrespective of the level of national income. The injections function is the vertical addition of the investment, government expenditure and export functions, each of which is a horizontal straight line.

The assumption that injections are independent of national income makes the theory simpler. (It is possible to drop this assumption, however, without destroying the theory.) But is the assumption sufficiently realistic? Let us examine each of the injections in turn.

Investment

There are four major determinants of investment.

Increased consumer demand. Investment is to provide extra capacity. This will only be necessary, therefore, if consumer demand increases. The bigger the increase in consumer demand, the more investment will be needed.

You might think that, since consumer demand depends on the level of national income, investment must too, and that therefore our assumption that investment is independent of national income is wrong. But we are not saying that investment depends on the *level* of consumer demand; rather it depends on *how much it has risen*. If income and consumer demand are high but *constant*, there will be no point in firms expanding their capacity: no point in investing.

The relationship between investment and *increased* consumer demand is examined by the 'accelerator theory'. We will look at this theory in section 16.4.

Expectations. Since investment is made in order to produce output for the future, investment must depend on firms' expectations about future market conditions.

KI 10 p62

Definition

Marginal propensity to withdraw The proportion of an increase in national income that is withdrawn from the circular flow: $mpw = \Delta W/\Delta Y$, where $mpw = mps + mpt + mpm$.

The cost and efficiency of capital equipment. If the cost of capital equipment goes down or machines become more efficient, the return on investment will increase. Firms will invest more. Technological progress is an important determinant here.

The rate of interest. The higher the rate of interest, the more expensive it will be for firms to finance investment, and hence the less profitable will the investment be. Just how responsive total investment in the economy is to changes in interest rates is a highly controversial issue and we will return to it later.

So if these are the main determinants of investment, does it mean that investment is totally independent of the level of national income? Not quite. Replacement of worn-out or outdated equipment *will* depend on the level of national income. The higher the current level of national income, the greater will be the stock of capital and therefore the more will need replacing each year. It is also possible that, if the level of national income is high and firms' profits are high, they will be able to *afford* more investment. However, it is not a gross distortion of reality to assume that investment and the level of national income are independent, at least in the short run.

Government expenditure

Government expenditure in any year is independent of the level of national income. The reason is as follows. In the months preceding the Budget each year, spending departments make submissions about their needs in the coming year. These are discussed with the Treasury and a sum is allocated to each department. That then (save for any unforeseen events) fixes government expenditure on goods and services for the following financial year.

Thus, again, for our purposes we can take government expenditure as independent of national income in the short term. Even if tax revenues turn out to be more or less than expected, this will not influence that year's government spending. The government can end up running either a budget surplus ($T > G$) or a budget deficit ($G > T$).

Over the longer term, however, government expenditure *will* depend on national income. The higher the level of national income, the higher is the amount of tax revenue that the government receives, and hence the more it can afford to spend. The governments of richer nations clearly spend much more than those of developing countries.

Exports

Exports are sold to people abroad, and thus depend largely on *their* incomes, not on incomes at home. Nevertheless, there are two indirect links between a country's national income and its exports:

- Via other countries' circular flows of income. If domestic incomes rise, more will be spent on imports. But this will cause a rise in other countries' incomes and lead them to buy more imports, part of which will be this country's exports.
- Via the exchange rate. A rise in domestic incomes will lead to a rise in imports. Other things being equal, this will lead to a depreciation in the exchange rate. This will make it cheaper for people in other countries to buy this country's exports. Export sales will rise.

However, it is useful in simple Keynesian models to assume that exports are determined independently of domestic national income.

Note that, although the injections function is assumed to be constant with respect to income and is drawn as a horizontal straight line, this does not mean that it will be constant *over time*. Investment can suddenly rise or virtually collapse as the confidence of business people changes. Exports can change too with shifts in the exchange rate or with speculation. The injections line, then, is constantly shifting up and down.

Section summary

1. In the simple Keynesian model, equilibrium national income is where withdrawals equal injections, and where national income equals the total expenditure on domestic products: where $W = J$ and where $Y = E$.
2. The relationships between national income and the various components of the circular flow of income can be shown on a 45° line diagram. In the diagram, C, C_d and W are endogenous variables. Each one rises as income rises. The relationships can also be expressed in terms of marginal propensities. The marginal propensity is given by $\Delta V/\Delta Y$ (where V is the variable in question).
3. Apart from being determined by national income, consumption is determined by wealth, taxation, the availability and cost of credit, expectations about future prices and incomes, the distribution of income, tastes and attitudes, and the average age of durables. Consumption of domestic product (C_d) is total consumption minus imports of goods and services and minus indirect taxes and plus subsidies on goods and services.
4. Like consumption, withdrawals (S, T and M) vary with national income. Net saving is also determined by the various factors that determine consumption: if these factors cause consumption to rise, then,

continued

CASE STUDIES AND APPLICATIONS

BUSINESS EXPECTATIONS AND THEIR EFFECT ON INVESTMENT

Recent European experience

In the boom years of the late 1980s, business optimism was widespread throughout Europe. Investment was correspondingly high, and with it there was a high rate of economic growth.

Surveys of European business expectations in the early 1990s, however, told a very different story. Pessimism was rife. Europe was in the grip of a recession, and output was falling (see Table (a)). Along with this decline in output and deteriorating levels of business and consumer confidence, there was a significant fall in investment.

Table (b) gives the indicator of industrial confidence in various EU countries and the indicator for the EU as a whole is plotted in Figure (a). The indicator shows the percentage excess of confident over pessimistic replies to business questionnaires: a negative figure means that there was a higher percentage of pessimistic responses. You can see that the indicator was strongly negative in 1993.

Not only was the total level of investment falling, but the proportion of that investment used to expand capacity was also falling. By contrast, the proportion of investment devoted to rationalisation schemes had risen. Firms were increasingly having to look for ways of cutting their costs through restructuring their operations. One of the consequences of this was a growth in structural unemployment (as well as in demand-deficient unemployment).

After 1993, pessimism began to decrease, and by the last quarter of 1994 the average EU industrial confidence indicator became positive. From 1995 to 2000, the indicator was mainly positive, as the European economy experienced growth rates averaging 2.6 per cent. Investment grew rapidly. Notice how the industrial confidence indicator mirrored the rate of economic growth. For example, both the rate of growth and the confidence indicator fell in 1996.

But then, in 2001, with the world economy slowing down and the 11 September attack on the World Trade Center in New York, industrial confidence plummeted, and so did investment, only to recover again as economic growth and business confidence returned.

Another useful indicator of the state of the economy is the degree of industrial capacity utilisation. The lower this is, the greater the slack in the economy. Figure (b) shows the percentage capacity utilisation in manufacturing industry in the EU. You can see how this mirrors industrial confidence (and hence economic growth).

(a) Macroeconomic indicators for the EU countries

	1989	1990	1991	1992	1993	1994	1995	1996	1997	1998	1999	2000	2001	2002	2003	2004	2005
GDP growth (%)	3.5	3.0	1.8	1.1	–0.4	2.8	2.4	1.6	2.5	2.9	2.9	3.6	1.7	1.1	0.9	2.3	2.2
Investment (% change)	6.9	3.6	–0.6	–0.4	–5.8	2.8	2.8	1.9	3.1	6.5	5.4	4.9	0.4	–1.5	–0.1	2.9	3.6
Unemployment (%)	7.8	7.3	7.8	8.9	10.1	10.5	10.1	10.2	10.0	9.4	8.6	7.8	7.4	7.7	8.1	8.1	8.1

Source: based on data in *European Economy Statistical Annex* (Commission of the European Communities).

(b) Industrial confidence indicator

Country	1989	1991	1993	1995	1996	1997	1998	1999	2000	2001	2002	2003	2004
Belgium	0	–15	–29	–9	–18	–3	–8	–9	2	–14	–12	–15	–3
Denmark	4	–8	–12	5	–8	6	–1	–13	6	–2	–4	–6	4
France	8	–20	–35	–2	–18	–5	5	–2	12	–4	–9	–9	–3
Germany	5	0	–34	–6	–21	–10	–5	–14	–2	–15	–18	–17	–8
Ireland	10	–9	–13	7	–1	3	3	5	10	–8	–7	–9	–4
Italy	8	–13	–17	6	–12	0	0	–4	12	–3	–3	–4	–2
Netherlands	1	–5	–10	2	–2	3	2	0	4	–4	–3	–8	–3
UK	–2	–32	–11	3	–5	–1	–16	–14	–7	–15	–15	–17	–2
EU	4	–14	–26	–1	–14	–4	–3	–8	4	–9	–11	–11	–4

Source: based on data in *Business and Consumer Surveys* (Commission of the European Communities).

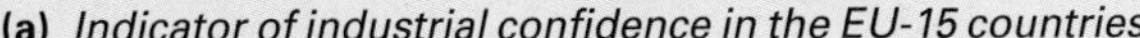

BOX 16.3

If the economy expands and firms respond by investing, there will be a time lag before this can be reflected in increased industrial capacity, since capital takes a time to build and/or install. In the meantime, the percentage utilisation of capacity could expand very rapidly, as existing slack is taken up. Then, as new capacity comes on line, the percentage capacity utilisation figure could rapidly cease rising, or even fall, depending on the rate of growth of consumer demand.

?

1. ***How is the existence of surveys of business confidence likely to affect firms' expectations and actions?***
2. ***Why, if the growth in output slows down (but is still positive), is investment likely to fall (i.e. the growth in investment be negative)? If you look at Table (a), you will see that this happened in 1991 and 1992. (We will examine this question in section 16.4 when we look at the accelerator theory.)***

(a) *Indicator of industrial confidence in the EU-15 countries*

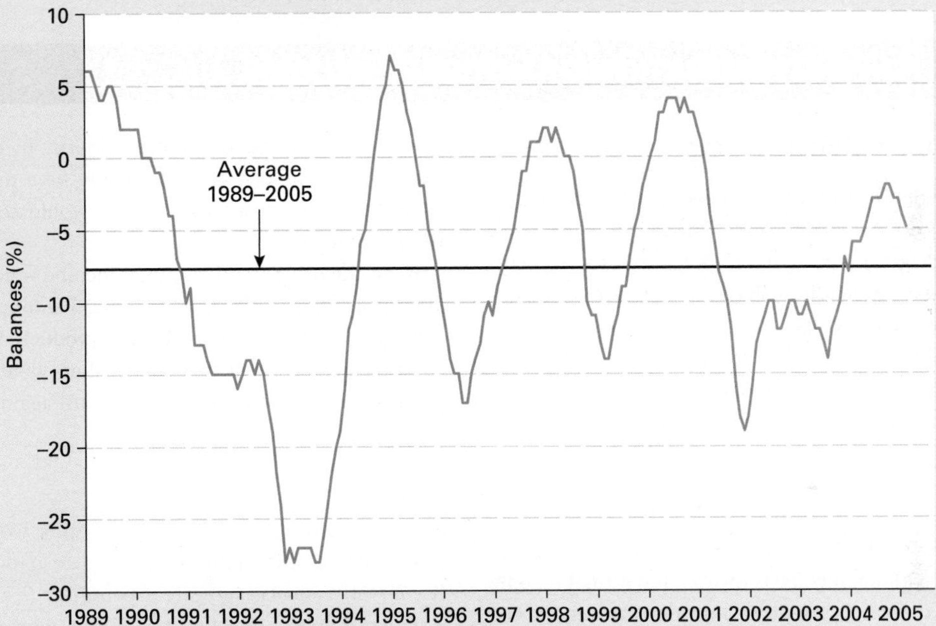

KI 31
p368

(b) *Indicator of the percentage of capacity utilisation in the EU-15 countries*

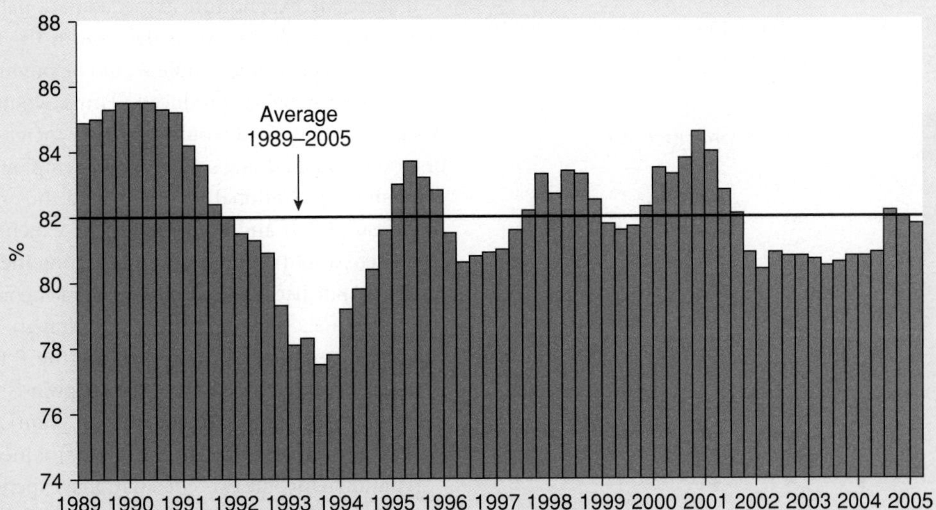

Source: based on data in *Business and Consumer Surveys* (Commission of the European Communities).

except in the case of a cut in income taxes, they will cause saving to fall and vice versa. Net tax revenues, apart from being dependent on incomes, depend on the rates of tax and benefits that the government sets and how progressive or regressive they are. Imports depend on the relative prices and quality of domestic and foreign goods, total consumption and tastes.

5. In the simple Keynesian model, injections are assumed to be exogenous variables. They are therefore drawn as a horizontal straight line in the 45° line diagram. In practice, there will be *some* relationship between injections and national income. Replacement investment depends to some extent on the level of output; government expenditure depends to some extent on the level of tax revenues; and exports depend on exchange rates and foreign incomes, both of which will depend on the level of imports. Nevertheless, in the short run it is reasonable to assume that injections are independent of national income.
6. The determinants of investment include the rate of interest, the size of increases in consumer demand, the cost and efficiency of capital equipment, and expectations about prices, consumer demand, interest rates and other costs.

16.2 THE DETERMINATION OF NATIONAL INCOME

Equilibrium national income

We can now put the various functions together on one diagram. This is done in Figure 16.7. Note that there is a new line on the diagram that we have not looked at so far. This is the aggregate expenditure (i.e. the aggregate demand) function. We defined aggregate expenditure as $C_d + J$. Graphically, then, the E function is simply the C_d function shifted upwards by the amount of J.

Equilibrium national income can be found in either of two ways.

$W = J$

Withdrawals equal injections at point x in the diagram. Equilibrium national income is thus Y_e. If national income were below this level, say at Y_1, injections would exceed withdrawals (by an amount $a - b$). This additional net expenditure injected into the economy would encourage firms to produce more and hence cause national income to rise. But as people's incomes rose, so they would save more, pay more taxes and buy more imports. In other words, withdrawals would rise. There would be a movement up along the W function. This process would continue until $W = J$ at point x.

If, on the other hand, national income were at Y_2, withdrawals would exceed injections (by an amount $c - d$). This deficiency of demand would cause production and hence national income to fall. As it did so, there would be a movement down along the W function until again point x was reached.

Figure 16.7 Equilibrium national income

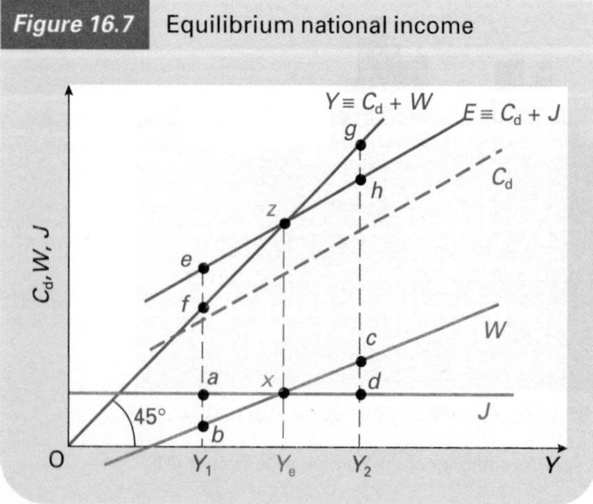

$Y = E$

If $W = J$, then $C_d + W = C_d + J$. In other words, another way of describing equilibrium is where national income ($Y \equiv C_d + W$) equals aggregate expenditure ($E \equiv C_d + J$). This is shown at point z in Figure 16.7. This is where the expenditure function ($C_d + J$) crosses the 45° line ($C_d + W$).

If aggregate expenditure exceeded national income, say at Y_1, there would be excess demand in the economy (of $e - f$). In other words, people would be buying more than was currently being produced. Firms would find their stocks dwindling and would therefore increase their level of production. In doing so, they would employ more factors of production. National income would thus rise. As it did so, consumption and hence aggregate expenditure would rise. There would be a movement up along the expenditure function. But because not all the extra income would be consumed (i.e. some would be withdrawn), expenditure would rise less quickly than income (the E line is flatter than the Y line). As income rises towards Y_e, the gap between Y and E gets smaller. Once point z is reached, $Y = E$. There is then no further tendency for income to rise.

If national income exceeded national expenditure, at say Y_2, there would be insufficient demand for the goods and services currently being produced. Firms would find their stocks of unsold goods building up. They would thus respond by producing less and employing fewer factors of production. National income would thus fall and go on falling until Y_e was reached.

Why do a – b = e – f, and c – d = g – h?

The multiplier: the withdrawals and injections approach

When injections rise (and continue at the higher level), this will cause national income to rise. But by how much?

In fact, national income will rise by *more* than injections: *Y* rises by a *multiple* of the rise in *J*.

$$\Delta Y > \Delta J$$

The number of times that the increase in income (ΔY) is greater than the increase in injections (ΔJ) is known as the ***multiplier*** (k).

$$k = \Delta Y/\Delta J$$

Thus if a £10 billion rise in injections caused a £30 billion rise in national income, the multiplier would be 3.

What causes the multiplier effect? The answer is that, when extra spending is injected into the economy, it will then stimulate further spending, which in turn will stimulate yet more spending and so on. For example, if firms decide to invest more, this will lead to more people being employed and hence more incomes being paid to households. Households will then spend part of this increased income on domestically produced goods (the remainder will be withdrawn). This increased consumption will encourage firms to produce more goods to meet the demand. Firms will thus employ more people and other factors of production. This leads to even more incomes being paid out to households. Consumption will thus increase yet again. And so the process continues.

The multiplier is an example of an important principle in economics: that of ***cumulative causation*** (see page 441). This is the last of our 15 threshold concepts (see panel).

THINKING LIKE AN ECONOMIST — ***THRESHOLD CONCEPT 15***

CUMULATIVE CAUSATION: ECONOMIC EFFECTS CAN SNOWBALL

Once an economy starts to expand, growth is likely to gather pace. Once it starts slowing down, this can gather pace too and end up in a recession. There are many other examples in economics of things getting 'onto a roll'. A rising stock market is likely to breed confidence in investors and encourage them to buy. This 'destabilising speculation' (see page 64) will then lead to further rises in share prices. A fall in stock market prices can lead to panic selling of shares. The booming stock market of the late 1990s and the falls in the early 2000s are good examples of this.

This phenomenon of things building on themselves is known as 'cumulative causation' and occurs throughout market economies. It is a *threshold concept* because it helps us to understand the built-in instability in many parts of the economy and in many economic situations.

Central to explaining cumulative causation is people's psychology. Good news creates confidence and this optimism causes people to behave in ways that build on the good news. Bad news creates pessimism and this leads to people behaving cautiously, which tends to reinforce the bad news.

Take two regions of an economy: an expanding region and a declining region. The expansion of the first region encourages workers to move there in search of jobs. The optimism in the area causes long-term investment as firms have confidence in an expanding market. This encourages house building and other forms of investment in infrastructure and services. And so the region thrives. Meanwhile the declining region suffers from deprivation as unemployment rises. This encourages people to move away and businesses to close. There is a further decline in jobs and further migration from the region.

Cumulative causation occurs not just at a macro level. If a company is successful, it is likely to find raising extra finance easier and that it can use its power more effectively to out-compete rivals. Giant companies, such as Microsoft, can gain all sorts of economies of scale, including network economies (see Box 6.4), all of which help the process of building their power base. Success breeds success.

1. ***How might cumulative causation work at the level of an individual firm that is losing market share?***
2. ***Are there any market forces that work against cumulative causation? For instance, how might markets help to arrest the decline of a depressed region of the economy and slow down the expansion of a booming region?***

Definitions

(Injections) multiplier The number of times by which a rise in income exceeds the rise in injections that caused it: $k = \Delta Y/\Delta J$.

Principle of cumulative causation An initial event can cause an ultimate effect that is much larger.

TC 12 p374

Note that in this simple Keynesian theory we are assuming that prices are constant (i.e. that there is no inflation) and hence that any increase in income is a *real* increase in income matched by extra production. So when we talk about extra injections into the economy causing extra spending, it is the extra *output* that this spending generates that we are concerned with. If the multiplier were 3, for example, this would mean that an injection of £1 of expenditure into the economy would lead to an increase in *output* of £3.

But even if there were limitless resources, an increase in injections would not cause national income to go on rising for ever: the multiplier is not infinite. Each time people receive extra income, they will save some of it, pay some of it in taxes and spend some of it on imports: in other words, withdrawals will rise. Eventually, as income goes on rising, all the extra injections will have leaked away into the three withdrawals. At that point, the multiplier process will have ceased; a new equilibrium will have been reached.

What determines the size of the multiplier? This can be shown graphically using either withdrawals and injections or income and expenditure. The income/expenditure approach will be examined shortly. For now we will use the withdrawals/injections approach. This is illustrated in Figure 16.8.

Assume that injections rise from J_1 to J_2. Equilibrium will move from point a to point b. Income will thus rise from Y_{e_1} to Y_{e_2}. The multiplier is therefore:

$$\frac{Y_{e_2} - Y_{e_1}}{J_2 - J_1} \quad \left(\text{i.e. } \frac{\Delta Y}{\Delta J}\right)$$

It can be seen that the size of the multiplier depends on the *slope of the W function*. Remember that the slope of the W function is given by the marginal propensity to withdraw ($\Delta W/\Delta Y$). The flatter the line (and hence the lower the *mpw*), the bigger will be the rise in national income: the bigger will be the multiplier.

? *Try this simple test of the above argument. Draw a series of W lines of different slopes, all crossing the J line at the same point. Now draw a second J line above the first. Mark the original equilibrium and all the new ones corresponding to each of the W lines. It should be quite obvious that the flatter the W line is, the more Y will have increased.*

Figure 16.8 The multiplier: a shift in injections

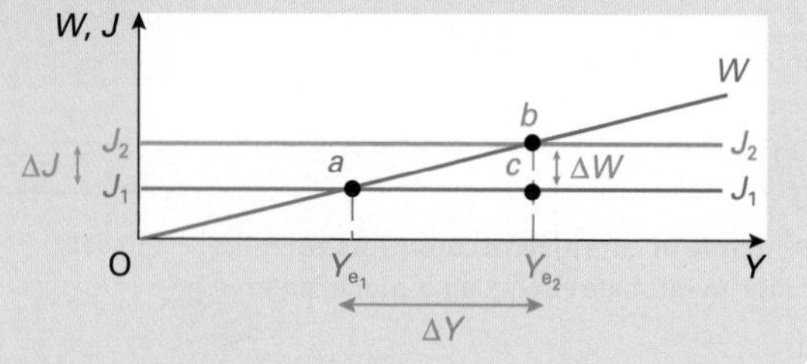

The point here is that the less is withdrawn each time extra income is generated, the more will be recirculated and hence the bigger will be the rise in national income. The size of the multiplier thus varies inversely with the size of the *mpw*. The bigger the *mpw*, the smaller the multiplier; the smaller the *mpw*, the bigger the multiplier. In fact, the ***multiplier formula*** simply gives the multiplier as the inverse of the *mpw*:

$$k = 1/mpw$$

or alternatively, since $mpw + mpc_d = 1$ and thus $mpw = 1 - mpc_d$:

$$k = 1/(1 - mpc_d)$$

Thus if the *mpw* were $^1/_4$ (and hence the mpc_d were $^3/_4$), the multiplier would be 4. So if J increased by £10 billion, Y would increase by £40 billion.

But why is the multiplier given by the formula $1/mpw$? This can be illustrated by referring to Figure 16.8. The *mpw* is the slope of the W line. In the diagram, this is given by the amount $(b - c)/(c - a)$. The multiplier is defined as $\Delta Y/\Delta J$. In the diagram, this is the amount $(c - a)/(b - c)$. But this is merely the inverse of the *mpw*. Thus the multiplier equals $1/mpw$.[3]

*LOOKING AT THE MATHS

The multiplier can be expressed as the first derivative of national income with respect to injections.

$$k = \frac{dY}{dJ}$$

Since $J = W$, it is also the first derivative of income with respect to withdrawals. Thus:

$$k = \frac{dY}{dW}$$

The slope of the withdrawals curve is found by differentiating the withdrawals function, $dW/dY = mpw$. Thus:

$$k = \frac{1}{mpw}$$

The algebra of the multiplier is explored on the book's website in Maths Case 16.1, which does not use calculus, and Maths Case 16.2, which does.

[3] In some elementary textbooks, the formula for the multiplier is given as $1/mps$. The reason for this is that it is assumed (for simplicity) that there is only one withdrawal, namely saving and only one injection, namely investment. As soon as this assumption is dropped, $1/mps$ becomes the wrong formula.

Definition

(Injections) multiplier formula The formula for the multiplier is $k = 1/mpw$ or $1/(1 - mpc_d)$.

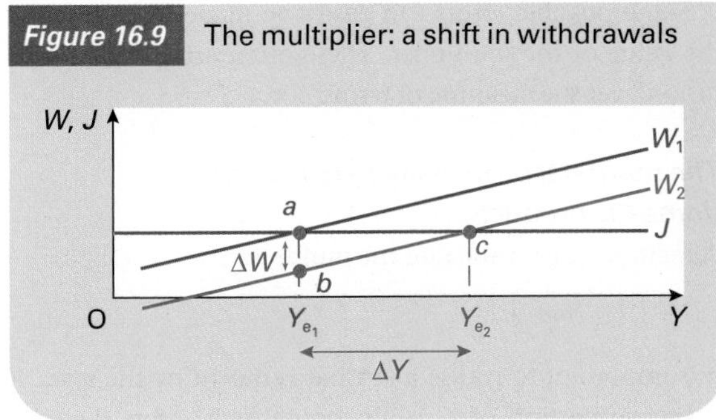

Figure 16.9 The multiplier: a shift in withdrawals

A shift in withdrawals

A multiplied rise in income can also be caused by a fall in withdrawals. This is illustrated in Figure 16.9.

The withdrawals function shifts from W_1 to W_2. This means that, at the old equilibrium of Y_{e_1}, injections now exceed withdrawals by an amount $a - b$. This will cause national income to rise until a new equilibrium is reached at Y_{e_2} where $J = W_2$. Thus a downward shift of the withdrawals function of $a - b$ (ΔW) causes a rise in national income of $c - a$ (ΔY). The multiplier in this case is given by $\Delta Y/\Delta W$: in other words, $(c - a)/(a - b)$.

Why is the 'withdrawals multiplier' strictly speaking a negative figure?

The multiplier: a numerical illustration

The multiplier effect does not work instantaneously. When there is an increase in injections, whether investment, government expenditure or exports, it takes time before this brings about the full multiplied rise in national income.

Consider the following example. Let us assume for simplicity that the *mpw* is ½. This will give an mpc_d of ½ also. Let us also assume that investment (an injection) rises by £160 million and stays at the new higher level. Table 16.2 shows what will happen.

As firms purchase more machines and construct more factories, the incomes of those who produce machines and those who work in the construction industry will increase by £160 million. When this extra income is received by households, whether as wages or profits, half will be withdrawn (mpw = ½) and half will be spent on the goods and services of domestic firms. This increase in consumption thus generates additional incomes for firms of £80 million over and above the initial £160 million (which is still being generated in each time period). When this additional £80 million of incomes is received by households (round 2), again half will be withdrawn and half will go on consumption of domestic product. This increases national income by a further £40 million (round 3). And so each time we go around the circular flow of income, national income increases, but by only half as much as the previous time (mpc_d = ½).

If we add up the additional income generated in each round (assuming the process goes on indefinitely), the total will be £320 million: twice the rise in injections. The multiplier is 2.

The bigger the mpc_d (and hence the smaller the *mpw*), the more will expenditure rise each time national income rises, and hence the bigger will be the multiplier.

Table 16.2 The multiplier 'round'

Round	ΔJ (£m)	ΔY (£m)	ΔC_d (£m)	ΔW (£m)
1	160	160	80	80
2	–	80	40	40
3	–	40	20	20
4	–	20	10	10
5	–	10	5	5
6	–	5	.	.
.		.	.	.
$1 \rightarrow \infty$		320	160	160

The multiplier: the income and expenditure approach

The multiplier can also be demonstrated using the income/expenditure approach. Assume in Figure 16.10 that the aggregate expenditure function shifts to E_2. This could be due either to a rise in one or more of the three injections, or to a rise in the consumption of domestically produced goods (and hence a fall in withdrawals). Equilibrium national income will rise from Y_{e_1} to Y_{e_2}.

What is the size of the multiplier? The initial rise in expenditure was $b - a$. The resulting rise in income is $c - a$. The multiplier is thus $(c - a)/(b - a)$.

The effect is illustrated in Table 16.3. Consumption of domestic product (C_d) is shown in column 2 for various levels of national income (Y). For every £100 billion rise in Y, C_d rises by £80 billion. Thus the mpc_d = 0.8. Assume initially that injections equal £100 billion at all levels of

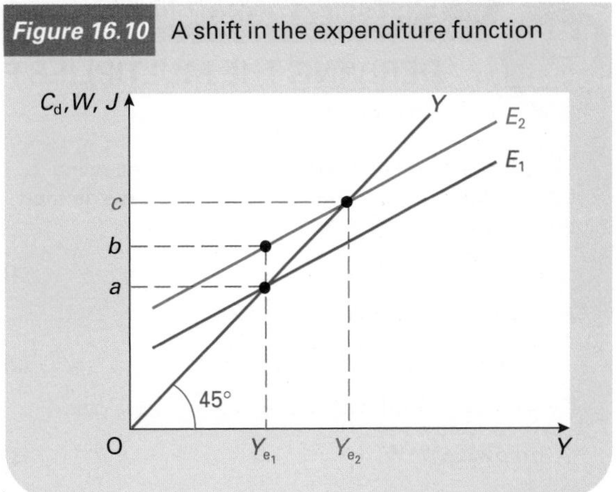

Figure 16.10 A shift in the expenditure function

Table 16.3 The effect of an increase in aggregate expenditure (£ billions)

Y	C_d	J (old)	E (old)	J (new)	E (new)
500	440	100	540	120	560
600	520	100	620	120	640
700	600	100	**700**	120	720
800	680	100	780	120	**800**
900	760	100	860	120	880

national income. Aggregate expenditure (column 4) equals $C_d + J$. Equilibrium national income is £700 billion. This is where $Y = E$.

Now assume that injections rise by £20 billion to £120 billion. Aggregate expenditure is now shown in the final column and is £20 billion higher than before at each level of national income (Y). At the original equilibrium national income (£700 billion), aggregate expenditure is now £720 billion. This excess of E over Y of £20 billion will generate extra incomes and continue doing so as long as E remains above Y. Equilibrium is reached at £800 billion, where once more $Y = E$. The initial rise in aggregate expenditure of £20 billion (from £700bn to £720bn) has led to an eventual rise in both national income and aggregate expenditure of £100 billion. The multiplier is thus 5 (i.e. £100bn/£20bn). But this is equal to $1/(1 - 0.8)$ or $1/(1 - mpc_d)$.

?

1. What determines the slope of the E function?
2. How does the slope of the E function affect the size of the multiplier? (Try drawing diagrams with E functions of different slopes and see what happens when they shift.)

*The multiplier: some qualifications

(This section examines the multiplier formula in more detail. You may omit it without affecting the flow of the argument.)

Some possible errors can easily be made in calculating the value of the multiplier. These often arise from a confusion over the meaning of terms.

The marginal propensity to consume domestic product

Remember the formula for the multiplier:

$$k = 1/(1 - mpc_d)$$

It is important to realise just what is meant by the mpc_d. It is the proportion of a rise in households' gross (i.e. pre-tax-and-benefit) income that actually accrues to domestic firms. It thus excludes that part of consumption that is spent on imports and that part which is paid to the government in VAT and other indirect taxes.

Up to now we have also been basing the *mpc* on gross income. As Web Case 16.1 shows, however, the *mpc* is often based on *disposable* (i.e. post-tax-and-benefit) income. After all, when consumers decide how much to spend, it is their disposable income rather than their gross income that they will consider. So how do we derive the mpc_d (based on gross income) from the *mpc* based on disposable income (mpc')? To do this, we must use the following formula:

$$mpc_d = mpc'(1 - t_E)(1 - t_Y) - mpm$$

where t_Y is the marginal rate of income tax, and t_E is the marginal rate of expenditure tax.

To illustrate this formula consider the following effects of an increase in national income of £100 million. It is assumed that $t_Y = 20$ per cent, $t_E = 10$ per cent and $mpc = 7/8$. It is also assumed that the *mps* (from gross income) = 1/10 and the *mpm* (from gross income) = 13/100. Table 16.4 sets out the figures.

Gross income rises by £100 million. Of this, £20 million is taken in income tax ($t_Y = 20$ per cent). This leaves a rise in disposable income of £80 million. Of this, £10 million is saved ($mps = 1/10$) and £70 million is spent. Of this, £7 million goes in expenditure taxes ($t_E = 10$ per cent) and

EXPLORING ECONOMICS **BOX 16.4**

DERIVING THE MULTIPLIER FORMULA

An algebraic proof

The formula for the multiplier can be derived using simple algebra. First of all, remember how we defined the multiplier:

$$k \equiv \Delta Y/\Delta J \quad (1)$$

and the marginal propensity to withdraw:

$$mpw \equiv \Delta W/\Delta Y \quad (2)$$

If we now take the inverse of equation (2), we get:

$$1/mpw \equiv \Delta Y/\Delta W \quad (3)$$

But in equilibrium we know that $W = J$. Hence any change in injections must be matched by a change in withdrawals and vice versa, to ensure that withdrawals and injections remain equal. Thus:

$$\Delta W = \Delta J \quad (4)$$

Substituting equation (4) in equation (3) gives:

$$1/mpw = \Delta Y/\Delta J \ (= k)$$

i.e. the multiplier equals $1/mpw$.

Table 16.4 Calculating the mpc_d

	ΔY	–	ΔT_Y	=	ΔY_{dis}		
(£m)	100		20		80		
	ΔY_{dis}	–	ΔS	=	ΔC		
(£m)	80		10		70		
	ΔC	–	ΔT_E	–	ΔM	=	ΔC_d
(£m)	70		7		13		50

£13 million leaks abroad (mpm = 13/100). This leaves £50 million that goes on the consumption of domestic product (mpc_d = 50/100 = ½). Substituting these figures in the above formula gives:

$$mpc_d = mpc\,(1 - t_E)(1 - t_Y) - mpm$$
$$= 7/8(1 - 1/10)(1 - 2/10) - 13/100$$
$$= 7/8 \,.\, 9/10 \,.\, 8/10 - 13/100$$
$$= 63/100 - 13/100 = 50/100 = 1/2$$

Note that the mpc_d, mps, mpm and mpt are all based on the rise in *gross* income, not disposable income. They are 50/100, 10/100, 13/100 and 27/100 respectively.

Maths Case 16.3 on the book's website derives the multiplier formula when the propensities to consume, save and import are all based on *disposable* as opposed to gross income.

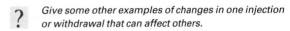

Assume that the rate of income tax is 15 per cent, the rate of expenditure tax is 12½ per cent, the mps is 1/20, the mpm is 1/8 and the mpc (from disposable income) is 16/17. What is the mpc_d? Construct a table like Table 16.4 assuming again that national income rises by £100 million.

The effects of changes in injections and withdrawals on other injections and withdrawals

In order to work out the size of a multiplied rise or fall in income, it is necessary to know first the size of the initial *total* change in injections and/or withdrawals. The trouble is that a change in one injection or withdrawal can affect others. For example, a rise in income taxes will reduce not only consumption, but also saving, imports and the revenue from indirect taxes. Thus the total rise in withdrawals will be *less* than the rise in income taxes.

? *Give some other examples of changes in one injection or withdrawal that can affect others.*

The relationship between the 45° line diagram and the aggregate demand and supply diagram

We have used two diagrams to show the determination of equilibrium national income: the aggregate demand and supply diagram and the 45° line diagram. The first shows

EXPLORING ECONOMICS — BOX 16.5

THE PARADOX OF THRIFT

When prudence is folly

The classical economists argued that saving was a national virtue. More saving would lead via lower interest rates to more investment and faster growth. Keynes was at pains to show the opposite. Saving, far from being a national virtue, could be a national vice.

KI 12 p80 Remember the fallacy of composition (see Box 3.5). Just because something is good for an individual, it does not follow that it is good for society as a whole. This fallacy applies to saving. If individuals save more, they will increase their consumption possibilities in the future. If society saves more, however, this may *reduce* its future income and consumption. As people save more, they will spend less. Firms will thus produce less. There will thus be a multiplied *fall* in income. The phenomenon of higher saving leading to *lower* national income is known as 'the paradox of thrift'.

But this is not all. Far from the extra saving encouraging more investment, the lower consumption will *discourage* firms from investing. If investment falls, the *J* line will shift downwards. There will then be a further multiplied fall in national income. (This response of investment to changes in consumer demand is examined in section 16.4 under the 'accelerator theory'.)

The paradox of thrift had in fact been recognised before Keynes, and Keynes himself referred to various complaints about 'underconsumption' that had been made back in the sixteenth and seventeenth centuries:

> In 1598 Laffemas . . . denounced the objectors to the use of French silks on the grounds that all purchasers of French luxury goods created a livelihood for the poor, whereas the miser caused them to die in distress. In 1662 Petty justified 'entertainments, magnificent shews, triumphal arches, etc.', on the ground that their costs flowed back into the pockets of brewers, bakers, tailors, shoemakers and so forth . . . In 1695 Cary argued that if everybody spent more, all would obtain larger incomes 'and might then live more plentifully'.[4]

But despite these early recognitions of the danger of underconsumption, the belief that saving would increase the prosperity of the nation was central to classical economic thought.

Is an increase in saving ever desirable?

[4] J. M. Keynes, *The General Theory of Employment, Interest and Money* (Macmillan, 1967), pp. 358–9.

aggregate demand dependent on the price level. The second shows aggregate demand (i.e. aggregate expenditure (E)) dependent on the level of national income. Figure 16.11 shows the multiplier effect simultaneously on the two diagrams. Initially, equilibrium is at Y_{e_1} where aggregate demand equals aggregate supply and where the aggregate expenditure line crosses the 45° line.

Now assume that there is an autonomous increase in expenditure. For example, increased business confidence results in increased investment. In diagram (b), the E line shifts to E_2. There is a multiplied rise in income to Y_{e_2}. In diagram (a), the aggregate supply curve is drawn as a horizontal straight line between Y_{e_1} and Y_{e_2}. This means that an increase in aggregate demand from AD_1 to AD_2 will raise income to Y_{e_2} with no increase in prices.

TC 15 p463

But what if the economy is approaching full employment? Surely we cannot expect the multiplier process to work in the same way as when there is plenty of slack in the economy? In this case, the aggregate supply curve will be upward sloping. This means that an increase in aggregate demand will raise prices and not just output. How do we analyse this with the 45° line diagram? We examine this in the next section.

Figure 16.11 Showing the multiplier effect on the 45° line and *AD*/*AS* diagrams

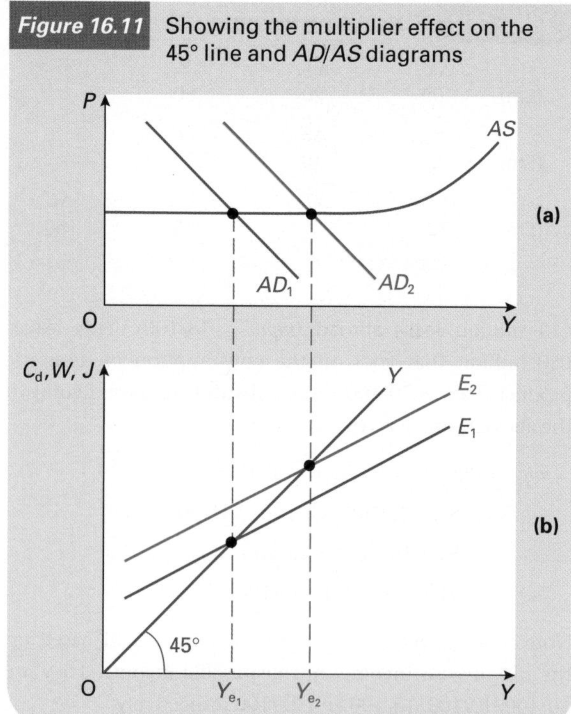

Section summary

1. Equilibrium national income can be shown on the 45° line diagram at the point where $W = J$ and $Y = E$.
2. If there is an increase in injections (or a reduction in withdrawals), there will be a multiplied rise in national income. The multiplier is defined as $\Delta Y/\Delta J$.
3. The size of the multiplier depends on the marginal propensity to withdraw (*mpw*). The smaller the *mpw*, the less will be withdrawn each time incomes are generated round the circular flow, and thus the more will go round again as *additional* demand for domestic product. The multiplier formula is $k = 1/mpw$ or $1/(1 - mpc_d)$.

*4. When working out the size of the multiplier, you must be careful to identify clearly the mpc_d (which is based on *gross* income and only includes expenditure that actually accrues to domestic firms) and not to confuse it with the *mpc* based on *disposable* income (which includes consumption of imports and the payment of indirect taxes). It is also necessary to identify the *full* changes in injections and withdrawals on which any multiplier effect is based.

5. The multiplier effect can also be illustrated on an aggregate demand and supply diagram.

16.3 THE SIMPLE KEYNESIAN ANALYSIS OF UNEMPLOYMENT AND INFLATION

'Full-employment' national income

The simple Keynesian theory assumes that there is a maximum level of national output, and hence real income, that can be obtained at any one time. If the equilibrium level of income is at this level, there will be no deficiency of aggregate demand and hence no disequilibrium unemployment. This level of income is referred to as the ***full-employment level of national income***. (In practice, there would still be some unemployment at this level because of equilibrium unemployment – structural, frictional and seasonal.)

Governments of the 1950s, 1960s and early 1970s aimed to achieve this full-employment income (Y_f), if inflation and the balance of payments permitted. To do this, they attempted to manipulate the level of aggregate demand. This approach was also adopted by the George W. Bush

Definition

Full-employment level of national income The level of national income at which there is no deficiency of demand.

administration in the USA in 2001, when attempts were made to stimulate aggregate demand through the use of fiscal and monetary policy in order to pull the US economy out of recession.

The deflationary gap

If the equilibrium level of national income (Y_e) is below the full-employment level (Y_f), there will be excess capacity in the economy and hence demand-deficient unemployment.

There will be what is known as a ***deflationary gap***. This is illustrated in Figure 16.12.

The full-employment level of national income (Y_f) is represented by the vertical line. The equilibrium level of national income is Y_e, where $W = J$ and $Y = E$. The deflationary gap is $a - b$: namely, the amount that the E line is below the 45° line at the full-employment level of income (Y_f). It is also $c - d$: the amount that injections fall short of withdrawals at the full-employment level of income.

TC 15 p463

Note that the size of the deflationary gap is *less* than the amount by which Y_e falls short of Y_f. This provides another illustration of the multiplier. If injections were raised by $c - d$, income would rise by $Y_f - Y_e$. The multiplier is thus given by:

$$\frac{Y_f - Y_e}{c - d}$$

In this simple Keynesian model, then, the cure for demand-deficient unemployment is to close the deflationary gap. This could be achieved by an expansionary *fiscal* policy of increasing government expenditure or lowering taxes, or by an expansionary *monetary* policy of increasing the amount of money in the economy and reducing interest rates, thereby encouraging extra consumption and investment. Either way, if the deflationary gap is successfully closed, there will be a multiplied rise in income of $Y_f - Y_e$. Equilibrium national income will be restored to the full-employment level.

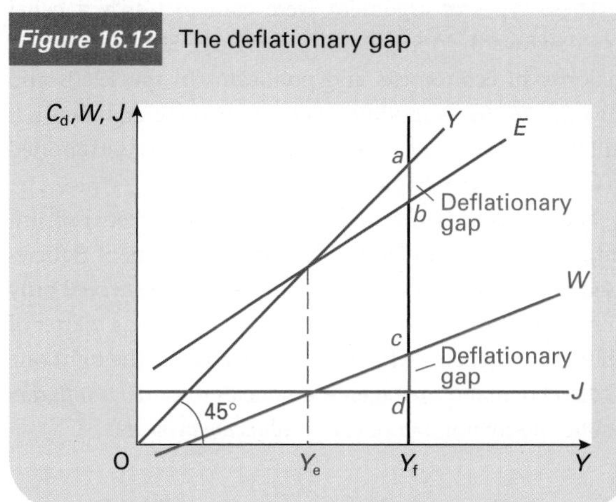

Figure 16.12 The deflationary gap

The inflationary gap

If, at the full-employment level of income, aggregate expenditure exceeds national income, there will be a problem of *excess* demand. Y_e will be above Y_f. The problem is that Y_f represents a real ceiling to output. In the short run, real national income *cannot* expand beyond this point.[5] Y_e cannot be reached. The result will therefore be demand-pull inflation.[6]

TC 12 p374

This situation involves an ***inflationary gap***. This is the amount by which aggregate expenditure exceeds national income or injections exceed withdrawals at the full-employment level of national income. This is illustrated by the gaps $e - f$ and $g - h$ in Figure 16.13.

To eliminate this inflation, the inflationary gap must be closed by either raising withdrawals or lowering injections or some combination of the two until Y_e equals Y_f. This can be done by a deliberate government policy of deflation. This could be either a contractionary *fiscal* policy of lowering government expenditure or raising taxes, or a contractionary *monetary* policy of reducing the amount of money in the economy and raising interest rates.

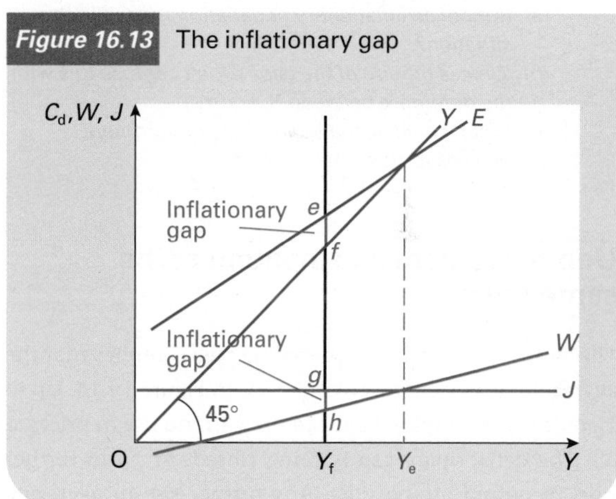

Figure 16.13 The inflationary gap

[5] Except with increased overtime working. In this simple model, we assume that this is not posssible.

[6] Note that the horizontal axis in the 45° line diagram represents *real* national income. If incomes were to rise by, say, 10 per cent but prices also rose by 10 per cent, real income would not have risen at all. People could not buy any more than before. In such a case, there will have been no rightward movement along the horizontal axis.

Definitions

Deflationary gap The shortfall of national expenditure below national income (and injections below withdrawals) at the full-employment level of national income.

Inflationary gap The excess of national expenditure over income (and injections over withdrawals) at the full-employment level of national income.

Even if the government does not actively pursue a deflationary policy, the inflationary gap may still close automatically. If the rich are better able than the poor to defend themselves against inflation, there will be a redistribution from the poor to the rich. But the rich tend to have a higher marginal propensity to save than the poor. Thus saving will rise and consumption will fall. This will swing the *W* line up and the *E* line down, thus narrowing the inflationary gap.

Inflation will also tend to worsen the balance of payments. Higher money incomes at home will lead to more imports being purchased. Higher domestic prices will lead to fewer exports being sold and more imports being bought in preference to the now dearer home-produced goods. The effect of this will be to shift the *W* line up and the *J* and *E* lines down, thus helping to close the inflationary gap.

Finally, as money incomes go up, people will tend to find themselves paying higher rates of tax (unless the government increases tax bands and allowances in line with inflation). This will shift the *W* line up and the *E* line down.

?

The present level of a country's exports is £12 billion; investment is £2 billion; government expenditure is £4 billion; total *consumer spending (not C_d) is £36 billion; imports are £12 billion; and expenditure taxes are £2 billion. The economy is currently in equilibrium. It is estimated that an income of £50 billion is necessary to generate full employment. The mps is 0.1, the mpt is 0.05 and the mpm is 0.1.*

(a) Is there an inflationary or deflationary gap in this situation?

(b) What is the size of the gap? (Don't confuse this with the difference between Y_e and Y_f.)

(c) What would be the appropriate government policies to close this gap?

Unemployment and inflation at the same time

The simple analysis of the preceding pages implies that the aggregate supply curve looks like AS_1 in Figure 16.14. Up to Y_f, output and employment can rise with no rise in prices at all. The deflationary gap is being closed. At Y_f no further rises in output are possible. Any further rise in aggregate demand is entirely reflected in higher prices. An inflationary gap opens. In other words, this implies that either inflation *or* unemployment can occur, but not both simultaneously.

Two important qualifications need to be made to this analysis to explain the occurrence of both unemployment *and* inflation at the same time.

First, there are *other* types of inflation and unemployment not caused by an excess or deficiency of aggregate demand: for example, cost-push and expectations-generated inflation; frictional and structural unemployment.

Thus, even if a government could manipulate national income so as to get Y_e and Y_f to coincide, this would not eliminate all inflation and unemployment – only demand-pull inflation and demand-deficient unemployment.

Figure 16.14 Unemployment *and* inflation

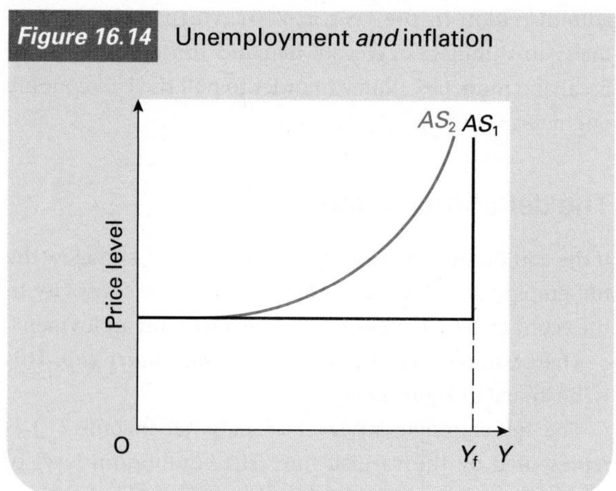

Keynesians argue, therefore, that governments should use a whole package of policies, each tailored to the specific type of problem. But certainly one of the most important of these policies will be the management of aggregate demand.

Second, not all firms operate with the same degree of slack. Thus a rise in aggregate demand can lead to *both* a reduction in unemployment *and* a rise in prices: some firms responding to the rise in demand by taking up slack and hence increasing output; other firms, having little or no slack, responding by raising prices; others doing both. Similarly, labour markets have different degrees of slack and therefore the rise in demand will lead to various mixes of higher wages and lower unemployment. Thus the *AS* curve will look like AS_2 in Figure 16.14.

?

How does the above argument about firms' responses to a rise in demand relate to the shape of their marginal cost curves?

These types of argument were used to justify a belief in a downward-sloping Phillips curve (see Box 14.5) by the majority of economists and politicians in the 1960s and into the 1970s. A modified version of these arguments is still used today by Keynesian economists. This is examined in more detail in Chapter 20.

The problem is that if there is a trade-off between unemployment and inflation, demand management policies used to make one of the objectives better will succeed only in making the other one worse. It then becomes a matter of political judgement which of the objectives is the right one to direct demand management policies towards. Is *inflation* public enemy number one, or is it *unemployment*? KI 32 p369

The relationship between the *AD*/*AS* diagram and the 45° line diagram

Now that we have introduced the argument that inflation can begin to occur *before* the full-employment level of income is reached, how does this affect the relationship between our two models: the *AD*/*AS* model and the 45° line model? This is examined in Figure 16.15. Initial equilibrium

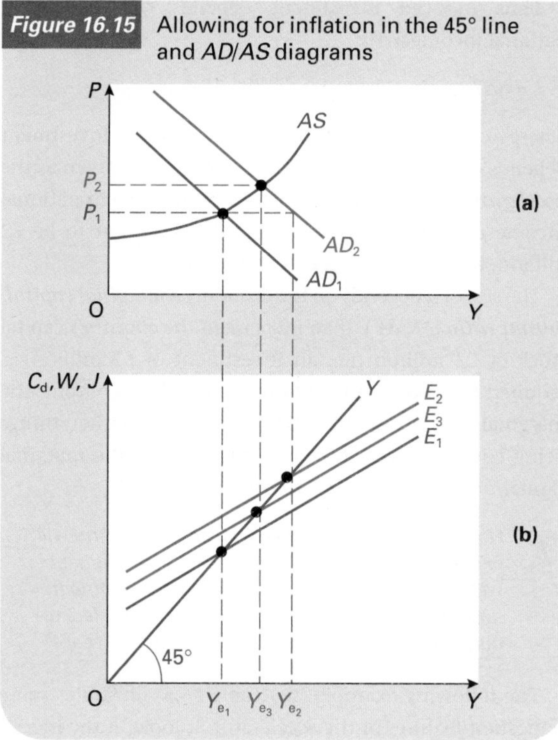

Figure 16.15 Allowing for inflation in the 45° line and *AD*/*AS* diagrams

is at Y_{e_1} in both parts of the diagram, where $AD_1 = AS$ and where E_1 crosses the 45° line.

Now let us assume that there is a rise in aggregate demand. The E line shifts initially to E_2 in diagram (b). If this rise in demand were to lead to a full multiplied rise in real income, equilibrium income would rise to Y_{e_2}. But we are now assuming that inflation can occur *before* the full-employment level of income is reached. In other words, we are assuming that the AS curve is upward sloping (not horizontal as it was in Figure 16.11).

In diagram (a), the rise in aggregate demand has shifted the AD curve from AD_1 to AD_2. Part of this increase in demand is reflected in higher prices – the price level rises to P_2 – and only *part* is reflected in higher output. Equilibrium real income therefore rises only to Y_{e_3} and not Y_{e_2}. In other words, it does not rise by the full extent of the multiplier.

In diagram (b), the effect of the higher prices is to reduce the real value of expenditure (E). In other words, a given amount of money buys fewer goods. If there is no compensating increase in money supply (which would shift the AD curve further to the right in diagram (a)), the E line must fall to the point where it intersects the 45° line at a real income of Y_{e_3}: the E line must fall to E_3. TC 12 p374

What is the mechanism that drives down the expenditure function from E_2 to E_3?

- The shortage of money drives up interest rates. This reduces investment and encourages saving.
- Higher prices reduce the real value of people's savings. They may therefore save more to compensate for this.
- Higher prices of domestic goods reduce exports and increase imports.
- Given the progressive nature of the tax system, higher money incomes lead to increased taxes.
- Inflation is likely to redistribute income from the poor to the rich, who have a higher *mps*.

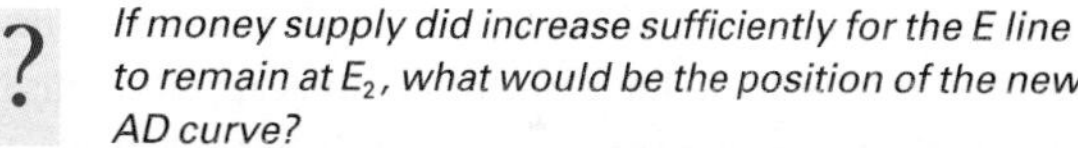

?

If money supply did increase sufficiently for the E line to remain at E_2, what would be the position of the new AD curve?

Section summary

1. If equilibrium national income (Y_e) is below the full-employment level of national income (Y_f), there will be a deflationary gap. This gap is equal to $Y - E$ or $W - J$ at Y_f. This gap can be closed by expansionary fiscal or monetary policy, which will then cause a multiplied rise in national income (up to a level of Y_f) and will eliminate demand-deficient unemployment.
2. If equilibrium national income exceeds the full-employment level of income, the inability of output to expand to meet this excess demand will lead to demand-pull inflation. This excess demand gives an inflationary gap, which is equal to $E - Y$ or $J - W$ at Y_f. This gap can be closed by deflationary policies.
3. This simple analysis tends to imply that the AS curve is horizontal up to Y_f and then vertical. In practice, the AS curve is likely to be upward sloping but getting steeper as full employment is approached and as bottlenecks increasingly occur.
4. An initial rise in aggregate demand (and an upward shift in the E curve) will be eroded to the extent that inflation reduces the real value of this demand: the E curve will shift back downwards again somewhat, unless there is a further boost to demand.

16.4 THE KEYNESIAN ANALYSIS OF THE BUSINESS CYCLE

TC 13 p381 Keynesians blame fluctuations in output and employment on fluctuations in aggregate demand. Theirs is therefore a 'demand-side' explanation of the business cycle. In the upturn (phase 1), aggregate demand starts to rise. It rises rapidly in the expansionary phase (phase 2). It then slows down and may start to fall in the peaking-out phase (phase 3). It then falls or remains relatively stagnant in the recession (phase 4) (see Figure 13.3 on page 380).

Keynesians seek to explain why aggregate demand fluctuates, and then to devise appropriate stabilisation policies to iron out these fluctuations. A more stable economy, they argue, provides a better climate for investment. With more investment, *potential* output grows more rapidly. This, given appropriate demand management policy, then allows a faster growth in actual output to be maintained.

KI 31 p368

Instability of investment: the accelerator

One of the major factors contributing to the ups and downs of the business cycle is the instability of investment.

When an economy begins to recover from a recession, investment can rise very rapidly. When the growth of the economy slows down, however, investment can fall dramatically, and during a recession it can all but disappear. Since investment is an injection into the circular flow of income, these changes in investment will cause multiplied changes in income and thus heighten a boom or deepen a recession.

The theory that relates investment to *changes* in national income is called the ***accelerator theory***. The term 'accelerator' is used because a relatively modest rise in national income can cause a much larger percentage rise in investment.

When there is no change in income and hence no change in consumption, the only investment needed is a relatively small amount of replacement investment for machines that are wearing out or have become obsolete. When income and consumption increase, however, there will have to be *new* investment in order to increase production capacity. This is called ***induced investment*** (I_i). Once this has taken place, investment will fall back to mere replacement investment (I_r) unless there is a further rise in income and consumption.

Thus induced investment depends on *changes* in national income (ΔY):

$$I_i = \alpha \Delta Y$$

where α is the amount by which induced investment depends on changes in national income. α is known as the ***accelerator coefficient***. Thus if a £1 million *rise* in national income caused the *level* of induced investment to be £2 million, the accelerator coefficient would be 2.

The size of α depends on the economy's ***marginal capital/output ratio*** ($\Delta K/\Delta Y$). If an increase in the country's capital stock of £2 million (i.e. an investment of £2 million) is required to produce £1 million extra national output, the marginal capital/output ratio would be 2. Other things being equal, the accelerator coefficient and the marginal capital/output ratio will therefore be the same.

?

How is it that the cost of an investment to a firm will exceed the value of the output that the investment will yield? Surely that would make the investment unprofitable? (Clue: the increase in output refers to output over a specific time period, usually a year.)

The following example (see Table 16.5) illustrates some important features of the accelerator. It looks at the investment decisions made by a firm in response to changes in the demand for its product. The firm is taken as representative of firms throughout the economy. The example is based on various assumptions:

- The firm's machines last exactly 10 years and then need replacing.
- At the start of the example, the firm has 10 machines in place, one 10 years old, one 9 years old, one 8 years old, one 7, one 6 and so on. Thus one machine needs replacing each year.

Table 16.5 The accelerator effect

	Year						
	0	1	2	3	4	5	6
Quantity demanded by consumers (sales)	1000	1000	2000	3000	3500	3500	3400
Number of machines required	10	10	20	30	35	35	34
Induced investment (I_i) (extra machines)		0	10	10	5	0	0
Replacement investment (I_r)		1	1	1	1	1	0
Total investment ($I_i + I_r$)		1	11	11	6	1	0

Definitions

Accelerator theory The level of investment depends on the rate of change of national income, and as a result tends to be subject to substantial fluctuations.

Induced investment Investment that firms make to enable them to meet extra consumer demand.

Accelerator coefficient The level of induced investment as a proportion of a rise in national income: $\alpha = I_i/\Delta Y$.

Marginal capital/output ratio The amount of extra capital (in money terms) required to produce a £1 increase in national output. Since $I_i = \Delta K$, the marginal apital/output ratio $\Delta K/\Delta Y$ equals the accelerator coefficient (α).

- Machines produce exactly 100 units of output per year. This figure cannot be varied.
- The firm always adjusts its output and its stock of machinery to match consumer demand.

The example shows what happens to the firm's investment over a six-year period when there is first a substantial rise in consumer demand, then a levelling off and then a slight fall. In year 2, consumer demand shoots up from 1000 units to 2000 units. In year 3, it goes up by a further 1000 units to 3000 units. In year 4, the rise begins to slow down: demand goes up by 500 units to 3500 units. In year 5, demand is constant at 3500 units. In year 6, it falls slightly to 3400 units. This example illustrates the following features of the accelerator.

Investment will rise when the growth of national income (and hence consumer demand) is rising ($\Delta Y_{t+1} > \Delta Y_t$). The rise in consumer demand is zero in year 1 and 1000 units in year 2. Investment rises from 1 to 11 machines. The growth in investment may be considerably greater than the growth in consumer demand, giving a large accelerator effect. Between years 1 and 2, consumer demand doubles but investment goes up by a massive 11 times!

Investment will be constant even when national income is growing, if the increase in income this year is the same as last year ($\Delta Y_{t+1} = \Delta Y_t$). In years 2 to 3, consumer demand continues to rise by 1000 units, but investment is constant at 11 machines.

Investment will fall even if national income is still growing, if the rate of growth is slowing down ($\Delta Y_{t+1} > \Delta Y_t$). In years 3 to 4, consumer demand rises by 500 units (rather than the 1000 units last year). Investment falls from 11 to 6 machines.

If national income is constant, investment will be confined to replacement investment only. In years 4 to 5, investment falls to the one machine requiring replacement.

If national income falls, even if only slightly, investment can be wiped out altogether. In years 5 to 6, even though demand has only fallen by 1/35, investment will fall to zero. Not even the machine that is wearing out will be replaced.

In practice, the accelerator will not be as dramatic and clear cut as this. The effect will be extremely difficult to predict for the following reasons:

- Many firms may have spare capacity and/or carry stocks. This will enable them to meet extra demand without having to invest.

- The willingness of firms to invest will depend on their confidence in *future* demand (see Box 16.3). Firms are not going to rush out and spend large amounts of money on machines that will last many years if it is quite likely that next year demand will fall back again.
- Firms may make their investment plans a long time in advance and may be unable to change them quickly. KI 30 p306
- Even if firms do decide to invest more, the producer goods industries may not have the capacity to meet a sudden surge in demand for machines.
- Machines do not as a rule suddenly wear out. A firm could thus delay replacing machines and keep the old ones for a bit longer if it was uncertain about its future level of demand.

All these points tend to reduce the magnitude of the accelerator and to make it very difficult to predict. Nevertheless the effect still exists. Firms still take note of changes in consumer demand when deciding how much to invest.

Box 16.6 shows how, from 1976 to 2005, fluctuations in investment were far more severe than fluctuations in national income. This tends to suggest that there was a substantial accelerator effect operating during the period.

The multiplier/accelerator interaction

If there is an initial change in injections or withdrawals, then theoretically this will set off a chain reaction between the multiplier and accelerator. For example, if there is a rise in government expenditure, this will lead to a multiplied rise in national income. But this *rise* in national income will set off an accelerator effect: firms will respond to the rise in income and the resulting rise in consumer demand by investing more. But this rise in investment constitutes a further rise in injections and thus will lead to a second multiplied rise in income. If this rise in income is larger than the first, there will then be a second rise in investment (the accelerator), which in turn will cause a third rise in income (the multiplier). And so the process continues indefinitely.

But does this lead to an exploding rise in national income? Will a single rise in injections cause national income to go on rising for ever? The answer is no, for two reasons. The first is that national income, in real terms, cannot go on rising faster than the growth in potential output. It will bump up against the ceiling of full employment, whether of labour or of other resources.

A second reason is that, if investment is to go on rising, it is not enough that national income should merely go on *rising*: instead, national income must *rise faster and faster*. Once the growth in national income slows down, investment will begin to fall, and then the whole process will be reversed. A fall in investment will lead to a fall in national income, which will lead to a massive fall in investment. The multiplier/accelerator interaction is shown more formally in Table 16.6. A numerical example is given in Web Case 16.3.

Table 16.6 The multiplier/accelerator interaction

Period t	$J\uparrow \rightarrow Y\uparrow$	(Multiplier)
Period $t+1$	$Y\uparrow \rightarrow I\uparrow$	(Accelerator)
	$I\uparrow \rightarrow Y\uparrow$	(Multiplier)
Period $t+2$	If $\uparrow Y_{t+1} > \uparrow Y_t$ then $I\uparrow$ If $\uparrow Y_{t+1} = \uparrow Y_t$ then I stays the same If $\uparrow Y_{t+1} < \uparrow Y_t$ then $I\downarrow$ This in turn will have a multiplied upward effect, no effect, or a multiplied downward effect respectively on national income.	(Accelerator)
Period $t+3$	This will then lead to a further accelerator effect and so on ...	

CASE STUDIES AND APPLICATIONS **BOX 16.6**

HAS THERE BEEN AN ACCELERATOR EFFECT OVER THE PAST 30 YEARS?

Investment is highly volatile. It is subject to far more violent swings than national income. If we look at the period from 1976 to 2005, the maximum annual rise in GDP was 5.6 per cent and the maximum fall was 3.8 per cent. By contrast, the maximum annual rise in investment was 19.4 per cent and the maximum fall was 10.9 per cent.

If we focus on *manufacturing* investment, the swings were even greater. The maximum annual rise in manufacturing investment in plant and machinery was 20 per cent and the maximum fall was 28 per cent, and in new buildings and works the maximum annual rise was a massive 59 per cent and the maximum fall was 39 per cent.

These figures are consistent with the accelerator theory, which argues that the *level* of investment depends on the *rate of change* of national income. A relatively small percentage change in national income can give a much bigger percentage change in investment.

The ups and downs in GDP and investment do not completely match because there are additional factors that determine investment other than simple changes in national income. These factors include interest rates, exchange rates and business expectations of future demand.

1. ***Can you identify any time lags in the graph? Why might there be time lags?***
2. ***Why does investment in construction and producer goods industries tend to fluctuate more than investment in retailing and the service industries?***

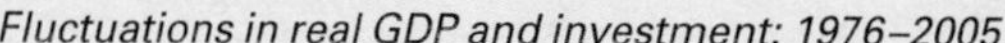

Fluctuations in real GDP and investment: 1976–2005

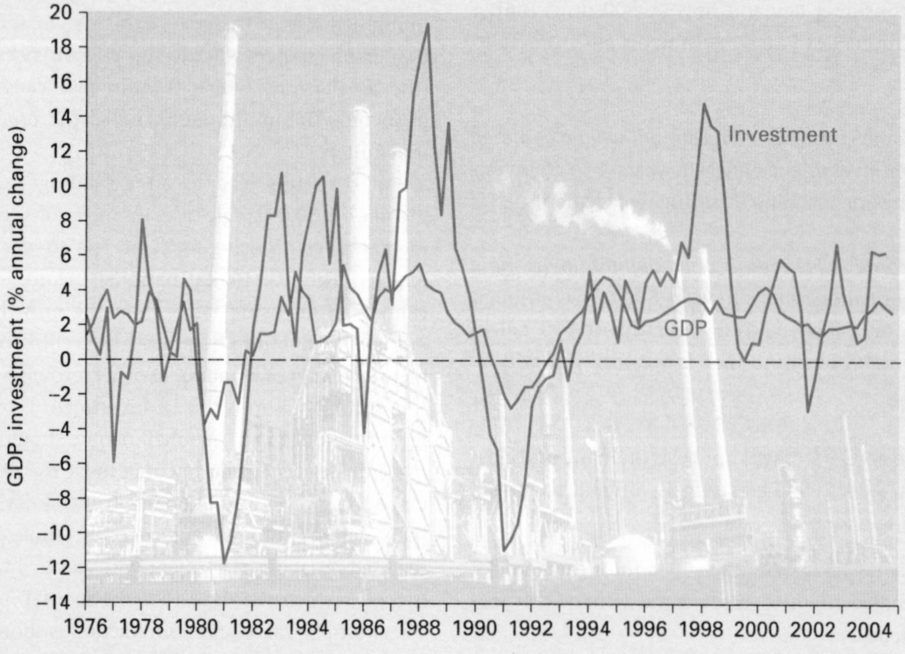

Source: based on data in *National Statistics*.

KI 31 p368

Fluctuations in stocks

Firms hold stocks (inventories) of finished goods. These stocks tend to fluctuate with the course of the business cycle, and these fluctuations in stocks themselves contribute to fluctuations in output.

Imagine an economy that is recovering from a recession. At first, firms may be cautious about increasing production. Doing so may involve taking on more labour or making additional investment. Firms may not want to make these commitments if the recovery could soon peter out. They may, therefore, run down their stocks rather than increase output. Initially the recovery from recession will be slow.

If the recovery does continue, however, firms will start to gain more confidence and will increase production. Also, they will find that their stocks have got rather low and will need building up. This gives a further boost to production, and for a time the growth in output will exceed the growth in demand. This extra growth in output will then, via the multiplier, lead to a further increase in demand.

Once stocks have been built up again, the growth in output will slow down to match the growth in demand. This slowing down in output will, via the accelerator and multiplier, contribute to the ending of the expansionary phase of the business cycle.

As the economy slows down, firms will find their stocks building up. Unless they cut back on production immediately, this increase in stocks cushions the effect of falling demand on output and employment.

If the recession continues, however, firms will be unwilling to go on building up stocks. But as firms attempt to reduce their stocks back to the desired level, production will fall *below* the level of sales, despite the fact that sales themselves are lower. This could lead to a dramatic fall in output and, via the multiplier, to an even bigger fall in sales.

Eventually, once stocks have been run down to the minimum, production will have to rise again to match the level of sales. This will contribute to a recovery and the whole cycle will start again.

Determinants of the course of the business cycle

We are now in a position to paint a more complete Keynesian picture of the business cycle. We need to answer two key questions: (a) why do booms and recessions last for several months or even years, and (b) why do they eventually come to an end – what determines their turning points? Let us examine each in turn.

Why do booms and recessions persist?

Time lags. It takes time for changes in injections and withdrawals to be fully reflected in changes in national income, output and employment. The multiplier process takes time. Moreover, consumers, firms and government may not all respond immediately to new situations.

TC 9 p101

'Bandwagon' effects. Once the economy starts expanding, expectations become buoyant. People think ahead and adjust their expenditure behaviour: they consume and invest more *now*. Likewise in a recession, a mood of pessimism may set in. The effect is cumulative. The multiplier and accelerator interact: they feed on each other.

Why do booms and recessions come to an end?

Ceilings and floors. Actual output can go on growing more rapidly than potential output only as long as there is slack in the economy. As full employment is approached and as more and more firms reach full capacity, so a ceiling to output will be reached.

At the other extreme, there is a basic minimum level of consumption that people tend to maintain. During a recession, people may not buy many luxury and durable goods, but they will continue to buy food and other basic goods. There is thus a floor to consumption.

The industries supplying these basic goods will need to maintain their level of replacement investment. Also, there will always be some minimum investment demand as firms feel the need to install the latest equipment. There is thus a floor to investment too.

Echo effects. Durable consumer goods and capital equipment may last several years, but eventually they will need replacing. The replacement of goods and capital purchased in a previous boom may help to bring a recession to an end.

The accelerator. For investment to continue rising, consumer demand must rise at a *faster and faster* rate. If this does not happen, investment will fall back and the boom will break.

Random shocks. National or international political, social or natural events can affect the mood and attitudes of firms, governments and consumers, and thus affect aggregate demand.

Changes in government policy. In a boom, a government may become most worried by inflation and balance of payments deficits and thus pursue contractionary policies. In a recession, it may become most worried by unemployment and lack of growth and thus pursue expansionary policies. These government policies, if successful, will bring about a turning point in the cycle.

Keynesians argue that governments should attempt to reduce cyclical fluctuations by using active stabilisation policies. A more stable economy will encourage investment and allow a faster growth in output to be maintained. The policy most favoured by Keynesians is *fiscal policy*. This is the subject of Chapter 19.

An analysis of the factors contributing to each of the four phases of the business cycle is given in Web Case 16.5.

Section summary

1. Keynesians explain cyclical fluctuations in the economy by examining the causes of fluctuations in the level of *aggregate demand*.
2. A major part of the Keynesian explanation of the business cycle is the instability of investment. The accelerator theory explains this instability. It relates the level of investment to *changes* in national income and consumer demand. An initial increase in consumer demand can result in a very large percentage increase in investment; but as soon as the rise in consumer demand begins to level off, investment will fall; and even a slight fall in consumer demand can reduce investment to virtually zero.
3. The accelerator effect will be dampened by the carrying of stocks, the cautiousness of firms, forward planning by firms and the inability of producer goods industries to supply the capital equipment.
4. The interaction of the multiplier and accelerator will cause cycles.
5. Keynesians identify other causes of cyclical fluctuations, such as cycles in the holding of stocks, time lags, 'bandwagon' effects, ceilings and floors to output, echo effects, swings in government policy and random shocks.

END OF CHAPTER QUESTIONS

1. An economy is currently in equilibrium. The following figures refer to elements in its national income accounts.

	£ billions
Consumption (total)	60
Investment	5
Government expenditure	8
Imports	10
Exports	7

(a) What is the current equilibrium level of national income?

(b) What is the level of injections?

(c) What is the level of withdrawals?

(d) Assuming that tax revenues are £7 billion, how much is the level of saving?

(e) If national income now rose to £80 billion and, as a result, the consumption of domestically produced goods rose to £58 billion, what is the mpc_d?

(f) What is the value of the multiplier?

(g) Given an initial level of national income of £80 billion, now assume that spending on exports rises by £4 billion, spending on investment rises by £1 billion, whilst government expenditure falls by £2 billion. By how much will national income change?

(h) Given this new level of national income, assume that full employment is achieved at a national income of £100 billion. Is there an inflationary or a deflationary gap?

(i) What is the size of this gap?

2. What is the relationship between the *mpc*, the mpc_d and the *mpw*?
3. Why will the short-run consumption function be different from the long-run consumption function?
4. Construct a table similar to Table 16.2 (on page 465), only this time assume that the mpc_d is 3/4. Show that national income will increase by £640 million.
5. Assume that the multiplier has a value of 3. Now assume that the government decides to increase aggregate demand in an attempt to reduce unemployment. It raises government expenditure by £100 million with no increase in taxes. Firms, anticipating a rise in their sales, increase investment by £200 million, of which £50 million consists of purchases of foreign machinery. How much will national income rise? (Assume *ceteris paribus*.)
6. What factors could explain why some countries have a higher multiplier than others?
7. How can the interaction of the multiplier and accelerator explain cyclical fluctuations in national income?
8. Why is it difficult to predict the size of the accelerator?

Additional case studies on the book's website (www.pearsoned.co.uk/sloman)

16.1 **Keynes' views on the consumption function.** An analysis of how the assumptions made by Keynes affect the shape of the consumption function.

16.2 **The relationship between income and consumption.** This examines three different theories of the consumption function – the absolute income hypothesis, the relative income hypothesis and the permanent income hypothesis. Each one is based on different assumptions about consumer behaviour.

16.3 **The multiplier/accelerator interaction.** A numerical example showing how the interaction of the multiplier and accelerator can cause cycles in economic activity.

16.4 **Heavenly cycles.** An examination of the claim by Jevons in the late nineteenth century that the business cycle depends on the sunspot cycle!

16.5 **The phases of the business cycle.** A demand-side analysis of the factors contributing to each of the four phases.

WEBSITES RELEVANT TO CHAPTERS 15 AND 16

Numbers and sections refer to websites listed in the Web Appendix and hotlinked from this book's website at www.pearsoned.co.uk/sloman.

- For news articles relevant to this and the previous chapter, see the *Economics News Articles* link from the book's website.
- For general news on national economies and the international economy, see websites in section A, and particularly A1–5. See also links to newspapers worldwide in A38, 39, 43 and 44, and the news search feature in Google at A41. See also links to economics news in A42.
- For information on the development of ideas, see C12, 18; also see links under *Methodology and History of Economic Thought* in C14; links to economists in I4 and 17. See also sites I7 and 11 > *Economic Systems and Theories > History of Economic Thought.*
- For data on economic growth, employment and the business cycle, see links in B1 or 2; also see B4 and 12. For UK data, see B3, 34 and 36. For EU data, see G1 > *The Statistical Annex.* For US data, see *Current economic indicators* in B5 and the *Data* section of B17. For international data, see B15, 21, 24, 31, 33 and 35. For links to data sets, see B28; I14.
- For a model of the economy (based on the Treasury model), see *The Virtual Economy* (site D1). In addition to the model, where you can devise your own Budget, there are worksheets and outlines of theories and the work of famous economists. See also *The Virtual Chancellor* (D10).
- For student resources relevant to this chapter, see sites C1–7, 9, 10, 19.

Chapter 17

Money and Interest Rates

In this chapter and the next, we are going to look at the special role that *money* plays in the economy. Changes in the amount of money can have a powerful effect on all the major macroeconomic indicators, such as inflation, unemployment, economic growth, interest rates, exchange rates and the balance of payments.

But why do changes in the money supply affect the economy? The answer is that the supply of money and the demand for money between them determine the *rate of interest*, and this has a crucial impact on aggregate demand and the performance of the economy generally. In section 17.5 we shall see just how this process works.

First we define what is meant by money and examine its functions. Then in sections 17.2 and 17.3 we look at the operation of the financial sector of the economy and its role in determining the supply of money.

We then turn to look at the demand for money. Here we are not asking how much money people would like. The answer to that would probably be 'as much as possible'! What we are asking is: how much of people's assets do they want to hold in the form of money?

Finally, we put supply and demand together to see how interest rates are determined.

CHAPTER MAP

17.1 THE MEANING AND FUNCTIONS OF MONEY

Before going any further we must define precisely what we mean by 'money' – not as easy a task as it sounds. Money is more than just notes and coin. In fact the main component of a country's money supply is not cash, but deposits in banks and other financial institutions. Only a very small proportion of these deposits are kept by the banks in their safes or tills in the form of cash. The bulk of the deposits appear merely as bookkeeping entries in the banks' accounts.

This may sound very worrying. Will a bank have enough cash to meet its customers' demands? The answer is yes. Only a small fraction of a bank's total deposits will be withdrawn at any one time, and banks always make sure that they have the ability to meet their customers' demands. The chances of banks running out of cash are practically nil. What is more, the bulk of all but very small transactions are not conducted in cash at all. By the use of cheques, credit cards and debit cards, most money is simply transferred from the purchaser's to the seller's bank account without the need for first withdrawing it in cash.

What items should be included in the definition of money? To answer this we need to identify the *functions* of money.

The functions of money

The main purpose of money is for buying and selling goods, services and assets: i.e. as a 'medium of exchange'. It also has three other important functions. Let us examine each in turn.

A medium of exchange

In a subsistence economy, where individuals make their own clothes, grow their own food, provide their own entertainments, etc., people do not need money. If people want to exchange any goods, they will do so by barter. In other words, they will do swaps with other people.

The complexities of a modern developed economy, however, make barter totally impractical for most purposes (see Web Case 17.1). Someone may have something you want, but they may not want what you have to offer them in return. What is more, under a system of capitalism where people are employed by others to do a specialist task, it would be totally impractical for people to be paid in food, clothes, cars, electrical goods, etc. What is necessary is a ***medium of exchange*** that is generally acceptable as a means of payment for goods and services and as a means of payment for labour and other factor services. 'Money' is any such medium.

Money as a medium of exchange is in effect being used as a 'means of settling a debt'. When you buy a good or service, you thereby incur a debt. This must be settled with a money payment. The debt can be settled immediately (e.g. when you buy something in a shop with cash) or later (e.g. when you buy something on credit and make the payment, say, at the end of the month).

To be a suitable physical means of exchange, money must be light enough to carry around, must come in a number of denominations, large and small, and must not be easy to forge (the attributes of money are explored in Web Case 17.2). Alternatively, money must be in a form that enables it to be transferred *indirectly* through some acceptable mechanism.

Definition

Medium of exchange Something that is acceptable in exchange for goods and services.

EXPLORING ECONOMICS — BOX 17.1

MONEY SUPPLY, NATIONAL INCOME AND NATIONAL WEALTH

Don't confuse the supply of money with the money value of national income. National income is a *flow* concept. It measures the value of the nation's output per year. Money supply, by contrast, is a *stock* concept. At any one point in time, there is a given amount of money in the economy.

But what if the money supply increases? Will the national income increase by that amount? No, because the extra money will usually be spent more than once on final goods and services. The rise in national income would thus be greater than the rise in money supply. On the other hand, some of the extra spending may simply result in higher prices. *Real* national income will rise by less than national income measured at current prices.

So if money supply is not the same as national *income*, is it the same as national *wealth*? After all, wealth is a stock concept. Again the answer is no. The nation's wealth consists of its *real* assets: land, buildings, capital equipment, works of art, etc. People may well hold part of their wealth in the form of money, it is true, but this is not wealth as far as the nation is concerned: if it were, the government could make us all wealthier by simply printing more money! Money represents wealth to the individual only to the extent that it represents a claim on *real* goods and services. It has nothing to do with national wealth.

For example, money in the form of bookkeeping entries in bank accounts can be transferred by the use of cheques, debit cards, standing orders and direct debits.

A means of storing wealth

People need a means whereby the fruits of *today's* labour can be used to purchase goods and services in the *future*. People need to be able to store their wealth: they want a means of saving. Money is one such medium in which to hold wealth. It can be saved.

A means of evaluation

Money allows the value of goods, services or assets to be compared. The value of goods is expressed in terms of prices, and prices are expressed in money terms. Money also allows dissimilar things, such as a person's wealth or a company's assets, to be added up. Similarly, a country's GDP is expressed in money terms. Money thus serves as a 'unit of account'.

Why may money prices give a poor indication of the value of goods and services?

A means of establishing the value of future claims and payments

People often want to agree *today* the price of some *future* payment. For example, workers and managers will want to agree the wage rate for the coming year. Firms will want to sign contracts with their suppliers specifying the price of raw materials and other supplies. Money prices are the most convenient means of measuring future claims.

What should count as money?

What items, then, should be included in the definition of money? Unfortunately, there is no sharp borderline between money and non-money.

Cash (notes and coin) obviously counts as money. It readily meets all the functions of money. Goods (fridges, cars and cabbages) do not count as money.

But what about various financial assets, such as bank accounts, building society accounts and stocks and shares? Do they count as money? The answer is 'It depends': it depends on how narrowly money is defined.

Narrow definitions of money include only items that can be spent directly, such as cash and current accounts in banks (since they can be spent directly by using cheques or debit cards). Note that cheques, debit cards and credit cards, although they are used to pay for goods directly, do not themselves count as money. Rather it is the balance in the account on which they are drawn that counts as money.

Broad definitions of money also include various items such as deposit and savings accounts in banks that cannot be spent directly, but which can nevertheless be readily converted into cash.

In terms of the broad definition of money, would a deposit account passbook count as money?

In order to understand the significance of different measures of the money supply and the ways in which money supply can be controlled, it is first necessary to look at the various types of account in which money can be held and at the various financial institutions involved.

Section summary

1. Money's main function is as a medium of exchange. In addition, it is a means of storing wealth, a means of evaluation and a means of establishing the value of future claims and payments.
2. Narrow definitions of money include items that can be directly spent: cash and money in cheque-book and debit-card accounts. Broad definitions of money also include items that cannot be directly spent but can, nevertheless, be readily converted into cash.

17.2 THE FINANCIAL SYSTEM

The role of the financial sector

Banks and other financial institutions are known as ***financial intermediaries***. They all have the common function of providing a link between those who wish to lend and those who wish to borrow. In other words, they act as the mechanism whereby the supply of funds is matched to the demand for funds. In this process, they provide four important services.

KI 21 p 207

Expert advice

Financial intermediaries can advise their customers on financial matters: on the best way of investing their funds

Definitions

Narrow definitions of money Items of money that can be spent directly (cash and money in cheque-book / debit-card accounts).

Broad definitions of money Items in narrow definitions plus other items that can be readily converted into cash.

Financial intermediaries The general name for financial institutions (banks, building societies, etc.) which act as a means of channelling funds from depositors to borrowers and on alternative ways of obtaining finance. This should help to encourage the flow of savings and the efficient use of them.

Expertise in channelling funds

Financial intermediaries have the specialist knowledge to be able to channel funds to those areas that yield the highest return. This too encourages the flow of savings as it gives savers the confidence that their savings will earn a good rate of interest. Financial intermediaries also help to ensure that projects that are potentially profitable will be able to obtain finance. They help to increase allocative efficiency.

Maturity transformation

Many people and firms want to borrow money for long periods of time, and yet many depositors want to be able to withdraw their deposits on demand or at short notice. If people had to rely on borrowing directly from other people, there would be a problem here: the lenders would not be prepared to lend for a long enough period. If you had £100 000 of savings, would you be prepared to lend it to a friend to buy a house if the friend was going to take 25 years to pay it back? Even if there was no risk whatsoever of your friend defaulting, most people would be totally unwilling to tie up their savings for so long. This is where a bank or building society comes in. It borrows money from a vast number of small savers, who are able to withdraw their money on demand or at short notice. It then lends the money to house purchasers for a long period of time by granting mortgages (typically these are paid back over 20 to 30 years). This process whereby financial intermediaries lend for longer periods of time than they borrow is known as ***maturity transformation***. They are able to do this because with a large number of depositors it is highly unlikely that they would all want to withdraw their deposits at the same time. On any one day, although some people will be withdrawing money, others will be making new deposits.

Risk transformation

You may be unwilling to lend money directly to another person in case they do not pay up. You are unwilling to take the risk. Financial intermediaries, however, by lending to large numbers of people, are willing to risk the odd case of default. They can absorb the loss because of the interest they earn on all the other loans. This spreading of risks is known as ***risk transformation***. What is more, financial intermediaries may have the expertise to be able to assess just how risky a loan is.

Which of the above are examples of economies of scale?

In addition to channelling funds from depositors to borrowers, certain financial institutions have another important function. This is to provide a means of transmitting payments. Thus by the use of cheques, debit cards, credit cards, standing orders, etc., money can be transferred from one person or institution to another without having to rely on cash.

The banking system

Types of bank

By far the largest element of money supply is bank deposits. It is not surprising, then, that banks play an absolutely crucial role in the monetary system. Banks can be divided into two main groups: *retail banks* and *wholesale banks*.

Retail banks. ***Retail banks*** are the familiar high street banks, such as Barclays, Lloyds/TSB, HSBC and National Westminster, and ex-building societies such as the Abbey National and HBOS (Halifax). They specialise in providing branch banking facilities to members of the general public, but they also lend to business, albeit often on a short-term basis.

Their business is in ***retail deposits and loans***. These are deposits and loans made through their branch network at published rates of interest. The branches are like 'retail outlets' for banking services.

Wholesale banks. The other major category of banks are the ***wholesale banks***. These include *investment banks* such as Morgan Stanley, Rothschild, S G Hambros and Goldman Sachs. They often act as 'brokers', arranging loans for companies from a number of different sources. They also offer financial advice to industry and provide assistance to firms in raising new capital through the issue of new shares.

Wholesale banks also include many overseas banks, especially Japanese and American. These have expanded their business in the UK and the rest of Europe enormously in recent years. Their major specialism is the finance of

Definitions

Maturity transformation The transformation of deposits into loans of a longer maturity.

Risk transformation The process whereby banks can spread the risks of lending by having a large number of borrowers.

Retail banks 'High street banks'. Banks operating extensive branch networks and dealing directly with the general public with published interest rates and charges.

Retail deposits and loans Deposits and loans made through bank/building society branches at published interest rates.

Wholesale banks Banks specialising in large-scale deposits and loans and dealing mainly with companies.

international trade and capital movements, and they deal extensively in the foreign exchange market. Most of their deposits are in foreign currencies.

They also include *finance houses*, which specialise in lending to businesses and in providing hire-purchase finance for the purchase of consumer durables, such as cars, furniture and electrical goods.

They are called wholesale banks because they specialise in receiving large deposits from and making large loans to industry and other financial institutions (normally of a minimum of £250 000): these are known as ***wholesale deposits and loans***. These may be for short periods of time to account for the non-matching of a firm's payments and receipts from its business. They may be for longer periods of time, for various investment purposes. These wholesale deposits and loans are very large sums of money. Banks thus compete against each other for them and negotiate individual terms with the firm to suit the firm's particular requirements. The rates of interest negotiated will reflect the current market rates of interest and the terms of the particular loan/deposit. Very large loans to firms are often divided ('syndicated') among several banks.

Banks also lend and borrow wholesale funds to and from each other. Banks that are short of funds borrow large sums from others with surplus funds, thus ensuring that the banking sector as a whole does not have funds surplus to its requirements. The rate at which they lend to each other is known as the IBOR (inter-bank offer rate). The IBOR has a major influence on the other rates that banks charge. In the eurozone, the IBOR is known as Euribor. In the UK, it is known as LIBOR (where 'L' stands for 'London').

Building societies

These UK institutions specialise in granting loans (mortgages) for house purchase. They compete for the savings of the general public through a network of high street branches. Unlike retail banks, they are not public limited companies, their 'shares' being the deposits made by their investors. In recent years, many of the building societies have converted to banks (including all the really large building societies except the Nationwide).

In the past, there was a clear distinction between banks and building societies. Today, however, they have become much more similar, with building societies now offering current account facilities and cash machines, and retail banks granting mortgages. This is all part of a trend away from the narrow specialisation of the past and towards the offering of a wider and wider range of services. This has been helped by a process of ***financial deregulation***. Inevitably, as this trend continues, the services offered by the various institutions will increasingly overlap.

Deposit taking and lending

KI 23 p251

Banks are in the business of deposit taking and lending. To understand this, we must distinguish between banks' *liabilities* and *assets*. The total liabilities and assets for the UK banks are set out in a balance sheet in Table 17.1.

Liabilities

Customers' deposits in banks (and other deposit-taking institutions such as building societies) are ***liabilities*** to these institutions. This means simply that the customers have the claim on these deposits and thus the institutions are liable to meet the claims.

There are four major types of deposit: sight deposits, time deposits, certificates of deposit and 'repos'.

Sight deposits. ***Sight deposits*** are any deposits that can be withdrawn on demand by the depositor without penalty. In the past, sight accounts did not pay interest. Today, however, there are some sight accounts that do.

The most familiar form of sight deposits are current accounts at banks. Depositors are issued with cheque books and/or debit cards (e.g. Switch or Connect) that enable them to spend the money directly without first having to go to the bank and draw the money out in cash. In the case of debit cards, the person's account is electronically debited when the purchase is made and the card is 'swiped' across the machine. This process is known as EFTPOS (electronic funds transfer at point of sale).

An important feature of current accounts is that banks often allow customers to be overdrawn. That is, they can draw on their account and make payments to other people in excess of the amount of money they have deposited.

Time deposits. ***Time deposits*** require notice of withdrawal. However, they normally pay a higher rate of interest than sight accounts. With some types of account, a depositor can withdraw a certain amount of money on demand, but there will be a penalty of so many days' lost interest. They are not cheque-book or debit-card accounts, although

Definitions

Wholesale deposits and loans Large-scale deposits and loans made by and to firms at negotiated interest rates.

Financial deregulation The removal of or reduction in legal rules and regulations governing the activities of financial institutions.

Liabilities All legal claims for payment that outsiders have on an institution.

Sight deposits Deposits that can be withdrawn on demand without penalty.

Time deposits Deposits that require notice of withdrawal or where a penalty is charged for withdrawals on demand.

Table 17.1 Balance sheet of UK banks: January 2005

Sterling liabilities	£bn	%	Sterling assets	£bn	%
Sight deposits		(35.7)	Notes and coin	5.3	(0.2)
UK banks, etc.	120.3		Balances with Bank of England		(0.1)
UK public sector	9.9		Operational deposits	0.9	
UK private sector	567.2		Cash ratio deposits	1.8	
Non-residents	71.6		Market loans		(24.8)
Time deposits		(34.6)	UK banks, etc.	362.1	
UK banks, etc.	234.9		CDs, etc.	62.6	
UK public sector	10.8		Non-residents	110.9	
UK private sector	320.9		Bills of exchange	15.4	(0.7)
Non-residents	178.1		Reverse repos	148.2	(6.9)
Certificates of deposit (CDs)	163.3	(7.6)	Investments	158.9	(7.4)
Repos	157.7	(7.3)	Advances	1213.2	(56.2)
Other	318.6	(14.8)	Miscellaneous	79.1	(3.7)
Total sterling liabilities	**2153.3**	(100.0)	**Total sterling assets**	**2158.4**	(100.0)
Liabilities in other currencies	2791.8		Assets in other currencies	2786.7	
Total liabilities	4945.1		Total assets	4945.1	

Source: based on data in Table B1.2 of *Bankstats* (Bank of England).

some allow customers to use cash cards. The most familiar form of time deposits are the deposit and savings accounts in banks and the various savings accounts in building societies. No overdraft facilities exist with time deposits.

A substantial proportion of time deposits are from the *banking sector*: i.e. other banks and other financial institutions. Inter-bank lending has grown over the years as money markets have become deregulated and as deposits are moved from one currency to another to take advantage of different rates of interest between different countries. A large proportion of overseas deposits are from foreign banks.

Certificates of deposit. ***Certificates of deposit*** are certificates issued by banks to customers (usually firms) for large deposits of a fixed term (e.g. £100 000 for 18 months). They can be sold by one customer to another, and thus provide a means whereby the holders can get money quickly if they need it without the *banks* that have issued the CD having to supply the money. (This makes them relatively 'liquid' to the depositor but 'illiquid' to the bank: see below and Box 17.2.) The use of CDs has grown rapidly in recent years. Their use by firms has meant that, at a wholesale level, sight accounts have become *less* popular.

Sale and repurchase agreements (repos). If banks have a temporary shortage of funds, they can sell some of their financial assets to other banks or to the central bank – the Bank of England in the UK and the European Central Bank in the eurozone (see below) – and later repurchase them on some agreed date, typically a fortnight later. These ***sale and repurchase agreements (repos)*** are in effect a form of loan – the bank borrowing for a period of time using some of its financial assets as the security for the loan. The most usual assets to use in this way are government bonds, normally called 'gilt-edged securities' or simply 'gilts' (see below). Sale and repurchase agreements involving gilts are known as *gilt repos*. As we shall see, gilt repos play a vital role in the operation of monetary policy.

Assets

A bank's financial ***assets*** are its claims on others. There are three main categories of assets.

Cash and operational balances in the central bank (Bank of England in the UK, ECB in the eurozone). Banks need to hold a certain amount of their assets as cash. This is largely used to meet the day-to-day demands of customers. They also keep 'operational balances' in the central bank.

Definitions

Certificates of deposit (CDs) Certificates issued by banks for fixed-term interest-bearing deposits. They can be resold by the owner to another party.

Sale and repurchase agreements (repos) An agreement between two financial institutions whereby one in effect borrows from another by selling its assets, agreeing to buy them back (repurchase them) at a fixed price and on a fixed date.

Assets Possessions, or claims held on others.

These are like the banks' own current accounts and are used for clearing purposes (i.e. for settling the day-to-day payments between banks). They can be withdrawn in cash on demand. In the UK, banks are also required to deposit a small fraction of their assets as 'cash ratio deposits' with the Bank of England. These cannot be drawn on demand.

Both cash and operational balances, however, earn no interest for banks. The vast majority of banks' assets are therefore in the form of various types of loan – to individuals and firms, to other financial institutions and to the government. These are 'assets' because they represent claims that the banks have on other people. Loans can be grouped into two types: short and long term.

Short-term loans. These are in the form of *market loans*, *bills of exchange* or *reverse repos*. The market for these various types of loan is known as the ***money market***.

- ***Market loans*** are made primarily to other banks or financial institutions. They consist of (a) money lent 'at call' (i.e. reclaimable on demand or at 24 hours' notice); (b) money lent 'at short notice' (i.e. money lent for a few days); (c) CDs (i.e. certificates of deposits made in other banks or building societies).
- ***Bills of exchange*** are loans either to companies (***commercial bills***) or to the government (***Treasury bills***). These are, in effect, an IOU, with the company issuing them (in the case of commercial bills), or the Bank of England on behalf of the government (in the case of Treasury bills), promising to pay the holder a specified sum on a particular date (the 'maturity date'), typically three months later. Since bills do not pay interest, they are sold below their face value (at a 'discount') but KI 24 p 253 redeemed on maturity at the face value. This enables the purchaser, in this case the bank, to earn a return.

  The price paid for bills will depend on demand and supply. For example, the more Treasury bills that the Bank of England offers for sale at its weekly tender of bills (i.e. the higher the supply), the lower will be their equilibrium price, and hence the higher will be their rate of return (i.e. their rate of interest, or 'rate of discount').

  Normally, a bank will buy *commercial* bills only if they have been first 'accepted' by another financial institution (typically an investment bank). This means that the investment bank will redeem the bill (i.e. pay up) on the maturity date, if the firm issuing the bill defaults on payment. Of course the investment bank charges for this insurance (or 'underwriting'). Bills that have been accepted in this way are known as ***bank bills***.
- ***Reverse repos***. When a sale and repurchase agreement is made, the financial institution *purchasing* the assets (e.g. gilts) is, in effect, giving a short-term loan. The other party agrees to buy back the assets (i.e. pay back the loan) on a set date. The assets temporarily held by the bank making the loan are known as 'reverse repos'.

Longer-term loans. These consist primarily of loans to customers, both personal customers and businesses. These loans, also known as *advances*, are of four main types: fixed-term (repayable in instalments over a set number of years – typically, six months to five years), overdrafts (often for an unspecified term), outstanding balances on credit-card accounts and mortgages (typically for 25 years).

Banks also make *investments*. These are partly in government bonds (gilts), which are effectively loans to the government. The government sells bonds, which then pay a fixed sum each year as interest. Once issued, they can then be bought and sold on the stock exchange. Banks are normally only prepared to buy bonds that have less than five years to maturity (the date when the government redeems the bonds). Banks also invest in various subsidiary financial institutions and in building societies.

Liquidity and profitability

As we have seen, banks keep a range of liabilities and assets. The balance of items in this range is influenced by two important considerations: profitability and liquidity.

Profitability. Profits are made by lending money out at a higher rate of interest than that paid to depositors. The average interest rate received by banks on their assets is greater than that paid by them on their liabilities.

Definitions

Money market The market for short-term loans and deposits.

Market loans Short-term loans (e.g. money at call and short notice).

Bills of exchange Certificates promising to repay a stated amount on a certain date, typically three months from the issue of the bill. Bills pay no interest as such, but are sold at a discount and redeemed at face value, thereby earning a rate of discount for the purchaser.

Commercial bills Bills of exchange issued by firms.

Treasury bills Bills of exchange issued by the Bank of England on behalf of the government. They are a means whereby the government raises short-term finance.

Bank bills Bills that have been accepted by another financial institution and hence insured against default.

Reverse repos Gilts or other assets that are purchased under a sale and repurchase agreement. They become an asset to the purchaser.

Liquidity The ease with which an asset can be converted into cash without loss.

EXPLORING ECONOMICS **BOX 17.2**

SECONDARY MARKETING

Or how to make illiquid assets liquid

Banks have the two conflicting aims of liquidity and profitability. They must hold sufficient liquid assets to be able to meet any demands from their customers and avoid a crisis of confidence. But they want to hold illiquid assets in order to make a profit – after all, the less liquid the asset, the greater the interest the bank is likely to be able to charge. The greater their ratio of illiquid assets to liquid ones, the greater their profit.

This conflict can be put another way. This is in terms of the size of the gap between the average maturity of a bank's assets and liabilities.

For reasons of profitability, the banks will want to 'borrow short' and 'lend long'. In other words, they will want to receive deposits that can be withdrawn instantly (like current accounts) or at only short notice. The benefits of liquidity to their customers will involve banks only having to pay out low rates of interest (or in the case of certain types of current account, none at all). But banks will want to grant *loans* with a much longer maturity (e.g. two-year personal loans), since these are charged at much higher interest rates than banks have to pay to their depositors. The difference in the average maturity of loans and deposits is known as the *maturity gap*.

For reasons of *profitability*, the banks will want a large maturity gap between loans and deposits. For reasons of *liquidity*, however, banks will want a relatively small gap: if there is a sudden withdrawal of deposits, banks will need to be able to call in enough loans.

The obvious way of reconciling the two conflicting aims of liquidity and profitability is by compromise: to hold a mixture of liquid and illiquid assets – to have a 'reasonable' maturity gap.

There is another way, however, whereby banks can reconcile these aims, whereby they can close the gap for *liquidity* purposes, but maintain the gap for *profitability* purposes. This is by the *secondary marketing* of assets.

Certificates of deposit (CDs) are a good example of secondary marketing. CDs are issued for fixed-period deposits in a bank (e.g. one year) at an agreed interest rate. The bank does not have to repay the deposit until the year is up. CDs are thus illiquid liabilities for the bank, and they allow it to increase the proportion of illiquid assets without having a dangerously high maturity gap. But the holder of the CD in the meantime can sell it to someone else (through a broker). It is thus liquid to the holder.

Because CDs are liquid to the holder, they can be issued at a relatively *low* rate of interest and thus allow the bank to increase its profitability.

Another example is when a bank sells some of its assets to another bank. The advantage to the first bank is that it gains liquidity. The advantage to the second bank is that it gains profitable assets (assuming that it has spare liquidity).

The effect of secondary marketing is to reduce the liquidity ratio that banks feel they need to keep. It has the effect of increasing their maturity gap.

There are dangers to the banking system, however, from secondary marketing. To the extent that banks individually feel that they can operate with a lower liquidity ratio, so this will lead to a lower *national* liquidity ratio. This may lead to an excessive expansion of credit (illiquid assets) in times of economic boom. Also, there is an increased danger of banking collapse. If one bank fails, this will have a knock-on effect on those banks that have purchased its assets.

Is it possible to argue that secondary marketing allows a lower safe average liquidity ratio? (Clue: the answer has to do with risk transformation.)

Liquidity. The ***liquidity*** of an asset is the ease with which it can be converted into cash without loss. Cash itself, by definition, is perfectly liquid.

Some assets, such as money lent at call to other financial institutions, are highly liquid. Although not actually cash, these assets can be converted into cash on demand with no financial penalty.

Other assets, such as gilts, can be converted into cash straight away by selling them on the Stock Exchange, but with the possibility of some financial loss, given that their market price fluctuates. Such assets, therefore, are not as liquid as money at call.

Other assets are much less liquid. Personal loans to the general public or mortgages for house purchase can be redeemed by the bank only as each instalment is paid. Other advances for fixed periods are repaid only at the end of that period.

Banks must always be able to meet the demands of their customers for withdrawals of money. To do this, they must hold sufficient cash or other assets that can be readily turned into cash. In other words, banks must maintain sufficient liquidity.

?

1. *If a bank buys a £500 000 Treasury bill at the start of its 91-day life for £480 000, at roughly what price could it sell it to another financial institution after 45 days? Why is it not possible to predict that precise price when the bill is first purchased?*
2. *Suppose there were a sudden surge in demand for cash from the general public. Would the existence of inter-bank market loans help to meet the demand in any way?*

The balance between profitability and liquidity

Profitability is the major aim of banks and most other financial institutions. However, the aims of profitability and liquidity tend to conflict. In general, the more liquid an asset, the less profitable it is, and vice versa. Personal and business loans to customers are profitable to banks, but highly illiquid. Cash is totally liquid, but earns no profit. Thus financial institutions like to hold a range of assets with varying degrees of liquidity and profitability.

The ratio of an institution's liquid assets to total assets is known as its ***liquidity ratio***. For example, if a bank had £100 million of assets, of which £10 million were liquid and £90 million were illiquid, the bank would have a 10 per cent liquidity ratio. If a financial institution's liquidity ratio is too high, it will make too little profit. If the ratio is too low, there will be the risk that customers' demands may not be able to be met: this would cause a crisis of confidence and possible closure. Institutions thus have to make a judgement as to what liquidity ratio is best – one that is neither too high nor too low.

Balances in the central bank, short-term loans (i.e. those listed above) and government bonds with less than 12 months to maturity would normally be regarded as liquid assets.

? *Why are government bonds that still have 11 months to run regarded as liquid, whereas overdrafts granted for a few weeks are not?*

The central bank

The Bank of England is the UK's central bank. The European Central Bank (ECB) is the central bank for the countries using the euro. The Federal Reserve Bank of America (the Fed) is the USA's central bank. All countries have a central bank and they fulfil two vital roles in the economy.

The first is to oversee the whole monetary system and ensure that banks and other financial institutions operate as stably and as efficiently as possible.

Definition

Liquidity ratio The proportion of a bank's total assets held in liquid form.

The second is to act as the government's agent, both as its banker and in carrying out monetary policy. The Bank of England traditionally worked in very close liaison with the Treasury, and there used to be regular meetings between the Governor of the Bank of England and the Chancellor of the Exchequer. Although the Bank may have disagreed with Treasury policy, it always carried it out. With the election of the Labour government in 1997, however, the Bank of England was given independence to decide the course of monetary policy. In particular, this meant that the Bank of England and not the government would now decide interest rates.

Another example of an independent central bank is the European Central Bank, which operates the monetary policy for the eurozone countries. Similarly, the Fed is independent of both the President and Congress, and its chairman is generally regarded as having great power in determining the country's economic policy. Although the degree of independence of central banks from government varies considerably around the world, there has been a general move in recent years to make central banks more independent.

If the UK adopts the euro, there will be a much reduced role for the Bank of England. At present, however, within its two broad roles, it has a number of different functions. Although we will consider the case of the Bank of England, the same principles apply to other central banks.

It issues notes

The Bank of England is the sole issuer of banknotes in England and Wales. (In Scotland and Northern Ireland, retail banks issue notes.) The issue of notes is done through the Issue Department, which organises their printing. This is one of two departments of the Bank of England. The other is the Banking Department. Table 17.2 shows the balance sheets of these two departments on 26 January 2005. As you can see from the balance sheet for the Issue Department, the note issue is backed by government and other securities.

The amount of banknotes issued by the Bank of England depends largely on the demand for notes from the general

Table 17.2 Balance sheet of the Bank of England: 26 January 2005

Liabilities	£m	Assets	£m
Issue Department			
Notes in circulation	35 192	Government securities	13 370
Notes in Banking Department	8	Other securities	21 830
	35 200		35 200
Banking Department			
Public deposits	769	Government securities	1 808
Bankers' deposits	2 586	Advances and other accounts	13 788
Reserves and other accounts	19 359	Premises, equipment, etc.	7 124
		Notes and coin from Issue Department	9
	22 729		22 729

Source: based on data in Table B1.1, *Bankstats* (Bank of England).

public. If people draw more cash from their bank accounts, the banks will have to draw more cash from their balances in the Bank of England. These balances are held in the Banking Department. The Banking Department will thus have to acquire more notes from the Issue Department, which will simply print more in exchange for extra government or other securities supplied by the Banking Department. Thus the amount of notes in circulation is always more at Christmas time.

It acts as a bank

To the government. It keeps the two major government accounts: the 'Exchequer' and the 'National Loans Fund'. Taxation and government spending pass through the Exchequer. Government borrowing and lending pass through the National Loans Fund. The government tends to keep its deposits in the Bank of England (the *public deposits* item in the balance sheet) to a minimum. If the deposits begin to build up (from taxation), the government will probably spend them on paying back government debt. If, on the other hand, it runs short of money, it will simply borrow more.

To banks. The *bankers' deposits* item in the balance sheet refers to banks' cash ratio and operational balances (see Table 17.1). As we have seen, the operational balances are used for clearing purposes between the banks and to provide them with a source of liquidity.

To overseas central banks. These are deposits of sterling (or euros in the case of the ECB) made by overseas authorities as part of their official reserves and/or for purposes of intervening in the foreign exchange market in order to influence the exchange rate of their currency.

It manages the government's borrowing programme

Whenever the government runs a budget deficit (i.e. spends more than it receives in tax and other revenues), it will have to finance that deficit by borrowing. It can borrow by issuing bonds (gilts), National Savings certificates or Treasury bills. The Bank of England organises this borrowing. Even when the government runs a budget surplus, the Bank of England will still have to manage the national debt (the accumulated borrowing from the past). The reason is that old bonds will be maturing and new issues of bonds will probably be necessary to replace them.

When an old issue of bonds is approaching maturity, the Bank of England will probably enter the market to buy them back over a number of weeks or months, rather than waiting to the maturity date and then suddenly releasing a large amount of liquidity into the economy.

When a new issue of bonds is made, the Bank of England will set a minimum price somewhat below the £100 face value and then invite tenders for these bonds above or at the minimum price. It will allocate them in descending order from the highest-priced bid to the lowest. Any unsold bonds (known as 'tap stock') will then be released on to the market in an orderly way at a price set by the Bank of England. Any temporary shortfall of money for the government is met by issuing Treasury bills.

The issuing of bonds and bills will also depend on the operation of monetary policy. This is examined in Chapter 19.

It oversees the activities of banks and other financial institutions

It advises banks on good banking practice. It discusses government policy with them and reports back to the government. It requires all recognised banks to maintain adequate liquidity: this is called ***prudential control***. Since May 1997, the Bank of England has ceased to be responsible for the detailed supervision of banks' activities. This responsibility has passed to the Financial Services Authority (FSA).

It provides liquidity, as necessary, to banks

It ensures that there is always an adequate supply of liquidity to meet the legitimate demands of depositors in banks. As we shall see below, it does this through the discount and repo markets.

It operates the government's monetary and exchange rate policy

Monetary policy. The Bank of England's Monetary Policy Committee (MPC) sets interest rates (the rate on gilt repos) at its monthly meetings. This nine-member committee consists of four experts appointed by the Chancellor of the Exchequer and four senior members of the Bank of England, plus the Governor in the chair. By careful management of the issue and repurchasing of gilts and Treasury bills, the Bank of England then keeps interest rates at the level decided by the MPC. It also, in the process, influences the size of the money supply. Details of this are given in Chapter 19.

Exchange rate policy. The Bank of England manages the country's gold and foreign currency reserves on behalf of the Treasury. This is done through the ***exchange equalisation account***. The Treasury sets the Bank an annual Remit for the management of the account (for example, setting a limit on changes in the level of reserves). By buying and selling foreign currencies on the foreign exchange market,

Definitions

Prudential control The insistence by the Bank of England that recognised banks maintain adequate liquidity.

Exchange equalisation account The gold and foreign exchange reserves account in the Bank of England

CASE STUDIES AND APPLICATIONS **BOX 17.3**

CHANGES IN THE BANKING INDUSTRY

Is bigger better?

There are considerable economies of scale in banking. These have resulted in a wave of mergers and takeovers. The process has been hastened by increasing deregulation in the banking industry, which has permitted banks to take on a whole range of functions.

The economies arise in the process of financial intermediation. Remember that intermediation involves providing a link between those who want to deposit money and those who want to borrow it. It involves matching the supply of funds to the demand for them.

If there were many small banks, much of their business would be in dealing with each other: in balancing inflows and outflows of funds between them. Even with computers, this would be a costly process and involve the banks having to maintain substantial reserves in case outflows exceeded inflows. With fewer bigger banks, however, an increased proportion of the flow of funds would be between their *own* customers and thus would not involve dealing with other banks. Thus reserves could be smaller as a percentage of total assets.

Also, as banks get bigger and the number of customers increases, so *net* withdrawals (positive or negative) diminish as a proportion of total deposits held. This, again, means that banks need to hold a smaller proportion of reserves: they can operate with a lower liquidity ratio. This increases banks' profitability, since cash reserves earn banks no money, and money at call earns a low rate.

Banks also benefit from economies of scope (see page 133). This means that they gain economies by diversifying into different but related activities. Thus traditional retail banks, such as Barclays and NatWest, have diversified into wholesale banking, stockbroking, discounting bills, insurance, foreign exchange dealing and a whole range of financial services to the corporate sector. This diversification not only reduces average costs, since customers can receive more than one service from the same premises, or through the same Internet site or telephone service, but it also reduces risk. If one part of the business became less profitable, this could be offset by increased profits from another.

Today it makes more sense to talk of retail or wholesale banking *activity*, rather than retail or wholesale banks. After all, the same banks are involved in both types of activity – and many more.

?

1. ***Are there any circumstances where diversification could lead to*** **increased** ***risks?***
2. ***To what extent are the lower costs associated with Internet banking attributable to economies of scale?***

the Bank of England can affect the exchange rate. For example, if there were a sudden selling of sterling (due, say, to bad trade figures and a resulting fear that the pound would depreciate), the Bank of England could help to prevent the pound from falling by using reserves to buy up pounds on the foreign exchange market. Intervention in the foreign exchange market is examined in detail in Chapter 24.

?

1. *Would it be possible for an economy to function without a central bank?*
2. *What effect would a substantial increase in the sale of government bonds and Treasury bills have on interest rates?*

The role of the London money market

It is through the London money market that the Bank of England exercises its control of the economy. The market deals in short-term lending and borrowing. It is normally divided into the 'discount' and 'repo' markets and the 'parallel' or 'complementary' market.

The discount and repo markets

The markets for bills of exchange (the discount market) and for repos play a crucial role in ensuring that banks have sufficient liquidity to meet all their needs.

Assume that bank customers start drawing out more cash. As a result, banks find themselves short of liquid assets. What can they do? The answer is that they borrow from the Bank of England. There are two ways in which this can be done.

The first is to enter a repo agreement, whereby the Bank of England buys gilts from the banks (thereby supplying them with money) on the condition that the banks buy the gilts back at a fixed price and on a fixed date, typically two weeks later. The repurchase price will be above the sale price. The difference is the equivalent of the interest that the banks are being charged for having what amounts to a loan from the Bank of England. The repurchase price (and hence the 'repo rate') is set by the Bank of England to reflect the rate chosen by the MPC (see section 19.2).

The second method is to sell Treasury bills back to the Bank of England before they have reached maturity (i.e. before the three months are up). This process is known as ***rediscounting***. The Bank of England will pay a price below

Definition

Rediscounting bills of exchange Buying bills before they reach maturity.

the face value, thus effectively charging interest to the banks. The price is set so that the 'rediscount rate' reflects the interest rate set by the Monetary Policy Committee.

In being prepared to rediscount bills or provide money through gilt repos, the Bank of England is thus the ultimate guarantor of sufficient liquidity in the monetary system and is known as ***lender of last resort***.

The need for banks to acquire liquidity in this way is not uncommon. It is generally a deliberate policy of the Bank of England to create a shortage of liquidity in the economy to force banks to obtain liquidity from it. But why should the Bank of England do this? It does it as a means of controlling interest rates. If the banks are forced to obtain liquidity from the Bank of England, they will be borrowing at the Bank of England's *chosen rate* (i.e. the repo rate). The banks will then have to gear their other rates to it, and other institutions will gear their rates to those of the banks.

The way in which the Bank of England creates a shortage of liquidity and the way in which it forces through changes in interest rates are examined in section 19.2 and Box 19.5 in particular.

The parallel money markets

The parallel money markets include the following:

- The inter-bank market (wholesale loans from one bank to another from one day to up to several months).
- The market for certificates of deposit.
- The inter-companies deposit market (short-term loans from one company to another arranged through the market).
- The foreign currencies market (dealings in foreign currencies deposited short term in London).
- The finance house market (short-term borrowing to finance hire purchase).
- The building society market (wholesale borrowing by the building societies).
- The commercial paper market (borrowing in sterling by companies, banks and other financial institutions by the issue of short-term (less than one year) 'promissory notes'. These, like bills of exchange, are sold at a discount and redeemed at their face value, but in the interim can be traded on the market at any time).

The parallel markets have grown in size and importance in recent years. The main reasons for this have been (a) the opening-up of markets to international dealing, given the abolition of exchange controls in 1979, (b) the deregulation of banking and money market dealing and (c) the volatility of interest rates and exchange rates, and thus the desire of banks to keep funds in a form that can be readily switched from one form of deposit to another, or from one currency to another. The main areas of growth have been in inter-bank deposits, certificates of deposit and the foreign currency markets.

Although the Bank of England does not deal directly in the parallel markets and does not provide 'last resort' lending facilities, it nevertheless closely monitors the various money market rates of interest and if necessary seeks to influence them, through its dealings in the discount and repo markets.

Why should Bank of England determination of the rate of interest in the discount and repo markets also influence rates of interest in the parallel markets?

Definition

Lender of last resort The role of the Bank of England as the guarantor of sufficient liquidity in the monetary system.

Section summary

1. Financial intermediaries include retail and wholesale banks and building societies. Between them they provide the following important functions: giving expert advice, channelling capital to areas of highest return, maturity transformation, risk transformation and the transmission of payments.
2. Banks' liabilities include both sight and time deposits. They also include certificates of deposit and repos. Their assets include: notes and coin, balances with the Bank of England, market loans, bills of exchange (Treasury bills and commercial bills), reverse repos, advances to customers (the biggest item – including overdrafts, personal loans, credit card debt and mortgages) and investments (government bonds and inter-bank investments).
3. Banks aim to make profits, but they must also maintain sufficient liquidity. Liquid assets, however, tend to be relatively unprofitable and profitable assets tend to be relatively illiquid. Banks therefore need to keep a balance of profitability and liquidity in their range of assets.
4. The Bank of England is the UK's central bank. It issues notes; it acts as banker to the government, to banks and to various overseas central banks; it manages the government's borrowing programme; it ensures sufficient liquidity for the financial sector; it operates the country's monetary and exchange rate policy.
5. The money market is the market in short-term deposits and loans. It consists of the discount and repo markets and the parallel money markets.
6. The Bank of England operates in the repo and discount markets. By buying (rediscounting) bills and through gilt repos, it provides liquidity to the banks at the rate of interest chosen by the Monetary Policy Committee. It is always prepared to lend in this way in order to ensure adequate liquidity in the economy.
7. The parallel money markets consist of various markets in short-term finance between various financial institutions.

17.3 THE SUPPLY OF MONEY

Definitions of the money supply

If money supply is to be monitored and possibly controlled, it is obviously necessary to measure it. But what should be included in the measure? Here we need to distinguish between the *monetary base* and *broad money*.

The ***monetary base*** (or 'high-powered money') consists of cash (notes and coin) in circulation outside the central bank. Thus, in the eurozone, the monetary base is given by cash (euros) in circulation outside the ECB.

In the UK, it is sometimes referred to as the 'narrow monetary base' to distinguish it from the ***wide monetary base***, which also includes banks' balances with the Bank of England. In the UK, the wide monetary base is known as *M0*.

But the monetary base gives us a very poor indication of the effective money supply, since it excludes the most important source of liquidity for spending: namely, bank deposits. The problem is which deposits to include. We need to answer three questions:

- Should we include just sight deposits, or time deposits as well?
- Should we include just retail deposits, or wholesale deposits as well?
- Should we include just bank deposits, or building society (savings institution) deposits as well?

In the past there has been a whole range of measures, each including different combinations of these accounts. However, financial deregulation, the abolition of foreign exchange controls and the development of computer technology have led to huge changes in the financial sector throughout the world. This has led to a blurring of the distinctions between different types of account. It has also made it very easy to switch deposits from one type of account to another. For these reasons, the most usual measure that countries use for money supply is ***broad money***, which in most cases includes both time and sight deposits, retail and wholesale deposits, and bank and building society (savings institution) deposits.

In the UK this measure of broad money is known as *M4*. In most other European countries and the USA it is known as *M3*. There are, however, minor differences between countries in what is included. (Official UK and eurozone measures of money supply are given in Box 17.4.)

As we have seen, bank deposits of one form or another constitute by far the largest component of (broad) money supply. To understand how money supply expands and contracts, and how it can be controlled, it is thus necessary to understand what determines the size of bank deposits. Banks can themselves expand the amount of bank deposits, and hence the money supply, by a process known as 'credit creation'.

The creation of credit: the simplest case

To illustrate this process in its simplest form, assume that banks have just one type of liability – deposits – and two types of asset – balances with the central bank (to achieve liquidity) and advances to customers (to earn profit).

Banks want to achieve profitability while maintaining sufficient liquidity. Assume that they believe that sufficient liquidity will be achieved if 10 per cent of their assets are held as balances with the central bank. The remaining 90 per cent will then be in advances to customers. In other words, the banks operate a 10 per cent liquidity ratio.

Assume initially that the combined balance sheet of the banks is as shown in Table 17.3. Total deposits are £100 billion, of which £10 billion (10 per cent) are kept in balances with the central bank. The remaining £90 billion (90 per cent) are lent to customers.

KI 23 p 251

Now assume that the government spends more money – £10 billion, say, on roads or hospitals. It pays for this with cheques drawn on its account with the central bank. The people receiving the cheques deposit them in their banks. Banks return these cheques to the central bank and their

Table 17.3 Banks' original balance sheet

Liabilities	£bn	Assets	£bn
Deposits	100	Balances with the central bank	10
		Advances	90
Total	100	Total	100

Definitions

Monetary base Notes and coin outside the central bank.

Wide monetary base Notes and coin outside the central bank plus banks' operational deposits with the central bank.

Broad money Cash in circulation plus retail and wholesale bank and building society deposits.

CASE STUDIES AND APPLICATIONS

BOX 17.4

UK AND EUROZONE MONETARY AGGREGATES

How long is a piece of string?

UK measures

There are two main measures of the money supply in the UK: M0 and M4. M0 is referred to as the 'wide monetary base' and M4 is referred to as 'broad money' or simply as 'the money supply'. In addition, there is a measure called 'Retail deposits and cash in M4' (previously known as M2). This measure excludes wholesale deposits.

The definitions are as follows:

M0. Cash in circulation with the public and cash held by banks and building societies + banks' operational balances with the Bank of England.

Retail deposits and cash in M4. Cash in circulation with the public (but not cash in banks and building societies) + private-sector *retail* sterling deposits in banks and building societies.

M4. *Retail deposits and cash in M4* + private-sector wholesale sterling deposits in banks and building societies + sterling certificates of deposit.

Table (a) gives the figures for these three aggregates for the end of January 2005.

Why is cash in banks and building societies included in the UK's M0 measure, but not in the other two measures?

Eurozone measures

Although the ECB uses three measures of the money supply, they are different from those used by the Bank of England. The narrowest definition (M1) includes overnight deposits (i.e. call money) as well as cash, and is thus much broader than the UK's M0 measure. The broadest eurozone measure (M3) is again broader than the UK's broadest measure (M4), since the eurozone measure includes various other moderately liquid assets. The definitions of the three eurozone aggregates are:

M1. Cash in circulation with the public + overnight deposits

M2. M1 + deposits with agreed maturity up to 2 years + deposits redeemable up to 3 months' notice

M3. M2 + repos + money-market funds and paper + debt securities with residual maturity up to 2 years

Table (b) gives the figures for UK money supply for each of these three ECB measures – again, for the end of January 2005.

What are the benefits of including these additional items in the broad measure of money supply?

(a) UK monetary aggregates, end January 2005

TC 15 p463

		£ million
	Cash outside Bank of England	42 621
+	Banks' operational deposits with Bank of England	79
=	**M0**	**42 700**
	Cash outside banks (i.e. in circulation with the public and non-bank firms)	34 499
+	Private-sector retail bank and building society deposits	807 586
=	**Retail deposits and cash in M4**	**842 085**
+	Private-sector wholesale bank and building society deposits + CDs	330 285
=	**M4**	**1 172 370**

(b) UK money supply using ECB measures: end January 2005

		£ million
	Currency in circulation	35 213
+	Overnight deposits	642 652
=	**M1**	**677 865**
+	Deposits with agreed maturity up to 2 years	88 696
+	Deposits redeemable up to 3 months' notice	328 908
=	**M2**	**1 095 469**
+	Repos	114 344
+	Money market funds and paper	61 031
+	**M3**	**1 270 844**

Source: based on data in *Bankstats*, Tables A1.1, A2.2.1 and A2.3 (Bank of England).

Table 17.4 The initial effect of an additional deposit of £10 billion

Liabilities	£bn	Assets	£bn
Deposits (old)	100	Balances with the central bank (old)	10
Deposits (new)	10	Balances with the central bank (new)	10
		Advances	90
Total	110	Total	110

Table 17.5 The full effect of an additional deposit of £10 billion

Liabilities	£bn	Assets	£bn
Deposits (old)	100	Balances with the central bank (old)	10
Deposits (new: initial)	10	Balances with the central bank (new)	10
(new: subsequent)	90	Advances (old)	90
		Advances (new)	90
Total	200	Total	200

balances correspondingly increase by £10 billion. The combined banks' balance sheet now is shown in Table 17.4.

But this is not the end of the story. Banks now have surplus liquidity. With their balances in the central bank having increased to £20 billion, they now have a liquidity ratio of 20/110, or 18.2 per cent. If they are to return to a 10 per cent liquidity ratio, they need only retain £11 billion as balances at the central bank (£11 billion/£110 billion = 10 per cent). The remaining £9 billion they can lend to customers.

Assume now that customers spend this £9 billion in shops and the shopkeepers deposit the cheques in *their* bank accounts. When the cheques are cleared, the balances in the central bank of the *customers'* banks will duly be debited by £9 billion, but the balances in the central bank of the *shopkeepers'* banks will be credited by £9 billion, *leaving overall balances in the central bank unaltered*. There is still a surplus of £9 billion over what is required to maintain the 10 per cent liquidity ratio. The new deposits of £9 billion in the shopkeepers' banks, backed by balances in the central bank, can thus be used as the basis for *further* loans: 10 per cent (i.e. £0.9 billion) must be kept back in the central bank, but the remaining 90 per cent (i.e. £8.1 billion) can be lent out again. When the money is spent and the cheques are cleared, this £8.1 billion will still remain as surplus balances in the central bank and can therefore be used as the basis for yet more loans. Again, 10 per cent must be retained and the remaining 90 per cent can be lent out. This process goes on and on until eventually the position is as shown in Table 17.5.

The initial increase in balances with the central bank of £10 billion has allowed banks to create new advances (and hence deposits) of £90 billion, making a total increase in money supply of £100 billion.

This effect is known as the ***bank (or deposits) multiplier***. In this simple example with a liquidity ratio of 1/10 (i.e. 10 per cent), the bank multiplier is 10. An initial increase in deposits of £10 billion allowed total deposits to rise by £100 billion. In this simple world, therefore, the bank multiplier is the inverse of the liquidity ratio (l).

TC 15 p463

Bank multiplier $= 1/l$

?

If banks choose to operate a 20 per cent liquidity ratio and receive extra cash deposits of £10 million:
(a) How much credit will ultimately be created?
(b) By how much will total deposits have expanded?
(c) What is the size of the bank multiplier?

*LOOKING AT THE MATHS

The process of credit creation can be expressed mathematically as the sum of an infinite series. If a is the proportion of any deposit that is lent by banks, where $a = 1 - l$, then total deposits will expand by:

$$D_T = D_0(1 + a + a^2 + a^3 + \ldots)$$
$$= D_0(1/1 - a) \quad (1)$$
$$= D_0(1/l)$$

Thus if there were an initial additional deposit (D_0) of £100 and if $a = 0.8$, giving a liquidity ratio (l) of 0.2, total deposits would expand by £100 × 1/0.2 = £500. The bank multiplier is 5.

Proof of equation (1) is given in Maths Case 17.1 on the book's website.

Note that the maths of the bank multiplier is very similar to that of the Keynesian expenditure multiplier of section 16.2 (see Maths Case 16.1 on the book's website). The economics, however, is quite different. The Keynesian multiplier is concerned with the effects of increased demand on real national output. The bank multiplier is simply concerned with monetary creation.

TC 12 p374

Definition

Bank (or deposits) multiplier The number of times greater the expansion of bank deposits is than the additional liquidity in banks that causes it: $1/l$ (the inverse of the liquidity ratio).

The creation of credit: the real world

In practice, the creation of credit is not as simple as this. There are three major complications.

Banks' liquidity ratio may vary

Banks may choose a different liquidity ratio. At certain times, banks may decide that it is prudent to hold a bigger proportion of liquid assets. If Christmas or the summer holidays are approaching and people are likely to make bigger cash withdrawals, banks may decide to hold more liquid assets.

On the other hand, there may be an upsurge in consumer demand for credit. Banks may be very keen to grant additional loans and thus make more profits, even though they have acquired no additional assets. They may simply go ahead and expand credit, and accept a lower liquidity ratio.

Customers may not want to take up the credit on offer. Banks may wish to make additional loans, but customers may not want to borrow. There may be insufficient demand. But will the banks not then lower their interest rates, thus encouraging people to borrow? Possibly, but it is not as simple as this. Banks must keep all their interest rates in line with other financial institutions in order to remain competitive. If banks lower the interest rates they charge to borrowers, they must also lower the rate they pay to depositors. But then depositors may switch to other institutions such as building societies.

How will an increased mobility of savings and other capital between institutions affect this argument?

Banks may not operate a simple liquidity ratio

The fact that banks hold a number of fairly liquid assets, such as money at call, bills of exchange and certificates of deposit, makes it difficult to identify a simple liquidity ratio. For example, if banks use £1 million in cash to purchase £1 million of bills, can we assume that the liquidity ratio has remained exactly the same? In other words, can we assume that ***near money*** assets, such as bills, are just as liquid as cash? If we assume that they are not, then has the liquidity ratio fallen? If so, by how much?

Banks do not see a clear-cut dividing line between liquid and non-liquid assets. They try to maintain a rough balance across the liquidity range, but the precise composition of assets will vary as interest rates on the various assets vary, and as the demands for liquidity vary.

In practice, therefore, the size of the bank multiplier will vary and is thus difficult to predict in advance.

Is the following statement true: 'The greater the number of types of asset that are counted as being liquid, the smaller will be the bank multiplier'?

Some of the extra cash may be withdrawn by the public

If extra cash comes into the banking system, and as a result extra deposits are created, part of them may be held by households and firms (known in this context as the ***non-bank private sector***) as cash *outside* the banks. In other words, some of the extra cash leaks out of the banking system. This will result in an overall multiplier effect that is smaller than the full bank multiplier. This overall multiplier is known as the ***money multiplier***. It is defined as the rise in total money supply expressed as a proportion of the rise in the monetary base that caused it: $\Delta M_s/\Delta M_b$ (where M_s is total broad money supply and M_b is the monetary base). The precise value will, of course, depend on how the broad money supply and the monetary base are defined. In the UK, the money multiplier is usually given by ΔM4/ΔM0. In the eurozone it is given by ΔM3/Δcurrency. Box 17.5 shows how the money multiplier is calculated.

What causes money supply to rise?

There are four sets of circumstances in which the money supply can rise.

Banks choose to hold a lower liquidity ratio

If banks collectively choose to hold a lower liquidity ratio, they will have surplus liquidity. The banks have tended to choose a lower liquidity ratio over time because of the increasing use of direct debits, cheques and debit-card and credit-card transactions.

Surplus liquidity can be used to expand advances, which will lead to a multiplied rise in broad money supply (e.g. M4).

An important trend in recent years has been the growth in *inter-bank lending*. Table 17.1 showed that short-term loans to other banks (including overseas banks) and CDs are now the two largest elements in banks' liquid assets. These assets may be used by a bank as the basis for expanding loans and thereby starting a chain of credit creation. But although these assets are liquid to an *individual bank*, they do not add to the liquidity of the banking system *as*

Definitions

Near money Highly liquid assets (other than cash).

Non-bank private sector Households and non-bank firms. In other words, everyone in the country other than banks and the government (central and local).

Money multiplier The number of times greater the expansion of money supply is than the expansion of the monetary base that caused it: ΔMs/ΔMb.

EXPLORING ECONOMICS *BOX 17.5

CALCULATING THE MONEY MULTIPLIER

The money multiplier (m) is the rise in total money supply (ΔM_s) divided by the rise in the monetary base (ΔM_b):

$$m = \Delta M_s / \Delta M_b \quad (1)$$

The total money supply (M_s) consists of deposits in banks and building societies (D) plus cash held by the public (C). Thus a rise in money supply would be given by:

$$\Delta M_s = \Delta D + \Delta C \quad (2)$$

The monetary base (M_b) consists of bank and building society reserves (R) plus cash held by the public (C). Thus a rise in the monetary base would be given by:

$$\Delta M_b = \Delta R + \Delta C \quad (3)$$

Thus, by substituting equations (2) and (3) into equation (1), the money multiplier is given by:

$$m = \frac{\Delta D + \Delta C}{\Delta R + \Delta C} \quad (4)$$

Assume now that banks wish to hold a given fraction (r) of any rise in deposits in the form of reserves, i.e.

$$r = \Delta R / \Delta D \quad (5)$$

and that the public wishes to hold a given fraction (c) of any rise in its deposits as cash, i.e.

$$c = \Delta C / \Delta D \quad (6)$$

If we now divide the top and bottom of equation (4) by ΔD, we get:

$$m = \frac{\Delta D/\Delta D + \Delta C/\Delta D}{\Delta R/\Delta D + \Delta C/\Delta D} = \frac{1 + c}{r + c} \quad (7)$$

Thus if c were 0.2 and r were 0.1, the money multiplier would be:

$$(1 + 0.2)/(0.1 + 0.2) = 1.2/0.3 = 4$$

i.e. $\Delta M_s = 4 \times \Delta M_b$.

1. ***If c were 0.1 and r were 0.01, by how much would money supply expand if the monetary base rose by £1 million?***
2. ***Money supply (M4) includes wholesale as well as retail deposits. Given that firms will wish to keep only a very small fraction of a rise in wholesale deposits in cash (if any at all), how will a change in the balance of wholesale and retail deposits affect the value of c and hence of the money multiplier?***

a whole. By using them for credit creation, the banking system is operating with a lower *overall* liquidity ratio.

What effects do debit cards and cash machines (ATMs) have on (a) banks' prudent liquidity ratios; (b) the size of the bank multiplier?

The non-bank private sector chooses to hold less cash

Households and firms may choose to hold less cash. Again, the reason may be a greater use of cards, direct debits, etc. (see Box 17.6). This means that a greater proportion of the cash base (M0) will be held as deposits in banks rather in people's wallets, purses or safes outside banks. The extra cash deposits allow banks to create more credit.

The above two reasons for an expansion of broad money supply (M4) are because more credit is being created for a given monetary base (M0). The other two reasons for an expansion of money supply are reasons why the monetary base itself might expand.

An inflow of funds from abroad

If the government intervenes in the foreign exchange market to maintain a rate of exchange *below* the equilibrium, there will be an excess demand for sterling (see Figure 14.14 on page 421). To maintain the exchange rate at this level, the Bank of England has to buy up the excess foreign currencies on offer with *extra* pounds, thereby building up the foreign currency reserves. When this sterling is used to pay for UK exports and is then deposited back in the banks by the exporters, credit will be created on the basis of it, leading to a *multiplied* increase in money supply.

The money supply will also expand if depositors of *sterling* in banks overseas then switch these deposits to banks in the UK. This is a *direct* increase in the money supply. In an open economy like the UK, movements of sterling and other currencies into and out of the country can be very large, leading to large fluctuations in the money supply.

A public-sector deficit

The public-sector net cash requirement (PSNCR) is the difference between public-sector expenditure and public-sector receipts. To meet this deficit, the government has to borrow money by selling interest-bearing securities (Treasury bills and gilts). In general, the bigger the PSNCR, the greater will be the growth in the money supply. Just how the money supply will be affected, however, depends on who buys the securities.

Such securities could be sold to the Bank of England. In this case, the Bank of England credits the government's account to the value of the securities it has purchased. When the government spends the money, it pays with cheques drawn on its account with the Bank of England. When the recipients of these cheques pay them into their bank accounts, the banks will present the cheques to the Bank of England and their balances there will be duly credited. These additional balances will then become the basis for credit creation. There will be a multiplied expansion of the money supply.

Similarly, if the government borrows through additional Treasury bills, and if these are purchased by the banking sector, there will be a multiplied expansion of the money supply. The reason is that, although banks' balances at the central bank will go down when the banks purchase the bills, they will go up again when the government spends the money. In addition, the banks will now have additional liquid assets (bills), which can be used as the basis for credit creation.

If, however, the government securities are purchased by the 'non-bank private sector' (the name given to the general public and non-bank firms), the money supply will remain unchanged. When people buy the bonds or bills, they will draw money from their banks. When the government spends the money, it will be redeposited in banks. There is no increase in money supply. It is just a case of existing money changing hands.

The government could attempt to minimise the boost to money supply by financing the PSNCR through the sale of gilts, since, even if these were partly purchased by the banks, they could not be used as the basis for credit creation.

Note that if there is a public-sector *surplus* (a negative PSNCR), this will either reduce the money supply or have no effect, depending on what the government does with the surplus. The fact that there is a surplus means that the public sector is spending less than it receives in taxes, etc. The initial effect, therefore, is to reduce the money in the economy: it is being 'retired' in the central bank.

If, however, the government then uses this money to buy back securities from the non-bank private sector, the money will merely return to the economy, and there will be no net effect on money supply.

? *If the government borrows* but does not spend the proceeds, *what effect will this have on the money supply if it borrows from*
(a) the banking sector;
(b) the non-bank private sector?

The flow-of-funds equation

KI 23 p 251

All these effects on money supply can be summarised using a ***flow-of-funds equation***. This shows the components of a *change* in money supply (ΔM_s). The following flow-of-funds equation is the one most commonly used in the UK, that for M4. It consists of four items (or 'counterparts' as they are known):

ΔM4	*equals*	PSNCR	(Item 1)
	minus	Sales of public-sector debt to (or *plus* purchases of public-sector debt from) the non-bank private sector	(Item 2)
	plus	Banks' and building societies' sterling lending to the UK private sector	(Item 3)
	plus	External effect	(Item 4)

Public-sector borrowing (item 1) will lead to a direct increase in the money supply, but not if it is funded by selling bonds and bills to the non-bank private sector. Such sales (item 2) have therefore to be subtracted from the PSNCR. But conversely, if the government buys back old bonds from the non-bank private sector, this will further increase the money supply.

The initial increase in liquidity from the sale of government securities to the banking sector is given by item 1. This increase in their liquidity will enable banks to create credit. To the extent that this extra lending is to the UK private sector (item 3), money supply will increase, and by a multiple of the initial increase in liquidity (item 1). Bank lending may also increase (item 3) even if there is no increase in liquidity or even a reduction in liquidity (item 1 is zero or negative), if banks respond to increases in the demand for loans by accepting a lower liquidity ratio.

Finally, if there is a net inflow of funds from abroad (item 4), this too will increase the money supply.

The flow-of-funds equation that we have just described is a simplified version of the one actually used in official statistics to analyse the components of changes in M4. The equation can easily be modified to show changes in retail deposits in M4 or the eurozone measure of M3.

Table 17.6 shows the components of changes in M4 for 2000 and 2004. It is interesting to compare the two years. In 2004 there was a large public-sector deficit (PSNCR) (item 1), which therefore had the effect of increasing the money supply. The effect was compounded by a large increase in bank lending (item 3) but was offset somewhat by substantial sales of government stock (item 2) and an outflow of funds abroad (item 4). By contrast, in 2000 there was a large public-sector surplus (a negative PSNCR), which, other things being equal, would have reduced the money supply. But as you can see quite clearly from the table, other things were not equal: there was again a large increase in bank lending (item 3), compounded by the use of some of the public-sector surplus to purchase government stock (item 2) and a substantial inflow of funds from abroad (item 4).

Definition

Flow-of-funds equation The various items making up an increase (or decrease) in money supply.

Table 17.6 Counterparts to changes in M4 (£m)

	PSNCR (+) (Public-sector net cash requirement) (1)	Sales (–)/purchases (+) of public-sector debt to/from non-bank private sector (2)	Banks' and building societies' sterling lending to UK private sector (less increases in bank's capital) (3)	External effect: inflows (+) outflows (–) (4)	Total ΔM4
2000	–37 525	+13 536	+80 279	+10 689	= +66 979
2004	+41 150	–26 298	+86 000	–4 249	= +96 603

Source: *Bank of England Financial Statistics* (Bank of England).

The relationship between money supply and the rate of interest

Simple monetary theory often assumes that the supply of money is totally independent of interest rates. This is illustrated in Figure 17.1. The money supply is ***exogenous***. It is assumed to be determined by government: what the government chooses it to be, or what it allows it to be by its choice of the level and method of financing the PSNCR.

More complex models, and especially Keynesian models, assume that higher interest rates will lead to higher levels of money supply, as in Figure 17.2. The reasons for this are as follows:

- Increases in money supply may occur as a result of banks expanding credit in response to the demand for credit. This assumes that banks have surplus liquidity in the first place. Higher demand for credit will drive up interest rates, making it more profitable for banks to supply more credit.
- Higher interest rates may encourage depositors to switch their deposits from sight accounts (earning little or no interest) to time accounts. Since money is less likely to be withdrawn quickly from time accounts, banks may feel the need to hold less liquidity, and therefore may decide to increase credit, thus expanding the money supply.
- Higher interest rates attract deposits from overseas. This increases the money supply to the extent that the Bank of England does not allow the exchange rate to appreciate in response.

An upward-sloping supply curve assumes that interest rates are determined by the market: by the interaction of supply and demand for money. An increase in demand for money raises interest rates, which in turn increases the supply of money (see sections 17.4 and 17.5). Supply is merely reflecting demand and is thus ***endogenously*** determined.

Figure 17.1 The supply of money curve: exogenous money supply

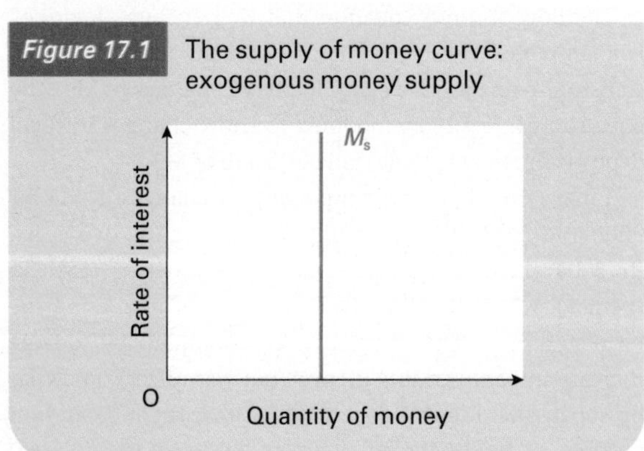

Figure 17.2 The supply of money curve: endogenous money supply

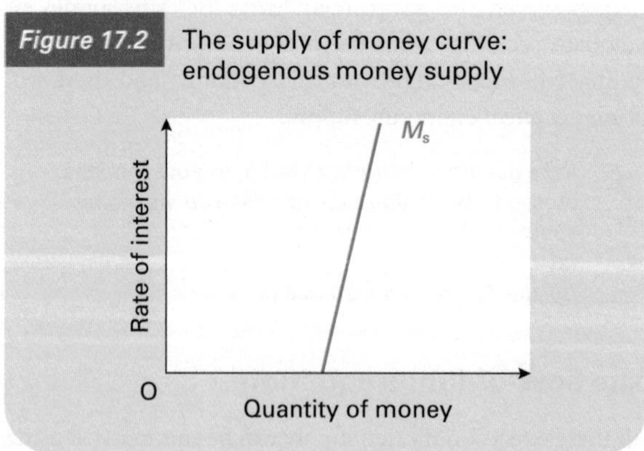

Definitions

Exogenous money supply Money supply that does not depend on the demand for money but is set by the authorities.

Endogenous money supply Money supply that is determined (at least in part) by the demand for money.

Section summary

1. Money supply can be defined in a number of different ways, depending on what items are included. A useful distinction is between narrow money and broad money. Narrow money includes just cash, and possibly banks' balances at the central bank. Broad money also includes deposits in banks and possibly various other short-term deposits in the money market. In the UK, M4 is the preferred measure of broad money. In the eurozone it is M3.
2. Bank deposits are a major proportion of broad money supply. The expansion of bank deposits is the major element in the expansion of the money supply.
3. Bank deposits expand through a process of credit creation. If banks' liquid assets increase, they can be used as a base for increasing loans. When the loans are redeposited in banks, they form the base for yet more loans, and thus takes place a process of multiple credit expansion. The ratio of the increase of deposits to an expansion of banks' liquidity base is called the 'bank multiplier'. It is the inverse of the liquidity ratio.
4. In practice, it is difficult to predict the precise amount by which money supply will expand if there is an increase in cash. The reasons are that banks may choose to hold a different liquidity ratio; customers may not take up all the credit on offer; there may be no simple liquidity ratio given the range of near money assets; and some of the extra cash may leak away into extra cash holdings by the public.
5. Money supply will rise if (a) banks choose to hold a lower liquidity ratio and thus create more credit for an existing amount of liquidity; (b) there is a net inflow of funds from abroad; (c) the government runs a PSNCR and finances it by borrowing from the banking sector or from abroad.
6. The flow-of-funds equation shows the components of any change in money supply. A rise in money supply equals the PSNCR *minus* sales of public-sector debt to the non-bank private sector, *plus* banks' lending to the private sector (less increases in banks' capital), *plus* inflows of money from abroad.
7. Simple monetary theory assumes that the supply of money is independent of interest rates. In practice, a rise in interest rates (in response to a higher demand for money) will often lead to an increase in money supply.

17.4 THE DEMAND FOR MONEY

The motives for holding money

The demand for money refers to the desire to *hold* money: to keep your wealth in the form of money, rather than spending it on goods and services or using it to purchase financial assets such as bonds or shares. It is usual to distinguish three reasons why people want to hold their assets in the form of money.

The transactions motive. Since money is a medium of exchange, it is required for conducting transactions. But since people receive money only at intervals (e.g. weekly or monthly) and not continuously, they require to hold balances of money in cash or in current accounts.

The precautionary motive. Unforeseen circumstances can arise, such as a car breakdown. Thus individuals often hold some additional money as a precaution. Firms too keep precautionary balances because of uncertainties about the timing of their receipts and payments. If a large customer is late in making payment, a firm may be unable to pay its suppliers unless it has spare liquidity.

TC 9 p101

The speculative or assets motive. Certain firms and individuals who wish to purchase financial assets such as bonds, shares or other securities, may prefer to wait if they feel that their price is likely to fall. In the meantime, they will hold money balances instead. This speculative demand can be quite high when the price of securities is considered certain to fall. Money when used for this purpose is a means of temporarily storing wealth.

Similarly, people who will require foreign currency at some time in the future (people such as importers, holiday makers, or those thinking of investing abroad or in foreign securities) may prefer to wait before exchanging pounds into the relevant foreign currencies if they believe that the sterling price of these currencies is likely to fall (the pound is likely to *appreciate*).

The transactions and precautionary demand for money: L_1

The transactions plus precautionary demand for money is termed L_1. 'L' stands for ***liquidity preference***: that is, the

Definition

Liquidity preference The demand for holding assets in the form of money.

CASE STUDIES AND APPLICATIONS — BOX 17.6

ARE THE DAYS OF CASH NUMBERED?

EFTPOS versus ATMs

Banking is becoming increasingly automated, with computer debiting and crediting of accounts replacing the moving around of pieces of paper. What was once done by a bank clerk is often now done by computer.

One possible outcome of this replacement of labour by computers is the gradual elimination of cash from the economy – or so some commentators have claimed.

The most dramatic example of computerisation in recent years has been EFTPOS (electronic funds transfer at the point of sale). This is where you pay for goods in the shops by means of a credit or debit card. When the card is swiped across the machine and the amount entered, your card is then automatically debited and the shop's account credited.

The advantage of this system is that it does away with the processing by hand of pieces of paper. In particular, it does away with the need for (a) credit-card slips when used in conjunction with credit cards and (b) cheques. Both cheques and credit-card slips have to be physically moved around and then read and processed by *people*. If cards were to become more extensively used for *small* transactions, they could well reduce the need for cash.

So are we moving towards a cashless society? Probably not. Cash is still the simplest and most efficient way of paying for a host of items, from your bus ticket to a newspaper to a packet of mints. What is more, another technical innovation is moving us in the direction of using *more* cash, not less! This is the cash machine – or *ATM* (automated teller machine), to give it its official title. The spread of cash machines to virtually every bank and building society branch and to many larger stores and supermarkets has been rapid in recent years. The sheer simplicity of obtaining cash at all hours from these machines, not only from your current account but also on your credit card, is obviously a huge encouragement to the use of cash.

So are we using more cash or less cash? The evidence suggests that, until recent years, there was a gradual decline in cash in circulation as a proportion of GDP. It fell from just over 5 per cent of GDP in 1980 to just over 3 per cent in the mid-1990s. Since then it has risen slightly. By 2005 the figure was 3.6 per cent.

But although the effects of EFTPOS and ATMs may be quite different in terms of the use of cash, they both have the same advantage to banks: they reduce the need for bank staff and thereby reduce costs.

Under what circumstances are cheques more efficient than cash and vice versa? Would you get the same answer from everyone involved in transactions: individuals, firms and banks?

desire to hold assets in liquid form. Money balances held for these two purposes are called ***active balances***: money to be used as a medium of exchange. What determines the size of L_1?

The major determinant of L_1 is *nominal national income* (i.e. national income at current prices). The bigger people's money income, the greater their expenditure and the bigger their demand for active balances. The *frequency with which people are paid* also affects L_1. The less frequently they are paid, the greater the level of money balances they will require to tide them over until the next payment.

Will students in receipt of a grant or an allowance who are paid once per term have a high or a low transactions demand for money relative to their income?

The *rate of interest* has some effect on L_1, albeit rather small (see Figure 17.3). At high rates of interest, people may choose to spend less and save more of their income, e.g. by buying shares. The effect is likely to be bigger on the pre-

Figure 17.3 The demand for money

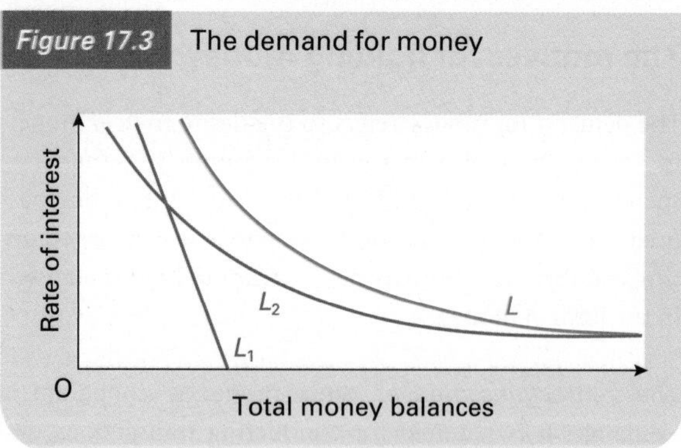

cautionary demand: a higher interest rate may encourage people to risk tying up their money. Firms' active balances are more likely to be sensitive to changes in *r* than those of individuals.

Other determinants of L_1 include the season of the year: people require more money balances at Christmas, for example. Also, any other factors that affect consumption will affect L_1.

The increased use of credit cards in recent years has reduced both the transactions and precautionary demands. Paying once a month for goods requires less money on average than paying separately for each item purchased.

Definition

Active balances Money held for transactions and precautionary purposes.

Moreover, the possession of a credit card reduces or even eliminates the need to hold precautionary balances for many people. On the other hand, the increased availability of cash machines, the convenience of debit cards and the ability to earn interest on current accounts have all encouraged people to hold more money in bank accounts. The net effect has been an increase in the demand for money.

The speculative (or assets) demand for money: L_2

The speculative demand for money balances is termed L_2. Money balances held for this purpose are called ***idle balances***.

People who possess wealth, whether they are wealthy or simply small savers, have to decide the best form in which to hold that wealth. Do they keep it in cash in a piggy bank, or in a current account in a real bank; or do they put it in some interest-bearing time account; or do they buy stocks and shares or government bonds; or do they buy some physical asset such as a car or property?

TC 1 p8

In making these decisions, people will have to weigh up the relative advantages and disadvantages of the various alternative assets. Assets can be compared according to two criteria: *liquidity* and the *possibility of earning income*. Just as we saw in the case of a bank's assets, these two criteria tend to conflict. The more liquid an asset is, the lower is likely to be the income earned from holding it. Thus cash is totally liquid to the holder: it can be used to buy other assets (or spent on goods) instantly, but it earns no interest. Stocks and shares, on the other hand, are not very liquid since they cannot be sold instantly *at a guaranteed price*. (They *can* be sold pretty well instantly, but if share prices are depressed, a considerable loss may be incurred in so doing. In other words, they are a *risky* means of holding wealth.) But stocks and shares have the *potential* of earning quite a high income for the holder, not only in terms of the dividends paid out of the firms' profits, but also in terms of the capital gain from any increase in the shares' prices.

KI 11 p66

?

Buying something like a car is at the other end of the spectrum from holding cash. A car is highly illiquid, but yields a high return to the owner. In what form is this 'return'?

KI 10 p62

There are three major determinants of the speculative demand for money. Let us examine each in turn.

The rate of interest (or rate of return) on assets

The higher the rate of return on assets, such as shares and bonds, the greater the opportunity cost of holding money and therefore the lower the speculative demand for money.

> **Definition**
>
> **Idle balances** Money held for speculative purposes: money held in anticipation of a fall in asset prices.

The rate of return on assets varies inversely with their price. Take the case of a government bond (which pays a fixed sum of money throughout its life). Assume that the government issued a £100 bond at a time when interest rates were 10 per cent. Thus the bond must pay £10 per year. Although the government will not redeem bonds until their maturity date, which could well be 20 years from when they were issued, holders can sell bonds at any time on the stock market. Their market price will reflect market rates of interest. Assume, for example, that interest rates fall to 5 per cent. What will happen to the market price of the bond paying £10 per year? It will be driven up to £200. At that price, the £10 per year is worth the current market rate of 5 per cent. Thus the market price of bonds varies inversely with the rate of interest.

Expectations of changes in the prices of securities and other assets

If people believe that share prices are about to rise rapidly on the stock market, they will buy shares and hold smaller speculative balances of money. If they think that share prices will fall, they will sell them and hold money instead. Some clever (or lucky) individuals anticipated the 2000–3 stock market decline. They sold shares and 'went liquid'.

As we have just seen, if the market price of securities is high, the rate of interest (i.e. the rate of return) on these securities will be low. Potential purchasers of these securities will probably wait until their prices fall and the rate of interest rises. Similarly, existing holders of securities will probably sell them while the price is high, hoping to buy them back again when the price falls, thus making a capital gain. *In the meantime, therefore, large speculative balances of money will be held.* L_2 is high.

If, on the other hand, the rate of interest is high, then L_2 is likely to be low. To take advantage of the high rate of return on securities, people buy them now instead of holding on to their money.

Would the demand for securities be low if their price was high, but was expected to go on rising*?*

The relationship between L_2 and the rate of interest (r) is again shown in Figure 17.3. The inverse relationship between r and L_2 gives a downward-sloping curve.

Speculative demand and the exchange rate

In an open economy like the UK where large-scale movements of currencies across the foreign exchanges take place, expectations about changes in the exchange rate are a major determinant of the speculative demand for money.

If people believe that the pound is likely to appreciate, they will want to hold sterling until it does appreciate. For example, if the current exchange rate is £1 = \$1.50 and speculators believe that it will shortly rise to £1 = \$1.75, then if they are correct they will make a 25c per £1 profit by holding sterling. The more quickly is the exchange rate expected to rise, the more will people want to hold sterling (as money). If, however, people believe that it will be a slow rise over time, they will want to buy sterling assets (such as UK government bonds) rather than money, since such assets will also earn the holder a rate of interest.

Conversely, if people believe that the exchange rate is likely to fall in the near future, they will economise on their holdings of sterling, preferring to hold their liquid assets in some other currency – the one most likely to appreciate against other currencies.

Graphically, changes in expectations about the exchange rate will have the effect of shifting the L_2 curve in Figure 17.3.

There is a further complication here. Expectations about changes in the exchange rate will themselves be influenced by the interest rate (relative to overseas interest rates). If the UK rate of interest goes up, people will want to deposit their money in the UK. This will increase the demand for sterling on the foreign exchange market: there will be a short-term financial inflow into the UK (the financial account of the balance of payments will go into surplus). The effect will be to drive up the exchange rate. Thus if people believe that the UK rate of interest will rise, they will *also* believe that the rate of exchange will appreciate, and they will want to hold larger speculative balances of sterling.

The introduction of the 'foreign exchange dimension' into our analysis will have two effects on the L_2 curve. First, the curve will become more elastic. If the rate of interest is low and is thought likely to rise, the speculative demand is likely to be *very* high. Not only will people hold money in anticipation of a fall in security prices, but they will also hold money (sterling) in anticipation of an appreciation of the exchange rate.

Second, the curve will become more unstable. Expectations of changes in the exchange rate do not just depend on current domestic interest rates. They depend on the current and anticipated future state of the balance of trade, the rate of inflation, the current and anticipated levels of interest rates in other major trading countries, the price of oil, and so on. If any of these cause people to expect a lower exchange rate, the speculative demand for money will fall: L_2 will shift to the left.

?

Which way is the L_2 curve likely to shift in the following cases?

(a) The balance of trade moves into deficit.
(b) People anticipate that foreign interest rates are likely to rise substantially relative to domestic ones.
(c) The domestic rate of inflation falls below that of other major trading countries.
(d) People believe that the pound is about to depreciate.

The total demand for money: $L_1 + L_2$

Figure 17.3 also shows the total demand for money balances (L). This is found by the horizontal addition of curves L_1 and L_2. This curve is known as the 'liquidity preference curve' or simply the demand for money curve.

Any factor, other than a change in interest rates, that causes the demand for money to rise will shift the L curve to the right. For example, a rise in national income will cause L_1 to increase, and thus L will shift to the right.

Additional effects of expectations

We have talked about expectations and their importance in determining the speculative demand for money. In particular, we have looked at (a) the effect of interest rates on people's anticipations of future security prices and (b) the effect of expectations about exchange rate movements. There are two other ways in which expectations can influence the demand for money, and make it more unstable.

Expectations about prices. If people expect *prices* to rise, they may reduce their money balances and purchase goods and assets now, before prices do rise. This will tend to shift L to the left. (Note, though, that once prices *have* risen, people will need more money to conduct the same amount of transactions.)

Expectations of interest rate levels over the longer term. If people come to expect that interest rates will normally be higher than they used to be, then any given interest rate

*LOOKING AT THE MATHS

The demand for money (L) can be expressed by the following function:

$$\begin{aligned} L &= L_1 + L_2 \\ &= l_1(PY,f,i) + l_2(i,er^e) \qquad (1) \\ &= l_1(PY,f,(r+\pi^e)) + l_2((r+\pi^e),er^e) \end{aligned}$$

This states that L_1 is a function l_1 of nominal national income (i.e. real national income (Y) multiplied by the price index (P)), the frequency with which people are paid (f) and the (nominal) rate of interest (i), which equals the real rate of interest (r) on alternative assets to money plus the expected rate of inflation (π^e). L_2 is a function of the nominal rate of interest (i) and the expected value of the exchange rate er^e.

The advantage of specifying a relationship in this way is that it gives a simple way of representing a situation where something depends on a number of determinants. It is a convenient shorthand. Indeed, a more complex function could easily be specified where the demand for money depends on a longer list of variables. The one above, however, identifies the main determinants.

By putting plus and minus signs under each of the terms, we could also identify whether the relationship with each of the determinants is a positive or negative one (i.e. whether the respective partial derivative is positive or negative). Equation (1) could thus be written:

$$L = l_1(\underset{+}{PY},\underset{-}{f},\underset{-}{i}) + l_2(\underset{-}{i},\underset{+}{er^e}) \qquad (2)$$

This merely states that the demand for money will rise as PY and er^e rise and f and i fall.

will seem lower relative to the 'normal' rate than it used to be. People will be more inclined to hold speculative balances of money in anticipation of a rise in interest rates. This will tend to shift L upwards.

In an era of uncertainty about inflation, interest rates and exchange rates, people's expectations will be hard to predict. They will be volatile and susceptible to rumours and political events. In such circumstances, the L curve itself will be hard to predict and will be subject to considerable shifts. Generally, it is likely that the greater the uncertainty, the greater will be the preference for liquidity, and the greater the risk of tying wealth up in illiquid assets.

Section summary

1. The three motives for holding money are the transactions, precautionary and speculative (or assets) motives.
2. The transactions-plus-precautionary demand for money (L_1) depends primarily on the level of nominal national income, the frequency with which people are paid and institutional arrangements (such as the use of credit or debit cards). It also depends to some degree on the rate of interest.
3. The speculative demand for money (L_2) depends on the rate of return on assets and on anticipations about future movements in security prices (and hence their rate of return) and future movements in exchange rates. If security prices are anticipated to fall or the exchange rate to rise, people will hold more money balances.
4. The demand for money is also influenced by expectations of price changes and the levels of interest rates over the longer term.

17.5 EQUILIBRIUM

Equilibrium in the money market

TC 4 p22 Equilibrium in the money market is where the demand for money (L) is equal to the supply of money (M_s). This equilibrium is achieved through changes in the rate of interest.

In Figure 17.4, equilibrium is achieved with a rate of interest r_e and a quantity of money M_e. If the rate of interest were above r_e, people would have money balances surplus to their needs. They would use these to buy shares, bonds and other assets. This would drive up the price of these assets and drive down the rate of interest. As the rate of interest fell, so there would be a contraction of the money supply (a movement down along the M_s curve) and an increase in the demand for money balances, especially speculative balances (a movement down along the liquidity preference curve). The interest rate would go on falling until it reached r_e. Equilibrium would then be achieved.

Similarly, if the rate of interest were below r_e, people would have insufficient money balances. They would sell securities, thus lowering their prices and raising the rate of interest until it reached r_e.

A shift in either the M_s or the L curve will lead to a new equilibrium quantity of money and rate of interest at the new intersection of the curves. For example, a rise in the supply of money will cause the rate of interest to fall.

In practice, there is no *one* single rate of interest. Different assets have different rates of interest. Table 17.7 gives examples of the rates of interest on various assets in the UK in January 2002.

Figure 17.4 Equilibrium in the money market

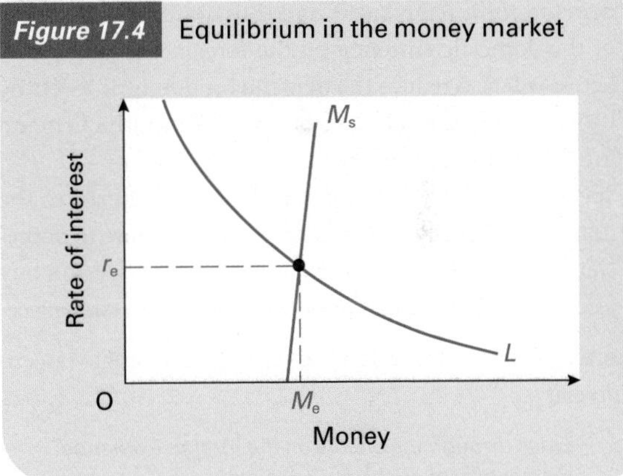

Equilibrium in the money markets, therefore, will be first where the *total* demand for and supply of money are equal. This is achieved by adjustments in the average rate of interest. Second, it will be where demand and supply of *each type* of financial asset separately balance. If, for example, there were excess demand for short-term loans (like money at call) and excess supply of money to invest in long-term assets (like bonds), short-term rates of interest would rise relative to long-term rates.

Equilibrium in the foreign exchange market

Changes in the money supply also affect the foreign exchange market. In a free foreign exchange market, TC 4 p22

Table 17.7 Selected rates of interest: January 2005

Asset	Period of loan	Rate of interest (% per annum)
Call money	Overnight	4.70
Gilt repos	2 weeks	4.72
Inter-bank loans	1 month	4.77
Treasury bills	3 months	4.66
Long-dated government bonds	20 years	4.44
Building society mortgage	Variable (25 years typical)	6.11
Ordinary shares (dividend yield of FTSE 100)	≃	3.20
(Banks' base rate = Bank of England repo rate)	≃	4.75

Source: *Bankstats* (Bank of England).

equilibrium will be achieved by changes in the exchange rate. Assume that the money supply increases. This has three direct effects:

- *Part* of the excess money balances will be used to purchase foreign assets. This will therefore lead to an increase in the supply of domestic currency coming on to the foreign exchange markets.
- The excess supply of money in the domestic money market will push down the rate of interest. This will reduce the return on domestic assets below that on foreign assets. This, like the first effect, will lead to an increased demand for foreign assets and thus an increased supply of the domestic currency on the foreign exchange market. It will also reduce the demand for domestic assets by those outside the country, and thus reduce the demand for the domestic currency.
- TC 9 p101 Speculators will anticipate that the higher supply of the domestic currency will cause the exchange rate to depreciate. They will therefore sell domestic currency and buy foreign currencies now, before the depreciation takes place.

The effect of all three is to cause the exchange rate to depreciate.

? *Trace through the effects on the foreign exchange market of a* fall *in the money supply.*

*LOOKING AT THE MATHS

Equilibrium in the money market is where demand and supply of money are equal. From Box 17.5, the money supply (M_s) equals the monetary base (M_b) multiplied by the money multiplier:

$$M_s = M_b\left(\frac{1+c}{rs+c}\right)$$

Note that this is the more complex version of the money multiplier that we examined in Box 17.5, not the simple bank multiplier developed in the text.

From the 'Looking at the maths' panel on page 500, the demand for money (L) is given by:

$$L = l_1(PY,f,(r+\pi^e)) + l_2((r+\pi^e),er^e)$$

Thus, in equilibrium:

$$M_s = L$$

$$\text{i.e. } M_b\left(\frac{1+c}{rs+c}\right) = l_1(PY,f,(r+\pi^e)) + l_2((r+\pi^e),er^e) \qquad (1)$$

At first sight, this equation looks quite daunting, but what we have done is to bring together money supply and demand, each of which has been separately derived in a set of simple stages. In one single equation (equation (1)) we have completed a jigsaw made up of several simple parts.

Section summary

1. Equilibrium in the money market is where the supply of money is equal to the demand. Equilibrium will be achieved through changes in the rate of interest.
2. A rise in money supply causes money supply to exceed money demand. This causes interest rates to fall and a movement down along both the supply of money curve and the demand for money curve until money supply is equal to money demand.
3. Equilibrium in the foreign exchange market is where the demand and supply of a currency are equal. A rise in money supply causes interest rates to fall. The rise in money supply plus the fall in interest rates causes an increased supply of domestic currency to come on to the foreign exchange market and a reduced demand for the domestic currency. This causes the exchange rate to depreciate.

END OF CHAPTER QUESTIONS

1. Imagine that the banking system receives additional deposits of £100 million and that all the individual banks wish to retain their current liquidity ratio of 20 per cent.
   (a) How much will banks choose to lend out initially?
   (b) What will happen to banks' liabilities when the money that is lent out is spent and the recipients of it deposit it in their bank accounts?
   (c) How much of these latest deposits will be lent out by the banks?
   (d) By how much will *total* deposits (liabilities) eventually have risen, assuming that none of the additional liquidity is held outside the banking sector?
   (e) How much of these are matched by (i) liquid assets; (ii) illiquid assets?
   (f) What is the size of the bank multiplier?
   (g) If one half of any additional liquidity is held *outside* the banking sector, by how much less will deposits have risen compared with (d) above?
2. What is meant by the terms *narrow money* and *broad money*? Does broad money fulfil all the functions of money?
3. How does money aid the specialisation and division of labour?
4. What enables banks safely to engage in both maturity transformation and risk transformation?
5. Why do banks hold a range of assets of varying degrees of liquidity and profitability?
6. If the government reduces the size of its public-sector net cash requirement, why might the money supply nevertheless increase more rapidly?
7. Why might the relationship between the demand for money and the rate of interest be an unstable one?
8. What effects will the following have on the equilibrium rate of interest? (You should consider which way the demand and/or supply curves of money shift.)
   (a) Banks find that they have a higher liquidity ratio than they need.
   (b) A rise in incomes.
   (c) A growing belief that interest rates will rise from their current level.

Additional case studies on the book's website (www.pearsoned.co.uk/sloman)

17.1 **Barter: its use in Russia in the 1990s.** When barter was used as an alternative to money.

17.2 **The attributes of money.** What distinguishes it from other assets?

17.3 **From coins to bank deposit money.** This case traces the evolution of modern money.

17.4 **Gresham's law.** This examines the famous law that 'bad money drives good money out of circulation'.

17.5 **German banking.** This case compares the tradition of German banks with that of UK retail banks. Although the banks have become more similar in recent years, German banks have a much closer relationship with industry.

17.6 **Making money grow.** A light-hearted illustration of the process of credit creation.

WEBSITES RELEVANT TO THIS CHAPTER

See sites listed at the end of Chapter 18 on page 527.

Chapter 18

The Relationship between the Money and Goods Markets

In Chapter 16 we saw how equilibrium national output was determined. In other words, we looked at macroeconomic equilibrium in goods markets. In Chapter 17 we saw how equilibrium was determined in the money market. In this chapter we combine the analysis of the two chapters.

In section 18.1 we examine how changes in money supply affect real national income. In other words, we see how changes in money markets are transmitted through to goods markets: how monetary changes affect real output. Then, in section 18.2, we look at things the other way round. We examine the effects on money markets and interest rates of changes in the goods market. For example, if aggregate demand increases and firms start to produce extra goods, to what extent will money markets act as a constraint on this process?

Then, in section 18.3, we combine goods and money market analysis into one model: the *ISLM* model. This helps us to see how the two markets interact and how an overall macroeconomic equilibrium is determined.

Finally we look at the interaction of goods and money markets when the central bank targets the rate of inflation: a common practice around the world today.

Although economists agree on many things, there is no complete agreement in macroeconomics. The debates between Keynesians (of various types), monetarists and new classicists (see section 15.5) have evolved, but have not been settled. As we go through this chapter, we will see the places where economists agree, and where they still differ.

CHAPTER MAP

18.1 THE EFFECTS OF MONETARY CHANGES ON NATIONAL INCOME

In this section we examine the impact on the economy of changes in money supply and interest rates: how they affect aggregate demand and how this, in turn, affects national income. A simple way of understanding the issues is in terms of the *quantity theory of money*.

The quantity theory of money

In section 15.2 (page 434), we looked at the following version of the quantity equation:

$$MV = PY$$

In case you did not study Chapter 15, let us state the theory again. First a definition of the terms: M is the supply of money; V is the income velocity of circulation (the number of times money is spent per year on national output (GDP)); P is the price index (where the index = 1 in the base year); and Y is the real value of national income (= national output) for the year in question (i.e. GDP measured in base-year prices).

MV is the total spending on national output. For example, if total money supply was £100 billion and each pound was spent on average five times per year on national output, then total spending on national output (MV) would equal £500 billion for that year. MV is thus simply (nominal) aggregate demand, since total spending on national output consists of the four elements of aggregate demand: consumer spending (C), investment expenditure (I), government spending (G) and expenditure on exports less expenditure on imports ($X - M$), all measured in current prices.

PY is the money value of national output: in other words, GDP measured at *current* prices. For example, if real national income (i.e. in base-year prices) was £200 billion, and the price index was 2.5 (in other words, prices were 2½ times higher than in the base year), then the value of national output in current prices would be £500 billion.

Because of the way we have defined the terms, MV must equal PY. A simple way of looking at this is that MV and PY are both ways of measuring GDP. MV measures it in terms of national expenditure. PY measures it in terms of the value of what is produced.

The effect of a rise in money supply

If money supply (M) rises, how will it affect the other three elements of the quantity equation? Will it simply lead to a rise in prices (P), or will there be a rise in real national income (Y)? What will happen to the velocity of circulation? Can we assume that it will remain constant, or will it change?

Clearly the relationship between money supply and prices depends on what happens to V and Y. What happens to them has been the subject of considerable debate over the years between economists. Keynesians have generally had different views from monetarists and new classical economists.

In this chapter we will focus on the effects of a change in money supply on aggregate demand. Will an increase in the amount of money in the economy lead to an increase in spending, and if so, how much? In other words, we will focus on the variability of V.

In Chapter 20 we will look at the effects of changes in aggregate demand on aggregate supply. Will a rise in aggregate demand lead to increased employment and output (Y), or will it simply lead to higher prices (P). In other words, we will look at the variability of Y.

1. *If V is constant, will (a) a £10 million rise in M give a £10 million rise in MV; (b) a 10 per cent rise in M give a 10 per cent rise in MV?*
2. *If both V and Y are constant, will (a) a £10 million rise in M lead to a £10 million rise in P; (b) a 10 per cent rise in M lead to a 10 per cent rise in P?*

Effects of changes in money supply on aggregate demand: the interest rate transmission mechanism

One way in which changes in money supply affect aggregate demand and national income is via changes in the rate of interest. It is a three-stage process. This is illustrated in Figure 18.1: KI 5 p21

- Diagram (a) shows the money market. A rise in money supply from M to M' leads to a surplus of money at r_1, and hence a fall in the rate of interest from r_1 to r_2.
- Diagram (b) shows the relationship between investment (I) and the rate of interest. A fall in the rate of interest from r_1 to r_2 leads to a rise in investment (and any other interest-sensitive expenditures) from I_1 to I_2.
- Diagram (c) is the Keynesian withdrawals and injections diagram. A rise in investment leads to a multiplied rise in national income (from Y_1 to Y_2).

The rise in income will be less than that shown in diagram (c), however, since any rise in income will lead to a rise in the transactions demand for money, L_1. L will shift to the right in diagram (a), and thus r will not fall as much as illustrated. Thus investment (diagram (b)) and national income (diagram (c)) will not rise as much as illustrated either.

The overall effect of a change in money supply on national income will depend on the size of the effect in each of the three stages. This will depend on the shapes of the curves in each of the three diagrams and whether they are likely to shift. The effect will be bigger:

Figure 18.1 Effect of a rise in money supply: the interest rate transmission mechanism

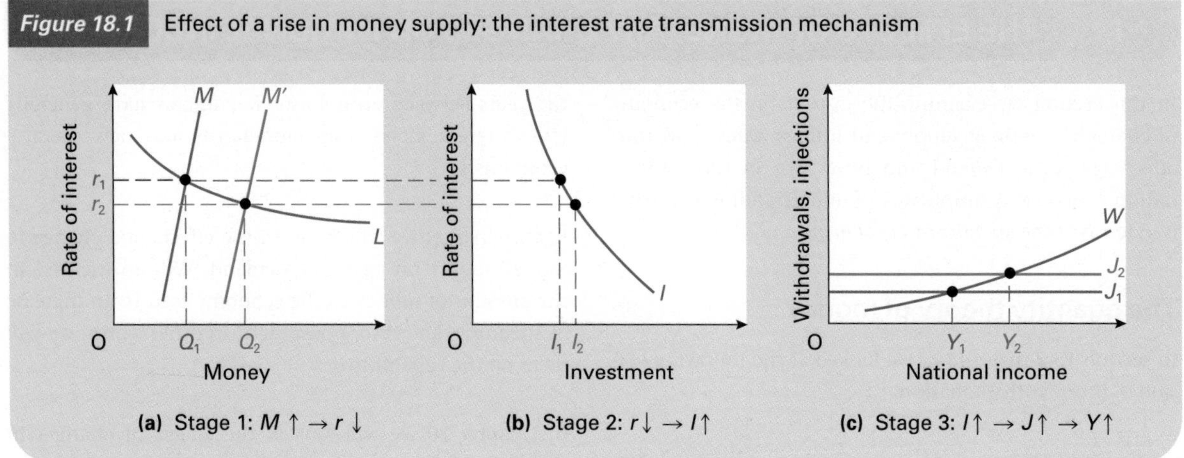

- The less elastic the liquidity preference curve (L): this will cause a bigger change in the rate of interest.
- The more interest elastic the investment curve (I): this will cause a bigger change in investment.
- The lower the marginal propensity to withdraw (*mpw*), and hence the flatter the withdrawals function: this will cause a bigger multiplied change in national income and aggregate demand.

The problem is that stages 1 and 2 may be both weak and unreliable, especially in the short run. This problem is stressed by Keynesians.

KI 9 p58

Problems with stage 1: the money–interest link

An interest-elastic demand for money. According to Keynesians, the speculative demand for money is highly responsive to changes in interest rates. If people believe the rate of interest will rise, and thus the price of bonds and other securities will fall, few people will want to buy them. Instead there will be a very high demand for liquid assets (money and near money). The demand for money will therefore be very elastic in response to changes in interest rates. The demand for money curve (the liquidity preference curve, L) will be shallow and may even be infinitely elastic at some minimum interest rate. This is the point where everyone believes interest rates will rise, and therefore no one wants to buy bonds. Everyone wants to hold their assets in liquid form.

TC 9 p101

With a very shallow L curve (as in Figure 18.2), a rise in money supply from M to M' will lead to only a small fall in the rate of interest from r_1 to r_2. Once people believe that the rate of interest will not go any lower, any further rise in money supply will have no effect on r. The additional money will be lost in what Keynes called the ***liquidity trap***. People simply hold the additional money as idle balances.

Keynes himself saw the liquidity trap as merely a special case: the case where the economy is in deep recession. In such a case, an expansion of money supply would have no effect on the economy. In more normal times, an expansion of money supply would be likely to have *some*

Figure 18.2 An elastic liquidity preference curve

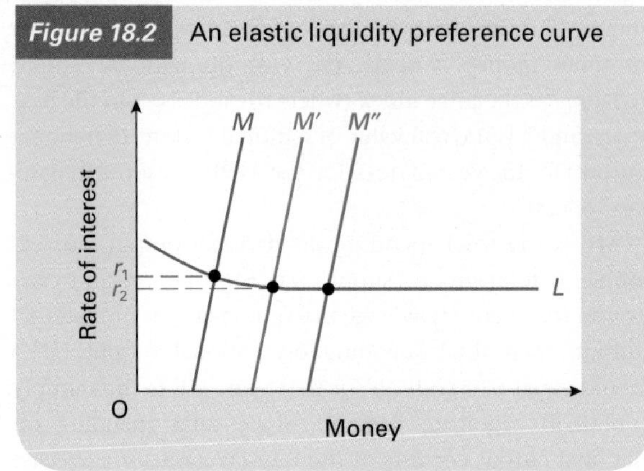

effect on interest rates. Nevertheless, the problem could be severe in times of recession. The Japanese economy suffered from a prolonged recession from the early 1990s to the early 2000s (see Box 19.2). The government and central bank expanded the money supply, but people seemed unwilling to spend. They preferred to hold idle balances. What is more, with interest rates already being virtually zero, there was little incentive to buy bonds or other assets. Thus any extra money was simply kept in idle balances – lost in the liquidity trap.

An unstable demand for money. A more serious problem for most countries is that the liquidity preference curve (L) is *unstable*. People hold speculative balances when they anticipate that interest rates will rise (security prices will fall). But it is not just the current interest rate that affects people's expectations of the future direction of interest rates. Many factors could affect such expectations:

KI 31 p368

TC 9 p101

Definition

Liquidity trap The absorption of any additional money supply into idle balances at very low rates of interest, leaving aggregate demand unchanged.

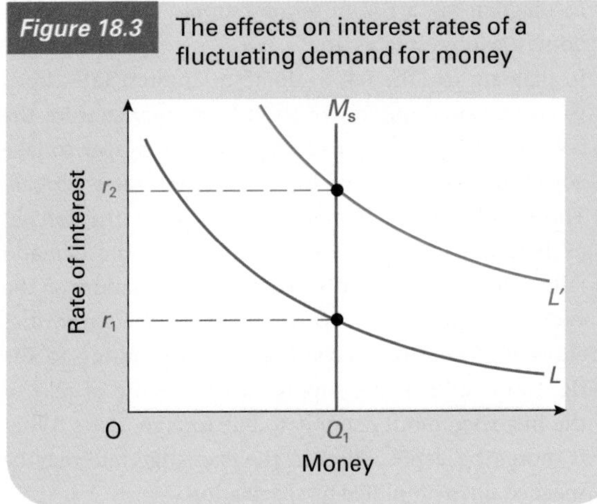

Figure 18.3 The effects on interest rates of a fluctuating demand for money

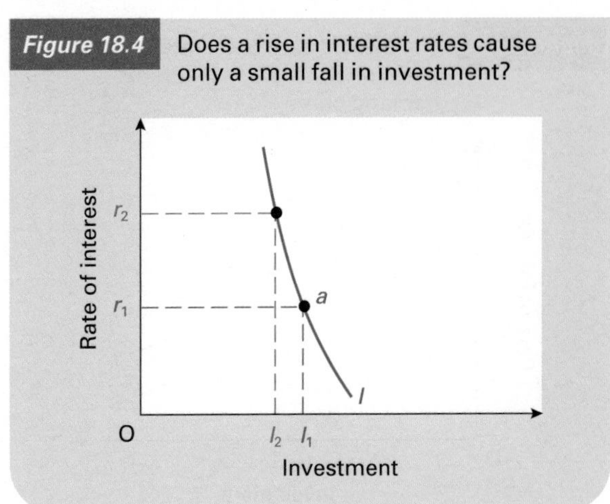

Figure 18.4 Does a rise in interest rates cause only a small fall in investment?

- Changes in foreign interest rates. Domestic interest rates would have to follow suit if the authorities wished to maintain a stable exchange rate.
- Changes in exchange rates. With a falling exchange rate, the authorities may raise interest rates to prevent it depreciating further.
- Statements of government intentions on economic policy.
- Good or bad industrial news. With good news, people tend to buy shares.
- Newly published figures on inflation or money supply. If inflation or the growth in money supply is higher than anticipated, people will expect a rise in interest rates in anticipation of a tighter monetary policy.

Thus the L curve can be highly volatile. With an unstable demand for money, it is difficult to predict the effect on interest rates of a change in money supply.

A policy of *targeting* money supply can be criticised for similar reasons. A volatile demand for money can cause severe fluctuations in interest rates if the supply of money is kept constant (see Figure 18.3). These fluctuations will cause further uncertainty and further shifts in the speculative demand for money. Targeting the money supply can therefore add to the volatility of the velocity of circulation (V).

Problems with stage 2: the interest rate–investment link

An interest-inelastic investment demand. In the 1950s and 1960s, many Keynesians argued that investment was unresponsive to interest rate changes: that the I curve in Figure 18.1(b) was steep. In these circumstances, a very large change in interest rates would be necessary to have any significant effect on investment and aggregate demand.

Investment, it was argued, depends on confidence of future markets. If confidence is high, firms will continue to invest even if interest rates are high. They can always pass the higher costs on to the consumer. If confidence is low, firms will not invest even if interest rates are low and borrowing is cheap. Evidence seemed to confirm the interest inelasticity of investment demand.

Few Keynesians hold this extreme position today. The evidence for an inelastic investment demand has been challenged. Just because investment was not significantly lower on occasions when interest rates were high, it does not follow that investment is unresponsive to interest rate changes. There may have been changes in *other* factors that helped to *maintain* investment: in other words, the I curve shifted to the right. For example, a rise in consumer demand would both cause the high interest rate *and* encourage higher investment.

Figure 18.4 shows a steep investment demand curve. If the rate of interest rises from r_1 to r_2, there is only a small fall in investment from I_1 to I_2. Now draw a much more elastic I curve passing through point a. Assume that this is the true I curve. Show how the rate of interest could still rise to r_2 and investment still only fall to I_2 if this curve were to shift.

Even if fixed investment in plant and machinery is not very interest sensitive, other components of aggregate demand may well be: for example, investment in stocks, consumer demand financed through credit cards, bank loans or hire purchase, and the demand for houses financed through mortgages.

An unstable investment demand. Today the major worry about the interest–investment link is not that the investment curve is inelastic, but rather that it shifts erratically with the confidence of investors.

Assume in Figure 18.5 that the initial investment demand curve is given by I_1. Now assume that the central bank reduces interest rates from r_0 to r_1. Other things being equal, the level of investment will rise from Q_0 to Q_1. If, however, firms believe that the economy will now pull out of recession, their confidence will increase. The investment curve will shift to I_2 and investment will increase quite markedly to Q_2. If, on the other hand, firms believe that inflation will now rise, which in turn will later force the central bank to raise interest rates again, their confidence may well decrease. The investment curve will shift to I_3 and the level of investment will actually fall to Q_3.

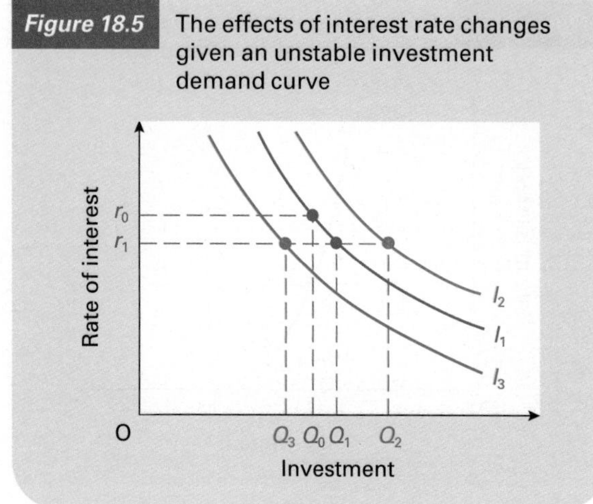

Figure 18.5 The effects of interest rate changes given an unstable investment demand curve

Monetary policy is likely to be effective, therefore, only if people have confidence in its effectiveness. This *psychological* effect can be quite powerful. It demands considerable *political* skill, however, to manipulate it.

The exchange rate transmission mechanism

KI 5 p21

There is another mechanism that backs up the interest rate mechanism. This includes the exchange rate as an intermediate variable between changes in the money supply and changes in aggregate demand. There are four stages in this exchange rate transmission mechanism (see Figure 18.6):

- In diagram (a), a rise in money supply causes a fall in domestic interest rates from r_1 to r_2.
- In diagram (b), the fall in domestic interest rates leads to an increased outflow of short-term finance from the country and a reduced inflow, as depositors seek to take advantage of relatively higher interest rates abroad. The supply of the domestic currency on the foreign exchange market rises from S_1 to S_2 and the demand falls from D_1 to D_2. This causes a depreciation of the exchange rate from er_1 to er_2 (assuming the authorities allow it). There is a second factor contributing to the rightward shift in the supply curve: the use of part of the increased money supply to buy foreign assets. What is more, the depreciation in the exchange rate may be speeded up or amplified by speculation.
- In diagram (c), the depreciation of the exchange rate causes a rise in demand for exports (X), since they are now cheaper for people abroad to buy (there is a movement down along the X curve). It also causes a fall in demand for imports (M), since they are now more expensive (there is a movement up along the M curve). Note that the rise in exports and fall in imports gives a current account balance of payments surplus. This is matched by the financial account deficit resulting from the lower interest rate encouraging people to buy foreign assets and people abroad buying fewer of this country's assets.
- In diagram (d), the rise in exports (an injection) and a fall in imports (a withdrawal) will cause a multiplied rise in national income.

Figure 18.6 The exchange rate transmission mechanism

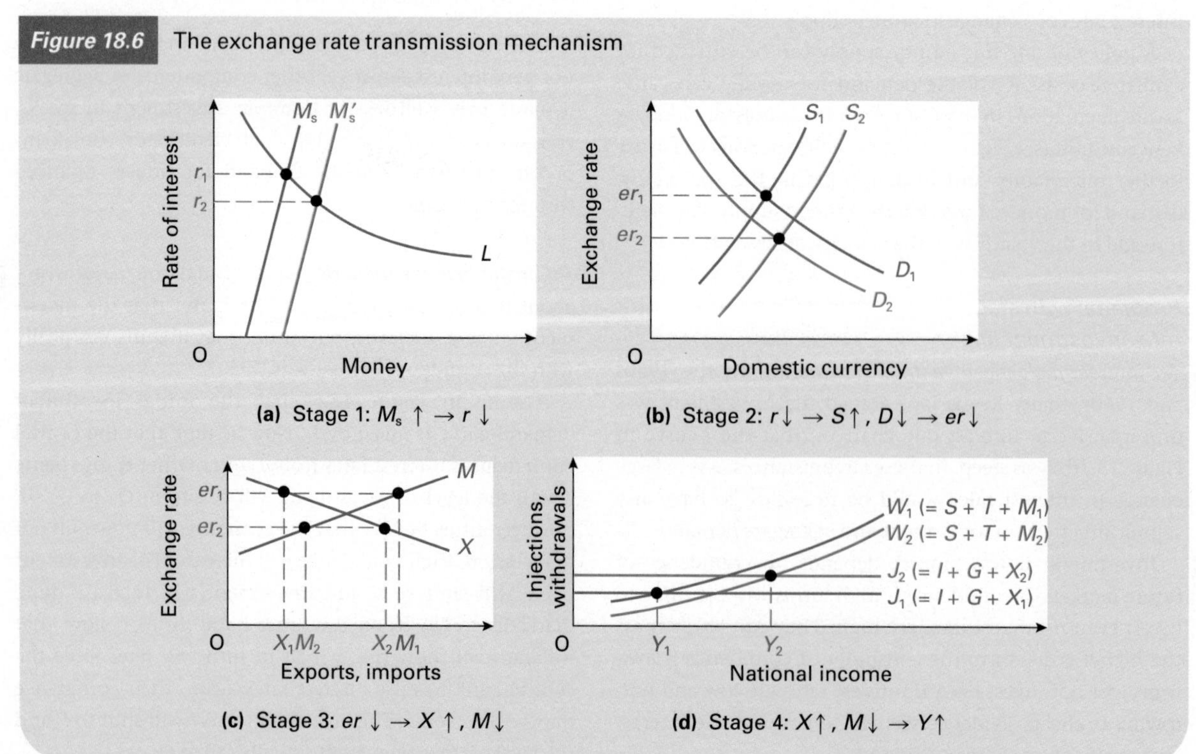

EXPLORING ECONOMICS BOX 18.1

CHOOSING THE EXCHANGE RATE OR THE MONEY SUPPLY

You can't choose both

If the government expands the money supply, then interest rates will fall and aggregate demand will tend to rise. With a floating exchange rate, this will cause the currency to depreciate.

But what if the government attempts to maintain a fixed exchange rate? To do this it must keep interest rates comparable with world rates. This means that it is no longer free to choose the level of money supply. The money supply has become endogenous.

The government can't have it both ways. It can choose the level of the money supply (providing it has the techniques to do so) and let interest rates and the exchange rate be what they will. Or it can choose the exchange rate, but this will then determine the necessary rate of interest and hence the supply of money. These issues are explored in Chapter 24.

Can the government choose both the exchange rate and the money supply if it is prepared to use the reserves to support the exchange rate?

Stage 1 will tend to be more powerful than in a closed economy. The liquidity preference curve will tend to be less elastic because, as interest rates fall, people may fear a depreciation of sterling and switch to holding other currencies. Just how strong stage 1 will be depends on *how much* people think the exchange rate will depreciate.

Stage 2 is likely to be very strong indeed. Given the openness of international financial markets, international financial flows can be enormous in response to interest rate changes. Only a relatively small change in interest rates is necessary to cause a relatively large financial flow. Monetarists and new classical economists stress the importance of this effect. Any fall in interest rates, they argue, will have such a strong effect on international financial flows and the exchange rate that the rise in money supply will be relatively quickly and fully transmitted through to aggregate demand.

Stage 3 may be quite strong in the long run. Given time, both the demand by consumers abroad for this country's exports and the domestic demand for imports may be quite elastic. In the short run, the effect may be rather limited. However, the size of the effect depends on people's expectations of exchange rate movements. If people think that the exchange rate will fall further, importers will buy *now* before the rate does fall. Exporters, on the other hand, will hold back as long as possible before shipping their exports. These actions will tend to push the exchange rate down. But such speculation is very difficult to predict as it depends on often highly volatile expectations.

? *If importers and exporters believe that the exchange rate has 'bottomed out', what will they do?*

Stage 4 is the familiar multiplier, only this time triggered by a change in imports and exports.

Note that, as with the interest rate transmission mechanism, the full effect will not be as large as that illustrated. This is because the increased national income will cause an increased *transactions* demand for money. This will shift the L curve to the right in diagram (a), and thus lead to a smaller fall in the rate of interest than that illustrated. The overall effect can be quite strong, but the precise magnitude is usually highly unpredictable.

The effects of changes in money supply will depend also on just how free the exchange rate is. If the government intervenes to 'peg' (i.e. fix) the exchange rate or to prevent excessive fluctuations, the transmission mechanism will not work in the way described. Alternative exchange rate systems (or 'regimes', as they are called) are examined in Chapter 23.

Portfolio balance: a more direct transmission mechanism

Monetarists stress a more direct transmission mechanism. If money supply increases, people will have more money than they require to hold. They will spend this surplus. Much of this spending will go on goods and services, thereby directly increasing aggregate demand:

$$M_s \uparrow \rightarrow M_s > M_d \rightarrow AD \uparrow$$

The theoretical underpinning for this is given by the *theory of* ***portfolio balance***. People have a number of ways of holding their wealth: as money, or as financial assets such as bills, bonds and shares, or as physical assets such as houses, cars and televisions. In other words, people hold a whole portfolio of assets of varying degrees of liquidity – from cash to central heating.

If money supply expands, people will find themselves holding more money than they require: their portfolios are unnecessarily liquid. Some of this money will be used to purchase financial assets, and some to purchase *goods*

Definition

Portfolio balance The balance of assets, according to their liquidity, that people choose to hold in their portfolios.

CASE STUDIES AND APPLICATIONS BOX 18.2

THE STABILITY OF THE VELOCITY OF CIRCULATION

What is the evidence?

How stable is the velocity of circulation (V) in practice? Does the evidence support the monetarist case that it is relatively stable or the Keynesian case that it fluctuates unpredictably, at least in the short run? Unfortunately, the facts do not unequivocally support either side.

The evidence

How has V behaved over time? To answer this we need to measure V. A simple way of doing this is to use the formula $V = PY/M$ (rearranging the terms in the quantity equation $MV = PY$). Thus we need to measure PY and M. PY is simply the money value of national output: in other words, GDP at current prices. The value of M (and hence V) will depend on which measure of the money supply we use.

The diagram shows how the velocities of circulation in the UK of both M4 and M0 have changed over the years.

The long run. As far as M4 is concerned, long-term increases in its velocity from 1973 to 1979 are explained by the increase in money substitutes and credit cards, and thus smaller holdings of money balances. The decrease after 1980 is explained by falling inflation and nominal interest rates, with people being increasingly prepared to hold money in sight accounts; by the growth in wholesale deposits (which earn interest); and by people putting a larger proportion of their savings into bank and building society accounts, attracted by higher *real* interest rates and new types of high-interest instant-access account. As the pace of these changes slowed down, so the fall in velocity became much more gentle after 1990.

As far as M0 is concerned, its velocity more than doubled between 1974 and 1993. One reason for this is the increased use of credit and debit cards, which has reduced the amount of cash people need to hold.

M0 and M4 velocities of circulation

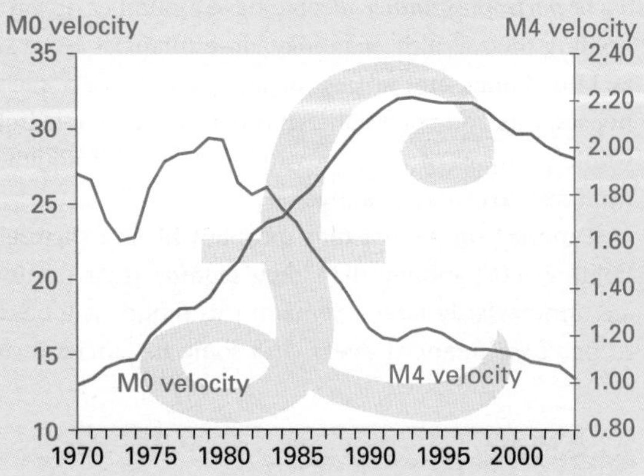

The growth of cash machines has also reduced the need to hold so much cash, given that people can easily obtain more 24 hours per day. The relatively smaller amount of cash thus circulates faster. But, as with M4, these changes in M0's velocity ceased in the early 1990s and since 1993 it has fallen slightly. Part of the reason has been a slowing down in the growth of credit and debit cards, and part has been lower inflation, which has reduced the opportunity cost of holding cash.

The point made by monetarists is that these changes are predictable and gradual and do not, therefore, undermine the close relationship between M and PY.

The short run. Evidence shows that the velocity of circulation is relatively *stable* in the short run, especially in recent years. However, this is largely because changes in money supply have not been used to manipulate aggregate demand and hence national income. If they had been, the attempt may well have been unsuccessful and V *would* have fluctuated.

KI 30 p306

The direction of causality

Monetary and real changes often work together – especially in the long run. An expansionary fiscal policy over a number of years will increase the PSNCR, which in turn will lead to an increase in money supply (M). If the fiscal policy increases nominal national income (PY), V may well as a result remain constant. But it does not follow from this that it was the growth in M that *caused* the growth in PY. On the few occasions when fiscal and monetary policy work in opposite directions, the evidence is unclear as to which has the bigger effect – especially as the time period is rarely long enough for the full effects to be identified.

What we are concerned about here is the direction of causality. Changes in aggregate demand may go together with changes in money supply. But is it higher money supply causing higher aggregate demand, or the other way round, or the two simply occurring simultaneously?

Monetarists argue that increases in money supply cause aggregate demand to expand (with a lag of perhaps a few months). For them money supply is exogenous: determined independently by the central bank. Keynesians, by contrast, argue that higher aggregate demand causes an increased demand for bank loans, and banks are only too happy to create the necessary credit, thus expanding the money supply. For them, money supply is endogenous.

Why might it be difficult to establish the direction of causality from the evidence?

and services. As more assets are purchased, this will drive up their price. This will effectively reduce their 'yield'. For bonds and other financial assets, this means a reduction in their rate of interest. For goods and services, this means a reduction in their marginal utility/price ratio: a higher level of consumption will reduce their marginal utility and drive up their price. The process will stop when a balance has been restored in people's portfolios. In the meantime, there will have been extra consumption and hence a rise in aggregate demand.

? *Do you think that this is an accurate description of how people behave when they acquire extra money?*

This mechanism has been criticised by Keynesians. Just how is the extra money injected into people's portfolios in the first place? There are two possible means in the short term.

Extra government expenditure or tax cuts financed by an increased money supply. This will lead to people receiving more money from the government, but what is causing the rise in aggregate demand? It could be argued that it is the extra government expenditure or the rise in people's disposable *incomes* that has directly caused the rise in aggregate demand, not the rise in people's money balances.

The use of monetary techniques. As we shall see in the next chapter, the central bank may release extra money into the economy by buying back bills and bonds (since they will pay for them with extra money). But the resulting extra money in people's portfolios has not involved any increase in wealth. People have more money, but fewer bonds and bills. Even if they buy more shares or physical assets with the extra money, this will largely merely offset the lower bond and bill holding. In the *short run*, therefore, the direct mechanism may be weak. The subsequent effects, however, when the banks use their newly acquired balances to grant loans and hence initiate a process of credit creation, will be stronger.

Portfolio balance and the interest rate mechanism

The holding of a range of assets in people's portfolios can strengthen the interest rate transmission mechanism by making the liquidity preference curve less elastic (curve L in Figure 18.1(a) is relatively steep). The reason is that speculative balances of money may now have a much smaller role. But why?

A reduction in the rate of interest (r) following an increase in the money supply may well make bond holding less attractive, but this does not mean that the extra money will be mainly held in idle balances. Again, it can be used to purchase other assets such as property. Idle balances may expand only slightly.

? *Redraw the three diagrams of Figure 18.1 with a steeper L curve. Show how an increase in money supply will have a larger effect on national income.*

How stable is the velocity of circulation?

Short-run variability of V. Most economists agree that there is some variability of the velocity of circulation (V) in the short run if the money supply is changed. To the extent that interest rates and yields do fall with an expansion of the money supply, people may well hold somewhat larger money balances: after all, the interest sacrificed by not holding bonds, etc. has been reduced. If people hold relatively more money, the velocity of circulation is thereby reduced, thus reducing the effect on aggregate demand. Furthermore, the direct mechanism may take time to operate. In the meantime, V will fall.

Also, the demand for money can shift unpredictably in the short run with changing expectations of prices, interest rates and exchange rates. Thus V is unpredictable in the short run, and so is the effect of monetary policy on aggregate demand. For these reasons, changing the money supply may not be an effective means of short-run demand management.

TC 9 p101

Long-run stability of V. The main claim of monetarists is that the velocity of circulation (V) is relatively stable over the longer run, and any changes that do occur are the predictable outcome of institutional changes, such as the increased use of credit cards (see Box 18.2).

One explanation of why V remains relatively stable in the long run, despite an increase in money supply, is that sufficient time has elapsed for the direct mechanism to have worked fully through.

Another explanation is the effect on inflation and consequently on interest rates. This works as follows.

Assume an initial increase in money supply. Interest rates fall. V falls. But if money supply goes on rising and hence expenditure goes on rising, inflation will rise. This will drive up *nominal* interest rates (even though *real* interest rates will stay low). But in choosing whether to hold money or to buy assets, it is the *nominal* rate of interest that people look at, since that is the opportunity cost of holding money. Thus people economise on money balances and V rises back again.

In extreme cases V will even rise to levels higher than before. This is likely if people start speculating that prices will rise further. People will rush to buy goods and assets before their prices rise further. This action will help to push the prices up even more. This form of destabilising speculation took place in the hyperinflation of Germany in the 1920s, as people spent their money as quickly as possible (see Box 14.2).

With a predictable V in the longer run, monetarists have claimed that monetary policy is the essential means of controlling long-term aggregate demand. For this reason, they have favoured a longer-term approach to monetary policy, including targets for the growth of the money supply (see page 560).

Today, most governments adopt a policy of setting a target for the rate of inflation. This involves the central bank then controlling aggregate demand by choosing an appropriate rate of interest. In these circumstances, the money supply must be *passively* adjusted to ensure that the chosen rate of interest is the equilibrium rate. This means expanding the money supply in line with the increase in real national income (Y) and the targeted increase in the price level (P).

We explore inflation targeting and its effects in section 18.4. We explore the operation of monetary policy in section 19.2.

Section summary

1. The quantity equation $MV = PY$ can be used to analyse the possible relationship between money and prices. Whether and how much increases in money supply (M) affect the price level (P) depends on whether the velocity of circulation (V) and the level of real national income (Y) are independent of money supply (M).
2. The interest rate transmission mechanism works as follows: (a) a rise in money supply causes money supply to exceed money demand; interest rates fall; (b) this causes investment to rise; (c) this causes a multiplied rise in national income; but (d) as national income rises, so the transactions demand for money rises, thus preventing quite such a large fall in interest rates.
3. The effect will be weak if the demand-for-money curve (L) is elastic and the investment demand curve is inelastic. The effects may also be unreliable because of an unstable and possibly inelastic investment demand.
4. The exchange rate transmission mechanism works as follows: (a) a rise in money supply causes interest rates to fall; (b) the rise in money supply plus the fall in interest rates causes an increased supply of domestic currency to come on to the foreign exchange market; this causes the exchange rate to fall; (c) this causes increased exports and reduced imports, and hence a multiplied rise in national income.
5. According to the theory of portfolio balance, if people have an increase in money in their portfolios, they will attempt to restore portfolio balance by purchasing assets, including goods. Thus an increase in money supply is transmitted directly into an increase in aggregate demand.
6. The demand for money is more stable in the long run than in the short run. This leads to a greater long-run stability in V (unless it changes as a result of other factors, such as institutional arrangements for the handling of money).

18.2 THE MONETARY EFFECTS OF CHANGES IN THE GOODS MARKET

If there is an expansion in one of the components of aggregate demand (C, I, G or $X - M$), what will be the monetary effects? Will the current level of money supply act as a constraint on the growth in national income? In other words, will an expansion of one component of aggregate demand, such as government expenditure, be at the expense of another component, such as investment?

The monetary effects of an increase in injections

Let us assume that business confidence grows and that, as a result, the level of investment increases. Let us also assume that there is a given quantity of money in the economy. Will the rise in investment lead to a full multiplier effect on national income?

The effect of the rise in investment is illustrated in Figure 18.7. In Figure 18.7(a), the rise in investment leads to a rise in injections to J_2. Other things being equal, national income would rise to Y_2. But this increase in national income also leads to a rise in the transactions demand for money. In Figure 18.7(b), the demand-for-money curve shifts from L to L'.

If the central bank does not allow money supply to rise, the higher demand for money will drive up interest rates to r_2. The effect of the higher interest rates is to reduce the level of investment. The overall rise in injections will be smaller than the rise from J_1 to J_2. Also net saving (i.e. saving minus borrowing) will rise as the higher interest rate acts as both an incentive for households to save and a disincentive for them to borrow. This causes an upward shift in the W curve. The result is that national income will not rise as far as Y_2. In the extreme case, there would be no rise in national income at all.

If, however, the central bank responded to the increase in investment by expanding the money supply to M_s', there would be no change in the rate of interest and hence no dampening effect on either investment or consumption.

?

Assume that the government cuts its expenditure and thereby runs a public-sector surplus.
(a) What will this do initially to equilibrium national income?
(b) What will it do to the demand for money and initially to interest rates?
(c) Under what circumstances will it lead to
(i) a decrease in money supply;
(ii) no change in money supply?
(d) What effect will (i) and (ii) have on the rate of interest compared with its original level?

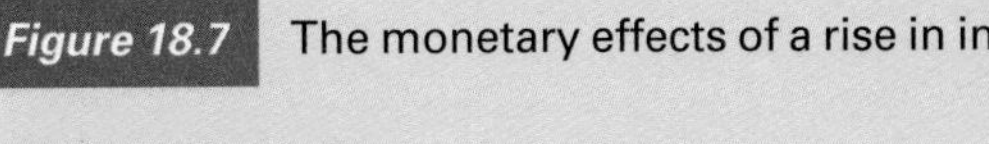

Figure 18.7 The monetary effects of a rise in injections

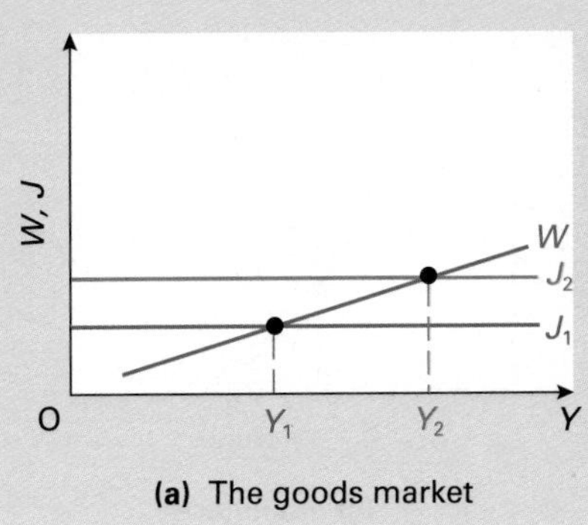

(a) The goods market

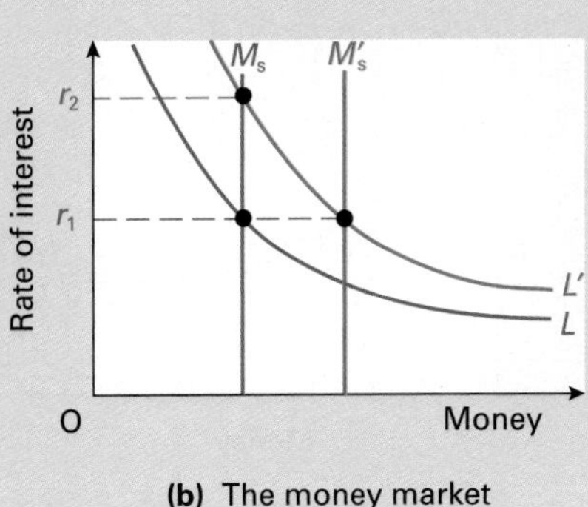

(b) The money market

Crowding out

Another example of the monetary constraints on expansion in the goods market is the phenomenon known as ***financial crowding out***. This is where an increase in public-sector spending reduces private-sector spending.

To illustrate the effects, assume that previously the government has had a balanced budget, but that now it chooses to expand the level of government expenditure without raising additional taxes. As a result, it runs a budget deficit ($G > T$). But this deficit will have to be financed by borrowing. The resulting public-sector net cash requirement will lead to an increase in the money supply if it is financed by borrowing from the central bank through the issue of bonds (gilts), or by the sale of Treasury bills to the banking sector. Alternatively, if it is financed by selling bills or bonds outside the banking sector, there will be no increase in the money supply.

The effect can once more be shown in Figure 18.7. The rise in government expenditure will cause injections to rise to J_2 and, other things being equal, national income will rise to Y_2. But, as with the case of increased investment, this increase in national income will lead to a rise in the demand for money. In Figure 18.7(b), the demand for money curve shifts from L to L'. If the PSNCR is financed in such a way as to allow money supply to expand to M'_s, there will be no change in the interest rate and no crowding-out effect. If, however, the money supply is not allowed to expand, interest rates will rise to r_2. This in turn will reduce investment: crowding out will occur. Injections will fall back again below J_2. In the extreme case, injections could even fall back to J_1 and thus national income return to Y_1. Here crowding out is total.

Definition

Financial crowding out Where an increase in government borrowing diverts money away from the private sector.

EXPLORING ECONOMICS — BOX 18.3

CROWDING OUT IN AN OPEN ECONOMY

Taking exchange rate effects into account

Will fiscal policy be crowded out in an open economy with floating exchange rates? Assume that the government increases its expenditure but does not allow the money supply to expand: a case of pure fiscal policy. What will happen?

- The increased government expenditure will increase the demand for money (see Figure 18.7(b)).
- This will drive up interest rates – the amount depending on the elasticity of the liquidity preference curve.
- This will lead to an inflow of finance from abroad, which in turn will lead to an appreciation of the exchange rate.
- The higher exchange rate will reduce the level of exports (an injection) and increase the level of imports (a withdrawal). This will add to the degree of crowding out.

Thus in an open economy with floating exchange rates, an expansionary fiscal policy will be crowded out not only by higher interest rates, but also by a higher exchange rate.

? ***We have argued that the short-term inflow of finance following a rise in the rate of interest will drive up the exchange rate. Are there any effects of expansionary fiscal policy on the demand for imports (and hence on the current account) that will go some way to offsetting this?***

Figure 18.8 Different views on the demand for money

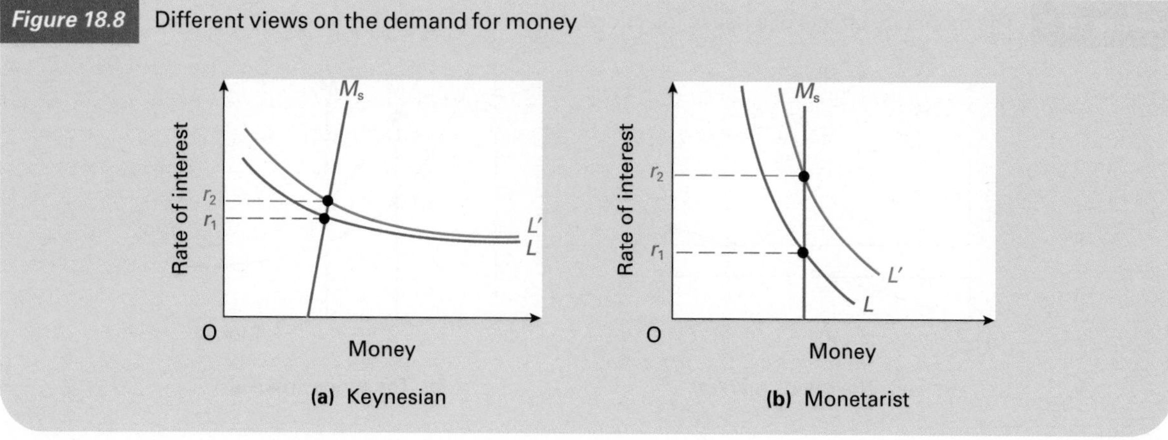

The extent of crowding out

Just how much crowding out will occur when there is an expansionary fiscal policy, but when money supply is *not* allowed to expand, depends on two things.

KI 9 p 58

The responsiveness (elasticity) of the demand for money to a change in interest rates. If the demand is relatively *elastic* (as in Figure 18.8(a)), the increase in demand, represented by a *horizontal* shift in the liquidity preference curve from *L* to *L*′, will lead to only a small rise in interest rates. If, however, the demand is relatively *inelastic* (as in Figure 18.8(b)), the same horizontal shift will lead to a bigger rise in interest rates.

As we saw in section 18.1, Keynesians generally see the liquidity preference curve as being more elastic than do monetarists. Thus, unlike monetarists, they argue that a rise in money demand normally leads to only a relatively modest rise in interest rates.

The responsiveness (elasticity) of investment to a change in interest rates. Keynesians argue that investment is relatively *unresponsive* to changes in interest rates. Business people are much more likely to be affected by the state of the market for their product than by interest rates. Thus in Figure 18.9(a), there is only a small fall in investment. Monetarists argue that investment is relatively *responsive* to changes in interest rates. Thus in Figure 18.9(b), there is a bigger fall in investment.

In the Keynesian case, therefore, the rise in demand for money arising from an expansionary fiscal policy will have only a small effect on interest rates and an even smaller effect on investment. Little or no crowding out takes place. In fact, the expansion of demand might cause an increase in investment through the accelerator effect (see pages 472–4).

TC 15 p463

Monetarists argue that interest rates will rise significantly and that there will be a severe effect on investment. Crowding out is substantial. For this reason, they argue that, if money supply is to be kept under control to prevent inflation rising, it is vital for governments to reduce the size of their budget deficit. They argue that, in the long run, crowding out is total, given the long-run stability of the velocity of circulation.

Figure 18.9 Different views on the demand for investment

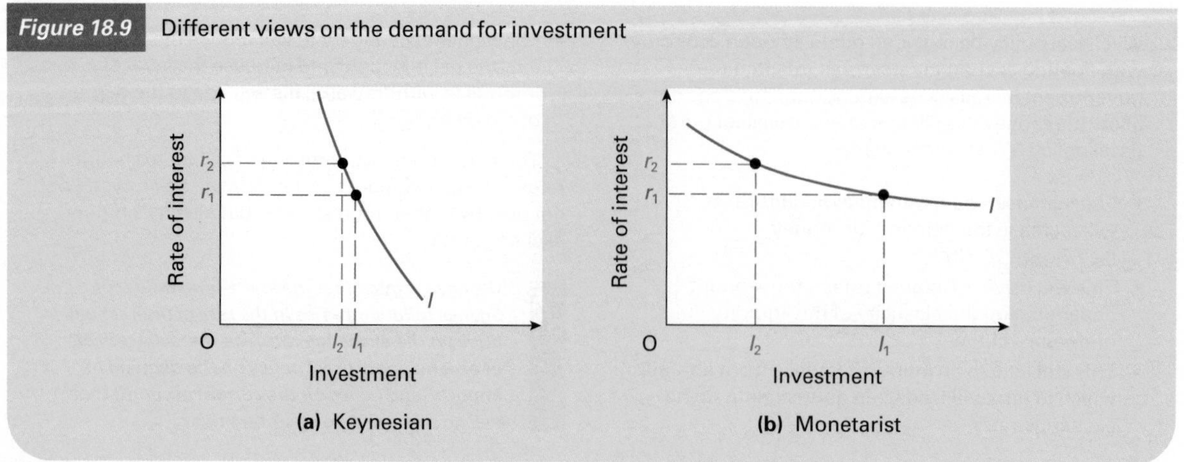

Is money supply exogenous or endogenous?

Money supply is *exogenous* (independently determined) if it can be fixed by the authorities and if it does not vary with aggregate demand and interest rates. In Figure 18.7(b) the *M* 'curve' would be vertical. It would shift only if the government or central bank *chose* to alter the money supply.

Money supply is *endogenous* (determined within the model) if it is determined by aggregate demand and hence the demand for money: banks simply expanding or contracting credit in response to customer demand. In such a case, the money supply curve would be upward sloping. The more that money supply expands in response to an increase in aggregate demand, the more gently upward sloping the money supply curve would be.

The more elastic the money supply curve, the less will money act as a constraint on expansion in the goods market, and the less will a rise in government expenditure crowd out private expenditure. In other words, the less will interest rates rise in response to a rise in the demand for money.

The extreme monetarist position is that money supply is wholly exogenous. The extreme Keynesian position is that money supply is wholly endogenous. Money simply passively expands to meet the demand for money.

In reality, money supply is partly exogenous and partly endogenous. The authorities are able to influence money supply, but banks and other financial institutions have considerable scope for creating credit in response to demand. If control of the money supply is adopted as the basis for policy, the authorities must reduce the endogenous element to a minimum.

As we shall see in the next chapter, the authorities in many countries recognise the difficulties in controlling the money supply directly. They therefore influence the supply of money indirectly by controlling interest rates and hence the demand for money.

Section summary

1. Changes in injections or withdrawals will have monetary implications. If there is a rise in investment with no change in the money supply, the increased demand for money will drive up interest rates and reduce both investment and consumption. The resulting rise in income will be smaller.
2. Similarly, if there is a fiscal expansion and *no* change in the money supply, the increased demand for money will again drive up the interest rate. This will to some extent crowd out private expenditure and thus reduce the effectiveness of the fiscal policy.
3. The extent of crowding out will depend on the shape of the liquidity preference curve and the investment demand curve. The less elastic the demand for money, and the more elastic the investment demand, the more crowding out will take place, and the less effective will fiscal policy be.
4. If there is a rise in aggregate demand, money supply may rise in response to this. The more elastic the supply of money curve, the less crowding out will take place.

*18.3 *ISLM* ANALYSIS: THE INTEGRATION OF THE GOODS AND MONEY MARKET MODELS

The goods and money markets

In this chapter, we have shown that there are two key markets in the economy at macroeconomic level, and that these two markets interact. The first is the goods market; the second is the money market. Each of these two markets has been analysed by using a model.

In the case of the goods market, the model is the Keynesian injections/withdrawals model. Any change in injections or withdrawals will cause national income to change. For example, a rise in government expenditure shifts the *J* line upwards and causes a rise in equilibrium national income. In other words, an increase in the demand for goods and services causes a (multiplied) rise in the output of goods and services (assuming that there are sufficient idle resources).

In the case of the money market, the model is the one showing the demand for money (*L*) and the supply of money (*M*) and their effect on the rate of interest. A change in the supply or demand for money will cause the equilibrium rate of interest to change. Monetary policy operates directly in this market, either by affecting the supply of money or by operating on interest rates.

What we have shown in this chapter is that the two markets *interact*: that changes in one market cause changes in the other. Take the case of an increase in investment: it has a direct effect in the goods markets, but also an indirect effect in money markets. We illustrated this in Figure 18.7. The goods market effect was shown in Figure 18.7(a). The rise in injections led to a multiplied rise in income to Y_2. The money market effect was shown in Figure 18.7(b). The rise in income led to a rise in the transactions demand for money and a resulting rise in interest rates to r_2. This in turn had an effect back in the goods market, with a higher interest rate dampening investment and consumption somewhat and reducing the final rise in income.

The effect of a rise in money supply in the two markets was shown in Figures 18.1 and 18.6 (on pages 506 and 508). The rise in money supply reduces interest rates. This then, via an increase in investment (or a reduction in the exchange rate and a resulting increase in exports and a reduction in imports), leads to a multiplied rise in income in the goods market. This in turn has an effect back in the money market, with a higher income leading to a higher demand for money, thus limiting the fall in interest rates.

The trouble with our analysis so far is that we have needed at least two diagrams. What we are going to look at in this section is a model which *combines* these two markets, which means that we will need only one diagram. The model is known as the ***ISLM model***.

The model allows us to examine the effects of changes originating in one of the two markets on *both* national income *and* interest rates: it shows what the equilibrium will be in both the goods and the money markets simultaneously. The model, as its name suggests, consists of two curves: an *IS* curve and an *LM* curve. The *IS* curve is based on equilibrium in the goods market; the *LM* curve is based on equilibrium in the money market.

Let us examine these two curves in turn.

The *IS* curve

Deriving the IS curve

To explain how the *IS* curve is derived, let us examine Figure 18.10, which as you can see is in two parts. The top part shows the familiar Keynesian injections and withdrawals diagram, only in this case, for simplicity, we are assuming that saving is the only withdrawal from the circular flow of income, and investment the only injection. Thus in equilibrium $I = S$ (i.e. $J = W$). The bottom part of the diagram shows the *IS* curve. This shows all the various combinations of interest rates (r) and national income (Y) at which $I = S$.

Let us assume that initially interest rates are at r_1. Both investment and saving are affected by interest rates, and thus, other things being equal, an interest rate of r_1 will give particular investment and saving schedules. Let us say that, in the top part of the diagram, these are shown by the curves I_1 and S_1. Equilibrium national income will be where $I = S$, i.e. at Y_1. Thus in the lower part of the diagram, an interest rate of r_1 will give a level of national income of Y_1. Thus point *a* is one point on the *IS* curve. At an interest rate of r_1 the goods market will be in equilibrium at an income of Y_1.

Figure 18.10 Goods market equilibrium: deriving the *IS* curve

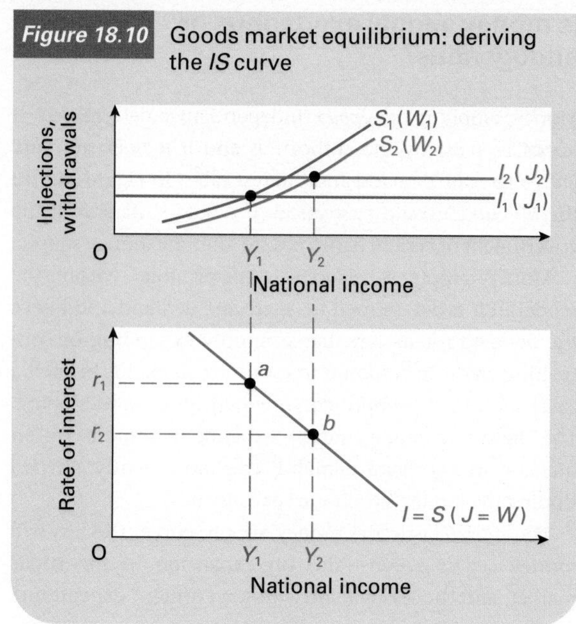

Now what will happen if the rate of interest changes? Let us assume that it falls to r_2. This will cause a rise in investment and a fall in saving. A rise in investment is shown in the top part of Figure 18.10 by a shift in the investment line to I_2. Likewise a fall in saving is shown by a shift in the saving curve to S_2. This will lead to a multiplied rise in income to Y_2 (where $I_2 = S_2$). This corresponds to point *b* in the lower diagram, which therefore gives a second point on the *IS* curve.

Thus *lower* interest rates are associated with *higher* national income, if equilibrium is to be maintained in the goods market ($I = S$).

The elasticity of the IS curve

KI 9 p 58

The elasticity of the *IS* curve (i.e. the responsiveness of national income to changes in interest rates) depends on two factors.[1]

The responsiveness of investment and saving to interest rate changes. The more investment and saving respond to a change in the rate of interest, the bigger will be the vertical shift in the *I* and *S* curves in the top part of the diagram, and thus the bigger will be the effect on national income. The bigger the effect on national income, the more elastic will be the *IS* curve.

Definition

ISLM model A model showing simultaneous equilibrium in the goods market ($I = S$) and the money market ($L = M$).

[1] Note that, as with demand and supply curves, the elasticity of the *IS* curve will vary along its length. Therefore we should really talk about the elasticity at a particular point on the curve, or between two points.

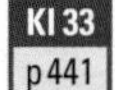
KI 33 p441

The size of the multiplier. This is given by $1/mps$ (i.e. $1/mpw$ in the full model). The *mps* is given by the slope of the *S* curve. The flatter the curve, the bigger the multiplier. The larger the value of the multiplier, the bigger will be the effect on national income of any rise in investment and fall in saving, and the more elastic therefore will be the *IS* curve. Thus the flatter the *S* curve in the top part of the diagram, the flatter the *IS* curve in the bottom part.

? *In a complete model where there were three injections (I, G and X) and three withdrawals (S, T and M), what else would determine the shape of the 'JW' curve?*

Keynesians argue that the *IS* curve is likely to be fairly inelastic. The reason they give is that investment is not very responsive to changes in interest rates: the demand for investment curve in Figure 18.1(b) on page 506 is relatively inelastic. Saving also, claim Keynesians, is unresponsive to interest rate changes. The effect of this is that there will only be a relatively small shift in the *I* and *S* curves in response to a change in interest rates, and thus only a relatively small change in national income.

Monetarists, by contrast, argue that investment and saving are relatively responsive to changes in interest rates and that therefore the *IS* curve is relatively elastic.

Shifts in the IS curve

A change in interest rates will cause a movement *along* the *IS* curve. As we saw in Figure 18.10, a reduction in interest rates from r_1 to r_2 causes a movement *along* the *IS* curve from point *a* to point *b*.

A change in any *other* determinant of investment or saving, however, will *shift* the whole curve. The reason is that it will change the equilibrium level of national income at any given rate of interest.

An increase in investment, other than as a result of a fall in interest rates, will shift the *IS* curve to the *right*. This could happen, for example, if there were an increase in business confidence. A rise in business confidence *at the current interest rate* will cause an upward shift of the *I* curve in the top diagram of Figure 18.10, which will cause a multiplied rise in income. Thus in the lower part of the diagram a higher equilibrium income is now associated with each level of the interest rate: the *IS* curve has shifted to the right. Likewise, for any given interest rate, a fall in saving, and hence a rise in consumption, would also shift the *IS* curve to the right.

In a complete model (with three injections and three withdrawals), where the *IS* curve was a '$J = W$' curve rather than a simple '$I = S$' curve, similar shifts would result from changes in other injections or withdrawals. Thus an expansionary fiscal policy that increased government expenditure (*G*) or cut taxes (*T*) would shift the '*IS*' curve (i.e. the *JW* curve) to the right.

? *In a complete JW model, what else would cause the JW curve (a) to shift to the right; (b) to shift to the left?*

The *LM* curve

The *IS* curve is concerned with equilibrium in the goods market. The *LM* curve is concerned with equilibrium in the money market. The *LM* curve shows all the various combinations of interest rates and national income at which the demand for money (*L*) equals the supply (*M*).

Deriving the LM curve

To explain how the *LM* curve is derived, we again use a diagram in two parts (see Figure 18.11), only this time they are side by side (the reason being that we use the same *vertical* axis (*r*) this time, whereas in Figure 18.10 we used the same horizontal axis (*Y*)). The left-hand part of the diagram is the familiar money market diagram, showing a liquidity preference (demand for money) curve (*L*) and a supply of money curve (*M*).

At any given level of national income, there will be a particular level of transactions-plus-precautionary demand for money, and hence a given overall demand for money curve (*L*). Let us assume that, when national income is at a level of Y_1 in the right-hand diagram of Figure 18.11, the demand for money curve is *L'*. With the given money supply curve M_s, the equilibrium rate of interest will be r_1. Thus point *c* is one point on the *LM* curve. At a level of national income Y_1, the money market will be in equilibrium at a rate of interest of r_1.

Figure 18.11 Money market equilibrium: deriving the *LM* curve

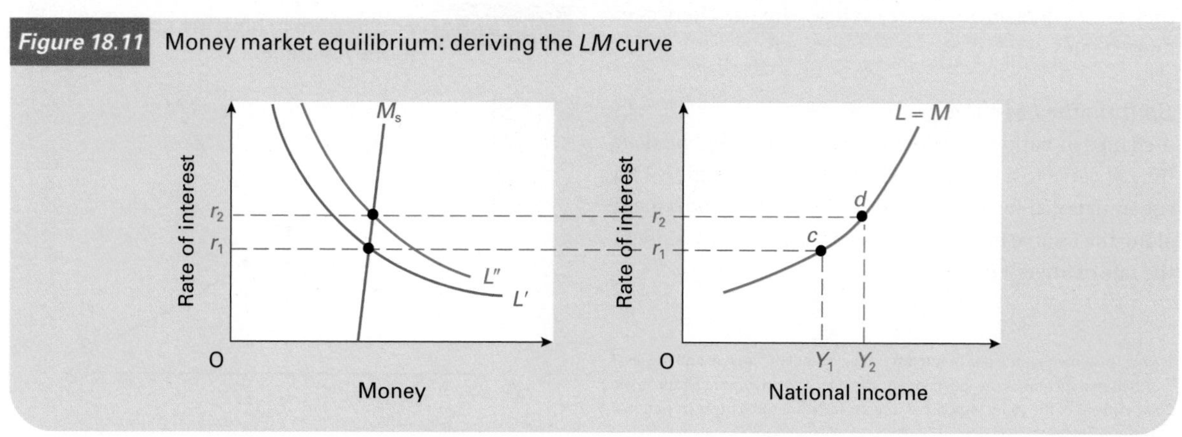

Now what will happen if the level of national income changes? Let us assume that national income rises to Y_2. The effect is to increase the transactions-plus-precautionary demand for money. The *L* curve shifts to the right: to, say, *L*″. This will cause the rate of interest to rise to the new equilibrium level of r_2. This therefore gives us a second point on the *LM* curve (point *d*).

Thus *higher* national income leads to a greater demand for money and hence *higher* interest rates if equilibrium is to be maintained in the money market. The *LM* curve is therefore upward sloping.

The elasticity of the LM curve

KI 9 p 58

The elasticity of the *LM* curve (i.e. the responsiveness of interest rate changes to a change in national income)[2] again depends on two factors.

The responsiveness of the demand for money to changes in national income. The greater the marginal propensity to consume, the more will the transactions demand for money rise as national income rises, and thus the more will the *L* curve shift to the right. Hence the more will the equilibrium interest rate rise, and the steeper will be the *LM* curve.

The responsiveness of the demand for money to changes in interest rates. The more the demand for money responds to a change in interest rates, the flatter will be the liquidity preference curve in the left-hand diagram. The flatter the *L* curve, the less will the equilibrium interest rate change for any given horizontal shift in the *L* curve (arising from a change in *Y*). The less the equilibrium interest rate changes, the flatter will be the *LM* curve.

The Keynesian and monetarist views on the shape of the *LM* curve reflect their views on the elasticity of the *L* curve. Keynesians argue that the *L* curve is likely to be relatively flat given the responsiveness of the speculative demand for money to changes in interest rates. They thus argue that the *LM* curve is correspondingly flat (depending, of course, on the scales of the axes). Monetarists, on the other hand, argue that the *LM* curve is relatively steep. This is because they see the demand for money as insensitive to changes in interest rates.

Shifts in the LM curve

A change in national income will cause a movement *along* the *LM* curve to a new interest rate. Thus in Figure 18.11 a rise in national income from Y_1 to Y_2 leads to a movement along the *L* curve from point *c* to point *d* and hence a rise in the rate of interest from r_1 to r_2.

A change in any *other* determinant of the demand and supply of money will *shift* the whole curve. The reason is that it will change the equilibrium level of interest associated with any given level of national income.

An increase in the demand for money, other than as a result of a rise in income, will shift the *L* curve to the *right*. This could be due to people being paid less frequently, or a greater use of cash, or increased speculation that the price of securities will fall. This increased demand for money will raise the equilibrium rate of interest at the current level of national income. The *LM* curve will shift upwards.

An increased supply of money will shift the M_s curve to the right. This will lower the rate of interest (in the left-hand part of Figure 18.11). This will shift the *LM* curve downwards: a lower rate of interest will be associated with any given level of national income.

Draw a diagram like Figure 18.11, only with just one L curve. Assume that the current level of national income is Y_1. Now assume that the supply of money decreases. Show the effect on

(a) the rate of interest;

(b) the position of the LM curve.

Equilibrium

KI 8 p 43

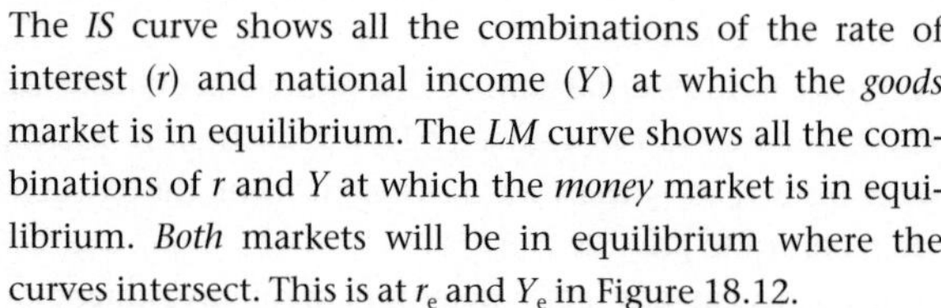

The *IS* curve shows all the combinations of the rate of interest (*r*) and national income (*Y*) at which the *goods* market is in equilibrium. The *LM* curve shows all the combinations of *r* and *Y* at which the *money* market is in equilibrium. *Both* markets will be in equilibrium where the curves intersect. This is at r_e and Y_e in Figure 18.12.

But what would happen if both markets were not simultaneously in equilibrium? How would equilibrium be achieved?

KI 5 p 21

Let us suppose that the current level of national income is Y_1. This will create a demand for money that will lead to an equilibrium interest rate of r_1 (point *a* on the *LM* curve). But at this low interest rate, the desired level of investment and saving would generate an income of Y_2 (point *b* on the *IS* curve). Thus national income will rise. But as national income rises, there will be a movement up along the *LM*

Figure 18.12 Equilibrium in both the goods and money markets

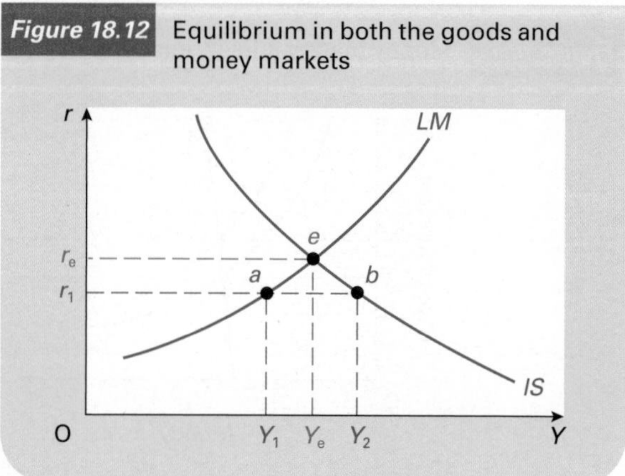

[2] Note this time that the rate of interest is the dependent variable and the level of national income is the independent variable. Thus the more elastic is the *LM* curve (i.e. the more responsive interest rates are to changes in national income), the *steeper* will it be.

curve from point *a*, since the higher income will generate a higher demand for money and hence push up interest rates. And as interest rates rise, so the desired level of investment will fall and the desired level of saving will rise so as to reduce the equilibrium level of national income below Y_2. There will be a movement back up along the *IS* curve from point *b*. Once the interest rate has risen to r_e, the actual level of income will be at the equilibrium level (i.e. *on* the *IS* curve). Both markets will now be in equilibrium.

? *Assume that national income is initially at Y_2 in Figure 18.12. Describe the process whereby equilibrium in both markets will be achieved.*

*LOOKING AT THE MATHS

Equilibrium in the *ISLM* model is where the two functions, *IS* and *LM*, are equal. The simplest mathematical representation of this is where both *IS* and *LM* are simple linear (i.e. straight-line) functions. The *IS* function could be expressed as:

$$r = a - bY \quad (1)$$

In other words, the higher the real rate of interest (*r*), the lower will be the level of aggregate demand and hence national income (*Y*).[3] This is consistent with a downward-sloping *IS* curve.

The *LM* function can be written as:

$$r = g + hY \quad (2)$$

In other words, the higher the level of real national income (and hence the higher the demand for money), the higher will be the real rate of interest. This is consistent with an upward-sloping *LM* curve.

We can then solve for *Y* by setting the two equations equal. Thus:

$$a - bY = g + hY$$

$$\text{i.e. } bY + hY = a - g$$

$$\text{giving } Y = \frac{a-g}{h+b}$$

More complex *IS* and *LM* functions. In practice, neither function is likely to be linear. Both *IS* and *LM* are likely to be curves rather than straight lines. To understand why, we need to look at the other determinants of *Y* in the case of the *IS* curve and of *r* in the case of the *LM* curve. Let us first examine the *IS* function.

Real national income consists of five elements:

$$Y = C + I + G + X - M \quad (3)$$

$$\text{or } Y = C(Y,T,r,\pi^e) + I(r,\pi^e,\Delta Y) + G + X(er) - M(Y,T,r,\pi^e er) \quad (3a)$$

Equation (3a) is simply an expansion of equation (3) listing the key determinants of each of the variables in equation (3), where *T* is taxes, π^e is expected inflation and *er* is the exchange rate. Investment being a function of changes in national income (ΔY) is the accelerator effect. Thus an *IS* function could be expressed as:

$$Y = IS(\underset{-}{r},\underset{-}{T},\underset{+}{\pi^e},\underset{+}{\Delta Y},\underset{+}{G},\underset{-}{er}) \quad (4)$$

All the variables in this function are contained in equation (3a). It is highly likely that the relationship between *Y* and most, if not all, these variables is non-linear (i.e. contains squared or higher power terms).

The sign under each of the variables indicates the direction in which *Y* changes when the variable changes. For example, the negative sign under the *T* term means that a rise in taxes would lead to a *fall* in *Y*. Put another way, the sign indicates the sign of the partial derivative of *Y* with respect to each variable. For example, the positive sign under the expected inflation term (π^e) means that when you differentiate *Y* with respect to π^e, you end up with a positive number. This simply means that a rise in π^e leads to a *rise* in *Y*.

Note that a change in *r* would lead to a movement along the *IS* curve. A change in any of the other determinants in equation (4) would shift the curve. A rise in any of the determinants with a positive sign would result in a rightward shift in the curve; a rise in any of the determinants with a negative sign would result in a leftward shift.

Turning to the *LM* function, this can be expressed as:

$$r = LM(\underset{+}{Y},\underset{-}{\frac{M_s}{P}},\underset{+}{\pi^e},\underset{+}{er^e},\underset{-}{f}) \quad (5)$$

where M_s/P is the real money supply, π^e is the expected rate of inflation, er^e is the expected exchange rate and *f* is the frequency with which people are paid. The *LM* curve assumes equilibrium in the money market. It therefore represents all the combinations of *r* and *Y* where the real demand for money is equal to the real supply. The real supply of money is given by the term M_s/P and the real demand for money depends on the other terms in equation (5) (see page 500). TC 12 p374

A rise in *Y* would cause a movement up along the *LM* curve. A rise in any of the other determinants would shift the curve: upwards in the case of the determinants with a positive sign; downwards in the case of those with a negative sign.

As with the *IS* function, it is highly likely that the relationship between *r* and most, if not all, the variables in the *LM* function is likely to be non-linear.

Maths Case 18.1 shows how equilibrium in the *ISLM* model can be derived from specific *IS* and *LM* functions.

[3] Note that although equation (1) shows *r* as a function of *Y*, the model in fact has *Y* as the dependent variable. In other words, *r* determines *Y*. We express equation (1) this way to make it consistent with equation (2), where *r* is the dependent variable.

Full effects of changes in the goods and money markets

KI 5 p21

ISLM analysis can be used to examine the full effects of changes in the goods market. Such changes are illustrated by a shift in the *IS* curve. Likewise, the full effects of changes in the money market can be illustrated by a shift in the *LM* curve.

EXPLORING ECONOMICS

ENVIRONMENTALLY SUSTAINABLE MACROECONOMIC EQUILIBRIUM

***Introducing an environmental constraint into the ISLM model*[4]**

In Box 13.6 we saw that economic growth, as conventionally measured using GDP figures, is not necessarily desirable. One reason for this is that economic growth can damage the environment.

Can we amend macroeconomic models to take the environment into account? The answer is yes. Here we show how it could be incorporated into the *ISLM* model.

We start with two simple propositions:

- *Using current technology, there will be a maximum level of national income that is environmentally sustainable.* If national income rises above this level, environmental degradation will occur. A higher level of national income *could* be sustained, however, if a cleaner technology was used.
- *Generally, more capital-intensive techniques are cleaner than more labour-intensive techniques.* This is mainly because capital-intensive techniques tend to be more modern and make a less wasteful use of resources, or have tighter environmental safeguards (e.g. emission levels) built into the technology. Generally, then, by using capital-intensive techniques, a higher level of national income can be sustained. One major factor that will encourage the use of more capital-intensive technology is a lower rate of interest (since the rate of interest represents the price of capital).

We can illustrate these two propositions graphically. The *EE* line in Figure (a) shows the various combinations of the maximum level of national income and interest rates that are environmentally sustainable. Any point on the line or to the left of it would be environmentally sustainable. Any point to the right of it would represent an environmentally unsustainable level of national income: it would cause environmental degradation to occur. Why is the curve negatively

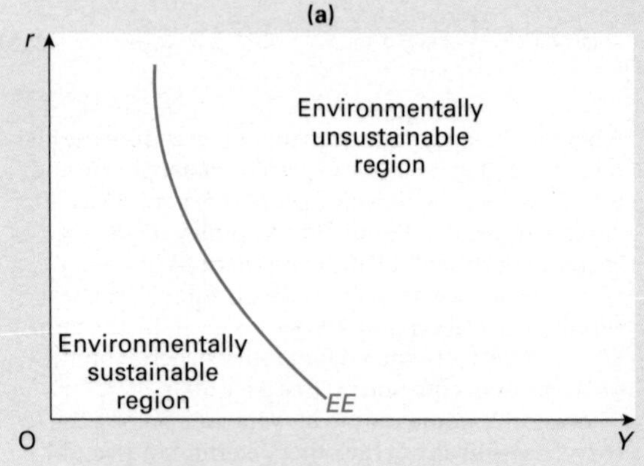

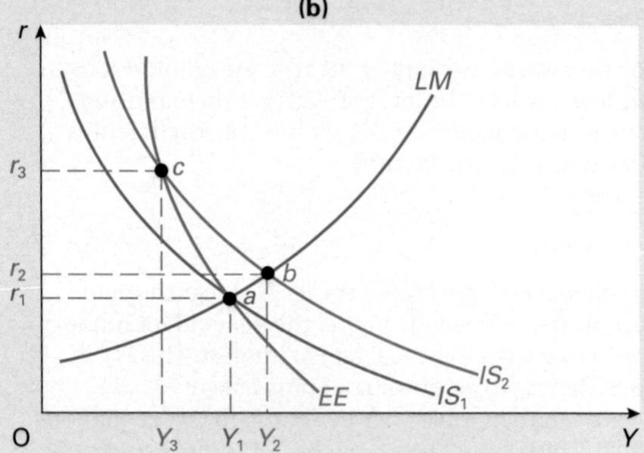

Changes in the goods market

Assume that business confidence rises and firms decide to increase their investment. The rise in injections leads to a rightward shift in the *IS* curve. This is illustrated in Figure 18.13(a). It is assumed that there is no exogenous increase in the money supply and that, therefore, the *LM* curve does not shift. Income rises to Y_2, but interest rates also rise (to r_2).

The rise in the rate of interest to r_2 restricts the rise in national income, since the higher interest rate dampens both investment and consumption. The net rise in injections is less than the original rise in investment. The steeper the *LM* curve, the less will national income rise.

If, however, money supply is expanded passively to meet the extra demand for money, then interest rates will not have to rise. This is illustrated in Figure 18.13(c). The rightward shift in the *IS* curve is matched by a downward shift in the *LM* curve. The rate of interest remains at r_1 and there is a full multiplied rise in national income to Y_4.

Changes in the money market

Assume that there is an increase in money supply. The *LM* curve shifts downwards. This is illustrated in Figure 18.13(b). Interest rates fall and this encourages an increase in borrowing and hence an increase in investment and consumption. This is shown by a movement down along the *IS* curve. National income rises. Equilibrium is reached at a rate of interest of r_3 and a national income of Y_3.

The fall in the rate of interest means that some of the extra money is absorbed in idle balances and is not all used to finance additional expenditure and this reduces the resulting increased national income. The effect on national income also depends on the elasticity of the *IS* curve. The steeper the *IS* curve, the less will national income rise. This will be the case when investment is relatively insensitive to cuts in interest rates.

If, however, the rise in money supply is accompanied by an autonomous rise in injections (for example, a rise in government expenditure), then the effect can be much

***BOX 18.4**

sloped? This shows that a lower rate of interest, by encouraging the use of more capital-intensive (i.e. cleaner) technology, would allow a higher level of environmentally sustainable national income.

We can now superimpose this line on an *ISLM* diagram. This is done in Figure (b), and we assume that the initial level of national income (Y_1), given by the point where the IS_1 and *LM* curves cross, is on the *EE* line (point *a*): i.e. is just environmentally sustainable.

If there is now an expansionary fiscal policy, the *IS* curve will shift to the right. This is illustrated by a shift in the *IS* curve from IS_1 to IS_2. The new equilibrium is at point *b*. But this is not environmentally sustainable. In fact, to restore sustainability, given the new *IS* curve, there would have to be a movement to point *c*. This would necessitate shifting the *LM* curve to the left through a contractionary monetary policy. The result, however, would be a *lower* level of national income than originally.

?

Going back to point a, show how an expansionary monetary policy (combined with a contractionary fiscal policy) would allow a higher level of environmentally sustainable national income.

If national income does rise into the environmentally unsustainable region, what will happen? Are there any forces that will restore sustainability? In fact there are forces pulling in opposite directions.

On the one hand, if current levels of national income cause environmental degradation, there will be political pressures to protect the environment, perhaps through controls or through market instruments, such as green taxes. Either way, firms will have the incentive to adopt greener technology and consumers will have the incentive to switch to greener products. The *EE* curve will shift to the right.

On the other hand, if the economy is currently to the right of *EE*, the environmental degradation will reduce the *future* capacity of the environment to absorb pollution. This will have the effect of shifting the *EE* curve to the left. The further to the right of the *EE* line the current position is, the faster will the *EE* line shift to the left.

Whether the *EE* line will actually shift to the right or left depends on which of these two forces is the stronger. Clearly, (a) the greener governments are and the more active their environmental policies and (b) the less far to the right of the *EE* line the current position is, the more likely the *EE* curve is to shift to the right: the more likely is the environment to be able to cope with economic growth.

?

1. ***What will determine the slope of the EE curve?***
2. ***Draw an IS-LM-EE diagram with the EE curve shallower than the IS curve. Now illustrate the effect of an expansionary fiscal policy. Given this fiscal expansion, illustrate by a shift in the LM curve the monetary policy that would be necessary to restore sustainability. Is national income now higher or lower than it was originally?***

[4] This box is based on A. Heyes, *A Proposal for Greening of Textbook Macro: 'IS-LM-EE'* (Royal Holloway College, University of London working paper, 1998).

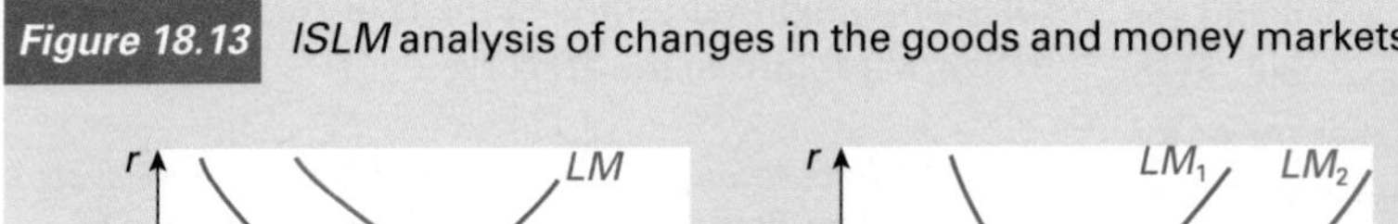

Figure 18.13 *ISLM* analysis of changes in the goods and money markets

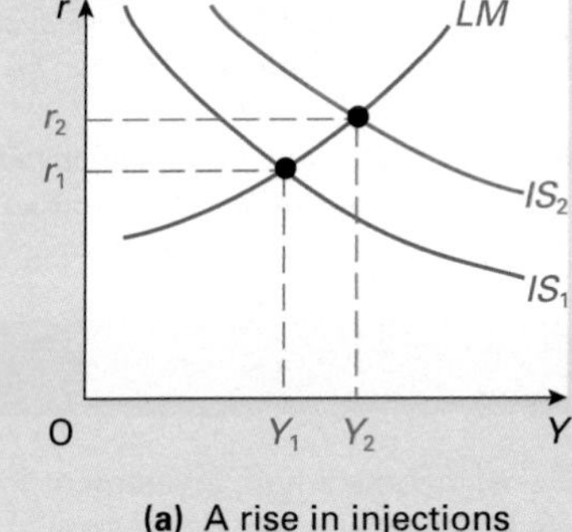

(a) A rise in injections

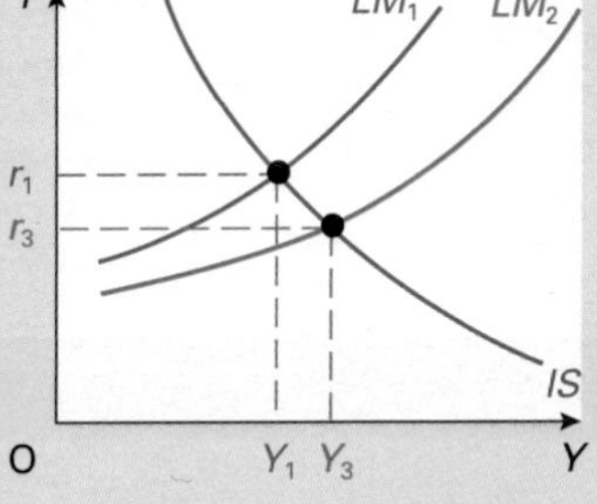

(b) A rise in money supply

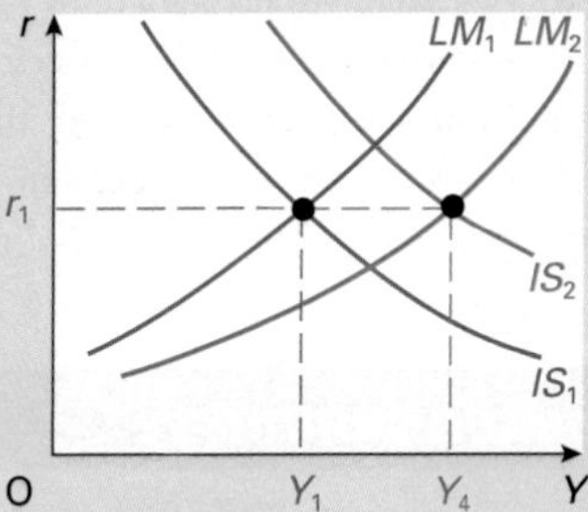

(c) A rise in both injections and the money supply

bigger. If the downward shift in the *LM* curve is matched by a rightward shift in the *IS* curve, then the effect is once more illustrated in Figure 18.13(c).

To summarise: the effect on national income of a change in either market depends on the slope of the *IS* and *LM* curves.

- The effect of a shift in the *IS* curve will be bigger when the *LM* curve is shallow and the *IS* curve is steep. When *LM* is shallow, a rightward shift in *IS* will lead to only a small rise in the rate of interest (r). If *IS* is steep, this rise in r will lead to only a small curtailing of investment. In these two circumstances, the dampening effect on investment and consumption is limited. There will be a large increase in national income (Y).
- The effect of a shift in the *LM* curve will be bigger when the liquidity preference curve (L) (e.g. in Figure 18.11(a)) is steep and the *IS* curve is shallow. When L is steep, there will be a relatively large downward shift in the *LM* curve for any given increase in the money supply and hence a relatively large fall in r. When *IS* is shallow, this fall in r will lead to a relatively large increase in investment and hence Y.
- The effect of a shift in either curve will be bigger if matched by a similar shift in the other curve.

?

On a diagram similar to Figure 18.12, trace through the effects of (a) a fall in investment and (b) a fall in the money supply. On what does the size of the fall in national income depend?

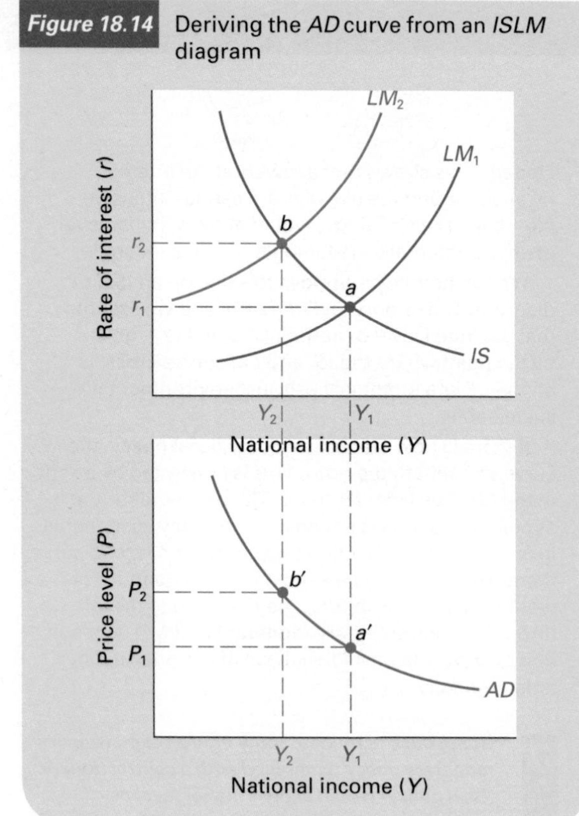

Figure 18.14 Deriving the *AD* curve from an *ISLM* diagram

Deriving an *AD* curve from the *ISLM* model

In section 14.2, we saw why the aggregate demand curve is downward sloping. Now we have looked at the *ISLM* model, we can give a more formal explanation of the shape of the *AD* curve.

Figure 18.14 shows both an *ISLM* diagram and an *AD* curve. In the top diagram, both goods and money markets are in equilibrium at point a (the point where the *IS* and *LM* curves cross). National income is Y_1 and the rate of interest is r_1. Turning to the bottom diagram, let us assume that with national income at Y_1, the price level happens to be P_1. The aggregate demand curve thus passes through point a'.

TC 12 p374

Now let us assume that the price level rises to P_2. The effect of the higher price is to raise the demand for (nominal) money balances: after all, people will need bigger money balances if they are to pay higher prices for goods. The higher demand for money balances will raise the equilibrium rate of interest at the current level of national income. In the top diagram, the *LM* curve will shift upwards. Assuming that the *LM* curve shifts to LM_2, equilibrium will now be at point b. National income will fall to Y_2. Thus a rise in the price level to P_2 has caused national income to fall to Y_2. In the bottom diagram, the *AD* curve must now pass through point b'.

If the *IS* curve shifts, or if the *LM* curve shifts other than as a result of a change in the price level, the *AD* curve must shift. For example, if investment rises, the *IS* curve will shift to the right. National income will rise for any given price level, and hence the *AD* curve must shift to the right. To summarise: rightward shifts in the *IS* or *LM* curve will lead to rightward shifts in the *AD* curve.

?

1. *Trace through the effects of a fall in the price level to show how a further point on the AD curve can be derived.*
2. *Explain what could cause a downward shift in the LM curve and how this would affect the AD curve.*

Section summary

1. The *ISLM* model allows equilibrium to be shown in both goods and money markets simultaneously. The model shows the relationship between national income and interest rates.
2. Equilibrium in the goods market is shown by the *IS* curve. This shows all the combinations of the rate of interest and national income where investment (I) equals saving (S) (or, in a complete Keynesian model, where injections equal withdrawals). As the rate of interest rises, so investment will fall and saving will rise: thus equilibrium national income will fall. The *IS* curve is thus downward sloping.

continued

3. A change in interest rates will cause a movement along the *IS* curve. A change in anything else that affects national income (i.e. a change in injections or withdrawals other than as a result of a change in interest rates) will cause a shift in the *IS* curve.
4. Equilibrium in the money market is shown by the *LM* curve. This shows all the combinations of national income and the rate of interest where the demand for money (*L*) equals the supply (*M*). As national income rises, so the demand for money will rise: thus the equilibrium rate of interest in the money market will rise. The *LM* curve is thus upward sloping.
5. A change in national income will cause a movement along the *LM* curve. A change in anything else that affects interest rates (i.e. a change in the demand or supply of money other than as a result of a change in national income) will shift the *LM* curve.
6. Simultaneous equilibrium in both goods and money markets (i.e. the equilibrium national income *and* the equilibrium rate of interest) is where *IS* = *LM*.
7. A change in injections or withdrawals will shift the *IS* curve. A rise in injections will shift it to the right. This will cause a rise in both national income and the rate of interest. The rise in income will be bigger and the rise in the rate of interest smaller, the steeper the *IS* curve and the flatter the *LM* curve.
8. A rise in money supply will shift the *LM* curve downwards. This will cause a fall in interest rates and a rise in national income. The rise in national income will be larger, the flatter the *IS* curve and the steeper the liquidity preference curve (*L*) and hence the bigger the downward shift in the *LM* curve for any given increase in the money supply.
9. An *AD* curve can be derived from an *ISLM* diagram. A higher price level will shift the *LM* curve upwards. This will lead to a lower level of national income. The higher price level and lower national income gives a new point on the *AD* curve.

18.4 TAKING INFLATION INTO ACCOUNT

Keeping inflation down

Since the early 1990s, most developed countries have experienced relatively low inflation. Inflation rates of between 0 and 3 per cent are typical of those experienced today. The average inflation rate for the G7[5] countries from 1997 to 2005 was just 1.2 per cent and for the OECD countries as a whole it was 2.0 per cent.

Part of the reason for this is the process of globalisation. Trade barriers between countries have been reduced; international price comparisons have been made easier through the Internet; competition legislation around the world has been tightened; labour markets have become more flexible, and with it the power of labour to drive up wages has declined. This all bears down on inflation. Labour markets are increasingly competitive and companies are increasingly wary about raising prices for fear of losing market share.

The other major reason for low inflation is the deliberate policy of targeting a low rate of inflation. As we shall see in section 19.5, using interest rates to achieve a target rate of inflation has become the prime focus of monetary policy in many countries (including the UK) and an important element in monetary policy in many others. In both the UK and the eurozone, the target inflation rate is 2 per cent.

If actual inflation is above target, the central bank raises real interest rates (i.e. interest rates after taking the higher inflation into account) so as to dampen aggregate demand and thereby reduce inflation. If actual inflation is below target, the central bank lowers real interest rates, thereby boosting aggregate demand and pushing inflation back up to target.

Such policies have been generally successful. What is more, as inflation targets are met, so this feeds through into people's expectations. People expect inflation to be at approximately its target level and hence wage and price setting reflect this. As a result, inflation remains at its target level.

In a world of inflation targets, how does this affect the relationship between the goods and money markets? What will be the effect of a change in aggregate demand? In this section, we explore these questions.

Aggregate demand and supply plotted against inflation

To illustrate the impact of changes in aggregate demand or supply in an economy with inflation targets, we can use a variant of the aggregate demand and supply model. This new version is illustrated in Figures 18.15 and 18.16.

In this version, the horizontal axis, as before, measures real national income (*Y*). The vertical axis, however, measures the *rate of inflation*, not the *level* of prices. The aggregate demand and supply curves are labelled *ADI* and *ASI* to distinguish them from the curves in the normal aggregate demand and supply diagram. We also add a line showing the target rate of inflation.

[5] The Group of Seven countries: Canada, France, Germany, Italy, Japan, UK, USA.

Figure 18.15 AD plotted against inflation

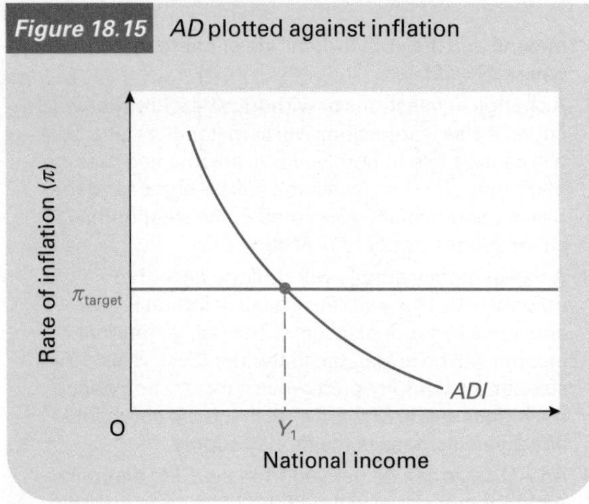

Before we look at the properties of the model, let us examine each of the three lines in turn. The first two are illustrated in Figure 18.15.

The inflation target line

This is simply a horizontal line at the target rate of inflation. If inflation is above target, real interest rates will be raised by the central bank. If it is below target, real interest rates will be cut.

If the government or central bank changes the target, the line will shift to the new target rate.

The aggregate demand/inflation curve

As with the normal *AD* curve, the *ADI* curve is downward sloping. In other words, a higher rate of inflation leads to a lower level of aggregate demand. But why?

The reason is simple. It consists of a two-stage process.

1. If the rate of inflation (π) goes above the target level, the central bank will raise the *real* rate of interest (i). In other words it will raise the nominal rate *more* than the rise in inflation. Thus if inflation goes up from a targeted 2 per cent to 3 per cent, the nominal interest rate must rise by more than 1 percentage point in order to achieve a rise in the real interest rate.
2. The higher real rate of interest will then reduce (real) aggregate demand (*AD*), through both the interest rate mechanism and the exchange rate mechanism (see pages 505–11).

To summarise:

$$\pi\uparrow \rightarrow i\uparrow \rightarrow AD\downarrow$$

Similarly, a fall in the rate of inflation will cause the central bank to lower the real rate of interest. This will then lead to an increase in aggregate demand.

The slope of the ADI curve. The slope of the *ADI* curve depends on the strength of the two stages. The curve will be relatively shallow:

- The more real interest rates respond to a change in inflation. Interest rate changes will be larger, the quicker the central bank wants to get inflation back to its target level and the less concerned it is about cutting back on aggregate demand and hence output and employment.
- The more responsive investment, consumption and exports (i.e. the components of aggregate demand) are to a change in interest rates.

A movement along the ADI curve. This will be caused by a change in the rate of inflation. If inflation rises, there will be a movement up the curve as the central bank raises the real rate of interest and this causes real income to fall. When *inflation* begins to fall in response to the higher rate of interest, there will be a movement back down the curve again.

The position of the ADI curve. A given *ADI* curve represents a given monetary policy. The particular *ADI* curve in Figure 18.15 intersects with the inflation target line at a real income of Y_1. This means that if inflation is on target, real national income will be Y_1. The central bank will need to consider whether this is consistent with long-term equilibrium in the economy: in other words, whether Y_1 is the *sustainable* level of national income (see Box 13.4 on page 382). If it is, then the monetary policy it has chosen is appropriate.

A shift in the ADI curve. Any factor that causes aggregate demand to change, other than the central bank responding to inflation being off target, will cause the *ADI* curve to shift. A rightward shift represents an increase in aggregate demand. A leftward shift represents a decrease.

Examples of a rightward shift include: cuts in tax rates, an increase in government expenditure and a rise in consumer or business confidence. The *ADI* curve will also shift to the right if the government or central bank sets a higher target rate of inflation. The reason is that this will lead to lower interest rates at every level of inflation.

The curve will also shift if the central bank changes its monetary policy, such that it no longer wants Y_1 to be the equilibrium level of national income. For example, if Y_1 in Figure 18.15 were below the sustainable level, and there was therefore demand-deficient unemployment, the central bank would want to reduce real interest rates in order to achieve a higher level of aggregate demand at the target rate of inflation. This will shift the *ADI* curve to the right. In other words, each level of inflation along this new *ADI* curve would correspond to a lower real rate of interest (i) and hence a higher level of aggregate demand.

But what determines the level of *Y*? This is determined by the interaction of aggregate demand and aggregate supply. To show this we introduce a third line: the *ASI* curve.

The aggregate supply/inflation curve

The *ASI* curve, like the normal *AS* curve, is upward sloping. In the short run it will be relatively shallow. In the long

Figure 18.16 *AD* and *AS* plotted against inflation

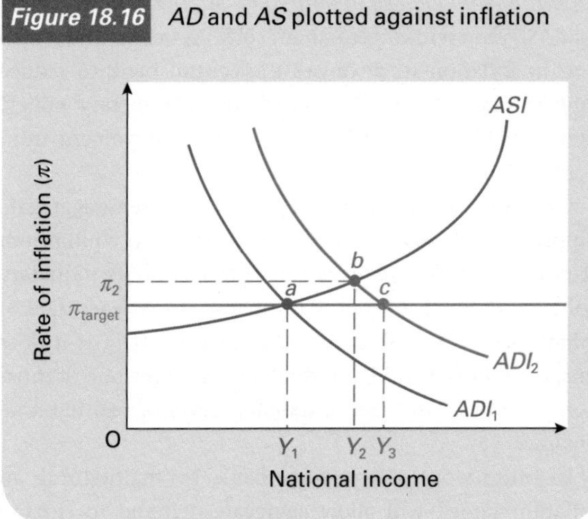

run it will be relatively steep, if not vertical at the sustainable level of national income. The curve illustrated in Figure 18.16 is the short-run *ASI* curve. But why is it shaped this way? Why will a higher rate of inflation lead to higher real national income?

Assume that the economy is currently generating a real national income of Y_1 and that inflation is on target (π_{target}). Equilibrium is at point *a*. Assume also that Y_1 represents the long-run sustainable level of output.

Now assume that consumer confidence rises, and that, as a result, the *ADI* curve shifts to ADI_2. Firms will respond to the higher aggregate demand partly by raising prices more than the current (i.e. target) rate of inflation and partly by increasing output: there is a movement along the *ASI* curve. Equilibrium moves to point *b*, where *ADI* = *ASI*.

KI 30 p306

But why will firms raise output as well as prices? The reason is that wage rises lag behind price rises. This is because of the time it takes to negotiate new wage rates and the fact that people were probably anticipating that inflation would stay at its target level. The higher prices now charged by firms will generate bigger profit margins for them, and thus they will be willing to supply more.

Over time, however, if the higher demand persists, wage rises would get higher. This would be the result of firms trying to obtain more labour to meet the higher demand and of unions seeking wage increases to compensate for the higher rate of inflation. Thus, assuming no increase in productivity, the *ASI* curve would shift upwards and continue doing so until real national income returned to the sustainable level Y_1. The long-run *ASI* curve would be vertical through point *a*.

Response to changes in aggregate demand and supply

A rise in aggregate demand

Assume, in Figure 18.16, that there has been a rise in real aggregate demand and that the *ADI* curve has shifted to ADI_2. Assume also that Y_1 is the sustainable level of national income. If inflation remained at its target level, the economy would move to point *c*, with national income increasing to Y_3. But as firms respond partly by increasing prices more rapidly, equilibrium is reached at point *b*. In other words, there has been a movement up along the *ASI* curve from point *a* to point *b* and back up along the new *ADI* curve from point *c* to point *b*. This movement along curve ADI_2 is the result of the higher interest rates imposed by the central bank in response to inflation rising to π_2.

But equilibrium at point *b* is above the target rate. This is unsustainable, even in the short run. One of two things must happen. The first option is for the central bank (or government) to accept a higher target rate of inflation: i.e. π_2. But if it does this, real income can only remain above its sustainable level in the short run. Soon, higher prices will feed through into higher wages and back into higher prices, and so on. The *ASI* curve will shift upwards.

The second option – the only effective option in the long run – is for the central bank to reduce aggregate demand back to ADI_1. This will mean changing monetary policy, such that a higher real rate of interest is chosen for each rate of inflation. This tighter monetary policy shifts the *ADI* curve to the left.

In other words, if the central bank is adhering strictly to an inflation target, any rise in real aggregate demand can have only a temporary effect, since the higher inflation that results will force the central bank to bring aggregate demand back down again.

The one exception to this would be if the higher aggregate demand encouraged firms to invest more. When the effects of this on aggregate supply began to be felt in terms of higher output, the short-term *ASI* curve itself would shift to the right, leading to a new equilibrium to the right of point *a*. In such a case, there would have been a long-term increase in output, even though the central bank was sticking to an inflation target.

Using a graph similar to Figure 18.16, trace through the effect of a reduction in aggregate demand.

A rise in aggregate supply

Assume now that aggregate supply rises. This could be a temporary 'supply shock', such as a cut in oil prices or a good harvest, or it could be a permanent increase caused, say, by technical progress. Let us take each in turn.

A temporary supply shock. In Figure 18.17, initial equilibrium is at point *a*, with curves ADI_1 and ASI_1 intersecting at the target rate of inflation. The rise in aggregate supply causes the *ASI* curve temporarily to shift from ASI_1 to ASI_2. Inflation thus falls below the target rate. As a result, the central bank reduces the real rate of interest (*i*). The effect is to increase aggregate demand. This is shown by a movement *along* curve ADI_1 from point *a* to point *d*. Inflation has fallen to π_3 and real national income has risen to Y_4. Since this is only a temporary increase in aggregate supply, the

Figure 18.17 The effects of an increase in aggregate supply

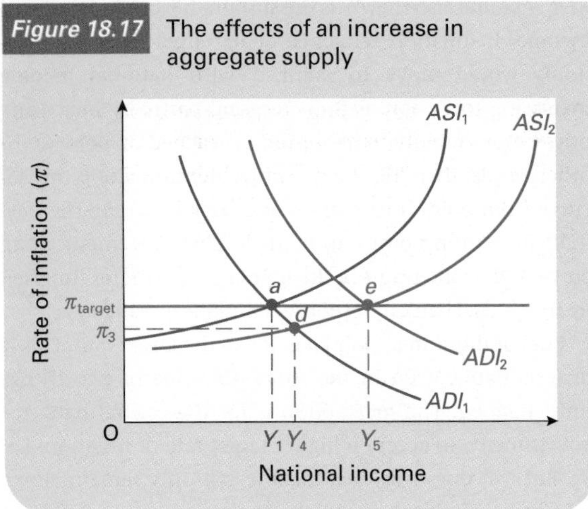

central bank will not change its monetary policy. The *ADI* curve, therefore, will not shift.

As the supply shock subsides, aggregate supply will fall again. The *ASI* curve will shift back from ASI_2 to ASI_1, causing inflation to rise again. The result is a move back up the ADI_1 curve from point *d* to point *a*.

?

1. *Trace through the effect of an adverse supply shock, such as a rise in oil prices.*
2. *What determines the amount that national income fluctuates when there is a temporary shift in the ASI curve?*

A permanent increase in aggregate supply. Now assume that ASI_2 represents a permanent shift. As before, the reduction in inflation to π_3 causes the central bank to reduce interest rates. If there is no change in monetary policy, there would be simply be, once more, a movement from point *a* to point *d*.

Once the central bank realises that the rise in aggregate supply is permanent, it will want to move to equilibrium at point *e*. To do this it will have to *change* its monetary policy and adopt a lower real interest rate at each rate of inflation. This will shift the *ADI* curve to ADI_2. If it does this, equilibrium will be restored at the target rate of inflation. Y_5 will be the new sustainable level of real national income.

In other words, the central bank, by maintaining an inflation target, will allow aggregate demand to expand sufficiently to accommodate the full rise in aggregate supply.

In the next chapter we explore policies to control aggregate demand. In the final section of that chapter (section 19.5), we look at whether it is best for a central bank to target inflation or whether it should adopt an alternative target. We also look at the more general issue of whether governments ought to set targets and stick to them, or whether they should allow themselves more discretion in managing the economy.

Section summary

1. Today, most countries have low rates of inflation compared with the past. Part of the reason for this is the deliberate targeting of low inflation by governments and central banks.
2. The effects of adhering to an inflation target can be illustrated in a modified version of the aggregate demand and supply diagram. Inflation, rather than the price level, is plotted on the vertical axis. The aggregate demand curve in this diagram (labelled *ADI*) is downward sloping. This is because higher inflation encourages the central bank to raise interest rates and this leads to a fall in real national income.
3. The aggregate supply (*ASI*) curve in the short run is upward sloping. This is because wage rises lag behind price rises and thus firms are encouraged to supply more in response to a rise in demand knowing that their profits will increase.
4. If aggregate demand rises, the *ADI* curve will shift to the right. Inflation will rise above its target level. This is shown by a movement up the *ASI* curve and back up the new *ADI* curve to the new intersection point (as in Figure 18.16). The movement up the new *ADI* curve is in response to the higher interest rate now set by the central bank as it attempts to bring inflation back down to its target level.
5. Since the new equilibrium is above the target rate of inflation, the central bank must change to a tighter monetary policy and raise the real rate of interest. This shifts the *ADI* curve back to the left and equilibrium is restored back at its original level. The rise in aggregate demand (unless accompanied by a rightward shift in aggregate supply) has had only a temporary effect on real national income.
6. A rise in aggregate supply (unless merely a temporary supply shock) will have a permanent effect on real national income. A rightward shift in aggregate supply will lead to an initial equilibrium at a rate of inflation below target and some rise in real national income as the rate of interest is reduced (as in Figure 18.17). The equilibrium is now below the target rate of inflation. The central bank must therefore change to a looser monetary policy and reduce the real rate of interest. This will shift the *ADI* curve to the right, causing a further rise in real national income that now fully reflects the rise in aggregate supply.

END OF CHAPTER QUESTIONS

1. Using one or more diagrams like Figures 18.1, 18.6, 18.7, 18.8 and 18.9, illustrate the following:
   (a) The effect of a contraction in the money supply on national income. Refer to both the interest-rate and the exchange-rate transmission mechanisms and show how the shapes of the curves affect the outcome.
   (b) The effect of a fall in investment on national income. Again show how the shapes of the curves affect the outcome. Specify your assumptions about the effects on the *supply* of money.
2. Controlling the money supply is sometimes advocated as an appropriate policy for controlling inflation. What implications do different assumptions about the relationships between *M* and *V*, and *M* and *Y* in the equation *MV* = *PY* have for the effectiveness of this policy?
3. Why may an expansion of the money supply have a relatively small effect on national income? Why may any effect be hard to predict?
4. Why does the exchange-rate transmission mechanism strengthen the interest-rate transmission mechanism?
5. Explain how the holding of a range of assets in people's portfolios may help to create a more direct link between changes in money supply and changes in aggregate demand.
6. Explain how financial crowding out can reduce the effectiveness of fiscal policy. What determines the magnitude of crowding out?

*7. What determines the shape of the *IS* and *LM* curves?

*8. Under what circumstances will (a) a rise in investment and (b) a rise in money supply cause a large rise in national income?

*9. Using *ISLM* analysis, explain what would cause the aggregate demand curve to be steep.

10. What would cause (a) a steep *ADI* curve; (b) a shallow *ADI* curve? Compare the short-run and long-run effects of (i) a temporary adverse supply shock and (ii) a permanent supply reduction under each of (a) and (b).
11. Under what circumstances would a rightward shift in the *ADI* curve lead to a *permanent* increase in real national income?

Additional case studies on the book's website (www.pearsoned.co.uk/sloman)

18.1 Crowding out. This case looks at a different version of crowding out from that analysed in section 18.2.

WEBSITES RELEVANT TO CHAPTERS 17 AND 18

Numbers and sections refer to websites listed in the Web Appendix and hotlinked from this book's website at www.pearsoned.co.uk/sloman.

- For news articles relevant to this and the previous chapter, see the *Economics News Articles* link from the book's website.
- For general news on money and banking, see websites in section A, and particularly A1–5, 7–9, 20–22, 25, 26, 31, 36. See also links to economic and financial news in A42.
- For monetary and financial data (including data for money supply and interest rates), see section F and particularly F2. Note that you can link to central banks worldwide from site F17. See also the links in B1 or 2.
- For monetary targeting in the UK, see F1 and E30. For monetary targeting in the eurozone, see F6 and 5.
- For links to sites on money and monetary policy, see the *Financial Economics* sections in I4, 7, 11, 17.
- For student resources relevant to Chapters 17 and 18, see sites C1–7, 9, 10, 12, 13, 19. See also '2nd floor – economic policy' in site D1. See also site D11 (*The virtual bank of Biz/ed*).

Chapter 19

Fiscal and Monetary Policy

The purpose of both fiscal and monetary policy is similar: to control aggregate demand. Excessive growth in aggregate demand can cause unsustainable short-term growth and inflation. Too little aggregate demand can result in a recession, with negative growth and rising unemployment.

Fiscal policy seeks to control aggregate demand by altering the balance between government expenditure (an injection into the circular flow of income) and taxation (a withdrawal). Monetary policy seeks to control aggregate demand by directly controlling the money supply or by altering the rate of interest and then backing this up by any necessary change in money supply. A reduction in interest rates will encourage more borrowing and hence raise aggregate demand. A rise in interest rates will dampen aggregate demand.

The first two sections of this chapter examine fiscal and monetary policy in turn: how they work and how effective they are. The third (optional) section shows how *ISLM* analysis can be used to compare the relative effectiveness of the two policies. The final two sections look at how the policies have been used in the UK and at whether governments should adopt fixed targets for policy (e.g. inflation targets) or whether they should adjust policies according to circumstances.

CHAPTER MAP

19.1 FISCAL POLICY

Fiscal policy has two possible roles. The first is to remove any severe deflationary or inflationary gaps. In other words, expansionary fiscal policy could be used to prevent an economy experiencing a severe or prolonged recession, such as that experienced in the Great Depression of the 1930s or in east and south-east Asia, Russia and Brazil in the late 1990s. It has also been used for this purpose in Japan in recent years, and to a lesser extent in the USA in 2001/2. Likewise, deflationary fiscal policy could be used to prevent rampant inflation, such as that experienced in the 1970s. To summarise: this first role is to prevent the occurrence of *fundamental* disequilibrium in the economy. Keynesians argue that fiscal policy can have a powerful effect here, but not all economists agree with this.

TC 15 p463

TC 13 p381

The second role is to smooth out the fluctuations in the economy associated with the business cycle. This involves reducing government expenditure or raising taxes when the economy begins to boom. This will dampen down the expansion and prevent 'overheating' of the economy, with its attendant problems of rising inflation and a deteriorating current account balance of payments. Conversely if a recession looms, the government should cut taxes or raise government expenditure in order to boost the economy. If these stabilisation policies are successful, they will amount merely to 'fine tuning'. Problems of excess or deficient demand will never be allowed to get severe. Any movement of aggregate demand away from a steady growth path would be immediately 'nipped in the bud'. Virtually no economist argues that perfect fine tuning is possible. There will always be some fluctuations in aggregate demand. Nevertheless many Keynesians argue that the careful use of fiscal policy can make the economy much more stable than it would otherwise be.

Before we look at just how fiscal policy can be used, it is important to understand some of the terminology of government spending and taxation.

Government finances: some terminology

Central government

Central government deficits and surpluses. Since an expansionary fiscal policy will involve raising government expenditure and/or lowering taxes, this will have the effect of either increasing the ***budget deficit*** or reducing the ***budget surplus***. A budget deficit in any one year is where central government's expenditure (including benefits) exceeds its revenue from taxation. A budget surplus is where tax revenues exceed central government expenditure. For most of the last 50 years, governments around the world have run budget deficits. In recent years, however, many countries, the UK included, have made substantial efforts to reduce their budget deficits, and some have achieved budget surpluses for periods of time.

To finance a deficit, the government will have to borrow (e.g. through the issue of bonds (gilts) or Treasury bills). As we saw in section 17.3, this will lead to an increase in the money supply to the extent that the borrowing is from the banking sector. The purchase of bonds or Treasury bills by the (non-bank) private sector, however, will not lead to an increase in the money supply.

The national debt. The budget deficit refers to the debt that the government incurs in one year. If the government runs persistent deficits over many years, these debts will accumulate. The accumulated debt is known as the ***national debt***. Note that the national debt is *not* the same thing as the country's overseas debt. In the case of the UK, only a relatively small fraction of national debt is owed overseas. The bulk of it is owed to UK citizens. In other words, the government finances its budget deficits largely by borrowing at home and not from abroad.

The whole public sector

The PSNCR. So far we have looked at merely the *central* government deficit or surplus. To get a more complete view of public finances, we would need to look at the deficit or surplus of the entire public sector: namely, central government, local government and public corporations. If the public sector spends more than it earns (through taxes and the revenues of public corporations, etc.), the amount of this deficit is known as the ***public-sector net cash requirement (PSNCR)*** (previously known as the 'public-sector borrowing requirement'). It is defined as public-sector expenditure minus public-sector receipts.

The reason for the name 'public-sector net cash requirement' is simple. If the public sector runs a deficit in the current year of, say, £1 billion, then it will have to borrow £1 billion in money this year in order to finance it.

If the public sector runs a surplus (a negative PSNCR), it will be able to repay some of the public-sector debts that have accumulated from previous years. Table 19.1 shows

Definitions

Budget deficit The excess of central government's spending over its tax receipts.

Budget surplus The excess of central government's tax receipts over its spending.

National debt The accumulated budget deficits (less surpluses) over the years: the total amount of government borrowing.

Public-sector net cash requirement (PSNCR) or public-sector borrowing requirement The (annual) deficit of the public sector, and thus the amount that the public sector must borrow.

Table 19.1 UK public-sector deficits (+)/surpluses(–): selected years, 1982–2004

Year	1982	1984	1986	1988	1990	1992	1994	1996	1998	2000	2002	2004
PSNCR (£bn)	5.3	10.3	2.6	–11.5	–1.3	28.6	39.4	24.8	–6.4	–37.5	18.3	41.2
% of GDP	1.9	3.2	0.7	–2.4	–0.2	4.7	5.8	3.3	–0.7	–3.9	1.8	3.6

Source: National Statistics.

Table 19.2 General government deficits/surpluses and debt as percentage of GDP

Country	General government deficits (–) or surpluses (+)			General government debt		
	Average 1991–5	Average 1996–2000	Average 2001–5	Average 1991–5	Average 1996–2000	Average 2001–5
Belgium	–6.5	–1.3	+0.1	139.2	125.2	105.9
France	–4.7	–2.6	–3.2	51.2	68.3	71.0
Germany	–2.9	–1.7	–3.6	46.6	61.6	64.8
Greece	–11.2	–4.0	–4.2	99.3	108.9	112.1
Ireland	–2.5	+2.1	+0.2	90.8	55.8	31.4
Italy	–9.9	–3.1	–2.7	127.6	131.0	120.8
Japan	–1.6	–5.8	–6.9	75.0	113.2	156.5
Netherlands	–3.5	–0.2	–2.2	91.6	79.6	64.3
Sweden	–7.4	+1.1	+0.8	74.9	76.9	61.7
UK	–6.0	–0.3	–2.2	44.7	50.9	42.6
USA	–4.5	0.0	–3.5	73.8	66.9	61.8
Euro area	–5.2	–2.1	–2.5	70.9	80.8	77.4

the PSNCR for selected years from 1982 to 2004. As you can see, in most years it has been positive (i.e. the public sector was running a deficit and had to borrow).

General government

A final category is 'general government'. This includes central and local government, but excludes public corporations. Thus we can refer to ***general government deficits and surpluses*** and ***general government debt***. Table 19.2 shows government deficits/surpluses and debt for selected countries averaged over three five-year periods. They are expressed as a proportion of GDP.

As you can see, all of them experienced deficits in the first period. But, with the exception of Japan, all experienced a reduction of these deficits in the second period and two countries experienced a surplus. Most countries, however, experienced an increase in deficits or a reduction in surpluses in the latest period. We explain this pattern in the next section.

Public-sector deficits and surpluses and the government's 'fiscal stance'

The government's ***fiscal stance*** refers to whether it is pursuing an expansionary or contractionary fiscal policy. Does the fact that there was a public-sector deficit in the UK right from 1971 to 1986 mean that the government's fiscal stance was expansionary throughout this period? Would the mere existence of a surplus mean that the stance was contractionary? The answer is no. Whether the economy expands or contracts depends on the balance of *total* injections and *total* withdrawals.

What we need to focus on is *changes* in the size of the deficit or surplus. If the deficit this year is lower than last year, then (*ceteris paribus*) aggregate demand will be lower this year than last. The reason is that either government expenditure (an injection) must have fallen, or tax revenues (a withdrawal) must have increased, or a combination of the two.

The fiscal stance and the state of the economy

Another problem is that the size of the deficit or surplus is not entirely due to deliberate government policy. It may not give a very good guide, therefore, to government intentions. The size of the deficit or surplus is influenced by

Definitions

General government deficit (or surplus) The combined deficit (or surplus) of central and local government.

General government debt The combined accumulated debt of central and local government.

Fiscal stance How expansionary or contractionary the Budget is.

the state of the economy. If the economy is booming with people earning high incomes, the amount paid in taxes will be high. In a booming economy the level of unemployment will be low. Thus the amount paid out in unemployment benefits will also be low. The combined effect of increased tax revenues and reduced benefits is to give a public-sector surplus (or a reduced deficit). By contrast, if the economy were depressed, tax revenues would be low and government expenditure on benefits would be high. The public-sector deficit would thus be high.

This relationship between the budget deficit or surplus and the state of the economy is illustrated in Figure 19.1. The tax revenue function is upward sloping. Its slope depends on tax rates. The government expenditure function (which in this diagram includes benefits) is drawn as downward sloping, showing that at higher levels of income and employment less is paid out in benefits. As can be clearly seen, there is only one level of income (Y_1) where there is a public-sector financial balance. Below this level of income there will be a public-sector deficit. Above this level there will be a surplus. The further income is from Y_1, the bigger will be the deficit or surplus. This is illustrated in Table 19.2. During the boom that was experienced in Europe and North America between 1996 and 2000, deficits fell. Japan, by contrast, was experiencing a prolonged recession. Its deficit rose, partly as a result of falling tax revenues and partly from a deliberately expansionary fiscal policy (see Box 19.2).

To conclude, the size of the deficit or surplus is a poor guide to the stance of fiscal policy. A large deficit *may* be due to a deliberate policy of increasing aggregate demand, but it may be due simply to the fact that the economy is depressed.

Figure 19.1 National income and the size of the public-sector deficit or surplus

G, T
Tax revenue
SURPLUS
DEFICIT
Government expenditure (including benefits)
O
Y_1
Y

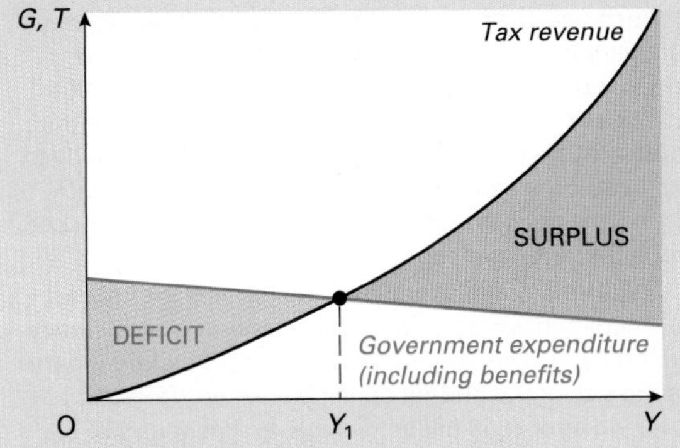

The structural balance

The public-sector deficit or surplus that would arise if the economy were producing at the 'sustainable' level of national income (see Box 13.4 on page 382) is termed the ***structural deficit or surplus***. Remember that the sustainable level of national income is where there is no excess or deficiency of aggregate demand. In Figure 19.1, if sustainable national income were below the intersection point of the two lines, there would be structural deficit.

If the economy is producing above or below the sustainable level of national income, there will be a cyclical component of the public-sector deficit or surplus. Thus the government could aim for a *structural* balance ($G = T$ at the sustainable level of national income), but be prepared to accept a deficit if the economy was in a recession, or a surplus if it was experiencing a boom.

Automatic fiscal stabilisers

We saw from Figure 19.1 that the size of the public-sector surplus or deficit will automatically vary according to the level of national income. The effect of this will be to reduce the level of fluctuations in national income without the government having to take any deliberate action.

Taxes whose revenues rise as national income rises and benefits that fall as national income rises are called ***automatic stabilisers***. They have the effect of reducing the size of the multiplier, reducing both upward and downward movements of national income. Thus, in theory, the business cycle should be dampened by such built-in stabilisers. The more taxes rise or benefits fall, the bigger will be the *mpt* (the net marginal tax propensity). Remember that we defined this as the proportion of any rise in income going in taxes and reduced benefits. The bigger the *mpt*, the smaller will be the multiplier and the greater will be the stabilising effect.

?

Draw an injections and withdrawals diagram, with a fairly shallow W curve. Mark the equilibrium level of national income. Now draw a second steeper W curve passing through the same point. This second W curve would correspond to the case where tax rates were higher. Assuming now that there has been an increase in injections, draw a second J line above the first. Mark the new equilibrium level of national income with each of the two W curves. You can see that national income rises less with the steeper W curve. The higher tax rates are having a dampening effect on the multiplier.

Definitions

Structural deficit (or surplus) The public-sector deficit (or surplus) that would occur if the economy were operating at the sustainable level of national income.

Automatic fiscal stabilisers Tax revenues that rise and government expenditure that falls as national income rises. The more they change with income, the bigger the stabilising effect on national income.

The effectiveness of automatic stabilisers

Automatic stabilisers have the obvious advantage that they act instantly as soon as aggregate demand fluctuates. By contrast, it may take some time before the government can institute discretionary changes in taxes or government expenditure, especially if forecasting is unreliable.

Nevertheless automatic stabilisers can never be the complete answer to the problem of fluctuations. Their effect is merely to reduce the multiplier – to reduce the severity of fluctuations, not to eliminate them altogether.

In addition, they tend to suffer two specific drawbacks: adverse effects on aggregate supply and the problem of 'fiscal drag'. Let us examine each in turn.

TC 3 p21

Adverse supply-side effects

High tax rates may discourage effort and initiative. The higher the marginal tax rate (*mpt*), the greater the stability provided by the tax system. But the higher tax rates are, the more likely they are to create a disincentive to work and to invest. For example, steeply progressive income taxes may discourage workers from doing overtime or seeking promotion. A higher marginal rate of income tax is equivalent to a higher marginal cost of working. People may prefer to work less and substitute leisure for income. The substitution effect of more progressive taxes may thus outweigh the income effect. These issues were examined in detail in section 10.2 (see pages 282–3).

KI 7 p35

High unemployment benefits may increase equilibrium unemployment. High unemployment benefits, by reducing the hardship of being unemployed, may encourage people to spend longer looking for the 'right' job rather than taking the first job offered. This has the effect of increasing unemployment and thus of shifting the Phillips curve to the right. This is because a longer average period of job search represents a higher level of *friction* in the economy and thus a higher *natural* (or *equilibrium*) level of unemployment.

High income-related benefits may create a poverty trap. The higher the level of income-related benefits and the more steeply they taper off, the greater will be the problem of the 'poverty trap'. What is the point in unemployed people seeking jobs, or people in very low-paid jobs seeking better ones, if as a result they lose their benefits and end up being little or no better off than before? The more that people are discouraged in this way, the lower will be the level of aggregate supply. (The question of the poverty trap was also examined in Chapter 10 (see page 287).)

The problem of fiscal drag

Automatic stabilisers help to reduce upward and downward movements in national income. This is fine if the current level of income is the *desirable* level. But suppose that there is currently a deep recession in the economy, with mass unemployment. Who would want to stabilise the economy at this level?

CASE STUDIES AND APPLICATIONS **BOX 19.1**

MANAGING THE US ECONOMY

To fiscal stimulate or not to fiscal stimulate, that is the question

Since the start of 2001, the US Federal Reserve, led by Alan Greenspan, had been fighting a sharp slowdown in the US economy. Interest rates had been cut seven times from their level of $6\frac{1}{2}$ per cent at the beginning of the year to $3\frac{1}{2}$ per cent in August. By September 2001, the economy seemed to be starting to recover.

The terrorist attacks on 11 September brought this modest recovery to an abrupt halt. At this point, many analysts were suggesting that it might be necessary to lower rates close to zero in order to kick-start the economy. Even then the success of such a strategy was not guaranteed.

At this point, it was decided that a measure of discretionary fiscal policy was required in order to help reduce pressure on the Federal Reserve and its use of interest rates to pump-prime the economy.

Following a meeting at the end of September 2001, Alan Greenspan advised Congress that a fiscal stimulus of $100 billion, or 1 per cent of US GDP, was advisable. The Stimulus Bill proposed cutting personal taxation from 27 to 25 per cent, and offering tax exemption to business on moneys used for new investment. The Democrats were opposed to the personal tax cuts, which would go largely to the rich. A compromise was reached in March 2002 when a stimulus package of $51 billion passed into law, consisting mainly of tax incentives to business.

Such was the delay in passing the Stimulus Bill that recovery began to occur without it. With continued reductions in interest rates, which by December 2001 had been cut 11 times and, at $1\frac{3}{4}$ per cent, were at the lowest level since the presidency of John F. Kennedy in the 1960s, the economy seemed to be bouncing back. Economic growth was 1.9 per cent in 2002, 3.0 per cent in 2003 and 4.4 per cent in 2004.

But it was not just the Stimulus Bill and the interest rate cuts that were boosting the economy. Fiscal policy generally was becoming more and more expansionary as the size of the budget deficit increased. Tax cuts totalling over $650 billion were given between 2001 and 2004 (71.7 per cent of which went to the richest 20 per cent, 26.4 per cent to the richest 1 per cent and just 0.2 per cent to the poorest 20 per cent). In 2004, the total tax cuts during this period had the effect of increasing the budget deficit from 1.6 to 4.2 per cent of GDP.

Which is likely to give a bigger boost to aggregate demand: tax cuts of a given amount targeted to (a) the rich, or (b) the poor?

In these circumstances, if the economy began to recover, the automatic stabilisers would act as a drag on the expansion. This is known as ***fiscal drag***. By reducing the size of the multiplier, the automatic stabilisers reduce the magnitude of the recovery. Similarly, they act as a drag on discretionary policy: the more powerful the automatic stabilisers are, the bigger the change in *G* or *T* that would be necessary to achieve a given change in national income.

Discretionary fiscal policy

Automatic stabilisers cannot prevent fluctuations. They merely reduce their magnitude. If there is a fundamental disequilibrium in the economy or substantial fluctuations in other injections and withdrawals, the government may choose to *alter* the level of government expenditure or the rates of taxation. This is known as ***discretionary fiscal policy***. It involves *shifting* the *J* and *W* lines.

In the UK, changes in taxation and some changes in government expenditure are announced by the Chancellor of the Exchequer in the Budget (which usually takes place in March). Some of these changes apply to the coming financial year (April to March); some apply to the next financial year or even the one after that.

Since Budgets are normally held only once per year, 'fine-tuning' aggregate demand on a week-by-week or month-by-month basis is left to monetary policy – to changes in interest rates (see section 19.2).

Note that discretionary changes in taxation or government expenditure, as well as being used to alter the level of aggregate demand (fiscal policy), are also used for other purposes, including the following:

- Altering aggregate supply. Examples include tax incentives to encourage people to work more, or increased government expenditure on training or on transport infrastructure (e.g. roads and railways). We look at such 'supply-side policies' in Chapter 22.
- Altering the distribution of income. As Chapter 10 explained, taxation and benefits are the government's major means of redistributing incomes from the rich to the poor.

Let us now compare the relative effects of changing government expenditure and changing taxes. Will a £100 million increase in government expenditure have the same effect as a £100 million cut in taxes? Will the multiplier be the same in each case?

Definitions

Fiscal drag The tendency of automatic fiscal stabilisers to reduce the recovery of an economy from recession.

Discretionary fiscal policy Deliberate changes in tax rates or the level of government expenditure in order to influence the level of aggregate demand.

Discretionary fiscal policy: changing G

If government expenditure on goods and services (roads, health care, education, etc.) is raised, this will create a full multiplied rise in national income. The reason is that all the money gets spent and thus all of it goes to boosting aggregate demand.

Show the effect of an increase in government expenditure by using (a) the injections and withdrawals diagram; (b) the income/expenditure diagram (see Figures 16.8 and 16.10 on pages 464 and 465).

Discretionary fiscal policy: changing T

Cutting taxes by £1 million will have a smaller effect on national income than raising government expenditure on goods and services by £1 million. The reason is that cutting taxes increases people's *disposable* incomes, of which only *part* will be spent. Part will be withdrawn into extra savings, imports and other taxes. In other words, not all the tax cuts will be passed on round the circular flow of income as extra expenditure.

The proportion of the cut in taxes that will be withdrawn is given by the *mpw*, and the proportion that will circulate round the flow is given by the mpc_d. Thus if the mpc_d were 4/5, the tax multiplier would only be 4/5 of the normal multiplier. If the mpc_d were 2/3, the tax multiplier would only be 2/3 of the normal multiplier, and so on. The formula for the tax multiplier (k_t) becomes:[1]

$$k_t = mpc_d \times k$$

Thus if the normal multiplier were 5 (given an mpc_d of 4/5), the tax multiplier would be $4/5 \times 5 = 4$. If the normal multiplier were 4 (given an mpc_d of 3/4), the tax multiplier would be $3/4 \times 4 = 3$, and so on. It should be obvious from this that the tax multiplier is always 1 less than the normal multiplier:

$$k_t = k - 1$$

Since the tax multiplier is smaller than the government expenditure multiplier, to achieve a given rise in income through tax cuts would therefore require a bigger budget deficit than if it were achieved through increased government expenditure. In other words, the required tax cut would be bigger than the required government expenditure increase.

Why will the multiplier effect of government transfer payments such as child benefit, pensions and social security be less than the full *multiplier effect given by government expenditure on goods and services? Will this 'transfer payments multiplier' be the same as the tax multiplier? (Clue: will the recipients of such benefits have the same mpc_d as the average person?)*

[1] Strictly speaking, the tax multiplier is negative, since a *rise* in taxes causes a *fall* in national income.

The effectiveness of discretionary fiscal policy

How successful will discretionary fiscal policy be? Can it 'fine tune' demand? Can it achieve the level of national income that the government would like it to achieve?

TC 15 p463

There are two main problem areas with discretionary fiscal policy. The first concerns the *magnitude* of the effects. If G or T is changed, how much will *total* injections and withdrawals change? What will be the size of the multiplier? How much will a change in aggregate demand affect output and employment, and how much will it affect prices?

KI 30 p306

The second concerns the *timing* of the effects. How quickly can policy be changed and how quickly will the changes affect the economy?

Problems of magnitude

KI 15 p101

Before changing government expenditure or taxation, the government will need to calculate the effect of any such change on national income, employment and inflation. Predicting these effects, however, is often very unreliable for a number of reasons.

Predicting the effect of changes in government expenditure

A rise in government expenditure of £x may lead to a rise in total injections (relative to withdrawals) that is smaller than £x. This will occur if the rise in government expenditure *replaces* a certain amount of private expenditure. For example, a rise in expenditure on state education may dissuade some parents from sending their children to private schools. Similarly an improvement in the national health service may lead to fewer people paying for private treatment.

Crowding out. If the government relies on ***pure fiscal policy*** – that is, if it does not finance an increase in the budget deficit by increasing the money supply – it will have to borrow the money from the non-bank private sector. It will thus be competing with the private sector for finance and will have to offer higher interest rates. This will force the private sector also to offer higher interest rates, which may discourage firms from investing and individuals from buying on credit. Thus government borrowing *crowds out* private borrowing. In the extreme case, the fall in consumption and investment may completely offset the rise in government expenditure, with the result that aggregate demand does not rise at all.

Figure 19.2 illustrates the extent of crowding out. (It is the same as Figure 18.7 on page 513.) The rise in government expenditure shifts the injections line from J_1 to J_2 in the left-hand diagram. The full multiplier effect of this would be a rise in national income to Y_2. However, the increased government expenditure leads to an increased demand for money. In the right-hand diagram, the liquidity preference curve shifts to L'. This raises the interest rate to r_2. Note that we are assuming that the money supply is purely exogenous – i.e. does not vary with the demand for money – and that, therefore, the money supply 'curve' is a vertical straight line (M_s).

The higher rate of interest reduces investment. The injections line falls below J_2, and, as a result, national income does not rise as far as Y_2. The amount by which actual income falls short of Y_2 measures the extent of crowding out.

The amount of crowding out from pure fiscal policy depends on three things:

- The shape of the L curve. The flatter the curve, the less will interest rates rise. A greater amount of liquidity will be released from idle balances and there will be a bigger increase in the velocity of circulation.
- Whether money supply is exogenous. If the extra demand for money leads to banks creating extra credit, the money supply curve will be upward sloping, not vertical. The more money is created, the flatter will be the M_s curve, the less interest rates will rise and the less will be the crowding out.

Definition

Pure fiscal policy Fiscal policy that does not involve any change in money supply.

Figure 19.2 The monetary effects of a rise in injections

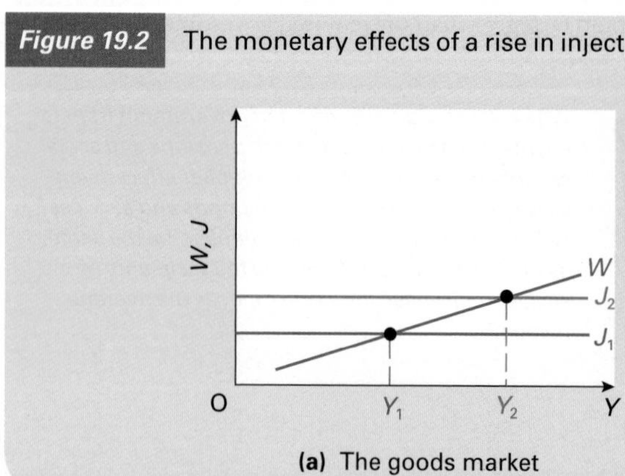

(a) The goods market

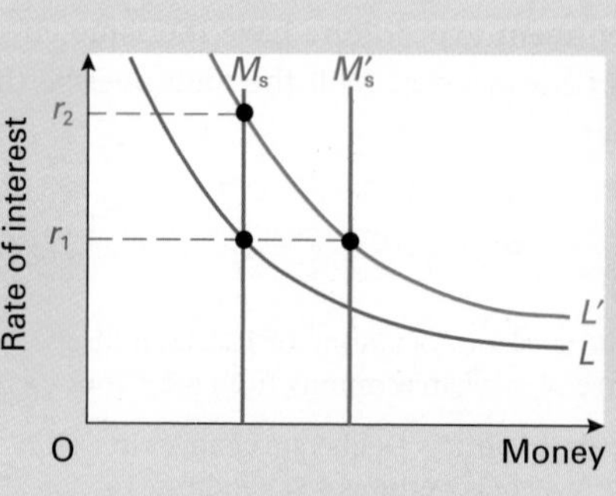

(b) The money market

- The responsiveness of investment (and consumption) to a change in interest rates. The more responsive investment is to a rise in interest rates, the more will the *J* curve shift downwards and the bigger will be the crowding-out effect.

If the fiscal policy is not *pure* fiscal policy, if the extra government borrowing is financed by borrowing from the banking sector, then the supply of money curve will shift to the right. If it were to shift as far as M_s', the rate of interest would remain at r_1 and there would be no crowding out.

How do people's expectations influence the extent of crowding out?

Predicting the effect of changes in taxes

A cut in taxes, by raising people's real disposable income, increases not only the amount they spend but also the amount they save. The problem is that it is not easy to predict the relative size of these two increases. In part it depends on whether people feel that the cut in tax is only temporary, in which case they may simply save the extra disposable income, or permanent, in which case they may adjust their consumption upwards.

Do theories of the long-run and short-run consumption function help us to understand consumer reactions to a change in taxes? (See section 16.1 and Web Cases 16.1 and 16.2.)

Predicting the resulting multiplied effect on national income

Even if the government *could* predict the net initial effect on injections and withdrawals, the extent to which national income will change is still hard to predict for the following reasons:

- The size of the multiplier may be difficult to predict. This is because the mpc_d and *mpw* may fluctuate. For example, the amount of a rise in income that households save or consume will depend on their expectations about future price and income changes.
- Induced investment through the accelerator is also extremely difficult to predict. It may be that a relatively small fiscal stimulus will be all that is necessary to restore business confidence, and that induced investment will rise substantially. In such a case, fiscal policy can be seen as a 'pump primer'. It is used to *start* the process of recovery, and then the *continuation* of the recovery is left to the market. But for pump priming to work, business people must *believe* that it will work. Business confidence can change very rapidly and in ways that could not have been foreseen a few months earlier.
- Multiplier/accelerator interactions. If the initial multiplier and accelerator effects are difficult to estimate, their interaction will be virtually impossible to estimate. Small divergences in investment from what was initially predicted will become magnified as time progresses.

Random shocks

Forecasts cannot take into account the unpredictable, such as the attack on the World Trade Center in New York in September 2001. Unfortunately, unpredictable events do occur and may seriously undermine the government's fiscal policy.

Give some examples of these random shocks.

Problems of timing

KI 30 p306

Fiscal policy can involve considerable time lags. If these are long enough, fiscal policy could even be *de*stabilising. Expansionary policies taken to cure a recession may not come into effect until the economy has *already* recovered and is experiencing a boom. Under these circumstances, expansionary policies are quite inappropriate: they simply worsen the problems of overheating. Similarly, contractionary policies taken to prevent excessive expansion may not take effect until the economy has already peaked and is plunging into recession. The contractionary policies only deepen the recession.

This problem is illustrated in Figure 19.3. Path (a) shows the course of the business cycle without government intervention. Ideally, with no time lags, the economy should be

Figure 19.3 Fiscal policy: stabilising or destabilising?

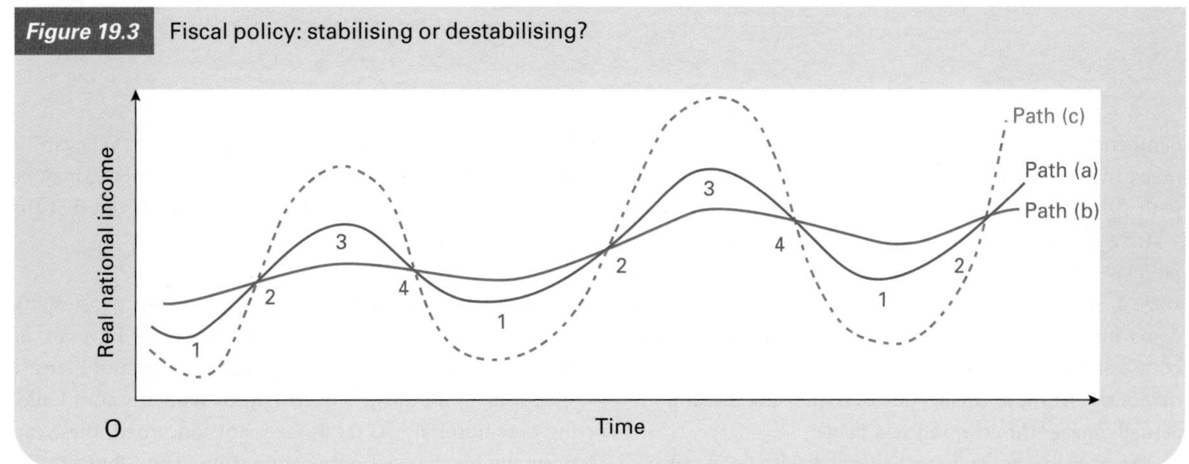

CASE STUDIES AND APPLICATIONS

DISCRETIONARY FISCAL POLICY IN JAPAN

Attempts to jumpstart the economy

1991–6

After experiencing an average annual economic growth rate of nearly 4 per cent from 1980 to 1991, it was a shock for the Japanese when the growth rate plummeted to 1.0 per cent in 1992, followed by a mere 0.2 per cent in 1993.

In response to the slowdown, the Japanese government injected into the economy a sequence of five public spending packages over the period 1992–6 totalling ¥59 500 billion (£330 billion): an average increase in government spending of 7 per cent a year in real terms. There were also substantial cuts in taxes. This, combined with the economic slowdown, moved the public-sector finances massively into deficit. A general government surplus of 0.8 per cent of GDP in 1992 was transformed into a deficit of over 5 per cent of GDP by 1996 (see the table). Japan's general government debt rose from 68.7 per cent of GDP in 1992 to 93.9 per cent by 1996.

In addition to this fiscal stimulus, the government reduced interest rates nine times, to a record low of 0.5 per cent by 1996. It also pursued a policy of business deregulation, especially within the service and financial sectors. Yet despite all these measures, it was not until 1996 that significant economic growth resumed (see the table).

Why did such an expansionary fiscal (and monetary) policy prove to be so ineffective? The answer can be found in the behaviour of the other components of aggregate demand.

In previous decades, the prosperity of Japanese business was built upon an export-led growth strategy. If there was a lack of demand at home, surplus capacity in the economy could simply be exported. But this option was no longer so easy. Since 1985 there had been a massive appreciation of the exchange rate: the yen rose by over 150 per cent against the US dollar in the ten years up to 1995. This, plus growing competition from other Asian exporters, meant that Japanese firms were finding it harder to export.

As far as investment was concerned, the slowdown in the economy and sluggish export sales, plus high levels of debt from the expansion of the late 1980s, reduced profits to near record lows and created a climate of business pessimism. After increases in

Japanese macroeconomic indicators: 1980–2005

	1980–91	1992	1993	1994	1995	1996	1997	1998	1999	2000	2001	2002	2003	2004	2005[a]
% annual growth in real GDP	3.8	1.0	0.2	1.1	1.9	3.4	1.9	−1.1	0.1	2.8	0.4	−0.3	2.5	2.6	2.1
General government budget balance as % of GDP	−1.1	0.8	−2.4	−3.8	−4.7	−5.1	−3.8	−5.5	−7.2	−7.5	−6.1	−7.9	−7.7	−6.5	−6.4
General government debt as % of GDP		68.7	74.9	79.7	87.1	93.9	100.3	112.2	125.7	134.1	142.3	149.3	157.5	163.5	170.0
Inflation	2.1	1.7	1.3	0.7	−0.1	0.1	1.7	0.7	−0.3	−0.7	−0.7	−0.9	−0.3	−0.1	0.1
Exchange rate index (1995 = 100)	35.6	65.0	80.4	93.4	100.0	87.2	83.3	86.6	99.3	108.1	99.7	94.6	94.8	97.0	

[a] Forecast.

Source: OECD data in various tables.

dampened in stage 2 and stimulated in stage 4. This would make the resulting course of the business cycle more like path (b), or even, if the policy were perfectly stabilising, a straight line. With time lags, however, contractionary policies taken in stage 2 may not come into effect until stage 4, and expansionary policies taken in stage 4 may not come into effect until stage 2. In this case, the resulting course of the business cycle will be more like path (c). Quite obviously, in these circumstances 'stabilising' fiscal policy actually makes the economy less stable.

There are five possible lags associated with fiscal policy.

Time lag to recognition. Since the business cycle can be irregular and forecasting unreliable, governments may be unwilling to take action until they are convinced that the problem is serious.

Time lag between recognition and action. Most significant changes in government expenditure have to be planned well in advance. The government cannot increase spending on motorways overnight or suddenly start building new hospitals. As far as taxes are concerned, these can normally be changed only at the time of the Budget, and

BOX 19.2

investment averaging 10 per cent per year from 1987 to 1990, investment fell for three successive years after 1991.

Consumers too were in a pessimistic mood. Even with a ¥5000 billion cut in taxation in 1994, consumer spending on domestic goods and services grew only marginally, whereas *saving* increased sharply, as did *imports*.

Even though the total fiscal stimulus over the period was large, the incremental nature of the government's action failed on each occasion to stimulate business and consumer activity to any significant degree.

1997–

The recovery of 1996 was short lived. With other countries, such as Thailand and Indonesia, experiencing a large economic downturn in 1997, and with a growing mood of pessimism across the region, the Japanese economy plunged into recession. By 1998, amidst bank failures and speculative outflows of money from the country, the Japanese economy was in a state of crisis. The government's response was once more to resort to fiscal policy.

A ¥16 000 billion (£80 billion) expansionary fiscal package in April 1998, was followed six months later by another package worth ¥24 000 billion (£120 billion). This second package included over ¥8000 billion on public works projects and cuts in the maximum rate of income tax from 65 per cent to 50 per cent (worth ¥4200 billion) and substantial cuts in corporate taxes. One novel feature of the package was the distribution of shopping vouchers to 35 million citizens: the elderly and families with young children. These free vouchers were worth ¥700 billion (£3.5 billion).

One of the biggest problems in stimulating the economy was the very high marginal propensity to save. Given the continuing pessimism of workers about the security of their jobs, many people responded to tax cuts by saving more, especially given that prices were stable or falling and hence the value of money saved would not be eroded by inflation. Even the shopping voucher scheme had limited success, as people used them to replace existing expenditure and saved the money that they no longer needed to use.

Another problem was the mood of businesses. With banks collapsing under the weight of bad debt, with loans to industry consequently cut, with Japanese companies eager to cut costs, and with business pessimism about consumer and export demand, investment was being cut back. Reductions in business taxes were not enough to reverse this.

A modest recovery was under way in 2000 (see the table), but in 2001, with the USA slipping into recession and with the European economy slowing down, Japanese exports began to fall and a mood of pessimism rapidly returned. The government had hoped that supply-side reforms to make the economy more competitive would work, but these are long-term policies and the problem was immediate.

So what could be done? The answer was very little. With interest rates of virtually zero, there was little scope for an expansionary monetary policy, and with a general government deficit of over 6 per cent and a debt of over 140 per cent of GDP and rising, there was now little scope for fiscal policy either. All that could be done was to wait for the recovery in the world economy and for the supply-side reforms to begin to work to make Japanese industry more competitive.

By 2003, the Japanese economy at last seemed to be recovering and for the next two years it managed to achieve moderate economic growth (but with a decline in output in the last half of 2004). But consumer spending remained hesitant and a persistently high value of the yen curbed a growth in exports.

If tax cuts are largely saved, should an expansionary fiscal policy be confined to increases in government spending?

will not be instituted until the new financial year or at some other point in the future. As Budgets normally occur annually, there could be a considerable time lag if the problems are recognised a long time before the Budget.

Time lag between action and changes taking effect. A change in tax rates may not immediately affect tax payments as some taxes are paid in arrears and new rates may take a time to apply.

Time lag between changes in government expenditure and taxation and the resulting change in national income, prices and employment. The multiplier round takes time. Accelerator effects take time. The multiplier and accelerator go on interacting. It all takes time.

Consumption may respond slowly to changes in taxation. The short-run consumption function tends to be flatter than the long-run function.

If the fluctuations in aggregate demand can be forecast, and if the lengths of the time lags are known, then all is not lost. At least the fiscal measures can be taken early and their delayed effects can be taken into account. Fiscal policy could go *some* way to reducing fluctuations, especially if forecasting techniques are improved and measures are used which involve the minimum of time lags.

Steady as you go

Given the problems of pursuing active fiscal policy, many governments today take a much more passive approach. Instead of changing the policy as the economy changes, a rule is set for the level of public finances. This rule is then applied year after year, with taxes and government expenditure being planned to meet that rule. For example, a target could be set for the PSNCR, with government expenditure and taxes being adjusted to keep the PSNCR at or within its target level. Box 19.4 looks at some examples of fiscal targets.

Postscript: the relative merits of changing government expenditure and changing taxes

Let us assume that, despite all the problems of fiscal policy, the government still wants to go ahead and use it to control aggregate demand. Which should it change: government expenditure, taxation or some combination of the two? It will need to take various things into account in making this decision.

The first consideration will probably be in its overall political objectives. Does it generally favour a larger or smaller public sector?

The political left tends to argue that market economies like the UK suffer from too little public expenditure. While private expenditure by the relatively wealthy on fast cars,

EXPLORING ECONOMICS — BOX 19.3

RIDING A SWITCHBACK

A parable for Chancellors

Imagine that you are driving a car along a straight but undulating road. These undulations are not regular: some of the hills are steep, some are gentle; some are long, some are short.

You are given the instruction that you must keep the car going at a constant speed. To do this, you will need to accelerate going up the hills and brake going down them.

There is a serious problem, however. The car is no ordinary car. It has the following distinctly unusual features:

- The front windscreen and side windows are blacked out, so you cannot see where you are going! All you can see is where you have *been* by looking in your rearview mirror.
- The brake and accelerator pedals both work with a considerable and unpredictable delay.
- The car's suspension is so good that you cannot feel whether you are going up or downhill. You can only judge this by looking in your mirror.
- Finally (you are relieved to know), the car has a special sensor and automatic steering that keep it in the correct lane.

As you are going along, you see that the road behind you is higher, and you realise that you are going downhill. The car gets faster and faster. You brake – but nothing happens. In your zeal to slow the car down, you put your foot down on the brake as hard as you can.

When the brake eventually does come on, it comes on very strongly. By this time, the car has already reached the bottom of the hill. As yet, however, you do not realise this and are still braking. But now the car is going up the next hill with the brakes still on. Looking in your mirror, you eventually realise this. You take your foot off the brake and start accelerating. But the pedals do not respond. The car is still slowing down rapidly, and you only just manage to reach the top of the hill.

Then, as you start going down the other side, the brakes eventually come off and the accelerator comes on . . .

This famous parable – first told by Frank Paish, Professor of Economics at the LSE, over 30 years ago – demonstrates how 'stabilising' activity can in fact be destabilising. When applied to fiscal policy, long and uncertain time lags can mean that the government can end up stimulating the economy in a boom and contracting it in a slump.

KI 30 p 306

So what should be done? One alternative, of course, would be to try to reduce the time lags and to improve forecasting. But failing this, the best policy may be to do nothing: to take a 'steady as you go' or 'fixed throttle' approach to running the economy. Going back to the car analogy, a fixed throttle will not prevent the car from going faster downhill and slower uphill, but at least it will not make the speed even *more* irregular.

?

1. ***Could you drive the car at a steady speed if you knew that all the hills were the same length and height, and if there were a constant 30-second delay on the pedals?***
2. ***What would a fixed throttle approach to fiscal policy involve?***

designer jeans, junk food and home security continues to grow rapidly, the public sector is deprived of resources. State education is squeezed; the streets are dirty; the environment is threatened; crime increases; the lot of the poor and homeless deteriorates. Private affluence goes side by side with public poverty.

The political right argues that the solution to social and economic problems does not lie in a growth of the 'nanny state', which stifles individual initiative. It is better, so the argument goes, to encourage attitudes where people take responsibility for the social consequences of their own actions, rather than leaving it up to the state.

Even if left and right agree on how much to dampen or stimulate the economy by fiscal policy, they will disagree over the means. The left would tend to favour increasing government expenditure to stimulate demand, and increasing taxes to reduce it. The right, by contrast, would tend to favour cutting taxes to stimulate aggregate demand, and cutting government expenditure to reduce it.

Apart from ideological considerations, there are the practical questions of which policies are the most effective and which suffer the fewer drawbacks.

Changing government expenditure has the advantage that it affects aggregate demand directly and has a bigger multiplier effect. Changes in government expenditure can be more specifically targeted than changes in taxation. For example, government expenditure can be directed to regions of high unemployment or to specific sectors, such as transport. Taxes cannot be used so selectively. Also, in the case of contractionary policy, higher taxes may act as a disincentive to effort (see pages 282–3) and may initially make inflation worse by adding to costs.

Nevertheless, the government can alter the balance between income and expenditure tax, or between personal income tax and corporation tax. It can also use taxes to alter the distribution of income. What is more, changes in taxes can usually be brought about more speedily than changes in government expenditure, and are thus more suitable for stabilising the economy.

Section summary

1. The government's fiscal policy influences the size of the budget deficit or surplus and the size of the PSNCR. The size of these alone, however, is a poor guide to the government's fiscal stance. A large deficit, for example, may simply be due to the fact that the economy is in recession and therefore tax receipts are low. A better guide is whether the change in the deficit or surplus will be expansionary or contractionary.
2. Automatic fiscal stabilisers are tax revenues that rise and benefits that fall as national income rises. They have the effect of reducing the size of the multiplier and thus reducing cyclical upswings and downswings.
3. Automatic stabilisers take effect as soon as aggregate demand fluctuates, but they can never remove fluctuations completely. They also create disincentives and act as a drag on recovery from recession.
4. Discretionary fiscal policy is where the government deliberately changes taxes or government expenditure in order to alter the level of aggregate demand. Changes in government expenditure on goods and services have a full multiplier effect. Changes in taxes and benefits, however, have a smaller multiplier effect as some of the tax/benefit changes merely affect other withdrawals and thus have a smaller net effect on consumption of domestic product. The tax multiplier has a value 1 less than the full multiplier.
5. There are problems in predicting the magnitude of the effects of discretionary fiscal policy. Expansionary fiscal policy can act as a pump primer and stimulate increased private expenditure, or it can crowd out private expenditure. The extent to which it acts as a pump primer depends crucially on business confidence – something that is very difficult to predict beyond a few weeks or months. The extent of crowding out depends on monetary conditions and the government's monetary policy.
6. There are five possible time lags involved with fiscal policy: the time lag before the problem is diagnosed, the lag between diagnosis and new measures being announced, the lag between announcement and implementation, the lag while the multiplier and accelerator work themselves out, and the lag before consumption fully responds to new economic circumstances.
7. The choice of which to change – government expenditure, taxation or a bit of both – depends partly on the government's political objectives: whether it wants to increase or decrease the size of the public sector. It also depends on their relative effectiveness in changing aggregate demand. Changes in *G* tend to have a bigger multiplier effect than changes in *T*. Changes in *T*, however, can usually be implemented more quickly than changes in *G*.

CASE STUDIES AND APPLICATIONS

FOLLOWING THE GOLDEN RULE

Fiscal policy in a straitjacket?

If the government persistently runs a budget deficit, the national debt will rise. If it rises faster than GDP, it will account for a growing proportion of GDP. There is then likely to be an increasing problem of 'servicing' this debt: i.e. paying the interest on it. The government could find itself having to borrow more and more to meet the interest payments, and so the national debt could rise faster still. As the government borrows more and more, so it has to pay higher interest rates to attract finances. If it is successful in this, borrowing and hence investment by the private sector could be crowded out (see pages 513 and 534).

Recognising these problems, many governments in recent years have attempted to reduce their debts.

Preparing for EMU

In signing the Maastricht Treaty in 1992, the EU countries agreed that to be eligible to join the single currency (i.e. the euro), they should have sustainable deficits and debts. This was interpreted as follows: the general government deficit should be no more than 3 per cent of GDP and general government debt should be no more than 60 per cent of GDP, or should at least be falling towards that level at a satisfactory pace.

But in the mid-1990s, several of the countries that were subsequently to join the euro had deficits and debts substantially above these levels (see Table 19.2 on page 530). Getting them down proved a painful business. Government expenditure had to be cut and taxes increased. Fiscal policy, unfortunately, proved to be powerful! Unemployment rose and growth remained low.

The EU Stability and Growth Pact

In June 1997, at the European Council in Amsterdam, the EU countries agreed that governments adopting the euro should seek to balance their budgets (or even aim for a surplus) averaged over the course of the business cycle, and that deficits should not exceed 3 per cent of GDP in any one year. A country's deficit is permitted to exceed 3 per cent only if its GDP has declined by at least 2 per cent (or 0.75 per cent with special permission from the Council of Ministers). Otherwise, countries with deficits exceeding 3 per cent are required to make deposits of money with the European Central Bank. These then become fines if the excessive budget deficit is not eliminated within two years.

There are two main aims of targeting a zero budget deficit over the business cycle. The first is to allow automatic stabilisers to work without 'bumping into' the 3 per cent deficit ceiling in years when economies are slowing. The second is to allow a reduction in government debts as a proportion of GDP (assuming that GDP grows on average at around 2–3 per cent per year).

The main criticism of aiming for a zero deficit over the cycle was initially that this would mean a further reduction in deficits, which by the start of the euro in 1999 were typically only just meeting the 3 per cent

(a) *Getting budget deficits down*

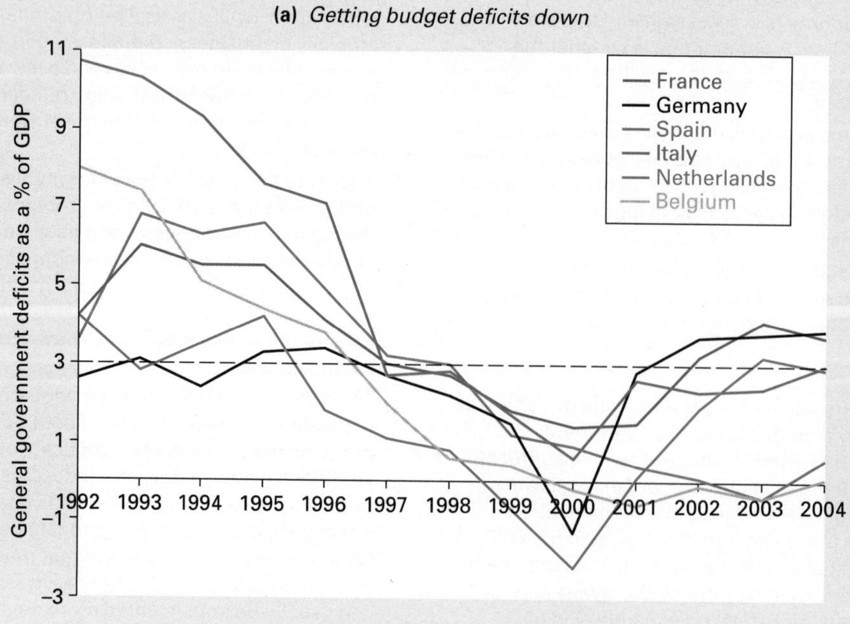

BOX 19.4

ceiling. In other words, meeting the zero deficit target would mean further deflationary fiscal policies: something that most political leaders in Europe felt to be inappropriate at a time when there were fears of a world recession.

Later the criticisms turned on whether the Pact was flexible enough. From 2002, both Germany and France breached the 3 per cent ceiling (see Figure (a)). This was partly the result of slow growth and rising unemployment, and hence falling tax revenue and rising benefit payments. Not surprisingly, both countries were reluctant to cut government expenditure to bring the deficit in line for fear of dampening an already sluggish economy. Despite various promises by the two countries to rein in expenditure, they continued to have deficits in excess of 3 per cent.

Eventually, in March 2005 a deal was reached between European finance ministers. This allowed Germany to exclude reunification costs and France to exclude military and aid costs from the calculation of government expenditure. This compromise brought the deficits of the two countries below the 3 per cent ceiling and allowed them to escape having to adopt tighter fiscal policy.

Labour's golden rule

The Labour government in the UK has adopted a similar approach to that of the Stability and Growth Pact. Under its 'golden rule', the government pledges that over the economic cycle, it will borrow only to invest (e.g. in roads, hospitals and schools) and not to fund current spending (e.g. on wages, administration and benefits). Investment is exempted from the zero borrowing rule because it contributes towards the growth of GDP. Indeed, in its 1998 'Comprehensive Spending Review', the government announced that government investment expenditure would double as a percentage of GDP. The government has also set itself the target of maintaining a stable public-sector debt/GDP ratio below 40 per cent.

To allow the golden rule to operate, government departments are set three-year spending limits and each has separate current and capital (investment) budgets.

As with the Stability and Growth Pact, the argument is that by using an averaging rule over the cycle, automatic stabilisers will be allowed to work. Deficits of receipts over current spending can occur when the economy is in recession or when growth is sluggish (as in 2001–3), helping to stimulate the economy. Surpluses can occur in boom periods (as in 1998–2000), helping to dampen the economy (see Figure (b)). As with the Stability and Growth Pact, however, a major criticism is whether the policy provides too much of a straitjacket. Does it prevent the government using substantial discretionary boosts to the economy at times of serious economic slowdown?

What effects will government investment expenditure have on public-sector debt (a) in the short run; (b) in the long run?

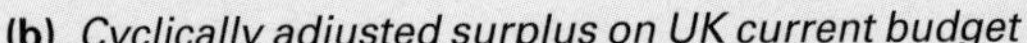

(b) *Cyclically adjusted surplus on UK current budget*

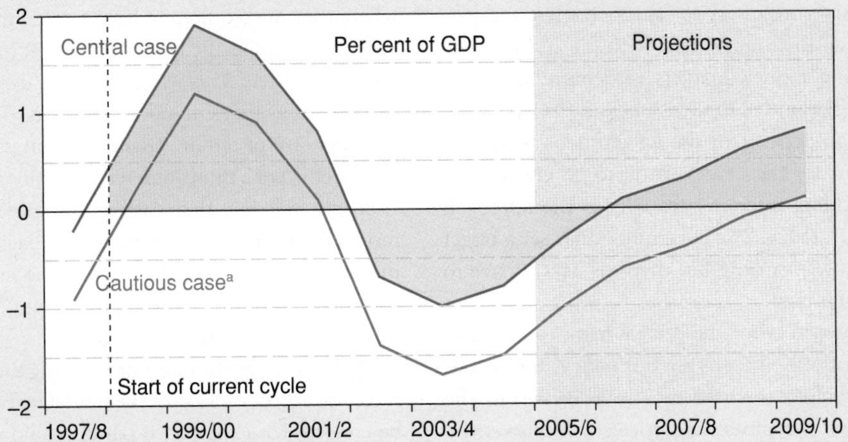

[a] Cautious case assumes trend output one percentage point lower in relation to actual output than in the central case.

Source: *Financial Statement and Budget Report* (HM Treasury, 2005).

19.2 MONETARY POLICY

Each month the Bank of England's Monetary Policy Committee (MPC) meets to set interest rates. The event gets considerable media coverage. Pundits, for two or three days before the meeting, try to predict what the MPC will do and economists give their 'considered' opinions about what the MPC *ought* to do.

The fact is that changes in interest rates have gained a central significance in macroeconomic policy. And it is not just in the UK. Whether it is the European Central Bank setting interest rates for the eurozone countries, or the Federal Reserve Bank setting US interest rates, or any other central bank around the world choosing what the level of interest rates should be, monetary policy is seen as having a major influence on a whole range of macroeconomic indicators.

But is monetary policy just the setting of interest rates? In reality, it involves the central bank intervening in the money market to ensure that the interest rate announced is also the *equilibrium* interest rate.

The policy setting

In framing its monetary policy, the government must decide on what the goals of the policy are. Is the aim simply to control inflation, or does the government wish also to affect output and employment, or does it want to control the exchange rate?

The government must also decide where monetary policy fits into the total package of macroeconomic policies. Is it seen as the major or even sole macroeconomic policy instrument, or is it merely one of several?

In the first, the government both sets the policy and decides the measures necessary to achieve it. Here the government would set the interest rate, with the central bank simply influencing money markets to achieve this rate. This first approach was used in the UK before 1997.

The second approach is for the government to set the policy *targets*, but for the central bank to be given independence in deciding interest rates. This is the approach adopted in the UK today. The government has set a target rate of inflation of 2 per cent, but then the MPC is free to choose the rate of interest.

The third approach is for the central bank to be given independence not only in carrying out policy, but in setting the policy targets themselves. The ECB, within the statutory objective of maintaining price stability over the medium term, decides on (a) the target rate of inflation – currently that inflation for the eurozone should be kept close to 2 per cent – and (b) the target rate of growth in money supply. It then sets interest rates to meet these targets.

Finally, there is the question of whether the government or central bank should take a long-term or short-term perspective. Should it adopt a target for inflation or money supply growth and stick to it come what may? Or should it adjust its policy as circumstances change and attempt to 'fine tune' the economy?

We will be looking primarily at *short-term* monetary policy: that is, policy used to keep to a set target for inflation or money supply growth, or policy used to smooth out fluctuations in the business cycle. It is important first, however, to take a longer-term perspective. Governments generally want to prevent an excessive growth in the money supply over the longer term. If money supply does grow rapidly, then inflation is likely to be high.

Control of the money supply over the medium and long term

There are two major sources of monetary growth: (a) banks choosing to hold a lower liquidity ratio (probably in response to an increase in the demand for loans); (b) public-sector borrowing financed by borrowing from the banking sector. If the government wishes to restrict monetary growth over the longer term, it could attempt to control either or both of these.

Banks' liquidity ratio

The central bank could impose a statutory ***minimum reserve ratio*** on the banks, *above* the level that banks would otherwise choose to hold. Such ratios come in various forms. The simplest is where the banks are required to hold a given minimum percentage of deposits in the form of cash or deposits with the central bank. Other versions are where they are required to hold a given minimum percentage of certain specified types of deposit in the form of various liquid assets. This was the system used in the UK up to 1981. Various types of liquid asset had to add up to at least $12\frac{1}{2}$ per cent of certain 'eligible liabilities'.

The effect of a minimum reserve ratio is to prevent banks choosing to reduce their cash or liquidity ratio and creating more credit. This was a popular approach of governments in many countries in the past. Some countries imposed very high ratios indeed in their attempt to slow down the growth in the money supply.

They also have the effect of reducing the bank multiplier, since, for any expansion of the monetary base, *less* credit can be created. For example, if banks would otherwise choose

Definition

Minimum reserve ratio A minimum ratio of cash (or other specified liquid assets) to deposits (either total or selected) that the central bank requires banks to hold.

a 10 per cent cash ratio, and if the central bank imposes a 20 per cent cash ratio, the bank multiplier is reduced from 10 (= 1/ $^1/_{10}$) to 5 (= 1/ $^1/_5$).

A major problem with imposing restrictions of this kind is that banks may find ways of getting round them. After all, banks would like to lend and customers would like to borrow. It is very difficult to regulate and police every single part of countries' complex financial systems.

Public-sector deficits

As we saw in section 17.3, government borrowing tends to lead to an increase in money supply. To prevent this, the public-sector net cash requirement (PSNCR) must be financed by selling *bonds* (as opposed to bills, which could well be taken up by the banking sector, thereby increasing money supply). However, to sell extra bonds the government will have to offer higher interest rates. This will have a knock-on effect on private-sector interest rates. The government borrowing will thus crowd out private-sector borrowing and investment.

If governments wish to reduce monetary growth and yet avoid financial crowding out, they must therefore reduce the level of the PSNCR. Monetarism, which reached its high point in the 1980s, advocates governments making reductions in the PSNCR (as a proportion of national income) the central part of their medium- and longer-term monetary strategy. Not only is this desirable as a means of restricting monetary growth, but, if it involves cutting government expenditure (as opposed to increasing taxes), it will also increase the size of the private sector relative to the public sector – and it is the private sector that monetarists see as the main source of long-term growth in output and employment.

In the UK, the Conservative government's medium-term financial strategy, introduced in 1980, attempted to do just this (see section 19.4). As well as setting targets for the growth of money supply, it also set targets for the PSNCR as a percentage of GDP.

How could long-term monetary growth come about if the government persistently ran a public-sector surplus (a negative PSNCR)?

Issues with medium- and long-term monetary control

Once inflation is at or near its target level, longer-term control of the monetary base is largely a matter of ensuring that government borrowing is kept in check (see Box 19.4). Keeping bank lending under control is achieved by *short-term* measures to keep inflation at its target rate (see below).

In the early years, however, when a government is embarking on a policy of bringing inflation down there can be serious problems. When the Thatcher government in 1980 adopted a policy of medium-term monetary control, inflation was 18 per cent.

The higher inflation is initially, and the more rapidly the government wishes to reduce it, the bigger the problems can be. The government must cut the PSNCR, but this will be a contractionary *fiscal* policy. This could lead to a recession, given that inflation may be slow to fall.

Adverse effects of automatic stabilisers. In a recession, automatic fiscal stabilisers come into force that will tend to push the PSNCR back up again. Lower incomes and lower expenditure will mean that less taxes are paid. At the same time, higher unemployment will involve increased government expenditure on unemployment benefits. This was a major problem in the UK in the early 1980s, and again in the early 1990s, when the severe recession turned a public-sector surplus of £12 billion in 1988 into a massive deficit of £43 billion by 1993. Attempts to cut the size of the PSNCR by tax increases (e.g. VAT on domestic fuel) and cuts in government expenditure served only to prolong the recession.

It is for this reason that, under the Stability and Growth Pact (see Box 19.4), eurozone countries are required to aim for a zero government deficit over the business cycle, so that in times of economic slowdown the deficit will not exceed 3 per cent: the limit set for deficits under the Pact.

Similarly, in the UK, the Chancellor pursues the 'golden rule' of fiscal policy. This is that, over the course of the business cycle, the government will borrow only to invest. In other words, leaving investment aside, there is a long-term target for the PSNCR of zero.

Political problems. Cutting the PSNCR involves raising taxes and/or cutting government expenditure. Both are unpopular with the electorate. The Thatcher government, as soon as it came into office, met considerable opposition in Parliament, from public opinion, from local authorities and from various pressure groups, to 'cuts'. Moreover, much of government expenditure is committed a long time in advance and cannot easily be cut. As a result, the government may find itself forced into refusing to sanction *new* expenditure. But this will mean cuts in capital projects such as roads, housing, schools and sewers, with a resulting decline in the country's infrastructure and long-term damage to the economy.

The operation of monetary policy in the short term

Inflation may be off target. Alternatively, the government (or central bank) may wish to alter its monetary policy. Assume, for example, that it wishes to operate a tighter monetary policy in order to reduce aggregate demand and inflation. What can it do?

For any given supply of money (M_s) there will be a particular equilibrium rate of interest at any one time: where the supply of money (M_s) equals the demand for money (L). This is shown as r_1 in Figure 19.4.

Figure 19.4 The demand for and supply of money

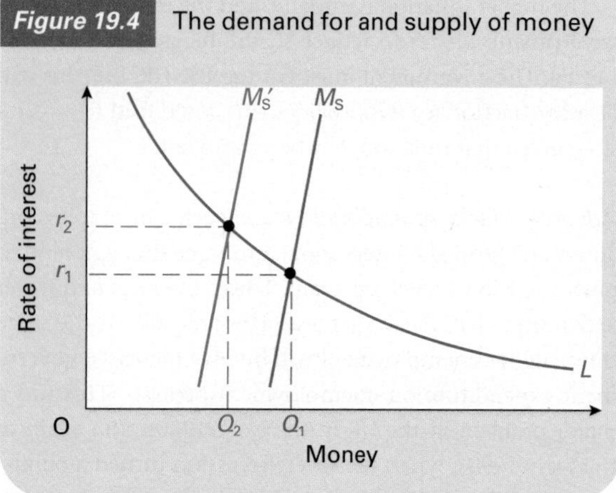

Table 19.3 Reducing the money supply

Liabilities		Assets	
Deposits	£10m ↓	Cash	£1m ↓
		Advances	£9m ↓

Thus to operate a tighter monetary policy, the authorities can do the following:

- Reduce money supply and accept whatever equilibrium interest rate results. Thus if money supply is reduced to Q_2 in Figure 19.4, a new higher rate of interest, r_2, will result.
- First raise interest rates to r_2 and then manipulate the money supply to reduce it to Q_2.

There are two other possibilities. The first is to keep interest rates low (at r_1), but also reduce money supply to a level of Q_2. The trouble here is that the government cannot both control the money supply *and* keep interest rates down without running into the problem of disequilibrium. Since the demand for money now exceeds the supply by $Q_1 - Q_2$, some form of credit rationing would have to be applied.

Credit rationing was widely used in the past, especially during the 1960s. The aim was to keep interest rates low, so as not to discourage investment, but to restrict credit to more risky business customers and/or to consumers. In the UK the Bank of England could order banks to abide by such a policy, although in practice it always relied on persuasion. The government also, from time to time, imposed restrictions on hire-purchase credit, by specifying minimum deposits or maximum repayment periods.

Such policies are not used today. They stifle competition and prevent efficient banks from expanding. Hire-purchase controls may badly hit certain industries (e.g. cars and other consumer durables), whose products are bought largely on hire-purchase credit. What is more, with the deregulation and globalisation of financial markets, it would be virtually impossible to ration credit. If one financial institution was controlled, borrowers could simply go elsewhere.

The other possibility is not primarily monetary policy. This is to reduce the demand for money (i.e. *shift* the demand for money curve (*L*) to the left). A contractionary fiscal policy is probably necessary here. This would reduce aggregate demand directly and thus reduce the transactions demand for money. Money supply could be reduced without raising interest rates or having to ration credit.

The following sections look at the two major approaches to monetary policy: (a) controlling the money supply and (b) controlling interest rates.

Techniques to control the money supply

There are two broad approaches to controlling the money supply.

The first is alter the level of liquidity in the banking system, on which credit is created. Suppose, for example, that banks operate a rigid 10 per cent cash ratio and have just two types of asset: cash and advances. Suppose also that the authorities are able to reduce cash in banks by £1 million. With a bank multiplier of 10 (= 1/cash ratio), advances must be reduced by £9 million, and hence money supply by £10 million (see Table 19.3).

TC 15 p463

If banks operated a rigid 5 per cent cash ratio and the government reduced cash in banks by £1 million, how much must credit contract? What is the bank multiplier?

The second approach is to alter the size of the bank multiplier, by altering the ratio of reserves to deposits. Thus if the bank multiplier can be reduced, credit will have to be reduced for any given reserve base.

Before they can actually apply techniques of monetary control, the authorities must make two preliminary decisions:

- Should a statutory minimum reserve or a minimum liquidity ratio be imposed on the banks, or should the banks be allowed to choose whatever ratios they consider to be prudent?
- Should the authorities attempt to control a range of liquid assets, or should they focus on controlling just the monetary base?

There are four techniques that a central bank could use to control the money supply. Assume in each case that the central bank wishes to reduce money supply.

Open-market operations ***Open-market operations*** are the most widely used of the four techniques around the world. They alter the monetary base (M0 in the UK). This then affects the amount of credit that banks can create and hence the level of broad money (M4 in the UK).

Definition

Open-market operations The sale (or purchase) by the authorities of government securities in the open market in order to reduce (or increase) money supply.

Open-market operations involve the sale or purchase by the central bank of government securities (bonds or bills) in the open market. These sales or purchases are *not* in response to changes in the PSNCR, and are best understood in the context of an unchanged PSNCR.

If the central bank wishes to *reduce* the money supply, it sells more securities. When people buy these securities, they pay for them with cheques drawn on banks. Thus banks' balances with the central bank are reduced. If this brings bank reserves below their prudent ratio (or statutory ratio, if one is in force), banks will reduce advances. There will be a multiple contraction of credit and hence of (broad) money supply.

The effect will be limited if the extra securities are bills (as opposed to bonds) and if some are purchased by banks. The reduction in one liquid asset (balances with the central bank) will be offset to some extent by an increase in another liquid asset (bills). Open-market operations are more likely to be effective in reducing the money supply, therefore, when conducted in the bond market.

?

1. *Explain how open-market operations could be used to* increase *the money supply.*
2. *Why would it be difficult for a central bank to predict the precise effect on money supply of open-market operations?*

Reduced central bank lending to the banks The central bank in most countries is prepared to provide extra money to banks (through rediscounting bills, gilt repos or straight loans). If banks obtain less money in this way, they will have to cut back on lending. Less credit will be created and broad money supply will thereby be reduced.

CASE STUDIES AND APPLICATIONS **BOX 19.5**

THE DAILY OPERATION OF MONETARY POLICY

What goes on at Threadneedle Street?

The Bank of England (the 'Bank') does not attempt to control money supply directly. Instead it seeks to control short-term interest rates by conducting open-market operations in the discount and gilt 'repo' markets (see page 488). These operations, as we shall see, determine short-term interest rates, which then have a knock-on effect on longer-term rates, as returns on different forms of assets must remain competitive with each other.

Let us assume that the Monetary Policy Committee (MPC) of the Bank of England is worried that inflation is set to rise, perhaps because there is excessive growth in the money supply. At its monthly meeting, therefore, it decides to raise interest rates. What does the Bank do?

The first thing is that it will *announce* a rise in interest rates. But it must do more than this. It must back up the announcement by using open-market operations to ensure that its announced interest rate is the *equilibrium rate*. In fact, it has to conduct open-market operations every day to keep interest rates at the level it chooses.

How do these open-market operations work? In general, the Bank of England seeks to keep banks short of liquidity. It achieves this through its weekly sales of Treasury bills to the banks and other financial institutions (collectively known as the Bank's 'counterparties').

The counterparties will thus have to borrow from the Bank of England. They do this by entering into sale and repurchase agreements (repos). This entails them selling gilts to the Bank, with an agreement that they will repurchase them from the Bank at a fixed date in the future (typically two weeks). The difference between the sale and repurchase prices is set by the Bank of England to reflect its chosen rate of interest. By the Bank determining the repo rate in this way, there will be a knock-on effect on other interest rates throughout the banking system.

Each morning at 9.45 the Bank of England forecasts that day's liquidity shortage. Unless the shortage is too small to necessitate action, it then provides liquidity through open-market operations: i.e. through repos (normally for two weeks) or the repurchasing of bills. The rate charged is that set by the MPC. At 2.30, the Bank revises its forecasts of the market's liquidity shortage and, if necessary, undertakes a further round of open-market operations.

Then at 3.30, it publishes a final update for the day's liquidity shortage, and if necessary makes a further repo facility available, normally on an overnight basis and normally at 1 per cent above the rate set by the MPC. The rate is higher because the Bank expects its counterparties to obtain liquidity at the 9.45 and 2.30 rounds. The 3.30 round is designed to cater for any unforeseen late shortage.

Finally, at 4.20, after the market has closed, banks may apply for additional overnight liquidity through repos to allow the process of clearing to be completed. The Bank will charge them anything from the MPC's agreed repo rate to 1½ per cent above that rate.

Although there is usually a shortage of liquidity in the banking system, on some days there may be a *surplus*. To prevent this driving market interest rates down, the Bank will invite its counterparties to bid for outright purchase of short-dated Treasury bills (i.e. ones part-way through their life) at prices set by the Bank to reflect its current (above equilibrium) interest rate: i.e. at prices lower than the market would otherwise set. At such prices, the Bank has no difficulty in selling them and hence in 'mopping up' the surplus liquidity.

Assume that the Bank of England wants to reduce interest rates. Trace through the process during the day by which it achieves this.

Whether or not banks *choose* to obtain extra money from the central bank depends on (a) the rate of interest charged by the central bank (i.e. its discount rate, repo rate or lending rate); and (b) its willingness to lend (or repurchase securities).

In some countries, it is the policy of the central bank to keep its interest rate to banks *below* market rates, thereby encouraging banks to borrow (or sell back securities) whenever such facilities are available. By controlling the amount of money it is willing to provide at these low rates, the central bank can control the monetary base. By cutting back the amount it provides, it can reduce the money supply.

In other countries, such as the UK and the eurozone countries, it is not so much the amount of money made available that is controlled, but rather the rate of interest (or discount). The higher this rate is relative to other market rates, the less will banks be willing to borrow, and the lower, therefore, will be the monetary base. Raising this rate, therefore, has the effect of reducing the money supply.

In some countries, central banks operate two rates: a main repo rate (or 'refinancing rate') on a set amount of money that the central bank wants to be made available, and a higher rate (a penal rate) used for 'last-resort' lending to banks short of liquidity. The European Central Bank operates such a system (see Box 19.7). Its higher rate is known as the 'marginal lending facility rate'.

Funding Rather than focusing on controlling the monetary base (as in the case of the above two techniques), an alternative is for the central bank to attempt to alter the overall liquidity position of the banks. An example of this approach is a change, by the central bank, in the balance of ***funding*** the national debt. To reduce money supply the central bank issues more bonds and fewer bills. Banks' balances with the central bank will be little affected, but to the extent that banks hold fewer bills, there will be a reduction in their liquidity and hence a reduction in the amount of credit created. Funding is thus the conversion of one type of government debt into another.

? *If the Bank of England issues £1 million of extra bonds and buys back £1 million of Treasury bills, will there automatically be a reduction in credit by a set multiple of £1 million?*

Variable minimum reserve ratios If banks are required to maintain a statutory minimum reserve ratio and if the central bank is free to alter this ratio, it can use it as a means of controlling the money supply. It does this by affecting not the monetary base, but the size of the bank multiplier.

Assume that there are just two types of asset: cash and advances, and that banks are required to maintain a minimum 10 per cent cash ratio (a ratio above that which the banks would have chosen for reasons of prudence). The bank multiplier is thus 10 (= $1/{}^{1}/_{10}$). Assume that banks' total assets are £100 billion, of which £10 billion are cash reserves and £90 billion are advances. This is illustrated in the first part of Table 19.4.

Now assume that the central bank raises the minimum reserve ratio to 20 per cent. Banks still have £10 billion cash reserves, and so they have to reduce their advances to £40 billion (giving total assets of £50 billion, of which the £10 million cash is the required 20 per cent). This is shown in the second part of Table 19.4. The bank multiplier has been reduced to 5 (= $1/{}^{1}/_{5}$).

In the past, central banks that imposed minimum reserve ratios on the banks tended to vary them in this way as a means of altering the money supply for any given monetary base. For example, several of the EU countries used this technique before joining the euro. Increasingly, countries that still have minimum reserve ratios are relying on open-market operations or direct lending to banks, rather than on varying the ratio. This is the case with the ECB. The USA, however, still uses variable minimum reserve ratios in this way (see Box 19.6).[2]

A version of variable minimum reserves was used in the UK up to 1981. Banks could be required to deposit a given percentage of their deposits in a special account at

[2] In one sense, it could be argued that the imposition of a minimum reserve ratio is a *form* of credit rationing. It restricts the ability of banks to expand credit as much as they would like for the amount of reserves they hold. In Figure 19.4, however, higher minimum reserves would still shift the *supply* curve, given that this curve measures broad money and not the monetary base. It is for this reason that we considered minimum reserve ratios under the heading of 'techniques to control the money supply'.

Definition

Funding Where the authorities alter the balance of bills and bonds for any given level of government borrowing.

Table 19.4 Effect of raising the minimum reserve ratio from 10% to 20%

Initial position: 10% reserve ratio				New position: 20% reserve ratio			
Liabilities		**Assets**		**Liabilities**		**Assets**	
Deposits	£100bn	Reserve assets	£10bn	Deposits	£50bn	Reserve assets	£10bn
		Advances, etc.	£90bn			Advances, etc.	£40bn
Total	£100bn	Total	£100bn	Total	£50bn	Total	£50bn

CASE STUDIES AND APPLICATIONS — BOX 19.6

CENTRAL BANKING AND MONETARY POLICY IN THE USA

How the 'Fed' works

The central bank in the USA is called the Federal Reserve System (or 'Fed'). It was set up in 1913 and consists of 12 regional Federal Reserve Banks, each of which is responsible for distributing currency and regulating banks in its region. But despite its apparent regional nature, it is still a *national* system. The Federal Reserve Board, based in Washington, decides on monetary policy and then the Federal Open Market Committee (FOMC) decides how to carry it out. The FOMC meets eight times a year. The Fed is independent of both the President and the Congress, and its chairman is generally regarded as having great power in determining the country's economic policy.

Its macroeconomic objectives include low inflation, sustainable economic growth, low unemployment and moderate long-term interest rates. Of course, these objectives may well conflict from time to time. In such a case, the objective of low inflation normally dominates.

When, however, there is no threat of rising inflation, the Fed may use monetary policy aggressively to pursue these other goals. Thus, from January to December 2001, with the US economy moving into recession, the FOMC cut interest rates ten times. In January the rate was 6 per cent; by December it was down to 1.75 per cent.

To carry out these objectives, the FOMC has three policy instruments. The most important one is open-market operations. These are conducted through the Federal Reserve Bank of New York, which buys and sells Treasury bills and government bonds. For example, if the FOMC wishes to reduce money supply, the New York Fed will sell more of these securities. The purchasers, whether they be banks, corporations or individuals, will pay for them with cheques drawn on bank accounts. When these cheques are cleared, banks' reserves with the Fed will be reduced and hence there will be a multiple contraction of credit.

The second policy instrument is the *discount rate*. Known as the 'federal funds rate', this is the rate of interest at which the Fed is willing to lend to banks, thereby providing them with liquidity on which they can create credit. By raising this rate, banks are discouraged from borrowing, and credit is thereby squeezed. Since 1995, the FOMC has published its target federal funds rate. Sometimes this rate merely mirrors other market rates and is not, therefore, an active instrument of policy. On other occasions, however, the Fed changes it ahead of other market rates in order to signal its intentions to tighten (or loosen) monetary policy.[3]

The final instrument is variable minimum reserves. Banks are legally required to hold a certain minimum percentage of various assets in the form of non-interest-bearing reserves. These percentages vary from around 10 per cent for sight accounts to zero for personal savings accounts. The Fed can vary these percentages within set limits. Thus it could raise the minimum reserve ratio to as high as 14 per cent on sight accounts ('checking accounts'). Given that any change in the reserve ratio causes a multiplied effect on advances, changes are made only occasionally and by a small amount.

In what ways is the Fed's operation of monetary policy (a) similar to and (b) different from the Bank of England's?

[3] For details of the Fed's interest rate policy see: http://www.federalreserve.gov/fomc/fundsrate.htm.

the Bank of England. These ***special deposits*** were frozen, and could not be drawn on until the authorities chose to release them. They provided a simple means of reducing banks' liquidity and hence their ability to create credit.

Difficulties in controlling money supply

The authorities may experience considerable difficulties in controlling the money supply. Difficulties occur whether they focus on the monetary base or on a wider range of liquid assets.

Problems with monetary base control. Assume that the authorities seek to control the monetary base (M0 in the UK). This could be done by imposing a statutory 'cash' ratio on banks (where 'cash' is notes and coin and banks' balances with the central bank). Assume that a statutory ratio of 10 per cent is imposed. Then provided the authorities control the supply of 'cash' by, say, open-market operations, it would seem that they can thereby control the creation of credit and hence deposits. There would be a bank multiplier of 10. For every £1 million decrease in cash held by the banks, money supply would fall by £10 million. There are serious problems, however, with this form of ***monetary base control***:

- Banks could hold cash in excess of the statutory minimum. For a time, therefore, they could respond to any restriction of cash by the authorities by simply reducing their cash ratio towards the minimum, rather than having to reduce credit.
- Unless cash ratios were imposed on every single financial institution, the control of certain institutions' lending

Definitions

Special deposits Deposits that the banks can be required to make in the Bank of England. They remain frozen there until the Bank of England chooses to release them.

Monetary base control Monetary policy that focuses on controlling the monetary base (as opposed to broad liquidity).

CASE STUDIES AND APPLICATIONS

MONETARY POLICY IN THE EUROZONE

The role of the ECB

The European Central Bank (ECB) is based in Frankfurt and is charged with operating the monetary policy of those EU countries that have adopted the euro. Although the ECB has the overall responsibility for the eurozone's monetary policy, the central banks of the individual countries, such as the Bank of France and Germany's Bundesbank, have not been abolished. They are responsible for distributing euros and for carrying out the ECB's policy with respect to institutions in their own countries. The whole system of the ECB and the national central banks is known as the European System of Central Banks (ESCB).

In operating the monetary policy of a 'euro economy' roughly the size of the USA, and in being independent from national governments, the ECB's power is enormous and is equivalent to that of the Fed (see Box 19.6). So what is the structure of this giant on the European stage, and how does it operate?

The structure of the ECB

The ECB has two major decision-making bodies: the Governing Council and the Executive Board.[4]

- The Governing Council consists of the members of the Executive Board and the governors of the central banks of each of the eurozone countries. The Council's role is to set the main targets of monetary policy and to take an oversight of the success (or otherwise) of that policy.
- The Executive Board consists of a president, a vice-president and four other members. Each serves for an eight-year, non-renewable term. The Executive Board is responsible for implementing the decisions of the Governing Council and for preparing policies for the Council's consideration. Each member of the Executive Board has a responsibility for some particular aspect of monetary policy.

The targets of monetary policy

The overall responsibility of the ECB is to achieve price stability in the eurozone. The target is a rate of inflation below, but close to, 2 per cent over the medium term. It is a weighted *average* rate for all 12 members, not a rate that has to be met by every member individually.

The ECB also sets a reference value for the annual growth of M3, the broad measure of the money supply (see Box 17.4 on page 491). This was set at 4½ per cent at the launch of the euro in 1999 and was still the same value in 2005. The reference value is not a rigid target, but is used as a guide to whether monetary policy is consistent with long-run price stability. In setting the reference value, three things are taken into account: the target for inflation, assumptions about the rate of growth of GDP (assumed to have a trend growth rate of 2 to 2½ per cent per year) and the velocity of circulation of M3 (assumed to be declining at a rate of between ½ and 1 per cent per year). The reference value is reviewed in December each year.

On the basis of its inflation target and M3 reference value, the ECB then sets the rates of interest. In March 2005, the rates were as follows: 2.00 per cent for the main 'refinancing operations' of the ESCB (i.e. the minimum rate of interest at which liquidity is offered once per week to 'monetary financial institutions' (MFIs) by the ESCB); a 'marginal lending' rate of 3.00 per cent (for providing overnight support to the MFIs); and a 'deposit rate' of 1.00 per cent (the rate paid to MFIs for depositing overnight surplus liquidity with the ESCB).

Interest rates are set by the Governing Council by simple majority. In the event of a tie, the president has the casting vote.

The operation of monetary policy

The ECB sets a minimum reserve ratio. It argues that this gives greater stability to the system and reduces

would merely shift business to other uncontrolled institutions, including overseas ones. Banks operate in a global market. Thus UK banks can do business with UK borrowers using money markets abroad, thereby diverting potentially profitable business away from London. This is an example of Goodhart's law (see Box 19.8).

KI 34 p552

- Alternatively, if those banks subject to statutory cash requirements were short of cash, they could attract cash away from the uncontrolled institutions.

The switching of business away from controlled banks is known as ***disintermediation***. To avoid this problem and to allow the greatest freedom of competition between financial institutions, the alternative is to use monetary base control with no *statutory* cash ratio.

But two major problems with monetary base control, with or without a statutory cash ratio, are the most serious of all. The first is that central banks, as lenders of last resort, *are always prepared to increase the monetary base, through repos or rediscounting, if it is demanded*. This makes it virtually impossible to have a precise control of the monetary base.

The second is the size and variability of the money multiplier. As we saw in section 17.3 (page 493), the money multiplier is the number of times greater the rise in (broad) money supply is than the rise in the monetary base (i.e.

Definition

Disintermediation The diversion of business away from financial institutions that are subject to controls.

BOX 19.7

the need for day-to-day intervention by the ECB. The ECB argues that, if there were no minimum reserves, with banks free to use as much of their reserves with the ESCB as they chose, then they would do so if there were an upsurge in demand from customers. After all, the banks know that they can always *borrow* from the ESCB to meet any liquidity requirements. In such a situation, the ECB would be forced to rely much more on open-market operations to prevent excessive lending by banks to their customers, and hence excessive borrowing from the ESCB, and this would mean much greater fluctuations in interest rates.

> Without the use of a minimum reserve system, the ESCB would be faced with a relatively high volatility of money market rates, which would require the frequent use of open market operations for fine-tuning purposes. Such a situation would have clear disadvantages in practical terms and could undermine the operational efficiency of monetary policy, as central bank signals may become blurred if markets have difficulty distinguishing policy signals from technical adjustments.[5]

The minimum reserve ratio is not designed to be used to make *changes* in monetary policy. In other words, it is not used as a *variable* minimum reserves ratio, and for this reason it is set at a low level. Since 1999 the ratio has been 2 per cent of key liquid and relatively liquid assets.

The main instrument for keeping the ECB's desired interest rate as the equilibrium rate is open-market operations in government bonds and other recognised assets, mainly in the form of repos. These repo operations are conducted by the national central banks, which must ensure that the repo rate does not rise above the marginal overnight lending rate or below the deposit rate.

ECB independence

The ECB is one of the most independent central banks in the world. It has very little formal accountability to elected politicians. Although its president can be called before the European Parliament, the Parliament has virtually no powers to influence the ECB's actions. Also, its deliberations are secret. Unlike meetings of the Bank of England's Monetary Policy Committee, the minutes of the Council meetings are not published.

There is one area, however, where the ECB's power is limited by politicians and this concerns the exchange rate of the euro. Under the Maastricht Treaty, EU finance ministers have the responsibility for deciding on exchange rate policy (even though the ECB is charged with carrying it out). If the finance ministers want to stop the exchange rate of the euro rising, in order to prevent putting EU exporters at a competitive disadvantage, this will put pressure on the ECB to lower interest rates, which might run directly counter to its desire to meet its inflation and money supply targets. This is another example of the principle of 'targets and instruments'. If you have only one instrument (the rate of interest), it cannot be used to achieve two targets (the exchange rate and inflation) if these two targets are in conflict.

More details of monetary policy in the eurozone and the role of the ECB are give in Web Case 19.4.

What are the arguments for and against publishing the minutes of the meetings of the ECB's Governing Council and Executive Board?

[4] See http://www.ecb.int/ecb/orga/decisions/govc/html/index.en.html.

[5] *The use of a minimum reserve system by the European System of Central Banks in Stage Three* (http://www.ecb.int/press/pr/date/1998/html/pr981013_3.en.html).

$\Delta M4/\Delta M0$ in the UK). In the mid-2000s, the money multiplier in the UK was around 28 and *highly* variable. In other words, controlling the monetary base (M0) would have a highly unpredictable effect on the money supply (M4).

For these reasons, the support for monetary base control has waned in recent years.

?

1. *Trace through the effects of a squeeze on the monetary base from an initial reduction in cash to banks' liquidity being restored through gilt repos. Will this restoration of liquidity by the central bank totally nullify the initial effect of reducing the supply of cash? (Clue: what is likely to happen to the rate of interest?)*
2. *Given the difficulties of monetary base control, would you expect M0 and broader measures of the money supply, such as M4, to rise and fall by the same percentage as each other?*

Problems with controlling broad money supply. One solution to the problems of monetary base control would be for the authorities to attempt to control broader money supply. In the UK, targets for the growth in broad money were an important part of monetary policy from 1976 to 1985. The UK has not targeted money supply growth since the 1980s, however. The European Central Bank has a 'reference value' of $4^1/_2$ per cent for M3 growth of the euro (see Box 17.4 on page 491 for a definition of M3). This, however, is only a guideline and not a strict target.

How would such a policy work? Assume that the authorities want to operate a tight monetary policy. They sell bonds on the open market. Banks, now short of cash, obtain money from the central bank through rediscounting bills or through repos. Thus although the central bank has been obliged to restore the amount of cash it had withdrawn from the system, there has been a decrease in bills and short-term bonds held by the banks. Banks' *overall* liquidity has thus been reduced. Such measures could be backed up by funding.

But, as with monetary base control, there are problems with attempting to control broad money supply. Banks may be prepared to reduce their liquidity ratio. This is likely if they already have surplus liquidity, or if their customers are prepared to switch from sight to time accounts (for which banks require fewer cash reserves). This will involve offering higher interest rates on time accounts, and hence charging higher interest rates on bank loans. But if the demand for loans is relatively insensitive to interest rate changes, this will have little effect on credit and hence overall deposits.

The use of open-market operations or funding to reduce money supply involves selling more bonds. But if potential purchasers believe interest rates will rise in the future (highly likely when the government is attempting to operate a tighter monetary policy), they will hold off buying bonds now and may even attempt to sell bonds before bond prices fall. Thus the authorities may be forced into a large immediate increase in bond interest rates.

Perhaps the biggest problem is the effect on interest rates.

TC 9 p101

The effect on interest rates. A policy of controlling money supply can lead to severe fluctuations in interest rates. This can cause great uncertainty for business and can be very damaging to long-term investment and growth.

The problem is more acute if the overall demand for money is inelastic and is subject to fluctuations. In Figure 19.5, with money supply controlled at M_s, even a fairly moderate increase in demand from L to L' leads to a large rise in interest rates from r to r_1.

And yet, if the authorities are committed to controlling money supply, they will have to accept that equilibrium interest rates may well fluctuate in this way.

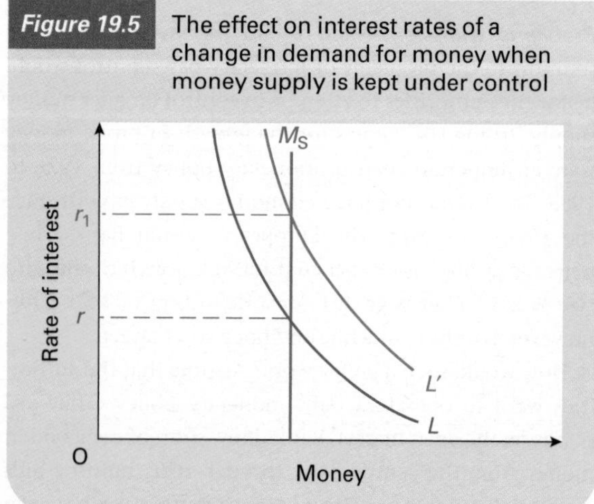

Figure 19.5 The effect on interest rates of a change in demand for money when money supply is kept under control

Because of the above difficulties in controlling the money supply directly, countries have become increasingly reliant on controlling interest rates (backed up, normally, by open-market operations).

Techniques to control interest rates

The approach to monetary control today in many countries is to focus directly on interest rates. Normally an interest rate change will be announced, and then open-market operations will be conducted by the central bank to ensure that the money supply is adjusted so as to make the announced interest rate the *equilibrium* one. Thus, in Figure 19.4 (on page 544), the central bank might announce a rise in interest rates from r_1 to r_2 and then conduct open-market operations to ensure that the money supply is reduced from Q_1 to Q_2.

In the UK, since the Bank of England was made independent in 1997, interest rate changes have been made by the Bank's Monetary Policy Committee (MPC) at its monthly meetings. These are then backed up through the Bank's operations in the discount and gilt repo markets. Similarly in the eurozone, the ECB's Governing Council sets interest rates at its fortnightly meetings.

Let us assume that the central bank decides to raise interest rates. What does it do? In general, it will seek to keep banks short of liquidity. This will happen automatically on any day when tax payments by banks' customers exceed the money they receive from government expenditure. This excess is effectively withdrawn from banks and ends up in the government's account at the central bank. Even when this does not occur, sales of bills by the central bank will effectively keep the banking system short of liquidity.

This 'shortage' can then be used as a way of forcing through interest rate changes. Banks will obtain the necessary liquidity from the central bank through gilt repos or by selling it back bills. The central bank can *choose the rate of interest to charge* (i.e. the gilt repo rate or the bill rediscount rate). This will then have a knock-on effect on other interest rates throughout the banking system.

The effects can be illustrated in Figure 19.6. Both parts of the diagram assume that the central bank wishes to raise the interest rate (the repo or discount rate) from r_1 to r_2.

In Figure 19.6(a), it is assumed that banks are short of liquidity and are seeking to sell gilts to the central bank on a repo basis. It is assumed that the central bank will supply as much cash (i.e. demand as many gilts through repos) as banks choose, but only at the central bank's chosen repo rate. The demand for gilts is thus perfectly elastic at the central bank's repo rate. The supply curve of gilts by the banks represents their demand for cash from the central bank, and hence is *downward* sloping: the lower the repo rate, the cheaper it is for the banks to obtain cash. If the central bank raises the repo rate to r_2, banks will supply fewer gilts (i.e. demand less cash from the central bank). If there is less liquidity in the banking system, the money supply will fall.

Figure 19.6 Central bank operations in the gilt repo and bill markets to affect interest rates

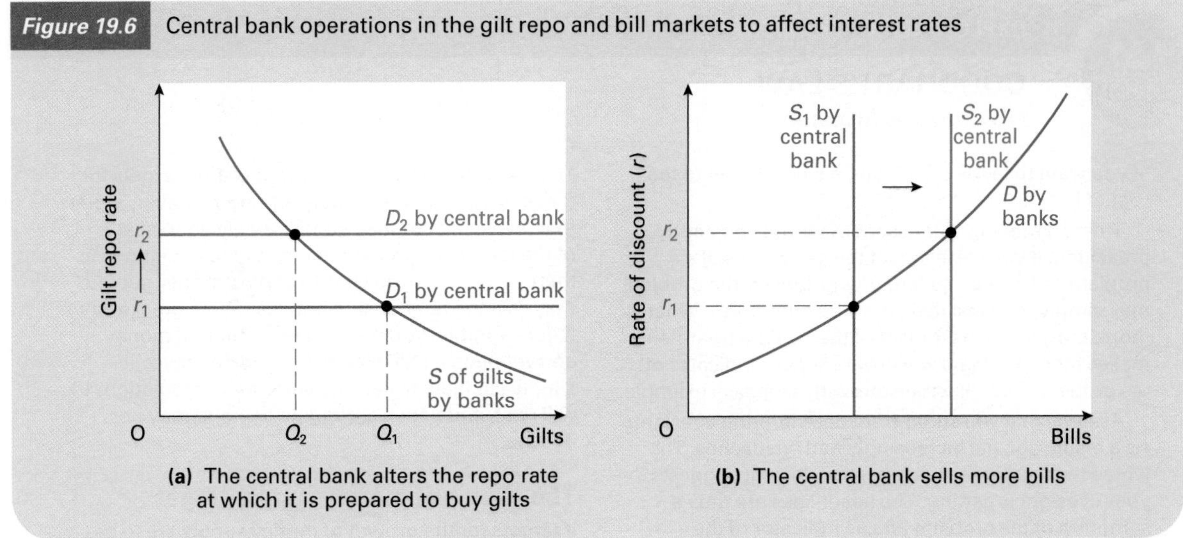

(a) The central bank alters the repo rate at which it is prepared to buy gilts

(b) The central bank sells more bills

In the event of banks having a surplus of liquidity, Figure 19.6(b) applies. Here banks are seeking to use their surplus liquidity to *buy* bills from the central bank. Their demand curve is *upward* sloping: the higher the rate of discount (i.e. the lower the price that banks have to pay for bills), the more the banks will demand. In this case, the central bank can raise the rate of discount by offering more bills for sale. By increasing the supply of bills from S_1 to S_2, it can increase the equilibrium rate from r_1 to r_2.

In both cases, the central bank will first decide on the repo rate (or discount rate) and then adjust the supply or demand of gilts or bills to ensure that the chosen rate is the equilibrium rate (see Boxes 19.5, 19.6 and 19.7 for details of how the Bank of England, the Fed and the ECB do this in practice).

A change in the repo rate will then have a knock-on effect on other interest rates. For example, in the UK, banks automatically adjust their base rates (to which they gear their other rates) when the Bank of England announces a change in the repo rate. Thus a 0.25 percentage point rise in the Bank of England's repo rate will mean a 0.25 percentage point rise in banks' deposit rates, overdraft rates, etc.

Problems with controlling interest rates

Even though central bank adjustment of the repo rate is the current preferred method of monetary control in most countries, it is not without its difficulties. The problems centre on the nature of the demand for loans. If this demand is (a) unresponsive to interest rate changes or (b) unstable because it can be significantly affected by other determinants (e.g. anticipated income or foreign interest rates), it will be very difficult to control by controlling the rate of interest.

TC 8 p 59 *Problem of an inelastic demand for loans.* If the demand for loans is inelastic, as in Figure 19.7, any attempt to reduce demand (e.g. from Q_1 to Q_2) will involve large rises in interest rates (r_1 to r_2). The problem will be compounded if the demand curve shifts to the right, due, say, to a consumer spending boom. High interest rates lead to the following problems:

- They may discourage long-term investment (as opposed to current consumption) and hence long-term growth.
- They add to the costs of production, to the costs of house purchase and generally to the cost of living. They are thus cost inflationary.
- They are politically unpopular, since the general public do not like paying higher interest rates on overdrafts, credit cards and mortgages.
- The necessary bond issue to restrain liquidity will commit the government to paying high rates on these bonds for the next 20 years or so.
- High interest rates encourage inflows of money from abroad. This makes it even more difficult to restrain bank lending.
- Inflows of money from abroad drive up the exchange rate. This can be very damaging for export industries and

Figure 19.7 An inelastic demand for loans

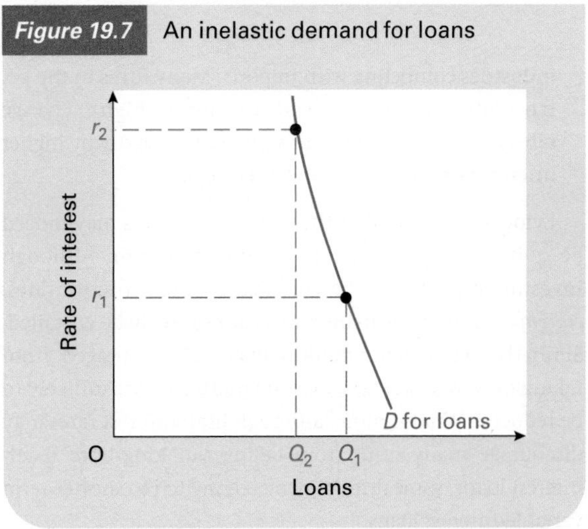

EXPLORING ECONOMICS BOX 19.8

GOODHART'S LAW

'To control is to distort'

'If you want to tackle a problem, it's best to get to the root of it.'

This is a message that economists are constantly preaching. If you merely treat the *symptoms* of a problem rather than its *underlying causes*, the problem may simply manifest itself in some other form. What is more, the symptoms (or lack of them, if the treatment makes them go away) will now be a poor indicator of the problem. Let's illustrate this with a medical example.

Assume that you suffer from deteriorating eyesight. As a result, you get increasingly bad headaches. The worse the headaches become, the worse it suggests your eyesight is getting. The headaches are thus a symptom of the problem and an indicator of the problem's magnitude. So what do you do? One approach is to treat the symptoms. You regularly take aspirins and the headaches go away. But you haven't treated the underlying problem – by getting stronger glasses, or perhaps even having eye surgery – all you have done is to treat the symptoms. As a result, headaches (or rather the lack of them) are now a poor indicator of your eyesight.

If you control the indicator rather than the underlying problem, the indicator ceases to be a good indicator. 'To control [the indicator] is to distort [its use as an indicator].' This is ***Goodhart's law*** and it has many applications in economics, especially in the field of monetary policy.

Goodhart's law. Controlling a symptom (i.e. an indicator) of a problem will not cure the problem. Instead, the indicator will merely cease to be a good indicator of the problem.

Money as an indicator of aggregate demand

Monetarists argue that the level of money supply determines the level of aggregate demand and prices. They therefore argue in favour of setting targets for the growth of money supply. Critics, however, argue that the level of money supply is only an *indicator* of the level of aggregate demand (and a poor one at that). As soon as you start to *control* money supply, they say, the relationship between them breaks down. If, for example, you restrict the amount of money and yet people still want to borrow, money will simply circulate faster (the velocity of circulation (V) will rise), and hence aggregate demand may not decline.

The choice of money supply target

If targets for the growth of money supply are to be set, which measure of money supply should be chosen? Goodhart's law suggests that whichever measure is chosen it will, by virtue of its choice, become a poor indicator. If the government targets M0 and directs its policy to reducing the amount of notes and coin in the economy, banks may try to reduce their customers' demand for cash by, say, increasing the charges for cash advances on credit cards. As a result, M0 may well be constrained, but all the other measures of money supply are likely to go on rising.

The choice of institutions

If bank advances are a good indicator of aggregate demand, the government may choose to control bank lending. But as soon as it does so, bank lending will become a poor indicator. If people's demand for loans is still high and *bank* loans are becoming difficult to obtain, people will simply go elsewhere to borrow money. If you regulate *part* of the financial system, you are likely to end up merely diverting business to other parts which are unregulated.

Give some everyday examples of Goodhart's law.

industries competing with imports. Many firms in the UK have suffered badly in recent years from a high exchange rate (see Table 14.7 on page 420) induced partly by higher interest rates than those in the eurozone.

Evidence suggests that the demand for loans may indeed be quite inelastic, especially in the short run. Although investment *plans* may be curtailed by high interest rates, *current* borrowing by many firms cannot easily be curtailed. Similarly, while householders may be discouraged from taking on *new* mortgages, existing mortgages are unlikely to be reduced. What is more, although high interest rates may discourage many firms from taking out long-term fixed-interest loans, some firms may merely switch to shorter-term variable-interest loans.

Problem of an unstable demand. Accurate monetary control requires the authorities to be able to predict the demand curve for money. Only then can they set the appropriate level of interest rates. Unfortunately, the demand curve may shift unpredictably, making control very difficult. The major reason is *speculation*:

Definition

Goodhart's law Controlling a symptom of a problem or only one part of the problem will not cure the problem: it will simply mean that the part that is being controlled now becomes a poor indicator of the problem.

EXPLORING ECONOMICS 

USING INTEREST RATES TO CONTROL BOTH AGGREGATE DEMAND AND THE EXCHANGE RATE

A problem of one instrument and two targets

Assume that the central bank is worried about excessive growth in the money supply and rising inflation. It thus decides to raise interest rates. One effect of these higher interest rates is to attract deposits into the country (causing a financial account surplus) and thus drive up the exchange rate. This makes imports cheaper and exports less competitive. This will result in a current account deficit, which will match the financial (plus capital) account surplus.

Now let us assume that the central bank becomes worried about the damaging effect on exports and wants to reduce the exchange rate. If it uses interest rates as the means of achieving this, it will have to *lower* them: lower interest rates will cause deposits to flow out of the country, and this will cause the rate of exchange to depreciate.

But there is a dilemma here. The central bank wants *high* interest rates to contain inflation, but *low* interest rates to help exporters. If interest rates are the only policy instrument, one objective will have to be sacrificed for the other.

Another example, but this time the reverse case, was when the UK was forced out of the 'exchange rate mechanism' (ERM) in September 1992. As we shall see in section 25.2, the ERM was a system of semi-fixed exchange rates between European currencies. The UK joined the ERM in 1990 at a relatively high rate of exchange. In its attempt to stay in the ERM and prevent speculation driving down the exchange rate, it had to keep interest rates at very high levels. But the economy was deep in recession and a lower interest rate would have helped to stimulate investment and aggregate demand generally. On this occasion the government wanted *high* interest rates to support the exchange rate, but *low* interest rates to revive the economy. Once the country had left the ERM and the pound was allowed to float, interest rates were reduced. There was no longer any conflict.

These examples illustrate a rule in economic policy: you must have at least as many instruments as targets. If you have two targets (e.g. low inflation and a low exchange rate), you must have at least two policy instruments (e.g. interest rates and one other).

?

1. ***Give some other examples of the impossibility of using one policy instrument to achieve two policy objectives simultaneously.***
2. ***If the central bank wanted to achieve a lower rate of inflation and also a* higher *exchange rate, could it under these circumstances rely simply on the one policy instrument of interest rates?***

- If people think interest rates will rise and bond prices fall, in the meantime they will demand to hold their assets in liquid form. The demand for money will rise.
- If people think exchange rates will rise, they will demand sterling while it is still relatively cheap. The demand for money will rise.
- If people think inflation will rise, the transactions demand for money may rise. People spend now while prices are still relatively low.
- If people think the economy is going to grow faster, the demand for loans will increase as firms seek to increase their investment.

TC 9 p101 It is very difficult for the authorities to predict what people's speculation will be. Speculation depends largely on world political events, rumour and 'random shocks'.

If the demand curve shifts very much, and if it is inelastic, monetary control will be very difficult. Furthermore, the authorities will have to make frequent and sizeable adjustments to interest rates. These fluctuations can be very damaging to business confidence and may discourage long-term investment.

? *Why does an unstable demand for money make it difficult to control the* supply *of money?*

The net result of an inelastic and unstable demand for money is that substantial interest rate changes may be necessary to bring about the required change in aggregate demand. An example occurred in 2001, when the US Federal Reserve, seeing the economy moving rapidly into recession, had to cut interest rates several times. At the beginning of 2001, the US 'federal funds rate' was 6 per cent. By the end of the year it had been reduced to 1.75 per cent (see Box 19.6 on page 547).

Using monetary policy

It is impossible to use monetary policy as a precise means of controlling aggregate demand. It is especially weak when it is pulling against the expectations of firms and consumers, and when it is implemented too late. However, if the authorities operate a tight monetary policy firmly enough and long enough, they should eventually be able to reduce lending and aggregate demand. But there will inevitably be time lags and imprecision in the process.

An expansionary monetary policy is even less reliable. If the economy is in recession, no matter how low interest rates are driven, people cannot be forced to borrow if they do not wish to. Firms will not borrow to invest if they predict a continuing recession.

A particular difficulty in using interest rate reductions to expand the economy arises if the repo rate is nearly zero but this is still not enough to stimulate the economy. The problem is that (nominal) interest rates cannot be negative, for clearly nobody would be willing to lend in these circumstances. Japan was in such a situation in the early 2000s. It was caught in the 'liquidity trap' (see page 506).

Despite these problems, changing interest rates can be quite effective. After all, they can be changed very rapidly. There are not the time lags of implementation that there are with fiscal policy. Indeed, since the early 1990s, most governments or central banks have used interest rate changes as the major means of keeping aggregate demand and inflation under control.

In the UK, the eurozone and many other countries, the government or central bank sets a target for the rate of inflation. In the UK, the target is $2\frac{1}{2}$ per cent. In the eurozone, it is a ceiling of 2 per cent. If forecasts suggest that inflation is going to be off-target, interest rate changes are announced, and then appropriate open-market operations are conducted to support the new interest rate. The use of such targets is examined in section 19.4.

One important effect of changing interest rates in this very public way is that it sends a clear message to people that inflation *will* be kept under control. People will therefore be more likely to adjust their expectations accordingly and keep their borrowing in check. KI 10 p62

Section summary

1. Control of the growth in the money supply over the longer term will normally involve governments attempting to restrict the size of the PSNCR. Whilst this is relatively easy once inflation has been brought under control, it can lead to serious problems if inflation is initially high. Increases in taxes and cuts in government expenditure are not only politically unpopular, but could also result in a recession.
2. In the short term, the government can use monetary policy to restrict the growth in aggregate demand in one of two major ways: (a) reducing money supply directly, (b) reducing the demand for money by raising interest rates.
3. The money supply can be reduced directly by using open-market operations. This involves the central bank selling more government securities and thereby reducing banks' reserves when their customers pay for them from their bank accounts. Alternatively, the central bank can reduce the amount of lending or rediscounting it is prepared to do (other than as a last-resort measure). Rather than controlling the monetary base in either of these two ways, the central bank could use funding. This involves increasing the sale of bonds relative to bills, thereby reducing banks' liquid assets. Finally, it could operate a system of variable minimum reserve ratios. Increasing these would force banks to cut back the amount of credit they create.
4. Controlling either the monetary base or broad liquidity, however, is difficult given that central banks, as lender of last resort, are always prepared to provide liquidity to the banks on demand. If the government is successful in controlling the money supply, there then arises the problem of severe fluctuations in interest rates if the demand for money fluctuates and is relatively inelastic.
5. The current method of control in the UK and many other countries involves the central bank influencing interest rates by its operations in the gilt repo and discount markets. The central bank keeps banks short of liquidity and then supplies them with liquidity, largely through gilt repos, at its chosen interest rate (gilt repo rate). This then has a knock-on effect on interest rates throughout the economy.
6. With an inelastic demand for loans, however, changes in interest rates may have to be very large to bring the required changes in monetary growth. High interest rates are politically unpopular and discriminate against those with high borrowing commitments. They also drive up the exchange rate, which can damage exports. Controlling aggregate demand through interest rates is made even more difficult by fluctuations in the demand for money. These fluctuations are made more severe by speculation against changes in interest rates, exchange rates, the rate of inflation, etc.
7. It is impossible to use monetary policy as a precise means of controlling aggregate demand in the short term. Nevertheless, controlling interest rates is a rapid way of responding to changing forecasts, and can be an important signal to markets that inflation will be kept under control, especially when, as in the UK and the eurozone, there is a firm target for the rate of inflation.

*19.3 *ISLM* ANALYSIS OF FISCAL AND MONETARY POLICY

ISLM analysis can be used to examine the effects of fiscal and monetary policy, taking both goods and money market effects into account simultaneously.

Assume that the economy is in recession and that the government wishes to raise the level of national income. Figure 19.8 illustrates the policy alternatives.

Figure 19.8(a) shows the effect of an increase in government expenditure (G) or a cut in taxes (T), but with no increase in money supply. The *IS* curve shifts to the right. Income rises to Y_2, but interest rates also rise (to r_2). Thus some crowding out occurs.

Figure 19.8 *ISLM* analysis of fiscal and monetary policy

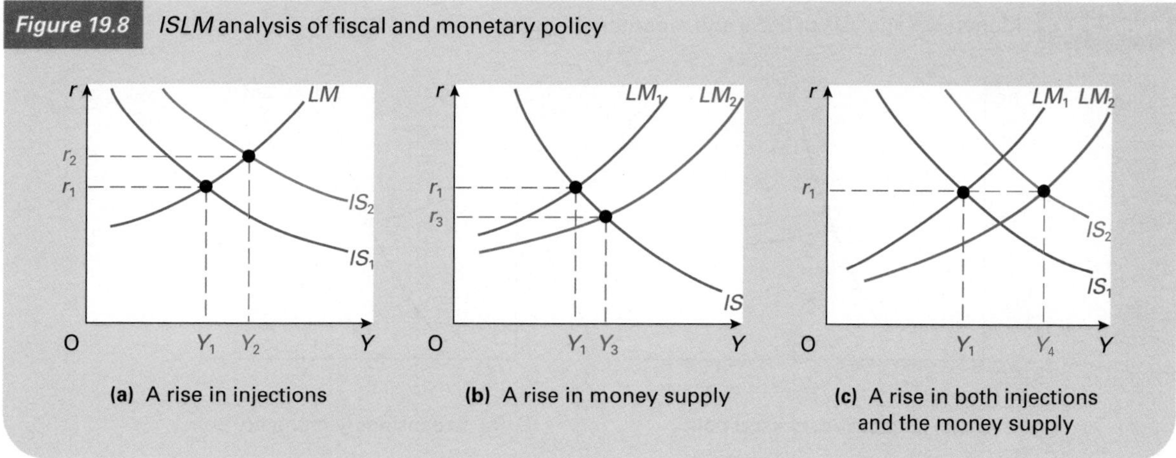

(a) A rise in injections

(b) A rise in money supply

(c) A rise in both injections and the money supply

Figure 19.8(b) shows the effect of an increase in money supply. The *LM* curve shifts downwards. Interest rates fall to r_3 and this encourages an increase in investment. As a result of this, income rises to Y_3.

Figure 19.8(c) shows what happens when the government finances higher government expenditure or lower taxes by increasing the money supply. There is no rise in interest rates, and thus no crowding out. National income rises by a greater amount than in (a) or (b), to Y_4.

The effectiveness of fiscal and monetary policy depends on the slope of the two curves. Fiscal policy is most effective when the *LM* curve is shallow and the *IS* curve is steep. When *LM* is shallow, a rightward shift in *IS* will lead to only a small rise in the rate of interest (*r*). If *IS* is steep, this rise in *r* will lead to only a small curtailing of investment. In these two circumstances, crowding out is minimised. There will be a large increase in national income (*Y*).

Monetary policy, by contrast, is most effective when the *LM* curve is steep and the *IS* curve is shallow. When *LM* is steep, a rightward shift in *LM* will lead to a relatively large fall in *r*. When *IS* is shallow, this fall in *r* will lead to a relatively large increase in investment and hence *Y*.

Fiscal and monetary policies will be most effective when applied simultaneously, as in Figure 19.8(c).

The Keynesian position

Keynesian analysis has traditionally made the following assumptions.

The LM curve is relatively shallow. This is because the liquidity preference curve (*L*) is relatively shallow, due to the important role of the speculative demand for money (see Figure 18.8(a) on page 514).

The IS curve is relatively steep. This is because the investment demand curve is relatively inelastic, due to the unresponsiveness of investment to changes in interest rates (see Figure 18.9(a) on page 514). Also, saving is relatively unresponsive to interest rate changes.

Under these circumstances, fiscal policy is more effective than monetary policy in controlling aggregate demand. Figure 19.9(a) shows a bigger increase in national income with expansionary fiscal policy, than does Figure 19.9(b) with expansionary monetary policy. Monetary policy is weak because increases in money supply lead to substantially increased holdings of idle balances and hence only a small fall in interest rates and a small downward shift in the *LM* curve.

Figure 19.9 Keynesian analysis of fiscal and monetary policy

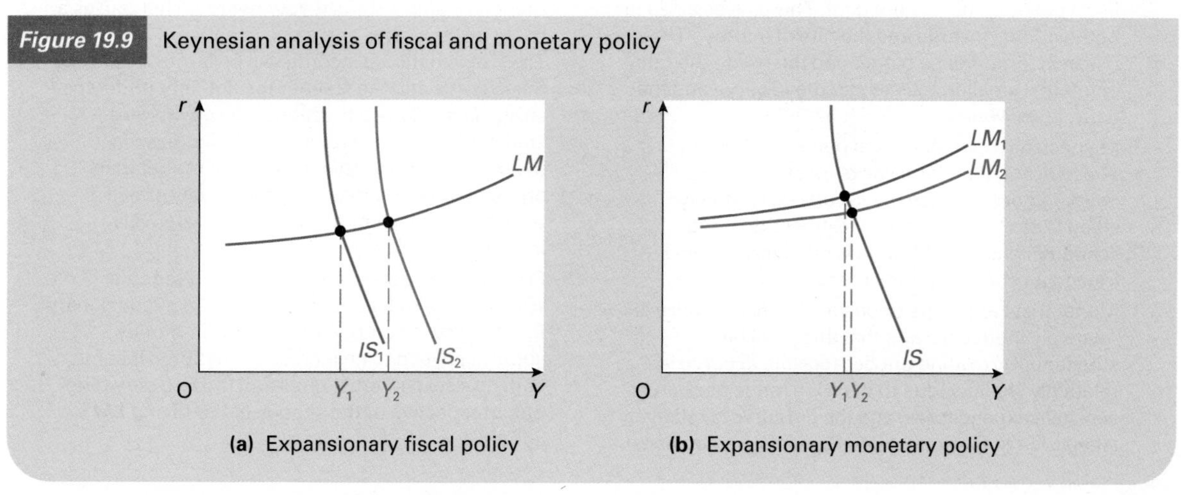

(a) Expansionary fiscal policy

(b) Expansionary monetary policy

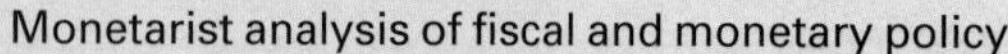

Figure 19.10 Monetarist analysis of fiscal and monetary policy

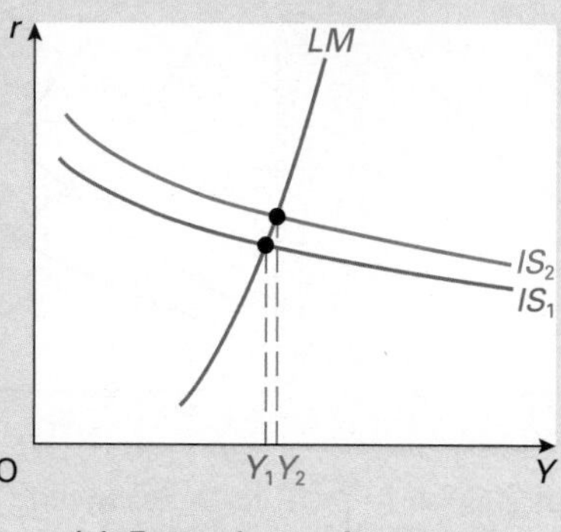

(a) Expansionary fiscal policy

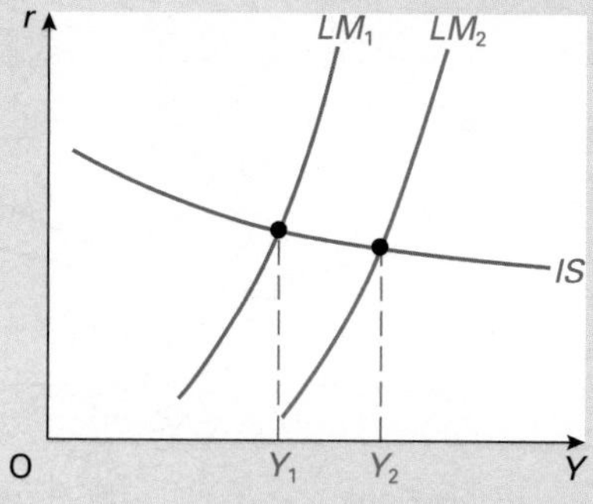

(b) Expansionary monetary policy

? *According to Keynesians, which will have a bigger effect on national income and employment: (unforeseen) fluctuations in investment or (unforeseen) fluctuations in the money supply?*

If money supply is endogenous, fiscal policy will be more effective still. A relatively elastic supply of money curve in the left-hand diagram of Figure 18.11 (on page 517) will give an even shallower *LM* curve.

Keynesians also stress that the *IS* curve tends to be *unstable* (for example, as investment fluctuates with business confidence). Fluctuations in a steep *IS* curve will lead to substantial fluctuations in national income (Y). To avoid this, argue Keynesians, active demand management (fiscal) policy will be required.

The monetarist position

Monetarist analysis has traditionally made the following assumptions.

The LM curve is relatively steep. This is because the *L* curve is relatively steep (see Figure 18.8(b)), due to the relatively small role of speculative balances of money, and the general interest inelasticity of the demand for money.

The IS curve is relatively shallow. This is because the *I* curve is relatively shallow (see Figure 18.9(b)), due to the wide range of interest-sensitive expenditures.

Under these circumstances, monetary policy is more effective than fiscal policy. Figure 19.10(b) shows a bigger increase in income with expansionary monetary policy than does Figure 19.10(a) with expansionary fiscal policy.

According to these assumptions, fiscal policy is weak because of crowding out. This is illustrated in Figure 19.10(a) by the steepness of the *LM* curve. The increased transactions demand resulting from a rise in income will lead to a large rise in interest rates. The reason is that there are few speculative holdings of money, and therefore a large rise in interest rates will be necessary to release sufficient money balances to meet the new higher transactions demand.

Section summary

1. Fiscal policy shifts the *IS* curve. An expansionary fiscal policy shifts it to the right. This causes a rise in both national income and the rate of interest. The rise in income will be bigger and the rise in the rate of interest smaller, the steeper the *IS* curve and the flatter the *LM* curve.
2. Keynesians argue that fiscal policy is relatively effective and that there will be relatively little crowding out because the *IS* curve is relatively steep (due to an inelastic investment demand schedule) and the *LM* curve is relatively shallow (due to an elastic liquidity preference curve).
3. Monetarists argue the opposite: that fiscal policy is relatively ineffective and that there will be substantial crowding out because the *IS* curve is relatively shallow (due to the wide range of interest-sensitive expenditures) and the *LM* curve is relatively steep (due to the small role of speculative balances).
4. Monetary policy shifts the *LM* curve. An expansionary monetary policy shifts it downwards. This causes a fall in interest rates and a rise in national income. The rise in national income will be larger, the flatter the *IS* curve and the steeper the liquidity preference curve (*L*) and hence the bigger the downward shift in the *LM* curve for any given increase in the money supply. This means that monetarists argue that monetary policy is relatively effective, whereas Keynesians argue that it is relatively ineffective.
5. Fiscal and monetary policy operating together will have the most powerful effect. An expansionary fiscal policy accompanied by a rise in money supply can lead to an increase in national income with no rise in interest rates and thus no crowding out, irrespective of the shapes of the *IS* and *LM* curves.

19.4 FISCAL AND MONETARY POLICY IN THE UK

This historical section is optional and may be omitted without loss of continuity, or you may prefer to look just at the final part of this section dealing with the most recent period.

Attitudes towards demand management

The history of demand management in the UK since the 1950s has mirrored debates between different schools of thought. Economists and politicians calling themselves 'Keynesian' advocated active fiscal policy as a means of stabilising aggregate demand. Others, calling themselves 'monetarist', argued in favour of using monetary policy rather than fiscal policy as a means of controlling inflation, seeing inflation as purely the consequence of excessive growth in the money supply.

TC 7 p 26

Debates over the control of demand have shifted ground somewhat in recent years. There is now less debate over the relative merits of fiscal and monetary policy. There is general agreement that a *combination* of fiscal and monetary policies will have a more powerful effect on demand than either used separately.

The debate today is much more concerned with whether the government ought to pursue an active demand management policy at all, or whether it ought merely to adhere to a set of policy rules.

Those in the Keynesian tradition prefer discretionary policy – changing policy as circumstances change. Those in the monetarist tradition prefer to set firm rules (e.g. targets for inflation, the PSNCR or growth in the money supply) and then stick to them. We examine the current debate in section 19.5. For the remainder of this section we will see how fiscal and monetary policies have evolved over the past 50 or more years.

Keynesian demand management in the 1950s and 1960s

During the 1950s and 1960s, both Labour and Conservative governments in the UK embraced Keynesian ideas. They pursued active demand management policies in an attempt to smooth out cyclical fluctuations and to keep national income as close as possible to the full-employment level.

The main policy instrument was changes in tax rates. But use was also made of government expenditure changes. Monetary policy was generally thought to be ineffective, because of both the insensitivity of demand to interest rate changes, and the difficulties in controlling overall liquidity through open-market operations. In the 1960s, however, increasing use was made of credit rationing to back up fiscal policy and to keep interest rates down.

Table 19.5 UK macroeconomic performance: 1921–2005

	Unemployment (% of labour force)[a]	Inflation (% increase in RPI)[b]	Growth (% increase in real GDP)[b]
1921–38	13.4	−1.5	2.1
1950–69	1.6	4.0	2.8
1970–99	7.6	8.0	2.0
2000–05	5.2	2.5	2.6

[a] Average.
[b] Average annual.

The overall performance of the economy

Economic performance during the 1950s and 1960s compares very favourably with the periods both before and after (see Figure 19.11 and Table 19.5).

Unemployment was considerably lower in the 1950s and 1960s than either before or after. *Inflation*, although averaging 4 per cent, and thus above the negative rates of the inter-war years, was nevertheless very modest compared with later years. *Growth* in the 1950s and 1960s was at a higher level than in the periods before or up to the mid-1980s. Also there was no deep or prolonged recession like those of the early 1920s, the early 1930s, 1979–82 and 1990–3.

However, there were still fluctuations in the economy, albeit of shorter duration and lower intensity than before or since. Also, although growth was relatively high by UK standards, it was significantly lower than in West Germany, France and Japan.

The balance of payments

Throughout the 1950s and 1960s, the UK was operating on a fixed exchange rate system. The exchange rate was pegged at $2.80 to the pound from 1949 until 1967 when it was devalued to $2.40. A fixed exchange rate constrained the government in its demand management policy. If the economy expanded too fast, the balance of payments went into deficit. The government would then pursue a deflationary policy, both to reduce the demand for imports directly, and to reduce inflation in order to increase the competitiveness of UK goods. If the balance of payments went into surplus, the government would reflate the economy. As a result of this, demand management was often referred to as ***stop–go policy***. The most common weapon used in times of balance of payments crisis was Bank rate.

KI 32 p 369

Definition

Stop–go policies Alternate deflationary and reflationary policies.

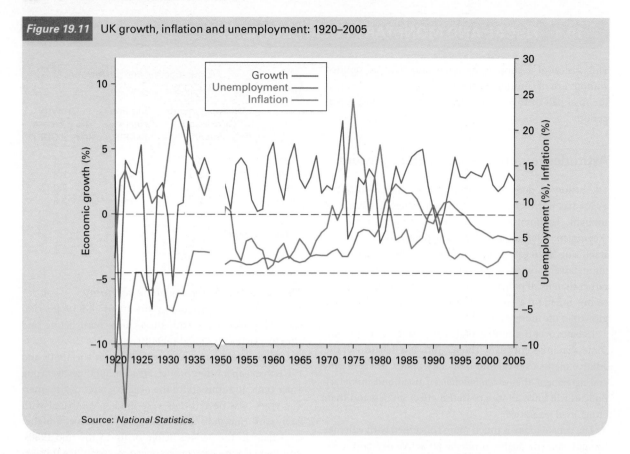

Figure 19.11 UK growth, inflation and unemployment: 1920–2005

Source: *National Statistics*.

This was the rate of interest set by the Bank of England, to which all the banks had to gear their rates. Bank rate rose quite steeply on several occasions.

During the 1960s, however, the maintenance of balance of payments equilibrium and of growth at full employment became increasingly incompatible objectives. Stop–go policy was thus perceived as swinging from one objective (correction of balance of payments deficits with 'stop' policy) to the other (stimulating growth and employment with 'go' policy). The underlying problem was that UK goods were becoming increasingly uncompetitive in world markets, due to a decline in the relative quality of UK goods and their higher relative prices.

Under a fixed exchange rate system there was therefore a long-term tendency for the balance of payments to deteriorate, and for governments to deflate. Eventually in 1967, with mounting pressure on sterling, the UK was forced to devalue the pound.

Monetarist criticisms of the policies of the 1950s and 1960s

Monetarists made two major criticisms of the Keynesian policies pursued during the 1950s and 1960s. First, they actually served to make the economy more unstable for the following reasons:

- Forecasting was bad. Frequently, the forecasters failed to foresee exogenous changes to demand, or wrongly predicted the magnitude and timing of their effects.
- Governments as a result were hesitant to take action until the economy was clearly either booming (or in balance of payments crisis) or in recession.
- When governments did take action, they tended to overreact in their attempt to speed up the correction of the problem.

Second, inflation was kept fairly low in this period *despite* attempts to fine tune the economy. The reason for this was the fixed exchange rate, which forced governments to deflate whenever inflation threatened the balance of payments. If there had been no such constraint, Keynesian governments would have pursued much more expansionist policies, which would have driven up the rate of inflation.

Would a floating exchange rate have imposed no constraint at all on expansionist policies?

The Keynesian response

In reply, Keynesians argued that the economy was relatively stable, and that there was a good record of achieving the various macroeconomic objectives.

However, they admitted that if there had been more flexibility in the exchange rate, or at least an earlier devaluation, this would have reduced the need for stop–go measures. There could then have been a more sustained expansion of the economy. This in turn would have boosted business confidence, increased investment and thereby increased long-term growth potential.

Provided demand was prevented from expanding too rapidly, any tendency for inflation to increase would be more due to cost-push or structural factors. These would be much better dealt with by using interventionist supply-side policies, such as ***prices and incomes policy*** to prevent cost-push inflation, and selective investment grants and infrastructure projects to relieve bottlenecks.

Finally, improvements in forecasting techniques and the swifter implementation of policies would help to reduce time lags and allow finer tuning.

Answer these points from a monetarist perspective.

The demise of fine tuning in the 1970s: the problem of stagflation

Fine tuning became impossible in the 1970s because of the rising problem of ***stagflation***: a combination of stagnation (low growth and high unemployment) and high inflation (see Figure 19.11). Demand management policies were still used, but they could no longer achieve an acceptable combination of inflation and unemployment. The Phillips curve had broken down.

Economists are not agreed on the causes of this stagflation, but there were a number of possible contributing factors.

The approach to monetary control. In an attempt to move to a more market-based form of monetary control, all ceilings on bank credit were abandoned; the liquidity ratio that banks were required to hold was reduced; all special deposits were released; and banks were no longer required to set their interest rates in accordance with Bank rate (a rate set by the Bank of England). The effect was to make it much more difficult to prevent an expansion of credit and there was a mushrooming of new banks and credit institutions.

Highly reflationary budgets in 1972 and 1973. The Heath government (1970–4) was committed to a rapid rate of economic growth. This was to be achieved by sharply expansionary fiscal policy. The effect was a rapid increase in the PSNCR. This, combined with more lax monetary control, led to a very rapid growth in money supply in 1972 and 1973 (see Table 19.6). Growth in aggregate demand could only in small part be met by increased output and employment.

Statutory controls over wages and prices, first introduced in November 1972, kept price rises in check for a while. But with a miners' strike being seen as a direct challenge to this prices and incomes policy, the government called an election in February 1974 and was defeated. The incoming Labour government abolished the prices and incomes policy, but this allowed the pent-up demand to feed straight through into price and wage increases. Inflation soared. By 1975 price inflation was nearly 25 per cent and wage inflation was over 30 per cent.

Table 19.6 Selected monetary indicators: 1969–2004

	Change in M4 (%) (1)	PSNCR (£bn) (2)	Inflation[a] (%) (3)	Nominal interest rate[b] (%) (4)	Real interest rate (4) − (3) (5)
1969	5.1	−0.5	5.4	9.1	3.7
1970	11.5	−0.2	6.4	9.2	2.9
1971	16.0	1.2	9.4	8.9	−0.5
1972	23.7	1.8	7.1	9.0	1.7
1973	22.3	4.1	9.2	10.7	1.6
1974	11.1	6.4	16.0	14.8	−1.2
1975	12.4	10.2	24.2	14.4	−9.8
1976	11.2	8.9	16.5	14.4	2.1
1977	14.7	5.5	15.8	12.7	−3.2
1978	15.0	8.4	8.3	12.5	4.2
1979	14.1	12.5	13.4	13.0	−0.4
1980	17.2	11.4	18.0	13.8	−4.2
1981	20.9	10.6	11.9	14.7	2.8
1982	12.1	5.3	8.6	12.9	4.3
1983	12.7	11.1	4.6	10.8	6.2
1984	13.2	10.3	5.0	10.7	5.7
1985	13.0	7.6	6.1	10.6	4.5
1986	15.6	2.6	3.4	9.9	6.5
1987	16.7	−1.2	4.2	9.5	5.3
1988	17.3	−11.4	4.9	9.4	4.5
1989	18.0	−9.1	7.8	9.6	1.8
1990	11.8	−1.3	9.5	11.1	1.6
1991	5.8	7.0	5.9	9.9	4.0
1992	3.6	28.6	3.7	9.1	5.4
1993	4.6	43.7	1.6	7.9	6.3
1994	4.7	39.4	2.4	8.1	5.7
1995	9.9	35.4	3.5	8.3	4.8
1996	9.5	24.8	2.4	8.1	5.7
1997	11.9	11.9	3.1	7.1	4.0
1998	8.3	−6.4	3.4	5.5	2.1
1999	4.2	−1.8	1.5	4.7	3.1
2000	8.2	−37.5	3.0	4.7	1.8
2001	6.7	−2.9	1.8	4.8	2.4
2002	7.3	18.3	1.7	4.8	2.5
2003	7.3	39.0	2.9	4.6	1.9
2004	8.9	41.2	3.0	4.8	2.8

[a] Based on the retail price index (RPI), the main measure of consumer prices inflation prior to 2003.
[b] Annual average on 20-year bonds.

Source: www.statistics.gov.uk.

Definitions

Prices and incomes policy When the government seeks to restrain price and wage increases. This may be in the form of a voluntary agreement with firms and/or unions, or there may be statutory limits imposed.

Stagflation A term used in the 1970s to refer to the combination of stagnation (low growth and high unemployment) and high inflation.

The adoption of floating exchange rates. In June 1972 a fixed exchange rate with the dollar was abandoned. A floating pound reduced the need to pursue deflationary policies in response to a balance of payments deficit. Instead the exchange rate could be allowed to depreciate. This removed a major constraint on the growth in money supply. This applied not just in the UK but throughout the world as countries moved over to floating exchange rates.

Oil prices. Between 1973 and 1974 the price of oil rose from \$3 to \$12 per barrel, and between 1978 and 1980 it rose from \$13 to \$31 per barrel. This not only raised costs and thus caused cost-push inflation, but also caused recessions in 1975 and 1979–81 as governments throughout the world deflated in response to the inflation and balance of payments crises.

Domestically generated cost-push pressures. Cost-push inflationary pressures increased as a result of the following: growing union power and militancy; the desire for real wage increases each year in excess of the economy's real growth; the increasing monopoly power of firms, as increased mergers led to a growth in industrial concentration; and low productivity growth and hence a lack of price competitiveness of UK goods.

Increased import penetration and a decline in the UK's share of world exports. Increasing competition from foreign imports and a lack of quality of UK goods led to a poor balance of payments, low growth, structural unemployment, and inflation caused by a falling exchange rate (necessary to restore price competitiveness of UK exports).

Technological change. The microchip revolution and other labour-displacing technology created unemployment. There was insufficient aggregate demand to create new jobs elsewhere.

Expectations of inflation. High and volatile inflation rates fuelled expectations of high inflation, which then made inflation worse.

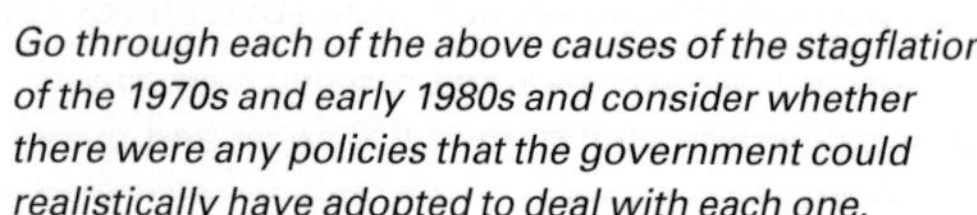

Go through each of the above causes of the stagflation of the 1970s and early 1980s and consider whether there were any policies that the government could realistically have adopted to deal with each one.

The response to stagflation

Several of these problems were problems of cost and supply, rather than excess or deficient demand. It was increasingly realised that, in addition to fiscal and monetary policies, there would have to be significant 'supply-side' policies.

The Keynesian response was to recommend supplementing demand management with interventionist supply-side policies, such as prices and incomes policy, regional policy, import restrictions and retraining policies (see section 22.1).

The Labour government of 1974–9 responded to the rise in both inflation and unemployment by reintroducing prices and incomes policy in the summer of 1975 (see Web Case 22.3). Inflation began to fall in 1976 and growth re-emerged. The government let the exchange rate fall to help stimulate the demand for exports, but the falling pound caused speculation and a sterling crisis in late 1976. The government was forced to borrow from the International Monetary Fund to support the pound, and in return had to pursue tough monetary and fiscal policies, including setting targets for the growth in money supply.

This accorded with the views of monetarists, who recommended abandoning discretionary demand management of the stop–go variety altogether, and moving to a 'steady-as-you-go' policy of sticking to monetary targets. In addition, they advocated the use of market-orientated supply-side policies such as tax reform, union reform, the abandonment of minimum wage rates, and lower unemployment benefits (see section 22.2).

From 1976 to 1979 growth was steady at between $2\frac{1}{2}$ and 3 per cent, unemployment was steady at between 5 and $5\frac{1}{2}$ per cent, and inflation was falling. But growing resentment at incomes restraint led to the 'winter of discontent' of 1978–9, when several groups of workers attempted to defy the incomes policy. The government lost the 1979 election.

Monetarism under Thatcher

With the election of the Conservatives in 1979, the UK for the first time had a government committed to monetarist policies.

On the supply side, the government pursued policies to free up the market. The prices and incomes policy was abandoned; legislation was introduced to curb trade union power; foreign exchange controls were lifted; the standard rate of income tax was cut from 33 per cent to 30 per cent (with VAT being raised to compensate for the loss of revenue); the government made it clear that it would not bale out 'lame duck' industries; and later on, it pursued a comprehensive policy of privatisation.

On the demand side, discretionary demand management in an attempt to fine tune the economy was totally abandoned. Instead, each year progressively descending targets were adopted for money supply growth for the following four years. This was known as the 'medium-term financial strategy'. These targets combined with statements that inflation was 'public enemy number one', were designed to reduce people's expectations of inflation, and hence the level of wage settlements. Money supply was to be kept on target in the short term by changes in interest rates, brought about by Bank of England operations in the discount market. All other forms of monetary control were abandoned. Foreign exchange controls were abolished in 1979 as were all forms of credit rationing; statutory reserve requirements were abolished in 1981.

In the medium term, the achieving of money supply targets would require a progressive reduction in the PSNCR as a proportion of GDP (if crowding out was to be avoided). Indeed, targeted reductions in the PSNCR were part of the medium-term financial strategy. Thus tight monetary policy was backed up by tight fiscal policy. In the public mind, the government's monetarist policy became synonymous with 'cuts'.

Demand-side policies in the early 1980s

1979–81. The abandoning of incomes policy, the rise in oil prices from 1979 to 1981 and a rise in VAT from 7 per cent to 15 per cent led to a rise in inflation from 8.3 per cent in 1978 to 18 per cent in 1980. At the same time, fiscal and monetary policy had a highly deflationary effect. Interest rates rose rapidly, reaching 17 per cent in late 1979. The high interest rates, plus an improving balance of payments due to North Sea oil, led to a rapid rise in the exchange rate, fuelled by speculation of further rises.

The combination of low demand, high interest rates, a high exchange rate and rapidly rising costs led to a severe recession – the deepest since the 1930s. Unemployment rocketed from just over 5 per cent in 1979 to nearly 10 per cent in 1981.

1982–5. The continuing tight monetary policy with high real interest rates allowed only a slow recovery from recession. Recovery was, however, helped somewhat by a fall in the exchange rate between 1981 and 1985. This was in part a response to the strength of the dollar, which was due to high US interest rates resulting from a large and growing US budget deficit. Growth re-emerged from 1982 and inflation fell back to around 5 per cent. The growth in demand, however, was insufficient to prevent the continuing rise in unemployment, which reached 12 per cent in 1984.

Exogenous factors such as consumer and business expectations made it difficult to keep money supply on target, but there was a relatively consistent attempt to pursue a steady-as-you-go demand management policy. Rules had replaced discretion (see section 19.5).

Assessing the monetarist experiment

Was the government able to carry through its monetarist intentions? On the plus side, after an initial upsurge (1979–81) the growth of money supply was reduced and inflation fell (see Table 19.6). But despite this there were a number of problems.

- The PSNCR proved very difficult to control and was above target in several years.
- From 1983 onwards, the recorded level of the PSNCR was artificially reduced by the sale of public-sector assets (British Telecom, British Gas, etc.). This allowed the government to pursue a more expansionary fiscal policy while *appearing* to maintain a tight monetary policy.
- The growth in money supply was also above target in several years despite a wide target range. The eventual reduction in its growth after 1981 was achieved at the cost of very high real interest rates.
- The government was forced to raise the target ranges in 1982, despite its commitment in the MTFS to a progressive lowering of them.
- Although it eventually managed to get its chosen measure of the money supply (M3) under control, other measures of money supply went on growing – an example of Goodhart's law.  KI 34 p552
- Allowing sterling to float more freely brought problems. High interest rates and North Sea oil caused the pound to soar in 1980, reaching $2.45 at the peak, with consequent damage to the export sector. But the government was afraid of intervening to lower the exchange rate because that would have increased the money supply (through reducing interest rates or having a net inflow of funds from abroad).
- The opposite problem was faced in January/February 1985, when the pound fell dramatically against a strong US dollar (reaching $1.04 at the lowest point). As the pound approached $1, the government felt obliged to intervene and interest rates were raised dramatically.

Despite all these difficulties, the government consistently saw inflation as 'public enemy number one', and the means of getting it down was a tight monetary policy and adherence to monetary targets.

A return to discretionary policies after 1985

As the 1980s progressed, although monetary targets were almost being achieved, their importance was waning. With unemployment over 3 million, the government was putting less emphasis on the desirability of a generally tight monetary policy and instead was becoming more pragmatic.

With the effective abandonment of money supply targets after 1985, demand management policy reverted to a more traditional stop–go pattern. Discretion seemed to be replacing rules.

The period from 1985 to 1988 can be summarised as a period of unbalanced fiscal and monetary policy. Monetary policy was expansionary. With inflation still relatively low after the recession, interest rates were lowered to stimulate economic growth, reduce unemployment and prevent further rises in the exchange rate (and the consequent damage to exports). Fiscal policy, on the other hand, remained relatively tight. Although the government made several cuts in tax rates, the now rapid growth in incomes caused tax *revenues* to increase. At the same time, the government continued to try to reduce its expenditure as a proportion of national income. The net result was that a public-sector deficit of over £11 billion in 1983 was turned into a surplus of over £11 billion by 1988.

This resulted in an imbalance in the impact of the policy. The extra money was spent largely on property and consumer durables (a large proportion of which were imported). House prices soared as mortgages were easy to obtain. Car sales boomed, as did the sales of electrical goods, furniture and foreign holidays.

Monetary policy was relatively expansionary throughout the world, and part of the extra money went into stocks and shares. The resulting increase in share prices was faster than the increase in profits and dividends. Eventually, in October 1987, 'the bubble burst' and share prices crashed. To avoid a collapse of confidence by firms and a plunge into recession, monetary policy was further relaxed. Aggregate demand grew more rapidly. Unemployment fell more rapidly and output grew more rapidly; but inflation began to rise and the balance of payments on current account plunged into a record deficit (see Figure 14.13 on page 418).

In response to this crisis, interest rates were raised several times in the last part of 1988 and during 1989. Banks' base rate rose from 7.5 per cent in May 1988 to 15 per cent by October 1989, and then remained at this level until October 1990 when the UK joined the exchange rate mechanism (ERM) of the European Monetary System (see section 25.2). It was clear that the government was pursuing a stop–go monetary policy, depending on how bad were the problems of inflation, the balance of payments and a depreciating exchange rate.

? *In what way was the stop–go policy of the late 1980s different from the stop–go policies pursued during the 1950s and 1960s?*

Targeting the exchange rate

Shadowing the German mark

Targets were not completely abandoned after 1985. There was a growing belief that, with closer links being forged with Europe, and with the desirability of a stable exchange rate between the pound and other European currencies, the exchange rate ought to be targeted. But as we saw in Box 19.9, the problem with effectively having only one instrument (interest rates) was that the government could not use it at one and the same time to control both the level of aggregate demand (and hence inflation) *and* the rate of exchange. In 1988, high interest rates were required to control the rapidly expanding credit, but low interest rates were required to prevent the exchange rate from rising above its target level of around £1 = 3.00 German marks: a rise that would be damaging to exports. The debate, however, resolved itself. With a *falling* pound in 1989, high interest rates were desirable for both exchange rate and counter-inflationary reasons.

? *Will targeting the exchange rate help to reduce inflation? Does it depend on the rate of inflation in the countries to whose currencies the pound is fixed?*

Fiscal policy was largely confined to the role of improving the *supply* side of the economy. This would be achieved by reducing the size of the public sector (which was seen by the government to be less productive than the private sector), and by giving tax cuts to improve incentives. So did fiscal policy have no demand management role at all? It did, but only to the extent that the amount of tax cuts was influenced by demand considerations.

ERM membership: 1990–2

In October 1990 the UK joined the European ***exchange rate mechanism (ERM)***. This was a system, set up in 1979, of semi-fixed exchange rates. Participating EU countries' currencies were allowed to fluctuate against each other only within set bands (see section 25.2 for more details). The requirement to keep the pound within an exchange rate band of approximately 2.78–3.13 marks meant that there was now effectively an exchange rate target. But with essentially only one instrument of macroeconomic policy, namely the rate of interest, all other macroeconomic goals had to be subordinated to this target.

In a fixed exchange rate system, UK interest rates were governed largely by those of the other countries within the system. The reunification of Germany had involved a large expansion of German money supply. In response, the Bundesbank (the German central bank), in order to prevent inflation rising, raised interest rates. To maintain sterling's value within the ERM, the UK government therefore had to pursue a high interest rate policy. But since, in late 1990, the German inflation rate was still only 2.8 per cent and the UK inflation rate was over 10 per cent, UK interest rates had to be considerably above the German level.

Within a few months it was clear that the UK was plunging into recession. On domestic grounds alone, lower interest rates would have been desirable. But by mid-1991 the pound was again under pressure in the ERM and so monetary policy had to be kept tight. Inflation was now falling rapidly, but interest rates were reduced only slightly. This meant that *real* interest rates had risen (see Table 19.6 on page 559). In the 12 months after joining the ERM, UK inflation fell by 6 percentage points whereas nominal interest rates fell by only 4 percentage points. There was thus a growing policy conflict between the *external* requirement of maintaining the exchange rate and the internal requirement of reflating a depressed domestic economy. TC 12 p374 KI 32 p369

Throughout 1991 and the first part of 1992, the government stuck resolutely to maintaining sterling's value in the ERM. Ministers justified this as being the best means of continuing the fight against inflation. But, as we shall see in section 25.2, this rate was becoming increasingly untenable as speculators became convinced that interest

Definition

ERM (the exchange rate mechanism) A system of semi-fixed exchange rates used by most of the EU countries prior to adoption of the euro. Members' currencies were allowed to fluctuate against each other only within agreed bands. Collectively, they floated against all other currencies.

rates would have to fall and that sterling, as a result, would have to be devalued. Eventually, on 'Black Wednesday', 16 September 1992, after a 5 percentage point rise in interest rates was insufficient to stop the speculation, the UK left the ERM and the pound was allowed to float.

A return to domestic-orientated policies: targeting inflation

With the need to defend the value of the pound removed, the government could focus once more on the domestic situation. Within four months, interest rates had been reduced by 4 percentage points. This loosening of monetary policy gave a welcome boost to the economy, which was still only just beginning to pull out of recession.

The government was not worried that this would lead to an unwelcome growth in money supply and inflation. Indeed, the control of inflation was now to be the main objective of monetary policy. An initial target rate of inflation of 1–4 per cent was set, to be backed up by 'monitoring ranges' of 0–4 per cent for M0 and 3–9 per cent for M4 until 1997, by which time inflation should be between 1 and 2½ per cent.

Targeting inflation was based on the belief that monetary policy cannot influence *real* variables such as output and employment in the long run. It can only influence inflation. It is better, therefore, to focus on achieving low inflation in order to provide the best environment for businesses to thrive. But to achieve an inflation target meant doing two things.

First, given the time lags between changing interest rates and their effect on inflation, interest rates would have to be changed in response to inflation *forecasts*, rather than the current rate of inflation. Second, people would have to be made to believe that the government could and would achieve the target. To this end, a number of steps were taken:

- The Bank of England published inflation forecasts, which the government publicly used to assess whether policy was on target.
- The Chancellor and the Governor of the Bank of England met monthly to consider the necessary interest rate policy to keep inflation within the target range. The Bank would then determine the *timing* of any agreed changes.
- Minutes of these meetings were published six weeks later, in order to give transparency to the process.
- Each time interest rates were changed, a press notice would be issued explaining the reasons. The idea here was to show the government's commitment to keeping to the target.

Was the policy a success? Inflation remained within the target bands, and the government claimed that this was the result of the policy. In fact, the reduction in inflation from 1992 to 1994 was the lagged result of the tight monetary conditions during the previous two years when the UK was in the ERM. Indeed, the government *reduced* interest rates several times between September 1992 and February 1994. After 1994, however, the policy *did* help to keep inflation down, with the government raising interest rates whenever inflationary forecasts were adverse.

As far as fiscal policy was concerned, with the PSNCR in 1993 being a massive £43.2 billion (see Table 19.6 on page 559), there was a serious problem that, if monetary growth was kept in check, government borrowing would crowd out private-sector growth. The government thus saw the need to get a 'better' balance between fiscal and monetary policy. It therefore announced a series of tax increases to be phased in over the coming years. It also stated its intention to examine ways of reducing government expenditure.

If tax increases are 'phased in' as an economy recovers from recession, how will this affect the magnitude and timing of the recovery?

Policy of the Labour government (1997–)

Fiscal policy

In 1997, the incoming Labour government confirmed its election commitment to stick to the previous government's expenditure targets for two years and to continue bringing down the PSNCR. That, plus a reluctance to raise taxes, initially prevented it from spending money on various social programmes advocated by many of its supporters.

Given, however, that the economy grew by over 3 per cent in 1997, the PSNCR fell rapidly (see Table 19.6), and that enabled the government to plan for a *growth* in government expenditure from 1999 onwards. The plans, announced in 1998 in the government's Comprehensive Spending Review, set targets for government expenditure, not for just one year, but for a three-year period.

Did this mean, therefore, that fiscal policy as a means of adjusting aggregate demand had been abandoned? In one sense, this was the case. The government was now committed to following its 'golden rule' (see Box 19.4), whereby public-sector receipts should cover all current spending, averaged over the course of the business cycle. In fact, in supporting sticking to the golden rule, the Chancellor explicitly rejected Keynesian fine tuning:

> In today's deregulated, liberalised financial markets, the Keynesian fine tuning of the past, which worked in relatively sheltered, closed national economies and which tried to exploit a supposed long-term trade-off between inflation and unemployment, will simply not work.[6]

But despite this apparent rejection of short-term discretionary fiscal adjustments, there is still a role for *automatic* fiscal stabilisers: with deficits rising in a recession and falling in a boom. There is also still the possibility, within the

[6] Extract from the Chancellor's Mansion House speech, 11 June 1998.

golden rule, of financing additional *investment* by borrowing, thereby providing a stimulus to a sluggish economy.

The golden rule also permitted increased government expenditure (or tax cuts) if there was a budget surplus. Thus in the 2001 Budget, the government announced spending increases of 3.7 per cent per year for three years and also modest tax cuts. The effect was to turn a forecast surplus of £16 billion in 2000/1 into a forecast deficit of £10 billion by 2003/4 (when the economy was predicted to be mid-cycle). But this was in line with the golden rule, which permits borrowing against capital spending – and that was planned to be £18 billion by 2003/4.

As it turned out, the fiscal stimulus in the 2001 Budget was timely, as the world economy was slowing down: a slowdown hastened by the attack on the World Trade Center in New York in September of that year.

But the government's forecast of the size of the deficit turned out to be a considerable underestimate. By 2004, the deficit had risen to £41.2 billion and many economists cast doubt as to whether the golden rule could be maintained. In the 2005 Budget, however, the government was still maintaining that the current budget would be in surplus when averaged over the cycle 1998/9 to 2005/6 (see Figure (b) in Box 19.4 on page 541).

Monetary policy

As far as monetary policy was concerned, the Labour government continued its predecessor's approach of targeting inflation. The target rate was set initially at $2^1/_2$ per cent for RPI inflation. (This was changed to 2 per cent for CPI inflation in December 2003.[7]) Unlike its predecessor, however, the government decided to make the Bank of England independent. Indeed, this was the first action taken by the Chancellor when the government came to power.

But why did the government give up its right to set interest rates? First, there is the political advantage of taking 'blame' away from the government if interest rates need to be raised in order to prevent inflation rising above its target. Second, an independent central bank, free to set interest rates in order to achieve a clear target, is more likely to be consistent in pursuit of this objective than a government concerned about its popularity. Then there is the question of transparency in decision making.

> If inflation is more than 1 percentage point higher or lower than the target, an open letter will be sent by the Governor to the Chancellor so that the public is fully informed as to why the divergence has occurred; the policy action being taken to deal with it; the period within which inflation is expected to return to the target; and how this approach meets the government's monetary policy objectives. Monetary policy decision-making is now among the most transparent and accountable in the world.[8]

Transparency is enhanced by the publication of the minutes of the monthly meetings of Bank's Monetary Policy Committee (MPC), at which interest rates are set. One of the main purposes of transparency is to convince people of the seriousness with which the Bank of England will adhere to its targets. This, it is hoped, will keep people's *expectations* of inflation low: the lower expected inflation is, the lower will be the actual rate of inflation. (We will explore the relationship between expected and actual inflation in the next chapter.)

As it turned out, inflation targeting was successful in its prime purpose: keeping inflation at or near its target. For the whole period from 1997 to 2005, the chosen measure of inflation never diverged by more than 1 percentage point from the target. In the light of the history of macroeconomic management over the last 60 years, this would seem remarkable.

A rules-based approach to demand-side policy?

With monetary policy geared to an inflation target and fiscal policy geared to following the golden rule, there seems to be little scope for discretionary demand management policy. Rules appear to have replaced discretion.

> When there are ever more rapid financial flows across the world that are unpredictable and uncertain, the answer is to ensure stability through establishing the right long-term policy objectives and to build credibility in the policy through well-understood procedural rules that are followed for fiscal and monetary policy.[9]

There is, however, a new form of fine tuning: the frequent adjustment of interest rates, not to smoothe out the business cycle, but to make sure that the inflation rule is adhered to. Nevertheless, with automatic fiscal stabilisers still operating, and with interest rate changes to stabilise inflation also having the effect of stabilising aggregate demand, cyclical fluctuations have been less pronounced in recent years. In the 10 years to 2005, annual economic growth has not fallen below 1.8 per cent or risen above 3.9 per cent.

But is it a good idea that rules have replaced the discretion to change the target of policy, as economic (or political) circumstances change? We examine the arguments in the final section of this chapter.

?

1. *From 1998 to 2001 the exchange rate of sterling was very high (see Table 14.7 on page 420). This was largely the result of the MPC keeping interest rates above those in other countries in order to try to keep inflation down to its $2^1/_2$ per cent target. What are the arguments for and against a discretionary rise in the inflation target in such circumstances?*
2. *Why do 'ever more rapid financial flows across the world that are unpredictable and uncertain' make Keynesian discretionary fiscal (and monetary policy) less suitable?*

[7] The consumer prices index (CPI) is the measure used in the eurozone and gives a slightly lower inflation rate than the retail prices index (RPI). Thus the former $2^1/_2$ per cent target is equivalent to the current 2 per cent target.

[8] *The Government's Overall Economic Strategy* (http://www.hm-treasury.gov.uk/pub/html/e_info/overview/1_goes.html).

[9] Extract from the Chancellor's Mansion House speech, 11 June 1998.

Section summary

1. In the 1950s and 1960s, both Labour and Conservative governments pursued active demand management policies. The dominating constraints on these policies were the balance of payments and electoral considerations. Demand management was little more than stop–go policy dictated by the state of the balance of payments and the need to win elections.
2. The 1950s and 1960s was a period of relative economic success. But whether this was due to the pursuit of Keynesian demand management policies or to other factors such as a buoyant world economy and economic optimism is a matter of debate.
3. In the 1970s, stagflation became a major problem due to a number of factors, including expansionary fiscal and monetary policies in the early 1970s, the adoption of floating exchange rates, a large rise in oil prices, growing domestically generated cost-push pressures, a decline in the competitiveness of UK exports, technological change and increasingly pessimistic expectations.
4. As a result of the dilemma of rising inflation *and* rising unemployment, government policy swung violently from a 'dash for growth' in the early 1970s, to two sets of prices and incomes policies, to a tight monetary policy towards the end of the decade.
5. The Conservative government in the 1980s initially pursued a tight monetary policy and targeted the PSNCR and the growth in the money supply. The exchange rate rose and the economy plunged into a deep recession. The economy started to grow again after 1982, but for a time a tight monetary policy was retained (along with monetary targets) in order to keep a downward pressure on inflation.
6. Then, after 1985, targets for monetary growth were abandoned and for a time targeting the exchange rate became the main focus of monetary policy. But with only one instrument (interest rates) there was a conflict between keeping exchange rates down and controlling inflation. This conflict disappeared after 1988 when high interest rates were required both for keeping inflation down and for preventing a *fall* in the exchange rate.
7. The UK joined the ERM in October 1990 and the conflict between domestic and exchange rate policy soon re-emerged. The economy was moving rapidly into recession, but the government was unable to make substantial cuts in interest rates because of the need to defend the value of the pound. Eventually in September 1992, with huge speculation against sterling, the UK was forced to leave the ERM.
8. After 1992, there was a return to using interest rates to manage domestic demand in line with inflation targets. There was mounting concern, however, about the size of the PSNCR, and fiscal policy was tightened until the PSNCR had been sufficiently reduced.
9. The Labour government, elected in 1997, made the Bank of England independent. This now targets a 2 per cent rate of inflation, and adjusts interest rates in order to meet that target. The government has set a golden rule to balance its current (as opposed to capital) budget over the course of the business cycle. There is therefore now little scope for discretionary demand management policy.

19.5 RULES VERSUS DISCRETION

Central to debates over the control of aggregate demand is the question of rules versus discretion. Should monetary (and fiscal) rules be adhered to, or should governments exercise the discretion to change the policies as economic circumstances change?

The case for rules

KI 30 p306

The case against discretionary policy centres on the problem of time lags. Both fiscal and monetary policies can involve long and variable time lags, which can make the policy at best ineffective and at worst destabilising. Taking the measures *before* the problem arises, and thus lessening the problem of lags, is no answer since forecasting tends to be unreliable.

By setting and sticking to rules, and then not interfering further, the government can provide a sound monetary framework in which there is maximum freedom for individual initiative and enterprise, and in which firms are not cushioned from market forces and are therefore encouraged to be efficient. By the government setting a target for a steady reduction in the growth of money supply, or a target for the rate of inflation, and then resolutely sticking to it, people's expectations of inflation will be reduced, thereby making the target easier to achieve.

KI 15 p101

This sound and stable monetary environment, with no likelihood of sudden contractionary or expansionary fiscal or monetary policy, will encourage firms to take a longer-term perspective and to plan ahead. This could then lead to increased capital investment and long-term growth.

The optimum situation is for all the major countries to adhere to mutually consistent rules, so that their economies do not get out of line. This will create more stable exchange rates and provide the climate for world growth (we explore this issue in section 25.1).

EXPLORING ECONOMICS **BOX 19.10**

INFLATION TARGETING

The fashion of the age

More and more countries are turning to inflation targeting as their main macroeconomic policy. Part of the reason is the apparent failure of discretionary macroeconomic policies. Discretionary fiscal and monetary policies suffer from time lags, from being used for short-term political purposes and from failing to straighten out the business cycle. But if discretionary policies have seemed not to work, why choose an inflation target rather than a target for the money supply or the exchange rate?

Money supply targets were adopted by many countries in the 1980s, including the UK, and this policy too was largely a failure. Money supply targets proved very difficult to achieve. As we have seen, money supply depends on the amount of credit banks create and this is not easy for the authorities to control. Then, even if money supply is controlled, this does not necessarily mean that aggregate demand will be controlled: the velocity of circulation may change. Nevertheless, many countries do still target the money supply, although in most cases it is not the main target. In a study of 91 countries by the Bank of England in 1999, of the 55 that targeted inflation, 31 also targeted the money supply (see Web Case 19.10).

Exchange rate targets, as we shall see in Chapter 24, may have serious disadvantages if the equilibrium exchange rate is not the one that is being targeted. The main instrument for keeping the exchange rate on target is the rate of interest. For example, if the exchange rate target were £1 = $1.50, and the exchange rate were currently £1 = $1.40, then interest rates would be raised. This would cause an inflow of money into the economy and hence push up the exchange rate. But, as we saw in Box 19.9 (on page 553), if the rate of interest is being used to achieve an exchange rate target, it cannot be used for other purposes, such as controlling aggregate demand or inflation. Raising interest rates to achieve an exchange rate target may lead to a recession.

Inflation targets have proved relatively easy to achieve. There may be problems at first, if the actual rate of inflation is way above the target level. The high rates of interest necessary to bring inflation down may cause a recession. But once inflation has been brought down and the objective is then simply to maintain it at the target level, most countries have been relatively successful. And the more successful they are, the more people will expect this success to be maintained, which in turn will help to ensure this success.

So, are there any problems with inflation targeting? Ironically, one of the main problems lies in its success. With worldwide inflation having fallen, and with global trade and competition helping to keep prices down, there is now less of a link between inflation and the business cycle. Booms no longer seem to generate the inflation they once did. Gearing interest rate policy to maintaining low inflation could still see economies experiencing unsustainable booms, followed by recessions. Inflation may be controlled, but the business cycle may not be. KI 34 p 552

Why may there be problems in targeting (a) both inflation and money supply; (b) both inflation and the exchange rate?

Advocates of this point of view in the 1970s and 1980s were the monetarists, but in recent years support for the setting of targets has become widespread. As we have seen, in both the UK and the eurozone countries, targets are set for both inflation and public-sector deficits.

Would it be desirable for all countries to stick to the same targets?

The case for discretion

Keynesians reject the argument that rules provide the environment for high and stable growth. Demand, argue Keynesians, is subject to many and sometimes violent exogenous shocks: e.g. changes in expectations, domestic political events (such as an impending election), world economic factors (such as the world economic slowdown of 2001/2) or world political events (such as a war). The resulting shifts in injections or withdrawals cause the economy to deviate from a stable full-employment growth path.

Any change in injections or withdrawals will lead to a cumulative effect on national income via the multiplier and accelerator and via changing expectations. These endogenous effects take time and interact with each other, and so a process of expansion or contraction can last many months before a turning point is eventually reached.

Since the exogenous changes in demand occur at irregular intervals and are of different magnitudes, the economy is likely to experience cycles of irregular duration and of varying intensity.

Given that the economy is inherently unstable and is buffeted around by various exogenous shocks, Keynesians argue that the government needs actively to intervene to stabilise the economy. Otherwise, the uncertainty caused by unpredictable fluctuations will be very damaging to investment and hence to long-term growth in potential output (quite apart from the short-term effects of recessions on actual output and employment). KI 31 p 368

If demand fluctuates in the way Keynesians claim, and if the policy of having a money supply or inflation rule is adhered to, interest rates must fluctuate. But excessive fluctuations in interest rates will discourage long-term business planning and investment. What is more, the

Figure 19.12 *ADI* curves based on different Taylor rules

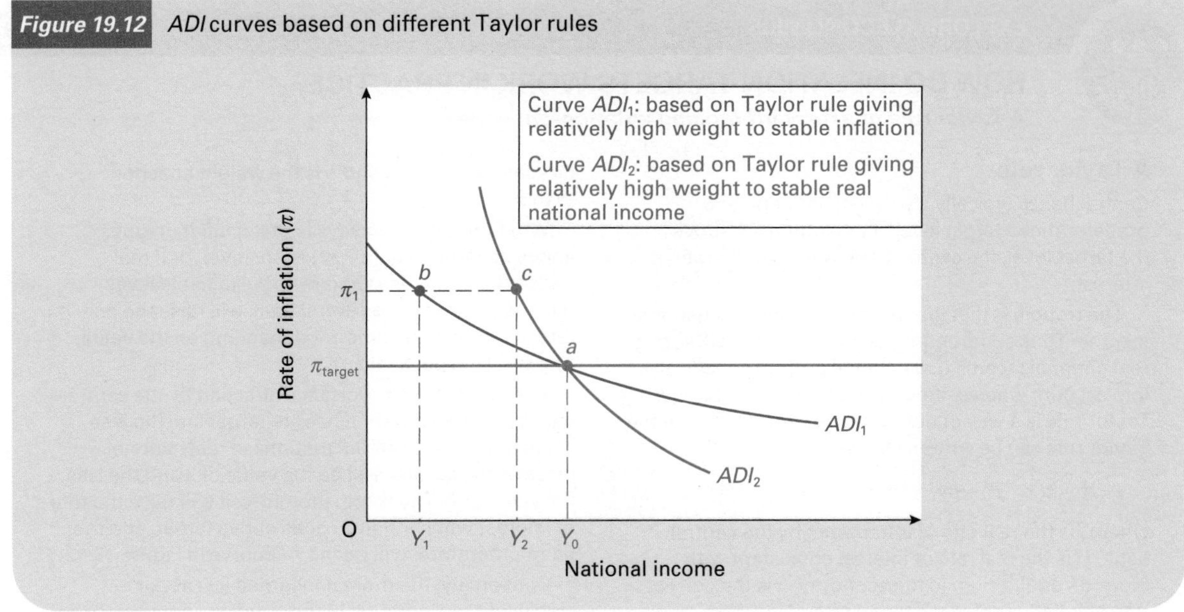

government may find it difficult to keep to its targets. This too may cause uncertainty and instability.

Difficulties with the choice of target

KI 34 p552 If the government is to adopt a target, which one should it choose? If a money supply measure is to be chosen, which one? They frequently do not grow at the same rate. What is more, the adoption of one measure as the target may lead to distortions as people switch the form of their holdings of liquidity and wealth (Goodhart's law).

If an inflation target is chosen, then again Goodhart's Law is likely to apply. Inflation may become a poor indicator of the state of the economy. If people believe that the central bank will be successful in achieving its inflation target, then those expectations will feed into their inflationary expectations, and not surprisingly the target will be met.

But that target rate of inflation may now be consistent with both a buoyant and a depressed economy. In other words, the Phillips curve may become horizontal. Similarly, in terms of Figure 18.17 (on page 526), the *ASI* curve will be horizontal (at least up to near full capacity in the economy). Shifts in the *ADI* curve will simply lead to changes in real national income. An example occurred in 2001/2 when the UK economy slowed down considerably and yet there was virtually no change in the rate of inflation. Thus achieving an inflation target may not tackle the much more serious problem of creating stable economic growth and an environment which will therefore encourage long-term investment.

For this reason, many economists have advocated the use of a ***Taylor rule***,[10] rather than a simple inflation target. A Taylor rule takes *two* objectives into account – (1) inflation and (2) either real national income or unemployment – and seeks to get the optimum degree of stability of the two. The degree of importance attached to each of the two objectives can be decided by the government or central bank. The central bank adjusts interest rates when either the rate of inflation diverges from its target or the level of real national income (or unemployment) diverges from its sustainable (or natural) level.

Take the case where inflation is above its target level. The central bank following a Taylor rule will raise the rate of interest. It knows, however, that this will reduce real national income. This, therefore, limits the amount that the central bank is prepared to raise the rate of interest. The more weight it attaches to stabilising inflation, the more it will raise the rate of interest. The more weight it attaches to stabilising real national income, the less it will raise the rate of interest.

This is illustrated in Figure 19.12. It shows two aggregate demand curves plotted against inflation (see Figure 18.15

[10] Named after John Taylor, from Stanford University, who proposed that for every 1 per cent that GDP rises above potential (sustainable) GDP, real interest rates should be raised by 0.5 percentage points and for every 1 per cent that inflation rises above its target level, real interest rates should be raised by 0.5 percentage points (i.e. nominal rates should be raised by 1.5 percentage points).

Definition

Taylor rule A rule adopted by a central bank for setting the rate of interest. It will raise the interest rate if (a) inflation is above target or (b) real national income is above the sustainable level (or unemployment is below the natural rate). The rule states how much interest rates will be changed in each case.

EXPLORING ECONOMICS

HOW DO INFLATION TARGETS WORK IN PRACTICE?

A Taylor rule or a forward-looking inflation-only rule?

A Taylor rule

Central banks typically try to keep inflation to a predetermined target level. If inflation rises above the target level, the central bank will raise the rate of interest.

The trouble is that this will also reduce real national income. Thus some countries, including the USA, take real national income (i.e. national output) specifically into account when setting interest rates. Adopting a Taylor rule is a way of doing this. A general form of the Taylor rule can be written as follows:

$$i = i^* + a(\pi - \pi^*) + by$$

where i is the real rate of interest set by the central bank; i^* is the real rate of interest consistent with long-run equilibrium in the economy; π is the current rate of inflation; π^* is the target rate of inflation, and so $a(\pi - \pi^*)$ is the divergence of actual inflation from the target rate weighted by an amount a; y is the percentage deviation of real national income from its sustainable level and b is the weight attached to this.

What this equation says is that if inflation goes above its target (i.e. $(\pi - \pi^*)$ is positive), or if real national income rises above its sustainable level (i.e. y is positive), the central bank will raise the real rate of interest, the amount depending on the values of a and b respectively.

The greater the importance attached by the central bank to getting inflation back to target and the less concerned it is about fluctuations in real national income, the greater will be the value of a and the less the value of b. The more, therefore, it will raise the rate of interest when inflation goes above target, and the flatter, therefore, will be the *ADI* curve in Figure 19.12.

Conversely, the more concerned it is about stabilising real national income and is prepared to see inflation deviate from its target, the greater will be the value of b and the less the value of a. The steeper, therefore, will be the *ADI* curve.

Fan chart of CPI inflation and GDP growth projections (made in 2005 Q1), based on market interest rate expectations

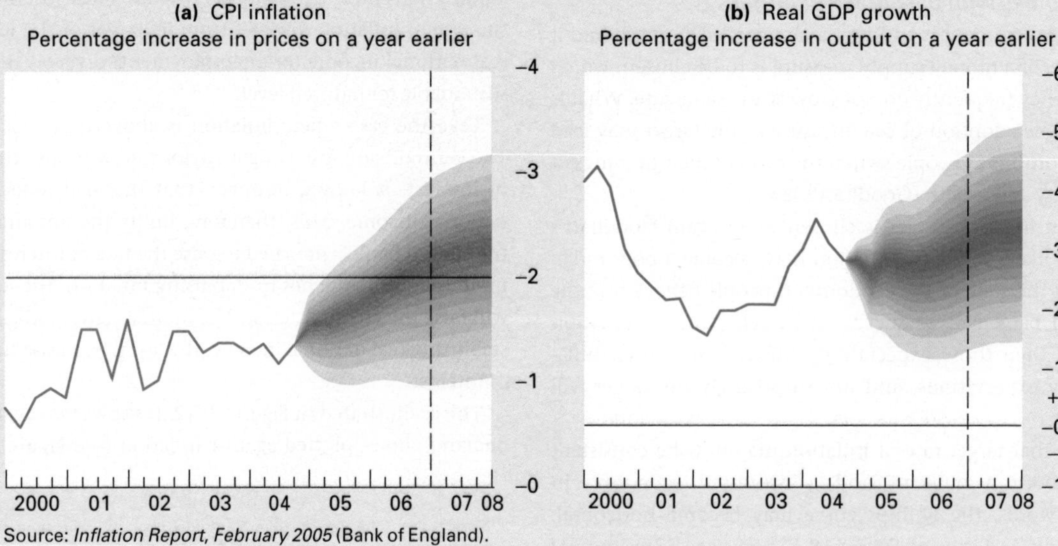

Source: *Inflation Report, February 2005* (Bank of England).

on page 524). Assume that the economy is currently at point a, with inflation on target and real national income at Y_0, which happens to be the sustainable level. Now assume that inflation rises to π_1. As this is above the target level, the central bank raises the rate of interest. This causes real national income to fall and is represented by a movement up along the *ADI* curve.

If the central bank puts a high weight on controlling inflation rather than on stabilising real national income, the curve will be relatively shallow, like ADI_1. It will be prepared to raise interest rates a lot and, as a result, see real national income fall a lot in the short term.

If, however, it puts a relatively high weight on stabilising real national income, the curve will be relatively steep, like ADI_2. It will not be prepared to see real national income fall very much and will thus only raise interest rates modestly.

Thus the central bank has to trade off inflation stability against real income stability. Its Taylor rule shows its optimum trade off and is illustrated by the slope of the *ADI* curve.

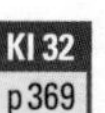

*BOX 19.11

The Bank of England rule

The Bank of England uses a rule that is apparently more simple than the Taylor rule, but in reality is more sophisticated. The Bank of England targets inflation alone; in this sense the rule is more simple. But the inflation figure on which it bases its interest rate decisions is the *forecast* rate of inflation, not the current rate; in this sense it is more sophisticated.

The Bank of England publishes a quarterly *Inflation Report*, which contains projections for inflation for the next three years. These projections assume that interest rates follow market expectations. They form the basis for the Monetary Policy Committee's monthly deliberations. If the projected inflation in 24 months' time is off target, the MPC will change interest rates accordingly.

Two key projections of the MPC are given in the Bank of England's *Inflation Report*, which is published each quarter. These are shown in the diagram. They are known as 'fan charts'. The first plots the forecast range of inflation. The second plots the forecast range of real GDP growth. In each case, the darkest central band represents a 10 per cent likelihood, as does each of the eight subsequent pairs of lighter areas out from the central band. Thus inflation or GDP growth are considered to have a 90 per cent probability of being within the fan. The bands get wider as the time horizon is extended, indicating increasing uncertainty about the outcome. Also, the less reliable the MPC considers the forecasts on which it bases its projections, the wider will be the fan.

The dashed line indicates the two-year target point. Thus in quarter 1 of 2005, the 2 per cent inflation target was for quarter 1 of 2007.

Although projections are made for GDP growth, these are to help inform the forecast for inflation. GDP growth is not itself an explicit target.

The inflation target rule can be written as follows:

$$i_t = a(\pi^e_{t+j} - \pi^*) + bx_t$$

where i_t is the real rate of interest (i) set by the central bank at the current time (t); π^e_{t+j} is the forecast rate of inflation (π^e) at some future point in time ($t+j$).

In the Bank of England's case, j is eight quarters (i.e. two years in the future). π^* is the target rate of inflation, and so $a(\pi^e_{t+j} - \pi^*)$ is the forecast divergence of the inflation rate from target weighted by an amount a; x_t is a set of other variables that the policy makers would like to be taken into account when setting interest rates, weighted by an amount b. These other variables could include expected inflation before and after time $t+j$ and the predicted speed of response of inflation to changes in interest rates. They could also include the percentage divergence of real income from the sustainable level if policy makers wanted to include this (making the Bank of England rule more like a forward-looking Taylor rule).

Comparing the two rules

The main difference between the two rules is that the Bank of England rule is based on forecasts. To the extent that these forecasts are accurate, this is a strength of the rule as it allows decisions to be made that can pre-empt changes in inflation and ensure that they do not occur.

By contrast, under the simple Taylor rule, interest rate decisions are based on the latest figures of actual inflation, which will already be out of date when they are published. There is thus likely to be a considerable time lag before inflation adjusts. Inflation is therefore likely to be far less stable than following a forward-looking rule.

On the other hand, the Bank of England rule does require inflation forecasts to be accurate if inflation is to be kept on target. Forecasts cannot predict the unpredictable, such as the 11 September 2001 attack on the World Trade Center and its dampening effect on aggregate demand. Likewise, supply-side shocks, such as oil price changes, are difficult to predict with any accuracy.

If people believe that the central bank will be successful in keeping inflation on target, does it matter which of the above two rules is used? Explain.

The Taylor rule is explored in more detail in Box 19.11 and is compared with the rule followed by the Bank of England of having an inflation target based on forecast inflation (rather than current inflation).

Difficulties with the target level

KI2 p8 When a target is first set, the short-term costs of achieving it may be too high. If expectations are slow to adjust downward and inflation remains high, then adherence to a tight monetary or inflation rule may lead to a very deep and unacceptable recession. This was a criticism made by many economists of monetarist policies between 1979 and 1982.

When a target has been in force for some time, it may cease to be the appropriate one. Economic circumstances might change. For example, a faster growth in productivity or a large increase in oil revenues may increase potential growth and thus warrant a faster growth in money supply. Or an extended period of relatively low inflation may warrant a lower inflation target. The government must at least have the discretion to *change* the rules, even if only occasionally. But if rules should not be stuck to religiously, does this mean that the government can engage in fine tuning? Keynesians today recognise that fine tuning may not be possible; nevertheless, significant and persistent excess or deficient demand *can* be corrected by demand management policy. For example, the actions taken in the USA by the Federal Reserve Bank in 2001 to cut interest rates substantially, and by the US government to increase its expenditure and to cut taxes, helped to stave off an even deeper recession in 2001 and 2002.

Improvements in forecasting, a willingness of governments to act quickly and the use of quick-acting policies can all help to increase the effectiveness of discretionary demand management.

? *Under what circumstances would adherence to money supply targets lead to (a) more stable interest rates and (b) less stable interest rates than pursuing discretionary demand management policy?*

Conclusions

The resolution of this debate will depend on the following factors:

- The confidence of people in the effectiveness of either discretionary policies or rules: the greater the confidence, the more successful is either policy likely to be.
- The degree of self-stabilisation of the economy (in the case of rules), or conversely the degree of inherent instability of the economy (in the case of discretion).
- The size and frequency of exogenous shocks to demand: the greater they are, the greater the case for discretionary policy.
- In the case of rules, the ability and determination of governments to stick to the rules and the belief by the public that they will be effective.
- In the case of discretionary policy, the ability of governments to adopt and execute policies of the correct magnitude, the speed with which such policies can be effected and the accuracy of forecasting.

Section summary

1. The case against discretionary policy is that it involves unpredictable time lags that can make the policy destabilising. Also, the government may ignore the long-run adverse consequences of policies designed for short-run political gain.
2. The case in favour of rules is that they help to reduce inflationary expectations and thus create a stable environment for investment and growth.
3. The case against sticking to money supply or inflation rules is that they may cause severe fluctuations in interest rates and thus create a less stable economic environment for business planning. Given the changing economic environment in which we live, rules adopted in the past may no longer be suitable for the present.
4. Although perfect fine tuning may not be possible, Keynesians argue that the government must have the discretion to change its policy as circumstances demand.

END OF CHAPTER QUESTIONS

1. The following table shows part of a country's national expenditure schedule (in £ billions):

National income (Y)	100	120	140	160	180	200	220
National expenditure (E)	115	130	145	160	175	190	205

(a) What is the government expenditure multiplier?

(b) What is the tax multiplier?

Assume that full employment is achieved at a level of national income of £200 billion.

(c) Is there an inflationary or a deflationary gap, and what is its size?

(d) By how much would government expenditure have to be changed in order to close this gap (assuming no shift in other injections or withdrawals)?

(e) Alternatively, by how much would taxes have to be changed in order to close the gap (again assuming no shift in other injections or withdrawals)?

(f) Alternatively, assuming that there were initially a balanced budget, and that the government wanted to maintain a balanced budget, by how much would both government expenditure and taxes have to be changed in order to close the gap?

2. What are the problems of relying on automatic fiscal stabilisers to ensure a stable economy at full employment?

continued

3. Does it matter if a country has a large national debt as a proportion of its national income?
4. If the government is running a budget deficit, does this mean that national income will increase?
5. What factors determine the effectiveness of discretionary fiscal policy?
6. Why is it difficult to use fiscal policy to 'fine tune' the economy?
7. Assume that a bank has the following simplified balance sheet, and is operating at its desired liquidity ratio:

Liabilities	(£m)	Assets	(£m)
Deposits	100	Balances with central bank	10
		Advances	90
	100		100

Now assume that the central bank repurchases £5 million of government bonds on the open market. Assume that the people who sell the bonds all have their accounts with this bank and keep a constant amount of cash outside the bank.

(a) Draw up the new balance sheet directly after the purchase of the bonds.

(b) Now draw up the eventual balance sheet after all credit creation has taken place.

(c) Would there be a similar effect if the central bank rediscounted £5 billion of Treasury bills?

(d) How would such open-market operations affect the rate of interest?

8. Is it possible for the government to target the money supply over the longer term without targeting the PSNCR?
9. What are the mechanics whereby the central bank raises the rate of interest?
10. What is Goodhart's law? How is it relevant to (a) monetary policy; (b) using assignment grades to assess a student's ability; (c) paying workers according to the amount of output they produce; (d) awarding local authority contracts to cleaning or refuse disposal companies on the basis of tendered prices?
11. 'It is easier to control the monetary base than broader money, but it is less relevant to do so.' Do you agree with this statement?

*12. Using diagrams like Figures 19.9 and 19.10, compare Keynesian and monetarist analyses of *contractionary* fiscal and monetary policy.

13. Is there a compromise between purely discretionary policy and adhering to strict targets?
14. Compare the relative merits of targeting (a) the money supply; (b) the exchange rate; (c) the rate of inflation.

Additional case studies on the book's website (www.pearsoned.co.uk/sloman)

19.1 The national debt. This explores the question of whether it matters if a country has a high national debt.

19.2 Fine tuning in 1959 and 1960. This looks at two Budgets in the era of Keynesian 'fine tuning'.

19.3 Trends in public expenditure. This case examines attempts to control public expenditure in the UK and relates them to the crowding-out debate.

19.4 Injections against the contagion. The use of discretionary fiscal policy in the late 1990s.

19.5 Monetary policy in the eurozone. This is a more detailed examination of the role of monetary policy and the ECB than that contained in Box 19.7.

19.6 Credit and the business cycle. This case traces cycles in the growth of credit and relates them to the business cycle. It also looks at some of the implications of the growth in credit.

19.7 Effective monetary policy versus banking efficiency and stability. This case examines potential conflicts between banking stability, efficiency and the effective operation of monetary policy.

19.8 Should central banks be independent of government? An examination of the arguments for and against independent central banks.

19.9 Managing the macroeconomy. This considers whether there have been conflicts of objectives in recent UK macroeconomic policy.

19.10 Monetary targeting: its use around the world. An expanded version of Box 19.10.

WEBSITES RELEVANT TO THIS CHAPTER

Numbers and sections refer to websites listed in the Web Appendix and hotlinked from this book's website at www.pearsoned.co.uk/sloman.

- For news articles relevant to this chapter, see the *Economics News Articles* link from the book's website.
- For general news on fiscal and monetary policies, see websites in section A, and particularly A1–5. See also links to newspapers worldwide in A38, 39 and 43, and the news search feature in Google at A41. See also links to economics news in A42.
- For information on UK fiscal policy and government borrowing, see sites E30, 36; F2. See also sites A1–8 at Budget time. For fiscal policy in the eurozone, see *Public Finances in EMU* in H1.
- For a model of the economy (based on the Treasury model), see *The Virtual Economy* (site D1). In addition to the model, where you can devise your own Budget, there are worksheets and outlines of theories and the work of famous economists.
- Sites I7 and 11 contain links to fiscal policy: go to *Macroeconomics > Macroeconomic Policy > Taxes and Taxation.*
- For monetary policy in the UK, see F1 and E30. For monetary policy in the eurozone, see F6 and 5. For monetary policy in the USA, see F8. For monetary policy in other countries, see the respective central bank site in section F.
- For links to sites on money and monetary policy, see the *Financial Economics* sections in I4, 7, 11, 17.
- For demand-side policy in the UK, see the latest Budget Report (e.g. section on maintaining macroeconomic stability) at site E30.
- For inflation targeting in the UK and eurozone, see sites F1 and 6.
- For student resources relevant to this chapter, see sites C1–7, 9, 10, 12, 13, 19. See also '2nd floor – economic policy' in site D1. Also see sites D10 (*The Virtual Chancellor*) and D11 (*The Virtual Bank of Biz/ed*).

Chapter 20

Aggregate Supply, Unemployment and Inflation

In the previous chapter, we focused on ways of managing aggregate demand. But what will be the *effects* of changes in aggregate demand on output, employment and prices? The answer depends on the responsiveness of aggregate *supply*.

We begin this chapter by examining what determines this responsiveness: in other words, we examine what determines the shape of the aggregate supply curve. As we shall see, there are different views on this. Also, the effect will be different in the long run from the short run.

Then we turn to the relationship between inflation and unemployment. Again, what is crucial here is the response of aggregate supply to a change in aggregate demand, in this case reflected in the shape of the Phillips curve. If aggregate supply responds to changes in aggregate demand, then a rise in aggregate demand should lead to a fall in unemployment, but probably a rise in inflation.

We examine three different views on the relationship between inflation and unemployment. One thing is clear: a simple Phillips curve does not exist beyond the short term.

CHAPTER MAP

20.1 AGGREGATE SUPPLY

The effect of an increase in aggregate demand on output, employment and prices is a crucial issue in macroeconomic policy and is at the heart of macroeconomic debate. The debate hinges on the shape of the aggregate supply curve and how it varies with time.

The extreme Keynesian and new classical positions are shown in Figure 20.1. Extreme Keynesians argue that up to full employment (Y_f), the aggregate supply (*AS*) curve is *horizontal*, at least in the short run. A rise in aggregate demand from AD_1 to AD_2 will raise output from Y_1 to Y_2, but there will be *no effect on prices* until full employment is reached. In this model, aggregate supply up to the full-employment level is determined entirely by the level of aggregate demand. But there is no guarantee that aggregate demand will intersect aggregate supply at full employment. Therefore governments should manage aggregate demand by appropriate fiscal and monetary policies to ensure production at Y_f.

Many economists argue that the aggregate supply curve is *vertical*, in the long run. New classicists argue that it is vertical in the short run too. Any rise in aggregate demand will have *no effect on output and employment*. It will merely lead to higher prices. Thus it is essential to control demand if *prices* are to be kept under control. To raise output and employment, however, will require supply-side policies: to shift the *AS* curve to the right.

If *AS* is somewhere between these two extremes, an increase in *AD* will have some effect on prices and some effect on output and employment (see Figure 20.1(c)).

Just what is the shape of the *AS* curve in practice, and what implications follow for policies to cure inflation and unemployment? How do economists differ in their answers to these questions? These are the topics for this chapter. First we must distinguish between short-run and long-run aggregate supply curves.

1. In the extreme Keynesian model, is there any point in supply-side policies?

2. In the new classical model, is there any point in using supply-side policies to tackle inflation?

Short-run aggregate supply

To understand the shape of the short-run *AS* curve, it is necessary to look at its microeconomic foundations. How will *individual* firms and industries respond to a rise in demand? What shape will their individual supply curves be?

KI 9 p58

In the short run, we assume that firms respond to the rise in demand for their product without considering the effects of a general rise in demand on their suppliers or on the economy as a whole. We also assume that the prices of inputs, including wage rates, are constant.

In the case of a profit-maximising firm under monopoly or monopolistic competition, there will be a rise in price and a rise in output. In Figure 20.2, profit-maximising output rises from where $MC = MR_1$ to where $MC = MR_2$. Just how much price changes compared with output depends on the slope of the marginal cost (*MC*) curve.

KI 17 p121

The nearer the firm is to full capacity, the steeper the *MC* curve is likely to be. Here the firm is likely to find diminishing returns setting in rapidly, and it is also likely to have to use more overtime with correspondingly higher unit labour costs. If, however, the firm is operating well below capacity, it can probably supply more with little or no increase in price. Its *MC* curve may thus be horizontal at lower levels of output.

Under oligopoly, where there is a tendency for prices to be more stable, firms may respond to an increase in demand without raising prices, even if their costs rise somewhat.

Figure 20.1 Contrasting views of the aggregate supply curve

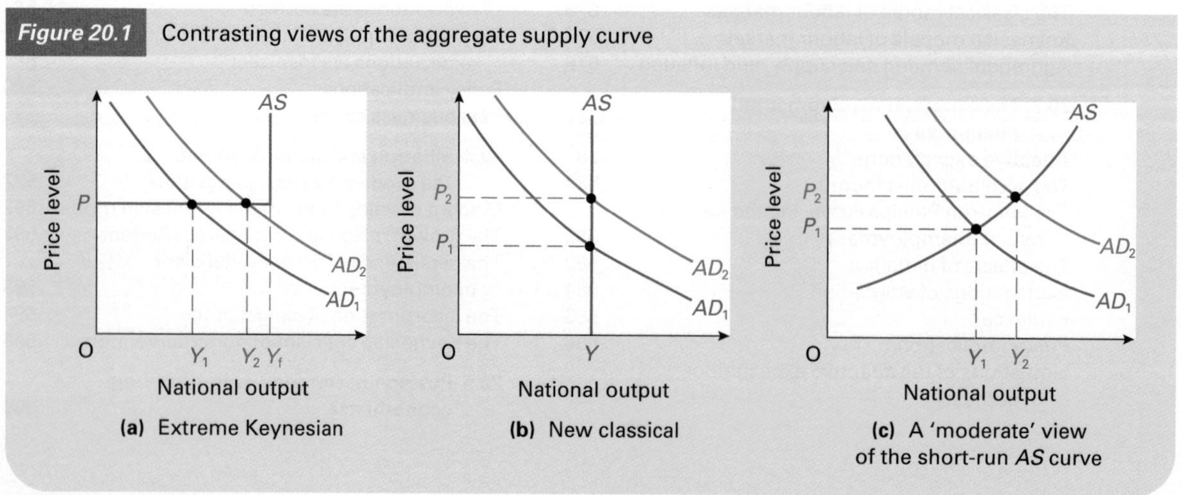

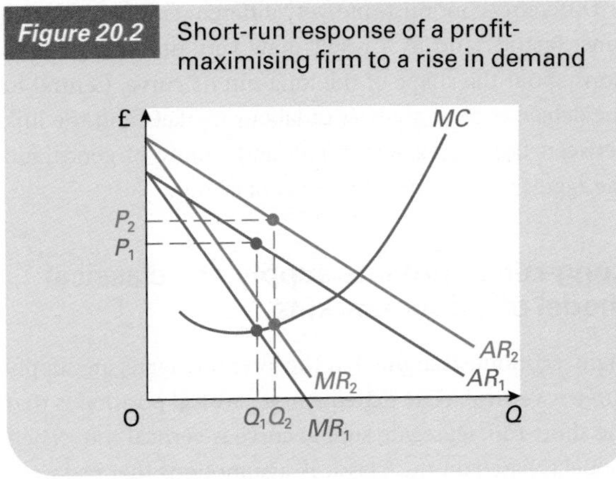

Figure 20.2 Short-run response of a profit-maximising firm to a rise in demand

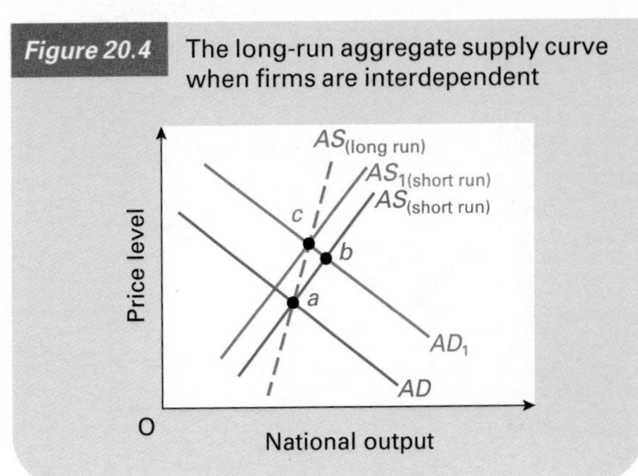

Figure 20.4 The long-run aggregate supply curve when firms are interdependent

When there is a general rise in demand in the economy, the *aggregate* supply response in the short run can be seen as simply the sum of the responses of all the individual firms. The short-run *AS* curve will look something like that in Figure 20.3. If there is generally plenty of spare capacity, a rise in aggregate demand (e.g. from AD_1 to AD_2) will have a big effect on output and only a small effect on prices. However, as more and more firms find their costs rising as they get nearer to full capacity, so the *AS* curve becomes steeper. Further increases in aggregate demand (e.g. from AD_2 to AD_3) will have bigger effects on prices and smaller effects on output. A general rise in prices, of course, means that individual firms were mistaken in assuming that a rise TC 12 p374 in price from P_1 to P_2 in Figure 20.2 was a *real* price rise (i.e. relative to prices elsewhere).

Long-run aggregate supply

Three important factors affect the *AS* curve in the long run.

The interdependence of firms

TC 10 p294 A rise in aggregate demand will lead firms throughout the economy to raise their prices (in accordance with the short-run *AS* curve). But as raw material and intermediate good producers raise their prices, this will raise the costs of production further up the line. A rise in the price of steel will raise the costs of producing cars and washing machines. At the same time, workers, experiencing a rise in demand for labour, and seeing the prices of goods rising, will demand higher wages. Firms will be relatively willing to grant these wage demands, since they are experiencing buoyant demand. The effect of all this is to raise firms' costs, and hence their prices. As prices rise for any given level of output, the short-run *AS* curve shifts upwards.

These long-run effects of a rise in aggregate demand are shown in Figure 20.4. Aggregate demand shifts to AD_1. The economy moves from point *a* to point *b* along the short-run *AS* curve. As costs rise and are passed on throughout the economy, the short-run *AS* curve shifts to AS_1, and the economy moves to point *c*. Thus the long-run *AS* curve passing through points *a* and *c* is steeper than the short-run *AS* curve. A rise in aggregate demand will therefore have a smaller effect on output and a bigger effect on prices in the long run than in the short run.

? *Under what circumstances would this interdependence of firms give a vertical long-run AS curve?*

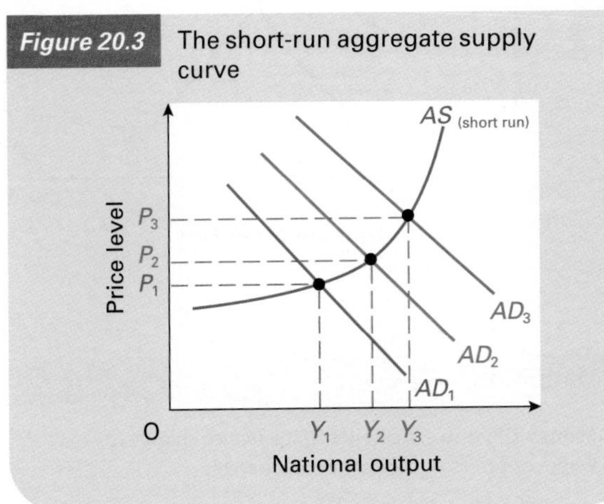

Figure 20.3 The short-run aggregate supply curve

Investment

With a rise in demand, firms may be encouraged to invest in new plant and machinery (the accelerator effect). In so doing, they may well be able to increase output significantly in the long run with little or no increase in their prices. Their long-run *MC* curves are much flatter than their short-run *MC* curves.

In Figure 20.5, the short-run *AS* curve shifts to the right.  KI 9 p58 Equilibrium moves from point *a* to *b* to *d*. In this case, the long-run *AS* curve joining points *a* and *d* is much more elastic than that in Figure 20.4. There is a relatively large increase in output and a relatively small increase in price.

The long-run *AS* curve will be flatter and possibly even downward sloping if the investment involves the introduction of new cost-reducing technology, or if firms generally experience economies of scale. It will be steeper if the extra investment causes significant shortages of materials,

Figure 20.5 Effect of investment on the long-run aggregate supply curve

machinery or labour. This is more likely when the economy is already operating near its full potential.

?
1. *Will the shape of the long-run AS curve here depend on just how the 'long' run is defined?*
2. *If a shift in the aggregate demand curve from AD to AD_1 in Figure 20.5 causes a movement from point a to point d in the long run, would a shift in aggregate demand from AD_1 to AD cause a movement from point d back to point a in the long run?*

TC 9 p101

Expectations

The effect of a rise in aggregate demand on output and prices will depend crucially on what effect people *expect* it will have.

If firms believe that it will lead to rapid economic growth, they will invest. The short-run *AS* curve will shift to the right.

If, on the other hand, people expect that a rise in demand will simply lead to higher prices, firms will not invest. Workers will demand higher wages to compensate for the higher costs of living. Firms will grant wage rises, knowing that they can pass on the rise in labour costs to the consumer. In these circumstances, the short-run *AS* curve will shift upwards (to the left).

If there is a fall in aggregate demand, the above three factors will operate in reverse; and again they will affect aggregate supply in different ways:

- The general reduction in costs will lead to the short-run *AS* curve shifting downwards (to the right).
- A fall in investment may lead to a decline in the capital stock and a leftward shift in the short-run *AS* curve.
- People may expect a recession and falling output (*AS* shifts to the left), or merely that prices will fall (*AS* shifts downwards to the right).

Depending on the relative strength of these three factors, the long-run *AS* curve could be shallow, steep or vertical. A fall in *AD* could thus lead to a deep recession with little effect on prices, or there could be little or no long-run reduction in output, but a significant reduction in prices.

Different economists put very different emphases on the three factors, and as a result draw very different conclusions about the shape of the long-run *AS* curve. Central to the debate is their analysis of labour markets and the link between the aggregate demand and supply of goods and the aggregate demand and supply of labour.

Long-run aggregate supply: the classical model of labour markets

Many economists argue that the long-run aggregate supply curve is vertical. (The extreme new classical position is that the short-run aggregate supply curve is vertical too.) Their model is based on the 'classical' assumptions that real wage rates are flexible in the long run and that people are fully aware of price and wage changes, and hence do not believe that they will be better off with a pay increase when prices are rising by the same percentage (i.e. they do not suffer from ***money illusion***). TC 12 p374

Figure 20.6 shows the aggregate demand and supply of labour. It is very similar to the diagram we looked at back on page 401. On the vertical axis we measure the average *real* wage rate (*W*/*P*): i.e. the wage rate after adjusting for prices. The aggregate demand for labour curve (AD_L) slopes downwards. This is merely an extension of the microeconomic demand for labour curve (see section 9.1) and is based on the assumption of diminishing returns to labour. For a given capital stock, the more people are employed, the lower their marginal productivity. Thus firms take on

Figure 20.6 The aggregate labour market

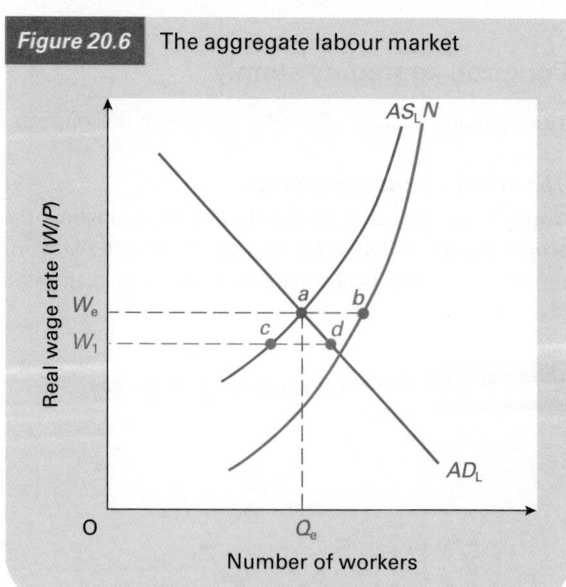

Definition

Money illusion The belief that a *money* change in wages or prices represents a *real* change.

more labour only if there is a fall in the real wage rate to compensate them for the lower output produced by the additional workers.

A higher real wage rate encourages more people to enter the labour market. For example, more married women may seek employment. The total number in the labour force (N) rises. The curve gets steeper as the limit of the potential labour force is reached.

There will, however, be some frictional and structural unemployment. Some workers will be searching for better jobs and others will have the wrong qualifications or live in the wrong location. The number of workers willing and able to accept jobs, therefore – the *effective aggregate supply of labour* (AS_L) – will be less than the total labour force.

KI 8 p43

The equilibrium real wage will be W_e, where $AD_L = AS_L$, with Q_e workers employed. There is no disequilibrium unemployment at this real wage rate, but there is some equilibrium or ***natural unemployment*** (i.e. frictional plus structural unemployment), shown by $(b - a)$.

With flexible prices and wage rates in the long run, *real* wage rates will also be flexible in the long run. This will ensure that long-run employment is kept at Q_e. Assume that aggregate demand (for goods) rises. Prices rise. This causes the real wage to fall below W_e, say to W_1 in Figure 20.6. But at this real wage rate there is an excess demand for labour of $d - c$. This will drive up the money wage rate until the *real* wage rate has returned to W_e. Thus equilibrium employment is at Q_e irrespective of changes in aggregate demand. Q_e would change only if there were some *exogenous* shift in the AD_L or AS_L curve (e.g. a growth in the working population would cause N and AS_L to shift to the right; a growth in labour productivity would cause AD_L to shift to the right).

? *Assume that there is a* fall *in aggregate demand (for goods). Trace through the short-run and long-run effect on employment.*

With long-run employment being at Q_e (the natural rate) irrespective of what happens to prices and *money* wages, the long-run aggregate supply curve will be vertical at the ***natural level of output***. (This is just another name for the *sustainable level of output* that we examined in Box 13.4.)

Some new classical economists argue that wage and price flexibility is very great, especially with increased part-time and short-term jobs. This flexibility is so great that both goods and labour markets clear virtually instantaneously, and the distinction between the short run and the long run breaks down. In such circumstances, the arguments above apply to the short run as well as to the long run. The effect is to give a vertical short-run aggregate supply curve as well as a vertical long-run one.

Long-run aggregate supply: Keynesian models of labour markets

Keynesian models of long-run aggregate supply take a very different view of labour markets.

Many labour markets exhibit considerable wage inflexibility. Employers bargain with unions and set wage rates usually for a whole year. If there is a fall in consumer demand, firms usually respond *not* by cutting wages, but rather by laying off workers, or by instituting early retirement, or by not replacing workers when they leave. In the short run, therefore, wages in many sectors of the economy are insensitive to a fall in demand.

In Figure 20.7, assume initially that with aggregate demand for labour at AD_{L_1}, the labour market is in equilibrium. The only unemployment is equilibrium unemployment of $b - a$. If there is a fall in the aggregate demand for goods, with prices sticky in the short run, the production of goods goes down, but real wage rates are little affected. The effect on the labour market is felt, therefore, by a fall in the aggregate demand for labour to AD_{L_2}, reflecting the lower demand for goods. But with wages sticky downwards, the real wage rate does not fall either. Instead, firms reduce employment from Q_1 to Q_2. There is now demand-deficient unemployment of $a - c$. *Total* unemployment is $b - c$.

This gives a short-run aggregate supply (of goods) curve that is highly elastic below the current wage. A fall in aggregate demand will lead to a large fall in output and only a KI 9 p58

Figure 20.7 Short-run response to a fall in the aggregate demand for labour: sticky wages

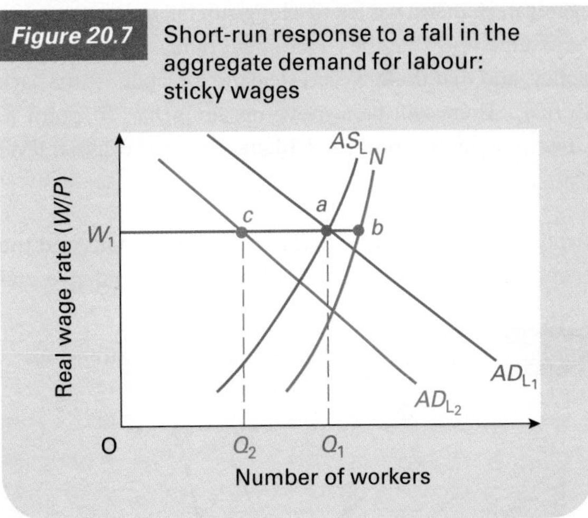

Definitions

Natural level of unemployment The level of equilibrium unemployment in monetarist analysis measured as the difference between the (vertical) long-run gross labour supply (N) and the (vertical) long-run effective labour supply (AS_L).

Natural level of output The level of output in monetarist analysis where the vertical long-run aggregate supply curve cuts the horizontal axis.

small fall in prices. The flatter are firms' marginal cost curves, the smaller will be the fall in prices.

But what about the *long* run? Clearly it depends on how long the long run is. Many Keynesians argue that prices and especially wages exhibit a degree of inflexibility over quite a long period of time, and over this period of time, therefore, the aggregate supply curve would not be vertical. What is more, Keynesians argue that the long-run *AS* curve is unlikely to be vertical for a number of other reasons.

KI 30 p 306

Hysteresis. As we saw on page 445, **hysteresis** refers to the lagging or persistence of an effect, even when the initial cause has been removed. In other words, an equilibrium position depends on the path taken to arrive there. In this context, hysteresis would be where long-run aggregate supply depends on what has been happening to aggregate demand and supply in the short run. Assume that the economy goes into recession, with a corresponding rise in demand-deficient unemployment and a fall in output. In Figure 20.8, aggregate demand has fallen from AD_{L_1} to AD_{L_2}. Demand-deficient unemployment is $a - b$ (the short-run effect).

As the recession persists, those previously laid off may not be readily re-employable, especially if they have been out of work for some time and have become deskilled and demoralised. The aggregate supply of labour curve has shifted to the left, perhaps as far as AS_{L_2}. In such a case, there would now no longer be an excess supply of labour that firms regard as 'employable' ($AD_{L_2} = AS_{L_2}$). There is no downward pressure on real wages: a long-run equilibrium has been reached. The implication of this is that the long-run aggregate supply (of goods) curve is *not* vertical. A leftward shift in aggregate demand has led to a long-run fall in output.

Assume now that the government pursues a reflationary policy, and that the aggregate demand for labour shifts back to AD_{L_1}. There will be a move up along AS_{L_2} to point *d*. Unemployment is now $e - d$, higher than the original level of $c - a$.

Expectations of output. If aggregate demand falls and the economy moves into recession, business confidence will fall and so will investment. The capital stock will therefore fall. This will reduce aggregate supply. Unless confidence quickly returns, and there is no guarantee that it will, the recession may be long lived. The reduction in aggregate supply will be *long* term.

The reduction in the capital stock will magnify the leftward shift in the aggregate demand for labour and increase the level of unemployment.

Long-run money illusion. The problem of demand deficiency will be compounded if there is long-run money illusion. Assume again that there is a fall in aggregate demand. Workers may be reluctant to accept a reduction in money wages, not appreciating that there is a corresponding fall in prices, thus leaving real wages unaffected. Thus real wages may be forced up, compounding the problem of disequilibrium unemployment.

Aggregate demand and supply, and inflation

Aggregate demand and supply analysis can be used to distinguish between demand-pull and cost-push inflation.

Demand-pull inflation

Assume that aggregate demand rises. In Figure 20.9(a), there is some increase in output, and the price level rises from P_0 to P_1. If demand goes on rising, so that the *AD* curve goes on shifting to the right, the price level will go on rising and there will be demand-pull inflation. There will be a movement from point *a* to *b* to *c* in Figure 20.9(b).

But sooner or later the short-run aggregate *supply* curve will start shifting. If the effects of rising costs and rising price expectations offset any stimulus to investment, the short-run *AS* curve will shift upwards. This will lead to a falling back of output but a further rise in prices as the economy moves to point *d*. If the government responds by giving a further boost to demand in order to keep expansion going, there will be a movement outward again to point *e*, but a further rise in prices. Then the *AS* curve will probably continue shifting upwards and the economy will move to point *f*.

If the government now makes the control of inflation its main policy objective, it may stop any further increases in aggregate demand. Aggregate supply may continue shifting upwards for a while as cost increases and expectations feed through. The economy moves to point *g*. In the extreme case, point *g* may be vertically above point *a*: the

Figure 20.8 The effect on wages and employment of a recovery from recession

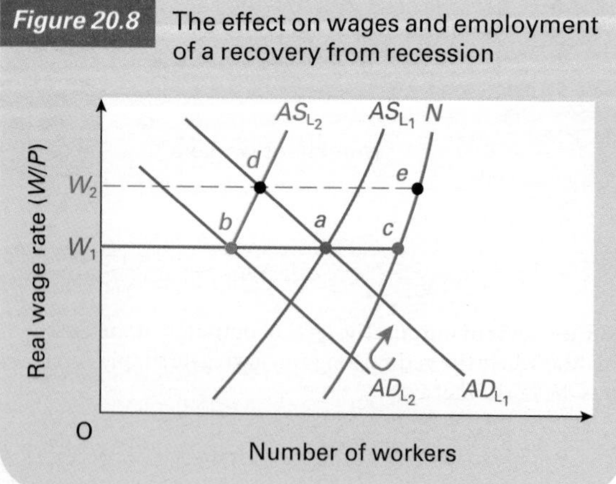

Definition

Hysteresis The persistence of an effect even when the initial cause has ceased to operate. In economics, it refers to the persistence of unemployment even when the demand deficiency that caused it no longer exists.

EXPLORING ECONOMICS

BOX 20.1

COST-PUSH INFLATION AND SUPPLY SHOCKS

It is important to distinguish a *single* supply shock, such as a rise in oil prices or an increase in VAT or excise duties, from a continuing upward pressure on costs, such as workers continually demanding increases in real wages above the level of labour productivity, or firms continually using their monopoly power to increase the real value of profits.

A single supply shock will give a *single* upward movement in the *AS* curve. Prices will move to a new higher equilibrium. Cost-push inflation in this case is a *temporary* phenomenon. Once the new higher price level has been reached, the cost-push inflation disappears. If, however, there is a continuous upward pressure on costs, cost-push inflation is likely to continue. It will get worse if the cost pressure intensifies.

Give some examples of single shocks and continuing changes on the demand side. Does the existence of multiplier and accelerator effects make the distinction between single shocks and continuing effects more difficult to make on the demand side than on the supply side?

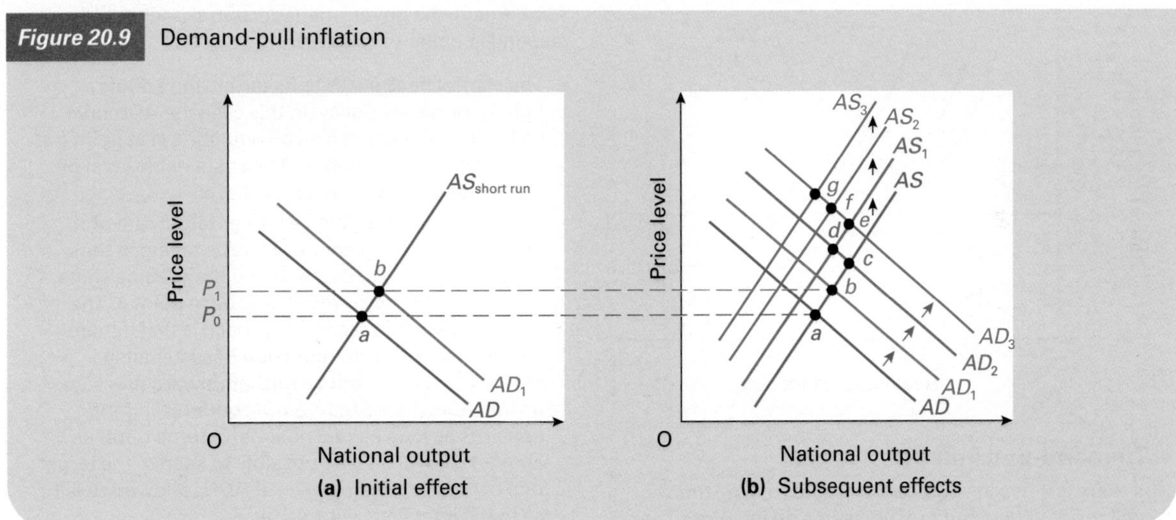

Figure 20.9 Demand-pull inflation

long-run aggregate supply curve is vertical. The only effect of the shift in *AD* to AD_3 has been inflation.

Note that, although costs in Figure 20.9(b) have increased and hence the *AS* curves have shifted upwards, this is not *cost-push* inflation because the rise in costs is the result of the rise in *demand*.

? *If point g is vertically above point a, does this mean that the long-run AS curve is vertical? Are there any circumstances where point g might be to the left of point a?*

Cost-push inflation

Assume that there is some exogenous increase in costs: a sharp increase in world oil prices, or an increase in wages due to increased trade union activity, or firms raising prices to cover the costs of a rise in interest rates. In Figure 20.10(a), the short-run *AS* curve shifts to AS_1. Prices rise to P_1 and there is a fall in national output.

If these increases in costs continue for some time, the *AS* curve will go on shifting upwards. Price rises will continue and there is cost-push inflation. The economy will move from point *a* to *b* to *c* in Figure 20.10(b). Continuous upward shifts in the *AS* curve are particularly likely if there is a continuing struggle between different groups (e.g. unions and employers' organisations) for a larger share of national income.

After a time, aggregate demand is likely to rise. This may be due to the government using expansionary fiscal and monetary policies to halt the falling output and employment. Or it may be due to money supply expanding endogenously as workers and firms need larger money balances to allow for increasingly costly transactions. Aggregate demand shifts to AD_1 and there is a movement to point *d*. There may be a further increase in costs and a movement to point *e*, and then a further increase in aggregate demand and so on.

Note again that, although demand has increased, this is not *demand-pull* inflation because the rise in demand is the result of the upward pressure on *costs*.

What causes inflation in practice?

Inflation targeting, with the use of interest-rate changes to achieve the target, implies that inflation is generally of the demand-pull variety. Forecasts of inflation (e.g. by the

EXPORING ECONOMICS

BOX 20.2

ANALYSING DEMAND-PULL AND COST-PUSH INFLATION USING THE *ADI/ASI* MODEL

Types of inflation under a policy of inflation targeting

We can use the *ADI/ASI* model to analyse the implications of demand-pull and cost-push pressures under a policy of inflation targeting. The diagram below is similar to Figure 18.17 (on page 526). Assume that the central bank operates with an inflation target of π_{target} and that the economy is currently in equilibrium at point *a* with aggregate demand and supply given by ADI_1 and ASI_1 respectively. Real national income is at the sustainable (or 'natural') level of Y_1.

Demand-pull and cost-push inflation

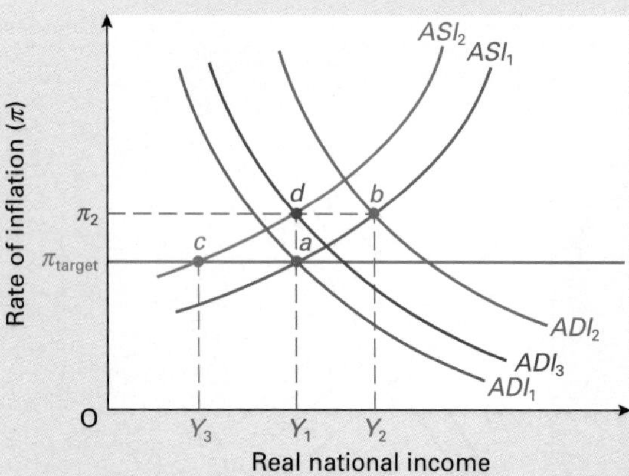

Demand-pull inflation

If there is a rise in aggregate demand to ADI_2, this will result in demand-pull pressures on inflation. The government or central bank could respond in either of two ways.

- Fiscal or monetary policy is tightened to shift the *ADI* curve back to ADI_1, thereby maintaining inflation at the target level.
- A new higher inflation target is adopted (e.g. π_2), allowing an equilibrium at point *b*. Note, however, that if the sustainable level of income remains at Y_1, Y_2 will not be sustainable. In the long run, the *ASI* curve will drift upwards, pushing inflation above the new higher target level. A tighter monetary policy (ADI_3) would then be needed to bring national income back down to the sustainable level, Y_1.

Cost-push inflation

If costs now rise faster than the rate of inflation (a *real* rise in costs), the *ASI* line will shift upwards (e.g. to ASI_2). Again, the government or central bank could respond in either of two ways.

- The central bank sticks to its target and adopts a tighter monetary policy. In this case the *ADI* curve will shift to the left to give an equilibrium at point *c* at the target rate of inflation. The sustainable level of output is now at the lower level of Y_3.
- The central bank is given a higher target rate of inflation (π_2) to prevent real income falling. It thus expands aggregate demand and the *ADI* line shifts to ADI_3. Equilibrium would now be at point *d*. The problem with this second approach is that if there has been a long-term reduction in sustainable output to Y_3, there will be further upward pressure on inflation: the *ASI* curve will continue shifting upwards as long as real national income remains above Y_3. It will only be possible to keep to the target rate of inflation, at any level, if *ADI* is allowed to fall so that it intersects with *ASI* at Y_3.

?

If cost-push pressures reduce the sustainable level of national income (e.g. from Y_1 to Y_3 in the diagram), why do demand-pull pressures not increase the sustainable level of real national income (e.g. from Y_1 to Y_2 in the diagram)?

Figure 20.10 Cost-push inflation

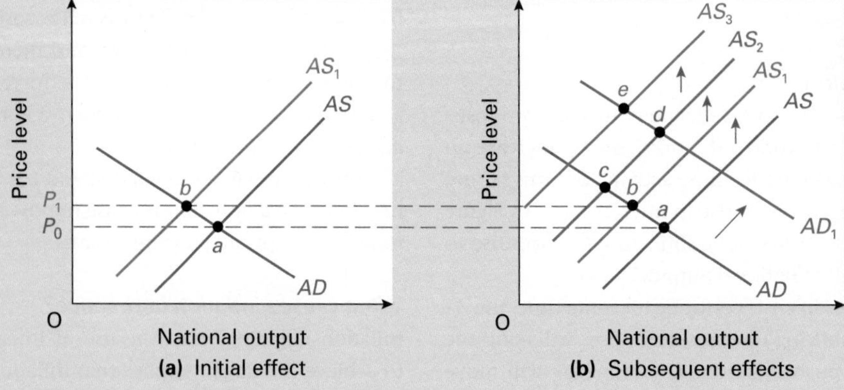

Bank of England) tend to concentrate on various factors affecting aggregate demand, such as the size of the PSNCR and business and consumer confidence. In most cases, changes in inflation are indeed caused by changes in the rate of growth of aggregate demand.

There are, however, occasions when there are exogenous changes in costs. In the short run, these can be shocks such as a rise in oil prices or a period of industrial unrest. In the longer term, technological changes can affect the rate of growth of aggregate supply. If this slows down, then for any given rate of growth in aggregate demand, there will be a higher rate of inflation. This rise in inflation could be described as 'cost push'. Under a policy of inflation targeting, however, the response to this problem would be one of slowing down the rate of growth in aggregate demand to match the slower growth in aggregate supply.

One of the key determinants of inflation is people's expectations. The higher inflation is expected to be, the higher it will be. In the remainder of the chapter we look at just how expectations affect inflation and how they affect the relationship between inflation and unemployment. In doing so we will look at theories that develop the old Phillips curve (see Box 14.5).

Section summary

1. The short-run aggregate supply curve depends on firms' short-run marginal cost curves. The more rapidly costs rise as output increases, the less elastic will the *AS* curve be.
2. The long-run *AS* curve will be less elastic (a) the more that cost increases are passed on from one part of the economy to another, (b) the less that increases in aggregate demand stimulate cost-reducing investment and (c) the more that people expect prices to rise as a result of the increase in demand.
3. Classical assumptions imply that the long-run aggregate supply curve is vertical. The key assumptions here are flexible prices and wages, and an absence of money illusion.
4. Keynesians argue that the long-run supply curve will not be vertical. It will be more elastic the greater the problem of hysteresis, the more that firms react to changes in aggregate demand by changing the level of investment and hence the size of the capital stock, and the greater the degree of long-run money illusion.
5. Demand-pull inflation occurs where there is a continuous rightward shift in the *AD* curve. Cost-push inflation occurs where there is a continuous upward shift in the *AS* curve. In practice, it is difficult to separate demand-pull and cost-push inflation as there are often exogenous and endogenous factors affecting both demand and costs simultaneously.

20.2 THE EXPECTATIONS-AUGMENTED PHILLIPS CURVE

A major contribution to the theory of unemployment and inflation was made by Milton Friedman (see Person Profile on the book's website) and others in the late 1960s. They incorporated people's expectations about the future level of prices into the Phillips curve. In its simplest form, this ***expectations-augmented Phillips curve*** may be expressed as:

$$\pi = f(1/U) + \pi^e + \kappa \quad (1)$$

This states that the rate of price inflation (π) depends on three things.

- First, it is a function (f) of the inverse of unemployment ($1/U$). This is simply the normal Phillips curve relationship. A rise in aggregate demand will lead to a fall in unemployment (a rise in $1/U$) and a rise in inflation: e.g. a movement from point *a* to point *b* in Figure 20.11.
- Second, the expected rate of inflation π^e must be added to the inflation that would result simply from the level of excess demand represented by ($1/U$).

Definition

Expectations-augmented Phillips curve A (short-run) Phillips curve whose position depends on the expected rate of inflation.

Figure 20.11 A Phillips curve

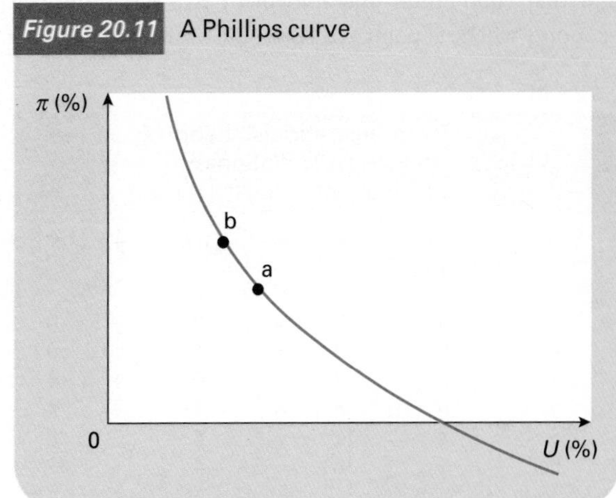

- Third, if there are any exogenous cost pressures on inflation (κ) (such as increases in international commodity prices), this must be added too.

Thus if people expected a 3 per cent inflation ($\pi^e = 3\%$) and if excess demand were causing demand-pull inflation of 2 per cent ($f(1/U) = 2\%$) and exogenous increases in costs were adding another 1 per cent to inflation ($\kappa = 1\%$), actual inflation would be $3 + 2 + 1 = 6$ per cent.

The model is developed in the framework of market clearing. Wages are not sticky downwards, at least not in the long run. There can be no long-run disequilibrium unemployment: no long-run deficiency of demand.

Adaptive expectations

What determines the expected rate of inflation (π^e)? In the model we are developing it depends on inflation rates *in the past*. This is known as the ***adaptive expectations hypothesis***. What this means is that people learn from experience. If last year they underpredicted the rate of inflation, then this year they will adapt: they will revise their expectations of inflation upwards.

In its simplest form, the adaptive expectations hypothesis assumes that the expected rate of inflation this year (π_t^e) will be the rate that inflation actually was last year (π_{t-1}):

$$\pi_t^e = \pi_{t-1} \qquad (2)$$

To keep the analysis straightforward, we will stick to this simple version of the adaptive expectations hypothesis.

The accelerationist theory

Let us trace the course of inflation and expectations over a number of years in an imaginary economy. To keep the analysis simple, assume there is no growth in the economy and no exogenous cost pressures on inflation ($\kappa = 0$ in equation (1)).

Year 1. Assume that at the outset, in year 1, there is no inflation of any sort; that none is expected; that $AD = AS$; and that equilibrium unemployment is 8 per cent. The economy will be at point *a* in Figure 20.12 and Table 20.1.

Table 20.1 The accelerationist theory of inflation and inflationary expectations

Year	Point on graph	π	=	$f(1/U)$	+	π^e
1	*a*	0	=	0	+	0
2	*b*	4	=	4	+	0
3	*c*	4	=	0	+	4
4	*d*	8	=	4	+	4
5	*e*	12	=	4	+	8
6	*f*	16	=	4	+	12

Figure 20.12 The accelerationist theory of inflation and inflationary expectations

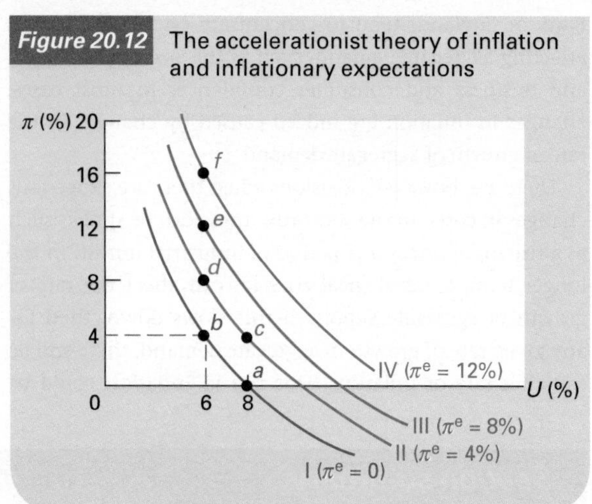

Year 2. Now assume that the government expands aggregate demand in order to reduce unemployment. Unemployment falls to 6 per cent. The economy moves to point *b* along curve I. Inflation has risen to 4 per cent, but people, basing their expectations of inflation on year 1, still expect a zero inflation. There is therefore no shift as yet in the Phillips curve. Curve I corresponds to an expected rate of inflation of zero. (See Web Case 20.1 for an explanation of why the short-run Phillips curve slopes downwards.)

Year 3. People now revise their expectations of inflation to the level of year 2. The Phillips curve shifts up by 4 percentage points to position II. If *nominal* aggregate demand (i.e. demand purely in monetary terms, irrespective of the level of prices) continues to rise at the same rate, the whole of the increase will now be absorbed in higher prices. *Real* aggregate demand will fall back to its previous level and the economy will move to point *c*. Unemployment will return to 8 per cent. There is no *demand-pull* inflation now, ($f(1/U) = 0$), but inflation is still 4 per cent due to expectations ($\pi^e = 4$ per cent). TC 12 p374

Year 4. Assume now that the government expands *real* aggregate demand again so as to reduce unemployment once more to 6 per cent. This time it must expand *nominal* aggregate demand by *more* than it did in year 2, because this time, as well as reducing unemployment, it also has to validate the 4 per cent expected inflation. The economy moves to point *d* along curve II. Inflation is now 8 per cent.

Definition

Adaptive expectations hypothesis The theory that people base their expectations of inflation on past inflation rates.

Year 5. *Expected* inflation is now 8 per cent (the level of actual inflation in year 4). The Phillips curve shifts up to position III. If at the same time the government now tries to keep unemployment at 6 per cent, it must expand nominal aggregate demand 4 per cent faster in order to validate the 8 per cent expected inflation. The economy moves to point *e* along curve III. Inflation is now 12 per cent.

Year 6 onwards. To keep unemployment at 6 per cent, the government must continue to increase nominal aggregate demand by 4 per cent more than the previous year. As the expected inflation rate goes on rising, the Phillips curve will go on shifting up each year.

Thus in order to keep unemployment below the initial equilibrium rate, price rises must go on *accelerating* each year. For this reason, the adaptive expectations theory of the Phillips curve is sometimes known as the ***accelerationist theory***.

The more the government reduces unemployment, the greater the rise in inflation that year, and the more the rise in expectations the following year and each subsequent year; and hence the more rapidly will price rises accelerate. Thus the true longer-term trade-off is between unemployment and the rate of *increase* in inflation.

$$\Delta\pi = f(1/U) \tag{3}$$

($\Delta\pi$ may be written $\dot{\pi}$.)

Note that the upward shift in the Phillips curve will be less rapid if expectations do not fully adjust to last year's inflation rate. The upward shift will be more rapid if expectations adjust to the rate of *increase* in inflation last year ($\Delta\pi_{t-1}$).

? *Construct a table like Table 20.1, only this time assume that the government wishes to reduce unemployment to 5 per cent. Assume that every year from year 1 onwards the government is prepared to expand aggregate demand by whatever it takes to do this. If this expansion of demand gives f(1/U) = 7 per cent, fill in the table for the first six years. Do you think that after a couple of years people might begin to base their expectations differently?*

The long-run Phillips curve and the natural rate of unemployment

KI 8 p43

As long as there are demand-pull pressures ($f(1/U) > 0$), inflation will rise as the expected rate of inflation (π^e) rises. In the long run, therefore, the Phillips curve will be *vertical* at the rate of unemployment where real aggregate demand equals *real* aggregate supply. This rate of unemployment is often called the ***natural rate*** (U_n). It is sometimes also known as the ***non-accelerating-inflation rate of unemployment (NAIRU)***.[1] In Figure 20.12, $U_n = 8$ per cent.

The implication for government policy is that expansionary monetary and fiscal policy can only reduce unemployment below U_n in the *short* run. In the long run, the effect will be purely inflationary.

? *What will determine the speed at which inflation accelerates?*

The effects of deflation

Let us now move on a few years from Table 20.1. Assume that the economy has returned to the natural rate of unemployment: $f(1/U) = 0$. The economy is therefore on the long-run Phillips curve. But, due to past excess demand, the expected rate of inflation is 20 per cent. The economy is thus at point *j* on short-run Phillips curve X in Figure 20.13.

The government now decides to make the control of inflation its main priority. It therefore reduces the growth of nominal aggregate demand *below* the rate of inflation. Real aggregate demand falls. Let us assume that there is a

Figure 20.13 The effects of deflation

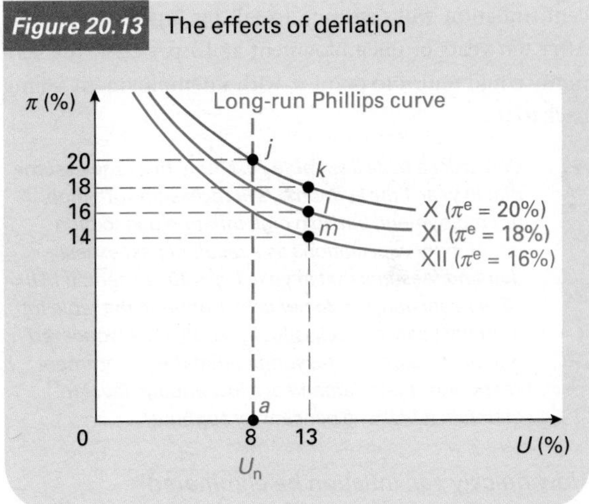

[1] Strictly speaking, the NAIRU is theoretically different from the natural rate in that it is based on the assumption of imperfect competition, price and wage stickiness and hysteresis: in other words, on Keynesian assumptions. The NAIRU is thus merely the rate of unemployment at which inflation is constant. We look at the NAIRU in section 20.4.

Definitions

Accelerationist theory The theory that unemployment can be reduced below the natural rate only at the cost of accelerating inflation.

Natural rate of unemployment or non-accelerating-inflation rate of unemployment (NAIRU) The rate of unemployment consistent with a constant rate of inflation: the rate of unemployment at which the vertical long-run Phillips curve cuts the horizontal axis.

EXPLORING ECONOMICS *BOX 20.3

BASING EXPECTATIONS ON THE PAST

More sophisticated adaptive expectations models

More complex adaptive expectations models assume that π^e is a weighted average of past rates of inflation:

$$\pi_t^e = a\pi_{t-1} + b\pi_{t-2} + c\pi_{t-3} \ldots + m\pi_{t-n} \quad (1)$$

where $a + b + c \ldots + m = 1$, and where $a > b > c$, etc.

In other words, people will base their expectations of inflation on the actual inflation rates over the last few years, but with last year's inflation having a bigger influence on people's expectations than the previous year's and so on.

In times of rapidly *accelerating* inflation, people may adjust their expectations of inflation upward by the amount that inflation *rose* last year ($\Delta\pi_{t-1}$). This gives:

$$\Delta\pi_t^e = \Delta\pi_{t-1} \quad (2)$$

Under what circumstances will term a in equation (1) be large relative to terms b, c etc?

2 per cent downward pressure on inflation: $f(1/U) = -2$. Inflation thus falls to 18 per cent. But unemployment rises, let us assume, from 8 per cent to 13 per cent. The economy moves along curve X to point *k*.

Next year the expected rate of inflation will fall to 18 per cent to match, and if real demand is still being deflated by the same amount ($f(1/U) = -2$), actual inflation will fall to 16 per cent. The economy moves to point *l* on curve XI.

If the government maintains unemployment at 13 per cent, inflation will continue to fall by 2 per cent a year. After ten years of unemployment at 13 per cent, the economy could return to point *a*, with unemployment falling back to U_n.

? *Construct a table like Table 20.1, only this time assume that in year 1 the economy is in recession with high unemployment, but also high inflation due to high inflationary expectations as a result of past excess demand. Assume that in year 1, $\pi = 30$ per cent, $f(1/U) = -6$ per cent and $\pi^e = 36$ per cent. Continue the table for as many years as it takes for inflation to be 'squeezed out' of the economy (assuming that the government keeps aggregate demand at a low enough level to maintain $f(1/U) = -6$ per cent throughout).*

How quickly can inflation be eliminated?

The short-run Phillips curve may be relatively shallow to the right of U_n. The more sticky downwards wages and prices are in the short run, the shallower the curve will be. Thus to get a relatively rapid fall in inflation, unemployment may have to be very high indeed.

According to the adaptive expectations model, there are two alternative routes to eliminating inflation.

The quick route. This involves a *severe* contraction. Unemployment rises to very high rates and the economy is plunged into a deep recession. However, the short-run Phillips curve shifts down fairly rapidly as the expected rate of inflation (π^e) falls quite quickly. Inflation may be squeezed out of the economy within two or three years. This approach could be called the 'short, sharp shock'.

The slow route. This involves a *mild* contraction. Unemployment rises perhaps one or two percentage points above the natural rate. Inflation falls only slightly in the first year, and thus π^e falls only slowly the next year and each subsequent year. Although less painful, this approach may take many years to eliminate inflation.

Explanations of stagflation

In the 1970s, many countries experienced 'stagflation' – the simultaneous rise in both unemployment and inflation. Monetarists used the adaptive expectations model to explain why this occurred. The explanation involved clockwise loops and rightward shifts in the long-run Phillips curve.

Clockwise Phillips loops

Consider a ten-year cycle. This is illustrated in Figure 20.14. The economy starts at position *a* in year 0. There is no inflation and the economy is at the natural rate of unemployment. The government over the next three years pursues an expansionary policy in order to reduce unemployment. The economy moves up through points *b*, *c* and *d*.

The government then starts worrying about inflation. It allows unemployment to rise somewhat, but being still

Figure 20.14 Clockwise Phillips loops

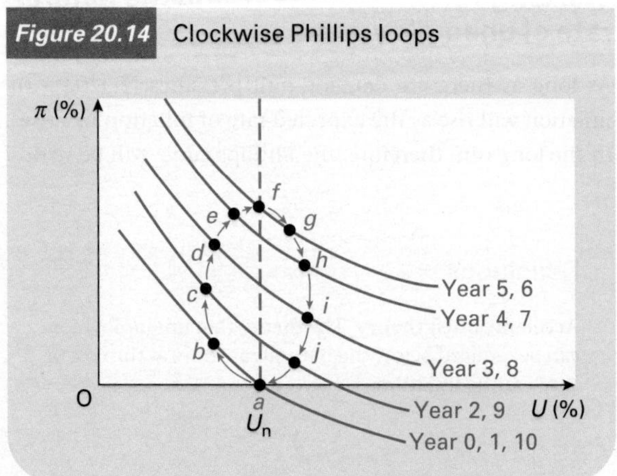

below U_n, there is still demand-pull inflation. The economy moves to point *e*. The government now allows unemployment to rise to U_n, but the Phillips curve still shifts up as expectations catch up with last year's inflation. The economy moves from point *e* to point *f*.

Thereafter the government allows unemployment to rise further, and the economy eventually returns to point *a*, via points *g*, *h*, *i* and *j*. The economy has thus moved through a clockwise loop.

Stagflation is easy to see. From points *d* to *f*, both unemployment *and* inflation are rising. What is more, several points are to the 'north-east' of other earlier points. For example, point *g* is north-east of point *c*. In other words, inflation *and* unemployment in year 6 (point *g*) are worse than in year 2 (point *c*).

? *Under what circumstances would a Phillips loop be (a) tall and thin; (b) short and wide?*

Rightward shifts in the long-run Phillips curve

If frictional or structural unemployment rises (due, say, to increased unemployment benefits), U_n will increase. The long-run Phillips curve will shift to the right.

Assume that the economy was initially on the long-run Phillips curve with $U_n = 8$ per cent and a stable inflation rate of 5 per cent. U_n now rises to 12 per cent. The government uses demand management policy to keep the rise in unemployment to only 10 per cent. But this is now *below* U_n and thus inflation will increase. Thus both inflation *and* unemployment have risen.

Evidence

The evidence for the UK since 1967 is consistent with the adaptive expectations model. (But note that it is consistent with other explanations too!) In Figure 20.15 loops can clearly be seen up to around 1993, when inflation targeting

Figure 20.15 Phillips loops in the UK?

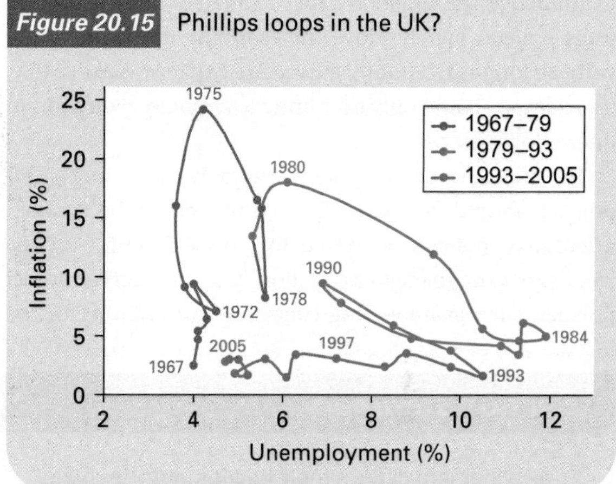

CASE STUDIES AND APPLICATIONS **BOX 20.4**

THE POLITICAL BUSINESS CYCLE (PART II)[2]

The art of looping the loop

Imagine that a politically naïve government has been fulfilling election promises to reduce unemployment, cut taxes and increase welfare spending. In Figure 20.14 this is shown by a move from points *a* to *b* to *c*.

To its dismay, by the time the next election comes, inflation is accelerating and unemployment is rising again. The economy is moving from point *d* to *e* to *f*. You would hardly be surprised to learn that it loses the election!

But now suppose a much more politically adroit government is elected. What does it do? The answer is that it does politically unpopular things at first, so that before the next election it can do nice things and curry favour with the electorate.

The first thing it does is to have a tough Budget. 'We are having to clear up the economic mess left by the last government.' It thus engineers a recession and begins to squeeze down inflationary expectations. The economy moves from point *f* to *g* to *h*.

But people have very short memories (despite opposition attempts to remind them). After a couple of years of misery, the government announces that the economy has 'begun to turn the corner'. Things are looking up. Inflation has fallen and unemployment has stopped rising. The economy has moved from point *h* to *i* to *j*.

'Thanks to prudent management of the economy', claims the Chancellor, 'I am now in a position to reduce taxes and to allow modest increases in government expenditure.' Unemployment falls rapidly; the economy grows rapidly; the economy moves from point *j* to *a* to *b*.

The government's popularity soars; the pre-election 'give-away' Budget is swallowed by the electorate who trustingly believe that similar ones will follow if the government is returned to office. The government wins the election.

Then comes the nasty medicine again. But who will be blamed this time?

?

1. ***Why might a government sometimes 'get it wrong' and find itself at the wrong part of the Phillips loop at the time of an election?***
2. ***Which electoral system would most favour a government being re-elected: the US fixed-term system with presidents being elected every four years, or the UK system where the government can choose to hold an election any time within five years of the last one?***

[2] See Box 14.7 on page 425 for part I.

began (see sections 18.4 and 19.5). At the same time, U_n would seem to have increased from about 4.5 per cent in the mid-1970s to around 11 per cent in the mid-1980s, and to have fallen to about 8 per cent in the late 1980s/early 1990s and to about 5 per cent in the mid-2000s.

Policy implications

The implications of the expectations-augmented Phillips curve are that monetary or fiscal policy can have no *long-run* effect on unemployment. They can only be used to influence the inflation rate. Ultimately, monetary and fiscal policies merely move the economy up or down the vertical long-run Phillips curve. An expansionary policy, for example, could only ever bring a *temporary* reduction in unemployment below U_n.

To reduce unemployment permanently, *supply-side* policies should be used. These could either be market-orientated policies of removing impediments to the working of the market (see section 22.2) or interventionist policies, such as improving education and training or the country's transport and communications infrastructure (see section 22.3). By reducing frictional and/or structural unemployment, such policies will shift the long-run Phillips curve back to the left.

Limitations of the adaptive expectations hypothesis

The adaptive expectations hypothesis suffers from a serious flaw: it assumes that people base their expectations on the past. So if inflation is on an upward trend, the future of inflation will always be underestimated. Similarly, inflation will always be overestimated if it is on a downward trend. Thus people will normally be wrong.

But people will soon realise that it is not rational to base their expectations blindly on the past. They will look at the *current* situation and what is likely to affect inflation. Thus, it is argued, adaptive expectations cannot be a rational basis of behaviour. An alternative view of price expectations was subsequently developed. We look at it in the next section.

Section summary

1. A refinement of the simple Phillips curve involves the incorporation of people's expectations about the rate of inflation. This gives an expectations-augmented Phillips curve. One explanation of how people form these expectations is given by the adaptive expectations hypothesis. In its simplest form, the hypothesis states that the expected rate of inflation this year is what it actually was last year: $\pi^e_t = \pi_{t-1}$.
2. If there is excess demand in the economy, producing upward pressure on wages and prices, initially unemployment will fall. The reason is that workers and firms will believe that wage and price increases represent *real* wage and price increases respectively. Thus workers are prepared to take jobs more readily and firms choose to produce more. But as people's expectations adapt upwards to these higher wages and prices, so ever-increasing rises in nominal aggregate demand will be necessary to maintain unemployment below the natural rate. Price and wage rises will accelerate: i.e. inflation will rise.
3. The Phillips curve, according to this analysis, is thus vertical at the natural rate of unemployment.
4. If an economy suffering from high inflation is deflated, initially unemployment will rise above the natural rate. But as expectations adapt downwards, so the short-run Phillips curve will shift downwards and inflation will fall. Eventually the economy will return to zero inflation at the natural rate of unemployment.
5. This position can be reached more quickly if the government deflates sharply, but then in the short run the rate of unemployment may rise substantially above the natural rate.
6. Stagflation can be explained in this model either by a movement from 9 o'clock to 12 o'clock round a clockwise Phillips loop, or by a rightward shift in the vertical Phillips curve combined with a mild expansionary policy.
7. The weakness of the adaptive expectations hypothesis is that people do not just base expectations of inflation on the past. They are also likely to base them on *current* events and conditions.

20.3 INFLATION AND UNEMPLOYMENT: THE NEW CLASSICAL POSITION

Economists of the ***new classical school*** conclude that the aggregate supply curve and Phillips curve are vertical not only in the long run, but in the short run too. Thus demand management can have no effect on output and employment even in the short run. The only likely effect of a rise in aggregate demand will be a rise in prices.

Definition

New classical school The school of economists which believes that markets clear virtually instantaneously and that expectations are formed 'rationally'.

There are two crucial assumptions in new classical macroeconomics:

- Prices and wages are flexible, and thus markets clear very rapidly.
- Expectations are 'rational', but are based on imperfect information.

Flexible wages and prices

New classical economists assume that markets clear virtually instantaneously. This is likely, they argue, in modern economies with flexible labour markets (see Box 9.8 on page 246) and facing global competition. There is thus no disequilibrium unemployment, even in the short run. All unemployment, therefore, is *equilibrium* unemployment, or 'voluntary unemployment' as new classical economists tend to call it. Increases in unemployment are therefore due to an increase in the natural level of unemployment, as people choose not to take jobs due to a lack of incentives to do so.

TC 10 p294 TC 3 p21

Rational expectations

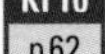

The analysis of the previous section was based on *adaptive* expectations. Expectations of inflation are based on *past* information and therefore take a time to catch up with changes in aggregate demand. Thus, for a short time, a rise in aggregate demand will raise output and employment above the natural level, while prices and wages are still relatively low.

The new classical analysis is based on ***rational expectations***. Rational expectations are not based on past rates of inflation. Instead they are based on the current state of the economy and the current policies being pursued by the government. Workers and firms look at the information available to them – at the various forecasts that are published, at various economic indicators and the assessments of them by various commentators, at government pronouncements, and so on. From this information they predict the rate of inflation as well as they can. It is in this sense that the expectations are 'rational': people use their reason to assess the future on the basis of current information.

But forecasters frequently get it wrong, and so do economic commentators! And the government does not always do what it says it will. Thus workers and firms base their expectations on *imperfect information*. Other versions assume that they may make very poor use of information. But either way, people frequently forecast incorrectly. The crucial point about the rational expectations theory, however, is that these errors in prediction are *random*. People's predictions of inflation are just as likely to be too high as too low.[3]

Definition

Rational expectations Expectations based on the current situation. These expectations are based on the information people have to hand. While this information may be imperfect and therefore people will make errors, these errors will be random.

Aggregate supply and the Phillips curve when expectations are correct

If people are correct in their expectations, and if the long-run aggregate supply and Phillips curves are vertical, so too will be the short-run curves. In the adaptive expectations model, the short-run *AS* curve is upward sloping (and the short-run Phillips curve downward sloping) only because expectations lag behind any changes in aggregate demand. Once expectations have adapted, the effect is felt purely in terms of price changes. Output and employment stay at the natural level in the long run.

In the new classical (rational expectations) model, there is *no* lag in expectations. If their information is correct, people will rationally predict that output and employment will stay at the natural level. They predict that any change in *nominal* aggregate demand will be reflected purely in terms of changes in prices, and that real aggregate demand will remain the same. If real aggregate demand remains the same, so will the demand for and supply of labour and the demand for and supply of goods. Thus, even in the *short* run, output and employment will stay at the natural level. TC 12 p374

Let us see how the adaptive expectations and the rational expectations models analyse the effects of an increase in aggregate demand. Figure 20.16 uses simple aggregate demand and supply curves. Diagram (a) gives the adaptive expectations analysis. Diagram (b) gives the rational expectations analysis.

In both diagrams, there is an initial equilibrium at point *a*. This is a long-run equilibrium, where aggregate demand (AD_1) equals long-run aggregate supply (*LRAS*). Price is stable and is at the level of P_1. The short-run supply curve with P_1 as the *expected* price level is given by $SRAS_1$. Note that this is upward sloping in *both* diagrams because it shows how much will be supplied *if* (and only if) people expect price to remain at P_1.

Now assume that the government raises aggregate demand to AD_2. What will happen to prices and output?

In Figure 20.16(a), people base their expectations of prices on the past. In other words, at first they expect the price level to stay at P_1. The economy thus moves to point *b*, where $AD_2 = SRAS_1$. Output rises to Q_2 and the price level rises to P_2. Then over time, as price expectations rise, the

[3] The rational expectations hypothesis can be stated as:

$$\pi_t = \pi_t^e + \epsilon_t \left(\sum_{t=1}^{t=\infty} \epsilon = 0 \right)$$

In other words, the rate of inflation for any time period (π_t) will be the rate that people expected in that time period (π_t^e) plus an error term (ϵ_t). This error term may be quite large but is equally likely to be positive or negative. Thus when you sum (Σ) the error terms over the years (strictly speaking, to infinity), the positive and negative values will cancel each other out and the sum will therefore be zero.

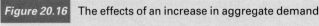

Figure 20.16 The effects of an increase in aggregate demand

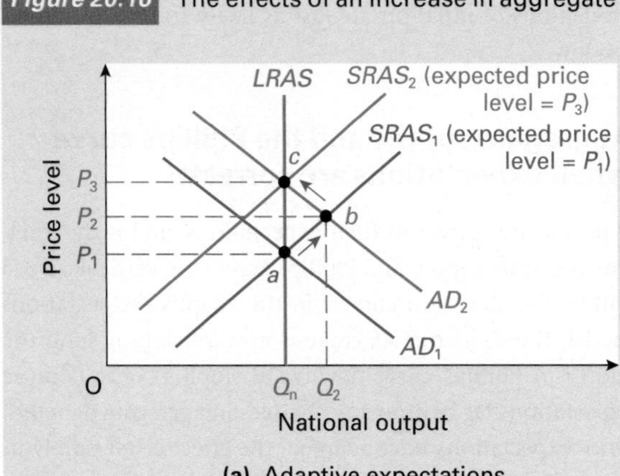

(a) Adaptive expectations

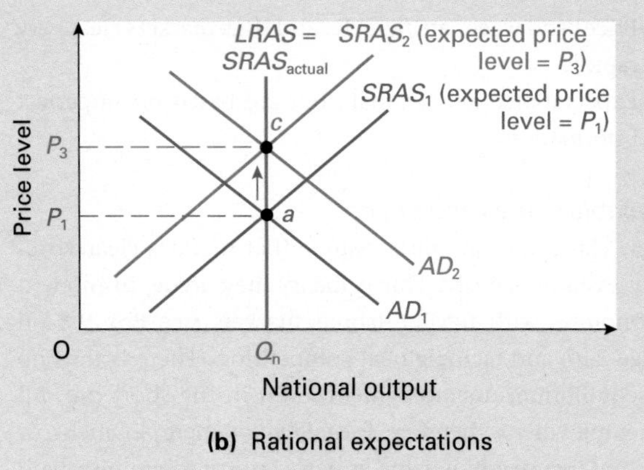

(b) Rational expectations

short-run aggregate supply curve shifts upwards, eventually reaching $SRAS_2$. Long-run equilibrium is thus at point *c*, where $AD_2 = LRAS$. In the short run, therefore, if the government expands aggregate demand, there will be a rise in output and employment. It is only in the long run that the effect is confined to higher prices. The actual length of time it takes to reach point *c* will depend on how quickly expectations adjust upwards.

In Figure 20.16(b), people correctly anticipate the full price effects of any increase in aggregate demand. The

EXPLORING ECONOMICS — BOX 20.5

THE RATIONAL EXPECTATIONS REVOLUTION

Trying to 'unfool' the economics profession

The rational expectations revolution swept through the economics profession in the 1970s in a way that no other set of ideas had done since Keynes. Although largely associated with the free-market, non-interventionist wing of economics, the rational expectations revolution has been far more wide reaching. Even economists implacably opposed to the free market have nevertheless incorporated rational expectations into their models.

The rational expectations revolution is founded on a very simple idea. People base their expectations of the future on the information they have available. They don't just look at the past, they also look at current information, including what the government is saying and doing and what various commentators have to say.

The new classical economists use rational expectations in the following context. If the *long-run* Phillips curve is vertical, so that an expansionary policy will in the end merely lead to inflation, it will be difficult for the government to fool people that this will not happen. If employers, unions, city financiers, economic advisers, journalists, etc. all expect this to happen, then it will: and it will happen in the *short run*. Why should firms produce more in response to a rise in demand if their costs are going to rise by just as much? Why should higher wages attract workers to move jobs, if wages everywhere are going up? Why should firms and unions not seek price and wage rises fully in line with the expected inflation?

But can the government not surprise people? The point here is that 'surprising' people really only means 'fooling' them – making them believe that an expansionary policy really *will* reduce unemployment. But why should the public be fooled? Why should people believe smooth-talking government ministers rather than the whole host of critics of the government, from the opposition, to economic commentators, to the next-door neighbour?

The rational expectations school revised the old saying, 'You can't fool all the people all the time' to 'You can hardly fool the people at all.' And if that is so, argue the new classical economists, unemployment can only momentarily be brought below its natural level.

Two of the most famous rational expectations economists are Robert Lucas and Thomas Sargent. Robert Lucas, like Milton Friedman and many other famous conservative economists, has his academic base in the University of Chicago, where he has been a professor since 1974. In 1995, like Milton Friedman in 1976, Lucas was awarded the Nobel prize in economics. Tom Sargent is professor of Economics at New York University and senior fellow at the Hoover Institution of Stanford University.

In recent years, they have gone beyond the simple context of the new classical world of perfect markets with instant market clearing, and have considered the role of rational expectations when markets are distorted. In this context, government policy *can* be effective. For example, supply-side policies can be directed to removing market distortions.

CASE STUDIES AND APPLICATIONS — BOX 20.6

FORECASTING THE WEATHER

An example of rational expectations

'What's the weather going to be like tomorrow?' If you are thinking of having a picnic, you will want to know the answer before deciding.

So what do you do? You could base your assessment on past information. Yesterday was fine; so was the previous day. Today is glorious. So, you think to yourself, it's a good bet that tomorrow will be fine too. If, on the other hand, the weather has been very changeable recently, you may feel that it's wiser not to take the risk. These 'forecasts' are examples of *adaptive* expectations: your forecasts are based on the actual weather over the last few days.

But would you really base such a crucial decision as to whether or not to have a picnic on something so unreliable? Wouldn't you rather take on board more information to help you make up your mind?

The first thing that might come to mind is the old saying that a British summer is three fine days and a thunder storm. We've just had the three fine days, you think to yourself, so perhaps we'd better stay at home tomorrow.

Or, being a bit more scientific about it, you turn on the weather forecast. Seeing loads of sunshine symbols all over the map, you decide to take a chance.

Basing your expectations in this way on current information (including even seeing whether there is a red sky that night) is an example of *rational* expectations.

So you go on your picnic and, guess what, it rains! 'I bet if we had decided to stay at home, it would have been fine', you grumble, as you eat your soggy sandwiches.

What you are acknowledging is that your decision was made on *imperfect* information. But the decision was still rational. It was still the best decision you could have made on the information available to you.

Weather forecasters make mistakes. But they are just as likely to get it wrong in predicting a sunny day as in predicting a wet day. It is still rational to base your decisions on their forecasts provided they are reasonably accurate.

Under what circumstances might weather forecasters have a tendency to err on the side of pessimism or optimism? If you knew this tendency, how would this affect your decisions about picnics, hanging out the washing or watering the garden?

short-run aggregate supply curve based on a particular price (e.g. $SRAS_1$ based on a price level P_1) cannot be moved along. The moment aggregate demand shifts to the right, people will correctly anticipate a rise in the price level. Thus the moment the economy begins to move up along $SRAS_1$ from point *a*, the whole *SRAS* curve will shift upwards. As a result, the economy moves *directly* to point *c*. Thus the *actual* short-run supply curve is vertical and, assuming expectations are correct, will be identical to the long-run 'curve'.

Show these effects of an increase in aggregate demand from both the adaptive expectations and rational expectations points of view, only this time show the effects on Phillips curves.

Aggregate supply and the Phillips curve when expectations are incorrect

Although over the years people's expectations are assumed to be correct on average, it is more than likely that in any one year they will be wrong. What implication does this have for output and employment?

The goods market

Assume that aggregate demand increases but that firms *under*predict the resulting rate of inflation: $\pi^e < \pi$. Firms do not realise that the increased expenditure on their product will be offset by an increase in costs. As a result, as profit maximisers, they decide to produce more. Thus if the government catches people unawares and unexpectedly boosts demand, then output will rise as firms, underpredicting the rate of inflation, believe that *real* demand has risen.

But in a rational expectations framework, this is just luck on the government's side. Firms might just as well have thought the government would give an even bigger boost to aggregate demand than it actually did. In this case, firms would have *over*predicted the rate of inflation, and as a result would have cut their output, believing that real demand had fallen. (A graphical analysis of these arguments is given in Web Case 20.3.)

The labour market

Let us assume that the government raises aggregate demand more than people expect, so that people underpredict the rate of inflation: $\pi^e < \pi$.

This means that workers will believe that they are getting a higher real wage (W/P) than they really are: $(W/P)^e > W/P$. They will supply more labour. In Figure 20.17, the labour supply curve shifts from AS_{L_1} to AS_{L_2}. Employment rises above the natural level Q_1 (where expectations are correct), to Q_2. If only labour (and not firms) underpredict the rate of inflation, this rise in employment to Q_2 is the only short-run effect.

Figure 20.17 Effects in the labour market of an underprediction of inflation

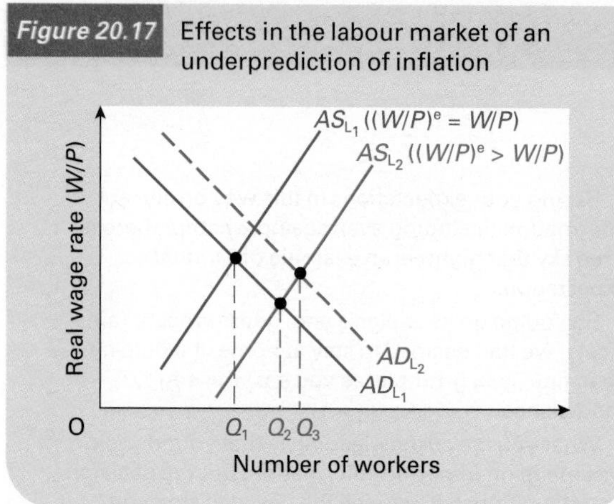

Figure 20.18 Short-run Phillips curves

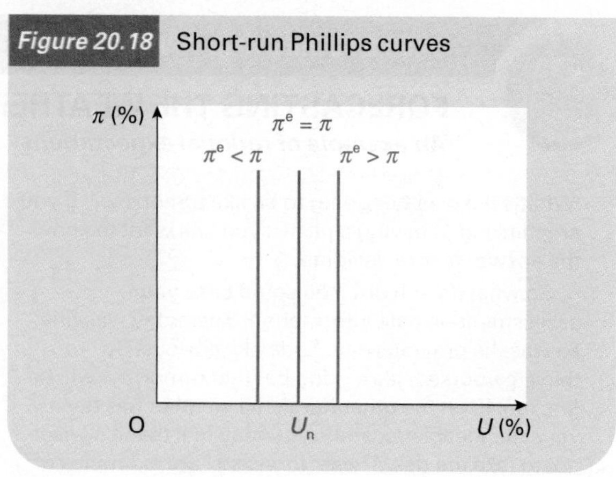

If, however, firms underpredict the rate of inflation too, the effect on employment will be more complicated. On the one level, as explained above, firms will want to produce more, and thus the demand for labour will tend to increase. For example, it might shift to AD_{L_2} in Figure 20.17, and thus employment would rise to Q_3. On the other hand, given that they are underpredicting the rate of inflation, they will believe that any given level of money wages (W) represents a higher level of *real* wages $(W/P)^e$ than it really does (W/P). They will tend, therefore, to employ fewer people at each wage rate, and the demand curve will shift to the left. Thus, depending on which way the demand curve shifts, firms could employ more or less labour than Q_2.

If people *over*predict the rate of inflation, employment will fall as workers believe that their real wage is lower than it really is and therefore work less; and output may well fall as firms believe their product's relative price has fallen.

Thus output and employment can vary from their natural level when people make errors in their predictions of inflation. But the short-run *AS* and Phillips curves will still be vertical because these errors are random. Errors in prediction simply shift the curves. This is shown in Figure 20.18. Underprediction of inflation shifts the short-run Phillips curve to the left (and the *AS* curve to the right) as unemployment temporarily falls below the natural level (and output rises above its natural level). Overprediction of inflation shifts the Phillips curve to the right (and the *AS* curve to the left). The average position for the short-run Phillips curve will be at U_n.

? *Should the government therefore simply give up as far as curing unemployment is concerned? (For the answer, see below.)*

Policy implications

If the new classical analysis is correct, anticipated changes in aggregate demand will have no effect on output and employment. *Un*anticipated changes in aggregate demand will have some effect, but only for as long as it takes people to realise their mistake and for their wages and prices to be corrected. Given rational expectations, people can be fooled in this way only by luck. There is no way that a government can *systematically* use demand management policy to keep output and employment above the natural level.

The new classical economists therefore totally reject Keynesian demand management policy, even in the short run. Monetary policy should be used to control inflation, but neither fiscal nor monetary policy can be used to increase output and employment. Similarly, there is no fear of a deflationary monetary policy reducing output and employment and leading to a recession. The reduction in aggregate demand will simply lead to lower inflation. Output and unemployment will remain at the natural level.

Thus for new classicists, the problems of inflation and unemployment are totally separate. Inflation is caused by excessive growth in the money supply and should be controlled by monetary policy. Unemployment will be at the natural rate and should be reduced by supply-side policies designed to increase the incentives to work.

To prevent unanticipated changes in aggregate demand and thus to prevent unemployment deviating from its natural level, new classical economists advocate the announcement of clear monetary rules and then sticking to them.

?

1. *If the government announced that it would, come what may, reduce the growth of money supply to zero next year, what (according to new classical economists) would happen? How might their answer be criticised?*
2. *For what reasons would a new classical economist support the policy of the Bank of England publishing its inflation forecasts and the minutes of the deliberations of the Monetary Policy Committee?*

Real business cycles

If unemployment and output fluctuate only *randomly* from the natural level, and then only in the short run, how can the new classical economists explain booms and

CASE STUDIES AND APPLICATIONS | BOX 20.7

THE BOY WHO CRIED WOLF

A government had better mean what it says

Do you remember the parable of the boy who cried, 'Wolf!'?

There was once this little village on the edge of the forest. The villagers used to keep chickens, but, when no one was around, wolves would come out of the forest and carry off the chickens. So one of the boys in the village was given the job of keeping a lookout for wolves.

One day for a joke the boy called out, 'Wolf, wolf! I see a wolf!' even though there was none. All the villagers came rushing out of their houses or back from the fields to catch the wolf. As you might expect, they were very angry to find that it was a false alarm.

The next day, thinking that this was great fun, the boy played the same trick again. Everyone came rushing out, and they were even more angry to find that they had been fooled again. But the boy just grinned.

The next day, when everyone was away in the fields, a wolf stalked into the village. The boy, spotting the animal, cried out 'Wolf, wolf! I see a wolf!' But the people in the fields said to each other, 'We're not going to be fooled this time. We've had enough of his practical jokes.' And so they carried on working. Meanwhile, back in the village, the wolf was killing all the chickens.

You can probably guess what the villagers said when they returned in the evening to find just a large pile of feathers.

A government says, 'We will take tough action to bring the rate of inflation down to 2 per cent.' Now of course this might be a 'joke' in the sense that the government doesn't really expect to succeed or even seriously to try, but is merely attempting to persuade unions to curb their wage demands. But if unions *believe* in both the government's intentions and its ability to succeed, the 'joke' may pay off. Some unions may well moderate their pay demands.

But some may not. What is more, the government may decide to give tax cuts to boost its popularity and stimulate growth, knowing that union pay demands are generally quite moderate. As a result, inflation soars.

But can the government get away with it a second or third time? It's like the boy who cried, 'Wolf!' After a time, people will simply not believe the government. If they see the government boosting aggregate demand, they will say to themselves, 'Here comes inflation. We'd better demand higher wages to compensate.'

Does this parable support the adaptive or the rational expectations hypothesis?

recessions? How can they explain the business cycle? Their answer, unlike Keynesians, lies not in fluctuations in aggregate demand. Rather it lies in shifts in aggregate *supply*. In a recession, the vertical short- and long-run aggregate supply curves will shift to the left (output falls) and the vertical short- and long-run Phillips curves will shift to the right (unemployment rises). The reverse happens in a boom. Since the new classical theory of cyclical fluctuations focuses on supply, it is known as ***real business cycle theory***.

But what makes aggregate supply shift in the first place, and why, after an initial shift, will the aggregate supply curve *go on* shifting, causing a recession or boom to continue?

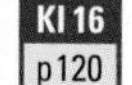

KI 16 p120

The initial shift in aggregate supply could come from a structural change: say, a shift in demand from older manufacturing industries to new service industries. Because of the immobility of labour, not all those laid off in the older industries will find work in the new industries. Structural unemployment (part of equilibrium unemployment) rises and output falls. *Aggregate* demand may be the same, but because of a change in its pattern, aggregate supply shifts to the left and the (vertical) Phillips curve shifts to the right.

Alternatively, the initial shift in aggregate supply could come from a change in technology. For example, a technological breakthrough in telecommunications could shift aggregate supply to the right. Or it could come from an oil price increase, shifting aggregate supply to the left.

But why, when a shift occurs, does the effect persist? Why is there not a single rise or fall in aggregate supply? There are two main reasons. The first is that several changes may take months to complete. For example, a decline in demand for certain older industries, perhaps caused by growing competition from abroad, does not take place overnight. Likewise, a technological breakthrough does not affect all industries simultaneously.

The second reason is that these changes affect the profitability of investment. If investment rises, this will increase firms' capacity and aggregate supply will shift to the right. If investment falls (as a result, say, of the election of a government less sympathetic to industry), aggregate supply will shift to the left. In other words, investment is causing changes in output not through its effect on aggregate *demand* (through the multiplier), but rather through its effect on aggregate *supply*.

Definition

Real business cycle theory The new classical theory which explains cyclical fluctuations in terms of shifts in aggregate supply, rather than aggregate demand.

So far we have seen how the theory of real business cycles explains persistent rises or falls in aggregate supply. But how does it explain *turning points*? Why do recessions and booms come to an end? The most likely explanation is that once a shock has worked its way through, aggregate supply will stop shifting. If there is then any shock in the other direction, aggregate supply will start moving back again. For example, after a period of recession, an eventual rise in business confidence will cause investment to rise and hence aggregate supply to shift back to the right. Since these 'reverse shocks' are likely to occur at irregular intervals, they can help to explain why real-world business cycles are themselves irregular.

?

Assume that there are two shocks. The first causes aggregate supply to shift to the left. The second, occurring several months later, has the opposite effect on aggregate supply. Show that if both these effects persist for some time, but gradually fade away, the economy will experience a recession that will bottom out and be followed in smooth succession by a recovery.

Section summary

1. The new classical theory assumes flexible prices and wages in the short run as well as in the long run. It also assumes that people base their expectations of inflation on a rational assessment of the *current* situation.
2. People may predict wrongly, but they are equally likely to underpredict or to overpredict. On average, over the years, they will predict correctly.
3. The rational expectations theory implies that not only the long-run but also the short-run *AS* and Phillips curves will be vertical. If people correctly predict the rate of inflation, they will correctly predict that any increase in nominal aggregate demand will simply be reflected in higher prices. Total output and employment will remain the same: at the natural level.
4. If people underpredict the rate of inflation, they will believe that there has been a *real* increase in aggregate demand, and thus output and employment will increase. But they are just as likely to overpredict the rate of inflation, in which case they will believe that real aggregate demand has fallen. The result is that output and employment will fall.
5. When the government adopts fiscal and monetary policies, people will rationally predict their effects. Given that people's predictions are equally likely to err on either side, fiscal and monetary policies are useless as means of controlling output and employment.
6. With a vertical aggregate supply curve, cyclical fluctuations must arise from shifts in aggregate supply, not shifts in aggregate demand. Real business cycle theory thus focuses on aggregate supply shocks, which then persist for a period of time. Eventually their effect will peter out, and supply shocks in the other direction can lead to turning points in the cycle.

20.4 INFLATION AND UNEMPLOYMENT: THE MODERN KEYNESIAN POSITION

Keynesians in the 1950s and early 1960s looked to aggregate demand to explain inflation and unemployment. Their approach was typically that of the inflationary/deflationary gap model. Although they recognised the existence of some cost-push inflation and some equilibrium unemployment, these factors were seen as relatively constant. As a result, there was thought to be a relatively stable inverse relationship between inflation and unemployment, as depicted by the Phillips curve. Governments could trade off inflation against unemployment by manipulating aggregate demand.

Modern developments of the Keynesian model

Keynesians still see aggregate demand as playing the crucial role in determining the level of inflation, output and employment. They still argue that the free market works inefficiently: it frequently fails to clear; price signals are distorted by economic power; most wages and many prices are 'sticky'; and most important, the free market is unlikely to settle at full employment.

They still argue, therefore, that it is vital for governments to intervene actively to prevent either a slump in demand or an overexpansion of demand.

Nevertheless the Keynesian position has undergone some major modifications in recent years. This has been in response to apparent shifts in the Phillips curve and the inability of the traditional Keynesian model to explain it.

The breakdown of the Phillips curve in the 1970s and the growing problem of 'stagflation' (see page 559) led many Keynesians to focus on cost-push causes of inflation. These causes included increased power and militancy of trade unions, a growing concentration of monopoly power in industry, and rising oil and other commodity prices. The effect was to push the short-run Phillips curve outwards.

Later, with a decline in industrial unrest in the 1990s and a growth of international competition keeping prices down, the Phillips curve apparently shifted inwards again. Keynesians attributed this partly to a *decline* in cost-push inflation. (These cost-push explanations are examined in Web Case 20.4.)

More recently, Keynesian analysis has incorporated three major modifications.

- An increased importance attached to equilibrium unemployment.
- A rationale for the persistence of demand-deficient unemployment.
- The incorporation of the theory of expectations: either adaptive or rational.

The growth in equilibrium unemployment

Higher structural unemployment

Most Keynesians include growth in equilibrium unemployment (NAIRU) as part of the explanation of the apparent rightward shift in the Phillips curve in the 1970s and 1980s. In particular, Keynesians highlight the considerable structural rigidities in the economy in a period of rapid industrial change. The changes include the following:

- Dramatic changes in technology. The microchip revolution, for example, made many traditional jobs obsolete.
- Competition from abroad. The introduction of new products from abroad, often of superior quality to domestic goods, or produced at lower costs, had led to the decline of many older industries: e.g. the textile industry.
- Shifts in demand away from the products of older labour-intensive industries to new 'high-tech' capital-intensive products.

Keynesians argue that the free market simply could not cope with these changes without a large rise in structural/technological unemployment. Labour is not sufficiently mobile – either geographically or occupationally – to move to areas where there are labour shortages or into jobs where there are skill shortages. A particular problem here is the lack of investment in education and training, with the result that the labour force is not sufficiently flexible to respond to changes in demand for labour.

?

1. *What effect will these developments have had on (a) the Phillips curve; (b) the aggregate supply curve?*
2. *What policy implications follow from these arguments?*

Hysteresis

If a recession causes a rise in unemployment which is not then fully reversed when the economy recovers, there is a problem of hysteresis (see page 578).

The recessions of the early 1980s and early 1990s created a growing number of people who were both deskilled and demotivated. Many in their forties and fifties who had lost their jobs were seen as too old by prospective employers. Many young people, unable to obtain jobs, became resigned to 'life on social security' or to doing no more than casual work. What is more, many firms, in an attempt to cut costs, cut down on training programmes. In these circumstances, a rise in aggregate demand again will not simply enable the long-term unemployed to be employed again. The effect has been a rightward shift in the Phillips curve: a rise in the NAIRU. To reverse this, argue Keynesians, the government should embark on a radical programme of retraining.

Recessions also cause a lack of investment. The reduction in their capital stock means that many firms cannot respond to a recovery in demand by making significant increases in output and taking on many more workers. Instead they are more likely to raise prices. Unemployment may thus fall only modestly and yet inflation may rise substantially. The NAIRU has increased: the Phillips curve has shifted to the right.

The persistence of demand-deficient unemployment

If there is demand-deficient unemployment, why will there not be a long-run fall in real wage rates so as to eliminate the surplus labour? Keynesians give two major explanations for the persistence of real wage rates above equilibrium.

Efficiency wages. The argument here is that wage rates fulfil two functions. The first is the traditional one of balancing the demand and supply of labour. To this Keynesians add the function of motivating workers. If real wage rates are reduced when there is a surplus of labour (demand-deficient unemployment), then those workers already in employment may become dispirited and work less hard. If, on the other hand, firms keep wage rates up, then by maintaining a well-motivated workforce, by cutting down on labour turnover and by finding it easier to attract well-qualified labour, firms may find their costs are reduced: a higher real wage rate is thus more profitable for them. The maximum-profit real wage rate (the ***efficiency wage rate***) is likely to be above the market-clearing real wage rate. Demand-deficient unemployment is likely to persist.

Insider power. If those still in employment (the insiders) are members of unions while those out of work (the

Definition

Efficiency wage rate The profit-maximising wage rate for the firm after taking into account the effects of wage rates on worker motivation, turnover and recruitment.

outsiders) are not, or if the insiders have special skills or knowledge that give them bargaining power with employers while the outsiders have no influence, then there is no mechanism whereby the surplus labour – the outsiders – can drive down the real wage rate and eliminate the demand-deficient unemployment.

These two features help to explain why real wage rates did not fall during the recessions of the early 1980s and early 1990s.

The incorporation of expectations

KI 10 p62

Some Keynesians incorporate adaptive expectations into their models. Others incorporate rational expectations. Either way, their models differ from new classical models in two important respects:

- Prices and wages are not perfectly flexible. Markets are characterised by various rigidities.
- Expectations influence *output* and *employment* decisions, not just pricing decisions.

Price and wage rigidities are likely to be greater downwards than upwards. It is thus necessary to separate the analysis of a decrease in aggregate demand from that of an increase.

Expansion of aggregate demand

Unless the economy is at full employment or very close to it, Keynesians argue that an expansion of demand *will* lead to an increase in output and employment, even in the long run after expectations have fully adjusted.

In Figure 20.19, assume that the economy has a fairly high level of unemployment (U_1) but at the same time some cost inflation. Inflation is constant at π_1, with expectations of inflation at π_1 also. The economy is at point *a*.

Now assume that the economy begins to recover. Aggregate demand rises. As there is plenty of slack in the economy, output can rise and unemployment fall. The economy moves to point *b* on short-run Phillips curve I.

Figure 20.19 The Keynesian analysis of reflationary policies

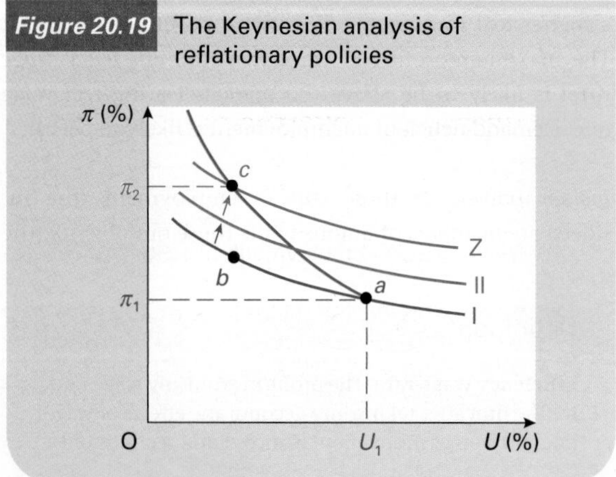

The rise in inflation will feed through into expectations. The short-run Phillips curve will shift upwards. With adaptive expectations, it will initially shift up, say, to curve II.

But will the short-run Phillips curve not go on shifting upwards as long as there is any upward pressure on inflation? Keynesians reject this argument for two reasons:

- If there is a gradual but sustained expansion of aggregate demand, firms, seeing the economy expanding and seeing their orders growing, will start to invest more and make longer-term plans for expanding their labour force. People will generally *expect* a higher level of output, and this optimism will cause that higher level of output to be produced. In other words, expectations will affect output and employment as well as prices. The Phillips curve will shift downwards to the left, offsetting (partially, wholly or more than wholly) the upward shift from higher inflationary expectations.
- If U_1 includes a considerable number of long-term unemployed, then the expansion of demand may be *initially* inflationary, since many of the newly employed will require some retraining (a costly exercise). But as these newly employed workers become more productive, their lower labour costs may offset any further upward pressure on wages from the expansion of demand. At the same time, the higher investment may embody new, more productive, techniques that will also help to prevent further acceleration in costs.

It is quite likely that these effects can prevent any further rises in inflation. Inflation can become stable at, say, π_2, with the economy operating at point *c*. The short-run Phillips curve settles at position Z. There is thus a long-run downward-sloping Phillips curve passing through points *a* and *c*.

Would it in theory be possible for this long-run Phillips curve to be horizontal or even upward sloping over part of its length?

If expectations are formed rationally rather than adaptively, there will merely be a quicker movement to this long-run equilibrium. If people rationally predict that the effect of government policy will be to move the economy to point *c*, then their predictions will bring this about. All rational expectations do is to bring the long run about much sooner! The theory of rational expectations on its own does not provide support specifically for either the new classical or the Keynesian position.

The lesson here for governments, however expectations are formed, is that a sustained, but moderate, increase in aggregate demand can lead to a sustained growth in aggregate supply. What should be avoided is an excessive and unsustainable expansion of aggregate demand, as occurred in the late 1980s in the UK and the late 1990s in the USA. This will lead to a boom, only to be followed by a 'bust' and a consequent recession.

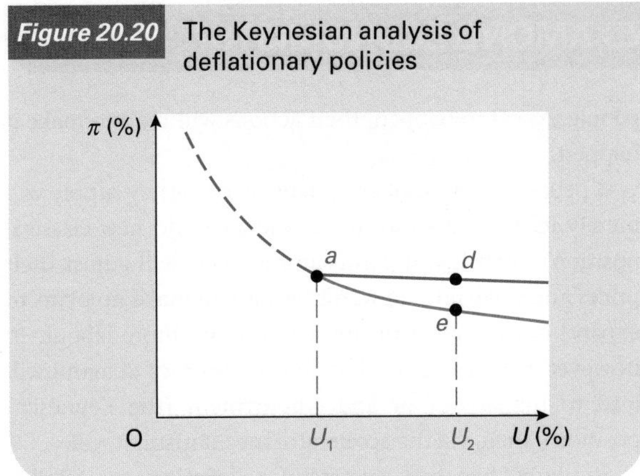

Figure 20.20 The Keynesian analysis of deflationary policies

Contraction of aggregate demand

Many Keynesians argue that the short-run Phillips curve is kinked at the current level of real aggregate demand. A reduction in real aggregate demand will have only a slight effect on inflation, since real wages are sticky downwards. Unions may well prefer to negotiate a reduction in employment levels, preferably by natural wastage (i.e. not replacing people when they leave), rather than accept a reduction in real wages. Thus in Figure 20.20, to the right of point *a*, the short-run Phillips curve is very shallow.

As long as this curve is not totally horizontal to the right of *a*, the introduction of expectations into the analysis will cause the short-run curve to shift downwards over time (if unemployment is kept above U_1) as people come to expect a lower rate of inflation.

With *adaptive* expectations, however, the curve could shift downwards very slowly indeed. If a movement from point *a* to point *d* represents only a 1 per cent reduction in inflation, and if it takes, say, two years for this to be fully reflected in expectations, then if unemployment is kept at U_2, inflation will reduce (i.e. the curve shift downwards) by only $^1/_2$ per cent a year. This may be totally unacceptable politically if inflation is already at very high levels, and if U_2 is also very high.

Even with *rational* expectations the response may be too slow. If there is a resistance from unions to receiving increases in wages below the current rate of inflation, or if they are attempting to 'catch up' with other workers, then even if they rationally predict the correct amount by which inflation will fall, inflation will fall only slowly. People will rationally predict the *resistance* to wage restraint, and sure enough, therefore, inflation will fall only slowly.

The worst scenario is when the government, in its attempt to eliminate inflation, keeps unemployment high for a number of years. As the core of long-term unemployed workers grows, an increasing number of workers become deskilled and therefore effectively unemployable. The effective labour supply is reduced, and firms find there is no longer a surplus of employable labour *despite* high unemployment. A long-term equilibrium is reached at, say, point *e* with still substantial inflation. The *long*-run Phillips curve too may thus be relatively shallow to the right of point *a*.

The Keynesian criticism of non-intervention

Keynesians are therefore highly critical of the new classical conclusion that governments should not intervene other than to restrain the growth of money supply. High unemployment may persist for many years and become deeply entrenched in the economy if there is no deliberate government policy of creating a steady expansion of demand.

Why is it important in the Keynesian analysis for there to be a steady *expansion of demand?*

Section summary

1. Modern Keynesians incorporate expectations into their analysis of inflation and unemployment. They also see an important role for cost-push factors and changes in equilibrium unemployment in explaining the position of the Phillips curve.
2. A growth in equilibrium unemployment in the 1970s and 1980s was caused by rapid changes in technology, greater competition from abroad and more rapid changes in demand patterns. It was also due to the persistence of unemployment beyond the recessions of the early 1980s and early 1990s, because of a deskilling of labour during the recessions (an example of hysteresis). The effect of increased equilibrium unemployment was to shift the Phillips curve to the right.
3. Demand-deficient unemployment may persist because real wage rates may be sticky downwards, even into the longer term. This stickiness may be the result of efficiency real wage rates being above market-clearing real wage rates and/or outsiders not being able to influence wage bargains struck between employers and insiders.
4. If expectations are incorporated into Keynesian analysis, the Phillips curve will become steeper in the long run (and steeper in the short run too in the case of rational expectations). It will not become vertical, however, since people will expect changes in aggregate demand to affect output and employment as well as prices.
5. If people expect a more rapid rise in aggregate demand to be sustained, firms will invest more, thereby reducing unemployment in the long run and not just increasing the rate of inflation. The long-run Phillips curve will be downward sloping.
6. The short- and long-run Phillips curves may be kinked. Reductions in real aggregate demand may have only a slight effect on inflation if real wage rates are sticky downwards.

20.5 POSTSCRIPT: COMMON GROUND AMONG ECONOMISTS?

Whilst there is some disagreement among economists over the nature of the aggregate supply and Phillips curves, and hence over the effects of changes in aggregate demand, it is important not to get the impression that economists disagree over everything. There is, in fact, quite a lot of common ground among the majority of economists over the issues that we have examined in this chapter.

If you look back to pages 447–9, we identified several areas where there is a high measure of agreement among economists. Let us restate three of these areas in the light of the theories we have covered in this chapter.

TC 13 p381

In the short run, changes in aggregate demand will have a major effect on output and employment. With the exception of extreme new classical economists, who argue that markets clear instantly and that expectations are formed rationally, all other economists would accept that the short-run aggregate supply curve is upward sloping, albeit getting steeper as potential output is approached. Similarly, they would argue that the short-run Phillips curve is downward sloping. There are two major implications of this analysis:

- Reductions in aggregate demand can cause reductions in output and increases in unemployment. In other words, too little spending will cause a recession.
- An expansion of aggregate demand by the government (whether achieved by fiscal or monetary policy, or both) will help to pull an economy out of a recession. There may be considerable time lags, however, before the economy responds fully to such expansionary policies.

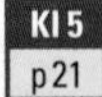

In the long run, changes in aggregate demand will have much less effect on output and employment and much more effect on prices. As we have seen, new classical economists and others argue that both the long-run aggregate supply curve and the long-run Phillips curve are vertical. Most Keynesian economists, while arguing that these curves are not vertical, would still see them as less elastic than the short-run curves. Nevertheless, many Keynesians argue that changes in aggregate demand *will* have substantial effects on long-term output and employment via changes in investment and hence in potential output (see Figure 20.5 on page 576).

KI 9 p58

Expectations have important effects on the economy. In fact, they are crucial in determining the success of government policy on unemployment and inflation. Whatever people expect to happen, their actions will tend to make it happen.

If people believe that an expansion of money supply will merely lead to inflation (the monetarist and new classical position), then it will. Firms and workers will adjust their prices and wage rates upwards. Firms will make no plans to expand output and will not take on any more labour. If, however, people believe that an expansion of demand will lead to higher output and employment (the Keynesian position), then, via the accelerator mechanism, it will.

Similarly, just how successful a deflationary policy is in curing inflation depends in large measure on people's expectations (but, as explained above, it also depends on the downward stickiness of real wages). If people believe that a deflationary policy will cause a recession, firms will stop investing and will cut their workforce. If they believe that it will cure inflation and restore firms' competitiveness abroad, firms may increase investment.

To manage the economy successfully, therefore, the government must convince people that its policies will work. This is as much a job of public relations as of pulling the right economic levers.

?

1. *If constant criticism of governments in the media makes people highly cynical about any government's ability to manage the economy, what effect will this have on the performance of the economy?*
2. *Suppose that, as part of the national curriculum, everyone in the country had to study economics up to the age of 16. Suppose also that the reporting of economic events by the media became more thorough (and interesting!). What effects would these developments have on the government's ability to manage the economy? How would your answer differ if you were a Keynesian from if you were a new classicist?*

One other area where there is considerable agreement among economists concerns the causes of longer-term growth. Although demand-side policy may be important for ensuring that economies achieve their potential output, only by increasing that potential itself can growth be sustained. To achieve higher rates of economic growth over the long term, therefore, the government should focus on means of getting potential output to grow more rapidly, and this requires an appropriate supply-side policy.

Chapter 21 examines long-term growth and Chapter 22 discusses various types of supply-side policy open to governments.

END OF CHAPTER QUESTIONS

1. Assume that inflation depends on two things: the level of aggregate demand, indicated by the inverse of unemployment ($1/U$), and the expected rate of inflation (π_t^e). Assume that the rate of inflation (π_t) is given by the equation:

$$\pi_t = (48/U - 6) + \pi_t^e$$

Assume initially (year 0) that the actual and expected rate of inflation is zero.

(a) What is the current (natural) rate of unemployment?

(b) Now assume in year 1 that the government wishes to reduce unemployment to 4 per cent and continues to expand aggregate demand by as much as is necessary to achieve this. Fill in the rows for years 0 to 4 in the following table. It is assumed for simplicity that the expected rate of inflation in a given year (π_t^e) is equal to the actual rate of inflation in the previous year (π_{t-1}).

Year	U	$48/U - 6$	+	π^e	=	π
0	...	...	+	...	=	...
1	...	...	+	...	=	...
2	...	...	+	...	=	...
3	...	...	+	...	=	...
4	...	...	+	...	=	...
5	...	...	+	...	=	...
6	...	...	+	...	=	...
7	...	...	+	...	=	...

(c) Now assume in year 5 that the government, worried about rising inflation, reduces aggregate demand sufficiently to reduce inflation by 3 per cent in that year. What must the rate of unemployment be raised to in that year?

(d) Assuming that unemployment stays at this high level, continue the table for years 5 to 7.

2. For what reasons might the long-run aggregate supply curve be (a) vertical; (b) upward sloping; (c) downward sloping?
3. How would you attempt to assess whether a particular period of inflation was the result of cost-push or demand-pull pressures?
4. What is the difference between adaptive expectations and rational expectations?
5. How can adaptive expectations of inflation result in clockwise Phillips loops? Why would these loops not be completely regular?
6. What implications would a vertical short-run aggregate supply curve have for the effects of demand management policy?
7. For what reasons may the NAIRU increase?
8. Given the Keynesian explanation for the persistence of high levels of unemployment after the early 1980s and early 1990s recessions, what policies would you advocate to reduce unemployment in the years following a recession?

Additional case studies on the book's website (www.pearsoned.co.uk/sloman)

20.1 Explaining the shape of the short-run Phillips curve. This shows how money illusion on the part of workers can explain why the Phillips curve is downward sloping.

20.2 The quantity theory of money restated. An examination of how the vertical long-run *AS* curve in the adaptive expectations model can be used to justify the quantity theory of money.

20.3 Getting predictions wrong. How incorrect predictions can lead to a rise or fall in output in the new classical model.

20.4 Cost-push factors in Keynesian analysis. How Keynesians incorporated cost-push inflation into their analysis of shifts in the Phillips curve.

WEBSITES RELEVANT TO THIS CHAPTER

See sites listed at the end of Chapter 22 on page 632.

Chapter 21
Long-term Economic Growth

In this chapter we turn our attention to the determinants of *long-run* economic growth. All developed countries have experienced economic growth over the past 60 years, but rates have differed significantly from one country to another. We look at some of these differences in section 21.1.

If an economy is to achieve sustained economic growth over the longer term, there must be a sustained increase in *potential* output. This means that there has to be a continuous rightward shift in aggregate supply.

The main ingredient in long-term economic growth is a growth in labour productivity. This, in turn, depends on two major factors: a growth in the amount of capital that workers use and technological progress. We can see these two elements if we look around us. Take a modern car factory, with its high-tech robot-driven equipment: it is no surprise that workers' productivity is much higher than it was, say, 30 years ago. Take a modern office, with powerful PCs: again it is no surprise that today's office staff are much more productive than their counterparts of years gone past.

In section 21.2 we look at the effects of an increase in the rate of capital investment when there is no change in technology. As we shall see, the effect will simply be growth to a new higher level of national income, not a permanently higher rate of economic growth.

If economic growth is to be higher over the long term, therefore, there must be an increase in the rate of technological progress. We look at how this affects economic growth in section 21.3. We also examine what *determines* the rate of invention, technological development and the use of new technology. It is important to understand this if the government is to develop appropriate supply-side policies – the subject of Chapter 22.

CHAPTER MAP

21.1 LONG-RUN ECONOMIC GROWTH IN INDUSTRIALISED COUNTRIES

Quite naturally, governments and individuals are concerned with the ups and downs of the business cycle. How does this year's economic performance compare with last year's? Are the various macroeconomic indicators such as growth, unemployment and inflation getting better or worse?

When we step back, however, and look at the longer span of history, these short-term fluctuations take on less significance. What we see is that economies tend to experience long-term economic growth, not long-term economic decline. Measured in terms of income per head (after adjusting for inflation), all developed nations are richer today than they were 50 years ago.

KI 2 p8 The picture, however, is not one of universal improvement. People are not necessarily happier; there are many stresses in modern living; the environment is in many respects more polluted; inequality has increased in most countries, especially over the last 20 years; for many people work is more demanding and the working day is longer than in the past; there is more crime and more insecurity. If you look back to Boxes 13.3 and 13.6, you will see that 'more' is not always 'better'.

Nevertheless, most people *want* more consumer goods; they want higher incomes. In this chapter, we examine what causes long-term economic growth, and how it can be increased. We leave you to judge whether a materially richer society is a better society.

Growth over the decades

Most developed countries experienced a recession in the early 1980s, the early 1990s and the early 2000s. Some experienced a minor recession in the mid-1970s. But these periods have been the exception. For the rest of the time since 1950, most countries have experienced sustained economic growth. Figure 21.1 shows UK GDP from 1950 to 2005. As you can see, the fluctuations in output appear minor compared with the long-term growth in output.

Such growth cannot be explained by a closing of the gap between actual and potential output: by an expansion of aggregate demand leading to a fuller use of resources. Instead, the explanation lies on the supply side. Countries' economic *capacity* has increased. There has been a growth in the average output per worker. Table 21.1 shows the average annual growth in output per employed person for several developed countries for the four decades from 1961 to 2000 and for the most recent period. The effect of an average annual growth in output of just 2 or 3 per cent builds up over the years to a substantial rise in output. Table 21.2 shows how many times greater output per worker in 2006 is compared with that in 1961.

Figure 21.1 UK GDP at market prices (2001 = 100)

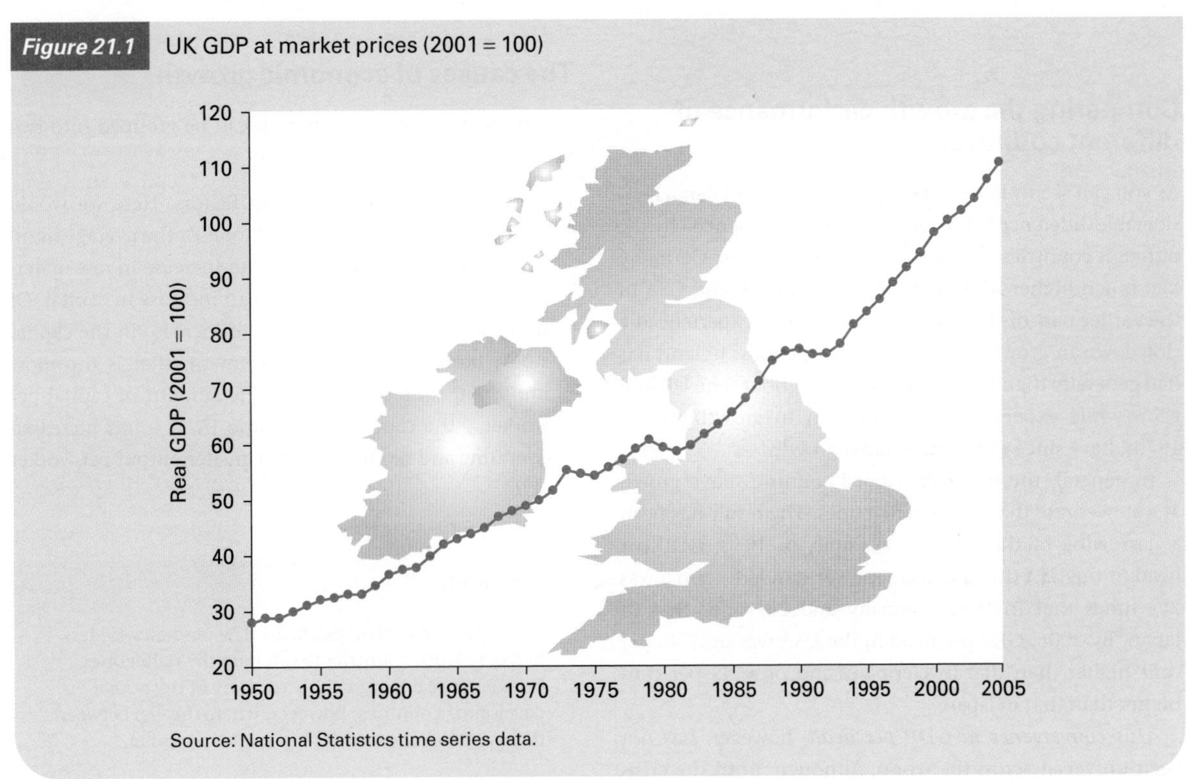

Source: National Statistics time series data.

Table 21.1 Average annual percentage growth rate in GDP per person employed

	1961–70	1971–80	1981–90	1991–2000	2001–6[b]	1961–2006[b]
France	4.9	2.8	2.3	1.5	1.1	2.6
Germany[a]	4.2	2.5	1.3	1.6	0.9	2.2
Italy	6.2	2.6	1.7	1.6	0.3	2.7
Ireland	4.2	3.7	3.8	3.4	3.0	3.7
Japan	8.6	3.7	3.0	1.1	2.0	3.8
Netherlands	3.8	2.7	1.6	1.2	1.1	2.2
UK	2.7	1.7	1.9	2.2	2.0	2.1
USA	2.3	1.2	1.3	1.7	2.4	1.7

[a] Up to 1991, figures are for West Germany only.
[b] 2006 projected.

Source: based on data in *European Economy* (Commission of the European Union).

Table 21.2 Output per person employed in 2006 relative to that in 1961

	Output per head in 2006/ output per head in 1961
France	3.3
Germany[a]	2.7
Italy	3.3
Ireland	5.3
Japan	5.6
Netherlands	2.7
UK	2.6
USA	2.2

[a] Up to 1991, West Germany only.

Source: based on data in *European Economy* (Commission of the European Union).

Comparing the growth performance of different countries

As you can see from these two tables, there has been a considerable difference in the rates of growth experienced by the different countries. Japan, Italy, France and West Germany had much higher rates of growth than the UK and USA in the earlier part of the period, but then they experienced a slowdown in growth rates in the later periods. Ireland has had generally high rates of growth throughout. The UK and USA, while experiencing a slowdown in growth in the 1970s, have since experienced faster growth.

In general, the richer developed countries have grown at a slower rate than the less rich ones. The result has been a narrowing of the gap. For example, in 1950, GDP per head in the USA (in purchasing-power standard terms) was 2½ times that in West Germany and 20 times that in Japan. By 2006, GDP per head in the USA was only 46 per cent higher than that in Germany and only 35 per cent higher than that in Japan.

This ***convergence in GDP per head***, however, has not been universal across the world. Although, until the crisis in the late 1990s, the Asian 'tigers' of Hong Kong, South Korea, Singapore and Taiwan were growing very rapidly, some of the poorest developing countries, and especially those in sub-Saharan Africa, have grown at pitifully slow rates, and in some cases GDP per head has declined. We examine the causes of low growth in developing countries in Chapter 26.

Although recent generations have come to expect economic growth, it is a relatively new phenomenon. For the majority of the last 2000 years, countries have experienced virtually static output per head over the long term. Economic growth has become significant only once countries have undergone an industrial revolution, and it is only with the technological advances of the twentieth and now the twenty-first centuries that long-term growth rates of 2 per cent or more have been achieved.

The causes of economic growth

The sources of economic growth can be grouped into two broad categories:

- An increase in the *quantity* of factors. Here we would include an increase in the workforce or the average number of hours that people work, an increase in raw materials (e.g. discoveries of oil) and an increase in capital. Of these, for most countries, it is an increase in the capital stock, brought about by investment, that is the most important source of growth. The amount of capital per worker – the capital/labour ratio (K/L) – has increased over time and has resulted in a greater output per worker (Y/L).

Definition

Convergence in GDP per head The tendency for less rich developed countries to catch up the richer ones. Convergence does not apply to many of the poorer developing countries, however, where the gap between them and richer countries has tended to widen.

- An increase in the *productivity* of factors. Here we would include an increase in the skills of workers, a more efficient organisation of inputs by management and more productive capital equipment. Most significant here is technological progress. Developments of computer technology, of new techniques in engineering, of lighter, stronger and cheaper materials, of digital technology in communications and of more efficient motors have all contributed to a massive increase in the productivity of capital. Machines today can produce much more output than machines in the past that cost the same to manufacture.

In the next two sections, we will examine these two sources of growth and focus first on capital accumulation (an increase in the *quantity* of capital) and then on technological progress (an increase in the *productivity* of factors).

Section summary

1. The determinants of economic growth in the long run lie primarily on the supply side.
2. Most developed countries have experienced average rates of economic growth of 2 per cent or more over the last 50 years, but there have been considerable differences between countries.
3. The income gap between developed countries has tended to narrow as the less rich ones have grown faster than the richer ones. Some of the poorest countries of the world, however, have experienced very low rates of growth, with the result that the gap between them and richer countries has widened.
4. The determinants of economic growth can be put into two broad categories: an increase in the quantity of factors and an increase in the productivity of factors.

21.2 ECONOMIC GROWTH WITHOUT TECHNOLOGICAL PROGRESS

Capital accumulation

An increase in capital per worker will generally increase output. In other words, the more equipment that is used by people at work, the more they are likely to produce. But to increase capital requires investment, and that investment requires resources – resources that could have been used for producing consumer goods. Thus more investment means diverting resources away from producing finished goods into producing machines, buildings and other capital equipment. This is the opportunity cost of investment. TC 1 p8

If we take a simple circular flow of income model, with saving as the only withdrawal and investment as the only injection, then saving will be equal to investment ($S = I$). An increase in saving, therefore, will enable more investment and more output for the future. Thus sacrifices today, in terms of more saving and less consumption, will mean more output and hence possibly more consumption for the future.

A model of economic growth

In Chapter 13, we looked at a simple growth model (see page 384). This stated that growth depends on the proportion of a rise in income that is saved and hence invested (i) and the marginal efficiency of capital (MEC):

$$g = i \times MEC$$

Thus if 15 per cent of national income is saved and invested ($i = 15\%$) and if a 1 per cent increase in the capital stock ($\Delta K = I$) leads to a $^1/_3$ per cent increase in annual output ($MEC = {}^1/_3$), then the rate of growth will be 5 per cent. For example, if national income is £100 billion, £15 billion will be invested ($i = 15\%$), and this will yield extra annual output of £5 billion ($MEC = {}^1/_3$). Thus national income has grown by 5 per cent (from £100 billion to £105 billion).

? *What would be the rate of economic growth if 20 per cent of national income were saved and invested and the marginal efficiency of capital were $^2/_5$?*

However, we need to make two qualifications to this simple model. The first is that the marginal efficiency of capital is likely to decline as the amount of capital per worker increases. This is because of diminishing returns to capital. The second is that a proportion of investment has to be used for replacing worn-out or obsolete equipment. The problem here is that, the larger the capital stock, the greater the proportion of investment that will be needed for replacement purposes, and the smaller the proportion that can be used for increasing the size of the capital stock.

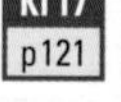

Growth to a long-run equilibrium level of national income

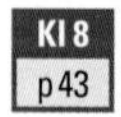

Let us now incorporate these two qualifications into a model of growth. This is known as the neoclassical or 'Solow' growth model, after the MIT economics professor and Nobel Prize winner, Robert Solow. In this model, we are assuming for simplicity that the size of the workforce is constant. Any increase in the capital stock, therefore, means an increase in the average amount of capital per worker.

Figure 21.2 Steady-state output

*LOOKING AT THE MATHS

Steady-state equilibrium in the Solow growth model is achieved where investment (I) equals depreciation (D). Investment is assumed to be a given fraction (s) of the level of national income Y, where national income is a function of the total capital stock (K): $Y = f(K)$. Thus:

$$I = sY$$
$$= s \times f(K) \qquad (1)$$

Depreciation in the model is assumed to be a fixed proportion (d) of the capital stock (K). Thus:

$$D = dK \qquad (2)$$

In steady-state equilibrium, given that $I = D$, from equation (1) and (2) we can write:

$$s \times f(K) = dK$$

Thus:

$$K = \frac{s \times f(K)}{d}$$

Thus if we know the production function ($Y = f(K)$), the saving rate (s) and the depreciation rate (d), we can solve for the steady-state equilibrium value of K and hence also for Y. Maths Case 21.1 on the book's website gives a worked example of this.

The model is illustrated in Figure 21.2. The size of the capital stock (K) is measured on the horizontal axis; the level of national output (Y) is measured on the vertical axis.

We start by looking at the effects of a growth in the capital stock on national output (i.e. on real national income (Y)). This is shown by the green output curve. As the capital stock increases, so output increases, but at a diminishing rate (the curve gets less and less steep). The reason for this is the law of diminishing returns: in this case, diminishing returns to capital. For example, if, in an office, you start equipping workers with PCs, at first output will increase very rapidly. But as more and more workers have their own PC rather than having to share, so the rate of increase in output slows down. When everyone has their own, output is likely to be at a maximum. Any additional PCs (of the same specification) will remain unused.

Increased output will mean increased saving and hence increased investment (the amount depending on the level of i). This is shown by the blue investment (I) curve. The vertical distance between the Y and I curves represents consumption ($C = Y - I$).

The magenta (D) line shows the amount of depreciation of capital that takes place, and hence the amount of replacement investment required. The bigger the capital stock, the larger the amount of replacement investment required.

KI 23 p251

Assume initially that the size of the capital stock is K_0. This will generate an output of Y_0 (point a). This output, in turn, will generate saving and investment of I_0, but of this, D_0 will have to be used for replacement purposes. The difference ($b - c$) will be available to increase the size of the capital stock. The capital stock will thus increase up to K_1 (point g). At this point, all investment will be required for replacement purposes. Output will therefore cease growing. Y_1 represents the ***steady-state level of national income***.

Effect of an increase in the saving rate

In the simple model, $g = i \times MEC$, an increase in the saving rate will increase i and hence the growth rate (g). When we take into account diminishing returns to capital and depreciation, however, an increase in the saving rate will lead to only a temporary increase in output, and to no long-term *growth* at all!

This is illustrated in Figure 21.3. If the saving rate increases, the investment curve will shift upwards. This is shown by a shift from I_1 to I_2. Investment is now above that which is necessary to maintain the capital stock at K_1. The capital stock will grow, therefore, and so will national income. But this growth is only temporary. Once the capital stock has risen to K_2, all the new higher level of investment will be absorbed in replacing capital ($I = D$ at point n). National income stops rising. Y_2 represents the new steady-state national income.

Does this mean, therefore, that there is no long-term gain from an increase in the saving rate? There *is* a gain, to the extent that income per worker is now higher (remember that we are assuming a constant labour force), and this higher income will be received not just once, but every year from now on as long as the saving rate remains at the new higher level. There is no increase in the long-term *growth rate*, however. To achieve that, we would have to look to the other determinants of growth.

Definition

Steady-state level of national income The long-run equilibrium level of national income. The level at which all investment is used to maintain the existing capital stock at its current level.

Figure 21.3 Effect of an increase in the rate of saving and investment

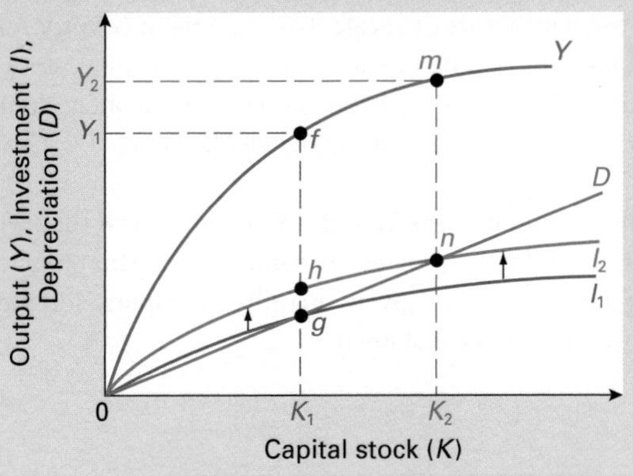

Figure 21.4 An optimum saving rate

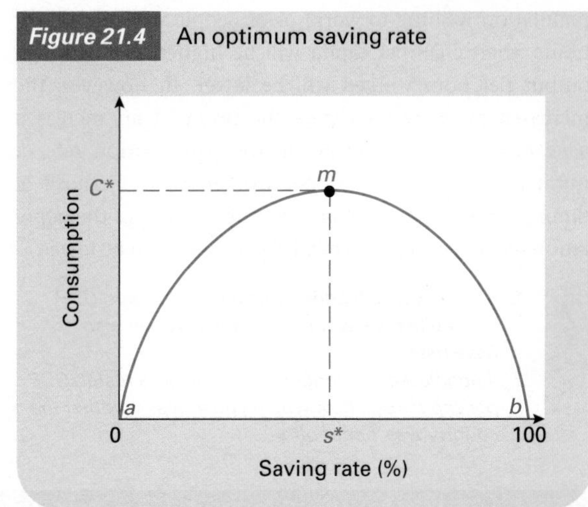

Human capital and education

The analysis of Figures 21.2 and 21.3 need not be confined to the stock of physical capital: machines, buildings, tools, etc. It can also apply to ***human capital***. Human capital, as we saw in Chapter 9, refers to the skills and expertise of workers that have been acquired through education and training. If part of saving is used for investment in education and training, then the productivity of workers will rise, and so will output. In Figures 21.2 and 21.3, therefore, the horizontal axis measures both physical and human capital. An increase in either has the effect of increasing the steady-state level of national income.

? *If there were a gradual increase in the saving rate over time, would this lead to sustained economic growth?*

An optimum rate of saving?

If an increase in the saving rate does at least lead to a higher level of output, is there an *optimum* level of saving? Clearly we would need to define 'optimum'. One definition would be where *consumption* per head is maximised.

Assuming a fixed population and a fixed workforce, higher saving will do two things. First, it will directly decrease consumption, since what is saved is not directly spent. Second, as we have seen, it will lead to higher output and hence higher income. So, with a higher saving rate, consumption will be a smaller proportion, but of a higher income. This implies that there will be some optimum saving rate at which consumption is maximised. This is illustrated in Figure 21.4.

If the saving rate is zero, the capital stock will be zero. Output and consumption will thus be zero (point *a*). As saving rises above zero, so the capital stock will grow, as will output and consumption. At the other extreme, if the saving rate were 100 per cent, although the capital stock would be high, all of the nation's income would go on maintaining that capital stock: there would be no consumption (point *b*). A saving rate somewhere between 0 and 100 per cent, therefore, will give the maximum consumption. In Figure 21.4, this is a rate of s^*, giving a level of consumption of C^* (point *m*). This is sometimes known as the ***golden-rule saving rate***.

Evidence suggests that all countries have saving rates below the golden-rule level. Thus increases in saving rates would result in increases in consumption.

? *If this is true, why do people not increase their rate of saving?*

An increase in the workforce

An increase in the workforce, or the number of hours worked by the existing workforce, will have the effect of shifting both the *Y* and *I* lines upwards in Figures 21.2 and 21.3. In other words, if a given amount of capital is used by more workers or for longer periods, output and hence saving and investment will increase. As more labour hours are used with any given amount of capital, diminishing returns to labour will set in. Output will grow, but at a diminishing rate. The marginal and average product of labour will fall (see Figure 5.1 on page 123). Thus although national output has risen (the new steady-state income is higher), the output per labour hour is less. KI 17 p121

The effect on GDP per head of the population

If the rise in total hours worked was the result of an increased ***participation rate*** (i.e. a greater proportion of the

Definitions

Human capital The qualifications, skills and expertise that contribute to a worker's productivity.

Golden-rule saving rate The rate of saving that maximises the level of long-run consumption.

Participation rate The percentage of the working-age population that is part of the workforce.

population wishing to work) or of people working longer hours, then GDP per capita will be higher, even though output per hour worked will be lower. If, however, the increased hours worked were the result of an increased *population*, with no increase in the participation rate or number of hours worked per worker, then, because of diminishing returns to labour, output per head of the population will have gone down: GDP per capita will be lower.

?

1. *If there were a higher participation rate and GDP per capita rose, would output per worker also have risen?*
2. *If people worked longer hours and, as a result, GDP per capita rose, how would you assess whether the country was 'better off'?*

If, however, there is an increase in both labour *and* capital, GDP per capita need not fall, even with the same number of hours worked per head. There are likely to be constant returns to scale. For example, if country A has double the population and double the capital stock of country B, its GDP is likely to be approximately double, and its GDP per head approximately the same.

What should be clear from the above analysis is that, without technological progress, or some other means of increasing output from a given quantity of inputs, long-term growth cannot be sustained.

Section summary

1. An increased saving rate will lead to higher investment and hence to an increase in the capital stock. This, in turn, will lead to a higher level of national income.
2. A larger capital stock, however, will require a higher level of replacement investment. Once this has risen to absorb all the extra investment, national income will stop rising: growth will cease. A steady-state level of national income has been achieved. An increased saving rate will therefore lead only to a rise in output, not to a long-term rise in the rate of growth.
3. An optimum rate of saving could be defined as one where consumption per head is maximised. This is sometimes known as the 'golden-rule saving rate'.
4. An increase in the workforce will lead to higher total output, but unless accompanied by an increase in the capital stock, it will generally lead to a reduction in output per worker.

21.3 ECONOMIC GROWTH WITH TECHNOLOGICAL PROGRESS

The effect of technological progress on output

Technological progress has the effect of increasing the output from a given amount of investment. This is shown in Figure 21.5. Initial investment and income curves are I_1 and Y_1; steady-state income is at a level of Y_1 (point f). A technological advance has the effect of shifting the Y line upwards, say to Y_2. The higher income curve leads to a higher investment curve (for a given *rate* of saving). This is shown by curve I_2. The new long-term equilibrium capital stock is thus K_2, and the new steady-state level of income is Y_2 (point p).

Figure 21.5 Effect of a technological advance

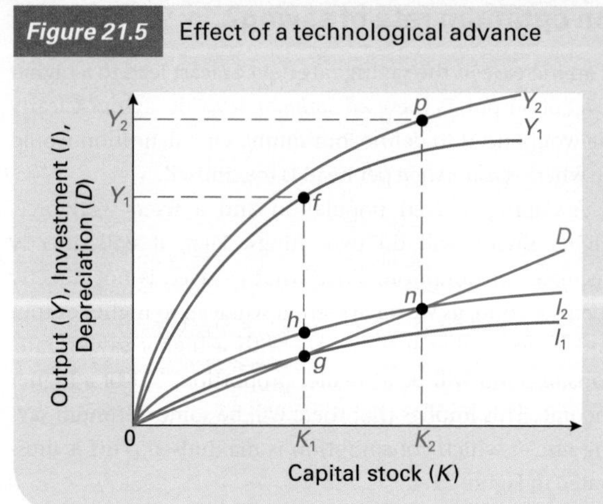

If there is a 'one-off' technological advance, the effect is the one we have just illustrated. Income rises to a higher level, but does not go on rising once the new steady-state level has been reached. But technological progress marches on over time. New inventions are made; new processes are discovered; old ones are improved. In terms of Figure 21.5, the Y curve *goes on* shifting upwards over time. The faster the rate of technological progress, the faster will the Y curve shift upwards and the higher will be the rate of economic growth. This is illustrated in Figure 21.6, which shows the increase in output over time. The faster the rate of technological progress, the higher the rate of growth of output.

Maths Case 21.2 explores the algebra of technological progress.

Figure 21.6 Effect of technological progress on growth rates

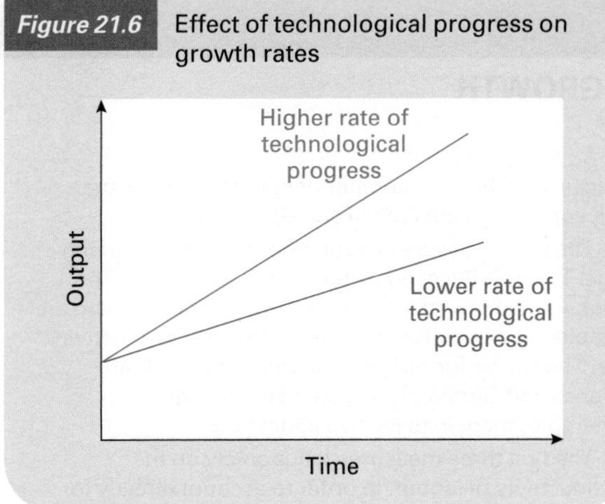

Figure 21.7 Effect of an increase in the saving rate, with a given rate of technological progress

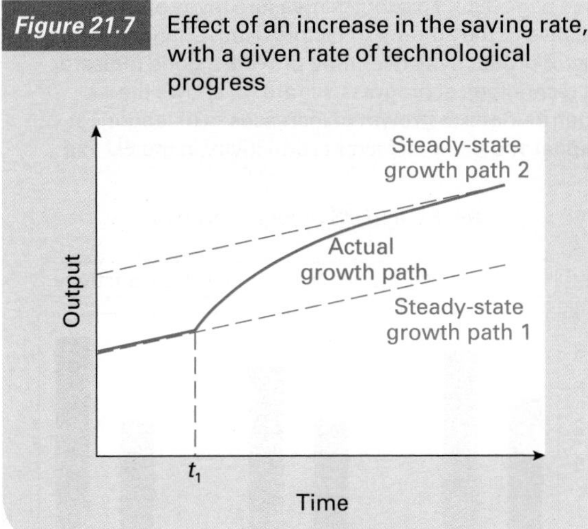

The effect of an increase in the saving rate with a given rate of technological progress

Figure 21.7 shows the combined effects of an increased saving rate and continuing technological progress. The rate of technological progress gives the slope of the ***steady-state growth path***. This is the growth path for any given saving rate. The saving rate determines the *position* (as opposed to slope) of the curve. Assume that the economy is on steady-state growth path 1. Then, at time t_1, there is an increase in the saving rate. This has the effect of increasing output and the economy will move towards steady-state growth path 2. But the full effect does not take place immediately, since new capital equipment takes time to plan and install and then to generate additional income, part of which will be used for more investment. Thus the actual growth path will follow the green line, gradually converging on steady-state growth path 2.

Endogenous growth theory

It should be clear from what we have argued that an increase in technological progress is essential if a country wants to achieve faster rates of growth in the long term. But is this purely in the lap of the scientists and engineers? In the Solow growth model that we have been considering up to now, this is the type of assumption made. In other words, technological progress is simply a 'given': it is exogenously determined.

But cannot governments adopt policies that encourage scientific breakthroughs and technological developments? What can be done to speed up the rate of innovation? Many economists argue that the rate of technological progress *can* be increased if more resources are devoted to research and development and to education and training, and if people are given appropriate incentives to innovate.

Once a discovery is made, its effects will depend on how widely the knowledge is dispersed. The more people can use the new technology and replicate and develop it, the greater will be the resulting increase in output.

What ***endogenous growth theory*** argues is that the rate of invention and technological development and the rate of diffusion of new technology depend on economic institutions, incentives and the role of government. All this suggests that appropriate policies can increase the rate of technological progress and hence increase the rate of economic growth.

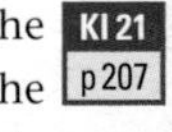
KI 21 p207

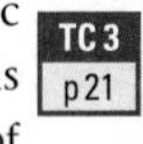
TC 3 p21

A model of endogenous technological progress

Endogenous growth models argue two things. The first is that technological progress is *dependent* on various economic factors such as the rate of investment in research and development. This could be included as an element in the investment (I) term, i.e.

$$I = I_n + I_c$$

where I_n is investment in research and development of new technology (it could also include investment in training) and I_c is investment in capital that uses current technology. The greater the value of I_n/I_c, the faster will the Y curve shift upwards in Figure 21.2 and the steeper will be the steady-state growth path in Figure 21.7. Any policy, then, that increases the proportion of national income being devoted

Definitions

Steady-state growth path The growth path for a given saving rate (where growth results from technological progress).

Endogenous growth theory A theory that the rate of growth depends on the rate of technological progress and diffusion, both of which depend on institutions, incentives and the role of government.

CASE STUDIES AND APPLICATIONS

PRODUCTIVITY AND ECONOMIC GROWTH

The key to a better standard of living?

KI 16 p120 Productive use of physical capital and labour are the two most important sources of a nation's material standard of living.[1]

There are four common ways of measuring productivity. The first is output per worker. This is the most straightforward measure to calculate. All that is required is a measure of total output and employment. Figure (a) shows the UK lagging behind the USA and France and slightly ahead of Germany.

The second measure is output per hour worked. This has the advantage that it is not influenced by the *number* of hours worked. So for an economy like the UK, with a very high percentage of part-time workers on the one hand, and long average hours worked by full-time employees on the other, such a measure would be more accurate in gauging worker efficiency. Here the UK lags behind all three countries. This is because of the high number of hours worked in the UK compared with France and Germany.

The third measure is output per person of working age. This is influenced by the employment rate. The higher the proportion of people of working age who are employed, the higher will this measure of productivity be. The UK performs better on this measure than France and Germany because of much higher unemployment in these two countries.

The first three measures focus solely on the productivity of labour. In order to account directly for the productivity of both labour *and* capital, we need to consider the growth in *total* factor productivity (*TFP*) (see page 386). This fourth measure gives output relative to the amount of factors used. Changes in total factor productivity over time provide a good indicator of technological progress. Figure (b) shows the contributions to growth of increases in (i) labour, (ii) capital and (iii) total factor productivity in the EU and

(a) *Productivity in selected countries: 2003 (UK = 100)*

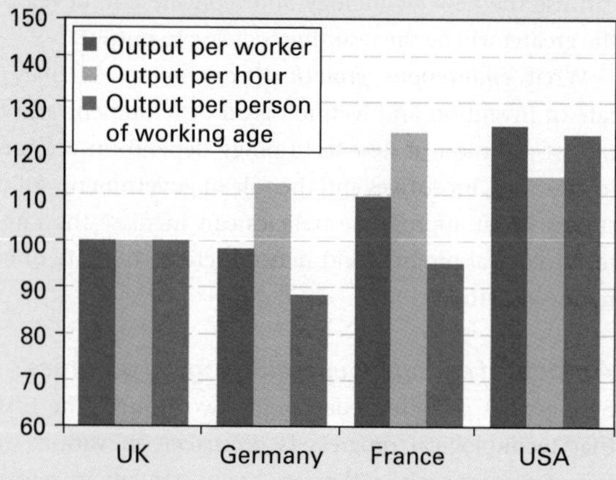

Source: *Economic and Fiscal Strategy Report*, Box 3.1 (HM Treasury, 2005).

(b) *EU and US potential growth*

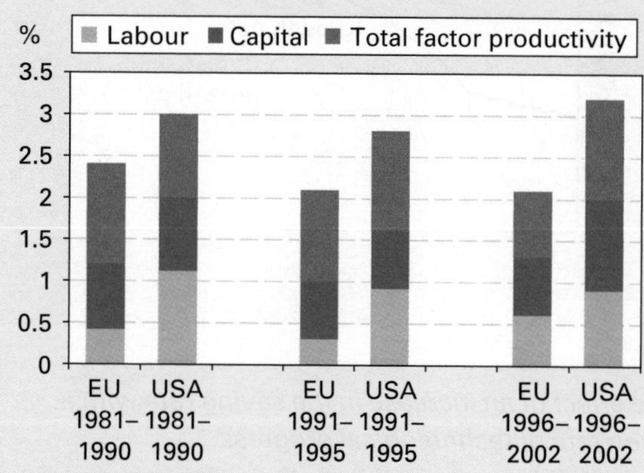

Source: *Advancing Long-term Prosperity: Economic Reform in an Enlarged Europe*, (HM Treasury, 2004), page 20.

to R&D and training will increase the long-run rate of economic growth.

The second factor is the responsiveness of Y to I_n. The greater the value of $\Delta Y/I_n$, the greater will be the rate of economic growth: the steeper will be the steady-state growth path.

KI 21 p207 The values of I_n and $\Delta Y/I_n$ depend on a range of factors, such as attitudes of business and financial institutions, tax incentives, government grants, a research infrastructure (laboratories, the number and skills of researchers, etc.), the degree of competition over the development of new products, and so on. In other words, they depend on structural and institutional factors within the economy and on the role of government.

Government policies to encourage R&D, innovation and risk taking are known as 'supply-side policies' and are the subject of the next chapter.

*LOOKING AT THE MATHS

The above endogenous growth model can be expressed algebraically as follows:

$$\Delta Y/Y = v(I_n/Y)$$

This states that the rate of economic growth ($\Delta Y/Y$) depends on the proportion of national income devoted to R&D and training (I_n/Y) by an amount v.

The higher the value of I_n/Y and the higher the value of v, the steeper will be the steady-state growth path.

BOX 21.1

the USA. It shows that, in the period 1996–2002, the USA's long-term growth was higher than the EU's for all three reasons: faster growth in the employment of labour, faster growth in the capital stock and faster growth in total factor productivity.

The importance of productivity

The higher the productivity of its factors of production, the higher will be a country's potential output; and the faster the rate of growth in productivity, the faster is likely to be the country's rate of economic growth. Any government seeking to raise the long-term growth rate in its country, therefore, must find ways of stimulating productivity growth.

On what does the growth of productivity depend? There are seven main determinants:

- Private investment in new physical capital (machinery and buildings) and in R&D.
- Public investment in education, R&D and infrastructure.
- Training and the development of labour skills.
- Innovation and the application of new technology.
- The organisation and management of factors of production.
- The rate of entry of new firms into markets: generally such firms will have higher productivity than existing firms.
- The business environment in which firms operate. Is there competition over the quality and design of products? Is there competitive pressure to reduce costs?

? ***Identify some policies that a government could pursue to stimulate productivity growth through each of the above means.***

But what are the mechanisms whereby productivity growth feeds through into growth of the economy?

- The capacity of the economy to grow will increase as productivity improvements extend potential output.
- Productivity improvements will drive prices downwards, stimulating demand and actual growth.
- With high returns from their investment, investors might be prepared to embark upon new projects and enterprises, stimulating yet further productivity growth and higher output.
- As labour productivity rises, so wages are likely to rise. The higher wages will lead to higher consumption, and hence, via the multiplier and accelerator, to higher output and higher investment, thereby stimulating further advances in productivity.
- In the longer term, businesses experiencing higher productivity growth would expect their lower costs, and hence enhanced competitiveness, to allow them to gain greater market share. This will encourage further investment and productivity growth.

It is clear that the prosperity of a nation rests upon its ability to improve its productivity. The more successful it is in doing this, the greater will be its rate of economic growth.

For an analysis of UK productivity, see Web Case 21.1.

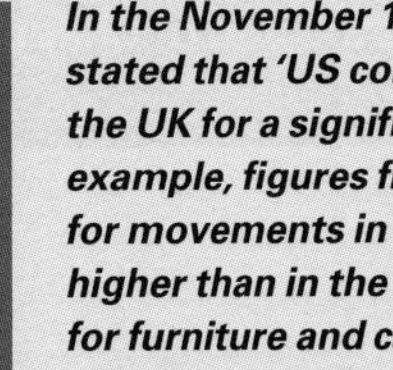

In the November 1998 pre-Budget Report[2] it was stated that 'US consumers pay less than those in the UK for a significant range of products. For example, figures from the OECD show, adjusting for movements in exchange rates, British prices are higher than in the US by an average of: 56 per cent for furniture and carpets; 54 per cent for hotels and restaurants; 29 per cent for cars.' Can productivity differences explain price differences?

[1] 'Capital productivity: why the US leads and why it matters', *The McKinsey Quarterly*, 1996, no. 3.

[2] http://archive.treasury.gov.uk/pub/html/prebudgetNov98/407603.htm, Box 3.3.

Section summary

1. A higher long-term rate of growth will normally require a faster rate of technological progress.
2. The rate of technological progress determines the slope of the steady-state growth path (i.e. the rate of steady-state growth). If there is a rise in the saving rate, this will shift the steady-state growth path upwards (parallel) and the actual growth path will gradually move from the lower to the higher path.
3. Endogenous growth theory argues that the rate of technological progress and its rate of diffusion depend on economic institutions and incentives. Supply-side policy could be used to alter these.

END OF CHAPTER QUESTIONS

1. For what reasons do countries experience very different long-run rates of economic growth from each other?
2. Why do developed countries experience a degree of convergence over time? Would you expect there to be total convergence of GDP per head?
3. If increased investment (using current technology) does not lead to increased long-run economic growth, does it bring any benefits?
4. What determines the rate of depreciation? What would happen if the rate of depreciation fell?
5. What is meant by the 'steady-state economic growth path'? What determines its slope?
6. What is the significance of the term 'endogenous' in endogenous growth theory? What, according to this theory, determines the long-run rate of economic growth?
7. Under what circumstances would a higher rate of investment lead to a higher rate of economic growth?
8. What determines the rate of growth in total factor productivity?

Additional case studies on the book's website (www.pearsoned.co.uk/sloman)

21.1 Productivity performance and the UK economy. A detailed examination of how the UK's productivity compares with that in other countries.

21.2 The USA: is it a 'new economy'? An examination of whether US productivity increases are likely to be sustained.

WEBSITES RELEVANT TO THIS CHAPTER

See sites listed at the end of Chapter 22 on page 632.

Chapter 22

Supply-side Policies

As we saw in the previous chapter, long-run economic growth can only be achieved through an increase in aggregate supply. This, in turn, requires an increase in productivity. But how can productivity be increased?

In this chapter we look at various policies to increase aggregate supply. We also examine how developments on the supply side can affect the other macroeconomic objectives of achieving low unemployment and low inflation. We start by looking at different approaches to supply-side policy and how they relate to the analysis of the economy. For example, we contrast Keynesian and new classical approaches.

Supply-side policies can be put into two broad categories: market orientated and interventionist. Market-orientated policies focus on 'freeing up' markets and improving market incentives. They involve policies such as tax cuts, privatisation and deregulation. We look at such policies in section 22.2.

Interventionist policies, by contrast, focus on ways of countering the inadequacies of markets through direct government provision of transport infrastructure, training or R&D, or financial support for private provision. We look at this type of policy in section 22.3.

Not surprisingly, the political right argues in favour of 'freeing up' the market; the left argues in favour of intervention.

The chapter closes by looking at the regional and urban balance of output and employment, and at various policies for improving the supply-side performance of less favoured parts of the economy.

CHAPTER MAP

22.1 APPROACHES TO SUPPLY-SIDE POLICY

Supply-side policies and the different macro objectives

Economic growth

As we saw in Chapter 21, economic growth over the long run depends primarily on technological progress. But a lot of technological progress is embodied in new capital equipment. In other words, you cannot have the new technology without having the equipment that uses it. To take advantage of new technology, therefore, firms often have to invest in new capital. Also, workers and management need the skills and flexibility to be able to take full advantage of technical innovations. This may require new working practices and new forms of organisation.

Thus supply-side policy to encourage more economic growth should focus not just on research and development, but also on investment, education and training, industrial organisation, work practices and the whole range of incentives that may be necessary to make optimum use of new techniques.

?

Why do Keynesians argue that, even in the long run, demand-side policies will still be required if faster growth in aggregate supply is to be achieved?

Unemployment

Supply-side policies can also be directed at other macroeconomic objectives. The cure for demand-deficient unemployment may lie on the demand side, but other types of unemployment require supply-side solutions.

Equilibrium unemployment – frictional, structural, etc. – is caused by rigidities or imperfections in the market. There is a mismatching of aggregate supply and demand, and vacancies are not filled despite the existence of unemployment. The problem is that labour is not sufficiently mobile, either occupationally or geographically, to respond to changes in the job market. Labour supply for particular jobs is too inelastic.

Supply-side policies aim to influence labour supply by making workers more responsive to changes in job opportunities. They may also aim to make employers more adaptable and willing to operate within existing labour constraints. Alternatively, they may seek to reduce the monopoly power of unions to drive real wages above the equilibrium.

Inflation and supply-side policies

If inflation is caused by cost-push pressures, supply-side policy can help to reduce it in three ways:

- By reducing the power of unions and/or firms (e.g. anti-monopoly legislation) and thereby encouraging more competition in the supply of labour and/or goods.
- By preventing people from exercising that power by some form of prices and incomes policy. (Such policies were used in the 1970s: see Web Case 22.3.)
- By encouraging increases in productivity through the retraining of labour, or by investment grants to firms, or by tax incentives, etc.

The new classical approach to supply-side policy

New classical economists argue that demand-side policy (by which they mean monetary policy) can only control inflation; it cannot affect growth and employment. Supply-side policy is the appropriate policy to increase output and reduce the level of unemployment.

Supply-side policy can be used to shift the aggregate supply curve to the right: to increase the amount that firms wish to supply at any given price. In Figure 22.1, output rises to Q_2 and prices fall to P_2. In the labour market, it can also reduce the natural rate of unemployment, and thus shift the vertical long-run Phillips curve to the left.

New classical economists advocate policies to 'free up' the market: policies that encourage private enterprise, or provide incentives and reward initiative. Section 22.2 examines these ***market-orientated supply-side policies***. TC 3 p21

This part of the new classical agenda has much in common with the ***neo-Austrian/libertarian school*** (see Box 11.6). The argument here is that a free market, with the absolute minimum of government interference, will provide the dynamic environment where entrepreneurs

Figure 22.1 Aggregate demand and supply: monetarist analysis

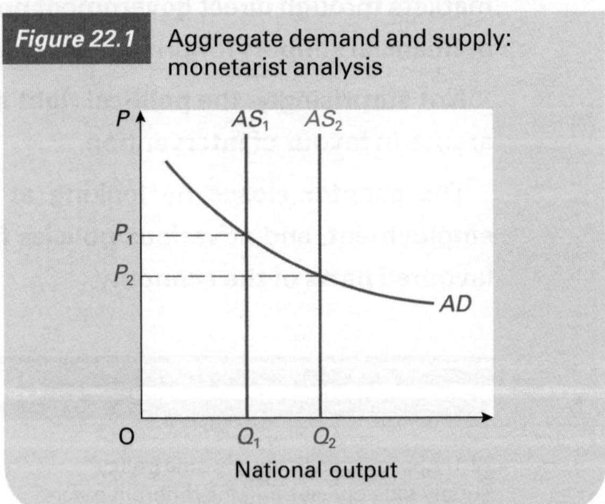

Definitions

Market-orientated supply-side policies Policies to increase aggregate supply by freeing up the market.

Neo-Austrian/libertarian school A school of thought that advocates maximum liberty for economic agents to pursue their own interests and to own property.

will be willing to take risks and develop new products and new techniques.

Unlike neoclassical economists, who concentrate on the desirability of achieving economic efficiency in competitive markets, the neo-Austrians take a longer-term perspective. They argue that the prospect of monopoly profits is often what provides a major motivation for firms to take risks. The search to achieve market advantages through new products and new techniques is just as important a part of competition, they argue, as competition in the market for existing goods. Thus private property rights are a key element in neo-Austrian thought: the right to keep the fruits of innovation and investment, with minimum taxation.

The Keynesian approach to supply-side policy

Modern Keynesians do not just advocate the management of demand. They too advocate supply-side policies, but generally of a more ***interventionist*** nature (e.g. training schemes, or policies to encourage firms to set up in areas of high unemployment).

The appropriate balance between demand- and supply-side policies depends on the degree of slack in the economy. In Figure 22.2, if output is below Q_1 with aggregate demand below AD_1, the immediate policy requirement is to increase aggregate *demand* rather than aggregate supply. If, however, the economy is approaching full employment with aggregate demand at AD_2 and output at Q_2, the most appropriate policy to increase output is a supply-side policy. This will shift the *AS* curve to the right (e.g. to AS_2) and raise output (e.g. to Q_3).

Figure 22.2 Aggregate demand and supply: Keynesian analysis

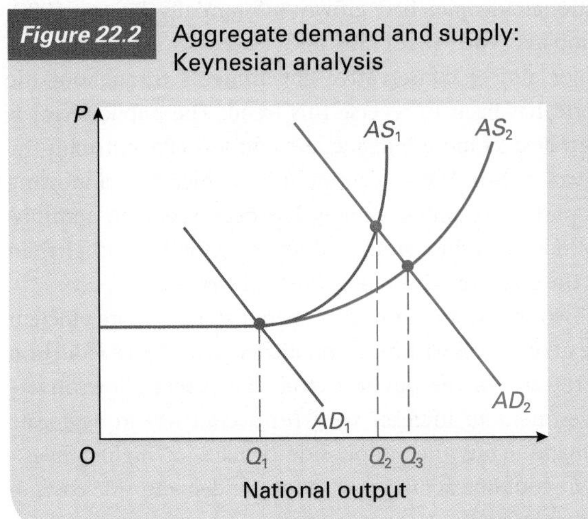

Definition

Interventionist supply-side policies Policies to increase aggregate supply by government intervention to counteract the deficiencies of the market.

Figure 22.3 Phillips curves

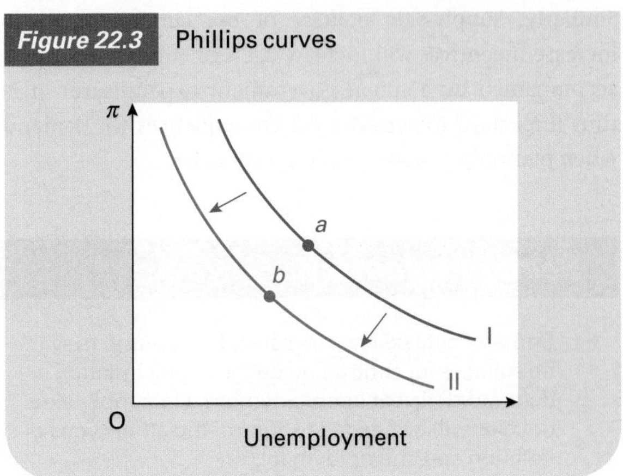

? *Does this mean that Keynesians would advocate using supply-side policies only at times of full employment?*

Keynesians also advocate supply-side policies to shift the Phillips curve to the left. If successful, such policies could lead simultaneously to lower unemployment and lower inflation. The economy could move from, say, point *a* to point *b* in Figure 22.3.

'Third Way' supply-side policies

With the election of the Blair government in the UK, there was much discussion of a 'Third Way' between the unfettered market system advocated by many of those on the right and the interventionist approach advocated by those on the left. The Third Way borrows from the right in advocating incentives, low taxes and free movements of capital. It also borrows from the left in advocating means whereby governments can improve economic performance and provide support for individuals.

Its main thrust is the concept of helping people to help themselves. Thus unemployment policies should be focused on helping the unemployed become employable, with unemployment benefits linked to the obligation actively to look for work. Growth policies should be a mixture of strengthening market incentives and keeping taxes low, regulation to encourage more competition and prevent monopoly abuse, and providing improved infrastructure and improved education and training.

The link between demand-side and supply-side policies

Policies can have both demand-side and supply-side effects. For example, many supply-side policies involve increased government expenditure: whether it be on retraining schemes, on research and development projects, or on industrial relocation. They will therefore cause a rise in aggregate demand (unless accompanied by a rise in taxes).

Similarly, supply-side policies of tax cuts designed to increase incentives will increase aggregate demand (unless accompanied by a cut in government expenditure). It is thus important to consider the consequences for demand when planning various supply-side policies.

Likewise, demand management policies often have supply-side effects. If a cut in interest rates boosts investment, there will be a multiplied rise in national income: a demand-side effect. But that rise in investment will also create increased productive capacity: a supply-side effect.

Section summary

1. Demand-side policies (fiscal and monetary) may be suitable for controlling demand-pull inflation or demand-deficient unemployment, but supply-side policies will be needed to control the other types of inflation and unemployment.
2. Supply-side policies, if successful, will shift the aggregate supply curve to the right, and possibly the Phillips curve downwards/to the left.
3. New classical and neo-Austrian economists favour market-orientated supply-side policies. Keynesians tend to favour interventionist supply-side policies. The Third Way advocates carefully targeted government intervention, regulation, welfare and education programmes to encourage people better to help themselves and markets to work more effectively.
4. Supply-side policies often have demand-side effects, and demand-side policies often have supply-side effects. It is important for governments to take these secondary effects into account when working out their economic strategy.

22.2 MARKET-ORIENTATED SUPPLY-SIDE POLICIES

Supply-side policies in the 1980s

TC 3 p21

Radical market-orientated supply-side policies were first adopted in the early 1980s by the Thatcher government in the UK and the Reagan administration in the USA. The essence of these policies was to encourage and reward individual enterprise and initiative, and to reduce the role of government; to put more reliance on market forces and competition, and less on government intervention and regulation. The policies were thus associated with the following:

- Reducing government expenditure so as to release more resources for the private sector.
- Reducing taxes so as to increase incentives.
- Reducing the monopoly power of trade unions so as to encourage greater flexibility in both wages and working practices and to allow labour markets to clear.
- Reducing the automatic entitlement to certain welfare benefits so as to encourage greater self-reliance.
- Reducing red tape and other impediments to investment and risk taking.
- Encouraging competition through policies of deregulation and privatisation.
- Abolishing exchange controls and other impediments to the free movement of capital.

Such policies were increasingly copied by other governments around the world. Today most countries have adopted some or all of the above measures.

Reducing government expenditure

The desire by many governments to cut government expenditure is not just to reduce the PSNCR and hence reduce the growth of money supply; it is also an essential ingredient of their supply-side strategy.

In most countries the size of the public sector, relative to national income, had grown substantially by the 1980s compared with the 1950s and 1960s (see Table 22.1). A major aim of conservative governments throughout the world has been to reverse this trend. The public sector is portrayed as more bureaucratic and less efficient than the private sector. What is more, it is claimed that a growing proportion of public money has been spent on administration and other 'non-productive' activities, rather than on the direct provision of goods and services.

Two things are needed, it is argued: (a) a more efficient use of resources within the public sector and (b) a reduction in the size of the public sector. This would allow private investment to increase with no overall rise in aggregate demand. Thus the supply-side benefits of higher investment could be achieved without the demand-side costs of higher inflation.

In practice, governments have found it very difficult to cut their expenditure without cutting services and the provision of infrastructure.

? *Why might a recovering economy (and hence a fall in government expenditure on social security benefits) make the government feel even more concerned to make discretionary cuts in government expenditure?*

Table 22.1 General government expenditure as a percentage of GDP at market prices (average annual)

	1961–70	1971–80	1981–5	1986–90	1991–5	1996–2000	2001–5
Belgium	33.7	50.0	61.5	55.3	54.0	50.8	50.4
Germany	37.0	45.3	48.2	46.0	48.2	48.6	48.0
France	38.3	42.4	51.5	50.2	53.0	54.0	53.7
Japan	–	26.8	33.2	31.5	33.2	38.9	38.9
Netherlands	39.9	49.3	59.5	55.0	53.0	47.4	48.1
Sweden	–	52.8	65.0	58.5	66.3	61.3	57.5
UK	36.5	41.2	44.6	39.8	42.5	40.3	42.6
USA	29.1	33.1	36.5	34.9	35.5	33.5	34.0

[a] Forecast.

Source: *European Economy* (Commission of the European Union).

CASE STUDIES AND APPLICATIONS — BOX 22.1

THE SUPPLY-SIDE REVOLUTION IN THE USA

'Reaganomics'

In both the UK and the USA, the 1980s proved to be years of radical political and economic change. Traditional economic and political practices were replaced by new and often controversial policies, although in theory many of the ideas advocated were based on old principles of *laissez-faire* capitalism.

In the USA, the era of 'Reaganomics' began in January 1981 when Ronald Reagan became President. With this new administration came a radical shift in policy aimed at directly tackling the supply side of the economy. This policy strategy involved four key strands:

- A reduction in the growth of Federal (central government) spending.
- A reduction in individual and corporate tax rates.
- A reduction in Federal regulations over private enterprise.
- A reduction in inflation through tight monetary policy.

On all four points, President Reagan was to achieve a degree of success. Federal spending *growth* was reduced even though military spending rocketed. Tax rates fell dramatically. Deregulation was speeded up. Inflation at first was stabilised and then fell sharply.

These supply-side measures were hailed as a great success by Republicans, and followers in both the UK and the USA were quick to advocate an even bigger reduction in the government's role.

Critics remained sceptical and pointed to the costs of Reaganomics. Huge budget deficits plagued the Reagan administration and the Bush Snr/Clinton and Bush Jnr administrations that followed. The massive tax cuts were not matched by an equivalent cut in public expenditure; nor did they produce a sufficiently high rate of economic growth, through which additional tax revenues were to balance the budget. In the 1980s, 'civilian' or welfare spending was cut repeatedly in preference to the huge military budget. This led to increasing social hardship.

And such hardship still exists under George W. Bush, 25 years later, and is getting no easier. The emphasis remains on cutting welfare and tightening requirements to receive state assistance. Critics claim that, even though the numbers on welfare may be falling, individuals and families remain in poverty, being forced to work for poverty wages as welfare support dwindles. The revolution is far from complete and its benefits to all social groups are far from even.

Tax cuts: the effects on labour supply and employment

Cutting the marginal rate of income tax was a major objective of the Thatcher and Major governments (1979–97), as it was of the Reagan administration. In 1979, the standard rate of income tax was 33 per cent, with higher rates rising to 83 per cent. By 1997 the standard rate was only 23 per cent and the top rate was only 40 per cent. The Blair government continued with this policy, so that by 2000 the standard rate was 22 per cent, with a starting rate of only 10 per cent.

Cuts in the marginal rate of income tax are claimed to have five beneficial effects: people work longer hours; more people wish to work; people work more enthusiastically; employment rises, unemployment falls. These are big claims. Are they true? TC 3 p21

People work longer hours

A cut in the marginal rate of income tax has a *substitution effect* inducing people to work more and also an *income effect* causing people to work less. (At this point, you should review the arguments about the incentive effects of tax cuts: see pages 282–3.) Evidence suggests that the two

effects will roughly cancel each other out. Anyway, for many people there is no such choice in the short run. There is no chance of doing overtime or working a shorter week. In the long run, there may be some flexibility in that people can change jobs.

More people wish to work

This applies largely to second income earners in a family, mainly women. A rise in after-tax wages may encourage more women to look for jobs. It may now be worth the cost in terms of transport, child care, family disruption, etc. The effects of a 1 or 2 per cent cut in income tax rates, however, are likely to be negligible. A more significant effect may be achieved by raising tax allowances. Part-time workers, especially, could end up paying no taxes. Of course, if unemployment is already high, the government will not want to increase the labour force.

People work more enthusiastically

There is little evidence to test this claim. The argument, however, is that people will be more conscientious and will work harder if they can keep more of their pay.

Employment rises

If wages are flexible, total employment will rise. This is illustrated in Figure 22.4. The *N* curve shows the total labour force. The AS_L curve shows the number of people who are actually qualified and willing to do the specific jobs they are offered at each (after-tax) wage rate. Equilibrium is where the aggregate demand for labour (AD_L) is equal to the labour cost to the employer (i.e. the pre-tax wage rate). Assume an initial income tax per worker of $a - b$. The equilibrium employment will be Q_1. Workers receive an after-tax wage W_1 and thus supply Q_1 labour. Employers' labour cost is the pre-tax wage lc_1. At this wage, they demand Q_1 labour.

If the income tax per worker now falls to $c - d$, equilibrium employment will rise to Q_2. Firms will employ more workers because their labour costs have fallen to lc_2. More workers will take up jobs because their after-tax wages have risen to W_2.

Figure 22.4 Effect of a tax cut on total unemployment

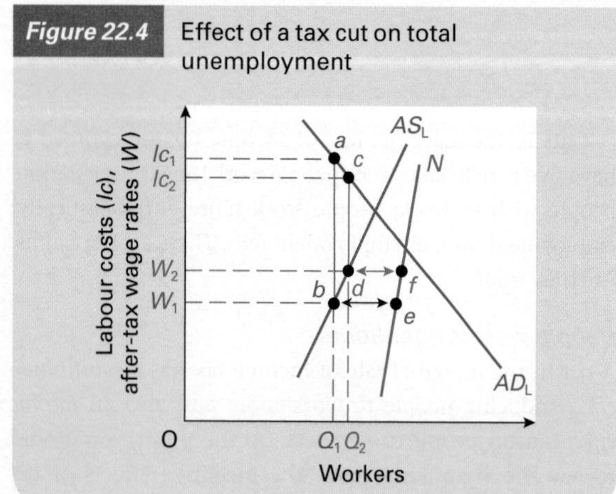

Unemployment falls

One of the causes of natural (equilibrium) unemployment highlighted by new classical economists is the cushioning provided by unemployment benefit. If income tax rates are cut, there will be a bigger difference between after-tax wage rates and unemployment benefit. More people will be motivated to 'get on their bikes' and look for work.

In Figure 22.4, the horizontal gap between *N* and AS_L represents equilibrium unemployment. With a cut in income tax per worker from $a - b$ to $c - d$, equilibrium unemployment will fall from $e - b$ to $f - d$.

? *What would happen to the AS_L curve and the level of unemployment if unemployment benefits were increased?*

Despite the cuts in marginal rates of income tax in many countries, it has been commonplace for these to be offset by significant increases in other taxes. For example, in the UK, VAT stood at only 8 per cent in 1979; in 2005 it was 17½ per cent. The marginal rate of national insurance contributions was 6½ per cent in 1979; in 2005 it was 11 per cent. The net effect was that taxes as a proportion of GDP rose from 34.2 per cent in 1979 to 37.3 per cent in 2005.

? *Does this mean that there were no positive incentive effects from the Conservative government's tax measures?*

To the extent that tax cuts do succeed in increasing take-home pay, there is a danger of 'sucking in' imports. In the UK, there is a high income elasticity of demand for imports. Extra consumer incomes may be spent on Japanese videos and hi-fi, foreign cars, holidays abroad and so on. Tax cuts can therefore have a serious effect on the current account of the balance of payments.

Tax cuts for business and other investment incentives

A number of financial incentives can be given to encourage investment. Selective intervention in the form of grants for specific industries or firms is best classified as an interventionist policy and will be examined later in this chapter. Market-orientated policies seek to reduce the general level of taxation on profits, or to give greater tax relief to investment. TC 3 p21

A cut in corporation tax (the tax on business profits) will increase after-tax profits. This will leave more funds for ploughing back into investment. Also the higher after-tax return on investment will encourage more investment to take place. In 1983 the main rate of corporation tax in the UK stood at 52 per cent. A series of reductions have taken place since then, and by 2005/6 the rate was 30 per cent for large companies and 19 per cent for small companies, with a zero per cent starting rate.

An alternative policy would be to increase investment allowances. Investment allowances are the system whereby the cost of investment can be offset against pre-tax profit, thereby reducing a firm's tax liability.

Reducing the power of labour

In Figure 22.5, if the power of unions to push wage rates up to W_1 were removed, then (assuming no change in the demand curve for labour) wage rates would fall to W_e. Disequilibrium unemployment ($Q_2 - Q_1$) would disappear. Employment would rise from Q_1 to Q_e.

Equilibrium unemployment, however, will rise somewhat as the gap between gross and effective labour supply widens. With the reduction in wage rates, some people may now prefer to remain 'on the dole'.

If labour costs to employers are reduced, their profits will probably rise. This could encourage and enable more investment and hence economic growth. If the monopoly power of labour is reduced, then cost-push inflation will also be reduced.

The Thatcher government took a number of measures to weaken the power of labour. These included restrictions on union closed shops, restrictions on secondary picketing, financial assistance for union ballots, and enforced secret ballots on strike proposals (see Chapter 9). It set a lead in resisting strikes in the public sector. Unlike previous Labour governments, it did not consult with union leaders over questions of economic policy. It was publicly very critical of trade union militancy and blamed the unions for many of the UK's economic ills. As a result, unions lost a lot of political standing and influence.

As labour markets have become more flexible, with increased part-time working and short-term contracts, and as the process of globalisation has exposed more companies to international competition, so this has further eroded the power of labour in many sectors of the economy.

? *Is the number of working days lost through disputes a good indication of (a) union power; (b) union militancy?*

Figure 22.5 Effect of reducing the power of labour

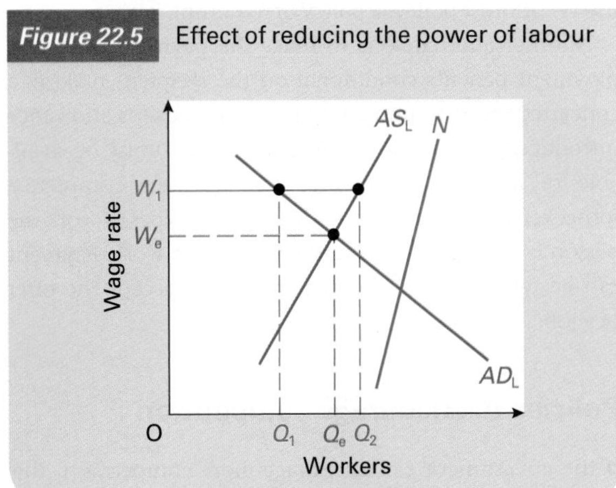

Reducing welfare

New classical economists claim that a major cause of unemployment is the small difference between the welfare benefits of the unemployed and the take-home pay of the employed. This causes voluntary unemployment (i.e. frictional unemployment). People are caught in a 'poverty trap': if they take a job, they lose their benefits (see page 287).

A dramatic solution to this problem would be to cut unemployment benefits. Unlike policies to encourage investment, this supply-side policy would have a very rapid effect. It would shift the effective labour supply curve to the right. In Figure 22.6, equilibrium unemployment would fall from $a - b$ to $c - d$ if real wage rates were flexible downwards; or from $a - b$ to $a - e$ if they were not flexible. In the case of non-flexible real wage rates, the reduction in equilibrium unemployment would be offset by a rise in disequilibrium unemployment ($e - b$).

Because workers would now be prepared to accept a lower wage, the average length of job search by the unemployed would be reduced. In Figure 22.7, the average duration of unemployment would fall from T_1 to T_2 (see page 403).

Figure 22.6 The effects of a cut in benefits on the number unemployed

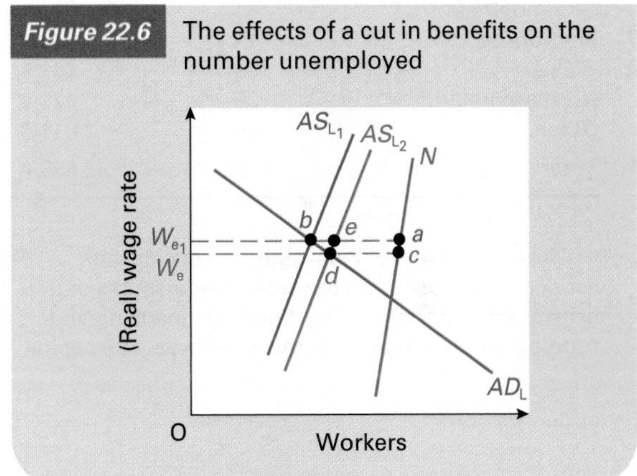

Figure 22.7 The effects of a cut in benefits on the average duration of unemployment

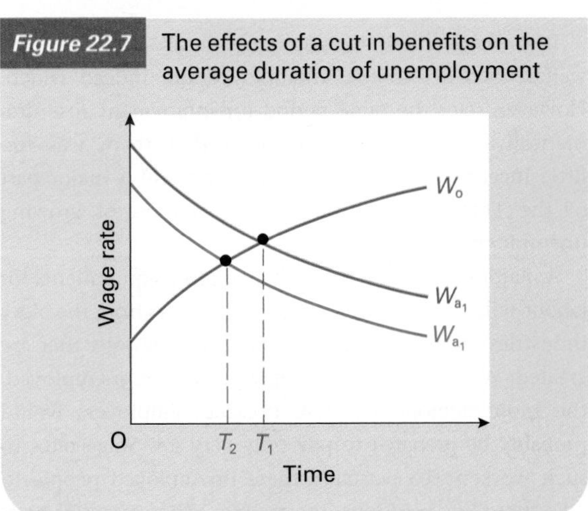

CASE STUDIES AND APPLICATIONS

ASSESSING PFI

A 'Third Way' solution to the provision of public services

The Private Finance Initiative (PFI), although introduced by the Conservative government in 1992, has become central to the Labour government's 'Third Way' approach of using the private sector to deliver public projects and services. It has become increasingly common for new schools, hospitals, roads, bridges, student accommodation, etc. to be funded and built by private companies under PFI contracts (see table and figure). Well-known examples include the Channel Tunnel rail link and capital investment in the London Underground.

PFI projects: total to January 2005

Department(s)	Number of signed projects	Capital value (£m)
Transport	45	21 432.1
Health	136	4 901.2
Defence	52	4 254.8
Education and Skills	121	2 922.8
Scotland	84	2 249.3
Work and Pensions	11	1 341.0
Home Office	37	1 095.8
Communities	61	972.1
Environment	13	632.7
Wales	33	551.3
Northern Ireland	39	528.8
Other	45	1 817.6
Total	677	42 699.4

The government or local authority decides the service it requires, and then seeks tenders from the private sector for designing, building, financing and running projects to provide these services. The capital costs are borne by the private sector, but then, if the provision of the service is not self-financing, the public sector pays the private firm for providing it. Thus instead of the public sector being an owner of assets and provider of services, it is merely an enabler, buying services from the private sector.

A key aim of PFI is to introduce competition (through the tendering process), private-sector expertise, innovation and the management of risk into the provision of public services.

> Under the Private Finance Initiative (PFI) the public sector contracts to purchase services on a long-term basis so as to take advantage of private sector management skills incentivised by having private finance at risk. The private sector has always been involved in the building and maintenance of public infrastructure, but PFI ensures that contractors are bound into long-term maintenance contracts and shoulder responsibility for the quality of the work they do. With PFI, the public sector defines what is required to meet public needs and ensures delivery of the outputs through the contract. Consequently, the private sector can be harnessed to deliver investment in better quality public services while frontline services are retained within the public sector.[1]

Clearly, there are immediate benefits to the public finances from using private, rather than public, funds to finance a project. Later, however, there is potentially an extra burden of having to buy the services from the private provider at a price that includes an element for profit. What is hoped is that the costs to the taxpayer of these profits will be more than offset by gains in efficiency.

? *Would a cut in benefits affect the W_0 curve? If so, with what effect?*

In the early 1980s, the gap between take-home pay and welfare benefits to the unemployed did indeed widen. However, over the same period unemployment rose dramatically. Nevertheless, the claim that there was too little incentive for people to work was still a major part of the Thatcher government's explanation of growing unemployment.

A major problem is that with changing requirements for labour skills, many of the redundant workers from the older industries are simply not qualified for new jobs that are created. What is more, the longer people are unemployed, the more demoralised they become. Employers would probably be prepared to pay only very low wage rates to such workers. To persuade these unemployed people to take these low-paid jobs, the welfare benefits would have to be slashed. A 'market' solution to the problem, therefore, may be a very cruel solution. A fairer solution would be an interventionist policy: a policy of retraining labour.

Another alternative is to make the payment of unemployment benefits conditional on the recipient making a concerted effort to find a job. In the jobseeker's allowance introduced in the UK in 1996, claimants must be available for, and actively seeking, work and must complete a Jobseeker's Agreement, which sets out the types of work the person is willing to do, and the plan to find work. Payment can be refused if the claimant refuses to accept the offer of a job.

Policies to encourage competition

If the government can encourage more competition, this should have the effect of increasing national output and

BOX 22.2

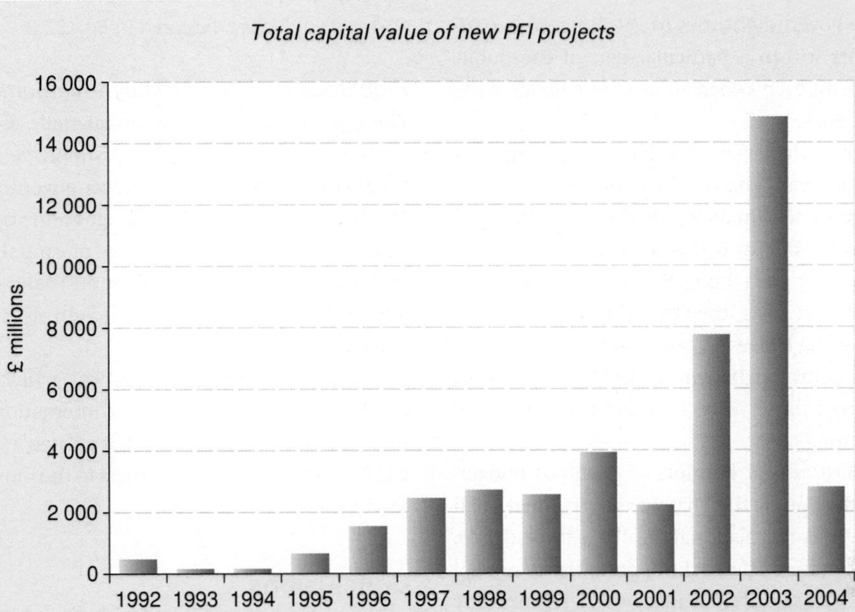

Critics, however, claim that PFI projects have resulted in poorer quality of provision and that cost control has often been poor, resulting in a higher burden for the taxpayer in the long term. What is more, many of the projects have turned out to be highly profitable, suggesting that the terms of the original contracts were too lax. Take the case of Carillion. It owns stakes in 18 PFI projects, including the new GCHQ communications centre at Cheltenham and the M6 toll road. In 2005, it announced that the net present value of its PFI investments was £83 million. This compared with an investment cost of just £29 million.

There is also the question of what happens if the private company runs into financial difficulties. In 2005, the engineering company Jarvis only just managed to avoid bankruptcy by securing refinancing on all 14 of its PFI deals. This involved selling a large amount of assets and renegotiating loans.

Do a news Web search for PFI projects and identify the issues currently surrounding the success or otherwise of PFI.

[1] *Financial Statement and Budget Report, Chapter C* (HM Treasury, 2005).

reducing inflation. Five major types of policy have been pursued under this heading.

Privatisation

If privatisation simply involves the transfer of a natural monopoly to private hands (e.g. the water companies), the scope for increased competition is limited. However, where there is genuine scope for competition (e.g. in the supply of gas and electricity), privatisation can lead to increased efficiency, more consumer choice and lower prices.

Alternatively, privatisation can involve the introduction of private services into the public sector (e.g. private contractors providing cleaning services in hospitals, or refuse collection for local authorities). Private contractors may compete against each other for the franchise. This may well lower the cost of provision of these services, but the quality of provision may also suffer unless closely monitored. The effects on unemployment are uncertain. Private contractors may offer lower wages and thus may use more labour. But if they are trying to supply the service at minimum cost, they may employ less labour.

KI 22 p 208

Deregulation

This involves the removal of monopoly rights. In 1979 the National Bus Corporation lost its monopoly of long-distance coach haulage. Private operators were now allowed to compete. This substantially reduced coach fares on a number of routes. In 1986 competition was allowed in providing local bus services (see Web Case 22.1).

An example in the private sector was the so-called 'Big Bang' on the Stock Exchange in 1986. Under this, the monopoly power of jobbers to deal in stocks and shares on the Stock Exchange was abolished. In addition, stockbrokers now compete with each other in the commission rates that they charge, and on-line share dealing has become commonplace.

Introducing market relationships into the public sector

This is where the government tries to get different departments or elements within a particular part of the public sector to 'trade' with each other, so as to encourage competition and efficiency.

The process often involves 'devolved budgeting'. For example, under the locally managed schools scheme (LMS), schools have become self-financing. Rather than the local authority meeting the bill for teachers' salaries, the schools have to manage their own budgets. The objective is to encourage them to cut costs, thereby reducing the burden on council tax payers. However, one result is that schools have tended to appoint inexperienced (and hence cheaper) teachers rather than those who can bring the benefits of their years of teaching.

Perhaps the most radical example of devolved budgeting was the introduction by the Thatcher government of an 'internal market' into the National Health Service (NHS). General practitioners were offered the opportunity to control their own budget. The size of the budget was determined by the number of patients and by their age and health profiles. GP fundholders purchased services directly from hospitals and had to cover their drugs bill. The suppliers of treatment, the hospitals, depended for much of their income on attracting the business of GP purchasers. They were thus put in competition with other hospitals.

Advocates of the internal market in the NHS argued that it created greater efficiency through competition. Critics, however, claimed that it led to growing inequalities of service between practices and between hospitals, and increased the administrative costs of the NHS.

The Labour government abolished the NHS internal market and replaced GP fundholding with a system of local primary care trusts, which co-ordinate health-care provision in a particular locality. They also purchase services for patients from hospitals with the objective of giving patients, through their GPs, more choice of where to be treated.

The government also introduced (in 2003) a system of 'foundation trusts'. Hospitals can apply for foundation trust status. If successful, they are given much greater financial autonomy in terms of purchasing, employment and investment decisions. Applications are judged by Monitor, the independent health regulator. By April 2005, there were 31 foundation trusts. Critics argue that funds have been diverted to foundation hospitals away from the less well-performing hospitals where greater funding could help that performance.

The Private Finance Initiative (PFI)

This is where a private company, after a competitive tender, is contracted by a government department or local authority to finance and build a project, such as a new road or a prison. The government then pays the company to maintain and/or run it, or simply rents the assets from the company. The public sector thus becomes a purchaser of services rather than a direct provider itself. The benefits and costs of PFI are explored in Box 22.2.

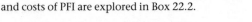

Free trade and free capital movements

The opening-up of international trade and investment is central to a market-orientated supply-side policy. One of the first measures of the Thatcher government (in October 1979) was to remove all exchange controls, thereby permitting the free inflow and outflow of capital, both long term and short term. Most other industrialised countries also removed or relaxed exchange controls during the 1980s and early 1990s.

The Single European Act of 1987, which came into force in 1993, was another example of international liberalisation. As we shall see in section 23.4, it created a 'single market' in the EU: a market without barriers to the movement of goods, services, capital and labour.

Conclusions

Although a number of supply-side measures have been taken in many countries during the last 20 years, many of the supply-side *effects* have been the result of changes in demand.

The recessions of the early 1980s and early 1990s caused many firms to fail. Those that survived were often able to do so only by increases in efficiency. Resistance from unions to the introduction of new labour-saving technology was weakened by high unemployment and the fear that, without the new technology, firms might be forced to close.

Similarly, demand had effects on the supply side during periods of expansion, like the late 1980s and late 1990s. Firms were encouraged to innovate and develop new products to take advantage of buoyant markets.

Even where supply-side changes cannot be traced directly to changes in aggregate demand, they often occur not as a result of government supply-side policy, but as a result of international competition and capital movements, new business practices, new inventions and new products.

Thus, although productivity in the UK and the USA grew more rapidly in the 1980s and 1990s than in the 1970s (see Table 21.1 on page 600), it is not clear to what extent this was the direct result of supply-side *policy*.

If supply-side measures led to a 'shake out' of labour and a resulting reduction in overstaffing, but also to a rightward shift in the Phillips curve, would you judge the policy as a success?

Section summary

1. Market-orientated supply-side policies aim to increase the rate of growth of aggregate supply by encouraging private enterprise and the freer play of market forces.
2. Reducing government expenditure as a proportion of GDP is a major element of such policies.
3. Tax cuts can be used to encourage more people to take up jobs, and people to work longer hours and more enthusiastically. They can be used to reduce equilibrium unemployment and encourage employers to take on more workers. Likewise tax cuts for businesses or increased investment allowances may encourage higher investment. The effects of tax cuts depend on how people respond to incentives. For example, people will work longer hours only if the substitution effect outweighs the income effect.
4. Reducing the power of trade unions by legislation could reduce disequilibrium unemployment and cost-push inflation. It could also lead to a redistribution of income to profits, which could increase investment and growth (but possibly lead to greater inequality).
5. A reduction in welfare benefits, especially those related to unemployment, will encourage workers to accept jobs at lower wages and thus decrease equilibrium unemployment.
6. Various policies can be introduced to increase competition. These include privatisation, deregulation, introducing market relationships into the public sector, public–private partnerships and freer international trade and capital movements.

22.3 INTERVENTIONIST SUPPLY-SIDE POLICY

TC 7 p 26

In this section, we look at the limitations of the market in stimulating supply-side improvements. We then look at ways in which the government can intervene to encourage more investment and a faster rate of economic growth. We will also assess the relative effectiveness of different types of interventionist policy.

Many of these policies come under the general heading of ***industrial policy***: the government taking an active role to support investment in industry and to halt the decline of the manufacturing sector (see Box 22.4).

The case against the market

TC 6 p 26

The basis of the case for government intervention is that the free market is likely to provide too little research and development, training and investment.

KI 28 p 300

There are potentially large external benefits from research and development (see page 301). Firms investing in developing and improving products, and especially firms engaged in more general scientific research, may produce results that provide benefits to many other firms. Thus the social rate of return on investment may be much higher than the private rate of return. Investment that is privately unprofitable for a firm may therefore still be economically desirable for the nation.

Similarly, investment in training may continue yielding benefits to society that are lost to the firms providing the training when the workers leave.

Investment often involves risks. Firms may be unwilling to take those risks, since the costs of possible failure may be too high. When looked at nationally, however, the benefits of investment might well have substantially outweighed the costs, and thus it would have been socially desirable for firms to have taken the risk. Successes would have outweighed failures.

Imperfections in the capital market. These may result in investment not being financed, even though it is privately profitable. Banks in the UK, unlike banks in France, Germany and Japan, have been reluctant to lend to firms for long-term investment.

Similarly, if firms rely on raising finance by the issue of new shares, this makes them very dependent on the stock market performance of their shares, which depends on current profitability and expected profitability in the near future, not on long-term profitability. Shareholders, who are mainly financial institutions, tend to demand too high a dividend rate from the companies in which they invest. This, in part, is due to competition between financial institutions to attract savers to buy their savings packages. The result is that there is less profit left over for ploughing back into investment. The fear of takeovers (the competition for corporate control) again makes managers overconcerned to keep shareholders happy. Finally, floating successful

Definition

Industrial policies Policies to encourage industrial investment and greater industrial efficiency.

CASE STUDIES AND APPLICATIONS

ALTERNATIVE APPROACHES TO TRAINING AND EDUCATION

It is generally recognised by economists and politicians alike that improvements in training and education can yield significant supply-side gains. Indeed, the UK's past failure to invest as much in training as many of its major competitors is seen as a key explanation for the country's poor economic performance until recent years.

Training and economic performance are linked in three main ways:

- *Labour productivity*. In various studies comparing the productivity of UK and German industry, education and training is seen as the principal reason for the productivity gap between the two countries (see diagram in Box 21.1).
- *Innovation and change*. A key factor in shaping a firm's willingness to introduce new products or processes will be the adaptability and skills of its workforce. If the firm has to spend a lot of money on retraining, or on attracting skilled workers away from other firms, the costs may prove prohibitive.
- *Costs of production*. A shortage of skilled workers will quickly create labour bottlenecks and cause production costs to increase. This will stifle economic growth.

If training is left to the employer, the benefits will become an externality if the workers leave to work elsewhere. Society has benefited from the training, but the firm has not. The free market, therefore, will provide a less than optimal amount of training. The more mobile the labour force, and the more 'transferable' the skills acquired from training, the more likely it is that workers will leave, and the less willing firms will be to invest in training.

In the UK, there is a high level of labour turnover. What is more, wage differentials between skilled and unskilled workers are narrower than in many other countries, and so there is less incentive for workers to train.

How can increased training be achieved? There are three broad approaches:

- Workers could be encouraged to stay with their employer so that employers would be more willing to invest in training. Externalities would be reduced.
- The government could provide subsidies for training. Alternatively, the government or some other agency could provide education and training directly.
- Firms could co-operate to prevent 'poaching' and set up industry-wide training programmes, perhaps in partnership with the government and unions.

Approaches to training in various countries

As far as the first approach is concerned, most countries have seen a movement towards *greater* labour mobility. The rise in the 'flexible firm' (see Box 9.8) has involved the employment of fewer permanent workers and more part-time and temporary workers. Some countries, such as Japan and Germany, however, have a generally lower rate of labour turnover than most. In Japan, the relationship between employer and employee has traditionally extended well beyond a simple short-term economic arrangement. Workers give loyalty and commitment to their employer, who in return virtually guarantees long-term employment and provides various fringe benefits (such as housing, child care, holiday schemes and health care). It is not surprising that Japanese firms invest highly in training.

In the USA, labour turnover is very high and yet there is little in the way of industry-wide training. Instead, the US government hopes, by having a high percentage of young people in further and higher education, that sufficient numbers and quality of workers are available for industry. Approximately 45 per cent of the US population enters higher education with 33 per cent of the population graduating, and only just over 0.2 per cent of GDP is spent on training.

In Germany, the proportion entering higher education is considerably lower (some 28 per cent, with just over 19 per cent of the population graduating), but expenditure on training accounts for 1.6 per cent of GDP. Most young people who do not enter higher education embark on some form of apprenticeship. They attend school for part of the week, and receive work-based training for the rest. The state, unions and employers' associations work closely in determining training provision, and they have developed a set of vocational qualifications based around the apprenticeship system. Given that virtually all firms are involved in training, the 'free-rider' problem of firms poaching labour without themselves paying for training is virtually eliminated. The result is that the German workforce is highly skilled. Many of the skills, however, are highly specific. This is a problem when the demand for particular skills declines and can result in high structural unemployment. KI 29 p303

companies on the Stock Exchange provides a large windfall gain to the original owners. This encourages entrepreneurs to *set up* companies, but discourages them from making *long-term* commitments to them. This all leads to the UK disease of 'short-termism': the obsession with short-term profits and the neglect of investment that yields profits only after a number of years.

Finally, in the case of ailing firms, if the government does not help finance a rescue investment programme, there may be substantial social costs from job losses. The avoidance of these social costs may make the investment socially profitable.

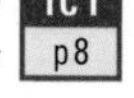

? *How would the radical right reply to these arguments?*

BOX 22.3

The UK approach

In the UK, the Conservative government's attitude towards training was initially influenced by its free-market approach to supply-side policy. Training was to be left largely to employers. However, with growing worries over the UK's 'productivity gap', the government set up Training and Enterprise Councils (TECs) in 1988. The TECs identified regional skills shortages, organised training and financed work-based training schemes.

The TECs were replaced in 2001 by the Learning and Skills Council (LSC). This has a budget of over £9 billion and is responsible for planning and funding training in sixth forms and further education colleges, work-based training for young people aged 16 to 24 ('Modern Apprenticeships'), adult and community learning, the provision of information, advice and guidance for adults, and developing links between education and business.

The LSC operates through 47 local arms, which have responsibility for co-ordinating plans for their area. The LSC also co-ordinates the activities of Centres of Vocational Excellence (CoVEs), which provide specialist vocational training, primarily in FE colleges, and which work closely with employers. It has also administered a series of Employer Training Pilots. These provide free or subsidised training to employees without a level 2 qualification, plus compensation to employers for giving workers time off to train.

In addition, a support service called 'Connexions' offers training and employment advice and support for young people between the ages of 13 and 19.

In 1991, the National Vocational Qualification (NVQ) was launched. Students work for an employer, and receive on-the-job training. They also attend college on an occasional basis. The NVQ is awarded when they have achieved sufficient experience. In addition, the government launched General National Vocational Qualifications (GNVQs). These further-education qualifications were aimed to bridge the gap between education and work, by ensuring that education was more work relevant.

The GNVQ system was modelled on that in France, where a clear vocational educational route is seen as the key to reducing skills shortages. At the age of 14, French students can choose to pursue academic or vocational education routes. The vocational route provides high-level, broad-based skills (unlike in Germany, where skills tend to be more job specific).

Another approach adopted by the Labour government in the UK has been to encourage 'lifelong learning'. Measures have included setting up the following:

- A University for Industry, which through its 'Learndirect' brand offers online courses in a range of business, technical and IT subjects.
- Some 700 UK Online centres. These offer access to the Internet, and helpers are on hand to provide basic IT, literacy and numeracy support.
- *Work-based Learning for Adults* in England and Wales and *Training for Work* in Scotland: two schemes to provide work-based training for people aged 25 and over who have been out of work for six months or more, with grants paid to employers.

Another measure, launched in England in 2001, was the introduction of two-year foundation degrees. These are offered by universities or higher education colleges. They are designed in conjunction with employers to meet various skill shortages. They are taken at the university or an associated college, normally on a part-time basis, and often include work-based study with local employers.

Critics of the UK strategy have argued that employers still face the threat of having newly trained labour poached; the regional activities of the LSC fail to account for national, long-term training issues; and NVQs often provide too narrow forms of training. Most importantly, the funding devoted to training is still low compared with most other industrialised countries. They claim that the UK system has the worst features of both the US and the German systems: too little training and too specific training.

?

1. ***Governments and educationalists generally regard it as desirable that trainees acquire transferable skills. Why may many employers disagree?***
2. ***There are externalities (benefits) when employers provide training. What externalities are there from the undergoing of training by the individual? Do they imply that individuals will choose to receive more or less than the socially optimal amount of training?***

KI 28 p300

The forms of intervention

Nationalisation. This is the most extreme form of intervention, and one that most countries have now rejected, given the worldwide trend of privatisation. Nevertheless, many countries have stopped short of privatising certain key transport and power industries, such as the railways and electricity generation. Having these industries under public ownership may result in higher investment than if they were under private ownership. Thus French governments have invested heavily in the state-owned railway system. This has resulted in fast, efficient rail services, with obvious benefits to rail users and the economy generally.

Grants. The government may sponsor research and development in certain industries (e.g. aerospace) or in specific fields (e.g. microprocessors). It may back investment programmes considered to benefit the economy as a whole.

Rationalisation. The government may encourage mergers or other forms of industrial reorganisation that will lead to greater efficiency and/or higher levels of investment. This could be done through government agencies or government departments.

Advice and persuasion. The government may engage in discussions with private firms in order to find ways to improve efficiency and innovation. It may bring firms together to exchange information and create a climate of greater certainty. It may bring firms and unions together to try to create greater industrial harmony.

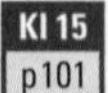

Information. The government may provide various information services to firms: technical assistance, the results of public research, information on markets, etc.

Direct provision. Improvements in infrastructure – such as a better motorway system – can be of direct benefit to industry. Alternatively, the government could provide factories or equipment to specific firms.

Planning

The most comprehensive approach to industrial policy is for the government to engage in national economic planning. This is not the 'command planning' of the former Soviet Union, where factories were issued with instructions on what to produce, what inputs to use and how much to invest (see Web Case 12.9). Rather, it is 'indicative planning'. Indicative planning works alongside the market. It does not replace it.

In a free market, there are likely to be many uncertainties for firms. Industries are highly interconnected. For example, if the electricity industry plans to expand, it will want to know the likely availability of coal or other fuels. Unless firms can know the plans of other firms, they may be cautious about taking investment decisions.

Indicative planning is where the government consults with industrialists to find out their intentions. It then seeks to co-ordinate the plans of firms, industries and sectors, and to recommend realistic and mutually consistent targets for output and investment. The government could also use persuasion or various financial incentives to obtain a consistent plan. The use of indicative planning in the UK is examined in Web Case 22.6.

Today in the UK and most other countries there is no comprehensive indicative planning at national level. Nevertheless, local authorities, regional development agencies (see page 627) and government departments do consult with industry and with chambers of commerce to improve the flow of information.

What instruments might a government use to 'persuade' firms to abide by a national plan? What are their advantages and disadvantages?

Selective intervention

Conservative governments have never favoured a comprehensive industrial strategy. Nevertheless, governments of both parties have intervened selectively in areas where they have felt that the market has provided inadequate investment.

Research and development (R&D)

Some 31 per cent of UK R&D is financed by the government, but around half of this has been concentrated in the defence, aerospace and nuclear power industries. As a result, there has been little government sponsorship of research in the majority of industry. Since the mid-1970s, however, there have been a number of government initiatives in the field of information technology. Even so, the amount of government support in this field has been very small compared with Japan, France and the USA. What is more, the amount of support declined between the mid-1980s and the late 1990s.

In 1999, however, the Labour government introduced a system of tax credits for small firms that invest in research and development. Then, in 2002, tax relief of 20 per cent of R&D expenditures by large firms was introduced.

Private-sector R&D is generally lower in the UK than in other major industrialised countries. Of the companies in the top 700 R&D spenders in the world in 2004, US companies' R&D as a percentage of sales was 4.9 per cent. For German companies the figure was 4.3 per cent, for Japanese companies it was 4.2 per cent, for French companies it was 3.1 per cent, while for UK companies it was only 2.3 per cent (see Web Case 22.2).

Industrial reorganisation

UK Labour governments in the past were concerned with encouraging efficiency and investment via rationalisation. For example, the Industrial Reorganisation Corporation (IRC) was set up in 1967 to provide loans to industry, and to arrange and finance mergers, where these were felt to lead to economies of scale and greater scope for investment. It was wound up in 1970 by the incoming Conservative government.

The main industrial reorganisation strategy pursued by the Conservative governments of the 1980s and 1990s was privatisation (see section 12.4 and page 617).

Assistance to small firms

UK governments in recent years have recognised the importance of small firms to the economy and have introduced

EXPLORING ECONOMICS — BOX 22.4

A NEW APPROACH TO INDUSTRIAL POLICY

As with many other areas of economic policy, industrial policy throughout most of the world has undergone a radical reorientation in recent years. The government's role has shifted from one of direct intervention in the form of subsidies and protecting industry from competition, to one of focusing upon the external business environment and the conditions that influence its competitiveness.

The reasons for such a change are both philosophical and structural:

- The rise of the political right in the 1980s led to a shift away from interventionist and towards market-based supply-side policy.
- Growing government debt, and a desire to curb public expenditure, acted as a key incentive to reduce the state's role in industrial affairs. This was argued to be one of the driving forces behind the European privatisation process since the 1980s.
- Industry, during the 1980s, became progressively more global in its outlook. As such, its investment decisions were increasingly being determined by external environmental factors, especially the technology, productivity and labour costs of its international competitors.

KI 21 p 207

The new approach to industrial policy, being widely adopted by many advanced countries, is to focus on improving those factors that shape a nation's competitiveness. This involves shifting away from particular sectors to targeting what are referred to as 'framework conditions for industry'. Policies include the following:

- The promotion of investment in physical and human capital. Human capital in particular, and the existence of a sound skills base, are seen as crucial for attracting global business and ensuring long-run economic growth.
- A reduction in non-wage employment costs, such as employers' social security and pension contributions. Many governments see these costs as too high and as a severe limitation on competitiveness and employment creation.
- The promotion of innovation and the encouragement of greater levels of R&D.
- Support for small and medium-sized enterprises. SMEs have received particular attention due to their crucial role in enhancing innovation, creating employment and contributing to skills development, especially in high-tech areas.
- The improvement of infrastructure. This includes both physical transport, such as roads and railways, as well as information highways.
- The protection of intellectual property by more effective use of patents and copyright. By reinforcing the law in these areas it is hoped to encourage firms to develop new products and commit themselves to research.

These policies, if they are to be truly effective, are likely to require co-ordination and integration, since they represent a radical departure from traditional industrial policy.

1. ***In what senses could these new policies be described as (a) non-interventionist; (b) interventionist?***
2. ***Does globalisation, and in particular the global perspective of multinational corporations, make industrial policy in the form of selective subsidies and tax relief more or less likely?***

various forms of advisory services, grants and tax concessions. For example, small firms pay a 19 per cent rate of corporation tax compared with 30 per cent for larger companies. In addition, small firms are subject to fewer planning and other bureaucratic controls than large companies.

Support to small firms in the UK is examined in Web Case 22.7.

Training

The government may set up training schemes, or encourage educational institutions to make their courses more vocationally relevant, or introduce new vocational qualifications (such as the GNVQs and NVQs in the UK). Alternatively, the government can provide grants or tax relief to firms which themselves provide training schemes. Alternative approaches to training in the UK, Germany, France and the USA are examined in Box 22.3.

The case against intervention

New classical economists, monetarists, neo-Austrian economists and others advocating the free market argue the following:

- A poor investment record may be due to managerial inertia and union restrictive practices. Forcing firms and unions to face up to competition in the market may be a better way of encouraging willingness to accept change. Government subsidies may simply allow firms to continue producing inefficiently.
- The government may not make an efficient use of taxpayers' money by giving investment grants. The money may well go to extravagant and unprofitable projects like Concorde or the Millennium Dome.
- A low investment record of private industry may be due to a low potential return on investment. If market

opportunities were good, firms would invest without the need of government support.

- UK investment has remained low in the past despite interventionist industrial policy.
- If the government is to help industry, it is best to reduce the tax burden generally, so as to increase the return on investment. The microeconomic allocation of investment resources will then still be provided by the market.

An example of a 'Third Way' approach to supply-side policy is the UK Labour government's 'welfare to work' policy (see Web Case 22.9). This provides benefits and other support to unemployed people and people currently outside the workforce to seek employment. It is interventionist to the extent that it targets support at particular people, but pro-market to the extent that it provides incentives for people to become more occupationally mobile.

 *Provide a critique of these arguments.*

Section summary

1. Those in favour of interventionist industrial policy point to failings of the market, such as the externalities involved in investment and training, the imperfections in the capital market and the short-term perspective of decision makers.
2. Intervention can take the form of grants, the encouragement of mergers and other forms of rationalisation, advice and persuasion, the provision of information and the direct provision of infrastructure.
3. Selective intervention can take the form of grants for research and development, encouragement of reorganisation, assistance to small firms and help for training.

22.4 REGIONAL AND URBAN POLICY

 Regional disparities in unemployment in the UK increased substantially during the early and mid-1980s, with the recession hitting the north, with its traditional heavy industries, much harder than the south. Table 22.2 shows unemployment rates for the various UK regions.

Similarly, there are regional disparities in average incomes, rates of growth and levels of prices, as well as in health, crime, housing, etc. Many of these disparities too grew wider in the 1980s. The magnitude of these problems in many parts of the north led to the 'north–south divide' becoming a major political issue.

In recent years, however, concern has shifted away from the problems of broad regions. Regional disparities of income still exist, but they narrowed dramatically during the recession of the early 1990s. The recession hit service industries, which are more concentrated in the south, harder than manufacturing industries, which are more concentrated in the north. Moreover, many industries today have less need

Table 22.2 Regional (claimant) unemployment rates (%): selected years

Region	Unemployment (%)							
	Jan 1979	Jan 1987	Jan 1990	Jan 1993	Jan 1996	Jan 1999	Jan 2002	Jan 2005
South East	2.4	6.8	2.6	9.0	5.5	2.5	1.6	1.7
South West	4.1	8.8	3.8	9.8	6.5	3.3	2.1	1.8
Eastern	2.8	8.1	3.1	9.7	6.4	3.2	2.1	2.1
East Midlands	3.4	9.7	4.9	10.0	7.0	4.0	3.1	2.6
North West	4.7	11.5	6.1	9.8	7.0	4.2	3.7	2.9
Yorkshire & Humberside	4.1	12.1	6.6	10.5	8.3	5.6	3.9	3.0
Wales	5.5	13.1	6.6	10.4	8.3	5.4	3.8	3.2
West Midlands	3.9	12.4	5.7	11.1	7.6	4.7	3.6	3.3
London	2.8	8.9	4.7	11.6	9.1	5.2	3.5	3.4
Scotland	5.7	13.8	8.4	9.9	7.8	5.5	4.2	3.6
Northern Ireland	7.8	16.9	13.0	14.0	11.2	7.3	4.9	3.6
North East	6.5	16.2	9.7	12.8	11.1	7.4	5.4	4.1
UK (average)	*4.1*	*10.8*	*5.6*	*10.5*	*7.7*	*4.6*	*3.2*	*2.8*

Source: National Statistics.

than in the past to be located in a specific region, and can therefore move to parts of the country where labour and other costs are lower. The problem today, therefore, is seen to be more one of specific *areas*, especially inner cities and urban localities subject to industrial decline.

Let us first, however, examine the causes of *regional* imbalance.

Causes of regional imbalance

If the market functioned perfectly, there would be no regional problem. If wages were lower and unemployment were higher in the north, people would simply move to the TC 10 p294 south. This would reduce unemployment in the north and help to fill vacancies in the south. It would drive up wages in the north and reduce wages in the south. The process would continue until regional disparities were eliminated.

The capital market would function similarly. New investment would be located in the areas offering the highest rate of return. If land and labour were cheaper in the north, capital would be attracted there. This too would help to eliminate regional disparities.

A similar argument applies between countries. With the expansion of the EU in 2004 to include east European countries (which have lower GDP per head), the effect should be labour migration from these countries to the richer EU countries and capital movements in the opposite direction.

In practice, the market does not always behave as just described. There are three major problems.

TC 8 p59 *Labour and capital immobility.* Labour may be geographically immobile. The regional pattern of industrial location may change more rapidly than the labour market can adjust to it. Thus jobs may be lost in the depressed areas more rapidly than people can migrate.

Similarly, existing capital stock is highly immobile. Buildings and most machinery cannot be moved to where the unemployed are! *New* capital is much more mobile. But there may be insufficient new investment, especially during a recession, to halt regional decline, even if some investors are attracted into the depressed areas by low wages and cheap land.

TC 15 p463 *Regional multiplier effects.* The continuing shift in demand may in part be due to ***regional multiplier effects*** (an example of cumulative causation: see Threshold Concept 15). In the prosperous regions, the new industries and the new workers attracted there create additional demand. This creates additional output and jobs, and hence more migration. There is a multiplied rise in income. In the depressed regions, the decline in demand and loss of jobs causes a multiplied downward effect. Loss of jobs in manufacturing leads to less money being spent in the local community; transport and other service industries lose custom. The whole region becomes more depressed.

There can be a similar process between countries. With free movement of capital in the EU, capital is attracted to the more prosperous regions of the Union, such as Germany, the northern half of France and the Benelux countries, and away from the less prosperous regions, such as Portugal, Greece and southern Italy.

Externalities. Labour migration imposes external costs on KI 28 p300 non-migrants. In the prosperous regions, the new arrivals compete for services with those already there. Services become overstretched; house prices rise; council house waiting lists lengthen; roads become more congested, etc. In the depressed regions, services decline, or alternatively local taxes must rise for those who remain if local services are to be protected. Dereliction, depression and unemployment cause emotional stress for those who remain.

Causes of urban decay

In recent decades there has been a general movement of people from the inner areas of the big cities to the suburbs, to smaller towns and cities, and to rural areas within easy commuting distance of towns. This movement has been paralleled by a decline in employment in the inner cities. But with an increasing number of urban jobs being taken by people commuting into the cities, the unemployment problem for those living in these areas grew dramatically. Moreover, many of the older manufacturing industries were located in the inner cities and it was these industries that were hardest hit by the recession of the early 1980s.

The run-down nature of many inner cities causes the TC 15 p463 more mobile members of the workforce to move away. Spending in these areas thus declines, causing a local multiplier effect. The jobs that poor people living in these areas do manage to find are often low-paid, unskilled jobs in the service sector (such as shops and the hotel and catering trade) or in petty manufacturing (like garment workshops).

Many of the newer industries prefer to locate away from the inner city areas on sites where land is cheaper, rates are lower and there is easy access to the motorway network. At the same time, for financial reasons, local authorities have found it difficult to offer inducements to firms to move into the inner cities. Nor can they afford to spend large amounts on improving the infrastructure of the blighted areas. Their council taxes are also higher, which again provides an inducement for more mobile workers to move

Definition

Regional multiplier effects When a change in injections into or withdrawals from a particular region causes a multiplied change in income in that region. The regional multiplier (k_r) is given by $1/mpw_r$, where the import component of mpw_r consists of imports into that region either from abroad or from other regions of the economy.

away as well as a disincentive for new firms to move into the area.

Approaches to regional and urban policy

Market-orientated solutions

Supporters of market-based solutions argue that firms are the best judges of where they should locate. Government intervention would impede efficient decision taking by firms. It is better, they argue, to remove impediments to the market achieving regional and local balance. For example, they favour either or both of the following.

Locally negotiated wage agreements. Nationally negotiated wage rates mean that wages are not driven down in the less prosperous areas and up in the more prosperous ones. This discourages firms from locating in the less prosperous areas. At the same time, firms find it difficult to recruit labour in the more prosperous ones, where wages are not high enough to compensate for the higher cost of living there.

Reducing unemployment benefits. A general reduction in unemployment and other benefits would encourage the unemployed in the areas of high unemployment to migrate to the more prosperous areas, or enable firms to offer lower wages in the areas of high unemployment.

The problem with these policies is that they attempt initially to *widen* the economic divide between workers in the different areas in order to encourage capital and labour to move. Such policies would hardly be welcomed by workers in the poorer areas!

?

1. Think of some other 'pro-market' solutions to the regional problem.
2. Do workers in the more prosperous areas benefit from pro-market solutions?

TC 7 p26

Interventionist policies

Interventionist policies involve encouraging firms to move. Such policies include the following.

KI 7 p35

Subsidies and tax concessions in depressed areas. These can have two beneficial effects: an income effect and a substitution effect. The income effect is where higher income for firms, as a result of subsidies, encourages them to produce more output and hence to employ more people. The substitution effect is where firms are encouraged to substitute labour for capital: i.e. to use more labour-intensive techniques.

- *General subsidies.* Grants or concessions for buildings, reduced rates of corporation tax, grants for firms to move, etc. would lead to an income effect as firms were attracted into the region. But the firms would not thereby be encouraged to use more labour-intensive techniques. There would be no substitution effect.
- *Employment subsidies.* Subsidies for employment, or reduced employers' national insurance contributions, would lead to both an income effect *and* a substitution effect. Firms would be attracted into the region and there would also be an encouragement to substitute (now cheaper) labour for capital.
- *Capital subsidies.* Grants for investment or other measures that reduce the cost of capital would lead to a positive income effect. The substitution effect, however, would be *negative*. Firms attracted to the area would be encouraged to use capital-intensive techniques, and would thus provide little employment.

In the short run, employment subsidies will have the largest effect on employment. In the long run, however, it is not so clear cut. Capital-intensive industries may require the services of local *labour*-intensive industries. Also, capital-intensive industries may be more profitable and have a higher rate of growth, thus generating more employment in the future.

If a Japanese car manufacturer were attracted into an unemployment blackspot and opened up a highly capital-intensive 'robot-line' car assembly plant, in what other local industries might employment be stimulated?

The provision of facilities in the depressed areas. The government or local authorities could provide facilities such as land and buildings at concessionary, or even zero, rents to incoming firms; or improve the infrastructure of the area (roads and communications, technical colleges, etc.).

The siting of government offices in depressed areas. The government could move some of its own departments out of London and locate them in areas of high unemployment. The siting of the vehicle licensing centre in Swansea is an example.

It is important to distinguish interventionist policies that merely seek to *modify* the market by altering market signals, from those that *replace* the market.

Regulation replaces the market, and unless very carefully devised and monitored may lead to ill-thought-out decisions being made. *Subsidies* and *taxes* merely modify the market, leaving it to individual firms to make their final local decisions. Taxes and subsidies in theory can internalise external costs and benefits, and can make actual prices reflect opportunity costs rather than market power. But if there are uniform tax or subsidy rates throughout a region, they will be higher than necessary in some cases and lower in others.

1. If you were the government, how would you set about deciding the rate of subsidy to pay a firm thinking of moving to a less prosperous area?
2. Should firms already located in less prosperous areas be paid a subsidy?

Regional policy in the UK

Certain areas are identified as requiring government financial assistance to boost their local economies. These are known as ***assisted areas*** (AAs) and cover around 29 per cent of the UK population. They are divided into two categories. Tier 1 areas are those suffering the most acute economic problems. There are four of these areas: Cornwall, South Yorkshire, Merseyside and much of Wales. Tier 2 areas include large parts of Scotland and the north-east of England and many smaller areas affected by economic decline.

The assistance comes from the UK government (the Department of Trade and Industry) for England, the Scottish Executive, the Welsh Assembly and the EU. It takes the form of Selective Finance for Investment (SFI) in England and Regional Selective Assistance in Scotland and Wales.

These consist of discretionary grants given to manufacturing firms or firms in the service sector that supply a national market. The grants are to establish a new business, or to expand or modernise an existing one. Grants are of at least £10 000 and are typically of 10–15 per cent of the capital value of the project, although this can be up to 35 per cent in Tier 1 areas and 20 per cent in certain Tier 2 areas (15 per cent in others). The grants are discretionary and a key criterion for assessing proposals is the extent to which they create skilled jobs.

Support under SFI is also available to small enterprises (employing less than 50 people) and medium-sized enterprises (employing from 50 to 250 people) in Tier 3 areas. These areas extend beyond Tiers 1 and 2, and include local authority districts with high unemployment rates and various rural development areas. Capital grants of up to 15 per cent for small enterprises and 7.5 per cent for medium-sized enterprises are available (with a ceiling of £100 000).

In 1998 the government set up eight ***Regional Development Agencies (RDAs)*** for the different regions of England (and a ninth for London in 2000). These, along with the Scottish Parliament and Welsh Assembly, are responsible for administering economic policies for their particular parts of the UK and for developing strategies for improving local infrastructure, encouraging inward investment and promoting investment in skills and training.

The largest amount of regional assistance comes from the European Regional Development Fund (ERDF). Since 1985 it has provided grants of up to 50 per cent for job-creating projects and projects to develop infrastructure. The money is available for use only in the assisted areas, and is intended to be *additional* to any supplied by member governments. However, some countries, including the UK, have tended to use ERDF grants to *replace* domestic assistance and have thus come into dispute with the EU. The bulk of ERDF grants are allocated to the poorer countries of the EU, such as Greece, Portugal and Spain. Box 22.5 gives more details of the allocation of ERDF grants and other structural funds between the member states.

In a consultation exercise for the period 2007–13, the EU Commission has proposed that assisted areas be reduced for the pre-2004 EU countries to allow for assistance being given to the new members, all of which have below average GDP per head. In the UK, the proportion of the population in assisted areas would fall from 30.9 per cent to 9.1 per cent.

The effectiveness of regional policy

The following tentative conclusions can be reached about the effectiveness of regional policy:

- A carefully targeted policy, which focuses on job creation (subject to efficiency criteria), is likely to be more cost-effective than general investment grants. Similarly, a policy that does not discriminate against the service sector, or small firms, is likely to be more cost-effective than one that concentrates on large-scale manufacturing.
- The government could focus its *national* expenditure more specifically on the depressed regions. The relocation of more government offices might help, as would the deliberate location of government spending and the targeting of infrastructure construction in the depressed regions.

High regional unemployment in the 1980s was in part a manifestation of the much higher levels of *national* unemployment than in the past. An expansion of economic activity throughout the whole country can go a long way towards easing the problems of the depressed regions. As you can see if you look back to Table 22.2 on page 624, unemployment in the UK in 2005 was highest in the north-east, at 4.1 per cent. But this was still considerably lower than the unemployment rate in the south-east in 1993, which at 9.0 per cent was the lowest in the country at that time!

Definitions

Assisted areas Areas of high unemployment qualifying for government regional selective assistance (RSA) and grants from the European Regional Development Fund (ERDF).

Regional Development Agencies (RDAs) Nine agencies, based in English regions, which initiate and administer regional policy within their area.

Urban policy in the UK

During the 1980s, the thrust of policy shifted away from regional and towards urban policy. Several new schemes were introduced involving the creation of various new categories of deprived area. Firms setting up in these areas were eligible for various grants or loans and were subject to fewer planning regulations.

CASE STUDIES AND APPLICATIONS

EU REGIONAL POLICY

Giving a helping hand to the poorer regions

With the signing of the Maastricht Treaty, which established the European Union in November 1993, member states agreed to work together to ensure that:

- The distribution of benefits from European unification were spread fairly.
- Economic and social development was speeded up in the less prosperous countries, so that they might play a fuller part in the EU's future development.
- Economic imbalances between countries did not distort the operation of the internal market between member states.

With the accession of 10 new members of the EU in 2004, regional policy was given more urgency, as all the new members have GDP below the EU average and several have regions with well below the EU average. Over 92 per cent of the population of the new member states live in regions with a GDP per head under 75 per cent of the EU-25 average, and 61 per cent of the population live in regions below 50 per cent.

The EU allocates just under one-third of its total budget to regional policy, and plans to spend some €336 billion on regional policy over the seven-year period 2007–13. In order to allocate these vast resources, the EU operates a series of four interrelated funds (collectively known as the Structural Funds), plus a Cohesion Fund.

The Structural Funds

The European Regional Development Fund (ERDF). This fund is managed by the Regional Policy Directorate-General. It primarily allocates its funding so as to reduce differences in levels of development between different regions. In particular, it focuses upon the following:

- Investment to create and maintain employment.
- Investment in infrastructure.
- Investments in education and health.
- Measures to enhance research and development.
- Collective measures to support economic activity.

The European Social Fund (ESF). The ESF is managed by the Employment and Social Affairs Directorate-General. It allocates funds to vocational training programmes, job creation and the adaptation of worker skills to industrial change.

The Guidance section of the European Agricultural Guidance and Guarantee Fund (EAGGF). The EAGGF is managed by the Agriculture Directorate-General. As we saw in section 3.4, the Guidance section allocates funds for the development and restructuring of agriculture and rural areas in general.

The Financial Instrument for Fisheries Guidance (FIFG). The FIFG is managed by the Fisheries Directorate-General. As with EAGGF, FIFG is concerned solely with one sector of the EU economy, namely fishing, and the problems faced by communities that rely on it.

Other funds

Cohesion Fund. This fund offers additional assistance to the poorest nations within the EU: those with GDP per head less than 90 per cent of the EU average. It applies to the ten new member states, plus Greece and Portugal. Up to 2006 it applied to Greece, Portugal, Spain and Ireland. Its aim is to support the development of infrastructure projects, and to enhance measures that help protect and improve the quality of the environment: for example, improving the quality of water supply and the treatment of waste.

The European Investment Bank (EIB). In addition to the Structural Funds, the EIB also offers support to the less prosperous regions within the EU (approximately two-thirds of its budget goes to such regions). However, unlike the Structural Funds, the EIB offers loans, not grants, and hence requires repayment. The EIB generally offers loans up to 50 per cent of the cost of the project, and these loans generally run for between 4 and 18 years. With only a small fee for administration, and with the EIB operating on a non-profit-making basis, interest rates charged by the EIB are low.

The allocation of Structural Funds

Given the diversity of funding alternatives, how are the resources available allocated? Support from the ERDF, ESF, EAGGF and FIFG focuses upon one or more of the following 'objectives':

- Objective 1: to promote the development and structural adjustment of regions that lag behind the rest of the EU. This receives by far the largest share of the Structural Funds budget (see chart). In order to achieve objective 1 status ('Tier 1' status), a region's per-capita GDP must be 75 per cent or less

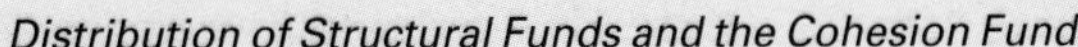

BOX 22.5

Distribution of Structural Funds and the Cohesion Fund

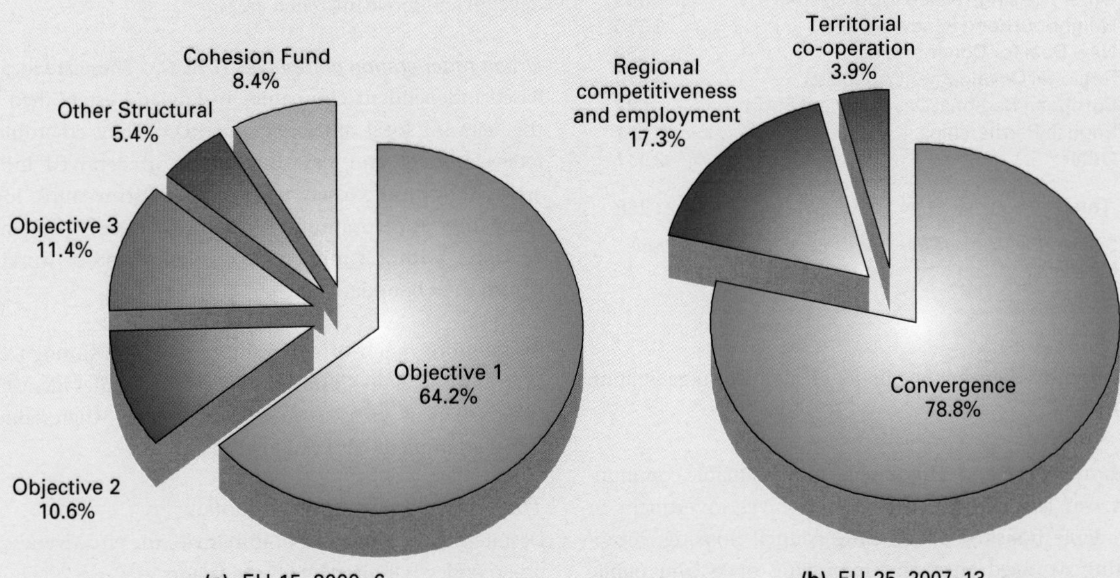

of the EU level for the last three years. This objective is funded by the ERDF, ESF and EAGGF.

- Objective 2: to support regions adversely affected by industrial and rural decline. In order to qualify for assistance under this objective, a region must have an unemployment rate above the EU average over the last three years. This objective is funded by the ERDF and ESF.
- Objective 3: to combat long-term unemployment, and help other groups excluded from the labour market, including help to those adapting to industrial change. This applies to all parts of the EU, but not to ERDF funding.
- Other: this includes 'Community Initiatives', innovative actions and technical assistance.

The distribution of the Structural Funds between these objectives plus the Cohesion Fund is shown in the chart.

Developments from 2007

From 2007, new allocations of funds will be made. These will include allocations to the ten new member states. Several regions of the 15 pre-2004 (EU-15) member states which previously received Objective 1 funding will now have a GDP per head *more* than 75 per cent of the average of the 25 EU countries. Their funding will thus be phased out from 2007 to 2013.

It is proposed to replace the categories shown in the chart with new ones. The Objective 1 and the Cohesion Fund regions/countries would continue to receive the bulk of the funding (78.8%) under a new 'Convergence' objective. Funding would be from the ERDF, ESF and Cohesion Fund.

Objectives 2 and 3 would be replaced by a new 'Regional competitiveness and employment' objective. The ERDF would fund regional programmes and the ESF would fund programmes at a national level that help develop a socially inclusive employment strategy.

The remainder of the funding would go to a 'European territorial co-operation' objective. This would support schemes in areas lying along and across the border with other member countries.

1. ***With 12 countries using the euro, how is the common currency likely to affect the distribution of income among the EU countries?***
2. ***What obstacles lie in the way of a growing convergence in output per head in the EU countries?***

Table 22.3 Funding for Sustainable Communities Projects: total 2003/4–2005/6

	£m
Investment in affordable housing and improving housing conditions	7 394
Other housing-related programmes	4 145
Neighbourhood Renewal Fund	1 375
New Deal for Communities	850
Regional Development Agencies	4 679
European Regional Development Fund	687
English Partnerships	521
Other	2 117
Total	21 768

Source: *The Communities Plan* (Office of the Deputy Prime Minister).

Currently there are five major elements of regeneration policy:

Communities Plan. This scheme for sustainable communities was launched in 2003 and involves investment in affordable housing, refurbishing council housing, regenerating deprived areas and improving parks and public spaces. The plan has a budget of £22 billion from 2002/3 to 2005/6: see Table 22.3 (note that this also includes some of the following items).

Neighbourhood Renewal Unit. This was set up in 2002 and oversees and supports local strategic partnerships in the 88 most deprived districts in England. It also runs the 'New Deal for Communities', which encourages and helps fund partnerships between local people, local businesses, community and voluntary organisations, local authorities and public agencies in the 39 most severely deprived neighbourhoods. The aim is to tackle problems of high unemployment, crime, educational under-achievement, poor health, poor housing and a poor physical environment.

Regional development agencies (RDAs). In addition to their regional policy role, the RDAs play an important part in urban regeneration schemes. They administer the *Single Regeneration Budget (SRB)*, a fund established in 1994 to encourage a partnership between government and the private sector (part of the Private Finance Initiative (PFI)) and to ensure that maximum benefit is gained from European Structural Funds. The RDAs provide grants for schemes that meet various local objectives, such as increased employment, training, new businesses, better housing, crime prevention and support for ethnic minorities. Moneys are allocated to partnerships drawn from local authorities, the Learning and Skills Council, and the private, community and voluntary sectors.

English Partnerships. Originally the *Urban Regeneration Agency* (URA), this aims to promote the reclamation and development of derelict or contaminated land. It acts as a partner with private firms, local authorities and the voluntary sector. It provides grants, loans, guarantees and partnership investment to encourage private companies to develop and move into such areas.

Urban regeneration companies (URCs). These are locally based independent companies in England established by the relevant local authority and RDA. They co-ordinate redevelopment and new investment in deprived urban areas. They work closely with English Partnerships, local companies and community groups. By 2005, there were 21 URCs, with 1.2 million people living and/or working within their boundaries.

In addition, much of the training provided through the Learning and Skills Council and the other bodies identified in Box 22.3 is focused on inner-city areas where educational attainment has been low.

The effectiveness of urban policy

Despite the large number of initiatives, the effectiveness of urban policy is limited by several factors:

- Government attempts to reduce local authority taxes have drastically reduced the ability of local authorities to provide the infrastructure and other incentives necessary to attract industry into their areas. This has been a particular problem for inner-city areas where the tax base has been low and the demands on expenditure have been high.
- The total amount of public money spent has been relatively low compared with other areas of government expenditure. In 2000/1 the total spent on grants for regeneration amounted to only 0.38 per cent of total government expenditure. With increased expenditures through the Communities Plan, however, this had risen to 1.49 per cent by 2005/6.
- It is questionable whether the jobs created by the various projects are in fact *new* jobs, or whether they would have been created anyway, either in that particular area or in a neighbouring (and possibly only marginally less deprived) area.
- Some of the new jobs created are filled not by residents of the areas, but by people commuting into them. The local residents often do not have sufficient skills to compete with outsiders.

Clearly the needs of the inner cities are great, and there is the danger that many of the initiatives may do little more than tinker with the problem. Unless sufficiently large amounts of *extra* money are available, it is unlikely that the effects of the policies will be substantial.

Section summary

1. Regional and local disparities arise from a changing pattern of industrial production. With many of the older industries concentrated in certain parts of the country and especially in the inner cities, and with an acceleration in the rate of industrial change, so the gap between rich and poor areas has widened.
2. Regional disparities can in theory be corrected by the market, with capital being attracted to areas of low wages and workers being attracted to areas of high wages.
3. In practice, regional disparities persist because of capital and labour immobility and regional multiplier effects.
4. The radical-right solution is to remove impediments to the market achieving regional balance. They favour such policies as local, rather than national, pay bargaining, reducing unemployment benefits, adopting uniform business rates and limiting local authority expenditure.
5. Interventionist solutions focus on measures to encourage firms to move to areas of high unemployment. These measures might include subsidies or tax concessions for firms that move, the provision of facilities and improved infrastructure in the depressed area, the siting of government offices in the depressed areas and the prevention of firms expanding in the prosperous ones. Employment subsidies will create more jobs than general subsidies, which in turn will create more jobs than capital subsidies.
6. In the UK there has been a movement away from general grants towards discretionary grants based on job creation. There are also regional grants from the EU and grants and initiatives for the regeneration of the inner cities.
7. The success of regional and urban policies has been limited by the relatively low level of government grants and by the fact that some of the money has gone to projects that would have gone ahead anyway.

END OF CHAPTER QUESTIONS

1. Define *demand-side* and *supply-side* policies. Sometimes it is said that Keynesians advocate demand-side policies and monetarists advocate supply-side policies. Is there any accuracy in this statement?
2. What is the relationship between 'successful' supply-side policies and unemployment in (i) the short run and (ii) the long run, according to (a) Keynesian and (b) monetarist assumptions?
3. Why might market-orientated supply-side policies have undesirable side-effects on aggregate demand?
4. What type of tax cuts are likely to create the greatest (a) incentives, (b) disincentives to effort?
5. Is deindustrialisation necessarily undesirable?
6. In what ways can interventionist industrial policy work *with* the market, rather than against it? What are the arguments for and against such policy?
7. Compare the relative merits of pro-market and interventionist solutions to regional decline.
8. What are the arguments for and against relying entirely on *discretionary* regional and urban policy?
9. Select a European country other than the UK and compare its regional and urban policy with that of the UK.

Additional case studies on the book's website (www.pearsoned.co.uk/sloman)

22.1 **Deregulating the UK bus industry.** Has this led to greater competition and improved services?

22.2 **The R&D Scoreboard.** An international comparison of spending by companies on R&D.

22.3 **Controlling inflation in the past.** This case study looks at the history of prices and incomes policies in the UK.

22.4 **UK industrial performance.** This examines why the UK has had a poorer investment record than many other industrial countries and why it has suffered a process of 'deindustrialisation'.

22.5 **Technology and economic change.** How to get the benefits from technological advance.

22.6 **Indicative planning in the UK.** Experiments with planning in the 1960s and 1970s.

22.7 **Assistance to small firms in the UK.** An examination of current government measures to assist small firms.

22.8 **Small-firm policy in the EU.** This looks at the range of support available to small and medium-sized firms in the EU.

22.9 **Welfare to work.** An examination of the UK Labour government's policy of providing support to people looking for work.

WEBSITES RELEVANT TO CHAPTERS 20, 21 AND 22

Numbers and sections refer to websites listed in the Web Appendix and hotlinked from this book's website at www.pearsoned.co.uk/sloman.

- For news articles relevant to these three chapters, see the *Economics News Articles* link from the book's website.
- For general news on unemployment, inflation, economic growth and supply-side policy, see websites in section A, and particularly A1–5. See also links to newspapers worldwide in A38 and 39, and the news search feature in Google at A41. See also links to economics news in A42.
- For data on unemployment, inflation and growth, see links in B1 or 2; also see B4 and 12. For UK data, see B3 and 34. For EU data, see G1 > *The Statistical Annex.* For US data, see *Current economic indicators* in B5 and the *Data* section of B17. For international data, see B15, 21, 24, 31, 33. For links to data sets, see B28; I14.
- For specific data on UK unemployment, see B1, *1. National Statistics* > the fourth link > *Labour Market* > *Labour Market Trends.* For international data on unemployment, see G1; H3 and 5.
- For information on the development of ideas, including information on classical, Keynesian, monetarist, new classical and new Keynesian thought, see C12, 18; also see links under *Methodology and History of Economic Thought* in C14; links to economists in I4 and 17. See also sites I7 and 11 > *Economic Systems and Theories* > *History of Economic Thought.*
- For the current approach to UK supply-side policy, see the latest Budget Report (e.g. sections on productivity and training) at site E30. See also sites E5 and 9.
- For support for a market-orientated approach to supply-side policy, see C17.
- For information on training in the UK and Europe, see sites D7; E5; G5, 14; and E34.
- For information on the support for small business in the UK, see site E38.
- For information on regional policy in the UK, see site E2; and in the EU, see site G12.
- For student resources relevant to these three chapters, see sites C1–7, 9, 10, 19. See also the *Labour market reforms* simulation in D3.

Part F: The World Economy

'Globalisation' is a word frequently used nowadays. But it neatly captures one of the key features of economics today: that it is global in nature. International trade has grown at a much faster rate than the levels of national output in any country. International financial flows have grown faster still. The result is that economies around the globe are intermeshed, and what happens in one country can have profound effects on others.

In Chapters 23 and 24 we look at the two key economic elements in this interdependence: international trade and international finance. Then in Chapter 25 we look at particular aspects of global interdependence. Finally we turn to the poorest countries of the world, whose development depends so much on the economic policies of the rich world.

Chapter 23

International Trade

Without international trade we would all be much poorer. There would be some items like pineapples, coffee, cotton clothes, foreign holidays and uranium that we would simply have to go without. Then there would be other items like wine and spacecraft that we could produce only very inefficiently. International trade has the potential to benefit *all* participating countries. This chapter explains why.

Totally free trade, however, may bring problems to countries or to groups of people within those countries. Many people argue strongly for restrictions on trade. Textile workers see their jobs threatened by cheap imported cloth. Car manufacturers worry about falling sales as customers switch to Japanese models or other east Asian ones. But are people justified in fearing international competition, or are they merely trying to protect some vested interest at the expense of everyone else? Section 23.2 examines these arguments and also looks at world attitudes towards trade restrictions.

A step on the road to freer trade is for countries to enter free-trade agreements with just a limited number of other countries. Examples include the EU and more recently the North American Free Trade Association (NAFTA – the USA, Canada and Mexico). We consider such 'preferential trading systems' in section 23.3. Finally, we look in more detail at the EU and the development of the 'single European market'.

CHAPTER MAP

This chapter may be studied after Chapter 11 or Chapter 12 if you prefer.

23.1 THE ADVANTAGES OF TRADE

The growth of world trade

World trade has grown rapidly over the past 60 years and at consistently higher rates than world GDP. Table 23.1 shows exports as a proportion of various countries' GDP. As you can see, in all cases the proportion was higher in 2005 than in 1965, and in some cases considerably higher.

The major industrial economies dominate world trade (see Figure 23.1). They account for 64 per cent of world exports and 67 per cent of world imports. The top ten trading nations account for over 55 per cent of world merchandise exports. The country with the highest share is Germany (10.0%), followed by the USA (9.6%), China (including Hong Kong) (8.8%) and Japan (6.3%).

Figure 23.1 Share of world exports (goods and commercial services), by value: 2003

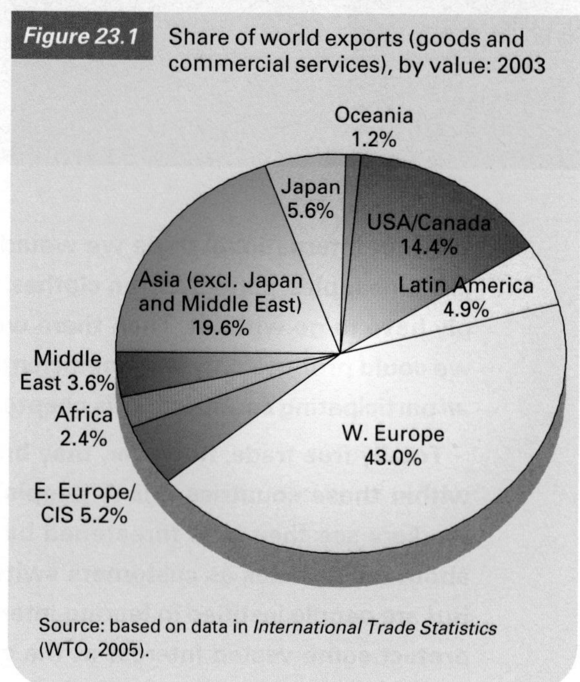

Source: based on data in *International Trade Statistics* (WTO, 2005).

Specialisation as the basis for trade

TC 1 p8 Why do countries trade with each other, and what do they gain from it? The reasons for international trade are really only an extension of the reasons for trade *within* a nation. Rather than people trying to be self-sufficient and do everything for themselves, it makes sense to specialise.

Firms specialise in producing certain goods. This allows them to gain economies of scale and to exploit their entrepreneurial and management skills and the skills of their labour force. It also allows them to benefit from their particular location and from the ownership of any particular capital equipment or other assets they might possess. With the revenues firms earn, they buy in the inputs they need from other firms and the labour they require. Firms thus trade with each other.

Countries also specialise. They produce more than they need of certain goods. What is not consumed domestically is exported. The revenues earned from the exports are used to import goods that are not produced in sufficient amounts at home.

Table 23.1 Exports as % of GDP

	1965	1985	2005
Belgium	43.0	71.8	86.5
France	12.7	22.9	26.3
Ireland	32.2	55.6	80.3
Japan	10.4	14.3	13.9
Luxembourg	85.0	114.4	142.2
Sweden	21.3	34.9	47.4
UK	18.4	28.8	25.7
USA	5.2	7.2	10.5
EU-15	18.7	31.0	36.2

Source: based on data in *Statistical Annex of European Economy* (Commission of the EU).

?

Why does the USA not specialise as much as General Motors or Texaco? Why does the UK not specialise as much as ICI? Is the answer to these questions similar to the answer to the questions, 'Why does the USA not specialise as much as Luxembourg?' and 'Why does ICI or Unilever not specialise as much as the local butcher?'

But which goods should a country specialise in? What should it export and what should it import? The answer is that it should specialise in those goods in which it has a *comparative advantage*. Let us examine what this means.

The law of comparative advantage

Countries have different endowments of factors of production. They differ in population density, labour skills, climate, raw materials, capital equipment, etc. These differences tend to persist because factors are relatively immobile between countries. Obviously land and climate are totally immobile, but even with labour and capital there are more restrictions on their international movement than on their movement within countries. Thus the ability to supply goods differs between countries.

What this means is that the relative costs of producing goods varies from country to country. For example, one

KI 2 p8 country may be able to produce 1 fridge for the same cost as 6 tonnes of wheat or 3 compact disc players, whereas another country may be able to produce 1 fridge for the same cost as only 3 tonnes of wheat but 4 CD players. It is these differences in relative costs that form the basis of trade.

At this stage, we need to distinguish between *absolute advantage* and *comparative advantage*.

Absolute advantage

When one country can produce a good with less resources than another country, it is said to have an ***absolute advantage*** in that good. If France can produce wine with less resources than the UK, and the UK can produce gin with less resources than France, then France has an absolute advantage in wine and the UK an absolute advantage in gin. Production of both wine and gin will be maximised by each country specialising and then trading with the other country. Both will gain.

Comparative advantage

The above seems obvious, but trade between two countries can still be beneficial even if one country could produce *all* goods with less resources than the other, providing the *relative* efficiency with which goods can be produced differs between the two countries.

Take the case of a developed country that is absolutely more efficient than a less developed country at producing both wheat and cloth. Assume that with a given amount of resources (labour, land and capital) the alternatives shown in Table 23.2 can be produced in each country.

Despite the developed country having an absolute advantage in both wheat and cloth, the less developed country (LDC) has a ***comparative advantage*** in wheat, and the developed country has a comparative advantage in cloth.

This is because wheat is relatively cheaper in the LDC: only 1 metre of cloth has to be sacrificed to produce 2 kilos of wheat, whereas 8 metres of cloth would have to be sacrificed in the developed country to produce 4 kilos of wheat (i.e. 2 metres of cloth for every 1 kilo of wheat). In other words, the opportunity cost of wheat is four times higher in the developed country (8/4 compared with 1/2). KI 2 p8

On the other hand, cloth is relatively cheaper in the developed country. Here the opportunity cost of producing 8 metres of cloth is only 4 kilos of wheat, whereas in the LDC 1 metre of cloth costs 2 kilos of wheat. Thus the opportunity cost of cloth is four times higher in the LDC (2/1 compared with 4/8).

Draw up a similar table to Table 23.1, only this time assume that the figures are: LDC 6 wheat or 2 cloth; DC 8 wheat or 20 cloth. What are the opportunity cost ratios now?

To summarise: countries have a comparative advantage in those goods that can be produced at a lower opportunity cost than in other countries.

If countries are to gain from trade, they should export those goods in which they have a comparative advantage and import those goods in which they have a comparative disadvantage. From this we can state a ***law of comparative advantage***:

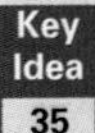

Key Idea 35 ***The law of comparative advantage.*** Provided opportunity costs of various goods differ in two countries, both of them can gain from mutual trade if they specialise in producing (and exporting) those goods that have relatively low opportunity costs compared with the other country.

See Web Case 23.1 for Ricardo's original statement of the law in 1817.

But why do they gain if they specialise according to this law? And just what will that gain be? We will consider these questions next.

The gains from trade based on comparative advantage

Before trade, unless markets are very imperfect, the prices of the two goods are likely to reflect their opportunity costs. For example, in Table 23.2, since the less developed country can produce 2 kilos of wheat for 1 metre of cloth, the *price* of 2 kilos of wheat will roughly equal the price of 1 metre of cloth.

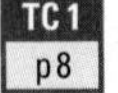

Table 23.2 Production possibilities for two countries

		Kilos of wheat		Metres of cloth
Less developed country	Either	2	or	1
Developed country	Either	4	or	8

Definitions

Absolute advantage A country has an absolute advantage over another in the production of a good if it can produce it with less resources than the other country.

Comparative advantage A country has a comparative advantage over another in the production of a good if it can produce it at a lower opportunity cost: i.e. if it has to forgo less of other goods in order to produce it.

The law of comparative advantage Trade can benefit all countries if they specialise in the goods in which they have a comparative advantage.

CASE STUDIES AND APPLICATIONS **BOX 23.1**

SHARING OUT THE JOBS

A parable of comparative advantage

Imagine that you and a group of friends are fed up with the rat race and decide to set up a self-sufficient community. So you club together and use all your savings to buy an old run-down farmhouse with 30 acres of land and a few farm animals.

You decide to produce all your own food, make your own clothes, renovate the farmhouse, make all the furniture, provide all your own entertainment and set up a little shop to sell the things you make. This should bring in enough income to buy the few items you cannot make yourselves.

The day comes to move in, and that evening everyone gathers to decide how all the jobs are going to be allocated. You quickly decide that it would be foolish for all of you to try to do all the jobs. Obviously it will be more efficient to specialise. This does not necessarily mean that everyone is confined to doing only one job, but it does mean that each of you can concentrate on just a few tasks.

But who is to do which job? The answer would seem to be obvious: you pick the best person for the job. So you go down the list of tasks. Who is to take charge of the renovations? Pat has already renovated a cottage, and is brilliant at bricklaying, plastering, wiring and plumbing. So Pat would seem to be the ideal person. Who is to do the cooking? Everyone agrees on this. Pat makes the best cakes, the best quiches and the best Irish stew. So Pat is everyone's choice for cook. And what about milking the sheep? 'Pat used to keep sheep', says Tarquin, 'and made wonderful feta cheese.' 'Good old Pat!' exclaims everyone.

It doesn't take long before it becomes obvious that 'clever-clogs' Pat is simply brilliant at everything, from planting winter wheat, to unblocking drains, to doing the accounts, to tie-dyeing. But it is soon realised that, if Pat has to do everything, nothing will get done. Even Chris, who has never done anything except market research, would be better employed milking the sheep than doing nothing at all.

So what's the best way of allocating the jobs so that the work gets done in the most efficient way? Sharon comes up with the solution. 'Everyone should make a list of all the jobs they could possibly do, and then put them in order from the one they are best at to the one they are worst at.'

KI 35 p637

So this is what everyone does. And then people are allocated the jobs they are *relatively* best at doing. Chris escapes milking the sheep and keeps the accounts instead. And Pat escapes with an eight-hour day!

If Pat took two minutes to milk the sheep and Tarquin took six, how could it ever be more efficient for Tarquin to do it?

Assume, then, that the pre-trade exchange ratios of wheat for cloth are as follows:

LDC	: 2 wheat for 1 cloth
Developed country	: 1 wheat for 2 cloth (i.e. 4 for 8)

TC 5 p24

Both countries will now gain from trade, provided the exchange ratio is somewhere between 2:1 and 1:2. Assume, for the sake of argument, that it is 1:1, that 1 wheat trades internationally for 1 cloth. How will each country gain?

The LDC gains by exporting wheat and importing cloth. At an exchange ratio of 1:1, it now only has to give up 1 kilo of wheat to obtain a metre of cloth, whereas before trade it had to give up 2 kilos of wheat.

The developed country gains by exporting cloth and importing wheat. Again at an exchange ratio of 1:1, it now has to give up only 1 metre of cloth to obtain 1 kilo of wheat, whereas before it had to give up 2 metres of cloth.

Thus both countries have gained from trade.

The actual exchange ratios will depend on the relative prices of wheat and cloth after trade takes place. These prices will depend on total demand for and supply of the two goods. It may be that the trade exchange ratio is nearer to the pre-trade exchange ratio of one country than the other. Thus the gains to the two countries need not be equal. (We will examine these issues below.)

?

1. *Show how each country could gain from trade if the LDC could produce (before trade) 3 wheat for 1 cloth and the developed country could produce (before trade) 2 wheat for 5 cloth, and if the exchange ratio (with trade) was 1 wheat for 2 cloth. Would they both still gain if the exchange ratio was (a) 1 wheat for 1 cloth; (b) 1 wheat for 3 cloth?*
2. *In question 1, which country gained the most from a trade exchange ratio of 1 wheat for 2 cloth?*

Simple graphical analysis of comparative advantage and the gains from trade: constant opportunity cost

The gains from trade can be shown graphically using production possibility curves. Let us continue with the example of the developed and less developed countries that we looked at in Table 23.2, where both countries produce just two goods: wheat and cloth.

For simplicity, assume that the pre-trade opportunity costs of cloth in terms of wheat in the two countries do not vary with output: i.e. there are *constant opportunity costs* of cloth in terms of wheat of 2/1 in the LDC and 1/2 in the developed country. Let us assume that the pre-trade production possibilities are as shown in Table 23.3.

For each 100 extra metres of cloth that the LDC produces, it has to sacrifice 200 kilos of wheat. For each extra

Table 23.3 Pre-trade production possibilities

	Less developed country			Developed country	
	Wheat (kilos m)	**Cloth (metres m)**		**Wheat (kilos m)**	**Cloth (metres m)**
a	1000	0	*g*	1200	0
b	800	100	*h*	1000	400
c	600	200	*i*	800	800
d	400	300	*j*	600	1200
e	200	400	*k*	400	1600
f	0	500	*l*	200	2000
			m	0	2400

200 kilos of wheat that the developed country produces, it has to sacrifice 400 metres of cloth. Straight-line pre-trade production possibility 'curves' can thus be drawn for the two countries with slopes of (minus) 2/1 and (minus) 1/2 respectively. These lines illustrate the various total combinations of the two goods that can be produced and hence consumed. They are shown as the blue lines in Figure 23.2.

Assume that before trade the LDC produces (and consumes) at point *e*: namely, 200 million kilos of wheat and 400 million metres of cloth; and that the developed country produces at point *k*: namely, 400 million kilos of wheat and 1600 million metres of cloth.

If they now trade, the LDC, having a comparative advantage in wheat, will specialise in it and produce at point *a*. It will produce 1000 million kilos of wheat and no cloth. The developed country will specialise in cloth and produce at point *m*. It will produce 2400 million metres of cloth and no wheat.

For simplicity, let us assume that trade between the two countries takes place at an exchange ratio of 1:1. This means that the two countries can now *consume* along the red lines in Figure 23.2: at, say, points *x* and *y* respectively. At point *x* the LDC consumes 400 million kilos of wheat (a gain of 200 million kilos over the pre-trade position) and 600 million metres of cloth (a gain of 200 million metres over the pre-trade position). At point *y* the developed country consumes 600 million kilos of wheat (a gain of 200 million kilos over the pre-trade position) and 1800 million metres of cloth (a gain of 200 million metres over the pre-trade position). Thus trade has allowed both countries to increase their consumption of both goods.

To summarise: before trade, the countries could only consume along their production possibility curves (the blue lines); after trade, they can consume along the higher red lines.

KI 35 p637

Note that in this simple two-country model the production and consumption of the two countries must match, since one country's exports are the other's imports. Thus if the LDC produces at point *a* and consumes at point *x*, the developed country, producing at point *m*, must consume at point *y*. The effects on trade of the two countries consuming at points *x* and *y* are shown in Table 23.4.

As complete specialisation has taken place in our example, the LDC now has to import all its cloth and the developed country has to import all its wheat. Thus, given the exchange ratio of 1:1, the LDC exports 600 million kilos of wheat in exchange for imports of 600 million metres of cloth. (These imports and exports are also shown in Figure 23.2.)

The final two columns of Table 23.4 show that trade has increased the total production and consumption of the two countries.

?

1. *If the opportunity cost ratio of* wheat *for* cloth *is 1/2 in the LDC, why is the slope of the production possibility curve 2/1? Is the slope of the production possibility curve always the reciprocal of the opportunity cost ratio?*
2. *Show (graphically) that, if the (pre-trade) opportunity cost ratios of the two countries were the same, there would be no gain from trade – assuming that the production possibility curves were straight lines and did not shift as a result of trade.*

Figure 23.2 Effect of trade on consumption possibilities

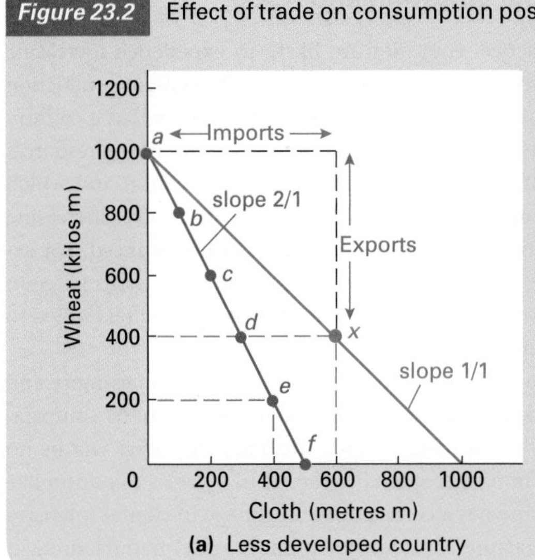

(a) Less developed country

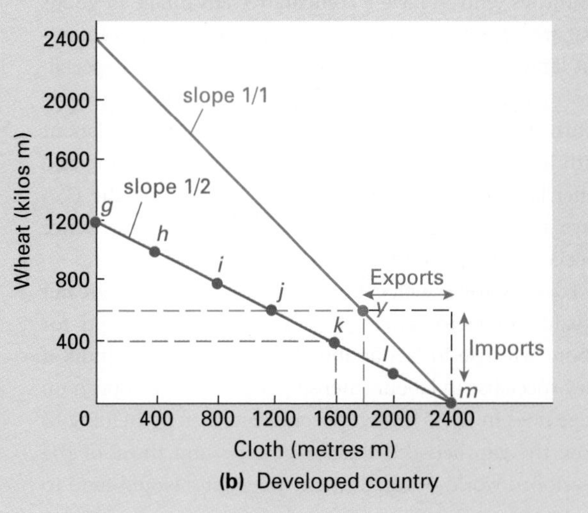

(b) Developed country

EXPLORING ECONOMICS — BOX 23.2

TRADE AS EXPLOITATION?

Does free trade exploit cheap labour abroad?

People sometimes question the morality of buying imports from countries where workers are paid 'pittance' wages. 'Is it right', they ask, 'for us to support a system where workers are so exploited?' As is often the case with emotive issues, there is some truth and some misunderstanding in a point of view like this.

KI 4 p11

First the truth. If a country like the UK trades with a regime that denies human rights, and treats its workers very badly, we may thereby be helping to sustain a corrupt system. We might also be seen to be lending it moral support. In this sense, therefore, trade may not help the cause of the workers in these countries. It is arguments like these that were used to support the imposition of trade sanctions against South Africa in the days of apartheid.

Now the misunderstanding. If we buy goods from countries that pay low wages, we are *not* as a result contributing to their low-wage problem. Quite the reverse. If countries like India export textiles to the West, this will help to *increase* the wages of Indian workers. If India has a comparative advantage in labour-intensive goods, these goods will earn a better price by being exported than by being sold entirely in the domestic Indian market. Provided *some* of the extra revenues go to the workers, they will gain from trade.

Under what circumstances would a gain in revenues by exporting firms* not *lead to an increase in wage rates?

Table 23.4 The production and consumption gains from trade

	Less developed country			Developed country			Total	
	Production	**Consumption**	**Imports (–) Exports (+)**	**Production**	**Consumption**	**Imports (–) Exports (+)**	**Production**	**Consumption**
No trade								
Wheat (kilos m)	200	200	0	400	400	0	600	600
Cloth (metres m)	400	400	0	1600	1600	0	2000	2000
With trade								
Wheat (kilos m)	1000	400	+600	0	600	–600	1000	1000
Cloth (metres m)	0	600	–600	2400	1800	+600	2400	2400

International trade and its effect on factor prices

Countries tend to have a comparative advantage in goods that are *intensive in their abundant factor*. Canada has abundant land and hence it is cheap. Therefore Canada specialises in grain production since grains are land intensive. South Asian countries have abundant supplies of labour with low wage rates, and hence specialise in clothing and other labour-intensive goods. Europe, Japan and the USA have relatively abundant and cheap capital, and hence specialise in capital-intensive manufactured goods.

Trade between such countries will tend to lead to greater equality in factor prices. For example, the demand for labour will rise in labour-abundant countries like India if they specialise in labour-intensive goods. This will push up wage rates in these low-wage countries, thereby helping to close the gap between their wage rates and those of the developed world. Without trade, wage rates would tend to be even lower.

Increasing opportunity costs and the limits to specialisation and trade

In practice, countries are likely to experience increasing opportunity costs (and hence have bowed-out production possibility curves). The reason for this is that, as a country increasingly specialises in one good, it has to use resources that are less and less suited to its production and which were more suited to other goods. Thus ever-increasing amounts of the other goods have to be sacrificed. For example, as a country specialises more and more in grain production, it has to use land that is less and less suited to growing grain.

These increasing costs as a country becomes more and more specialised lead to the disappearance of its comparative cost advantage. When this happens, there will be no point in further specialisation. Thus whereas a country like Germany has a comparative advantage in capital-intensive manufactures, it does not produce only manufactures. It would make no sense not to use its fertile lands to produce

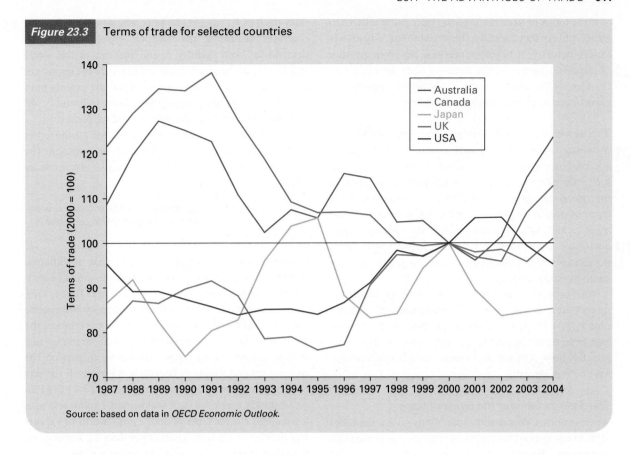

Figure 23.3 Terms of trade for selected countries

Source: based on data in *OECD Economic Outlook.*

food or its forests to produce timber. The opportunity costs of diverting all agricultural labour to industry would be very high.

Thus increasing opportunity costs limit the amount of a country's specialisation and hence the amount of its trade. There are also other limits to trade:

- Transport costs may outweigh any comparative advantage. A country may be able to produce bricks more cheaply than other countries, but their weight may make them too expensive to export.
- It may be the factors of production, rather than the goods, that move from country to country. Thus developed countries, rather than exporting finished goods to LDCs, may invest capital in LDCs to enable manufactures to be produced there. Also, labour may migrate from low-wage to high-wage countries.
- Governments may restrict trade (see section 23.2).

The terms of trade

What price will our exports fetch abroad? What will we have to pay for imports? The answer to these questions is given by the *terms of trade*.

To simplify matters, suppose there is only one exported good and only one imported good. In this case, the terms of trade are defined as P_x/P_m, where P_x is the price of the exported good and P_m is the price of the imported good. This is the reciprocal of the exchange ratio: for example, if 2x exchange for 1m (an exchange ratio of 2/1), the price of x will be half the price of m. The terms of trade will be 1/2.

1. *If 4x exchange for 3m, what are the terms of trade?*
2. *If the terms of trade are 3, how many units of the imported good could I buy for the money earned by the sale of 1 unit of the exported good? What is the exchange ratio?*

In the real world where countries have *many* exports and imports, the ***terms of trade*** are given by:

$$\frac{\text{Average price of exports}}{\text{Average price of imports}}$$

expressed as an index, where price changes are measured against a base year in which the terms of trade are assumed to be 100. Thus if the average price of exports relative to the average price of imports has risen by 20 per cent since the base year, the terms of trade will now be 120. The terms of trade for selected countries are shown in Figure 23.3 (with 2000 as the base year).

Definition

Terms of trade The price index of exports divided by the price index of imports and then expressed as a percentage. This means that the terms of trade will be 100 in the base year.

If the terms of trade rise (export prices rising relative to import prices), they are said to have 'improved', since fewer exports now have to be sold to purchase any given quantity KI 5 p21 of imports. Changes in the terms of trade are caused by changes in the demand for and supply of imports and exports, and by changes in the exchange rate.

The terms of trade and comparative advantage

KI 14 p99 Assuming there are two goods x and m, trade can be advantageous to a country as long as the terms of trade P_x/P_m are different from the opportunity cost ratios of the two goods, given by MC_x/MC_m. For example, if the terms of trade were greater than the opportunity cost ratio ($P_x/P_m > MC_x/MC_m$), it would benefit the country to pro- TC 11 p297 duce more x for export in return for imports of m, since the relative value of producing x (P_x/P_m) is greater than the relative cost (MC_x/MC_m).

With increasing opportunity costs, however, increasing specialisation in x will lead to MC_x rising (and MC_m falling), until $P_x/P_m = MC_x/MC_m$. At this point, there can be no more gain from further specialisation and trade: the maximum gain has been achieved and comparative cost advantages have been exhausted.

The determination of the terms of trade

When countries import and export many goods, the terms of trade will depend on the prices of all the various exports and imports. These prices will depend on the demand and supply of each traded good and their elasticities in the respective countries. Take the case of good g in which country A has a comparative advantage with respect to the rest of the world. This is illustrated in Figure 23.4.

Demand and supply curves of good g can be drawn for both country A and the rest of the world. (The upward-sloping supply curves imply increasing opportunity costs of production.) Before trade, country A has a low equilibrium price of P_1 and the rest of the world a high equilibrium price of P_2. After trade, price will settle at P_3 in both KI 8 p43 countries (assuming no transport costs), where total demand by both country A and the rest of the world together equals total supply, and thus where the imports of g into the rest of the world ($d - c$) equal the exports from country A ($b - a$). The position of P_3 relative to P_1 and P_2 will depend on the elasticities of demand and supply.

A similar analysis can be conducted for all the other traded goods – both exports and imports of country A. The resulting prices will allow country A's terms of trade to be calculated.

? *Draw a similar diagram to Figure 23.4 showing how the price of an individual good imported into country A is determined.*

The analysis is complicated somewhat if different national currencies are involved, since the prices in each country will be expressed in its own currency. Thus to convert one country's prices to another currency will require knowledge of the rate of exchange: e.g. for the USA and the UK it might be \$2 = £1. But under a floating exchange rate system, the rate of exchange will depend in part on the demand for and supply of imports and exports. If the rate of exchange were to depreciate – say, from \$2 = £1 to \$1.50 = £1 – the UK's terms of trade will worsen. Exports will earn less foreign currency per pound: e.g. £1 worth of exports will now be worth only \$1.50 rather than \$2. Imports, on the other hand, will be more expensive: e.g. \$6 worth of imports previously cost £3; they now cost £4.

? *Why will exporters probably welcome a 'deterioration' in the terms of trade?*

In a world of many countries and many goods, an individual country's imports and exports may have little effect on world prices. In the extreme case, it may face prices totally dictated by the external world demand and supply. The country in this case is similar to an individual firm

Figure 23.4 Determination of the price of an individual traded good

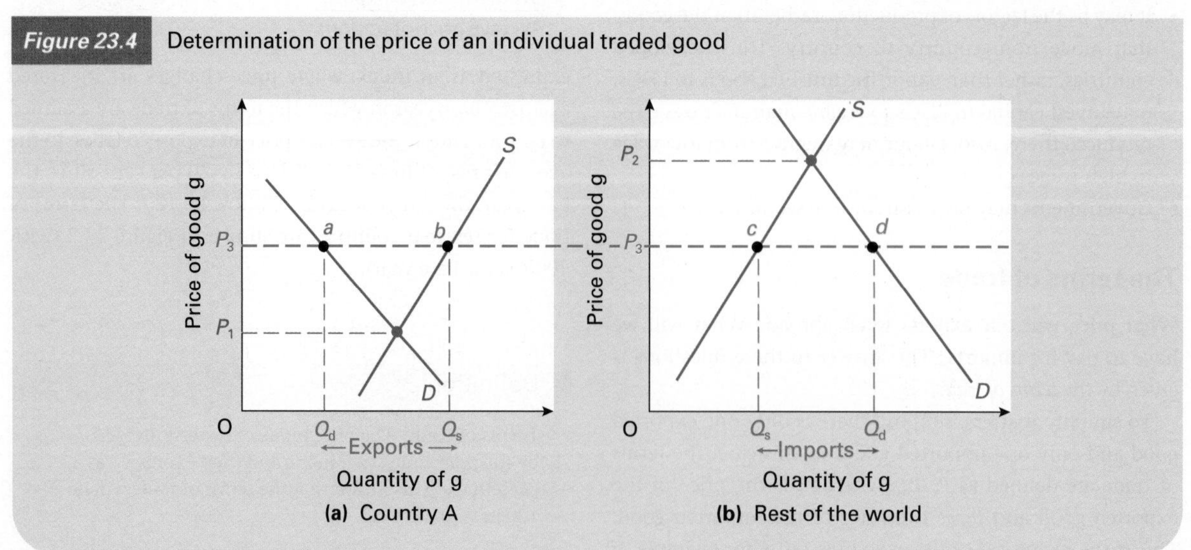

under perfect competition. The country is too small to influence world prices, and thus faces a horizontal demand curve for its exports and a horizontal supply curve for its imports. In foreign currency terms, therefore, the terms of trade are outside its control. Nevertheless, these terms of trade will probably be to its benefit, in the sense that the gains from trade will be virtually entirely received by this small country rather than the rest of the world. It is too small for its trade to depress the world price of its exports or drive up the price of its imports.

In general, a country's gains from trade will be greater the less elastic its own domestic demand and supply of tradable goods, and the more elastic the demand and supply of other countries. You can see this by examining Figure 23.4. The less elastic the domestic demand and supply, the bigger will be the effect of trade on prices faced by that country. The more the trade price differs from the pre-trade price, the bigger the gain.

Figure 23.5 Equilibrium before trade

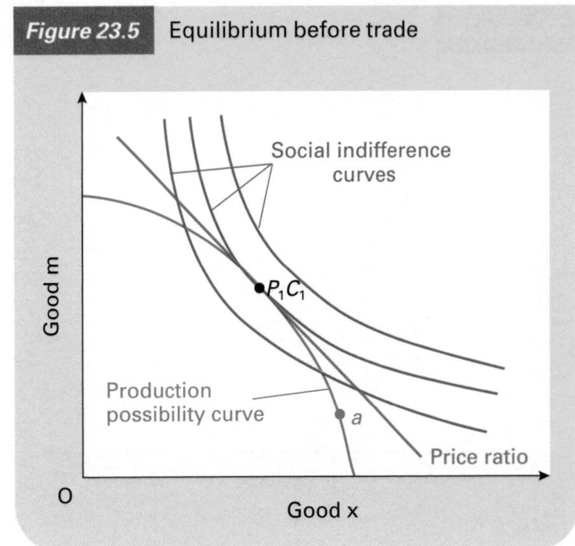

*Intermediate analysis of gains from trade

The analysis of section 11.1 (pages 297–9) can be used to demonstrate the welfare gains from trade and the limits to specialisation under conditions of increasing opportunity cost. A simple two-good model is used, and the pre-trade position is compared with the position with trade.

Pre-trade

Let us make the following simplifying assumptions:

- There are two goods, x and m.
- Country A has a comparative advantage in the production of good x.
- There are increasing opportunity costs in the production of both x and m. Thus the production possibility curve is bowed out.
- Social indifference curves can be drawn, each one showing the various combinations of x and m that give society in country A a particular level of utility.

Figure 23.5 shows the pre-trade position in country A. Production and consumption at P_1C_1 will give the highest possible utility. (All other points on the production possibility curve intersect with lower indifference curves.)

If there is perfect competition, production will indeed be at P_1C_1. There are four steps in establishing this:

- The slope of the production possibility curve ($-\Delta m/\Delta x$) is the marginal rate of transformation (*MRT*), and equals MC_x/MC_m (see page 298). For example, if the opportunity cost of producing 1 extra unit of x (Δx) was a sacrifice of 2 units of m ($-\Delta m$), then an extra unit of x would cost twice as much as an extra unit of m: i.e. $MC_x/MC_m = 2/1$, which is the slope of the production possibility curve, $-\Delta m/\Delta x$.
- The slope of each indifference curve ($-\Delta m/\Delta x$) is the marginal rate of substitution in consumption (*MRS*), and equals MU_x/MU_m. For example, if x had three times the marginal utility of m ($MU_x/MU_m = 3$), consumers would be willing to give up 3m for 1x ($-\Delta m/\Delta x = 3$).
- Under perfect competition:

$$\frac{MC_x}{MC_m} = \frac{P_x}{P_m} = \frac{MU_x}{MU_m}$$

- Thus the domestic pre-trade price ratio P_x/P_m under perfect competition must equal the slope of the production possibility curve (MC_x/MC_m) and the slope of the social indifference curve (MU_x/MU_m). This is the case at P_1C_1 in Figure 23.5.

1. *If production were at point a in Figure 23.5, describe the process whereby equilibrium at point P_1C_1 would be restored under perfect competition.*
2. *Why would production be unlikely to take place at P_1C_1 if competition were not perfect?*

With trade

If country A has a comparative advantage in good x, the price of x relative to m is likely to be higher in the rest of the world than in country A: i.e. world P_x/P_m > pre-trade domestic P_x/P_m. This is shown in Figure 23.6. The world price ratio is given by the slope of the line *WW*. With this new steeper world price ratio, the optimum production point will be P_2 where *MRT* (the slope of the production possibility curve) = world P_x/P_m (the slope of *WW*).

With production at P_2, the country can by trading consume *anywhere* along this line *WW*. The optimum consumption point will be C_2 where *MRS* (the slope of the indifference curve) = world P_x/P_m (the slope of *WW*). Thus trade has allowed consumption to move from point C_1 on the lower indifference curve I_1 to point C_2 on the higher indifference curve I_2. There has thus been a gain from trade. Perfect competition will ensure that this gain is realised, since production at P_2 and consumption at C_2 meet the equilibrium condition that:

Figure 23.6 Equilibrium with trade

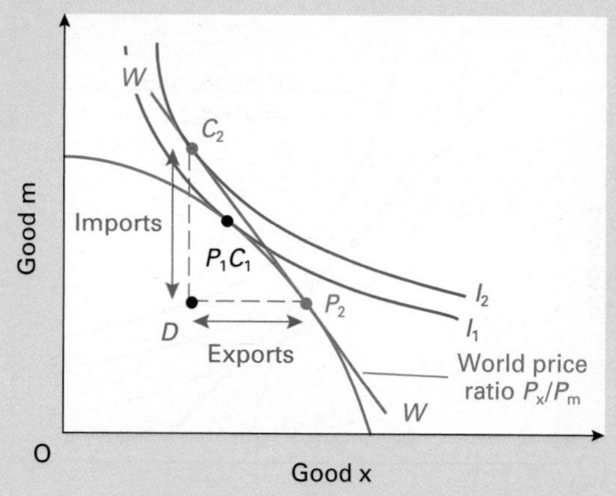

$$\frac{MC_x}{MC_m} = \frac{P_x}{P_m} = \frac{MU_x}{MU_m}$$

How much will be imported and how much will be exported? With production at P_2 and consumption at C_2, country A will import $C_2 - D$ of good m in exchange for exports of $P_2 - D$ of good x.

TC 10 p294

Similar diagrams to Figure 23.6 can be drawn for other countries. Since they show equilibrium for both imports and exports on the *one* diagram, economists refer to them as ***general equilibrium diagrams*** (see page 299 for another example).

> ?
> 1. *Draw a similar diagram to Figure 23.6, only this time assume that the two goods are good a measured on the vertical axis and good b measured on the horizontal axis. Assume that the country has a comparative advantage in good a. (Note that the world price ratio this time will be shallower than the domestic pre-trade price ratio.) Mark the level of exports of a and imports of b.*
> 2. *Is it possible to gain from trade if competition is not perfect?*

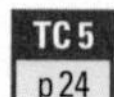

Other reasons for gains from trade

Decreasing costs. Even if there are no initial comparative cost differences between two countries, it will still benefit both to specialise in industries where economies of scale (either internal or external) can be gained, and then to trade. Once the economies of scale begin to appear, comparative cost differences will also appear, and thus the countries will have gained a comparative advantage in these industries.

> **Definition**
>
> **General equilibrium diagrams (in trade theory)** Indifference curve/production possibility curve diagrams that show a country's production and consumption of both imports and exports.

A similar argument applies to different models of the same product (e.g. different models of cars or electrical goods). Several countries, by specialising in just one or two models each, can gain the full economies of scale and hence a comparative advantage in their particular model(s). KI 35 p637 Then, through trade, consumers can gain from having a wider range from which to choose. Much of the specialisation that international trade permits is of this nature.

The decreasing cost reason for trade is particularly relevant for small countries where the domestic market is not large enough to support large-scale industries. Thus exports form a much higher percentage of GDP in small countries such as Singapore than in large countries such as the USA.

> ? *Would it be possible for a country with a comparative* dis*advantage in a given product at* pre-trade *levels of output to obtain a comparative advantage in it by specialising in its production and exporting it?*

Differences in demand. Even with no comparative cost differences and no potential economies of scale, trade can benefit both countries if demand conditions differ.

If people in country A like beef more than lamb, and people in country B like lamb more than beef, then rather than A using resources better suited for lamb to produce beef and B using resources better suited for producing beef to produce lamb, it will benefit both to produce beef *and* lamb and to export the one they like less in return for the one they like more.

Increased competition. If a country trades, the competition from imports may stimulate greater efficiency at home. This extra competition may prevent domestic monopolies/oligopolies from charging high prices. It may stimulate greater research and development and the more rapid adoption of new technology. It may lead to a greater variety of products being made available to consumers.

Trade as an 'engine of growth'. In a growing world economy, the demand for a country's exports is likely to grow, especially when these exports have a high income elasticity of demand. This provides a stimulus to growth in the exporting country.

Non-economic advantages. There may be political, social and cultural advantages to be gained by fostering trading links between countries.

Section summary

1. Countries can gain from trade if they specialise in producing those goods in which they have a comparative advantage: i.e. those goods that can be produced at relatively low opportunity costs. This is merely an extension of the argument that gains can be made from the specialisation and division of labour.
2. If two countries trade, then, provided that the trade price ratio of exports and imports is between the pre-trade price ratios of these goods in the two countries, both countries can gain. They can both consume *beyond* their production possibility curves.
3. With increasing opportunity costs there will be a limit to specialisation and trade. As a country increasingly specialises, its (marginal) comparative advantage will eventually disappear. Trade can also be limited by transport costs, factor movements and government intervention.
4. The terms of trade give the price of exports relative to the price of imports. Additional trade can be beneficial if the terms of trade (P_x/P_m) are greater than the relative marginal costs of exports and imports (MC_x/MC_m).
5. A country's terms of trade are determined by the demand and supply of imports and exports and their respective elasticities. This will determine the prices at which goods are traded and affect the rate of exchange. A country's gains from trade will be greater the less elastic its own domestic demand and supply of tradable goods, and the more elastic the demand and supply of other countries.

*6. Trade allows countries to achieve a higher level of utility by consuming on a higher social indifference curve. The maximum gain from trade is achieved by consuming at the point where the world price ratio is tangential to both the production possibility curve and a social indifference curve. This would be achieved under perfect competition.

7. Gains from trade also arise from decreasing costs (economies of scale), differences in demand between countries, increased competition from trade and the transmission of growth from one country to another. There may also be non-economic advantages from trade.

23.2 ARGUMENTS FOR RESTRICTING TRADE

KI 2 p8

Most countries have not pursued a policy of totally free trade. Their politicians know that trade involves costs as well as benefits. In this section, we will attempt to identify what these costs are, and whether they are genuine reasons for restricting trade.

Although countries may sometimes contemplate having completely free trade, they usually limit their trade. However, they certainly do not ban it altogether. The sorts of questions that governments pose are (a) should they have freer or more restricted trade and (b) in which sectors should restrictions be tightened or relaxed? Ideally, countries should weigh up the marginal benefits against the marginal costs of altering restrictions.

Methods of restricting trade

Tariffs (customs duties). These are taxes on imports and are usually ***ad valorem tariffs***: i.e. a percentage of the price of the import. Tariffs that are used to restrict imports are most effective if demand is elastic (e.g. when there are close domestically produced substitutes). Tariffs can also be used as a means of raising revenue, but in this case they are more effective if demand is inelastic. They can also be used to raise the price of imported goods to prevent 'unfair' competition for domestic producers.

Definition

Ad valorem tariffs Tariffs levied as a percentage of the price of the import.

Quotas. These are limits imposed on the quantity of a good that can be imported. Quotas can be imposed by the government, or negotiated with other countries which agree 'voluntarily' to restrict the amount of exports to the first country.

Exchange controls. These include limits on how much foreign exchange can be made available to importers (financial quotas), or to citizens travelling abroad, or for investment. Alternatively, they may take the form of charges for the purchase of foreign currencies.

Import licensing. The imposition of exchange controls or quotas often involves requiring importers to obtain licences. This makes it easier for the government to enforce its restrictions.

Embargoes. These are total government bans on certain imports (e.g. drugs) or exports to certain countries (e.g. to enemies during war).

CASE STUDIES AND APPLICATIONS BOX 23.3

FREE TRADE AND THE ENVIRONMENT

Do whales, rainforests and the atmosphere gain from free trade?

International trade provides an outlet for hardwood from the rainforests, for tiger parts for medicines, for chemicals and other industrial products produced with little regard for safety or environmental standards, and for products produced using electricity generated from low-cost, high-sulphur, highly polluting coal.

The problem is that countries are likely to export goods that they can produce at a relatively low opportunity cost. But these opportunity costs are *private* costs. They do not take into account externalities. This is a powerful argument against free trade based on free-market prices.

KI 28 p300

Surely, though, the developed countries use taxes, legislation and other means to prevent the abuse of the environment? They may do, but this does not stop them importing products from countries that do not.

In reply, the advocates of free trade argue that it is up to each country to decide its own environmental standards. If a poor country produces a product in a cheap polluting way, the gains from exporting it may more than offset the environmental damage done.

There is some strength in this argument provided (a) the government of that country has done a proper study of the costs and benefits involved, including the external costs; and (b) the externalities are confined to within the country's borders. Unfortunately, in many cases neither of these conditions holds. Much of the pollution generated from industrial production has global effects (e.g. global warming).

As countries such as China and India take an increasingly large share of world exports of industrial products, so these problems are likely to grow. Both countries have much lower environmental protection standards than in Europe and North America.

? ***Should the world community welcome the use of tariffs and other forms of protection by the rich countries against imports of goods from developing countries that have little regard for the environment?***

Export taxes. These can be used to increase the price of exports when the country has monopoly power in their supply.

Subsidies. These can be given to domestic producers to prevent competition from otherwise lower-priced imports. They can also be applied to exports in a process known as ***dumping***. The goods are 'dumped' at artificially low prices in the foreign market. (This, of course, is a means of artificially *increasing exports*, rather than reducing imports.)

Administrative barriers. Regulations may be designed to exclude imports. For example, in Germany all lagers not meeting certain purity standards are banned. Taxes may be imposed that favour local products or ingredients.

Procurement policies. This is where governments favour domestic producers when purchasing equipment (e.g. defence equipment).

TC 7 p26

Arguments in favour of restricting trade

Economic arguments having some general validity

The infant industry argument. Some industries in a country may be in their infancy, but have a potential comparative advantage. This is particularly likely in developing countries. Such industries are still too small to have gained economies of scale; their workers are inexperienced; they lack back-up facilities, such as communications networks and specialist suppliers. They may have only limited access to finance for expansion. Without protection, these ***infant industries*** will not survive competition from abroad.

Protection from foreign competition, however, will allow them to expand and become more efficient. Once they have achieved a comparative advantage, the protection can then be removed to enable them to compete internationally.

Similar to the infant industry argument is the *senile industry argument*. This is where industries with a potential comparative advantage have been allowed to run down and can no longer compete effectively. They may have considerable potential, but be simply unable to make enough profit to afford the necessary investment without some temporary protection. This is one of the most powerful arguments used to justify the use of special protection for the automobile and steel industries in the USA.

? *How would you set about judging whether an industry had a genuine case for infant/senile industry protection?*

Definitions

Dumping Where exports are sold at prices below marginal cost – often as a result of government subsidy.

Infant industry An industry that has a potential comparative advantage, but which is as yet too underdeveloped to be able to realise this potential.

To reduce reliance on goods with little dynamic potential. Many developing countries have traditionally exported primaries: foodstuffs and raw materials. The world demand for these, however, is fairly income inelastic, and thus grows relatively slowly. In such cases, free trade is not an engine of growth. Instead, if it encourages countries' economies to become locked into a pattern of primary production, it may prevent them from expanding in sectors like manufacturing that have a higher income elasticity of demand. There may thus be a valid argument for protecting or promoting manufacturing industry. (We explore these arguments in section 26.2.)

To prevent 'dumping' and other unfair trade practices. A country may engage in dumping by subsidising its exports. Alternatively, firms may practise price discrimination by selling at a higher price in home markets and a lower price in foreign markets in order to increase their profits. Either way, prices may no longer reflect comparative costs. Thus the world would benefit from tariffs being imposed to counteract such practices.

? *Does the consumer in the importing country gain or lose from dumping?*

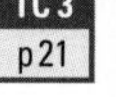

It can also be argued that there is a case for retaliating against countries that impose restrictions on your exports. In the *short* run, both countries are likely to be made worse off by a contraction in trade. But if the retaliation persuades the other country to remove its restrictions, it may have a longer-term benefit. In some cases, the mere threat of retaliation may be enough to get another country to remove its protection.

EXPLORING ECONOMICS — BOX 23.4

STRATEGIC TRADE THEORY

An argument for protection?

Lester Thurow is professor of Management and Economics at the Massachusetts Institute of Technology (MIT). He is also one of the USA's best-known and most articulate advocates of 'managed trade'.

Thurow (and others) have been worried by the growing penetration of US markets by imports from Japan and Europe and also from China and many other developing countries. Their response is to call for a carefully worked-out strategy of protection for US industries.

The *strategic trade theory* that they support argues that the real world is complex. It is wrong, they claim, to rely on free trade and existing comparative advantage. Particular industries will require particular policies of protection or promotion tailored to their particular needs:

- Some industries will require protection against unfair competition from abroad – not just to protect the industries themselves, but also to protect the consumer from the oligopolistic power that the foreign companies will gain if they succeed in driving the domestic producers out of business.
- Other industries will need special support in the form of subsidies to enable them to modernise and compete effectively with imports.
- New industries may require protection to enable them to get established – to achieve economies of scale and build a comparative advantage.
- If a particular foreign country protects or promotes its *own* industries, it may be desirable to retaliate in order to persuade the country to change its mind.

But, despite the enthusiasm of the strategic trade theorists, their views have come in for concerted criticism from economic liberals. If the USA is protected from cheap imports from Asia, they claim, all that will be achieved is a huge increase in consumer prices. The car, steel, telecommunications and electrical goods industries might find their profits bolstered, but this is hardly likely to encourage them to be more efficient.

Another criticism of managed trade is the difficulty of identifying just which industries need protection, and how much and for how long. Governments do not have perfect knowledge. What is more, the political lobbyists from various interested groups are likely to use all sorts of tactics – legal or illegal – to persuade the government to look favourably on them. In the face of such pressure, will the government remain 'objective'? No, say the liberals.

So how do the strategic trade theorists reply? If it works for Japan, they say, it can work for the USA. What is needed is a change in attitudes. Rather than industry looking on the government as either an enemy to be outwitted or a potential benefactor to be wooed, and government looking on industry as a source of votes or tax revenues, both sides should try to develop a partnership – a partnership from which the whole country can gain.

But whether sensible, constructive managed trade is possible in the US democratic system, or the UK for that matter, is a highly debatable point. 'Sensible' managed trade, say the liberals, is just pie in the sky.

? ***Airbus, a consortium based in four European countries, has received massive support from the four governments, in order to enable it to compete with Boeing, which until the rise of Airbus had dominated the world market for aircraft. To what extent are (a) air travellers; (b) citizens of the four countries likely to gain or lose from this protection? (See Web Case 23.9.)***

KI 19 p157

To prevent the establishment of a foreign-based monopoly. Competition from abroad, especially when it involves dumping, could drive domestic producers out of business. The foreign company, now having a monopoly of the market, could charge high prices with a resulting misallocation of resources.

All of the above arguments suggest that governments should adopt a 'strategic' approach to trade. ***Strategic trade theory*** (see Box 23.4) argues that protecting certain industries allows a net gain *in the long run* from increased competition in the market. This argument has been used to justify the huge financial support given to the aircraft manufacturer Airbus, a consortium based in four European countries. The subsidies have allowed it to compete with Boeing, which would otherwise have a monopoly in many types of passenger aircraft. Airlines and their passengers worldwide, it is argued, have benefited from the increased competition.

To spread the risks of fluctuating markets. A highly specialised economy – Zambia with copper, Cuba with sugar – is highly susceptible to world market fluctuations. Greater diversity and greater self-sufficiency can reduce these risks.

To reduce the influence of trade on consumer tastes. It is a mistake to assume that fixed consumer tastes dictate the pattern of production through trade. Multinational companies through their advertising and other forms of sales promotion may influence consumer tastes. Thus some restriction on trade may be justified in order to reduce this 'producer sovereignty'.

?

In what ways may free trade have harmful cultural effects on developing countries?

To prevent the importation of harmful goods. A country may want to ban or severely curtail the importation of things such as drugs, pornographic literature and live animals.

KI 28 p300

To take account of externalities. Free trade will tend to reflect private costs. Both imports and exports, however, can involve externalities. The mining of many minerals for export may damage the health of miners; the production of chemicals for export may involve pollution; the importation of juggernaut lorries may lead to structural damage to houses (see Box 23.3).

Definition

Strategic trade theory The theory that protecting/supporting certain industries can enable them to compete more effectively with large monopolistic rivals abroad. The effect of the protection is to increase long-run competition and may enable the protected firms to exploit a comparative advantage that they could not have done otherwise.

Economic arguments having some validity for specific groups or countries

The arguments considered so far are of general validity: restricting trade for such reasons could be of net benefit to the world. There are other arguments, however, that are used by individual governments for restricting trade, where their country will gain, but at the expense of other countries, such that there will be a net loss to the world. Such arguments include the following.

KI 19 p157

The exploitation of market power. If a country, or a group of countries, has market power in the supply of exports (e.g. South Africa with diamonds, OPEC with oil) or market power in the demand for imports (e.g. the USA or other large wealthy countries), it can exploit this power by intervening in trade.

Let us first take the case of a country, or a group of countries acting as a cartel, which has monopoly power in the sale of a particular export: for example, West African countries in the sale of cocoa. But let us assume that there are many individual producers that are therefore price takers and are thus not in a position to exploit the country's overall market power. In Figure 23.7, these price-taking firms will collectively produce at point *a* where $P = MC$. Market equilibrium is at a trade price of P_1 and an output of Q_1.

The country's profit, however, would be maximised at point *b* where $MC = MR$, with output at the lower level of Q_2. By imposing an export tax of $P_2 - P_3$, therefore, the country can maximise its gain from this export. Producers will receive P_3 and will therefore supply Q_2. Market price will be P_2.

?

1. *How much would be the total tax revenue for the government?*
2. *Will the individual producers gain from the export tax?*

Now let us take the case of a country that has *monopsony* power in the demand for an import. This is illustrated in Figure 23.8. Without intervention, equilibrium will be at point *d* where demand equals supply. Q_1 would be purchased at a price of P_1.

Figure 23.7 A country with a monopoly demand for an export

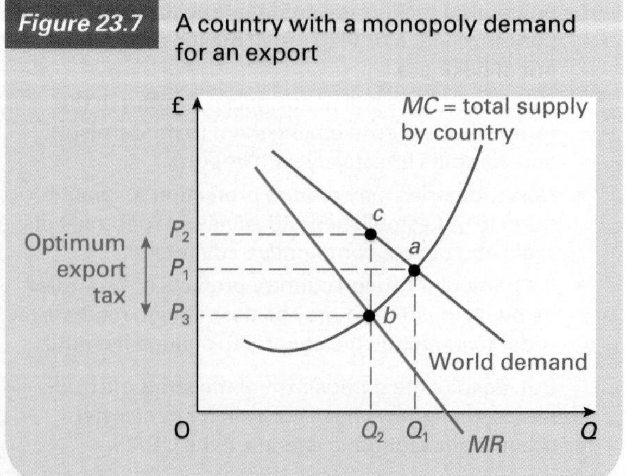

EXPLORING ECONOMICS *BOX 23.5

THE OPTIMUM TARIFF OR EXPORT TAX

Using calculus

The size of the optimum export tax depends on the price elasticity of demand ($P\epsilon_d$). You can see this if you imagine rotating the demand and *MR* curves in Figure 23.7. The less elastic the demand curve, the bigger will be the optimum export tax.

The formula for the optimum export tax rate is:

$$t = 1/P\epsilon_d$$

The proof of this is as follows.

In Figure 23.7, the optimum tax rate is:

$$(P_2 - P_3) \div P_2 \qquad (1)$$

From the point of view of the country (as opposed to individual producers) this is simply:

$$(P - MR) \div P \qquad (2)$$

Remember from Box 2.5 (on page 56) that price elasticity of demand is given by:

$$P\epsilon_d = \frac{-dQ}{dP} \times \frac{P}{Q} \qquad (3)$$

Remember also, from Box 5.9 (on page 152), that:

$$MR = \frac{dTR}{dQ} = \frac{d(P \cdot Q)}{dQ} \qquad (4)$$

From the rules of calculus:

$$\frac{d(P \cdot Q)}{dQ} = \frac{dP \cdot Q + dQ \cdot P}{dQ} \qquad (5)$$

$$\therefore P - MR = P - \frac{dP \cdot Q + dQ \cdot P}{dQ} \qquad (6)$$

and

$$\frac{P}{P - MR} = \frac{P}{P - \dfrac{dP \cdot Q + dQ \cdot P}{dQ}} \qquad (7)$$

$$= 1 - \frac{P}{\dfrac{dP \cdot Q + dQ \cdot P}{dQ}} \qquad (8)$$

Again from the rules of calculus:

$$= 1 - \left(\frac{dQ \cdot P}{dP \cdot Q} + \frac{dQ \cdot P}{dQ \cdot P}\right) \qquad (9)$$

$$= 1 - \frac{dQ \cdot P}{dP \cdot Q} - 1 \qquad (10)$$

$$= \frac{-dQ \cdot P}{dP \cdot Q} = P\epsilon_d \qquad (11)$$

∴ from equations (2) and (11):

$$\frac{P - MR}{P} = \textit{optimum tax rate} = \frac{1}{P\epsilon_d}$$

See if you can devise a similar proof to show that the optimal import tariff, where a country has monopsony power, is $1/P\epsilon_s$ (where $P\epsilon_s$ is the price elasticity of supply of the import).

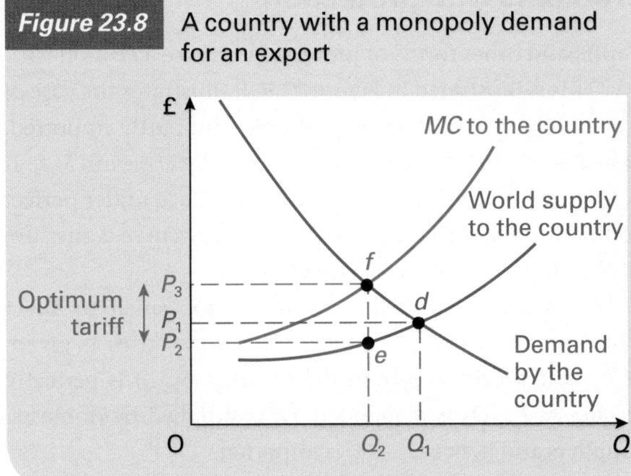

Figure 23.8 A country with a monopoly demand for an export

But the marginal cost of imports curve will be *above* the supply curve because, given the country's size, the purchase of additional imports would drive up their price. This means that the cost of additional imports would be the new higher price (given by the supply curve) *plus* the rise in expenditure on the imports that would previously have been purchased at a lower price. The country will maximise its gain from trade at point *f* by importing Q_2, where demand equals marginal cost. Consumption can be reduced to Q_2 if the government imposes a tariff of $P_3 - P_2$. This is known as the ***optimum tariff***. The country now only pays P_2 to importers. Consumers have to pay P_3 (i.e. P_2 plus the tariff).

The country gains from such intervention, but only at the expense of the other countries with which it trades.

To protect declining industries. The human costs of sudden industrial closures can be very high. In such circumstances, temporary protection may be warranted to allow industries that have lost comparative advantage to decline more slowly. Such policies will be at the expense of the consumer, who will be denied access to cheaper foreign imports.

Definition

Optimum tariff A tariff that reduces the level of imports to the point where marginal social cost equals marginal social benefit.

EXPLORING ECONOMICS BOX 23.6

GIVING TRADE A BAD NAME

Arguments that don't add up

'Why buy goods from abroad and deny jobs to workers in this country?' This is typical of the concerns that many people have about an open trade policy. However, these concerns are often based on arguments that do not stand up to close inspection. Here are four of them.

'Imports should be reduced since they lower the standard of living. The money goes abroad rather than into the domestic economy.' Imports are consumed and thus add directly to consumer welfare. Also, provided they are matched by exports, there is no net outflow of money. Trade, because of the law of comparative advantage, allows countries to increase their standard of living: to consume beyond their production possibility curve (see Figures 23.2 and 23.6).

'Protection is needed from cheap foreign labour.' Importing cheap goods from, say, Indonesia, allows more goods to be consumed. The UK uses less resources by buying these goods through the production and sale of exports than by producing them at home. However, there will be a cost to *certain* UK workers whose jobs are lost through foreign competition.

'Protection reduces unemployment.' At a microeconomic level, protecting industries from foreign competition may allow workers in those industries to retain their jobs. But if foreigners sell fewer goods to the UK, they will not be able to buy so many UK exports. Thus unemployment will rise in UK export industries. Overall unemployment, therefore, is little affected, and in the meantime the benefits from trade to consumers are reduced. *Temporary* protection given to declining industries, however, may help to reduce structural unemployment.

'Dumping is always a bad thing, and thus a country should restrict subsidised imports.' Dumping may well reduce world economic welfare: it goes against the law of comparative advantage. The importing country, however, may well *gain* from dumping. Provided the dumping is not used to drive domestic producers out of business and establish a foreign monopoly, the consumer gains from lower prices. The losers are the taxpayers in the foreign country and the workers in competing industries in the home country.

? ***Go through each of these four arguments and provide a reply to the criticisms of them.***

To improve the balance of payments. Under certain special circumstances, when other methods of balance of payments correction are unsuitable, there may be a case for resorting to tariffs (see Chapter 24).

'Non-economic' arguments

A country may be prepared to forgo the direct economic advantages of free trade – consumption at a lower opportunity cost – in order to achieve objectives that are often described as 'non-economic':

- It may wish to maintain a degree of self-sufficiency in case trade is cut off in times of war. This may apply particularly to the production of food and armaments.
- It may decide not to trade with certain countries with which it disagrees politically.
- It may wish to preserve traditional ways of life. Rural communities or communities based on old traditional industries may be destroyed by foreign competition.
- It may prefer to retain as diverse a society as possible, rather than one too narrowly based on certain industries.

Pursuing such objectives, however, involves costs. Preserving a traditional way of life, for example, may mean that consumers are denied access to cheaper goods from abroad. Society must therefore weigh up the benefits against the costs of such policies.

? *If economics is the study of choices of how to use scarce resources, can these other objectives be legitimately described as 'non-economic'?*

Problems with protection

Tariffs and other forms of protection impose a cost on society. This is illustrated in Figure 23.9. It illustrates the case of a good that is partly home produced and partly imported. Domestic demand and supply are given by D_{dom} and S_{dom}. It is assumed that firms in the country produce under perfect competition and that therefore the supply curve is the sum of the firms' marginal cost curves. 

Let us assume that the country is too small to affect world prices: it is a price taker. The world price is given, at P_w, and world supply to the country (S_{world}) is perfectly elastic. At P_w, Q_2 is demanded, Q_1 is supplied by domestic suppliers and hence $Q_2 - Q_1$ is imported.

Now a tariff is imposed. This shifts up the world supply curve to the country by the amount of the tariff. Price rises to $P_w + t$. Domestic production increases to Q_3, consumption falls to Q_4, and hence imports fall to $Q_4 - Q_3$.

This imposes a cost on society. Consumers are having to pay a higher price, and hence consumer surplus falls from *ABC* to *ADE*. The cost to consumers in lost consumer surplus is thus *EDBC* (i.e. areas 1 + 2 + 3 + 4). *Part* of this cost, however, is redistributed as a *benefit* to other sections in

Figure 23.9 The cost of protection

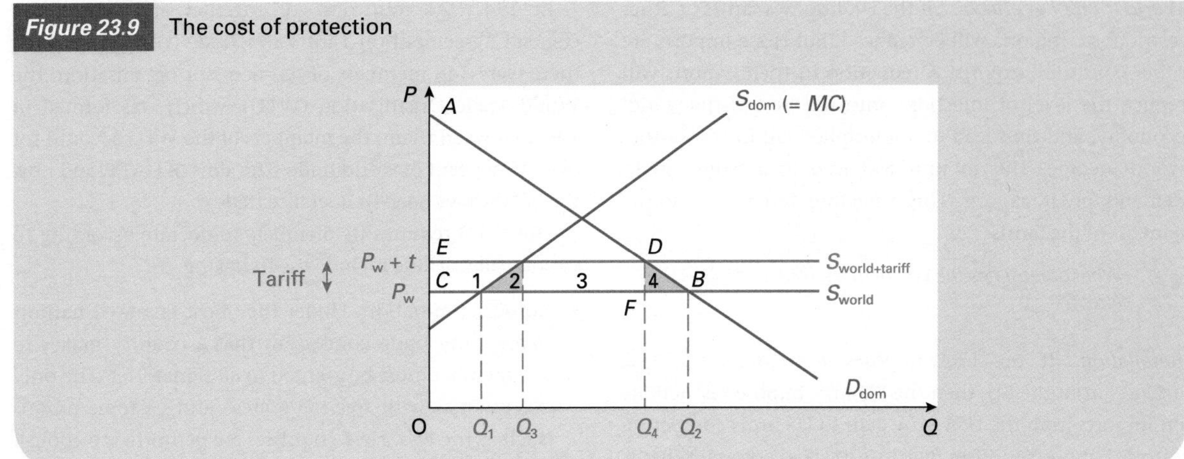

society. *Firms* face a higher price, and thus gain extra profits (area 1): where profit is given by the area between the price and the *MC* curve. The *government* receives extra revenue from the tariff payments (area 3): i.e. $Q_4 - Q_3 \times$ tariff. These revenues can be used, for example, to reduce taxes.

But *part* of this cost is not recouped elsewhere. It is a net cost to society (areas 2 and 4).

Area 2 represents the extra costs of producing $Q_3 - Q_1$ at home, rather than importing it. If $Q_3 - Q_1$ were still imported, the country would only be paying S_{world}. By producing it at home, however, the costs are given by the domestic supply curve (= *MC*). The difference between *MC* and S_{world} (area 2) is thus the efficiency loss on the production side.

Area 4 represents the loss of consumer surplus by the reduction in consumption from Q_2 to Q_4. Consumers have saved area FBQ_2Q_4 of expenditure, but have sacrificed area DBQ_2Q_4 of utility in so doing – a net loss of area 4.

The government should ideally weigh up such costs against any benefits that are gained from protection.

? *In this model, where the country is a price taker and faces a horizontal supply curve (the small country assumption), is any of the cost of the tariff borne by the overseas suppliers?*

Apart from these direct costs to the consumer, there are several other problems with protection. Some are direct effects of the protection; others follow from the reactions of other nations.

Protection as 'second best'. Many of the arguments for protection amount merely to arguments for some type of government intervention in the economy. Protection, however, may not be the best way of dealing with the problem, since protection may have undesirable side-effects. There may be a more direct form of intervention that has no side-effects. In such a case, protection will be no more than a *second-best* solution.

For example, using tariffs to protect old inefficient industries from foreign competition may help prevent unemployment in those parts of the economy, but the consumer will suffer from higher prices. A better solution would be to subsidise retraining and investment in those areas of the country in *new efficient* industries – industries with a comparative advantage. In this way, unemployment is avoided, but the consumer does not suffer.

Even if the *existing* industries were to be supported, it would still be better to do this by paying them subsidies than by putting tariffs on imports. This argument can be expressed in terms of Figure 23.9. As we have seen, a tariff imposes costs on the consumer of areas 1 + 2 + 3 + 4. In the current example, area 2 may be a cost worth paying in order to increase domestic output to Q_3 (and hence reduce unemployment). Areas 1 and 3, as argued above, are merely *redistributed* elsewhere (to firms and the government respectively). But this still leaves area 4. This is a side-effect cost *not* recouped elsewhere.

A *subsidy*, on the other hand, would not have involved this side-effect cost. In order to raise output to Q_3, a rate of subsidy the same as the tariff rate would have to be given to producers. This would raise the amount they receive per unit to $P_w + t$. They would choose to supply Q_3. The price to the consumer, however, would *remain at the world price* P_w. There would thus be no cost to the consumer. The cost of the subsidy to the taxpayer would be areas 1 + 2. Area 1 would be redistributed to firms as extra profit. Area 2, as argued above, may be worth paying to achieve the desirable output and employment consequences.

If the aim is to increase output, a *production* subsidy is the best policy. If the aim is to increase employment, an *employment* subsidy is the best policy. In either case, to use *protection* instead would be no more than second best, since it would involve side-effects.

To conclude: the best policy is to tackle the problem directly. Unless the aim is specifically to reduce imports (rather than help domestic industry), protection is an indirect policy, and hence never more than second best.

? *What would be the 'first-best' solution to the problem of an infant industry not being able to compete with imports?*

World multiplier effects. If the UK imposes tariffs or other restrictions, imports will be reduced. But these imports are other countries' exports. A reduction in their exports will reduce the level of injections into the 'rest-of-the-world' economy, and thus lead to a multiplied fall in rest-of-the-world income. This in turn will lead to a reduction in demand for UK exports. This, therefore, tends to undo the benefits of the tariffs.

What determines the size of this world multiplier effect?

Retaliation. If the USA imposes restrictions on, say, imports from the EU, then the EU may impose restrictions on imports from the USA. Any gain to US firms competing with EU imports is offset by a loss to US exporters. What is more, US consumers suffer, since the benefits from comparative advantage have been lost.

The increased use of tariffs and other restrictions can lead to a trade war: each country cutting back on imports from other countries. In the end, everyone loses.

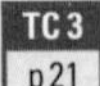
Protection may allow firms to remain inefficient. By removing or reducing foreign competition, protection may reduce firms' incentive to reduce costs. Thus if protection is being given to an infant industry, the government must ensure that the lack of competition does not prevent it 'growing up'. Protection should not be excessive and should be removed as soon as possible.

Bureaucracy. If a government is to avoid giving excessive protection to firms, it should examine each case carefully. This can lead to large administrative costs.

Corruption. Some countries that have an extensive programme of protection suffer from corruption. Home producers want as much protection as possible. Importers want as much freedom as possible. It is very tempting for both groups to bribe officials to give them favourable treatment.

The WTO

After the Wall Street crash of 1929, the world plunged into the Great Depression. Countries found their exports falling dramatically, and many suffered severe balance of payments difficulties. The response of many countries was to restrict imports by the use of tariffs and quotas. Of course, this reduced other countries' exports, which encouraged them to resort to even greater protectionism. The net effect of the Depression and the rise in protectionism was a dramatic fall in world trade. The volume of world trade in manufactures fell by more than a third in the three years following the Wall Street crash. Clearly there was a net economic loss to the world from this decline in trade.

After the Second World War there was a general desire to reduce trade restrictions, so that all countries could gain the maximum benefits from trade. There was no desire to return to the beggar-my-neighbour policies of the 1930s.

In 1947, 23 countries got together and signed the General Agreement on Tariffs and Trade (GATT). By 2005, there were 148 members of its successor organisation, the World Trade Organisation (WTO), which was formed in 1995. Between them, the members of the WTO account for over 97 per cent of world trade. The aims of GATT, and now the WTO, have been to liberalise trade.

The WTO requires its members to operate according to various rules. These include the following:

- Non-discrimination. Under the 'most favoured nations clause', any trade concession that a country makes to one member must be granted to *all* signatories. The only exception is with free-trade areas and customs unions (such as the EU). Here countries are permitted to abolish tariffs between themselves while still maintaining them with the rest of the world.
- Reciprocity. Any nation benefiting from a tariff reduction made by another country must reciprocate by making similar tariff reductions itself.
- The general prohibition of quotas.
- Fair competition. If unfair barriers are erected against a particular country, the WTO can sanction retaliatory action by that country. The country is not allowed, however, to take such action without permission.
- Binding tariffs. Countries cannot raise existing tariffs without negotiating with their trading partners.

Unlike the GATT, the WTO has the power to impose sanctions on countries breaking trade agreements. If there are disputes between member nations, these will be settled by the WTO, and if an offending country continues to impose trade restrictions, permission will be granted for other countries to retaliate.

For example, in March 2002, the Bush administration imposed tariffs on steel imports into the USA in order to protect the ailing US steel industry (see Web Case 23.7). The EU and other countries referred the case to the WTO, which in December 2003 ruled that they were illegal. This ruling made it legitimate for the EU and other countries to impose retaliatory tariffs on US products. President Bush consequently announced that the steel tariffs would be abolished.

Could US action to protect its steel industry from foreign competition be justified in terms of the interests of the USA as a whole (as opposed to the steel industry in particular)?

The greater power of the WTO has persuaded many countries to bring their disputes to it. In the first 10 years of its existence it had dealt with over 300 disputes (compared with 300 by GATT over the whole of its 48 years).

Trade rounds

Periodically, member countries have met to negotiate reductions in tariffs and other trade restrictions. There have been eight 'rounds' of such negotiations since the signing of GATT in 1947. The last major round to be completed was the Uruguay round, which began in Uruguay in 1986, continued at meetings around the world and culminated in a deal being signed in April 1994. By that time, the average tariff on manufactured products was 4 per cent and falling. In 1947 the figure was nearly 40 per cent. The Uruguay round agreement also involved a programme of phasing in substantial reductions in tariffs and other restrictions up to the year 2002 (see Web Case 23.2).

Despite the reduction in tariffs, many countries have still tried to restrict trade by various other means, such as quotas and administrative barriers. Also, barriers have been particularly high on certain non-manufactures. Agricultural protection in particular has come in for sustained criticism by developing countries. High fixed prices and subsidies given to farmers in the EU, the USA and other advanced

CASE STUDIES AND APPLICATIONS **BOX 23.7**

THE DOHA DEVELOPMENT AGENDA

A new direction for the WTO?

> Globalisation, based on the free play of comparative advantage, economies of scale and innovation, has produced a genuinely radical force, in the true sense of the word. It essentially amplifies and reinforces the strengths, but also the weaknesses, of market capitalism: its efficiency, its instability, and its inequality. If we want globalisation not only to be efficiency-boosting but also fair, we need more international rules and stronger multilateral institutions.[1]

In November 1999, the members of the World Trade Organisation met in Seattle in the USA. What ensued became known as the 'Battle of Seattle' (see Web Case 23.4). Anti-globalisation protesters fought with police; the world's developing economies fell out with the world's developed economies; and the very future of the WTO was called into question. The WTO was accused of being a free trader's charter, in which the objective of free trade was allowed to ride rough-shod over anything that might stand in its way. Whatever the issue – the environment, the plight of developing countries, the dominance of trade by multinationals – free trade was king.

At Seattle, both the protesters and developing countries argued that things had gone far enough. The WTO must redefine its role, they argued, to respect *all* stakeholders. More radical voices called for the organisation to be scrapped. As Pascal Lamy, the EU Trade Commissioner, made clear in the quote above, rules had to be strengthened, and the WTO had to ensure that the gains from trade were fairer and more sustainable.

The rebuilding process of the WTO began in Doha, Qatar, in November 2001. The meeting between the then 142 members of the WTO concluded with the decision to launch a new round of WTO trade talks, to be called the 'Doha Development Agenda'. The talks are designed to increase the liberalisation of trade. However, such a goal is to be tempered by a policy of strengthening assistance to developing economies.

> The Doha Development Agenda moves the WTO into a new era: one which allows the organisation to play a fuller role in the pursuit of economic growth, employment and poverty reduction, in global governance, and in the promotion of sustainable development, while maintaining its key function of increasing and improving the conditions for world-wide trade and investment.[2]

At Doha it was agreed that the new trade talks would address questions such as:

- Sustainable development and the environment. In the past, international trade agreements always seemed to take precedence over international environmental agreements, even though they are legally equivalent. In the new Doha round, this relationship is to be clarified. The hope is to achieve greater coherence between various areas of international policy making.
- Trade and development. The Doha round will attempt to address a number of issues of concern to developing countries as they become more integrated into the world's trading system. For example, it will seek to extend special provisions to developing economies to improve their access to markets in developed countries. It will also attempt to strengthen the current special treatment that developing countries receive, such as the ability to maintain higher rates of tariff protection.

Other areas identified for discussion include: greater liberalisation of agriculture; rules to govern foreign direct investment; the co-ordination of countries' competition policies; the use and abuse of patents on medicines; and the needs of developing countries.

The talks were originally scheduled for completion by January 2005, but this deadline was extended to December 2005 at the earliest, given difficulties in reaching agreements at meetings prior to that date.

Interim agreement was reached at talks in Geneva in July 2004. This involved commitment by the EU to end export subsides on agricultural products, although no date was set, and an agreement by the USA to 'prioritise' the 'cotton issue', whereby US farmers were given a $3 billion subsidy, the effect of which had been to flood the world market with cheap cotton, making it impossible for lower-cost west African producers to compete. The agreement was deliberately vague so as to appease both the developed and developing world.

Outline the advantages and drawbacks of adopting a free trade strategy for developing economies. How might the Doha Development Agenda go some way to reducing these drawbacks?

[1] 'Global policy without democracy' (speech by Pascal Lamy, EU Trade Commissioner, given in 2001).

[2] EU summary of Doha Ministerial Conference, http://trade-info.cec.eu.int/europa/2001newround/compas.htm.

countries mean that the industrialised world continues to export food to many developing countries that have a comparative advantage in food production! Farmers in developing countries often find it impossible to compete with subsidised food imports from the rich countries.

The latest round of trade negotiations began in Doha, Qatar, in 2001 (see Box 23.7). The negotiations are focusing on both trade liberalisation and measures to encourage development of poorer countries. In particular, the Doha Development Agenda, as it is called, is concerned with measures to make trade fairer so that its benefits are spread more evenly around the world. This will involve improved access for developing countries to markets in the rich world. The Agenda is also concerned with the environmental impacts of trade and development. The negotiations were originally due to be completed in 2005, but have since been extended.

Section summary

1. Countries use various methods to restrict trade, including tariffs, quotas, exchange controls, import licensing, export taxes, and legal and administrative barriers. Countries may also promote their own industries by subsidies.
2. Reasons for restricting trade that have some validity in a world context include the infant industry argument, the inflexibility of markets in responding to changing comparative advantage, dumping and other unfair trade practices, the danger of the establishment of a foreign-based monopoly, the problems of relying on exporting goods whose market is growing slowly or even declining, the need to spread the risks of fluctuating export prices, and the problems that free trade may adversely affect consumer tastes, may allow the importation of harmful goods and may not take account of externalities.
3. Often, however, the arguments for restricting trade are in the context of one country benefiting even though other countries may lose more. Countries may intervene in trade in order to exploit their monopoly/monopsony power. In the case of imports, the optimum tariff would be that which would reduce consumption to the level where price was equal to the country's marginal cost. In the case of exports, the optimum export tax would be that which reduced production to the level where the country's marginal revenue was equal to marginal cost. Other 'beggar-my-neighbour' arguments include the protection of declining industries and improving the balance of payments.
4. Finally, a country may have other objectives in restricting trade, such as remaining self-sufficient in certain strategic products, not trading with certain countries of which it disapproves, protecting traditional ways of life or simply retaining a non-specialised economy.
5. Arguments for restricting trade, however, are often fallacious. In general, trade brings benefits to countries, and protection to achieve one objective may be at a very high opportunity cost. Other things being equal, there will be a net loss in welfare from restricting trade, with any gain in government revenue or profits to firms being outweighed by a loss in consumer surplus. Even if government intervention to protect certain parts of the economy is desirable, restricting trade is unlikely to be a first-best solution to the problem, since it involves side-effect costs. What is more, restricting trade may have adverse world multiplier effects; it may encourage retaliation; it may allow inefficient firms to remain inefficient; it may involve considerable bureaucracy and possibly even corruption.
6. Most countries of the world are members of the WTO and in theory are in favour of moves towards freer trade. The Uruguay round brought significant reductions in trade restrictions, both tariff and non-tariff. Nevertheless, countries have been very unwilling to abandon restrictions if they believe that they can gain from them, even though they might be at the expense of other countries.

23.3 PREFERENTIAL TRADING

The world economy seems to have been increasingly forming into a series of trade blocs, based upon regional groupings of countries: a European region centred on the European Union, an Asian region on Japan, a North American region on the USA and a Latin American region. Such trade blocs are examples of ***preferential trading arrangements***. These arrangements involve trade restrictions with the rest of the world, and lower or zero restrictions between the members.

Although trade blocs clearly encourage trade between their members, many countries outside the blocs complain that they benefit the members at the expense of the rest of the world. For many developing economies, in need of access to the most prosperous nations in the world, this represents a significant check on their ability to grow and develop.

Definition

Preferential trading arrangements A trade agreement whereby trade between the signatories is freer than trade with the rest of the world.

Types of preferential trading arrangement

There are three possible forms of such trading arrangements.

Free trade areas

A ***free trade area*** is where member countries remove tariffs and quotas between themselves, but retain whatever restrictions *each member chooses* with non-member countries. Some provision will have to be made to prevent imports from outside coming into the area via the country with the lowest external tariff.

Customs unions

A ***customs union*** is like a free trade area, but in addition members must adopt *common* external tariffs and quotas with non-member countries.

Common markets

A ***common market*** is where member countries operate as a *single* market. Like a customs union, there are no tariffs and quotas between member countries and there are common external tariffs and quotas. But a common market goes further than this. A full common market includes the following features.

A common system of taxation. In the case of a *perfect* common market, this will involve identical rates of tax in all member countries.

A common system of laws and regulations governing production, employment and trade. For example, in a perfect common market, there would be a *single* set of laws governing issues such as product specification (e.g. permissible artificial additives to foods, or levels of exhaust emissions from cars), the employment and dismissal of labour, mergers and takeovers, and monopolies and restrictive practices.

Free movement of labour, capital and materials, and of goods and services. In a perfect common market, this will involve a total absence of border controls between member states, the freedom of workers to work in any member country and the freedom of firms to expand into any member state.

The absence of special treatment by member governments of their own domestic industries. Governments are large purchasers of goods and services. In a perfect common market, they should buy from whichever companies within the market offer the most competitive deal and not show favouritism towards domestic suppliers: they should operate a *common procurement policy*.

The definition of a common market is sometimes extended to include the following two features of *economic and monetary union*.

A fixed exchange rate between the member countries' currencies. In the extreme case, this would involve a single currency for the whole market.

Common macroeconomic policies. To some extent, this must follow from a fixed exchange rate, but in the extreme case it will involve a single macroeconomic management of the whole market, and hence the abolition of separate fiscal or monetary intervention by individual member states.

We will examine European economic and monetary union in section 25.3.

The direct effects of a customs union: trade creation and trade diversion

By joining a customs union (or free trade area), a country will find that its trade patterns change. Two such changes can be distinguished: trade creation and trade diversion.

Trade creation

KI 35 p637

Trade creation is where consumption shifts from a high-cost producer to a low-cost producer. The removal of trade barriers allows greater specialisation according to comparative advantage. Instead of consumers having to pay high prices for domestically produced goods in which the country has a comparative disadvantage, the goods can now be obtained more cheaply from other members of the customs union. In return, the country can export to them goods in which it has a comparative advantage.

For example, suppose that the most efficient producer in the world of good x is France. Assume that, before it joined the EU (then called the European Economic Community), the UK had to pay tariffs on good x from France. After joining the EU, however, it was then able to import good x from France without paying tariffs. There was a gain to UK

Definitions

Free trade area A group of countries with no trade barriers between themselves.

Customs union A free trade area with common external tariffs and quotas.

Common market A customs union where the member countries act as a single market with free movement of labour and capital, common taxes and common trade laws.

Trade creation Where a customs union leads to greater specialisation according to comparative advantage and thus a shift in production from higher-cost to lower-cost sources.

Figure 23.10 Trade creation

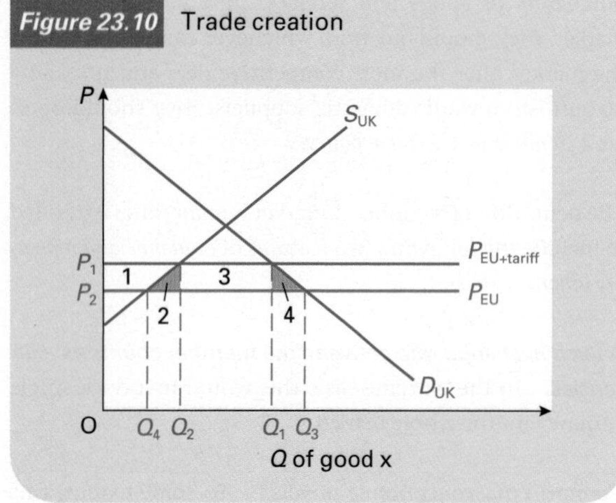

Figure 23.11 Trade diversion

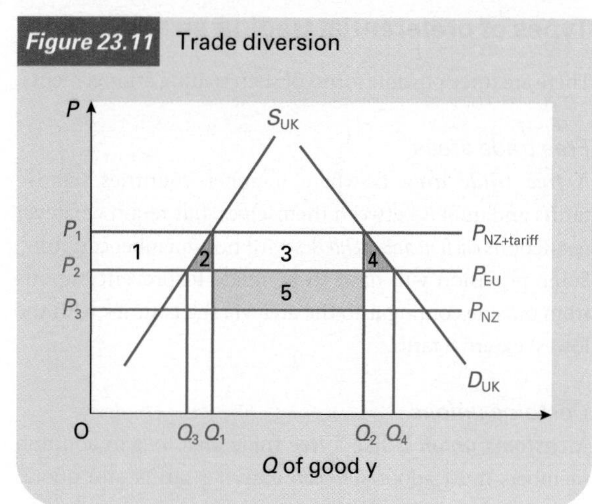

consumers. This gain is illustrated in Figure 23.10. The diagram assumes for simplicity that the UK is a price taker as an importer of good x from France: the EU price is given.

The diagram shows that, before joining the EU, the UK had to pay the EU price *plus* the tariff (i.e. P_1). At P_1 the UK produced Q_2, consumed Q_1 and thus imported $Q_1 - Q_2$. With the removal of tariffs, the price falls to P_2. Consumption increases to Q_3 and production falls to Q_4. Imports have thus increased to $Q_3 - Q_4$. Trade has been created.

The gain in welfare from the removal of the tariff is also illustrated in Figure 23.10. A reduction in price from P_1 to P_2 leads to an increase in consumer surplus of areas 1 + 2 + 3 + 4. On the other hand, there is a loss in profits to domestic producers of good x of area 1 and a loss in tariff revenue to the government of area 3. There is still a net gain, however, of areas 2 + 4.

The increased consumption of wine in the UK after joining the EU may be seen as trade creation.

Trade diversion

Trade diversion is where consumption shifts from a lower-cost producer outside the customs union to a higher-cost producer within the union.

Assume that the most efficient producer of good y in the world was New Zealand – outside the EU. Assume that, before membership, the UK paid a similar tariff on good y from any country, and thus imported the product from New Zealand rather than the EU.

After joining the EU, however, the removal of the tariff made the EU product cheaper, since the tariff remained on the New Zealand product. Consumption thus switched to a higher-cost producer. There was thus a net loss in world efficiency. As far as the UK was concerned, consumers still gained, since they were paying a lower price than before, but this time the loss in profits to domestic producers and the loss in tariff revenue to the governments might have been larger.

These benefits and costs are shown in Figure 23.11. For simplicity it assumes a constant New Zealand and EU price (i.e. that their supply curves are infinitely elastic). The domestic supply curve (S_{UK}) is upward sloping, and is assumed to be equal to marginal cost.

Before joining the EU, the UK was importing good y from New Zealand at a price P_1 (i.e. the New Zealand price plus the tariff). The UK thus consumed Q_2, produced Q_1 domestically and imported the remainder, $Q_2 - Q_1$. On joining the EU, it was now able to consume at the EU (tariff-free) price of P_2. (Note that this is above the tariff-free New Zealand price, P_3). What are the gains and losses?

- Consumers' gain: consumer surplus rises by areas 1 + 2 + 3 + 4.
- Producers' loss: UK producer surplus (profit) falls by area 1.
- Government's loss: previously tariffs of areas 3 + 5 were paid. Now no tariffs are paid. The government thus loses this revenue.

There is thus a net gain of areas 1 + 2 + 3 + 4 minus areas 1 + 3 + 5, i.e. areas 2 + 4 minus area 5. If, however, area 5 is bigger than area 2 + 4, there is a net loss.

When trade *diversion* takes place, therefore, there may still be a net gain, but there may be a net loss. It depends on circumstances.

TC 1 p8

Definition

Trade diversion Where a customs union diverts consumption from goods produced at a lower cost outside the union to goods produced at a higher cost (but tariff free) within the union.

?

Under which of the following circumstances is there likely to be a net gain from trade diversion? (Refer to Figure 23.11.) (a) A small difference between the EU price and the New Zealand pre-tariff price, and a large difference between the EU price and the New Zealand price with the tariff, or vice versa. (b) Elastic or inelastic UK demand and supply curves. (c) The UK demand and supply curves close together or far apart.

A customs union is more likely to lead to trade diversion rather than trade creation:

- When the union's external tariff is very high. Under these circumstances, the abolition of the tariff within the union is likely to lead to a large reduction in the price of goods imported from other members of the union.
- When there is a relatively small cost difference between goods produced within and outside the union. Here the abolition of even relatively low tariffs within the union will lead to internally produced goods becoming cheaper than externally produced goods.

Longer-term effects of a customs union

The problem with the above analysis is that it assumes *static* demand and supply curves: in other words, supply and demand curves that are unaffected by changes in trading patterns. In reality, if a country joins a customs union, the curves are likely to shift. Membership itself affects demand and supply – perhaps beneficially, perhaps adversely.

Longer-term advantages (economic)

- Increased market size may allow a country's firms to exploit (*internal*) *economies of scale*. This argument is more important for small countries, which have therefore more to gain from an enlargement of their markets.
- *External economies of scale*. Increased trade may lead to improvements in the infrastructure of the members of the customs union (better roads, railways, financial services, etc.). This in turn could bring bigger long-term benefits from trade between members, and from external trade too, by making the transport and handling of imports and exports cheaper.
- The bargaining power of the whole customs union with the rest of the world may allow member countries to gain *better terms of trade*. This, of course, will necessarily involve a degree of political co-operation between the members.
- *Increased competition* between member countries may stimulate efficiency, encourage investment and reduce monopoly power. Of course, a similar advantage could be gained by the simple removal of tariffs with any competing country.
- Integration may encourage a *more rapid spread of technology*.

Longer-term disadvantages (economic)

- *Resources may flow from the country* to more efficient members of the customs union, or to the geographical centre of the union (so as to minimise transport costs). This can be a major problem for a *common market* (where there is free movement of labour and capital). The country could become a depressed 'region' of the community, with adverse regional multiplier effects.
- If integration encourages greater co-operation between firms in member countries, it may also encourage *greater oligopolistic collusion*, thus keeping prices higher to the consumer. It may also encourage mergers and takeovers which would increase monopoly power.
- *Diseconomies of scale*. If the union leads to the development of very large companies, they may become bureaucratic and inefficient.
- The *costs of administering* the customs union may be high. This problem is likely to be worse, the more the intervention in the affairs of individual members.

It is extremely difficult to assess these arguments. To decide whether membership has been beneficial to a country requires a prediction of what things would have been like if it had not joined. No *accurate* predictions of this sort can be made, and they can never be tested. Also, many of the advantages and disadvantages are very long term, and depend on future attitudes, institutions, policies and world events, which again cannot be predicted.

In addition, some of the advantages and disadvantages are distinctly political, such as 'greater political power' or 'loss of sovereignty'. Assessment of these arguments cannot be made by economists.

How would you set about assessing whether or not a country had made a net long-term gain by joining a customs union? What sort of evidence would you look for?

Preferential trading in practice

Preferential trading has the greatest potential to benefit countries whose domestic market is too small, taken on its own, to enable them to benefit from economies of scale, and where they face substantial barriers to their exports. Most developing countries fall into this category, and as a result many have attempted to form preferential trading arrangements.

Examples in Latin America and the Caribbean include the Latin American Integration Association (LAIA), the Andean Community, the Central American Common Market (CACM) and the Caribbean Community (CARICOM). A Southern Common Market (MerCoSur) was formed in 1991, consisting of Argentina, Brazil, Paraguay and Uruguay. It has a common external tariff and most of its internal trade is free of tariffs.

In 1993, the six original ASEAN nations (Brunei, Indonesia, Malaysia, the Philippines, Singapore and Thailand) agreed to work towards an ASEAN Free Trade Area (AFTA). ASEAN (the Association of South-East Asian Nations) now has ten members (the new ones being Laos, Myanmar, Vietnam and Cambodia) and is dedicated to increased economic co-operation within the region. What progress has been made in achieving AFTA? By 2005 the original six members had reduced internal tariffs to an average of 3.8 per cent and had no tariffs on over 60 per cent of products. Plans are to eliminate all tariffs between these six by 2010 and for the remaining countries by 2015. ASEAN also plans to establish a common market, the ASEAN Economic Community (AEC), by 2020.

In Africa, the Economic Community of West African States (ECOWAS) has been attempting to create a common market between its members and to achieve the adoption of a single currency for most of its members by July 2005.

North American Free Trade Association (NAFTA)

Along with the EU, NAFTA is one of the two most powerful trading blocs in the world. It came into force in 1994 and consists of the USA, Canada and Mexico. These three countries have agreed to abolish tariffs between themselves in the hope that increased trade and co-operation will follow. Tariffs between the USA and Canada were phased out by 1999, and tariffs between Mexico and the other two countries will be by 2009. New non-tariff restrictions will not be permitted either, but many existing ones can remain in force, thus preventing the development of true free trade between the members. Indeed, some industries, such as textiles and agriculture, will continue to have major non-tariff restrictions.

NAFTA members hope that, with a market similar in size to the EU, they will be able to rival the EU's economic power in world trade. Other countries may join in the future, so NAFTA may eventually develop into a Western Hemisphere free trade association.

NAFTA is, however, at most only a free trade area and not a common market. Unlike the EU, it does not seek to harmonise laws and regulations. Member countries are permitted total legal independence, subject to the one proviso that they must treat firms of other member countries equally with their own firms – the principle of 'fair competition'. Nevertheless, NAFTA has encouraged a growth in trade between its members, most of which is trade creation rather than trade diversion.

Web Case 23.8 looks at the costs and benefits of NAFTA membership to the three countries involved.

Asia-Pacific Economic Co-operation forum (APEC)

The most significant move towards establishing a more widespread regional economic organisation in east Asia appeared with the creation of the Asia-Pacific Economic Association (APEC). APEC links NAFTA, Japan, China, Hong Kong China, Korea, Taiwan, Australia, New Zealand, Papua New Guinea, Russia, Chile, Peru and the seven Pacific economies of the ASEAN nations: in total 21 economies, which account for 34 per cent of the world's population and 60 per cent of world GDP. At the 1994 meeting of APEC leaders, it was resolved to create a free trade area across the Pacific by 2010 for the developed industrial countries, and by 2020 for the rest.

Unlike the EU and NAFTA, APEC is likely to remain solely a free trade area and not to develop into a customs union, let alone a common market. Within the region there exists a wide disparity in GDP per capita, ranging from Japan and the USA at over $34 000 to Vietnam at a mere $400. Such disparities create a wide range of national interests and goals. Countries are unlikely to share common economic problems or concerns. In addition, political differences and conflicts within the region are widespread, reducing the likelihood that any organisational agreement beyond a simple economic one would succeed.

The economic benefits from free trade, however, and the resulting closer regional ties, could be immense. If the whole of the US and Russian economies are included, then APEC accounts for nearly half of world trade – a truly massive trading zone.

The longest established and most comprehensive of preferential trading arrangements is the European Union. The remainder of this chapter is devoted to examining its evolution from a rather imperfect customs union to a common market (though still not perfect).

Section summary

1. Countries may make a partial movement towards free trade by the adoption of a preferential trading system. This involves free trade between the members, but restrictions on trade with the rest of the world. Such a system can be either a simple free trade area, or a customs union (where there are common restrictions with the rest of the world), or a common market (where in addition there is free movement of capital and labour, and common taxes and trade laws).
2. A preferential trading area can lead to trade creation where production shifts to low-cost producers within the area, or to trade diversion where trade shifts away from lower-cost producers outside the area to higher-cost producers within the area.
3. There is a net welfare gain from trade creation: the gain in consumer surplus outweighs the loss of tariff revenue and the loss of profit to domestic producers. With trade diversion, however, these two losses may outweigh the gains to consumers: whether they do depends on the size of the tariffs and on the demand for and supply of the traded goods.
4. Preferential trading may bring dynamic advantages of increased external economies of scale, improved terms of trade from increased bargaining power with the rest of the world, increased efficiency from greater competition between member countries, and a more rapid spread of technology. On the other hand, it can lead to increased regional problems for members, greater oligopolistic collusion and various diseconomies of scale. There may also be large costs of administering the system.
5. There have been several attempts around the world to form preferential trading systems. The two most powerful are the European Union and the North American Free Trade Association (NAFTA).

23.4 THE EUROPEAN UNION

Historical background

The European Economic Community was formed by the signing of the Treaty of Rome in 1957 and came into operation on 1 January 1958.

The original six member countries of the EEC (Belgium, France, Italy, Luxembourg, Netherlands and West Germany) had already made a move towards integration with the formation of the European Coal and Steel Community in 1952. This had removed all restrictions on trade in coal, steel and iron ore between the six countries. The aim had been to gain economies of scale and allow more effective competition with the USA and other foreign producers.

The European Economic Community extended this principle and aimed eventually to be a full common market with completely free trade between members in all products, and with completely free movement of labour, enterprise and capital.

All internal tariffs between the six members had been abolished and common external tariffs established by 1968. But this still only made the EEC a *customs union*, since a number of restrictions on internal trade remained (legal, administrative, fiscal, etc.). Nevertheless the aim was eventually to create a full common market.

In 1973 the UK, Denmark and Ireland became members. Greece joined in 1981, Spain and Portugal in 1986, and Sweden, Austria and Finland in 1995. The latest expansion came in May 2004, when Cyprus, the Czech Republic, Estonia, Hungary, Latvia, Lithuania, Malta, Poland, Slovakia and Slovenia joined. The EU now has 25 members.

The institutions of the European Union

The goal of some politicians is for the European Union (as it is now called) to become a complete political union, with a central federal government: a 'United States of Europe'. Although this is unlikely in the foreseeable future, there are some political and legal institutions that affect life in member countries.

European Commission. This consists of 25 commissioners appointed by the member countries (one each). The commissioners administer existing Union policy, propose new policies and are answerable to the European Parliament (see below). They are backed up by a civil service of 36 'Directorates-General' in Brussels, each responsible for a particular area, such as regional policy or agriculture.

European Council. This is the main decision-making body of the EU and consists of 25 senior ministers, one from each country. It receives proposals from the Commission, and has the power to decide on all EU issues. Which ministers are represented on the Council depends on the purpose of the meeting. Thus finance ministers represent their country on economic issues, agricultural ministers on farm policy, etc.

European Parliament. Constituencies in the member countries elect MEPs to serve in the European Parliament in Strasbourg. Its powers are rather limited in practice, but in theory both the Commission and the Council are answerable to it.

The European Court of Justice. This meets in Luxembourg and decides on areas of legal dispute arising from EU treaties, whether between governments, institutions or individuals.

From customs union to common market

The European Union is clearly a customs union. It has common external tariffs and no internal tariffs. But is it also a common market? For many years, there have been *certain* common economic policies.

The Common Agricultural Policy (CAP). The Union sets common high prices for farm products. This involves charging variable import duties to bring foreign food imports up to EU prices and intervention to buy up surpluses of food produced within the EU (see section 3.4).

Regional policy. EU regional policy provides grants to firms and local authorities in relatively deprived regions of the Union (Box 22.5).

Competition policy. EU policy here has applied primarily to companies operating in more than one member state (see section 12.3). For example, Article 81 of the Amsterdam Treaty prohibits agreements between firms which will adversely affect competition in trade between member states.

Harmonisation of taxation. VAT is the standard form of indirect tax throughout the EU. However, there are substantial differences in VAT rates between member states (see Box 23.9), as there are with other tax rates.

What would be the economic effects of (a) different rates of VAT, (b) different rates of personal income tax and (c) different rates of company taxation between member states if there were no other barriers to trade or factor movements?

Social policy. In 1989 the European Commission presented a *social charter* to the heads of state. This spelt out a series of worker and social rights that should apply in all member states (see Web Case 23.10). These rights were grouped under 12 headings covering areas such as the guarantee of decent levels of income for both the employed and the non-employed, freedom of movement of labour between member countries, freedom to belong to a trade union and equal treatment of men and women in the labour market. However, the charter was only a recommendation and each element had to be approved separately by the Council.

Then in December 1991 the Maastricht Treaty was signed. This set out a timetable for economic and monetary union for the EU (see section 25.3), but also included a 'social chapter', which attempted to move the Community forward in implementing the details of the social charter in areas such as maximum hours, minimum working conditions, health and safety protection, information and consultation of workers, and equal opportunities.

The UK Conservative government refused to sign this part of the Maastricht Treaty. It maintained that such measures would increase costs of production and make EU goods less competitive in world trade. Critics of the UK position argued that the refusal to adopt minimum working conditions (and also a minimum wage) would make the UK the 'sweatshop' of Europe. One of the first acts of the incoming Labour government in 1997 was to sign up to the social chapter.

Would the adoption of improved working conditions necessarily lead to higher labour costs per unit of output?

Non-tariff barriers

Despite these common policies, and despite the fact that tariffs between EU members had been eliminated long ago, there was still not free trade between member states. The 1980s saw a proliferation of *non-tariff* barriers. These included: high taxes on products not made in the country (e.g. taxes on wine by non-wine producing countries); giving subsidies or granting tax relief to domestic firms; special licences or permissions designed to favour domestic producers (e.g. granting national airlines the sole right to operate a given domestic route); governments giving contracts to domestic producers (e.g. for defence equipment and office supplies); various professions recognising only their own national qualifications; and restrictions on the right to sell financial services in other member countries.

The category often cited by businesses as being the most important single barrier was that of regulations and norms. In some cases, the regulations merely added to the costs of imports. But in the cases of many mechanical engineering and telecommunications products, technical and health-and-safety regulations sometimes ruled out foreign imports altogether.

Completing the internal market

The Single European Act of 1987, however, sought to remove these barriers and to form a genuine common market by the end of 1992 (see Box 23.9).

One of the most crucial aspects of the Act was its acceptance of the principle of ***mutual recognition***. This is the principle whereby if a firm or individual is permitted to do something under the rules and regulations of *one* EU country, it must also be permitted to do it in all other EU countries. This means that firms and individuals can choose the country's rules that are least constraining. It also means that individual governments can no longer devise special rules and regulations that keep out competitors from other EU countries (see Box 23.8). Here was the answer to the dilemma of how to get all EU countries to agree to common sets of rules and regulations. All that was required was that they recognised the rules and regulations applying in each other's countries. However, there was a danger that governments would end up competing against each other to provide the lightest set of regulations in order to attract firms to invest in their country. This could be to the detriment of consumers and workers.

Thus *some* common sets of rules and regulations were still required. One other feature of the Single European Act helped here. This was the institution of *majority* voting in questions of harmonisation of rules and regulations. Previously, unanimous approval had been necessary. This had meant that an individual country could veto the dismantling of barriers. This new system of majority voting, however, does not apply to the harmonisation of taxes.

The benefits and costs of the single market

It is difficult to quantify the benefits and costs of the single market, given that many occur over a long period, and that it is hard to know to what extent the changes that are taking place are the direct result of the single market.

One study conducted in 1998 did, nevertheless, estimate the benefits in terms of increased consumption (see Table 23.5). This found that the benefits to the smaller, lower-income countries, such as Portugal and Greece, were the greatest. Such estimates, however, do depend crucially on the assumptions made and are thus open to substantial error.

Even though the precise magnitude of the benefits is difficult to estimate, it is possible to identify the *types* of benefit that have resulted, many of which have been substantial.

Trade creation. Costs and prices have fallen as result of a greater exploitation of comparative advantage. Member

KI 35 p637

Definition

Mutual recognition The EU principle that one country's rules and regulations must apply throughout the EU. If they conflict with those of another country, individuals and firms should be able to choose which to obey.

CASE STUDIES AND APPLICATIONS — BOX 23.9

FEATURES OF THE SINGLE MARKET

Since 1 January 1993 trade within the EU has operated very much like trade within a country. In theory, there should be no more difficulty for a firm in Birmingham to sell its goods in Paris than in London. At the same time, the single market allows free movement of labour and involves the use of common technical standards.

The features of the single market are summed up in two European Commission publications:[3]

- Elimination of border controls on goods within the EU: no more long waits.
- Free movement of people across borders.
- Common security arrangements.
- No import taxes on goods bought in other member states for personal use.
- The right for everyone to live in another member state.
- Recognition of vocational qualifications in other member states: engineers, accountants, medical practitioners, teachers and other professionals able to practise throughout Europe.
- Technical standards brought into line, and product tests and certification agreed across the whole EU.
- Common commercial laws – making it attractive to form Europe-wide companies and to start joint ventures.
- Public contracts to supply equipment and services to state organisations now open to tenders across the EU.

So what does the single market mean for individuals and for businesses?

Individuals

Before 1993, if you were travelling in Europe, you had a 'duty-free allowance'. This meant that you could only take goods up to the value of €600 across borders within the EU without having to pay VAT in the country into which you were importing them. Now you can take as many goods as you like from one EU country to another, provided they are for your own consumption. But to prevent fraud, member states may ask for evidence that the goods have been purchased for the traveller's own consumption if they exceed specified amounts.

Individuals have the right to live and work in any other member state. Qualifications obtained in one member state must be recognised by other member states.

Firms

Before 1993 all goods traded in the EU were subject to VAT at every internal border. This involved some 60 million customs clearance documents at a cost of some €70 per consignment.[4]

This has all now disappeared. Goods can cross from one member state to another without any border controls: in fact, the concepts of 'importing' and 'exporting' within the EU no longer officially exist. All goods sent from one EU country to another will be charged VAT only in the country of destination. They are exempt from VAT in the country where they are produced.

One of the important requirements for fair competition in the single market is the convergence of tax rates. Although income tax rates, corporate tax rates and excise duties still differ between member states, there has been some narrowing in the range of VAT rates. There is now a lower limit of 15 per cent on the standard rate of VAT. What is more, the member states have agreed to abolish higher rates of VAT on luxury goods, and to have no more than two lower rates of at least 5 per cent on 'socially necessary' goods, such as food and water supply. The table shows VAT rates in 1988 and 2005.

In what ways would competition be 'unfair' if VAT rates differed widely between member states?

VAT rates (%) in the EU: 1988 and 2005

	1988		2005
	Standard rate	High rates	Standard rate
Austria			20
Belgium	19	25.3	21
Czech Republic			19
Cyprus			15
Denmark	22	–	25
Estonia			18
Finland			22
France	18.6	33.3	19.6
Germany	14	–	16
Greece	18	36	18
Hungary			25
Ireland	25	–	21
Italy	18	38	20
Latvia			18
Lithuania			18
Luxembourg	12	–	15
Malta			18
Netherlands	20	–	19
Poland			22
Portugal	16	30	19
Slovakia			19
Slovenia			20
Spain	12	33	16
Sweden			25
UK	15	–	17.5

[3] *A Single Market for Goods* (Commission of the European Communities, 1993); *10 Key Points about the Single European Market* (Commission of the European Communities, 1992).

[4] See *A Single Market for Goods* (Commission of the European Communities, 1993).

CASE STUDIES AND APPLICATIONS — BOX 23.10

THE INTERNAL MARKET SCOREBOARD

Keeping a tally on progress to a true single market

This success or otherwise of implementing EU internal market directives is measured by the Internal Market Scoreboard, which tracks the transposition (or 'implementation') deficit for each country. This is the percentage of directives that have failed to be implemented by their agreed deadline.

The Scoreboard has been published every six months since 1997 and, in addition to tracking the deficit for each country, also shows the average deficit across all 25 EU countries. The chart shows that the average deficit was falling until May 2002, but since then has risen somewhat. Part of the problem is that new directives are being issued as existing ones are being implemented.

According to the January 2005 Scoreboard:

> Member States persistently fail to transpose Internal Market rules correctly and on time. The transposition deficit for the EU has got significantly worse and now stands at 3.6%. This is a long way from the 1.5% interim target set by successive European Councils. And the real target is, of course, 0% because timely and correct transposition is a legal obligation.
>
> The deficit for the EU15 Member States is 2.9%, which represents a very significant step backwards after their progress in reducing the deficit since the Lisbon summit in 2000. When all 25 Member States are included in the calculation, the deficit rises to 3.6% – too high, but still considerably better than the 7.1% deficit at enlargement thanks to the sustained notification efforts of the new Member States. Concretely, this means that the Commission is still awaiting 1428 notifications of national implementing measures.
>
> Member States' failure is not only a breach of their legal obligations – it also deprives businesses and citizens in practice of their rights and undermines the day-to-day working of the Internal Market.
>
> . . . What is striking is that the performance of almost all EU15 Member States has deteriorated significantly since enlargement. Only Germany, France and the Netherlands have reduced their deficits since then.
>
> What is equally striking is that the 10 new Member States have significantly reduced their deficits since their EU accession. Many now have better records than EU15 Member States.

Transposition deficits vary considerably from one country to another. Thus in January 2005, Lithuania had a deficit of 1.0 per cent, followed by Spain with 1.3 per cent. At the other extreme, the Czech Republic had a deficit of 9.6 per cent. Of the EU-15 countries, Greece's deficit of 5.1 per cent was the highest.

?

1. ***What value are scoreboards for Member States and the European Commission?***
2. ***Why do you think that it is so important that legislation, such as that governing the Internal Market, is in place in all Member States at the same time?***

Internal Market Scoreboard: average transposition deficits

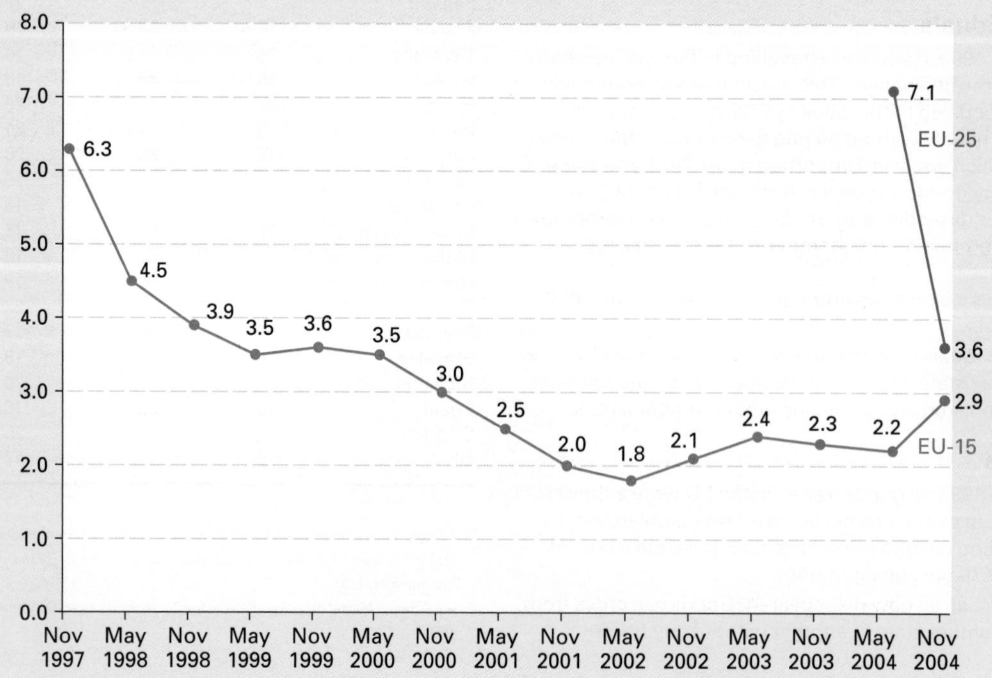

the deficit for the original 15 EU members had risen to 2.9 per cent.

If there have been clear benefits from the single market programme, why do individual member governments still try to erect barriers, such as new technical standards?

The effect of the new member states

Given the very different nature of the economies of many of the new entrants to the EU, and their lower levels of GDP per head, their potential gain from membership has been substantial. The gains come through trade creation, increased competition, technological transfer and inward investment, both from other EU countries and from outside the EU.

A study in 2004 concluded that Poland's GDP would rise by 3.4 per cent and Hungary's by almost 7 per cent.[5] Real wages would rise, with those of unskilled workers rising faster than those of skilled workers, in accordance with these countries' comparative advantage. There would also be benefits for the EU-15 countries from increased trade and investment, but these would be relatively minor in comparison to the gains to the new members.

In future years, now that the euro is used by at least 12 of the member states, trade within the EU is likely to continue to grow as a proportion of GDP. We examine the benefits and costs of the single currency and the whole process of economic and monetary union in the EU in section 25.3.

To examine the arguments about full monetary union, we need first to look at the question of exchange rate determination and alternative exchange rate systems. This is the subject of the next chapter.

[5] M. Maliszewska, *Benefits of the Single Market Expansion for Current and New Member States* (Centrum Analiz Społeczno-Ekonomicznych).

Section summary

1. The European Union is a customs union in that it has common external tariffs and no internal ones. But virtually from the outset it has also had elements of a common market, particularly in the areas of agricultural policy, regional policy, monopoly and restrictive practice policy, and to some extent in the areas of tax harmonisation and social policy.
2. Nevertheless, there have been substantial non-tariff barriers to trade within the EU, such as different tax rates, various regulations over product quality, licensing, state procurement policies, educational qualification requirements, financial barriers, various regulations and norms, and subsidies or tax relief to domestic producers.
3. The Single European Act of 1987 sought to sweep away these restrictions and to establish a genuine free market within the EU: to establish a full common market. Benefits from completing the internal market have included trade creation, cost savings from no longer having to administer barriers, economies of scale for firms now able to operate on a Europe-wide scale, and greater competition leading to reduced costs and prices, greater flows of technical information and more innovation.
4. Critics of the single market point to various changes in industrial structure that have resulted, bringing problems of redundancies and closures. They also point to adverse regional multiplier effects as resources are attracted to the geographical centre of the EU, to possible problems of market power with the development of giant 'Euro-firms', and to the possibilities of trade diversion.
5. The actual costs and benefits of EU membership to the various countries vary with their particular economic circumstances – for example, the extent to which they gain from trade creation, or lose from adverse regional multiplier effects – and with their contributions to and receipts from the EU budget.
6. These cost and benefits in the future will depend on just how completely the barriers to trade are removed, on the extent of monetary union and on any further enlargements to the Union.

END OF CHAPTER QUESTIONS

1. Imagine that two countries, Richland and Poorland, can produce just two goods, computers and coal. Assume that for a given amount of land and capital, the output of these two products requires the following constant amounts of labour:

	Richland	Poorland
1 computer	2	4
100 tonnes of coal	4	5

Assume that each country has 20 million workers.

(a) Draw the production possibility curves for the two countries (on two separate diagrams).

(b) If there is no trade, and in each country 12 million workers produce computers and 8 million workers produce coal, how many computers and tonnes of coal will each country produce? What will be the total production of each product?

(c) What is the opportunity cost of a computer in (i) Richland; (ii) Poorland?

(d) What is the opportunity cost of 100 tonnes of coal in (i) Richland: (ii) Poorland?

(e) Which country has a comparative advantage in which product?

(f) Assuming that price equals marginal cost, which of the following would represent possible exchange ratios?
(i) 1 computer for 40 tonnes of coal;
(ii) 2 computers for 140 tonnes of coal;
(iii) 1 computer for 100 tonnes of coal;
(iv) 1 computer for 60 tonnes of coal;
(v) 4 computers for 360 tonnes of coal.

(g) Assume that trade now takes place and that 1 computer exchanges for 65 tonnes of coal. Both countries specialise completely in the product in which they have a comparative advantage. How much does each country produce of its respective product?

(h) The country producing computers sells 6 million domestically. How many does it export to the other country?

(i) How much coal does the other country consume?

(j) Construct a table like Table 23.4 to show the no-trade and with-trade positions of each country.

(k) How much coal does the other country consume?

2. If capital moves from developed to less developed countries, and labour moves from less developed to developed countries, what effects will these factor movements have on wage rates and the return on capital in the two types of country?
3. What factors determine a country's terms of trade?
4. Go through each of the arguments for restricting trade (both those of general validity and those having some validity for specific countries) and provide a counter-argument for not restricting trade.
5. If countries are so keen to reduce the barriers to trade, why do many countries frequently attempt to erect barriers?
6. What factors will determine whether a country's joining a customs union will lead to trade creation or trade diversion?
7. Why is it difficult to estimate the magnitude of the benefits of completing the internal market of the EU?
8. Look through the costs and benefits that we identified from the completion of the internal market. Do the same costs and benefits arise from the enlarged EU of 25 members?

Additional case studies on the book's website (www.pearsoned.co.uk/sloman)

23.1 David Ricardo and the law of comparative advantage. The original statement of the law of comparative advantage by David Ricardo back in 1817.

23.2 The Uruguay round. An examination of the negotiations that led to substantial cuts in trade barriers.

23.3 The World Trade Organisation. This looks at the various opportunities and threats posed by this major international organisation.

23.4 The Battle of Seattle. This looks at the protests against the WTO at Seattle in November 1999 and considers the arguments for and against the free trade policies of the WTO.

23.5 Banana, banana. The dispute between the USA and the EU over banana imports.

23.6 Beyond bananas. Other US/EU trade disputes.

23.7 Steel barriers. This examines the use of tariffs by the George W. Bush administration in 2002 to protect the ailing US steel industry.

23.8 Assessing NAFTA. Who are the winners and losers from NAFTA?

23.9 Strategic trade theory. The case of Airbus.

23.10 The social dimension of the EU. The principles of the social charter.

23.11 The benefits of the single market. Evidence of achievements and the Single Market Action Plan of 1997.

WEBSITES RELEVANT TO THIS CHAPTER

Numbers and sections refer to websites listed in the Web Appendix and hotlinked from this book's website at www.pearsoned.co.uk/sloman.

- For news articles relevant to this chapter, see the *Economics News Articles* link from the book's website.
- For general news on international trade, see websites in section A, and particularly A1–5, 7–9, 24, 25, 31. See also links to newspapers worldwide in A38, 39 43 and 44, and the news search feature in Google at A41. See also links to economics news in A42.
- For international data on imports and exports, see site H16 >*Resources*> *Trade statistics.* See also *World Economic Outlook* in H4 and trade data in B23. See also the trade topic in I14. The ESDS International site (B35) has links to World Bank, IMF, OECD, UN and Eurostat datasets (but you will need an Athens password, available free to all UK higher education students).
- For details of individual countries' structure of imports and exports, see B32.
- For UK data, see B1, *1. National Statistics*> the fourth link > *Compendia and Reference*> *Annual Abstract*> *External trade and investment.* See also B3 and 34. For EU data, see G1 > *The Statistical Annex*> *Foreign trade and current balance.*
- For discussion papers on trade, see H4 and 7.
- For trade disputes, see H16.
- For various pressure groups critical of the effects of free trade and globalisation, see H12–14.
- For information on various preferential trading arrangements, see H20–22.
- For EU sites, see G1, 3, 7–14, 16–18.
- Sites I7 and 11 contain links to various topics in *International economics* (*International trade, International agreements, Economic co-operation* and *EU Economics*). Sites I4 and 17 have links to *International economics.*
- For student resources relevant to this chapter, see sites C1–7, 9, 10, 19.

Chapter 24

The Balance of Payments and Exchange Rates

We live in a world in which events in one country or group of countries can have profound effects on other countries. Look at what happened in 1997. A crisis in a few south-east Asian countries, such as Thailand and Indonesia, rapidly spread to other Asian countries such as Japan. As their economies contracted, so the contagion spread to other countries, such as Russia and Brazil.

As globalisation has increased, with trade and international financial movements growing much more rapidly than countries' GDP, and becoming much freer at the same time, so countries' vulnerability to balance of payments problems and exchange rate fluctuations has increased.

This chapter explores the relationships between a country's balance of payments and its exchange rate. In particular, we ask whether a country should allow its exchange rate to be determined entirely by market forces, with the possible instability that this brings; or should it attempt to fix its exchange rate to another currency (such as the US dollar), or at the very least attempt to reduce exchange rate fluctuations through central bank intervention in the foreign exchange market. We also look at the experience of countries in operating different types of exchange rate system.

CHAPTER MAP

24.1 ALTERNATIVE EXCHANGE RATE REGIMES

Policy objectives: internal and external

A country is likely to have various ***internal*** and ***external policy objectives***. *Internal* objectives include such things as economic growth, low unemployment and low inflation. *External* objectives include such things as avoiding current account balance of payments deficits, encouraging international trade and preventing excessive exchange rate fluctuations. Internal and external objectives may come into conflict, however.

KI 32 p 369

A simple illustration of potential conflict is with the objectives of *internal balance* and *external balance*.

Internal balance. ***Internal balance*** is where the economy is at the sustainable level of national income: i.e. where the output gap is zero (see Box 13.4 on page 382). This can be expressed in various ways, depending on the model of the economy and the policy objectives being pursued.

Thus, in the simple Keynesian model, internal balance is where the economy is at the *full-employment* level of national income: i.e. where Y_e (equilibrium national income) = Y_f (full-employment national income) (see Chapter 16). In the monetarist/new classical models, it would be where the economy is on the vertical Phillips curve with stable inflation. In the context of inflation targeting, it would be where meeting the inflation target is consistent with achieving sustainable national income: i.e. where the *ADI* crosses the *ASI* curve at the targeted inflation rate (see Figure 18.17 on page 526).

If there is initially internal balance and then aggregate demand falls, in the short run output will fall below the sustainable level and disequilibrium unemployment will occur. Internal balance will be destroyed. The stickier wages and prices are, the longer it will take for internal balance to be restored.

External balance. ***External balance*** is the term for a *balance of payments* equilibrium. In the context of floating exchange rates, it is normally used in the narrow sense of a current account balance, and therefore also a capital plus financial account balance.

In the context of a fixed exchange rate, or an exchange rate target, it is often used more loosely to refer merely to a *total currency flow balance*. This is where the total demand and supply of the currency are equal at the targeted exchange rate with *no need for intervention from the reserves*: in other words, where any current account deficit is matched by a surplus on the other two accounts, and vice versa.

Conflicts between internal and external balance

It may, however, be difficult to achieve internal and external balance simultaneously. This is illustrated in Figure 24.1.

> **Definitions**
>
> **Internal policy objectives** Objectives relating solely to the domestic economy.
>
> **External policy objectives** Objectives relating to the economy's international economic relationships.
>
> **Internal balance** Where the equilibrium level of national income is at the desired level.
>
> **External balance** Narrow definition: where the current account of the balance of payments is in balance (and thus also the capital plus financial accounts). Loose definition: where there is a total currency flow balance at a given exchange rate.

Figure 24.1 Internal and external balance

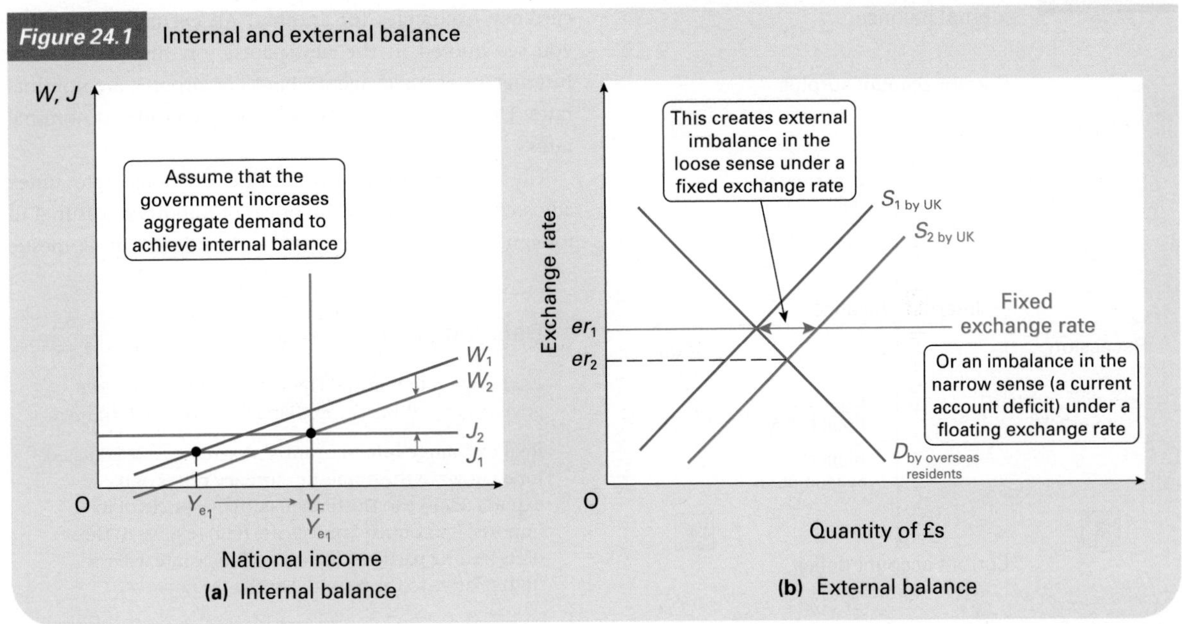

Assume in diagram (b) that the exchange rate is er_1. Currency demand and supply curves are given by D and S_1 and there is no central bank intervention. Thus er_1 is the *equilibrium* exchange rate and there is external balance in the loose sense. Assume also that there is external balance in the narrow sense: i.e. a current account balance.

Let us also assume, however, that there is a recession. This is illustrated in diagram (a). Equilibrium national income is Y_{e_1}, where W_1 equals J_1. There is a deflationary gap: Y_{e_1} is below the full-employment level, Y_F. There is no *internal* balance.

Now assume that the government expands aggregate demand through fiscal policy in order to close the deflationary gap and restore internal balance. It raises injections to J_2 and reduces withdrawals to W_2. National income rises to Y_{e_2}. But this higher national income leads to an increased demand for imports. The supply of sterling will shift to S_2 in diagram (b). There is now a current account deficit, which destroys external balance in the narrow sense. If the government maintains the exchange rate at er_1 (by buying sterling from the reserves), external balance will be destroyed in the loose sense too.

TC 4 p22 External balance in the loose sense could be restored by allowing the exchange rate to depreciate to er_2, so that the demand and supply of sterling are equated at the new lower exchange rate.

But will this also correct the current account deficit and restore external balance in the narrow sense? It will go *some* way to correcting the deficit, as the lower exchange rate will make imports relatively more expensive and exports TC 8 p59 relatively cheaper. The amount that imports fall and exports rise will depend on their price elasticity of demand.

But there may also be an effect on the financial account. The higher aggregate demand will lead to a higher demand for money. This will drive up interest rates unless money supply is allowed to expand to offset the higher demand for money. If interest rates rise, this will lead to an inflow of finance (a financial account surplus). In Figure 24.1(b), the supply curve of sterling would shift to the left and the demand curve to the right. The exchange rate would not fall as far, therefore, as er_2. If the positive effect of higher interest rates on the financial account was bigger than the negative effect of higher imports on the current account, the exchange rate would actually *appreciate*.

Either way, there will be a current account deficit and an equal and opposite financial plus capital account surplus. Narrow external balance has not been restored in the short term. (We explore the long-term current account balance under floating exchange rates in section 24.3.)

Figure 24.2 shows the effect of various 'shocks' that can affect both internal and narrow external balance.

?

1. *Assume that there is both internal and narrow external balance. Now assume that as a result of inflation being below target, the central bank cuts interest rates. Into which of the four quadrants in Figure 24.2 will the economy move?*
2. *Imagine that there is an inflationary gap, but a current account equilibrium. Describe what will happen if the government raises interest rates in order to close the inflationary gap. Assume first that there is a fixed exchange rate; then assume that there is a floating exchange rate.*

The ability of the economy to correct these imbalances depends on the ***exchange rate regime***. We examine alternative exchange rate regimes in the final part of this section, but first we must distinguish between nominal and real exchange rates.

Figure 24.2 Effects on internal and (narrow) external balance

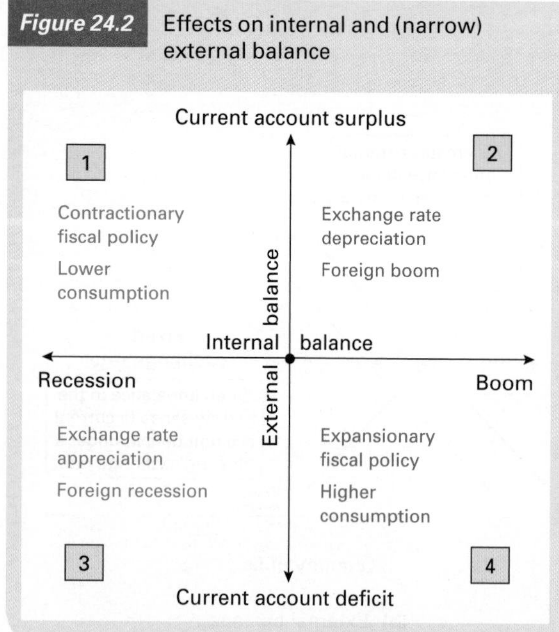

Nominal and real exchange rates

A nominal exchange rate is simply the rate at which one currency exchanges for another. All exchange rates that you see quoted in the newspapers, on the television or Internet, or at travel agents, banks or airports, are nominal rates. Up to this point we have solely considered nominal rates.

The ***real exchange rate*** is the exchange rate index adjusted for changes in the prices of imports (measured in foreign currencies) and exports (measured in domestic TC 12 p374

Definitions

Exchange rate regime The system under which the government allows the exchange rate to be determined.

Real exchange rate A country's exchange rate adjusted for changes in the domestic currency prices of its exports relative to the foreign currency prices of its imports. If a country's prices rise (fall) relative to those of its trading partners, its real exchange rate will rise (fall) relative to the nominal exchange rate.

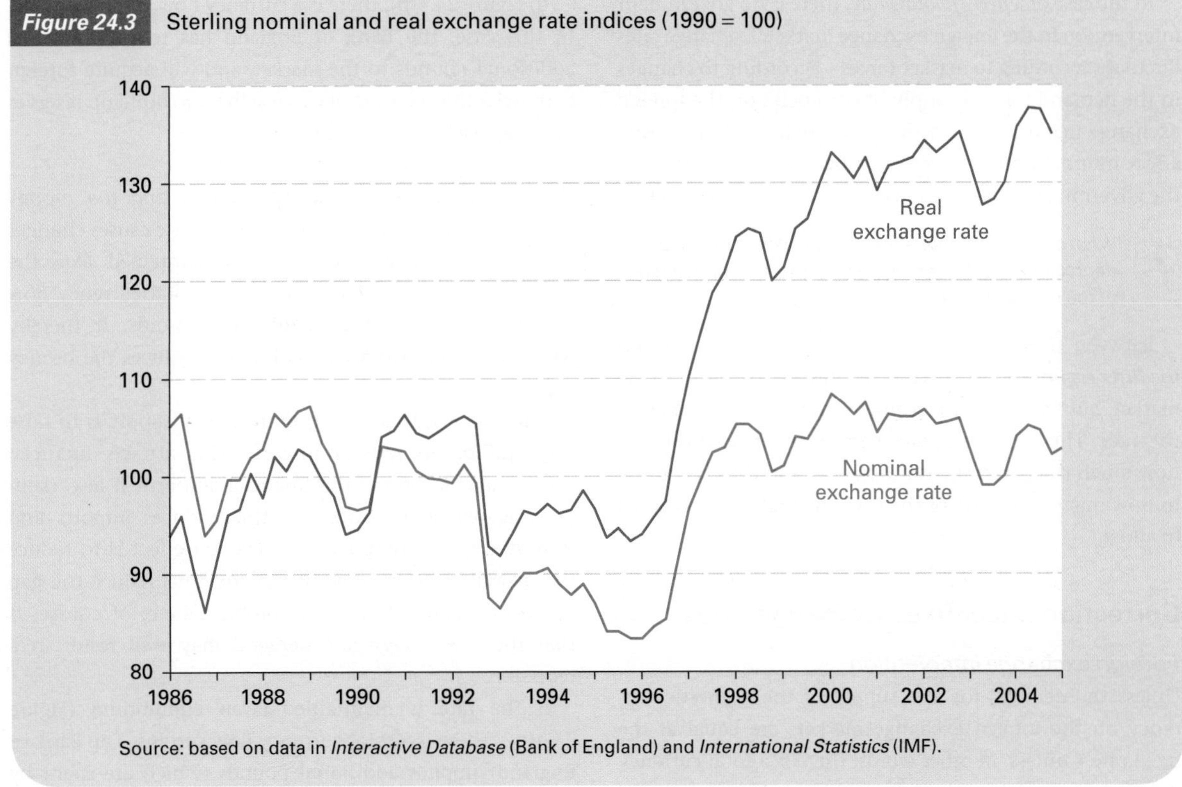

Figure 24.3 Sterling nominal and real exchange rate indices (1990 = 100)

Source: based on data in *Interactive Database* (Bank of England) and *International Statistics* (IMF).

prices): in other words, adjusted for the terms of trade. Thus if a country has a higher rate of inflation for its exports than the weighted average inflation of the imports it buys from other countries, its real exchange rate index (RERI) will rise relative to its nominal exchange rate index (NERI).

The real exchange rate index can be defined as:

$$\text{RERI} = \text{NERI} \times P_X/P_M$$

where P_X is the domestic currency price index of exports and P_M is the foreign currencies weighted price index of imports. Thus if (a) a country's inflation is 5 per cent higher than the trade weighted average of its trading partners (P_X/P_M rises by 5 per cent per year) and (b) its nominal exchange rate depreciates by 5 per cent per year (NERI falls by 5 per cent per year), its real exchange rate index will stay the same.

Take another example: if a country's export prices rise faster than the foreign currency prices of its imports (P_X/P_M rises), its real exchange rate will appreciate relative to its nominal exchange rate.

The real exchange rate thus gives us a better idea of the *quantity* of imports a country can obtain from selling a given quantity of exports. If the real exchange rate rises, the country can get more imports for a given volume of exports.

Figure 24.3 shows the nominal and real exchange rate indices of sterling. As you can see, the real exchange rate has risen over time relative to the nominal exchange rate. This is because the UK has had a higher rate of inflation than the weighted average of its trading partners.

The real exchange rate also gives a better idea than the nominal exchange rate of how competitive a country is. The lower the real exchange rate, the more competitive will the country's exports be. Figure 24.3 shows that the UK has become less competitive since 1996, thanks not only to a rise in the nominal exchange rate index, but also to higher inflation than its trading partners.

Alternative exchange rate regimes

There are a number of possible exchange rate regimes. They all lie somewhere between two extremes. These two extreme regimes are a ***totally fixed rate*** and a ***freely floating rate***.

In the case of a *fixed rate*, the government will almost certainly have to intervene in the foreign exchange market in order to maintain that rate, and will probably have to take internal policy measures too. KI 5 p21

Definitions

Totally fixed exchange rate Where the government takes whatever measures are necessary to maintain the exchange rate at some stated level.

Freely floating exchange rate Where the exchange rate is determined entirely by the forces of demand and supply in the foreign exchange market with no government intervention whatsoever.

In the case of a *freely floating rate*, there is no government intervention in the foreign exchange market. Exchange rates fluctuate according to market forces – according to changes in the demand for and supply of currencies on the foreign exchange market. Changes in the exchange rate may well affect internal policy objectives, however, and thus cause the government to take various internal policy measures.

TC 4 p22

?

What adverse internal effects may follow from (a) a depreciation of the exchange rate; (b) an appreciation of the exchange rate?

Between these extremes there are a number of ***intermediate regimes***, where exchange rates are partly left to the market, but where the government intervenes to influence the rate. These intermediate regimes differ according to how much the government intervenes, and thus according to how much flexibility of the exchange rate it is prepared to allow.

Correction under fixed exchange rates

Foreign exchange intervention

Unless the demand for and supply of the domestic currency on the foreign exchange markets are equal at the fixed rate – unless, in other words, there is a total currency flow balance – the central bank will have to intervene in the market and buy or sell the domestic currency to make up the difference. This is illustrated in Figure 24.4, which looks at the case of the UK.

Figure 24.4(a) shows the case of a currency flow deficit (an excess of pounds) of an amount $a - b$. The Bank of England thus has to purchase these excess pounds by drawing on its foreign exchange reserves, or by borrowing foreign currency from foreign banks.

Definition

Intermediate exchange rate regimes Where the government intervenes to influence movements in the exchange rate.

In Figure 24.4(b), there is a currency flow surplus of $c - d$. In this case, the Bank of England has to supply $c - d$ additional pounds to the market, and will acquire foreign currencies in exchange. It can use these to build up reserves or to pay back foreign loans.

Foreign exchange market intervention and the money supply. Maintaining a fixed exchange rate causes changes in the money supply. If the rate is maintained *above* the equilibrium (Figure 24.4(a)), there is a total currency flow deficit. The Bank of England buys pounds. It thereby withdraws them from circulation and reduces the money supply.

The effect of this reduction in money supply is to raise the equilibrium rate of interest. This attracts financial inflows and improves the financial account. It also dampens aggregate demand, and thus reduces imports and improves the current account. The net effect is to reduce the overall currency flow deficit and thus reduce the gap $a - b$ in Figure 24.4(a). The problem here, of course, is that the lower aggregate demand may well result in a recession.

If the rate is maintained *below* equilibrium (Figure 24.4(b)), there is a total currency flow surplus. The Bank of England supplies additional pounds (which are spent by people abroad on UK exports, etc. and are thus injected into the UK economy). It thereby increases the money supply.

The effect of the increased money supply is to reduce interest rates. This worsens the financial account and, by boosting aggregate demand, increases imports. The currency flow surplus is reduced. The gap $d - c$ narrows.

Sterlisation. If the Bank of England did not want the money supply to alter, it would have to counter these effects with other monetary measures: e.g. open-market operations. Thus when there is a deficit and money supply falls, the Bank of England could buy back government bonds from the general public, thereby restoring the money supply to its previous level. This will prevent the economy moving into recession.

Figure 24.4 Central bank intervention to maintain a fixed exchange rate

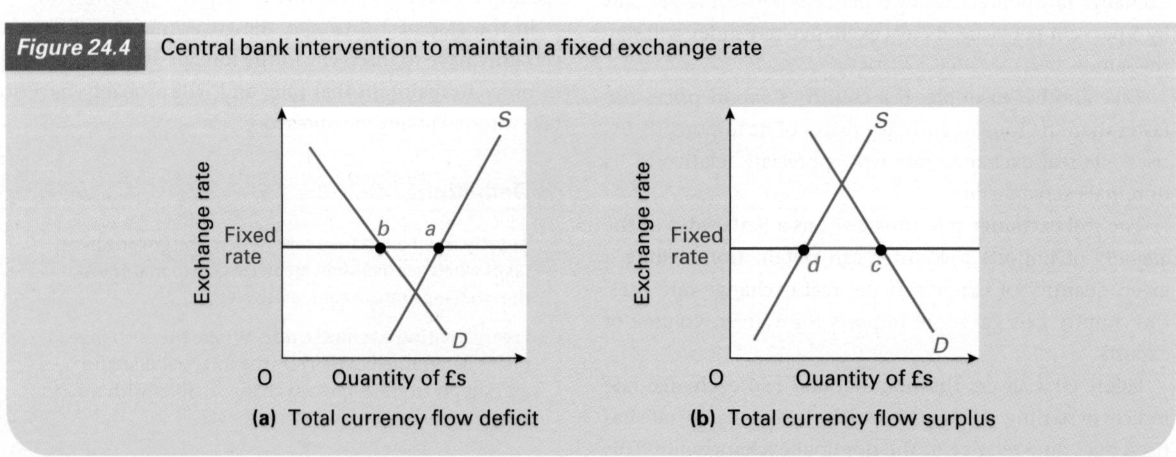

CASE STUDIES AND APPLICATIONS BOX 24.1

THE UK'S BALANCE OF PAYMENTS DEFICIT

A cyclical problem or a long-term trend?

In the late 1980s, the UK current account balance of payments moved sharply into deficit, as the diagram shows. In 1989 the current account deficit was 5 per cent of GDP – the highest percentage ever recorded. Opinions differed dramatically, however, as to how seriously we should have taken these figures. Not surprisingly, the government claimed that the problem was merely temporary and was not something to cause serious concern. The opposition parties (also not surprisingly) saw the figures as disastrous and a sign that the economy was badly off course.

So who was correct? In fact there was an element of truth in both these claims.

The government was correct to the extent that the severity of the deficit partly reflected the unprecedented boom of the late 1980s. An average growth rate of real GDP of 3.6 per cent between 1984 and 1988 had led to a huge increase in imports. Since the boom could not be sustained, the growth in imports was bound to slow down. Another factor contributing to the deficit was the fall in oil revenues caused by a fall in oil prices. Oil exports fell from £16.1 billion in 1985 to £5.9 billion in 1989. Again, this fall in oil revenues was unlikely to continue once oil prices began to rise again. The current account deficit was also a mirror image of the financial account surplus. This had been caused by a rise in interest rates, used to slow the economy down. As short-term finance flowed into the country to take advantage of the higher interest rate, so this drove the exchange rate up (see Table 14.7 on page 420). The higher exchange rate contributed to the fall in exports and the rise in imports.

But the opposition parties were also correct. The severity of the deficit reflected an underlying weakness of the UK's trading position. If the deficit had been merely a cyclical problem associated with the boom phase of the business cycle, the current account should have gone into *surplus* in the early 1990s as the economy moved into recession. But even in the depths of the recession in 1991, the current account deficit was still nearly 2 per cent of GDP.

The government, however, sought to place a large portion of the blame on a falling demand for exports as the rest of the world began to move into recession.

Subsequent events appeared to support the Conservative government's interpretation. The world economy was recovering in 1994 and the current account deficit virtually disappeared. But then, with a large appreciation of sterling from 1997, and an even larger appreciation of the real exchange rate (see Figure 24.3), the current account started to deteriorate again, as the diagram shows. By 2005, the trade in goods deficit had reached record levels. Optimists claimed that this was, once more, simply a temporary situation, caused by a high exchange rate and low growth in demand in the eurozone. Pessimists again saw it as a sign of a much deeper malaise in the UK exporting sector – that the supply-side reforms of the 1980s , 1990s and early 2000s had made too little difference.

So should we worry about balance of payments deficits? What effect do they have on exchange rates, inflation, growth, unemployment, etc.? What should the government do? These are questions we shall look at in this chapter.

UK balance of payments as a percentage of GDP, 1970–2007

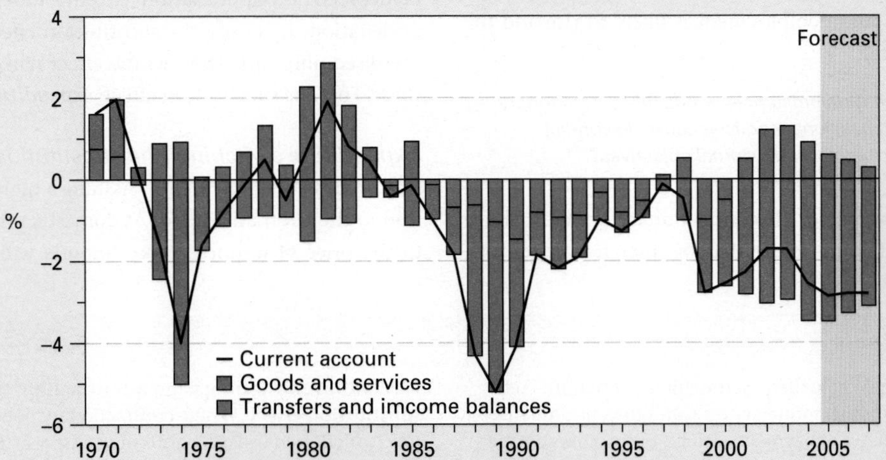

Source: *Financial Statement and Budget Report* (HM Treasury, 2005).

This process of countering the effects on money supply of a balance of payments deficit or surplus is known as ***sterilisation***.

?

Describe the open-market operations necessary to sterilise the monetary effects of a balance of payments surplus. Would this in turn have any effect on the current or financial accounts of the balance of payments?

There is a problem with sterilisation, however. If the money supply is not allowed to change, the currency flow deficit or surplus will persist. In the case of a deficit, a recession may be avoided, but the central bank will have to continue using reserves to support the exchange rate. But reserves are not infinite. Sooner or later they will run out! A recession may be inevitable.

Correcting the disequilibrium

If a balance of payments deficit persists, and reserves continue to dwindle or foreign debts mount, the government will have to tackle the underlying disequilibrium. If the exchange rate is to remain fixed, it must shift the demand and supply curves so that they intersect at the fixed exchange rate.

It can use contractionary fiscal and monetary policies for this purpose. Such policies have two main effects on the current account: an income effect (***expenditure reducing***) and a substitution effect between home and foreign goods (***expenditure switching***).

KI 7 p35

Expenditure reducing. Contractionary policy reduces national income. This in turn reduces expenditure, including expenditure on imports, shifting the supply of sterling curve to the left in Figure 24.4(a). The bigger the marginal propensity to import, the larger the shift.

There is a possible conflict here, however, between external and internal objectives. The balance of payments may improve, but unemployment is likely to rise and the rate of growth fall.

?

Under what circumstances would (a) contractionary and (b) expansionary policies cause no conflict between internal and external objectives?

Expenditure switching. If contractionary policies reduce the rate of inflation below that of foreign competitors, exports will become relatively cheaper compared with foreign competing goods and imports relatively more expensive compared with home-produced alternatives. Foreign consumers will switch to UK exports. The more elastic their demand, the bigger the switch. UK consumers will switch to home-produced goods. Again, the more elastic their demand, the bigger the switch. Demand in both cases will be more elastic the closer UK goods are as substitutes for foreign goods.

TC 8 p59

To the extent that contractionary policies result in expenditure switching rather than expenditure reducing, so this reduces the conflict between balance of payments and employment objectives.

Expenditure switching can also be achieved by placing restrictions on imports (tariffs and/or quotas) or the subsidising of exports. But this would conflict with the objective of free trade.

To the extent that fiscal and monetary policies affect interest rates, so this will affect the financial account of the balance of payments. Higher interest rates will increase the demand for sterling and will thus lead to an improvement on the financial account. (The implications of this are explored in section 24.2.)

Correction under free-floating exchange rates

Freely floating exchange rates should automatically and immediately correct any balance of payments deficit or surplus: by depreciation and appreciation respectively. Foreign exchange dealers simply adjust the exchange rate so as to balance their books – in line with demand and supply.

KI 5 p21

As with fixed rates, an income effect and a substitution effect of the correction process can be distinguished. But the nature of the income and substitution effects of depreciation/appreciation is quite different from that of deflation. It is only the substitution effect that corrects the disequilibrium. The income effect makes the problem *worse*! First the substitution effect: ***expenditure switching***.

Expenditure switching (the substitution effect)

KI 7 p35

The process of adjustment. Assume a higher rate of inflation in the UK than abroad. As domestic prices rise relative to the price of imports, more imports will be purchased.

Definitions

Sterilisation Where the government uses open-market operations or other monetary measures to neutralise the effects of balance of payments deficits or surpluses on the money supply.

Expenditure changing (reducing) from a contraction: the income effect Where contractionary policies lead to a reduction in national income and hence a reduction in the demand for imports.

Expenditure switching from a contraction: the substitution effect Where contractionary policies lead to a reduction in inflation and thus cause a switch in expenditure away from imports and towards exports.

Expenditure switching from depreciation: the substitution effect Where a lower exchange rate reduces the price of exports and increases the price of imports. This will increase the sale of exports and reduce the sale of imports.

Figure 24.5 Adjustment of the exchange rate to a shift in demand and supply

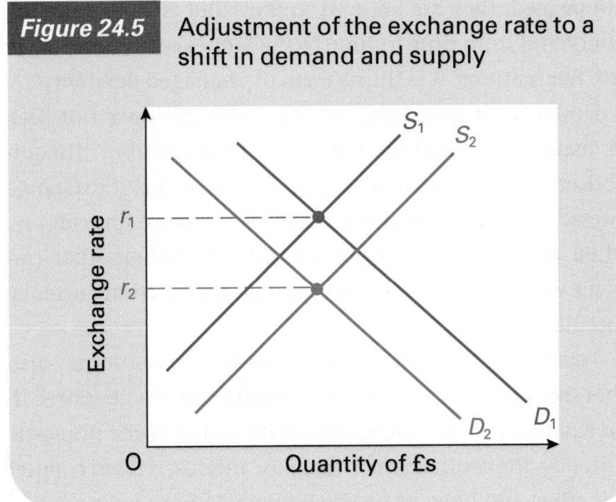

Figure 24.6 The income effect (stable prices)

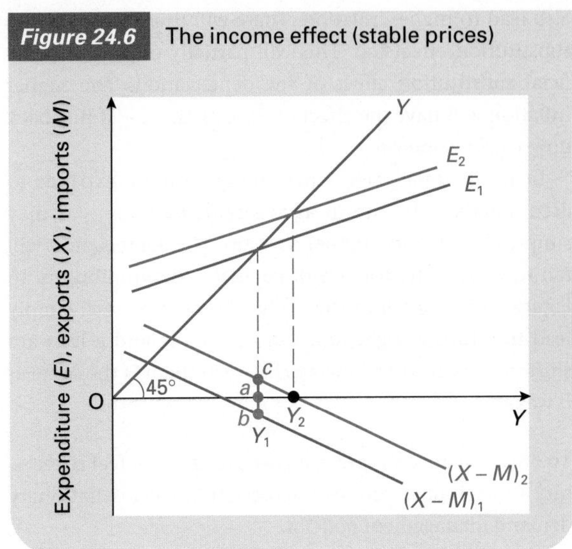

The supply of pounds curve will shift to the right (to S_2 in Figure 24.5). UK exports will now be relatively more expensive for foreigners. Less will be sold. The demand for pounds curve will shift to the left (to D_2).

Foreign exchange dealers will now find themselves with a glut of unsold pounds. They will therefore lower the exchange rate (to r_2 in Figure 24.5). The amount that the exchange rate has to change depends on:

- The amount that the curves shift. Thus large differences in international inflation rates or large differences in international interest rates will cause large shifts in the demand for and supply of currencies, and hence large movements in exchange rates.
- The elasticity of the curves. The less elastic the demand and supply curves of sterling, the greater the change in the exchange rate for any given shift in demand and supply.

But what determines the elasticity of the demand and supply curves. This is examined in Web Case 24.1.

KI 7 p35

Expenditure changing (the income effect)

Depreciation, as well as affecting relative prices, will affect national income. This will cause ***expenditure changing***.

We have already established that, as the exchange rate falls, so more exports will be sold and less imports purchased: this was the substitution effect. But this is only an initial effect.

Exports are an injection into, and imports a withdrawal from, the circular flow of income. There will thus be a multiplied rise in national income. This income effect (expenditure *increasing*) reduces the effectiveness of the depreciation. Two situations can be examined.

Definition

Expenditure changing (increasing) from depreciation: the income effect Where depreciation, via the substitution effect, will alter the demand for imports and exports, and this, via the multiplier, will affect the level of national income and hence the demand for imports.

A rise in national income and employment, but no change in prices. Assume that there are substantial unemployed resources, so that an increase in aggregate demand will raise output and employment but not prices. As national income rises, so imports rise (thereby tending to offset the initial fall), but exports are unaffected.

This is illustrated by the line $(X - M)_1$ in Figure 24.6. At low levels of national income, spending on imports is low; thus exports (X) exceed imports (M). $X - M$ is positive. As national income and hence imports rise, $X - M$ falls, and after a point becomes negative. Thus the $X - M$ line is downward sloping.

Assume an initial equilibrium national income at Y_1, where national income (Y) equals national expenditure (E_1), but with imports exceeding exports by an amount $a - b$. The exchange rate thus depreciates.

This will cause a substitution effect: exports rise and imports fall. The $X - M$ line therefore shifts upwards. But this in turn causes an income effect. Aggregate demand rises, and the E line shifts upwards.

An eventual internal and external equilibrium is reached at Y_2, where $Y = E_2$ and $(X - M)_2 = 0$.

The positive substitution effect of this depreciation is $c - b$. The negative income effect is $c - a$. The net effect is thus only $a - b$, which is the size of the initial deficit. Had it not been for this negative income effect, a smaller depreciation would have been needed.

At least in this case, the income effect is having a desirable *internal* consequence: reducing unemployment.

A rise in prices. If the economy is near full employment, the rise in aggregate demand from depreciation will make that depreciation even less effective. Not only will the higher demand lead directly to more imports, but it will also lead to higher inflation. There will thus be an adverse substitution effect too. This will partially offset the beneficial substitution effect of the depreciation. The higher inflation will have the effect of shifting the $X - M$ line back down again somewhat.

In the extreme case, where money supply expands to accommodate the rise in aggregate demand, $X - M$ may simply return to its original position. The depreciation will fail to correct the balance of payments disequilibrium. In Figure 24.5, the fall in the exchange rate to r_2 will simply lead to a further rightward shift in supply and a leftward shift in demand, until the gap between them is the same as it was at r_1.

To offset the income effect, a government may feel it necessary to back up a currency depreciation with deflationary demand management policies.

Intermediate exchange rate regimes

There are a number of possible intermediate systems between the two extremes of totally fixed and completely free-floating exchange rates.

Adjustable peg. The ***adjustable peg*** system is towards the fixed end of the spectrum. Exchange rates are fixed (or 'pegged') for a period of time – perhaps several years.

In the short and medium term, therefore, correction is the same as with a totally fixed system. Central banks have to intervene in the foreign exchange market to maintain the rate. If a deficit persists, then deflationary or other policies must be adopted to *shift* the currency demand and supply curves. This will be a problem, however, if there already exist substantial unemployed resources.

In the long term, if a fundamental disequilibrium occurs, the currency can be repegged at a lower or higher rate. Adjusting the peg downwards is known as ***devaluation***. Adjusting it upwards is known as ***revaluation***.

Alternatively, more frequent smaller adjustments could be made, thus moving the system away from the fixed end of the spectrum.

Managed floating. The ***managed floating*** system is towards the free-floating end of the spectrum. Exchange rates are not pegged: they are allowed to float. But the central bank intervenes from time to time to prevent excessive exchange rate fluctuations. It is thus a form of 'managed flexibility'.

Under such a system, the central bank does not seek to maintain a long-term or even medium-term disequilibrium rate. Rather it tries to allow an 'orderly' exchange rate adjustment to major changes in demand and supply, while preventing the violent short-term swings that can occur with a totally free float (swings arising from currency speculation).

To back up the central bank's use of reserves, it may also alter interest rates to prevent exchange rate fluctuations. If, for example, there were a large-scale selling of the domestic currency, the central bank could raise interest rates to counter this effect and prevent the exchange rate from falling.

? *How would raising interest rates in this way affect the balance between the current and financial accounts of the balance of payments?*

The degree of currency stability sought, and hence the degree of intervention required, will vary from country to country and from government to government. At one extreme, the government may intervene only if exchange rate fluctuations become very severe; at the other extreme, the government may try to maintain the exchange rate at some unofficial target level.

Crawling peg. The ***crawling peg*** system is midway between managed floating and the adjustable peg system. Instead of making large and infrequent devaluations (or revaluations), the government adjusts the peg by small amounts, but frequently – say, once a month, as the equilibrium exchange rate changes.

Joint float. Under a ***joint float*** a group of countries have a fixed or adjustable peg system between their *own* currencies, but *jointly float* against all other currencies.

Exchange rate band. With an ***exchange rate band*** the government sets a lower and an upper limit to the exchange rate: say, £1 = \$1.40 and £1 = \$1.60. It then allows the exchange rate to fluctuate freely within these limits. It will intervene, however, if the rate hits the floor or the ceiling.

Definitions

Adjustable peg A system whereby exchange rates are fixed for a period of time, but may be devalued (or revalued) if a deficit (or surplus) becomes substantial.

Devaluation Where the government repegs the exchange rate at a lower level.

Revaluation Where the government repegs the exchange rate at a higher level.

Managed floating A system of flexible exchange rates, but where the government intervenes to prevent excessive fluctuations or even to achieve an unofficial target exchange rate.

Crawling peg A system whereby the government allows a gradual adjustment of the exchange rate.

Joint float Where a group of currencies pegged to each other jointly float against other currencies.

Exchange rate band Where a currency is allowed to float between an upper and lower exchange rate, but is not allowed to move outside this band.

Figure 24.7 The crawling peg within exchange rate bands

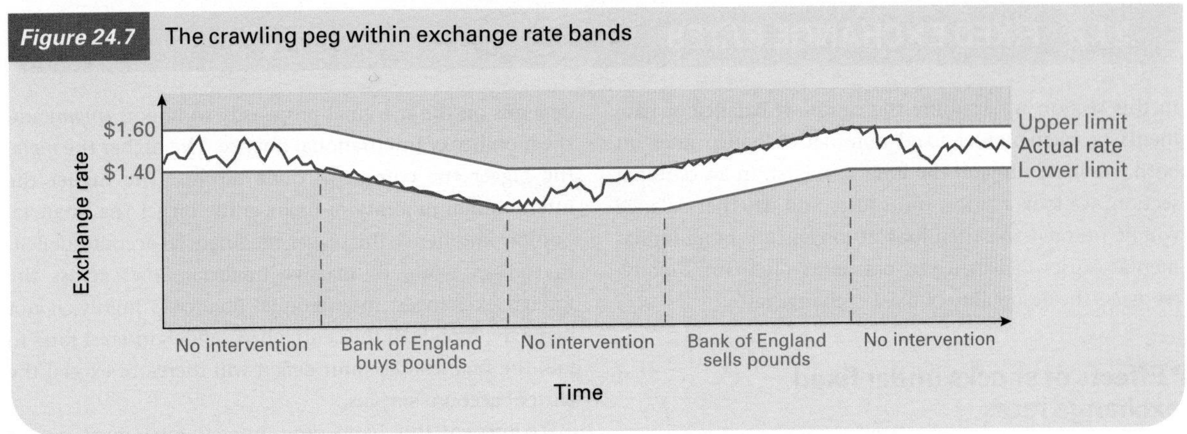

Exchange rate bands could be narrow (say ±1 per cent) or wide (say ±15 per cent).

Exchange rate bands can be incorporated in other systems – the band could be adjustable, crawling or fixed. For example, Figure 24.7 illustrates a crawling peg system with an exchange rate band.

The exchange rate mechanism (ERM) of the European Monetary System (EMS) was an example of a joint float against non-member currencies and an adjustably pegged exchange rate band with member currencies (see section 25.2). The ERM2 system for the ten new members of the EU is similar.

All these intermediate systems are attempts to achieve as many as possible of the advantages of both fixed and flexible exchange rates, with as few as possible of the attendant disadvantages. To assess any of these compromise systems, therefore, we must examine the advantages and disadvantages of fixed and flexible exchange rates. We do this in the next two sections.

Section summary

1. There may be a conflict in achieving both internal and external balance simultaneously. The nature of the conflict depends on the exchange rate regime that the country adopts.
2. Nominal exchange rates are simply the rates at which one currency exchanges for another. Real exchange rates take account of differences in inflation rates between import and export prices and are a measure of the competitiveness of a country's exports.
3. Under a fixed exchange rate system, the government will have to intervene whenever the equilibrium exchange rate ceases to coincide with the fixed rate. If the equilibrium rate falls below the fixed rate, the government will have to buy in the domestic currency on the foreign exchange market. This will have the effect of reducing the money supply. Likewise selling the domestic currency in order to prevent an appreciation will increase money supply. The government can prevent these changes in money supply by the use of appropriate open-market operations or other monetary measures. This is known as 'sterilisation'. Sterilisation, however, means that the disequilibrium is likely to go uncorrected.
4. If a deficit (or surplus) persists under a fixed rate, the government can attempt to shift the currency demand and supply curves. To cure a deficit, it can use contractionary fiscal or monetary policies. These have two effects. Deflation leads to a fall in national income (the income effect) and hence a fall in the demand for imports. It also leads to a fall in inflation and hence a switch in demand from foreign goods to home-produced goods (the substitution effect).
5. Correction under free-floating exchange rates also involves an income and a substitution effect. If there is a deficit, the exchange rate will depreciate. This will make imports more expensive and exports cheaper, and hence there will be a substitution effect as imports fall and exports rise.
6. The income effect of a depreciation, however, reduces its effectiveness. The rise in exports and fall in imports (i.e. the substitution effect of a depreciation) will lead to a multiplied rise in national income, which will cause imports to rise back again somewhat. The bigger this income effect, the bigger will be the depreciation necessary to achieve equilibrium in the foreign exchange market. Correction is made more difficult if any depreciation leads to increases in domestic prices and hence to a second substitution effect – only this time an adverse one.
7. There are intermediate exchange rate regimes between the extremes of fixed rates and free-floating rates. The exchange rate may be fixed for a period of time (the adjustable peg); or it may be allowed to change gradually (the crawling peg); or the government may merely intervene to dampen exchange rate fluctuations (managed floating); or the exchange rate may be allowed to fluctuate within a band, where the band in turn may be fixed, adjustable or crawling.

24.2 FIXED EXCHANGE RATES

In this section we examine the causes of balance of payments problems under fixed nominal exchange rates, in both the short run and the long run. First, in an optional section, we look at short-run causes and whether balance will be restored. We then look at longer-run, more fundamental causes of balance of payments problems. Finally, we assess the desirability of fixed exchange rates.

*Effects of shocks under fixed exchange rates

Under fixed exchange rates, it is unlikely that internal and external balance can persist for long without government intervention. Various macroeconomic 'shocks', such as changes in injections or withdrawals, or changes in international interest rates, are constantly occurring. These are likely to destroy either internal or external balance or both. Even with government intervention, it may still be very difficult, if not impossible, to restore both balances. Correction of balance of payments disequilibria will come into conflict with the other macroeconomic goals of growth, full employment and stable prices.

How the economy responds to shocks under fixed exchange rates, and which policy measures are most effective in dealing with the resultant disequilibria depends on two things: (a) whether the shocks are internal or external; (b) the flexibility of wages and prices, which, in turn, depends on the time period under consideration.

Response to an internal shock

Let us assume that there is a fall in aggregate demand, caused by a fall in consumer demand or investment, or by a rise in saving.

Short-run effect. In the short run, prices and especially wages tend to be relatively inflexible (this is a central assumption of Keynesian analysis). The fall in aggregate demand will lead to a recession. Internal balance will be destroyed. In a closed economy, the central bank would probably reduce interest rates to boost the economy, either to tackle the recession directly or because *forecast* inflation had fallen below its target level.

In an open economy under fixed exchange rates, however, this is not possible. But why?

The lower aggregate demand will lead to a fall in imports, resulting in a *current account* surplus. There is an opposite effect on the *financial account*, however. The reduced aggregate demand will lead to a fall in the demand for money and hence downward pressure on interest rates. If interest rates were allowed to fall, there would be a resulting financial outflow and hence a financial account deficit.

But which would be the larger effect: the current account surplus or the financial account deficit? This depends on the marginal propensity to import (*mpm*) and the mobility of international finance. The higher the *mpm*, the bigger the current account surplus. The higher the international mobility of finance, the bigger the financial outflow and hence the bigger the financial account deficit. In today's world of massive financial flows across the foreign exchanges, international finance is highly, if not perfectly, mobile. If the central bank allows interest rates to fall, the financial account deficit will therefore exceed the current account surplus.

To prevent this happening, interest rates must not be allowed to fall or, at least, must fall only very slightly – just enough for the resulting financial account deficit to match the current account surplus. With hardly any fall in interest rates, money supply must thus be allowed to contract to match the fall in the demand for money.

Thus to maintain the fixed exchange rate (without massively draining reserves) interest rates will be determined by the balance of payments. They cannot be used for domestic purposes, such as targeting inflation, targeting real national income or some combination (e.g. a Taylor rule: see page 567). Internal imbalance will persist in the short run.

Long-run effect. In the long run, there will be much greater, if not perfect, price and wage flexibility. Under new classical assumptions, such flexibility will exist in the short run too. This flexibility will ensure that internal balance is restored. The Phillips curve is vertical at the natural rate of unemployment.

But, with a fixed exchange rate, will it also ensure external balance? Again, let us assume that people decide to spend less and save more. As in the short run, this will lead to a *current account* surplus. This time, however, the effect is much bigger. In the short run, there was little or no price effect (i.e. no substitution effect) since there was little change in inflation. There was only an income effect from reduced imports caused by the recession. In the long run, however, the lower real aggregate demand reduces inflation. Assuming that inflation falls below that of trading partners, the *real* exchange rate falls. This makes exports relatively cheaper and imports relatively more expensive. This causes imports to fall and exports to rise.

The resulting rise in aggregate demand not only helps to eliminate the recession, but also helps to reduce the current account surplus.

Thus, despite a fixed *nominal* exchange rate, wage and price flexibility cause the *real* exchange rate to be flexible. This helps restore overall external balance. Nevertheless, a current account surplus may persist. Indeed, as the surplus is used to buy foreign assets, so, over time, these will yield an income, further crediting the current account.

TC 12 p374

But what is clear is that, although interest rates are determined by the need to maintain a fixed nominal exchange rate, wage and price flexibility in the long run will eventually restore internal balance. The question is, how long will the long run be? How long will the recession persist? If it is too long, and if interest rates cannot be cut, then can expansionary fiscal policy be used? We examine this in Box 24.2.

Response to an external shock

Assume now that there is a fall in demand for exports.

Short-run effect. The fall in exports causes the *current account* to go into deficit. It also reduces aggregate demand, causing a multiplied fall in national income. This reduces the demand for imports: the larger the *mpm*, the bigger the reduction in imports. Aggregate demand will go on falling until the lower injections are matched by lower withdrawals. But the current account deficit will not be eliminated, since the fall in withdrawals to match the fall in exports consists only partly of lower imports, but *partly* of lower saving and lower tax receipts.

TC 15 p463

The reduction in aggregate demand reduces the transactions demand for money, putting downward pressure on interest rates. This would result in a financial outflow and hence a *financial account* deficit, making the overall currency flow deficit worse. To prevent this happening, the central bank must prevent interest rates from falling by reducing the money supply (through open market operations). Indeed, given the current account deficit, interest rates may have to be slightly higher than they were originally in order to create a financial account surplus sufficient to offset the current account deficit. This will make the recession worse.

Long-run effect. The reduction in aggregate demand will put downward pressure on domestic inflation. This will help to reduce the *real* exchange rate and hence correct the current account deficit. It will also restore internal balance. Again, however, without fiscal policy, the long run may be some time in coming. The recession may persist.

? *Trace through the short-run and long-run internal and external effects (under a fixed exchange rate) of (a) a fall in domestic saving; (b) a rise in the demand for exports.*

Causes of longer-term balance of payments problems under fixed exchange rates

With moderately flexible prices, current account balance may eventually be restored after 'one-off' shocks. However, long-term continuing shifts in the demand and supply of imports and exports can make balance of payments problems persist. We will examine four causes of these long-term shifts.

Different rates of inflation between countries. If a country has persistently higher rates of inflation than the countries with which it trades, it will have a growing current account deficit. Exports and import substitutes will become less and less competitive as its *real* exchange rate appreciates.

Different rates of growth between countries. If a country grows faster than the countries with which it trades, its imports will tend to grow faster than its exports.

Income elasticity of demand for imports higher than for exports. If the income elasticity of demand for imports is relatively high, and the income elasticity of demand for exports is relatively low, then as world incomes grow, the country's imports will grow faster than its exports. This is a particular problem for many developing countries: they import manufactured goods and capital equipment, whose demand grows rapidly, and export primary products – food and raw materials – whose demand grows relatively slowly (see section 26.2).

KI 9 p58

Long-term structural changes

- Trading blocs may emerge, putting up tariff barriers to other countries. Australian and New Zealand exports were adversely affected when the UK joined the EEC.
- Countries may exercise monopoly power to a greater extent than previously. The OPEC oil price increases of 1973/4 and 1978/9 are examples.
- Countries may develop import substitutes. Thus plastics and other synthetics have in many cases substituted for rubber and metals, worsening the balance of payments of traditional primary exporters.
- The nature and quality of a country's products may change. Thus Japan has shifted from producing low-quality simple manufactured goods in the 1950s to producing high-quality sophisticated manufactured goods today. This has helped increase its exports.

To maintain a fixed exchange rate under such circumstances, governments have to take measures to correct the disequilibria. They can use demand-side policies (fiscal and monetary: see Box 24.2), supply-side policies or protectionist policies.

Advantages of fixed exchange rates

Many economists are opposed to fixed exchange rates, for the reasons examined shortly. Nevertheless, many business people are in favour of relatively rigid exchange rates. The following arguments are used.

Certainty. With fixed exchange rates, international trade and investment become much less risky, since profits are not affected by movements in the exchange rate.

Little or no speculation. Provided the rate is *absolutely* fixed – and people believe that it will remain so – there is no point in speculating. For example, between 1999 and

BOX 24.2

THE EFFECTIVENESS OF FISCAL AND MONETARY POLICIES UNDER FIXED EXCHANGE RATES

Monetary policy

Monetary policy is not very effective under fixed exchange rates.

Assume that the central bank, worried by rising inflation, wishes to reduce the growth in nominal aggregate demand. It thus reduces the rate of growth in money supply. This drives up interest rates and causes a fall in national income.

What effect will this have on the balance of payments? The lower national income reduces expenditure on imports and hence leads to a surplus on the current account. Also, the higher interest rates encourage an inflow of finance and hence a surplus on the financial account too. This balance of payments surplus will *increase* money supply again and reduce interest rates back towards the original level. Aggregate demand will rise back towards its original level. Monetary policy has been ineffective.

But rather than changing the *supply* of money, can the government not directly alter interest rates? The problem here is that, in order to maintain the rate of exchange at the fixed level, the government's room for manoeuvre is very limited. For example, if it raises interest rates, the resulting inflow of finance will cause a balance of payments surplus. The government could, for a period of time, simply build up reserves, but it may not want to do this indefinitely.

The problem is more serious if the economy is in recession and the central bank wants to *increase* aggregate demand by *reducing* interest rates. The financial outflow will force the central bank to buy in the domestic currency by using its reserves. But it can do this for only so long. Eventually, it will be forced to raise interest rates again in order to stem the drain on the reserves. In today's world, with little in the way of exchange controls and with massive amounts of short-term international liquidity, such flows can be enormous. This gives the central bank virtually no discretion over changing interest rates. Interest rates will have to be kept at a level so as to maintain the exchange rate. In the case of *perfect* mobility of international finance, interest rates must be kept at world rates. Monetary policy will be totally ineffective.

Fiscal policy

Fiscal policy is much more effective.

Assume that there is a recession and the government wishes to increase aggregate demand. It thus cuts taxes and/or raises government expenditure. This raises national income and increases expenditure on imports. Also, higher inflation raises the real exchange rate. This makes exports less competitive and imports relatively cheaper. The current account moves into deficit.

The increase in aggregate demand will raise the demand for money and hence put upward pressure on interest rates. This will lead to an inflow of finance and a financial account surplus. To prevent this swamping the current account deficit, the central bank must prevent interest rates from rising very much. In the case of an infinitely elastic supply of finance, interest rates must not be allowed to rise at all.

Thus money supply must be allowed to expand to keep interest rates down. This expansion of the money supply thus reinforces the expansionary fiscal policy and prevents crowding out.

Thus a high level of international financial mobility *enhances* the effectiveness of fiscal policy.

Suppose that under a managed floating system the central bank is worried about high inflation and wants to keep the exchange rate up in order to prevent import prices rising. To tackle the problem of inflation, it raises interest rates. What will happen to the current and financial accounts of the balance of payments?

2001, when the old currencies of the eurozone countries were still used, but were totally fixed to the euro, there was no speculation that the German mark, say, would change in value against the French franc or the Dutch guilder.

? *When the UK joined the ERM in 1990, it was hoped that this would make speculation pointless. As it turned out, speculation forced the UK to leave the ERM in 1992. Can you reconcile this with the argument that fixed rates discourage speculation?*

Automatic correction of monetary errors. If the central bank allows the money supply to expand too fast, the resulting extra demand and lower interest rates will lead to a balance of payments deficit. This will force the central bank to intervene to support the exchange rate. Either it must buy the domestic currency on the foreign exchange market, thereby causing money supply to fall again (unless it sterilises the effect), or it must raise interest rates. Either way this will have the effect of correcting the error.

Prevents governments pursuing 'irresponsible' macroeconomic policies. If a government deliberately and excessively expands aggregate demand – perhaps in an attempt to gain short-term popularity with the electorate – the resulting balance of payments deficit will force it to constrain demand again (unless it resorts to import controls).

Disadvantages of fixed exchange rates

The new classical view

New classicists make two crucial criticisms of fixed rates.

Fixed exchange rates make monetary policy ineffective. Interest rates must be used to ensure that the overall balance of payments balances. As a result, money supply must be allowed to vary with the demand for money in order to keep interest rates at the necessary level. Thus monetary policy cannot be used for domestic purposes (see Box 24.2). Inflation depends on world rates, which may be high and domestically unacceptable. If the central bank tries to reduce inflation by attempting to reduce money supply and raise interest rates, the current and financial accounts will go into surplus. Money supply will thus increase until domestic inflation rises back to world levels.

Fixed rates contradict the objective of having free markets. Why fix the exchange rate, when a simple depreciation or appreciation can correct a disequilibrium? In the new classical world where markets clear, and supply and demand are relatively elastic, why not treat the foreign exchange market like any other, and simply leave it to supply and demand?

The Keynesian view

In the Keynesian world, wages and prices are relatively 'sticky', and demand-deficient unemployment and cost-push inflation may persist. As such, there is no guarantee of achieving both internal and external balance simultaneously when exchange rates are fixed. This leads to the following problems.

Balance of payments deficits can lead to a recession. A balance of payments deficit can occur even if there is no excess demand. As we saw above, this could be caused by different rates of growth or different rates of inflation from trading partners, a higher income elasticity of demand for imports than for exports, and so on. If protectionism is to be avoided, and if supply-side policies work only over the long run, the government will be forced to reduce the rate of growth of aggregate demand. This will lead to higher unemployment and possibly a recession.

If wages and prices are sticky downwards, the contraction may have to be severe if a significant improvement in the *current* account is to be made. Here, reliance would have to be placed largely on lower *incomes* reducing the demand for imports. If the deflation is achieved through higher interest rates, however, an improvement on the *financial* account may remove the need for a severe deflation, especially given the high degree of financial mobility that exists nowadays. Nevertheless, the rate of interest may still be higher than that desired for purely internal purposes.

If a country has a *persistent* current account deficit, it may need to have persistently higher interest rates than its competitors and suffer persistently lower growth rates as a result. It will also tend to build up short-term debts, as money is put on deposit in the country to take advantage of the higher interest rates. This can make the problem of speculation much more acute if people come to believe that the fixed rate cannot be maintained (see below).

Competitive deflations leading to world depression. If deficit countries deflated, but surplus countries *reflated*, there would be no overall world deflation or reflation. Countries may be quite happy, however, to run a balance of payments surplus and build up reserves. Countries may thus competitively deflate – all trying to achieve a balance of payments surplus. But this is beggar-my-neighbour policy. Not all countries can have a surplus! Overall the world must be in balance. Such policies lead to general world deflation and a restriction in growth.

Problems of international liquidity. If trade is to expand, there must be an expansion in the supply of currencies acceptable for world trade (dollars, euros, gold, etc.): there must be adequate ***international liquidity***. Countries' reserves of these currencies must grow if they are to be sufficient to maintain a fixed rate at times of balance of payments disequilibrium. Conversely, there must not be excessive international liquidity. Otherwise the extra demand that would result would lead to world inflation. It is important under fixed exchange rates, therefore, to avoid too much or too little international liquidity. The problem is how to maintain adequate control of international liquidity. The supply of dollars, for example, depends largely on US policy, which may be dominated by its internal economic situation rather than by any concern for the well-being of the international community. Similarly, the supply of euros depends on the policy of the European Central Bank, which is governed by the internal situation in the eurozone countries.

? *Why will excessive international liquidity lead to international inflation?*

Speculation. If speculators believe that a fixed rate simply cannot be maintained, speculation is likely to be massive. If there is a huge deficit, there is no chance whatsoever of a *re*valuation. Either the rate will be devalued or it will remain the same. Speculators will thus sell the domestic currency. After all, it is a pretty good gamble: heads they

> **Definition**
>
> **International liquidity** The supply of currencies in the world acceptable for financing international trade and investment.

win (devaluation); tails they stay the same (no devaluation). This speculative selling will worsen the deficit, and may itself force the devaluation. Speculation of this sort had disastrous effects on some south-east Asian currencies in 1997 (see Web Case 24.4) and on the Argentinian peso in 2002 (see Web Case 24.6).

? *To what extent do Keynesians and new classicists agree about the role of fixed exchange rates?*

Postscript

An argument used in favour of fixed rates is that they prevent governments from pursuing inflationary policies. But if getting inflation down is desirable, why do governments not pursue an anti-inflationary policy directly? Today, many governments (or central banks) make inflation targeting the goal of monetary policy. Most, however, have floating exchange rates.

Section summary

*1. Macroeconomic shocks are constantly occurring. Whether internal and external balance will be restored under a fixed exchange rate, following a shock, depends on price and wage flexibility and on the time period.

*2. In the short run there is a degree of wage and price inflexibility. If there is a fall in aggregate demand, the resulting fall in national income will reduce the demand for imports. This will cause a current account surplus. The fall in aggregate demand will also reduce the demand for money and put downward pressure on interest rates. This will cause a financial account deficit. This effect can be large, given the high mobility of international finance. Interest rates are thus constrained by the need for the financial account to balance the current account.

*3. In the long run, with wage and price flexibility, the real exchange rate can change. This will help to restore both internal and external balance.

4. Over the longer term, balance of payments disequilibria under fixed exchange rates can arise from different rates of inflation and growth between countries, different income elasticities of demand for imports and exports, and long-term structural changes.

5. Under fixed exchange rates, monetary policy will not be very effective, but fiscal policy will be much more effective.

6. Fixed exchange rates bring the advantage of certainty for the business community, which encourages trade and foreign investment. They also help to prevent governments from pursuing irresponsible macroeconomic policies.

7. Both new classical and Keynesian economists, however, see important disadvantages in fixed exchange rates. New classical economists argue that they make monetary policy totally ineffective, and that they run counter to the efficiency objective of having free markets. Keynesians argue that fixed rates can lead to serious internal imbalance with perhaps a persistent recession; that with competitive deflations a recession can be worldwide; that there may be problems of excessive or insufficient international liquidity; and that speculation could be very severe if people came to believe that a fixed rate was about to break down.

24.3 FREE-FLOATING EXCHANGE RATES

Floating exchange rates and the freeing of domestic policy

With a freely floating exchange rate there can be no overall balance of payments disequilibrium. Foreign exchange dealers will constantly adjust the exchange rate to balance their books, so that the demand for and supply of any currency are equal.

This, therefore, removes the balance of payments constraint on domestic policy that exists under a fixed exchange rate. No reserves are required, since there is no central bank intervention to support the exchange rate. The government would seem free to pursue whatever domestic policy it likes. Any resulting effects on the balance of payments are simply and automatically corrected by a depreciation or appreciation of the exchange rate.

In reality, however, things are not quite so simple. Even under a totally free-floating exchange rate, some constraints on domestic policy may be imposed by the effects of these exchange rate movements. For example, a depreciation of the exchange rate increases the price of imports. If the demand for imports is relatively inelastic, this may lead to a higher rate of inflation.

Response to shocks under a floating exchange rate

Internal shocks

Let us assume that there is a rise in aggregate demand that causes inflation. For the moment, however, let us also assume that monetary policy maintains real interest rates at international levels. For simplicity, let us assume that there is no inflation abroad. How will a floating exchange rate system cope with this internal shock of a rise in aggregate demand? The exchange rate will simply depreciate to maintain the competitiveness of exports and import substitutes.

For example, assume an initial exchange rate of £1 = $2. A UK product costing $2 in the USA will earn £1 for the UK exporter. If UK inflation now causes prices to double, the exchange rate will roughly halve. If it falls to £1 = $1, then the same product costing $2 in the USA will now earn £2 for the UK exporter, which in *real* terms is the same amount as before. This is the ***purchasing-power parity theory***. This states that domestic price changes will be offset by (nominal) exchange rate changes, thereby maintaining the same relative prices between countries as before.

TC 12 p374

? *If this is the case, need firms worry about losing competitiveness in world markets if domestic inflation is higher than world inflation?*

If we now drop the assumption that real interest rates are maintained at the same level as abroad, the purchasing-power parity theory will break down. Let us assume that the rise in aggregate demand causes a rise in UK real interest rates. This could be either the effect of the higher demand for money pushing up interest rates, or it could be a deliberate act of the central bank to bring inflation back down to the target level.

There are now two effects on the exchange rate. The higher aggregate demand and higher inflation will cause the current account to move into deficit, thereby putting downward pressure on the exchange rate. The higher real interest rates, however, will cause the financial account to move into surplus as depositors choose to hold their money in pounds. This will put upward pressure on the exchange rate. Whether the exchange rate actually falls or rises depends on which of the two effects is the bigger. In today's world of huge international financial flows, the effect on the financial account is likely to be the larger one: the exchange rate will thus *appreciate*.

But either way, the new equilibrium exchange rate will be above the purchasing-power parity rate. This will adversely affect export industries, since the exchange rate has not fallen sufficiently (if at all) to compensate for their higher sterling price. It will also adversely affect domestic industries that compete with imports, since again the exchange rate has not fallen sufficiently to retain their competitiveness with imports. The current account thus remains in deficit, matched by an equal and opposite financial plus capital account surplus.

This has been the position in the UK for several years. The rate of inflation has been above that of major trading partners; the current account has been persistently in deficit (see Box 24.1) and the capital plus financial account has been persistently in surplus; interest rates have been persistently above interest rates in the USA and the eurozone. The result has been an appreciating real exchange rate (see Figure 24.3).

External shocks

Now let us assume that the rest of the world goes into recession (but with no change in international interest rates). The demand for UK exports will fall. This will lead to a depreciation of the exchange rate. This in turn will boost the demand for UK exports and domestic substitutes for imports. This boost to demand again will help to offset the dampening effect of the world recession.

Floating exchange rates thus help to insulate the domestic economy from world economic fluctuations.

? *Will there be* any *cost to the UK economy from a decline in the demand for exports resulting from a world recession?*

The path to long-run equilibrium

If there is a single shock, and if there is initially both internal balance and also external balance in the narrow sense (i.e. a current account balance), eventually both internal balance and current account balance will be restored. Current account balance will be restored by a change in the exchange rate that restores purchasing-power parity. This is illustrated in Figure 24.8.

Assume that the country experiences the same long-term rate of inflation as its trading partners and that, therefore, the nominal exchange rate follows the same path as the real exchange rate. Assume also that there are no *long-term* changes to cause an appreciation or depreciation and

Figure 24.8 Exchange rate path to long-run equilibrium after a shock at time t_1

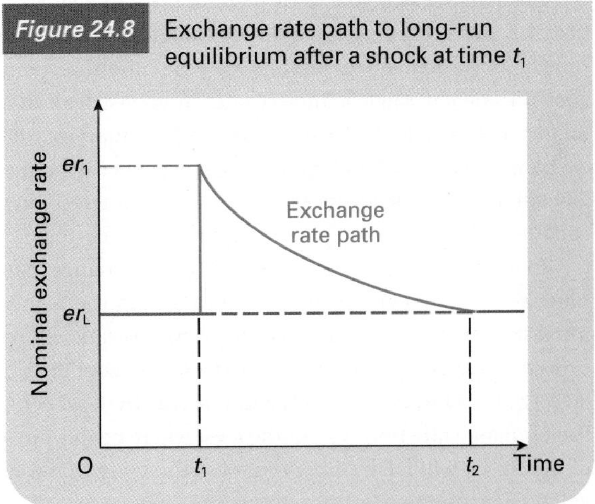

Definition

Purchasing-power parity theory The theory that the exchange rate will adjust so as to offset differences in countries' inflation rates, with the result that the same quantity of internationally traded goods can be bought at home as abroad with a given amount of the domestic currency.

CASE STUDIES AND APPLICATIONS

THE PRICE OF A BIG MAC

The Economist's *guide to purchasing-power parity rates*

Twice a year *The Economist* publishes its 'hamburger standard' exchange rates for currencies. It is a lighthearted attempt to see if currencies are exchanging at their purchasing-power parity rates. The test is the price at which a 'Big Mac' McDonald's hamburger sells in different countries!

The following extracts are from the June 2005 Big Mac report (9/6/05).

> Italians like their coffee strong and their currencies weak. That, at least, is the conclusion one can draw from their latest round of grumbles about Europe's single currency. But are the Italians right to moan? Is the euro overvalued?
>
> Our annual Big Mac index (see table) suggests they have a case: the euro is overvalued by 17% against the dollar. How come? The euro is worth about \$1.22 on the foreign-exchange markets. A Big Mac costs €2.92, on average, in the eurozone and \$3.06 in the United States. The rate needed to equalise the burger's price in the two regions is just \$1.05. To patrons of McDonald's, at least, the single currency is overpriced.

If the Big Mac is taken as representative of all goods and services, then the euro would, indeed, be overvalued by 17 per cent in PPP terms compared with the dollar. In other words, at the market exchange rate of €1 = \$1.22, a Big Mac would cost \$3.58 in the eurozone: 17 per cent more than the \$3.06 price in the USA.

The hamburger standard

	Big Mac price in dollars at current exchange rate	Under (–) / over (+) valuation against the dollar (%)
Iceland	6.67	+118
Norway	6.06	+98
Switzerland	5.05	+65
Denmark	4.58	+50
Sweden	4.17	+36
Eurozone[a]	3.58	+17
UK	3.44	+12
New Zealand	3.17	+4
USA[b]	3.06	0
Turkey	2.92	–5
Canada	2.63	–14
Mexico	2.58	–16
Australia	2.50	–18
Japan	2.34	–23
Czech Rep	2.30	–25
Singapore	2.17	–31
South Africa	2.10	–31
Poland	1.96	–36
Bulgaria	1.88	–39
Sri Lanka	1.75	–43
Argentina	1.64	–46
Egypt	1.55	–49
Russia	1.48	–52
Thailand	1.48	–52
Malaysia	1.38	–55
China	1.27	–59

[a] Weighted average of member countries.
[b] Average of New York, Chicago, San Francisco and Atlanta.

that, therefore, the long-term equilibrium exchange rate is constant over time. This is shown by the horizontal line at er_L.

Now assume, as before, that there is a rise in aggregate demand and a resulting rise in interest rates. This occurs at time t_1. As the demand for imports rises, the current account goes into deficit. Higher interest rates, however, lead to a financial inflow and an immediate appreciation of the exchange rate to er_1. But then, the exchange rate will gradually fall back to its long-run rate as the higher interest rates curb demand and interest rates can thus come back down.

What determines the level of er_1? This exchange rate must be high enough to balance the gain from the higher interest rate against the fact that the exchange rate will be expected to depreciate again back to its long-run equilibrium level er_L. For example, if the interest rate rises by 1 per cent, the exchange rate must rise to the level where people anticipate that it will fall by 1 per cent per year. Only that way will finance stop flowing into the country.

Describe the exchange rate path if there were a single shock that caused interest rates to fall. What determines the magnitude and speed of changes in the exchange rate in such a scenario?

Speculation

In the real world, shocks are occurring all the time. Also there is considerable uncertainty over the future course of the exchange rate path. What is more, things are made more complicated by the activities of speculators. As soon as any exchange rate change is anticipated, speculators will buy or sell the currency.

KI 10 p62

Assume, for example, that there is a rise in UK inflation above international rates. This causes a fall in the demand for exports and hence a fall in the demand for sterling (assuming a price elasticity of demand greater than 1), and a rise in imports and hence a rise in the supply of sterling. This is illustrated in Figures 24.9 and 24.10. The exchange

BOX 24.3

The table shows the degree of overvaluation or undervaluation in Big Mac PPP terms of a range of currencies. You can see that the pound is overvalued against the dollar by 12 per cent. In other words, for a Big Mac to cost the same in the UK as in the USA, the exchange rate would have to be 12 per cent lower, at £1 = $1.63, rather than the market rate of £1 = $1.83.

Our index shows that burger prices can certainly fall out of line with each other. If he could keep the burgers fresh, an ingenious arbitrageur could buy Big Macs for the equivalent of $1.27 in China, whose yuan is the most undervalued currency in our table, and sell them for $5.05 in Switzerland, whose franc is [one of] the most overvalued currencies. The impracticality of such a trade highlights some of the flaws in the PPP idea. Trade barriers, transport costs and differences in taxes drive a wedge between prices in different countries.

More important, the $5.05 charged for a Swiss Big Mac helps to pay for the retail space in which its served, and for the labour that serves it. Neither of these two crucial ingredients can be easily traded across borders. David Parsley, of Vanderbilt University, and Shang-Jin Wei, of the International Monetary Fund, estimate that non-traded inputs, such as labour, rent and electricity, account for between 55% and 64% of the price of a Big Mac.[1]

But even if we were to look purely at the *traded* component of goods, the purchasing-power parity exchange rate would be unlikely to be achieved.

Economists lost some faith in PPP as a guide to exchange rates in the 1970s, after the world's currencies abandoned their anchors to the dollar. By the end of the decade, exchange rates seemed to be drifting without chart or compass. Later studies showed that a currency's purchasing power does assert itself over the long run. But it might take three to five years for a misaligned exchange rate to move even halfway back into line.

The point here is that exchange rate movements, especially over the short and medium terms, reflect factors influencing the financial account of the balance of payments: factors such as actual and expected interest rate differentials, investment prospects and speculation about exchange rate movements.

?

1. ***If the Chinese yuan is undervalued by 59 per cent in PPP terms against the US dollar and the Icelandic króna overvalued by 118 per cent, what implications does this have for the interpretation of Chinese, Icelandic and US GDP statistics?***
2. ***Why do developing countries' currencies tend to be undervalued relative to those of developed countries (see table)?***
3. ***At the time the table was compiled, the Big Mac PPP rate for the Japanese yen was $1 = ¥81.7. What was the market exchange rate?***

[1] 'A prism into the PPP puzzles: the microfoundations of Big Mac real exchange rates', October 2004. Available at www2.owen.vanderbilt.edu/david.parsley/research.htm.

Figure 24.9 Stabilising speculation

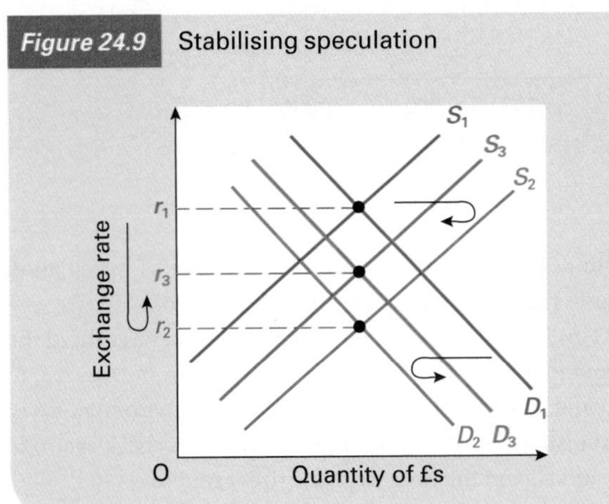

Figure 24.10 Destabilising speculation

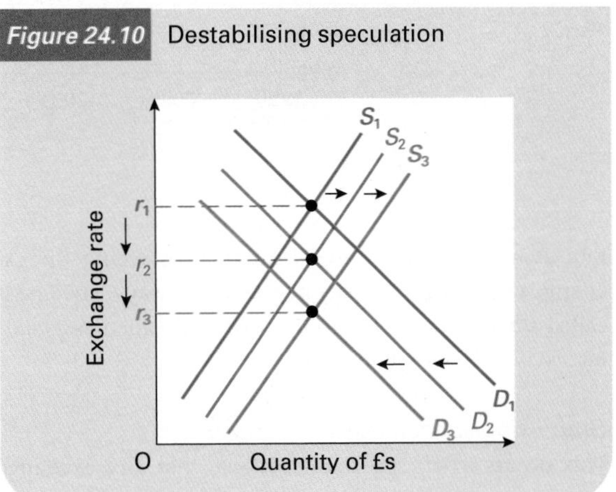

CASE STUDIES AND APPLICATIONS

THE EURO/DOLLAR SEESAW

Ups and downs in the currency market

For periods of time, world currency markets can be quite peaceful, with only modest changes in exchange rates. But with the ability to move vast sums of money very rapidly from one part of the world to another and from one currency to another, speculators can suddenly turn this relatively peaceful world into one of extreme turmoil.

In this box we examine the huge swings of the euro against the dollar since the euro's launch in 1999. In Web Case 24.4 we examine two other examples of currency turmoil: both from the 1990s.

First the down . . .

On 1 January 1999, the euro was launched and exchanged for $1.16. By October 2000 the euro had fallen to $0.85. What was the cause of this 27 per cent depreciation? The main cause was the growing fear that inflationary pressures were increasing in the USA and that, therefore, the Federal Reserve Bank would have to raise interest rates. At the same time, the eurozone economy was growing only slowly and inflation was well below the 2 per cent ceiling set by the ECB. There was thus pressure on the ECB to cut interest rates.

The speculators were not wrong. As the diagram shows, US interest rates rose, and ECB interest rates initially fell, and when eventually they did rise (in October 1999), the gap between US and ECB interest rates soon widened again.

In addition to the differences in interest rates, a lack of confidence in the recovery of the eurozone economy and a continuing confidence in the US economy encouraged investment to flow to the USA. This inflow of finance (and lack of inflow to the eurozone) further pushed up the dollar relative to the euro.

The low value of the euro meant a high value of the pound relative to the euro. This made it very difficult for UK companies exporting to eurozone countries and also for those competing with imports from the eurozone (which had been made cheaper by the fall in the euro).

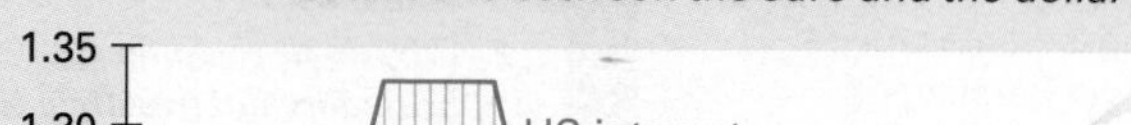

Fluctuations between the euro and the dollar

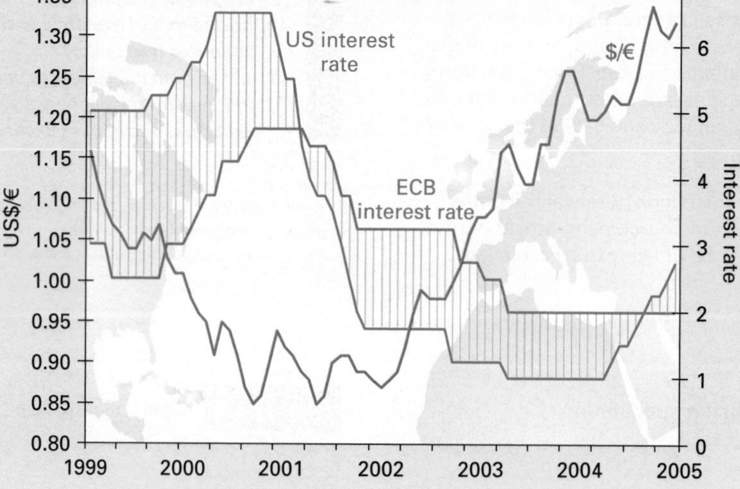

rate depreciates from r_1 to r_2. Speculators seeing the exchange rate falling can react in one of two ways. The first is called *stabilising speculation*; the second is called *destabilising speculation* (see section 2.5).

Stabilising speculation

This occurs when speculators believe that any exchange rate change will soon be reversed.

In our example, speculators may anticipate that the central bank will raise interest rates or take some other measure to reduce inflation. They thus believe that the exchange rate will appreciate again. As a result, they buy more pounds and sell fewer. But this very act of speculation causes the appreciation they had anticipated.

KI 10 p62

This is illustrated in Figure 24.9. Inflation has caused the demand for and supply of pounds to shift from D_1 and S_1 to D_2 and S_2, and the exchange rate to fall from r_1 to r_2. Stabilising speculation then shifts the curves back again, to D_3 and S_3, and the exchange rate rises again to r_3.

The action of speculators in this case, therefore, prevents excessively large exchange rate changes. In general, stabilising speculation occurs whenever speculators believe that the exchange rate has 'overreacted' to the current economic situation.

BOX 24.4

In October 2000, with the euro trading at around 85¢, the ECB plus the US Federal Reserve Bank (America's central bank), the Bank of England and the Japanese central bank all intervened on the foreign exchange market to buy euros. This arrested the fall, and helped to restore confidence in the currency. People were more willing to hold euros, knowing that central banks would support it.

. . . Then the up

The position changed completely in 2001. With the US economy slowing rapidly and fears of an impending recession, the Federal Reserve Bank reduced interest rates 11 times during the year: from 6 per cent at the beginning of the year to 1.25 per cent at the end (see the diagram). Although the ECB also cut interest rates, the cuts were relatively modest: from 4.75 at the beginning of the year to 3.25 at the end. With eurozone interest rates now considerably above US rates, the euro began to rise.

In addition, a massive deficit on the US current account, and a budget deficit nearing 4 per cent of GDP, made foreign investors reluctant to invest in the US economy. In fact, investors were pulling out of the USA. One estimate suggests that European investors alone sold $70 billion of US assets during 2002. The result of all this was a massive depreciation of the dollar and appreciation of the euro, so that by March 2005 the exchange rate had risen to $1.35: a 60 per cent appreciation since July 2001! By 2004, the US budget deficit had risen to 4.5 per cent of GDP – well above the budget deficits in France and Germany (see Box 19.4 on page 540).

The effects on business in the eurozone

So is a strong euro bad for European business? With over 20 per cent of the eurozone's GDP determined by export sales, and a large part of those exports going to the USA, the dollar/euro exchange rate will invariably be significant. The question is, how significant? The concern was that, with slow growth in the eurozone, the rise in the euro and the resulting fall in exports would slow growth rates even further. With the German economy on the brink of recession, the euro's rise might be simply too much for the German economy to bear. The investment bank Morgan Stanley estimated that for every 10 per cent rise in the value of the euro against the dollar, European corporate profits fall by 3 per cent.

And it was not just the fact that the euro was strong. What also worried European businesses was the *speed* at which the euro strengthened against the dollar. The question was whether they could adjust quickly enough to accommodate the rise.

However, the impact of the euro's rise on eurozone business was tempered by a number of other factors:

- Companies are increasingly using sophisticated management and operational systems, in which value creation is spread throughout a global value chain. Often procurement systems are priced in dollars.
- Firms hedge their currency risks. BMW, for example, uses forward exchange markets to agree to buy or sell currencies in the future at a price quoted *today* (this, of course, costs it a premium).
- Many European companies (again BMW is an example) have located some of their production facilities in the USA and use them to help meet demand in the US market. This helps to insulate them from the effects of the rise in the value of the euro.

Businesses in the eurozone seem initially to have accommodated the euro's rapid rise. However, if the value of the euro continues to strengthen on world markets, the achievement of even slow eurozone growth might prove increasingly difficult to maintain.

Find out what has happened to the euro/dollar exchange rate over the past 12 months. (You can find the data from the Bank of England's Statistical Interactive Database at www.bankofengland.co.uk/statisticsindex.htm). Explain why the exchange rate has moved the way it has.

? *Draw a similar diagram to Figure 24.9, showing how an initial appreciation of the exchange rate would similarly be reduced by stabilising speculation.*

Destabilising speculation

KI 31 p 368 This occurs when speculators believe that exchange rate movements will continue in the same direction.

In our example, speculators may believe that inflation will not be brought under control. They anticipate a continuing fall in the exchange rate and thus sell *now* before the exchange rate falls any further. In Figure 24.10, this speculation causes the demand and supply curves to shift further, to D_3 and S_3; and causes the exchange rate to fall further, to r_3.

Eventually, however, this destabilising speculation could cause ***overshooting***, with the exchange rate falling well

Definition

Exchange rate overshooting Where a fall (or rise) in the long-run equilibrium exchange rate causes the actual exchange rate to fall (or rise) by a greater amount before eventually moving back to the new long-run equilibrium level.

below the purchasing-power parity rate. At this point speculators, believing that the rate will rise again, will start buying pounds again. This causes the exchange rate to rise.

Obviously, governments prefer stabilising to destabilising speculation. Destabilising speculation can cause severe exchange rate fluctuations. The resulting uncertainty is very damaging to trade. It is very important, therefore, that governments create a climate of confidence. People must believe that the government can prevent economic crises from occurring.

Conclusion

Whatever speculators anticipate will happen to the exchange rate, their actions will help to bring it about. If they think the rate will fall, they will sell pounds, hence causing it to fall. Thus speculators as a whole will gain. This applies to both stabilising and destabilising speculation.

If speculators on average gain from their speculation, who loses?

Advantages of a free-floating exchange rate

The advantages and disadvantages of free-floating rates are to a large extent the opposite of fixed rates.

Automatic correction. The government simply lets the exchange rate move freely to the equilibrium. In this way, balance of payments disequilibria are automatically and instantaneously corrected without the need for specific government policies – policies that under other systems can be mishandled.

No problem of international liquidity and reserves. Since there is no central bank intervention in the foreign exchange market, there is no need to hold reserves. A currency is automatically convertible at the current market exchange rate. International trade is thereby financed.

Insulation from external economic events. A country is not tied to a possibly unacceptably high world inflation rate, as it is under a fixed exchange rate. It can choose its own inflation target. It is also to some extent protected against world economic fluctuations and shocks (see page 683).

Governments are free to choose their domestic policy. Under a fixed rate, a government may have to deflate the economy even when there is high unemployment. Under a floating rate, the government can choose whatever level of domestic demand it considers appropriate, and simply leave exchange rate movements to take care of any balance of payments effect. This is a major advantage, especially when the effectiveness of deflation is reduced by downward wage and price rigidity, and when competitive deflation between countries may end up causing a world recession.

Disadvantages of a free-floating exchange rate

Despite these advantages, there are still some serious problems with free-floating exchange rates.

Speculation. Short-run instability can be lessened by stabilising speculation, thus making speculation advantageous. If, due to short-run inelasticity of demand, a deficit causes a very large depreciation, speculators will *buy* pounds, knowing that in the long run the exchange rate will appreciate again. Their action therefore helps to lessen the short-run fall in the exchange rate.

Nevertheless, in an uncertain world where there are few restrictions on currency speculation, where the fortunes and policies of governments can change rapidly, and where large amounts of short-term deposits are internationally 'footloose', speculation can be highly destabilising in the short run. Considerable exchange rate overshooting can occur. As we shall see in section 25.1, there have been violent swings in exchange rates in recent years – even under a managed floating exchange rate system where governments have attempted to dampen such fluctuations!

The continuance of exchange rate fluctuations over a number of years is likely to encourage the growth of speculative holdings of currency. This can then cause even larger and more rapid swings in exchange rates.

KI 11 p66

Uncertainty for traders and investors. The uncertainty caused by currency fluctuations can discourage international trade and investment. To some extent, the problem can be overcome by using the ***forward exchange market***. Here traders agree with a bank *today* the rate of exchange for some point in the *future* (say, six months' time). This allows traders to plan future purchases of imports or sales of exports at a known rate of exchange. Of course, banks charge for this service, since they are taking upon themselves the risks of adverse exchange rate fluctuations.

This will not help long-term investment, however. The possibility of exchange rate appreciation may well discourage firms from investing abroad.

Why would banks not be prepared to offer a forward exchange rate to a firm for, say, five years' time?

Lack of discipline on the domestic economy. Governments may pursue irresponsibly inflationary policies. Also, unions and firms may well drive up wages and prices, without the same fear of losing overseas markets or of the government imposing deflationary policies. The depreciation resulting

Definition

Forward exchange market Where contracts are made today for the price at which a currency will be exchanged at some specified future date.

EXPLORING ECONOMICS BOX 24.5

THE EFFECTIVENESS OF MONETARY AND FISCAL POLICIES UNDER FLOATING EXCHANGE RATES

With a floating exchange rate, monetary policy is strong and fiscal policy is weak (the reverse of the case with fixed exchange rates).

Monetary policy

Assume that the economy is in recession and the central bank wishes to increase aggregate demand. It thus reduces interest rates. Three effects follow, each contributing to the effectiveness of the monetary policy.

1. *The expansionary monetary policy directly increases aggregate demand.* The size of the effect here depends on the amount that interest rates change and the elasticity of aggregate demand in response to the changes in interest rates.
2. *The exchange rate depreciates.* Higher aggregate demand increases imports and (via higher prices) reduces exports. This plus the lower interest rates reduce the demand for and increase the supply of domestic currency on the foreign exchange market. The exchange rate thus depreciates.

   This reinforces the increase in domestic demand. A lower exchange rate makes exports less expensive again and therefore increases their demand (an injection). Imports become more expensive again and therefore their demand falls (a withdrawal). There is thus a *further* multiplied rise in income.
3. *Speculation may cause initial exchange rate overshooting.* Lower interest rates cause speculative financial outflows in anticipation of the depreciation. This causes the exchange rate to fall below its eventual rate – to overshoot, thus causing a further rise in aggregate demand.

   This is only a short-term effect, however, since speculators will stop selling the domestic currency when the rate has gone so low that they feel it must rise again (back towards the purchasing-power parity level) sufficiently fast to offset the lower interest rates they are now getting. The greater the mobility of international finance and the better the information of the speculators, the shorter will the short run be.

Fiscal policy

Fiscal policy is relatively weak under a floating rate. Again let us assume that the objective is to raise aggregate demand to combat a recession. The government thus reduces taxes and/or increases its expenditure. The rise in aggregate demand raises imports and (via higher prices) reduces exports. This effect on the current account of the balance of payments puts downward pressure on the exchange rate.

The higher aggregate demand, however, increases the transactions demand for money and hence *raises* interest rates. These higher interest rates will lead to financial inflows. This will put upward pressure on the exchange rate, which is likely to swamp the downward pressure from the current account deficit. There will therefore be an *appreciation* of the exchange rate. This will increase imports and reduce exports, thus reducing aggregate demand again, and reducing the effectiveness of the fiscal expansion.

Compare the relative effectiveness of fiscal and monetary policies as means of reducing aggregate demand under a system of floating exchange rates.

from this inflation will itself fuel the inflation by raising the price of imports.

Conclusion

Neither fixed nor free-floating exchange rates are free from problems. For this reason, governments have sought a compromise between the two, the hope being that some intermediate system will gain the benefits of both, while avoiding most of their disadvantages.

One compromise was tried after the Second World War. This was the *adjustable peg*. Another is the system that replaced the adjustable peg in the early 1970s and continues for much of the world today. This is the system of *managed floating*. We examine these systems in the next section.

Section summary

1. Under a free-floating exchange rate, the balance of payments will automatically be kept in balance by movements in the exchange rate. This removes the *balance of payments* constraint on domestic policy. It does not, however, remove external constraints entirely.
2. According to the purchasing-power parity theory, any changes in domestic prices will simply lead to equivalent changes in the exchange rate, leaving the international competitiveness of home-produced goods unaffected. If, however, internal shocks cause changes in interest rates, there will be a change in

continued

the *financial* account balance. This will influence exchange rates and destroy the purchasing-power parity theory. The current account will go out of balance (in an equal and opposite way to the financial account).

3. External shocks will be reflected in changes in exchange rates and will help to insulate the domestic economy from international economic fluctuations.
4. Exchange rate movements are highly influenced by speculation. If speculators believe that an appreciation or depreciation is merely temporary, their activities will help to stabilise the exchange rate. If, however, they believe that an exchange rate movement in either direction will continue, their activities will be destabilising and cause a bigger movement in the exchange rate.
5. The advantages of free-floating exchange rates are that they automatically correct balance of payments disequilibria; they eliminate the need for reserves; and they give governments a greater independence to pursue their chosen domestic policy.
6. On the other hand, a completely free exchange rate can be highly unstable, made worse by destabilising speculation. This may discourage firms from trading and investing abroad. What is more, a flexible exchange rate, by removing the balance of payments constraint on domestic policy, may encourage governments to pursue irresponsible domestic policies for short-term political gain.

24.4 EXCHANGE RATE SYSTEMS IN PRACTICE

The adjustable peg system: 1945–73

After the collapse in 1931 of the fixed exchange rate system of the gold standard (see section 15.2), the huge scale of the initial disequilibria caused wild swings in exchange rates. Many countries resorted to protectionism, given the great uncertainties associated with free trade under fluctuating exchange rates.

The Bretton Woods system

In 1944 the allied countries met at Bretton Woods in the USA to hammer out a new exchange rate system: one that would avoid the chaos of the 1930s and encourage free trade, but that would avoid the rigidity of the gold standard. The compromise they worked out was an adjustable peg system that lasted until 1971.

Under the ***Bretton Woods system*** there was a totally fixed dollar/gold exchange rate ($35 per ounce of gold). The USA guaranteed that it would freely convert dollars into gold. It was hoped thereby to encourage countries to hold dollars as their major reserve currency. After all, if dollars were freely convertible into gold, they were as good as gold. All other countries pegged their exchange rate to the dollar.

To prevent temporary, short-term fluctuations in the exchange rate, central banks *intervened* on the foreign exchange markets using their foreign reserves. This enabled them to maintain the pegged rate within a 1 per cent band.

If the disequilibrium became more serious, governments were supposed to pursue policies of *deflation* or *reflation*. In the meantime, in the case of a deficit, the central bank might have insufficient reserves to maintain the exchange rate. The International Monetary Fund was set up to provide such liquidity. All countries were required to deposit a quota of funds with the IMF, depending on the size of their trade. The IMF would then lend to countries in balance of payments deficit to enable them to maintain their exchange rate. The more a country had to borrow from the IMF, the more the IMF would insist that it pursued appropriate deflationary policies to correct the disequilibrium.

If the deficit became severe, countries could *devalue*: the pegged rate could be adjusted (in consultation with the IMF).

? *Under this system, how would you expect countries to respond to a balance of payments surplus? Would a revaluation benefit such countries?*

Advocates of an adjustable peg system argue that the Bretton Woods arrangement made a significant contribution to the long boom of the 1950s and 1960s.

- Since rates were fixed for a long period of time – perhaps many years – uncertainty was reduced and trade was encouraged.
- Pegged rates, plus the overseeing role of the IMF, prevented governments from pursuing irresponsible policies, and helped to bring about an international harmonisation of policies. They kept world inflation in check.
- If a deficit became severe, countries could devalue. This prevented them being forced into a depression or into adopting protectionist policies. The IMF ensured an orderly process of devaluation.

However, there were two serious weaknesses with the system. These became more and more apparent during the 1960s, and eventually led to the system's downfall.

Definition

Bretton Woods system An adjustable peg system whereby currencies were pegged to the US dollar. The USA maintained convertibility of the dollar into gold at the rate of $35 to an ounce.

Problems of adjustment to balance of payments disequilibria

To avoid internal policy being governed by the balance of payments, and to avoid being forced into a depression, countries with a fundamental deficit were supposed to devalue. There were several difficulties here, however.

- Identifying whether a deficit was fundamental. Governments were frequently overoptimistic about the future balance of payments position.
- If devaluation did take place, it could be very disruptive to firms. A devaluation suddenly alters the costs and revenues of importers and exporters by a substantial amount. If a devaluation is felt to be imminent, it can cause great uncertainty and may make them reluctant to take on new trade commitments.

? *Would this uncertainty have a similar or a different effect on exporting companies and companies using imported inputs?*

- At first a devaluation might make a current account deficit *worse*: the ***J-curve effect***. The price elasticities of demand for imports and exports may be low in the short run (see Web Case 24.1). Directly after devaluation, few extra exports may be sold, and more will have to be paid for imports that do not have immediate substitutes. There is thus an initial deterioration in the balance of trade before it eventually improves. In Figure 24.11, devaluation takes place at time t_1. As you can see, the diagram has a J shape.

For these reasons, countries in deficit tended to put off devaluing until they were forced to by a crisis. The reluctance of countries to devalue caused other problems.

KI 31 p368 *Stop–go policies.* Countries had to rely much more on *deflation* as a means of curing deficits. The UK in particular found that, whenever the economy started to grow, the balance of payments went into deficit. This forced the government to curb demand again through fiscal and/or monetary policies.

Figure 24.11 The J-curve effect

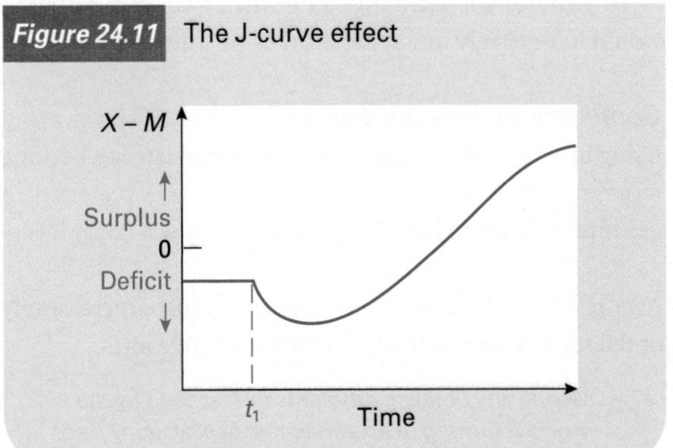

Speculation. If countries delayed devaluing until a deficit became really severe, an eventual large devaluation became inevitable. This provided a field day for speculators: they could not lose, and there was a high probability of a substantial gain.

Large-scale disruption. The delay in devaluing plus the build-up of speculative pressure could cause the devaluation to be very large when it eventually came. This could be highly disruptive.

Countries' balance of payments deficits could be reduced and adjustment made easier if surplus countries were willing to revalue. There was a reluctance to do this, however, by countries such as Japan. Revaluation was strongly opposed by exporters (and producers of import substitutes), who would find it suddenly more difficult to compete. What is more, there were not the same pressures for surplus countries to revalue as there were for deficit countries to devalue. A lack of reserves can force deficit countries to devalue. Surplus countries, however, may be quite happy to carry on building up reserves.

The USA was not allowed to devalue when in deficit. The onus was on other countries to revalue, which they were reluctant to do. Hence large US deficits persisted. The problem of these deficits was linked to the second major problem area: that of international liquidity.

Problems of international liquidity and the collapse of the system

With an adjustable peg system, there have to be sufficient stocks of internationally acceptable currencies or other liquid assets. This 'international liquidity' is necessary both to finance trade and to provide enough reserves for central banks to support their currencies whenever there is a currency flow deficit. Under the Bretton Woods system, there were three main sources of liquidity: gold, dollars and IMF quotas. But since IMF quotas were only in existing currencies, they were not a source of *additional* liquidity.

As world trade expanded, so deficits (and surpluses) were likely to be larger, and so more reserves were required. But the supply of gold was not expanding fast enough, so countries increasingly held dollars. After all, dollars earned interest. The willingness to hold dollars enabled the USA to run large balance of payments deficits. All the USA needed to do to pay for the deficits was to 'print' more dollars, which other countries were prepared to accept as reserves.

Definition

The J-curve effect Where a devaluation causes the balance of payments first to deteriorate and then to improve. The graph of the balance of payments over time thus looks like a letter J.

US balance of payments deficits in the 1960s got steadily worse. The financing of the Vietnam War, in particular, deepened the deficit. Dollars flooded out of the USA. World liquidity thus expanded rapidly, fuelling world inflation. Furthermore, the rapid growth in overseas dollar holdings meant that US gold reserves were increasingly inadequate to guarantee convertibility. Some countries, fearful that the USA might eventually be forced to suspend convertibility, chose to exchange dollars for gold. US gold reserves fell, creating a further imbalance and a deepening of the crises.

Despite various attempts to rescue the system with its overreliance on the dollar, it eventually collapsed. In June 1972 the pound was floated. Over the following year, other countries followed suit, and despite a further dollar devaluation the system was finally abandoned in 1973.

?

Why would the adjustable peg system have been less suitable in the world of the mid-1970s than it was back in the 1950s?

Managed floating

The world has been on a floating exchange rate system since the breakdown of the Bretton Woods system in the early 1970s. This allows adjustment to be made to the inevitable shifts in demand and supply, shifts that got more extreme in the early 1970s with a quadrupling of oil prices in 1973–4 and rapid changes in world trading patterns. Domestic policy has been largely freed from balance of payments constraints. At the same time, *managed* floating was claimed to allow adjustment to be more gentle, ideally avoiding wild swings in the exchange rate aggravated by speculation.

TC 7 p26

Some minor currencies remain pegged (but adjustable) to a major currency such as the dollar, but float along with it against other currencies. Other currencies are pegged to each other, but jointly float with the rest of the world. The most notable example of this were the currencies of the exchange rate mechanism of the European Monetary System (see section 25.2).

Some countries allow their currencies to float freely. Most countries, however, from time to time have attempted to stabilise their exchange rate, and have thus been operating a system of 'managed flexibility'.

If the country decides to adopt a managed floating system, how could the central bank prevent the exchange rate from falling? There are two main methods:

- Using reserves or foreign loans to purchase domestic currency on the foreign exchange market.
- Raising interest rates to attract short-term financial inflows.

Problems with managed floating since 1972

Managing the exchange rate involved problems, however. Governments needed to know when to intervene, what exchange rate level they should aim to maintain, and how persistently they should try to maintain that rate in the face of speculative pressure.

Predicting the long-term equilibrium exchange rate

Differing inflation rates between countries will require exchange rate adjustments to maintain purchasing-power parity. It is not correct, however, for governments to assume that this will be the *only* cause of shifts in the long-term equilibrium exchange rate. For example, the 1973–4 and 1979–80 oil crises caused fundamental and unpredictable changes in currency demand and supply. So too did other factors, such as the dismantling of trade barriers within the EU, protectionist measures adopted in different parts of the world, changes in technology and changes in tastes.

It is therefore very difficult for the government to predict what the long-term equilibrium will be, and what proportion of any exchange rate movement is therefore due to long-term and what proportion merely to short-term phenomena.

The growth in speculative financial flows

The OPEC oil price increase in 1973–4 caused huge balance of payments deficits for oil importers. The OPEC countries could not spend all of these surpluses on additional imports since (a) they did not have the capacity to consume such a huge increase in imports and (b) the oil-importing countries did not have the capacity to supply such a huge increase in exports. The surpluses were thus largely invested in short-term dollar and to a lesser extent other major currency assets. This created a large capacity for short-term loans by western banks. These moneys could be rapidly shifted from one world financial centre to another, depending on which country had the most favourable interest rates and exchange rates. This created a massive capacity for speculation, and thus made it difficult for countries to control exchange rates by currency sales alone.

Over the years, the scale of speculative flows has continued to increase. Some $2 trillion now passes across the international exchanges every day. Reserves and access to foreign loans are simply inadequate to prevent concerted speculative selling.

To manage the exchange rate, therefore, central banks would have to rely much more on using interest rates.

Conflicts with internal policy

Using interest rates to support the exchange rate has become more and more unpopular as countries have preferred to use interest rates to keep inflation at or below a target level.

As a result of these problems, countries have increasingly opted for a system of freely floating exchange rates.

Would any of these problems be lessened by the world returning to an adjustable peg system? If so, what sort of adjustable peg system would you recommend?

Figure 24.12 Dollar/sterling exchange rate and sterling exchange rate index: 1976–2005

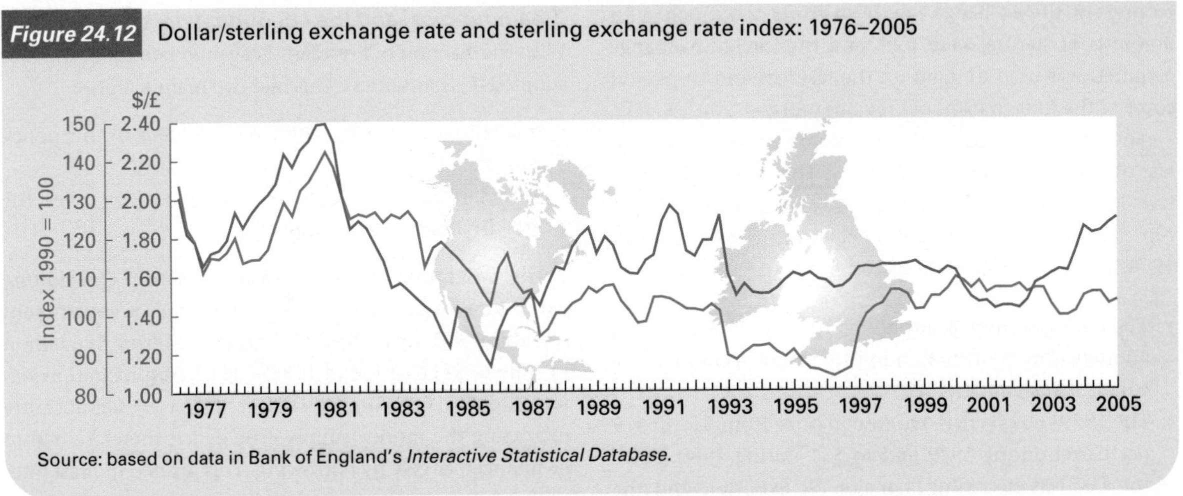

Source: based on data in Bank of England's *Interactive Statistical Database*.

Table 24.1 Exchange rate indices, averages for each period (1995 = 100)

	1970–3	1974–7	1978–81	1982–5	1986–9	1990–3	1994–6	1997–9	2000–2	2003–5
USA	61	58	57	80	77	86	101	121	133	124
Japan	17	19	25	30	51	64	94	90	96	91
Germany	36	44	53	58	71	82	97	98	94	103
UK	163	122	118	113	106	107	102	125	129	128
Italy	256	181	134	112	113	118	106	113	112	122

Source: based on data in *European Economy Statistical Annex* (Commission of the EU).

The UK experience of managed floating

Figure 24.12 shows the fluctuations in UK exchange rates since 1976, with respect to both the dollar and the more important trade-weighted average exchange rate with all other countries. As can be seen, the fluctuations have been large and often violent. Other countries have experienced similar fluctuations. Also, there have been clear long-term trends, as Table 24.1 shows.

But why have exchange rates changed so much? Part of the explanation lies in differences in countries' rates of inflation. This is the purchasing-power parity theory (see page 683). If a country's prices went up by 10 per cent more than the weighted average of its trading partners, its exchange rate would need to depreciate by 10 per cent to compensate. But this provides only part of the explanation. Other causes of exchange rate movements include changes in relative interest rates, various international shocks, longer-term shifts in demand and supply for imports and exports, and speculation.

The first oil crisis and its aftermath: 1973–6

The 1973–4 oil crisis, which followed large world commodity price increases over the previous two years, caused a major shock to the world economy. What were the UK and other industrialised countries to do?

Depreciation could not provide the solution. The demand for oil is highly price inelastic. The price increase had thus already caused a major inflationary shock to the world economy. Depreciation would probably have made things worse. What is more, deflationary policies, or a growth in protectionism, would have caused a major world recession.

The solution seemed to be to borrow: (a) to 'recycle' the oil revenue so as to prevent excessive deflation, and (b) to attempt to maintain reasonably stable exchange rates and avoid competitive depreciation. Until 1975 the UK was reasonably successful in this policy. A substantial proportion of the OPEC surpluses were deposited in the UK, and the government undertook large-scale foreign borrowing. The exchange rate was thus kept up by these financial inflows, and also by using reserves.

From early 1975, however, the exchange rate began falling, despite continued intervention. In 1976 it began to plummet, even though by now inflation was falling and the balance of payments was improving. Destabilising speculation set in. Many of the short-term financial deposits were withdrawn from the UK.

In November 1976, a major loan had to be negotiated with the IMF. The resulting rescue package included an insistence on deflationary measures such as higher interest rates. The exchange rate bottomed out at the end of 1976.

The second oil crisis and the rise of monetarism: 1976–81

The measures of late 1976, helped by the growing importance of North Sea oil, caused renewed confidence in sterling. Until autumn 1977, the Bank of England intervened to prevent the exchange rate from rising too much. Vast amounts of sterling were sold, and the foreign exchange acquired was used to build up the reserves and to pay off some of the foreign loans of previous years.

Then, from autumn 1977 to autumn 1981, the pound was allowed to float relatively freely. The result was a massive 30 per cent appreciation of the exchange rate (a 53 per cent appreciation in the PPP rate!) from its low point in 1976. There were four main reasons for this:

- The UK's growing oil surplus. North Sea oil was making an increasing contribution to the current account of the balance of payments.
- The 1979–80 oil crisis. Oil rose in price from $13 to $19 per barrel during 1979 and to $31 during 1980. Since the UK was becoming a major oil exporter, and the pound was now a 'petrocurrency', OPEC surpluses were attracted to London.
- The advent of monetarism. From 1977 the money supply was targeted. When the Thatcher government came to power in 1979, these monetarist policies were more rigorously applied. In order to keep to its monetary targets, the government drove up interest rates, with short-term interest rates reaching over 17 per cent in late 1979. Interest rates remained considerably higher than in competitor countries. But this simply encouraged further financial inflows. The exchange rate had to rise.
- The recession of 1980–2. These highly deflationary monetary policies caused a deep recession. The resulting decline in the demand for imports further contributed to a rising exchange rate.

The huge appreciation of sterling devastated large parts of UK industry. Many exporters simply could not compete, while imports were so cheap that they drove many firms out of business.

Keynesian critics argue that the government should have adopted a less restrictive fiscal and monetary policy. As far as fiscal policy is concerned, they argue that taxation from oil revenues could have been directly invested in infrastructure. Alternatively, significant tax cuts could have been given. As for monetary policy, they argue that the government should have adopted higher monetary targets. This would have kept interest rates down and lowered the exchange rate.

Keynesians argue that these policies would not have been inflationary because North Sea oil gave the UK an increase in *potential* income. A rise in aggregate demand to match this would simply have prevented a deflationary gap from opening.

?

1. *Were there any advantages of the high exchange rate?*
2. *Would there have been a danger of inflation rising if deflationary policies had not been used, even though there was a rise in potential income caused by North Sea oil?*

'Reaganomics' and the US budget deficit: 1981–5

With the election of President Reagan in late 1980, the USA adopted 'Reaganomics'. This had two main features:

- Increasing incentives. The major element in this policy was tax cuts.
- Monetarism. Tight control was to be kept over the growth of the money supply.

His commitment to increasing defence expenditure led to a rapid increase in the overall level of government spending, and the budget deficit increased from $76 billion in 1980 to $212 billion in 1985. The US administration was unwilling to finance the budget deficit by significantly increasing the money supply. The deficit therefore had to be financed largely by borrowing. This pushed interest rates well above those of other countries.

The high interest rates, however, attracted foreign finance to the USA and thus provided a financial account surplus. These financial movements were so large that they caused the dollar to appreciate, despite the current account deficit. This, in turn, worsened the current account deficit.

Other industrialised economies, and especially Japan, experienced the opposite effect. With its lower inflation and lower growth in domestic demand, Japan had a large current account surplus. This was more than offset, however, by a huge outflow of finance, encouraged by low Japanese interest rates. The yen *depreciated* (see Table 24.2).

The high dollar caused grave problems for US exporting industries and industries competing with imports. Large numbers of bankruptcies were suffered in both industry and agriculture. There were growing demands for protectionism, but President Reagan resisted them.

Sterling was particularly vulnerable as many of the OPEC oil revenues deposited in the UK were switched to the USA. As the dollar rose, so the pound fell (see Figure 24.12). Crisis was reached in January/February 1985 with the exchange rate dipping as low as £1 = $1.04 (see Web Case 24.3). This drove the main central banks of the world into concerted action to sell dollars, and the dollar started to fall.

Until early 1985, destabilising speculation had worked to drive the dollar up and other currencies, especially the pound, down. After February 1985, speculation went into reverse. With the dollar now falling, people sold dollars and bought other currencies.

?

1. *Why would the pound not have gone on falling indefinitely?*
2. *Could the UK have done anything to prevent the massive fall in the dollar/pound exchange rate from $2.40 in 1981 to only just above $1.00 in early 1985?*

Mixed fortunes for the pound: 1985–90

After February 1985 sterling at first appreciated. But then, with a falling price of oil (which affected sterling as a petrocurrency) and a more relaxed monetary policy in the run-up to the 1987 election, the pound depreciated again.

Table 24.2 US and Japanese exchange rates: 1980–5 (1980 = 100)

	1980	1981	1982	1983	1984	1985
US effective exchange rate (trade weighted)	100.0	112.7	125.9	133.2	143.7	150.2
Japanese effective exchange rate (trade weighted)	100.0	102.6	91.0	95.1	95.2	95.4

Source: *International Finance Statistics* (IMF).

However, in 1987 the pound began to rise. Oil prices were firmer; inflation had fallen to just over 3 per cent and interest rates were still very high relative to those of other countries. The Chancellor, Nigel Lawson, anxious to avoid repeating the damage to UK industry that was done by the high exchange rate of the early 1980s, was keen to prevent the pound rising. He was also keen to keep the exchange rate pegged as closely as possible to the German mark, hoping to pave the way for the UK joining the ERM (see section 25.2).

But how was he to keep the exchange rate from rising? The answer was to reduce interest rates. Between October 1986 and May 1988 interest rates fell from 11 per cent to $7^1/_2$ per cent. For several months the policy of shadowing the mark seemed to work. The exchange rate was effectively pegged; the economy grew and unemployment fell.

Keeping the exchange rate down through reductions in interest rates, plus a policy of reducing income taxes, was causing the economy to expand rapidly. The current account thus moved rapidly into deficit (see Box 24.1) and inflation began to rise sharply. Between 1985 and 1989 an annual current account surplus of £2.2 billion had been transformed into a deficit of £26.3 billion. In mid-1989, with the current account still deteriorating, the exchange rate began to fall.

The weakness of the pound and worries about rising inflation put growing pressure on the government to join the ERM. After all, the ERM countries had managed to secure much lower average rates of inflation than the UK, and there was a strong desire among the business community to be part of this 'low inflation club'. Eventually, in October 1990, Margaret Thatcher decided to join the ERM and sacrifice the monetary independence she had so long cherished. The era of a floating pound had apparently come to an end.

? *To what extent was there a conflict after 1988 between using interest rates to affect the rate of inflation and using them to maintain a given exchange rate? Explain under what circumstances there was and was not a conflict.*

Sterling in the 1990s

Between October 1990 and September 1992, sterling was in the ERM, at a central rate of £1 = 2.95 German marks, with permitted fluctuations of ±6 per cent against any other ERM currency (we will examine the ERM in section 25.2). As we saw in section 19.6 (page 562), this exchange rate proved unsustainably high and the UK, along with Italy, was forced out of the ERM by a massive wave of speculation. Within two months of this, sterling had depreciated by some 15 per cent.

Since 1992, the UK has adopted a virtually free-floating exchange rate. Between 1992 and 1996, fluctuations in the exchange rate were relatively minor. The government was now targeting inflation, and with inflation coming down, it was at first able to reduce interest rates. But this mirrored reductions in inflation and interest rates in other countries, and thus there was little need for exchange rate changes.

By the beginning of 1996, however, speculators began buying pounds, believing that the exchange rate would appreciate. They saw that the economy was now beginning to grow quite rapidly, and was likely to continue doing so, given that an election was coming up. Inflation was thus likely to rise and this would force the government to raise interest rates. Indeed, by mid-1996 interest rates bottomed out. When the new Labour government was elected in 1997 and the Bank of England was made independent, the Bank raised interest rates several times in order to bring inflation down to the target level. The effect was a large-scale appreciation of sterling. Between January 1996 and April 1998, the exchange rate index rose by 26 per cent, and with inflation still above the trade weighted average of the UK's trading partners, the real exchange rate index rose by a massive 34 per cent (see Figure 24.3). This clearly made it very difficult for UK exporters and industries competing with imports.

Since 1998, the pound has been well above its purchasing-power parity rate. This has been largely the result of UK interest rates being higher that eurozone rates. This has continued to put both the export and import competing sectors in the UK under great competitive pressure. The current account has remained in deficit.

With the high level of the exchange rate, and a high degree of volatility too, it is not surprising that large portions of the business community are anxious for the UK to adopt the euro. We shall be looking at the euro in the next chapter.

The volatility of exchange rates

Exchange rates have become extremely volatile. Currencies can gain or lose several percentage points in the space of a few days. These changes can then make all the difference between profit and loss for trading companies. There are a number of reasons for this volatility:

- Money supply or inflation targets. Central banks may have to make considerable changes to interest rates in order to keep to their targets. These in turn cause exchange rate fluctuations.
- A huge growth in international financial markets. This has encouraged the international transfer of money and capital.
- The abolition of exchange controls in most industrialised countries.
- The growth in information technology. The simple use of a computer can transfer capital and finance internationally in a matter of seconds.
- The preference for liquidity. With the danger of currency fluctuations, companies prefer to keep their financial capital as liquid as possible. They do not want to be locked into assets denominated in a declining currency.
- The growing speculative activities of trading companies. Many large companies have a team of dealers to help manage their liquid assets: to switch them from currency to currency in order to take advantage of market movements.
- The growing speculative activities of banks and other financial institutions.
- The growing belief that rumour and 'jumping on the bandwagon' are more important determinants of currency buying or selling than cool long-term appraisal. If people *believe* that speculation is likely to be destabilising, their actions will ensure that it is. Many companies involved in international trade and finance have developed a 'speculative mentality'.
- The growing belief that governments are powerless to prevent currency movements. As short-term capital (or 'hot money') grows relative to official reserves, it is increasingly difficult for central banks to stabilise currencies through exchange market intervention.

Although most governments and firms dislike highly volatile exchange rates, few today advocate a return to fixed exchange rates, or a Bretton Woods type system. Nevertheless, suggestions have been made for reducing volatility. We examine some of these in Chapter 25.

Section summary

1. Under the Bretton Woods system (1945–71), currencies were pegged to the US dollar. The rate was supported from countries' reserves and if necessary with loans from the IMF. If there was a moderate disequilibrium, countries were supposed to use deflationary/reflationary policies. If the disequilibrium became severe, they were supposed to devalue/revalue.
2. The system was claimed to bring certainty for business and a constraint on governments pursuing irresponsible fiscal and monetary policies, while avoiding the problem of a recession if a balance of payments deficit became severe.
3. However, it was sometimes difficult to identify whether a deficit was severe enough to warrant a devaluation; a devaluation itself could be very disruptive for firms; and devaluation at first could make the deficit worse (the J-curve effect). If a country was reluctant to devalue, it would have to rely on deflation and a possible recession to tackle a balance of payments deficit.
4. Problems for deficit countries were made worse by an unwillingness of surplus countries to revalue or reflate.
5. Dollars were the main source of international liquidity under the Bretton Woods system. The USA, by creating dollars to pay for balance of payments deficits, caused excessive liquidity. This caused worldwide inflation, a lack of confidence in the USA and an eventual collapse of the system.
6. Since the early 1970s the world has largely been on a managed floating exchange rate system. The degree of intervention varies from country to country and from time to time.
7. In theory, managed floating can give the necessary degree of exchange rate flexibility in a world where shifts in currency demand and supply have become much larger. It can also release domestic policy from being dominated by balance of payments considerations. At the same time, the intervention could (in theory) prevent violent exchange rate fluctuations and allow a more orderly adjustment to new equilibrium exchange rates.
8. Nevertheless, there are problems under managed floating of predicting long-term equilibrium exchange rates. What is more, with the massive growth in 'hot money' since the early 1970s, it has become increasingly difficult for countries on their own to counteract speculation. The main instrument of intervention has become the rate of interest. There may be a conflict, however, in using interest rates both to control exchange rates *and* to control the domestic economy.
9. Sterling exchange rates have shown considerable volatility over the years, with large divergences from the purchasing-power parity rate. For example, the rise in UK interest rates in 1997–8 caused a large appreciation of sterling, much to the consternation of exporters.
10. The volatility of exchange rates around the world has tended to grow. There are many reasons for this, including a growth in international financial markets and a liberalisation of international financial movements combined with easier computer transfer of funds, a growth in speculative activities and a growing belief in the impotence of governments acting on their own to stabilise rates.

*APPENDIX: THE OPEN ECONOMY AND *ISLM* ANALYSIS

In this appendix, we show how the *ISLM* analysis that we examined in section 19.3 can be extended to incorporate the open economy. We will first assume a fixed rate of exchange and then later a free-floating rate.

Analysis under a fixed exchange rate

The BP curve

We start by introducing a third curve, the *BP* (balance of payments) curve. This curve, like the *IS* and *LM* curves, plots a relationship between the rate of interest (r) and the level of national income (Y). All points along the *BP* curve represent a position of *balance of payments equilibrium*.

The curve slopes upwards from left to right (see Figure 24.13). Increases in the rate of interest (r) will cause the financial account to move into surplus as finance is attracted into the country. Increases in national income (Y), in contrast, will cause the current account to move into deficit as more imports are purchased. If the overall balance of payments is to stay in equilibrium, current account deficits must be matched by financial (plus capital) account surpluses and vice versa. Thus a rise in Y must be accompanied by a rise in r, and reductions in Y must be accompanied by reductions in r. The *BP* curve therefore slopes upwards. Any point below the *BP* line represents a position of overall deficit; any point above the line, a position of surplus.

The slope of the *BP* curve depends on two factors.

The marginal propensity to import (mpm = $\Delta M/\Delta Y$). The higher the *mpm*, the steeper will be the *BP* curve. The reason is that with a high *mpm* there will be a correspondingly large rise in imports for any given rise in national income. This will cause a large current account deficit. To maintain an overall balance of payments equilibrium, this will require a correspondingly large financial account surplus. This in turn will require a large rise in interest rates. Thus the bigger the *mpm*, the larger the rise in interest rates that will be necessary to restore balance of payments equilibrium, and hence the steeper will be the *BP* curve.

The elasticity of supply of international finance. The greater the elasticity of supply of international finance, the less will be the rise in interest rates necessary to attract an inflow of finance and thereby restore balance of payments equilibrium after a rise in national income, and hence the flatter will be the *BP* curve. In the case of a perfectly elastic supply of international finance, the *BP* curve will be horizontal at the world rate of interest.

KI 9 p58

Equilibrium in the model

If we now put the *BP* curve on an *ISLM* diagram, we have the position shown in Figure 24.14. Point *a* represents full equilibrium. At r_1 and Y_1, investment equals saving (point *a* is on the *IS* curve), the demand for money equals the supply (point *a* is also on the *LM* curve), and finally the balance of payments is in balance (point *a* is also on the *BP* curve).

KI 8 p43

But what is the mechanism that ensures that all three curves intersect at the same point? To answer this question, let us assume that the three curves just happen to intersect at the same point, and then let us examine the effects of changes in fiscal and monetary policies, which shift the *IS* and *LM* curves respectively. Will equilibrium be restored? The answer is yes, via a change in the money supply. Let us examine fiscal and monetary policy changes in turn.

Fiscal policy under fixed exchange rates

An expansionary fiscal policy, i.e. a rise in government spending and/or a reduction in tax, will have the effect of shifting the *IS* curve to the right (e.g. to IS_2 in Figure 24.15).

Figure 24.13 The *BP* curve

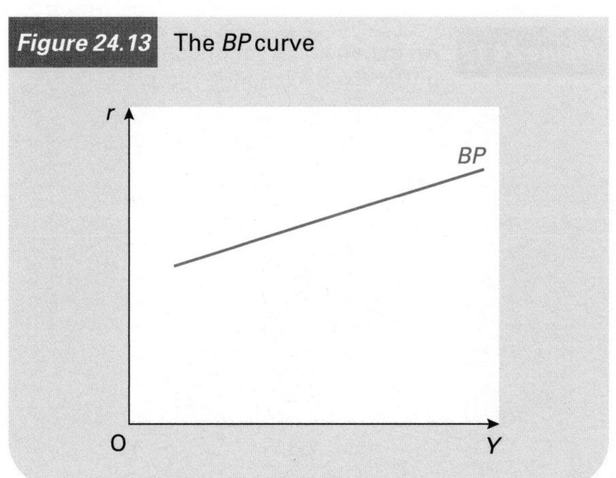

Figure 24.14 Full equilibrium in the goods, money and foreign exchange markets

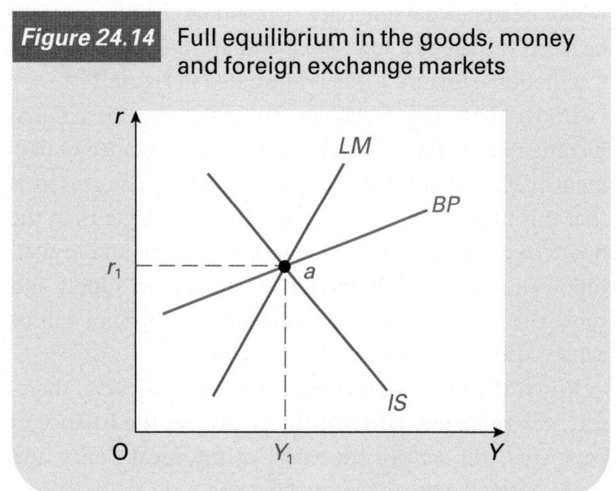

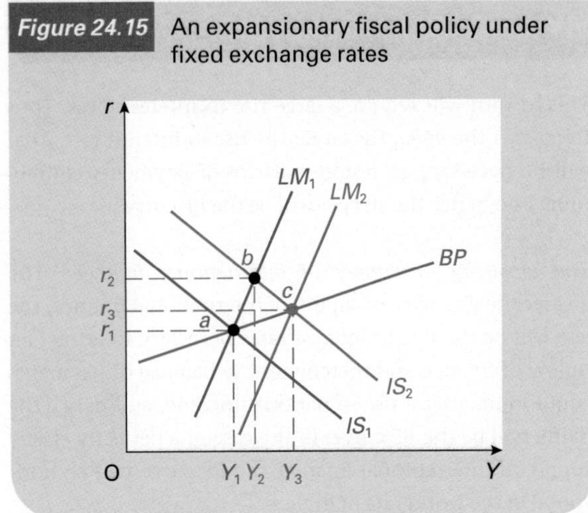

Figure 24.15 An expansionary fiscal policy under fixed exchange rates

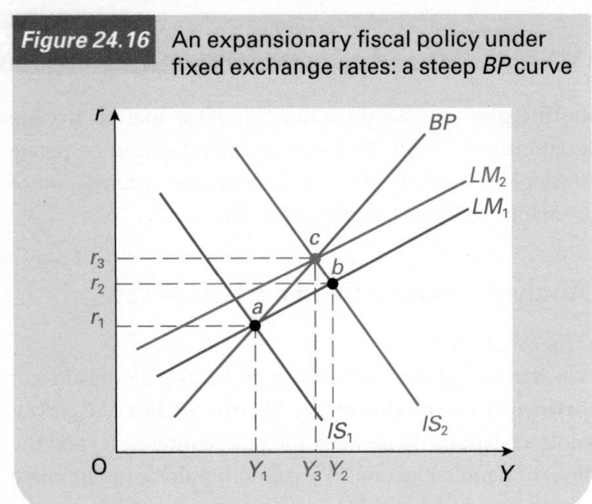

Figure 24.16 An expansionary fiscal policy under fixed exchange rates: a steep *BP* curve

The reason is that for any given rate of interest there will be a higher equilibrium level of national income than before.

This will increase national income, but the extra demand for money that results will drive up interest rates. In a *closed* economy, equilibrium would now be at point *b* (r_2, Y_2), where $IS_2 = LM_1$. But in our open economy model, this equilibrium is *above the BP curve*. There is a balance of payments surplus. The reason for this is that the higher interest rates have caused a financial account surplus that is bigger than the current account deficit that results from the higher national income.

Such a surplus will cause the money supply to rise as funds flow into the country. This will in turn cause the *LM* curve to shift to the right. Equilibrium will finally be achieved at point *c* (r_3, Y_3), where $IS_2 = LM_2 = BP$. Thus under these conditions, the monetary effect of the change in the balance of payments will *reinforce* the fiscal policy and lead to a bigger rise in national income.

What will be the effect of an expansionary fiscal policy on interest rates and national income if there is a perfectly elastic supply of international finance?

TC 8 p59 If the *BP* curve were steeper than the *LM* curve, the effect would be somewhat different. (Remember the *BP* curve will be steep if there is a high *mpm* and an inelastic supply of international finance.) This is illustrated in Figure 24.16.

Under these circumstances, an initial rise in national income to Y_2 (where $IS_2 = LM_1$) will cause a balance of payments *deficit* (point *b* is *below the BP curve*). The reason is that this time the current account deficit is bigger than the financial account surplus (due to a large *mpm* and a small inflow of finance). This will reduce the money supply and cause the *LM* curve to shift to the left. Equilibrium will be achieved at point *c*, where $LM_2 = IS_2 = BP$.

When the *BP* curve is steeper than the *LM* curve, therefore, the monetary effect of the change in the balance of payments will *dampen* the effect of the fiscal policy and lead to a smaller rise in national income.

Monetary policy under fixed exchange rates

An expansionary monetary policy will cause the *LM* curve to shift to the right (e.g. to LM_2 in Figure 24.17). The increased supply of money will drive down the rate of interest and increase national income. In a closed economy, equilibrium would now be at point *b* (r_2, Y_2), where $LM_2 = IS$. But in an open economy, this extra demand will have sucked in extra imports, and the lower interest rate will have led to net financial outflows. There will be a balance of payments deficit: point *b* is below the *BP* curve.

The balance of payments deficit will cause the money stock to fall as money flows abroad. This will cause the *LM* curve to shift back again to its original position. The economy will return to its initial equilibrium at point *a*.

Thus under a fixed exchange rate regime, monetary policy alone will have *no long-term effect* on national income and employment. Only when accompanied by an expansion in aggregate demand (either through fiscal policy or through an autonomous rise in investment or a fall in

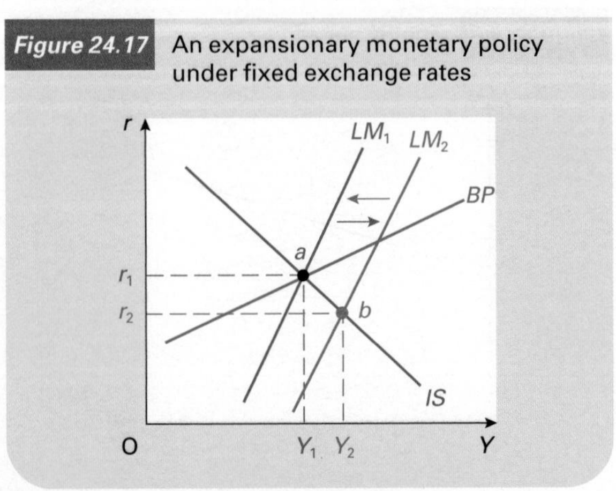

Figure 24.17 An expansionary monetary policy under fixed exchange rates

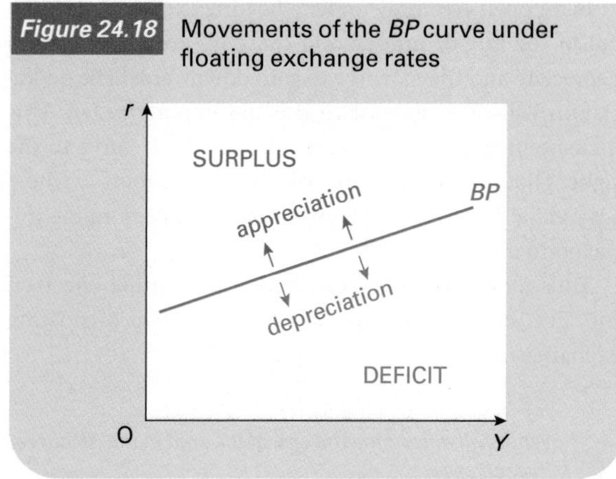

Figure 24.18 Movements of the *BP* curve under floating exchange rates

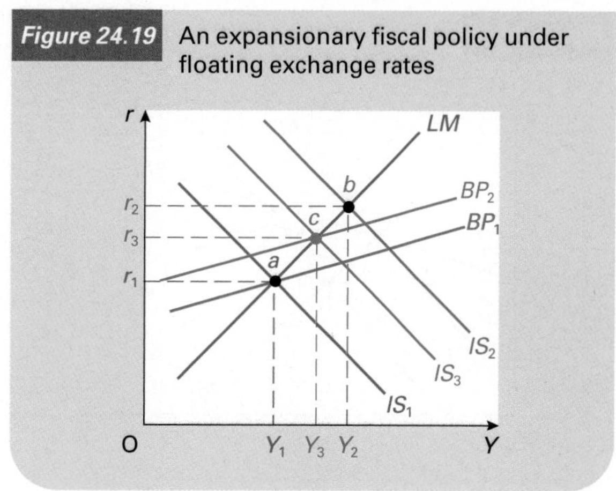

Figure 24.19 An expansionary fiscal policy under floating exchange rates

savings) will an expansion of money supply lead to higher national income.

> ?
> 1. *Why does this conclusion remain the same if the BP curve is steeper than the LM curve?*
> 2. *Trace through the effects of a fall in exports (thereby shifting the BP curve).*
> 3. *Show what will happen if there is (a) a rise in business confidence and a resulting increase in investment; (b) a rise in the demand for money balance (say, for precautionary purposes).*

Analysis under free-floating exchange rates

As the exchange rate changes, the *BP* curve will shift (see Figure 24.18). If the *IS* and *LM* curves intersect *above* the *BP* curve, there will be a balance of payments surplus. This will cause the exchange rate to appreciate. The appreciation will cause the surplus to disappear. This in turn will cause the *BP* curve to shift upwards.

Similarly, if the *IS* and *LM* curves intersect *below* the *BP* curve, the resulting balance of payments deficit will cause a depreciation and a downward shift of the *BP* curve. Thus the *BP* curve will always shift so that it intersects where the *IS* and *LM* curves intersect.

Fiscal policy under floating exchange rates

Assume that the government pursues a reflationary fiscal policy. The *IS* curve shifts to IS_2 in Figure 24.19.

At point *b*, where the *LM* curve and the new *IS* curve intersect, there is a balance of payments surplus (due to higher financial inflows attracted by the higher rate of interest). This causes the exchange rate to appreciate and the *BP* curve to shift upwards.

But the higher exchange rate will cause a fall in exports and a rise in imports. This fall in aggregate demand will cause the *IS* curve to shift back towards the left. The new equilibrium will be at a point such as *c*. This represents only a modest change from point *a*. Thus under a floating exchange rate the effects of fiscal policy may be rather limited.

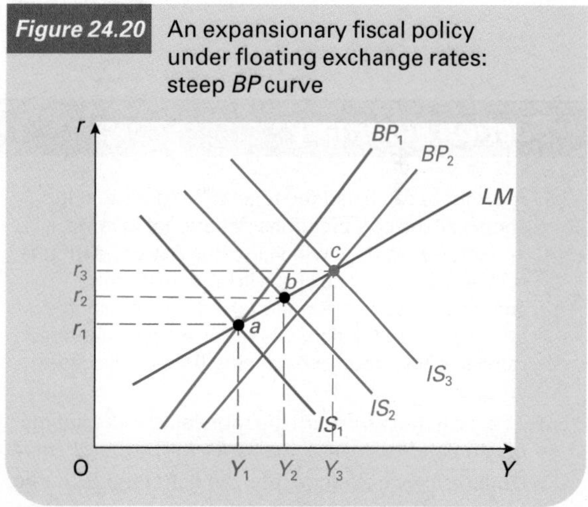

Figure 24.20 An expansionary fiscal policy under floating exchange rates: steep *BP* curve

The effect will be stronger, however, the steeper the *BP* curve. In Figure 24.20, the *BP* curve is steeper than the *LM* curve. This time a rise in the *IS* curve from IS_1 to IS_2 will lead to a balance of payments *deficit* and hence a *depreciation* of the exchange rate. The *BP* curve will shift *downwards*. The depreciation will cause a rise in exports and a fall in imports. This *rise* in aggregate demand will cause the *IS* curve to shift to the *right*. The new equilibrium will be at point *c*, which is at a higher level of national income, Y_3. Under these circumstances, the balance of payments effect makes fiscal policy stronger.

> ?
> *Under what circumstances would an expansionary fiscal policy have* no effect at all *on national income?*

Monetary policy under floating exchange rates

An expansionary monetary policy will shift the *LM* curve to the right, to LM_2 in Figure 24.21. In a closed economy, equilibrium would now be at point *b*.

Figure 24.21 An expansionary monetary policy under floating exchange rates

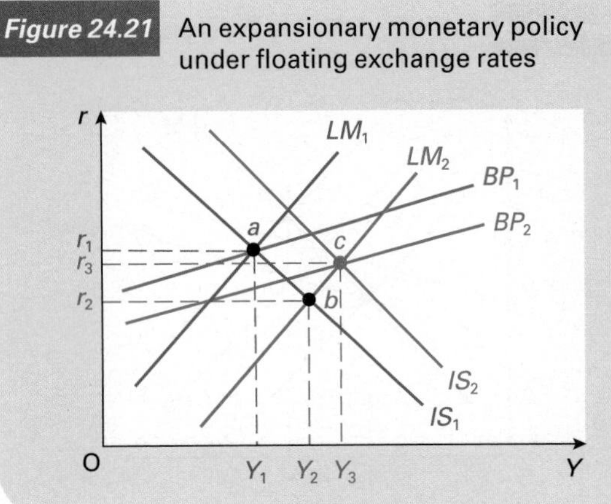

In an open economy under a floating exchange rate, the fall in the rate of interest will cause the exchange rate to depreciate and the *BP* curve to shift downwards. The depreciation will cause exports to rise and imports to fall. This increase in aggregate demand will shift the *IS* curve to the right. The new equilibrium will thus be at point *c*, where $LM_2 = IS_2 = BP_2$. This represents a large change from the initial point *a*.

Thus monetary policy can have a substantial effect on the level of national income under a system of floating exchange rates.

? *What will determine the size of the shift in the BP curve in each case?*

Section summary

1. A *BP* curve can be added to an *ISLM* diagram. It shows all the combinations of national income and interest rates at which the balance of payments is in equilibrium. The curve is upward sloping, showing that a rise in national income (causing a current account deficit) will require a rise in interest rates to give a counterbalancing financial account surplus.
2. The lower the *mpm* and the more elastic the supply of international finance, the flatter will be the *BP* curve.
3. Under a fixed exchange rate, the flatter the *BP* curve, the larger will be the effect on national income of an expansionary fiscal policy. Provided the *BP* curve is flatter than the *LM* curve, an expansionary fiscal policy will cause a balance of payments surplus (via its effect of increasing interest rates). The resulting increase in money supply will strengthen the initial effect of the fiscal policy.
4. Monetary policy under fixed exchange rates will have no effect on national income. Any expansion of money supply will, by depressing interest rates, simply lead to a balance of payments deficit and thus a reduction in the money supply again.
5. Under a floating exchange rate an appreciation will shift the *BP* curve upwards and a depreciation will shift it downwards.
6. If the *BP* curve is flatter than the *LM* curve, fiscal policy under a floating exchange rate will be dampened by the resulting changes in the exchange rate. An expansionary fiscal policy will lead to an appreciation (due to the effects of higher interest rates), which in turn will dampen the rise in aggregate demand.
7. Monetary policy will have a relatively large effect on aggregate demand under floating rates. A rise in money supply will reduce interest rates and raise aggregate demand. This will cause a balance of payments deficit and thus a depreciation. This in turn will lead to a further expansion of aggregate demand.

END OF CHAPTER QUESTIONS

1. Assume a free-floating exchange rate. Draw a diagram like Figure 24.6 (on page 675), only this time show an initial equilibrium national income with a balance of payments surplus.
   (a) Mark the size of the surplus.
   (b) Show the resulting shifts in the $(X - M)$ and the E curves.
   (c) Mark the eventual equilibrium.
   (d) Show the size of the income and substitution effects (of the change in the exchange rate).
   (e) Under what circumstances will the income effect be (i) 'desirable'; (ii) 'undesirable'?
   (f) Could the income effect of the change in the exchange rate ever be larger than the substitution effect?
2. Compare the relative effectiveness of fiscal and monetary policy under (a) fixed; (b) free-floating exchange rates. How is the effectiveness influenced by the elasticity of supply of international finance?
3. What will be the effects on the domestic economy under free-floating exchange rates if there is a rapid expansion in world economic activity? What will determine the size of these effects?
4. For what reasons might the exchange rate diverge from the purchasing-power parity rate over the longer term?
5. Why does exchange rate overshooting occur? What determines its magnitude?
6. Consider the argument that in the modern world of large-scale, short-term international capital movements, the ability of individual countries to affect their exchange rate is very limited.
7. If speculators had better information about future exchange rates, would their actions be more or less stabilising than at present?

*8. Using *ISLMBP* analysis, trace through the effect of (a) a deflationary fiscal policy and (b) a deflationary monetary policy under (i) a fixed exchange rate; (ii) a free-floating exchange rate.

Additional case studies on the book's website (www.pearsoned.co.uk/sloman)

24.1 The Marshall–Lerner condition. An analysis of the determinants of the elasticities of demand and supply of a currency.

24.2 The gold standard. A historical example of fixed exchange rates.

24.3 The sterling crisis of early 1985. When the pound fell almost to $1.00.

24.4 Currency turmoil in the 1990s. Two examples of speculative attacks on currencies: first on the Mexican peso in 1995; then on the Thai baht in 1997.

24.5 The euro, the US dollar and world currency markets. An analysis of the relationship between the euro and the dollar.

24.6 Argentina in crisis. The collapse of the Argentinian peso in 2001/2.

WEBSITES RELEVANT TO THIS CHAPTER

See sites listed at the end of Chapter 25 on page 719.

Chapter 25

Global and Regional Interdependence

One of the major causes of currency fluctuations is the very different conditions existing in different countries and the different policies they pursue. For example, an expansionary fiscal policy plus a tight monetary policy can lead to huge currency appreciation if other countries do not follow suit. This is what happened to the dollar in 1983 and 1984. Conversely, a persistent current account deficit, plus a policy of interest rate reductions in order to stimulate the economy, can lead to large-scale currency depreciation. This happened to sterling after it left the ERM in 1992.

Changes in exchange rates that result from such imbalances are then often amplified by speculation. And this problem is becoming worse. As we have seen, approximately $2 trillion per day passes across the foreign exchange markets. The scale of such movements makes any significant speculation simply too great for individual countries to resist. And on some occasions even the concerted action of groups of countries cannot maintain exchange rate stability.

In the first section, we explore the nature of the interdependence of economies and why countries are so vulnerable to international fluctuations. We then look at what can be done to create a greater co-ordination of international economic policies and consider the role of the G7 countries in this process.

The extreme solution to currency instability is for countries to adopt a common currency. In section 25.3, we look at the euro and how economic and monetary union (EMU) operates. The chapter finishes by looking at some alternative suggestions for reducing currency fluctuations.

CHAPTER MAP

25.1 GLOBALISATION AND THE PROBLEM OF INSTABILITY

We live in an interdependent world. Countries are affected by the economic health of other countries and by their governments' policies. Problems in one part of the world can spread like a contagion to other parts, with perhaps no country immune.

There are two major ways in which this process of 'globalisation' affects individual economies. The first is through trade. The second is through financial markets.

Interdependence through trade

So long as nations trade with one another, the domestic economic actions of one nation will have implications for those which trade with it. For example, if the US administration feels that the US economy is growing too fast, it might adopt various deflationary fiscal and monetary measures, such as higher tax rates or interest rates. US consumers will not only consume fewer domestically produced goods, but also reduce their consumption of imported products. But US imports are other countries' exports. A fall in these other countries' exports will lead to a multiplier effect in these countries. Output and employment will fall.

TC 15 p463

Changes in aggregate demand in one country thus send ripples throughout the global economy. The process whereby changes in imports into (or exports from) one country affect national income in other countries is known as the ***international trade multiplier***.

Assume that the US economy expands. What will determine the size of the multiplier effect on other countries?

The more open an economy, the more vulnerable it will be to changes in the level of economic activity in the rest of the world. This problem will be particularly acute if a nation is heavily dependent on trade with one other nation (e.g. Canada on the USA) or one other region (e.g. Switzerland on the EU).

International trade has been growing as a proportion of countries' national income for many years. This is illustrated in Figure 25.1, which shows the growth in world real exports and in real GDP. You can see that exports have been growing much more rapidly than GDP. From 1948 to 2002 the average annual growth in world output was 3.6 per cent, whereas the figure for world exports was 6.0 per cent. With most nations committed to freer trade, and with the WTO overseeing the dismantling of trade barriers, so international trade is likely to continue growing as a proportion of world GDP. This will increase countries'

> **Definition**
>
> **International trade multiplier** The effect on national income in country B of a change in exports (or imports) of country A.

Figure 25.1 Growth in world real GDP and world merchandise exports (volume)

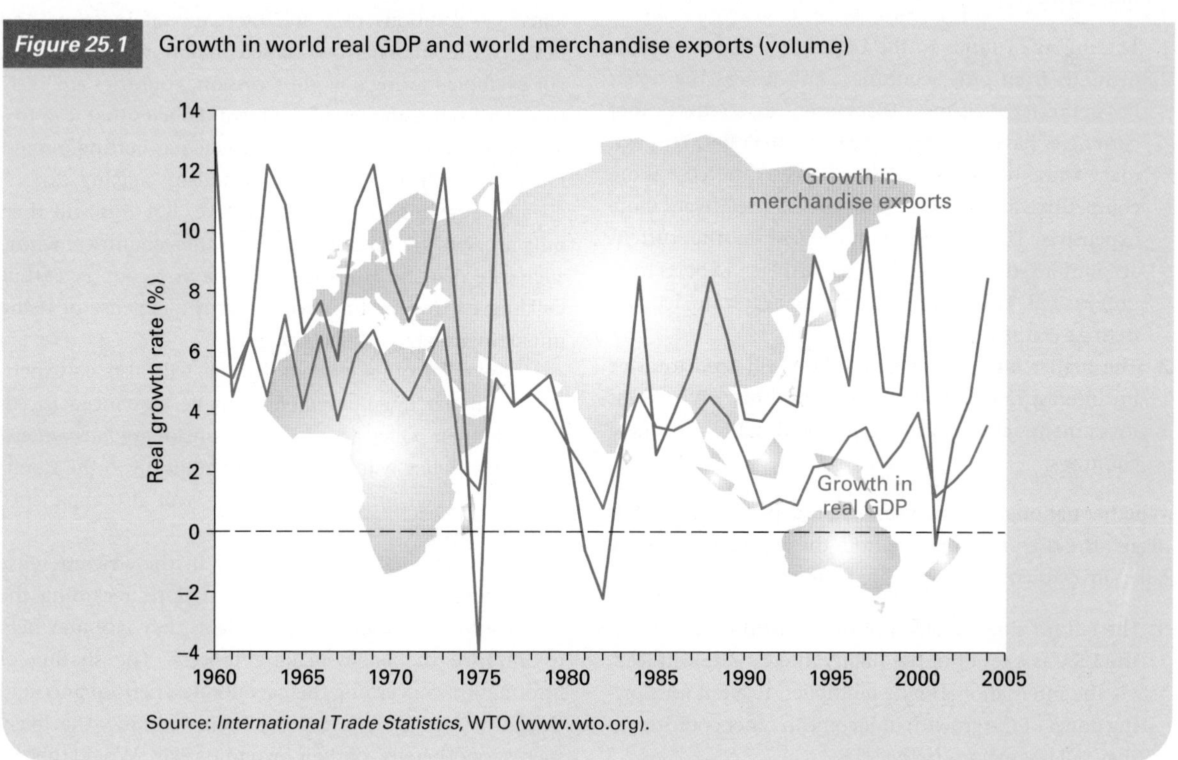

Source: *International Trade Statistics*, WTO (www.wto.org).

KI 31 p368 interdependence and their vulnerability to world trade fluctuations.

? *Are exports likely to continue growing faster than GDP indefinitely? What will determine the outcome?*

Financial interdependence

International trade has grown rapidly over the last 30 years, but international financial flows have grown much more rapidly. The value of banks' holdings of liabilities to foreign residents (individuals and institutions) has been increasing by an average of some 15 per cent per year over the past 30 years. The value of cross-border transactions in bonds and equities has increased by nearly 30 per cent per year over the same period. Even after taking inflation into account, this is still a very large real rate of increase.

Each day, some \$2 trillion of assets are traded across the foreign exchanges. Many of the transactions are short-term financial flows, moving to where interest rates are most favourable or to currencies where the exchange rate is likely to appreciate. This again makes countries interdependent.

Assume that the Federal Reserve Bank in the USA, worried about rising inflation, decides to raise interest rates. These higher interest rates will attract an inflow of funds from other countries. This will cause the dollar to appreciate. Knowing that this will happen, speculators will seek to buy dollars quickly before the exchange rate has finished appreciating. They may well buy dollars *before* the Fed raises interest rates, in anticipation that it will do so.

There will be three major effects of this on America's trading partners.

1. The inflow of funds to the USA represents an outflow of funds from other countries. And just as the dollar has appreciated against other currencies, so these other currencies have depreciated against the dollar. This will make these other countries' exports to the USA more competitive and imports from the USA relatively more expensive. There is an improvement in the current account of the USA's trading partners. Exports rise; imports fall. This represents a rise in aggregate demand in these countries.
2. The higher interest rate in the USA will tend to drive up interest rates in other countries. This will depress investment, and hence aggregate demand, in these countries.

Whether national income rises or falls depends on which is bigger: the rise in net exports from the depreciation or the fall in investment from the higher interest rates.

3. The fall (or slowing down of the growth) in income in the USA as a result of the higher interest rate will lead, via the international trade multiplier, to a fall (or slowing down of the growth) in income in other countries as they sell less exports to the USA.

There is a simple conclusion from the above analysis. The larger the financial flows, the more will interest rate changes in one country affect the economies of other countries: the greater will be the financial interdependence.

What will be the effect on the UK economy if the European Central Bank cuts interest rates?

The need for international policy co-ordination

There is an old saying: 'If America sneezes, the rest of the world catches a cold.' Viruses of a similar nature regularly infect the world economy. A dramatic example in recent years was the 'Asian contagion' of 1997–8. Economic crises spread rapidly round south-east and east Asia, then to Russia and then to Brazil (see Web Case 25.3). World leaders were seriously worried that the whole world would plunge into recession. What was needed was a co-ordinated policy response.

International business cycles

As a consequence of both trade and financial interdependence, the world economy, like the economy of any individual country, tends to experience periodic fluctuations in economic activity – an *international* business cycle. The implication of this is that countries will tend to share common problems and concerns at the same time. At one time, the most pressing problem may be world inflationary pressures; at another time, it may be a world recession. TC 13 p381

In order to avoid 'beggar-my-neighbour' policies, it is better to seek *common* solutions to these common problems: i.e. solutions that are international in scope and design rather than narrowly based on national self-interest. For example, during a world recession, countries are likely to suffer from rising unemployment. Policies that lead to a depreciation of the exchange rate (such as cutting interest rates) will help to stimulate demand by making exports cheaper and imports more expensive. But this will then only worsen the trade balance of other countries, whose aggregate demand will thus fall. The first country is thus tackling its own unemployment at the expense of rising unemployment in other countries.

However, if other nations (which will also be experiencing higher unemployment) can be convinced to co-ordinate their policy actions, an expansionary *international* economic policy will benefit all. In addition to the resulting rise in their imports, all nations will also experience rising export sales.

Even if national policies are not in the strictest sense co-ordinated, discussions between nations regarding the nature and magnitude of the problems they face may help to improve the policy-making process. The sharing of information concerning their economies' performance and their intended actions enables them to assess the likely success or otherwise of their own initiatives. Would they be

CASE STUDIES AND APPLICATIONS **BOX 25.1**

GLOBALISATION AND THE US TRADE IMBALANCE

Is the world paying for excessive American expenditure?

The USA has a huge current account deficit. In 2004, it was $666 billion (5.7 per cent of GDP), up from $531 billion (4.8 per cent of GDP) in 2003. The chart shows this deepening deficit since 1991.

The current account deficit is offset by an equal and opposite capital-plus-financial account surplus, much of which consists of the purchase of US government bonds and Treasury bills. These massive inflows to the USA represent some 80 per cent of the savings which the rest of the world invests abroad. These financial inflows have permitted the current account deficit to continue to deepen.

US current account deficits (as % of GDP)

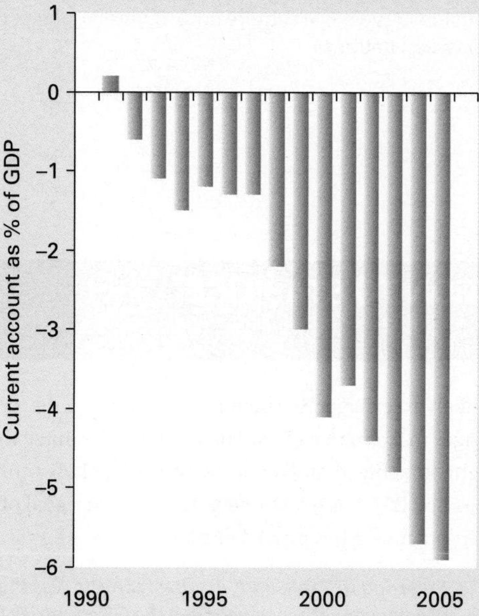

And yet US interest rates have been at historically low levels. Nominal interest rates from mid-2003 to mid-2004 were a mere 1 per cent (see chart in Box 24.4 on page 686) and real rates were −1.3 per cent! How is it, then, that with such low interest rates, the USA could maintain such a large financial account surplus?

An answer in Asia

Several Asian currencies, including the Chinese yuan (or 'renminbi') were pegged to the dollar and had been running large current account surpluses. Instead of letting their currencies appreciate against the dollar, Asian central banks were using their surpluses to buy dollars. These countries saw a triple advantage in this. First, it allowed them to build up reserves and thereby bolster their ability to resist any future speculative attacks on their currencies. Second, and more important, it kept their exchange rates low and thereby helped to keep their exports competitive. This helped to sustain their rapid rates of economic growth. Third, it helped to keep US interest rates down and therefore boost US spending on Asian exports.

From 2001 to 2005, Asian dollar reserves rose by $1.6 trillion. This accounted for nearly 70 per cent of the US current account deficit over the period. What is more, the annual rate of increase in these reserves from 2003 to 2005 was over 20 per cent. The effect was a huge increase in global liquidity and hence money supply.

Consequences of the imbalance

Can the USA simply continue with a massive current account deficit, financed by the acquisition of equally huge amounts of dollars by the rest of the world, and Asia in particular? Or must there be a correction of the current account imbalance?

A depreciation of the dollar. From mid-2004, US interest rates began to rise – but not fast enough to prevent the dollar's slide on the foreign exchange market. This depreciation did, however, help to arrest further deterioration in the current account.

Many commentators, however, have argued that the rate would need to fall another 20 to 30 per cent if the deficit was to be reduced to a sustainable size without injecting excessive liquidity into the world economy. This would mean an exchange rate of around $1.70 to the euro and $2.45 to the pound, which would have devastating effects on European exports and make sustained European recovery much more difficult.

The problem for the USA is not just on the current account. Inward investment slowed rapidly from 2001 to 2004. The current account deficit could only be financed, therefore, from overseas central bank purchases of dollars and by short-term inflows to the USA encouraged by higher interest rates. This simply made the need to reduce the current account deficit all the more pressing.

Overheating in China. A real danger for the Chinese and other Asian economies is that real increases in output may not match the increase in money supply. The result would then be inflation. Indeed, China's concern about the inflationary impact of increased money supply resulted in it raising interest rates in 2004, thereby helping to sterilise some of the currency flow surplus. The worry, however, was whether this would cause the rapid Chinese growth to falter.

Potential currency volatility. Perhaps the biggest long-term danger of the huge increase in international liquidity is the potential for large-scale selling of the dollar and consequent overshooting of the long-term equilibrium exchange rate. The USA would be forced to raise interest rates and this could trigger a recession that spreads around the globe. This would be aggravated by a decline in asset prices, particularly shares and property, which would cut consumer demand, further deepening the recession.

Examine the merits for the Chinese of (a) floating the yuan freely; (b) pegging it to a trade-weighted basket of currencies (a policy it adopted in mid-2005)

pursuing incompatible policy goals? Would the cumulative actions of individual nations cause the global economy to grow too fast? With such knowledge, fluctuations in international economic activity might be more effectively regulated, if not totally removed.

Although co-operation is the ideal, in practice discord often tends to dominate international economic relations. The reason is that governments are normally concerned with the economic interests of other countries only if they coincide with those of their own country. This, however, can create a prisoner's dilemma problem (see page 192). With *all* countries looking solely after their own interests, the world economy suffers and everyone is worse off.

In the next section, we shall consider how international economic policy tends to be conducted in practice.

? *Give some examples of beggar-my-neighbour policies.*

Section summary

1. Changes in aggregate demand in one country will affect the amount of imports purchased and thus the amount of exports sold by other countries and hence their national income. There is thus an international trade multiplier effect.
2. Changes in interest rates in one country will affect financial flows to and from other countries, and hence their exchange rates, interest rates and national income.
3. To prevent problems in one country spilling over to other countries and to stabilise the international business cycle will require co-ordinated policies between nations.

25.2 CONCERTED INTERNATIONAL ACTION TO STABILISE EXCHANGE RATES

International harmonisation of economic policies

The four main underlying causes of exchange rate movements are divergences in *interest rates*, *growth rates*, *inflation rates* and *current account balance of payments*. Table 25.1 shows the variation in the levels of these and other indicators for the seven major industrial countries. Although the divergences between the countries have narrowed somewhat since the early 1990s, they are still considerable.

For many years now, the leaders of these countries have met once a year at an economic summit conference (and more frequently if felt necessary). Top of the agenda in most of these 'Group of Seven' (G7) meetings has been how to generate world economic growth without major currency fluctuations. But to achieve this, it is important that there is a ***harmonisation*** of economic policies between nations. In other words, it is important that all the major countries are pursuing consistent policies aiming at common international goals.

But how can policy harmonisation be achieved? As long as there are significant domestic differences between the major economies, there is likely to be conflict, not harmony. For example, if one country, say the USA, is worried about the size of its budget deficit, it may be unwilling to respond to world demands for a stimulus to aggregate demand to pull the world economy out of recession. What is more, speculators, seeing differences between countries, are likely to exaggerate them by their actions, causing large changes in exchange rates. The G7 countries have therefore sought to achieve greater ***convergence*** of their economies. But as Box 25.2 shows, convergence may be a goal of policy, but in practice it has proved elusive.

? *Referring to Table 25.1, in what respects was there greater convergence between the G7 countries in the period 2001–5 than in the period 1996–2000?*

Because of a lack of convergence, there are serious difficulties in achieving international policy harmonisation:

- Countries' budget deficits and national debt may differ substantially as a proportion of their national income. This puts very different pressures on the interest rates necessary to service these debts.
- Harmonising rates of monetary growth or inflation targets would involve letting interest rates fluctuate with the demand for money. Without convergence in the

Definitions

International harmonisation of economic policies Where countries attempt to co-ordinate their macroeconomic policies so as to achieve common goals.

Convergence of economies When countries achieve similar levels of growth, inflation, budget deficits as a percentage of GDP, balance of payments, etc.

Table 25.1 Average annual difference between highest and lowest values of the G7 countries for various macroeconomic indicators

	1991–5	1996–2000	2001–5
Economic growth (% change in real GDP)	3.5	3.8	2.8
Output gap (%)	4.3	3.3	3.4
Unemployment (%)	8.5	7.4	4.6
Inflation (CPI) (%)	4.1	2.6	3.1
Short-term nominal interest rate (%)	7.9	6.5	4.5
Current account (% of GDP)	5.6	5.3	8.1
General government borrowing (% of GDP)	8.9	7.0	7.8
General government gross debt (% of GDP)	84	82	114
Effective exchange rate[a]	111	34	44

[a] Largest % relative appreciation of one currency against another over the five-year period.

Source: based on data in *Economic Outlook* (OECD).

demand for money, interest rate fluctuations could be severe.

- Harmonising interest rates would involve abandoning monetary, inflation and exchange rate targets (unless interest rate 'harmonisation' meant adjusting interest rates so as to maintain monetary or inflation targets or a fixed exchange rate).
- Countries have different internal structural relationships. A lack of convergence here means that countries with higher endemic *cost* inflation would require higher interest rates and higher unemployment if international inflation rates were to be harmonised, or higher inflation if interest rates were to be harmonised.
- Countries have different rates of productivity increase, product development, investment and market penetration. A lack of convergence here means that the growth in exports (relative to imports) will differ for any given level of inflation or growth.
- Countries may be very unwilling to change their domestic policies to fall in line with other countries. They may prefer the other countries to fall in line with them!

If any one of the four – interest rates, growth rates, inflation rates or current account balance of payments – could be harmonised across countries, it is likely that the other three would then not be harmonised.

Total convergence and thus total harmonisation may not be possible. Nevertheless most governments favour some movement in that direction: some is better than none.

? *If total convergence were achieved, would harmonisation of policies follow automatically?*

Greater exchange rate rigidity between groups of currencies: the European Monetary System

One means of achieving greater currency stability is for countries to group together into blocs, and to peg their exchange rates to each other, while floating against the rest of the world. This will have two potential advantages:

- Trade will be encouraged between the members of the bloc. The greater the harmonisation of policies within the bloc, and therefore the less frequent any adjustments of the pegged rates, the more will trade be encouraged.
- The combined reserves of all countries in the bloc can be used to prevent excessive fluctuations of the bloc's currencies with the rest of the world.

The *exchange rate mechanism* (ERM) of the *European Monetary System* (EMS) was an example of such an arrangement. The EMS came into existence in March 1979. Its aim was to create currency stability, monetary co-operation and the convergence of economic policies of the European Community (EC) countries. The ERM involved participants pegging their exchange rate to each other within bands, and jointly floating with the rest of the world.

Although the UK became a formal member of the EMS, it chose not to join the exchange rate mechanism. Spain joined the ERM in 1989. The UK eventually joined in 1990. Portugal joined in April 1992.

Then in September 1992, the UK and Italy indefinitely suspended their membership of the ERM, but Italy rejoined in November 1996 as part of its bid to join the single European currency (see section 25.3). Austria joined in 1995, Finland in 1996 and Greece in 1998. By the time the ERM was replaced by the single currency in 1999, only Sweden and the UK were outside the ERM.

The features of the ERM

Under the system, each currency was given a central exchange rate with each of the other ERM currencies in a grid. However, fluctuations were allowed from the central rate within specified bands. For most countries these bands were set at $\pm 2^1/_4$ per cent. The central rates could be adjusted from time to time by agreement, thus making the

CASE STUDIES AND APPLICATIONS **BOX 25.2**

'SEVEN MEN IN A BOAT'

Attempts at harmonisation

In recent years, governments of the major industrial nations have tried to come to terms with the ever-growing interdependence of their economies. Economic disruptions in one country (e.g. a worsening US budget or current account deficit or a unilateral decision by, say, the ECB or Japan to raise interest rates) can have profound effects on the world economy.

G7 meetings

As a result of the potentially highly unstable nature of economic relationships, finance ministers and heads of state of the *Group of Seven* (G7) countries – Canada, France, Germany, Italy, Japan, the UK and the USA (and more recently Russia, making it the G8) – have met on a regular basis to try to harmonise their policies. But the key problem in this has been the nations' overriding self-interest.

Problems with G7 agreements

There are two major problems with G7 agreements. The first is that they are not binding. If governments are not prepared to give up national sovereignty and submit to international control, they are always likely to put purely national interests first. For example, the USA may unilaterally cut interest rates in order to tackle domestic unemployment, or raise them to tackle inflation. Large and disruptive financial flows can result from such interest rate changes and there can be significant effects on exchange rates. In such cases, the rest of the world may suffer and countries may be forced to adjust their own interest rates.

Thus whilst G7 ministers may say 'the right things', in practice they may do little to implement their recommendations. For example, in the communiqué from the April 2005 meeting, ministers stated that vigorous action was needed to address global imbalances and foster growth. Such actions would include fiscal tightening in the USA and further structural reforms in the EU and Japan. As it turned out, there was little or no resulting change in domestic policy.

The second problem is the lack of international convergence. Successful policy co-ordination requires that serious imbalances in world trade should be kept to a minimum. But such is the size of the US current account deficit and the Japanese and Chinese surpluses that huge pressures are placed on the foreign exchange market. These imbalances also create massive financial flows and great uncertainty. As a result, speculation is likely to be a far more powerful determinant of events than any agreement made by finance ministers. Exchange rates can thus be highly volatile (see Box 24.4).

Response to the south-east Asian crisis

The need to establish greater co-operation was demonstrated by the south-east Asian crisis in 1997–8 (see Web Cases 25.3 and 25.4) and the shock waves it sent round the global economy. The fact that the crisis came as a total surprise to governments, international institutions, international financiers and speculators clearly revealed the need to monitor more closely, and when necessary, regulate the world economy.

Following weeks of negotiations with the IMF and World Bank, the finance ministers and central bank governors of the G7 countries met in October 1998 to agree a package of measures designed to prevent a repeat of the 'Asian contagion' and to restore greater stability to the international financial system. The agreement included the provision of credit facilities, through the IMF and the World Bank, for 'well-run' economies whose currencies were victims of speculative attack. The IMF would have $90 billion for this purpose. It also called for the establishment of closer links between national and international regulatory bodies, to provide more effective regulation of financial markets.

On the central issue of exchange rate regimes, however, the G7 had little to say, merely calling for 'consideration of the elements necessary for the maintenance of sustainable exchange rate regimes in emerging markets, including consistent macroeconomic policies'.

Harmonising attempts to reduce poverty

The Genoa Summit in 2001 was dominated by riots and protests, and it was these that made the news. However, the G8 made significant moves in extending help to the world's poorest countries. The G8's aim was to co-ordinate strategies more effectively over a wide range of development areas: debt relief, trade access, health and education.

At a subsequent meeting in Gleneagles, Scotland in July 2005, the G8 leaders agreed to cancel debts of 18 of the poorest developing countries, mainly in Africa (see page 747), owed to the IMF, the World Bank and the African Development Bank (but not private banks). It was also agreed to more than double the amount of aid to Africa by 2010 compared to 2004.

For many, the Gleneagles Summit was seen as a new dawn in international relations, with the world's wealthiest nations now set to work together for the good of all nations, rather than their own self-interest. Time will show whether such optimism was justified.

To what extent can international negotiations over economic policy be seen as a game of strategy? Are there any parallels between the behaviour of countries and the behaviour of oligopolists? (See the section on game theory in Chapter 7, pages 191–5.)

Table 25.2 History of the ERM

	Mar 1979	Sept 1979	Nov 1979	Mar 1981	Oct 1981	Feb 1982	June 1982	Mar 1983	July 1985	Apr 1986	Aug 1986	Jan 1987	Jun 1989	Jan 1990	Oct 1990	Apr 1992	Sept 1992	Sept 1992	Nov 1992	Jan 1993	May 1993	Aug 1993	Jan 1995	Mar 1995	Oct 1996	Nov 1996	Mar 1998	Jan 1999	Jan 2001
Belgian franc	En2¼%					–8.5		+1.5	+2.0	+1.0		+2.0										B15%						S	
Danish krone	En2¼%	–2.9	–4.8			–3.0		+2.5	+2.0	+1.0												B15%						B2¼%	
German mark	En2¼%	+2.0			+5.5		+4.25	+5.5	+2.0	+3.0		+3.0										B15%						S	
French franc	En2¼%				–3.0		–5.75	–2.5	+2.0	–3.0												B15%						S	
Irish punt	En2¼%							–3.5	+2.0		–8.0									–10.0		B15%					+3.0	S	
Italian lira	En6%			–6.0	–3.0		–2.75	–2.5	–6.0					B2¼%			–7.0	Ex	–	–	–	–	–	–		–En15%		S	
Dutch guilder	En2¼%				+5.5		+4.25	+3.5	+2.0	+3.0		+3.0										B15%						S	
UK pound	–	–	–	–	–	–	–	–	–	–	–	–	–		–En6%			Ex	–	–	–	–	–	–	–	–	–	–	
Spanish peseta	–	–	–	–	–	–	–	–	–	–	–		–En6%				–5.0		–6.0		–8.0	B15%		–7.0				S	
Portuguese escudo	–	–	–	–	–	–	–	–	–	–	–	–	–	–		–En6%			–6.0		–6.5	B15%		–3.5				S	
Austrian schilling	–	–	–	–	–	–	–	–	–	–	–	–	–	–	–	–	–	–	–	–	–		–En15%					S	
Finnish markka	–	–	–	–	–	–	–	–	–	–	–	–	–	–	–	–	–	–	–	–	–	–	–		–En15%			S	
Greek drachma	–	–	–	–	–	–	–	–	–	–	–	–	–	–	–	–	–	–	–	–	–	–	–	–	–	–	–En15%		S

– = % devaluation; + = % revaluation; B% = new band; En% = entry band; Ex = exit; S = join single currency

Source: *European Economy*.

ERM an 'adjustable peg' system. All the currencies floated jointly with currencies outside the ERM.

If a currency reached the upper or lower limit against *any* other ERM currency, intervention would take place to maintain the currencies within the band. This would take the form of central banks in the ERM selling the strong currency and buying the weak one. It could also involve the weak currency countries raising interest rates and the strong currency countries lowering them.

The ERM in practice

In a system of pegged exchange rates, countries should harmonise their policies to avoid excessive currency misalignments and the need for large devaluations or revaluations. There should be a convergence of their economies: they should be at a similar point on the business cycle and have similar inflation rates and interest rates.

The ERM in the 1980s. In the early 1980s, however, French and Italian inflation rates were persistently higher than German rates. This meant that there had to be several realignments (see Table 25.2). After 1983 realignments became less frequent, and then from 1987 to 1992 they ceased altogether. This was due to a growing convergence of members' internal policies.

By the time the UK joined the ERM in 1990, it was generally seen by its existing members as being a great success. It had created a zone of currency stability in a world of highly unstable exchange rates, and had provided the necessary environment for the establishment of a truly common market by the end of 1992.

Crisis in the ERM. Shortly after the UK joined the ERM, strains began to show. The reunification of Germany involved considerable reconstruction in the eastern part of the country. Financing this reconstruction was causing a growing budget deficit. The Bundesbank (the German central bank) thus felt obliged to maintain high interest rates in order to keep inflation in check. At the same time, the UK was experiencing a massive current account deficit (partly the result of entering the ERM at what many commentators argued was too high an exchange rate). It was thus obliged to raise interest rates in order to protect the pound, despite the fact that the economy was sliding rapidly into recession. The French franc and Italian lira were also perceived to be overvalued, and there were the first signs of worries as to whether their exchange rates within the ERM could be retained.

At the same time, the US economy was moving into recession and, as a result, US interest rates were cut. This led to a large outflow of capital from the USA. With high German interest rates, much of this capital flowed to Germany. This pushed up the value of the German mark and with it the other ERM currencies. In September 1992, things reached crisis point. First the lira was devalued. Then two days later, on 'Black Wednesday' (16 September), the UK and Italy were forced to suspend their membership of the ERM: the pound and the lira were floated. At the same time, the Spanish peseta was devalued by 5 per cent.

? *Under what circumstances may a currency bloc like the ERM (a) help to prevent speculation; (b) aggravate the problem of speculation?*

Turmoil returned in the summer of 1993. The French economy was moving into recession and there were calls for cuts in French interest rates. But this was possible only if Germany was prepared to cut its rates too, and it was not. Speculators began to sell francs and it became obvious that the existing franc/mark parity could not be maintained. In an attempt to rescue the ERM, the EU finance ministers agreed to adopt very wide ±15 per cent bands. The result was that the franc and the Danish krone depreciated against the mark.

The old ERM appeared to be at an end. The new ±15 per cent bands hardly seemed like a 'pegged' system at all. However, the ERM did not die. Within months, the members were again managing to keep fluctuations within a very narrow range (for most of the time, within ±2¼ per cent!).

The road to EMU

The EU countries were right to stress the importance of convergence of their economies. Certainly, if they were to progress from the ERM to eventual monetary union, with a single currency, then convergence was essential: not only between economic indicators, such as growth, interest rates, inflation rates and levels of government debt, but also between the policies of their governments and the structure of their economies and institutions.

As the 1990s progressed, so the economies of most of the EU countries were converging, and in May 1998 the decision was made that 11 of the 15 EU countries would proceed to economic and monetary union (EMU), with a single currency (the euro) in January 1999. EMU is the subject of the next section.

With the birth of the euro in January 1999, the only EU countries not joining were the UK, Sweden and Denmark. Denmark was alone in remaining in what became known as ERM2. The Danish krone was pegged to the euro within a ±2¼ per cent band.

In May 2004, ten new members joined the EU. They all stated their intention to join the euro, but to do so, they have to be members of ERM2 for at least two years. Estonia, Lithuania and Slovenia were the first to join ERM2 in June 2004, with the wide band of ±15 per cent.

Section summary

1. Currency fluctuations can be lessened if countries harmonise their economic policies. Ideally this will involve achieving compatible growth rates, inflation rates, balance of payments (as a percentage of GDP) and interest rates. The attempt to harmonise one of these goals, however, may bring conflicts with one of the other goals.
2. Leaders of the G7 countries meet at least annually to discuss ways of harmonising their policies. Usually, however, domestic issues are more important to the leaders than international ones, and frequently they pursue policies that are not in the interests of the other countries.
3. One means of achieving greater currency stability is for a group of countries to peg their exchange rates with each other and yet float jointly with the rest of the world.
4. The exchange rate mechanism of the European Monetary System was an example. Members' currencies had a central parity against each other and were allowed to fluctuate within a band. The band was ±2¼ per cent for the majority of the ERM countries, but originally Italy (up to 1990) and then the new members, Spain, the UK and Portugal, adopted a wider ±6 per cent.
5. The need for realignments seemed to have diminished in the late 1980s as greater convergence was achieved between the members' economies. Growing strains in the system, however, in the early 1990s, led to a crisis in September 1992. The UK and Italy left the ERM and realignments of the peseta, escudo and punt followed. There was a further crisis in July 1993 and the bands were widened to ±15 per cent, although in practice fluctuations were kept within ±2¼ per cent for most of the time from 1993 to the start of the euro in 1999.
6. The ERM was seen as an important first stage on the road to complete European monetary union.

25.3 EUROPEAN ECONOMIC AND MONETARY UNION (EMU)

The advent of EMU

Chapter 23 looked at the Single European Act and the intention to remove all trade barriers in the EU by 1993. But many advocates of a single market argued for much deeper economic integration. The result was the Treaty on European Union hammered out at Maastricht in the Netherlands in December 1991. The Maastricht Treaty also covered moves towards political and social union, but it is its plans for monetary union that concern us here. This was to be achieved in three stages. Countries that met five 'convergence criteria' by the end of stage 2 would be eligible to proceed to stage 3. This would involve the creation of a single European currency – a European ***currency union***. The UK and Denmark negotiated an 'opt-out' from the treaty. They do not have to adopt the single currency if they so choose.

Stage 1 was a preliminary stage, during which preparations were made for the establishment of a European Monetary Institute (EMI), an institution that would be the forerunner of a European central bank.

Definition

Currency union A group of countries (or regions) using a common currency.

Stage 2 began on 1 January 1994 with the establishment of the EMI. It attempted to co-ordinate monetary policy and encourage greater co-operation between EU central banks. During stage 2, the member states sought to meet five convergence criteria:

- Inflation: should be no more than $1^1/_2$ per cent above the average inflation rate of the three countries in the EU with the lowest inflation.
- Interest rates: the rate on long-term government bonds should be no more than 2 per cent above the average of the three countries with the lowest inflation rates.
- Budget deficit: should be no more than 3 per cent of GDP at market prices.
- National debt: should be no more than 60 per cent of GDP at market prices.
- Exchange rates: the currency should have been within the normal ERM bands for at least two years with no realignments or excessive intervention.

Before the end of stage 2, the Council of Ministers had to decide which countries had met the convergence criteria and would thus be eligible to progress to stage 3.

Stage 3 would commence at the latest on 1 January 1999. At the beginning of this stage, the countries that met the five criteria would fix their currencies permanently to the new single currency: the euro. The national currencies would therefore effectively disappear.

At the same time, a European System of Central Banks (ESCB) would be created, consisting of a European Central Bank (ECB) and the central banks of the member states. The ECB would be independent: independent from governments and also from EU political institutions. It would operate the monetary policy on behalf of the countries that had adopted the single currency.

In March 1998, the European Commission ruled that 11 of the 15 member states were eligible to proceed to EMU in January 1999. The UK and Denmark were to exercise their opt out and Sweden and Greece failed to meet one or more of the convergence criteria.

All 11 countries unambiguously met the interest rate and inflation criteria, but doubts were expressed by many 'Eurosceptics' as to whether they all genuinely met the other three criteria.

Exchange rates. Neither Finland nor Italy had been in the ERM for two years (Finland had joined the ERM in October 1996 and Italy had rejoined in November 1996), and the Irish punt was revalued by 3 per cent on 16/3/98. However, the Commission regarded these three countries as being sufficiently close to the reference value.

Government deficits. All 11 countries met this criterion, but some countries only managed to achieve a deficit of 3 per cent or below by taking one-off measures, such as a special tax in Italy and counting privatisation receipts in Germany. Yet, under the Stability and Growth Pact, eurozone countries would be required to keep their deficits within the 3 per cent limit (see Box 19.4). The concern was that countries that only just met this criterion at time of entry would find it difficult to keep within the limit in times of recession or slow growth. This proved to be the case with France and Germany from 2002 to 2005.

Government debt. Only four countries had debts that did not exceed 60 per cent (France, Finland, Luxembourg and the UK). However, the Maastricht Treaty allowed countries to exceed this value as long as the debt was 'sufficiently diminishing and approaching the reference value at a satisfactory pace.' Critics argued that this phrase was interpreted too loosely.

The euro came into being on 1 January 1999 (with Greece joining in 2001), but euro banknotes and coins were not introduced until 1 January 2002. In the meantime, national currencies continued to exist alongside the euro, but at irrevocably fixed rates. The old notes and coins were withdrawn a few weeks after the introduction of euro notes and coins.

Advantages of the single currency

EMU has several major advantages.

Elimination of the costs of converting currencies. With separate currencies in each of the EU countries, costs were incurred each time one currency was exchanged into another. The elimination of these costs, however, was probably the least important benefit from the single currency. The European Commission estimated that the effect was to increase the GDP of the countries concerned by an average of only 0.4 per cent. The gains to countries like the UK, which have well-developed financial markets, would be even smaller.

Increased competition and efficiency. Despite the advent of the single market, large price differences remained between member states. Not only does the single currency eliminate the need to convert one currency into another (a barrier to competition), but it brings more transparency in pricing, and puts greater downward pressure on prices in high-cost firms and countries.

Elimination of exchange rate uncertainty (between the members). Even with a narrow-banded ERM, realignments might still occur from time to time if separate currencies had remained. As the events of 1992 and 1993 showed, this could cause massive speculation if it was believed that currencies were out of line. Removal of this uncertainty has helped to encourage trade between the eurozone countries. Perhaps more importantly, it has encouraged investment by firms that trade between these countries, given the greater certainty in calculating costs and revenues from such trade.

Figure 25.2 Inward investment to EU countries (including from other EU countries) as a percentage of total EU countries

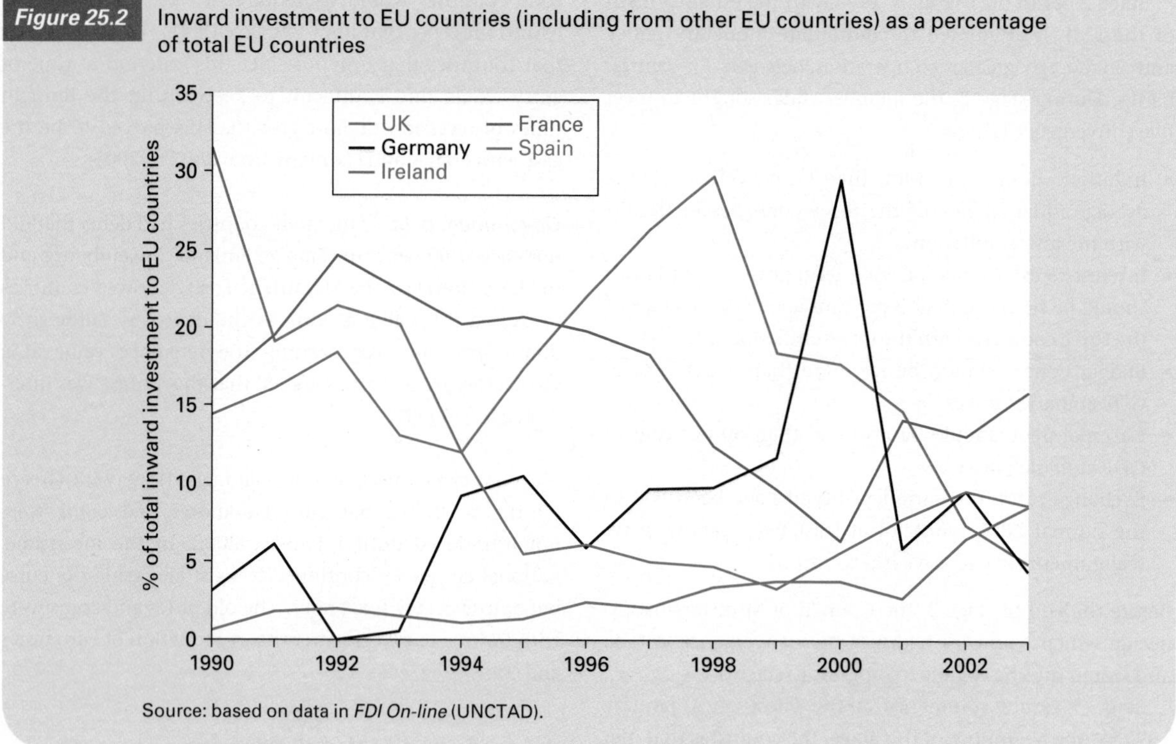

Source: based on data in *FDI On-line* (UNCTAD).

Increased inward investment. Investment from the rest of the world is attracted to a eurozone of some 310 million inhabitants, where there is no fear of internal currency movements. By contrast, the UK, by not joining, has found that inward investment has been diverted away to countries within the eurozone.

From 1990 to 1998, the UK's share of inward investment to EU countries (including from other EU countries) was nearly 22.2 per cent. From 1999 to 2003, it was 12.6 per cent, and it fell throughout this period, from 18.4 per cent in 1999 to 4.9 per cent in 2003 (see Figure 25.2).

Lower inflation and interest rates. A single monetary policy forces convergence in inflation rates (just as inflation rates are very similar between the different regions within a country). With the ECB being independent from short-term political manipulation, it has resulted in a low average inflation rate in the eurozone countries. This, in turn, has helped to convince markets that the euro will be strong relative to other currencies. The result is lower long-term rates of interest. This, in turn, further encourages investment in the eurozone countries, both by member states and by the rest of the world.

Opposition to EMU

Monetary union has been bitterly opposed, however, by certain groups. Many eurosceptics see within it a surrender of national political and economic sovereignty. The lack of an independent monetary and exchange rate policy is a serious problem, they argue, if an economy is at all out of harmony with the rest of the Union. For example, if countries like Italy and Spain have higher rates of inflation, how are they to make their goods competitive with the rest of the Union? With separate currencies these countries could allow their currencies to depreciate. With a single currency, however, they could become depressed 'regions' of Europe, with rising unemployment and all the other regional problems of depressed regions *within* a country. This might then require significant regional policies – policies that might not be in place or, if they were, would be seen as too interventionist by the political right.

? *How might multiplier effects (the principle of cumulative causation) lead to prosperous regions becoming more prosperous and less prosperous regions falling even further behind?* TC 15 p463

The reply given by proponents of EMU is that it is better to tackle the problem of high inflation in such countries by the disciplines of competition from other EU countries, than merely to feed that inflation by keeping separate currencies and allowing repeated devaluations, with all the uncertainty that they bring. If such countries become depressed, they argue, it is better to have a fully developed *fiscal* policy for the Union which will divert funds into investment in such regions. What is more, the high-inflation countries tend to be the poorer ones with lower wage levels (albeit faster wage *increases*). With the high mobility of labour and capital that will accompany the development of the single market, resources are likely

EXPLORING ECONOMICS BOX 25.3

OPTIMAL CURRENCY AREAS

When it pays to pay in the same currency

Imagine that each town and village used a different currency. Think how inconvenient it would be having to keep exchanging one currency into another, and how difficult it would be working out the relative value of items in different parts of the country.

Clearly, there are benefits of using a common currency, not only within a country but across different countries. The benefits include greater transparency in pricing, more open competition, greater certainty for investors and the avoidance of having to pay commission when you change one currency into another. There are also the benefits from having a single monetary policy if that is delivered in a more consistent and effective way than by individual countries.

So why not have a single currency for the whole world? The problem is that the bigger a single currency area gets, the more likely the conditions are to diverge in the different parts of the area. Some parts may have high unemployment and require reflationary policies. Others may have low unemployment and suffer from inflationary pressures. They may require *deflationary* policies.

What is more, different members of the currency area may experience quite different shocks to their economies, whether from outside the union (e.g. a fall in the price of one of their major exports) of from inside (e.g. a prolonged strike). These 'asymmetric shocks' would imply that different parts of the currency area should adopt different policies. But with a common monetary policy and hence common interest rates, and with no possibility of devaluation/revaluation of the currency of individual members, the scope for separate economic policies is reduced.

The costs of asymmetric shocks (and hence the costs of a single currency area) will be greater, the less the mobility of labour and capital, the less the flexibility of prices and wage rates, and the fewer the alternative policies there are that can be turned to (such as fiscal and regional policies).

So is the eurozone an optimal currency area? Certainly strong doubts have been raised by many economists.

- Labour is relatively immobile.
- There are structural differences between the member states.
- The transmission effects of interest rate changes are different between the member countries, given that countries have different proportions of borrowing at variable interest rates and different proportions of consumer debt to GDP.
- Exports to countries outside the eurozone account for different proportions of the members' GDP, and thus their economies are affected differently by a change in the rate of exchange of the euro against other currencies.
- Wage rates are relatively inflexible.
- Under the Stability and Growth Pact (see Box 19.4), the scope for using discretionary fiscal policy is curtailed.

This does not necessarily mean, however, that the costs of having a single European currency outweigh the benefits. Also, the problems outlined above should decline over time as the single market develops. Finally, the problem of asymmetric shocks can be exaggerated. European economies are highly diversified; there are often more differences *within* economies than between them. Thus shocks are more likely to affect different industries or localities, rather than whole countries. Changing the exchange rate, if that were still possible, would hardly be an appropriate policy in these circumstances.

Why is a single currency area likely to move towards becoming an optimal currency area over time?

to be attracted to such countries. This could help to narrow the gap between the richer and poorer member states.

The critics of EMU counter this by arguing that labour is relatively immobile, given cultural and language barriers. Thus an unemployed worker in Wales could not easily move to a job in Turin or Helsinki. What the critics are arguing here is that the EU is not an ***optimal currency area*** (see Box 25.3).

Perhaps the most serious criticism is that the same rate of interest must apply to all eurozone countries: the 'one-size-fits-all' problem. The trouble is that while one country might require a lower rate of interest in order to ward off recession (such as Germany in 2003–5), another might require a higher one to prevent inflation. As convergence between the member economies increases, however, this problem is likely to lessen.

Another problem for members of a single currency occurs in adjusting to a shock when that shock affects members to different degrees. These are known as ***asymmetric shocks***. For example, a sudden change in the price of oil would

Definitions

Optimal currency area The optimal size of a currency area is the one that maximises the benefits from having a single currency relative to the costs. If the area were increased or decreased in size, the costs would rise relative to the benefits.

Asymmetric shocks Shocks (such as an oil price increase or a recession in another part of the world) that have different-sized effects on different industries, regions or countries.

affect an oil-exporting country like the UK differently from oil importing countries. This problem is more serious, the less the factor mobility between member countries and the less the price flexibility within member countries.

This problem, however, should not be overstated. The divergences between economies are often the result of a lack of harmony between countries in their demand-management policies: something that is impossible in the case of monetary policy, and more difficult in the case of fiscal policy, for countries in the eurozone. Also, many of the shocks that face economies today are global and have similar (albeit not identical) effects on all countries. Adjustment to such shocks would often be better with a single co-ordinated policy, something that is much easier with a single currency and a single central bank.

Even when shocks are uniformly felt in the member states, however, there is still the problem that policies adopted centrally will have different impacts on each country. For example, in the UK, a large proportion of borrowing is at variable interest rates. In Germany, by contrast, much is at fixed rates. Thus if the European central bank were to raise interest rates, the deflationary effects would be felt disproportionately in the UK. Of course, were this balance to change – and there is some evidence that types of borrowing are becoming more uniform across the EU – this problem would diminish.

The problem for economists is that the issue of monetary union is a very emotive one. 'Europhiles' often see monetary union as a vital element in their vision of a united Europe. Many Eurosceptics, however, see EMU as a surrender of sovereignty and a threat to nationhood. In such an environment, a calm assessment of the arguments and evidence is very difficult.

?

1. *By what means would a depressed country in an Economic Union with a single currency be able to recover? Would the market provide a satisfactory solution to its problems or would (Union) government intervention be necessary, and if so, what form could that intervention take?*
2. *Is greater factor mobility likely to increase or decrease the problem of cumulative causation associated with regional multipliers? (See page 625.)*

The UK Labour government specified five convergence criteria that must be met before it would put the question of UK adoption of the euro to the electorate in a referendum. These are examined in Web Case 25.6.

Section summary

1. The euro was born on 1 January 1999. Twelve countries adopted it, having at least nominally met the Maastricht convergence criteria. Euro notes and coins were introduced on 1 January 2002, with the notes and coins of the old currencies withdrawn a few weeks later.
2. The advantages claimed for EMU are that it eliminates the costs of converting currencies and the uncertainties associated with possible changes in inter-EU exchange rates. This encourages more investment, both inward and by domestic firms. What is more, a common central bank, independent from domestic governments, provides the stable monetary environment necessary for a convergence of the EU economies and the encouragement of investment and inter-Union trade.
3. Critics claim, however, that it makes adjustment to domestic economic problems more difficult. The loss of independence in policy making is seen by such people to be a major issue, not only because of the loss of political sovereignty, but also because domestic economic concerns may be at variance with those of the Union as a whole. A single monetary policy is claimed to be inappropriate for dealing with asymmetric shocks. What is more, countries and regions at the periphery of the Union may become depressed unless there is an effective regional policy.

25.4 ACHIEVING GREATER CURRENCY STABILITY

One important lesson of recent years is that concerted speculation has become virtually unstoppable. This was made clear by the expulsion of the UK and Italy from the ERM in 1992, the dramatic fall of the Mexican peso and rise of the yen in 1995, the collapse of various south-east Asian currencies and the Russian rouble in 1997–8, and the collapse of the Argentinian peso in early 2002. In comparison with the vast amounts of short-term finance flowing across the foreign exchanges each day, the reserves of central banks seem trivial.

If there is a consensus in the markets that a currency will depreciate, there is little that central banks can do. For example, if there were a 50 per cent chance of a 10 per cent depreciation in the next week, selling that currency now would yield an 'expected' return of just over 5 per cent for the week (i.e. 50% of 10%): equivalent to more than 5000 per cent at an annual rate!

For this reason, many commentators have argued that there are only two types of exchange rate system that can work over the long term. The first is a completely free-floating exchange rate, with no attempt by the central bank to support the exchange rate. With no intervention, there is no problem of a shortage of reserves!

The second is to share a common currency with other countries: to join a common currency area, such as the eurozone, and let the common currency float freely. The country would give up independence in its monetary policy, but at least there would be no problem of exchange rate instability within the currency area. A similar alternative is to adopt a major currency of another country, such as the US dollar or the euro. Many smaller states have done this. For example, Kosovo has adopted the euro and Ecuador has adopted the US dollar.

An attempt by a country to peg its exchange rate is likely to have one of two unfortunate consequences. Either it will end in failure as the country succumbs to a speculative attack, or its monetary policy will have to be totally dedicated to maintaining the exchange rate.

So is there any way of 'beating the speculators' and pursuing a policy of greater exchange rate rigidity? Or must countries outside a currency union be forced to accept freely floating exchange rates, with all the uncertainty for traders that such a regime brings?

This section looks at two possible solutions. The first is to reduce international financial mobility, by putting various types of restriction on foreign exchange transactions. The second is to move to a new type of exchange rate regime that offers the benefits of a degree of rigidity without being susceptible to massive speculative attacks.

Controlling exchange transactions

Until the early 1990s, many countries retained restrictions of various kinds on financial flows. Such restrictions made it more expensive for speculators to gamble on possible exchange rate movements. It is not the case, as some commentators argue, that it is impossible to reimpose controls. Indeed, Malaysia did just that in 1998 when the ringgit was under speculative attack. Many countries in the developing world still retain controls, and the last ERM countries to give them up did so only in 1991. It is true that the complexity of modern financial markets provides the speculator with more opportunity to evade controls, but they will still have the effect of dampening speculation.

In September 1998, the IMF said that controls on inward movements of finance could be a useful tool, especially for countries that were more vulnerable to speculative attack. In its 1998 annual report, it argued that the Asian crisis of 1997–8 was the result not only of a weak banking system, but also of open financial accounts, allowing massive withdrawals of funds.

The aim of financial controls is not to prevent international flows of finance. After all, such flows are an important source of financing investment. Also, if finance moves from countries with a lower marginal productivity of capital to countries where it is higher, this will lead to an efficient allocation of world savings. The aim of financial controls must therefore be to prevent speculative flows that are based on rumour or herd instinct rather than on economic fundamentals.

Types of control

In what ways can movements of short-term finance be controlled? There are various alternatives, each one with strengths and drawbacks.

Quantitative controls. Here the authorities would restrict the amount of foreign exchange dealing that could take place. Perhaps financial institutions would be allowed to exchange only a certain percentage of their assets. Developed countries and most developing countries have rejected this approach, however, since it is seen to be far too anti-market.

The exception is the use of special emergency measures to restrict capital movements in times of a currency crisis. According to Article 57 of the Treaty of Amsterdam, the EU Council of Ministers may 'adopt measures on the movement of capital to or from third countries'. Article 59 allows 'safeguard measures' to be taken if 'in exceptional circumstances, movements of capital to or from third countries cause . . . serious difficulties for the operation of economic and monetary union'. Article 60 allows member states to take 'unilateral measures against a third country with regard to capital movements and payments'.

A 'Tobin' tax. This is named after James Tobin, who in 1972 advocated the imposition of a small tax of 0.1 to 0.5 per cent on all foreign exchange transactions, or on just financial account transactions.[1] This would discourage destabilising speculation (by making it more expensive) and would thus impose some 'friction' in the foreign exchange markets, making them less volatile.

Calls for the use of Tobin taxes have become more frequent in recent years (see Box 25.4), and in November 2001 the French National Assembly became the first national legislature to incorporate into law a Tobin tax of up to 0.1 per cent. This was followed by Belgium in 2002. The EU finance ministers ordered the European Commission to undertake a feasibility study of such a tax. In late 2001, the charity War on Want declared that 13 March 2002 would be international 'Tobin tax day'. Ironically, Tobin died on 11 March 2002.

A problem with such a tax is that it would penalise transactions that were for normal trading or investment purposes as well as those for speculative purposes. Another problem is that the tax might have to be quite high to prevent speculation in times of uncertainty, and this would be very damaging to trade and investment. A possibility here

[1] J. Tobin, 'A proposal for international monetary reform', *Eastern Economic Journal*, vol. 4, no. 3–4 (1978), pp. 153–9.

EXPLORING ECONOMICS

THE TOBIN TAX

A new panacea?

In the mid-1980s, the daily turnover in the world's foreign exchange markets was approximately $150 billion. By 2005, it had risen to a truly massive $2 trillion. But only some 5 per cent of this was used for trade in goods and services.

With the massive growth in speculative flows, it is hardly surprising that this can cause great currency instability and financial crises at times of economic uncertainty. Global financial markets have often been decisive in both triggering and intensifying economic crises. The ERM crisis in 1992, the Mexican peso crisis in 1994, the south-east Asian crisis in 1997, the Russian rouble meltdown in 1998 and the crisis in Argentina in 2001/2 are the most significant in a long list.

The main issue is one of volatility of exchange rates. If currency markets responded to shifts in economic fundamentals, then currency volatility would not be so bad. However, it is increasingly the case that vast quantities of money flow around the global economy on pure speculation, in which the herd instinct often drives speculative waves. Invariably, given the volume of speculative flows, exchange rates overshoot their natural equilibrium, intensifying the distortions created. Such currency movements are a huge destabilising force, not just for individual economies but for the global economy as a whole.

So is there anything countries can do to reduce destabilising speculation? One suggestion is the introduction of a Tobin tax.

The Tobin tax

Writing in 1972, James Tobin proposed a system for reducing exchange rate volatility without fundamentally impeding the operation of the market. This involved the imposition of an international tax of some 0.1 to 0.5 per cent payable on all spot or cash exchange rate transactions. He argued that this would make currency trading more costly and would therefore reduce the volume of destabilising short-term financial flows, which would invariably lead to greater exchange rate stability.

Tobin's original proposal suggested that the tax rate would need to be very low so as not to affect 'normal business'. Even if it was very low, speculators working on small margins would be dissuaded from regular movements of money, given that the tax would need to be paid per transaction. If a tax rate of 0.2 per cent was set, speculators who moved a sum of money once a day would face a yearly tax bill of approximately 50 per cent. An investor working on a weekly movement of money would pay tax of 10 per cent per annum, and a monthly movement of currency would represent a tax of 2.4 per cent for the year. Given that 40 per cent of currency transactions have only a two-day time horizon, and 80 per cent a time horizon of less than seven days, such a tax would clearly operate to dampen speculative currency movements.

In addition to moderating volatility and speculation, the Tobin tax might yield other benefits. It would, in the face of globalisation, restore to the nation state an element of control over monetary policy. In the face of declining governance over international forces, this might be seen as a positive advantage of the Tobin proposals.

The tax could also generate significant revenue. Estimates range from $150–300 billion annually. Many of the world's leading pressure groups, such as War on Want, have argued that the revenue from such an international tax could be used to tackle international problems, such as world poverty and environmental degradation. The World Bank estimates that some

would be to impose the tax only at times of exchange market turbulence, or to impose a higher tax at such times. At least a tax is far less distortionary than quantitative controls.

Non-interest-bearing deposits. Here a certain percentage of inflows of finance would have to be deposited with the central bank in a non-interest-bearing account for a set period of time. Chile in the late 1990s used such a system. It required that 30 per cent of all inflows be deposited with Chile's central bank for a year. This clearly amounted to a considerable tax (i.e. in terms of interest sacrificed) and had the effect of discouraging short-term speculative flows. The problem was that it meant that interest rates in Chile had to be higher in order to attract finance.

One objection to all these measures is that they are likely only to dampen speculation, not eliminate it. If speculators believe that currencies are badly out of equilibrium and will be forced to realign, then no taxes on financial movements or artificial controls will be sufficient to stem the flood.

There are two replies to this objection. The first is that, if currencies are badly out of line, exchange rates *should* be adjusted. The second is that dampening speculation is probably the ideal. Speculation *can* play the valuable role of bringing exchange rates to their long-term equilibrium more quickly. Controls are unlikely to prevent this aspect of speculation: adjustments to economic fundamentals. If they help to lessen the wilder forms of destabilising speculation, so much the better.

Exchange rate target zones

One type of exchange rate regime that has been much discussed in recent years is that proposed by John Williamson,

BOX 25.4

$225 billion is needed to eliminate the world's worst forms of poverty. The revenue from a Tobin tax would, in a relatively short period of time, easily exceed this amount.

Problems with the Tobin tax

How far would a tax on currency transactions restrict speculative movements of money? The issue here concerns the rate of return investors might get from moving their money. If a currency was to devalue by as little as 3 to 4 per cent, a Tobin tax of 0.2 per cent would do little to deter a speculative transaction based upon such a potential return. Given devaluations of 50 per cent in Thailand and Indonesia following the 1997 crash, and a 60 per cent appreciation of the euro against the dollar from 2002 to 2005, along with severe short-term fluctuations, a 3 to 4 per cent movement in the currency appears rather modest. Raising the rate of the Tobin tax would be no solution, as it would begin to impinge upon 'normal business'.

One response to such a situation has been proposed by a German economist, Paul Bernd Spahn. He suggests that a two-tier system is used. On a day-to-day basis, a minimal tax rate, as originally envisaged by Tobin, is charged against each transaction conducted. However, during periods when exchange rates are highly unstable, a tax surcharge is levied. This would be at a far higher rate, and would only be triggered once a currency moved beyond some predetermined band of exchange rate variation.

A further problem identified with the Tobin tax concerns the costs of its administration. However, given inter-linked computer systems and the progressive centralisation of foreign exchange markets – in terms of market places, traders and currencies – effective administration is becoming easier. Most foreign exchange markets are well monitored already and extending such monitoring to include overseeing tax collection would not be overly problematic.

Another problem is tax avoidance. For example, the Tobin tax is a tax payable on spot exchange rate transactions. This could encourage people to deal more in futures. Foreign exchange futures are a type of 'derivative' that allow people to trade currencies in the future at a price agreed today (see Box 2.6). These would be far more difficult to monitor, since no currency is exchanged *today*, and hence more difficult to tax. One solution would be to apply a tax on the notional value of a derivative contract. However, derivatives are an important way through which businesses hedge against future risk. Taxing them might seriously erode their use to a business and damage the derivatives market as a whole, making business more risky.

Even with avoidance, however, supporters of the Tobin tax argue that it is still likely to be successful. The main problem is the one of political will.

Although some countries, such as France and Belgium, have supported the introduction of a Tobin tax, most of the major economies are opposed to it. With reservations being expressed by the IMF, any concerted international action to control global financial movements will be difficult to put on the agenda, let alone put in place and administer.

? ***George Soros, multi-millionaire currency speculator, has referred to global capital markets as being like a wrecking ball rather than a pendulum, suggesting that such markets are becoming so volatile that they are damaging to all concerned, including speculators. What might lead Soros to such an observation?***

of Washington's Institute for International Economics.[2] Williamson advocates a form of crawling peg within broad exchange rate bands (see Figure 24.7 on page 677). This would have four major features:

- Wide bands. Currencies would be allowed to fluctuate by ±10 per cent of their central parity.
- Central parity set in *real* terms, at the 'fundamental equilibrium exchange rate' (FEER): i.e. a rate that is consistent with long-run balance of payments equilibrium.
- Frequent realignments. In order to stay at the FEER, the central parity would be adjusted frequently (say, monthly) to take account of the country's rate of inflation. If its rate of inflation were 2 per cent per annum above the trade-weighted average of other countries, the central parity would be devalued by 2 per cent per annum. Realignments would also reflect other changes in fundamentals, such as changes in the levels of protection, or major political events, such as German reunification.
- 'Soft buffers'. Governments would not be forced to intervene at the ±10 per cent mark or at some specified fraction of it. In fact, from time to time the rate might be allowed to move outside the bands. The point is that the closer the rate approached the band limits, the greater would be the scale of intervention.

There are two main advantages of this system. First, the exchange rate would stay at roughly the equilibrium level, and therefore the likelihood of large-scale devaluations or revaluations, and with them the opportunities for large-scale speculative gains, would be small. The reason why the narrow-banded ERM broke down in 1992 and 1993 was that the central parities were *not* equilibrium rates.

[2] See, for example, J. Williamson and M. Miller, 'Targets and indicators: a blue-print for the co-ordination of economic policy', *Policy Analyses in International Economics No. 22*, IIE, 1987.

Second, the wider bands would leave countries freer to follow an independent monetary policy: one that could therefore respond to domestic needs.

The main problem with the system is that it may not allow an independent monetary policy. If the rate of exchange has to be maintained within the zone, monetary policy may sometimes have to be used for that purpose rather than controlling inflation.

Nevertheless, crawling bands have been used relatively successfully by various countries, such as Chile and Israel, over quite long periods of time. What is more, in 1999 Germany's former finance minister, Oskar Lafontaine, argued that they might be appropriate for the euro relative to the dollar and yen. A world with three major currencies, each changing gently against the other two in an orderly way, has a lot to commend it.

?

1. *Would the Williamson system allow countries to follow a totally independent monetary policy?*
2. *If the euro were in a crawling peg against the dollar, what implications would this have for the ECB in sticking to its inflation target of no more than 2 per cent?*

Section summary

1. Many economists argue that, with the huge flows of short-term finance across the foreign exchanges, governments are forced to adopt one of two extreme forms of exchange rate regime: free floating or being a member of a currency union.
2. If financial flows could be constrained, however, exchange rates could be stabilised somewhat.
3. Forms of financial control include: quantitative controls, a tax on exchange transactions and non-interest-bearing deposits of a certain percentage of capital inflows with the central bank. Such controls can dampen speculation, but may discourage capital from flowing to where it has a higher marginal productivity.
4. An alternative means of stabilising exchange rates is to have exchange rate target zones. Here exchange rates are allowed to fluctuate within broad bands around a central parity, which is adjusted to the fundamental equilibrium rate in a gradual fashion.
5. The advantage of this system is that, by keeping the exchange rate at roughly its equilibrium level, destabilising speculation is avoided, and yet there is some freedom for governments to pursue an independent monetary policy. Monetary policy, however, may still from time to time have to be used to keep the exchange rate within the bands. The system also has the drawback of removing the pressure on governments to maintain a low rate of inflation.

END OF CHAPTER QUESTIONS

1. Under what circumstances does a growth in financial flows make exchange rates less stable?
2. Assume that countries in the eurozone decide to pursue a deflationary fiscal policy. What effect is this likely to have on the UK economy?
3. It is often argued that international convergence of economic indicators is a desirable objective. Does this mean that countries should all seek to achieve the same rate of economic growth, monetary growth, interest rates, budget deficits as a percentage of their GDP, etc?
4. Did the exchange rate difficulties experienced by countries under the ERM strengthen or weaken the arguments for progressing to a single European currency?
5. Assume that just some of the members of a common market like the EU adopt full economic and monetary union, including a common currency. What are the advantages and disadvantages to those members joining the full EMU and to those not?
6. Is the eurozone an optimal currency area? Explain your answer.
7. How are asymmetric shocks dealt with within a country? To what extent can this process be mirrored within the eurozone?
8. Would the world benefit from the general imposition of controls on the movement of international finance?

Additional case studies on the book's website (www.pearsoned.co.uk/sloman)

25.1 The new economy. Does globalisation bring economic success?

25.2 High oil prices. What is their effect on the world economy?

25.3 Crisis in south-east Asia. Causes of the severe recession in many south-east Asian countries in 1997/8.

25.4 The 1997/8 crisis in Asia: the role played by the IMF.

25.5 Converging on the euro. Did the 11 countries that adopted the euro in 1999 genuinely meet the convergence criteria?

25.6 The UK Labour government's convergence criteria for euro membership. An examination of the five tests set by the UK government that would have to be passed before the question of euro membership would be put to the electorate in a referendum.

WEBSITES RELEVANT TO CHAPTERS 24 AND 25

Numbers and sections refer to websites listed in the Web Appendix and hotlinked from this book's website at www.pearsoned.co.uk/sloman.

- For news articles relevant to this and the previous chapter, see the *Economics News Articles* link from the book's website.
- For general news on countries' balance of payments and exchange rates, see websites in section A, and particularly A1–5, 7–9, 20–25, 31. For articles on various aspects of economic development, see A27, 28; I9. See also links to newspapers worldwide in A38, 39, 43 and 44, and the news search feature in Google at A41. See also links to economics news in A42.
- For international data on balance of payments and exchange rates, see *World Economic Outlook* in H4 and *OECD Economic Outlook* in B21 (also in section 6 of B1). See also the trade topic in I14. The ESDS International site (B35) has links to World Bank, IMF, OECD, UN and Eurostat datasets (but you will need an Athens password, available free to all UK higher education students).
- For details of individual countries' balance of payments, see B32.
- For UK data on balance of payments, see B1, *1. National Statistics* > the fourth link > *Economy* > *United Kingdom Balance of Payments – the Pink Book.* See also B3, 34; F2. For EU data, see G1 > *The Statistical Annex* > *Foreign trade and current balance.*
- For exchange rates, see A3; B34; F2, 6, 8.
- For discussion papers on balance of payments and exchange rates, see H4 and 7.
- Sites I7 and 11 contain links to *Balance of payments and exchange rates* in *International economics.*
- For various pressure groups critical of the effects of free trade and globalisation, see H12–14.
- For information on EMU, see sites G1, 2, 3 and 6; F3–6 and 9.
- For student resources relevant to these two chapters, see sites C1–7, 9, 10, 19. See also *The trade balance and the exchange rate* in site D3.

Chapter 26 Economic Problems of Developing Countries

In this final chapter, we turn to the economic problems of the poorer countries of the world. These include all the countries of Africa and Latin America and most of the countries of Asia. More than three-quarters of the world's population lives in these countries. As Theodore Schultz said when accepting the Nobel Prize in Economics in 1979:

> ***Most of the people of the world are poor, so if we knew the economics of being poor we would know much of the economics that really matters.***

We start by looking at the nature and extent of their poverty and the means by which it can be measured. We then look at the trade relations between the poorer countries and the advanced industrialised world. As we shall see, most developing countries are highly dependent for their development, or lack of it, on their relationships with the rich world.

In section 26.3, the focus shifts to some of the internal problems faced by developing countries: problems such as the neglect of agriculture, the use of inappropriate technology and the rise in unemployment. The final section looks at one of the most serious problems facing poorer countries: the problem of huge international debts. We look at the growing calls for the debts of the poorest countries to be cancelled and at the response of the rich countries.

CHAPTER MAP

26.1 THE PROBLEM OF UNDERDEVELOPMENT

The gulf between rich and poor countries

The typical family in North America, western Europe, Japan and Australasia has many material comforts: plentiful food to eat; a house or apartment with electricity and running hot and cold water; an inside toilet connected to an underground sewerage system; access to free or affordable health care and education; numerous consumer durables; holidays away from home; visits to the cinema, concerts, sports events, etc. There are some people, it is true, who are very poor. But it is only a small minority that cannot afford the basics of life, such as adequate food, shelter and clothing.

KI 1 p4

In most of Africa and large parts of Asia and Latin America, the picture is quite different. The majority of people live in poverty. For them life is a daily struggle for survival. Affluence does exist in these countries, but here it is the fortunate few who can afford good food, good housing and the various luxury items that typify life in the industrialised world.

KI 17 p121

A large proportion of the inhabitants live in the countryside. For many, this means living in a family with many children and working on a small amount of land with too little income to buy adequate agricultural machinery, fertilisers or pesticides. With a rapid growth in population there is less and less land to go round. As land is passed on from generation to generation, it is divided up between the offspring into smaller and smaller plots. Many who cannot make ends meet are forced to sell their land to the local landlords. Then as landless labourers they have to accept very low-paid jobs on the large farms or plantations. Others try to survive by borrowing, hoping to be able to pay off their debts with future crop sales. But often the only source of finance is again the local landlord who charges exorbitant rates of interest. As a result, they end up in a state of 'debt bondage' where they can never pay off their debts, but year in year out have to give part of their crops to the landlord as interest.

Others come to the rapidly growing cities. In the cities, at least there are some jobs. But far more people migrate to the cities than there are jobs available. Thus the number of unemployed in the cities grows inexorably. People are forced to do anything to earn a living: selling wares on street corners, or working as casual labourers, domestic servants or shoe shiners; some resort to prostitution and crime, others merely beg. All round the outskirts of cities throughout the developing world, shanty towns mushroom as the poor flock in from the countryside. Families crowd into one- or two-roomed shacks, often with no electricity, no water and no sanitation. There are schools in these towns, but often parents cannot afford to allow their children to attend. Instead they have to send them out to work to supplement the family's meagre income.

Statistics cannot give the complete picture, but they can give us some indication of the gulf between rich and poor countries. Here are some examples:

- 85 per cent of the world's population lives in developing countries but earns only 20 per cent of the world's income.
- The GNY[1] per head of the 20 poorest countries of the world in 2003 averaged only $220. For the richest 20 it was $29 100.
- The average annual GNY-per-capita growth rate between 1975 and 2003 was 5.8 per cent in East Asia but was –0.5 per cent in Sub-Saharan Africa. It was 2.0 per cent in the advanced industrialised countries.
- The average life expectancy at birth in the 10 poorest countries of the world is 42 years. It is 79 years in the 10 richest countries.
- Developing countries tend to suffer higher rates of inflation than advanced industrial economies.

Table 26.1 gives more details.

The meaning of 'development'

Countries want to develop. But just what do we mean by 'development?' Clearly it is a normative concept. Its definition will depend on the goals that the economist assumes societies want to achieve. So how do economists define and measure development?

The basic needs approach

A starting point is to identify the basic needs that people have if they are to be able to realise their potential as human beings. Different economists have identified various lists of requirements, including the following items:

- Adequate food, shelter, warmth and clothing.
- Universal access to education.
- Availability of adequate health care.
- Availability of non-demeaning jobs.
- Sufficient free time to be able to enjoy social interaction.
- Freedom to make one's own economic decisions.
- Freedom for people to participate in the decisions of government and other bodies that affect their lives.

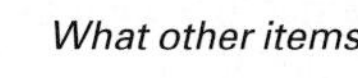

? *What other items might be included as basic needs?*

There are four major problems with defining development in terms of a basic list of requirements.

The first is in deciding *what to include*. Any definition of *economic* development would clearly include people's

[1] GNY (gross national income): see appendix to Chapter 13.

Table 26.1 Selected world statistics

	Low-income economies[a]	Sub-Saharan Africa	Lower-middle-income economies[b]	Upper-middle-income economies[c]	High-income economies[d]	All countries
Population (millions, 2003)	2310	703	2655	335	971	6272
GNY per capita ($ per annum, 2000)	450	490	1480	5340	28 550	5500
Population growth (average annual %, 1990–2003)	2.0	2.5	1.1	1.3	0.7	1.4
Growth in private consumption per capita (average annual %,1980–2003)	1.3	−0.3	2.8	1.4	1.9	1.2
Growth in exports of goods and services (average annual % 1980–2003)	5.5	2.6	5.4	7.8	5.5	5.6
Life expectancy at birth (years) (2002)	58	46	69	73	78	67
Number of doctors per 1000 people (1993–2000)	0.4	0.1	1.9	1.8	2.8	1.4
Under-5 mortality per 1000 (2002)	126	174	40	22	7	81
Adult literacy (%, 2002)						
Female	52	42	14	10	<2	27
Male	32	30	12	9	<2	20
Urban population as % of total population (2003)	30	36	50	76	76	48

[a] Those countries with a GNY per head in 2003 of $765 or less.
[b] Those countries with a GNY per head in 2003 of $766–$3035.
[c] Those countries with a GNY per head in 2003 of $3036–$9385.
[d] Those countries with a GNY per head in 2003 of over $9385.

Source: *World Development Indicators* (World Bank, 2005).

material standard of living. But should development include social and political factors such as 'self-esteem', freedom from servitude and freedom of religion?

The second problem is in *measuring each of the items*. It is possible to measure such things as income per head, literacy rates and mortality rates. It is much more difficult, however, to measure the achievement of social and political objectives such as self-esteem.

The third problem is in arriving at a *single measure* of the level of development. You cannot add the average calorific intake to the number of doctors and nurses to the percentage of homes having various basic amenities such as running water. You can meaningfully add things up only if they are expressed in the same units, or if appropriate *weights* are attached to each of the items. Clearly, the assigning of any such weights would be highly controversial.

The fourth problem is in deciding the importance of the *distribution* of the various items. If, say, the average calorific intake increases, but the poorest sections of the population have less to eat, has the country really experienced an increase in the level of development?

However, many economists argue that the basic needs approach does provide a useful 'checklist' to see whether a country's development is broadly based or confined to just one or two indicators.

Would it be possible with this basic needs approach to say (a) that one country was more developed than another; (b) that one country was developing faster than another?

Using GNY to measure development

The desire to have a single measure for development and thus to be able to make simple comparisons between countries has led to the universal use of real gross national income (GNY) per capita as the main indicator. It has some major advantages:

- It takes into account virtually all the goods and services produced in a country, and converts them into a single measure by the use of market prices.
- Although markets are by no means perfect, they do reflect the strength of demand and the opportunity costs of supply.

- The rules for the measurement of GNY are universally agreed.
- Virtually all countries compile GNY statistics.
- Although not every item that affects human welfare is included in GNY, a sustained rise in GNY is generally agreed to be a *necessary* condition for a sustained rise in welfare.
- There is a fairly close correlation between the level of per-capita GNY and other indicators such as mortality rates, literacy rates, and calorific and protein intake.

However, there are four fundamental criticisms of relying on simple GNY per capita as an indicator of development.

Many items are excluded. Much of production that does not get bought and sold will escape being recorded. This is a particular problem with rural societies that are largely subsistence based. People grow their own food, build their own houses, make their own clothes and provide their own entertainment. GNY statistics are therefore likely to *understate* the level of production in these societies.

On the other hand, as these societies 'develop', the size of the market sector is likely to grow. A larger proportion of people's consumption will be of items they have purchased and which therefore do enter into GNY statistics. Thus GNY figures will *overstate* the rate of growth of production and consumption.

As an economy becomes more urbanised, there is likely to be a growth in *external* costs of production and consumption, such as pollution and crime. Traditional ways of life will be destroyed; people may find themselves increasingly in a competitive, uncaring environment. Again the growth in GNY is likely to *overstate* the growth in human welfare. KI 28 p300

Market prices may be highly distorted. GNY is based on market prices, but these prices may be distorted. Markets are often highly fragmented, and there is little competition to ensure that prices reflect undistorted marginal costs. Companies often have considerable monopoly power to push up prices of manufactured goods; landlords often have power to push up rents; governments may impose price controls on food; employers with monopsony power may be able to pay very low wages.

? *How would a redistribution of income to the powerful be likely to affect GNY?*

Exchange rates may not reflect local purchasing power. GNY statistics are initially compiled in terms of the domestic currency. For purposes of international comparison they then have to be converted into a common currency – usually the US dollar – at the current exchange rate. But exchange rates reflect demand and supply of *traded* goods; they do not reflect the prices of *non-traded* goods.

Figure 26.1 GNY per head as a percentage of US GNY per head: 2003 (using purchasing-power parity exchange rates)

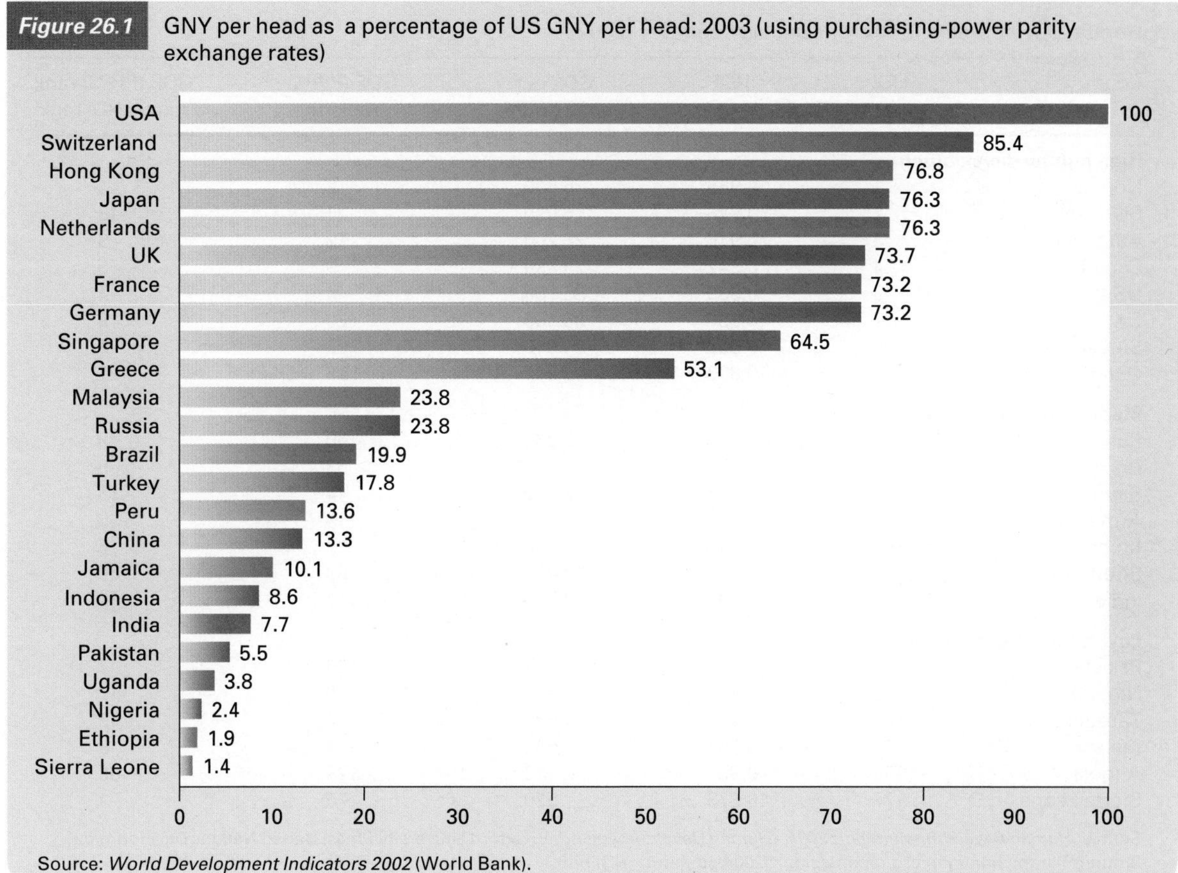

Source: *World Development Indicators 2002* (World Bank).

EXPLORING ECONOMICS 

THE HUMAN DEVELOPMENT INDEX (HDI)

A measure of human welfare?

Since 1990, the United Nations Development Program (UNDP) has published an annual Human Development Index (HDI). This is an attempt to provide a more broadly based measure of development than GDP or GNY. HDI is the average of three indices based on three sets of variables: life expectancy at birth, education (a weighted average of adult literacy (two-thirds) and average years of schooling (one-third)), and real GDP per capita, measured in US dollars at purchasing-power parity exchange rates. Countries are then placed in one of three groups according to their HDI: high human development (0.8 to 1.0), medium human development (0.5 to 0.799) and low human development (below 0.5).

For each of the three indices making up the HDI, a sophisticated formula is used. Thus the index for GDP attempts to measure material well-being by building in the assumption of a rapidly diminishing marginal utility of income above average world levels.

The table, based on the 2004 Human Development Report, gives the 2002 HDIs for selected countries and their rankings. It also gives rankings for GDP per capita. The final column shows the divergence between the two rankings. A positive number shows that a country has a higher ranking for HDI than GDP per capita. As can be seen, the rankings differ substantially in some cases between the two measures. For some countries, such as Sweden, Australia, Armenia and Nigeria, GDP understates their relative level of human development, whereas for others, such as Qatar, Saudi Arabia and South Africa, GDP per capita overstates their relative level of human development. Thus Angola's (PPP) GDP per capita is over three times that of Tanzania and yet its HDI is lower.

The point is that countries with similar levels of national income may use that income quite differently.

Recently, work has been done to adjust HDI figures for various other factors, such as overall income distribution, gender inequalities and inequalities by region or ethnic group. Thus the overall HDI can be adjusted downwards to reflect greater degrees of inequality. Alternatively, separate HDIs can be produced for separate regions, ethnic groups or women and men within a country.

1. ***For what reasons are HDI and per capita GDP rankings likely to diverge?***
2. ***Why do Qatar and Saudi Arabia have such a large negative figure in the final column of the table?***

Human Development Index for selected countries (2002)

Country	HDI ranking	HDI	GDP per head (PPP$)	GDP (PPP$) ranking	GDP (PPP$) rank minus HDI rank
High human development					
Norway	1	0.956	36 600	2	1
Sweden	2	0.946	26 050	21	19
Australia	3	0.946	28 260	12	9
Canada	4	0.942	29 480	9	5
USA	8	0.939	35 750	4	–4
UK	12	0.936	26 150	20	8
Singapore	25	0.902	24 040	22	–3
Qatar	47	0.833	19 844	26	–21
Medium human development					
Russia	57	0.796	8 230	60	3
Brazil	72	0.775	7 770	63	–9
Saudi Arabia	77	0.768	12 650	44	–33
Armenia	82	0.754	3 120	115	33
China	94	0.745	4 580	99	5
South Africa	119	0.666	10 070	53	–66
India	127	0.595	2 670	117	–10
Low human development					
Pakistan	142	0.497	1 940	135	–7
Nigeria	151	0.466	860	166	15
Tanzania	162	0.407	580	174	12
Malawi	165	0.388	580	174	9
Angola	166	0.381	2 130	128	–38
Sierra Leone	177	0.273	520	176	–1

Source: *Human Development Report 2004 – Human Development Index* (Oxford University Press, United Nations Development Program) (http://hdr.undp.org/reports/global/2004/pdf/hdr04_HDI.pdf).

Generally, the price of non-traded goods and services in developing countries will be lower than the price of similar goods and services in advanced countries. The *level* of GNY is therefore likely to *understate* the level of production in poor countries. If, on the other hand, the proportion of traded goods increases over time, the *growth* of GNY will again *overstate* the growth in production. It is much better, therefore, to estimate GNY using purchasing-power parity exchange rates. Even if this is done, however, massive differences remain in GNY per head between rich and poor countries. This is illustrated in Figure 26.1, which shows GNY per head at PPP exchange rates as a percentage of US GNY per head.

KI 4 p11 *Simple GNY per head ignores the distribution of income.* Since the early 1980s, many developing countries have achieved relatively rapid growth in per capita GNY as they have sought overseas investment, privatised their industries and cut the levels of public provision. But with a deepening of poverty, a growing inequality in the distribution of income and an increase in unemployment, few would argue that this constitutes genuine 'development'.

Many who have advocated the concentration on GNY and its rate of growth have argued that, while the rich may be the first to benefit from prosperity, gradually the benefits will 'trickle down' to the poor. In practice, the wealth has failed to trickle down in many countries. The rich have got richer while the poor have got poorer.

Given the weaknesses of GNY, but given the desirability of having a single measure of development, various composite indicators have been constructed. The most widely used is the ***Human Development Index (HDI)***, which is a combined measure of life expectancy, education and GDP per head at PPP exchange rates. This index is examined in Box 26.1.

Definition

Human Development Index (HDI) A composite index made up of three elements: an index for life expectancy, an index for school enrolment and adult literacy, and an index for GDP per capita (in PPP$).

Section summary

1. There are a number of ways of categorising countries according to their level of development.
2. The level of development of a country can be defined in terms of the extent to which it meets basic needs for human life. There is no universal agreement, however, about which items should be measured or about how to measure and weight them. Nevertheless, the approach provides a useful indicator of whether development is broadly based and how rapidly the most serious problems of poverty are being tackled.
3. The most widely used measure of development is GNY per head at PPP exchange rates. However, there are serious problems with using GNY: many items may be excluded, especially for a more subsistence-based society; prices may be highly distorted; and the statistics ignore the question of the distribution of income. Another widely used measure is the Human Development Index.

26.2 INTERNATIONAL TRADE AND DEVELOPMENT

The importance of international trade to developing countries

International trade is one of the most contentious issues in development economics. Should countries adopt an open trading policy with few if any barriers to imports? Should governments actively promote trade by subsidising their export sector? Or should they restrict trade and pursue a policy of greater self-sufficiency? These are issues that we will be looking at in this section.

Whether it is desirable that developing countries should adopt policies of more trade or less, trade is still vital. Certain raw materials, capital equipment and intermediate products that are necessary for development can be obtained only from abroad. Others *could* be produced domestically, but only at much higher cost.

Trade strategies

As they develop, countries' policies towards trade typically go through various stages.

Primary outward-looking stage

Traditionally, developing countries have exported primaries – minerals such as copper, cash crops such as coffee, and non-foodstuffs such as cotton – in exchange for manufactured consumer goods. Having little in the way of an industrial base, if they want to consume manufactured goods, they have to import them.

Secondary inward-looking stage

In seeking rapid economic development, most developing countries drew lessons from the experience of the advanced countries. The main conclusion was that industrialisation was the key to economic success.

But industrialisation required foreign exchange to purchase capital equipment. This led to a policy of ***import-substituting industrialisation***, which involved cutting back on non-essential imports and thereby releasing foreign exchange. Tariffs and other restrictions were imposed on those imports for which a domestic substitute existed, or which were regarded as unimportant.

Secondary outward-looking stage

Once an industry had satisfied domestic demand, it had to seek markets abroad if expansion was to continue. What is more, as we shall see, import substitution brought a number of serious problems for developing countries. The answer seemed to be to look outward again, this time to the export of manufactured goods. Many of the most economically successful developing countries (especially Hong Kong, Singapore, South Korea, Taiwan and, more recently, China) have owed their high growth rates to a rapid expansion of manufactured exports.

We will now examine the three stages in more detail.

Approach 1: Exporting primaries – exploiting comparative advantage

The importance of primary exports

Despite moves towards import substitution and secondary export promotion, many developing countries still rely heavily on primary exports. These constituted 72 per cent of total developing country exports in 1970. Although by 2002 this had fallen to 53 per cent for low-income countries and 40 per cent for middle-income countries, it was still much higher than the figure for advanced countries (18 per cent). For many of the poorest African countries, the figure was over 90 per cent.

The justification for exporting primaries

Three major arguments have been traditionally used for pursuing a policy of exporting primaries. In each case, the arguments have also been used to justify a policy of free or virtually free trade.

Exporting primaries exploits comparative advantage. Traditional trade theory implies that countries should specialise in producing those items in which they have a comparative advantage: i.e. those goods that can be produced at relatively low opportunity costs. For most developing countries, this means that a large proportion of their exports should be primaries.

KI 35 p637

The reasons for differences in comparative costs were examined by two Swedish economists, Eli Heckscher and Bertil Ohlin. They believed that comparative cost differences arise from differences in factor endowments. The ***Heckscher–Ohlin theory*** states that: *a country should specialise in those goods that are intensive in the country's abundant factor*. The more abundant a factor, the relatively cheaper it is likely to be, and thus the lower will be the opportunity cost of producing goods that are intensive in its use. Thus labour-abundant developing countries should specialise in labour-intensive products. By exporting these products, which will typically be primaries, they can earn the foreign exchange to import goods that use large amounts of capital and other resources that are in short supply.

According to this theory, international trade would lead not only to higher consumption, but also to ***factor price equalisation***: i.e. the erosion of income inequalities between trading nations. For example, if wage rates are low in developing countries, trade will increase the demand for their labour-intensive products and thereby push up wage rates. International trade will also erode income differentials *within* countries. The demand for exports will increase the demand for the relatively cheap factors, and imports will reduce the demand for the relatively expensive ones. Thus the cheap factors will go up in price and the expensive ones will come down.

1. *What effect will trade have on the price of capital in developing and developed countries?*
2. *It is sometimes claimed that trade with developing countries is unjust because it leads to the importation of goods produced at pitifully low wages. How can the Heckscher–Ohlin theory be used to refute this claim? Is there any validity in the claim? (See Box 23.2.)*

Exporting primaries provides a 'vent for surplus'. Trade offers a ***vent for surplus***: i.e. a means of putting to use resources that would otherwise not be used. These surpluses will occur where the domestic market is simply not big enough to consume all the available output of a particular

Definitions

Import-substituting industrialisation A strategy of restricting imports of manufactured goods and using the foreign exchange saved to build up domestic substitute industries.

Heckscher–Ohlin version of comparative advantage A country has a comparative advantage in those goods that are intensive in the country's relatively abundant factor.

Factor price equalisation The tendency for international trade to reduce factor price inequalities both between and within countries.

Vent for surplus Where international trade enables a country to exploit resources that would otherwise be unused.

good. There is far too little demand within Zambia to consume its potential output of copper. The same applies to Namibian uranium or Peruvian tin.

Exporting primaries provides an 'engine for economic growth'. According to this argument, developing countries benefit from the growth of the economies of the developed world. As industrial expansion takes place in the rich North, this will create additional demand for primaries from the poor South.

Traditional trade theory in the context of development

There are several reasons for questioning whether the above arguments justify a policy of relying on primary exports as the means to development.

Comparative costs change over time. Over time, with the acquisition of new skills and an increase in the capital stock, a developing country that once had a comparative advantage in primaries may find that it now has a comparative advantage in certain *manufactured* products, especially those that are more labour intensive and use raw materials of which the country has a plentiful supply. The market, however, cannot necessarily be relied upon to bring about a smooth transition to producing such products.

Concentrating on primary production may hinder growth. The theory of comparative advantage shows how trade allows a country to consume beyond its production possibility curve (see pages 636–40). As its economy grows, however, this production possibility curve will *shift outwards*. By concentrating on primaries, the curve may shift outwards more slowly than if the country had pursued a policy of industrialisation. In other words, economic growth may be slower from a policy of exporting primaries than from a policy of industrialisation.

The benefits from trade may not accrue to the nationals of the country. If a mine or plantation is owned by a foreign company, it will be the foreign shareholders who get the profits from the sale of exports. In addition, these companies may bring in their own capital and skilled labour from abroad. The benefits gained by the local people will probably be confined to the additional wages they earn. With these companies being in a position of monopsony power, the wages are often very low.

Why does this argument make GNY a better indicator of development than GDP? (See the appendix to Chapter 13.)

Trade may lead to less equality. Trade shifts income distribution in favour of those factors of production employed intensively in the export sector. If exports are labour intensive, greater equality will tend to result. But if they are land or raw material intensive, trade will redistribute income in favour of large landowners or mine-owners.

Exporting primary exports may involve external costs. KI 28 p300 Mining can lead to huge external costs, such as the despoiling of the countryside and damage to the health of miners. Mines and plantations can lead to the destruction of traditional communities and their values.

Trade may adversely influence tastes. The more freely a country trades, the more will people's aspirations for a 'better life' be fuelled. If people cannot afford to buy the goods imported from the affluent world, their frustrations are likely to increase.

These arguments cast doubt on whether a policy of relying on free trade in primary exports is the best way of achieving economic development. Various trends in the international economy have also worked against primary exporters, causing them serious balance of payments problems.

Balance of payments problems: long term

Long-term trends in international trade have caused problems for primary exporting countries in three ways: (a) exports have grown slowly; (b) imports have grown rapidly; (c) the terms of trade have moved against them.

Low income elasticity of demand for primary products. As world incomes grow, so a smaller proportion of these KI 9 incomes is spent on primaries. Since food is a necessity, p58 consumers, especially in rich countries, already consume virtually all they require. A rise in incomes, therefore, tends to be spent more on luxury goods and services, and only slightly more on basic foodstuffs. The exceptions are certain 'luxury' imported foodstuffs such as exotic fruits. In the case of raw materials, as people's incomes grow, they tend to buy more and more expensive products. The extra value of these products, however, arises not from the extra raw materials they might contain, but from their greater sophistication.

Agricultural protection in advanced countries. Faced with the problem of a slowly growing demand for food produced by their own farmers, advanced countries increasingly imposed restrictions on imported food. Reducing these restrictions has been one of the main aims of the Doha Development Agenda (the latest round of WTO trade negotiations: see Box 23.7 on page 653).

Technological developments. Synthetic substitutes have in many cases replaced primaries in the making of consumer durables, industrial equipment and clothing. Also, the process of miniaturisation, as microchips have replaced machines, has meant that less and less raw materials have been required to produce any given amount of output.

Rapid growth in imports. There tends to be a high income elasticity of demand for imported manufactures. This is the result partly of the better-off in developing countries being able to afford luxury goods, and partly of the development of new tastes as people are exposed to the products of the developed world – products such as Coca-Cola, Levi jeans, mobile phones and iPods. In fact, the whole process has been dubbed 'Coca-Colanisation'.

TC 8 p 59 *Deterioration in the terms of trade.* The slow growth in demand for primary exports and the rapid growth in demand for manufactured imports has led to chronic current account balance of payments problems for primary exporters. This has caused their exchange rates to depreciate and hence brought a decline in their terms of trade, where a country's terms of trade are defined as the average price of its exports divided by the average price of its imports (P_x/P_m).

This problem has been compounded by adverse movements in international prices of primaries and manufactures. The overall demand for primaries tends to be relatively price inelastic. There is no substitute for food, and in the short run there is often no substitute for minerals. On the other hand, the demand for any *one* primary product, and especially the demand for any one *country's* primary exports, will be very price elastic: there are plenty of other countries producing substitutes. This will encourage countries to produce as much as possible (as long as price remains above marginal cost), but as all countries do the same, the low overall price elasticity will depress primary product prices. Between 1980 and 2000, non-fuel primary product prices fell by 45 per cent (see Table 26.2).

Because of a lack of domestic substitutes, the price elasticity of demand for manufactured imports is also low. This gives market power to the overseas suppliers of these imports, which tends to raise their price relative to exports.

Balance of payments problems: short term

There are also problems for primary exporting countries in the *short term*.

The prices of primary products are subject to large fluctuations. This causes great uncertainty for primary exporters. The current account of the balance of payments fluctuates wildly, which tends to cause large swings in exchange rates or requires massive government intervention to stabilise them.

Price fluctuations are caused partly by the low price elasticity of demand and supply of primaries, which we have just considered. They are also caused by substantial *shifts* in their demand and supply.

Table 26.2 World primary commodity prices (1990 = 100)

	1960	1970	1980	1990	2003
Agricultural products	208	163	175	100	95
Metals and minerals	137	144	120	100	82
All non-fuel commodities	187	156	159	100	91
Oil	34	19	224	100	126

Source: *World Development Indicators 2005* (World Bank).

The demand for *food* is relatively stable, but that for minerals varies with the business cycle and tends to vary more than the demand for consumer goods. The reason is the *accelerator principle* (see section 16.4). Since the *level* of investment demand depends on the size of *changes* in consumer demand, investment will fluctuate much more than consumer demand. But since many minerals are inputs into *capital* equipment, their demand is also likely to fluctuate more than consumer demand. KI 31 p 368

The supply of minerals is relatively stable. The supply of cash crops, however, varies with the harvest. Many developing countries are subject to drought or flood, which can virtually wipe out their export earnings from the relevant crop.

If a disastrous harvest of rice were confined to a particular country, would (a) the world price and (b) its own domestic price of rice fluctuate significantly? What would happen to the country's export earnings and the earnings of individual farmers?

With a price-inelastic world demand and supply for primaries, shifts in either curve will lead to substantial fluctuations in world prices. The problem is most serious for countries that rely on just one or two primary products, such as Ghana on cocoa and the Congo on copper. Diversification into other primaries would help to reduce their exposure. TC 8 p 59

Approach 2: Import-substituting industrialisation (ISI)

Dissatisfaction with relying on primary exporting has led most countries to embark on a process of industrialisation. The newly industrialised countries (NICs), such as Malaysia and Brazil, are already well advanced along the industrialisation road. Other developing countries have not yet progressed very far, especially the poorest African countries. TC 7 p 26

The most obvious way for countries to industrialise was to cut back on the imports of manufactures and substitute them with home-produced manufactures. This could not be done overnight: it had to be done in stages, beginning with assembly, then making some of the components, and finally making all, or nearly all, of the inputs into production. Most developing countries have at least started on the first stage. Several of the more advanced developing countries have component-manufacturing industries. Only a few of the larger NICs, such as India, Brazil and South Korea, have built extensive capital goods industries.

The method most favoured by policy makers is ***tariff escalation***. Here tariff rates (or other restrictions) increase

Definition

Tariff escalation The system whereby tariff rates increase the closer a product is to the finished stage of production.

CASE STUDIES AND APPLICATIONS

BOX 26.2

WHEN DRIVING AND ALCOHOL DO MIX

A case of import substitution in Brazil

Two major changes in world trade hit Brazil in the 1970s. The first was the fourfold increase in world oil prices. Brazil has very little oil of its own. The second was the slump in the world sugar cane market as a result of northern countries' protection of their sugar beet industries. Brazil was a major cane sugar exporter.

Faced with a resulting large increase in its import bill and a slump in its sugar exports, the Brazilian government came up with an ingenious solution. It could use surplus sugar cane to make alcohol, which could then be used instead of petrol for cars. Large distilleries were set up to convert the sugar cane into alcohol. At the same time, cars were produced (e.g. VW Beetles) that could run on alcohol rather than petrol.

Thus by one measure two problems were alleviated.

Then with the decline in oil prices from the mid-1980s, the relative cost-efficiency of alcohol-powered cars declined: at times it was cheaper to import oil than to produce alcohol. This illustrates the danger of basing major schemes on terms of trade existing at a particular time. If these terms of trade subsequently change, the schemes could prove to be uneconomical.

A more flexible solution was found in 2003 with the introduction of dual-fuel cars that could run on either alcohol or petrol or a mixture of the two. This gave consumers the chance of using whichever fuel was the cheapest at the time. The popularity of these 'flexi-fuel' cars has given a much-welcomed boost to the sugar cane and alcohol fuel industries. By 2005, 50 per cent of Brazilian cars were dual fuel, and alcohol constituted 40 per cent of all vehicle fuel sold. By 2007 all new Brazilian cars should be able to run on alcohol.

In the mid-1990s, Brazil abolished subsidies on alcohol, but the industry is now well able to survive without. With oil prices at around $50 per barrel, alcohol can be produced at half the cost of petrol.

Since the 1970s, alcohol production has displaced some $120 billion of oil imports. Given this success of the alcohol programme, Brazil has now embarked on another import-substituting drive: to displace diesel fuel with vegetable oils from its huge soybean crop. Perhaps this 'biodiesel' will become the new dollar saver.

Could a case be made out for a flexible tax on oil imports to ensure that it was always profitable to produce alcohol?

as one moves from the raw materials to the intermediate product to the finished product stage. Thus finished goods have higher tariffs than intermediate products. This encourages assembly plants, which are protected by high tariffs from imported finished products, and are able to obtain components at a lower tariff rate.

One of the problems with ISI is that countries are desperately short of resources to invest in industry. As a result, a policy of ISI has usually involved encouraging investment by multinational companies. But even without specific 'perks' (e.g. tax concessions, cheap sites, the cutting of red tape), multinationals will still probably be attracted by the protection afforded by the tariffs or quotas.

Adverse effects of import substitution

Some countries, such as South Korea and Taiwan, pursued an inward-looking ISI policy for only a few years. For them it was merely a stage in development, rapidly to be followed by a secondary outward-looking policy. Infant industries were initially given protection, but when they had achieved sufficient economies of scale, the barriers to imports were gradually removed.

The countries that have continued to pursue protectionist ISI policies have generally had a poorer growth record. They have also tended to suffer from other problems, such as a deepening of inequality. The development of the modern industrial sector has often been to the detriment of the traditional sectors and also to the export sector.

The criticisms of ISI are numerous, and include the following.

It has run directly counter to the principle of comparative advantage. Rather than confining ISI to genuine infant industries and then gradually removing the protection, ISI has been applied indiscriminately to a whole range of industries. Countries are producing goods in which they have a comparative *disadvantage*.

If a country specialises in a good in which it has a comparative disadvantage, where will it be consuming with respect to its production possibility curve?

It has cushioned inefficient practices and encouraged the establishment of monopolies. Without competition from imports, many of the industries are highly inefficient and wasteful of resources. What is more, in all but the largest or most developed of the developing countries the domestic market for manufactures is small. If a newly established industry is to be large enough to gain the full potential economies of scale, it must be large relative to the market. This means that it will have considerable monopoly power.

KI 19 p157

It has involved artificially low real interest rates. To encourage capital investment in the import-substituting industries, governments have often intervened to keep interest rates low. This has encouraged the use of capital-intensive technology with a consequent lack of jobs. It has also starved other sectors (such as agriculture) of much-needed finance, and it has discouraged saving.

It has led to urban wages above the market-clearing level. Wage rates in the industrial sector, although still low compared with advanced countries, are often considerably higher than in the traditional sectors.

- They are pushed up by firms seeking to retain labour in which they have invested training.
- Governments, seeking to appease the politically powerful urban industrial working class, have often passed minimum wage laws.
- Trade unions, although less widespread in developing than in advanced countries, are mainly confined to the new industries.

Higher industrial wages again encourage firms to use capital-intensive techniques.

It has involved overvalued exchange rates. Restricting imports tends to lead to an appreciation of the exchange rate. This makes non-restricted imports cheaper. This then discourages the production of domestic goods, such as food and component parts, which compete with those imports. Also a higher exchange rate discourages exports. Exports tend to be priced in dollars. If the exchange rate appreciates, domestic currency will buy more dollars; or put another way, a dollar will exchange for less domestic currency. Thus exporters will earn less domestic currency as the exchange rate appreciates.

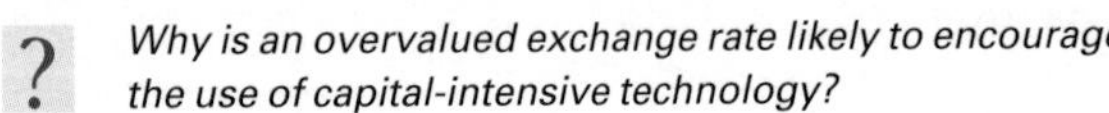

Why is an overvalued exchange rate likely to encourage the use of capital-intensive technology?

It does not necessarily save on foreign exchange. Many of the new industries are highly dependent on the importation of raw materials, capital equipment and component parts. These imported inputs, unlike imports of finished goods, are often supplied by a single firm, which can thus charge monopoly prices. What is more, a large proportion of the extra incomes generated by these industries tends to be spent on imports by the new urban élites.

Protection has not been applied evenly. Many different tariff rates have often been used in one country: in fact, a policy of tariff escalation demands this. In addition, governments have often used a whole range of other protectionist instruments, such as the licensing of importers, physical and value quotas, and foreign exchange rationing. The result is that protection has been highly uneven.

Economists have developed the concept of ***effective protection*** to measure the true degree of protection that an industry gets. Effective protection measures the extra domestic value added that protection gives an industry. By *domestic value added* we mean the difference between the world market price of the finished good and the cost of the imported inputs used to make the good.

The effective rate of protection is given by the formula:

$$\frac{V^* - V}{V} \times 100$$

where V is the free-trade domestic value added, and V^* is the value added after the imposition of tariffs. There are three variables that determine the rate of effective protection:

- The tariff rate on the finished good (the nominal rate of protection). The higher this is, the higher will be the value of V^* relative to V, and hence the higher will be the effective rate of protection.
- The tariff rate (or rates) on the inputs. The higher these are, the lower will be the value of V^* relative to V, and hence the lower will be the effective rate of protection.
- The level of value added as a proportion of the price of the finished good. The higher this is, the lower will be the effective rate of protection (assuming tariff escalation).

To demonstrate this last point, work out the effective rate of protection in the following three cases:
(a) Free-trade finished good price = £100; free-trade cost of imported inputs = £40.
(b) Free-trade finished good price = £100; free-trade cost of imported inputs = £80.
(c) Free-trade finished good price = £100; free-trade cost of imported inputs = £100.
In each case, assume that a 50 per cent tariff is imposed on the finished good and a 10 per cent tariff on the imported inputs.

In many countries, effective protective rates have varied massively from one industry to another. For example, according to World Bank estimates, in 1980 effective rates of protection in manufacturing ranged from –85 per cent to 219 per cent in Brazil and from –62 per cent to 1119 per cent in Nigeria! Clearly, such huge differences in effective protection impose massive distortions on the market.

Under what circumstances could the effective rate of protection be negative?

Income distribution is made less equal. Additional incomes generated by the modern sector tend to be spent on modern-sector goods and imported goods. Thus there is a multiplier effect *within* the modern sector, but virtually none between the sectors. Also, as we saw above, an overvalued exchange rate leads to a bias against agriculture, and thus further KI 4 p11

Definition

Effective rate of protection The percentage increase in an industry's domestic value added resulting from protection given to that industry.

Table 26.3 Growth rates and export performance of selected secondary outward-looking countries

	Average annual growth in real GDP (%)		**Share of manufactures in merchandise exports (%)**		**Average annual growth rate of merchandise exports (%)**	
	1960–90	**1991–2003**	**1970**	**2002**	**1960–90**	**1991–2003**
Brazil	5.5	1.8	13	55	14.1	5.8
Malaysia	6.8	6.5	7	80	13.4	9.4
South Korea	8.4	6.0	77	92	30.4	8.4
Singapore	9.2	6.3	28	85	16.3	7.4
Hong Kong	7.9	3.8	96	95	18.3	6.5
China	8.1	9.3	35	90	13.4	14.7
All developing countries	4.3	3.2	27	60	13.6	8.2

Sources: data drawn from *Handbook of Statistics* (UNCTAD) and *World Development Indicators* (World Bank).

deepens the divide between rich and poor. Finally, the relatively high wages of the modern sector encourage workers to migrate to the towns, where many, failing to get a job, live in dire poverty.

Social, cultural and environmental costs. A policy of ISI often involves imposing an alien set of values. Urban life can be harsh, competitive and materialistic. Moreover, the drive for industrialisation may involve major costs to the environment, as a result of waste products from new industries.

Finally, import substitution is necessarily limited by the size of the domestic market. Once that is saturated, ISI can come to an abrupt halt. At that stage, further expansion can come only from exporting; but if these industries have been overprotected, they will be unable to compete in world markets.

This has been a long list of problems and different economists put different emphases on them. Neo-classical economists stress the problems of market distortions, arguing that ISI leads to great inefficiency. Neo-Marxist economists, on the other hand, stress the problems of ***dependency***. Many of the new industries will be owned by multinational companies, which import unsuitable technologies. The countries will then become dependent on imported inputs and foreign sources of capital. (See Web Case 26.2.)

Approach 3: Exporting manufactures – a possible way forward?

The countries with the highest rates of economic growth are those that have successfully made the transition to being exporters of manufactures. Table 26.3 gives some examples.

> **Definition**
>
> **Dependency** Where the development of a developing country is hampered by its relationships with the industrialised world.

The transition from inward-looking to outward-looking industrialisation

How is a country to move from import substituting to being outward looking? One approach is to take it industry by industry. When an industry has saturated the home market and there is no further scope for import substitution, it should then be encouraged to seek markets overseas. The trouble with this approach is that, if the country is still protecting other industries, there will probably still be an overvalued exchange rate. Thus specific subsidies, tax concessions or other 'perks' would have to be given to this industry to enable it to compete. The country would still be highly interventionist, with all the distortions and misallocation of resources that this tends to bring.

The alternative is to wean the whole economy off protection. Three major things will need doing. There will need to be a devaluation of the currency in order to restore the potential profitability of the export sector. There will also need to be a dismantling of the various protective measures that had biased production towards the home market. Finally, there will probably need to be a removal or relaxing of price controls. But these are things that cannot be done 'at a stroke'. Firms may have to be introduced gradually to the greater forces of competition that an outward-looking trade policy brings. Otherwise there may be massive bankruptcies and a corresponding massive rise in unemployment.

The benefits from a secondary outward-looking policy

The advocates of outward-looking industrialisation make a number of points in its favour.

It conforms more closely to comparative advantage. Countries pursuing an open trade regime will be able to export only goods in which they have a comparative advantage. The resources used in earning a unit of foreign exchange from exports will be less than those used in

CASE STUDIES AND APPLICATIONS

THE CHINESE ECONOMIC MIRACLE

Riding the dragon

'China is amazing. It *is* capitalism, but at an unprecedented speed.' 'The talent of Chinese software engineers is unbelievable. I can't believe how effective they are.' *(Bill Gates, Chairman, Microsoft)*

'If your business isn't making money in China, it probably wouldn't make money anywhere else.' *(Carlos Ghosn, President, Nissan Motor Company)*[2]

On the basis of several indicators, China's economic performance is extraordinary. From 1990 to 2004 annual economic growth averaged 9.1 per cent. Its exports grew by an average of 16.5 per cent (see chart). In 2004 it overtook Japan to become the world's third largest exporter (after Germany and the USA). In PPP terms, China is the world's second biggest economy after the USA, or third if the eurozone is taken as a single economy.

And as China's economy and exports have boomed, so foreign investment has flooded into the country. In 1990 foreign direct investment (FDI) into China was $3.5 billion. By 2003 the figure had risen to $53.5 billion.

Chinese export-orientated growth has been based on three key factors: specialising in goods in which it has a comparative advantage; having an economy that is favourable to both domestic and inward investment; and having an exchange rate that is undervalued in PPP terms.

Specialisation

China has been industrialising rapidly. With the huge size of the domestic market and with an open policy towards exporting, China has specialised in goods that exploit its diverse but relatively well-trained labour force. Huge industrial complexes have sprung up along the coast from where it is easy to export.

Chinese firms have adapted to changing world markets and to their own changing comparative advantage. Twenty years ago, textiles and clothing were China's main export industry. These relatively labour-intensive industries were ideally suited to exploit the abilities of China's abundant labour. Today textiles and clothing account for a sixth of China's exports. Electronic goods, by contrast, account for more than a third and are growing at a rate three times as fast as textiles. Electronic goods exploit China's increasingly well-trained and well-educated workforce.

Investment

But why are foreign investors attracted to China? Is it simply that the economy is growing rapidly? Clearly that is part of the attraction, but it is more than that. For a start, the Chinese economy is huge. With a population of 1.3 billion and a GDP of $1.55 trillion in 2004, China represents a massive potential market. The government has also invested heavily in improving the

Growth in Chinese exports and GDP (%)

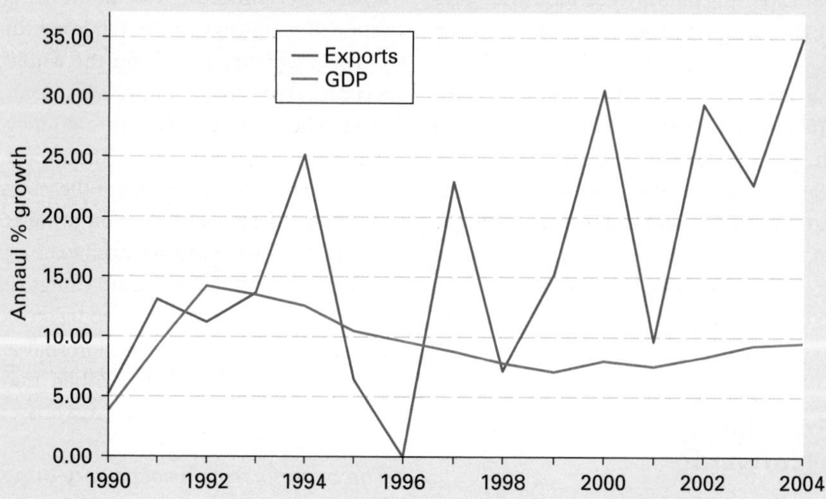

saving a unit of foreign exchange by replacing imports with home-produced goods. In other words, resources will be used more efficiently.

Economies of scale. If the home market is too small to allow a firm to gain all the potential economies of scale, these can be gained by expanding into the export market.

Increased competition. By having to compete with foreign companies, exporters will be under a greater competitive pressure than industries shielded behind protective KI 3 p11

BOX 26.3

country's transport, power and communications infrastructure.

What is more, much of the growth in income in the Chinese economy is concentrated in the hands of the middle class, which now constitutes 20 per cent of the population and 50 per cent of the urban population. According to the Chinese Academy of Social Sciences, the middle class constitutes households with assets between $18 000 and $36 000. The demand for consumer goods by these middle-class Chinese is very income elastic. As a result, sales of electrical goods, furniture, cars and fashion clothing are growing rapidly. Not only foreign manufacturers, but foreign retailers too are taking advantage of this. For example, by 2004, Wal-Mart had 28 Supercenters in China, sourcing 95 per cent of its merchandise from local suppliers. Carrefour, the French supermarket chain, had over 40 stores.

But foreign investors are attracted not only by the growing domestic Chinese market. They are also attracted by the opportunity to manufacture high-tech products with a highly skilled workforce.

> More and more companies become cutting edge and leapfrog foreign rivals. Whether games consoles, DVD recorders or flat-screen monitors, Chinese factories are grabbing high-tech market share.
>
> 'Ten years ago, China was about low cost,' says Infineon's Ulrich Schumacher. 'Now it is at the forefront of technical development. Infineon can develop twice as fast in China as anywhere else.'
>
> 'Engineers are working in three shifts, seven days a week,' enthuses Mr Schumacher. 'In Germany that would not be possible: there, engineers don't work on weekends.'
>
> Bill Gates is similarly impressed after his latest visit to Microsoft's research lab in Beijing, one of four in China and Hong Kong. 'The talent of the people there is unbelievable, I can't believe how effective they are,' he says.
>
> All this is worrying news for high-tech workers in industrialised countries, who hoped their skills would give them a competitive advantage in the globalised economy.[3]

An undervalued exchange rate

Despite the booming economy and export sector, and a massive current account surplus against the USA ($162 billion in 2004), the Chinese yuan remained pegged to the US dollar at $1 = 8.28 yuan from 1995 to 2005. This undervaluation of the yuan against the dollar has been a major contributing factor in the continued growth in Chinese exports.

The situation has become even more extreme with other countries. With the fall in the dollar in 2003/4 against the euro, yen and sterling, the dollar-pegged yuan thus also fell against these currencies. This made Chinese exports even cheaper in Europe and east Asia, further fuelling the trade imbalance.

The USA for some time had been pressing for a revaluation of the yuan or a floating of the yuan so that it can appreciate. Indeed, in 2005 the US Senate was pushing the Bush administration to adopt a 27.5 per cent tariff on all Chinese imports unless China revalued its currency.

China eventually, in 2005, moved to a pegged exchange rate with a basket of eleven currencies, each currency being weighted in the basket by the amount of trade with China. The effect was to bring a 2.1 per cent devaluation against the US dollar. The new system, it is hoped, will help to prevent the instability of the exchange rate with currencies other than the dollar.

Another issue facing the Chinese authorities is the perceived overheating of the economy. With worries about rising inflation and investment considerably outstripping consumption, the concern is that the boom is becoming unsustainable. The problem is exacerbated by the undervalued yuan. As finance flows into China, this puts upward pressure on the Chinese money supply.

If interest rates are raised or controls on investment tightened, this could cause the investment bubble to burst. The resulting slowing of the economy could then become excessive and lead to a decline in FDI. This could then send shock waves around the world economy, as did the south-east Asian crisis in 1997/8 (see Web Cases 25.3, 25.4 and 26.3). The task, then, is how to achieve a slight slowdown in growth to sustainable levels without triggering a crash.

1. ***In what ways does a booming Chinese economy benefit the rest of the world?***
2. ***Why may the Chinese be reluctant to adopt a freely floating exchange rate?***

[2] 'Is China a goldmine or minefield?' *BBC News Online*, 19 February 2004 (http://news.bbc.co.uk/1/hi/business/3494069.stm).

[3] Ibid.

barriers. This will encourage (a) resource saving in the short run, both through their better *allocation* and through reductions in X inefficiency (see Box 6.5), and (b) innovation and investment, as firms attempt to adopt the latest technology, often obtained from developed countries.

Increased investment. To the extent that outward-looking policies lead to a greater potential for economic growth, they may attract more foreign capital. To the extent that they involve an increase in interest rates, they will tend to encourage saving. To the extent that they lead to increased incomes, additional saving will be generated, especially given that the *marginal* propensity to save may be quite high. The extra savings can be used to finance extra investment.

It can lead to more employment and a more equal distribution of income. According to the Heckscher–Ohlin theory, the manufactured goods in which a country will have a comparative advantage are those produced by labour-intensive techniques. Export expansion will thus increase the demand for labour relative to capital, and create more employment. The increased demand for labour will tend to lead to a rise in wages relative to profits.

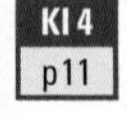

? *Will the adoption of labour-intensive techniques* necessarily *lead to a more equal distribution of income?*

TC3 p21 *It removes many of the costs associated with ISI.* Under a policy of ISI, managers may spend a lot of their time lobbying politicians and officials, seeking licences (and sometimes paying bribes to obtain them), adhering to norms and regulations or trying to find ways round them. If an outward-looking policy involves removing all this, managers can turn their attention to producing goods more efficiently.

Drawbacks of an export-orientated industrialisation strategy

The export of manufactures is seen by many developed countries as very threatening to their own industries. Their response has often been to erect trade barriers. These barriers have tended to be highest in the very industries (such as textiles, footwear and processed food) where developing countries have the greatest comparative advantage. Even if the barriers are *currently* low, developing countries may feel that it is too risky to expand their exports of these products for fear of a future rise in barriers. Recognising this problem, the World Trade Organisation is very keen to ensure fair access for developing countries to the markets of the rich world (see Box 23.7 on page 653).

? *Consider the arguments from the perspective of an* advanced country *for and against protecting its industries from imports of manufactures from developing countries.*

The successes of developing countries such as Malaysia and South Korea in exporting manufactures do not imply that other developing countries will have similar success. As additional developing countries attempt to export their manufactures, they will be facing more and more competition from each other.

Another problem is that, if a more open trade policy involves removing or reducing exchange and capital controls, the country may become more vulnerable to speculative attack. This was one of the major contributing factors to the east Asian crisis of the late 1990s (see Web Case 26.3). Gripped by currency and stock market speculation, and by banking and company insolvency, many countries of the region found that economic growth had turned into a major recession. The 'miracle' seemed to be over. Nevertheless, the countries with the fewest distortions fared the best during the crisis. Thus Singapore and Taiwan, which are open and relatively flexible, experienced only a slowdown, rather than a recession.

Exporting manufactures may thus be a very risky strategy for developing countries. Perhaps the best hope for the future may be for a growth in manufacturing trade *between* developing countries. That way they can gain the benefits of specialisation and economies of scale that trade brings, while at the same time producing for a growing market. The feasibility of this approach depends on whether developing countries can agree to free trade areas or even customs unions between themselves. There does, however, seem to be a strong movement in this direction (see pages 657–8).

Section summary

1. Trade is of vital importance for the vast majority of developing countries, and yet most developing countries suffer from chronic balance of trade deficits.
2. Developing countries have traditionally been primary exporters. This has allowed them to exploit their comparative advantage in labour-intensive goods and has provided a market for certain goods that would otherwise have no market at home.
3. However, with a low world income elasticity of demand for primary products, with the development of synthetic substitutes and with the protection of agriculture in developed countries, the demand for primary exports has grown only slowly. At the same time, the demand for manufactured imports into developing countries has grown rapidly. The result has been a worsening balance of trade problem; and with a *price*-inelastic demand for both imports and exports, the terms of trade have worsened too. There is also the danger that comparative costs may change over time; that most of the benefits from primary exports may accrue to foreign owners of mines and plantations, or to wealthy elites in the domestic population; that mines and plantations can involve substantial environmental and other external costs; and that export earnings can fluctuate, given instabilities in supply and unstable world prices.
4. Import-substituting industrialisation was seen to be the answer to these problems. This was normally achieved in stages, beginning with the finished goods stage and then working back towards the

continued

capital goods stage. ISI, it was hoped, would allow countries to benefit from the various dynamic advantages associated with manufacturing.

5. For many countries, however, ISI brought as many, if not more, problems than it solved. It often led to the establishment of inefficient industries, protected from foreign competition and facing little or no competition at home either. It led to considerable market distortions, with tariffs and other forms of protection haphazardly applied and with resulting huge variations in effective rates of protection; to overvalued exchange rates with a resulting bias against exports and the agricultural sector generally; to a deepening of inequalities and to large-scale social and environmental problems as the cities expanded and as poverty and unemployment grew. Finally, the balance of payments was in many cases made worse as the new industries became increasingly dependent on imported inputs and as growing urbanisation caused a growing demand for imported consumer goods.
6. The most rapidly growing of the developing countries are those that have pursued a policy of export-orientated industrialisation. This has allowed them to achieve the benefits of economies of scale and foreign competition. It has allowed them to specialise in goods in which they have a comparative advantage (i.e. labour-intensive goods) and yet which have a relatively high income elasticity of demand. Whether countries that have pursued ISI can successfully turn to an open, export-orientated approach depends to a large extent on the degree of competition they face, not only from rich countries, but also from other developing countries.

26.3 STRUCTURAL PROBLEMS WITHIN DEVELOPING COUNTRIES

The neglect of agriculture

The drive to industrialise by many developing countries has often been highly damaging to agriculture, especially in the poorest countries such as those of sub-Saharan Africa. With a backward and run-down agricultural sector, with little or no rural infrastructure, many countries today face a food crisis of immense proportions. Harrowing scenes of famine and death from countries like Ethiopia and the Sudan have become all too familiar.

Over the years, opinions have gradually changed. It is now realised that the relief of poverty, unemployment and the maldistribution of income can best be achieved by improving productivity and incomes in the rural sector. No longer is agriculture seen as a sector to be 'squeezed' like an orange. Rather it is seen as a sector that must be developed in harmony with the urban sector. Agricultural output must be increased for the benefit of rural and urban dwellers alike. At the same time, industrial output can be given new markets in the rural sector if rural incomes expand. The following are some of the possible ways forward.

Price reform. The price of food needs to be raised relative to the price of industrial goods. This may be achieved simply through the reduction of protection of manufactured products. Higher relative food prices increase the profitability of agricultural production and enables farmers to afford to invest in irrigation, agricultural implements, land improvement, etc.

TC 3 p21

Devaluation. If the currency is devalued, or allowed to depreciate, this increases the price of food imports and thus makes it easier for domestic food producers to compete. It also increases the profitability of food exports.

Government support for rural infrastructure projects. If food is to be marketed, there must be adequate rural infrastructure. Government road-building schemes and the setting-up of marketing boards can make a dramatic difference to the viability of commercial food production.

TC 7 p26

The provision of finance. Farmers need access to cheap finance and not to be forced to borrow at sky-high interest rates from local moneylenders. This can be achieved by setting up rural banks specialising in the provision of finance to small farmers. These could be nationalised institutions, or the government could give incentives to private banks to expand into the rural sector.

The adoption of new technologies and practices. There have been rapid advances in agricultural technology in recent years. The development of new fertilisers, pesticides, simple but effective agricultural machinery, and most of all of new high-yielding strains of grain, especially wheat and rice, have helped to transform traditional agriculture in certain developing countries such as India. There has been a *Green Revolution*.

Other countries, however, and especially those of sub-Saharan Africa, have made little progress in adopting these technologies. This is due partly to an inability to afford the new equipment, chemicals and seeds, partly to the lack of infrastructure to make them available, and partly to their unsuitability to the generally more arid African conditions. When the technologies are adopted, it is often only by large multinationals operating in plantations. For example, companies like Monsanto have been the main developers and users of genetically modified crops.

Governments can help by funding research into the best farming methods and inputs for local conditions. They can also help by providing finance for the adoption of the new methods.

Education and advice. Many farmers are simply unaware of new more efficient farming methods. Training schemes or rural advisers can help here.

KI 21 p207

Land reform. As population grows, land holdings are divided and subdivided as they are passed from generation to generation. Thus many farmers operate on tiny plots of land that can never yield an adequate income. Increasingly, they get into debt and are forced to mortgage their land to large landowners at high interest rates, or to sell it to them at low prices. The number of landless labourers or farmers in 'debt bondage' therefore grows.

A solution to this problem is the redistribution of land. Clearly, this cannot be done unless there is a government sympathetic to the rural poor and willing to take on the inevitable opposition from the large farmers. Often these large farmers are politically powerful and have the police on their side.

Two of the most successful newly industrialised countries, Taiwan and South Korea, despite having right-wing governments, underwent a radical redistribution of land from rich to poor in the late 1940s and early 1950s. In both countries, the growth of the agricultural sector has been rapid and yet continues to be egalitarian, based as it is on small, but not tiny, peasant holdings. In both countries extreme rural poverty has been virtually eliminated.

The encouragement of rural co-operatives. If small farmers get together and form co-operatives, they may be able to afford to share agricultural equipment such as tractors and harvesters, and undertake irrigation schemes; they may be able to set up input-purchasing and crop-marketing and distribution organisations, and gain easier access to credit. In many countries, national or local governments have actively encouraged such co-operatives by providing subsidies, tax incentives and advice, and by passing favourable legislation.

Inappropriate technology

The technology employed in a country depends on the type of development strategy it is pursuing. Some strategies lead to the adoption of relatively labour-intensive technologies, others to relatively capital-intensive ones.

Neo-classical theory suggests that countries should use techniques that are intensive in their abundant factor. This is simply an extension of the Heckscher–Ohlin theory, only this time it is applied to the choice of techniques rather than to the choice of goods. The theory implies that (labour-abundant) developing countries should adopt labour-intensive techniques; techniques that use relatively more of the cheap factor (labour) and relatively less of the expensive factor (capital).

With the advent of policies of industrialisation, however, came strong arguments for adopting capital-intensive technology. Capital-intensive technologies were seen to be more advanced. These were the technologies that were developed in rich countries, countries with sophisticated research facilities. The argument here was that, despite having a higher capital/labour ratio, these techniques nevertheless had a low capital/output ratio. The equipment might be expensive, but it would yield a very high output and would thus cost less *per unit* of output.

? *If a modern capital-intensive technique has a higher capital/labour ratio and a lower capital/output ratio than a traditional labour-intensive one, what can we say about its labour/output ratio relative to the traditional technique?*

A second argument was that, if multinationals were to be encouraged to invest in developing countries, they had to be allowed to bring with them their own technology – technology that was almost invariably capital intensive. In other words, the choice was not between more labour-intensive and more capital-intensive techniques, but rather between having *extra* capital (by allowing multinationals to invest) and not having it at all.

A final argument in favour of capital-intensive technology was that it provides a greater level of profit, and that this profit will then be reinvested, thereby causing a faster rate of economic growth.

Given these arguments, many governments of developing countries actively encouraged the use of capital-intensive techniques; some still do. But also there were other features of ISI that unintentionally led to biases in favour of capital-intensive technology. These included the following:

- Wage rates above the market-clearing level, driven up by minimum wage legislation, trade union activity, or firms trying to ensure that workers they had trained were not 'poached' by other firms.
- Low interest rates to encourage investment. The effect of this, plus relatively high wage rates in the expanding industries, is to encourage the substitution of capital for labour.
- An overvalued exchange rate. This lowers the relative price of imported inputs, which under a policy of tariff escalation have low tariffs. This encourages the use of import-intensive technology, which also tends to be capital intensive.
- The ignorance of many multinational companies of alternative efficient labour-intensive technology.
- The bias of engineers. It is engineers rather than economists who are often instrumental in deciding which production techniques a firm will use. Engineers tend to be biased in favour of *mechanically* efficient techniques, which tend to be capital intensive, rather than *economically* efficient techniques, which may well be labour intensive.

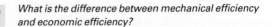

? *What is the difference between mechanical efficiency and economic efficiency?*

In recent years, with the criticism of ISI has come the criticism of capital-intensive technologies.

- Capital-intensive equipment may require more maintenance.
- It may have to be imported, and may use a high proportion of imported inputs. This will put a strain on the country's balance of trade. By using less domestic inputs, there will be less spread effect to other sectors of the economy: there will be a smaller multiplier effect.
- There may be problems of hold-ups, breakdowns and incorrect usage due to problems in obtaining parts and an absence of properly trained maintenance staff.
- Even if they do generate higher profits, there is no guarantee that these will be reinvested. They may simply flow abroad to foreign shareholders, or be spent largely on luxury consumption if the profits initially stay within the country (and a high proportion of luxury goods are imported anyway).
- Capital-intensive techniques often involve large-scale production. There have been many examples of countries opening up plants that are simply too large relative to the market. As a result, they never operate at full capacity, and thus may operate inefficiently.

In addition, capital-intensive technologies have other detrimental effects. As we shall see shortly, they worsen the unemployment problem. Also, as these are large-scale technologies, the firms using them usually locate in the cities. KI 4 p11 This tends to worsen the problem of ***dualism***. Inequality between urban and rural incomes tends to grow; and with relatively few workers being employed in these industries at relatively high wages, the gap between their wages and those of the urban poor tends to grow also.

KI 28 p300 The concentration of large-scale plants in cities can cause severe problems of pollution, especially if the government is not very strict in enforcing pollution control.

? *Why may governments of developing countries be less strict than developed countries in controlling pollution?*

So what can be done to encourage a more appropriate technology? Part of the solution lies in correcting market distortions: there will probably need to be a devaluation of the currency and a rise in interest rates. This would remove two of the key factors favouring capital-intensive industry.

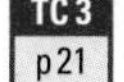

Then there will probably also need to be positive encouragement given to the invention or adoption of *efficient* labour-intensive technologies. This could involve government-sponsored research, information centres to provide details of the various techniques used around the world, education and training schemes for managers and workers, the provision of advice on production, marketing, distribution, etc., and incentives for inventions (such as subsidies or patent protection).

The government could help to encourage small businesses (which typically use more labour-intensive techniques) by, for example, setting up development banks that provide services specifically for small businesses (including farms and other rural businesses), and which grant loans at similar rates to those charged to large firms; encouraging the formation of co-operatives through tax concessions or subsidies, or by reducing the amount of red tape such organisations are likely to encounter; and providing small workshops at low or zero rent.

What difficulties is a government likely to encounter in encouraging the use of labour-intensive technology?

Unemployment

Imagine the choice of living in a large family in the countryside with too little land to be able to feed you and the other family members, or of seeking your fortune in the city where there are nowhere near enough jobs to go round. It is not much of a choice. But it is the sort of choice that millions of people are forced to make. Open unemployment rates in developing countries are generally much higher than in developed countries: rates in excess of 15 per cent are not uncommon.

But even these high rates grossly understate the true extent of the problem. With the system of extended families, where the family farm or the family trade occupies all the family members, people may not be out looking for jobs and are thus not openly unemployed, but their output is nevertheless very low. There is simply not enough work to occupy them fully. This is the problem of ***disguised unemployment***. Then there are those who manage to do a few hours' work each week as casual labourers or as petty traders. These people are ***underemployed***. When you add the problem of disguised unemployment and underemployment to the problem of open unemployment, the problem becomes overwhelming.

The causes of the unemployment problem are deep seated and complex, but four stand out as being particularly important in most developing countries.

Rapid population growth

With reductions in mortality rates (due to improved health care) that have not been matched by equivalent reductions in birth rates, populations in most developing countries have grown rapidly for many years now. The labour force has thus grown rapidly too. The growth in production has

Definitions

Dualism The division of an economy into a modern (usually urban) sector and a poor traditional (usually rural) sector.

Disguised unemployment Where the same work could be done by fewer people.

Underemployment Where people who want full-time work are only able to find part-time work.

EXPLORING ECONOMICS

UNEMPLOYMENT IN DEVELOPING COUNTRIES

Three simple models

In this box we will look at three models that have been developed to explain Third World unemployment.

Limited choice of techniques

The simplest version of this model assumes that there is only one technique available to firms and that just two factors of production are involved – labour and capital. Firms will thus face a right-angled isoquant (see section 5.3). This is illustrated in diagram (a).

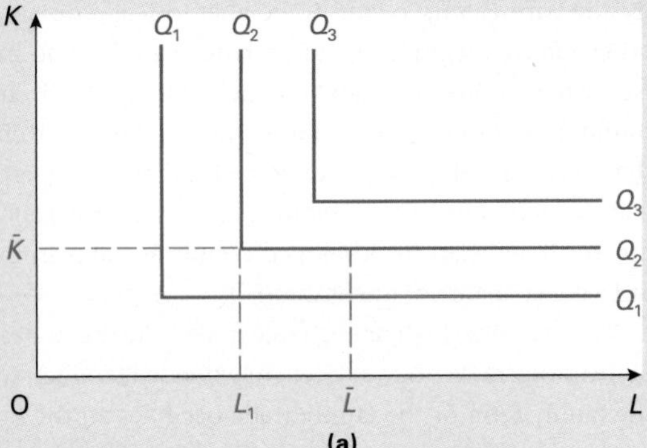

(a)

Each isoquant shows a *particular* level of output (Q). Given that there is only one choice of technique, involving a particular combination of labour and capital, then for each amount of capital used a *particular* amount of labour will be needed – no more and no less. Any extra labour will simply be idle.

For example, if each machine required one operative and if ten machines were available, then ten operatives would be required. An eleventh would add nothing to output. Similarly, if there were ten operatives available, an eleventh machine would be idle.

If, in diagram (a), the total supply of capital were $\bar{K}$, then firms would require L_1 of labour. But if the total labour force were $\bar{L}$, then $\bar{L} - L_1$ workers would be unemployed.

Thus the lack of availability of labour-intensive techniques means that there is not enough capital to employ everyone.

Capital-intensity bias

This model assumes that there *are* labour-intensive techniques available, but that firms choose not to use them. Assuming again that there are just the two factors, labour and capital, this time firms will face *curved* isoquants. In other words, the firm can choose to combine labour and capital in any proportions it chooses. This is illustrated in diagram (b).

Assume that the total supplies of capital and labour are $\bar{K}$ and $\bar{L}$ respectively. With a price ratio given by the slope of the isocost *AB*, the factor market will clear. All capital and all labour will be employed at point *d* on isoquant Q_1.

Managers, however, may have a bias in favour of capital-intensive techniques. Alternatively, the price of labour may be above the market-clearing level, or the price of capital may be below the market-clearing level, so that the isocost is steeper than *AB* (e.g. *CD*). In either case, if $\bar{K}$ capital is used, *less* than $\bar{L}$ labour will be employed. With an isocost of *CD*, only L_1 will be employed. $\bar{L} - L_1$ will be unemployed. There will also be a lower level of output, since production is now on the lower isoquant Q_2.

simply not been fast enough to create enough jobs for these extra workers.

Capital-intensity bias

As we have seen, import-substituting industrialisation has involved a bias in favour of capital-intensive technology. This has led to the production of goods and to the use of processes that provide only limited employment opportunities. As long as the relative price of capital to labour is kept low, or as long as there is a lack of modern efficient *labour-intensive* techniques available, or as long as multinational companies choose to bring in their own (capital-intensive) technology, so there will continue to be a lack of demand for labour.

Rural–urban migration

Throughout the developing world, people flock from the countryside to the towns and thereby swell the numbers of urban unemployed. Migration accounts for some 55 per cent of urban population growth in developing countries. But, if life in the shantytowns is wretched, what is the point? The point is that for most of the migrants there was no chance at all of getting another job in the countryside, whereas in the towns there is at least some chance. If one in five migrants gets a job, then you might be the lucky one.

The decision to migrate thus depends on four main factors:

- The income differential between the countryside and the town. The more that jobs in the town pay relative to what the migrant could earn by staying behind, the more the person is likely to migrate. If their decision was to be totally rational, they would also take into account the differences in the cost of living between the two areas.
- The chance of getting a job. The higher the rate of urban unemployment, the less the chance of getting a job and thus the less likely the person is to migrate.

*BOX 26.4

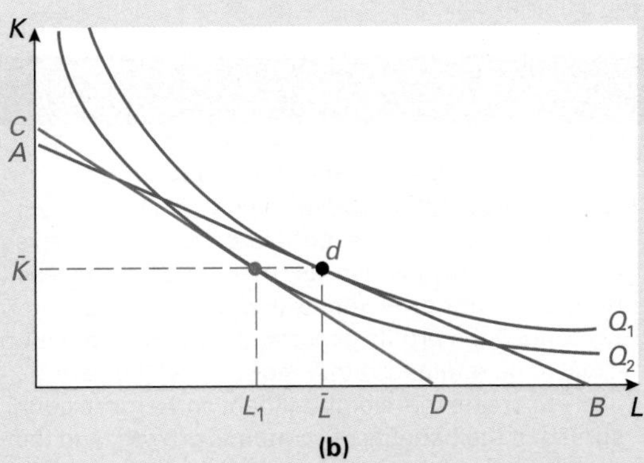

(b)

?

If there were three techniques available, what would the isoquant look like? Would it make any difference to the conclusions of this model?

Rural–urban migration

This model assumes that migration depends first on the difference between urban wages (W_u) and rural wages (W_r). The bigger the differential, the more will people wish to migrate. Second, it depends on the likelihood of getting a job. The more likely people are to find a job, the more likely they are to migrate.

These two can be combined in the concept of an *expected urban wage* (W_u^e). This is the *actual average* urban wage multiplied by the probability of getting a job. Thus if the average wage were £40 per week, and if there were a 50 per cent chance of getting a job, the expected urban wage would be £20. If the chance were only 25 per cent, the expected wage would be only £10, and so on. This can be expressed formally as:

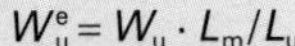

$$W_u^e = W_u \cdot L_m/L_u$$

where L_m is the total number of workers employed in the urban sector and L_u is the total labour supply (employed and unemployed). Thus L_m/L_u is the employment rate, which can be taken as an indication of the probability of getting a job.

So when will rural workers migrate to the towns? According to the model this will occur when:

$$W_u^e > (W_r + \alpha)$$

where α is a term representing the costs of migration. In other words, people will migrate when, after taking the cost of migrating into account, they can expect to earn more in the towns than in the countryside.

But as people migrate, W_r will tend to rise as the supply of rural labour falls, and W_u^e will tend to fall as the new arrivals in the towns increase L_u and thus reduce the likelihood of others getting a job. An equilibrium urban unemployment will be reached when:

$$W_u^e = W_r + \alpha$$

At that point, migration will stop.

Thus in this model, urban unemployment will be greater (a) the higher is the level of the actual urban wage (W_u), (b) the lower is the level of the rural wage (W_r) and (c) the lower are the costs of migrating (α).

If more jobs were created in the towns, how, in the rural–urban migration model, would this affect (a) the level of urban unemployment; (b) the rate of urban unemployment?

- The 'risk attitude' of the person: in other words, how willing potential migrants are to take the gamble of whether or not they will get a job.
- The degree of misinformation. People may migrate to the towns, attracted by the 'bright lights' of the city and the belief (albeit probably misplaced) that their prospects are much better there.

?

What would be the effect on the levels of migration and urban unemployment of the creation of jobs in the towns?

External influences

Most developing countries are highly dependent on international economic forces. If the world economy goes into recession, or world interest rates rise, or protectionist policies are pursued by developed countries, this will have a damaging effect on industry in developing countries. Their exports will fall and unemployment will rise.

There is no simple cure for unemployment in developing countries. Nevertheless, there are certain measures that governments can take which will help to reverse its growth:

- The government can encourage the use of more labour-intensive techniques by adopting the sorts of policy outlined earlier.
- It can help to reverse rural–urban migration by reducing the rural 'push'. This will involve policies of encouraging rural development and thereby providing jobs away from the big towns.
- It can provide jobs directly by embarking on labour-intensive infrastructure construction projects. For example, it can employ gangs of workers to build roads or dig irrigation ditches.
- It can adopt policies that help to reduce the rate of population growth: policies such as educational and propaganda programmes to persuade people to have smaller families, measures to raise the economic and social status

of women so that they have a freer choice over family size, and policies directed at tackling extreme poverty so that the very poor do not feel the need to have a large family as an insurance that they will be supported in their old age.

?

1. *Is there any potential conflict between the goals of maximising economic growth and maximising either (a) the level of employment or (b) the rate of growth of employment?*
2. *What is the relationship between unemployment and (a) poverty; (b) inequality?*

Section summary

1. The urban/industrial bias of many development programmes has led to the neglect of agriculture. The effect has been a deepening of rural poverty and a growing inability of the rural sector to feed the towns. Policies to reverse this trend include the raising of food prices, devaluation of the currency, government support for rural infrastructure projects, the provision of lower-interest finance to the rural sector, encouragement for the adoption of new labour-intensive techniques in farming and the use of new high-yielding seeds, land reform and the setting-up of rural co-operatives.
2. Development programmes have often encouraged the use of capital-intensive technology through policies of low interest rates, relatively high urban wages, an overvalued exchange rate or encouraging investment by multinational companies. These capital-intensive technologies were often seen as advantageous in that they yielded higher profits and thus more surplus for reinvestment. Often they were more sophisticated than labour-intensive techniques, and sometimes they had a lower capital/output ratio despite having a higher capital/labour ratio. Nevertheless, labour-intensive techniques may involve less maintenance and less reliance on imported inputs and foreign skilled personnel; the profits generated from them are more likely to be retained within the country; they are likely to create more employment and a more equal spread of the benefits of economic growth; and they may be less polluting.
3. Unemployment is a major problem for most developing countries, both in the countryside and in the ever-growing shantytowns surrounding the cities. The causes are complex, but include rapid population growth, biases towards the use of capital-intensive technology, and a vulnerability to world economic changes. Urban unemployment has grown rapidly as people have migrated from the countryside, attracted by the relatively higher wages, the 'bright lights of the city' and at least the *possibility* (however remote) of getting a job.

26.4 THE PROBLEM OF DEBT

A serious consequence of the oil shocks of the 1970s and the reactions of the developed world to these shocks was a major debt crisis in developing countries. Attempts to service these debts – to pay interest and instalments on capital repayments – have caused severe strains on the economies of many developing countries. By the early 1980s, the problem had become so severe that many developing countries found it virtually impossible to continue servicing their debt. There was a growing fear that countries would default on payment, thereby precipitating an international banking crisis.

Although today, from the perspective of the rich world, the debt problem is no longer seen as a 'crisis', this is largely because the world financial system has found ways of coping with the debt, and threats of default have subsided. From the perspective of the majority of poor countries, however, the problems are still acute. For many the debts are still mounting and the suffering of their people continues to grow. For others, total debt is falling, but still remains at levels where the costs of servicing it put huge strains on their economies and represent a massive transfer of moneys to the rich world. Table 26.4 shows the growth of debt from 1973 to 2003.

In this final section, we look first at the origins of the debt crisis and then at schemes that have been adopted to cope with it. We then turn finally to look at ways in which the problem of debt can be tackled.

Table 26.4 Growth in debt of developing countries (average annual)

	1973–1980	1981–1985	1986–1995	1996–2003
All developing countries	22.6	14.6	7.8	2.6
Low-income countries	16.5	17.5	9.5	−0.2
Middle-income countries	24.7	13.7	7.4	3.3
Sub-Saharan Africa	23.9	15.1	8.4	−0.5

Sources: based on data in *Global Development Finance* (World Bank, 2005).

The oil shocks of the 1970s

In 1973–4, oil prices quadrupled and the world went into recession. Oil imports cost much more and export demand was sluggish. The current account deficit of oil-importing developing countries rose from 1.1 per cent of GNY in 1973 to 4.3 per cent in 1975.

It was not difficult to finance these deficits, however. The oil surpluses deposited in commercial banks in the industrialised world provided an important additional source of finance. The banks, flush with money and faced with slack demand in the industrialised world, were very willing to lend. Bank loans to developing countries rose from $3 billion in 1970 to $12 billion in 1975. These flows enabled developing countries to continue with policies of growth.

The world recession was short lived, and with a recovery in the demand for their exports and with their debts being eroded by high world inflation, developing countries found it relatively easy to service these increased debts (i.e. pay interest and make the necessary capital repayments).

In 1979/80 world oil prices rose again (from $15 to $38 per barrel). This second oil shock, like the first one, caused a large increase in the import bills of developing countries. But the full effects on their economies this time were very much worse, given the debts that had been accumulated in the 1970s and given the policies adopted by the industrialised world after 1979.

Table 26.5 illustrates the worsening debt position after 1979, compared with that in 1974. These are averages for all developing countries. Some fared very much worse than this. For example, in 1984 the ratio of debt service (i.e. interest and capital repayments) to exports was 35 per cent for Kenya, 45 per cent for Brazil and Mexico, and 63 per cent for Bolivia.

But why were things so much worse this time?

- The world recession was deeper and lasted longer (1980–3), and when recovery came, it came very slowly. Developing countries' current account balance of payments deteriorated sharply. This was due both to a marked slowing down in the growth of their exports and to a fall in their export prices.
- The tight monetary policies pursued by the industrialised countries led to a sharp increase in interest rates, and the resulting fall in inflation meant, therefore, that there was a very sharp increase in *real* interest rates. This greatly increased developing countries' costs of servicing their debts (see Table 26.5).
- The problem was made worse by the growing proportion of debt that was at variable interest rates. This was largely due to the increasing proportion of debt that was in the form of loans from commercial banks.

After 1979, many developing countries found it increasingly difficult to service their debts. Then in 1982 Mexico, followed by several other countries such as Brazil, Bolivia, Zaire and Sudan, declared that it would have to suspend payments. There was now a debt crisis, which threatened not only the debtor countries, but also the world banking system.

Coping with debt: rescheduling

There are two dimensions to tackling the debt problems of developing countries. The first is to cope with difficulties in servicing their debt. This usually involves some form of rescheduling of the repayments. The second dimension is to deal with the causes of the problem. Here we will focus on rescheduling.

Rescheduling official loans

Official loans are renegotiated through the Paris Club. Industrialised countries are members of the club, which arranges terms for the rescheduling of their loans to developing countries. Agreements normally involve delaying the date for repayment of loans currently maturing, or spreading the repayments over a longer period of time. Paris Club agreements are often made in consultation with the IMF, which works out a programme with the debtor country for tackling its underlying economic problems.

The main recipients of official loans are low-income and lower-middle-income countries (the upper-middle-income countries relying largely on commercial bank loans). Between 1982 and 1987, demands by low-income countries for Paris Club renegotiations increased dramatically. By 1987 virtually all the sub-Saharan African countries had sought repeated Paris Club assistance. By 1987 it was becoming clear that the existing arrangements were inadequate for many countries.

Several attempts have been made since the mid-1980s to make rescheduling terms more generous, with longer periods before repayments start, longer to repay when they do start, and lower interest rates. In return, the developing countries have had to undertake various 'structural adjustment programmes' supervised by the IMF (see below).

Table 26.5 Debt ratios: average of all developing countries: selected years

	1974	1980	1984	1986	1988	1990	1994	1998	2000	2002	2003
Ratio of debt to GNY (%)	11	20	30	34	36	34	40	42	39	39	37
Ratio of debt to exports (%)	80	86	146	212	189	168	163	151	117	111	98
Ratio of debt service to exports (%)	12	14	20	26	24	19	17	19	19	18	15

Source: *Global Development Finance* (World Bank, 2005).

CASE STUDIES AND APPLICATIONS **BOX 26.5**

ARGENTINA IN CRISIS

Why did it all go so wrong?

In December 2001, the IMF refused a fresh loan of $1.3 billion to Argentina. This triggered a crisis in the country with mass rioting and looting. As the crisis deepened, Argentina announced that it was defaulting on its $166 billion of foreign debt. This hardly came as a surprise, however. For many commentators, it was simply a question of when.

The severity of Argentina's predicament was summed up by a 2001 report from Jubilee Plus, which stated:

> Argentina has to pay $75.3bn in foreign debt payments between now (September 2001), and the first quarter of 2003. This represents 27 per cent of her GDP; and 322 per cent of her annual export earnings. To repay these debts, Argentina has to triple exports; halt all imports and divert one quarter of GDP away from domestic consumption to foreign creditors. As this cannot conceivably be achieved, Argentina is effectively insolvent.[4]

Background to the crisis

Argentina's debt problem stretches back over many decades. Since it joined the IMF in 1956, in 34 of the succeeding years it has had to borrow money. Debt growth began to escalate with the military regimes of the 1970s and early 1980s. Foreign debt increased from $7.8 billion in 1975 to $46 billion in 1984. In more recent times, the rate of increase had declined, but debt continued to grow. In 1991, foreign debt stood at $65 billion; in 2001, it reached $160.2 billion.

In the 1980s, Argentina suffered hyperinflation, as the government simply printed money to pay for its expenditure and corruption was rife. By the end of the 1980s, prices were rising by some 200 per cent a month. In return for debt rescheduling, the government pursued policies of privatisation and liberalisation, but seemed unable to make significant cuts in the budget deficit.

Then in 1991, the decision was taken to peg the Argentine peso to the dollar at a rate of $1 = 1 peso. This move seemed to work as prices were effectively set in dollars. As the world economy pulled out of the recession of the early 1990s, and as foreign investment flowed into Argentina, it seemed as if things were set fair for the Argentine economy. From 1991 to 1994, economic growth averaged nearly 8 per cent.

Things took a massive turn for the worse in 1998/9, however, as Argentina suffered fallout from the south-east Asian crisis (see Web Cases 25.3, 25.4 and 26.3). The crisis had a bad effect on Brazil, with large-scale speculation against the Brazilian currency, the real. In 1999 the real plummeted, but the peso, being linked to the dollar, could not follow suit.

In the face of Argentina's overvalued peso, Brazil and many of its other rivals took the opportunity to capture Argentinean export markets. With declining foreign currency earnings from exports, debt management became progressively more difficult to the point of default.

Between 1998 and 2002, Argentina was in deep recession and debts were increasingly difficult to service. Although new rescheduling arrangements were made, these came with tough demands by the IMF that austerity measures were pursued. As part of these measures, wages were cut. Not surprisingly, the result was a collapse in consumer spending. As unemployment rose (estimated at 29 per cent in 2000), reducing the budget deficit became increasingly difficult. In the first half of November 2001, tax receipts dropped by 17 per cent.

Thus, in attempting to control its debt growth, and meet the conditionality imposed by the IMF, Argentina saw a collapse of its economy and a dramatic increase in inequality and poverty.

The default and its aftermath

Argentina's default on its debts in January 2001 was the biggest of its kind in history.

In a series of dramatic measures, the Argentine peso was unpegged from the dollar and a new rate set nearly 29 per cent lower. But even this fixed rate could not be maintained. Over the next three months, the peso depreciated a further 40 per cent. The economy seemed in free-fall. GDP fell by 11 per cent in 2002, and by the end of the year, income per head was 22 per cent below that of 1998. Unemployment was 18 per cent.

Then, however, the economy began to recover, helped by higher (peso) prices for exports as a result of the currency depreciation. In 2003 economic growth was 8.7 per cent and in 2004 it was 8.5 per cent. Equity markets rose rapidly as confidence returned.

But what of the debt? In 2005, Argentina successfully made a huge debt swap (see Box 26.7). A large proportion of its defaulted debt was in the form of bonds. It offered to swap the old bonds for new peso bonds, but worth only 35 per cent as much. By the deadline of 25 February, there was a 76 per cent take-up of the offer: clearly people thought that 35 per cent was better than nothing! At a stroke, bonds originally worth $104 billion now became worth just $36.2 billion.

After the massive default of 2001, will creditors be willing to lend to Argentina again? Surprising as it may seem, the answer seems to be yes. The apparent current strength of the Argentine economy is attracting foreign capital at only 3 to 4 per cent above rates on US bonds. Investors seem to have a short memory and/or a high level of optimism.

?

One solution proposed to help solve Argentina's weak financial position was that it should have abandoned the peso altogether as its unit of currency, and replaced it with the US dollar. What advantages and drawbacks might such a solution have for the Argentine economy both in the short and the long term?

[4] Ann Pettifor, Liana Cisneros and Alejandro Olmos Gaona, *It Takes Two to Tango* (Jubilee Plus report, 2001).

But despite the apparent advances made by the Paris Club in making its terms more generous, the majority of low-income countries failed to meet the required IMF conditions, and thus failed to have their debts reduced. What is more, individual Paris Club members were often reluctant to reduce debts unless they were first convinced that other members were 'paying their share'. Nevertheless, some creditor countries have unilaterally introduced more generous terms and even cancelled some debts.

The net effect of rescheduling, but only very modest debt forgiveness, can be seen in Table 26.5. By the mid-1990s average debt service ratios had fallen from the levels of the mid-1980s and yet the ratio of total debt to GNY was higher. There were thus growing calls for the cancellation of debts (see below).

Rescheduling commercial bank loans

After the declarations of Mexico and other countries of their inability to service their debts, there was fear of an imminent collapse of the world banking system. Banks realised that disaster could be averted only by collective action of the banks to reschedule debts. This has normally involved the creditor banks forming a Bank Advisory Committee (BAC) – a small committee that liaises with the country and the banks concerned. Such arrangements have sometimes been referred to as the 'London Club'. The BAC negotiates a rescheduling agreement with the debtor country. When all creditor banks have approved the agreement, it is signed by each of them.

The approach of banks in the 1980s was to reschedule some of the debts – the minimum necessary to avoid default – and to provide some additional loans in return for debtor countries undertaking structural adjustment (as described below). Additional loans, however, fell well short of the amount that was needed. Banks were unwilling to supply extra money to deal with current debt-servicing problems when they saw the problem as a long-term one of countries' inability to pay. Nevertheless, banks were increasingly setting aside funds to cover bad debt, and thus the crisis for the banks began to recede.

As banks felt less exposed to default, so they became less worried about it and less concerned to negotiate deals with debtor countries. Many of the more severely indebted countries, however, found their position still deteriorating rapidly. What is more, many of them were finding that the IMF adjustment programmes were too painful (often involving deep cuts in government expenditure) and were therefore abandoning them. Thus in 1989 US Treasury Secretary Nicholas Brady proposed measures to *reduce* debt.

The *Brady Plan* involved the IMF and the World Bank lending funds to debtor countries to enable them to repay debts to banks. In return for this instant source of liquidity, the banks would have to be prepared to accept repayment of less than the full sum (i.e. they would sell the debt back to the country at a discount). To benefit from such deals, the debtor countries would have to agree to structural adjustment programmes. Several such agreements were negotiated, with countries buying back their debt at discount rates ranging between 44 and 84 per cent. Much of the debt reduction has involved debt swaps of one sort or another (see Box 26.7).

What are the relative advantages and disadvantages to a developing country of rescheduling its debts compared with simply defaulting on them (either temporarily or permanently)?

Dealing with debt: structural reform within the developing countries

Before it is prepared to sanction the rescheduling of debts, the IMF frequently demands that debtor countries undertake severe market-orientated adjustment programmes. These include the following:

- Tight fiscal and monetary policies to reduce government deficits, reduce interest rates and reduce inflation.
- Supply-side reforms to encourage greater use of the market mechanism and greater incentives for investment.
- A more open trade policy and devaluation of the currency in order to encourage more exports and more competition.

These policies, however, can bring extreme hardship as countries are forced to deflate. Unemployment and poverty increase and growth slows down or becomes negative. Even though in the long run developing countries may emerge as more efficient and better able to compete in international trade, in the short run the suffering may be too great to bear. Popular unrest and resentment against the IMF and the country's government may lead to riots and the breakdown of law and order, and even to the overthrow of the government.

A more 'complete' structural adjustment would extend beyond simple market liberalisation and tough monetary policies to much more open access to the markets of the rich countries, to more aid and debt relief being channelled into health and education, and to greater research and development in areas that will benefit the poor (e.g. into efficient labour-intensive technology and into new strains of crops that are suitable for countries' specific climate and soil conditions, and which do not require large amounts of chemicals).

Dealing with debt: debt forgiveness

By the end of the 1990s, the debt burden of many of the poorest countries had become intolerable. Despite portions of their debt being written off under Paris Club terms, the debts of many countries were still rising. Between 1980 and 2000, the debt of sub-Saharan Africa had quadrupled, from $61 billion to $250 billion. Some countries, such as Ethiopia and Mozambique, were spending nearly half their export earnings on merely servicing their debt.

CASE STUDIES AND APPLICATIONS

'ECOCIDE'

Debt and the environment

Faced with mounting debts and the need to service them, many developing countries have attempted to increase their export earnings. One way of achieving this is through the intensified extraction of minerals and ores or intensified farming, often by multinational corporations. But a consequence of this may be massive environmental damage. Some examples include:

KI 28 p300

- long-term degradation of the soil from monoculture and from the increased use of chemical pesticides and fertilisers;
- overfishing of rivers and seas;
- chopping down forests for timber;
- clearing forests for grazing cattle or for growing cash crops;
- 'desertification', as a lack of forest cover leads to the encroachment of deserts in marginal areas;
- open-cast mining, with little concern for the direct effect on the environment, or for poisonous waste products tipped into rivers;
- burning highly polluting low-grade coal for electricity generation;
- building dams for electricity generation and irrigation which flood large areas of land and destroy communities.

An example of a country forced into what has been called 'ecocide' in response to its huge debt burden is Brazil. One of the most environmentally damaging of all Brazilian projects has been the Grande Carajas iron ore project. Proposed in 1980, the Carajas scheme cost some $62 billion and has involved massive deforestation of an area larger than France and Britain together. The Brazilian government has been willing to allow this environmental damage because Carajas is seen as a 'national export project'.

Another example of ecocide has occurred in Venezuela. The country has huge gold reserves (some 10 per cent of the world total), worth some $140 billion. With the fall in oil prices in the 1990s, and hence a fall in revenues for Venezuela, one of the world's leading oil exporters, the Venezuelan authorities sought to exploit the country's gold reserves more aggressively. By 1994, the state had contracted out some 436 sites, covering 12 839 km^2. By 2000, this had risen to 30 000 km^2 (an area the size of Belgium), earning revenue of some $250 million per year.

The extraction of gold, however, has wrought great environmental damage. The richest gold reserves are in the region of Guayana, which makes up part of the Amazon river basin. It is an area rich, and in many respects unique, in its biodiversity. The environmental impact of open-cast mining within the region is already being felt. One of the most serious consequences has been the poisoning of rivers with mercury (used to separate gold from other minerals). In addition to the destruction of the forests and rivers, there are many cases where indigenous peoples have had their human rights violated and have even been murdered to make way for the mines.

The misuse and destruction of rainforests caused dramatic effects in 1997. In large parts of Indonesia (another highly indebted country), it is normal practice to burn land after forests have been felled, either to clear it for crops or for replanting. In 1997, the El Niño effect on ocean currents had caused a major drought

Even with substantial debt rescheduling and some debt cancellation, highly indebted countries were being forced to make savage cuts in government expenditure, much of it on health, education and transport. The consequence was a growth in poverty, hunger, disease and illiteracy. African countries on average were paying four times more to rich countries in debt servicing than they were spending on health and education: it was like a patient giving a blood transfusion to a doctor! The majority of these countries had no chance of 'growing their way out of debt'. The only solution for them was for a more substantial proportion of their debt to be written off.

The heavily indebted poor countries (HIPC) initiative

In 1996 the World Bank and the IMF launched the HIPC initiative. A total of 42 countries, mainly in Africa, were identified as being in need of substantial debt relief. (This number was subsequently reduced to 38.) The object of the initiative was to reduce the debts of such countries to 'sustainable' levels by cancelling debts above 200–250 per cent of GDP (this was reduced to 150 per cent in 1999 and to a lower level still for five countries).

The HIPC process involves countries passing through two stages. In the first stage, eligible countries must demonstrate a track record of 'good performance'. This means that they must satisfy the IMF, World Bank and Paris Club that they are undertaking adjustment measures, such as cutting government expenditure and liberalising their markets. It also involves the countries preparing a Poverty Reduction Strategy Paper (PRSP) to show how they will use debt relief to tackle poverty, and especially how they will improve health and education. Once the IMF and World Bank are satisfied that the country is making sufficient progress, the 'decision point' is reached and the country enters the second stage.

During this second stage, some interim debt relief is provided. Meanwhile the country must establish a 'sound track record' by implementing policies established at the decision point and based on the PRSP. The length of this stage depends on how long it takes the country to implement the policies. At the end of the second stage, the

BOX 26.6

and the forest fires got out of hand. As a result, air pollution on a massive scale affected many countries in south-east Asia. Most of Indonesia, Malaysia and Singapore became covered with a haze of dense smoke. The international air pollutant index has a scale on which readings above 500 are considered extremely hazardous. In parts of Malaysia readings of 1200 were recorded – equivalent to smoking a couple of packs of cigarettes a day. Schools and airports were closed, and income from tourism was lost throughout the region.

In recent years, there has been growing international awareness of the scale of the environmental destruction that is taking place. In particular, the rich countries have begun to realise that they too might suffer from this destruction, with its consequences for global warming and the loss of many unique species of plants and animals. Increasingly, international agencies such as the IMF and the World Bank are taking ecological issues into account when considering appropriate development and adjustment programmes.

Many in the developed world now realise that development must be sustainable. It is no good trying to secure 'development' for the current generation if, in the process, the environment is damaged and future generations suffer. This is a message that has been well understood by indigenous peoples for countless generations, especially those living on marginal lands: from the Aborigines of the Australian outback to the tribes of the African bush. It is seen as a moral imperative that the land bequeathed by one's ancestors should be passed on in just as good a state to one's descendants (see page 330).

In 1992 in Rio de Janeiro, the United Nations Conference on Environment and Development (UNCED) put forward a programme for environmentally responsible development. In Agenda 21 it set out various policies that could be carried out by the international community. The policies, which were approved by 178 countries, included: targeting aid to projects that helped improve the environment (such as providing clean water); research into environmentally friendly farming methods; and programmes that help reduce population growth (such as family planning and education).

The test of such sentiments, however, is action. To monitor this, a Commission on Sustainable Development was established in December 1992. In 2003 it set out a programme until 2015. Every two years from 2004 there would be a particular focus for action. For example, in 2004 and 2005 the focus was on water, sanitation and human settlements; in 2006 and 2007, the focus is on energy for sustainable development, industrial development, air pollution and climate change.

?

1. ***If reductions in developing countries' debt are in the environmental interests of the whole world, then why have developed countries not gone much further in reducing or cancelling the debts owed to them?***
2. ***Would it be possible to devise a scheme of debt repayments that would both be acceptable to debtor and creditor countries and not damage the environment?***

country reaches the 'completion point' and debts are cancelled by the various creditors, on a pro rata basis, to bring the debt to the sustainable threshold.

Despite the welcome given to the HIPC initiative back in 1996, it has been heavily criticised:

- The qualifying period is too long. By 2005, only 18 countries had reached the completion point, with another 9 having reached the decision point. The total amount of relief committed by the end of 2004 was £32 billion out of an expected eventual total of £58 billion. Despite having a previous 'good track record', many countries still had to adhere to the full two-stage process, which could be very lengthy.
- The thresholds have been set too high, with the resulting reduction in debt servicing being quite modest, or in many cases zero. In response to this criticism and calls for creditor countries to do more, the G8 countries agreed at the Gleneagles summit in July 2005 to cancel the $40 billion worth of debt owed by these 18 countries to the World Bank, IMF and African Development Bank.
- Countries in arrears to multilateral agencies, such as the World Bank and IMF, have first to make the back payments due. For some of the poorest countries, particularly those which have suffered civil wars (such as the Republic of Congo), such a requirement is virtually impossible to meet. Individual donor countries have sometimes agreed to partial forgiveness of arrears, but this has generally been insufficient to allow enough funds to be diverted to clear arrears with multilateral agencies.
- The IMF reform programmes have been too harsh. The required reductions in government expenditure lead to deep cuts in basic health and education, and deflationary policies lead to reductions in investment. What is more, past experience shows that two-thirds of IMF programmes in the poorest countries break down within three years. If such experience were repeated, many countries would never receive HIPC relief!
- Many of the non-HIPCs are also suffering debts which divert a large percentage of their income from poverty relief. Just because non-HIPCs can manage to service their debts, it does not make it desirable that they should be forced to do so.

CASE STUDIES AND APPLICATIONS BOX 26.7

SWAPPING DEBT

A solution to developing countries' debt?

Faced with the inability of many developing countries to service, let alone repay, their debts, many banks have collaborated with debtor countries in ingenious schemes to convert debt into some other form. There are a number of types of these 'debt swaps', as they are called.

Debt-for-equity swaps

Banks sell a certain amount of a country's debt at a discount in the secondary market. The purchaser (a firm or a bank) then swaps the debt with the central bank of the developing country for local currency, which is then used to buy shares in one or more of the country's companies. Sometimes debt–equity swaps are part of a privatisation programme, the debt being swapped for shares in a newly privatised company.

As far as the debtor country is concerned, this has the benefit of both reducing the debt and increasing the amount of investment in domestic companies. It has the drawback, however, of increasing foreign ownership and control in the country.

Debt-for-cash swaps

This is where the banks allow a debtor country to 'buy back' (i.e. repay) its debt at a discount. In order to do this, the developing country will probably have to secure a loan from another source. The developing country gains from achieving a net reduction in its debt. The bank gains by achieving an instant repayment of a percentage of the original debt.

Debt-for-bonds swaps

Here debt is converted into lower-interest-rate or lower value bonds. The developing country gains by having to pay a lower rate of interest. The bank gains by having a greater certainty of payment. A version of this system was adopted by Argentina in 2005 (see Box 26.5) when it agreed to swap old bonds, on which it had defaulted, for new ones worth only 35 per cent of the old ones, but at least which would be honoured.

Debt-for-nature or development swaps

This is where debts are cancelled in return for investment in environmental projects. There are two types of scheme: bilateral and commercial.

In a bilateral swap, a creditor country agrees to cancel debt in return for the debtor country investing a proportion of the amount in environmental projects. By 2003 there had been 82 such swaps in 30 debtor countries. These resulted in $1.1 trillion paid into environmental projects on debts of $3.5 trillion.

In a commercial swap, the debt owed to banks is sold to an international environmental agency at a substantial discount (or sometimes even given away); the agency then agrees to cancel this debt in return for the country funding the agency to carry out various environmental projects. By 2003, some $170 billion of commercial debt had been bought by environmental agencies for under $50 billion, with debtor countries in return agreeing to fund some $115 billion of environmental projects overseen by the agencies.

Like debt-for-nature swaps, debt-for-development swaps involve the selling or donating of debt to an international development agency, which then cancels it in return for the country carrying out specific projects in the fields of education, transport infrastructure, health, agriculture, etc.

Debt-for-export swaps

Under these schemes, banks arrange for developing countries to sell exports that they would otherwise have difficulty in selling (perhaps because of industrial country protection), provided the revenues are used to pay off specific debt. Clearly, the developing country can gain from the development of new export markets, but there is a danger that, by being a form of 'export protection', it could encourage the production of goods in which the country has a comparative disadvantage, and encourage inefficiency in production.

Debt-to-local-debt swaps

This is where external debt is converted into debt in the local currency (usually indexed to the US dollar). The original creditor sells the debt to a company that requires local currency to finance a subsidiary operating in the debtor country. The company benefits from a cheap source of local currency. The country benefits from a reduction in the need for scarce foreign currency.

Would the objections of developing countries to debt–equity swaps be largely overcome if foreign ownership were restricted to less than 50 per cent in any company? If such restrictions were imposed, would this be likely to affect the 'price' at which debt were swapped for equity?

According to many charities, such as Oxfam, a much better approach would be to target debt relief directly at poverty reduction, with the resources released being used for investment in fields such as health, education, rural development and basic infrastructure. The focus, they argue, should be on what countries can afford to pay *after* essential spending on poverty relief and human development.

?

Imagine that you are an ambassador of a developing country at an international conference. What would you try to persuade the rich countries to do in order to help you and other poor countries overcome the debt problem? How would you set about persuading them that it was in their own interests to help you?

Should all debt be cancelled and aid increased?

In recent years there have been growing calls for the cancellation of debts and a significant increase in aid, especially for the poorest developing countries, many ravaged by war, drought or AIDS. The United Nations has for many years called on wealthy countries to give 0.7 per cent of their GDP in aid. In practice they give only a little over 0.2 per cent.

As we have seen, the G8 meeting in Gleneagles in 2005 agreed to cancel 100 per cent of the $40 billion worth of debts owed to multilateral agencies such as the World Bank and IMF by the 18 HIPC countries that had reached the completion point. This was still, however, only a tiny proportion of the $520 billion of debt owed by poor countries. What is more, most of the $40 billion would have been cancelled anyway under the original HIPC terms. Then there is the plight of many non-HIPC countries, such as Kenya, which could be argued to be in greater need of debt relief than some HIPC countries.

At the summit France, Germany, Italy and the UK also committed themselves to meeting the 0.7 per cent of GDP aid target by 2015. The G8 as a whole agreed to increase aid to Africa by $25 billion a year by 2010 – a more than doubling of aid compared to 2004.

The argument against debt cancellation and a substantial increase in aid is that this could represent a 'moral hazard' (see Box 4.5 on page 104). Once the burden of debt had been lifted and aid had been increased, countries might be tempted to squander the money. It might also encourage them to seek further loans, which might again be squandered.

If, however, moneys were paid into national 'Poverty Funds', which could be monitored by civil society, Parliament and possibly multilateral agencies, this might help to ensure that the money would be used to fund key poverty-reducing projects, such as health, education, clean water and other basic infrastructure projects. (Web Case 26.6 examines some of the issues surrounding aid.)

Section summary

1. After the 1973 oil crisis, many developing countries borrowed heavily in order to finance their balance of trade deficits and to maintain a programme of investment. Despite this increase in debt, a combination of low real interest rates, a recovery in the world economy and high international rates of inflation allowed developing countries to sustain moderate rates of economic growth after 1975.
2. After the 1979 oil price rises, however, there was a much deeper world recession than in the mid-1970s, and real interest rates were much higher. Debt increased dramatically, and much of it at variable interest rates.
3. Although the problem for middle-income countries is now less serious, the situation has deteriorated for many of the poorest countries.
4. Rescheduling can help developing countries to cope with increased debt in the short run. During the 1980s and early 1990s there were several initiatives to encourage rescheduling programmes. Official loans are renegotiated through the Paris Club. This will normally involve some combination of longer repayment periods, grace periods in which payments may be delayed and either lower interest rates or partial cancellation of debts. Commercial bank loans have also frequently been renegotiated through a Bank Advisory Committee of the banks concerned. This has normally involved delaying paying loans for a period of time and the extension of the repayment period. In addition, under the Brady Plan, countries have borrowed from the World Bank and other international institutions to buy back their debt from banks at a discount.
5. If the problem is to be tackled, however, then either debts have to be written off – something that banks have been increasingly forced to do – or the developing countries themselves must take harsh corrective measures. The IMF favours 'structural adjustment' policies of deflation and market-orientated supply-side policies. An alternative is to pursue a more interventionist policy of restricting imports and encouraging investment in import-substituting sectors of the economy.
6. In 1996 the World Bank and IMF launched the HIPC initiative to help reduce the debts of heavily indebted poor countries to sustainable levels. HIPC relief has been criticised, however, for being made conditional on the debtor countries pursuing excessively tough IMF adjustment programmes, for having an excessively long qualifying period and debt sustainability thresholds that are too high, and for delays in its implementation. A better approach might be to target debt relief directly at programmes to help the poor.

END OF CHAPTER QUESTIONS

1. Compare the relative merits of using GNY statistics with those of various basic needs indicators when assessing both the level and the rate of a country's economic development.
2. If a developing country has a comparative advantage in primary products, should the government allow market forces to dictate the pattern of trade?
3. What are the advantages and disadvantages for a developing country of pursuing a policy of ISI?
4. Should all developing countries aim over the long term to become *exporters* of manufactured products?
5. How would you attempt to assess whether the technology used by an industry in a developing country was 'inappropriate'?
6. What policies could be adopted to reduce urban unemployment in developing countries?
7. To what extent was the debt crisis of the early 1980s caused by inappropriate policies that had been pursued by the debtor countries?
8. What are the advantages and disadvantages of debt swapping as a means of reducing the debts of developing countries?

Additional case studies on the book's website (www.pearsoned.co.uk/sloman)

26.1 **Theories of development.** This looks at different approaches to the analysis of poverty and development.

26.2 **Multinational corporations and developing countries.** This examines whether multinational investment is a net benefit to developing countries.

26.3 **A miracle gone wrong.** Lessons from east Asia.

26.4 **Ethical business.** An examination of the likelihood of success of companies which trade fairly with developing countries.

26.5 **The great escape.** This case examines the problem of capital flight from developing countries to rich countries.

26.6 **Economic aid.** Does aid provide a solution to the debt problem?

WEBSITES RELEVANT TO THIS CHAPTER

Numbers and sections refer to websites listed in the Web Appendix and hotlinked from this book's website at www.pearsoned.co.uk/sloman.

- For news articles relevant to this chapter, see the *Economics News Articles* link from the book's website.
- For news on various aspects of economic development, see A27, 28; I9. See also links to newspapers worldwide in A38, 39, 43 and 44, and the news search feature in Google at A41. See also links to economics news in A42.
- For links to a range of development sites, see sites I9 and 10.
- For data on developing countries, see sites B1, 19, 23, 31, 32, 33 and especially 35.
- For data on debt and development, see B24 and 35 (*Global Development Finance*) and B31. Also see debt section in I14.
- For information on trade and developing countries, see H4, 7, 9, 10, 16, 17.
- For information on debt and developing countries, see H4, 7, 9, 10, 12–14, 17–19.
- Sites I7 and 11 contain links to *Capital flows and aid* and *Trade and trade policy* in *Economic Development.* Site I4 has links to *International economics*, *Development economics* and *Economic development.* Site I17 has links to *Trade policy* and *Development economics.*
- For student resources relevant to this chapter, see sites C1–7, 9, 10, 19. See also *Virtual Developing Country* in *Virtual Worlds* in site C2.

Postscript: The Castaways or Vote for Caliban

The Pacific Ocean –
A blue demi-globe.
Islands like punctuation marks.

A cruising airliner,
Passengers unwrapping pats of butter.
A hurricane arises,
Tosses the plane into the sea.

Five of them flung onto an island beach,
Survived.

Tom the reporter.
Susan the botanist.
Jim the high-jump champion.
Bill the carpenter.
Mary the eccentric widow.

Tom the reporter sniffed out a stream of drinkable water.
Susan the botanist identified a banana tree.
Jim the high-jump champion jumped up and down and gave them each a bunch.
Bill the carpenter knocked up a table for their banana supper.
Mary the eccentric widow buried the banana skins,
But only after they had asked her twice.

They all gathered sticks and lit a fire.
There was an incredible sunset.

Next morning they held a committee meeting.
Tom, Susan, Jim and Bill
Voted to make the best of things.
Mary, the eccentric widow, abstained.

Tom the reporter killed several dozen wild pigs.
He tanned their skins into parchment
And printed the Island News with the ink of squids.

Susan the botanist developed new strains of banana
Which tasted of chocolate, beefsteak, peanut butter,
Chicken and bootpolish.

Jim the high-jump champion organised organised games
Which he always won easily.

Bill the carpenter constructed a wooden water wheel
And converted the water's energy into electricity.
Using iron ore from the hills, he constructed lampposts.

They all worried about Mary, the eccentric widow,
Her lack of confidence and her –
But there wasn't time to coddle her.

The volcano erupted, but they dug a trench
And diverted the lava into the sea
Where it formed a spectacular pier.
They were attacked by pirates but defeated them
With bamboo bazookas firing
Sea-urchins packed with home-made nitro-glycerine.
They gave the cannibals a dose of their own medicine
And survived an earthquake thanks to their skill in jumping.

Tom had been a court reporter
So he became a magistrate and solved disputes.
Susan the botanist established
A university which also served as a museum.
Jim the high-jump champion
Was put in charge of law enforcement –
Jumped on them when they were bad.
Bill the carpenter built himself a church,
Preached there every Sunday.

But Mary the eccentric widow . . .
Each evening she wandered down the island's main street,
Past the Stock Exchange, the Houses of Parliament,
The prison and the arsenal.
Past the Prospero Souvenir Shop,
Past the Robert Louis Stevenson Movie Studios,
Past the Daniel Defoe Motel
She nervously wandered and sat on the end of the pier of lava.

Breathing heavily,
As if at a loss,
As if at a lover,
She opened her eyes wide
To the usual incredible sunset.

Adrian Mitchell

1. *Had the castaways reduced their problem of scarcity by the end of the poem?*
2. *Could the 'usual incredible sunset' be described as an economic good?*

Educational Health Warning! Adrian Mitchell asks that none of his poems be used in connection with any examination whatsoever.

Appendix 1: Some Techniques of Economic Analysis

As you will see if you flick back through the pages, there are many diagrams and tables and several equations. But this does not mean that there are many mathematical techniques that you will have to master in order to study this book. In fact there are relatively few techniques, but they are ones which we use many times in many different contexts. You will find that if you are new to the subject, you will very quickly become familiar with these techniques. If you are not new to the subject, perhaps you could reassure your colleagues who are!

On some university courses, however, you will take mathematics to a higher level. To meet your needs there are a number of optional 'Looking at the Maths' sections scattered throughout the book. These use maths to express arguments that have just been covered in words or diagrams. Most of these 'Looking at the Maths' sections also refer to 'Maths Cases' on the book's website. These cases consist of worked examples and also have a question at the end for you to test your understanding of the relevant technique. The answers to these questions are also on the website.

But please note that the 'Looking at the Maths' sections are purely optional and will not be suitable for many courses. In such cases you can simply ignore them.

Diagrams as pictures

On many occasions, we use diagrams simply to provide a picture of a relationship. Just as a photograph in a newspaper can often depict an event much more vividly than any verbal account, so too a diagram in economics can often picture a relationship with a vividness and clarity that could never be achieved by words alone.

For example, we may observe that as people's incomes rise, they spend a lot more on entertainment and only a little more on food. We can picture this relationship very nicely by the use of a simple graph.

In Figure A1.1, an individual's income is measured along the horizontal axis and expenditure on food and entertainment is measured up the vertical axis. There are just two lines on this diagram: one showing how the expenditure on entertainment rises as income rises, the other how the expenditure on food rises as income rises. Now we could use a diagram like this to plot actual data. But we may simply be using it as a sketch – as a picture. In this case we do not necessarily need to put figures on the two axes. We are simply showing the relative *shapes* of the two curves. These shapes tell us that the person's expenditure on entertainment rises more quickly than that on food, and that above

Figure A1.1 Effect of a rise in an individual's income on his or her expenditure on food and entertainment

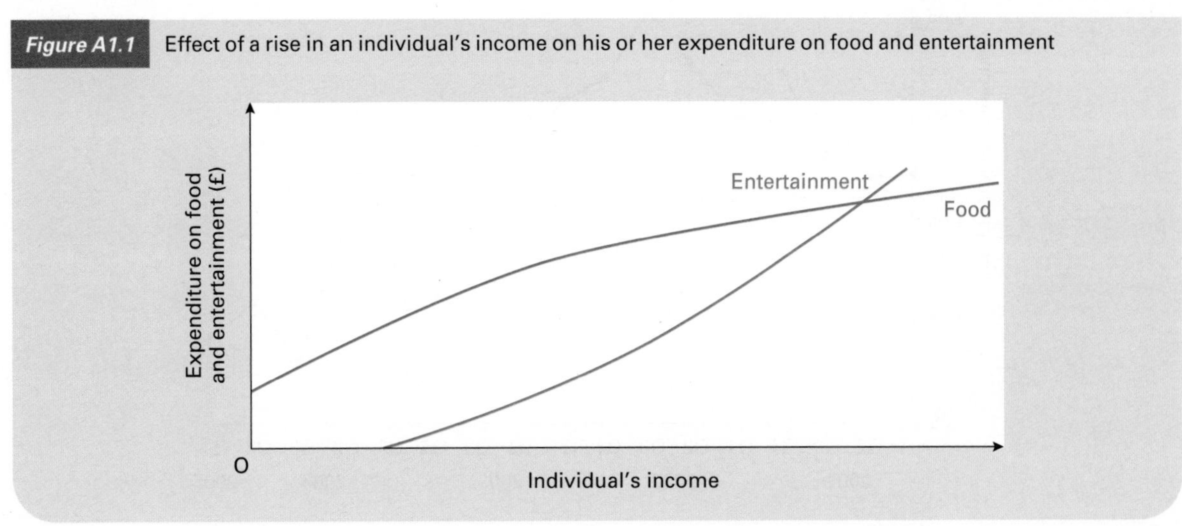

Table A1.1 UK unemployment, 2001 Q1–2005 Q1

	2001				2002				2003				2004				2005
	Q1	Q2	Q3	Q4	Q1	Q2	Q3	Q4	Q1	Q2	Q3	Q4	Q1	Q2	Q3	Q4	Q1
Unemployment (millions)	1.47	1.47	1.48	1.52	1.50	1.53	1.55	1.52	1.51	1.48	1.49	1.47	1.42	1.45	1.38	1.41	1.39

Source: based on *Time Series Data* (National Statistics, 2005).

a certain level of income the expenditure on entertainment becomes greater than that on food.

? *What else is the diagram telling us?*

Representing real-life statistics

In many cases, we will want to depict real-world data. We may want to show, for example, how unemployment has changed over the years in a particular country, or how income is distributed between different groups in the population. In the first we will need to look at *time-series* data. In the second we will look at *cross-section* data.

Time-series data

Table A1.1 shows the level of UK unemployment between the first quarter of 2001 and the first quarter of 2005. A table like this is a common way of representing ***time-series data***. It has the advantage of giving the precise figures, and is thus a useful reference if we want to test any theory and see if it predicts accurately.

Notice that in this particular table the figures are given quarterly. Depending on the period of time over which we want to see the movement of a variable, it may be more appropriate to use a different interval of time. For example, if we wanted to see how unemployment had changed over the past 50 years, we might use annual figures or even average figures for longer periods of time. If, however, we wanted to see how unemployment had changed over the course of a year, we would probably use monthly or even weekly figures.

? *The table in Box 1.2 shows time-series data for four different variables for four different countries. Would there have been any advantage in giving the figures for each separate year? Would there have been any disadvantage?*

Time-series data can also be shown graphically. In fact the data from a table can be plotted directly on to a graph. Figure A1.2 plots the data from Table A1.1. Each dot on the graph corresponds to one figure from the table. The dots

Definition

Time-series data Information depicting how a variable (e.g. the price of eggs) changes over time.

Figure A1.2 UK unemployment: 2001 Q1–2005 Q1

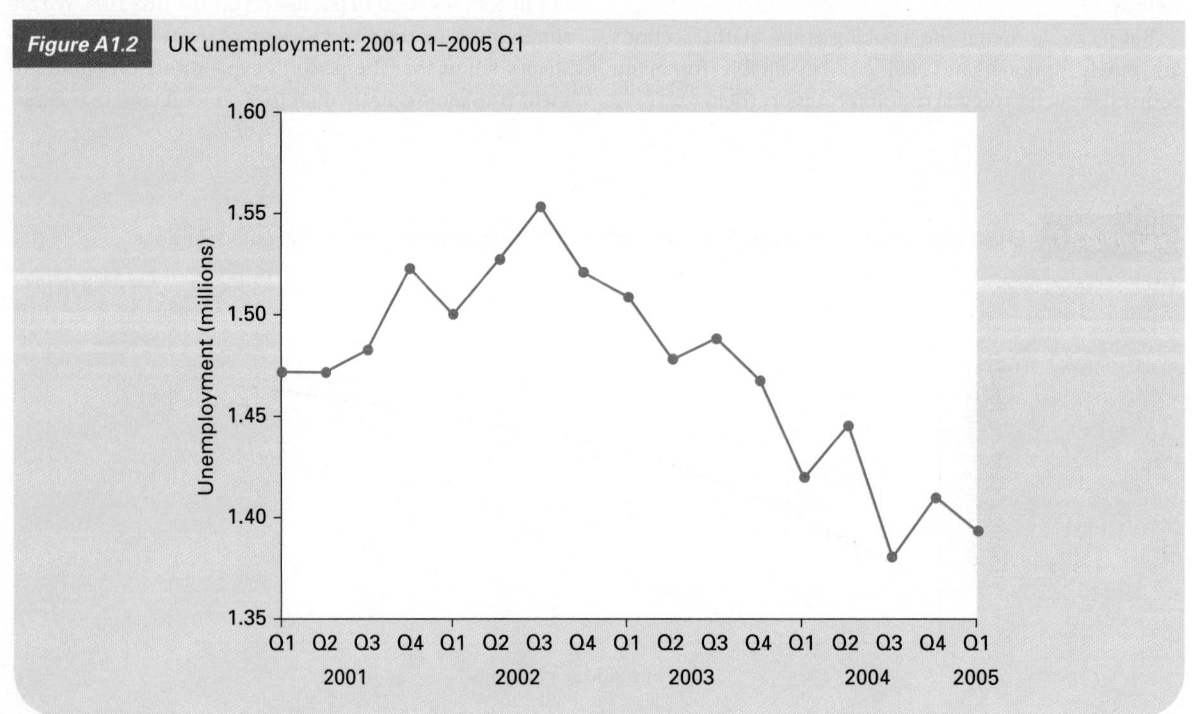

Table A1.2 UK economic growth, 2001 Q1–2005 Q1 (% increase over equivalent quarter in previous year)

	2001				2002				2003				2004				2005
	Q1	Q2	Q3	Q4	Q1	Q2	Q3	Q4	Q1	Q2	Q3	Q4	Q1	Q2	Q3	Q4	Q1
Economic growth (%)	2.6	2.4	2.1	2.2	1.7	1.5	1.9	1.9	2.0	2.0	2.1	2.7	3.0	3.6	3.1	2.9	2.8

Source: based on *Time Series Data* (National Statistics, 2005).

are then joined up to form a single line. Thus if you wanted to find the level of unemployment at any time between 2001 Q1 and 2005 Q1, you would simply find the appropriate date on the horizontal axis, read vertically upward to the line you have drawn, then read across to find the level of unemployment.

Although a graph like this cannot give you quite such an accurate measurement of each point as a table does, it gives a much more obvious picture of how the figures have moved over time and whether the changes are getting bigger (the curve getting steeper) or smaller (the curve getting shallower). We can also read off what the likely figure would be for some point *between* two observations.

? *What was the level of unemployment midway between quarter 2 and quarter 3 2004?*

It is also possible to combine *two* sets of time-series data on one graph to show their relative movements over time. Table A1.2 shows the figures for UK economic growth for the same time period. Figure A1.3 plots these data along with those from Table A1.1. This enables us to get a clear picture of how unemployment and the rate of economic growth moved in relation to each other over the period in question. Note that we use a different vertical scale for the two variables. This is inevitable given that they are measured in different units.

? *How would it be possible to show three different lines on the same diagram?*

All developed countries publish time-series data for the major macroeconomic variables such as national income, prices, employment and unemployment, interest rates, and imports and exports. Microeconomic data on the distribution of income, the performance of particular industries, the distribution of household expenditure and so on also appear in the official government statistics. Firms, consumers' associations, charities and other organisations also publish microeconomic statistics.

Appendix 2 looks at the range of readily available microeconomic and macroeconomic statistics. The statistical sources are arranged by subject headings.

There are also several sources of data freely available on the Internet. Section B of Appendix 2 at the end of the book gives a number of websites containing data sets. These websites can be accessed directly from the hotlinks section of this book's own website (www.pearsoned.co.uk/sloman).

Figure A1.3 UK unemployment and economic growth: 2001 Q1–2005 Q1

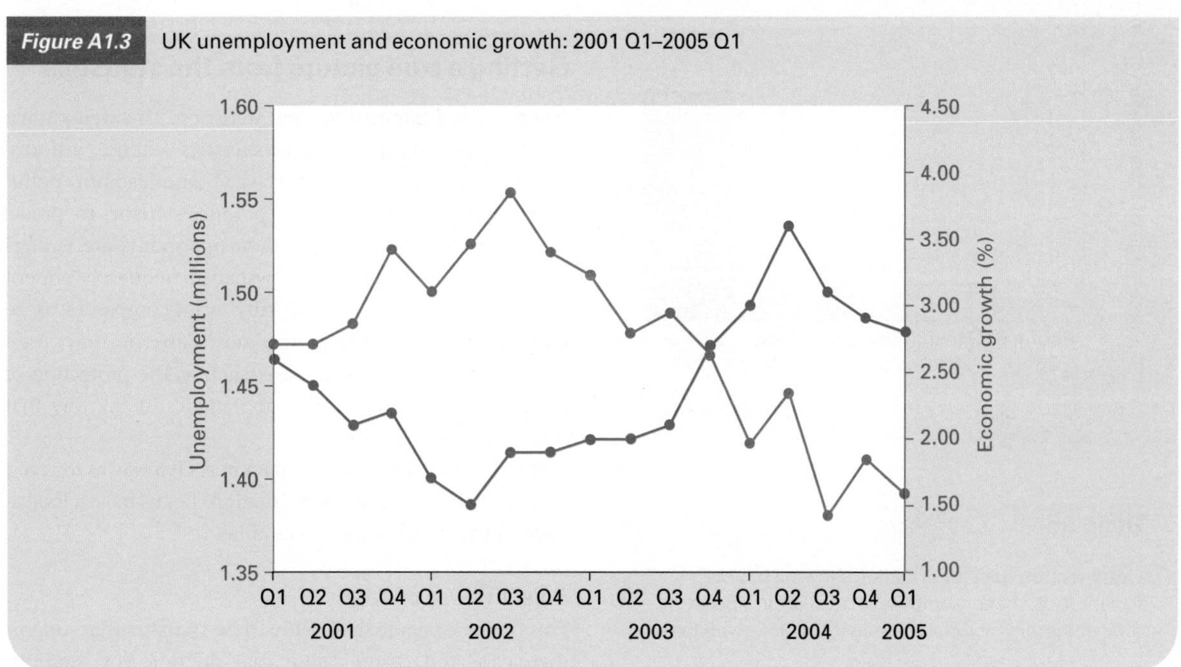

Table A1.3 Income before taxes and benefits

	Quintile groups of households					
	Bottom 20%	**Next 20%**	**Middle 20%**	**Next 20%**	**Top 20%**	**Total**
1977	4	10	18	26	42	100
2002/3	3	7	15	25	50	100

Source: *Social Trends* (National Statistics, 2005).

Cross-section data

Cross-section data show different observations made at the same point in time. For example, they could show the quantities of food and clothing purchased at various levels of household income, or the costs to a firm or industry of producing various quantities of a product.

Table A1.3 gives an example of cross-section data. It shows the distribution of household income in the UK before the deduction of taxes and the addition of benefits. It puts households into five equal-sized groups (or 'quintiles') according to their income. Thus the poorest 20 per cent of households are in one group, the next poorest 20 per cent are in the next and so on. Looking just at the 2002/3 figures, they show that the poorest 20 per cent earned just 3 per cent of total household incomes, whereas the richest 20 per cent earned 50 per cent.

Cross-section data like these are often represented in the form of a chart. Figure A1.4 shows the data as a *bar chart*, and Figure A1.5 as a *pie chart*.

Figure A1.5 The distribution of UK pre-tax income (2002/3): the use of a pie chart

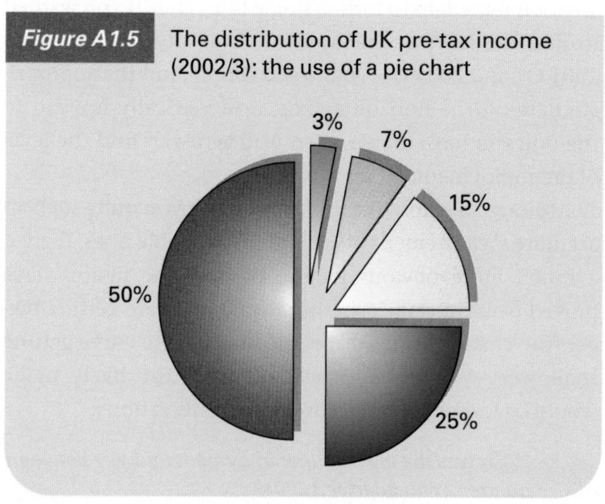

Figure A1.4 The distribution of UK pre-tax income (2002/3): the use of a bar chart

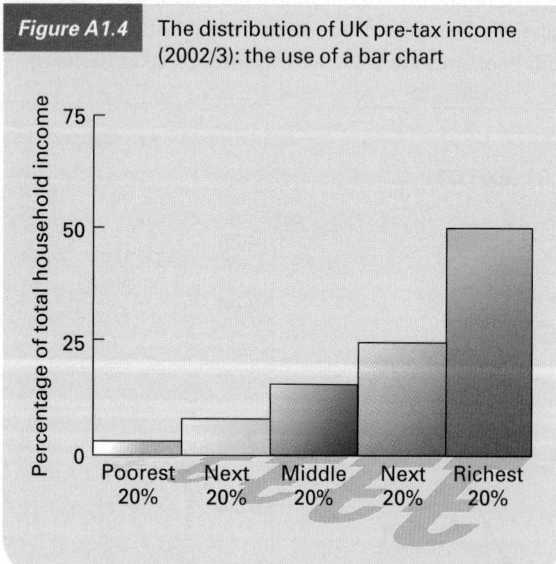

Definition

Cross-section data Information showing how a variable (e.g. the consumption of eggs) differs between different groups or different individuals at a given time.

It is possible to represent cross-section data at two or more different points in time, thereby presenting the figures as a time series. In Table A1.3, figures are given for just two time periods. With a more complete time series we could graph the movement of the shares of each of the five groups over time.

? *Could bar charts or pie charts be used for representing time-series data?*

Getting a true picture from the statistics

'There are lies, damned lies and statistics.' This well-known saying highlights the abuse of statistics – abuse, unfortunately, that is commonplace. Have you noticed how politicians always seem to be able to produce statistics to 'prove' that they are right and that their opponents are wrong? And it's not just politicians. Newspapers frequently present statistics in the most 'newsworthy' way; companies try to show their performance in the most flattering way; pressure groups fighting for a cause (such as the protection of the environment) again present statistics in the way that best supports their case.

It is not difficult to present data in such a way as to give a grossly distorted picture of a situation. Let us have a look at some of the most common examples.

Selective use of data

This is where people select only those statistics that support their case and ignore those that do not. For example,

Figure A1.6 The relationship between consumer income and the consumption of a particular foodstuff, using graphs with different scales

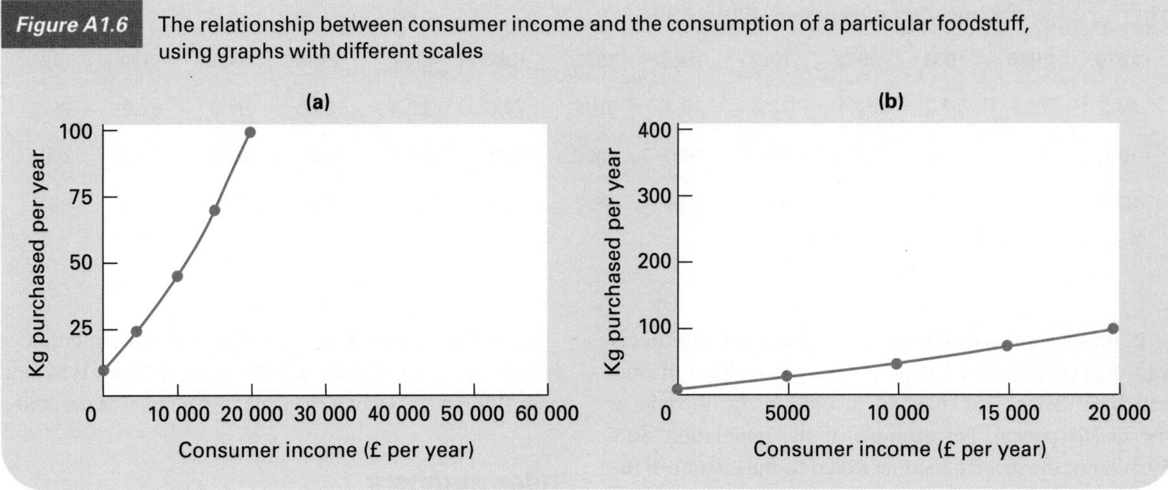

assume that unemployment has risen but inflation has fallen. The government highlights the inflation statistics to show how successful its policies have been. The opposition parties do the opposite: they concentrate on the unemployment statistics to demonstrate the failure of government policy.

Graphical presentation of data

Two graphs may present exactly the same data and yet convey a quite different impression about them. Figure A1.6 shows how the amount that people buy of a particular foodstuff varies with their income. It is based on the information in Table A1.4.

Diagram (a) shows *exactly the same* information as diagram (b), and yet at a glance it would seem from diagram (a) that people buy a lot more as their incomes rise, whereas from diagram (b) it would seem that people only buy a little more.

Clearly the choice of *scales* for the two axes will determine the shape of the graph.

?

1. *If the vertical scale for Figure A1.2 ran from 0 to 5 million, how would this alter your impression of the degree to which unemployment had changed?*
2. *What are the advantages and disadvantages of presenting data graphically with the axes starting from zero?*

Table A1.4 Annual purchases per person of a particular foodstuff

Consumer income (£ per year)	0	5000	10 000	15 000	20 000
Foodstuff purchased per person (kg per year)	10	25	45	70	100

Use of absolute or proportionate values

'People are paying more taxes now than they did when the government came to office', claims the opposition.

'Since coming into office we have cut taxes substantially', claims the government.

So who is right? Do we pay more or less tax? Quite possibly they are both right. If incomes have risen, we probably do pay more tax in total. After all, the more we earn, the greater the sum of money we will be paying in income tax; and the more we spend, the more we will be paying out in VAT. Thus in *absolute* terms we probably are paying more in taxes.

On the other hand, if the government has cut the rates of tax, we may be paying a smaller *proportion* of our income. In other words, a smaller proportion of a larger total can still represent an absolute increase.

Ignoring questions of distribution

'The average person has become better off under this government', claims a minister.

'Poverty has increased steeply under this government', claims the opposition. 'More than half the population are worse off now than when the government came to office.'

Surely, this time one of the claims must be wrong? But again, both could be right. The term 'average' normally refers to the ***mean***. The mean income is simply the total national income divided by the number in the population: i.e. income *per head*. If this is what is meant by the average, then the government may well be correct. Income per head may have risen.

Definition

Mean (or arithmetic mean) The sum of the values of each of the members of the sample divided by the total number in the sample.

Table A1.5 UK manufacturing output (2001 = 100)

1979	1980	1981	1982	1983	1984	1985	1986	1987	1988	1989	1990	1991
84.2	76.9	72.2	72.1	73.6	76.4	78.6	79.6	83.4	89.5	93.0	92.9	88.3
1992	**1993**	**1994**	**1995**	**1996**	**1997**	**1998**	**1999**	**2000**	**2001**	**2002**	**2003**	**2004**
88.2	89.5	93.7	95.1	95.8	97.6	98.2	98.9	101.4	100.0	96.9	97.4	98.8

Source: *Economic Trends* (National Statistics).

If, however, a relatively few people have got a lot richer and the rest have got a little poorer, the ***median*** income will have fallen. The median income is the income of the *middle* person. For example, if the population were 50 million, the median income would be the income of the twenty-five millionth richest person. This person's income may have fallen.

Real or nominal values

'Incomes have risen by 5 per cent this last year', claims the government.

'The standard of living has fallen', claims the opposition.

One of the most common abuses of statistics is deliberately switching between real and nominal figures, depending on what message you want to give your audience. ***Nominal*** figures are the simple monetary values at the prices ruling at the time. For example, if you earned a wage of £100 per week last year and are earning £105 per week this year, then in nominal terms your wage has risen by 5 per cent.

But what if prices have risen by 8 per cent? Your 5 per cent increase in wages will in fact buy you 3 per cent *less* goods. Your ***real*** wages have gone down by 3 per cent. In other words, to show how much better or worse off a person or nation is, the nominal figure must be corrected for inflation.

Key Idea 36

The distinction between nominal and real figures. Nominal figures are those using current prices, interest rates, etc. Real figures are figures corrected for inflation.

Thus:

Real growth = Nominal growth − Inflation

1. *If a bank paid its depositors 3 per cent interest and inflation was 5 per cent, what would be the* real *rate of interest?*
2. *Has your real income gone up or down this last year?*

The time chosen for comparison

'Between 1982 and 1990, Britain's real growth rate averaged 3.5 per cent per year', boasted the Conservative government of the time.

'Between 1979 and 1993, Britain could only manage a real growth rate of 1.6 per cent per year', chided the opposition.

Again both were correct, but they had chosen either to include or to ignore the periods from 1979 to 1982 and from 1990 to 1993 when the real growth rate was negative.

Index numbers

Time-series data are often expressed in terms of ***index numbers***. Consider the data in Table A1.5. It shows index numbers of manufacturing output in the UK from 1979 to 2004.

One year is selected as the ***base year*** and this is given the value of 100. In our example this is 2001. The output for other years is then shown by their percentage variation from 100. For 1981 the index number is 72.2. This means that manufacturing output was 27.8 per cent lower in 1981 than in 2001. The index number for 2000 is 101.4. This means that manufacturing output was 1.4 per cent higher in 2000 than in 2001.

Does this mean that the value of manufacturing output in 2000 was 1.4 per cent higher in money terms?

The use of index numbers allows us to see clearly any upward and downward movements and to make an easy comparison of one year with another. For example, Table A1.5 shows quite clearly that manufacturing output fell from 1979 to 1982 and did not regain its 1979 level until 1988.

Using index numbers to measure percentage changes

To find the annual percentage growth rate in any one year we simply look at the percentage change in the index from

Definitions

Median The value of the middle member of the sample.

Nominal values Money values measured at *current* prices.

Real values Money values corrected for inflation.

Index number The value of a variable expressed as 100 plus or minus its percentage deviation from a base year.

Base year (for index numbers) The year whose index number is set at 100.

Table A1.6 Constructing a weighted average index

Industry	Weight	Year 1		Year 2	
		Index	Index times weight	Index	Index times weight
A	0.7	100	70	90	63
B	0.2	100	20	110	22
C	0.1	100	10	130	13
Total	1.0		100		98

the previous year. To work this out we use the following formula:

$$\left(\frac{I_t - I_{t-1}}{I_{t-1}}\right) \times 100$$

where I_t is the index in the year in question and I_{t-1} is the index in the previous year.

Thus to find the growth rate in manufacturing output from 1987 to 1988 we first see how much the index has risen ($I_t - I_{t-1}$). The answer is 89.5 − 83.4 = 6.1. But this does *not* mean that the growth rate is 6.1 per cent. According to our formula, the growth rate is equal to:

$$\frac{89.5 - 83.4}{83.4} \times 100$$

$$= 6.1/83.4 \times 100$$

$$= 7.3\%$$

What was the growth rate in manufacturing output from (a) 1982 to 1983; (b) 2000 to 2001?

The price index

Perhaps the best known of all price indices is the ***consumer prices index (CPI)***. It is an index of the prices of goods and services purchased by the average household. Movements in this index, therefore, show how the cost of living has changed. Annual percentage increases in the CPI are the commonest definition of the rate of inflation. Thus if the CPI went up from 100 to 110 over a twelve-month period, we would say that the rate of inflation was 10 per cent.

If the CPI went up from 150 to 162 over twelve months, what would be the rate of inflation?

Definitions

Consumer prices index (CPI) An index of the prices of goods bought by a typical household.

Weighted average The average of several items where each item is ascribed a weight according to its importance. The weights must add up to 1.

The use of weighted averages

The CPI is a ***weighted average*** of the prices of many items. The index of manufacturing output that we looked at previously was also a weighted average, an average of the output of many individual products.

To illustrate how a weighted average works, consider the case of a weighted average of the output of just three industries, A, B and C. Let us assume that in the base year (year 1) the output of A was £7 million, of B £2 million and of C £1 million, giving a total output of the three industries of £10 million. We now attach weights to the output of each industry to reflect its proportion of total output. Industry A is given a weight of 0.7 because it produces seven-tenths of total output. Industry B is given a weight of 0.2 and industry C a weight of 0.1. We then simply multiply each industry's index by its weight and add up all these figures to give the overall industry index.

The index for each industry in year 1 (the base year) is 100. This means that the weighted average index is also 100. Table A1.6 shows what happens to output in year 2. Industry A's output falls by 10 per cent, giving it an index of 90 in year 2. Industry B's output rises by 10 per cent and industry C's output rises by 30 per cent, giving indices of 110 and 130, respectively. But as you can see from the table, despite the fact that two of the three industries have had a rise in output, the total industry index has *fallen* from 100 to 98. The reason is that industry A is so much larger than the other two that its decline in output outweighs their increase.

The consumer prices index is a little more complicated. This is because it is calculated in two stages. First, products are grouped into categories such as food, clothing and services. A weighted average index is worked out for each group. Thus the index for food would be the weighted average of the indices for bread, potatoes, cooking oil, etc. Second, a weight is attached to each of the groups in order to work out an overall index.

Functional relationships

Throughout economics we examine how one economic variable affects another: how the purchases of cars are affected by their price; how consumer expenditure is affected by taxes, or by incomes; how the cost of producing washing machines is affected by the price of steel; how the rate of unemployment is affected by the level of government expenditure. These relationships are called ***functional relationships***. We will need to express these relationships in a precise way, preferably in the form of a table or a graph or an equation.

Simple linear functions

These are relationships which produce a straight line when plotted on a graph. Let us take an imaginary example of the relationship between total value added tax receipts in an economy (V) and the level of consumer expenditure (C). This functional relationship can be written as:

$$V = f(C)$$

This is simply shorthand for saying that VAT receipts are a function of (i.e. depend on) the level of consumer expenditure.

If we want to know just *how much* VAT revenue will be at any given level of consumer expenditure, we will need to spell out this functional relationship. Let us do this in each of the three ways.

As a table. Table A1.7 gives a selection of values of C and the corresponding level of V. It is easy to read off from the table the level of VAT receipts at one of the levels of consumer expenditure listed. It is clearly more difficult to work out the level of VAT receipts if consumer expenditure is £23.4 billion or £47.6 billion.

As a graph. Figure A1.7 plots the data from Table A1.7. Each of the dots corresponds to one of the points in the table. By joining the dots up into a single line we can easily read off the value for VAT receipts at some level of consumption other than those listed in the table. A graph also has the advantage of allowing us to see the relationship at a glance.

It is usual to plot the *independent variable* (i.e. the one that does not depend on the other) on the horizontal or x-axis, and the *dependent variable* on the vertical or y-axis. In our example, VAT receipts *depend* on consumer expenditure. Thus VAT receipts are the dependent variable and consumer expenditure is the independent variable.

Table A1.7 A VAT function

Consumer expenditure (£bn per year)	VAT receipts (£bn per year)
0	0
10	2
20	4
30	6
40	8
50	10

Figure A1.7 A graph of the VAT function: $V = 0.2C$

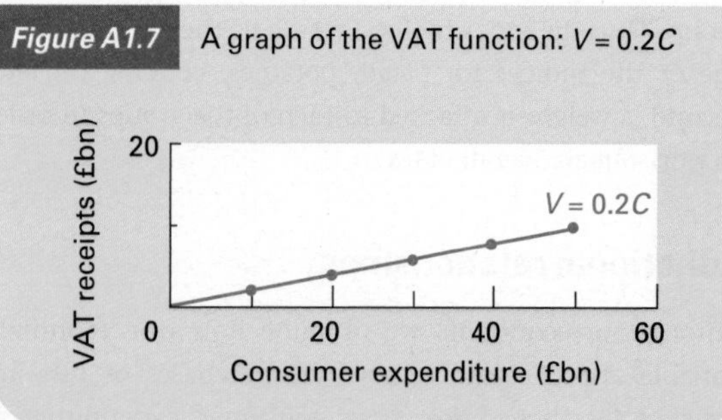

As an equation. The data in the table can be expressed in the equation:

$$V = 0.2C$$

This would be the equation if the VAT rate were 20 per cent on all goods and services.

An equation has the major advantage of being precise. We could work out *exactly* how much would be paid in VAT at any given level of consumption.

This particular function starts at the origin of the graph (i.e. the bottom left-hand corner). This means that when the value of the independent variable is zero, so too is the value of the dependent variable.

When a graph does not pass through the origin its equation will have the form:

$$y = a + bx$$

where y stands for the dependent variable and x for the independent variable, and a and b will have numbers assigned in an actual equation. For example, the equation might be:

$$y = 4 + 2x$$

This would give Table A1.8 and Figure A1.8.

Table A1.8 $y = 4 + 2x$

x	y
0	4
1	6
2	8
3	10
4	12
5	14
.	.
.	.

Definition

Functional relationships The mathematical relationships showing how one variable is affected by one or more others.

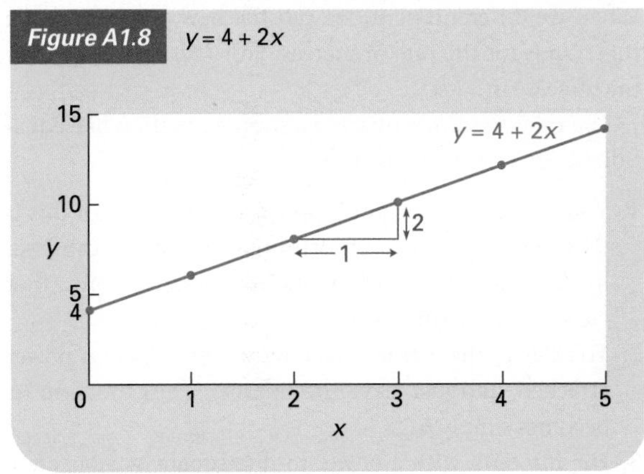

Figure A1.8 $y = 4 + 2x$

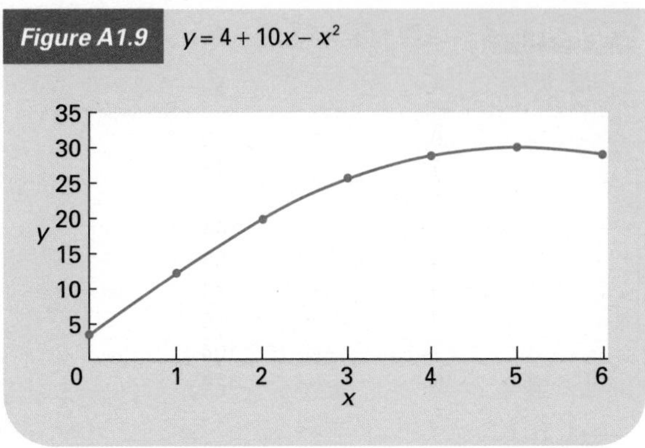

Figure A1.9 $y = 4 + 10x - x^2$

Notice two things about the relationship between the equation and the graph:

- The point where the line crosses the vertical axis (at a value of 4) is given by the constant (a) term. If the a term is negative, the line will cross the vertical axis *below* the horizontal axis.
- The slope of the line is given by the b term. The slope is 2/1: for every 1 unit increase in x there is a 2 unit increase in y.

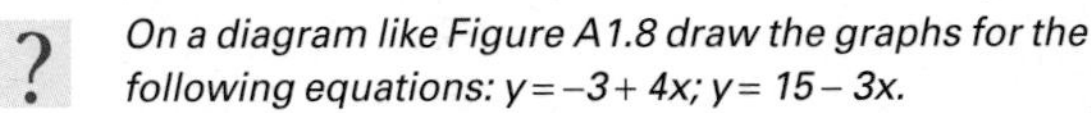

? *On a diagram like Figure A1.8 draw the graphs for the following equations:* $y = -3 + 4x$; $y = 15 - 3x$.

Note that in the second equation of the question, the x term is negative. This means that y and x are *inversely related*. As x increases, y decreases.

Non-linear functions

With these functions the equation involves a squared term (or other power terms). Such functions will give a curved line when plotted on a graph. As an example, consider the following equation:

$$y = 4 + 10x - x^2$$

Table A1.9 and Figure A1.9 are based on it.

As you can see, y rises at a decelerating rate and eventually begins to fall. This is because the negative x^2 term is becoming more and more influential as x rises and eventually begins to outweigh the $10x$ term.

Table A1.9 $y = 4 + 10x - x^2$

x	y
0	4
1	13
2	20
3	25
4	28
5	29
6	28
7	25
.	.
.	.

? *What shaped graph would you get from the equations:*

$$y = -6 + 3x + 2x^2; \quad y = 10 - 4x + x^2$$

(If you cannot work out the answer, construct a table like Table A1.9 and then plot the figures on a graph.)

*Elementary differentiation

In several starred boxes and *Looking at the Maths* sections we will be using some elementary calculus. The part of calculus we will be using is called ***differentiation***. This is a technique to enable us to calculate the rate of change of a variable. The purpose of this section is not to explain why differentiation involves the procedures it does, but simply to state the rules that are necessary for our purposes. You will need to consult a maths book if you want to know how these rules are derived.

First, let us see when we would be interested in looking at the rate of change of a variable. Take the case of a firm thinking of expanding. It will want to know how much its costs will increase as its output increases. It will want to know the rate of change of costs with respect to changes in output.

Let us assume that it faces a cost function of the form:

$$C = 20 + 5Q + Q^2 \qquad \textbf{(1)}$$

where C is the total cost of production and Q is the quantity produced. Table A1.10 and Figure A1.10 are derived from this equation.

The rate of increase in its costs with respect to increases in output is given by the *slope* of the cost curve in Figure A1.10. The steeper the slope, the more rapidly costs

> **Definition**
>
> **Differentiation** A mathematical technique to find the rate of change of one variable with respect to another.

Table A1.10 $C = 20 + 5Q + Q^2$

x	y
0	20
1	26
2	34
3	44
4	56
5	70
6	86
7	104
8	124
.	.
.	.

Figure A1.10 A total cost function: $C = 20 + 5Q + Q^2$

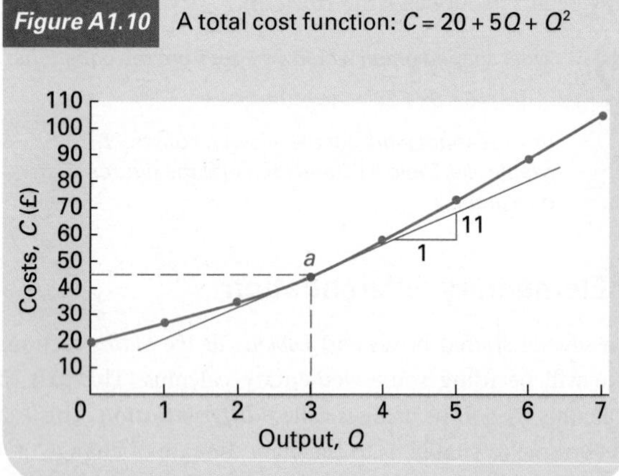

increase. At point *a* the slope of the curve is 11. This is found by drawing the tangent to the curve and measuring the slope of the tangent. At this point on the curve, what we are saying is that for each one unit increase in output there is an £11 increase in costs. (Obviously as the graph is curved, this rate of increase will vary at different outputs.)

This rate of increase in costs is known as the ***marginal cost***. It is the same with other variables that increase with quantity: their rate of increase is known as *marginal*. For example, *marginal revenue* is the rate of increase of sales revenue with respect to output.

We can use the technique of differentiation to derive a marginal from a total equation: in other words, to derive the slope of the total curve. Let us assume that we have an equation:

$$y = 10 + 6x - 4x^2 + 2x^3 \qquad (2)$$

Definition

Marginal cost The rate of increase in costs with respect to output.

When we differentiate it, we call the new equation dy/dx: this stands for the rate of increase in y (dy) with respect to the increase in x (dx).

The rules for differentiating a simple equation like equation (2) are very straightforward.

1. You delete the constant term (10). The reason for this is that, being constant, by definition it will not cause an increase in y as x increases, and it is the *increase* in y that we are trying to discover.
2. You delete the x from the x term which has no power attached, and just leave the number. Thus the term $6x$ becomes simply 6.
3. For any term with a power in it (a square, a cube, etc.), its value should be *multiplied* by the power term and the power term reduced by one. Thus in the term $4x^2$, the 4 would be multiplied by 2 (the power term), and the power term would be reduced from 2 to 1 (but x to the power of 1 is simply x). After differentiation, therefore, the term becomes $8x$. In the term $2x^3$, the 2 would be multiplied by 3 (the power term), and the power term would be reduced from 3 to 2. After differentiation, therefore, the term becomes $6x^2$.

Applying these three rules to the equation:

$$y = 10 + 6x - 4x^2 + 2x^3 \qquad (2)$$

gives:

$$dy/dx = 6 - 8x + 6x^2 \qquad (3)$$

To find the rate of change of y with respect to x at any given value of x, therefore, you simply substitute that value of x into equation (3).

Thus when $x = 4$, $dy/dx = 6 - (8 \times 4) + (6 \times 16) = 70$. In other words, when $x = 4$, for every 1 unit increase in x, y will increase by 70.

Returning to our cost function in equation (1), what is the marginal cost equation? Applying the three rules to the equation:

$$C = 20 + 5Q + Q^2 \qquad (1)$$

gives:

$$dC/dQ = 5 + 2Q \qquad (4)$$

Thus at an output of 3, the marginal cost (dC/dQ) is $5 + (2 \times 3) = 11$, which is the slope of the tangent to point *a*.

?
What would be the marginal cost equation if the total cost equation were:

$$C = 15 + 20Q - 5Q^2 + Q^3?$$

What would be the marginal cost at an output of 8?

Finding the maximum or minimum point of a curve

The other important use we can make of calculus is to find the maximum or minimum point of a curve. This has a number of important applications. For example, a firm may want to know the minimum point on its average cost curve (a curve which shows how costs per unit of output vary as

ISSUES AND APPLICATIONS *BOX A1.1

WHEN IS GOOD NEWS REALLY GOOD?

Are things getting better or merely getting worse more slowly?

From the second quarter of 1990 unemployment rose continuously for many quarters. By the third quarter of 1991 unemployment had increased by some 0.75 million. What good news could the government possibly draw from this?

Governments, always in search of any glimmer of good economic news, proclaimed that unemployment was rising more slowly (in other words, that the rate of increase in unemployment was falling). This was perfectly correct.

To show this let us assume that *N* is the number of people out of work. The rate of change of unemployment is therefore given by dN/dt (where t is time). A positive figure for dN/dt represents a rise in unemployment, a negative figure a fall. Its value is given by the slope of the green line in the diagram. From the second quarter of 1990 this figure was positive. Bad news!

But the government sought a rosier interpretation. By using a second-order derivative, d^2N/dt^2, it could show that the rate of increase in unemployment from early 1991 had been falling. The value of this is given by the slope of the red line in the diagram. The government proclaimed that this was evidence that the economy was beginning to recover. Good news!

The use of calculus in this manner is a two-edged sword and such statistical sophistry is open to the political opposition, who could at a later date, if they so wished, claim that a fall in unemployment was bad economic news. Dare they?

If the opposition were indeed to claim that a fall in unemployment was bad news, what would have to be the value of d^2N/dt^2: positive or negative?

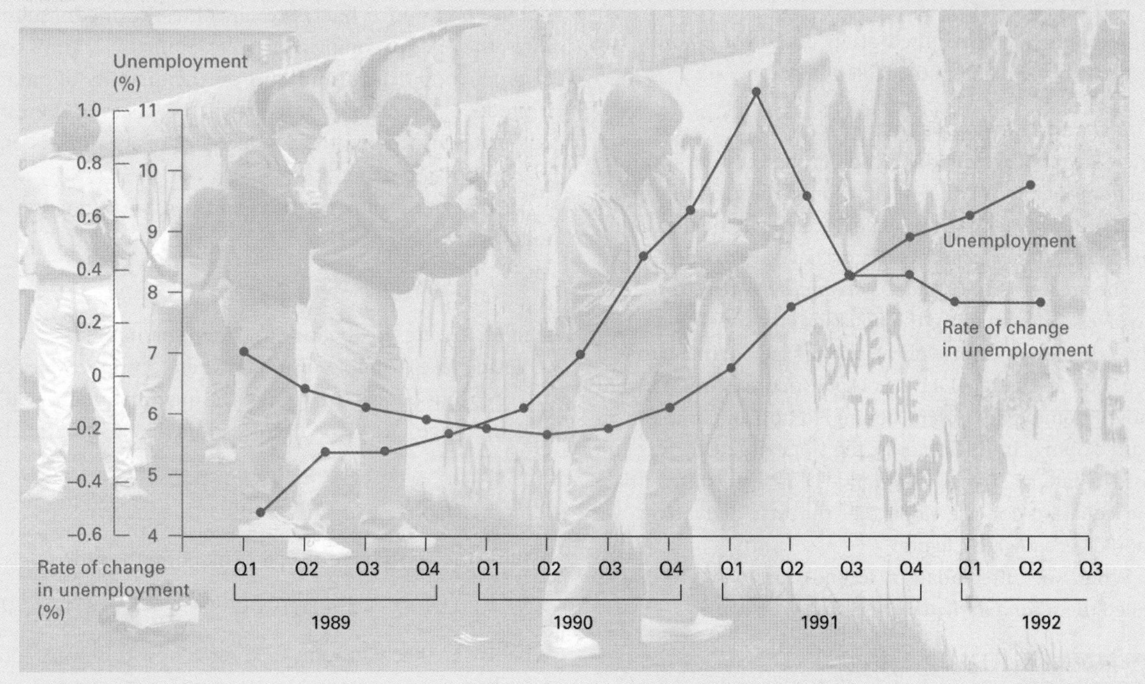

output increases). Also it is likely to want to know the output at which it will earn maximum profit. Let us examine this particular case.

Assume that the equation for total profit (Π) is:

$$\Pi = -20 + 12Q - Q^2 \quad (5)$$

This gives profit at various outputs as shown in Table A1.11. The corresponding graph is plotted in Figure A1.11.

? *What is the meaning of a negative profit?*

Figure A1.11 A total profit function: $\Pi = -20 + 12Q - Q^2$

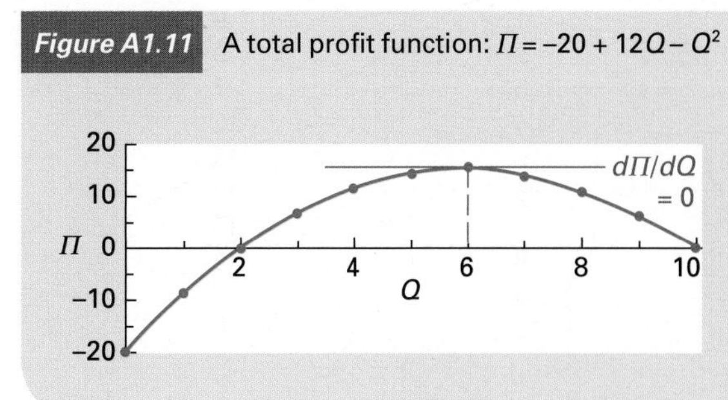

It can be seen at a glance that profits are maximised at an output of 6 units. But we could have worked this out directly from the profit equation without having to draw up a table or graph. How is this done?

Remember that when we differentiate a curve, the equation we get (known as 'the first derivative') gives us the slope of the curve. You can see that at the point of maximum profit (the top of the curve) its slope is zero: the tangent is horizontal. So all we have to do to find the top of the curve is to differentiate its equation and set it equal to zero.

Given that:

$$\Pi = -20 + 12Q - Q^2 \quad (5)$$

then:

$$d\Pi/dQ = 12 - 2Q \quad (6)$$

Setting this equal to zero gives:

$$12 - 2Q = 0$$

$$\therefore 2Q = 12$$

$$\therefore Q = 6$$

Thus profits are maximised at an output of 6 units: the result we obtained from the table and graph.

The second derivative test

There is a problem with this technique, however. How can we tell from equation (6) that we have found the *maximum* rather than the *minimum*? The problem is that *both* the maximum *and* the minimum points of a curve have a zero slope.

The answer is to conduct a ***second derivative test***. This involves differentiating the equation a second time. This gives the rate of change of the *slope* of the original curve. If you look at Figure A1.11, as output increases, the tangent moves from being upward sloping, to horizontal, to downward sloping. In other words, the slope is getting less and less. Its rate of change is *negative*. Thus if we differentiate the equation for the slope (i.e. the first derivative), we should get a negative figure.

When we differentiate a second time we get what is called the ***second derivative***. It is written d^2y/dx^2.

Table A1.11 $\Pi = -20 + 12Q - Q^2$

Q	Π
0	−20
1	−9
2	0
3	7
4	12
5	15
6	16
7	15
8	12
9	7
10	0
.	.

If we differentiate equation (6):

$$d\Pi/dQ = 12 - 2Q \quad (6)$$

we get:

$$d^2\Pi/dQ^2 = -2 \quad (7)$$

(Note that the rules for differentiating a second time are the same as for the first time.) Given that the second derivative in this case is negative, we have demonstrated that we have indeed found the maximum profit point (at $Q = 6$), and not the minimum.

? *Given the following equation for a firm's average cost (AC), i.e. the cost per unit of output (Q):*

$$AC = 60 - 16Q + 2Q^2$$

(a) At what output is AC at a minimum?

(b) Use the second derivative test to prove that this is a minimum and not a maximum.

Partial differentiation

Many relationships in economics involve more than two variables. For example, the demand for a product depends not just on its price, but also on income, the price of substitutes, the price of complements, etc. Similarly, a firm's cost of production depends not just on the quantity of output it produces, but also on wage rates, the prices of the various materials it uses, the productivity of its workers and machinery, and so on.

Such relationships can be expressed as a function as follows:

$$y = f(x_1, x_2, x_3, \ldots x_n)$$

where x_1, x_2, etc. are the various determinants of y.

Let us take a simple example where a firm's total cost (TC) depends on just two things: the quantity produced (Q) and the wage rate (W). The cost function will be of the form:

$$TC = f(Q, W)$$

Assume that in the case of a particular firm the function is:

$$TC = 20 + 10Q - 4Q^2 + 2Q^3 + 6W \quad (8)$$

What we are likely to want to know is how this firm's total cost changes as quantity changes, assuming the wage rate is held constant. Alternatively we may wish to know how its total cost changes as the wage rate changes, assuming that output is held constant. To do this we use the technique of

Definitions

Second derivative test If on differentiating an equation a second time the answer is negative (positive), the point is a maximum (minimum).

Second derivative The rate of change of the first derivative, found by differentiating the first derivative.

partial differentiation. This involves the same technique as simple differentiation but applied to just the one variable that is not held constant.

Thus to find the rate of change of costs with respect to quantity in equation (8), we differentiate the equation with respect to Q and ignore the W term. We ignore it as it is held constant and is thus treated like the constant (20) term in the equation. Using the rules of differentiation, the ***partial derivative*** is thus:

$$\frac{\partial TC}{\partial Q} = 10 - 8Q + 6Q^2 \tag{9}$$

Note that instead of using the symbol 'd' that we used in simple differentiation, we now use the symbol '∂'. Apart from that, the rules for partial differentiation are exactly the same as with simple differentiation.

If we now wanted to see how this firm's costs vary with the wage rate for any given output, then we would partially differentiate equation (8) with respect to W, giving:

$$\frac{\partial TC}{\partial W} = 6$$

In other words, for each £1 rise in the wage rate, total cost would rise by £6.

Assume that the demand for a product is given by the following function

$$Q_D = 1000 - 50P + 2P^2 + 10P_S + P_S^2$$

where Q_D is the quantity demanded, P is the price of the good and P_S is the price of a substitute good. What is the partial derivative of this demand function with respect to (a) the price of the good; (b) the price of the substitute good? Interpret the meaning of each partial derivative.

Definitions

Partial differentiation A mathematical technique used with functions containing two or more independent variables. The technique is used to find the rate of change of the dependent variable with respect to a single independent variable assuming that the other independent variables are held constant.

Partial derivative The partial derivative of a function of two or more independent variables is the derivative with respect to just one of those variables, while holding the others constant.

Appendix summary

1. Diagrams in economics can be used as pictures: to sketch a relationship so that its essentials can be perceived at a glance.
2. Tables, graphs and charts are also used to portray real-life data. These can be time-series data or cross-section data or both.
3. In order to get a true picture from economic data it is important to be aware of various ways that statistics can be abused: these include a selective use of data, a choice of axes on a graph to make trends seem more or less exaggerated or to make a curve more or less steep, confusing absolute and relative values, ignoring questions of distribution, confusing nominal and real values, and selecting the time period to make the statistics look the most favourable or unfavourable.
4. Presenting time-series data as index numbers gives a clear impression of trends and is a good way of comparing how two or more series (perhaps originally measured in different units) have changed over the same time period. A base year is chosen and the index for that year is set at 100. The percentage change in the value of a variable is given by the percentage change in the index (I). The formula is:

   $$\left(\frac{I_t - I_{t-1}}{I_{t-1}}\right) \times 100$$

   Several items can be included in one index by using a weighted value for each of the items. The weights must add up to 1, and each weight will reflect the relative importance of that particular item in the index.
5. Functional relationships can be expressed as an equation, a table or a graph. In the linear (straight-line) equation $y = a + bx$, the a term gives the vertical intercept (the point where the graph crosses the vertical axis) and the b term gives the slope. When there is a power term (e.g. $y = a + bx + cx^2$), the graph will be a curve.

*6. Differentiation can be used to obtain the rate of change of one variable with respect to another. The rules of differentiation require that in an equation of the form:

   $$y = a + bx + cx^2 + dx^3$$

   the a term disappears, the bx term simply becomes b, the cx^2 term becomes $2cx$, the dx^3 becomes $3dx^2$ and so on, with each extra term being multiplied by its power term and its power term being reduced by 1.

*7. To find the value of the x term at which the y term is at a maximum or minimum, the equation should be differentiated and set equal to zero. To check which it is – maximum or minimum – the second derivative should be calculated. If it is negative, then setting the first derivative equal to zero has yielded a maximum. If the second derivative is positive, then setting the first derivative to zero has yielded a minimum value.

Appendix 2: Websites

All the following websites can be accessed from this book's own website (http://www.pearsoned.co.uk/sloman). When you enter the site, click on **Hot Links**. You will find all the following sites listed. Click on the one you want and the 'hot link' will take you straight to it.

The sections and numbers below refer to the ones used in the Web icons throughout the text. Thus if the icon contained the number A21, this would refer to the Money World site.

(A) General news sources

As the title of this section implies, the websites here can be used for finding material on current news issues or tapping into news archives. Most archives are offered free of charge. However, some do require you to register. As well as key UK and American news sources, you will also notice some slightly different places from where you can get your news, such as the St Petersburg Times and Kyodo News (from Japan). Check out sites number 38 My Virtual Newspaper, 43 Guardian World News Guide and 44 Online newspapers for links to newspapers across the world. Try searching for an article on a particular topic by using site number 41 Google News Search.

1. BBC news
2. The Economist
3. The Financial Times
4. The Guardian
5. The Independent
6. ITN
7. The Observer
8. The Telegraph
9. The Times, Sunday Times
10. The New York Times
11. Fortune
12. Time Magazine
13. The Washington Post
14. Moscow Times (English)
15. St Petersburg Times (English)
16. Straits Times
17. New Straits Times
18. The Scotsman
19. The Herald
20. Euromoney
21. Money World
22. Market News International
23. BusinessWeek online
24. Ananova
25. CNN Money
26. Wall Street Journal
27. Asia related news
28. allAfrica.com
29. Greek News Agencies (English)
30. Kyodo News: Japan (English)
31. RFE/RL News
32. The Australian
33. Sydney Morning Herald
34. Japan Times
35. Reuters
36. Bloomberg
37. David Smith's Economics UK.com
38. My Virtual Newspaper (links to a whole range of news sources)
39. Newspapers on World Wide Web
40. Economics in the News from Gametheory.net
41. Google News Search
42. Moreover
43. Guardian World News Guide
44. Online newspapers

(B) Sources of economic and business data

Using websites to find up-to-date data is of immense value to the economist. The data sources below offer you a range of specialist and non-specialist data information. Universities have free access to the MIMAS and ESDS sites, which are huge databases of statistics. Site 34, the Treasury Pocket Data Bank, is a very useful source of key UK and world statistics, and is updated monthly. It comes as an Excel file.

1. Economics Network gateway to economic data
2. Biz/ed Gateway to economic and company data
3. National Statistics
4. Data Archive (Essex)
5. Econ Links
6. Economic Resources (About)
7. Nationwide House Prices Site
8. House Web (data on housing market)
9. Incomes Data Services
10. Keynote Publications Ltd.
11. Land Registry (house prices, etc)
12. Manchester Information and Associated Services (MIMAS)
13. Global Financial Data
14. PACIFIC International trade and business reference page
15. Economagic
16. Groningen Growth and Development Centre
17. Resources for economists on the Internet
18. Joseph Rowntree Foundation
19. Social Science Information Gateway (SOSIG)
20. Central European Business Daily
21. OECD Statistics
22. CIA world statistics site
23. UN Millennium Country Profiles
24. World Bank statistics

25. Japanese Economic Foundation
26. Ministry of International Trade and Industry (Japan)
27. Nomura Research Institute (Japan)
28. Nanyang Technological University, Singapore: Statistical Data Locators
29. Richard Tucker's Data Resources site
30. Oanda Currency Converter
31. World Economic Outlook Database (IMF)
32. Economist Country Briefings
33. OFFSTATS links to data sets
34. Treasury Pocket Data Bank (source of UK and world economic data)
35. Economic and Social Data Service (ESDS)
36. The official yearbook of the UK

(C) Sites for students and teachers of economics

The following websites offer useful ideas and resources to those who are studying or teaching economics. It is worth browsing through some just to see what is on offer. Try out the first four sites, for starters. The Internet Economist is a very helpful tutorial for economics students on using the Internet.

1. Economics Network of the UK Higher Education Academy
2. Biz/ed
3. Ecedweb
4. Econ Links: student resources
5. Economics and Business Education Association
6. Tutor2U
7. Economics America
8. The Internet Economist (tutorial on using the Web)
9. Oxford School of Learning
10. Teaching resources for economists
11. Resources for University Teachers of Economics (University of Melbourne)
12. Federal Reserve Bank of San Francisco: Economics Education
13. Federal Reserve Bank of Minneapolis Economic Education
14. WebEc resources
15. BibEc papers
16. Online Opinion (Economics)
17. The Idea Channel
18. History of Economic Thought
19. Resources For Economists on the Internet (RFE)
20. Classroom Expernomics
21. VCE Economics (Economics teaching resources – Australian)
22. Paul Krugman Website
23. JokEc: economics jokes!
24. Veconlab: Charles Holt's classroom experiments

(D) Economic models and simulations

Economic modelling is an important aspect of economic analysis. There are a number of sites that offer access to a model for you to use, e.g. Virtual economy (where you can play being Chancellor of the Exchequer). Using such models can be a useful way of finding out how economic theory works within an environment that claims to reflect reality.

1. Virtual economy
2. Virtual factory
3. Virtual Learning arcade
4. About.com Economics
5. Estima (statistical analysis)
6. SPSS (statistical analysis)
7. National Institute of Economic and Social Research
8. Software available on the Economics Network site
9. RFE: Software
10. Virtual Chancellor
11. Virtual Bank of Biz/ed
12. Virtual Farm

(E) UK government and UK organisations' sites

If you want to see what a government department is up to, then look no further than the list below. Government departments' websites are an excellent source of information and data. They are particularly good at offering information on current legislation and policy initiatives.

1. Gateway site (Directgov)
2. Office of the Deputy Prime Minister
3. Central Office of Information
4. Competition Commission
5. DfES
6. Department for International Development
7. DfT
8. Department of Health
9. DWP
10. DTI
11. Environment Agency
12. UK euro information site
13. Low Pay Unit
14. DEFRA
15. Office of Communications (Ofcom)
16. Office of Gas and Electricity Markets (Ofgem)
17. Official Documents OnLine
18. Office of Fair trading (OFT)
19. Office of Rail Regulation (ORR)
20. The Takeover Panel
21. Sustainable Development Commission
22. OFWAT
23. National Statistics (NS)
24. National Statistics Time Series Data
25. Strategic Rail Authority (SRA)
26. Patent Office
27. Parliament Website
28. Scottish Executive
29. Scottish Environment Protection Agency
30. Treasury
31. Equal Opportunities Commission
32. Trades Union Congress (TUC)
33. Confederation of British Industry
34. Adam Smith Institute
35. Royal Institute of International Affairs
36. Institute of Fiscal Studies
37. Advertising Standards Authority
38. Small Business Service

(F) Sources of monetary and financial data

As the title suggests, here are listed useful websites for finding information on financial matters. You will see that the list comprises mainly central banks, both within Europe and further afield.

1. Bank of England
2. Bank of England Monetary and Financial Statistics
3. Banque de France
4. Bundesbank (German central bank)
5. Central Bank of Ireland
6. European Central Bank

7. Eurostat
8. US Federal Reserve Bank
9. Netherlands Central Bank
10. Bank of Japan
11. Reserve Bank of Australia
12. Bank Negara Malaysia (English)
13. Monetary Authority of Singapore
14. National Bank of Canada
15. National Bank of Denmark (English)
16. Reserve Bank of India
17. Links to central banks from the Bank for International Settlements
18. The London Stock Exchange

(G) European Union and related sources

For information on European issues, the following is a wide range of useful sites. The sites maintained by the European Union are an excellent source of information and are provided free of charge.

1. Economic and Financial Affairs: (EC DG)
2. European Central Bank
3. EU official Web site
4. Euromonitor
5. Eurostat
6. Site for information on the euro and EMU
7. Enterprise: (EC DG)
8. Competition: (EC DG)
9. Agriculture: (EC DG)
10. Energy and Transport: (EC DG)
11. Environment: (EC DG)
12. Regional Policy: (EC DG)
13. Taxation and Customs Union: (EC DG)
14. Education and training: (EC DG)
15. European Patent Office
16. European Commission
17. European Parliament
18. European Council

(H) International organisations

This section casts its net beyond Europe and lists the Web addresses of the main international organisations in the global economy. You will notice that some sites are run by pressure groups, such as Jubilee Research, while others represent organisations set up to manage international affairs, such as the International Monetary Fund and the United Nations.

1. Food and Agricultural Organisation
2. International Air Transport Association (IATA)
3. International Labour Organisation (ILO)
4. International Monetary Fund (IMF)
5. Organisation for Economic Co-operation and Development (OECD)
6. OPEC
7. World Bank
8. World Health Organisation
9. United Nations
10. United Nations Industrial Development Organisation
11. Friends of the Earth
12. Jubilee Research
13. Oxfam
14. Christian Aid (reports on development issues)
15. European Bank for Reconstruction and Development (EBRD)
16. World Trade Organisation (WTO)
17. United Nations Development Programme
18. UNICEF
19. EURODAD – European Network on Debt and Development
20. NAFTA
21. South American Free Trade Areas
22. ASEAN
23. APEC

(I) Economics search and link sites

If you are having difficulty finding what you want from the list of sites above, the following sites offer links to other sites and are a very useful resource when you are looking for something a little bit more specialist. Once again, it is worth having a look at what these sites have to offer in order to judge their usefulness.

1. Gateway for UK official sites
2. Alta Plana
3. Data Archive Search
4. Inomics (search engine for economics information)
5. International Digital Electronic Access Library
6. Estima: Links to economics resources sites
7. Social Science Information Gateway (SOSIG)
8. WebEc
9. One World (link to economic development sites)
10. Economic development sites (list) from One World.net
11. Biz/ed Internet catalogue
12. Web links for economists from the Economics Network
13. Yahoo's links to economic data
14. OFFSTATS links to data sets
15. UniGuide academic guide to the Internet (Economics)
16. Internet Resources for Economists
17. Google Web Directory: Economics
18. Resources for Economists on the Internet

(J) Internet search engines

The following search engines have been found to be useful.

1. Google
2. Altavista
3. Overture
4. Excite
5. Infoseek
6. Search.com
7. MSN
8. UK Plus
9. Yahoo
10. Teoma
11. Kartoo

Threshold Concepts and Key Ideas

THRESHOLD CONCEPTS

KEY IDEAS

28. **Externalities are spillover costs or benefits.** Where these exist, even an otherwise perfect market will fail to achieve social efficiency. 300
29. **The free-rider problem.** People are often unwilling to pay for things if they can make use of things that other people have bought. This problem can lead to people not purchasing things that would be to the benefit of them and other members of society to have. 303
30. **The problem of time lags.** Many economic actions can take a long time to take effect. This can cause problems of instability and an inability of the economy to achieve social efficiency. 306
31. **Economies suffer from inherent instability.** As a result, economic growth and other macroeconomic indicators tend to fluctuate. 368
32. **Societies face trade-offs between economic objectives.** For example, the goal of faster growth may conflict with that of greater equality; the goal of lower unemployment may conflict with that of lower inflation (at least in the short run). This is an example of opportunity cost: the cost of achieving more of one objective may be achieving less of another. The existence of trade-offs means that policy-makers must make choices. 369
33. **The principle of cumulative causation.** An initial event can cause an ultimate effect that is much larger. 441
34. **Goodhart's law.** Controlling a symptom (i.e. an indicator) of a problem will not cure the problem. Instead, the indicator will merely cease to be a good indicator of the problem. 552
35. **The law of comparative advantage.** Provided opportunity costs of various goods differ in two countries, both of them can gain from mutual trade if they specialise in producing (and exporting) those goods that have relatively low opportunity costs compared with the other country. 637
36. **The distinction between nominal and real figures.** Nominal figures are those using current prices, interest rates, etc. Real figures are figures corrected for inflation. A:6

Glossary

Absolute advantage A country has an absolute advantage over another in the production of a good if it can produce it with less resources than the other country can.

Accelerationist theory The theory that unemployment can only be reduced below the natural rate at the cost of accelerating inflation.

Accelerator coefficient The level of induced investment as a proportion of a rise in national income: $\alpha = I_i/\Delta Y$.

Accelerator theory The *level* of investment depends on the *rate of change* of national income, and as result tends to be subject to substantial fluctuations.

Active balances Money held for transactions and precautionary purposes.

Actual growth The percentage annual increase in national output actually produced.

***Ad valorem* tariffs** Tariffs levied as a percentage of the price of the import.

***Ad valorem* tax** A tax on a good levied as a percentage of its value. It can be a single-stage tax or a multi-stage tax (such as VAT).

Adaptive expectations hypothesis The theory that people base their expectations of inflation on past inflation rates.

Adjustable peg A system whereby exchange rates are fixed for a period of time, but may be devalued (or revalued) if a deficit (or surplus) becomes substantial.

Adverse selection The tendency of those who are at greatest risk to take out insurance.

Aggregate demand Total spending on goods and services made in the economy. It consists of four elements, consumer spending (C), investment (I), government spending (G) and the expenditure on exports (X), less any expenditure on imports of goods and services (M): $AD = C + I + G + X - M$.

Aggregate demand for labour curve A curve showing the total demand for labour in the economy at different levels of real wage rates.

Aggregate supply of labour curve A curve showing the total number of people willing and able to work at different average real wage rates.

Aggregate supply The total amount of output in the economy.

Allocative efficiency A situation where the current combination of goods produced and sold gives the maximum satisfaction for each consumer at their current levels of income. Note that a redistribution of income would lead to a different combination of goods that was allocatively efficient.

Alternative theories of the firm Theories of the firm based on the assumption that firms have aims other than profit maximisation.

Ambient-based standards Pollution control that requires firms to meet minimum standards for the environment (e.g. air or water quality).

Appreciation A rise in the free-market exchange rate of the domestic currency with foreign currencies.

Arbitrage Buying an asset in a market where it has a lower price and selling it again in another market where it has a higher price and thereby making a profit.

Arc elasticity The measurement of elasticity between two points on a curve.

Assets Possessions, or claims held on others.

Assisted areas Areas of high unemployment qualifying for government regional selective assistance (RSA) and grants from the European regional development fund (ERDF).

Asymmetric information Where one party in an economic relationship (e.g. an agent) has more information than another (e.g. the principal).

Asymmetric shocks Shocks (such as an oil price increase or a recession in another part of the world) that have different-sized effects on different industries, regions or countries.

Authorised institutions The institutions comprising the monetary (or banking) sector.

Automatic fiscal stabilisers Tax revenues that rise and government expenditure that falls as national income rises. The more they change with income, the bigger the stabilising effect on national income.

Average (total) cost Total cost (fixed plus variable) per unit of output: $AC = TC/Q = AFC + AVC$.

Average cost pricing or **mark-up pricing** Where firms set the price by adding a profit mark-up to average cost.

Average fixed cost Total fixed cost per unit of output: $AFC = TFC/Q$.

Average physical product Total output (TPP) per unit of the variable factor in question: $APP = TPP/Q_v$.

Average rate of income tax Income taxes as a proportion of a person's total (gross) income: T/Y.

Average revenue Total revenue per unit of output. When all output is sold at the same price average revenue will be the same as price: $AR = TR/Q = P$.

Average variable cost Total variable cost per unit of output: $AVC = TVC/Q$.

Balance of payments account A record of the country's transactions with the rest of the world. It shows the country's payments to or deposits in other countries (debits) and its receipts or deposits from other countries (credits). It also shows the balance between these debits and credits under various headings.

Balance of payments on current account The balance on trade in goods and services plus net investment income and current transfers.

Balance on trade in goods Exports of goods minus imports of goods.

Balance on trade in goods and services (or balance of trade) Exports of goods and services minus imports of goods and services.

Balance on trade in services Exports of services minus imports of services.

Balancing item (in the balance of payments) A statistical adjustment to ensure that the two sides of the balance of payments account balance. It is necessary because of errors in compiling the statistics.

Bank (or deposits) multiplier The number of times greater the expansion of bank deposits is than the additional liquidity in banks that causes it: $1/L$ (the inverse of the liquidity ratio).

Bank bills Bills that have been accepted by another institution and hence insured against default.

Barometric firm price leadership Where the price leader is the one whose prices are believed to reflect market conditions in the most satisfactory way.

Barriers to entry Anything that prevents or impedes the entry of firms into an industry and thereby limits the amount of competition faced by existing firms.

Barter economy An economy where people exchange goods and services directly with one another without any payment of money. Workers would be paid with bundles of goods.

Base year (for index numbers) The year whose index number is set at 100.

Basic needs approach The attempt to measure development in terms of a country's ability to meet the basic requirements for life.

Basic rate of tax The main marginal rate of tax, applying to most people's incomes.

Behavioural theories of the firm Theories that attempt to predict the actions of firms by studying the behaviour of various groups of people within the firm and their interactions under conditions of potentially conflicting interests.

Benefit principle of taxation The principle that people ought to pay taxes in proportion to the amount they use government services.

Benefits in kind Goods or services which the state provides directly to the recipient at no charge or at a subsidised price. Alternatively, the state can subsidise the private sector to provide them.

Bilateral monopoly Where a monopsony buyer faces a monopoly seller.

Bill of exchange A certificate promising to repay a stated amount on a certain date, typically three months from the issue of the bill. Bills pay no interest as such, but are sold at a discount and redeemed at face value, thereby earning a rate of discount for the purchaser.

Black markets Where people ignore the government's price and/or quantity controls and sell illegally at whatever price equates illegal demand and supply.

Bretton Woods system An adjustable peg system whereby currencies were pegged to the US dollar. The USA maintained convertibility of the dollar into gold at the rate of $35 to an ounce.

Broad definitions of money Items in narrow definitions plus other items that can be readily converted into cash.

Broad money in UK (M4) Cash in circulation plus retail and wholesale bank and building society deposits.

Budget deficit The excess of central government's spending over its tax receipts.

Budget line A graph showing all the possible combinations of two goods that can be purchased at given prices and for a given budget.

Budget surplus The excess of central government's tax receipts over its spending.

Buffer stocks Stocks of a product used to stabilise its price. In years of abundance, the stocks are built up. In years of low supply, stocks are released on to the market.

Business cycle or **Trade cycle** The periodic fluctuations of national output round its long-term trend.

Capital All inputs into production that have themselves been produced: e.g. factories, machines and tools.

Capital account of the balance of payments The record of the transfers of capital to and from abroad.

Cartel A formal collusive agreement.

Central bank Banker to the banks and the government.

Centrally planned or command economy An economy where all economic decisions are taken by the central authorities.

Certificates of deposit (CDs) Certificates issued by banks for fixed-term interest-bearing deposits. They can be resold by the owner to another party.

Ceteris paribus Latin for 'other things being equal'. This assumption has to be made when making deductions from theories.

Change in demand This is the term used for a shift in the demand curve. It occurs when a determinant of demand *other* than price changes.

Change in supply The term used for a shift in the supply curve. It occurs when a determinant *other* than price changes.

Change in the quantity demanded The term used for a movement along the demand curve to a new point. It occurs when there is a change in price.

Change in the quantity supplied The term used for a movement along the supply curve to a new point. It occurs when there is a change in price.

Claimant unemployment Those in receipt of unemployment-related benefits.

Clearing system A system whereby inter-bank debts are settled.

Closed shop Where a firm agrees to employ only union members.

Coase theorem By sufferers from externalities doing deals with perpetrators (by levying charges or offering bribes), the externality will be 'internalised' and the socially efficient level of output will be achieved.

Collusive oligopoly Where oligopolists agree (formally or informally) to limit competition between themselves. They may set output quotas, fix prices, limit product promotion or development, or agree not to 'poach' each other's markets.

Collusive tendering Where two or more firms secretly agree on the prices they will tender for a contract. These prices will be above those which would be put in under a genuinely competitive tendering process.

Command-and-control (CAC) systems The use of laws or regulations backed up by inspections and penalties (such as fines) for non-compliance.

Commercial bills Bills of exchange issued by firms.

Common market A customs union where the member countries act as a single market with free movement of labour and capital, common taxes and common trade laws.

Comparative advantage A country has a comparative advantage over another in the production of a good if it can produce it at a lower opportunity cost: i.e. if it has to forgo less of other goods in order to produce it.

Competition for corporate control The competition for the control of companies through takeovers.

Complementary goods A pair of goods consumed together. As the price of one goes up, the demand for both goods will fall.

Compounding The process of adding interest each year to an initial capital sum.

Compromise strategy One whose worst outcome is better that the maximax strategy and whose best outcome is better than the maximin strategy.

Conglomerate merger When two firms in different industries merge.

Consumer durable A consumer good that lasts a period of time, during which the consumer can continue gaining utility from it.

Consumer sovereignty A situation where firms respond to changes in consumer demand without being in a position in the long run to charge a price above average cost.

Consumer surplus The excess of what a person would have been prepared to pay for a good (i.e. the utility) over what that person actually pays.

Consumers' share of a tax on a good The proportion of the revenue from a tax on a good that arises from an increase in the price of the good.

Consumption The act of using goods and services to satisfy wants. This will normally involve purchasing the goods and services.

Consumption function The relationship between consumption and national income. It can be expressed algebraically or graphically.

Consumption of domestically produced goods and services (C_d) The direct flow of money payments from households to firms.

Convergence in GDP per head The tendency for less rich developed countries to catch up the richer ones. Convergence does not apply to many of the poorer developing countries, however, where the gap between them and richer countries has tended to widen.

Convergence of economies When countries achieve similar levels of growth, inflation, budget deficits as a percentage of GDP, balance of payments, etc.

Core workers Workers, normally with specific skills, who are employed on a permanent or long-term basis.

Cost–benefit analysis The identification, measurement and weighing up of the costs and benefits of a project in order to decide whether or not it should go ahead.

Cost-plus pricing (full-cost pricing) When firms price their product by adding a certain profit 'mark-up' to average cost.

Cost-push inflation Inflation caused by persistent rises in costs of production (independently of demand).

Countervailing power When the power of a monopolistic/oligopolistic seller is offset by powerful buyers who can prevent the price from being pushed up.

Cournot equilibrium Where the outputs chosen by each firm are consistent with each other: where the two firms' reaction curves cross.

Cournot model of duopoly A model where each firm makes its price and output decisions on the assumption that its rival will produce a particular quantity.

Crawling peg A system whereby the government allows a gradual adjustment of the exchange rate.

Credible threat (or promise) One that is believable to rivals because it is in the threatener's interests to carry it out.

Cross-price elasticity of demand The percentage (or proportionate) change in quantity demanded of one good divided by the percentage (or proportionate) change in the price of another.

Cross-price elasticity of demand (arc formula) $\Delta Q_{Da}/\text{average } Q_{Da} \div \Delta P_b/\text{average } P_b$.

Cross-section data Information showing how a variable (e.g. the consumption of eggs) differs between different groups or different individuals at a given time.

Cross-subsidise To use profits in one market to subsidise prices in another.

Crowding out Where increased public expenditure diverts money or resources away from the private sector.

Cumulative causation (principle of) When an initial change causes an eventual change that is larger.

Currency union A group of countries (or regions) using a common currency.

Current account balance of payments Exports of goods and services minus imports of goods and services plus net incomes and current transfers from abroad. If inflows of money (from the sale of exports, etc.) exceed outflows of money (from the purchase of imports, etc.) there is a 'current account surplus' (a positive figure). If outflows exceed inflows there is a 'current account deficit' (a negative figure).

Customs union A free trade area with common external tariffs and quotas.

Deadweight loss of an indirect tax The loss of consumers' plus producers' surplus from the imposition of an indirect tax.

Deadweight welfare loss The loss of consumers' plus producers' surplus in imperfect markets (when compared with perfect competition).

Debit card A card that has the same use as a cheque. Its use directly debits the person's current account.

Debt servicing Paying the interest and capital repayments on debt.

Deciles Divisions of the population into ten equal-sized groups (an example of a quantile).

Decision tree (or game tree) A diagram showing the sequence of possible decisions by competitor firms and the outcome of each combination of decisions.

Debentures (company bonds) Fixed-interest loans to firms. These assets can be traded on the stock market and their market price is determined by demand and supply.

Deduction Using a theory to draw conclusions about specific circumstances.

Deflationary gap The shortfall of national expenditure below national income (and injections below withdrawals) at the full-employment level of national income.

Deflationary policy Fiscal or monetary policy designed to reduce the rate of growth of aggregate demand.

Demand curve A graph showing the relationship between the price of a good and the quantity of the good demanded over a given time period. Price is measured on the vertical axis; quantity demanded is measured on the horizontal axis. A demand curve can be for an individual consumer or group of consumers, or more usually for the whole market.

Demand function An equation which shows the mathematical relationship between the quantity demanded of a good and the values of the various determinants of demand.

Demand management policies Demand-side policies (fiscal and/or monetary) designed to smooth out the fluctuations in the business cycle.

Demand schedule (market) A table showing the different total quantities of a good that consumers are willing and able to buy at various prices over a given period of time.

Demand schedule for an individual A table showing the different quantities of a good that a person is willing and able to buy at various prices over a given period of time.

Demand-deficient or **cyclical unemployment** Disequilibrium unemployment caused by a fall in aggregate demand with no corresponding fall in the real wage rate.

Demand-pull inflation Inflation caused by persistent rises in aggregate demand.

Demand-side policies Policies designed to affect aggregate demand: fiscal policy and monetary policy.

Demand-side policy Government policy designed to alter the level of aggregate demand, and thereby the level of output, employment and prices.

Dependency Where the development of a developing country is hampered by its relationships with the industrialised world.

Depreciation (of a currency) A fall in the free-market exchange rate of the domestic currency with foreign currencies.

Depreciation (of capital) The decline in value of capital equipment due to age, or wear and tear.

Deregulation Where the government removes official barriers to competition (e.g. licences and minimum quality standards).

Derived demand The demand for a factor of production depends on the demand for the good which uses it.

Destabilising speculation Where the actions of speculators tend to make price movements larger.

Devaluation Where the government re-pegs the exchange rate at a lower level.

Differentiation A mathematical technique to find the rate of change of one variable with respect to another.

Diminishing marginal rate of substitution The more a person consumes of good X and the less of good Y, the less additional Y will that person be prepared to give up in order to obtain an extra unit of X: i.e. $\Delta Y/\Delta X$ diminishes.

Diminishing marginal returns When one or more factors are held fixed, there will come a point beyond which the extra output from additional units of the variable factor will diminish.

Diminishing marginal utility As more units of a good are consumed, additional units will provide less additional satisfaction than previous units.

Diminishing marginal utility of income Where each additional pound earned yields less additional utility.

Direct monetary transmission mechanism A change in money supply having a direct effect on aggregate demand.

Direct taxes Taxes on income and wealth. Paid directly to the tax authorities on that income or wealth.

Dirty floating (managed flexibility) A system of flexible exchange rates but where the government intervenes to prevent excessive fluctuations or even to achieve an unofficial target exchange rate.

Discounting The process of reducing the value of future flows to give them a present valuation.

Discretionary fiscal policy Deliberate changes in tax rates or the level of government expenditure in order to influence the level of aggregate demand.

Diseconomies of scale Where costs per unit of output increase as the scale of production increases.

Disequilibrium unemployment Unemployment resulting from real wage rates in the economy being above the equilibrium level.

Disguised unemployment Where the same work could be done by fewer people.

Disintermediation The diversion of business away from financial institutions which are subject to controls.

Disposable income Household income after the deduction of taxes and the addition of benefits.

Distribution of income by class of recipient Measurement of the distribution of income between the classes of person who receive it (e.g. homeowners and non-homeowners or those in the North and those in the South).

Diversification This is where a firm expands into new types of business.

Dominant firm price leadership When firms (the followers) choose the same price as that set by a dominant firm in the industry (the leader).

Dominant strategy game Where the *same* policy is suggested by different strategies.

Dualism The division of an economy into a modern (usually urban) sector and a poor traditional (usually rural) sector.

Dumping When exports are sold at prices below marginal cost – often as a result of government subsidy.

Duopoly An oligopoly where there are just two firms in the market.

Econometrics The science of applying statistical techniques to economic data in order to identify and test economic relationships.

Economic discrimination When workers of identical *ability* are paid different wages or are otherwise discriminated against because of race, age, sex, etc.

Economic efficiency A situation where each good is produced at the minimum cost and where individual people and firms get the maximum benefit from their resources.

Economic model A formal presentation of an economic theory.

Economic rent The excess that a factor is paid over the amount necessary to keep it in its current employment.

Economies of scale When increasing the scale of production leads to a lower cost per unit of output.

Economies of scope When increasing the range of products produced by a firm reduces the cost of producing each one.

ECU (European Currency Unit) The predecessor to the euro: a weighted average of EU currencies. It was used as a reserve currency and for the operation of the exchange rate mechanism (ERM).

Effective rate of protection The percentage increase in an industry's domestic value added resulting from protection given to that industry.

Efficient (capital) market hypothesis The hypothesis that new information about a company's current or future performance will be quickly and accurately reflected in its share price.

Efficiency wage hypothesis The hypothesis that the productivity of workers is affected by the wage rate that they receive.

Efficiency wage rate The profit-maximising wage rate for the firm after taking into account the effects of wage rates on worker motivation, turnover and recruitment.

Elastic demand (with respect to price) Where quantity demanded changes by a larger percentage than price. Ignoring the negative sign, it will have a value greater than 1.

Elasticity A measure of the responsiveness of a variable (e.g. quantity demanded or quantity supplied) to a change in one of its determinants (e.g. price or income).

EMS (The European Monetary System, mark 1) A system whereby EC countries co-operated to achieve greater exchange rate stability. It involved use of the exchange rate mechanism (the ERM).

Endogenous growth theory A theory that the rate of economic growth depends on the rate of technological progress and diffusion, both of which depend on institutions, incentives and the role of government.

Endogenous money supply Money supply that is determined (at least in part) by the demand for money.

Endogenous variable A variable whose value is determined by the model of which it is part.

Engel curve A line showing how much of a good people will demand at different levels of income.

Entrepreneurship The initiating and organising of the production of new goods, or the introduction of new techniques, and the risk taking associated with it.

Envelope curve A long-run average cost curve drawn as the tangency points of a series of short-run average cost curves.

Environmental charges Charges for using natural resources (e.g. water or national parks), or for using the environment as a dump for waste (e.g. factory emissions or sewage).

Equation of exchange $MV = PY$. The total level of spending on GDP (MV) equals the total value of goods and services produced (PY) that go to make up GDP.

Equilibrium A position of balance. A position from which there is no inherent tendency to move away.

Equilibrium price The price where the quantity demanded equals the quantity supplied: the price where there is no shortage or surplus.

Equilibrium unemployment ('natural') unemployment The difference between those who would like employment at the current wage rate and those willing and able to take a job.

Equi-marginal principle Consumers will maximise total utility from their incomes by consuming that combination of goods where $MU_a/P_a = MU_b/P_b = MU_c/P_c \ldots = MU_n/P_n$.

Equities Company shares. Holders of equities are owners of the company and share in its profits by receiving dividends.

Equity A distribution of income that is considered to be fair or just. Note that an equitable distribution is not the same as an equal distribution and that different people have different views on what is equitable.

ERM (the exchange rate mechanism) A system of semi-fixed exchange rates used by most of the EU countries prior to adoption of the euro. Members' currencies were allowed to fluctuate against each other only within agreed bands. Collectively they floated against all other currencies.

Excess burden (of a tax on a good) The amount by which the loss in consumer plus producer surplus exceeds the government surplus.

Excess capacity (under monopolistic competition) In the long run, firms under monopolistic competition will produce at an output below their minimum-cost point.

Exchange equalisation account The gold and foreign exchange reserves account in the Bank of England.

Exchange rate The rate at which one national currency exchanges for another. The rate is expressed as the amount of one currency that is necessary to purchase *one unit* of another currency (e.g. \$1.60 = £1).

Exchange rate band Where a currency is allowed to float between an upper and lower exchange rate, but is not allowed to move outside this band.

Exchange rate index A weighted average exchange rate expressed as an index where the value of the index is 100 in a given base year. The weights of the different currencies in the index add up to 1.

Exchange rate overshooting Where a fall (or rise) in the long-run equilibrium exchange rate causes the actual exchange rate to fall (or rise) by a greater amount before eventually moving back to the new long-run equilibrium level.

Exchange rate: real A country's exchange rate adjusted for changes in the domestic currency prices of its exports relative to the foreign currency prices of its imports. If a country's prices rise (fall) relative to those of its trading partners, its real exchange rate will rise (fall) relative to the nominal exchange rate.

Exchange rate regime The system under which the government allows the exchange rate to be determined.

Exogenous money supply Money supply that does not depend on the demand for money but is set by the authorities.

Exogenous variable A variable whose value is determined independently of the model of which it is part.

Expansion path The line on an isoquant map that traces the minimum-cost combinations of two factors as output increases. It is drawn on the assumption that both factors can be varied. It is thus a long-run path.

Expectations-augmented Phillips curve A (short-run) Phillips curve whose position depends on the expected rate of inflation.

Expenditure changing (increasing) from depreciation: the income effect Where depreciation, via the substitution effect, will alter the demand for imports and exports, and this will, via the multiplier, affect the level of national income and hence the demand for imports.

Expenditure changing (reducing) from deflation: the income effect Where deflationary policies lead to a reduction in national income and hence a reduction in the demand for imports.

Expenditure switching from deflation: the substitution effect Where deflationary policies lead to a reduction in inflation and thus cause a switch in expenditure away from imports and also towards exports.

Expenditure switching from depreciation: the substitution effect Where a lower exchange rate reduces the price of exports and increases the price of imports. This will increase the sale of exports and reduce the sale of imports.

Explicit costs The payments to outside suppliers of inputs.

External balance (in the economy) Narrow definition: where the current account of the balance of payments is in balance (and thus also the capital plus financial accounts). Loose definition: where there is a total currency flow balance at a given exchange rate.

External benefits Benefits from production (or consumption) experienced by people *other* than the producer (or consumer).

External costs Costs of production (or consumption) borne by people *other* than the producer (or consumer).

External diseconomies of scale Where a firm's costs per unit of output increase as the size of the whole *industry* increases.

External economies of scale Where a firm's costs per unit of output decrease as the size of the whole *industry* grows.

External policy objectives Objectives relating to the economy's international economic relationships.

Externalities Costs or benefits of production or consumption experienced by society but not by the producers or consumers themselves. Sometimes referred to as 'spillover' or 'third-party' costs or benefits.

Factor price equalisation The tendency for international trade to reduce factor price inequalities both between and within countries.

Factors of production (or resources) The inputs into the production of goods and services: labour, land and raw materials, and capital.

Fallacy of composition What applies to the individual does not necessarily apply to the whole.

Financial account of the balance of payments The record of the flows of money into and out of the country for the purposes of investment or as deposits in banks and other financial institutions.

Financial crowding out When an increase in government borrowing diverts money away from the private sector.

Financial deregulation The removal of or reduction in legal rules and regulations governing the activities of financial institutions.

Financial flexibility Where employers can vary their wage costs by changing the composition of their workforce or the terms on which workers are employed.

Financial intermediaries The general name for financial institutions (banks, building societies, etc.) which act as a means of channelling funds from depositors to borrowers.

Fine tuning The use of demand management policy (fiscal or monetary) to smooth out cyclical fluctuations in the economy.

First-best solution The solution of correcting a specific market distortion by ensuring that the whole economy operates under conditions of social efficiency (Pareto optimality).

First-degree price discrimination Where a firm charges each consumer for each unit the maximum price which that consumer is willing to pay for that unit.

First-mover advantage When a firm gains from being the first one to take action.

Fiscal drag The tendency of automatic fiscal stabilisers to reduce the recovery of an economy from recession.

Fiscal policy Policy to affect aggregate demand by altering the balance between government expenditure and taxation.

Fiscal stance How deflationary or reflationary the Budget is.

Fixed costs Total costs that do not vary with the amount of output produced.

Fixed exchange rate (totally) Where the government takes whatever measures are necessary to maintain the exchange rate at some stated level.

Fixed factor An input that cannot be increased in supply within a given time period.

Flat organisation Where the senior management communicate directly with those lower in the organisational structure, bypassing middle management.

Flexible firm A firm that has the flexibility to respond to changing market conditions by changing the composition of its workforce.

Floating exchange rate When the government does not intervene in the foreign exchange markets, but simply allows the exchange rate to be freely determined by demand and supply.

Flow An amount of something occurring over a *period of time*: e.g. production per week, income per year, demand per week. (Contrasts with *stock*.)

Flow-of-funds equation The various items making up an increase (or decrease) in money supply.

Forward exchange market Where contracts are made today for the price at which currency will be exchanged at some specified future date.

Franchising Where a firm is given the licence to operate a given part of an industry for a specified length of time.

Free trade area A group of countries with no trade barriers between themselves.

Freely floating exchange rate Where the exchange rate is determined entirely by the forces of demand and supply in the foreign exchange market with no government intervention whatsoever.

Free-market economy An economy where all economic decisions are taken by individual households and firms and with no government intervention.

Free-rider problem When it is not possible to exclude other people from consuming a good that someone has bought.

Frictional (search) unemployment Unemployment that occurs as a result of imperfect information in the labour market. It often takes time for workers to find jobs (even though there are vacancies) and in the meantime they are unemployed.

Full-employment level of national income The level of national income at which there is no deficiency of demand.

Functional distribution of income Measurement of the distribution of income according to the source of income (e.g. from employment, from profit, from rent, etc.).

Functional flexibility Where employers can switch workers from job to job as requirements change.

Functional relationships The mathematical relationship showing how one variable is affected by one or more others.

Funding Where the authorities alter the balance of bills and bonds for any given level of government borrowing.

Future price A price agreed today at which an item (e.g. commodities) will be exchanged at some set date in the future.

Futures or forward market A market in which contracts are made to buy or sell at some future date at a price agreed today.

Gaia philosophy The respect for the rights of the environment to remain unharmed by human activity. Humans should live in harmony with the planet and other species. We have a duty to be stewards of the natural environment, so that it can continue to be a self-maintaining and self-regulating system.

Game theory (or the theory of games) The study of alternative strategies oligopolists may choose to adopt, depending on their assumptions about their rivals' behaviour.

GDP (gross domestic product at market prices) The value of output (or income or expenditure) in terms of the prices actually paid. GDP = GVA + taxes on products – subsidies on products.

General equilibrium A situation where all the millions of markets throughout the economy are in a simultaneous state of equilibrium.

General equilibrium diagrams (in trade theory) Indifference curve/production possibility curve diagrams that show a country's production and consumption of both imports and exports.

General government debt The combined accumulated debt of central and local government.

General government deficit (or surplus) The combined deficit (or surplus) of central and local government.

Geographical immobility The lack of ability or willingness of people to move to jobs in other parts of the country.

Giffen good An inferior good whose demand increases as its price increases as a result of a positive income effect larger than the normal negative substitution effect.

Gini coefficient The area between the Lorenz curve and the 45° line divided by the total area under the 45° line.

GNY (gross national income) GDP plus net income from abroad.

Gold standard The system whereby countries' exchange rates were fixed in terms of a certain amount of gold and whereby balance of payments deficits were paid in gold.

Golden-rule saving rate The rate of saving that maximises the level of long-run consumption.

Goodhart's Law Controlling a symptom of a problem or only one part of the problem will not *cure* the problem: it will simply mean that the part that is being controlled now becomes a poor indicator of the problem.

Government bonds or 'gilt-edged securities' A government security paying a fixed sum of money each year. It is redeemed by the government on its maturity date at its face value.

Government surplus (from a tax on a good) The total tax revenue earned by the government from sales of a good.

Grandfathering Where each firm's emission permit is based on its *current* levels of emission (e.g. permitted levels for all firms could be 80 per cent of their current levels).

Green tax A tax on output designed to charge for the adverse effects of production on the environment. The socially efficient level of a green tax is equal to the marginal environmental cost of production.

Gross domestic product (GDP) The value of output produced within the country over a 12-month period.

Gross national income (GNY) GDP plus net income from abroad.

Gross value added at basic prices (GVA) The sum of all the values added by all industries in the economy over a year. The figures exclude taxes on products (such as VAT) and include subsidies on products.

Growth maximisation An alternative theory that assumes that managers seek to maximise the growth in sales revenue (or the capital value of the firm) over time.

Heckscher–Ohlin version of comparative advantage A country has a comparative advantage in those goods that are intensive in the country's relatively abundant factor.

H-form organisation (holding company) Where the parent company holds interests in a number of subsidiary companies.

Historic costs The original amount the firm paid for factors it now owns.

Hit-and-run competition When a firm enters an industry to take advantage of temporarily high profits and then leaves again as soon as the high profits have been exhausted.

Horizontal equity The equal treatment of people in the same situation.

Horizontal merger When two firms in the same industry at the same stage in the production process merge.

Households' disposable income The income available for households to spend: i.e. personal incomes after deducting taxes on incomes and adding benefits.

Human capital The qualifications, skills and expertise that contribute to a worker's productivity.

Human Development Index (HDI) A composite index made up of three elements: an index for life expectancy, an index for school enrolment and adult literacy, and an index for GDP per capita (in PPP$).

Hysteresis The persistence of an effect even when the initial cause has ceased to operate. In economics, it refers to the persistence of unemployment even when the demand deficiency that caused it no longer exists.

Identification problem The problem of identifying the relationship between two variables (e.g. price and quantity demanded) from the evidence when it is not known whether or how the variables have been affected by *other* determinants. For example, it is difficult to identify the shape of a demand curve simply by observing price and quantity when it is not known whether changes in other determinants have *shifted* the demand curve.

Idle balances Money held for speculative purposes: money held in anticipation of a fall in asset prices.

Imperfect competition The collective name for monopolistic competition and oligopoly.

Implicit costs Costs which do not involve a direct payment of money to a third party, but which nevertheless involve a sacrifice of some alternative.

Import-substituting industrialisation (ISI) A strategy of restricting imports of manufactured goods and using the foreign exchange saved to build up domestic substitute industries.

Incidence of tax The distribution of the burden of tax between sellers and buyers.

Income effect (of a price change) The effect of a change in price on quantity demanded arising from the consumer becoming better or worse off as a result of the price change.

Income effect of a rise in wage rates Workers get a higher income for a given number of hours worked and may thus feel they need to work *fewer* hours as wage rates rise.

Income effect of a tax rise Tax increases reduce people's incomes and thus encourage people to work more.

Income elasticity of demand The percentage (or proportionate) change in quantity demanded divided by the percentage (or proportionate) change in income.

Income elasticity of demand (arc formula) ΔQ_D/average $Q_D \div \Delta Y$/average Y.

Income–consumption curve A line showing how a person's optimum level of consumption of two goods changes as income changes (assuming the price of the goods remains constant).

Increasing opportunity costs of production When additional production of one good involves ever increasing sacrifices of another.

Independence (of firms in a market) Where the decisions of one firm in a market will not have any significant effect on the demand curves of its rivals.

Independent risks Where two risky events are unconnected. The occurrence of one will not affect the likelihood of the occurrence of the other.

Index number The value of a variable expressed as 100 plus or minus its percentage deviation from a base year.

Indifference curve A line showing all those combinations of two goods between which a consumer is indifferent: i.e. those combinations that give the same level of utility.

Indifference map A graph showing a whole set of indifference curves. The further away a particular curve is from the origin, the higher the level of satisfaction it represents.

Indifference set A table showing the same information as an indifference curve.

Indirect monetary transmission mechanism A change in money supply affecting aggregate demand indirectly via some other variable.

Indirect taxes Taxes on expenditure (e.g. VAT). They are paid to the tax authorities, not by the consumer, but indirectly by the suppliers of the goods or services.

Indivisibilities The impossibility of dividing a factor into smaller units.

Induced investment Investment firms make to enable them to meet extra consumer demand.

Induction Constructing general theories on the basis of specific observations.

Industrial policies Policies to encourage industrial investment and greater industrial efficiency.

Inelastic demand (with respect to price) Where quantity demanded changes by a smaller percentage than price. Ignoring the negative sign, it will have a value less than 1.

Infant industry An industry that has a potential comparative advantage, but which is as yet too underdeveloped to be able to realise this potential.

Inferior goods Goods whose demand *decreases* as consumer incomes increase. Such goods have a negative income elasticity of demand.

Inflationary gap The excess of national expenditure over income (and injections over withdrawals) at the full-employment level of national income.

Informal sector The parts of the economy that involve production and/or exchange, but where there are no money payments.

Infrastructure (industry's) The network of supply agents, communications, skills, training facilities, distribution channels, specialised financial services, etc. that supports a particular industry.

Injections (J) Expenditure on the production of domestic firms coming from outside the inner flow of the circular flow of income. Injections equal investment (I) plus government expenditure (G) plus expenditure on exports (X).

Input–output analysis This involves dividing the economy into sectors where each sector is a user of inputs from and a supplier of outputs to other sectors. The technique examines how these inputs and outputs can be matched to the total resources available in the economy.

Insiders Those in employment who can use their privileged position (either as members of unions or because of specific skills) to secure pay rises despite an excess supply of labour (unemployment).

Interdependence (under oligopoly) One of the two key features of oligopoly. Each firm will be affected by its rivals' decisions. Likewise its decisions will affect its rivals. Firms recognise this interdependence. This recognition will affect their decisions.

Intermediate exchange rate regimes Where the government intervenes to influence movements in the exchange rate.

Internal balance (of an economy) Where the equilibrium level of national income is at the desired level.

Internal policy objectives (national) Objectives relating solely to the domestic economy.

Internal rate of return The rate of return of an investment: the discount rate that makes the net present value of an investment equal to zero.

International harmonisation of economic policies Where countries attempt to co-ordinate their macroeconomic policies so as to achieve common goals.

International liquidity The supply of currencies in the world acceptable for financing international trade and investment.

International trade multiplier The effect on national income in Country B of a change in exports (or imports) of Country A.

Intervention price (in the CAP) The price at which the EU is prepared to buy a foodstuff if the market price were to be below it.

Interventionist supply-side policies Policies to increase aggregate supply by government intervention to counteract the deficiencies of the market.

Investment The production of items that are not for immediate consumption.

***ISLM* model** A model showing simultaneous equilibrium in the goods market ($I = S$) and the money market ($L = M$).

Isocost A line showing all the combinations of two factors that cost the same to employ.

Isoquant A line showing all the alternative combinations of two factors that can produce a given level of output.

J-curve effect Where a devaluation causes the balance of trade first to deteriorate and then to improve. The graph of the balance of trade over time thus looks like a letter J.

Joint float Where a group of currencies pegged to each other jointly float against other currencies.

Joint supply Where the production of more of one good leads to the production of more of another.

Just-in-time methods Where a firm purchases supplies and produces both components and finished products as they are required. This minimises stock holding and its associated costs.

Kinked demand theory The theory that oligopolists face a demand curve that is kinked at the current price, demand being significantly more elastic above the current price than below. The effect of this is to create a situation of price stability.

Labour All forms of human input, both physical and mental, into current production.

Labour force The number employed plus the number unemployed.

Land (and raw materials) Inputs into production that are provided by nature: e.g. unimproved land and mineral deposits in the ground.

Law of comparative advantage Trade can benefit all countries if they specialise in the goods in which they have a comparative advantage.

Law of demand The quantity of a good demanded per period of time will fall as price rises and will rise as price falls, other things being equal (*ceteris paribus*).

Law of diminishing (marginal) returns When one or more factors are held fixed, there will come a point beyond which the extra output from additional units of the variable factor will diminish.

Law of large numbers The larger the number of events of a particular type, the more predictable will be their average outcome.

Lender of last resort The role of the Bank of England as the guarantor of sufficient liquidity in the monetary system.

Liabilities All legal claims for payment that outsiders have on an institution.

Libertarian school A school of thought that advocates maximum liberty for economic agents to pursue their own interests and to own property.

Limit pricing Where a monopolist (or oligopolist) charges a price below the short-run profit maximising level in order to deter new entrants.

Liquidity The ease with which an asset can be converted into cash without loss.

Liquidity preference The demand for holding assets in the form of money.

Liquidity ratio The proportion of a bank's total assets held in liquid form.

Liquidity trap The absorption of any additional money supply into idle balances at very low rates of interest, leaving aggregate demand unchanged.

Lock-outs Union members are temporarily laid off until they are prepared to agree to the firm's conditions.

Long run The period of time long enough for *all* factors to be varied.

Long run under perfect competition The period of time that is long enough for new firms to enter the industry.

Long-run average cost curve A curve that shows how average cost varies with output on the assumption that *all* factors are variable. (It is assumed that the least-cost method of production will be chosen for each output.)

Long-run marginal cost The extra cost of producing one more unit of output assuming that all factors are variable. (It is assumed that the least-cost method of production will be chosen for this extra output.)

Long-run profit maximisation An alternative theory of the firm which assumes that managers aim to *shift* cost and revenue curves so as to maximise profits over some longer time period.

Long-run shut-down point This is where the *AR* curve is tangential to the *LRAC* curve. The firm can just make normal profits. Any fall in revenue below this level will cause a profit-maximising firm to shut down once all costs have become variable.

Lorenz curve A curve showing the proportion of national income earned by any given percentage of the population (measured from the poorest upwards).

Macroeconomics The branch of economics that studies economic aggregates (grand totals): e.g. the overall level of prices, output and employment in the economy.

Managed flexibility (dirty floating) A system of flexible exchange rates but where the government intervenes to prevent excessive fluctuations or even to achieve an unofficial target exchange rate.

Marginal benefit The additional benefit of doing a little bit more (or 1 unit more if a unit can be measured) of an activity.

Marginal capital/output ratio The amount of extra capital (in money terms) required to produce a £1 increase in national output. Since $I_i = \Delta K$, the marginal capital/output ratio $\Delta K/\Delta Y$ equals the accelerator coefficient (α).

Marginal consumer surplus The excess of utility from the consumption of one more unit of a good (*MU*) over the price paid: $MCS = MU - P$.

Marginal cost (of an activity) The additional cost of doing a little bit more (or 1 unit more if a unit can be measured) of an activity.

Marginal cost (of production) The cost of producing one more unit of output: $MC = \Delta TC/\Delta Q$.

Marginal disutility of work The extra sacrifice/hardship to a worker of working an extra unit of time in any given time period (e.g. an extra hour per day).

Marginal efficiency of capital or **internal rate of return** The rate of return of an investment: the discount rate that makes the net present value of an investment equal to zero.

Marginal physical product The extra output gained by the employment of one more unit of the variable factor: $MPP = \Delta TPP/\Delta Q_v$.

Marginal productivity theory The theory that the demand for a factor depends on its marginal revenue product.

Marginal propensity to consume The proportion of a rise in national income that goes on consumption: $mpc = \Delta C/\Delta Y$.

Marginal propensity to import The proportion of an increase in national income that is spent on imports: $mpm = \Delta M/\Delta Y$.

Marginal propensity to save The proportion of an increase in national income saved: $mps = \Delta S/\Delta Y$.

Marginal propensity to withdraw The proportion of an increase in national income that is withdrawn from the circular flow: $mpw = \Delta W/\Delta Y$, where $mpw = mps + mpt + mpm$.

Marginal rate of factor substitution The rate at which one factor can be substituted by another while holding the level of output constant: $MRS = \Delta F_1/\Delta F_2 = MPP_{F2}/MPP_{F1}$.

Marginal rate of income tax The income tax rate. The rate paid on each *additional* pound earned: $\Delta T/\Delta Y$.

Marginal rate of substitution (between two goods in consumption) The amount of one good (Y) that a consumer is prepared to give up in order to obtain one extra unit of another good (X): i.e. $\Delta Y/\Delta X$.

Marginal revenue The extra revenue gained by selling one more unit per time period: $MR = \Delta TR/\Delta Q$.

Marginal revenue product (of a factor) The extra revenue a firm earns from employing one more unit of a variable factor: $MRP_{factor} = MPP_{factor} \times MR_{good}$.

Marginal tax propensity The proportion of an increase in national income paid in tax: $mpt = \Delta T/\Delta Y$.

Marginal utility The extra satisfaction gained from consuming one extra unit of a good within a given time period.

Market The interaction between buyers and sellers.

Market clearing A market clears when supply matches demand, leaving no shortage or surplus.

Market for loanable funds The market for loans from and deposits into the banking system.

Market loans Short-term loans (e.g. money at call and short notice).

Market-orientated supply-side policies Policies to increase aggregate supply by freeing-up the market.

Mark-up A profit margin added to average cost to arrive at price.

Marshall–Lerner condition Depreciation will improve the balance of payments only if the sum of the price elasticities of demand for imports and exports is greater than 1.

Maturity transformation The transformation of deposits into loans of a longer maturity.

Maximax The strategy of choosing the policy which has the best possible outcome.

Maximin The strategy of choosing the policy whose worst possible outcome is the least bad.

Maximum price A price ceiling set by the government or some other agency. The price is not allowed to rise above this level (although it is allowed to fall below it).

Mean (or arithmetic mean) The sum of the values of each of the members of the sample divided by the total number in the sample.

Means-tested benefits Benefits whose amount depends on the recipient's income or assets.

Median The value of the middle member of the sample.

Medium of exchange Something that is acceptable in exchange for goods and services.

Medium-term financial strategy (MTFS) The policy of the Conservative government in Britain during the 1980s of setting targets for the PSBR and the growth of money supply for the following four years.

Menu costs of inflation The costs associated with having to adjust price lists or labels.

Merit goods Goods which the government feels that people will underconsume and which therefore ought to be subsidised or provided free.

M-form (multi-divisional form) of corporate organisation Where the firm is split into a number of separate divisions (e.g. different products or countries), with each division then split into a number of departments.

Microeconomics The branch of economics that studies individual units: e.g. households, firms and industries. It studies the interrelationships between these units in determining the pattern of production and distribution of goods and services.

Minimum price A price floor set by the government or some other agency. The price is not allowed to fall below this level (although it is allowed to rise above it).

Minimum reserve ratio A minimum ratio of cash (or other specified liquid assets) to deposits (either total or selected) that the central bank requires banks to hold.

Mixed command economy A planned economy that nevertheless makes some use of markets.

Mixed economy An economy where economic decisions are made partly by the government and partly through the market.

Mixed market economy A market economy where there is some government intervention.

Mobility of labour The willingness and ability of labour to move to another job.

Monetarists Those who attribute inflation solely to rises in money supply.

Monetary base Notes and coin outside the central bank.

Monetary base control Monetary policy that focuses on controlling the monetary base (as opposed to broad liquidity).

Monetary policy Policy to affect aggregate demand by altering the supply or cost of money (rate of interest).

Money illusion When people believe that a money wage or price increase represents a *real* increase: in other words, they ignore or underestimate inflation.

Money market The market for short-term loans and deposits.

Money multiplier The number of times greater the expansion of money supply is than the expansion of the monetary base that caused it: $\Delta Ms/\Delta Mb$.

Monopolistic competition A market structure where, like perfect competition, there are many firms and freedom of entry into the industry, but where each firm produces a differentiated product and thus has some control over its price.

Monopoly A market structure where there is only one firm in the industry.

Monopsony A market with a single buyer or employer.

Moral hazard The temptation to take more risk when you know that other people (e.g. insurers) will cover the risks.

Multiplier (injections multiplier) The number of times a rise in income exceeds the rise in injections that caused it. $k = \Delta Y/\Delta J$.

Multiplier effect An initial increase in aggregate demand of £*x*m leads to an eventual rise in national income that is greater than £*x*m.

Multiplier formula (injections multiplier) The formula for the multiplier is $k = 1/mpw$ or $1/(1 - mpc_d)$.

Mutual recognition The EU principle that one country's rules and regulations must apply throughout the EU. If they conflict with those of another country, individuals and firms should be able to chose which to obey.

Narrow definitions of money Items of money that can be spent directly (cash and money in cheque-book/debit-card accounts).

Nash equilibrium The position resulting from everyone making their optimal decision based on their assumptions about their rivals' decisions. Without collusion, there is no incentive for any firm to move from this position.

National debt The accumulated budget deficits (less surpluses) over the years: the total amount of government borrowing.

National expenditure on domestic product (*E*) Aggregate demand in the Keynesian model: i.e. $C_d + J$.

Nationalised industries State-owned industries that produce goods or services that are sold in the market.

Natural level of output The level of output in monetarist analysis where the vertical long-run aggregate supply curve cuts the horizontal axis.

Natural level of unemployment The level of equilibrium unemployment in monetarist analysis measured as the difference between the (vertical) long-run gross labour supply curve (N) and the (vertical) long-run effective labour supply curve (AS_L).

Natural monopoly A situation where long-run average costs would be lower if an industry were under monopoly than if it were shared between two or more competitors.

Natural rate of unemployment The rate of unemployment at which there is no excess or deficiency of demand for labour.

Natural wastage When a firm wishing to reduce its workforce does so by not replacing those who leave or retire.

Near money Highly liquid assets (other than cash).

Negative income tax A combined system of tax and benefits. As people earn more they gradually lose their benefits until beyond a certain level they begin paying taxes.

Neo-Austrian/libertarian school A school of thought that advocates maximum liberty for economic agents to pursue their own interests and to own property.

Net investment Total investment minus depreciation.

Net national product (NNY) GNY minus depreciation.

Net present value of an investment The discounted benefits of an investment minus the cost of the investment.

Network economies The benefits to consumers of having a network of other people using the same product or service.

New classical school The school of economists which believes that markets clear virtually instantaneously and that expectations are formed 'rationally'.

New Keynesians Economists who seek to explain the downward stickiness of real wages and the resulting persistence of unemployment.

Nominal national income National income measured at current prices.

Nominal values Money values measured at *current* prices.

Non-accelerating-inflation rate of unemployment (NAIRU) The rate of unemployment consistent with a constant rate of inflation. (In monetarist analysis this is the same as the natural rate of unemployment: the rate of unemployment at which the vertical long-run Phillips curve cuts the horizontal axis.)

Non-bank private sector Households and non-bank firms: in other words, everyone in the country other than banks and the government (central and local).

Non-collusive oligopoly Where oligopolists have no agreement between themselves either formal, informal or tacit.

Non-excludability Where it is not possible to provide a good or service to one person without it thereby being available for others to enjoy.

Non-price competition Competition in terms of product promotion (advertising, packaging, etc.) or product development.

Non-rivalry Where the consumption of a good or service by one person will not prevent others from enjoying it.

Normal goods Goods whose demand increases as consumer incomes increase. They have a positive income elasticity of demand. Luxury goods will have a higher income elasticity of demand than more basic goods.

Normal profit The opportunity cost of being in business: the profit that could have been earned in the next best alternative business. It is counted as a cost of production.

Normal rate of return The rate of return (after taking risks into account) that could be earned elsewhere.

Normative statement A value judgement.

Numerical flexibility Where employers can change the size of their workforce as their labour requirements change.

Occupational immobility The lack of ability or willingness of people to move to other jobs irrespective of location.

Oligopoly An market structure where there are few enough firms to enable barriers to be erected against the entry of new firms.

Oligopsony A market with just a few buyers or employers.

Open economy One that trades with and has financial dealings with other countries.

Open-market operations The sale (or purchase) by the authorities of government securities in the open market in order to reduce (or increase) money supply or influence interest rates.

Opportunity cost Cost measured in terms of the best alternative forgone.

Optimal currency area The optimal size of a currency area is the one that maximises the benefits from having a single currency relative to the costs. If the area were increased or decreased in size, the costs would rise relative to the benefits.

Optimum tariff A tariff that reduces the level of imports to the point where the country's marginal social cost equals marginal social benefit.

Organisational slack Where managers allow spare capacity to exist, thereby enabling them to respond more easily to changed circumstances.

Outsiders Those out of work or employed on a casual, part-time or short-term basis, who have little or no power to influence wages or employment.

Overheads Costs arising from the general running of an organisation, and only indirectly related to the level of output.

Pareto improvement Where changes in production or consumption can make at least one person better off without making anyone worse off.

Pareto optimality Where all possible Pareto improvements have been made: where, therefore, it is impossible to make anyone better off without making someone else worse off.

Partial derivative The partial derivative of a function of two or more independent variables is the derivative with respect to just one of those variables, while holding the others constant.

Partial differentiation A mathematical technique used with functions containing two or more independent variables. The technique is used to find the rate of change of the dependent variable with respect to a single independent variable assuming that the other independent variables are held constant.

Participation rate The percentage of the working-age population that is part of the workforce.

Partnership A firm owned by two or more people. They each have unlimited liability for the firm's debts.

Peak-load pricing Price discrimination (second or third degree) where a higher price is charged in peak periods and a lower price in off-peak periods.

Perfect competition A market structure where there are many firms; where there is freedom of entry into the industry; where all firms produce an identical product; and where all firms are price takers.

Perfectly contestable market A market where there is free and costless entry and exit.

Phillips curve A curve showing the relationship between (price) inflation and unemployment. The original Phillips curve plotted *wage* inflation against unemployment for the years 1861–1957.

Picketing When people on strike gather at the entrance to the firm and attempt to persuade workers or delivery vehicles from entering.

Plant economies of scale Economies of scale that arise because of the large size of the factory.

Point elasticity The measurement of elasticity at a point on a curve. The formula for price elasticity of demand using the point elasticity method is: $dQ/dP \times P/Q$, where dQ/dP is the inverse of the slope of the tangent to the demand curve at the point in question.

Poll tax A lump-sum tax per head of the population. Since it a fixed *amount*, it has a marginal rate of zero with respect to both income and wealth.

Polluter pays principle The principle that polluters ought to be charged (e.g. through green taxes) for the external environmental costs that they generate.

Portfolio balance The balance of assets, according to their liquidity, that people choose to hold in their portfolios.

Positive statement A value-free statement which can be tested by an appeal to the facts.

Post-Keynesians Economists who stress the importance of institutional and behavioural factors, and the role of business confidence in explaining the state of the economy. They argue that firms are more likely to respond to changes in demand by changing output rather than prices.

Potential growth The percentage annual increase in the capacity of the economy to produce.

Potential output The output that could be produced in the economy if there were a full employment of resources (including labour).

Poverty trap (for developing countries) When countries are too poor to save and invest enough to achieve real per capita growth.

Poverty trap (for individuals) Where poor people are discouraged from working or getting a better job because any extra income they earn will be largely taken away in taxes and lost benefits.

Predatory pricing Where a firm sets its prices below average cost in order to drive competitors out of business.

Preferential trading arrangements A trade agreement whereby trade between the signatories is freer than trade with the rest of the world.

Present value approach to appraising investment This involves estimating the value *now* of a flow of future benefits (or costs).

Price benchmark A price which is typically used. Firms, when raising prices will usually raise it from one benchmark to another.

Price discrimination Where a firm sells the same product at different prices.

Price elasticity of demand (arc formula) ΔQ/average $Q \div \Delta P$/average P. The average in each case is the average between the two points being measured.

Price elasticity of demand ($P\epsilon_D$) The percentage (or proportionate) change in quantity demanded divided by the percentage (or proportionate) change in price: $\%\Delta Q_D \div \%\Delta P$.

Price elasticity of supply ($P\epsilon_S$) The percentage (or proportionate) change in quantity supplied divided by the percentage (or proportionate) change in price: $\%\Delta Q_S \div \%\Delta P$.

Price elasticity of supply (arc formula) ΔQ_S/average $Q_S \div \Delta P$/average P.

Price mechanism The system in a market economy whereby changes in price in response to changes in demand and supply have the effect of making demand equal to supply.

Price taker A person or firm with no power to be able to influence the market price.

Price-cap regulation Where the regulator puts a ceiling on the amount by which a firm can raise its price.

Price–consumption curve A line showing how a person's optimum level of consumption of two goods changes as the price of one of the two goods changes (assuming that income and the price of the other good remain constant).

Prices and incomes policy When the government seeks to restrain price and wage increases. This may be in the form of a voluntary agreement with firms and/or unions, or there may be statutory limits imposed.

Primary labour market The market for permanent full-time core workers.

Primary market in capital Where shares are sold by the issuer of the shares (i.e. the firm) and where, therefore, finance is channelled directly from the purchasers (i.e. the shareholders) to the firm.

Principal–agent problem Where people (principals), as a result of lack of knowledge, cannot ensure that their best interests are served by their agents.

Principle of cumulative causation An initial event can cause an ultimate effect that is much larger.

Prisoners' dilemma Where two or more firms (or people), by attempting independently to choose the best strategy for whatever the other(s) are likely to do, end up in a worse position than if they had co-operated in the first place.

Private efficiency Where a person's marginal benefit from a given activity equals the marginal cost.

Private limited company A company owned by its shareholders. Shareholders' liability is limited to the value of their shares. Shares can only be bought and sold privately.

Producers' share of a tax on a good The proportion of the revenue from a tax on a good that arises from a reduction in the price to the producer (after the payment of the tax).

Product differentiation When one firm's product is sufficiently different from its rivals' to allow it to raise the price of the product without customers all switching to the rivals' products. A situation where a firm faces a downward-sloping demand curve.

Production The transformation of inputs into outputs by firms in order to earn profit (or meet some other objective).

Production function The mathematical relationship between the output of a good and the inputs used to produce it. It shows how output will be affected by changes in the quantity of one or more of the inputs.

Production possibility curve A curve showing all the possible combinations of two goods that a country can produce within a specified time period with all its resources fully and efficiently employed.

Productive efficiency A situation where firms are producing the maximum output for a given amount of inputs, or producing a given output at the least cost. The least-cost combination of factors for a given output.

Productivity deal When, in return for a wage increase, a union agrees to changes in working practices that will increase output per worker.

Profit (rate of) Total profit ($T\Pi$) as a proportion of the total capital employed (K): $r = T\Pi/K$.

Profit satisficing Where decision makers in a firm aim for a target level of profit rather than the absolute maximum level.

Profit-maximising rule Profit is maximised where marginal revenue equals marginal cost.

Progressive tax A tax whose average rate with respect to income rises as income rises.

Proportional tax A tax whose average rate with respect to income stays the same as income rises.

Prudential control The insistence by the Bank of England that recognised banks maintain adequate liquidity.

Public good A good or service that has the features of non-rivalry and non-excludability and as a result would not be provided by the free market.

Public limited company A company owned by its shareholders. Shareholders' liability is limited to the value of their shares. Shares may be bought and sold publicly – on the Stock Exchange.

Public-sector borrowing requirement (PSBR) or **Public-sector net cash requirement (PSNCR)** The (annual) deficit of the public sector (central government, local government and public corporations), and thus the amount that the public sector must borrow.

Public-sector debt repayment (PSDR) or **Public-sector surplus** The (annual) surplus of the public sector, and thus the amount of debt that can be repaid.

Purchasing-power parity theory The theory that the exchange rate will adjust so as to offset differences in countries' inflation rates, with the result that the same quantity of internationally traded goods can be bought at home as abroad with a given amount of the domestic currency.

Pure fiscal policy Fiscal policy which does not involve any change in money supply.

Quantiles Divisions of the population into equal-sized groups.

Quantity demanded The amount of a good a consumer is willing and able to buy at a given price over a given period of time.

Quantity theory of money The price level (P) is directly related to the quantity of money in the economy (M).

Quasi-rent Temporary economic rent arising from short-run supply inelasticity.

Quintiles Divisions of the population into five equal-sized groups (an example of a quantile).

Quota (set by a cartel) The output that a given member of a cartel is allowed to produce (production quota) or sell (sales quota).

Random walk Where fluctuations in the value of a share away from its 'correct' value are random: i.e. have no systematic pattern. When charted over time, these share price movements would appear like a 'random walk': like the path of someone staggering along drunk!

Rate of discount The rate that is used to reduce future values to present values.

Rate of economic growth The percentage increase in output over a 12-month period.

Rate of inflation The percentage increase in the level of prices over a 12-month period.

Rate of profit Total profit ($T\Pi$) as a proportion of the capital employed (K): $r = T\Pi/K$.

Rational choices Choices that involve weighing up the benefit of any activity against its opportunity cost.

Rational consumer A person who weighs up the costs and benefits to him or her of each additional unit of a good purchased.

Rational consumer behaviour The attempt to maximise total consumer surplus.

Rational economic behaviour Doing more of activities whose marginal benefit exceeds their marginal cost and doing less of those activities whose marginal cost exceeds their marginal benefit.

Rational expectations Expectations based on the *current* situation. These expectations are based on the information people have to hand. Whilst this information may be imperfect and therefore people will make errors, these errors will be random.

Rational producer behaviour When a firm weighs up the costs and benefits of alternative courses of action and then seeks to maximise its net benefit.

Rationalisation The reorganising of production (often after a merger) so as to cut out waste and duplication and generally to reduce costs.

Rationing Where the government restricts the amount of a good that people are allowed to buy.

Reaction function (or curve) This shows how a firm's optimal output varies according to the output chosen by its rival (or rivals).

Real balance effect As the price level rises, so the value of people's money balances will fall. They will therefore *spend* less in order to increase their money balances and go some way to protecting their real value.

Real business cycle theory The new classical theory which explains cyclical fluctuations in terms of shifts in aggregate supply, rather than aggregate demand.

Real exchange rate A country's exchange rate adjusted for changes in the domestic currency prices of its exports relative to the foreign currency prices of its imports. If a country's prices rise (fall) relative to those of its trading partners, its real exchange rate will rise (fall) relative to the nominal exchange rate.

Real income Income measured in terms of how much it can buy. If your *money* income rises by 10 per cent, but prices rise by 8 per cent, you can only buy 2 per cent more goods than before. Your *real* income has risen by 2 per cent.

Real national income National income after allowing for inflation: i.e. national income measured in constant prices: i.e. in terms of the prices ruling in some base year.

Real values Money values corrected for inflation.

Real-wage unemployment Disequilibrium unemployment caused by real wages being driven up above the market-clearing level.

Recession A period where national output falls for six months or more.

Recognised banks Banks licensed by the Bank of England. All financial institutions using the word 'bank' in their title have to be recognised by the Bank of England. This requires them to have paid-up capital of at least £5 million and to meet other requirements about their asset structure and range of services.

Rediscounting bills of exchange Buying bills before they reach maturity.

Reflationary policy Fiscal or monetary policy designed to increase the rate of growth of aggregate demand.

Regional Development Agencies (RDAs) Nine agencies, based in English regions, which initiate and administer regional policy within their area.

Regional multiplier effects When a change in injections into or withdrawals from a particular region causes a multiplied change in income in that region. The regional multiplier (k_r) is given by $1/mpw_r$, where the import component of mpw_r consists of imports into that region either from abroad or from other regions of the economy.

Regional unemployment Structural unemployment occurring in specific regions of the country.

Regression analysis A statistical technique which allows a functional relationship between two or more variables to be estimated.

Regressive tax A tax whose average rate with respect to income falls as income rises.

Regulatory capture Where the regulator is persuaded to operate in the industry's interests rather than those of the consumer.

Relative price The price of one good compared with another (e.g. good X is twice the price of good Y).

Replacement costs What the firm would have to pay to replace factors it currently owns.

Resale (or retail) price maintenance Where the manufacturer of a product (legally) insists that the product should be sold at a specified retail price.

Restrictive practice Where two or more firms agree to adopt common practices to restrict competition.

Retail banks 'High street banks'. Banks operating extensive branch networks and dealing directly with the general public, with published interest rates and charges.

Retail deposits and loans Deposits and loans made through bank/building society branches at published interest rates.

Retail price index (RPI) An index of the prices of goods bought by a typical household.

Revaluation Where the government re-pegs the exchange rate at a higher level.

Reverse repos When gilts or other assets are *purchased* under a sale and repurchase agreement. They become an asset to the purchaser.

Risk When an outcome may or may not occur, but its probability of occurring is known.

Risk averse Where a person is not prepared to take a gamble even if the odds of gaining are favourable.

Risk loving Where a person is willing to take a gamble even if the odds of gaining are unfavourable.

Risk neutral Where a person is willing to take a gamble if the odds are favourable and is unwilling if the odds are unfavourable.

Risk transformation The process whereby banks can spread the risks of lending by having a large number of borrowers.

Sale and repurchase agreement (repos) An agreement between two financial institutions whereby one in effect borrows from another by selling it assets, agreeing to buy them back (repurchase them) at a fixed price and on a fixed date.

Sales revenue maximisation An alternative theory of the firm based on the assumption that managers aim to maximise the firm's short-run total revenue.

Say's law Supply creates its own demand. In other words, the production of goods will generate sufficient demand to ensure that they are sold.

Scarcity The excess of human wants over what can actually be produced to fulfil these wants.

Search theory This examines people's behaviour under conditions of ignorance where it takes time to search for information.

Seasonal unemployment Unemployment associated with industries or regions where the demand for labour is lower at certain times of the year.

Second best (problem of) The difficulty of working out the best way of correcting a specific market distortion if distortions in other parts of the market continue to exist.

Second derivative The rate of change of the first derivative: found by differentiating the first derivative.

Second derivative test If on differentiating an equation a second time the answer is negative (positive), the point is a maximum (minimum).

Secondary action Industrial action taken against a company not directly involved in a dispute (e.g. a supplier of raw materials to a firm whose employees are on strike).

Secondary labour market The market for peripheral workers, usually employed on a temporary or part-time basis, or a less secure 'permanent' basis.

Secondary market in capital Where shareholders sell shares to others. This is thus a market in 'second-hand' shares.

Second-best solution The solution to a specific market distortion that recognises distortions elsewhere and seeks to minimise the overall distortionary effects to the economy of tackling this specific distortion.

Second-degree price discrimination Where a firm charges a consumer so much for the first so many units purchased, a different price for the next so many units purchased, and so on.

Self-fulfilling speculation The actions of speculators tend to cause the very effect that they had anticipated.

Semi-strong efficiency (of share markets) Where share prices adjust quickly, fully and accurately to publicly available information.

Sensitivity analysis Where a range of possible values of uncertain costs and benefits are given to see whether the project's desirability is sensitive to these different values.

Set aside A system in the EU of paying farmers not to use a certain proportion of their land.

Shares (equities) A part ownership of a company. Companies' distributed profits are paid to shareholders in the form of dividends according to the number of shares held.

Short run (in production) The period of time over which at least one factor is fixed.

Short run under perfect competition The period during which there is too little time for new firms to enter the industry.

Short-run shut-down point This is where the *AR* curve is tangential to the *AVC* curve. The firm can only just cover its variable costs. Any fall in revenue below this level will cause a profit-maximising firm to shut down immediately.

Short-termism Where firms and investors take decisions based on the likely short-term performance of a company, rather than on its long-term prospects. Firms may thus sacrifice long-term profits and growth for the sake of a quick return.

Sight deposits Deposits that can be withdrawn on demand without penalty.

Size distribution of income Measurement of the distribution of income according to the levels of income received by individuals (irrespective of source).

Social benefit Private benefit plus externalities in consumption.

Social cost Private cost plus externalities in production.

Social efficiency A situation of Pareto optimality: where all possible Pareto improvements have been made: where, therefore, it is impossible to make anyone better off without making someone else worse off.

Social efficiency (improvement in) A Pareto improvement: where changes in production or consumption can make at least one person better off without making anyone worse off.

Social rate of discount A rate of discount that reflects *society's* preferences for present benefits over future ones.

Social-impact standards Pollution control that focuses on the effects on people (e.g. on health or happiness).

Sole proprietorship A firm owned by one person. That person has unlimited liability.

Special deposits Deposits that the banks can be required to make in the Bank of England. They remain frozen there until the Bank of England chooses to release them.

Special Drawing Rights (SDRs) Additional liquidity created by the IMF. SDRs give countries the right to borrow a certain amount of additional funds from the IMF, with no requirement for extra deposits (quotas).

Specialisation and division of labour Where production is broken down into a number of simpler, more specialised tasks, thus allowing workers to acquire a high degree of efficiency.

Specific tax A tax on a good levied at a fixed amount per unit of the good, irrespective of the price of that unit.

Speculation Where people make buying or selling decisions based on their anticipations of future prices.

Speculators People who buy (or sell) commodities or financial assets with the intention of profiting by selling them (or buying them back) at a later date at a higher (lower) price.

Spot price The current market price.

Spreading risks (for an insurance company) The more policies an insurance company issues and the more independent the risks of claims from these policies are, the more predictable will be the number of claims.

Stabilising speculation Where the actions of speculators tend to reduce the magnitude of price fluctuations.

Stagflation A term used in the 1970s to refer to the combination of stagnation (low growth and high unemployment) and high inflation.

Stakeholders (in a company) People who are affected by a company's activities and/or performance (customers, employees, owners, creditors, people living in the neighbourhood, etc.). They may or may not be in a position to take decisions, or influence decision taking, in the firm.

Standardised unemployment rate The measure of the unemployment rate used by the ILO and OECD. The unemployed are defined as persons of working age who are without work, available to start work within two weeks and either have actively looked for work in the last four weeks or are waiting to take up an appointment.

Steady-state growth path The growth path for a given saving rate (where growth results from technological progress).

Steady-state level of national income The long-run equilibrium level of national income. The level at which all investment is used to maintain the existing capital stock at its current level.

Sterilisation When the government uses open-market operations or other monetary measures to neutralise the effects of balance of payments deficits or surpluses on the money supply.

Stock An amount of something (inputs, goods, money, etc.) existing at a point of time. (Contrasts with *flow*.)

Stock (or inventory) appreciation The increase in monetary value of stocks due to increased prices. Since this does not represent increased output it is not included in GDP.

Stop–go policies Alternate deflationary and reflationary policies to tackle the currently most pressing of the four problems which fluctuate with the business cycle.

Strategic trade theory The theory that protecting/supporting certain industries can enable them to compete more effectively with large monopolistic rivals abroad. The effect of the protection is to increase long-run competition and may enable the protected firms to exploit a comparative advantage that they could not have done otherwise.

Strong efficiency (of share markets) Where share prices adjust quickly, fully and accurately to all available information, both public and that only available to insiders.

Structural unemployment Unemployment that arises from changes in the pattern of demand or supply in the economy. People made redundant in one part of the economy cannot immediately take up jobs in other parts (even though there are vacancies).

Structuralists Economists who focus on specific barriers to development and how to overcome them.

Subsistence production Where people produce things for their own consumption.

Substitute goods A pair of goods which are considered by consumers to be alternatives to each other. As the price of one goes up, the demand for the other rises.

Substitutes in supply These are two goods where an increased production of one means diverting resources away from producing the other.

Substitution effect of a price change The effect of a change in price on quantity demanded arising from the consumer switching to or from alternative (substitute) products.

Substitution effect of a rise in wage rates Workers will tend to substitute income for leisure as leisure now has a higher opportunity cost. This effect leads to *more* hours being worked as wage rates rise.

Substitution effect of a tax rise Tax increases reduce the opportunity cost of leisure and thus encourage people to work less.

Sunk costs Costs that cannot be recouped (e.g. by transferring assets to other uses).

Supernormal profit (also known as **pure profit, economic profit, abnormal profit**, or simply **profit**). The excess of total profit above normal profit.

Supply curve A graph showing the relationship between the price of a good and the quantity of the good supplied over a given period of time.

Supply schedule A table showing the different quantities of a good that producers are willing and able to supply at various prices over a given time period. A supply schedule can be for an individual producer or group of producers, or for all producers (the market supply schedule).

Supply-side economics An approach which focuses directly on aggregate supply and how to shift the aggregate supply curve outwards.

Supply-side policy Government policy that attempts to alter the level of aggregate supply directly (rather than through changes in aggregate demand).

Sustainability (environmental) The ability of the environment to survive its use for economic activity.

Sustainable output The level of national output corresponding to no excess or deficiency of aggregate demand.

Tacit collusion Where oligopolists take care not to engage in price cutting, excessive advertising or other forms of competition. There may be unwritten 'rules' of collusive behaviour such as price leadership.

Takeover bid Where one firm attempts to purchase another by offering to buy the shares of that company from its shareholders.

Takeover constraint The effect that the fear of being taken over has on a firm's willingness to undertake projects that reduce distributed profits.

Target real wage theory The theory that unions bargain for target real wage increases each year irrespective of the level of real growth in the economy.

Tariff escalation The system whereby tariff rates increase the closer a product is to the finished stage of production.

Tariffs (or import levies) Taxes on imported products: i.e. customs duties.

Tax allowance An amount of income that can be earned tax-free. Tax allowances vary according to a person's circumstances.

Tax avoidance The rearrangement of one's affairs so as to reduce one's tax liability.

Tax evasion The illegal non-payment of taxes (e.g. by not declaring income earned).

Technological unemployment Structural unemployment that occurs as a result of the introduction of labour-saving technology.

Technology-based standards Pollution control that requires firms' emissions to reflect the levels that could be achieved from using the best available pollution control technology.

Terms of trade The price index of exports divided by the price index of imports and then expressed as a percentage. This means that the terms of trade will be 100 in the base year.

Third-degree price discrimination When a firm divides consumers into different groups and charges a different price to consumers in different groups, but the same price to all the consumers within a group.

Tie-in sales Where a firm is only prepared to sell a first product on the condition that its customers by a second product from it.

Time deposits Deposits that require notice of with-drawal or where a penalty is charged for withdrawals on demand.

Time-series data Information depicting how a variable (e.g. the price of eggs) changes over time.

Total consumer expenditure on a product (*TE*) (per period of time) The price of the product multiplied by the quantity purchased: $TE = P \times Q$.

Total consumer surplus The excess of a person's total utility from the consumption of a good (TU) over the amount that person spends on it (TE): $TCS = TU - TE$.

Total cost The sum of total fixed costs and total variable costs: $TC = TFC + TVC$.

Total currency flow on the balance of payments The current plus capital plus financial account balance but excluding the reserves.

Total physical product The total output of a product per period of time that is obtained from a given amount of inputs.

Total (private) surplus Total consumer surplus ($TU - TE$) plus total producer surplus ($TR - TVC$).

Total producer surplus (*TPS*) Total revenue minus total variable cost ($TR - TVC$): in other words, total profit plus total fixed cost ($T\Pi + TFC$).

Total revenue A firm's total earnings from a specified level of sales within a specified period: $TR = P \times Q$.

Total revenue (*TR*) (per period of time) The total amount received by firms from the sale of a product, before the deduction of taxes or any other costs. The price multiplied by the quantity sold. $TR = P \times Q$.

Total social surplus Total benefits to society from consuming a good minus total costs to society from producing it. In the absence of externalities, total social surplus is the same as total (private) surplus.

Total utility The total satisfaction a consumer gets from the consumption of all the units of a good consumed within a given time period.

Tradable permits Each firm is given a permit to produce a given level of pollution. If less than the permitted amount is produced, the firm is given a credit. This can then be sold to another firm, allowing it to exceed its original limit.

Trade creation Where a customs union leads to greater specialisation according to comparative advantage and thus a shift in production from higher-cost to lower-cost sources.

Trade cycle or **Business cycle** The periodic fluctuations of national output round its long-term trend.

Trade diversion Where a customs union diverts consumption from goods produced at a lower cost outside the union to goods produced at a higher cost (but tariff free) within the union.

Traditional theory of the firm The analysis of pricing and output decisions of the firm under various market conditions, assuming that the firm wishes to maximise profit.

Transfer payments Moneys transferred from one person or group to another (e.g. from the government to individuals) without production taking place.

Treasury bills Bills of exchange issued by the Bank of England on behalf of the government. They are a means whereby the government raises short-term finance.

U-form (unitary form) of corporate organisation Where the managers of the various departments of a firm are directly responsible to head office, normally to a chief executive.

Uncertainty When an outcome may or may not occur and its probability of occurring is not known.

Underemployment Where people who want full-time work are only able to find part-time work.

Unemployment The number of people who are actively looking for work but are currently without a job. (Note that there is much debate as to who should officially be counted as unemployed.)

Unemployment rate The number unemployed expressed as a percentage of the labour force.

Unit elastic demand Where quantity demanded changes by the same percentage as price. Ignoring the negative sign, it will have a value equal to 1.

Universal benefits Benefits paid to everyone in a certain category irrespective of their income or assets.

Util An imaginary unit of satisfaction from the consumption of a good.

Value added tax (VAT) A tax on goods and services, charged at each stage of production as a percentage of the value added at that stage.

Variable costs Total costs that vary with the amount of output produced.

Variable factor An input that can be increased in supply within a given time period.

Velocity of circulation The number of times annually that money on average is spent on goods and services that make up GDP.

Vent for surplus When international trade enables a country to exploit resources that would otherwise be unused.

Vertical equity The redistribution from the better off to the worse off. In the case of taxes, this means the rich paying proportionately more taxes than the poor.

Vertical merger When two firms in the same industry at different stages in the production process merge.

Vertical restraints Conditions imposed by one firm on another which is either its supplier or its customer.

Wage–price spiral Wages and prices chasing each other as the aggregate demand curve continually shifts to the right and the aggregate supply curve continually shifts upwards.

Wage taker An employer or employee who has no power to influence the market wage rate.

Wages councils Independent bodies which used to set rates of pay in certain low pay industries.

Weak efficiency (of share markets) Where share dealing prevents cyclical movements in shares.

Weighted average The average of several items where each item is ascribed a weight according to its importance. The weights must add up to 1.

Wholesale banks Banks specialising in large-scale deposits and loans and dealing mainly with companies.

Wholesale deposits and loans Large-scale deposits and loans made by and to firms at negotiated interest rates.

Wide monetary base (M0) Notes and coin outside the central bank plus banks' operational deposits with the central bank.

Withdrawals (*W*) (or leakages) Incomes of households or firms that are not passed on round the inner flow. Withdrawals equal net saving (S) plus net taxes (T) plus expenditure on imports (M): $W = S + T + M$.

Working to rule Workers do the bare minimum they have to, as set out in their job descriptions.

Yield on a share The dividend received per share expressed as a percentage of the current market price of the share.

Index

Page numbers in red indicate definitions